The Rough Guide to

Scandinavia

There are more than one hundred and fifty Rough Guide titles
covering destinations from Amsterdam to Zimbabwe

Forthcoming titles include

Argentina • Croatia • Ecuador • Southeast Asia

Rough Guide Reference Series

Classical Music • Country Music • Drum 'n' Bass • English Football
European Football • House • The Internet • Jazz • Music USA • Opera
Reggae • Rock Music • Techno • Unexplained Phenomena • World Music

Rough Guide Phrasebooks

Czech • Dutch • Egyptian Arabic • European Languages • French • German
Greek • Hindi & Urdu • Hungarian • Indonesian • Italian • Japanese
Mandarin Chinese • Mexican Spanish • Polish • Portuguese • Russian
Spanish • Swahili • Thai • Turkish • Vietnamese

Rough Guides on the Internet

www.roughguides.com

ROUGH GUIDE CREDITS

Text editor: Gavin Thomas
Series editor: Mark Ellingham
Editorial: Martin Dunford, Jonathan Buckley, Jo Mead, Kate Berens, Amanda Tomlin, Ann-Marie Shaw, Paul Gray, Helena Smith, Judith Bamber, Orla Duane, Olivia Eccleshall, Ruth Blackmore, Sophie Martin, Geoff Howard, Claire Saunders, Alexander Mark Rogers, Polly Thomas, Joe Staines, Lisa Nellis, Andrew Tomičić, Claire Fogg, Richard Lim, Duncan Clark, Peter Buckley (UK); Andrew Rosenberg, Mary Beth Maioli, Don Bapst, Stephen Timblin (US)
Cartography: Melissa Baker, Maxine Repath, Nichola Goodliffe, Ed Wright

Production: Susanne Hillen, Andy Hilliard, Link Hall, Helen Ostick, Julia Bovis, Michelle Draycott, Katie Pringle, Robert Evers, Niamh Hatton, Mike Hancock, Robert McKinlay
Picture research: Louise Boulton, Sharon Martins
Online editor: Kelly Cross (US)
Finance: John Fisher, Gary Singh, Edward Downey, Mark Hall, Tim Bill
Marketing & Publicity: Richard Trillo, Niki Smith, David Wearn, Jemima Broadbridge (UK); Jean-Marie Kelly, Myra Campolo, Simon Carloss (US)
Administration: Tania Hummel, Charlotte Marriott, Demelza Dallow

ACKNOWLEDGEMENTS

Paul Karr: special thanks to Martha L. Coombs. Also to Britt S. Lightbody, Lillian Hess, Anne Marie Barsoe, Anne Sofie Bølling, Charlotte Krogh, Sally Schmidt, Lena Abskildov, Helen Tharsgaard, Poul Brundto, Irene Banke Jensen, Ulla Madsen, Susanne Jensen, Kaj Lawsen, Hanne M. Østergaard, Dorte Husted, Mette Langhoff Gregersen, Joan Jensen, Louise Thomsen and Johnny Anthonsen.
Phil Lee: thanks to Tom Ingebrigtsen, Anette Slettbakk, Roy Owen and Siri Giil; to Rob Duckett for hiking round in wet weather bearing a determined grin; and especially to Ruth Rigby for her careful assistance and cheery company in Oslo.
James Proctor: Per Henriksson in Stockholm for fantastic times; Åsa Ericson for her expert knowledge of Swedish train tickets; the entire tourist office in Västerås for their good humour; and Ann-Charlotte Carlsson at the Swedish Travel and Tourism Council in London for last-minute information.
Neil Roland: for friendship, inspiration and unexpected levels of kindness: Ingvar Grimberg, Erik Söderlund, Inger

Eide-Jensen and Stigake Berkin in Gothenburg, Christer Hagström in Helsingborg, Charlotte Lindell in Lund, Torbjorn Persson in Malmö, Kalle Sundin in Öland, Anders Karlson in Norrköping, Peter Doolk in Gotland, Jonas Alsen in Linköping.
Andrew Spooner: Kaarina Pelkonen for superlative support; Mikko, Darin, Timpa and Ari for fellowship; Rafael Rybczynski for Helsinki nightlife; Petronella Perret for rally driving; Eno for Finnish proofreading; Charlie for moral support; Peterjon Cresswell for contacts; and all the many members of staff at the very helpful Finnish Tourist Board offices around the country.
The **editor** would also like to thank: Link Hall for typesetting (and patience); Ed Wright, Nichola Goodliffe and Mandy Muggridge for maps; Alistair McDermott and Nick Thomson for Basics research; Sharon Martins for pictures; Russell Walton for eagle-eyed proofreading; Helena Smith for indexing; Richard Lim for Swedish trivia; and Kate Berens for editorial wisdom.

PUBLISHING INFORMATION

This fifth edition published June 2000 by
  Rough Guides Ltd, 62–70 Shorts Gardens,
  London WC2H 9AB.
Distributed by the Penguin Group:
Penguin Books Ltd, 27 Wrights Lane, London W8 5TZ
Penguin Putnam, Inc. 375 Hudson Street, New York NY 10014, USA
Penguin Books Australia Ltd, 487 Maroondah Highway, PO Box 257, Ringwood, Victoria 3134, Australia
Penguin Books Canada Ltd, 10 Alcorn Avenue, Toronto, Ontario, Canada M4V 1E4
Penguin Books (NZ) Ltd, 182–190 Wairau Road, Auckland 10, New Zealand
Typeset in Linotron Univers and Century Old Style to an original design by Andrew Oliver.
Printed in England by Clays Ltd, St Ives PLC.

Illustration in Part One and Part Three by Edward Briant.
Illustration on p.1 by Tommy Yamaha
© Rough Guides Ltd 2000
No part of this book may be reproduced in any form
  without permission from the publisher except for the
  quotation of brief passages in reviews.
768pp – Includes index
A catalogue record for this book is available from the
  British Library
ISBN 1-85828-517-8

The publishers and authors have done their best to
  ensure the accuracy and currency of all the information
  in *The Rough Guide to Scandinavia*, however, they can
  accept no responsibility for any loss, injury, or
  inconvenience sustained by any traveller as a result of
  information or advice contained in the guide.

The Rough Guide to

Scandinavia

written and researched by

Jules Brown, Paul Karr, Phil Lee, James Proctor, Neil Roland, Mick Sinclair and S. Andrew Spooner

ROUGH GUIDES

THE ROUGH GUIDES

TRAVEL GUIDES • PHRASEBOOKS • MUSIC AND REFERENCE GUIDES

 We set out to do something different when the first Rough Guide was published in 1982. Mark Ellingham, just out of university, was travelling in Greece. He brought along the popular guides of the day, but found they were all lacking in some way. They were either strong on ruins and museums but went on for pages without mentioning a beach or taverna. Or they were so conscious of the need to save money that they lost sight of Greece's cultural and historical significance. Also, none of the books told him anything about Greece's contemporary life – its politics, its culture, its people, and how they lived.

So with no job in prospect, Mark decided to write his own guidebook, one which aimed to provide practical information that was second to none, detailing the best beaches and the hottest clubs and restaurants, while also giving hard-hitting accounts of every sight, both famous and obscure, and providing up-to-the-minute information on contemporary culture. It was a guide that encouraged independent travellers to find the best of Greece, and was a great success, getting shortlisted for the Thomas Cook travel guide award,

and encouraging Mark, along with three friends, to expand the series.

The Rough Guide list grew rapidly and the letters flooded in, indicating a much broader readership than had been anticipated, but one which uniformly appreciated the Rough Guide mix of practical detail and humour, irreverence and enthusiasm. Things haven't changed. The same four friends who began the series are still the caretakers of the Rough Guide mission today: to provide the most reliable, up-to-date and entertaining information to independent-minded travellers of all ages, on all budgets.

We now publish more than 150 titles and have offices in London and New York. The travel guides are written and researched by a dedicated team of more than 100 authors, based in Britain, Europe, the USA and Australia. We have also created a unique series of phrasebooks to accompany the travel series, along with an acclaimed series of music guides, and a best-selling pocket guide to the Internet and World Wide Web. We also publish comprehensive travel information on our web site:

www.roughguides.com

HELP US UPDATE

We've gone to a lot of effort to ensure that the fifth edition of *The Rough Guide to Scandinavia* is accurate and up-to-date. However, things change – places get "discovered", opening hours are notoriously fickle, restaurants and rooms raise prices or lower standards. If you feel we've got it wrong or left something out, we'd like to know, and if you can remember the address, the price, the time, the phone number, so much the better.

We'll credit all contributions, and send a copy of the next edition (or any other Rough Guide if you prefer) for the best letters. Please mark letters: "Rough Guide Scandinavia Update" and send to:
Rough Guides, 62–70 Shorts Gardens, London WC2H 9AB, or Rough Guides, 4th Floor, 345 Hudson St, New York, NY 10014.
Or send email to: mail@roughguides.co.uk
Online updates about this book can be found on Rough Guides' Web site at www.roughguides.com

READERS' LETTERS

Thanks to all the readers who wrote in with comments and suggestions about the last edition: K. Baer, Adrian Banfield, Phil Beeson, Jan Best, Gillian Bolton, Kymmene Brereton, Jon Paul Buchmeyer, Victoria Burford, Julie Coleman, Nigel Drury, T. Ford, Mike Gerrard, Bruce Gilsen, Nicholas Gorrill, Robert Dale Hajek, R. Haworth, Sally Heaphy, Peter Hubble, Scott Huegel, Hara Iliopoulou, John Jacobs, Philip King, Niels Larsen, Eija Lietoff, Gill Manns, Tony Manns, Marc Mills, Peter Mitchell, Peter Kuipers Munneke, M.R. Neil, Martin Nossel, Marguerite Osborne, Martyn Perkins, Marc Phillips, D.G. Price, Mark Rosen, Edward Rowland, Abby Rudland, Stewart Russell, Peter Shapiro, Joseph J. Shore, Richard Stephens, M. Stoneman, Monica S. Straaf, Guido Sutermeister, Tada Taku, Madeleine Tyack, Sarah Westlake, Kathleen A. Williams, Sharon Williams.

CONTENTS

Introduction xii

PART FOUR SWEDEN 359

PART FIVE FINLAND   609

Introduction 611 / Getting there from the rest of Scandinavia 612 / Costs, money and banks 613 / Mail and telecommunications 613 / The media 614 / Getting around 615 / Accommodation 617 / Food and drink 619 / Directory 623 / History 624 / Finnish language 636

- # CHAPTER 17: OSTROBOTHNIA, KAINUU AND LAPLAND 709–731

LIST OF MAPS

MAP SYMBOLS

═══	Motorway	∴	Ruin
═══	Major road	♦	General point of interest
═══	Minor road	▲	Mountain peak
-----	Path	ⓘ	Tourist office
━━━	Railway	✉	Post office
▪▪▪▪	Wall	©	Telephone
— —	Ferry route	P	Parking
───	Waterway	☻	Swimming pool
┴┴┴┴	Canal	✿	Synagogue
━ ━ ━	Chapter division boundary	★	Bus stop
■━■━■	International boundary	▬	Building
▬ ▪ ▪ ▬	County boundary	✚	Church (town maps)
✈	Airport	⊡	Cemetery
◉	Accommodation	▦	Park
♜	Castle	▨	National Park
⛫	Stately home	▧	Forest
⸸	Church	▦	Sand/beach
♟	Museum	⛆	Glacier

INTRODUCTION

Scandinavia – Denmark, Norway, Sweden and Finland – conjures resonant images: wild, untamed lands, reindeer and the Midnight Sun; wealthy, healthy, blue-eyed blondes enjoying life in a benevolent welfare state. Yet it's a picture that's only partially accurate. Certainly, by Western European standards Scandinavia is affluent, with a high standard of living and the near eradication of poverty. And for travellers it holds some of Europe's most unspoilt terrain. But it's by no means paradise: there's a social conformity that can be stifling, and the problems of other industrialized countries – drug addiction, racism, street violence – are beginning to make themselves felt. The larger part of the population clusters in the south, where there's all the culture, nightlife and action you'd expect. But no one capital fully reflects its society. With the exception of Denmark these are large, often physically inhospitable countries and rural traditions remain strong, not least in the great tracts of land above the Arctic Circle, where the Sami (Lapps) survive as they have done for thousands of years – by reindeer herding, hunting and fishing.

Historically, the Scandinavian countries have been closely entwined, though in spite of this they remain strikingly individual. For visitors, the efficient and well-organized tourist infrastructure lessens the shock of getting about in what are, after all, Europe's most expensive countries. **Denmark** is the geographical and social bridge between Europe and Scandinavia – easy to reach and the best known of the Scandinavian countries. The Danes are much the most gregarious of the Nordic peoples, something manifest in the region's most relaxed and appealing capital, Copenhagen, and the decidedly more permissive attitude to alcohol.

Norway features great mountains, a remote and bluff northern coast and the mighty western fjords: raw, often inaccessible landscapes which can demand long, hard travel. Even by Scandinavian standards the country is sparsely populated, and people live in small communities along a coastline which stretches from the lower reaches of the North Sea right up to the Russian border.

Sweden is the most "Scandinavian" country in the world's eyes: affluent and with a social system and consensus politics that are considered an enlightened model, though confidence in the country's institutions has been shaken of late with the collapse of the economy and the fragmentation of old alliances; crime and unemployment are rising, too. Travelling is simple enough, although Sweden has Scandinavia's least varied landscape – away from the southern cities and coastal regions an almost unbroken swath of lakes, forests and hills, in which every Swede has a second, peaceful, weekend home.

Finland is perhaps the least known of the mainland Scandinavian countries. Ruled for hundreds of years by the Swedes and then the Russians, it became independent only at the beginning of the twentieth century and has grown into a vibrant, confident nation. Its vast coniferous forests and great lake systems have produced an empathy between the Finns and their country and its nature which is hard to ignore. Also, though Finland is undeniably Scandinavian and looks to the West for its lifestyle, there are, historically and culturally, a number of similarities between Finland and Eastern Europe.

Connections and costs

Travelling in Scandinavia is easy. Public transport is efficient and well co-ordinated, there are a minimum of border formalities between the countries and excellent connections between all the main towns and cities: indeed, it's perfectly feasible to visit sev-

eral, if not all, of the mainland countries on one trip. From Western Europe it's simplest to enter Denmark, from where you can continue northwards into Norway (by boat) or Sweden (by boat or train), the two countries separated by a long north–south border. From Sweden's east coast there are ferries across to Finland, as well as a land border between the two in the far north.

As for **costs**, the Scandinavian countries are expensive by north European standards, but not excessively so. Their reputation for high prices is largely based on the cost of consumables – from books to meals and beer – rather than more substantial items, particularly accommodation, where first-rate budget opportunities are ubiquitous.

When to go

Deciding **when to go** isn't easy since, except for Denmark, Scandinavia experiences intense seasonal changes. The short summers (roughly mid-June to mid-August) can be as hot as in any southern European resort, with high temperatures regularly recorded in Denmark, southern Norway and Sweden, and the Baltic islands. Even the northern areas of each country are temperate, and the whole of the Norwegian west coast, for example, is warmed by the Gulf Stream. Rain, though, is regular, and in the far north of Norway especially – and to a lesser extent in Sweden and Finland – summer temperatures can plunge extremely low at night, so campers need decent equipment for extended spells of sleeping out. One bonus this far north, though not exactly a boon to sleep, is the almost constant daylight provided by the Midnight Sun.

The **summer** is celebrated everywhere with a host of outdoor events and festivities, and is the time when all the facilities for travellers (tourist offices, hotel and transport discounts, summer timetables) are functioning. However, it's also the most crowded time to visit, as the Scandinavians are all on holiday too: go either side of summer (late May/early June or September), when the weather is still reasonable, and you'll benefit from more peace and space. Autumn, especially, is a beautiful time to travel, with the trees and hillsides turning golden brown in a matter of days.

In **winter**, from November to around late May, only Denmark retains a semblance of Western European weather, while the other countries suffer long, dark and extremely cold days. The cold may be severe, but it's crisp and sharp, never damp, and if you're well wrapped up the cities at least needn't be off-limits – though, unless you're exceptionally hardy, the far north is best left to its own, gloomy devices. You'll find broad climatic details in the introductions to each country; for mean temperatures all year round, check the **temperature chart** below.

AVERAGE TEMPERATURE °F											
	Jan	Feb	March	April	May	June	July	Aug	Sept	Oct	Nov	Dec
Denmark												
Copenhagen	32	32	35	44	53	60	64	63	57	49	42	36
Norway												
Oslo	23	25	30	41	52	59	63	61	52	43	34	28
Bergen	35	35	37	43	50	55	59	59	54	46	41	37
Tromsø	26	25	28	32	38	48	54	54	45	37	32	28
Sweden												
Stockholm	27	30	30	39	53	57	64	62	51	45	40	34
Östersund	18	26	22	33	50	52	59	54	44	39	30	27
Haparanda	14	21	15	30	48	56	61	55	44	36	25	22
Finland												
Helsinki	22	21	26	37	48	58	63	61	53	43	35	28
Tampere	17	17	23	35	47	56	61	59	50	40	32	25
Ivalo	8	8	16	27	39	49	56	52	42	31	21	14

Note that these are *average temperatures*. The Gulf Stream can produce some very temperate year-round weather and, in summer, southern Scandinavia can be blisteringly hot. In winter, on the other hand, temperatures of -40°F are not unknown in the far north.

What to take

It's as well to give some thought as to **what to take** – and worth packing that bit more to stave off hardship later. Expect occasional rain throughout the summer and take a waterproof jacket and a spare sweater. A small, foldaway umbrella is useful too. If camping, a warm sleeping bag and good walking shoes are vital (and useful, too, in sprawling cities and the flat southern lands). Mosquitoes are a pest in summer, especially further north and in lake regions, and some form of protective cream is essential. For winter travel, take as many layers as you can pack. Gloves, a hat or scarf that covers your face, thick socks and thermal underwear are all obligatory.

PART ONE
THE
BASICS

GETTING THERE FROM BRITAIN

The section below covers routes from Great Britain to Denmark, Norway, Sweden and Finland. For details on getting to Scandinavia from Ireland, see p.11. For connections within Scandinavia itself, see the "Getting There" sections for each individual country.

BY PLANE

Air fares from the UK to Scandinavia continue to drop as new operators join the fray. The best starting point for cheap deals is often the **classified sections** in the Sunday newspapers (*The Sunday Times* especially) or, if you live in London, *Time Out* magazine or the *Evening Standard*. Special offers are often advertised in many newspapers' weekend travel supplements, or, if you can travel at short notice, Ceefax lists a large number of travel agents touting last-minute discounted tickets. Better still, all major airlines have **Web sites** giving up-to-the-minute information about timetables, fares and special offers, or check the very useful Cheapflights (*www.cheapflights.co.uk*), which will signpost you to the booking agent or airline offering the lowest current prices. Failing that, go straight to a **discount flight agent** like STA Travel or usit CAMPUS (see box on p.5); they specialize in youth flights, and generally have good deals if you're under 26 or a student, as well as ordinary discounted tickets if you're not. It's worth checking their Web sites for special offers too.

It's also worth contacting the major **airlines** – British Airways, SAS (the airline of Denmark, Norway and Sweden) or Finnair – directly. All offer various discounts and special deals, such as SAS's "Rock Bottom" and (slightly more expensive) "Super Saver" tickets, plus discounted fares for under-26s and over-65s, though the latter is only available on certain destinations. Discount tickets do, however, tend to carry restrictions: they must often be booked at least seven days in advance, you must stay abroad at least one Saturday night, and you can't usually change your return flight date.

Special offers and discounted tickets apart, the **scheduled fares** of the major airlines are pretty well matched; the cheaper seats tend to be found on smaller carriers such as Maersk and British Midland. Low-cost carriers such as Go and Ryanair offer the best deals, but serve only a limited number of destinations. It's also worth noting that the cheapest airlines often don't fly to a city's main airport, which can in some cases mean a two-hour bus ride to the city centre – Ryanair flights to Oslo, for example, land at Sandefjord airport, over one hundred kilometres from the capital. When no direct flights are available, airlines can usually offer you **connections** to Scandinavian airports via a Scandinavian partner (British Midland with SAS, or British Airways with Sun Air, for example).

You might also consider buying an **air pass**, usually sold only in conjunction with tickets from Britain, which can be useful for getting around the vast expanses of Scandinavia. SAS (in conjunction with Lufthansa and British Midland) run the **Yes Pass**, which allows under-26s (or students under 30) to take between four and ten flights using these three airlines' European services. Itineraries are booked when buying the pass, though dates can be changed for about £20 per flight. Each flight coupon costs £39 (plus taxes), whilst the outward and return legs from the UK, where you must begin your itinerary, cost £59 each. Another option from SAS is the **Visit Scandinavia Air Pass**, which allows flights between and within Denmark, Norway, Sweden and Finland with a raft of airlines including SAS, Maersk Air, Skyways and Air Botnia. Each flight requires a coupon costing £50–80, depending on the route; they're only available in conjunction with special fares from the UK flying with SAS.

TO DENMARK

Denmark is the Scandinavian country closest to – and best served by plane from – Britain. SAS fly around seven times daily **from London** Heathrow and Stansted **to Copenhagen** (1hr 45min), and also have daily flights from Heathrow **to Århus**, while British Airways operate five daily from Heathrow to Copenhagen and two daily from Heathrow **to Billund** (in Central Jutland). Go have three daily flights from Stansted to Copenhagen and Maersk offer three daily flights from Gatwick to Billund and two daily from Gatwick to Copenhagen. Ryanair have twice-daily flights from London Stansted to Århus, while the Brazilian airline Varig fly from Heathrow three times a week to Copenhagen.

There are also services to Denmark from various **regional airports** in the UK, including from **Aberdeen** to Esbjerg (with British Midland), **Birmingham** to Copenhagen (Maersk), **Glasgow** to Copenhagen (British Midland), **Manchester** to Copenhagen (SAS), and **Newcastle** to Copenhagen (British Airways). All these carriers operate at least one flight a day, though services may be reduced at weekends.

The lowest regular **fares** at present are with Go and Ryanair, at around £100 return; otherwise, expect to pay in the region of £150 including tax for a discounted return ticket from Britain to Denmark bought directly from SAS, British Midland or British Airways (though watch out for occasional offers that bring fares down below £100 return).

TO NORWAY

There's a good choice of flights **from London** Heathrow to **Oslo**, with both SAS and British Airways operating about five flights daily, while British Airways also have six Oslo flights a week from Gatwick. From Stansted, KLM UK fly twice daily to both Oslo and **Bergen**, while Ryanair fly twice daily to Oslo (Sandefjord). SAS also have twice-daily services from Stansted to Oslo, and from Heathrow to **Stavanger**. The other Norwegian destination connected directly to London is **Kristiansand**, with six Maersk Air flights a week from Gatwick.

If you're heading directly to the fjords, there are fast and regular flights from regional airports. From **Aberdeen**, KLM UK fly three times daily to Stavanger and daily to Bergen, whilst SAS have two or three flights daily to Stavanger. From

Newcastle, Braathens SAFE flies to Bergen and Oslo more or less daily. SAS flies between **Manchester** and Oslo daily except Saturday, and British Airways have twice-daily flights on the same route.

The cheapest **fares** at present are to Oslo with Ryanair (from as low as £60 return) and KLM UK from Stansted (about £90 return). Expect to spend around £150 inclusive of taxes to Oslo on most other carriers, and to pay more if flying from regional airports. As ever, you'll need to book well in advance and have flexible arrangements to take advantage of the cheapest fares.

TO SWEDEN

Flying to Sweden, the choice of routes is not as wide as you might expect, though routes from

London to Stockholm and Gothenburg are well served. There are ample flights **to Stockholm**, with SAS (about 7 daily from Heathrow and Stansted), Finnair (3 daily from Gatwick, 5 daily from Heathrow), and British Airways (8 daily from Heathrow, 2–3 daily from Gatwick), while Ryanair have once-daily services to Stockholm and **Malmö** from Stansted. To **Gothenburg**, SAS operate two flights daily from Heathrow, with British Airways offering three daily from Heathrow and another three out of Gatwick. KLM UK have flights (daily except Sat) from London City Airport to Malmö. Apart from London, only **Manchester** has direct flights to Sweden, with Finnair and British Airways offering twice-daily and SAS daily (except Sat) flights to Stockholm.

The cheapest **fares** are currently with Ryanair

DISCOUNT FLIGHT AGENTS

Alpha Flights, 37 Kings Exchange, Tile Yard Rd, London N7 9AH (☎020/7609 8188).

APA Travel, 138 Eversholt St, London NW1 1BL (☎020/7387 5337).

Benz Travel, 83 Mortimer St, London W1N 7PV (☎020/7462 0000).

North South Travel, Moulsham Mill Centre, Parkway, Chelmsford, Essex CM2 7PX (☎01245/492 882). Friendly, competitive travel agency, offering discounted fares worldwide – profits are used to support projects in the developing world.

STA Travel (*www.statravel.co.uk*), 86 Old Brompton Rd, London SW7 3LH; 117 Euston Rd, London NW1 2SX; 38 Store St, London WC1 (☎020/7361 6161); 25 Queens Rd, Bristol BS8 1QE (☎0117/929 4399); 38 Sidney St, Cambridge CB2 3HX (☎01223/366 966); 75 Deansgate, Manchester M3 2BW (☎0161/834 0668); 88 Vicar Lane, Leeds LS1 7JH (☎0113/244 9212); 36 George St, Oxford OX1 2OJ (☎01865/792 800); and branches in Birmingham, Canterbury, Cardiff, Coventry, Durham, Glasgow, Loughborough, Nottingham, Warwick and Sheffield. Worldwide specialists in low-cost flights and tours for students and under-26s.

Strata Travel, 9 Central Parade, Green St, Enfield, Middlesex EN3 7HG (☎020/8805 1555). Cheap charter and scheduled flights to Scandinavia.

Trailfinders (*www.trailfinders.com*), 42–50 Earls Court Rd, London W8 6FT (☎020/7937 5400); 194

Kensington High St, London W8 7RG (☎020/7938 3939); 58 Deansgate, Manchester M3 2FF (☎0161/839 6969); 254–284 Sauchiehall St, Glasgow G2 3EH (☎0141/353 2224); 22–24 The Priory, Queensway, Birmingham B4 6BS (☎0121/236 1234); 48 Corn St, Bristol BS1 1HQ (☎0117/929 9000). One of the best informed and most efficient agents.

Travel Bug, 125a Gloucester Rd, London SW7 4SF (☎020/7835 2000); 597 Cheetham Hill Rd, Manchester M8 5EJ (☎0161/721 4000). Large range of discounted tickets.

Travel CUTS, 295a Regent St, London W1R 7YA (☎020/7255 1944); 33 Prince's Square, London W2 4NG (☎020/7792 3770). British branch of Canada's main youth and student travel specialist.

usit CAMPUS (*www.usitcampus.co.uk*), 52 Grosvenor Gardens, London SW1W 0AG (☎020/7730 3402); 541 Bristol Rd, Selly Oak, Birmingham B29 6AU (☎0121/414 1848); 61 Ditchling Rd, Brighton BN1 4SD (☎01273/570 226); 39 Queen's Rd, Clifton, Bristol BS8 1QE (☎0117/929 2494); 5 Emmanuel St, Cambridge CB1 1NE (☎01223/324 283); 53 Forrest Rd, Edinburgh EH1 2QP (☎0131/668 3308); 105–106 St Aldates, Oxford OX1 1BU (☎01865/484 730); plus branches in YHA shops and on university campuses all over Britain. Student and youth travel specialists.

Usit Council, 28a Poland St, London W1V 3DB (☎020/7437 7767). Flights and student discounts.

(from £60 return to Malmö and from £100 return to Stockholm). Otherwise, barring special offers, which may bring prices down to about £130 return, minimum fares are around £200. Discount agents may be able to offer small savings on these.

TO FINLAND

Finnair offer a good choice of flights to Finland, with four daily services **from London** Heathrow **to Helsinki**, and another two from Gatwick. British Airways also fly to Helsinki (5 daily from Heathrow; 2 daily from Gatwick). There are also twice-daily services with Buzz from London Stansted to Helsinki. From **Manchester** there are twice-daily services to Helsinki on Finnair and British Airways. No other British airports have direct flights to Finland, though you can arrange connecting flights through SAS, British Midland and British Airways, among others.

The cheapest **fares** to Helsinki are with Buzz – from around £120 return. Otherwise, discount fares go for around £200 return, though special offers may bring this figure down to as low as £130 at certain times of the year (usually Jan–March). There are also charter flights to Lapland during the winter, particularly around Christmas – check with the specialist tour operators listed on p.9.

BY TRAIN

Taking a train can be a relaxed way of getting to Scandinavia, though it may not work out a lot, if at all, cheaper than flying, especially if you're over 26. Most train tickets also allow you to break your journey – travelling to Oslo, for instance, you could stop off at Brussels, Hamburg, Copenhagen and Gothenburg.

Planning your journey, however, can be a headache, since through-ticketing arrangements are very limited. **Rail Europe** (see box opposite) offer routings via the fast but relatively expensive Eurostar to Paris and Brussels and then onto Scandinavia. If you want to go more cheaply using a cross-channel ferry your options are strictly limited: through-ticketing is available from just one outlet in the UK, **Wasteels** (see opposite), all of whose routings are via the Dover–Ostend crossing. You could, with careful planning, organize your own train and ferry tickets, although this is obviously a complicated, if potentially money-saving, process (for ferry operators see "By Car and Ferry", p.8. For train travel in the UK call National

Rail Enquiries (see box opposite), or visit *www.thetrainline.com*).

A number of deals involving **rail passes** make it possible to cut costs, however. If you have no clear itinerary, the **InterRail pass** might be the best bet. The pass gives you free travel on most state railways in mainland Europe (though supplements are payable on some express trains, and you only get a 34 percent discount in the country where you buy the pass rather than free travel) as well as discounts on many private railways, buses and ferries (including those from Harwich to Esbjerg and from southern England to mainland Europe, as well as several in Scandinavia and between Scandinavia and Germany – some of the very short ones are free). To be eligible, you have to provide proof that you've been resident for at least six months in one of the countries covered by the pass. Passes are valid in up to eight zones covering most of Europe, the British Isles, Turkey and Morocco, and last for a month (except single-zone passes, which are valid for 22 days only). If you're **under 26**, a pass covering one zone is £159, two zones £209, three zones £229, four or more £259. Norway, Sweden and Finland are all in Zone B; Denmark is in Zone C, along with Germany, Switzerland and Austria. Depending on your route, you may have to buy a pass that covers Zone E (France, Belgium, the Netherlands and Luxembourg) too. The passes are available from many train stations as well as youth and student travel agencies. If you are **over 26**, you can still buy a pass, though prices are roughly £80 higher.

If you're 60 or over, the **Rail Europe Senior Card** gives up to 30 percent discount on any journeys which cross international frontiers (but not on journeys within countries) in most of Western Europe, including Scandinavia. To obtain it, you must first have a Senior Citizen Rail Card (£16 from any train station) and then pay an extra £5 at any British Rail Travel Centre or travel agent specializing in European rail travel.

For details of the **Eurail** pass (not available to residents of Europe), see p.15 and p.19. For rail passes for use within Scandinavia, such as the **ScanRail** and **EuroDomino** passes, see "Getting around", p.27. There are also certain individual country passes available; for more on these, see the relevant country's "Getting Around" section. Anyone thinking of travelling extensively by train would be wise to pick up a copy of the latest monthly **Thomas Cook European Rail Timetable** (the red volume),

TRAIN COMPANIES AND TICKET AGENTS

Deutsche Bahn UK, 18 Conduit St, London W1R 9TD (☎020/7317 0919). European rail tickets and passes including ScanRail.

Eurostar, Eurostar House, Waterloo Station, London SE1 8SE (☎0345/303 030, www.eurostar.com). Services to Paris and Brussels. For through-tickets on to Scandinavia contact Rail Europe.

National Rail Enquiries, telephone information only (☎0345/484 950, www.railtrack.co.uk). Train times and ticket prices within the UK, but no ticket sales.

Rail Europe, 179 Piccadilly, London W1V 0BA (☎08705/848 848). Through-tickets using Eurostar, plus Eurail and ScanRail passes.

Wasteels, by platform 2, Victoria Station, London SW1V 1JY (☎020/7834 7066) Youth-ticket specialists with most current rail passes also available. They offer the only through-ticketing service v a cross-channel ferry, though expect a long wait if visiting their office. Their phone service is also very patchy.

www.thetrainline.com Comprehensive online booking service and timetable information for all UK train services.

COACH COMPANIES

Eurolines, 52 Grosvenor Gardens, London SW1W 0AU (☎0990/143 219).

National Express, 164 Buckingham Palace Rd, London SW1W 9TP (☎08705/808 808, www.nationalexpress.co.uk).

which contains schedules of all major train and ferry routes throughout Europe.

TO DENMARK

There are two trains **from London** Charing Cross daily via Dover and Ostend **to Copenhagen**, the quickest being the late-morning train with changes at Brussels and Hamburg. The journey takes 24 hours – couchettes and sleeping berths are available (supplement payable) on the Brussels–Hamburg leg of the trip. Through-tickets are only available on this route from Wasteels. Fares are currently £143 single and £277 return to Copenhagen (under-26s £117/£187). Supplements may also be payable for seat reservations. If you break your journey make sure your ticket is stamped at the station where it's broken.

The fastest and priciest route is **via the Channel Tunnel on Eurostar**, travelling from Waterloo via either Paris or Brussels and taking roughly twenty hours. Fares start at £235 single and £382 return (under-26s £186/363). Tickets are available from Rail Europe; book well in advance for the cheapest fares. Rail Europe can sell you through-tickets from most UK starting points. As always, check for special offers.

ON TO NORWAY, SWEDEN AND FINLAND

Getting to Norway, Sweden or Finland by train from Britain involves first travelling to Copenhagen, as described above, and then taking an onward service. Unfortunately connections aren't necessarily convenient. From Copenhagen to **Stockholm**, there is only one direct overnight service (although there are almost hourly indirect services). The only through-ticket available to Stockholm from the UK must be bought at Wasteels, travelling via Dover–Ostend with a quickest journey time of 31 hours. Fares are £192 single, £375 return (under-26s £160/274).

For **Oslo** there are two through-ticketing options, one from Wasteels via Ostend and Copenhagen (34 hours), the other from Rail Europe travelling from London Waterloo on the Eurostar to Brussels then on via Cologne. The fare via Ostend is £207 single, £404 return (under-26s £173/300). The Eurostar route direct is a slightly complicated though – surprisingly – cheaper option, thanks to Rail Europe's long-term special offer to Cologne of £89 return. This ticket has certain restrictions (no stopovers are allowed apart from a 24hr break in Brussels). Rail Europe then sell you another ticket from Cologne via Hamburg and Copenhagen to Oslo, which has a different set of restrictions, though you're allowed to break your journey during this leg. The total cost is £164 single, £239 return (no youth fares). This route also requires some very quick changes at Brussels, Cologne, Hamburg and Copenhagen if you want the quickest journey time of 24 hours.

No through-ticketing is available to **Finland** from the UK, though it's possible to connect with the Silja line ferry to Helsinki in Stockholm.

BY COACH

A coach journey to Scandinavia can be an endurance test, and with airfares to Scandinavia falling it can actually prove more expensive than flying. Only if time is no object and price all-important, or if you specifically do not want to fly, is it really worth taking the bus.

Eurolines run two direct services weekly from London to **Copenhagen** (20hr), plus four involving a change of bus at Amsterdam (24hr); all continue to **Gothenburg** (25–29hr), where they connect with services to **Stockholm** (30–34hr) and **Oslo** (31–37hr). The two direct weekly buses from London connect at Gothenburg with buses for **Vanesborg** (28hr) and **Karlstad** (30hr). Buses also run twice weekly from London direct to **Hirtshals** (22hr) via **Århus** (20hr) and **Aalborg** (21hr). There are no through-ticketed coach arrangements between Britain and Finland. **Fares** to all Danish destinations are £68 one-way, £97 return. Oslo costs £108/173; Stockholm £103/149. If you are **under 26**, expect to save between £5 to £20 on each fare. In the peak summer months fares increase slightly.

Another option is the **Euroline Pass**, which offers unlimited coach travel throughout much of Europe, including Denmark and Sweden but excluding Norway and Finland. The pass is valid either for 30 days (under-26s £199, over-26s £229) or 60 days (£249/279).

There are no through services from anywhere in Britain outside London, though **National Express** connect with Eurolines buses in London from all over the British Isles.

BY CAR AND FERRY

Ferry connections out of Harwich and Newcastle link Britain with Denmark, western Sweden and southern Norway. Fares aren't cheap, but discounts and special deals, such as DFDS Seaways' "All in one car" midweek return fares, can cut costs greatly. There are also 25 percent discounts on all fares for senior citizens and students. Unless otherwise stated, we've quoted the cheapest fares for a one-way passage. Not surprisingly, fares are usually at their lowest during the winter months.

An alternative to travelling directly by ferry to Scandinavia is to take a ferry **to Germany** or **Holland** (or even Belgium or France), and drive from there. DFDS Seaways' crossings from Harwich to Hamburg and Stena Line's from Harwich to the Hook of Holland are probably the most convenient options if you're heading straight for Scandinavia. **Hitching** is generally possible in Belgium, the Netherlands and, especially, Germany, but notoriously bad in Scandinavia itself.

TO SCANDINAVIA FROM BRITAIN

From the UK **to Denmark**, DFDS Seaways sail from **Harwich to Esbjerg** three or four times a week, a trip of nearly 20 hours. Fares in low season start at £49 one-way/£84 return, plus £45 each way for a car (£163/292 for an "All in one car" fare covering 1 car and up to 4 people), rising to £98/166 plus £65 each way for a car (£349/611 "All in one car") in high season; for unreserved weekend fares a £10 supplement is payable. All prices include a berth in a sleeping cabin.

For most of the year, the only services from Britain to **Norway** are the two or three sailings each week with Fjord Line from **Newcastle to Stavanger** (20hr), **Haugesund** (23hr) and **Bergen** (27hr). Tickets cost the same to all three ports, with a minimum fare in winter of £41 each

---

FERRY OPERATORS

DFDS Seaways (*www.scansea.com*), Scandinavia House, Parkeston Quay, Harwich, Essex CO12 4QG (☎0990/333 000); 15 Hanover St, London W1R 9HG (☎020/7409 6060); Tyne Commission Quay, North Shields NE29 6EA (☎0191/296 0101). Harwich to Esbjerg; Newcastle to Gothenburg and Kristiansand.

Fjord Line, International Ferry Terminal, Royal Quays, North Shields, Tyne and Wear NE29 6EG (☎0191/296 1313). Newcastle to Stavanger, Haugesund and Bergen.

P&O North Sea Ferries, King George Dock, Hedon Rd, Kingston-upon-Hull HU9 5QA (☎01482/377 177). Hull to Rotterdam.

P&O Scottish Ferries, PO Box 5, Jamieson's Quay, Aberdeen AB11 5NP (☎01224/589 111). Aberdeen to Lerwick offering through-ticketing on the Smyril Line service from Lerwick to Bergen.

Stena Line, Charter House, Park St, Ashford, Kent TN24 8EX (☎0990/707 070). Harwich to the Hook of Holland.

way (including cabin berth), plus £60 for a car, rising in summer to £62 each way and £85 per car. During the summer months reclining seats are available instead of a cabin for £48. Motorbikes are carried for £30 each way year-round, while bicycles cost £5 in winter and £10 in summer each way Students, senior citizens and registered disabled people get a 50 percent discount except during parts of June, July and August – check with the company for specific dates. The DFDS Seaways ferry from Newcastle to Gothenburg also stops in **Kristiansand** (see overleaf). From May to September, P&O Scottish Ferries run a weekly service from **Aberdeen** to **Lerwick** in Shetland and offer through-ticketing to connect with the Smyril Line service to **Bergen**. Through fares start at £89 each way for a reclining seat plus £90 per car (motorbikes £34, bicycles £6) from Aberdeen, £47 plus £38 per car from Lerwick (Smyril Lines service, bookable through P&O Scottish Ferries), with 10 percent discounts for students and senior citizens. The journey from Aberdeen to Bergen takes about three days in all and involves a stopover in Lerwick.

SPECIALIST TOUR OPERATORS

Aeroscope, Scope House, Morerton-in-the-Marsh, Gloucestershire GL56 0BQ (☎01608/650 103). One- and two-centre city breaks.

Anglers' World Holidays, 46 Knifesmith Gate, Chesterfield, Derbyshire S40 1RQ (☎01246/221 717). Angling holidays in Denmark and Sweden.

Arctic Experience/Discover the World, 29 Nork Way, Banstead, Surrey SM7 1PB (☎01737/218 800, www.arctic-discover.co.uk). Specialist adventure tours including whale-watching in Norway and dog-sledging in Lapland.

Ashley Tours, "Cleve", Well Lane, Little Witley, Worcester WR6 6LN (☎01886/888 335). Annual tours to the Gothenburg Jazz Festival.

Branta, 7 Wingfield St, London SE15 4LN (☎020/7635 5812). Bird-watching tours.

Crystal Holidays, Crystal House, Arlington Rd, Surbiton, Surrey KT6 6BW (☎020/8399 5144, www.crystalholidays.co.uk). City breaks, country tours and skiing holidays.

DA Study Tours, Williamson House, Low Causeway, Culross, Fife KY12 8HL (☎01383/882 200). Coach tours for culture vultures.

DFDS Seaways, Scandinavia House, Parkeston Quay, Harwich, Essex CO12 4QG (☎0990/333 111, www.scansea.com). Breaks in Denmark and Sweden, including two nights on board ship and two or three nights abroad – good deals out of season.

Finman Travel International, 87–89 Church St, Leigh, Manchester WN7 1AZ (☎01942/262 662, pamela@finmantravel.co.uk). Tailor-made Finnish and Swedish holidays, Helsinki city breaks, cruises and winter trips to Lapland.

Inntravel, Park St, Hovingham, York YO62 4JZ (☎01653/629 010). Outdoor holidays in Norway including skiing, walking, fjord cruises, and whale- and reindeer-watching.

Insight, 15 Grosvenor Place, London SW1X 7HH (☎0990/143 433, www.insighttours.com). Coach tours and tailor-made holidays.

King's Angling Holidays, 27 Minster Way, Hornchurch, Essex RM11 3TH (☎01708/453 043, valerieking@lineone.net). Angling in Denmark and Sweden.

Norvista, 227 Regent St, London W1R 8PD (☎020/7409 7334, www.norvista.com). Finland specialists with a variety of tours and holidays, plus some in Sweden.

Scandinavian Travel Service, 2 Berghem Mews, Blythe Rd, London W14 0HN (☎020/7559 6666, sales@scantravel.com). City breaks, tours and cruises.

ScanMeridian, 28b High St, Hampstead, London NW3 1QA (☎020/7431 5322). Scandinavia specialists offering city breaks, fly-drive, cottage holidays, cruises and tailor-made holidays.

Scantours, 45 Whitcomb St, London WC2H 7DH (☎020/7839 2927, www.scantoursuk.com). Scandinavia specialists with a wide range of packages and tailor-made holidays.

Specialised Tours, 4 Copthorne Bank, Copthorne, Crawley, West Sussex RH10 3QX (☎01342/712 785). City breaks and tailor-made holidays.

Taber Holidays, 30a Bingley Rd, Saltaire, Shipley, West Yorkshire, BD18 4RS (☎01274/594 642, info@taberhols.co.uk). Norwegian specialists with dozens of options, including self-catering holidays, fjord cruises, motoring tours and guided coach tours.

To Sweden, DFDS Seaways operate a twice-weekly service from **Newcastle to Gothenburg** (26hr) which stops in Norway at **Kristiansand** (18hr) en route. Prices to both destinations are the same and start at £54 one-way in low season, £93 return. The "All in one car" fare is £175 one-way, £313 return. Expect to pay more in the spring and summer months, and supplements at weekends. All fares include a cabin berth.

There are no direct passenger ferries from Britain to **Finland**.

TO SCANDINAVIA FROM OTHER COUNTRIES

There are numerous ferry links to Scandinavia from other European countries. The main routes are given below – note that there are also minor connections to the Danish islands. More details can be obtained from ferry companies and travel agents, and in the relevant "Travel Details" sections of the guide.

From **Germany**, the most useful route is the hour-long crossing from Puttgarten to Rødby, on the way to Copenhagen. Ferries run half-hourly round the clock all year. Other routes include Rostock to Gedser (9–11 daily; 2hr), Kiel to Oslo (1 daily; 19hr 30min), Kiel to Gothenburg (1 daily; 14hr), Rostock to Trelleborg (ferry: 4–5 daily; 5hr 30min–7hr; catamaran: 2–3 daily; 2hr 45min) and Sassnitz to Trelleborg (4–5 daily; 3hr 30min). From Travemünde, you can get ferries to Rødby (1 daily; 2hr 30min), Malmö (2 daily; 9hr) and Trelleborg (2–6 daily; 7–8hr), and there are also services from Travemünde and Lubeck to Helsinki (1–3 weekly; 22hr and 36hr respectively).

From **Poland**, ferries run from Swinoujscie to Copenhagen (5 weekly; 9hr 15min), Malmö (1–2 daily; 9hr) and Ystad (1 daily; 6hr 45min), Gdansk to Oxelosund (3–6 weekly; 18hr 30min), and Gdynia to Karlskrona (6 weekly; 10hr 30min). They also run from Tallinn, the capital of **Estonia**, to Helsinki (ferry: 6 daily; 3hr 30min–6hr 45min; hydrofoil: 4–6 daily; 1hr 30min; catamaran: 2–3 daily; 1hr 45min) and Stockholm (1 daily; 15hr).

PACKAGE TOURS

Don't be put off by the idea of an **inclusive package**. In such an expensive part of Europe, it can be the cheapest way to do things, and may also be the only way to reach remote parts of the region at inhospitable times of year. If you just want to see one city and its environs, then **city breaks** invariably work out cheaper than arranging the same trip independently. Prices include return travel, usually by plane, and accommodation (with breakfast), with most operators offering a range from hostel to luxury-class hotel. As a broad guide, two-night hotel stays in Copenhagen or Stockholm start at around £250 per person out of season; in Oslo, prices start at around £280, while two nights in Helsinki will cost from £260. If you stay for a week in any of these places, rates per night fall considerably.

There are also an increasing number of operators offering **special-interest holidays** to Scandinavia, from camping tours to Arctic cruises (see box overleaf. Prices for these are a good deal higher, but are generally excellent value for money.

GETTING THERE FROM IRELAND

The easiest route to Scandinavia from Ireland is on one of the three daily SAS flights from Dublin to Copenhagen, from where you can connect to virtually anywhere in the region. You can also fly direct with Aer Lingus to Stockholm, Helsinki and Copenhagen (about five weekly in summer; fewer in winter).

Official **fares** to Copenhagen start at around IR£180 plus tax for a midweek rock-bottom economy

AIRLINES

Aer Lingus, 40 O'Connell St, Dublin 1 (☎01/844 4777); 46–48 Castle St, Belfast BT1 1HB (☎0845/973 7747); 2 Academy St, Cork (☎021/327 155); 136 O'Connell St, Limerick (☎061/474 239). Dublin to Copenhagen, Helsinki and Stockholm.

British Airways (*www.british-airways.com*), 1 Fountain Centre, Fountain St, Belfast BT1 6HR (☎0345/222 111); in the Republic c/o Aer Lingus (addresses above; reservations ☎1800/626 747).

British Midland (*www.britishmidland.com*), Nutley, Merrion Rd, Dublin 4 (☎01/283 8833); Suite 2, The Fountain Centre, College St, Belfast (☎0345/554 554).

Ryanair, Phoenix House, Conyngham Rd, Dublin (☎01/609 7800, *www.ryanair.com*). Dublin to Oslo, Stockholm and Malmö via London Stansted.

SAS, Terminal Building, Dublin Airport (☎01/844 5440, *www.flysas.co.uk* or *www.sas.se*). Dublin to Copenhagen.

DISCOUNT AGENTS

Joe Walsh Tours, 8 Lower Baggot St, Dublin (☎01/676 3053); 69 Upper O'Connell St, Dublin (☎01/872 2555). General budget fares agent.

Student & Group Travel, 71 Dame St, Dublin 2 (☎01/677 7834). Student specialists.

Trailfinders, 4–5 Dawson St, Dublin (☎01/677 7888).

Travel Shop, 35 Belmont Rd, Belfast 4 (☎028/9047 1717).

usit NOW, O'Connell Bridge, 19–21 Aston Quay, Dublin 2 (☎01/679 8833); Fountain Centre, Belfast BT1 6ET (☎028/9032 4073); 10–11 Market Parade, Patrick St, Cork (☎021/270 900); 33 Ferryquay St, Derry (☎01504/371 888); Victoria Place, Eyre Square, Galway (☎091/565 177); Central Buildings, O'Connell St, Limerick (☎061/415 064). Ireland's main student and youth travel specialists.

FERRY COMPANIES

Irish Ferries, Ferry Port, Alexandra Rd, Dublin (from the Republic ☎1890/313131; from Northern Ireland ☎0800/018 2211); St Patrick's Bridge, Cork (☎021/551 995). Irish agents for DFDS Seaways.

P&O European Ferries, The Terminal Building, Larne Harbour, Co. Antrim BT40 5AQ (☎0870/242 4777).

TOUR OPERATORS

Crystal Holidays, 5 Merrion Row, Dublin 2 (☎01/676 4806). One- and two-centre city breaks, plus skiing holidays.

Falcon Travel, 2 Winder Place, Dublin (☎01/287 0070); 19 Lower Camden St, Dublin 2 (☎01/478 0533). City breaks and cruises.

Thomas Cook, 11 Donegall Place, Belfast (☎028/9055 0232); 118 Grafton St, Dublin (☎01/677 1721). Package-holiday and flight agent, with occasional discount offers.

fare, although special offers are sometimes available, and a discount agent such as USIT (see box overleaf) may have youth, student or discounted tickets for even less. To really do it on the cheap you could find one of the numerous special deals to London and then take advantage of the more competitive airfares available there. Ryanair also offer through-ticketing, with a change of planes at London Stansted to Stockholm, Malmö and Oslo, with prices starting at about IRE200. SAS passengers flying from the Republic can also purchase the Visit Scandinavia Air Pass (see "Getting there from Britain", p.3).

From Belfast, there are no direct flights to Scandinavia, and your best bet is probably to fly via London or Dublin with British Airways, British Midland or SAS. **Fares** to Copenhagen, Stockholm or Oslo usually start at about £200 for an economy return, £250 to Helsinki, but special offers can take these as low as £155 return to Copenhagen, and just over £200 to other Scandinavian capitals. Failing that, you should be

able to get a reasonable deal through a discount agent, either in Northern Ireland or in mainland Britain.

If you are planning to travel from Ireland **by train**, the best option by far is to buy an InterRail pass (see "Getting there from Britain", p.6). Getting to Scandinavia **by coach** involves going to London and picking up a connection there. For motorists, combined **ferry** fares covering Celtic Sea and North Sea crossings are generally available through Irish Ferries from the Republic or P&O from the North (see box overleaf for addresses).

Not many operators run **package tours** to Scandinavia from Ireland, although where available these may be the cheapest way to travel, and sometimes the only way to reach remote parts of the region at inhospitable times of year. Likewise, city-break packages may well work out cheaper than arranging the same trip independently. British operators are listed on p.9, those based in Ireland are given in the box on p.11.

GETTING THERE FROM NORTH AMERICA

From North America, Scandinavia is well served by numerous American and European airlines, though only SAS, American, Delta and Finnair provide direct flights. If you are visiting more than one country, an air pass might be your best bet.

SHOPPING FOR TICKETS

Barring special offers, the cheapest of the airlines' published fares is usually an **Apex** (Advance Purchase Excursion) ticket, although this will carry certain restrictions: you may have to book – and pay – at least 21 days before departure, spend at least seven days abroad

(maximum stay three months), and you tend to get penalized if you change your schedule. On transatlantic routes, there are also winter **Super Apex** tickets, sometimes known as "Eurosavers" – slightly cheaper than an ordinary Apex, but limiting your stay to between seven and 21 days. Some airlines also issue **Special Apex** tickets to under-24s, often with a maximum stay of a year. Many airlines offer youth or student fares to under-26s; a passport or driver's licence is sufficient proof of age, though these tickets are subject to availability and can have eccentric booking conditions. It's worth remembering that most cheap return fares involve spending at least one Saturday night away and that many will only give a percentage refund if you want to cancel or alter your journey – check the restrictions carefully before buying a ticket.

You can normally cut costs further by going through a **specialist flight agent** – either a **consolidator**, who buys up blocks of tickets from the airlines and sells them at a discount, or a **discount agent**, who in addition to dealing with discounted flights may also offer special student and youth fares and a range of other travel-related services such as travel insurance, rail passes, car rental, tours and the like. Bear in mind, though, that penalties for changing your plans on discounted tickets can be stiff. Remember too that these companies make their money by dealing in bulk – don't expect them to answer lots of questions. Some agents specialize in **charter flights**, which may be cheaper than anything available on a scheduled flight, but again departure dates are fixed and withdrawal penalties are high (check the refund policy). If you travel a lot, **discount travel clubs** are another option – the annual membership fee may be worth it for benefits such as cut-price air tickets and car rental.

Don't automatically assume that tickets purchased through a travel specialist will be cheapest – once you get a quote, check with the airlines and you may turn up an even better deal. Be advised also that the pool of travel companies is swimming with sharks – exercise caution and never deal with a company that demands cash up front or refuses to accept payment by credit card.

Students might be able to find cheaper flights through the major student travel agencies, such

---

DISCOUNT TRAVEL COMPANIES IN NORTH AMERICA

Airtech, Suite 204, 588 Broadway, New York NY 10012 (☎1-800/575-TECH or 212/219-7000, www.airtech.com). Standby seat broker; also deals in consolidator fares and courier flights.

Airtreks.com, High Adventure Travel, 442 Post St, 4th Floor, San Francisco CA 94102 (☎1-800/350-0612 or 415/912-5600, www.airtreks.com). Round-the-World tickets. Web site features interactive database that lets you build and price your own RTW itinerary.

Cheap Tickets Offices nationwide (☎1-800/377-1000 or 212/570-1179, www.cheaptickets.com). Travel store dealing in discounted fares.

Council Travel, 205 E 42nd St, New York NY 10017 (☎1-800/226-8624 or 212/822-2700, www.counciltravel.com); plus branches in many other US cities. Student/budget travel agency.

Educational Travel Center, 438 N Frances St, Madison WI 53703 (☎1-800/747-5551 or 608/256-5551, www.edtravel.com). Student/youth and consolidator fares.

Mister Cheaps, Suite 307, 74 Varick St, New York NY 10013 (☎1-888/37-CHEAPS or 212/431-1616, www.mistercheaps.com). Consolidator.

Skylink, 265 Madison Ave, 5th Floor, New York NY 10016 (☎1-800/892-0027, www.pltravel.com). Branches also in Chicago, Los Angeles, Montréal, Toronto and Washington DC. Consolidator.

STA Travel, 10 Downing St, New York NY 10014 (☎1-800/777-0112 or 212/627-3111, www.statravel.com); plus branches in Los Angeles, San Francisco, Miami, Chicago, Seattle, Philadelphia, Washington DC and Boston. Worldwide discount travel firm specializing in student/youth fares, student IDs, travel insurance, car rental, rail passes, etc.

Student Flights, Suite A104, 5010 E Shea Blvd, Scottsdale AZ 85254 (☎1-800/255-8000 or 602/951-1177, www.isecom). Student/youth fares, student IDs and rail passes.

TFI Tours International, 34 W 32nd St, New York NY 10001 (☎1-800/745-8000 or 212/736-1140). Consolidator.

Travac Tours, 989 6th Ave, New York NY 10018 (☎1-800/872-8800 or 212/563-3303, www.thetravelsite.com). Consolidator and charter broker. You can have a list of fares faxed to you by calling toll-free on ☎888/872-8327.

Travel Avenue, Suite 1404, 10 S Riverside Plaza, Chicago IL 60606 (☎1-800/333-3335 or 312/876-6866, www.travelavenue.com). Discount travel agent.

Travel CUTS, 187 College St, Toronto ON M5T 1P7 (☎1-800/667-2887 or 416/979-2406, www.travelcuts.com); plus other branches throughout Canada. Student travel organization specializing in student fares, IDs and other travel services.

Travelers Advantage, 311 W Superior St, Chicago IL 60610 (☎1-800/255-0200, www.travelersadvantage.com). Travel club; annual membership fee.

UniTravel, Suite 120, 11737 Administration Drive, St Louis MO 63146 (☎1-800/325-2222 or 314/569-2501). Consolidator.

Worldtek Travel, 111 Water St, New Haven CT 06511 (☎1-800/243-1723 or 203/772-0470, www.worldtek.com). Discount travel agency.

Worldwide Discount Travel Club, 1674 Meridian Ave, Miami Beach FL 33139 (☎305/534-2082). Travel club with discounts on package holidays only. Annual membership fee.

as Council Travel, STA Travel or, for Canadian students, Travel CUTS (see box overleaf for addresses and phone numbers).

A further possibility is to see if you can arrange a **courier flight**, although the hit-or-miss nature of these makes them most suitable for the single traveller who travels light and has a very flexible schedule. In return for shepherding a parcel through customs and possibly giving up your baggage allowance, you can expect to get a significantly discounted ticket. At present, however, the only courier flights to Scandinavia are on the New York–Copenhagen route. For information about

courier flights contact the Air Courier Association (☎1-800/822-0888, *www.aircourier.org*) or the International Association of Air Travel Couriers (☎561/582-8320, *www.courier.org*). For more options, consult *A Simple Guide to Courier Travel* (Pacific Data Sales Publishing).

If you are travelling to Scandinavia as part of a longer trip, consider buying a **Round-the-World** (RTW) ticket, although since Scandinavia is not one of the more obvious destinations for round-the-world travellers, you would probably have to have a custom-designed RTW ticket (more expensive than an "off-the-shelf" RTW ticket) assem-

---

AIRLINES

Air Canada Canada ☎1-888/247-2262, US ☎1-800/776-3000, *www.aircanada.ca*. Daily from Toronto (with connections from Vancouver) to Frankfurt and Zurich, and 5–7 weekly to Paris, with onward connections to major Scandinavian cities.

Air France US ☎1-800/237-2747, Canada ☎1-800/667-2747, *www.airfrance.fr*. Daily from many North American cities to Paris, with connecting flights to major Scandinavian cities.

American Airlines ☎1-800/433-7300, *www.aa.com*. Flights daily from Chicago direct to Stockholm.

British Airways US ☎1-800/247-9297, Canada ☎1-800/668-1059, *www.british-airways.com*. Daily flights from 22 North American cities to London, with onward connections to major Scandinavian cities.

Continental Airlines ☎1-800/231-0856, *www.continental.com*. Daily between various major North American and European cities, with connecting flights to Scandinavia.

Delta Air Lines US ☎1-800/241-4141, Canada ☎1-800/221-1212, *www.delta-air.com*. Daily non-stop from New York (JFK) to Stockholm, with connections from most major North American cities.

Finnair US ☎1-800/950-5000, Canada ☎1-800/461-8651, *www.finnair.com*. Direct flights to Helsinki from New York (daily except for the winter months when they fly every day except Tues) and Miami (frequency varies according to season).

Icelandair ☎1-800/223-5500, *www.icelandair.com*. Daily direct flights to Reykjavik from New York, Baltimore, Boston and Minneapolis, plus two weekly from Orlando and

Halifax (Nova Scotia), with onward connections to Oslo, Stockholm and Helsinki. Some flights allow a three-night stopover in Reykjavik.

Lufthansa US ☎1-800/645-3880, Canada ☎1-800/563-5954, *www.lufthansa.com*. Daily flights from major North American cities via Frankfurt to Scandinavia.

Northwest/KLM ☎1-800/447-4747, *www.nwa.com*. Flights from major North American cities to Scandinavia via Amsterdam.

Sabena ☎1-800/955-2000, *www.sabena.com*. Direct flights from Atlanta, Boston, Chicago, Cincinnati, New York, Washington DC and Montréal to Brussels, with connections to Scandinavia.

SAS ☎1-800/221-2350, *www.flysas.com* or *www.scandinavian.net*. Daily direct flights to Copenhagen, Stockholm and Oslo from New York (Newark); to Stockholm and Copenhagen from Chicago; and to Copenhagen from Seattle. Connections with most major cities in North America via a domestic carrier.

Swissair US ☎1-800/221-4750, Canada ☎1-800/267-9477, *www.swissair.com*. Daily to Zurich from Atlanta, Boston, Chicago, Cincinnati, Los Angeles, Miami, Newark, New York (JFK) and Montréal, with connections to Scandinavia.

TWA ☎1-800/892-4141, *www.twa.com*. Daily to Paris from many major cities in North America, with connecting flights to Scandinavia.

US Airways ☎1-800/622-1015, *www.usairways.com*. Daily from Philadelphia, Pittsburgh or Charlotte to several European cities, with onward connections to Scandinavia.

Virgin Atlantic Airways ☎1-800/862-8621, *www.fly.virgin.com*. Daily from various US cities to London, with connections to Scandinavia.

bled for you by a travel agent, which can be quite expensive. Another source of cheap airfares is **the Internet**. There are a number of Web sites where you can look up fares and even book tickets. Search the travel sections of your Web browser or try Travelocity at *www.travelocity.com*, FLIFO Cyber Travel Agent at *www.flifo.com*, or make a bid for a fare at *www.priceline.com*.

FLIGHTS FROM THE USA AND CANADA

The majority of flights to Scandinavia from North America involve **changing planes** in London, Reykjavik, Brussels, Amsterdam, Paris, Frankfurt or Zurich – and if you don't live in one of the gateway cities for flights in North America, you might have to change planes more than once. **Direct flights**, of which there are a few, are obviously preferable, and if you can be fairly flexible with your departure dates you should be able to take advantage of the special promotional fares that are offered regularly by the airlines. **Fares** to Copenhagen, Oslo and Stockholm are fairly similar, whichever carrier you choose, though it's still worth shopping around. Flights to Helsinki tend to be more expensive, unless you fly with Finnair, in which case the difference is minimal. Fares also depend on what time of year you fly: they're most expensive during high season (roughly June–Aug and around Christmas and New Year) and cheapest during low season (Nov–March, excluding Christmas and New Year); the remaining months are classified as shoulder season, with fares somewhere in between.

From New York you can fly direct to Copenhagen, Stockholm and Oslo on SAS, to Helsinki on Finnair, and to Stockholm on Delta (journey time from 7hr 30min to over 10hr on an indirect flight). Fares are around US$800–900 round-trip (high season), US$380–420 (low). **From Chicago**, American Airlines fly direct to Stockholm (journey time from 8hr 30min to at least 11hr on an indirect flight), while SAS fly direct to both Stockholm and Copenhagen. Fares are around US$930–1020 round-trip (high season), US$440–490 (low). **From Seattle**, SAS fly direct to Copenhagen; fares are around US$1070–1270 (high season), US$550–600 (low). Fares are similar **from Los Angeles and San Francisco**, though there are no direct flights from here to Scandinavia.

There are no direct flights **from Canada**, and flying time can vary between 9–13hr from Toronto, and 13–18hr from Vancouver, depending on connections. You might consider taking a cheap flight to New York or Chicago and continuing from there. Fares from Toronto or Montréal are around CDN$1500–1650 (high season), CDN$900–1200 (low). From Vancouver, fares are around CDN$1950 (high season), CDN$1250 (low). It's worth remembering the direct SAS flight from Seattle to Copenhagen, which currently works out at about CDN$1600 (high season , CDN$900 (low).

If you're thinking about getting around Scandinavia by air, check out the **Visit Scandinavia Air Pass** offered by SAS. This comes in the form of discount coupons for air travel within Norway, Sweden, Denmark and Finland. It can only be purchased in conjunction with a round-trip ticket on SAS. The coupons are valid for three months from arrival and cost $75 per segment for travel between most cities ($145 to a few particularly distant ones).

TRAVELLING VIA EUROPE

If fares seem high you might want to consider flying to **London**, one of the cheapest European cities to get to, and taking a flight, train or ferry on to Scandinavia (see "Getting there from Britain", p.3). If you're visiting Scandinavia as part of a wider tour of Europe, it may be worth buying a **Eurail pass** (they're only available to non-residents of Europe, although you can buy them in London at the Rail Europe office – see box, p.7), which can get you by train to Scandinavia from anywhere in Europe. Allowing unlimited first-class train travel in seventeen European countries, the basic Eurail pass costs US$554 for 15 days, US$718 for 21 days, US$880 for one month, $1260 for two months and US$1558 for three months. The **Eurail Flexipass** is cheaper if you're not planning to travel every day of your stay: US$654 for ten days of travel within two months; US$862 for fifteen days in two months. **Under-26s** are eligible for the even better value **Eurail Youthpass** (US$388 for 15 days, US$623 for one month, US$882 for two months), while the **Under-26 Flexipass** costs US$458 for ten days of travel within two months and US$599 for fifteen days in two months. Note, however, that the youth passes are only valid for second-class travel.

If you're planning to travel by train only once you've arrived in Scandinavia, then you're better off with a Scandinavia-wide **ScanRail pass** (see p.27), or a single-country train pass (see the relevant country's "Getting Around" section). The Web site **www.railpass.com** is a useful source

TOUR OPERATORS

Abercrombie and Kent (☎1-800/323-7308, *www.abercrombiekent.com*). Upmarket company offering Scandinavian and Baltic coach tours and cruises.

Above the Clouds Trekking (☎1-800/233-4499, *www.aboveclouds.com*). Week-long walking tour of Norway's mountains and fjords, with hotel accommodation.

Adventure Center (☎1-800/227-8747, *www.adventurecenter.com*). Fifteen-day camping tour of Norway, Sweden and Finland.

Adventures Abroad (☎1-800/665-3398, *www.adventures-abroad.com*). Canadian-based company with a variety of Scandinavian packages, specializing in small group tours.

American Express Vacations (☎1-800/241-1700, *www.americanexpress.com*). Flight-plus-hotel packages to major Scandinavian cities.

Backroads (☎1-800/462-2848, *www.backroads.com*). Norwegian holidays including a seven-day cycling trip in the Vesteralen and Lofoten Islands and an eight-day hiking tour of the mountains, glaciers and fjords.

Bennett Tours (☎1-800/221-2420, *www.bennett-tours.com*). Cheap winter weekend breaks or bus tours (May to early Sept) throughout Scandinavia.

Borton Overseas (☎1-800/843-0602, *www.bortonoverseas.com*). Adventure-vacation specialists, with biking, hiking, rafting, bird-watching, dog-sledging and cross-country skiing tours, plus farm and cabin stays.

Brekke Tours (☎1-800/437-5302, *www.brekketours.com*). Sightseeing and cultural tours of Scandinavia. Call for a brochure.

Contiki Tours (☎1-800/CONTIKI, *www.contiki.com*). Tours of Scandinavia and Russia for 18- to 35-year-olds. Campsite/cabin accommodation.

Euro-Bike & Walking Tours (☎1-800/321-6060, *www.eurobike.com*). Summer cycling tours of Sweden and Denmark.

EuroCruises (☎1-800/688-3876, *www.eurocruises.com*). Cruises of the Baltic Sea, the fjords of Norway and the canals of Sweden.

Euroseven (☎1-800/890-3876, *www.euroseven.com*). Hotel-plus-flight packages from New York, Baltimore or Boston to Scandinavia.

International Gay and Lesbian Travel Association (☎1-800/448-8550, *www.iglta.org*). Trade group with lists of gay-owned or gay-friendly travel agents, accommodation and other travel services.

Loma Travel (☎1-888/665-9899). Canadian tour operator offering cheap flights, tours and cruises.

Nordique Tours (☎1-800/995-7997, *www.ptla.com/nordique*). Scandinavian package tours with emphasis on the Norwegian fjords.

Norvista Travel Services (☎1-800/529-4929, *www.norvista.net*). Tour department of Finnair. Air/hotel deals to Helsinki, plus other Scandinavian city packages.

Norwegian Coastal Voyage – Bergen Line Services (☎1-800/323-7436, *www.coastalvoyage.com*). Norwegian coastal cruises, Swedish canal cruises and Scandinavian ferry services.

Passage Tours (☎1-800/548-5960, *www.passagetours.com*). Scandinavian specialist offering tours, ski packages and cheap weekend breaks.

Saga Holidays (☎1-800/343-0273, *www.sagaholidays.com*). Specialists in group travel for seniors offer a cruise and coach tour of Sweden, Norway and Finland.

SAS (☎1-800/221-2350 ext 4, *www.scandinavian.net*). Scandinavian airline tour desk. Agents for specialist tour operators.

Scanam World Tours (☎1-800/545-2204, *www.scanamtours.com*). Scandinavian specialist with group and individual tours and cruises, plus cheap weekend breaks.

Scand-America Tours (☎1-800/886-8428 or 727/939-1505, *www.scandamerica.com*). Offers a wide variety of packages – everything from dog-sledging to garden tours – throughout Scandinavia.

Scanditours (☎1-800/432-4176, *www.scanditours.com*). Canadian Scandinavian specialist with wide range of travel options. Offices in Toronto and Vancouver.

Scantours (☎1-800/223-7226, *www.scantours.com*). Major Scandinavian holiday specialists offering vacation packages and customized itineraries, including cruises and city sightseeing tours.

Special Interest Travel Gallery Website (*www.sitravel.com*). Online resource for special-interest tours in Scandinavia.

Vantage Deluxe World Travel (☎1-800/322-6677, *www.vantagetravel.com*). Deluxe group tours and cruises in Scandinavia.

of information and up-to-the-minute fares for all these passes.

PACKAGES AND ORGANIZED TOURS

There are a number of companies operating **organized tours** of Scandinavia, ranging from deluxe cruises to cycling holidays. Group tours can be very expensive, and occasionally don't include the airfare, so check what you are getting. If your visit is centred on cities you could simply book a hotel-plus-flight package (which can work out cheaper than booking the two separately). Bennett Tours, Euroseven, Scanam and Passage Tours offer very reasonable weekend deals in the low season (see box opposite). Tour reservations can often be made through your local travel agent.

GETTING THERE FROM AUSTRALIA AND NEW ZEALAND

There are no direct flights from Australia or New Zealand to Scandinavia; instead you'll have to fly to either a European or Asian gateway city, from where you can get a connecting flight or other onward transport. Fares are pretty steep, so if you're on a tight budget it's worth flying to London (see "Getting there from Britain", p.3), Amsterdam or Frankfurt first, and picking up a cheap flight from there. If you intend to take in a

DISCOUNT AGENTS

Anywhere Travel, 345 Anzac Parade, Kingsford, Sydney (☎02/9663 0411, anywhere@ozemail.com.au).

Budget Travel, 16 Fort St, Auckland (☎0800/808 040 or 09/366 0061, www.budgettravel.co.nz).

CIT, 422 Collins St, Melbourne (☎03/9650 5510); 263 Clarence St, Sydney (☎02/9267 1255); plus branches in Brisbane, Adelaide and Perth.

Destinations Unlimited, 3 Milford Rd, Milford, Auckland (☎09/373 4033).

European Travel Office (ETO), 122 Rosslyn St, West Melbourne (☎03/9329 8844); 20th Floor, 133 Castlereagh St, Sydney (☎02/9267 7727).

Flight Centre (www.flightcentre.com). Australia: branches nationwide (☎131600 for nearest branch). New Zealand: National Bank Towers, 205–225 Queen St (☎0-800/354443), plus branches nationwide.

Harvey World Travel, 631 Princes Highway, Kogarah, Sydney (☎132757 or 02/9567 6099, www.harveyworld.com.au), plus branches nationwide.

Northern Gateway, 22 Cavenagh St, Darwin (☎08/8941 1394).

STA Travel, Australia (☎1300/360 960 for nearest branch, www.statravel.com.au): 256 Flinders St, Melbourne (☎03/9654 7266); 855 George St, Sydney (☎1800/637 444 or 02/9212 1255); plus other offices in state capitals and major universities. New Zealand (www.statravel.co.nz): Travellers' Centre, 10 High St, Auckland (☎09/309 0458); 90 Cashel St, Christchurch (☎03/379 9098); 130 Cuba St, Wellington (☎04/385 0561); plus offices in Dunedin, Palmerston North, Hamilton and major universities.

Thomas Cook, Australia: 257 Collins St, Melbourne (☎131771 or 03/9282 0222); 175 Pitt St, Sydney (☎1800/801 002 or 02/9231 2877); plus branches in other state capitals. New Zealand: 159 Queen St, Auckland (☎0800/353 535 or 09/379 3924).

Topdeck Travel, 65 Glenfell St, Adelaide (☎08/8232 7222).

Trailfinders, 8 Spring St, Sydney (☎02/9247 7666, www.trailfinders.com.au).

Travel.com, 80 Clarence St, Sydney (☎02/9290 1500, www.travel.com.au).

Tymtro Travel, 428 George St, Sydney (☎02/9223 2211).

UTAG Travel, 122 Walker St, North Sydney (☎131398 or 02/9956 8399, www.utag.com.au).

number of other European countries on your trip, it might be worth buying a Eurail pass before you go.

Airfares to Europe vary significantly with the **season**: low season runs from mid-January to the end of February and during October and November; high season runs from mid-May to the end of August and from December to mid-January; the rest of the year is counted as shoulder season. Tickets purchased direct from the **airlines** tend to be expensive, with published fares ranging from A$2000/NZ$2500 (low season) to A$2500–3000/NZ$3000–3600 (high). Travel agents offer better deals on fares and have the latest information on special deals, such as free stopovers en route and fly-drive-accommodation packages. Flight Centre and STA (see box overleaf for addresses) generally offer the best discounts, especially for students and those under 26. For a discounted ticket to Scandinavia from **Sydney**, **Melbourne**, or **Auckland**, expect to pay A$1600–2500/NZ$2000–2700. Fares from

Perth and **Darwin** are slightly cheaper via Asia, rather more expensive via Canada and the US. Fares from **Christchurch** and **Wellington** are around NZ$150–300 more than those from Auckland.

Airlines flying out of Australia and New Zealand often use SAS and Finnair for connecting services on to cities in Sweden, Norway, Denmark and Finland. For flights to other **European cities**, the lowest fares are with Britannia to London, during its limited charter season (Nov–March), when you can expect to pay A$1000–1600/ NZ$1200–1900. For a scheduled flight, count on paying A$1500–2260/NZ$1900–2800 on Alitalia or KLM; A$1900–2500/NZ$2280–3000 on SAS, Thai Airways and Lufthansa; A$2400–2850/ NZ$2700–3400 on British Airways, Qantas, Singapore Airlines, Air New Zealand and Canadian Airways depending on the season. See the box below for a full rundown of airlines and routes.

Air passes which allow for discounted flights within Europe and Scandinavia, such as the SAS

AIRLINES

Air New Zealand (*www.airnz.com*), 5 Elizabeth St, Sydney (☎132476); 139 Queen St, Auckland (☎0800/737 000). Daily flights from Aukland to London or Frankfurt via Los Angeles. Onward connections with SAS to Scandinavia.

Alitalia/KLM (*www.alitalia.com*), 5 Elizabeth St, Sydney (☎1300/653 757); 229 Queen St, Auckland (☎09/379 4457). Six flights weekly from Sydney (with Ansett connections from other state capitals) to major Scandinavian cities via Amsterdam or Milan.

Britannia Airways (*www.ukflightshop.com.au*), c/o UK Flight Shop, 7 Macquarie Place, Sydney (☎02/9247 4833); c/o World Aviation, Trustbank Building, 229 Queen St, Auckland (☎09/308 3355). Charter flights to London.

British Airways (*www.british-airways.com*), Level 4, 50 Franklin St, Melbourne (☎03/9603 1133); 70 Hunter St, Sydney (☎02/8904 8800); 154 Queen St, Auckland (☎09/356 8690). Daily to London from Sydney, Perth or Brisbane with onward connections to Scandinavian cities.

Cathay Pacific (*www.cathaypacific.com*), 8 Spring St, Sydney (☎131747); 205 Queen St, Auckland (☎09/379 0861). Several flights weekly from Australia and New Zealand to Hong Kong, with onward connections to Scandinavia.

Lufthansa (*www.lufthansa.com*), 143 Macquarie St, Sydney (☎1300/655 727); 36 Kitchener St, Auckland (☎0800/945 220). Daily flights from major cities via Bangkok or Singapore and Frankfurt.

Qantas (*www.qantas.com*), 70 Hunter St, Sydney (☎131313); 154 Queen St, Auckland (☎09/357 8900 or 0800/808 767). Daily from state capitals via Asia or Europe to Scandinavia.

SAS (*www.flysas.com*), Level 15, 31 Market St, Sydney (☎02/9299 9800). No flights from Australia or New Zealand, but can organize connections to Scandinavia via Bangkok, Beijing, Singapore or Tokyo.

Singapore Airlines (*www.singapore-airlines.com*), 17 Bridge St, Sydney (☎131011); West Plaza Building, cnr Fanshawe and Albert streets, Auckland (☎09/303 2129 or 0800/808 909). Daily service from major Australian and New Zealand cities to Scandinavia via Singapore.

Thai Airways (*www.thai-airways.com*), 75 Pitt St, Sydney (☎1300/651 960); 22 Fanshawe St, Auckland (☎09/377 3886). Three flights weekly to Stockholm from Auckland and Sydney via Bangkok.

SPECIALIST TOUR OPERATORS

Adventure World, 73 Walker St, North Sydney (☎02/9956 7766 or 1800/221 931, *www.adventureworld.com.au*), plus branches in Brisbane and Perth; 101 Great South Rd, Remuera, Auckland (☎09/524 5118, *www.adventureworld.co.nz*).

Bentours, Level 11, 2 Bridge St, Sydney (☎02/9241 1353). Ferry, rail, bus and hotel passes and a host of scenic tours throughout Scandinavia including fjord-travel, cycling in Denmark and a four-day ferry journey down the Göta Canal between Stockholm and Gothenburg.

CIT *www.cittravel.com.au*), 422 Collins St, Melbourne (☎03/9650 5510); 263 Clarence St, Sydney (☎02/9267 1255); plus branches in Brisbane, Adelaide and Perth. City tours and accommodation packages.

Explore Holidays, Level 2, 55 Blaxland Rd, Ryde, Sydney (☎02/9857 6200). Stockholm mini-stays and 21-day adventure tour through central and northern Sweden and coastal Norway.

USIT Beyond, cnr Shortland St and Jean Batten Place, Auckland (☎09/379 4224; *www.usitbeyond.co.nz*); plus branches in Hamilton, Palmerston North, Wellington and Christchurch.

YHA Travel Centres (*www.yha.com.au*), 38 Stuart St, Adelaide (☎08/3231 5583); 154 Roma St, Brisbane (☎07/3236 1680); 191 Dryandra St, O'Connor, Canberra (☎02/6248 0177); 69a Mitchell St, Darwin (☎08/8981 2560); 28 Criterion St, Hobart (☎03/6234 9617); 83 Hardware Lane, Melbourne (☎03/9670 9611); 236 William St, Northbridge, Perth (☎08/9227 5122); 422 Kent St, Sydney (☎02/9261 1111). Budget accommodation throughout Scandinavia for YHA members.

"Visit Scandinavia Pass" and British Airways–Qantas "One World Explorer", are available in conjunction with a flight to Scandinavia, and must be bought at the same time. Expect to pay A$2400–2850/NZ$2600–3000. For extended trips, **Round-the-World** tickets, valid up to a year, can be good value. Tickets that take in Scandinavia include the Star Alliance package (bookable through Ansett and Air New Zealand; around A$2800/NZ$3350) based on miles travelled (open-jaw travel and backtracking permitted), and the One World Alliance "Global Explorer" (bookable through Qantas; A$2400–2900/NZ$2900–3400).

There are very few **package holidays** to Scandinavia. Your best bet is Bentours (see box above for details), who will put together a package for you, and who are about the only agents who offer skiing holidays. Alternatively, wait until you get to Europe, where there's a greater choice of holidays and prices (see "Getting there from Britain").

If you're planning to travel a lot **by train**, or use trains to get to Scandinavia from another European country, it's worth considering a train pass. **Eurail passes**, which come in numerous versions (see p.15 for a rundown) are available from most travel agents, or from branches of CIT or Thomas Cook (see box p.17 for addresses). There's also a specific pass for Scandinavia, the **ScanRail** pass, which is sold by Bentours – further details on p.27.

RED TAPE AND VISAS

European Union, US, Canadian, Australian and New Zealand citizens need only a valid passport to enter Denmark, Norway, Sweden or Finland for up to three months. All other nationals should consult the relevant embassy about visa requirements. For longer stays, EU nationals can apply for a residence permit while in the country, which, if it's granted, may be valid for up to five years. Non-EU nationals can only apply for residence permits before leaving home, and must be able to prove they can support themselves without working. Contact the relevant embassy in your country of origin.

In spite of the lack of restrictions, **checks** are frequently made on travellers at the major points of entry. If you're young and are carrying a rucksack, be prepared to prove that you have enough money to support yourself during your stay. You may also be asked how long you intend to stay and why. Be polite. It's the only check that will be made, since once you get into Scandinavia there are few passport controls between the individual countries.

SCANDINAVIAN EMBASSIES AND CONSULATES

AUSTRALIA
Denmark 15 Hunter St, Yarralumla, Canberra 2600 (☎02/6273 2195 or 6273 2196); **Finland** 10 Darwin Ave, Yarralumla, Canberra 2600 (☎02/6273 3800); **Norway** 17 Hunter St, Yarralumla, Canberra 2600 (☎02/6273 3444); **Sweden** 5 Turrana St, Yarralumla, Canberra 2600 (☎02/6270 2700).

CANADA
Denmark 47 Clarence St, Suite 450, Ottawa, ON, K1N 9K1 (☎613/562-1811); **Finland** 55 Metcalfe St, Suite 850, Ottawa, ON K1P 6L5 (☎613/236-2389); **Norway** Royal Bank Center, 90 Sparks St, Suite 532, Ottawa, ON, K1P 5B4 (☎613/238-6571); **Sweden** 377 Dalhousie St, Ottawa, ON K1N 9N8 (☎613/241-8553).

IRELAND
Denmark 121–122 St Stephen's Green, Dublin 2 (☎01/475 6404); **Finland** Russell House, Stokes Place, St Stephen's Green, Dublin 2 (☎01/478 1344); **Norway** 34 Molesworth St, Dublin 2 (☎01/662 1800); **Sweden** 13–17 Dawson St, Dublin 2 (☎01/671 5822).

NEW ZEALAND
Denmark Level 7, 45 Johnston St, Wellington (☎04/471 0520); **Finland** 4th Floor, BNZ Building, 137 Armagh St, Christchurch (☎03/366 1653); **Norway** Level 38, Coopers & Lybrand Tower, 23–29 Albert St, Auckland (☎09/355 1830); **Sweden** 13th Floor, Vogel Building, Aitken St, Thorndon, Wellington (☎04/499 9895).

UK
Denmark 55 Sloane St, London SW1X 9SR (☎020/7235 1255); **Finland** 38 Chesham Place, London SW1X 8HW (☎020/7235 9531); **Norway** 25 Belgrave Square, London SW1X 8QD (☎020/7591 5500); **Sweden** 11 Montagu Place, London W1 2AL (☎020/7917 6400).

USA
Denmark 3200 Whitehaven St NW, Washington, DC 20008 (☎202/234-4300); **Finland** 3301 Massachusetts Ave NW, Washington, DC 20008 (☎202/298-5800); **Norway** 2720 34th St NW, Washington, DC 20008 (☎202/333-6000); **Sweden** 1501 M St NW, Washington, DC 20005 (☎202/467-2600).

MONEY AND BANKS

Of Scandinavia's currencies, Denmark and Norway use kroner, Sweden kronor – abbreviated respectively as Dkr, Nkr and Skr, or as DKK, NOK and SEK.

In this guide, we've abbreviated each as "kr", except where it's not clear to which country's money we're referring, in which case we've prefixed it with an "S" (Swedish), "D" (Danish) or "N" (Norwegian). Though they share a broadly similar exchange rate (currently 8–10kr to £1, 5–7kr to US$1), the currencies are not interchangeable. Finland uses the markka, abbreviated as Fmk or just mk – the rate at the time of writing was 9mk to £1, 6mk to US$1.

TRAVELLER'S CHEQUES AND CREDIT CARDS

It's easiest and safest to carry money as **traveller's cheques**, available for a small commission (usually 1 percent of the amount ordered) from any bank and some building societies, whether or not you have an account. In Britain, banks also issue current account holders with a **Eurocheque card** and cheque book, with which you can get cash from most banks in Scandinavia; you'll pay a few pounds service charge a year but usually no commission on transactions.

The major **credit and charge cards** – Visa, MasterCard, American Express and Diners Club – are accepted almost everywhere in Scandinavia, while credit-card holders (and holders of some other bank cards) can use them to withdraw local currency from cashpoint machines (ATMs).

EXCHANGING MONEY

Exchanging money is easy but usually expensive. Banks have standard exchange rates, but commissions can vary enormously and it's always worth shopping around. Post offices often provide good exchange rates too. Some places charge per transaction, others per cheque, so it makes sense to carry large denomination cheques, or to try to change several people's money at once.

Banking hours vary from country to country – check each country under "Costs, Money and Banks". Outside those times, and especially in more remote areas, you'll often find that you can change money at hostels, hotels, campsites, tourist offices, airports and ferry terminals – though usually at worse rates than at the bank.

MAIL AND TELECOMMUNICATIONS

Post office opening hours and more specific information on how to use the mail and telephone systems is given under each individual country's section on "Mail and Telecommunications".

You can have letters sent **poste restante** to any post office in Scandinavia by addressing them "Poste Restante", followed by the name of the town and country. When picking mail up you'll need to take your passport; make sure to check under middle names and initials, as letters often get misfiled.

Phone boxes are plentiful, and almost always work; English instructions are normally posted inside. To make a collect call, dial the operator,

INTERNATIONAL DIALLING CODES

To Scandinavia:
Dial your country's international access code, then

Denmark ☎45	Norway ☎47	Sweden ☎46	Finland ☎358
From Denmark to:	**From Norway to:**	**From Sweden to:**	**From Finland to:**
Britain ☎00-44	Britain ☎00-44	Britain ☎009-44	Britain ☎00-44
US & Canada ☎00-1	US & Canada ☎00-1	US & Canada ☎009-1	US & Canada ☎00-1
Australia ☎00-61	Australia ☎00-61	Australia ☎009-61	Australia ☎00-61
New Zealand ☎00-64	New Zealand ☎00-64	New Zealand ☎009-64	New Zealand ☎00-64
Ireland ☎00-353	Ireland ☎00-353	Ireland ☎009-353	Ireland ☎00-353

who will speak English. To make a **direct call** to Britain or North America, dial the international access and country code, wait for the tone, then dial the area code, omitting the first 0 if there is one, and subscriber number.

There's no shortage of places in Scandinavia to send and receive **email**. Cybercafés have now begun to appear in most of the region's cities and there's also plentiful online access in public libraries, often free.

HEALTH

Health care in Scandinavia is excellent and widely available. Language is rarely a problem and the nearest tourist office will be able to recommend local doctors and hospitals.

EU nationals can take advantage of health services in **Denmark**, **Sweden** and **Finland** under the same terms as residents of the country. To do this you'll need form E111, which you can get over the counter at the post office or by applying on form SA30 by post, one month in advance, to any DSS office in Britain. Norway also has a **reciprocal health agreement** with Britain, which is detailed below.

North American visitors will find that medical treatment is far less expensive than they're accustomed to in the United States, but even so it's essential to take out travel insurance. In the case of an emergency, you should go to a hospital, since this will prove less expensive than a doctor's visit. Prescription drugs are also cheap, but pharmacies will only supply prescriptions written by EU doctors.

HEALTH PROBLEMS

In **Denmark**, tourist offices and health offices (*Kommunes Social og Sundhedforvaltning*) have lists of doctors. If the doctor decides you need hospital treatment, it'll be arranged for free, but always take your E111 with you. For doctors' consultations and prescriptions (available from an *Apotek*, or pharmacy) you'll have to pay the full cost on the spot, but keep a receipt and take this together with your E111 and passport to the local Danish health office for a refund – sometimes a long and frustrating process. Health care in Denmark is free for American visitors, provided it doesn't look like you've come to the country with the intention of having a serious illness treated for free.

In **Norway**, hotels and tourist offices have lists of local doctors and dentists, and there'll usually be an emergency department you can go to outside surgery hours. You'll pay about 120kr for an appointment, but EU citizens will be reimbursed for part of the cost of any treatment; ambulance travel and hospital stays are free. Get a receipt (*Legeregning*) at the time of payment, and take it and your passport to the social insurance office (*Trygdekasse*) of the district where treatment was obtained. For prescription drugs, go to a pharmacy (*Apotek*); late-opening ones in the main cities are detailed in the listings sections of the Guide.

In **Sweden** there is no local doctor system: go to the nearest hospital with your passport and they'll treat you for a fee of around 140kr. If you need medicine you'll get a prescription to take to a pharmacy (*Apotek*), for which the maximum charge is normally around 100kr. Hospital stays cost 80kr per day; the emergency department is called the *Akutmottagning*.

In **Finland**, treatment at a doctor's surgery (*Terveyskeskus*), found in all towns and villages, is free, but medicines have to be paid for at a pharmacy (*Apteekki*) – although, provided you have your passport, you won't be charged any more than Finns. Hospitals levy charges whether you stay in a bed or are treated as an outpatient.

INSURANCE

Most people will want to take out some kind of comprehensive travel insurance. Bank

and credit cards often have certain levels of medical or other insurance included, especially if you use them to pay for your trip. This can be quite comprehensive, anticipating anything from lost luggage to missed connections. Similarly, if you have a good all-risks home insurance policy it may well cover your possessions against loss or theft even when overseas, and many private medical schemes also cover you when abroad – make sure you know the procedure and the helpline number.

If you plan to participate in **winter sports**, or do some **hiking**, you'll probably have to pay an extra premium; check carefully that any insurance policy you are considering will cover you in case of an accident. Check also exactly what is

TRAVEL INSURANCE SUPPLIERS

AUSTRALIA AND NEW ZEALAND
Cover More Australia: ☎02/9202 8000, *www.covermore.com.au*
Ready Plan Australia: ☎03/9771 4000 or 1300/555 018; New Zealand: ☎09/300 5333
Travel.com *www.travel.com.au*

BRITAIN AND IRELAND
Columbus Travel Insurance ☎020/7375 0011, *www.columbusdirect.co.uk*
Endsleigh Insurance ☎020/7436 4451, *www.endsleigh.co.uk*
Frizzell Insurance ☎01202/292 333, *www.frizzell.co.uk*
STA ☎020/7361 6262. *www.statravel.co.uk*
usit Northern Ireland: ☎028/9032 4073; Eire: ☎01/679 8833, *www.usitcampus.co.uk*

usit CAMPUS ☎020/7730 8111, *www.usitcampus.co.uk*

USA AND CANADA
Access America ☎1-800/284-8300, *www.accessamerica.com*
Carefree Travel Insurance ☎1-800/323-3149, *www.carefreetravel.com*
Desjardins Travel Insurance (Canada only) ☎1-800/463-7830, *www.avdl.com*
STA Travel ☎1-800/777-0112 or 212/627-3111, *www.statravel.com*
Travel Guard ☎1-800/826-1300, *www.noelgroup.com*
Travel Insurance Services ☎1-800/937-1387, *www.travelinsure.com*

and isn't covered, and make sure the per-article limit will cover your most valuable possession. Note that very few insurers will arrange on-the-spot payments in the event of a major expense or loss; you will usually be reimbursed only after going home. In all cases of **loss** or **theft** of goods, you will have to contact the local **police** to have a **report** made out so that your insurer can process the claim; for **medical claims**, you'll need to provide supporting bills. Keep photocopies of everything you send to the insurer and note any time period within which you must lodge claims.

BRITISH AND IRISH COVER

In Britain and **Ireland**, travel insurance schemes (from around £23 a month) are sold by many **travel agents**, **banks** and by **specialist insurance companies**. Policies issued by Campus Travel or STA, Endsleigh Insurance, Frizzell Insurance, usit CAMPUS or Columbus Travel Insurance are all good value. Columbus also do an annual multitrip Europe-wide policy which offers twelve months' basic cover for £49.

US AND CANADIAN COVER

Before buying an insurance policy, check that you're not already covered. **Canadian provincial health plans** typically provide some overseas medical coverage, while holders of official **student/teacher/youth cards** are entitled to accident coverage and hospital inpatient benefits.

Students may also find that their **student health coverage** extends during the vacations and for one term beyond the date of last enrolment. **Bank and credit cards** (particularly American Express) often provide certain levels of medical or other insurance, and travel insurance may also be included if you use a major credit or charge card to pay for your trip. **Homeowners' or renters' insurance** often covers theft or loss of documents, money and valuables while overseas.

After exhausting the possibilities above, you might want to contact a **specialist travel insurance company**; your travel agent can usually recommend one, or see the box overleaf. The best **premiums** are usually to be had through student/youth travel agencies – the current rates for STA policies, for example, are $35 (7 days); $55 (8–15 days); $115 (1 month); $180 (2 months); plus $55 for each extra month.

AUSTRALIAN AND NEW ZEALAND COVER

Travel insurance is available from most **travel agents** or direct from **insurance companies** by phone or over the Internet. Most policies are similar in premium and coverage, although they're generally cheaper when purchased over the Internet: a typical policy covering medical costs, lost baggage and personal liability for Scandinavia will start at about A$100/NZ$110 for two weeks, A$170/NZ$190 for one month; add about A$30/NZ$40 for insurance bought over the counter.

INFORMATION AND MAPS

Before you leave, it's worth contacting the national tourist boards for free maps, timetables, accommodation listings and brochures – though don't go mad, since much of what you'll need can easily be obtained later in Scandinavia.

TOURIST OFFICES

Once in Scandinavia, every town (and even some villages) has a **tourist office**, where you can pick up free town plans and information, brochures and other bumph. Many book private rooms (sometimes youth hostel beds), rent bikes, sell local dis-

SCANDINAVIA ONLINE

Abba

www.abbasite.com

Official shrine to Stockholm's fab four, with picture galleries, sound clips and assorted Eurovision trivia.

City.net

www.city.net/countries

Click on your country for easy-to-use introductions to all of Scandinavia's larger towns and cities, with up-to-the minute weather reports and masses of other useful info.

Denmark

www.visitdenmark.com

Official homepage of the Danish Tourist Board, featuring reams of practical and cultural information, attractively presented. For Copenhagen, have a look at *www.woco.dk*, the stylish site of the Wonderful Copenhagen office.

Finland

www.finland-tourism.com

Bundles of Finnish info in a functional layout. For Helsinki, check out *www.hel.fi/english*, a comprehensive city site with maps, timetables and listings.

Lego

www.lego.com

Lots of games, virtual plastic bricks and information about the original Legoland at Billund, Denmark.

Norway

www.visitnorway.com

Links to all things Norwegian. The less tourist-oriented *www.norway.org* is also a good source of general information and links. There's a decent Oslo city site at *www.oslopro.no*.

Sami

www.itv.se/boreale/samieng.htm

Comprehensive introduction to the Sami people and their culture, with features on history, music, art and reindeer.

Santa Claus

www.santaclausoffice.fi

Email Santa directly at his office in Finnish Lapland.

Saunas

www.sauna.fi

Home of the Finnish Sauna Society, with indispensible practical advice on sauna dos and don'ts.

Scandinavia

www.goscandinavia.com

General introduction to Scandinavia, with links to individual country sites.

Sweden

www.visitsweden.com

Links to Swedish tourist, transport and accommodation resources, with a useful search engine. For Stockholm, *www.whattodo.com* has good listings and other info

Yahoo!

www.yahoo.com/regional_information/countries

Over ten thousand links, clearly labelled, to Scandinavian sites.

count cards and change money. During summer, they're open daily until late evening; out of high season, shop hours are more usual, and in winter they're sometimes closed at weekends. You'll find full details of individual offices throughout the text.

MAPS

The **maps** in this book should be adequate for most purposes, but drivers, cyclists and hikers will require something more detailed. Tourist offices often give out reasonable road maps and town plans, but anything better you'll have to buy. There's a list of specialist map shops in the box overleaf.

For **Scandinavia** as a whole, Kümmerley & Frey produce a road map on a scale of 1:1,000,000; Rand McNally produce a good road atlas of Scandinavia. For really detailed plans of the **capital cities**, the fold-out Falk maps are excellent and easy to use.

MAP OUTLETS

AUSTRALIA AND NEW ZEALAND
Map Land, 372 Little Bourke St, Melbourne (☎03/9670 4383).

The Map Shop, 16a Peel St, Adelaide (☎08/8231 2033).

Map World, 371 Pitt St, Sydney (☎02/9261 3601).

Perth Map Centre, 884 Hay St, Perth (☎09/9322 5733).

Speciality Maps, 58 Albert St, Auckland (☎09/307 2217).

Travel Bookshop, Shop 3, 175 Liverpool St, Sydney (☎02/9261 8200).

Worldwide Maps and Guides, 187 George St, Brisbane (☎07/3221 4330).

BRITAIN
Daunt Books, 83 Marylebone High St, London W1 (☎020/7224 2295).

John Smith and Sons, 57–61 St Vincent St, Glasgow G2 5TB (☎0141/221 7472).

National Map Centre, 22–24 Caxton St, London SW1 (☎020/7222 2466).

Stanfords, 12–14 Long Acre, London WC2 (☎020/7836 1321); smaller outlets at 52 Grosvenor Gardens, London SW1W 0AG and 156 Regent St, London W1R 5TA. Online orders at *www.stanfords.co.uk*.

The Travel Bookshop, 13–15 Blenheim Crescent, London W11 2EE (☎020/7229 5260). Online orders at *www.thetravelbookshop.co.uk*.

CANADA
International Travel Maps & Books, 552 Seymour St, Vancouver, BC V6B 3J5 (☎604/687-3320, *www.itmb.com*).

Open Air Books and Maps, 25 Toronto St, Toronto, ON M5C 2R1 (☎1-800/360-9185 or 416/363-0719).

Ulysses Travel Bookshop, 4176 St-Denis, Montréal, PQ H2W 2M5 (☎514/843-9447, *www.ulysses.ca*).

IRELAND
Easons Bookshop, 80 Middle Abbey St, Dublin 1 (☎01/873 3811).

Fred Hanna's Bookshop, 27–29 Nassau St, Dublin 2 (☎01/677 1255).

Waterstones, Queens Building, 8 Royal Ave, Belfast BT1 1DA (☎028/9024 7355).

USA
The ADC Map and Travel Center, 1636 I St NW, Washington, DC 20006 (☎1-800/544-2659 or 202/628-2608).

Book Passage, 51 Tamal Vista Blvd, Corte Madera, CA 94925 (☎1-800/999-7909 or 415/927-0960, *www.bookpassage.com*).

The Complete Traveler Bookstore, 3207 Fillmore St, San Francisco, CA 94123 (☎415/923-1511, *www.completetraveler.com*).

The Complete Traveller Bookstore, 199 Madison Ave, New York, NY 10016 (☎212/685-9007).

Elliott Bay Book Company, 101 S Main St, Seattle, WA 98104 (☎1-800/962-5311 or 206/624-6600, *www.elliottbaybook.com*).

Map Link Inc., 30 S La Patera Lane, Unit 5, Santa Barbara, CA 93117 (☎805/692-6777, *www.maplink.com*).

Phileas Fogg's Books & Maps, #87 Stanford Shopping Center, Palo Alto, CA 94304 (☎1-800/533-FOGG, *www.foggs.com*).

Rand McNally (☎1-800/234-0679 for nearest branch and direct mail order, *www.randmcnally.com*), 444 N Michigan Ave, Chicago, IL 60611 (☎312/321-1751); 150 E 52nd St, New York, NY 10022 (☎212/758-7488); 595 Market St, San Francisco, CA 94105 (☎415/777-3131); plus branches nationwide.

Travel Books & Language Center, 4437 Wisconsin Ave, Washington, DC 20016 (☎1-800/220-2665).

Sierra Club Bookstore, 6014 College Ave, Oakland, CA 94618 (☎510/658-7470, *www.sierraclubbookstore.com*).

For individual countries, maps of **Denmark** are produced by Kümmerley & Frey (1:300,000), Ravenstein (1:500,000), and Baedeker (1:400,000); **Finland** is covered by Kümmerley & Frey (1:1,000,000). For **Norway**, you're best off with the Kümmerley & Frey (1:1,000,000) or the Roger Lascelles 1:800,000 map, which also has a place name index. For **Sweden** as a whole,

the best maps are produced by Terrac and Hallwag.

If you're staying in one area for a long time, or are **hiking**, you'll need something more detailed still – a minimum scale of 1:400,000; much larger (1:50,000) if you're doing any serious trekking. The larger tourist offices also sometimes have decent hiking maps of the local area. For **Norway**, the

NATIONAL TOURIST BOARD OFFICES

AUSTRALIA
No tourist board office, but the various embassies (see p.20) handle tourist information.

BRITAIN
Denmark: 55 Sloane St, London SW1 (☎020/7259 5958); **Norway**: Charles House, 5–11 Lower Regent St, London SW1 (☎020/7839 2650); **Sweden**: 11 Montagu Place, London W1 (☎020/7724 5868); **Finland**: 30–35 Pall Mall, London SW1 (☎020/7839 4048).

CANADA
Contact the tourist board in the USA.

IRELAND
No tourist board office, but the embassies (see p.20) handle tourist information.

NEW ZEALAND
Again, the embassies (see p.20) supply tourist information.

USA
Scandinavian Tourist Board, 655 3rd Ave, New York, NY 10017 (☎212/885-9700).

1:400,000 Kümmerley & Frey regional maps are very good, while the government agency, Statens Kartverk, produce a series of high-quality 1:50,000 maps covering the entire country: these are widely available from tourist offices and bookshops, and also from the national hiking organization, DNT, Stortingsgate 28, Oslo. For **Sweden** there's the 1:300,000 Esselte Kartor series and the 1:400,000 Kartförlaget series; Sweden's hiking organization, STF, can be contacted at Box 25, S-101 20 Stockholm. In **Finland**, Kümmerley & Frey produce a number of regional maps of Finland at a scale of 1:400,000; the best source of hiking maps is Aleksi, Unioninkatu 32, Helsinki. The provinces of **Denmark** are covered by the 1:200,000 Kort og Matrykelstyren series.

GETTING AROUND

Public transport systems are good throughout Scandinavia. Denmark, Norway, Sweden and Finland have a fairly comprehensive rail network which runs as far north
as it dares before plentiful buses take over. Fjords and inordinate amounts of water – lakes, rivers and open sea – make ferries a major form of transport too.

For further information see each country's individual "Getting Around" section, and the "Travel Details" at the end of every chapter.

RAIL PASSES

Nowhere does travel come cheap, but a number of **passes** can ease the burden. If you're travelling to and around the region by train, the InterRail or Eurail passes (see "Getting there", p.6 and p.15) can cut costs. If you're planning to travel by train only within Scandinavia itself, it's well worth considering a **ScanRail** pass, which covers all four countries and is available to all, although you'll have to buy it before you leave home (for details of outlets in the UK and Ireland, North

America and Australasia, see p.7, p15 and p.19 respectively). The regular ScanRail pass is available for travel on any five days in a fifteen-day period (adult £139/US$187; under-26s £105/US$140), any ten days in a month (adult £187/US$301; youth £141/US$226) and 21 consecutive days (adult £212/US$340; youth £160/US$256). Over-60s get a discount of about fifteen percent on the full price of the pass. There's also an eight-day **ScanRail Drive Pass**, which allows five days of train travel and three days of car rental, with the option of adding additional car days. Note that a small supplement is charged for certain inter-city, express trains.

The pass also gives 50 percent discount on a number of ferry routes. You need to buy it before leaving home: see the "Getting There" sections for addresses of train ticket and specialist agents.

Another possibility is the **EuroDomino Pass** (only available to those who have been resident in Europe for six months), valid for between three and eight days, which offers unlimited train travel within any one of 25 European countries including Sweden, Denmark, Finland and Norway. Like

the ScanRail pass, you'll have to buy it before you leave home. You have to buy a separate pass for each country, which comes in under-26 standard-class, over-26 standard-class and first-class versions, with varying prices for different countries. Denmark is the cheapest, with three days' travel within a month costing £49/59/119 (under-26/over-26/first class), eight days £89/109/179. Sweden is the most expensive, with three days costing £99/119/159, eight days £159/199/259. The prices for Finland and Norway fall somewhere between.

FLIGHTS

Internal Scandinavian **flights** can be a surprisingly good bargain, and may save a great deal of time, particularly if you're heading for the far-northern reaches. During the summer – usually July and the early part of August – SAS usually has cheap set-price tickets to anywhere in mainland Scandinavia except Finland, plus other discounts for families and young people. Contact SAS offices in Denmark, Norway and Sweden for

CAR RENTAL FIRMS

AUSTRALIA
Avis ☎1800/225 533 or 136333, *www.avis.com*
Budget ☎1300/362 848, *www.budget.com.au*
Hertz ☎1800/550 067 or 133039,
www.hertz.com

BRITAIN
Avis ☎0990/900 500, *www.avis.co.uk*
Budget ☎0800/181 181, *www.budget.com*
Europcar/InterRent ☎0345/222 525,
www.europcar.co.uk
Hertz ☎0990/996 699, *www.hertz.co.uk*
Holiday Autos ☎0990/300 400,
www.holidayautos.co.uk
National Car ☎01895/233 300,
www.nationalcar-europe.com

IRELAND
Avis ☎01/605 7500, *www.avis.co.uk*
Budget Rent-A-Car ☎01/837 9611,
www.budget.com

Europcar ☎01/874 5844, *www.europcar.co.uk*
Hertz ☎01/660 2255, *www.hertz.co.uk*
Holiday Autos ☎01/454 9090,
www.holidayautos.co.uk

NEW ZEALAND
Avis ☎09/526 2847, *www.avis.com*
Budget ☎09/375 2222, *www.budget.co.nz*
Hertz ☎09/309 0989 or 0800/655 955,
www.hertz.com

NORTH AMERICA
Auto Europe ☎1-800/223-5555,
www.autoeurope.com
Avis ☎1-800/331-1084, *www.avis.com*
Budget ☎1-800/527-0700,
www.drivebudget.com
Europcar ☎1-800/800-6000, *www.europcar.com*
Hertz US ☎1-800/654-3001, Canada ☎1-800/263-0600, *www.hertz.com*
Kemwel Holiday Autos ☎1-800/422-7737,
www.kemwel.com

[For addresses of car rental firms in Scandinavia, see the "Listings" sections of major cities.]

the latest deals – they're detailed under "Listings" in the accounts of the capital cities. Also. check out the **air passes** on offer before leaving home (see "Getting there" p.3, p.15 and p.18 for details of outlets and offers in, respectively, the UK and Ireland, North America, and Australasia).

CAR RENTAL

Car rental is pricey, although some tourist offices do arrange summer deals which can bring the cost down a little. On the whole, expect to pay at least £350/US$480 a week for a small car plus

fuel; see each country's "Getting Around" section for specific prices and details of rules of the road and documentation.

You may well find it cheaper, especially if you're travelling from North America, to arrange car hire before you go; airlines sometimes have special deals with rental companies if you book your flight and car through them. Alternatively, if you don't want to be tied down, try an agency such as Holiday Autos, who will arrange advance booking through a local agent and can usually undercut the big companies considerably (see the box opposite for phone numbers).

ACCOMMODATION

Accommodation is going to be your major daily expense in Scandinavia. If you plan ahead, however, there are a number of ways you can avoid paying over the (already high) odds. Youth hostels, campsites and cabins are the obvious budget options, and not just for tourists – they're popular with Scandinavians, too. There's also a series of discount passes available, for use in hotel chains all over Scandinavia.

HOTELS

Scandinavian **hotels** aren't as expensive as you might think; certainly not if you compare them with equivalent accommodation in, say, London or New York. Lots of Scandinavian hotels, usually dependent on business travellers, drop their prices drastically at weekends and during the summer holiday period, so it's always worth enquiring in the tourist office about special local

deals. The major cities also feature cheap "packages", usually involving a night's hotel accommodation and a free city discount card. More details, and a guide to prices, are given under each country's "Accommodation" section, as well as under the specific town and city accounts.

In addition, some Scandinavia-wide hotel chains operate a discount or **hotel cheque system** which you can organize before you leave. You either purchase cheques in advance, redeemable against a night's accommodation in any hotel belonging to the particular chain, or you buy a **hotel pass** which entitles you to a hefty discount on normal room rates. There are a bewildering number of schemes available, but most only operate from June to September and all offer basically the same deal: consult your travel agent, or one of the national tourist boards.

YOUTH HOSTELS

Joining the **Hostelling International** (HI) association gives you access to what is sometimes the only budget accommodation available in Scandinavia. Non-members can use most of the hostels but will pay slightly more – the difference may add up to a sizeable sum over a couple of weeks considering the low cost of annual membership. You'll also need a **sheet sleeping bag**, the only kind allowed in HI hostels. They can either be rented at the hostels or bought at camping shops; alternatively, you can simply stitch a

YOUTH HOSTEL ASSOCIATIONS

AUSTRALIA
Australian Youth Hostels Association, Level 3, 10 Mallett St, Camperdown, NSW 2050 (☎02/9565 1699, *www.yha.org.au*). A$47 for first year's membership, A$29 yearly thereafter.

CANADA
Hostelling International/Canadian Hostelling Association, Room 400, 205 Catherine St, Ottawa, ON K2P 1C3 (☎613/237-7884 or 1-800/663-5777, *www.hostellingintl.ca*). Annual membership costs CDN$25 for adults, CDN$12 for under-18s.

ENGLAND AND WALES
Youth Hostel Association (YHA), Trevelyan House, 8 St Stephen's Hill, St Alban's, Herts AL1 2DY (☎01727/855 215, *www.yha.org.uk*). London information office: 14 Southampton St, London WC2 7HY (☎020/7379 0597). Annual membership £11.

IRELAND
Youth Hostel Association of Northern Ireland, 22–32 Donegall Rd, Belfast BT12 5JN

(☎028/9032 4733); **An Oige**, 61 Mountjoy St, Dublin 7 (☎01/830 4555). Annual membership costs £8 in Northern Ireland, IR£10 in the Republic.

NEW ZEALAND
New Zealand Youth Hostels Association of New Zealand, PO Box 436, Christchurch (☎03/379 9970, *www.yha.co.nz*). Annual membership NZ$40.

SCOTLAND
Scottish Youth Hostel Association, 7 Glebe Crescent, Stirling FK8 2JA (☎01786/891 400). Annual membership £6.

USA
Hostelling International-American Youth Hostels (HI-AYH), 733 15th St NW, Suite 840, Washington, DC 20005 (☎202/783-6161, *www.hiayh.org*). Annual membership adults US$25, over-55s US$15, under-17s free.

---

couple of old sheets together and take a pillowcase. If you're planning to cook for yourself using youth hostel kitchens, bear in mind that many don't provide pots, pans and utensils – take at least the basic equipment with you.

You can join Hostelling International either at home (for addresses, see box above) or in Scandinavia itself (the addresses of the relevant national hostelling organizations are given in each country's "Accommodation" section). For a complete listing of Scandinavian hostels, consult *Hostelling International: Europe and the Mediterranean*.

CAMPING

Camping is hugely popular in Scandinavia. Further details are given in each country's "Accommodation" section, but a number of points common to all the countries of the region are worth noting. In order to use certain sites you may need a camping carnet, which you can buy at the first site you visit; camping rough is, with certain exceptions, legal in Norway and Sweden; and most campsites have furnished **cabins**, though if you intend to use these take a sleeping bag, as bedding is not usually provided.

POLICE AND CRIME

Scandinavia is one of the most peaceful corners of Europe. You will find that most public places are well lit and secure, most people genuinely friendly and helpful, and street crime and hassle relatively rare.

PETTY CRIME AND MINOR OFFENCES

It would be foolish, however, to assume that problems don't exist. The capital cities have their share of **petty crime**, fuelled by a growing number of drug addicts and alcoholics after easy money. Keep tabs on your cash and passport (and don't leave anything visible in your car when you leave it) and you should have little reason to visit the **police**. If you do, you'll find them courteous, concerned, and, most importantly, usually able to speak English. If you have something stolen, make sure you get a **police report** – essential if you are to make an insurance claim.

As for **offences** you might commit, **nude sunbathing** is universally accepted in all the major resorts (elsewhere there'll be no one around to care); and **camping rough** is a tradition enshrined in law in Norway and Sweden, and tolerated in Finland, though in Denmark it's more difficult. Being **drunk** on the streets can get you arrested, and **drinking and driving** is treated especially rigorously. **Drug** offences, too, meet with the same harsh attitude that prevails throughout the rest of Europe.

SEXUAL HARASSMENT & THE WOMEN'S MOVEMENT

In general, the social and economic position of women in Scandinavia is more advanced than in almost all other European countries – something which becomes obvious after a short time there. Many women are in traditionally male occupations, and sexual harassment is less of a problem than elsewhere in Europe.

You can walk almost everywhere in comparative comfort and safety, and although in the capital cities you can expect to receive occasional unwelcome attentions, it's very rarely with any kind of violent intent. Needless to say, travelling alone on the underground systems in Copenhagen, Oslo, Stockholm and Helsinki late at night is unwise. If you do have any problems, the fact that almost everyone understands English makes it easy to get across an unambiguous response.

WOMEN'S ORGANIZATIONS

Denmark's women's movement is in a state of flux: the once prominent *Rødstrømper* (Red Stockings) – the Radical Feminists – are now less active. But there are lots of feminist groups around the country, and in Copenhagen a couple of active women's centres: Dannerhuset, Nansersgade 1 (☎33 14 16 76), and Kvindehuset, Gothersgade 37 (☎33 14 28 04).

Norway's women's movement is highly developed, assisted by progressive government and a 1986–89 Labour administration led by a woman, Dr Gro Harlem Brundtland, which endeavoured to even out parliamentary representation by promoting women into the cabinet. Contacts in Oslo can be made through the Norsk Kvinnesaksforening (☎22 60 42 27).

In **Sweden**, the women's movement is also strongly developed, riding on the back of the social-welfare reforms introduced by the Social Democratic governments of the last forty years. You'll find women's centres in most major towns, such as Grupp 8 at Snickarbacken 10, Stockholm, an active socialist-feminist group.

The women's movement in **Finland** is lagging behind the rest of Scandinavia, and there have been fewer reforms to benefit the lot of women over the years. The major feminist organization,

Unioni, first established in 1892 in Helsinki, is the best place for up-to-date information (Bulevardi 11A; ☎09 64 31 58; closed mid-June to July).

GAY SCANDINAVIA

Scandinavia comprises some of the most liberated and tolerant countries in Europe. Gays are rarely discriminated against in law, and the age of consent is almost uniformly the same as for heterosexuals – usually fifteen or sixteen. However, in all four mainland countries you'll not find much of a scene outside the capitals.

ATTITUDES AND THE LAW

Denmark used to have a reputation for being the gay pornography capital of the world, and although this is no longer so, there is a very good gay scene in Copenhagen. As far as the law goes, in 1989 the Danish parliament voted to make a form of homosexual marriage legal, and it has continued to investigate other ways of eliminating discrimination against gays. For more information contact the Landsforeningen for Bøsser og Lebiske, in Copenhagen at Teglgårdsstræde 13 (☎33 13 19 48), or in Århus at Jægergårdsgade 42 (☎86 13 19 48). They also maintain a Web site at *www.lbl.dk*.

Norway was one of the first countries in the world – in 1981 – to pass a law making discrimi-

nation against homosexuals illegal, and Norwegian society is reasonably tolerant of homosexuality. There is a strong and effective gay and lesbian organization, with a national HQ in Oslo (LLH, PO Box 68, 38 St Olavsplass; ☎22 36 19 48, fax 22 11 47 45) and branches throughout the country.

In **Sweden** gay marriage is now legal. However, there are very few gay bars, and gay saunas and video shops with cubicles have been outlawed since mid-1987. The national organization, the RFSL, can be contacted at Sveavägen 57–59, 10126 Stockholm (☎08/736 02 13, fax 30 47 30, *www.rfsl.se*).

From a legal point of view, there is some discrimination against gays in **Finland**. The country's penal code forbids the public encouragement of homosexuality, although nobody has ever been convicted for breaking the anti-gay laws. SETA (Organization for Sexual Equality in Finland), at Hietalahdenkatu 16, 3rd floor, Helsinki (☎09/612 3233, *www.seta.fi*), can provide further information – on Helsinki and elsewhere – and publishes a bimonthly nationwide magazine; during the summer they also print useful pages of information in English for foreign visitors to Helsinki.

TRAVELLERS WITH DISABILITIES

Scandinavia is, in many ways, a model of awareness for the disabled traveller: wheelchair access, other facilities and help are generally available at hotels, hostels, museums and public places. Getting there, too, is getting easier: DFDS ferries have specially adapted cabins, and Silja Line offer discounts for disabled passengers.

PLANNING A HOLIDAY

There are **organized tours and holidays** specifically for people with disabilities – the contacts in the box below will be able to put you in touch with specialists for trips to Scandinavia. It's important to know where you may expect help

and where you must be self-reliant, especially regarding transportation and accommodation. It's also vital to be honest with travel agencies, insurance companies and travel companions. It's worth thinking about your limitations and making sure others know them, too. If you don't use a wheelchair all the time but your walking capabilities are limited, remember that you are likely to need to cover greater distances while travelling (sometimes over rougher terrain and in hotter/colder temperatures than you are used to. If you use a wheelchair, it is always wise to have it serviced before you go and carry a repair kit.

People with a pre-existing medical condition are sometimes excluded from travel **insurance policies**, so read the small print carefully. To

TRAVELLERS WITH DISABILITIES

AUSTRALIA AND NEW ZEALAND

Barrier Free Travel, 36 Wheatley St, North Eellingen, NSW 2454 (☎02/6655 1733).

DPA (Disabled Persons Assembly), Level 4 Wellington Trade Centre, 173–175 Victoria St; PO Box 27–524 Wellington (☎04/801 9100).

Wheelchair Travel, 29 Ranelagh Drive, Mt Eliza, VIC 3930 (☎1800/674 468 or 03/9787 8861, www.travelability.com).

BRITAIN

Access Travel, 6 The Hillock, Astley, Lancs M29 7GW (☎01942/888844, fax 891811). The sole licensed UK tour operator dealing specifically with travellers with disabilities.

Holiday Care Service, 2nd floor, Imperial Building, Victoria Rd, Horley, Surrey RH6 7PZ (☎01293/774 535, fax 784 647. Minicom 776 943, holiday.care@virgin.net).

RADAR (Royal Association for Disability and Rehabilitation), 12 City Forum, 250 City Rd, London EC1V 8AF (☎020/7250 3222, Minicom 7250 4119). A good source of advice on holidays and travel abroad.

Tripscope, The Courtyard, Evelyn Rd, London W4 5JL (☎020/8994 9294, fax 8994 3618, Minicom ☎0845/758 5641, tripscope@cableinet.co.uk). Information service offering free advice on UK and international transport for those with limited mobility.

IRELAND

Disability Action Group, 2 Annadale Ave, Belfast BT7 3JH (☎028/9049 1011).

Irish Wheelchair Association, Blackheath Drive, Clontarf, Dublin (☎01/833 8241, fax 833 3873, iwa@iol.ie).

US AND CANADA

Mobility International USA, PO Box 10767, Eugene, OR 97440 (voice & TDD ☎541/343-1284, www.miusa.org). Their Web site has useful travel tips and listings of disabled-friendly accommodation and sights, plus information on foreign exchange programmes for the disabled.

Society for the Advancement of Travel for the Handicapped (SATH), 347 5th Ave, Suite 610, New York. NY 10016 (☎212/447-7284, www.sittravel.com). Non-profit travel-industry referral service that passes queries on to its members as appropriate; allow plenty of time for a response.

Travel Information Service (☎215/456-9603). Telephone information and referral service.

Twin Peaks Press, PO Box 129, Vancouver, WA 98666 (☎360/694-2462 or 1-800/637-2256). Publisher of the *Directory of Travel Agencies for the Disabled*, listing more than 370 agencies worldwide; *Travel for the Disabled*; the *Directory of Accessible Van Rentals* and *Wheelchair Vagabond*, loaded with personal tips.

make your journey simpler, ask your travel agent to notify airlines or bus companies, who can cope better if they are expecting you. A **medical certificate** of your fitness to travel, provided by your doctor, is also extremely useful; some airlines or insurance companies may insist on it. Make sure that you have extra supplies of drugs – carried with you if you fly – and a prescription including the generic name in case of emergency. Carry spares of any clothing or equipment that might be hard to find; if there's an association representing people with your disability, contact them early in the planning process.

FACILITIES IN SCANDINAVIA

In **Denmark**, facilities are generally outstanding. The Danish Tourist Board (see p.27 for addresses) publishes the comprehensive 100-page *Access in Denmark – a Travel Guide for the Disabled*, which covers everything from airports to zoos.

The **Norwegian** Tourist Board uses the wheelchair symbol throughout its publications to denote accessibility. Transport is not too much of a problem: Norwegian State Railways have special carriages on most main routes with wheelchair space, hydraulic lifts and a disabled toilet;

new ships on the Hurtigrute Coastal Express route have lifts and cabins for disabled people; and new fjord ferries also have lifts from the car deck to the lounge and toilets. According to Norwegian law, all new public buildings must be accessible to disabled people. For further information, contact the Norwegian Association of the Disabled, PO Box 9217, Gronland, N-0134 Oslo (☎22 17 02 55, fax 22 17 61 77).

In **Sweden**, many hotels are provided with specially adapted rooms, and camping-cabin holidays are not beyond wheelchair users either, as some chalet-villages have cabins with wheelchair access. The Stockholm T-bana system has elevators at most stations, and there are specially converted minivans and taxis for hire. A useful holiday guide with more information is available from Swedish tourist offices, or contact the Swedish Federation of Disabled Persons (DHR), Katrinebergsvägen 6, S-117 43 Stockholm (☎08/18 91 00, fax 645 65 41).

Finland is as welcoming to the disabled traveller as the other Scandinavian countries. The Finnish Tourist Board issues a free leaflet, *Tourist Services for the Disabled*, giving a brief overview of facilities; further information can be obtained from Mr Jens Gellin, Rullaten ry, Vartiokyläntie 9, 00950 Helsinki (☎09/322 069).

OUTDOOR ACTIVITIES

Scandinavia is a wonderful place if you love the great outdoors, with great hiking, fishing and, of course, skiing opportunities. Best of all you won't find the countryside overcrowded – there's plenty of space to get away from it all, especially in the north. As you might expect, any kind of hunting is forbidden without a permit, and fishing usually requires a special licence, available from local tourist offices.

HIKING

Scandinavia offers the ultimate in hiking experiences – a landscape of rugged mountains, icy glaciers and deep green fjords, much of it far from the nearest road. Many of the best hiking areas have been set aside as **national parks**, with information centres, lodges and huts dotted along well-

marked trails. Huts are usually run by national or local hiking organizations, and you will have to become a member to be able to use them. See "Maps and Information" p.26 for map suppliers, and note also that **tourist offices** in the hiking areas supply maps and leaflets describing local routes. Where hiking routes are covered in the Guide we've listed the best source of local information. It's essential to plan your route thoroughly before setting out, taking into account weather conditions, and not to overestimate what you can manage in the time. In many areas solo hiking is advised against strongly.

As far as **equipment** goes, for day walking you'll need warm clothing and gloves, waterproofs, and sun and mosquito protection; on all but the easiest and shortest hikes, a compass is a good idea – as long as you know how to use it. For long-distance treks you'll also need a sleeping bag, medical kit and a torch, plus a pair of sturdy, comfortable boots. Note that Camping Gaz is only available from selected outlets in Scandinavia – details from national tourist boards – so take your own supply. For hiking campers, a plastic survival bag keeps you and your pack dry. And take a torch.

Especially if you're planning to camp, you should be aware of some specific **ground rules**. The landscape is there for everyone's use and camping rough is legal much of the time – but the Scandinavians are concerned to protect the environment both from the damage caused by excessive tourism and the potential disasters that can result from ignorance or thoughtlessness.

Don't **light fires** anywhere other than at designated spots – and even these shouldn't be used in times of drought. **Tents** may only be placed on marked sites or, on some hikes, in other designated areas. When camping, do not break tree branches or leave **rubbish**; and try not to disturb nesting **birds**, especially in the spring.

In the northern reaches of Scandinavia, be wary of frightening **reindeer herds**, since if they scatter it can mean several extra days' work for the herder; also, avoid tramping over moss-covered stretches of moorland – the reindeer's staple diet. **Picking flowers, berries and mushrooms** is also usually prohibited in the north. If you are going to pick and eat anything, however, it's a wise idea, post-Chernobyl, to check on the latest advice from the authorities – tourist offices should know the score.

Glaciers are slow-moving masses of ice in constant, if normally imperceptible, motion, and are therefore potentially dangerous. Never climb a glacier without a guide, never walk under one and always heed the instructions at the site. Guided crossings can be terrific; local tourist offices and hiking organizations have details – see the relevant accounts in the Guide.

WINTER SPORTS

Aside from the cities, which maintain their usual roster of activities and attractions, though sometimes with reduced opening hours, the big incentive for coming to Scandinavia in winter is the range of **winter sports** available – from ice fishing to dog-sledging. Although you're not likely to come on a skiing package to Scandinavia (it's nearly always cheaper to go to other European resorts), it's easy to arrange a few days **cross-country skiing** wherever you are – even in Oslo and Stockholm there are ski runs within the city boundaries, and plenty of places to rent equipment.

WORK

Norway, Sweden and Finland in particular are extremely suspicious of potential foreign workers, and you may have to prove

on entry that you are not there to seek work (by showing return tickets and sufficient cash, for instance). The chances of finding casual work are, in any case, decidedly slim.

THE PAPERWORK

If you're serious about **working**, and an EU citizen, **Denmark** and **Sweden** are the best options, though for other than relatively low-paid bar/restaurant/hotel work you really need to speak the language. You can stay for up to three months while you look for work, and, if you find it, a residence permit should be granted. Fast-food restaurants and larger hotels have a fairly high turnover of foreign staff, and private employment agencies can sometimes place unskilled foreign workers. Non-EU citizens are not allowed to look for work after arriving and need to set up employment before leaving home.

OTHER OPTIONS

The best-paid opportunity to live and work in Scandinavia for a short period is by **working on a farm**. You live with a farming family, work incredibly hard and receive board and lodging and pocket money in return. Vacancies are usually for the spring and summer, although some jobs stay open for a full year. Serious vacancies (ie for young farmers and/or people with experience) are dealt with by the International Farm Experience Programme, YFC Centre, National Agricultural Centre, Kenilworth, Warwickshire CV8 2LG. For summer farm work (no experience necessary), 18- to 30-year-olds should contact the Norwegian Youth Council (Landsradet for Norske Ungdomsorganisasjoner), Working Guest Programme, Rolf Hofmosgate 18, Oslo 6, Norway (apply by April 15).

If you would like to do **voluntary work** in mainland Scandinavia, send an SAE to International Voluntary Service, Ceresole House, 53 Regent Rd, Leicester LE1 6YL. They organize international work camps two to three weeks long, with food and accommodation provided. You must be at least 18 and pay your own travel expenses. In the USA, contact the Council on International Educational Exchange, 205 E 42nd St, New York, NY 10017 (☎1-888/COUNCIL or 212/822-2600) or check their Web site (*www.councilexchanges.org*).

INFORMATION

For more information about working in Scandinavia – paid or voluntary – consult the series of books published in Britain by Vacation Work – *The International Directory of Voluntary Work*, *Summer Jobs Abroad* and *Work Your Way Around the World* – all of which have sections on the Scandinavian countries.

BOOKS

There are surprisingly few books on Scandinavia in English: few travellers have written well (or indeed at all) about the region, and historical or political works tend to concentrate almost exclusively on the Vikings.

However, more and more Scandinavian literature is appearing in translation – notably the Icelandic Sagas and selected modern novelists – and it's always worth looking out for a c.1900 *Baedeker's Norway and Sweden*, if only for the phrasebook, from which you can learn the Swedish and Norwegian for "When does the washerwoman come?" and "We must tie our-

selves together with rope to cross this glacier."

Of the publishers, Peter Owen and Forest Books regularly produce fine new translations of modern Scandinavian novels. Norvik Press, too, is a good source of new translations of old and new Scandinavian writing; for their catalogue write to them at EUR/University of East Anglia, Norwich NR4 7TJ, UK. Titles go in and out of print regularly; if your library doesn't have copies, your local bookshop may be able to order them for you. Publishers in the listings below are given in the format UK/US. Where only one publisher is given, this covers both the UK and US, unless otherwise specified; o/p means out of print.

SCANDINAVIA

TRAVEL AND GENERAL

Jeremy Cherfas, *The Hunting of Whale* (o/p). Subtitled "A tragedy that must end", this is a convincing condemnation of whaling and all those – like Norway – involved in it.

Tom Cunliffe, *Topsail and Battleaxe* (Merlin Press/Sheridan House). The intertwined stories of the tenth-century Vikings who sailed from Norway, past the Faroes and Iceland to North America, and the author's parallel trip in 1983 – made in a 75-year-old pilot cutter. Enthusiastically written, with good photos.

John McCormick, *Acid Earth* (Earthscan, UK). Good for background on the burning issue of acid rain, of which the Scandinavian countries are net recipients – especially from Britain.

Christoph Ransmayr, *The Terrors of Ice and Darkness* (Grove Press, US). Clever mingling of fact and fiction as the book's main character follows the route of the 1873 Austro-Hungarian expedition to the Arctic. A story of obsession and, ultimately, madness.

Mary Wollstonecraft, *A Short Residence in Sweden, Norway and Denmark* (Penguin). A searching account of Wollstonecraft's three-month solo journey through southern Scandinavia in 1795.

HISTORY, MYTHOLOGY AND ART

Johannes Brøndsted, *The Vikings* (o/p). Classic and immensely readable account of the Viking period, with valuable sections on social and cultural life, art, religious beliefs and customs.

H.R. Ellis Davidson, *The Gods and Myths of Northern Europe* (Penguin). A handy Saga companion, this is a *Who's Who* of Norse mythology, including some useful reviews of the more obscure gods. Displaces the classical deities and their world as the most relevant mythological framework for northern and western European culture.

P.V. Glob, *The Bog People* (Faber & Faber, UK). A fascinating study of the various Iron Age bodies discovered fully preserved in northwestern European peat-bogs, most of them in Denmark. Excellent, if ghoulish, photographs.

Gwyn Jones, *A History of the Vikings* (Oxford UP). Probably the best book on the subject: a superb, thoughtful and thoroughly researched account of the Viking period.

F. Donald Logan, *The Vikings in History* (Routledge). Scholarly – and radical – re-examination of the Vikings' impact on medieval Europe, indispensable for the Viking fan.

Geoffrey Parker, *The Thirty Years' War* (Routledge). One of the more recent accounts of this turbulent period, acknowledged as an authoritative, if dry, read.

Else Roesdahl, *The Vikings* (Penguin). A lucid account of the 300-year reign of Scandinavia's most famous (and most misunderstood) cultural ambassadors, and the traces that they've left throughout northern Europe.

DENMARK

HISTORY AND PHILOSOPHY

Inga Dahlsgård, *Women in Denmark, Yesterday and Today* (o/p). A refreshing presentation of Danish history from the point of view of its women.

W. Glyn Jones, *Denmark: A Modern History* (o/p). A valuable account of the twentieth century (up until 1984), with a commendable outline of pre-twentieth-century Danish history. Strong on politics, useful on social history and the arts, but disappointingly brief on recent grassroots movements.

Søren Kierkegaard, *Either/Or* (Penguin). A new translation of Kierkegaard's most important work, packed with wry and wise musings on love, life and death in nineteenth-century Danish society; includes the (in)famous "Seducer's Diary".

Roger Poole and Henrik Stangerup (eds), *A Kierkegaard Reader* (Fourth Estate, UK). By far the best and most accessible introduction to this notoriously difficult nineteenth-century Danish philosopher and writer, with a sparkling introductory essay.

LITERATURE AND BIOGRAPHY

Hans Christian Andersen (ed. Naomi Lewis), *Hans Andersen's Fairy Tales* (Oxford UP). Still the most internationally prominent figure of Danish literature, Andersen's fairy-tales are so widely translated and read that the full clout of their allegorical content is often overlooked: interestingly, his first collection of such tales (published in 1835) was condemned for its 'violence and questionable morals". *A Visit to Germany, Italy and Malta, 1840–1841* (Peter Owen, UK) is the most enduring of his travel works, while his autobiography, *The Fairy Tale of My Life* (o/p), is a fine alternative to the numerous sycophantic portraits which have appeared since.

Steen Steensen Blicher, *Diary of a Parish Clerk; Twelve Stories* (Athlone Press). Blicher was a keen observer of Jutish life, writing stark, realistic tales in local dialect and gathering a seminal collection of Jutish folk tales – published as *E Bindstouw* in 1842.

Karen Blixen (Isak Dinesen), *Out of Africa; Letters from Africa; Seven Gothic Tales* (Penguin). *Out of Africa*, the account of Blixen's attempts to run a coffee farm in Kenya after divorce from her husband, is a lyrical and moving tale. But it's in *Seven Gothic Tales* that Blixen's fiction was at its zenith: a flawlessly executed, weird, emotive work, full of twists in plot and strange, ambiguous characterization.

Tove Ditlevsen, *Early Spring* (Seal Press). An autobiographical novel of growing up in the working-class Vesterbro district of Copenhagen during the 1930s. As an evocation of childhood and early adulthood, it's totally captivating.

Martin A. Hansen, *The Liar* (Sun & Moon Press, UK). An engaging novel, showing why Hansen was one of Denmark's most perceptive – and popular – authors during the postwar period. Set in the 1950s, the story examines the inner thoughts of a lonely schoolteacher living on a small Danish island.

Peter Høeg, *Miss Smilla's Feeling for Snow*. A worldwide bestseller (published in the US as *Miss Smilla's Sense of Snow*) (Harvill/Delta), this compelling thriller deals with Danish colonialism in Greenland and the issue of cultural identity.

Dea Trier Mørch, *Winter's Child* (Nebraska UP). A wonderfully lucid sketch of modern Denmark as seen through the eyes of several women in the maternity ward of a Copenhagen hospital. See also *Evening Star*, which deals with the effect of old age and death on a Danish family.

Judith Thurman, *Isak Dinesen: The Life of Karen Blixen* (Penguin, UK). The most penetrating biography of Blixen, elucidating details of the farm period not found in the two "Africa" books.

NORWAY

HISTORY AND SOCIOLOGY

Oddvar K. Hoidal, *Quisling: A Study in Treason* (o/p). A comprehensive biography of the twentieth century's most famous traitor, Vidkun Quisling, presented in all his unpleasant fullness.

Gwyn Jones, *The Norse Atlantic Saga* (o/p). An excellent account of the (mainly Norwegian) discovery and settlement of Iceland, Greenland and North America, interspersed with extracts from the Sagas.

Francois Kersaudy, *Norway 1940* (Bison Books, US). A short but well-informed history of the Norwegian resistance – in 1940 – to the Nazi invasion, including accounts of the British forces who helped the Norwegians in their fight.

Magnús Magnússon and Hermann Palsson (trans.), *The Vinland Sagas: The Norse Discovery of America* (Penguin/Viking). An account, in contemporary reportage, of the Viking Norwegians' discovery of North America in the tenth century.

LITERATURE AND ART

Knut Faldbakken, *The Sleeping Prince* (Peter Owen, UK). Story of the fantasy created in the mind of a middle-aged spinster as she awaits her sleeping prince – an absorbing and spirited novel by one of Norway's finest writers. Other Faldbakken novels in print include *Insect Summer* and the less accessible *Adam's Diary* (both Peter Owen, UK).

Jostein Gaarder, *Sophie's World* (Dolphin/Berkeley). Detective story meets the history of philosophy in this unusual but thoroughly enjoyable book.

Janet Garton and Henning Sehmsdorf, *New Norwegian Plays* (Dufour Editions, US). Four plays written between 1979 and 1983, including work by the feminist writer Bjørg Vik and a Brechtian analysis of Europe in the nuclear age by Edvard Hoem.

Knut Hamsun, *Hunger* (Rebel Inc./Noonday Press); *The Wanderer* (o/p); *Mysteries* (Souvenir Press/Noonday Press); *The Women at the Pump* (Souvenir Press/Sun & Moon Press); *Wayfarers* (Souvenir Press/Sun & Moon Press); *Growth of the Soil* (Souvenir Press/Random House); *Pan* (Alkin Books/Noonday Press). Hamsun's novels are enjoying a resurgence of interest after a backlash caused by his pro-Nazi sympathies during the last war. They're thoughtful, lyrical works on the whole, deliberately simple in style but with an underlying, sometimes sinister, ambivalence.

Henrik Ibsen, *Ibsen Plays*, Vols 1–6 (Heinemann). The key international figure of Norwegian literature, Ibsen was a social dramatist, keen through his characters to portray contemporary society in all its forms and hypocrisies. All his major plays are contained in this six-volume set.

Jonas Lie, *The Seer* (Forest Books/Dufour Editions). The celebrated nineteenth-century Norwegian writer – who spent over thirty years living abroad – is represented here by his first great success, the novella *The Seer*, and eight other short stories.

Øystein Lønn, *Tom Reber's Last Retreat* (Marion Boyars, US). A recent novel by one of Norway's best-known contemporary writers, examining a businessman's past and his increasingly complicated present in typically tense style.

Sigbjørn Obstfelder, *A Priest's Diary* (o/p). The last, uncompleted work of a highly regarded Norwegian poet who died of consumption in 1900 aged 33. A moodily intense piece, it forms only a segment of an ambitious work that Obstfelder intended to be his life's major undertaking.

Cora Sandel, *Alberta and Jacob; Alberta and Freedom; Alberta Alone* (Women's Press/Ohio UP). The celebrated *Alberta* trilogy follows the struggle of a young woman to prove herself in a hostile environment. With its depth of insight and contemporary detail, it ranks as a key work of twentieth-century Norwegian literature. Also available in English are Sandel's *Krane's Café* (o/p), *The Leech* (o/p) and *The Silken Thread* (Peter Owen/Ohio UP).

Amalie Skram, *Betrayed* (o/p). A psychological study of nineteenth-century sexual mores, concerning the marriage of a shy young bride to an older sea captain.

Bjørg Vik, *Aquarium of Women* (Norvik Press, UK). A collection of nine connected short stories by one of Norway's best-known feminist writers.

CRITICISM AND BIOGRAPHY

J.P. Hodin, *Edvard Munch* (Thames & Hudson). The best available general introduction to Munch's life and work, with lots of interesting historical detail.

Michael Meyer, *Ibsen on File* (o/p). The best brief introduction to Ibsen's work for the general reader. For more depth, Meyer's biography, *Ibsen* (Abacus, UK), is invaluable, and a marvellous read to boot.

SWEDEN

HISTORY AND POLITICS

Eric Elstob, *Sweden: A Traveller's History* (o/p). An introduction to Swedish history from the year dot, with useful chapters on art, architecture and cultural life.

Alan Palmer, *Bernadotte* (o/p). First English biography for over fifty years of Napoleon's marshal, later Sweden's King Karl Johan XIV. It's lively and comprehensive, though probably for enthusiasts only.

Michael Roberts, *The Early Vasas: A History of Sweden 1523–1611* (o/p). This general account of the period is complemented by Roberts' more recent *Gustavus Adolphus and the Rise of Sweden* (Addison Wesley), which, more briefly and enthusiastically, covers the period from 1612 to the king's death in 1632.

LITERATURE

Sigrid Cambüchen, *Byron* (o/p). A highly regarded Swedish literary critic, Cambüchen has taken as her starting point the exhumation of the poet Byron's body by devotees in the 1930s – developing this into a brilliantly realized biography.

Stig Dagerman, *The Games of Night* (Quartet). Intense short stories by a prolific young writer who had written four novels, four plays, short stories and travel sketches by the time he was 26. He committed suicide in 1954 at the age of 31. This is some of the best of his work.

Robert Fulton (trans.), *Preparations for Flight* (Forest Books/Dufour Editions). Eight Swedish short stories from the last 25 years, including two rare prose outings from the poet Niklas Rådström.

P.C. Jersild, *A Living Soul* (Norvik Press/Dufour Editions). Social satire based around the "experiences" of an artificially produced, bodiless human brain floating in liquid. Entertaining, provocative reading from one of Sweden's best novelists.

Sara Lidman, *Naboth's Stone* (Dufour Editions, US). A novel set in 1880s Västerbotten, in Sweden's far north, charting the lives of settlers and farmers as the industrial age – and the railway – approaches.

Agneta Pleijel, *The Dog Star* (Peter Owen/Dufour Editions). Powerful tale of a young girl's approach to puberty. One of Pleijel's finest novels, full of fantasy and emotion.

Clive Sinclair, *Augustus Rex* (o/p). August Strindberg dies in 1912 – and is then brought back to life by the Devil in 1960s Stockholm. Bawdy, imaginative and very funny treatment of Strindberg's well-documented neuroses.

Bent Söderberg, *The Mysterious Barricades* (Peter Owen/Dufour Editions). Leading Swedish novelist writes of the Mediterranean during the wars – a part of the world he's lived in for over thirty years.

Hjalmar Söderberg, *Short Stories* (Norvik Press/Dufour Editions. Twenty-six short stories from the stylish pen of Söderberg (1869–1941). Brief, ironic and eminently ripe for dipping into.

August Strindberg, *Strindberg Plays: Two* (Methuen, UK); *Strindberg Plays: Three* (Methuen, UK); *Three Plays* (Penguin); *Inferno/From an Occult Diary* (Penguin), *By the Open Sea* (Penguin/Haskell House). Strindberg is now seen as a pioneer in both his subject matter and style. His early plays were realistic in a manner not then expected of drama, and confronted themes that weren't considered suitable viewing at all, with psychological examinations of the roles of the sexes both in and out of marriage. A fantastically prolific writer, only a fraction of his sixty plays, twelve historical dramas, five novels, short stories, numerous autobiographical volumes and poetry has ever been translated into English.

CRITICISM AND BIOGRAPHY
Peter Cowie, *Ingmar Bergman* (Limelight Editions, US). New edition of a well-written and sympathetic account of the director's life and career.

Michael Meyer, *Strindberg on File* (o/p). A useful brief account of Strindberg's life and work, though for a more stirring biography the same author's *Strindberg* (o/p) is the best and most approachable source.

ART AND ARCHITECTURE
Henrik O. Andersson and Frederic Bedoure, *Svensk Arkitektur* (o/p). Seminal book on Swedish architectural history from 1640 to 1970, with text in English and Swedish. Colour plates illustrate the works of each architect. One to borrow from the library.

Barbro Klein and Mats Widbom (eds), *Swedish Folk Art – All Tradition Is Change* (o/p). Lavishly produced volume on the folk art movement, illustrating the influences of local culture on art and design up to and including IKEA.

Roger Tanner (trans.), *A History of Swedish Art* (o/p). Covers architecture, design, painting and sculpture, ranging from prehistoric rock carvings to postmodernism. Well illustrated.

FINLAND

HISTORY
D.G. Kirby, *Finland in the Twentieth Century – A History and Interpretation* (C. Hurst, UK). By far the best insight into contemporary Finland and the reshaping of the nation after independence.

Fred Singleton, *A Short History of Finland* (Cambridge UP). A very readable and informative account of Finland's past. It lacks the detail of most academic accounts, but is an excellent starting point for general readers.

LITERATURE
Tove Jansson, The *Moomin* books (Puffin/Sunburst). Enduring children's tales, with evocative descriptions of Finnish nature.

Matti Joensuu, *Harjunpää and the Stone Murders* (o/p). The only one of the Harjunpää series, involving the Helsinki detective, Timo Harjunpää, to have been translated into English. It's set in contemporary Helsinki during a bout of teenage gang warfare.

Christer Kihlman, *The Rise and Fall of Gerdt Bladh* (o/p). Supremely evocative study of personal anguish set against a background of Finland's ascent from rural backwater to prosperous modern nation.

Väinö Linna, *The Unknown Soldier* (o/p). Using his experiences fighting in the Winter War, Linna triggered immense controversy with this book, depicting for the first time Finnish soldiers not as "heroes in white" but as drunks and womanizers.

Elias Lönnrot, *Kalevala* (Oxford UP). The classic tome of Finnish literature, this collection of folk tales was transcribed over twenty years by Lönnrot, a rural doctor. Set in an unspecified point in the past, the plot centres on a state of war between the mythical region of Kalevala (probably northern Karelia) and Pohjola (possibly Lapland) over possession of a talisman called the Sampo. The story is regarded as quintessentially Finnish, but it's not an easy read, due mainly to its length (some 22,750 lines), and the nonlinear course of the plot. Its influence on Finnish literature is huge, though, and it was a linchpin of the Finnish nationalist and language movements.

Oscar Parland, *The Year of the Bull* (Peter Owen/Dufour Editions). Absorbing look at the civil war-torn Finland of 1918 through the eyes of a young boy.

Kirsti Simonsuuri (ed.), *Enchanting Beasts* (Forest Books/Dufour Editions). A slender but captivating tome, and one of the few English translations of the best of Finland's modern female poets.

DIRECTORY

ADDRESSES In Scandinavia addresses are always written with the number after the street name. In multi-floored buildings the ground floor is always counted as the first floor, the first the second, and so on.

ALCOHOL Except in Denmark, alcohol is very expensive throughout Scandinavia. For spirits especially, you'll find it cheaper to exceed your duty-free limit and pay the duty than buying when you get there.

ARCTIC CIRCLE This, an imaginary line drawn at 66° 33' latitude, stretches across three mainland Scandinavian countries – Norway, Sweden and Finland – and denotes the limit beyond which there is at least one day in the year on which the sun never sets, and one on which it never rises.

BOOKS You'll find English-language books in almost every bookshop, though at about twice the price you'd pay at home.

BRING An alarm clock is useful for early-morning buses and ferries, mosquito repellent and anti-septic cream handy (vital in the far north), and a raincoat or foldaway umbrella more or less essential.

LEFT LUGGAGE There are luggage lockers in most train stations, ferry terminals and long-distance bus stations.

MUSEUMS AND GALLERIES As often as not there's a charge to get in, though other than for the really major collections it's rarely very much; ISIC cards are valid for reductions at most. Opening times vary greatly: in winter they are always reduced; the likely closing day is Monday.

NEWSPAPERS You'll find British newspapers on sale in every capital city – often on the day of issue – as well as in many other large towns. Your only other choices are likely to be the *International Herald Tribune* and *USA Today*.

NORTHERN LIGHTS (Aurora Borealis) A shifting coloured glow visible during winter in the northern parts of Scandinavia, usually above the Arctic Circle, and caused by the solar wind bringing electronically charged particles into contact with the Earth's atmosphere. You'll need to be in luck to see a really good display.

TIME Denmark, Sweden and Norway are one hour ahead of the UK; Finland is two hours ahead. Denmark, Sweden and Norway are six to nine hours ahead of the eastern US; Finland is seven to ten hours ahead.

WORLD SERVICE You can keep in touch with British and world events by listening to the BBC World Service, which is broadcast to all of mainland Scandinavia. Frequencies vary according to area and usually change every few months. For the latest details write for the free *Programme Guide* to BBC External Services Publicity, Bush House, PO Box 76, Strand, London WC2.

PART TWO

DENMARK

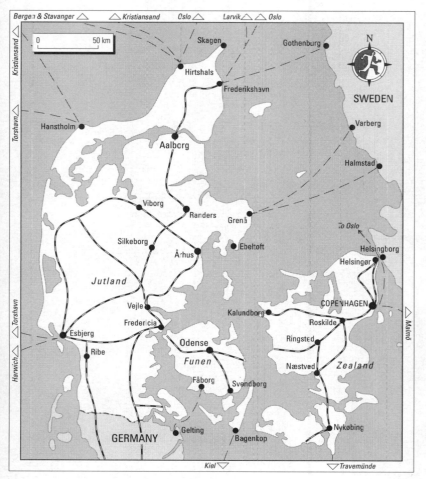

Introduction

Delicately balanced between Scandinavia proper and mainland Europe, **Denmark** is a difficult country to pin down. In many ways it shares the characteristics of both regions: it's an EU member, and has prices and drinking laws that are broadly in line with the rest of Europe. But Danish social policies and style of government are distinctly Scandinavian: social benefits and the standard of living are high, and its politics are very much that of the consensus.

It may seem hard to believe, but it wasn't so long ago that tiny Denmark ruled a good chunk of northern Europe. Since imperialist times, however, the country's energies have been turned inwards, towards the development of a well-organized but rarely over-bureaucratic society that does much to foster a pride in Danish arts and culture and uphold the freedoms of the individual. Indeed, once here, it becomes easy to share the Danes' puzzlement as to why other small, formerly Empire-owning nations haven't followed their example.

■ Where to go

While Denmark is the easiest Scandinavian country in which to travel – both in terms of cost and distance – the landscape itself is the region's least dramatic: largely green, flat and rural farmland punctuated by innumerable fairy-tale half-timbered villages, with surprisingly few urban settlements. Apart from a scattering of small islands, the country is made up of three main landmasses – the islands of Zealand and Funen and the peninsula of Jutland, which extends northwards from Germany.

The vast majority of visitors make for **Zealand** (Sjælland) and, more specifically, **Copenhagen**, the country's one truly large city and an atmospheric and exciting focal point. The compact capital really has everything: a beautiful old centre, a good array of museums – both national collections and smaller oddball establishments – and a boisterous nightlife. But Copenhagen has little in common with the rest of Zealand, which is largely quiet and rural – much like the rest of the country. Zealand's smaller neighbour, **Funen** (Fyn), has only one urban draw in **Odense**, and is otherwise sedate, renowned for the cuteness of its villages, the sandy beaches of its southern coast – a major holiday destination – and numerous explorable small islands.

Only **Jutland** (Jylland) is far enough away from Copenhagen to enjoy a truly individual flavour, as well as Denmark's most varied scenery, ranging from soft green hills to desolate heathlands. In **Århus**, Jutland also has the most lively and enjoyable city outside the capital.

■ When to go

Copenhagen attracts visitors all year round, but the intake peaks during July and August – which means May, early June and September are probably the most pleasant times to be there, although there's plenty happening in the city throughout the year. Anywhere else is enjoyably crowd-free all year round except for July, the Danish vacation month, when the population heads en masse for the countryside and the coastal strips – though, even then, only the most popular areas are uncomfortably crowded. Many outdoor events – from big rock festivals to local folk dance displays – take place between mid-June and mid-August, when all tourist facilities and transport services (including the more minor ferry links) are operating in full. In more isolated areas things begin to slacken off in September.

Denmark has the least extreme **climate** of the Scandinavian countries, but due to the proximity of the sea the weather can fluctuate rapidly. A wet day will as likely be followed by a sunny one and vice versa, and stiff breezes are common, especially along Jutland's west coast, where they can be particularly strong. **Summer** is on the whole sunny and clear: throughout July the temperature averages 20°C (68°F), often reaching 26°C (78°F). **Winter** conditions are cold but not severe: there's usually a snow covering from December to early February, and the temperature can at times drop as low as -15°C (5°F), but generally it hovers around or just below freezing point.

Getting there from the rest of Scandinavia

One look at a map will show you there'll be few problems getting to Denmark from the other Scandinavian countries. Links by rail, sea and air are fast and frequent all year round and, generally speaking, the journey to Denmark can be a rewarding part of your trip rather than a chore.

■ By train

Copenhagen is a major junction for **trains** between Europe and the rest of Scandinavia. There are usually several daily services to Copenhagen from the major Scandinavian cities – Stockholm,

Gothenburg, Oslo, Bergen, Turku and Helsinki – and less frequent links (usually one a day in summer) with remoter spots in the far north, such as Narvik (in Norway) and Kiruna (in Sweden). InterRail and Eurail passes are valid on all the international routes into Denmark (see Basics).

■ By bus

There are several direct **bus** links between the major Danish cities and the rest of Scandinavia, using the ferry routes outlined below. To Copenhagen from Sweden there are usually two buses a day from Halmstad, and nine a day from Malmö and Lund. For long-distance enthusiasts, there's also a bus to Helsinki twice a week in summer, travelling from Copenhagen via Stockholm.

■ By ferry

Precise details of the numerous **ferries** into Zealand and Jutland from Norway and Sweden are best checked in the ferry companies' latest brochures or at any tourist office, since timetables and prices fluctuate constantly. There are sometimes reductions for holders of railcards (see Basics), and fares are usually a lot cheaper outside the peak period from the end of June to early August – though bear in mind that services are likely to be less frequent out of season, and possibly nonexistent in winter. Even if you're heading for Copenhagen, don't disregard the possibility of a quicker, and cheaper, crossing into north Jutland – an interesting part of Denmark, with easy rail links to the capital; or, from Sweden, reaching Denmark by way of the interesting island of Bornholm.

From Sweden

The quickest route **from Sweden** to Denmark is the twenty-minute Scandlines crossing from Helsingborg to Helsingør (32Skr return), which runs round the clock; you can walk or cycle straight on board. Some Stockholm–Copenhagen trains use this ferry for part of the journey, completing the trip to Copenhagen fifty minutes later, but a newly constructed rail link from Copenhagen to Malmö (Sweden) has reduced crossing times between Denmark and Sweden on other services. Two other operators make the same crossing – see the Helsingør section (p.100) for details.

Another inexpensive link is the ferry service from Limhamn to Dragør (30Skr, cars from 395Skr), which takes just under an hour and leaves you a half-hour's bus ride (bus #30 or #33) from central Copenhagen. The most direct link to Copenhagen, however, is the 45-minute catamaran journey with Flygbåtarna from Malmö, though this is comparatively expensive at 97Skr one-way. A cheaper option is the catamaran operated by Pilen on the same route (20Skr one-way). None of the ferries run when the sea is frozen – which is extremely possible between mid-November and mid-March.

With time to spare, you could reach Denmark proper by way of Bornholm, a sizeable Danish island that's actually nearer to Sweden. A ferry runs several times daily between Ystad and Rønne, while in summer there are several daily catamaran crossings from Simrishamn to Allinge. From Rønne, you can take the twice-daily (once in winter) ferry to Copenhagen.

Stena has luxury boats sailing several times a day in summer from Gothenburg to Frederikshavn in Jutland (3–4 hours; 64Skr one-way, cars from 395Skr; ScanRail holders half-price), and there's also the hydrofoil SeaCat, which takes just two hours and costs 70Skr (cars 490Skr). Lion Ferry sail daily from Halmstad and Varberg to Grenå (for Århus) for a basic fare of 80Dkr one-way (cars 395Dkr).

From Norway

The only direct connection **from Norway** to Copenhagen is on the DFDS crossing from Oslo (315–760Dkr), though you'll save a lot of money by taking one of the numerous routes to either Frederikshavn or Hirtshals in Jutland. From Oslo to Frederikshavn there are four to seven crossings a week with Stena (250–350Dkr one-way), and a similar number with the slightly cheaper Color Line, which also sails to Hirtshals (150–370Dkr). There are also connections from Larvik and Moss to Frederikshavn (with Stena and Larvik Lines), and from Kristiansand to Hirtshals with Color Line (140–350Dkr) – any of which should save money over the fare from Oslo, except perhaps on a summer weekend when all the lines are at their most expensive.

■ By plane

SAS (☎70 10 30 00 or 32 32 68 00) operate around ten **flights** daily into Copenhagen from Oslo and Stockholm, five daily from Helsinki; Finnair (☎33 36 45 45) fly several times daily to Copenhagen from Helsinki. Contact a tourist office or travel agent to find out about special reduced fare deals between the Scandinavian capitals – there are usually several each summer.

Copenhagen is very much the Danish hub of the SAS network (Århus is a poor second) and international arrivals often dovetail with domestic flights to other Danish cities, which cost little extra on top of the international fare. The smaller Maersk Air (☎32 31 45 45) links Copenhagen with smaller Danish cities and islands.

SAS and other companies sometimes run daily flights from Bergen and Stavanger to Aalborg and Århus; one-way fares are upwards of 1500Dkr, but under-26s can enjoy substantial discounts – sometimes paying as little as 500Dkr. Again, check with a travel agent. For flights between Denmark and Finland check with SAS or Finnair (☎33 36 45 45), both of whom have offices in central Copenhagen.

Costs, money and banks

Costs for virtually everything – eating, sleeping, travelling and entertainment – are far lower in Denmark than in any other Scandinavian country. If you come for just a few days, stay in youth hostels or on campsites and don't eat out, it's possible to survive on £15/US$22 a day. Otherwise, moving around the country, combining campsites or hostels with cheap hotel accommodation, visiting museums, eating a full meal each day plus a few snacks and going for a drink in the evening, you can expect to spend a minimum of £25–30/$38–45 per day.

Danish currency is the krone (plural kroner), made up of 100 øre, and it comes in notes of 1000kr, 500kr, 100kr, 50kr and 20kr, and coins of 20kr, 10kr, 5kr, 1kr, 50øre and 25øre.

Banks are the best places to change traveller's cheques and foreign cash; there's a uniform commission of 20kr per transaction – so change as much as is feasible in one go. Banking hours are Mon–Wed & Fri 9.30am–4pm, Thurs 9.30am–6pm. Most international airports and ferry ports have late-opening exchange facilities. Alternatively, the red Kontanten high-street **cash machines** give cash advances on Visa and Eurocheque cards – depending on your banking arrangements these can work out cheaper than changing cash or traveller's cheques.

Mail and telecommunications

Like most other public bodies in the country, the Danish **post office** runs an exceedingly tight ship. Anything you post is almost certain to arrive within two days. You can buy **stamps** from most newsagents, and from post offices, most of which are open Mon–Fri 9am–6pm, Sat 9am–1pm, with reduced hours in smaller communities. **Poste restante** is available at any post office, and many hotels, youth hostels and campsites will hold mail ahead of your arrival.

The old-style Danish **public telephones** frustratingly keep one of your coins even if the number is engaged, which obviously means you should only insert the minimum amount – two 1kr coins – to start with. The newer phones give refunds and change – don't insert any money until the call is answered. **Cardphones** are becoming more common in the bigger cities; you can buy phonecards (telekort) in 20kr, 50kr and 100kr denominations from post offices. Most hotel rooms have a phone but it's much cheaper to make calls from the public phone at reception. Youth hostels and campsites generally have public phones; if not, the warden will probably let you use the house one for a payphone fee.

One thing to remember when dialling Danish numbers is always, even if you're already within the area concerned, to use the **area code** – a two-figure number which precedes the six-figure subscriber number.

Calling from abroad, the **international code** for Denmark is ☎45; codes for international calls from Denmark are given on p.22. To make a **collect international call**, dial ☎141 for the operator and ask to be connected to the operator in your own country, who will put through the collect call – full instructions for this "Country Direct" system are displayed in phone booths. Be warned that **directory enquiries** (international ☎113, domestic ☎118) are expensive, with a minimum charge of 5–20kr per call, plus a per-minute accumulating charge that climbs ridiculously high whilst the operator puzzles out your request. Try a phone book or Internet terminal first. It's also possible to enquire about Danish phone numbers from outside Denmark by calling ☎45/80 20 20 20 or looking up the national phone company's Web site www.teledanmark.dk.

It can be quite difficult at present finding **Internet** and **email** access in Denmark, though new cafés are beginning to spring up. In Copenhagen, try Babel, at Frederiksborggade 33 (☎33 33 93 38), or the free email service at the Use-t tourist office on Rådhusstraede.

Finally, in an **emergency**, dial ☎112 from any phone box for a fast free connection to the emergency services.

The media

For a country of its size, Denmark has an impressive number of newspapers and freesheets. By the lowest-common-denominator standards of the modern global media, the **Danish press**, with its predominantly serious and in-depth coverage of worthy issues, can't help but seem a little anachronistic. If you can read Danish your choices among the main newspapers (each costing 7–10kr) are *Politiken*, a reasonably impartial newssheet with strong arts features; *Berlingske Tidende*, conservative/centrist; *Aktuelt*, a trade union paper; *Kristeligt Dagblad*, a Christian paper; *Jyllands-Posten*, a well-respected right-wing paper; and *Information*, left-wing and intellectual. The weekly *Weekendavisen*, published on Fridays, has excellent background features. The best sports coverage can be found in the two tabloids – *B.T.*, which has a conservative bias, and *Ekstra Bladet*. You'll find excellent **entertainment listings** in both *Jyllands-Posten* and *Politiken*, and every Thursday *Information* has a section devoted to listings too. The free Danish **rock music** paper, the monthly *Gaffa*, lists most of the bigger rock shows, and innumerable similar regional papers do the same for their areas – find them in cafés, record shops and the like. You can keep in touch with global current affairs with the **overseas newspapers**, sold in all the main towns: most UK weekday titles cost 15kr and are available the day after publication at train stations and the bigger newsagents, which are also likely to stock recent issues of *USA Today*. There's also a very short "News In English" each morning at 8.30am on Radio Denmark (93.8MHz in Copenhagen, 91.7MHz in Århus).

On first acquaintance, **Danish television** seems as outmoded as the national press. There are three national channels: the non-commercial Channel 1 and DR 2, and the commercial Channel 2 – though, apart from the advertising, you'll probably struggle to spot the difference between them. The fourth station, Channel 3, a cable channel, is shared with Sweden and Norway. None of these start up until mid-afternoon, and all close down before midnight; the evening news programmes begin at 7pm and 7.30pm. If you're staying in a hotel, or a youth hostel with a TV room, you may also have the option of German and Swedish channels – plus a handful of cable and satellite stations.

Getting around

Despite being made up largely of islands, Denmark is a swift and easy country in which to travel. All types of public transport – trains, buses and the essential ferries – are punctual and efficient, and where you need to switch from one type to another, you'll find the timetables impressively well integrated. And with Denmark being such a small country, you can get from one end to the other in half a day; even if, as is more likely, you're planning to see it all at leisure, you'll rarely need to do more than an hour's daily travelling. Besides being small, Denmark is also very flat, with scores of villages linked by country roads – ideal for effortless cycling.

■ Trains

Trains are easily the best way to get about. Danske Statsbaner (DSB) – Danish State Railways – run an exhaustive and reliable network. InterRail, Eurail and ScanRail passes are valid on all routes except the few private lines that operate in some rural areas. There are just a few out-of-the-way regions that trains fail to penetrate, though these can be easily crossed by buses, which often run in conjunction with local train connections. Some of these buses are operated privately, some by DSB, in which case train passes are valid (for more on buses, see below).

Trains range from **inter-city expresses (ICs)**, which have six-seat compartments and a buffet car, to smaller **local trains (regionaltog)**, with open-plan carriages. Departure times are listed on notices both on station concourses and the platforms (departures in yellow, arrivals in white), and announced over the loudspeaker. On the train, each station is usually called a few minutes before you arrive. Watch out for *forstillekupé* – special quiet compartments where loud talking is discouraged and for which you pay extra (unless you have a first-class ticket) on top of the normal fare.

Tickets should be bought in advance from the station – on IC and international trains (see below) you must also usually purchase an advance seat reservation (15–30kr) – although you can buy tickets for *regionaltog* on board. One-way tickets allow you to break your journey once, but travel must be completed on a single day. All trains have an inspector who checks tickets: he/she is almost certain to speak English and will normally be able to answer questions about routes and times. **Fares** are calculated on a zonal system. Copenhagen–Odense, for example, costs 190kr one-way by IC train; Copenhagen–Århus, 263kr – both these fares include the cost of a mandatory seat reservation. Slower trains don't require advance reservations, but equally there's no guarantee that you'll get a seat. The price of a return ticket is no cheaper than two one-ways, but avoiding travelling on a Monday, Friday or Sunday could save you 30–40kr over a long trip.

If you don't have a rail pass but are a **student**, there are various other discounts of up to 50 percent available through DIS, the Danish student travel organization. Those **over 65** qualify for 30–50 percent discounts on certain routes, and people travelling in a group of three or more are also entitled to discounts of up to 50 percent – get details from any Danish tourist office.

Seat reservations, costing 30kr from the station ticket office, can be a good idea on busy routes – typically those to and from ferry terminals, and in and out of major cities at holiday times; ask at a tourist office or station for advice. Reservations are compulsory on crossings of the Store Bælt, the sea dividing Zealand from Funen and Jutland. If you're taking a *regionaltog* on this route, you can buy one from the inspector on board; in the unlikely event of there being no spare seats, you'll be turfed off at the ferry port and will have to wait for the next train.

As for **timings**, DSB's *Køreplan* (30kr from any newsagent) details all DSB train, bus and ferry services inside (and long-distance routes outside) the country, including the local Copenhagen S-train system and all private services, and is a sound investment if you're planning to do a lot of travelling within the country. If you're not, smaller **timetables** detailing specific routes can be picked up for free at tourist offices and station ticket offices.

■ Buses

There are only a handful of **long-distance bus** services in Denmark: Århus–Copenhagen (about 170–190kr), Århus–Aalborg (about 100kr), Aalborg–Copenhagen (about 200kr) and Frederikshavn–Esbjerg (about 200kr). These fares represent quite a saving over full train fares but, while just as efficient, long-distance buses are much less comfortable than trains. Where buses really come into their own, however, is in the few areas where trains are scarce or connections

complicated. Much of Funen and northeast Jutland are barely touched by trains, for example, and if you're travelling from Esbjerg to Frederikshavn or Aalborg you save several hours – and a lot of timetable reading – by taking the bus. Companies worth checking out are Abildskous Rutebiler (☎86 78 48 88), Fjerritslev-København (☎98 11 66 00) and, around Jutland, X-busser (☎98 90 09 00). Buses are also often the best way of getting to smaller outlying towns and your best source of information is the local tourist office or bus station.

■ Ferries

Ferries connect all the Danish islands, and vary in size from the train-carrying DSB ferries linking Zealand, Funen and Jutland, to raft-like affairs serving tiny, isolated settlements a few minutes off the (so-called) mainland. Where applicable, train and bus fares include the cost of ferry crossings (although you can also pay at the terminal and walk on), while the smaller ferries commonly charge 10–40kr for foot passengers. Contact the nearest tourist office for full details.

■ Planes

Domestic flights operated by SAS, are hardly essential in somewhere of Denmark's size, but can be handy if you're in a rush: from Copenhagen it's less than an hour's flying time to anywhere in the country. There are three kinds of fare: "red departures" (returns valid on weekdays); "green departures" (weekend returns, slightly pricier); and "blue departures" (valid for travel at any time and therefore the most expensive). A blue one-way ticket costs the same as a red return. If you're **under 26** or **over 60**, regular airfares can be cut with the 300kr **standby ticket**; get details from an SAS desk or tourist office. Adding a domestic connection onto an SAS flight to Denmark from abroad is also usually economical.

■ Driving and hitching

Given the excellent public transport system, the size of the country, and the comparatively high price of petrol, **driving** isn't really economical unless you're in a group. **Car rental** is expensive too, though it's worth checking the cut-price deals offered by some ferry lines. You'll need an international driving licence and must be aged at least

20 to take to the roads, although many firms won't rent vehicles to anyone under 25. Danes drive on the right, and there's a speed limit in towns of 50kph, 80kph in open country and 110kph on motorways. As in Sweden and Finland, headlights need to be used at all times. There are random breath tests for suspected drunken drivers, and the penalties are severe. When parked in a town, not on a meter, a parking-time disc must be displayed; get one from a tourist office, police station or bank. You set the time when you've parked on the hands of the clock, then return before your allotted time (indicated by signs) is up. As for **hitching**, this is illegal on motorways, but otherwise is a fairly easy and reasonably safe way to get around.

■ Cycling

Cycling is the best way to appreciate Denmark's pastoral, and mostly flat, landscape, as well as being a good method of getting about in the towns. Traffic is sparse on most country roads and all large towns have cycle tracks – though watch out for sometimes less-than-careful drivers on main roads. Bikes can be **rented** at nearly all youth hostels and tourist offices, at most bike shops and some train stations for around 40–50kr per day or 200kr per week, plus there's often a 200kr deposit. For long-distance cycling, **plan your route** taking into account the frequent westerly winds – pedalling is easier facing east than west.

If the wind gets too strong, or your legs get too tired, you can take your bike on all types of public transport except city buses. Unless you're travelling more than 100km, however, you can't use ICs and will have to take the slower local trains – and pay 12–30kr for your machine. The brochure *Cykler i tog* (free from train stations) lists rates and rules in full. For a similar fee, long-distance buses have limited cycle space, while ferries let bikes on free or for a few kroner. Domestic flights charge around 100kr for airlifting your bike.

Accommodation

While less costly in Denmark than in other Nordic countries, **accommodation** is still going to be your major daily expense and you should plan it carefully. Hotels, however, are by no means off limits if you seek out the better offers, and both youth hostels and campsites are plentiful – and of a uniformly high standard.

■ Hotels and private rooms

Coming to Denmark on a standard package trip (see Basics) is one way to stay in a **hotel** without spending a fortune. Another way is simply to be selective. Most Danish hotels charge a steep 600kr for a double room (singles from around 380kr) with a bathroom, TV and phone, but going without the luxuries can result in big savings. In most large towns you'll find several hotels offering rooms without bathrooms for as little as 300kr for a double (200kr for a single), and some **inns** (called *kro*) in country areas match this price – sometimes for rooms with full facilities. Other advantages of staying in a hotel or inn are the lack of a curfew (common in hostels in big cities) and the inclusion of an all-you-can-eat breakfast – so large you won't need to buy lunch.

Only in peak season will you need to make **reservations** in advance, although obviously for the cheaper places you should book as early as you can. Danish tourist offices overseas (see p.27) will give you a free list of hotels (and approximate prices) throughout the country, though much more accurate and extensive information can be found at local tourist offices – often the best way to locate what's currently on offer is simply to phone the local tourist office and ask, then call the hotel directly. Tourist offices get no commission so they're unbiased. Local tourist offices will also have details of **private rooms** in someone's home, vaguely akin to British-style bed and breakfast (often without the breakfast). These vary greatly but reckon on paying 200–300kr a double. An increasingly popular option is to stay on a **farm** (*bondegårdsferie*) – information from Ferie på Landet, Sandegade 26, 8700 Horsens (☎70 10 41 90).

■ Youth hostels

Youth hostels (*vandrerhjem*) are the cheapest option under a roof. Every town has one, they're much less pricey than hotels, and they have a high degree of comfort thanks to a campaign by the Danish hostelling association (Danmarks Vandrerhjem) to raise their profile and attract families. Most hostels offer a choice of various sizes of private room, often with toilets and showers, and all have dormitory accommodation; nearly all have cooking facilities. **Rates** generally range from around 95kr for a dormitory bed to 100–200kr per person in a private room. It's rare for hostels other than those in major towns or ferry ports to be full, but during the summer it's

ACCOMMODATION PRICE CODES

The Danish hotels listed throughout the Guide have been graded according to the following price bands, based on the **cheapest rate for a double room in summer**.

① Under 300kr   ② 300–400kr   ③ 400–500kr   ④ 500–650kr

⑤ 650–900kr   ⑥ 900–1300kr   ⑦ Over 1300kr

always wise to phone ahead to make a reservation, and to check on the hostel's location – some are several kilometres outside the town centre.

As with all Scandinavian hostels, sleeping bags are not allowed, so you need to bring either a sheet sleeping bag or rent hostel linen – which can become expensive over a long stay. It's a good idea, too, to get an **HI card**, since without one you'll be hit with the cost of either an overnight card (25kr) or a year-long Danish membership card (50kr). If you're intent on doing a lot of hostelling, it's worth contacting Danmarks Vandrerhjem, Vesterbrogade 39, DK-1620, Copenhagen V (☎33 31 36 12, fax 33 31 36 26), for their guide to Danish hostels (*Vandrerhjem i Danmark*; free, but there's a charge for postage) – published in several languages, including English.

Sometimes cheaper still, and occasionally free, are **Sleep-Ins**, run by local authorities and usually open for a two-week period during July or August. Copenhagen has several well-established and city-approved Sleep-Ins which operate all summer, offering bed, shower and breakfast for around 100kr, while Århus's Sleep-In is good too; most other towns have downmarket versions, often no more than a mattress on the floor. You need your own sleeping bag, sometimes only one night's stay is permitted and there may be an age restriction (typically 16- to 24-year-olds only, although this may not be strictly enforced). Sleep-ins come and go, so check the current situation at a local tourist office, or with Use-It in Copenhagen (see p.71).

■ **Camping**

If you don't already have an International Camping Card from a camping organization in your own country, you'll need a **Visitor's Pass** to camp in Denmark, which costs 24kr per person (48kr for a family) from any campsite and is valid on all official sites until the end of the year. **Camping rough** without the landowner's permission is illegal, but possible if you stay out of sight; a dim view is taken of camping on beaches and an

on-the-spot fine may well be imposed. In a few rural spots, the local tourist office will be able to inform you about a corner of a nearby field that's been assigned for rough camping.

Campsites (*camping plads*) can, in any case, be found virtually everywhere. All sites are open in June, July and August, many are open from April through to September, and a few operate all year round. There's a rigid grading system: one-star sites have drinking water and toilets, two-star sites have, in addition, kitchen, showers, laundry and a food shop within a kilometre, while three-star sites (by far the majority) have all the above plus a TV room, on-site shop, cafeteria, and perhaps other facilities. Prices vary only slightly, three-star sites charging 32–42kr per person, the others a few kroner less. Many sites also have **cabin accommodation**, usually with cooking facilities, which at 50–70kr a night represents massive savings for several people sharing, although on busy sites cabins are often booked up throughout the summer. Bear in mind that city camping sites, or those in other particularly popular locations, will charge more – perhaps as much as 400kr in extreme cases – for a cabin. Any Danish tourist office can give you a free leaflet listing all the sites and the basic camping rules, or there's an official guide, *Camping Danmark*, available from kiosks, bookshops and tourist offices (70kr). For further information, contact the Dansk Camping Union, Gl Kongevej 74D, DK-1850 Frederiksberg C (☎31 21 06 00).

Food and drink

Although good food can cost a lot, there are plenty of ways to eat affordably and healthily in Denmark, and with plenty of variety too. Much the same applies to drink: the only Scandinavian country free of social drinking taboos, Denmark is an imbiber's delight – both for its huge choice of tipples, and for the number of places where they can be sampled.

■ Food

Traditional Danish **food** is centred on meat and fish: beef, veal, chicken and pork are frequent menu items – though rarely bacon, which is mainly exported – along with various forms of salmon, herring, eel, plaice and cod. Combinations of these are served with potatoes and another, usually boiled, vegetable. Ordinary restaurant meals can be expensive, especially in the evening, and are often no-go areas for vegetarians – but there are other ways to eat Danish food that won't ruin your budget or your diet.

Breakfast

Breakfast (*morgenmad*) can be the tastiest and is certainly the healthiest (and most meat-free) Danish meal. Almost all hotels offer a sumptuous breakfast as a matter of course, and if you're staying in a rural youth hostel you can often attack a help-yourself table laden with cereals, bread, cheese, fruit juice, milk and tea for around 38kr – though city hostels' breakfasts tend to be less exciting. Breakfast elsewhere will be far less substantial: many cafés offer a very basic one for around 20kr, but you're well advised to hold out until lunchtime.

Lunch and snacks

You can track down an excellent-value **lunch** (*frokost*) simply by walking around and reading the signs chalked up outside any café, restaurant or *bodega* (a kind of bar that also sells basic food). On these notices, put out between 11.30am and 2.30pm, you'll often see the word *tilbud*, which refers to the "special" priced dish, or *dagens ret*, meaning "dish of the day" – a plate of chilli con carne or lasagne for around 45kr, or a two-course set lunch for about 60kr. Some restaurants carry a fixed-price (75–90kr) three-course lunch where you can pick from a selection of dishes. A variation on this idea is a choice of *smørrebrød*, or open sandwiches: slices of rye bread heaped with meat (commonly either ham, beef or liver pâté), fish (salmon, eel, caviar, cod roe, shrimp or herring) or cheese, and generously piled with assorted trimmings (mushrooms, cucumber, pickles or slices of lemon). A selection of three or four of these costs about 75kr.

Elsewhere, the American **burger** franchises are as commonplace and as popular as you'd expect, as are **pizzerias**, which are dependable and affordable at any time of day, many offering special deals such as all-you-can-eat-salad with a basic pizza for 45kr, or a more exotic dish or pizza topping for 45–70kr. You can also get a very ordi-

nary self-service meat, fish or omelette lunch in a **supermarket cafeteria** for 40–75kr.

Most Danes buy **snacks** from the very popular fast-food stands (*pølsevogn*) found on all main streets and at train stations. These serve various types of **hot sausage** (*pølser*) for 12–20kr: the long thin *wiener*, the fatter *frank-furter*, or the *franske*, a sausage inside a cylindrical piece of bread. Alternatives include a **toasted ham and cheese sandwich** (*pariser-toast*) for 15kr – vegetarians can ask for the ham to be left out – and **chips** (*pommes frites*), which come in big (*store*) and small (*lille*) forms. All of the above come with various types of ketchup and mustard to order.

If you just want a cup of **coffee** (always fresh) or **tea** (usually a fairly exotic teabag brew), drop into the nearest café, where either will cost 10–14kr. You help it down with a **Danish pastry** (*wienerbrød*), tastier and much less sweet than the imitations sold abroad under the same name.

Dinner

Dinner (*aftensmad*) in Denmark presents as much choice as lunch, but the cost is likely to be much higher. Pizzerias and similar places (see opposite keep their prices unchanged from lunchtime, and many youth hostels serve simple but filling evening meals for up to 60kr, though you have to order it in advance – as with breakfast, the best tend to be in rural areas. The most cost-effective dinners (80–100kr), however, are usually found in **ethnic restaurants** (most commonly Chinese or Middle Eastern, with a smaller number of Indian, Indonesian and Thai), which, besides à la carte dishes, often have a help-yourself table – ideal for gluttonous over-indulgence – and you usually get soup and a dessert thrown in as well. Often the same **Danish restaurants** that are promising for lunch turn into expense-account affairs at night, offering an atmospheric, candle-lit setting for the slow devouring of immaculately prepared meat or fish, where you'll be hard pushed to spend less than 200kr per person.

Shops and markets

An especially tight budget may well leave you dependent on **shopping** for food. Brugsen, Føtex and Irma are the most commonly found **supermarkets** (usually open Mon–Fri 9am–5.30pm, later on Thurs & Fri, Sat 9am–5pm), and there's little difference in price, although you'll also come across Netto, which can be slightly cheaper but is mostly

GLOSSARY OF DANISH FOOD AND DRINK TERMS

Basics

Brød	Bread	*Nogle småkager*	Biscuits	*Sødmælk*	Full cream milk
Bøfsandwich	Hamburger	*Ostebord*	Cheese board	*Sukker*	Sugar
Chokolade (varm)	Chocolate (hot)	*Pølser*	Frankfurters/ sausages	*Te*	Tea
Det kolde bord	Help-yourself cold buffet	*Sildebord*	A selection of spiced and	*Wienerbrød*	"Danish" pastry
Is	Ice cream		pickled herring	**Egg (æg) dishes**	
Kaffe (med fløde)	Coffee (with cream)	*Skummetmælk*	Skimmed milk	*Kogt æg*	Boiled egg
Letmælk	Low-fat milk	*Smør*	Butter	*Omelet*	Omelette
Mælk	Milk	*Smørrebrød*	Open sandwiches	*Røræg*	Scrambled eggs
				Spejlæg	Fried eggs

Fish (*Fisk*)

Ål	Eel	*Krabbe*	Crab	*Røget Sild*	Kipper
Forel	Trout	*Krebs*	Crayfish	*Sardiner*	Sardines
Gedde	Pike	*Laks*	Salmon	*Sild*	Herring
Helleflynder	Halibut	*Makrel*	Mackerel	*Søtunge*	Sole
Hummer	Lobster	*Rejer*	Shrimp	*Stør*	Sturgeon
Karpe	Carp	*Rogn*	Roe	*Store rejer*	Prawns
Klipfisk	Salt cod	*Rødspætte*	Plaice	*Torsk*	Cod

Meat (*Kød*)

And(ung)	Duck(ling)	*Hare*	Hare	*Lever*	Liver
Bøf	Beef	*Kalkun*	Turkey	*Rensdyr*	Reindeer
Dyresteg	Venison	*Kanin*	Rabbit	*Skinke*	Ham
Fasan	Pheasant	*Kylling*	Chicken	*Svinekød*	Pork
Gås	Goose	*Lam*	Lamb		

Vegetables (*Grøntsager*)

Artiskokker	Artichokes	*Kartofler*	Potatoes	*Ris*	Rice
Asparges	Asparagus	*Linser*	Lentils	*Rødbeder*	Beetroot
Blomkål	Cauliflower	*Løg*	Onions	*Rødkål*	Red cabbage
Champignons	Mushrooms	*Majs*	Sweetcorn	*Rosenkål*	Sprouts
Grønne bønner	Runner beans	*Majskolbe*	Corn on the cob	*Salat*	Lettuce, salad
Gulerødder	Carrots	*Nudler*	Noodles	*Salatgurk*	Cucumber
Hvide bønner	Kidney beans	*Feberfrugt*	Peppers	*Selleri*	Celery
Hvidløg	Garlic	*Persille*	Parsley	*Spinat*	Spinach
Julesalat	Chicory	*Porrer*	Leeks	*Turnips*	Turnips

Fruit (*Frugt*)

Æbler	Apples	*Citron*	Lemon	*Pærer*	Pears
Abrikoser	Apricots	*Ferskner*	Peaches	*Rabarber*	Rhubarb
Ananas	Pineapple	*Grapefrugt*	Grapefruit	*Rosiner*	Raisins
Appelsiner	Orange	*Hindbær*	Raspberries	*Solbær*	Blackcurrants
Bananer	Bananas	*Jordbær*	Strawberries	*Stikkelsbær*	Gooseberries
Blommer	Plums	*Kirsebær*	Cherries	*Svesker*	Prunes
Blåbær	Blueberries	*Mandariner*	Tangerines	*Vindruer*	Grapes
Brombær	Blackberries	*Melon*	Melon		

continued overleaf . . .

GLOSSARY OF DANISH FOOD AND DRINK TERMS (contd)

Danish specialities

Æbleflæsk	Smoked bacon with onions and sautéed apple rings	Medisterpølse	A spiced pork sausage, usually served with boiled potatoes or stewed vegetables
Æggekage	Scrambled eggs with onions, chives, potatoes and bacon pieces	Røget sild	Smoked herring on rye bread garnished with a raw egg yolk, radishes and chives
Ålesuppe	Sweet and sour eel soup		
Boller i karry	Meatballs in curry sauce served with rice	Sild i karry	Herring in curry sauce
		Skidne æg	Poached or hard-boiled eggs in a cream sauce, spiced with fish mustard and served with rye bread, decorated with sliced bacon and chives
Flæskesteg	A hunk of pork with red cabbage, potatoes and brown sauce		
Frikadeller	Pork rissoles		
Grillstegt kylling	Grilled chicken with salad		
Hakkebøf	Minced beef rolled into balls and fried with onions	Skipper labskovs	Danish stew: small squares of beef boiled with potatoes, peppercorns and bay leaves
Kalvebryst i frikasseé	Veal boiled with vegetables and served in a white sauce with peas and carrots	Stegt med stuvede kartofler	Fried eel with diced potatoes and white sauce
Kogt torsk	Poached cod in mustard sauce with boiled potatoes		

Drink (*Drikke*)

Æblemost	Apple Juice	Fadøl	Draught beer	Mineralvand	Tomato juice
Appelsinvand	Orangeade	Guldøl	Strong beer	Øl	Beer
Citronvand	Lemonade	Husets vin	House wine	Rødvin	Red wine
Eksport-Øl	Export beer (very strong lager)	Hvidvin	White wine	Tomatjuice	Soda Water
		Kærnemælk	Buttermilk	Vin	Wine

filled with freezer food. Smaller supermarkets may be open shorter hours, especially on Saturday, when they close at 1 or 2pm except on the first Saturday of the month. Late-night shopping is generally impossible, although in bigger towns, the DSB supermarket at the train station is likely to be open until midnight.

The best spots for fresh fruit and veg are the Saturday and (sometimes) Wednesday **markets** held in most towns, and you can buy smørrebrød (see opposite) for 15–40kr a piece from special smørrebrød shops, at least one of which will be open until 10pm.

■ Drink

If you've arrived from near-teetotal Norway or Sweden, you're in for a shock. Not only is alcoholic **drink** entirely accepted in Denmark, it's quite common to see people strolling along the pedestrianized streets swigging from a bottle of beer, and although extreme drunkenness is frowned upon, alcohol is widely consumed throughout the day by most types of people.

Although you can buy booze more cheaply from supermarkets, the most sociable **places to drink** are pubs and cafés, where the emphasis is on beer – although you can also get spirits and wine (or tea and coffee). There are also bars and bodegas (see opposite), in which, as a very general rule, the mood tends to favour wines and spirits, and the customers are a bit older than those found in cafés.

The cheapest type of beer is **draught beer** (fadøl), half a litre of which costs 15–20kr. Draught is a touch weaker than **bottled beer**, which costs 17–18kr for a third of a litre, and a great deal less potent than the **export beers** (guldøl or eksport-øl), costing 25–30kr per bottle. All Danish beer is lager-style, the most common brands being Carlsberg and Tuborg, and although a number of towns have their own locally brewed rivals, you'll need a finely tuned palate to spot much difference between them. One you will notice the taste of is Lys Pilsner, a very low-alcohol lager.

Most international **wines and spirits** are widely available, a shot of the hard stuff costing 18–20kr in a bar, a glass of wine upwards of 15kr. While in the country you should investigate the many varieties of the schnapps-like **Akvavit**, which Danes consume as eagerly as beer, especially with meals; more than two or three turn most non-Danes pale. A tasty relative is the gloriously hot and strong Gammel Dansk Bitter Dram – Akvavit-based but made with bitters – only ever drunk with food at breakfast time.

Directory

EMERGENCIES ☎112. Ask for fire, police or ambulance.

FISHING Well stocked with bream, dace, roach, pike trout, zander and much more, Denmark's lakes and rivers are a fishing enthusiast's dream. The only problem is bringing enough bait (more expensive than you might expect) to cope with the inevitably large catch. The time to come is in early or late summer, and the prime areas are in central Jutland, around Randers and Viborg, and slightly further north around Silkeborg and Skanderborg. For specialist angling trips, see the "Getting There" sections in Basics.

MARKETS Virtually every town has a market, usually on Wednesday and Saturday mornings.

PUBLIC HOLIDAYS All shops and banks are closed on the following days, and public transport and many museums run to Sunday schedules: January 1, Maundy Thursday, Good Friday, Easter Monday, Prayer Day (fourth Friday after Easter), Ascension Day (around mid-May), Whit Monday, the afternoons of May 1 and June 5 (Constitution Day), December 24 (afternoon only), December 25 and December 26.

SALES TAX A tax of 25 percent is added to almost everything you'll buy – but it's always included in the marked price.

SHOPS Shop hours are Mon–Thurs 9am–5.30pm, Fri 9am–7 or 8pm, Sat 9am–1 or 2pm, Sun closed. On the first Saturday of the month shops stay open until 5pm.

TIPPING Unless you're in the habit of having porters carry your luggage, you'll never be expected to tip – restaurant bills include a 15 percent service charge.

History

Spending much time in Denmark soon makes you realize that its history is entirely disproportionate

to its size. Nowadays a small – and often overlooked – nation, Denmark has nonetheless played an important role in key periods of European history, firstly as home-base of the Vikings, and later as a medieval superpower. Markers to the past, from prehistory to the wartime resistance movement, are never hard to find. Equally easy to spot are the benefits stemming from some of the earliest welfare state systems and some of western Europe's most liberal social policies.

■ Early settlements

Traces of human habitation, such as deer bones prised open for marrow, have been found in central Jutland and dated at 50,000 BC, but it is unlikely that any settlements of this time were permanent, as much of the land was still covered by ice. From 14,000 BC tribes from more southerly parts of Europe arrived during the summer to hunt reindeer for meat and antlers, which provided raw material for axes and other tools. The melting ice caused the shape of the land to change and the warmer climate enabled vast forests to grow in Jutland. From about 4000 BC, settlers with agricultural knowledge arrived: they lived in villages, grew wheat and barley and kept animals, and buried their dead in **dolmens** or megalithic graves.

The earliest metal and bronze finds are from 1800 BC, the result of trade with southern Europe. The richness of some pieces indicates an awareness of the cultures of Crete and Mycenae. By this time the country was widely cultivated and densely populated. Battles for control over individual areas saw the emergence of a ruling warrior class, and, around 500 AD, a tribe from Sweden calling themselves **Danes** migrated southwards and took control of what became known as **Denmark**.

■ The Viking era

Around 800 AD, under **King Godfred**, the Danish boundaries were marked out. However, following Charlemagne's conquest of the Saxons in Germany, the Franks began to threaten the Danes' territory, and they had to prepare an opposing force. They built fast, seaworthy vessels and defeated Charlemagne easily. Then, with the Norwegians, they attacked Spanish ports and eventually invaded Britain. By 1033, the Danes controlled the whole of England and Normandy and dominated trade in the Baltic.

In Denmark itself, which then included much of what is now southern Sweden, the majority of people were farmers: the less wealthy paid taxes to the king and those who owned large tracts of land provided the monarch with military forces. In time, a **noble class** emerged, expecting and receiving privileges from the king in return for their support. Law-making was the responsibility of the *ting*, a type of council consisting of district noblemen. Above the district *ting* there was a provincial *ting*, charged with the election of the king. The successful candidate could be any member of the royal family, which led to a high level of feuding and bloodshed.

In 960, with the baptism of King **Harald ("Bluetooth")**, Denmark became officially Christian – principally, it's thought, to stave off imminent invasion by the German emperor. Nonetheless, Harald gave permission to a Frankish monk, **Ansgar**, to build the **first Danish church**, and Ansgar went on to take control of missionary activity throughout Scandinavia. Harald was succeeded by his son **Sweyn I ("Forkbeard")**. Sweyn was a pagan but he tolerated Christianity, even though he suspected the missionaries of bringing a German influence to bear in Danish affairs. In 990 he joined with the Norwegians in attacking Britain, whose king was the well-named Ethelred "the Unready". Sweyn's son, **Knud I ("the Great")** – King Canute of England – married Ethelred's widow, took the British throne and soon controlled a sizeable empire around the North Sea – the zenith of Viking power.

■ The rise of the Church

During the eleventh and twelfth centuries, Denmark was weakened by violent internal struggles, not only between different would-be rulers but also among the Church, nobility and monarchy. Following the death of **Sweyn II** in 1074, two of his four sons, Knud and Harald, fought for the throne – Harald, supported by the peasantry and the Church, emerging victorious. A mild and introspective individual, Harald was nonetheless a competent monarch, and introduced the first real Danish currency. He was constantly derided by Knud and his allies, however, and after his death in 1080 his brother became **Knud II**. He made generous donations to the Church, but his introduction of higher taxes and the absorption of all unclaimed land into the realm enraged the nobility. The farmers of North Jutland revolted in 1086, forcing Knud to flee to Odense, where he was slain on the high altar of Skt Alban's Kirke. The ten-year period of poor harvests that ensued was taken by many to be divine wrath, and there were reports of miracles occurring in Knud's tomb, leading to the murdered king's canonization in 1101.

The battles for power continued, and eventually, in 1131, a **civil war** broke out that was to simmer for two decades, various claimants to the throne and their offspring slugging it out with the support of either the Church or nobility. During this time the power of the clergy escalated dramatically thanks to **Bishop Eskil**, who enjoyed a persuasive influence on the eventual successor, Erik III. Following Erik's death in 1143, the disputes went on, leading to the division of the kingdom between two potential rulers, Sweyn and Knud. Sweyn's repeated acts of tyranny resulted in the death of Knud in Roskilde, but Knud's wounded aide, Valdemar, managed to escape and raise the Jutlanders in revolt at the battle of Grathe Heath, south of Viborg.

■ The Valdemar era

Valdemar I ("the Great") assumed the throne in 1157, strengthening the crown by ending the elective function of the *ting*, and shifting the power to choose the monarch to the Church. Technically the *ting* still influenced the choice of king, but in practice hereditary succession became the rule.

After Bishop Eskil's retirement, **Absalon** became Archbishop of Denmark, erecting a fortress at the fishing village of **Havn** (later to become København – Copenhagen). Besides being a zealous churchman, Absalon possessed a sharp military mind and came to dominate Valdemar I and his successor, Knud IV. During this period, Denmark saw some of its best years, expanding to the south and east, and taking advantage of internal strife within Germany. In time, after Absalon's death and the succession of **Valdemar II**, Denmark controlled all trade along the south coast of the Baltic and in the North Sea east of the Ejder. Valdemar II was also responsible for subjugating Norway, and in 1219 he set out to conquer Estonia and take charge of Russian trade routes through the Gulf of Finland. According to Danish legend, the national flag, the Dannebrog, fell down from heaven during a battle in Estonia in 1219.

However, in 1223 Valdemar II was kidnapped by Count Henry of Schwerin (a Danish vassal) and forced to give up many Danish possessions. There was also a redrawing of the southern boundary of Jutland, which caused the Danish population of the region to be joined by a large number of Saxons from Holstein.

Within Denmark, the years of expansion had brought great prosperity. The rules of the *ting* were written down as the **Jutlandic Code**, thus unifying laws all over the country – an act which had the effect of concentrating powers of justice in the person of the monarch, rather than the *ting*. The increasingly affluent nobles demanded greater rights if they were to be counted on to support the new king. The Church was envious of the growing power of the nobles and much bickering ensued in the following years, resulting in the eventual installation of Valdemar II's son, Christoffer I, as monarch.

Christoffer died suddenly in Ribe when his only son Erik was two years old; Queen Margrethe took the role of regent until **Erik V** came of age. Erik's overbearing manner and penchant for German bodyguards annoyed the nobles, and they forced him to a meeting at Nyborg in 1282 where his powers were limited by a *håndfæstning*, or charter, that included an undertaking for annual consultation with a Danehof, or forum of nobles. In 1319 **Christoffer II** became king, after agreeing to an even sterner charter, which allowed for daily consultations with a *råd* – a council of nobles. In 1326, in lieu of a debt which Christoffer had no hope of repaying, Count **Gerd of Holstein** occupied a large portion of Jutland. Christoffer fled to Mecklenburg and Gerd installed the twelve-year-old Valdemar, Duke of Schleswig, as a puppet king.

As they proceeded to divide the country among themselves, the Danish nobles became increasingly unpopular with both the Church and the peasantry. Christoffer attempted to take advantage of the internal discord to regain the crown in 1329 but was defeated in battle by Gerd. Under the peace terms Gerd was given Jutland and Funen, while his cousin, Count Johan of Plön, was granted Zealand, Skåne and Lolland-Falster. In 1332 Skåne, the richest Danish province, inflicted a final insult on Christoffer when its inhabitants revolted against Johan and transferred their allegiance to the Swedish king, Magnus.

Gerd was murdered in 1340. The years of turmoil had taken their toll on all sections of Danish society: from Christoffer's death in 1332, the country had been without a monarch and it was felt that a re-establishment of the crown was essential to restoring stability. The throne was given to **Valdemar IV** and the monarchy strengthened by the taking back of former crown lands that had been given to nobles. Within twenty years Denmark had regained its former territo-

ry, with German forces driven back across the Ejder. The only loss was Estonia, a Danish possession since 1219, which was sold to the Order of Teutonic Knights.

In 1361, the buoyant king attacked and conquered Gotland, much to the annoyance of the Hanseatic League, who were using it as a Baltic trading base. A number of anti-Danish alliances sprang up and the country was slowly plundered until peace was agreed in 1370 under the **Treaty of Stralsund**. This guaranteed trade for the Hanseatic partners by granting them control of castles along the west coast of Skåne for fifteen years. It also laid down that the election of the Danish monarch had to be approved by the Hanseatic League – the peak of their power.

■ The Kalmar Union

Valdemar's daughter Margrethe forced the election of her five-year-old son, Olav, as king in 1380, installing herself as regent. Following his untimely death after only a seven-year reign, Margrethe became Queen of Denmark and Norway, and later of Sweden as well – the first ruler of a united Scandinavia. In 1397, a formal document, the **Kalmar Union**, set out the rules of the union of the countries, which allowed for a Scandinavian federation under the same monarch and foreign policy, within which each country had its own internal legislation. It became evident that Denmark was to be the dominant partner within the union when Margrethe placed Danish nobles in civic positions in Norway and Sweden but failed to reciprocate with Swedes and Norwegians in Denmark.

Erik VII ("of Pomerania") became king in 1396, and was determined to remove the Counts of Holstein who had taken possession of Schleswig. In 1413 he persuaded a meeting of the Danehof to declare the whole of Schleswig to be crown property, and three years later war broke out with the German-influenced nobility of the region. Initially the Hanseatic League supported the king, unhappy with the Holstein privateers who were interfering with their trade. But Erik also introduced important economic reforms within Denmark, ensuring that foreign goods reached Danish people through Danish merchants instead of coming directly from Hanseatic traders. This led to a war with the League, after which, in 1429, Erik imposed the **Sound Toll** (*Øresundstolden*) on shipping passing through the narrow strip of sea off the coast of Helsingør.

The conflicts with the Holsteiners and the Hanseatic League had, however, badly drained financial resources. Denmark still relied on hired armies to do its fighting, and the burden of taxation had caused widespread dissatisfaction, particularly in Sweden. With the Holstein forces gaining ground in Jutland, Erik fled to Gotland, and in 1439 Swedish and Danish nobles elected in his place **Christoffer III**, who acquiesced to the nobles' demands and ensured peace with the Hanseatic League by granting them exemption from the Sound Toll.

His sudden death in 1448 left – after internal struggle – **Christian I** to take the Danish throne. Following the death of his uncle and ally, the Count of Holstein, he united Schleswig and Holstein at Ribe in 1460 and became Count of Holstein and Duke of Schleswig. In Denmark itself he also instigated the *stændermøde*: a council of merchants, clergy, freehold peasants and nobility, forging a powerful position for the crown – a policy that was continued by his successor, Hans.

Hans died in 1513 and **Christian II** came to the throne, seeking to re-establish the power of the Kalmar Union and reduce the trading dominance of the Hanseatic League. He invaded Sweden in 1520 under the guise of protecting the Church, but soon crowned himself King of Sweden at a ceremony attended by the cream of the Swedish nobility, clergy and the merchant class – an amnesty being granted to those who had opposed him. It was, however, a trick. Once inside the castle, 82 of the "guests" were arrested on charges of heresy, sentenced to death, and executed – an event that became known as the **Stockholm Bloodbath**. This was supposed to subdue Swedish hostility to the Danish monarch but in fact had the opposite effect. Gustavus Vasa, previously one of six Swedish hostages held by Christian in Denmark, became the leader of a revolt that ended Christian's reign in Sweden and finished the Kalmar Union.

Internally, too, Christian faced a revolt, to which he responded with more brutality. At the end of 1522, a group of Jutish nobles banded together with the intention of overthrowing him, joining up with Duke Frederik of Holstein-Gottorp (heir to half of Schleswig-Holstein), who also regarded the Danish king with disfavour. The following January, the nobles renounced their royal oaths and, with the support of forces from Holstein, gained control of all of Jutland and Funen. As they prepared to invade Zealand, Christian fled to Holland, hoping to assemble an army and return. In his absence, Frederik of Holstein-Gottorp became **Frederik I**.

■ The Reformation

At the time of Frederik's acquisition of the crown there was a growing unease with the role of the Church in Denmark, especially with the power – and wealth – of the bishops. Frederik was a Catholic but refused to take sides in religious disputes and did nothing to prevent the destruction of churches, being well aware of the groundswell of peasant support for Lutheranism. Frederik I died in 1533 and the fate of the Reformation hinged on which of his two sons would succeed him. The elder and more obvious choice was Christian, but his open support for Lutheranism set the bishops and nobles against him. The younger son, Hans, was just 12 years old, but was favoured by the Church and the nobility. The civil war that ensued became known as the **Counts' War**, and ended in 1536 with Christian III on the throne and the establishment of the new Danish Lutheran Church, with a constitution placing the king at its head.

■ Danish–Swedish conflicts

New trading routes across the Atlantic had reduced the power of the Hanseatic League, and Christian's young and ambitious successor, **Frederik II**, saw this as a chance for expansion. Sweden, however, had its own expansionist designs, and the resulting **Seven Years War** (1563–1570) between the two countries caused widespread devastation and plunged the Danish economy into crisis.

The crisis turned out to be short-lived: price rises in the south of Europe led to increasing Danish affluence, reflected in the building of the elaborate castle of Kronborg in Helsingør. By the time **Christian IV** came to the throne in 1596, Denmark was a solvent and powerful nation. Christian's reign was to be characterized by bold new town layouts and great architectural works. Copenhagen became a major European capital, acquiring many of the buildings which still grace the city today, including Rosenborg, Børsen and Rundetårnet.

To stem the rise of Swedish power after the Seven Years War, Christian IV took Denmark into the abortive **Thirty Years War** in 1625, in which Danish defeat was total, and the king was widely condemned for his lack of foresight. The war led to increased taxes, inflation became rampant, and a number of merchants displayed their anger by petitioning the king over tax exemptions and other privileges enjoyed by nobles.

In 1657 Sweden occupied Jutland, and soon after marched across the frozen sea to Funen with the intention of continuing to Zealand. Hostilities ceased with the signing of the **Treaty of Roskilde**, under which Denmark finally lost all Swedish provinces. Sweden, however, was still suspicious of possible Danish involvement in Germany, and broke the terms of the treaty, commencing an advance through Zealand towards Copenhagen. The Dutch, to whom the Swedes had been allied, regarded this as a precursor to total Swedish control of commercial traffic through the Sound and sent a fleet to protect Copenhagen. This, plus a number of local uprisings within Denmark and attacks by Polish and Brandenburg forces on Sweden, halted the Swedes' advance and forced them to seek peace. The **Treaty of Copenhagen**, signed in 1660, acknowledged Swedish defeat but allowed the country to retain the Sound provinces acquired under the Treaty of Roskilde, so preventing either country from monopolizing trade through the Sound.

■ Absolute monarchy

In Denmark, the financial power of the nobles was fading as towns became established and the new merchant class grew. The advent of firearms caused the king to become less dependent on the foot-soldiers provided by the nobles, and there was a general unease about the privileges – such as exemption from taxes – that the nobles continued to enjoy. Equally, few monarchs were content with their powers being limited by *håndfæstning*.

During the Swedish siege of Copenhagen, the king had promised special concessions to the city and its people, in the hope of encouraging them to withstand the assault. Among these was the right to determine their own rate of tax. A meeting of the city's burghers decided that everyone, including the nobility, should pay taxes. The nobles had little option but to submit. Sensing their power, the citizens went on to suggest that the crown become hereditary and end the *håndfæstning* system. Frederik III accepted and, with a full-scale ceremony in Copenhagen, was declared hereditary monarch. The task of writing a new constitution was left to the king and its publication, in 1665, revealed that he had made himself absolute monarch, bound only to uphold the Lutheran faith and ensure the unity of the kingdom. The king proceeded to rule, aided by a Privy Council in which seats were drawn mainly from the top posts within the civil service. The noble influence on royal decision-making had been drastically cut.

Christian V, king from 1670, instigated a broad system of royal honours, creating a new class of landowners who enjoyed exemptions from tax, and whose lack of concern for their tenants led Danish peasants into virtual serfdom. In 1699 **Frederik IV** set about creating a Danish militia to make the country less dependent on foreign mercenaries. While Sweden turned its allegiances towards Britain and Holland, Denmark re-established relations with the French, a situation which culminated in the **Great Northern War** (1709–1720). One result of this was the emergence of Russia as a dominant force in the region, while Denmark emerged with a strong position in Schleswig, and Sweden's exemption from the Sound Toll was ended.

The two decades of peace that followed saw the arrival of **Pietism**, a form of Lutheranism which strove to renew the devotional ideal. Frederik embraced the doctrine towards the end of his life, and it was adopted in full by his son, **Christian VI**, who took the throne in 1730. He prohibited entertainment on Sunday, closed down the Royal Theatre, and made court life a sombre affair: attendance at church on Sundays became compulsory and confirmation obligatory.

■ The Enlightenment

Despite the beliefs of the monarch, Pietism was never widely popular, and by the 1740s its influence had waned considerably. The reign of **Frederik V**, from 1746, saw a great cultural awakening: grand buildings such as Amalienborg and Frederikskirke were erected in Copenhagen (though the latter's completion was delayed for twenty years), and there was a new flourishing of the arts. The king, perhaps as a reaction to the puritanism of his father, devoted himself to a life of pleasure and allowed control of the nation effectively to pass to the civil service. **Neutrality** was maintained and the economy benefited as a consequence.

In 1766, **Christian VII** took the crown. His mental state was unstable, his moods ranging from deep lethargy to rage and drunkenness. By 1771 he had become incapable of carrying out even the minimum of official duties. The king's council, filled by a fresh generation of ambitious young men, insisted that the king effect his own will – under guidance from them – and disregard the suggestions of his older advisers.

Decision-making became dominated by a German court physician, **Johann Friedrich Struensee**, who had accompanied the king on a tour of England and had gained much of the credit for the good behaviour of the unpredictable monarch. Struensee combined personal arrogance with a sympathy for many of the ideas then fashionable elsewhere in Europe; he spoke no Danish (German was the court language) and had no concern for Danish traditions. Through him a number of sweeping **reforms** were executed: the Privy Council was abolished, the Treasury became the supreme administrative organ, the death penalty was abolished, the moral code lost many of its legal sanctions, and the press was freed from censorship.

There was opposition from several quarters. Merchants complained about the freeing of trade, and the burghers of Copenhagen were unhappy about their city losing its autonomy. In addition, there were well-founded rumours about the relationship between Struensee and the queen. Since nothing was known outside the court of the king's mental state, it was assumed that the monarch was being held prisoner. Struensee was forced to reintroduce censorship of the press as their editorials began to mount attacks on him. The Royal Guards mutinied when their disbandment was ordered, while at the same time a coup was being plotted by Frederik V's second wife, Juliane Marie of Brunswick, and her son, Frederik. After a masked ball at the palace in 1772, Struensee was arrested and tried, and soon afterwards beheaded. The dazed king was paraded before his cheering subjects.

The court came under the control – in ascending order of influence – of Frederik, Juliane, and a minister, **Ove Høegh-Guldberg**. All those who had been appointed to office by Struensee were dismissed, and while Høegh-Guldberg eventually incurred the wrath of officials by operating in much the same arrogant fashion as Struensee had, he recognized – and exploited – the anti-German feelings that had been growing for some time. Danish became the language of command in the army and later the court language, and in 1776 it was declared that no foreigner should be given a position in royal office.

In the wider sphere, the country prospered through dealings in the Far East, and Copenhagen consolidated its role as the new centre of Baltic trade. The outbreak of the American War of Independence provided neutral Denmark with fresh commercial opportunities. In 1780 Denmark joined the **League of Armed Neutrality** with Russia, Prussia and Sweden, which had the effect of maintaining trading links across the Atlantic until the end of the war.

Faced with the subsequent conflict between Britain and revolutionary France, Denmark joined the second armed neutrality league with Russia and Sweden, until a British naval venture into the Baltic during 1801 obliged withdrawal. British fears that Denmark would join Napoleon's continental blockade resulted in a British attack led by Admiral Nelson, which destroyed the Danish fleet in Copenhagen. The pact between France and Russia left Denmark in a difficult situation. To oppose this alliance would leave them exposed to a French invasion of Jutland. To oppose the British and join with the French would adversely affect trade. As the Danes tried to stall for time, the British lost patience, occupying Zealand and commencing a three-day bombardment of Copenhagen. Sweden had aligned with the British and was demanding the ceding of Norway if Denmark were to be defeated – which, under the **Treaty of Kiel**, is exactly what happened.

■ The Age of Liberalism

The Napoleonic Wars destroyed Denmark's international prestige and left the country bankrupt, and the period up until 1830 was spent in recovery. Meanwhile, in the arts, a **national romantic movement** was gaining pace. The sculptor Thorvaldsen and the writer-philosopher Kierkegaard are perhaps the best-known figures to emerge from the era, but the most influential domestically was a theologian called **N.F.S. Grundtvig**, who, in 1810, developed a new form of Christianity – one that was free of dogma and drew on the virtues espoused by the heroes of Norse mythology. In 1825 he left the intellectual circles of Copenhagen and travelled the rural areas to guide a religious revival, eventually modifying his earlier ideas in favour of a new faith in the wisdom of "the people" – something that was to colour the future liberal movement.

On the political front, there was trouble brewing in Danish-speaking **Schleswig** and German-speaking **Holstein**. The Treaty of Kiel had compelled Denmark to relinquish Holstein to the Confederation of German States – although, confusingly, the Danish king remained duke of the province. He promised to set up a consultative assembly for the region, while within Holstein a campaign sought to pressure the king into granting the duchy its own constitution. The campaign was suppressed, but the problems of the region were not resolved. Further demands called for a complete separation from Denmark, with the duchies being brought together as a single independent state. The establishment of consultative assemblies in both Holstein and Schleswig eventually came about in 1831, though they lacked any real political muscle.

Although absolutism had been far more benevolent towards the ordinary people in Denmark than elsewhere in Europe, interest was growing in the liberalism that was sweeping through the continent. In Copenhagen a group of scholars proffered the idea that Schleswig be brought closer to Danish affairs, and in pursuit of this they formed the Liberal Party and brought pressure to bear for a new liberal constitution. As the government wavered in its response, the liberal movement grew and its first newspaper, *Fædrelandet*, appeared in 1834.

In 1837 the crown agreed to the introduction of elected town councils and, four years later, to elected bodies in parishes and counties. Although the franchise was restricted, many small farmers gained political awareness through their participation in the local councils.

In 1839, **Christian VIII** came to the throne. As Crown Prince of Norway, Christian had approved a liberal constitution in that country, but surprised Danish liberals by not agreeing to a similar constitution at home. In 1848 he was succeeded by his son **Frederik VII**. Meanwhile, the liberals had organized themselves into the **National Liberal Party**, and the king signed a **new constitution** that made Denmark the most democratic country in Europe, guaranteeing freedom of speech, freedom of religious worship, and many civil liberties. Legislation was to be put in the hands of a Rigsdag elected by popular vote and consisting of two chambers: the lower Folketing and upper Landsting. The king gave up the powers of an absolute monarch, but his signature was still required before bills approved by the Rigsdag could become law. And he could select his own ministers.

Within Schleswig-Holstein, however, there was little faith that the equality granted to them in the constitution would be upheld. A delegation

from the duchies went to Copenhagen to call for Schleswig to be combined with Holstein within the German Confederation. A Danish compromise suggested a free constitution for Holstein with Schleswig remaining as part of Denmark, albeit with its own legislature and autonomy in its internal administration. The Schleswig-Holsteiners rejected this and formed a provisional government in Kiel.

The inevitable war that followed was to last for three years and, once Prussia's support was withdrawn, it ended in defeat for the duchies. The Danish prime minister, C.C. Hall, drew up a fresh constitution that excluded Holstein from Denmark. Despite widespread misgivings within the Rigsdag, the constitution was narrowly voted through. Frederik died before he could give the royal assent and it fell to **Christian IX** to put his name to the document that would almost certainly trigger another war.

It did and under the peace terms Denmark ceded both Schleswig and Holstein to Germany, leaving the country smaller than it had been for centuries. The blame was laid firmly on the National Liberals, and the new government, appointed by the king and drawn from the country's affluent landowners, saw its initial task as replacing the constitution, drawn up to deal with the Schleswig-Holstein crisis, with one far less liberal in content. The election of 1866 resulted in a narrow majority in the Rigsdag favouring a new constitution. When this came to be implemented, it retained the procedure for election to the Folketing, but made the Landsting franchise dependent on land and money and allowed twelve of the 64 members to be selected by the king.

The landowners worked in limited co-operation with the National Liberals and the Centre Party (a less conservative version of the National Liberals). In opposition, a number of interests, encompassing everything from leftist radicals to followers of Grundtvig, were shortly combined into the **United Left**, which put forward the first political manifesto seen in Denmark. It called for equal taxation, universal suffrage in local elections, more freedom for the farmers, and contained a vague demand for closer links with the other Scandinavian countries. The United Left became the majority within the Folketing in 1872.

The ideas of **revolutionary socialism** had begun percolating through the country around 1871 via a series of pamphlets edited by Louis

Pio, who attempted to organize a Danish Internationale. In April 1872, Pio led 1200 brick-layers into a strike, announcing a mass meeting on May 5. The government banned the meeting and had Pio arrested: he was sentenced to five years in prison and the Danish Internationale was banned. The workers began forming trade unions and workers' associations.

The intellectual left also became active. A series of lectures delivered by Georg Brandes in Copenhagen cited Danish culture, in particular its literature, as dull and lifeless compared to that of other countries. He called for fresh works that questioned and examined society, instigating a bout of literary attacks on institutions such as marriage, chastity and the family. As a backlash, conservative groups in the government formed themselves into the **United Right** under Prime Minister **J.B.S. Estrup**.

The left did their best to obstruct the government but gradually lost influence, while the strength of the right grew. In 1889, the left issued a manifesto calling for reductions in military expenditure, a declaration of neutrality, the provision of old age pensions, sick pay, a limit to working hours, and votes for women. The elections of 1890 improved the left's position in the Folketing, and also saw the election of two **Social Democrats**. With this, the left moved further towards moderation and compromise with the right. The trade unions, whose membership escalated in proportion to the numbers employed in the new industries, grew in stature, and were united as the Association of Trade Unions in 1898. The Social Democratic Party grew stronger with the support of the industrial workers, although it had no direct connection with the trade unions.

■ Parliamentary democracy and World War I

By the end of the century the power of the right was in severe decline. The elections of 1901, under the new conditions of a secret ballot, saw them reduced to the smallest group within the Folketing and heralded the beginning of **parliamentary democracy**.

The government of 1901 was the first real democratic government, assembled with the intention of balancing differing political tendencies – and it brought in a number of reforms. Income tax was introduced on a sliding scale, and free schooling beyond the primary level began. As

years went by, Social Democrat support increased, while the left, such as it was, became increasingly conservative. In 1905 a breakaway group formed the **Radical Left** (Det Radikale Venstre), politically similar to the English Liberals, calling for the reduction of the armed forces to the status of coastal and border guards, greater social equality, and votes for women.

An alliance between the Radicals and Social Democrats enabled the two parties to gain a large majority in the Folketing in the election of 1913, and a year later conservative control of the Landsting was ended. Social advances were made, but further domestic progress was halted by international events as Europe prepared for war.

Denmark had enjoyed good trading relations with both Germany and Britain in the year preceding **World War I** and was keen not to be seen to favour either side in the hostilities. On the announcement of the German mobilization, the now Radical-led cabinet, with the support of all the other parties, issued a **statement of neutrality** and was able to remain clear of direct involvement in the conflict.

At the conclusion of the war, attention was turned again towards Schleswig-Holstein, and under the **Treaty of Versailles** it was decided that Schleswig should be divided into two zones for a referendum. In the northern zone a return to unification with Denmark was favoured by a large percentage, while the southern zone elected to remain part of Germany. A new German–Danish border was drawn up just north of Flensburg.

High rates of unemployment and the success of the Russian Bolsheviks led to a series of strikes and demonstrations, the unrest coming to a head with the **Easter crisis** of 1920. During March of that year, a change in the electoral system towards greater proportional representation was agreed in the Folketing but the prime minister, **CTh Zahle**, whose Radicals stood to lose support through the change, refused to implement it. The king, Christian X, responded by dismissing him and asking **Otto Liebe** to form a caretaker government to oversee the changes. The royal intervention, while technically legal, incensed the Social Democrats and the trade unions, who were already facing a national lockout by employers in response to demands for improved pay rates. The unions, perceiving the threat of a right-wing coup, began organizing a general strike to begin after the Easter holiday. There was a large republican demonstration outside Amalienborg.

On Easter Saturday, urgent negotiations between the king and the existing government concluded with an agreement that a mutually acceptable caretaker government would oversee the electoral change and a fresh election would immediately follow. Employers, fearful of the power the workers had shown, met many of the demands for higher wages.

The next government was dominated by the Venstre. They fortified existing social policies, and increased state contributions to union unemployment funds. But a general economic depression continued, and there was widespread industrial unrest as the krone declined in value and living standards fell. A month-long **general strike** followed and a workers' demonstration in Randers was subdued by the army.

Verstre and the Social Democrats jostled for position over the next decade, though under the new electoral system no one party could achieve enough power to undertake major reform. The economy did improve, however, and state influence spread further through Danish society than ever before. Enlightened reforms were put on the agenda, too, making a deliberately clean break with the moral standpoints of the past – notably on abortion and illegitimacy. Major public works were funded, such as the bridge between Funen and Jutland over the Lille Bælt, and the Stormstrømsbro, linking Zealand to Falster.

■ The Nazi occupation

While Denmark had little military significance for the Nazis, the sea off Norway was being used to transport iron ore from Sweden to Britain, and the fjords offered good shelter for a fleet engaged in a naval war in the Atlantic. To get to Norway, the Nazis planned an invasion of Denmark. At 4am on April 9, 1940, the German ambassador in Copenhagen informed Prime Minister Stauning that German troops were preparing to cross the Danish border and issued the ultimatum that unless Denmark agreed that the country could be used as a German military base – keeping control of its own affairs – Copenhagen would be bombed. To reject the demand was considered a postponement of the inevitable, and to save Danish bloodshed the government acquiesced at 6am. "They took us by telephone," said a Danish minister.

A national coalition government was formed which behaved according to protocol but gave no unnecessary concessions to the Germans.

Censorship of the press and a ban on demonstrations were imposed, ostensibly intended to prevent the Nazis spreading propaganda. But these measures, like the swiftness of the initial agreement, were viewed by some Danes as capitulation and were to be a thorn in the side of the Social Democrats for years to come.

The government was reshuffled to include non-parliamentary experts, one of whom, **Erik Scavenius**, a former foreign minister, conceived an ill-fated plan to gain the confidence of the Germans. He issued a statement outlining the government's friendly attitude to the occupying power, and even praised the German military victory – which upset the Danish public and astonished the Germans, who asked whether Denmark would like to enter into commercial agreement immediately rather than wait until the end of the war. Scavenius was powerless to do anything other than agree, and a deal was signed within days. Under its terms, the krone was to be phased out and German currency made legal tender.

Public reaction was naturally hostile, and Scavenius was, not surprisingly, regarded as a traitor. Groups of Danes began a systematic display of antipathy to the Germans. Children wore red, white and blue 'RAF caps', Danish customers walked out of cafés when Germans entered, and the ban on demonstrations was flouted by groups who gathered to sing patriotic songs. On September 1, 1940, an estimated 739,000 Danes around the country gathered to sing the same song simultaneously. The king demonstrated his continued presence by riding on horseback each morning through Copenhagen.

Meanwhile, the Danish government continued its balancing act, knowing that failure to co-operate at least to some degree would lead to a complete Nazi takeover. It was with this in mind that Denmark signed the Anti-Comintern Pact making communism illegal, but insisted on the insertion of a clause that allowed only Danish police to arrest Danish communists.

Vilhelm Buhl, who was appointed prime minister on May 3, 1942, had been an outspoken opponent of the signing of the Anti-Comintern Pact and it was thought he might end the apparent appeasement. Instead, the tension between occupiers and occupied was to climax with Hitler's anger at the curt note received from Christian X in response to the Führer's birthday telegram. Although it was the king's standard reply, Hitler took the mere "thank you" as an insult and immediately replaced his functionaries in Denmark with hardliners who demanded a new pro-German government.

Scavenius took control and, in 1943, elections were called in an attempt to show that freedom of political expression could exist under German occupation. The government asked the public to demonstrate faith in national unity by voting for any one of the four parties in the coalition, and received overwhelming support in the largest ever turnout for a Danish election.

Awareness that German defeat was becoming inevitable stimulated a wave of strikes throughout the country. Berlin declared a state of emergency in Denmark, and demanded that the Danish government comply – which it refused to do. Germany took over administration of the country, interning many politicians. The king was asked to appoint a cabinet from outside the Folketing, and Germans were free for the first time to round up Danish Jews. Resistance was organized under the leadership of the **Danish Freedom Council**. Sabotage was carefully co-ordinated, and an underground army, soon comprising over 43,000, prepared to assist in the Allied invasion. In June 1944, rising anti-Nazi violence led to a curfew being imposed in Copenhagen and assemblies of more than five people being banned, to which workers responded with a spontaneous general strike. German plans to starve the city had to be abandoned after five days.

■ The postwar period

After the German surrender in May 1945, a **liberation government** was created, composed equally of prewar politicians and members of the Danish Freedom Council, with Vilhelm Buhl as prime minister. Its internal differences earned the administration the nickname "the debating club".

While the country had been spared the devastation seen elsewhere in Europe, it still found itself with massive economic problems and it soon became apparent that the liberation government could not function. In the ensuing election there was a swing to the Communists, and a minority Venstre government was formed. The immediate concern was to strengthen the economy, although the resurfacing of the southern Schleswig issue began to dominate the Rigsdag.

Domestic issues soon came to be overshadowed by the **international situation** as the Cold War began. Denmark had unreservedly joined the United Nations in 1945, and had joined the IMF and World Bank to gain financial help in restoring its economy. In 1947 Marshall Plan aid brought further assistance. As world power became polarized between East and West, the Danish government at first tried to remain impartial, but in 1947 agreed to join NATO – a total break with the established concept of Danish neutrality (though, to this day, the Danes remain opposed to nuclear weapons).

The years after the war were marked by much political manoeuvring among the Radicals, Social Democrats and Conservatives, resulting in many hastily called elections and a number of ineffectual compromise coalitions distinguished mainly by the level of their infighting. Working-class support for the Social Democrats steadily eroded, and support for the Communists was largely transferred to the new, more revisionist, Socialist People's Party.

Social reforms, however, continued apace, not least in the 1960s, with the abandoning of all forms of censorship and the institution of free abortion on demand. Such measures are typical of more recent social policy, though Denmark's odd position between Scandinavia and the rest of mainland Europe still persists. A referendum held in 1972 to determine whether Denmark should join the EC resulted in a substantial majority in favour, making Denmark the first Scandinavian member of the community – Sweden, the second, didn't join until 1995 – though public enthusiasm remained lukewarm.

■ The 1970s and 1980s

Perhaps the biggest change in the 1970s was the foundation – and subsequent influence – of the new **Progress Party** (Fremskridtspartiet), headed by Mogens Glistrup, who claimed to have an income of over a million kroner but to be paying no income tax through manipulation of the tax laws. The Progress Party stood on a ticket of immigration curbs and drastic tax cuts, and Glistrup went on to compare tax avoidance with the sabotaging of Nazi railway lines during the war. He also announced that if elected he would replace the Danish defence force with an answering machine saying "we surrender" in Russian. He was eventually imprisoned after an investigation by the Danish tax office; released in 1985, he set himself up as a tax consultant.

What the success of the Progress Party pointed to was dissatisfaction with both the economy and the established parties' strategies for dealing with its problems. In September 1982, **Poul Schlüter** became the country's first Conservative prime minister of the twentieth century, leading the widest-ranging coalition yet seen — including Conservatives, the Venstre, Centre Democrats and Christian People's Party. In keeping with the prevailing political climate in the rest of Europe, the prescription for Denmark's economic malaise was seen to be spending cuts, not sparing the social services, and with an extension of taxation into areas such as pension funds. These policies continued until the snap election of 1987, which resulted in a significant swing to the left. Nevertheless, Schlüter was asked to form a new government, which he did in conjunction with the Progress Party in order to gain a single-seat working majority. A further election, in May 1988, largely served to affirm the new Schlüter-led government, if only, perhaps, because of the apparent lack of any workable alternative.

■ Towards the millennium

In January 1993 Schlüter's government was forced to resign over a political scandal, when it was revealed that asylum had been denied to Sri Lankan Tamil refugees in the late 1980s and early 1990s in contravention of Danish law. The Social Democrats, led by **Poul Nyrup Rasmussen**, took power and formed a four-party coalition. For the first time in ten years Denmark was ruled by a majority government. Since the 1994 election Nyrup Rasmussen has presided over a centre-left majority coalition, which has been criticized for its weak policies on tax reform, the welfare state and the thorny issue of **European union**.

Though traditionally a reluctant member of the EC, Denmark was carried into the European **Exchange Rate Mechanism** (or ERM, widely viewed as the first step towards a single European currency) by Schlüter at the start of the 1990s, a move that transformed the Danish economy into one of the strongest in Europe and made its inflation rate the lowest of any EC member. The price for this, however was soaring unemployment and further cuts in public spending.

The outcome of the **referendum on the Maastricht treaty** (the blueprint for European political and monetary union) in June 1992, however, provided an unexpected upset to the Schlüter apple cart. Despite calls for a "Yes" vote not only from the government but also from the opposition Social Democrats, over 50 percent of Danes rejected the treaty — severely embarrass-

ing the prime minister and sending shivers down the spine of every western European government. The government and other pro-Europe parties didn't give up, however, but set to work on a revised version of the Maastricht Treaty, with the emphasis on protecting national interests — it included a pledge allowing the Danish people to reject citizenship of a United Europe.

A **second referendum** in May 1993 was a triumph for the government, with almost 57 percent of the Danish population voting in favour of the new Treaty. Anti-European feelings, already intense, reached boiling point, and the night after the referendum young left-wingers and anarchists came together in central Copenhagen to declare the area an "EU-free zone". The police moved in to break up the demonstration, battles with the demonstrators ensued, and for the first time ever the Danish police opened fire against a crowd of civilians. Fortunately nobody died, but the incident sparked off a major investigation into the actions of the police, and while Denmark avoided the risk of economic isolation in an increasingly integrated European community, doubts among the Danish people remain, along with a continuing dissatisfaction at the way the yes vote was achieved.

Rasmussen and the Social Democrats retained the largest share of the vote in subsequent elections in 1998 and, as the new millennium dawned, the country was well placed for life in a new Europe. Danes were ranked at the top of the newly created "European Future Readiness Index", which measures social costs and problems such as environmental quality, healthcare costs, poverty and unemployment while the organization Transparency International revealed that Denmark had been chosen as the world's **least corrupt nation**: of 99 countries surveyed, only the Danes received a perfect score on its "Anti-Corruption Index". All was not absolutely well, however. In 1999, crime and poverty in Copenhagen were becoming a serious worry for the first time in many years. Things came to a head during a November **riot** in the city when police used teargas to quell more than one hundred protesters — the first such disturbance since the 1993 anti-Maastricht demonstrations. This time vandals wielded crowbars, bricks and bombs as they broke shop windows and set fires to protest the extradition of a Danish hoodlum from Turkey. City officials were hoping dearly that it would not be the precursor of further violence to come.

A BRIEF GUIDE TO DANISH

Danish in some ways is similar to German, but there are significant differences in pronunciation, Danes tending to swallow the ending of many words and leave certain letters silent. English is widely understood, as is German; young people especially often speak both fluently. And if you can speak Swedish or Norwegian then you should have little problem making yourself understood – all three languages share the same root. A handy phrasebook to take is *Traveller's Scandinavia* (Pan) – which, as well as Danish, covers Norwegian and Swedish.

PRONUNCIATION

In **pronunciation**, unfamiliar **vowels** include:

æ when long between **ai**r and t**ai**lor. When short like g**e**t. When next to "**r**" sounds more like h**a**t.

å when long like s**a**w, when short like **o**n.

ø like f**u**r but with the lips rounded.

e, when long, is similar to pl**a**te, when short somewhere between pl**a**te and h**i**t; when unstressed it's as in **a**bove.

Consonants are pronounced as in English, except:

d at the end of a word after a vowel, or between a vowel and an unstressed "e" or "i", like **th**is. Sometimes silent at the end of a word.

g at the beginning of a word or syllable as in **g**o. At the end of a word or long vowel, or before an unstressed e, usually like **y**et but sometimes like the Scottish lo**ch**. Sometimes mute after an a, e, or o.

hv like **v**iew

hj like **y**et

k as English except between vowels, when it's as in **g**o.

p as English except between vowels, when it's as in **b**it.

r pronounced as in French from the back of the throat but often silent.

sj as in **sh**eet

t as English except between vowels, when it's as in **d**o. Often mute when at the end of a word.

y between b**ee** and p**oo**l

BASICS

Do you speak English?	*Taler De engelsk?*	Goodnight	*Godnat*
Yes	*Ja*	Goodbye	*Farvel*
No	*Nej*	Yesterday	*I går*
I don't understand	*Jeg forstår det ikke*	Today	*I dag*
I understand	*Jeg forstår*	Tomorrow	*I morgen*
Please	*Værså venlig*	Day after	*I overmorgen*
Thank you	*Tak*	tomorrow	
Excuse me	*Undskyld*	In the morning	*Om morgenen*
Good morning	*Godmorgen*	In the afternoon	*Om eftermiddagen*
Good afternoon	*Goddag*	In the evening	*Om aftenen*

SOME SIGNS

Entrance	*Indgang*	Arrival	*Ankomst*
Exit	*Udgang*	Departure	*Afgang*
Push/pull	*Skub/træk*	Police	*Politi*
Danger	*Fare*	No Smoking	*Rygning forbudt/Ikke rygere*
Gentlemen	*Herrer*	No Entry	*Ingen adgang*
Ladies	*Damer*	No Camping	*Campering forbudt*
Open	*Åben*	No Trespassing	*Adgang forbudt for*
Closed	*Lukket*		*uvedkommende*

QUESTIONS AND DIRECTIONS

Where is?	*Hvor er?*	Near/far	*Er det nær/fjern*
When?	*Hvornår?*	Left/right	*Venstre/højre*
What?	*Hvad?*	Straight ahead	*Ligeud*
Why?	*Hvorfor?*	I'd like. . .	*Jeg vil gerne ha. . .*
Who?	*Hvem?*	Where is the youth	*Hvor er vandrerhjemmet?*
How much?	*Hvor meget?*	hostel?	
How much does it	*Hvad koster det?*	Can we camp here?	*Må vi campere her?*
cost?		It's too expensive	*Det er for dyrt*
Here	*Her*	Where are the toilets?	*Hvor er toiletterne ?*
There	*Der*	How far is it to. . .?	*Hvor langt er der til. . .?*
Good/bad	*God/dårlig*	Where can I get a	*Hvor kan jeg tage/*
Cheap/expensive	*Billig/dyr*	train/bus/ferry to. . .?	*bussen/færgen til. . .?*
Hot/cold	*Varm/kold*	At what time does. . .?	*Hvornår går. . .?*
Better/bigger/cheaper	*Bedre/større/billigere*	Ticket	*Billet*

NUMBERS

0	*Nul*	9	*Ni*	18	*Atten*	80	*Firs*
1	*En*	10	*Ti*	19	*Nitten*	90	*Halvfems*
2	*To*	11	*Elleve*	20	*Tyve*	100	*Hundrede*
3	*Tre*	12	*Tolv*	21	*Enogtyve*	101	*Hundrede og et*
4	*Fire*	13	*Tretten*	30	*Tredive*	151	*Hundrede og*
5	*Fem*	14	*Fjorten*	40	*Fyrre*		*enoghalvtreds*
6	*Seks*	15	*Femten*	50	*Halvtreds*	200	*To hundrede*
7	*Syv*	16	*Seksten*	60	*Tres*	1000	*Tusind*
8	*Otte*	17	*Sytten*	70	*Halvfjerds*		

DAYS AND MONTHS

Monday	*mandag*	January	*januar*	July	*juli*
Tuesday	*tirsdag*	February	*februar*	August	*august*
Wednesday	*onsdag*	March	*marts*	September	*september*
Thursday	*torsdag*	April	*april*	October	*oktober*
Friday	*fredag*	May	*maj*	November	*november*
Saturday	*lørdag*	June	*juni*	December	*december*
Sunday	*søndag*				

(Days and months are never capitalised)

GLOSSARY OF DANISH TERMS AND WORDS

Banegård	Railway station	*Herregård*	Manor house	*Rutebilstation*	Bus station
Bakke	Hill or ridge	*Jernebane*	Railway	*Rådhus*	Town hall
Domkirke	Cathedral	*Kirke*	Church	*Skov*	Wood or forest
Gammel or	Old	*Klint*	Cliff	*Stue*	Room
Gamle		*Kloster*	Monastery	*Sø*	Lake
Hav	Sea	*Kro*	Inn	*Torvet*	Market square
Havn	Harbour	*Plads*	Square	*Tårn*	Tower
				Vand	Water

CHAPTER ONE

ZEALAND

As the largest of Denmark's islands, and home to its capital, **Zealand** (Sjælland) is Denmark's most important – and most visited – region. Though not an especially big city, Copenhagen dominates much of the island; the nearby towns, while far from being drab suburbia, tend inevitably to be dormitory territory. Only much further away, towards the west and south, does the pace become more provincial.

It would be perverse to come to Zealand and not visit **Copenhagen** – easily the most extrovert and cosmopolitan place in the country, and as lively by night as it is by day. But once there you should make at least a brief journey into the country to see how different the rest of Denmark can be. Woods and expansive parklands appear almost as soon as you leave the city – and even if you don't like what you find, the swiftness of the metropolitan transport network, which covers almost half the island, means that you can be back in the capital in easy time for an evening drink.

North of Copenhagen, the coastal road passes the outstanding modern art museum of **Louisiana** and the absorbing Karen Blixen museum at **Rungsted** before reaching **Helsingør**, site of the renowned **Kronborg Slot** (better known as Elsinore Castle), an impressive fortification that nevertheless quite unfairly steals the spotlight from **Frederiksborg Slot**, an even more eye-catching fort in nearby **Hillerød**. West of Copenhagen and on the main route to Funen is **Roskilde**, a former capital with an extravagant cathedral that's still the last resting place for Danish monarchs, and with a gorgeous location on the Roskilde fjord – from where five Viking boats were salvaged that are now restored and displayed in a specially built museum. **South** of Copenhagen, at the end of the urban S-train system, is **Køge**, which – beyond the industrial sites that flank it – has a well-preserved medieval centre and long, sandy beaches lining its bay.

Further out from the sway of Copenhagen, Zealand's towns are appreciably smaller, more scattered, and far less full of either commuters or day-trippers. **Ringsted**, plumb in the heart of the island, is another one-time capital, a fact recalled by the twelfth- and thirteenth-century royal tombs in its church. Further south, **Næstved**, surrounded by lush countryside, gives access to three smaller islands just off the coast: **Lolland**, **Falster** and **Møn**. Each of these is busy during the summer, but outside high season you'll find them green and peaceful, with Lolland offering a leisurely backdoor route, via Langeland, to Funen.

Not part of Zealand, but conveniently reached by a ferry from Copenhagen, is the island of **Bornholm**. A huge slab of granite in the Baltic, it houses a few small fishing communities and has some fine beaches and an unusual history, making a stimulating

---

ACCOMMODATION PRICE CODES

The hotels and guest houses listed in this chapter have been graded according to the following price bands, based on the **cheapest rate for a double room in summer**.

   ① Under 300kr   ② 300–400kr   ③ 400–500kr   ④ 500–650kr
       ⑤ 650–900kr   ⑥ 900–1300kr   ⑦ Over 1300kr

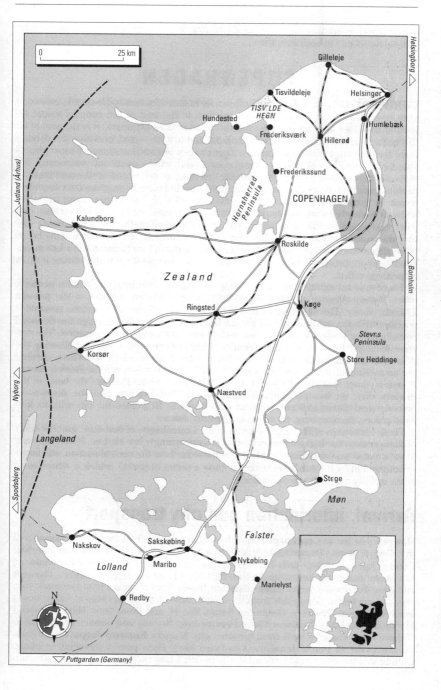

detour if you're heading for Sweden – it's nearer Sweden than Denmark, with regular ferry connections to both countries.

COPENHAGEN

COPENHAGEN, as any Dane will tell you, is no introduction to Denmark; indeed, a greater contrast with the sleepy provincialism of the rest of the country would be hard to find. Despite that, the city completely dominates Denmark: it is the seat of all the nation's institutions – political, financial and artistic – and provides the driving force for the country's social reforms. Copenhagen is also Scandinavia's most affordable capital, and one of Europe's most user-friendly cities: small and welcoming, it's a place where people rather than cars set the pace, as evidenced by the multitude of pavement cafés and the number of thoroughfares that have been given over to pedestrians. In summer especially there's a varied range of lively street entertainment, while at night there are plenty of cosy bars and an intimate club and live-music network that could hardly be bettered. This is not to mention the city's beckoning history museums and galleries of Danish and international art, as well as a worthy batch of smaller collections. If you're intent on heading north into Scandinavia's less populated (and pricier) reaches, you'd certainly be wise to spend a few days living it up in Copenhagen first.

There was no more than a tiny fishing settlement here until the twelfth century, when Bishop Absalon oversaw the building of a castle on the site of the present Christiansborg. The settlement's prosperity grew after Erik of Pomerania granted it special privileges and imposed the Sound Toll on vessels passing through the Øresund strait between Denmark and Sweden, which was then under Danish control. The revenue from the tolls enabled a self-confident trading centre to flourish. Following the demise of the Hanseatic ports, the city became the Baltic's principal harbour, earning the name København ("merchant's port"), and in 1443 it was made the Danish capital. A century later, Christian IV began the building programme that was the basis of the modern city: up went Rosenborg Slot, Børsen, Rundetårnet, and the districts of Nyboder and Christianshavn, while in 1669 Frederik III graced the city with its first royal palace, Amalienborg, for his queen, Sophie Amalie.

These structures still exist, like much of the Copenhagen of that time, and the taller of them remain the highest points in what is a refreshingly low skyline. It's an easy city to get around: you're unlikely to need to venture far from the central section, still largely hemmed in by the medieval ramparts (now a series of parks), which is where most of the activity and sights are contained.

Arrival, information and city transport

However you get to Copenhagen you'll be within easy reach of the centre. **Trains** pull into Central Station (Hovedbanegården), near Vesterbrogade. Downstairs, the InterRail Centre (July to mid-Sept daily 7am–1am), restricted to InterRail or Eurail pass holders, is a useful refuge for long-distance travellers, with large left-luggage lockers, showers and even microwave ovens. **Long-distance buses** from other parts of Denmark stop only a short bus or S-train ride from the centre: buses from Århus stop at Valby; buses from Aalborg at Ryparken Station on S-train line H; and those from Hanstholm and Fjerritsslev on Hans Knudsens Plads. **Ferries** from Norway and Sweden dock close to Nyhavn, a few minutes' walk from the inner city. Modern **Kastrup Airport**, 8km from the city, is the air hub of Scandinavia and your likely entry point if travelling by plane. Getting into the city from here couldn't be easier: a new rail line, one of the fastest air-

ONWARD TRAVEL TO SWEDEN AND NORWAY

If you're travelling on to Sweden and Norway, a brand new rail link connecting Copenhagen Central Station with Malmö and – via fast train (reservations always required) – Stockholm, Gothenburg and Oslo was scheduled to open in June 2000. Using this new link, the ride across the Øresund via tunnel and bridge should now take 35 minutes (around half an hour quicker than the old ferry–shuttle combination) and cost 65kr. Contact DSB (Danish Railways) on ☎70 13 14 15 for up-to-the-minute information.

port-to-city links in Europe, runs directly to Central Station every twenty minutes (12min; 18kr). There's also a slower but cheaper city bus (#32; 16.50kr) to Rådhuspladsen.

Information

Once you've arrived, your first stop should be **Use-It**, centrally placed at the back of the Huset complex at Rådhusstræde 13 in the heart of Indre By (mid-June to mid-Sept daily 9am–7pm; mid-Sept to mid-June Mon–Fri 10am–4pm; ☎33 15 65 18). They provide full details of budget accommodation, eating, drinking and entertainment, a free city map, will hold mail and store luggage, and in summer issue *Playtime*, a small but extremely useful free newspaper. There's also a Wonderful Copenhagen **tourist office** near Central Station at Bernstorffsgade 1 (May Mon–Fri 9am–5pm, Sat 9am–2pm, Sun 9am–1pm; June to mid-Sept daily 9am–6pm; mid-Sept to April Mon–Fri 9am–5pm, Sat 9am–noon; ☎33 11 13 25), which provides countrywide information and distributes the free *Copenhagen This Week*, an up-to-date news and listings magazine.

If you plan to visit many museums, either in Copenhagen or in nearby towns like Helsingør, Roskilde and Køge, the **Copenhagen Card** is valid for transport on the entire metropolitan system (which includes the towns mentioned above) and also gives entry to virtually every museum in the area. Obviously its worth will depend on your itinerary, but the three-day card (320kr) can certainly save money if well used – especially since it also gets you twenty- to fifty-percent discounts on some car hire and ferry rides, and on certain museum entry prices across the sound in southern Sweden. It's available from the tourist office, travel agents, hotels and most train stations in the metropolitan region.

City transport

The best way to see most of Copenhagen is simply to **walk**: the inner city is compact and much of the central area pedestrianized. There is, however, an integrated zonal network of buses and electric "S-trains" (*S-tog*) covering Copenhagen and the surrounding areas, which run about every ten to fifteen minutes between 5am and 12.30am, after which a night bus (*Natbusserne*) system comes into operation – less frequent, but still with services once or twice an hour. The **S-train** network is a bit erratic, running some odd routes and being occasionally plagued by inexplicable delays, but it's still the fastest way to reach outlying points. Stations are marked by red hexagonal signs with a yellow "S" inside them. All thirteen lines stop at Central Station, but after this they diverge confusingly. Study a map before boarding the train or you could end up some way from your intended destination.

Buses can sometimes be a swifter way to get around, once you get the hang of finding the stops – marked by yellow placards on signposts – so long as you avoid the rush hour. The city's main bus stand is adjacent to City Hall in the big open square called Rådhuspladsen), a block from both Central Station and the Tivoli Gardens.

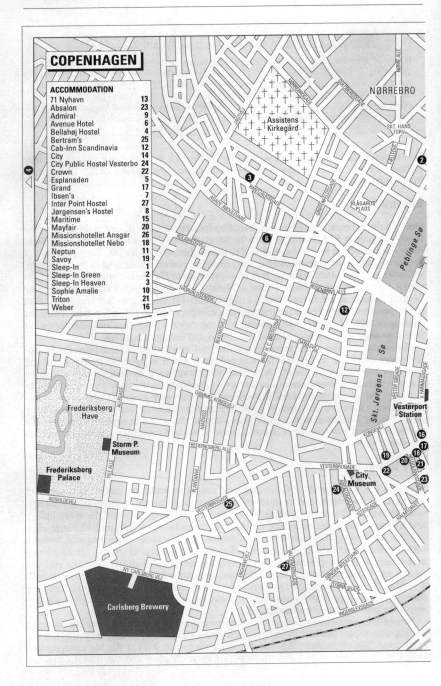

COPENHAGEN

ACCOMMODATION

71 Nyhavn	13
Absalon	23
Admiral	9
Avenue Hotel	6
Bellahøj Hostel	4
Bertram's	25
Cab-Inn Scandinavia	12
City	14
City Public Hostel Vesterbo	24
Crown	22
Esplanaden	5
Grand	17
Ibsen's	7
Inter Point Hostel	27
Jørgensen's Hostel	8
Maritime	15
Mayfair	20
Missionshotellet Ansgar	26
Missionshotellet Nebo	18
Neptun	11
Savoy	19
Sleep-In	1
Sleep-In Green	2
Sleep-In Heaven	3
Sophie Amalie	10
Triton	21
Weber	16

NØRREBRO

Assistens
Kirkegård

SKT. HANS
TORV

BLÅGÅRDS
PLADS

Peblinge Sø

Skt. Jørgens
Sø

Vesterport
Station

Frederiksberg
Have

Storm P.
Museum

Frederiksberg
Palace

ROSKILDEVEJ

City
Museum

Carlsberg Brewery

NY CARLSBERG VEJ

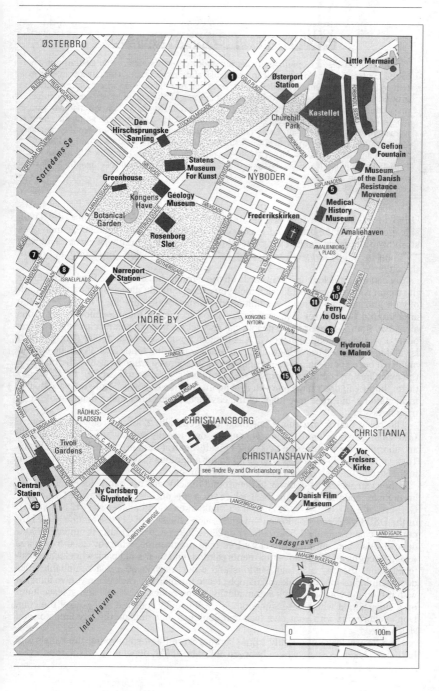

UNDERGROUND AND OVERDUE

The idiosyncrasies of Copenhagen's S-train and bus routes means that getting quickly to the centre from the outskirts can be a frustrating experience. The city's transit system will be getting a much-needed boost, however, in 2002 or 2003 when its first underground line finally opens. The evidence of this work is obvious all over the city centre, disrupting views and traffic in high-visibility areas such as Christianshavn and Nørreport. But there is a light at the end of the tunnel. By 2003 the plan is to run a light railway or underground train every couple of minutes during rush hour, linking central Copenhagen not just to its own suburbs but also with the new Øresund bridge to Sweden and with Kastrup Airport. Underground stops will be conveniently located in Christianshavn, at Kongens Nytorv (the huge square/traffic circle beside Nyhavn canal), and on Strøget.

Other useful buses leave from Central Station's Vesterport side entrance, the Tivoli side entrance and the bridge at the end of the tracks (including the #550S, which goes straight to the ferry docks every ten minutes). Night bus numbers always end with "N", and the stops are well marked by yellow signs on major routes into and out of the city.

You can use InterRail or Eurail cards on the S-trains, but otherwise the best option is the **ticket** with ten stamps (80kr), which you cancel individually according to the length of your journey: one stamp gives unlimited transfers within one hour in one zone (the area around the centre), two stamps are good for ninety minutes and three stamps allow two hours – two or more people can use tickets from the same carnet simultaneously. For a short single journey of less than an hour, use a Grundbillet (11kr), which is valid for unlimited transfers within two zones within that time. Tickets can be bought on board buses or at train stations and should be stamped when boarding the bus or in the machines on station platforms. Except on buses, it's rare to be asked to show your ticket, but if you don't have one you face an instant fine of 250kr. Route maps cost 10kr from stations, but most free maps of the city include bus lines and a diagram of the S-train network.

The basic **taxi** fare within Copenhagen is generally 22kr plus 8kr per kilometre (rates increase after 6pm and at weekends) – only usually worthwhile if several people are sharing. There's a useful taxi rank outside Central Station, or phone Københavns Taxa (☎35 35 35 35 for a cab, ☎35 39 35 35 for a minibus). Alternatively, just hail a cab in the street that's showing a green "Fri" sign on top.

Bikes can also be a good way to get around the city, and are handy for exploring the immediate countryside. The best place to rent one is Københavns Cyklebørs, Gothersgade 157 (☎33 14 07 17), or try Cykeltanken, Godthåbsvej 247 (☎31 87 14 23), or the DSB Cykelcenter on Reventlowsgade, along the side of Central Station. Bike hire normally costs around 40–50kr per day or 200–250kr per week, plus a refundable 200kr deposit. Also bear in mind the city's free bike programme, whereby 2500 free bikes (easily recognized by the advertisements painted onto their solid back wheels) are scattered about the city at S-train stations and other busy locations; a refundable 20kr deposit unlocks one. The rules are simple: leave the bike in a rack when you've finished with it (you get your coin back automatically as you relock the bike), or just leave it out on a sidewalk, in which case someone else will happily return it and pocket the coin. Don't secure one with your own lock and don't take one outside the city limits or you risk a fine.

Boat tours leave frequently from Gammel Strand and sail around the canals and harbour. Tickets cost anywhere between 40kr and 120kr, depending on the tour.

Accommodation

Whether it's a hostel bed or a luxury hotel suite, **accommodation** of all kinds is easy to come by in Copenhagen, and almost all of it is centrally located. If you're going to be arriving late or during July and August – the busiest time of year – it's wise, especially if you're looking for a cheap place, to book in advance, if only for the first night.

Hotels

You won't find a grotty **hotel** in Copenhagen, though the cheaper ones often forgo the pleasures of private bathroom, phone and TV. Prices do, however, almost always include breakfast. Most of the budget hotels are just west of the inner centre, around Istedgade – a slightly seedy (though rarely dangerous) area on the far side of the train station. This area is also home to a number of mid-range hotels, and there are further mid-price hotels around Nyhavn canal, on the other side of Indre By, and out towards the quiet suburb of Frederiksberg. If you arrive without a reservation, Wonderful Copenhagen's main tourist information office at Bernstorffsgade 1 (☎33 25 38 44) will find you a hotel room, although queues for this service can be lengthy during high season, and it costs 40kr.

Absalon, Helgolandsgade 15 (☎33 24 22 11, fax 33 24 34 11). Clean and modern, with soundproofing that makes it extremely quiet and relaxing. ⑤.

Admiral, Toldbodgade 24–28 (☎33 11 82 82, fax 33 32 55 42). A 200-year-old granary beside the harbour, converted into comfortable wood-beamed rooms ⑥.

Avenue, Åboulevard 29 (☎35 37 31 11, fax 35 37 34 86, *avenue@get2net.dk*). A comfortable place to stay, on a main suburban boulevard that's surprisingly close to downtown Copenhagen. ⑥.

Bertrams, Vesterbrogade 107 (☎33 25 04 05, fax 33 25 04 02). Newish two-star between Central Station and the Carlsberg Brewery, and quite affordable. ④.

Cab-Inn Scandinavia, Vodroffsvej 57 (☎35 36 11 11, fax 35 36 11 14). In a quiet suburb very close to city centre. You'll feel like a passenger on an overnight boat with the flip-up tables and tiny showers, but it's clean and safe, and the free breakfast, fun crowd, pleasant staff and unbeatably low price make it easily the top budget hotel in town. ④. There's a second branch close by at Danasvej 32 with similar – although slightly more expensive (⑤) – rooms (☎33 21 04 00, fax 33 21 74 09). Take bus #8, #12, #13, or #29 to either hotel.

City, Peder Skramsgade 24 (☎33 13 06 66, fax 33 13 06 67). Decent three-star in the Nyhavn area, though you pay for the location. ⑥.

Crown, Vesterbrogade 41 (☎33 21 21 66, fax 33 21 00 66). Yet another three-star near Central Station, better than many of the others. ⑤.

Esplanaden, Bredgade 78 (☎33 91 32 00, fax 33 91 32 39). Cheaper but also further from the centre than its sister hotel the *Neptun* (see overleaf). ⑥.

Grand, Vesterbrogade 9A (☎33 31 61 00, fax 33 31 33 50). Very popular with British travellers, and quite close to both the Tivoli Gardens and a row of British- and American-style pubs and restaurants. ⑦.

Ibsens, Vendersgade 23 (☎33 13 19 13, fax 33 13 19 16, *hotel@ibsenshotel.dk*). The staff can be lukewarm at times, but the central location and recently renovated rooms still make it a winner. A bounteous Danish breakfast spread of cereal, yogurt, bread and cheese is included. ⑥.

Maritime, Peder Skramsgade 19 (☎33 13 48 82, fax 33 15 03 45). Affordable three-star hotel off Nyhavn, close to many attractions, and all rooms have cable television. ⑤.

Mayfair, Helgolandsgade 3 (☎33 31 48 01, fax 33 23 96 86). Old Danish-style elegance coupled with every modern convenience. ⑥.

Missionshotellet Ansgar, Colbjørnsensgade 29 (☎33 21 21 96, fax 33 21 61 91). Compact and tidy, this place actually lowers its prices in high season. No alcohol served. ⑤.

Missionshotellet Nebo, Istedgade 6 (☎33 21 12 17, fax 33 23 47 74). Small, cheap and friendly, and one of the best deals in this part of the city, though it's located on one of the city's famously sleazy streets and alcohol isn't served. ④.

Neptun, Skt Annæ Plads 14–20 (☎33 13 89 00, fax 33 14 12 50). Expensive business hotel in an 1856 building, its main drawcard is a prime location across the Nyhavn canal from scores of cafés. ⑦.

71 Nyhavn, Nyhavn 71 (☎33 11 85 85, fax 33 93 15 85). New hotel right on the famous canals, above a good restaurant. Central to the action and classy, but the 84 rooms come at a price. ⑦.

Savoy, Vesterbrogade 34 (☎33 26 75 00, fax 33 26 75 01). Nice and quiet three-star on a lane off the main street. ⑤.

Sophie Amalie, Skt Annæ Plads 21 (☎33 13 34 00, fax 33 11 77 07). Large luxurious rooms, right by the harbour. ⑥.

Triton, Helgolandsgade 7–11 (☎35 21 80 50, fax 35 31 69 70). A showpiece of contemporary Danish design, well-suited to a cosy stay. ⑥.

Weber, Vesterbrogade 11b (☎33 31 14 32, fax 33 31 14 41). Plush, cosy and full of charm – but you pay for it. ⑦.

Hostels, pensions and student accommodation

For those on a tighter budget, Copenhagen has a great selection of **hostel** accommodation, where a dormitory bed costs 80–100kr (less in the official HI hostels). Space is only likely to be a problem in the peak summer months from June to August, during which you should call ahead or turn up as early as possible. For the most up-to-date information ask at Use-It (see p.71), or check the accommodation reviews in *Playtime* (see p.71).

If you're around for more than couple of weeks, subletting a room in a **student hall** or **shared flat**, or renting a **private room** in someone's home (generally 130–175kr per person per day – ask at Use-It) can be a money-saving option. You can also arrange private rooms through the tourist office at Bernstorffsgade 1 for a fee of 40kr, though you can only do so in person, not over the phone. This office cannot book rooms in advance, only on the day itself; if you want something a confirmed booking before you arrive, Bed & Breakfast in Denmark, Postboks 53, DK 2900 Hellerup (☎39 61 04 05, fax 39 61 05 25), can make advance arrangements for you.

Hostels

Bellahøj, Herbergvejen 8, in the Brønshøj district (☎38 28 97 15). More homely than its rivals, situated in a distant residential part of the city, with cheap beds. Simple to reach, too: about 15min from the city centre on bus #2 or #11 (night bus #82N) to Herbergsvejen. Buses #8, #63 and #68 also stop close by. Reception is open 24hr and there's no curfew, although there's a dormitory lockout from 10am–1pm. Closed Dec.

City Public Hostel Vesterbro, Absalonsgade 8 (☎33 31 20 70). Handily placed, ten minutes' walk from Central Station between Vesterbrogade and Istedgade. There's a noisy sixty-bed dormitory on the lower floor, but less crowded conditions (dormitories of 4–20 beds) on other levels. Also has kitchen. Reports vary, but the atmosphere is easy-going and there's no curfew. Bed linen is 30kr extra. Buses #6 and #28 stop close by. Open May to mid-Aug.

Inter Point, Valdemarsgade 15 (☎33 31 15 74). Run by the Danish YMCA/YWCA, dorm beds here are cheap, but there are only 28 to be had and there's a 12.30am curfew. About ten minutes' walk from Central Station, or take bus #3, #6 or #16. Open July to mid-Aug.

Jørgensens, Rømersgade 11 (☎33 13 81 86). Hotel that in summer turns into a hostel with dormitory accommodation (4–14 beds per dormitory), including breakfast and televisions in each room. Those without a sleeping bag can rent blankets for 30kr. Very central, near both Nørreport station and Strøget; take bus #5.

Sleep-In, Blegdamsvej 132 (☎35 26 50 59). A vast hall divided into four-bed compartments. Nice, if busy, atmosphere, with a young and friendly staff and sporadic free gigs by local bands; no curfew. Beds 80kr, breakfast 30kr; if you don't have a sleeping bag you can rent sheets for 30kr (plus 40kr deposit). Bus #1, #6, #14, #85N or #95N from Rådhuspladsen or the train station. Open July–Aug.

Sleep-In Green, Ravnsborggade 18 (☎35 37 77 77). Ecological hostel right in hip Nørrebro, featuring organic snacks, good all-volunteer staff and bright rooms of ten, twenty and 38 beds. It also looks onto a pretty interior courtyard, which is unfortunately off-limits to the guests. There are extra charges for bedding (70kr) and breakfast (30kr) and a noon–4pm lockout. Take bus #5, #16, #81N or #84N. Open late May to Sept.

Sleep-In Heaven, 7th floor, Struenseegade 7 (☎35 35 46 48, *sleepinheaven@get2net.dk*). Another big hostel, with four- and eight-bed dorms, in Nørrebro outside the city centre. Also has lockers, Internet access, and takes credit cards. Catch #8, #12, #13 buses from Central Station or #85N night bus from Rådhauspladsen. Closed Jan to mid-Feb.

Campsites

Of Copenhagen's various campsites, only one is close to the city centre, although the others are fairly easily reached by public transport. There's little difference in price among them.

Absalon, Korsdalsvej 132, Rødovre (☎36 41 06 00; June–Aug). About 9km to the southwest of the city and open all year. Take S-train line B to Brøndbyøster.

Bellahøj, on Hvidkildevej (☎38 10 11 50). Near the *Bellahøj* youth hostel this is the most central but least comfortable option, with long queues for the showers and cooking facilities. Buses #2, #8, #63 and #68.

Charlottenlund Strandpark, Strandvejen 144B, Charlottenlund (☎39 62 36 88; May–Sept). Beautifully situated at Charlottenlund Beach, 8km south of the city centre; take bus #6.

Nærum on Ravnebakken (☎45 80 19 57; mid-April to mid-Sept). Around 20km from the centre, but very pleasant: take a train to Jægersborg, then private train (InterRail and Eurail not valid) to Nærum. Cabins also available.

Strandmøllen, Strandmøllevej 2 (☎45 80 94 45; mid-May to Aug). Around 14km north of the city, a twenty-minute ride away on S-train line C (to Klampenborg), then bus #188 towards Helsingør.

Tangloppen, in Ishøj Havn (☎43 54 07 67). Some 17km south of city centre, but close to some good and popular beaches. Take any train to Ishøj, then bus #128.

The City

Exploring Copenhagen is supremely easy. Most of what you're likely to want to see can be found in the city's relatively small – and effortlessly walkable – centre, between the long inlet of the inner harbour (Inder Havnen) on the east and a semicircular series of lakes on the west. Within this area the divisions are well defined. **Indre By** forms the city's inner core, an intricate maze of streets, squares and alleys whose pleasure lies as much in its general daily bustle as in specific sights. The area **northeast of Indre By**, beyond the major thoroughfare of Gothersgade, is quite different, a boldly proportioned grid-pattern of streets and avenues built to accommodate the dwellings of the Danish nobility in the seventeenth century and reaching a pinnacle of affluence with the palaces of Amalienborg and Rosenborg. The far end of this stretch is guarded, now as three hundred years ago, by the Kastellet, which lies within the fetching open spaces of Churchill Park.

Separated by a moat from Indre By, **Christiansborg** is the administrative centre for the whole country, housing the national parliament and government offices as well as a number of museums and the ruins of Bishop Absalon's original castle. **Christianshavn**, facing Christiansborg across the inner harbour, provides further contrast, with its tightly proportioned and traditionally working-class streets and a pretty waterfront lined by Dutch-style dwellings. A few blocks to the east lies the "free city" of **Christiania**, an area colonized by the young and homeless in the early 1970s, whose alternative society remains an enduring controversy in Danish life – and merits at least a quick look. **West of the city centre**, Vesterbrogade is the prime thoroughfare, beginning at the carefree delights of the Tivoli Gardens and running to the city fringes at Frederiksberg Have.

Indre By

The natural place from which to begin exploring Indre By (though not actually in it) is the buzzing open space of **Rådhuspladsen**. Here, the **Rådhus**, or City Hall (Mon–Fri 10am–3pm; free), has a spacious and elegant main hall that retains many of its original early twentieth-century features, not least the sculptured banisters heading up from the first floor; there's also a lift up to the bell tower (at 10am, noon & 2pm; 10kr) for a not madly impressive view over the city. More interesting is **Jens Olsen's World Clock** (Mon–Fri 10am–4pm, Sat 10am–1pm; 10kr), in a side room close to the entrance. What looks like a mass of inscrutable dials is an astronomical timepiece which took 27 years to perfect and contains a 570,000-year calendar plotting eclipses of the moon and sun, solar time, local time and various planetary orbits – all with incredible accuracy. At no. 57 on Rådhuspladsen, and with an appeal of an entirely different kind, **Ripley's Believe It Or Not!** (June–Aug daily 10am–10pm; Sept–May Mon–Thurs & Sun 10am–4pm, Fri & Sat 10am–8pm; 62kr) is collection of oddities based on the cartoons of American Robert L. Ripley – a life-size model of the world's tallest man and a bicycle made from matchsticks are just two of hundreds of exhibits.

Along Strøget

Indre By proper begins with **Strøget** (literally "level measure"), the series of streets – Vesterbrogade, Frederiksberggade, Nygade, Vimmelskaftet Amagertorv and Østergade – which run east–west across the district, lined by pricey stores and graceless fast-food dives. Very much the public face of Copenhagen, it's hard to imagine anything unpleasant ever happening here, and the strip is perfectly suited to stress-free ambling amongst the crowds of locals and street entertainers who parade along it. The most active part is usually around **Gammeltorv** and **Nytorv**, two adjacent squares ("old" and "new") flanking Strøget, where there's a morning fruit-and-vegetable market, stalls selling handmade jewellery and bric-a-brac, and frequent political rallies. It was between these squares that the fifteenth-century Rådhus stood before it was destroyed by fire in 1795. A new Rådhus was erected on Nytorv a century later, and this is now the city's **Domhuset**, or Law Courts, marked by a suitably forbidding row of Neoclassical columns.

Just east of here is the **Helligåndskirken** (daily 11am–4pm), one of the oldest churches in the city, founded in the fourteenth century though largely rebuilt from 1728 onwards. While it's still in use as a place of worship, there are often art shows and other free exhibitions inside which provide a good excuse for a peek at the church's vaulted ceiling and slender granite columns. Of equally low-key appeal is the tobacco shop directly across Strøget which holds the **W.Ø. Larsens Tobaksmuseet** (Mon–Fri 9.30am–5pm, Sat 9am–1pm; free) and its briefly diverting clutter of vintage pipes, ornate cigar holders and every conceivable smoking accessory, plus paintings and drawings satirizing the deadly habit. Just beyond, a path leads south off Strøget, through Højbro Plads and on to the grandiose **Skt Nikolai Kirke** (no longer used for services), whose upper floors are employed primarily as an exhibition space for contemporary artists, while at ground level there's a daytime café.

The final section of Strøget is Østergade, where you'll find another international tourist pull: the **Guinness World of Records Museum** (June–Aug daily 10am–10pm; Sept–May Mon–Thurs 10am–6pm, Fri & Sat 10am–8pm; 62kr). It's much as you'd expect, with family-oriented exhibits on the world's tallest, fastest and smallest. Beyond, Østergade flows past the swish and chic *Hotel d'Angleterre* into the biggest of the city squares, **Kongens Nytorv**. Built on what was the edge of the city in medieval times, the square has an equestrian statue of its creator, Christian V, in its centre and a couple of grandly ageing structures around two of its shallow angles. One of these, the Kongelige Teater or **Royal Theatre**, dates from 1874; the other, **Charlottenborg**, next door, was finished in 1683, at the same time as the square itself, for a son of Frederik III. It was later sold to Queen Charlotte Amalie, but since 1754 has been the home of the Royal Academy of Art, which uses some of the spacious rooms for eclectic art exhibitions. Drop in if the building's open – hours and admission prices depend on what's on show – if only to glimpse the elegant interior.

The Latin Quarter and around

There's more interest among the tangle of buildings and streets **north of Strøget**. Crossing Gammeltorv and following Nørregade leads to the old university area, sometimes called the **Latin Quarter**, parts of which retain an academic function, which accounts for the book-carrying students milling around. The old university building is overlooked by Copenhagen's cathedral, **Vor Frue Kirke** (Mon–Thurs 9am–4.30pm, Fri 9–10.30am & 12.30–4.30pm, Sat 9am–4.30pm, Sun noon–1pm & 3–4pm). Built on the site of a twelfth-century church, the present structure dates only from 1829, when it was erected amidst the devastation caused by the British bombardment in 1807. The weighty figure of Christ behind the altar and the solemn statues of the apostles, some crafted by Bertel Thorvaldsen (for more on whom, see p.84), others by his pupils, merit a quick call. From the cathedral, dodge across Skindergade into **Gråbrødretorv**, a charming cobbled square, filled with good cafés and restaurants and often crowded with buskers. The square dates back to 1238, when the city's first monastery was built here; today, it's a gathering place for locals in the know, who come in good weather to dine well. Just north of here is the **Rundetårn** (June–Aug Mon–Sat 10am–8pm, Sun noon–8pm; Sept–May Mon–Sat 10am–5pm, Sun noon–5pm), a round tower with a gradually ascending spiral ramp winding to its summit, built by Christian IV as an **observatory** – and perhaps also to provide a vantage point from which his subjects could admire his additions to the city. Today the best views are of the more immediate hive of medieval streets and the pedestrians filling them. Legend has it that Tsar Peter the Great sped to the top on horseback in 1715, pursued by the Tsarina in a six-horse carriage – a smoother technique than descending the cobbles on a skateboard, a short-lived fad in more recent times. If you're not quite up to trying that, look in on the contemporary art gallery part of the way up instead, with changing temporary exhibitions.

After leaving the Rundetårn, you could easily spend half an hour browsing the bookshops of Købmagergade, or visit the **Museum Erotica** (May–Aug daily 10am–11pm; Sept–April daily 10am–6pm), which lurks along here at no. 24, a shrine to the erotic (and the just plain pornographic) through the ages. For something more traditional, the **Musical History Museum**, just off Kultorvet at Åbenrå 30 (May–Sept Mon–Wed & Fri–Sun 1–3.50pm; Oct–April Mon, Wed, Sat & Sun 1–3.50pm; 15kr), has an impressive quantity of musical instruments and sound-producing devices spanning the globe and the last thousand years. Naturally the bulk come from Denmark, and there are some subtle insights into the social fabric of the nation to be gleaned from the yellowing photos of country dances and other get-togethers hung alongside the instruments. There are also recordings to listen to, and a weekly guided tour in English (Wed 11am; other times by request).

Less musical sounds are provided by the cars hurtling along Nørre Voldgade, at the top of Kultorvet, which marks the edge of the pedestrianized streets of the old city. There are two reasons to queue up at the traffic lights and cross over: the first is the fruit-and-vegetable **market** – and Saturday flea market – on Israel Plads; the second is the **Workers' Museum** at Rømersgade 22 (Arbejdermuseet; Tues–Fri 10am–3pm, Sat & Sun 11am–4pm; 25kr), an engrossing and thoughtful guide to working-class life in Copenhagen from the 1930s to the 1950s. Entering the museum, you walk down a reconstructed Copenhagen street – complete with passing tram and a shop window hawking the consumer durables of the day – and continue, via a backyard where washing hangs drying, through a printing works subsidized by the Marshall Plan and into a coffee shop, which sells an old-fashioned coffee and chicory blend by the cup. Elsewhere, mock-up house interiors contain family photos, newspapers and TVs showing newsreels of the time. The permanent displays are backed up by some outstanding temporary exhibitions from labour movements around the world.

Finally, take a peek inside the Filmhuset, at Gothersgade 55, the home base of the national film industry and also the location of the **Danish Film Museum** (Mon, Tues, Thurs & Fri noon–4pm, Sept–May Tues until 9pm; free). Here the dust is kept off the cameras, props and other remnants of an early film industry that, before Hollywood and the advent of the talkies, was among the world's most advanced and successful. You can watch screenings of classic and experimental films here, then have a drink afterwards in the café.

North of Gothersgade

There's a profound change of mood once you cross **Gothersgade**, the road marking the northern perimeter of Indre By. The congenial medieval alleyways of the old city give way to long, broad streets and a number of proud, aristocratic structures. There's a whole group of these in the **harbour area** near Nyhavn, although perhaps the most impressive building of all is Rosenborg Slot, a short way to the west away from the harbour and close to several major museums.

From Nyhavn to Esplanaden

Running from Kongens Nytorv to the waterfront, **Nyhavn** is a wide but quite short street, its two sides divided by a slender canal, which was until recently frequented by sailors but is now in the advanced stages of gentrification. One or two of the old tattoo shops remain, now looking decidedly artificial and increasingly outnumbered by small but expensive restaurants and antique shops. The canalside is quite picturesque, even so, with yachts moored on the water and well preserved eighteenth-century houses lining the street, three of which (numbers 18, 20 and 67) were lived in at various times by Hans Christian Andersen. This is perhaps the city's most attractive area, with an astounding variety of restaurants crammed into a single line of brightly painted town houses running alongside the canal that visually connects the huge square of Kongens Nytorv to the city's ferry port. Real fishing and pleasure boats fill the canal with activity during the days, and a nightly ritual brings hundreds of young city residents to sit by the canal and drink "hand beers", facing off against the well-heeled tourists and locals dining at the area's extravagant restaurants and bars. The far end of Nyhavn is the departure point for the hydrofoil to Malmö, boats to Rønne and, a block away at the end of Skt Annæ Plads, ferries for Oslo.

From Skt Annæ Plads, Amaliegade leads under a colonnade into the cobbled **Amalienborg Plads**. The statue of Frederik V in its centre reputedly cost more than all four of the identical Rococo palaces that flank it thanks to French sculptor, Jacques Saly, who spent thirty years in Copenhagen at the court's expense creating it. Dating from the mid-eighteenth century, this quartet of imposing palaces provides a sudden burst of welcome symmetry into the city's generally haphazard layout. Two of them now serve as royal residences and there's a changing of the guard each day at noon when Queen Margarethe II is at home – generally attended by gangs of camera-toting tourists.

Between the square and the harbour are the lavish gardens of **Amaliehaven**, while in the opposite direction, on Bredgade, looms the great dome of **Frederikskirken**, also known as the "Marmorkirken", or "Marble Church" (Mon–Sat 11am–2pm; free guided tours Sat 11am). Modelled on – and intended to rival – St Peter's in Rome, the church was begun in 1749, but because of its enormous cost lay unfinished until a century and a half later, when its most prominent feature (one of Europe's largest domes) was completed with Danish (rather than the more expensive Norwegian) marble. If you can time your visit to coincide with the guided tour, the reward is the chance to climb first to the whispering gallery and then out onto the rim of the dome itself. From here there's a stunning, and usually blustery, view over the sharp geometry of Amalienborg and across the sea to the factories of Malmö in Sweden.

Further along Bredgade, at no. 22, the former Danish Surgical Academy now holds the **Medical History Museum** (guided tours only; in English on Wed, Thurs, Fri & Sun at 2pm; free) – not a place to visit if you've spent the morning on a brewery binge, since the enthusiastically presented hour-long tour features aborted foetuses, straitjackets, syphilis treatments, amputated feet, eyeballs and a dissected head.

The Kastellet and around

A little way beyond the Medical History Museum, Bredgade concludes at Esplanaden, facing the green space of Churchill Park. To the right, the German armoured car that was commandeered by Danes and used to bring news of the Nazi surrender marks the entrance to the **Museum of the Danish Resistance Movement** (Frihedsmuseet; May to mid-Sept Tues–Sat 10am–4pm, Sun 10am–5pm; mid-Sept to April Tues–Sat 11am–3pm, Sun 11am–4pm; free). Initially, the Danes put up little resistance to the

German invasion, but later the Nazis were given a systematically wretched time. The museum records the growth of the organized response and has a special section on the youths from Aalborg who formed themselves into the "Churchill Club". Feeling the adults weren't doing enough, this gang of 15-year-olds set about destroying German telegraph cables, blowing up cars and trains and stealing weapons. There's also a small, but inevitably moving, collection of artworks and handicrafts made by concentration camp inmates.

The road behind the museum crosses into the grounds of the **Kastellet** (daily 6am–10pm; free), a fortress built by Christian IV and expanded by his successors through the seventeenth century, after the loss of Danish possessions in Skåne had put the city within range of Swedish cannonballs. It's now occupied by the Danish army and its buildings are closed to the public. The tall arches and gateways, however, are an enjoyable setting for a stroll, as are the grassy slopes beside the moat. In a corner of the park, perched on some rocks just off the harbour bank – though you can't get there directly from the military compound, and must swing back to the road to find it – the **Little Mermaid** (*Den Lille Havfrue*) exerts an inexplicable magnetism on tourists. Since its unveiling in 1913, this bronze statue of a Hans Christian Andersen character, sculpted by Edvard Erichsen and paid for by the boss of the Carlsberg brewery, has become the best-known emblem of the city – a fact which has led to it being the victim of several subversive pranks: the original head disappeared in 1964, a cow's head was forced over the replacement in 1986, and more recently one of its arms was stolen. A hundred metres away is the far more spectacular **Gefion Fountain**, created by Anders Bundgaard and showing the goddess Gefion with her four sons, whom she's turned into oxen, having been promised in return as much land as she can plough in a single night. The legend goes that she ploughed a chunk of Sweden, then picked it up (creating Lake Vänern) and tossed it into the sea – where it became Zealand.

West from the harbour: Rosenborg Slot and the museums

Just southwest of the Kastellet lies **Nyboder**, a curious area of short, straight and narrow streets lined with rows of compact yellow dwellings. Although some of these are recently erected apartment blocks, the original houses, on which the newer constructions are modelled, were built by Christian IV to encourage his sailors to live in the city. The area at one time declined into a slum, but recent and vigorous revamping has made it an increasingly sought-after district. The oldest (and prettiest) houses can be found along Skt Pauls Gade.

Across Sølvgade from Nyboder is the main entrance to **Rosenborg Slot** (May & Sept to mid-Oct daily 11am–3pm; June–Aug daily 10am–4pm; mid-Oct to April Tues, Fri & Sun 11am–2pm; 45kr), a Dutch Renaissance palace and one of the most elegant buildings bequeathed by Christian IV to the city. Though intended as a country residence, Rosenborg served as the main domicile of Christian IV (he died here in 1648) and, until the end of the nineteenth century, the monarchs who succeeded him. It became a museum as early as 1830 and in the main building you can still see the rooms and furnishings used by the regal occupants. The highlights, though, are in the treasury downstairs, which displays the rich accessories worn by Christian IV (and his horse), the crown of absolute monarchs and the present crown jewels. Outside, the splendidly neat squares of Rosenborg Have can be reached by leaving the palace itself and using the park's main entrance on the corner of Østervoldgade and Sølvgade. On the west side of the Slot is Kongens Have, the city's oldest public park and a popular place for picnics, and, close by, the **Botanical Garden** (Botaniske Have; daily April–Sept 8.30am–6pm; Oct–March 8.30am–4pm; free).

Opposite Rosenborg Slot, and marked by a few runic stones, is the **Geology Museum** (Tues–Sun 10am–5pm; 20kr), which has a great meteorite section but is otherwise quite missable unless you're a mineral freak. Only slightly more worthwhile is the neighbouring National Gallery, the **Statens Museum for Kunst**, Sølvegade 48–50 (Tues–Sun 10am–5pm; 30kr, free Wed), a mammoth collection that's too large to take in on a short visit and too dull to warrant a longer one. While all the big cheeses have their patch – there are some minor Picassos and more major works by Matisse and Braque, Modigliani, Dürer and El Greco – it's the creations of Emil Nolde, with their bloated ravens, hunched figures and manic children, that best capture the mood of the place. This museum recently doubled in size, adding a new building for modern art (including contemporary Danish and other European work), a restaurant, a children's room and views of Kongens Have in an effort to keep up with the times.

Art fans will find greater things across the park behind the museum, in the fine **Den Hirschsprungske Samling** (Mon & Thurs–Sun 11am–4pm, Wed 11am–9pm; 25kr) on Stockholmsgade. Heinrich Hirschsprung was a late-nineteenth-century tobacco baron who sunk some of his profits into the patronage of emerging Danish artists, including the Skagen artists (see p.158). It was Hirschsprung's wish that on his death the collection – which also features Eckersburg, Købke and lesser names from the Danish mid-nineteenth-century Golden Age – would be given to the nation, but the government of the day vetoed the plan, and Hirschsprung set up his own gallery.

Christiansborg

Christiansborg sits on the island of Slotsholmen, connected to Indre By by several short bridges: a mundane part of the city, but administratively – and historically – an important one. It was here, in the twelfth century, that Bishop Absalon built the castle that was the origin of the city, and the drab royal palace, completed in 1916, that occupies the site is nowadays given over primarily to government offices and the state parliament or **Folketinget** (guided tours in English: July & Aug daily on the hour 10am–4pm; Sept–June Sun same times; free). Close to the bus stop on Christiansborg Slotsplads is the entrance to the **Ruins under Christiansborg** (May–Sept daily 9.30am–3.30pm; Oct–April Tues, Thurs & Sun 9.30am–3.30pm; 40kr), where a staircase leads down to the remains of Bishop Absalon's original castle. The first fortress suffered repeated mutilations by the Hanseatic League, and Erik of Pomerania had a replacement erected in 1390, into which he moved the royal court. This in turn was pulled down by Christian IV and another castle built between 1731 and 1745. The stone and brick walls that comprise the ruins, and the articles from the castles stored in an adjoining room, are surprisingly absorbing, the mood enhanced by the semi-darkness and lack of external noise.

There are a number of other, less captivating museums in and around Christiansborg Slotsplads – the main courtyard within Christiansborg – to which the information office close to the ruins' entrance can provide directions – the confusing array of buildings makes it easy to get lost. That said, you could probably sniff your way to the **Royal Stables** (May–Oct Fri–Sun 2–4pm; Nov–April Sat & Sun 2–4pm; 10kr), one of the country's least essential collections, focusing on all things equine. Nearby, the **Theatre Museum** (Wed 2–4pm, Sat & Sun noon–4pm; 20kr) is more interesting, housed in what was the eighteenth-century Court Theatre and displaying original costumes, set-models and the old dressing rooms and boxes. Exiting the courtyard and walking through Tøjhusgade takes you past the **Armoury Museum** (Tøjhusmuseet; Tues–Sun noon–4pm; 20kr), where you can view weaponry from Christian IV's arsenal and a host of crests and coats of arms. A few strides further on, a small gateway leads into the gorgeous tree-lined grounds of the **Royal Library** – an excellent venue for a picnic. The library (Mon–Fri 9am–7pm) contains original manuscripts by Hans Christian Andersen, Karen Blixen and Søren Kierkegaard (of whom there's a statue in the gardens), though you can only get to see them if you can convince the staff at reception that you're a bona fide scholar (a student card should suffice). The big black extension at Christian's Brygge 8 on the waterfront – known as the "Black Diamond" – doubled the library's capacity and added a concert hall, conference rooms and restaurants. Finally, adjacent to Christiansborg Slotsplads sits the long, low form of the seventeenth-century **Børsen**, or Stock Exchange – with its spire of four entwined dragons' tails, it's one of the most distinctive buildings in the city and worth seeking out.

Thorvaldsen's Museum and National Museum

On the far side of Slotsholmen, **Thorvaldsen's Museum** (Tues–Sun 10am–5pm; 20kr; guided tours in English July & Aug Sun 3pm) is home to an enormous collection of work and memorabilia (and the body) of Denmark's most famous sculptor. Despite negligible schooling, Bertel Thorvaldsen (1770–1844) drew his way into the Danish Academy of Fine Arts before moving onto Rome, where he perfected the heroic, classical figures for which he became famous. Nowadays he's not widely known outside Denmark, although in his day he enjoyed international renown and won commissions all over Europe.

Other than a selection of early works in the basement, the labels of the great, hulking statues read like a roll-call of the famous and infamous: Vulcan, Adonis, John Russell, Gutenberg, Pius VII and Maximilian; while the Christ Hall contains the huge casts of the statues of Christ and Apostles which can be seen in Vor Frue Kirke (see p.79). A prolific and gifted sculptor, Thorvaldsen was something of a wit too. Asked by the Swedish artist J.T. Sergel how he managed to make such beautiful figures, he held up the scraper with which he was working and replied, "With this".

There's another major collection a short walk away over the Slotsholmen moat to the west: the **National Museum** (Tues–Sun 10am–5pm; 40kr), which has an ethnographic section in a separate wing at Ny Vestergade 10, but is really strongest (as you'd expect) on Danish history; if you've any interest at all in the subject you could spend a couple of hours here. Much of the early stuff, ranging from prehistory to the Viking days, comes from Jutland – jewellery, bones and even bodies, all remarkably well preserved and much of it only discovered after wartime fuel shortages led to large-scale digging of the Danish peat bogs. Informative explanatory texts help clarify the Viking section, whose best exhibits – apart from the familiar horned helmets – are the sacrificial gifts, among them the Sun Chariot, a model horse carrying a sun disc with adornments of gold and bronze. Further floors store a massive collection of almost anything and everything that featured in Christian-era Denmark up to the nineteenth century – finely engraved wooden altarpieces, furniture, clothing and more – as well as a good section on peasant life.

Christianshavn

From Christiansborg, a bridge crosses the Inder Havnen to the island of Amager and into **Christianshavn**, built by Christian IV as an autonomous new town in the early sixteenth century to provide housing for workers in the shipbuilding industry. It was given features more common to Dutch port towns of the time, even down to a small canal (Wilders Kanal), and in parts the area is more redolent of Amsterdam than Copenhagen. Although its present inhabitants are fairly well-off, as evidenced by some immaculately preserved houses along Overgaden oven Vandet, Christianshavn still has the mood of a working-class quarter, with a group of secondhand shops along the district's main street, Torvegade.

Poking skywards through the trees near Torvegade is the blue-and-gold spire of **Vor Frelsers Kirke** (May–Oct 10am–4.30pm; March–April & Nov Mon–Sun 11am–2.30pm; Dec–Feb 11am–2pm; spire 20kr), on the corner of Prinsessegade and Skt Annæ Gade. The spire, with its helter-skelter outside staircase, was added to the otherwise plain church in the mid-eighteenth century, instantly becoming one of the more recognizable features on the city's horizon. Climbing the spire is fun, but not entirely without risk (though the rumour that the builder fell off it and died, while plausible, is untrue). To get to the spire, go through the church and up to a trap door which opens onto the platform where the external steps begin: there are four hundred of them, slanted and slippery (especially after rain) and gradually becoming smaller. The reward for reaching the top is a great view of Copenhagen and beyond.

Christiania

A few streets east of Vor Frelsers Kirke, **Christiania** occupies an area that was for centuries used as a barracks, before the soldiers moved out and it was colonized by young and homeless people. It was declared a "free city" on September 24, 1971, with the aim of operating autonomously from Copenhagen, and its continued existence has fuelled one of the longest-running debates in Danish (and Scandinavian) society. One byproduct of its idealism and the freedoms assumed by its residents (and, despite recent lapses, generally tolerated by successive governments and the police) was to make Christiania a refuge for petty criminals and shady individuals from all over the city. But the problems have inevitably been overplayed by Christiania's critics, and a surprising number of Danes – of all ages and from all walks of life – do support the place, not least because Christiania has performed usefully, and altruistically, when established bodies have been found wanting. An example has been in the weaning of heroin addicts off their habits (once, a 24-hour cordon was thrown around the area to prevent dealers reaching the addicts inside: reputedly the screams – of deprived junkies and suppliers being "dealt with" – could be heard all night). And Christiania residents have stepped in to provide free shelter and food for the homeless at Christmas when the city administration declined to do so.

The population of around one thousand is swelled in summer by the curious and the sympathetic – although the residents ask people not to camp here, and tourists not to point cameras at the weirder-looking inhabitants. The craft shops and restaurants are – partly because of their refusal to pay any kind of tax – fairly cheap, and nearly all are good, as are a couple of innovative music and performance art venues. These, and the many imaginative dwellings, including some built on stilts in a small lake, make a visit worthwhile. Additionally, there are a number of alternative political and arts groups based in Christiania; for information on these – and on the district generally – call in to Galopperiet (daily noon–5pm), to the left of the area's main entrance on the corner of Bådsmandsstræde and Prinsessegade. Two-hour guided tours of Christiania operate in summer (information on ☎32 57 96 70; 20kr).

Christiania is also the gateway to **Holmen**, once a forgotten naval station but now a complex of four art schools – the National School of Architecture, the National School of Theatre, the National Film School and the Rhythmical Music Conservatory – which the city plans to continue developing in coming years. Check the area for current developments – change is in the air and it's quickly becoming Europe's latest industrial zone to be taken over by artists and revellers. There's a wildly popular and fun restaurant with a military theme, *Holmen Base Camp* (see p.90), here as well.

Along Vesterbrogade

Hectic **Vesterbrogade** begins on the far side of Rådhuspladsen from Strøget, and its first attraction is Copenhagen's most famous after the Little Mermaid: the **Tivoli Gardens** (May–Sept & mid-Nov to late Dec daily 11am–midnight; 44kr). This park of many bland amusements, which first flung open its gates in 1843, was modelled on the Vauxhall Gardens in London, and in turn became the model for the Festival Gardens in London's Battersea Park. The name is now synonymous with Copenhagen at its most innocently pleasurable, and the opening of the gardens each year on May 1 is taken to mark the beginning of summer. There are fairground rides (about 15kr each), fountains and fireworks (Wed, Fri & Sat nights), and nightly entertainment in the central arena, encompassing everything from acrobats and jugglers to the mid-Atlantic tones of various fixed-grin crooners. Naturally, it's overrated and overpriced, but an evening spent wandering among the revellers of all ages indulging in the mass consumption of ice cream is an experience worth having – once, at any rate. Close to the gardens' Vesterbrogade entrance is the predictable **Holography Museum** (daily: mid-April to mid-Sept 10am–midnight; mid-Sept to mid-April 10am–6pm; 32kr) – once you've seen through one hologram you've seen through them all – and the abysmal **Louis Tussaud's Wax Museum** (mid-April to mid-Sept 10am–11pm; mid-Sept to mid-April 10am–6pm; 48kr).

Behind the Tivoli, across Tietgensgade towards the harbour, is the dazzling **Ny Carlsberg Glyptotek**, Dantes Plads 7 (Tues–Sun 10am–4pm; 30kr, free Wed & Sun), opened in 1897 by brewer Carl Jacobsen as a venue for ordinary people to see classical art exhibited in classical style. Its centrepiece is the conservatory: "Being Danes", said Jacobsen, "we know more about flowers than art, and during the winter this greenery will make people pay a visit; and then, looking at the palms, they might find a moment for the statues." It's an idea that succeeded, and even now the gallery is well-used – and not just by art lovers: there's a programme of electronic music daily at 1pm, as well as a seasonal roster of other free events; pick up a schedule at the entrance.

As for the contents, this is by far Copenhagen's finest gallery, with a stirring array of Greek, Roman and Egyptian art and artefacts, as well as what is reckoned to be the biggest (and best) collection of Etruscan art outside Italy. There are excellent examples of nineteenth-century European art too, including a complete collection of Degas casts made from the fragile working sculptures he left at his death, Manet's *Absinthe Drinker*, and two small cases containing tiny caricatured heads by Honore Daumier. Easily missed, but actually the most startling room in the place, is an antechamber with just a few pieces – early works by Man Ray, some Chagall sketches and a Picasso pottery plate. There's a new French wing containing Impressionist art and work from Danish painting's so-called "Golden Age" (1800–1850), plus a French café on a balcony overlooking greenhouses of palm trees.

Finally, if you're at all interested in Denmark's world-class tradition of design, don't leave this area without at least looking in on the new **Danish Design Centre**, 27–29 Hans Christian Andersens Boulevard. The building, designed by Danish architect Henning Larsen, serves as an exhibit hall, research facility and showcase for industrial design.

Beyond the Tivoli Gardens

Just west of the train station, the streets between Vesterbrogade and **Istedgade** used to be Copenhagen's token red-light area, and the only part of the city where you might have felt unsafe. Over recent years, the low rents have attracted students and a large number of immigrant families: walk along Istedgade and you're likely to find dreadlocked rastas and Turks sipping tea from tulip glasses, plus a number of diverse (but well-priced) ethnic eateries.

At Vesterbrogade 59 is the **City Museum** (Københavns Bymuseum; May–Sept 10am–4pm; Oct–April 1–4pm; closed Tues; 20kr), which has reconstructed ramshackle house exteriors and tradesmen's signs from early Copenhagen. Looking at these, the impact of Christian IV becomes resoundingly apparent. There's a large room recording the form and cohesion that this monarch and amateur architect gave the city, even including a few of his own drawings. The rest of the city's history is told by paintings – far too many paintings, in fact. Head upstairs for the room devoted to Søren Kierkegaard, filled with bits and bobs – furniture from his home, paintings of his girl-

Kierkegaard is inextricably linked with Copenhagen, yet his championing of individual will over social conventions and his rejection of materialism did little to endear him to his fellow Danes. Born in 1813, Kierkegaard believed himself set on an "evil destiny" – partly the fault of his father, who is best remembered for having cursed God on a Jutland heath. Kierkegaard's first book, *Either/Or*, published in 1843, was inspired by his love affair with one Regine Olsen; she failed to understand it, however, and married someone else. Few other people understood *Either/Or*, in fact, and Kierkegaard, though devastated by the broken romance, came to revel in the enigma he had created, becoming a "walking mystery in the streets of Copenhagen" (he lived in a house on Nytorv). He was a prolific author, sometimes publishing two books on the same day and often writing under pseudonyms. His greatest philosophical works were written by 1846 and are often claimed to have laid the foundations of existentialism.

friend Regine Olsen, jewellery, books and manuscripts – that form an intriguing footnote to the life of this nineteenth-century Danish writer and philosopher, and much the most interesting part of the museum (see box above).

A few minutes to the north of Vesterbrogade, at Gammel Kongevej 10, on the corner with Vester Søgade, is the **Tycho Brahe Planetarium** (daily 10.30am–9pm; 70kr), the biggest in Scandinavia, named after the world-famous Danish astronomer who invented instruments to accurately plot the sun, planets and stars for the first time.

West to the Carlsberg Brewery and Frederiksberg Have

Way out west along Vesterbrogade (save your legs by taking bus #6 or #18 to Valby Langgade and crossing the street), down Enghavevej and along Ny Carlsberg Vej, you'll find the **Carlsberg Brewery**'s new Visitor Centre at Gamle Carlsberg Vej 11. Note also the fine Elephant Gate: four elephants carved in granite supporting the building that spans the road.

Vesterbrogade finishes up opposite the **Frederiksberg Have**, which contains the Frederiksberg Palace, now used as a military academy and closed to the public. Throughout the eighteenth century, the city's top nobs came here to mess about in boats along the network of canals that dissect the copious lime-tree groves, and its pleasant surrounds are now a popular weekend picnic spot for locals. While here, you might call in at the entertaining **Storm P. Museum** (May–Sept Tues–Sun 10am–4pm; Oct–April Wed, Sat & Sun 10am–4pm; 20kr), by the gate facing Frederiksberg Allé, packed with the satirical cartoons that made "Storm P." (Robert Storm Petersen) one of the most popular bylines in Danish newspapers from the 1920s. Even if you don't understand the Danish captions, you'll leave the museum with an insight into the national sense of humour.

Beyond the Frederiksberg Palace, at Roskildevej 32 (buses #6, #28, #39 and #550S), is Copenhagen's **Zoo**, which has the usual array of caged lions, elephants and monkeys, plus a special children's section (June–Aug daily 9am–6pm; April–May Mon–Fri 9am–5pm, Sat & Sun 9am–6pm; Sept–Oct daily 9am–5pm; Nov–March daily 9am–4pm; 60kr).

Out from the centre

Unlike many other major European cities, Copenhagen has only a few miles of drab housing estates on its periphery before the countryside begins. There are a number of things worth venturing out for, although none of them need keep you away from the main action for long.

Just outside the inner city, only a few minutes on foot from Indre By, is **Assistens Kirkegård**, a cemetery built to cope with the dead from the 1711–12 plague. More interestingly, it contains the graves of Hans Christian Andersen and Søren Kierkegaard – both well signposted, although not from the same entrance. If you get lost, look at the handy catalogue by the gate on Kapelvej. The cemetery is off Nørrebrogade in the district of Nørrebro: walk from the Nørreport station along Frederiksborggade and over the lake. Alternatively, buses #5, #7, #16 and #18 run along the graveyard's edge. Slightly further out is **Grundtvigs Kirke** (mid-May to mid-Sept Mon–Sat 9am–4.45pm, Sun noon–4pm; mid-Sept to mid-May Mon–Sat 9am–4pm, Sun noon–1pm), an astonishing yellow-brick creation whose gabled front resembles a massive church organ which rises upwards and completely dwarfs the row of terraced houses that share the street. The church, named after and dedicated to the founder of the Danish folk high schools, was designed by Jensens Klint and his son in 1913, but was not finished until 1926. To reach it from the city centre takes about twenty minutes on bus #10, #16, #19 or #21. Get off in the small square of Bispetorv soon after passing the Bispebjerg Hospital; the church itself is in På Bjerget.

South

If the weather's good, take a trip south to the **Amager beaches**, about half an hour away by bus #12 along Øresundsvej (ask for Helgoland). On the other side of the airport from the beaches (take bus #30) lies the village of **DRAGØR**, an atmospheric cobbled fishing village from where ferries depart for Limhamn in Sweden. There are a couple of good local history collections in the **Dragør Museum** by the harbour (May–Sept Tues–Fri 2–5pm, Sat & Sun noon–6pm; 15kr), and the **Amager Museum** (June–Aug Wed–Sun 11am–3pm; Sept–May Wed & Sun 11am–3pm; 15kr), a few minutes' walk away.

Further out, on the road to Køge, the southern suburb of **Ishøj** is home to many ethnic communities, mainly from the Middle East, and an excellent museum of modern art, **Arken** (Tues 10am–5pm, Wed 10am–9pm, Thurs–Sat 10am–5pm; 40kr). Looking very much like a ship, this sleek museum rises from Ishøj beach and houses excellent temporary exhibitions, plus a glassed-in restaurant overlooking the bay that serves herring specialities for lunch. From central Copenhagen take the S-train to Ishøj station and then bus #128, a 45-minute journey altogether.

North

If you're tired of history, culture and the arts, you might fancy a guided tour around the **Eksperimentarium** (Mon–Fri 9am–6pm, Tues & Thurs until 9pm, Sat & Sun 11am–6pm; 69kr, children 49kr). Located in a former beer-bottling hall, this workshop-museum attempts to raise scientific awareness through some interesting and entertaining hands-on exhibits, such as a disco which beats to your biorhythms. There's a new pavilion area for young children as well, with trick mirrors, a Fairy-Tale Room, and the chance to build a house using "superlight" bricks.

Just outside the city limits, reached by bus #6, **CHARLOTTENLUND** has a lovely beach, good for sunbathing – as long as you can ignore the smoke-belching chimneys in the background. Its main attraction these days is the **Danish Aquarium** (Danmarks Akvarium; daily 10am–4pm; 45kr), with its impressive collection of tropical fish, sharks, crocodiles and turtles. Nearby **Charlottenlund Fort** (open 24hr; free) has a few abandoned cannons and is only worth bothering with for the great views over the city and out to sea. You're better off making for **Charlottenlund Slotshave**, a former manor house with a gorgeous park (open 24hr; free) perfect for strolling and picnicking.

If you're in the mood for an amusement park but can't face (or afford) Tivoli, venture out to **Bakken** (late March to late Aug daily noon–midnight; free), close to the

Klampenborg stop at the end of line C on the S-train network. Set in a corner of Kongens Dyrehave (the Royal Deer Park), it's possibly more fun than its city counterpart – and certainly more down-to-earth – and besides the usual swings and rollercoasters offers easy walks through oak and beech woods. Strolling back towards Klampenborg along Christiansholmsvej, a left turn at the restaurant *Peter Lieps Hus* gives superb views over the Øresund.

Finally, half an hour's bus journey (#184) to the north is the village of **LYNGBY**, and its **Open-Air Museum** (Frilandsmuseet; April–Nov Tues–Sun 10am–5pm; 30kr), set inside a large park and comprising restored seventeenth- to mid-nineteenth-century buildings, drawn from all over Denmark and its former territories. A walk through the park leads to the Sorgenfri Palace, one-time home of Frederik V (closed to the public). Take S-train line A or C to Sorgenfri.

Eating

Whether you want a quick coffee and croissant, or to sit down to a five-course gourmet dinner, you'll find more choice – and lower prices – in Copenhagen than in any other Scandinavian capital. Many of the city's innumerable **cafés** offer good-value, filling lunches, and there are plenty of **pizzerias**, again many with daily specials and all-you-can-eat salad deals. Most **restaurants** are open for lunch and dinner: prices tend to be higher in the evenings, but there are generally good-value deals at lunchtime, so those on a budget needn't deprive themselves of a blowout.

If you're stocking up for a **picnic** – or a trip to Sweden or Norway – take advantage of the numerous outlets selling *smørrebrød* (open sandwiches); Smørrebrødskunsten, on the corner of Magstræde at Rådhusstræde, and Københavns Smørrebrød, Vesterbrogade 6c, are two of the most central. For more general food shopping, use one of the **supermarkets**: ISO at Vesterbrogade no. 23, Irma at Vesterbrogade 1 and Superbrugsen at Borgergade 28 (off Gothersgade), are cheaper than their counterparts along Strøget.

Cafés and pizzerias

Amagertorv, Amagertorv 6. Tearoom serving coffees, cocoa and Danish pastries, as well as finger sandwiches.

Bar Bar Bar, Vesterbrogade 51. A stylish and relaxed place for a coffee, drink or light snack.

Café Amokka, Dag Hammarskjolds Allé 38–40. Popular coffee house in the Østerbro neighbourhood, with great desserts to go with the good coffee plus some eclectic food and a special children's menu.

Café au lait, Nørre Voldgade 27. Opposite the Nørreport S-train station, a pleasantly unflustered place for a coffee or snack. There are other branches at Gothersgade 11, Vesterbrogade 16 and Vornedamsvej 16.

Café Sonja, Saxogade 86. Pasta and salad main courses for under 50kr.

Caféen i Nikolaj, Nikolaj Plads 22. Nibble a light lunch or pastry and then tour the rest of this former church, which now houses an art gallery. Closed Sun.

Floras Kaffebar, Blågårdsgade 27. Daily specials at 45kr, plus soups and cakes, served in an easygoing atmosphere. Come back at night for cheaper-than-average beer.

Juice & Java, Kronprinsensgade 11. Good spot for a quick sandwich and juice in the heart of a hip downtown area.

Kaffe Salonen, Peblinge Dosserling 6. Super-hip coffee house in Nørrebro with outdoor tables locking out onto a canal, and a waterside terrace on a floating dock too; coffee, beer, ice creams, some food. Paddleboats for rent on the dock.

Klaptræet, Kultorvet 13. Very cheap breakfasts and good-value eating throughout the day.

Shawarwa, Strøget, close to Rådhuspladsen. Excellent Middle-Eastern snacks: shawarmas, pitta bread with falafels and kebabs, starting at 22kr.

Tim's Cookies, 41 Nørrebrogade. One of the cheapest lunch places in town. Sandwiches on tasty bread, plus bagels, brownies, and cookies too, all between 10kr and 35kr.

Toppoli Pizza, Rantzausgasse 8A. Daily lunch specials and small pizzas at 25kr, plus Italian ices and sandwiches.

Vagabondo's Cantina, Vesterbrogade 70. The most central of several branches of this dependable pizza chain, with pizza and pasta dishes from 50kr.

Restaurants

Many of the city's Danish restaurants knock out affordable (around 80kr) and high-quality lunches, either from a set menu or from an open buffet. Dinner will always be more expensive, although Copenhagen's growing band of ethnic restaurants are making it increasingly affordable – many have adopted the Scandinavian open-table idea, offering all-you-can-eat meals from around 60kr, but don't plan a night's dancing after wading through one. These are also usually the best bet for finding vegetarian food.

As a rule, Danes tends to finish dining early, if they dine out at all – most actually prefer eating at home. As a result, most restaurants in the city cater to tourists and stay open until 11.00pm or midnight. Roughly half the city's restaurants don't open at all on Sunday, and those that do keep shorter hours, usually opening for dinner only. Most Danish *smørrebrød* restaurants serve lunch only, but open seven days a week.

Finally, Danes are keen on reserving tables in advance, and while you're unlikely to have to wait long for a place, it's still a good idea to ring ahead at the city's more popular spots. We've given telephone numbers for those restaurants where reservations are advisable.

Danish restaurants

Bagatallen, Tivoli Gardens (☎33 75 07 51). This restaurant continues to win admirers for its good Danish and French food and drinks, served within the walls of the famous amusement park.

Café Kunstforeningen, Gammel Strand 48, near Christiansborg Palace. Danish lunches in a basement or at pavement tables, with museum views in good weather. Good Sunday brunches.

Café Petersborg, Bredgade 76 (☎33 12 50 16). In an eighteenth-century building between Nyhavn and Kongens Nytorv, the food here favours Danish cooking – lots of *smørrebrød* choices on the menu.

Café Rosenkælderen, Rosengården 5. A couple of minutes' walk from Nørreport Station on a tiny street north of Strøget, this central and cheap café has stacks of daily specials and lunch and dinner plates starting at around 50kr.

Divan 1, Tivoli Gardens. New place serving Danish/French food on a big terrace overlooking the Tivoli lawn and stages.

DSB Bistro, Banegårdspladsen 7. Believe it or not, it's here inside Central Station that you'll get a broad, comparatively low-cost, introduction to Danish food. Allow a couple of hours to explore the massive cold buffet served from 11.30am to 9.30pm for 139kr; there are far cheaper daily specials too.

Els, Store Strandstræde 3 (☎33 14 13 41). Very plush, with a game-oriented menu and walls lined with elegant mid-nineteenth-century Danish art. A full meal will set you back around 300kr.

Holmen Base Camp, Building 148, Halvtolv 12 (☎70 23 23 18). Cavernous and fun place on the former Holmen naval base, a 600-seat compound with patio, live-music club and children's playroom; sand floors simulate a beach atmosphere as you dine on Danish, French, Spanish and other cuisines.

Huset med det grønne træ, Gammeltorv 20 (☎33 12 87 86). The "House with the Green Tree" does indeed have a tree – and some of the finer Danish lunches in the downtown area. Main courses go for around 80–100kr.

Langelinie Pavillonen, Langelinie (☎33 12 12 14). New owner, new style, but still serving good Danish and French meals. It's facing the water close to The Little Mermaid.

Nyhavns Færgekro, Nyhavn 5. Unpretentious and thoroughly tasty traditional food, either from the lunchtime fish-laden buffet (80kr) or the à la carte restaurant upstairs.

Peder Oxe, Gråbrødre Torv 11 (☎33 11 00 77). Very popular steakhouse on a small square off Strøget, especially worthwhile at lunchtime when prices are lower; bookings advisable. Main courses from 80kr to 170kr. Also has a lively wine cellar.

Skt Gertruds Kloster, Hauser Plads 32 (☎33 14 66 30). Smoulderingly romantic haunt in the vaults of a medieval cloister, though you'll spend a fortune. It's next to Kultorvet, close to Nørreport Station.

Spisehuset, Rådhusstræde 13. In the Huset building, with a varied but always wholesome and fairly cheap menu, including 70kr daily specials.

Spiseloppen, Bådsmandsstræde 43, Christiania. Superb food that won't break the bank.

Thorvaldsen, Gammel Strand 34 (☎33 32 04 00). Across the canal from the Christiansborg Palace, this place serves a strange combination of Danish and Spanish food, but somehow it all works well enough.

Traktørstet på Rosenborg, Øster Voldgade 44 (☎33 15 76 20). Rather expensive place on lawn and terrace just outside Rosenborg castle. Good food, but you pay for the location.

Ethnic restaurants

A/S Bananrepublikken, Nørrebrogade 13. Right on Nørrebro's main thoroughfare, this restaurant serves ethnic foods with a modern Danish edge, including great tapas, from around 100kr. See also "Drinking and nightlife", p.94.

Ayuttaya, Griffenfeldsgade 39, Nørrebro (☎35 37 38 68). Without question one of the city's top Thai restaurants, and consequently usually packed – reservations aren't a bad idea.

Bali, Lille Kongensgade 4, southeast of Kongens Nytorv (☎33 11 08 08). Tread carefully around the bamboo plants and you'll find a fine Indonesian restaurant; the house special is *rijsttafel*, costing 128kr.

Bastionen & Løven, Voldgade 50, Christianshavn (☎32 95 09 40). Restaurant set in a converted windmill, with a view of the moat that once defended the city. Known for its 90kr all-you-can-eat buffet, with a little bit of everything in it.

Bonobo, Store Kongensgade 44. A strange and fun eatery: French food served in what's basically a shrine to monkeys. Children love this place for the decor and atmosphere, while adults savour the food.

Burgery & Bakery, Godthåbsvej 109A. Out in Frederiksberg, but it comes highly recommended by locals as an informal but good dinner choice. Mostly burgers and pastries, as you'd expect from the name.

Café Bjørg, Vester Volgade 19. Caribbean restaurant on busy street corner in city centre, near the gay district. Open late.

Café Latino, Gothersgade 113. A tiny and likeable restaurant serving Latin American dishes from 50kr. Seems to periodically close down and change hands, but a good choice if it's open.

Era Ora, Torvegade 62 (☎32 54 06 93). Top-flight Italian fare, good enough to earn a Michelin star, and priced as you'd expect. Near (but not actually in) Christiania.

Hercegovina, Bernstoffsgade 3 (☎33 15 63 63). With one entrance facing the train station and another inside Tivoli, this classy Croatian restaurant is easy to find and always popular for its portions and its unusual offerings.

Kashmir, Nørrebrogade 35. Right in the middle of Nørrebro, this Indian restaurant's 39kr lunch is the best value for miles.

Kate's Joint, Blågardsgade 12. Spicy Thai and Caribbean-influenced meals in ultra-hip and homely spot.

KGB, Dronningens Tværgade 22 (☎33 36 07 70). A vodka bar and one of the city's few Russian restaurants. Main courses around 60–85kr.

Koh-i-Noor, Vesterbrogade 33. A mix of Indian, Pakistani and halal cuisines, with vegetarian dishes available; the set dinner costs 89kr. Also variously known as *Le Mirage* and the *Blue Star*.

La Mer, Blågards Plads 10 (☎35 37 22 24). One of the city's best fish restaurants on one of its nicest squares up in Nørrebro. Fish and chips for 42kr, plus more elegant meals of grilled fish. Closed July.

L'Education Nationale, Larsbjørnsstræde 12 (☎33 91 53 60). Well-done French meals for 70–120kr.

Merhaba, Abel Cathrinesgade 7 (☎33 22 77 21). Good Turkish food just west of Central Station, with prices starting at 50kr. There's sometimes a three-course set meal on offer for 69kr.

Mexicali, Åboulevard 12, Nørrebro. Decent Mexican food from around 80kr.

O's American Breakfast & Barbecue, Øster Farimagsgade. American-style Southern cooking northwest of the Botanic Gardens (bus #40). Serves big breakfasts until late afternoon, then switches to barbecue meals for dinner.

Pasta Basta, Valhendorfsgade 22 (☎33 11 21 31). An array of fish and meat pasta dishes and pasta salads from which you can help yourself for 69kr. Open until 5am, this is a favourite final stop for late-night groovers and wildly popular with locals anytime. On a road parallel with and to the north of Strøget.

Riz-Raz, Kompagnistræde 20, Christiania. A Middle-Eastern vegetarian buffet place, with all you can eat for 49kr at lunchtime, 59kr in the evenings. Popular with backpackers.

Shezan, Viktoriagade 22, Vesterbro (☎33 24 78 88). Excellent Pakistani dishes. There's another branch near the Malmö catamaran terminal at Havnegade.

Souls Kitchen, Vesterbrogade 3, Vesterbo. New Cajun-American restaurant not far from the centre of town and Central Station. Expect spices.

Sticks 'n' Sushi, Nansensgade 59, Nørreport (☎33 11 14 07). New, but already among the city's favourite Japanese eateries. It's a block south of the Peblinge Sø canal.

Taco Shop, 57–59 Nørre Farimagsgade, Nørreport. Serves 40–60kr tacos and burritos, and stays open much later – until 10pm each night, including Sundays – than is usual in this city. A block north of Israel Plads, near Nørreport Station.

Vegetarian and organic

Cap Horn, Nyhavn 21 (☎33 12 85 04). Expensive, but worth splashing out on if you're wanting high-quality cooking with organic ingredients.

Den Grønne Kælder, Pilestræde 48, at junction with Vendersgade (☎33 93 01 40). Close to Strøget, this vegetarian place has a variety of healthy lunches and organic wines. Closed Sun.

Govindas, Nørre Farimagsgade 82. Krishna-run restaurant producing mediocre but affordable lacto-vegetarian meals for 35kr (45kr after 3pm). Closed Sun.

Naturbageri Sativa, corner of Frederiksborggade and Nørre Farimagsgade. Good little organic bakery in the heart of Nørrebro.

Økologiske Café, Griffenfeldsgade 17. Nørrebro gathering place for Greens, with meat and fish served on one day of every week. Closed weekends.

Picnic, Fælledvej 22B, Norrebrø. Tiny, friendly sandwich and lunch place on Skt Hans Torv, with very little seating.

LATE NIGHT FOOD

For late-night eating, as well as *Pasta Basta*, listed above, and the late-opening cafés mentioned under "Nightlife", you might want to join the thespians munching fresh bread and rolls in *Herluf Trolle*, on Herluf Trolles Gade, just behind the Royal Theatre.

Drinking, nightlife and entertainment

An almost unchartable network of **cafés and bars** covers Copenhagen. You can get a drink – and usually a snack too – in any of them, although some are especially noted for their congeniality and ambience, and it's these we've listed below. Almost all the better cafés and bars are in – or close to – either Indre By or the Nørrebro and Nørreport districts just to the north, and it's no hardship to sample several on the same night, though bear in mind that Fridays and Saturdays are very busy, and you'll probably need to queue before getting in anywhere.

Another area the city excels in is **live music**. Major international names visit regularly, but it's with its small-scale shows that Copenhagen really stands out. Minor gigs early in the week in cafés and bars are often free, making it a cheap and simple business to take in several places until you find something to your liking; later in the week there may be modest cover charge. There are also a number of medium-size halls that host the best of Danish and overseas rock, jazz, hip-hop and funk. Things normally kick off around 10pm and, if not free, admission is 25–75kr. Throughout the summer, there are many **free concerts** in the city parks, some featuring leading Danish bands. You can find out who's playing where by reading the latest copy of *Gaffa*, free from music and record shops, or *Huset*, a free monthly magazine available from the Huset building at Rådhusstræde 13, which lists what's on at its own three music venues. New **film** releases, often in English with Danish subtitles, are shown all over the city; more esoteric fare is screened at Græsshoppen in Huset, the Delta Bio, Kompagnistræde 19, or the Park Bio, on Østergade (☎35 38 33 62). Full listings are printed in all newspapers. For kids, there's a special cinema, Tivoli Bio for Børn, by the main entrance to Tivoli Gardens.

With the plethora of late-opening cafés and bars, you'll never have to choose between going to a **club** and going to bed. If you do get a craving for a dance floor fling, however, you'll find the discos much like those in any major city, although they're generally more concerned with having a good time than defining the cutting edge of fashion. You'll be dancing alone if you turn up much before midnight; after that time, especially on Fridays and Saturdays, they fill rapidly – and stay open until 5am. Another plus is that drink prices are seldom hiked up and admission is fairly cheap at 25–45kr. For full **listings** of events and all kinds of entertainment, check out the free monthly tourist magazines, *Copenhagen This Week* and *Cope City Guide*, and keep an eye out for notices in Use-It and city cafés.

Bars and cafés

Bang & Jensen, Istedgade 130, Vesterbro. Former chemist's shop, now a popular breakfast spot that turns into a late-opening bar. Saturday night is cocktail night.

Barcelona, Fælledvej 21, Nørrebro. Near Skt Hans Torv, this chic venue is very much the place to be seen, though you pay over the odds for the privilege. Restaurant (☎31 35 76 11) serves medium-priced Danish and French food as well, despite the name.

Café Blågårds Apotek, Blågårds Plads 20, Nørrebro. Pretty, candlelit café on a Nørrebro square with lots of wines and draught beers; a good spot for a drink.

Café Dan Turell, Store Regnegade 3. Something of an institution with the artier student crowd (it takes its name from a famous Danish writer) and a fine central place for a sociable tipple. Spot it by the rows of bicycles parked outside, a few blocks north of Kongens Nytorv.

Café Rust, Guldbergsgade 8. A late-night rock 'n' roll bar, lively and popular, and less than a block north of Skt Hans Nytorv.

Café Sommersko, Kronprinsensgade 6. Sizeable, but crowded most nights, with Parisian-style food and drink and free live music on Sunday afternoons to soothe away hangovers. A block north of Strøget.

Foley's Irish Pub, Lille Kannikestræde 3. Authentic Irish pub a few blocks north of Strøget, often the final stop for local Irish after a night of pub-crawling. Decent food too.

Globe Irish Pub, Nørregade 43–45, Nørreport. Loud and flashy pub near Nørreport station with lots of televised sports, although your fellow drinkers are more likely to be tourists than expat Irish.

Hard Rock Café, Vesterbrogade 3, next to Tivoli Gardens. As seen on a million T-shirts; it's as popular and bland as you'd expect. Occasional live music.

Krasnapolsky, Vestergade 10, near the Rådhus. The Danish avant-garde art hanging on the wall reflects the trendsetting reputation of this ultramodern watering hole. Come here at least once, if only to drink at the very long bar.

Peder Hvitfeldt, P. Hvitfeldtsstræde 15. Spit-and-sawdust-type place on a short street one block south of Kultorvet, immensely popular with a youthful crowd. Come early if you want to sit down.

Pussy Galore's Flying Circus, Skt Hans Torv 30, Nørrebro. Trendy cocktail bar with burgers and outdoor seating on one of Nørrebro's hippest squares – definitely one of the places to be seen. Arne Jakobsen's trademark Danish chairs decorate the interior of the bar, which is often used as a pre-club stop.

Sabines Cafeteria, Teglgårdsstræde 4. Where the young and good-looking begin their evening's drinking.

Sebastopol, Guldbergsgade 2. Another good brasserie on the side of hip Skt Hans Torv.

Universitetscaféen, Fiolstræde 2, Nørreport. A prime central location directly south of Nørreport Station. Open until 5am, and a good spot to hit, early or late, for a leisurely beer.

Live music

A/S Bananrepublikken, Nørrebrogade 13, Nørrebro (☎35 36 08 30). One of the best places in town to hear world music; also has a good range of ethnic foods (see p.91).

Café Rust, Guldbergsgade 8, Nørrebro (☎35 35 00 33). One of the best-known places in town, on the edge of busy Skt Hans Torv and always packed. Bands play at weekends and often on Thursdays too, either indoors or on a very popular outdoor patio.

Club Blue Note, Studiestræde 31, Vesterport (☎33 13 08 06). A jazz, techno and house club that's perfectly positioned itself for the late, late-night set. Sometimes stays open past when other clubs empty out, remaining open all morning until breakfast. Between Vesterport Station and Vor Frue Kirke.

Copenhagen Jazz House, Niels Hemmingsensgade 10 (☎33 15 26 00). The country's premier jazz venue, featuring international names and Denmark's finest. Can be pricey, but students get substantial discounts. Closed Sun & Mon. Near Amagertorv

Femøren, Amager. Large open-air rock concerts from June to August. Bus #12 or #13.

Ideal Bar, Enghavevej 40, Vesterbro (☎33 25 80 12). Latin and swing music, part of the immensely popular *Vega* (see below).

La Fontaine, Kompagnistræde 11. City-centre jazz club open seven days a week, from 10pm right through to 6am. Not far from the Use-It office.

Loppen (Bådsmandsstræde 43, Christiania (☎35 57 84 22). On the edge of the "free city" and a suitably cool warehouse setting for both established and experimental Danish rock, jazz and performance artists, and quite a few British and American ones too. Also does disco nights.

Musikcaféen, Rådhusstræde 13. Sizeable hall, near Use-It office, but small enough to have plenty of atmosphere on good nights – of which there are several most weeks.

Musikloppen, Christiania. Rock 'n' roll or Danish pop plays here, mainly at weekends.

Pavillonen, inside Fælledparken park, Borgemester Jensens Allée 45, Nørrebro (☎35 26 01 11). In summer, this open-air venue serves a barbecue Thurs–Sat nights and follows it up with a diverse selection of Danish rock bands.

Pumpehuset, Studiestræde, Vesterport (☎33 93 19 60). Offers a broad sweep of middle-of-the-road rock, hip-hop and funk groups from Denmark and around the world about three times a month. Between Vesterport Station and Vor Frue Kirke.

Sofies Kælder, Sofiegade, Christianshavn. Hosts rock bands in the evenings, with a jazz concert every Saturday afternoon (3–6pm).

Tex, Vestergade 7, near the Rådhus (☎33 91 39 13). Live music and dodgy "theme jams" in the style of Metallica, Lenny Kravitz and the like. Its posters are plastered all over town, so you'll always know what's on.

Vega, Enghavevej 40 (☎33 25 80 12). In a former union hall, this newish club retains its 1950s and 1960s decor – zigzag tiles and suchlike – while showcasing plenty of modern underground rock.

Clubs

Club Mantra, Tivoli Gardens. Right beside Tivoli Gardens in a former jazz club, this is one of the best and most central disco/house music nightspots in town. The decor features leather sofas and a gorgeous panoramic mural of the city.

Discotek IN, Nørregade 1, Nørreport. The gimmick here is the free drinks you get with the expensive entry charge of 100–150kr. Bland pop, but always crowded and raucous due to the flowing alcohol. Just south of Nørreport Station.

Park Diskotek, Østerbrogade 79, Østerbro (☎35 42 62 48). Jammed club with disco and house music, a bar, café and more. A fun mixed crowd jams the place, especially the open deck during summer.

Q-House og dance, Axeltorv 5 (☎33 11 19 15). You can't miss this multicoloured dance club, easily reachable (and visible) from central Copenhagen and not far from Central Station, either. A bit staid, with an older clientele, but fine if you're looking to tango until dawn.

Stengade 30, Stengade 18 (☎35 36 09 38). Nørrebro club with live rock acts six nights a week, followed by all-night dance parties.

Stereo Bar, Linnésgade 16, Nørreport (☎33 13 61 13). *The* place for retro 1970s music, illuminated by lava lamps – they also do Latino, jazz and world-music nights.

Subsonic, Skindergade 45 (☎33 13 26 25). A very funky place with big dance floor and copy of an old SAS airport lounge – including original airplane seats – and a beer cellar too. The DJs pump out an Eighties groove. It's a short block north of, and parallel to, Strøget.

Woodstock, Vestergade 12 (☎33 11 20 71). Pulls a large, fun-loving crowd eager to dance to anything with a beat – though the music is predominantly 1960s. Close to the Rådhus.

Gay and lesbian Copenhagen

Copenhagen has a lively **gay scene**, which includes a good sprinkling of gay bars and clubs, a bookshop and a sauna, though no, at the time of writing, specifically gay hotels. For **contacts and information**, ignore the misleadingly named "Copenhagen Gay Centre" (no more than a glorified sex emporium) and contact the **National Organization for Gay Men and Women** (Landsforeningen for Bøsser og Lesbiske, or LBL), based at Teglgårdsstræde 13 (☎33 13 19 48). They provide information and advice, along with a bookshop, travel agency and café (Tues & Sun 1pm–3am, Wed & Thurs 1pm–4am, Fri 1pm–5am, Sat 1pm–6am). There's also a **gay switchboard** (☎33 13 01 12), and further information can be gleaned from *Pan* magazine – in Danish, but easily understood – which doesn't have listings but does have ads announcing the latest happenings. The **Gay Liberation Movement** (BBF) meets each Monday at 8pm in the Bøssehuset in Christiania at Karlsvognen and Refshalevej.

Bars and clubs

Amigo Bar, Schønbergsgade 4. Frequented by gay men of all ages; serves snacks too.

Café Babooshka, Turesensgade 6. Lesbian-only café; open Fri & Sat 9am–2pm, sometimes other nights as well.

Café Intime, Allegade 25. Not the most interesting crowd, but a piano player and live acts keep things moving along.

Can Can, Mikkel Bryggersgade 11. A favourite late-drinking spot for gay men. One block northwest of Rådhus.

Centralhjornet, Kattesundet 18. An ordinary and somewhat dreary place, with only history – it's Copenhagen's oldest gay bar – on its side. It's in the city centre, just northeast of *Can Can*.

Club Amigo, Studiestræde 31A, Vesterport. Enormous club with bar, cinemas, sauna and solarium, pool room, video room and much more. Gay men only. One of several gay venues in Studiestræde, between Vesterport Station and Vor Frue Kirke.

Cosy Bar, Studiestræde 24, Vesterport. Gets busy late, mainly with clones and motorbike boys, and stays open right through until morning.

Masken Bar, Studiestræde 33, Vesterport. Relatively staid bar popular with an older clientele.

Men's Bar, Teglgårdsstræde 3. The city's most macho bar, popular with leather and motorbike types; monthly Sunday brunches are well attended.

Pan Klub Disco, Knabrostræde 3. A new three-storey behemoth right in the centre of the city, just off Strøget, this place is the unquestioned hub of the city's gay nightlife and is always buzzing. The *Pan 2 Dance Bar*, on the upstairs level, also opens Wed 8pm–6am.

Sebastian, Hyskenstræde 10. A bright and popular late-night café-restaurant with touches of culture – art, magazines, live music – as well as a pool table. One block south of Strøget.

Size Bar, Vimmelskaffet 41F. A two-floor café-bar that's rapidly becoming another of the city's prime gay nightspots. Very central location, right off Strøget. Fri–Sat 8pm–5am.

Listings

Airlines British Airways, Rådhuspladsen 16 (☎80 20 80 22); Finnair, Nyropsgade 47 (☎33 36 45 45); SAS, Hammerichsgade 1–5 (☎70 10 30 00 or 32 32 68 00).

Banks and exchange Central services include American Express, 3rd floor, 7A Nørregade (Mon–Fri 9am–5pm, Sat 9am–2pm), and Det Danske Bank, Amagertorv 12 (Mon–Fri 9.30am–4pm, Thurs until 6pm). For changing money outside bank hours – at bank rates – there are bureaux at Central Station (daily 7am–9pm), the airport arrival hall (6.30am–10pm) and departure hall (6.30am–8.30pm), and at the seasonal Tivoli office (May to mid-Sept 10am–11pm).

Bookshops Most of the city's bookshops are in the area around Fiolstræde and Købmagergade. The Book Trader, Skindergade 23 (☎33 12 06 69), has a varied selection of old and new books in English; Kupeen DIS Rejser, Skindergade 28 (☎33 11 00 44), has guidebooks and maps for budget travellers. Chief places for new books are GAD (☎33 15 05 58), at Vimmelskaftet 32 (on Strøget) and also inside Central Station; Arnold Busck, Købmagergade 49 (with a discount branch at Østergade 16); and Boghallen i Politikens Hus, Rådhuspladsen 37 (☎33 47 25 60).

Car parks Usually pay and display, with different rates depending on zone colour: in descending level of expense, zones are coloured red (20kr per hour), yellow (12kr), green (9kr), blue (5kr) and white (free). Downtown car parks are thin on the ground, but there's a handy one at the Statoil petrol station in Israel Plads (12kr for 1hr, 65kr per day) and another attached to the Q8 station near Vesterport Station at Nyropsgade 42 (7–10kr per hour, 55kr per day).

Car rental Avis, Kampmannsgade 1 (☎33 15 22 99); Hertz, Ved Vesterport (☎33 17 90 20); Europcar, Gyldenløvesgade 17 (☎33 11 62 00).

Dentist Tandlægevagten, Oslo Plads 14 (☎35 38 02 51). Open nightly for emergencies only 8–9.30pm, Sat & Sun also 10am–noon. Turn up and be prepared to pay at least 150kr on the spot.

Doctors Call ☎33 93 63 00 Mon–Fri 8am–4pm and you'll be given the name of a doctor in your area. There's a night fee of around 300kr to be paid in cash. For non-urgent treatment, get a list of doctors from the tourist office, Use-It, or a local health department (Kommunens social og sundhedsforvaltning).

Email and Internet It's currently rather difficult to find public Internet access in Copenhagen, but expect that to change rapidly. For the moment, try Babel, Frederiksborggade 33 (☎33 33 93 38) or the free email service at the Use-It office on Rådhusstræde.

Embassies Australia, Strandboulevarden 122 (☎39 29 20 77); Canada, Kristen Bernikows Gade 1 (☎33 48 32 00); Ireland, Østbanegade 21 (☎35 42 32 33); New Zealand (use UK); UK, Kastelsvej 40 (☎35 44 52 00); USA, Dag Hammerskjölds Allé 24 (☎35 55 31 44).

Emergencies ☎112 for police or ambulance.

Hitching First check the car-share notices on Use-It notice boards. If they don't deliver anything, use the following routes (and remember you're not supposed to hitch on motorways). Heading south to Germany, take S-train line A or bus #16 to Ellebjerg station, which leaves you by the ring road, near the start of motorway E20. Going north to Helsingør and Sweden, take S-train line B or F to Ryparken (or bus #6, #24 or #84 to Hans Knudsen Plads) and hitch along Lyngbyvej (for the E4). West for Funen and Jutland, take S-train line B to Tåstrup, then walk along Køgevej and hitch from Roskildevej (A1).

Hospitals The local emergency department is at Rigshospitalet, Blegdamsvej 9 (☎35 45 35 45); free treatment for EU and Scandinavian nationals, though others are unlikely to have to pay.

Late-opening shops The supermarket at Central Station is open daily from 8am until midnight.

Laundry Central places to do washing include Alaska Vask & Rens, Borgergade 2; Møntvask, Istedgade 29; Quickvask, Istedgade 45; and Vasketeria, Dronningensgade 42. An average load costs about 40kr.

Left luggage The DSB Garderobe office downstairs in Central Station stores luggage for 20kr per day per pack, and there are small and large lockers for 25–35kr per day as well. There are also lockers in the InterRail Centre in Central Station and at Use-It, Rådhusstræde 13.

Library Hovedbiblioteket, Krystalgade 15–17 (Mon–Fri 10am–7pm, Sat 10am–2pm), is the main city library, with mostly Danish books and magazines. Huset, Rådhusstræde 13, also has a very well-stocked reading room, with international magazines and newspapers.

Lost property The police department's lost property office is at Slotherrensvej 113, Vanløse (☎38 74 88 22). Otherwise, for things lost on a bus, contact the bus information line on ☎33 13 14 15; lost on a train, the DSB office at Central Station (☎33 16 21 10; Mon–Fri 9am–4pm, Thurs until 6pm); lost on a plane, contact Kastrup Airport (☎32 47 47 47 or 32 31 32 31).

Markets There's a good flea market at Israel Plads on Saturday mornings May–Sept (bus #5 or #16), and a Salvation Army market, selling bric-a-brac and old clothes, at Hørhusvej (Tues–Thurs 1–5pm, Fri 1–6pm, Sat 9am–1pm); take bus #30, #3 or #4 to Brydes Allé. Try also the various summertime markets that pop up around Christiania's fruit-and-veg markets, and the Saturday-morning market held from mid-April until mid-October behind Frederiksberg Rådhus (bus #1 or #14).

Newspapers and news in English Overseas newspapers are sold at the stall in Rådhuspladsen and some newsagents along Strøget. News in English is broadcast daily at 8.30am on Radio Denmark (93.8MHz in Copenhagen).

Pharmacy Steno Apotek, Vesterbrogade 6 is open 24 hours.

Post offices Main office at Tietgensgade 39, right behind Central Station (Mon–Fri 11am–6pm, Sat 9am–1pm). Also at Central Station (Mon–Fri 8am–10pm, Sat & Sun 9am–4pm). Poste restante at Use-It, Rådhusstræde 13, 1466 Copenhagen K, or any named post office.

Saunas There are public saunas at Borgergade 12, Sjællandsgade 12 and Sofiegade 15. Generally open Mon–Fri 8am–6.30pm, Sat 8am–2pm; 30kr per person.

Travel agents KILROY Travels, Skindergade 28 (☎33 11 00 44), can give advice on travelling around Denmark, the rest of Scandinavia and Europe.

AROUND ZEALAND

It's easy to see more of Zealand by making day-trips out from the capital, although, depending on where you're heading next, it's often a better idea to pack your bags and leave the city altogether. Transport links are excellent throughout the region, making much of northern and central Zealand commuter territory for the capital; but that's hardly something you'd notice as you pass through dozens of tiny villages and large forests on the way to historic centres such as **Helsingør**, **Køge** and – an essential call if you're interested in Denmark's past – **Roskilde**. Except for the memorable vistas of the **northern coast**, and the explorable smaller **islands** off southern Zealand and **Bornholm** to the east, however, you'll find the soft green terrain varies little; and, unless you're a true nature lover, you'll soon want to push on (which is easily done) to the bigger cities in Funen and Jutland.

North Zealand

The **coast north of Copenhagen**, as far as Helsingør, rejoices under the tag of the "Danish Riviera", a label which neatly describes its line of tiny one-time fishing hamlets, now inhabited almost exclusively by the super-wealthy. It's best seen on the hour-long bus journey (#188) north to Helsingør from Klampenborg, itself the last stop on line C of the S-train system – the views of beckoning beaches are lovely. There's also a frequent train service between Copenhagen and Helsingør; it's slightly quicker than the bus, but you won't see much unless you break the journey, since views from the train are obscured by trees almost the entire way.

The Karen Blixen Museum, Humlebæk and Louisiana

There are two good reasons to stop before Helsingør. The **Karen Blixen Museum** (May–Sept daily 10am–5pm; Oct–April Wed–Fri 1–4pm, Sat & Sun 11am–4pm; 30kr) is a fifteen-minute walk or a short ride on bus #388 from Rungsted Kyst train station on the *regionaltog* train line going north towards Helsingør. The museum is housed in the family home of the writer who, while long a household name in Denmark for her short stories (often written under the pen-name of Isak Dinesen) and outspoken opinions, enjoyed a resurgence of international popularity during the mid-1980s when the film *Out of Africa* – based on her 1937 biographical account of running a coffee plantation in Kenya – was released. After returning from Africa, Blixen lived here until her death in 1962, and much of the house is maintained as it was during her final years. Texts describing Blixen's eventful life (her father committed suicide and she married the twin brother of the man she loved, among other things) line the walls, while exhibits include a collection of first editions and the tiny typewriter she used in Africa. Even if you've never read a word of Blixen, it's hard not to be impressed by accounts of her spirit and strength, which shine through the museum. After seeing the house, make for the well-tended flower garden, where Blixen's simple grave lies beneath a protective beech tree.

In Humlebæk, the next community of any size, you'll find **Louisiana** (daily 10am–5pm, Wed until 10pm; 55kr), a modern-art museum on the northern edge of the village at Gammel Strandvej 13, a short walk from the train station. Even if you go nowhere else outside Copenhagen, it would be a shame to miss this: the setting alone is worth the journey, harmoniously combining art, architecture and landscape. The entrance is in a nineteenth-century villa, from which lead two carefully designed modern corridors containing the indoor collection, their windows giving views of the sculpture park and Øresund outside.

It seems churlish to mention individual items, but the museum's American section, in the south corridor, includes some devastating pieces by Edward Kienholz, Malcolm Morley's scintillatingly gross *Pacific Telephone Los Angeles Yellow Pages*, in which the telephone directory cover expands to monstrous proportions and coffee stains rib the city skyline like a weird metallic grid, and (in the reading room) Jim Dines' powerful series *The Desire*. You'll also find some of Giacometti's gangly figures haunting a room of their own off the north corridor, and an equally affecting handful of sculptures by Max Ernst, squatting outside the windows and leering inwards. Except for some collages by Arthur Køpcke and paintings by various Danish luminaries of the CoBrA group, homegrown artists have a rather low profile, although their work is often featured in temporary exhibitions.

Helsingør

First impressions of **HELSINGØR** are none too enticing. The bus stops outside the noisy train station, outside which Havnepladsen is usually full of transit passengers loitering around fast-food stalls before making for the ferry terminal, 100m distant. Away from the hustle, though, Helsingør is a quiet and likeable town. Strategically positioned on the four-kilometre strip of water linking the North Sea and the Baltic, the town's wealth was founded on the Sound Toll of 1429, which was levied on passing ships right up until the nineteenth century. Shipbuilding subsequently restored some of the town's fortunes after the toll was abolished, but today it's once again the sliver of water between Denmark and Sweden, and the ferries across it to Helsingborg, which account for most of Helsingør's livelihood.

The Town

The town's main draw, on a sandy curl of land extending seawards, is **Kronborg Slot** (May–Sept daily 10.30am–5pm; April & Oct Tues–Sun 11am–4pm; Nov–March Tues–Sun 11am–3pm; 30kr, 45kr joint ticket with Maritime Museum), famous principally as the setting – under the name of Elsinore Castle – for Shakespeare's *Hamlet*. Actually, the playwright never visited Helsingør, and his hero was based on one Amleth

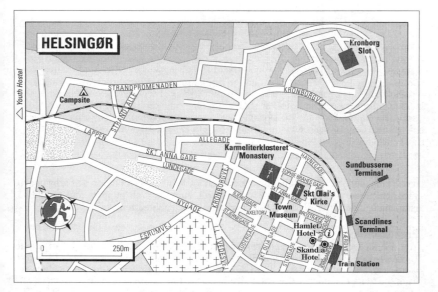

(or Amled), a tenth-century character lost in the mists of Danish mythology who certainly predated the castle – none of which has affected the castle's thriving trade in Hamlet souvenirs nor the hundreds of requests asking for the whereabouts of "Hamlet's bedroom". During winter, guided tours leave from the entrance every half-hour, during summer the number of visitors make this impossible – instead, well-informed attendants hover in every room ready to answer questions.

Construction of the present castle, built on the site of Erik of Pomerania's fortress, was instigated during the sixteenth century by Frederik II. Frederik commissioned the Dutch architects Van Opbergen and Van Paaschen, who took their ideas from the buildings of Antwerp. Various bits have been destroyed and rebuilt since, but it remains a grand affair, enhanced immeasurably by its setting, and with an interior, the royal chapel in particular, that is spectacularly ornate – though appreciation is hampered by the steady flow of tourists. Crowds are less of a problem in the labyrinthine cellars, which can be seen on a half-hourly guided tour (departing from the cellar entrance). The body of Holger Danske, a mythical hero from the legends of Charlemagne, is said to lie beneath the castle, ready to wake again when Denmark needs him, although the tacky Viking-style statue depicting the legend detracts somewhat from the cellars' authentic aura of decay. The castle also houses the national **Maritime Museum**, an uninteresting collection of model ships and nautical knick-knacks.

Away from Kronborg and the harbour area, Helsingør has a well-preserved **medieval quarter**. **Stengade** is the main pedestrianized street, linked by a number of narrow alleyways to **Axeltorv**, the town's small market square and a good spot to linger over a beer – alternatively, stroll into nearby **Brostræde**, a street that's famous for the immense ice creams made with traditional ingredients sold here. Near the corner of Stengade and Skt Annagade, the spired Skt Olai's Kirke is connected to the **Karmeliterklosteret Monastery**, which served originally as a hospital, during which time it prided itself on its brain operations. The unnerving tools of this profession are still on show next door at the **Town Museum** (daily noon–4pm; 10kr), together with diagrams of the corrective insertions made into patients' heads. For something less

---

FERRIES TO SWEDEN

Three **ferry lines** cross from Helsingør to Helsingborg in Sweden, though only two take foot passengers. The main one, and probably the best option, is the Scandlines boat leaving from the main terminal by the train station (32kr return). The Sundbusserne crossing, by small craft which are often heavily buffeted by the choppy waters, also costs 32kr return. The third line, Sundbroen, takes cars only. It's perfectly feasible, and on a sunny day very enjoyable, to rent a **bike** from the courtyard behind the tourist office (40kr a day) and cross to Helsingborg for a day's cycling along the Swedish coast. But take food and especially drink with you – both tend to be more expensive in Sweden than in Denmark, alcohol exorbitantly so.

---

disturbing, seek out the oddball **Journeymen's Club** (Naverhulen) in a nearby court-yard, cluttered with souvenirs of world travel, such as crab puppets and armadillo lampshades. Act interested and you might get a free guided tour.

Practicalities

You can pick up a free map and information on Helsingør from the **tourist office** at Havnepladsen 3 (June–Aug Mon–Sat 9am–7pm, Sun 9am–noon; Sept–May Mon–Fri 9am–5pm, Sat 9am–1pm; ☎49 21 13 33), across Strandgade from the train station, or from the tourist counter in the station itself. Due to the numbers of visiting tourists, the closest thing to a cheap **hotel** in town is the *Skandia*, Bramstræde 1 (☎49 21 09 02; ②), which is decent and clean. If you can afford it, treat yourself to the "Hamlet" or "Ophelia" suites at the *Hotel Hamlet*, Bramstræde 5 (☎49 21 05 91, fax 49 26 01 30, *HotelHamlet@internet.dk*; ⑤), a handsome white three-star with a fish and steak restau-rant. There's also a **youth hostel** (☎49 21 16 40; Feb–Nov), with doubles (①), literally on the beach, a twenty-minute walk to the north along the coastal road (Ndr. Strandvej), or take bus #340 from the station and get off just after the sports stadium. The *Helsingør Camping* **campsite**, at Campingvej 1 (☎49 21 58 56), is closer to town and also by a beach, between the main road Lappen (which begins where Skt Annagade ends) and the sea.

For **eating**, the usual pizza and fast-food outlets are two-a-penny around Stengade. A little more expensively, there's fine Danish food in the small, atmospheric *Bixen*, Hovedvagtsstræde 7, across from the train station (☎49 21 67 54), and a good café, the *Kronborg Havbad*, right next to Kronborg Slot. Given the proximity of the capital, nightlife of note is a rare commodity, but for an evening drink, stroll the streets on either side of Stengade, where there are several decent bars. Rowdier boozing goes on at the top end of Axeltorv, popular with Swedes taking advantage of Denmark's more liberal licensing laws.

Onwards from Helsingør: the North Zealand coast

Some of the best beaches in Zealand and several attractive fishing villages are within easy reach of Helsingør, either by bike, local buses or a network of private trains (on which the Copenhagen Card is valid, although InterRail and Eurail are not). No one par-ticular place has the power to hold you for long, but the region as a whole is hard to beat for a few days' relaxation.

Hellebæk and Hornbæk

A string of fine beaches can be found simply by following Ndr. Strandvej from Helsingør towards the sleepy village of **HELLEBÆK**, some 5km north. At Hellebæk itself, part of the beach is a well-known, if unofficial, venue for rude bathing. Trains from Helsingør stop at Hellebæk and then continue for 7km to the moderately larger **HORNBÆK**, blessed with excellent beaches and fabulous views over the sea towards Kullen, the rocky promontory jutting out from the Swedish coast. Though fast becoming a playground for yacht-owners and their cronies, Hornbæk is a lovely spot to stay over. In a library just off the main street, the **tourist office** (Mon, Tues & Thurs 2–7pm, Wed & Fri 10am–5pm, Sat 10am–2pm; ☎49 70 47 47) can find you private rooms and summer cottages. Or, from June to August, try the inexpensive pension *Ewaldsgården*, Johannes Ewalds Vej 5 (☎ & fax 49 70 00 82; ④), close by the train station, with single, double and family rooms. Just a few minutes' walk away is Hornbæk's exceptionally inexpensive campsite (☎49 70 02 23; mid-April to mid-Sept).

Gilleleje and Tisvildeleje

From Hornbæk, trains continue along the coast to **GILLELEJE**, twenty minutes further on, another appealing fishing village that does a roaring tourist trade. It's a good place for a short stopover, though unfortunately accommodation tends to be booked up far in advance and the only hotel in town is the Swiss-chalet-style *Strand*, Vesterbrogade 4B (☎ & fax 48 30 05 12; ⑤). The budget option is the all-year campsite, just outside the village at Bregnerødvej 21 (☎49 71 97 55). An alternative is to head west to the youth hostel in Tisvildeleje (see below).

While in Gilleleje, negotiate at least some of the footpath that runs along the top of the dunes, where, in 1835, **Søren Kierkegaard** took lengthy contemplative walks, later recalling: "I often stood there and reflected over my past life. The force of the sea and the struggle of the elements made me realize how unimportant I was." Ironically, so important would Kierkegaard become that a monument to him now stands on the path bearing his maxim: "Truth in life is to live for an idea."

From Gilleleje, bus #343 largely follows the coast to **TISVILDELEJE** (a 30min journey), where there are yet more beaches and Tisvilde Hegn (locally called simply "Hegn"), a forest of wind-tormented trees planted here during the eighteenth century to prevent sand drifts. The **youth hostel** (☎48 70 98 50) is part of a holiday complex, the *Sankt Helene Centeret*, at Bygmarken 30, and has forty-odd family rooms – including affordable doubles (②).

Inland from the coast

It's hard to continue along the coast without first detouring inland, and in any case the effort is barely worthwhile. Trains from both Tisvildeleje and Gilleleje run to Hillerød, in the heart of north Zealand, which – thanks to its magnificent castle – is the place to make for. On the way, though, you might spend a few hours at another royal residence, **Fredensborg Slot**, built by Frederik IV to commemorate the 1720 Peace Treaty with Sweden. The castle is only open in July (noon–5pm; guided tours 10kr), but even outside this month its grand, statue-lined gardens (open all year; free), stretching down to an expansive lake, are distinctly appealing.

Hillerød: Frederiksborg Slot

HILLERØD is half an hour by train from Helsingør, and a similar distance from Copenhagen (last stop on line E of the S-train network). Here is a castle which easily pushes the more famous Kronborg into second place, **Frederiksborg Slot** (daily: April–Oct 10am–5pm; Nov–March 11am–3pm; 40kr), which lies decorously across three small islands within an artificial lake. Buses #701 and #703 run from the train station to the castle, or it's a twenty-minute walk, following the signs (*Slottet*) through the town centre.

The castle was the home of Frederik II and birthplace of his son Christian IV. At the turn of the seventeenth century, under the auspices of Christian, rebuilding began in an unorthodox Dutch Renaissance style. It's the unusual aspects of the design – a prolific use of towers and spires, Gothic arches and flowery window ornamentation – that still stand out, despite the changes wrought by fire and restoration.

You can see the exterior of the castle for free simply by walking through the main gates, across the seventeenth-century S-shaped bridge, and into the central courtyard. Since 1882, the interior has functioned as a **museum of Danish history**, largely funded by the Carlsberg brewery magnate Carl Jacobsen in an attempt to create a Danish Versailles, and to heighten the nation's sense of history and cultural development. It's a good idea to buy the illustrated guide (25kr) to the museum, since without it the contents of the sixty-odd rooms are barely comprehensible. Many of the rooms are surprisingly free of furniture and household objects, and attention is drawn to the ranks of portraits along the walls – a motley crew of flat-faced kings and thin consorts who between them ruled and misruled Denmark for centuries, giving way in later rooms to politicians, scientists and writers.

Two rooms deserve special mention. The **chapel**, where monarchs were crowned between 1671 and 1840, is exquisite, its vaults, pillars and arches gilded and embellished, and the contrasting black marble of the gallery riddled with gold lettering. The shields, in tiered rows around the chapel, are those of the knights of the Order of the Elephant, who sat with the king in the late seventeenth century. The **Great Hall**, above the chapel, is a reconstruction, but this doesn't detract from its beauty. It's bare but for the staggering wall and ceiling decorations: tapestries, wall reliefs, portraits and a glistening black-marble fireplace. In Christian IV's day the hall was a ballroom, and the polished floor still tempts you to some fancy footwork as you slide up and down its length.

Away from the often crowded interior, the **gardens**, on the far side of the lake, have some photogenic views of the castle from their stepped terraces and are a good spot for a rest. The quickest way to them is through the narrow Mint Gate to the left of the main castle building, which adjoins a roofed-in bridge leading to the King's Wing. In summer you can also cross the lake on the hourly *M/F Frederiksborg* ferry (May–Sept daily).

Though Frederiksborg is the main reason to come to Hillerød, while here you could also visit the **Money Historical Museum** (open during banking hours; free) at Slotsgade 16–18. During the reigns of Frederik II and Christian IV all Danish coins were minted in Hillerød. Besides samples of these, the place displays currencies from all over the world.

If you do want **to stay**, try the three-star *Hillerød*, Milnersvej 41 (☎48 24 08 00, fax 48 24 08 74; ⑤). The only budget option is the **campsite** at Blytækkervej 18 (☎42 26 48 54; Easter to mid-Sept). The **tourist office** at Slotsgade 52 (June–Aug Mon–Fri 9am–6pm, Sat 10am–5pm; Sept–May Mon–Fri 9am–4pm, Sat 10am–1pm; ☎42 26 28 52) can arrange private rooms.

West from Copenhagen: Roskilde and beyond

There's very little between Copenhagen and the West Zealand coast to see and explore except for the ancient former Danish capital of **ROSKILDE**, less than half an hour by train from the big city. There's been a community here since prehistoric times, and later the Roskilde fjord provided a route to the open sea that was used by the Vikings. But it was the arrival of Bishop Absalon in the twelfth century that made the place the base of the Danish church – and, as a consequence, the national capital. Roskilde's importance waned after the Reformation, and it came to function mainly as a market for the neighbouring rural communities – much as it does today, as well as serving as dormitory territory for Copenhagen commuters. In high season, especially, it can be

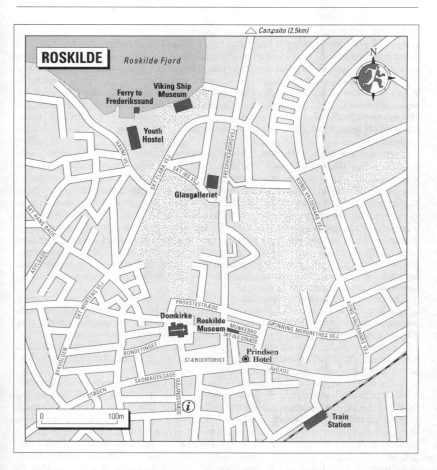

crammed with day-trippers seeking the dual blasts from the past supplied by its royal tombs and Viking boats; while the first week of each July sees a massive influx of visitors when it hosts the **Roskilde Festival** – northern Europe's biggest open-air rock event. Yet at any other time the ancient centre is one of Denmark's most appealing towns, and the surrounding countryside quiet and unspoilt.

The Town

The major pointer to the town's former status is the fabulous **Roskilde Domkirke** (April & Sept Mon–Fri 9am–4.45pm, Sat 11.30am–4.45pm, Sun 12.30–4.45pm; May–Aug Mon–Sat 9am–4.45pm, Sun 12.30–4.45pm; Oct–March Mon–Sat 10am–3.45pm, Sun 12.30–3.45pm; 6kr), founded by Bishop Absalon in 1170 on the site of a tenth-century church erected by Harald Bluetooth, and finished during the fourteenth century – although portions have been added right up to the twentieth. The result is a mishmash of architectural styles, though one that hangs together with surprising neatness. Every square inch seems adorned by some curious mark or etching, but it's the claustrophobic collection of coffins containing the regal remains of twenty kings and seventeen queens in four large **royal chapels** that really catch the eye. The most richly endowed chapel is that of Christian IV, a previously austere resting place jazzed-up – in typical early nineteenth-century Romantic style – with bronze statues, wall-length frescoes and vast paintings of scenes from his reign. A striking contrast is provided by the simple red-brick chapel just outside the cathedral where Frederik IX was laid to rest in 1972. Try to get to the cathedral just before the hour to see and hear the animated medieval clock above the main entrance: a model of St Jørgen gallops forward on his horse to wallop the dragon and the hour is marked by the creature's squeal of death.

From one end of the cathedral, a roofed passageway, the **Arch of Absalon**, feeds into the yellow **Bishop's Palace**. The incumbent bishop nowadays confines himself to one wing, while the others have been turned into showplaces for (predominantly) Danish art. The main building houses the **Museum for Contemporary Art** (Museet for Samtidskunst; Mon–Fri 11am–5pm, Sat & Sun noon–4pm; free), whose diverse temporary exhibitions often reflect current trends. The theme continues in the west wing, where the **Palæhøjen** gallery (Tues–Fri & Sun noon–4pm, Sat 10am–2pm; free), run by the local arts society, extends outdoors, turning up a collection of striking sculpture beneath the fruit trees of the bishop's garden. The less compelling **Palace Collections** (May–Sept daily 11am–4pm; Oct–April Sat & Sun 1–3pm; 5kr) are made up of paintings, furniture and other artefacts belonging to the wealthiest Roskilde families of the eighteenth and nineteenth centuries.

The **Roskilde Museum**, close to the cathedral at Skt Ols Gade 18 (June–Aug daily 11am–5pm; Sept–May Mon–Fri & Sun 2–5pm; 10kr), is a little more enticing, with strong sections on medieval pottery and toys. Look out for the strange photos that satirist Gustav Wied (who lived in Roskilde for many years and whose rooms are reconstructed here) took of his family. The museum extends to Ringstedgade 6, a shop kitted out in early twentieth-century style, where locals dutifully turn up to buy traditional salted-herring and sugar loaves.

More absorbing, and better known, is the **Viking Ship Museum** in Strandengen (Vikingeshibshallen; daily: April–Oct 9am–5pm; Nov–March 10am–4pm; 30kr), on the banks of the fjord ten minutes' walk north of the centre. This is one of Denmark's most interesting little museums, with five excellent specimens of Viking shipbuilding given the space they deserve: there's a deep-sea trader, a merchant ship, a man-of-war, a ferry and a longship, each retrieved from the fjord where they had been sunk to block invading forces. Together, they give an impressive indication of the Vikings' nautical versatility, their skills in boat-building, and their far-ranging travels to places as various as Paris, Hamburg and North America. The material here tries hard to convince you that the Vikings sailed abroad not only to rape and pillage, but also to find places where they could quietly settle down and farm. Boat-building and sail-making demonstrations sometimes take place outdoors – the Vikings' sails were spun from a special wool produced from wild Norwegian sheep – and there's a decent gift shop and café as well.

From the adjacent docks, the **cruise boat** *M/F Harald Blåtand* sails three times daily up the pretty fjord to Frederikssund and back (☎46 35 87 50, fax 46 35 81 89; 70kr one way), a journey of a little less than two hours each way. You can also do either the outbound or return leg of the trip by bus, which takes the same amount of time but costs about half as much.

Whilst in town, take a moment to inspect the **Glasgalleriet**, Skt Ibs Vej 12 (daily noon–4.30pm; free), a good little glasswork gallery in the old Roskilde Gasworks building between the harbour and the city's central green park. This park, quiet and soothing and with views of the fjord, was once the central stronghold of Viking power – a spot now marked by a hard-to-find plaque and a walking path to town, but nothing else.

THE ROSKILDE FESTIVAL

The **Roskilde Festival** has grown from humble beginnings into a weekend of live rock that now attracts some 80,000 people annually. The festival takes place over the last weekend in June and there's a special free camping ground beside the festival site, to which shuttle buses run from the train station every ten minutes. Tens of thousands of tickets are sold in advance – contact the tourist office for more information. If you want to get into the hostel or campsite you'll have to book a long way in advance.

Practicalities

Copenhagen is less than an hour's drive east of Roskilde, but if you're heading towards Funen or further south in Zealand it's easiest **to stay** here for the night. This is now a cheaper proposition than it once was, with a brand new **youth hostel** recently opened on the harbour, ideally located next to the Viking Museum at Vindeboder 7 (☎46 35 21 84, fax 46 32 66 90) – there are dorms, double rooms (②), a kitchen and a view of the water. If that's full, there's a **campsite** (☎46 75 79 96; mid-April to mid-Sept) on the wooded edge of the fjord around 2km north of town – an appealing setting that means it gets very crowded at peak times; it's linked to the town centre by bus #602. There's also the pricey *Prindsen* hotel at Algade 13 (☎ & fax 46 35 80 10. ⑥). For more information, or to arrange a private room, call in at Roskilde's **tourist office** at Gullandstræde 15 (April–June Mon–Fri 9am–5pm, Sat 10am–1pm; July & Aug Mon–Fri 9am–5pm, Sat 9am–3pm, Sun 10am–2pm; Sept–March Mon–Thurs 9am–5pm, Fri 9am–4pm, Sat 10am–1pm; ☎46 35 27 00).

Eating isn't a problem in Roskilde, with plenty of options. One of the best spots in town for a quick and inexpensive bite is the cafeteria of the Viking Museum – they do sandwiches and daily specials for no more than 35kr, and stock reasonably priced beers. Also on the waterfront, *Havne Caféen*, Havne Vej 43, north across the docks from the museum, does pizza and fish specials from 50kr. There's also a good little park with views of the town at the top of the stairs behind the café. Other options include loads of mainstream restaurants, cafés and pubs lining Skomagergade, just south of the Domkirke, and the maze of streets branching off it; for a quick bite, pop into the *No. 44 Sandwich Bar* at 44 Skomagergade, where sandwiches go for around 40kr, or use the Strandberg supermarket on Skt Ols Stræde, by the Roskilde Museum.

Evening entertainment in Roskilde amounts to visiting the sprinkling of bars around the town centre, taking in the occasional free event in the town park, or a pleasant walk along the banks of the fjord. Serious revellers head for Copenhagen.

Lejre Historical-Archeological Centre

Iron Age Denmark is kept alive and well at the **Lejre Historical-Archeological Centre**, 12km west of Roskilde, by volunteer families who spend the summer living in a reconstructed Iron Age settlement, farming and carrying out domestic chores using implements – and wearing clothes – copied from those of the period. Modern-day visitors are welcome (May–Sept daily 10am–4pm; 50kr), and can try their hand at grinding corn, paddling a dugout canoe and cooking pancakes. The serious scientific purpose is to gain an understanding of family life in Denmark 2500 years ago, but the centre can be a lot of fun to visit as a day-trip. To get here, take a local train from Roskilde to the village of Lejre; from Lejre station, bus #233 covers the 4km to the historical centre's entrance.

Beyond Roskilde: western Zealand

Beyond Roskilde, western Zealand is flat and bland. You might find yourself travelling through on the way to **Kalundborg**, from where ferries depart for Århus and the island of Samsø, or to **Korsør**, the other main town on the west coast, from where ferries leave for the island of Langeland and to Nyborg on Funen. Apart from these, the area's only real interest lies in the **Hornsherred Peninsula**, which divides the Roskilde fjord and Isefjord. There are long, quiet beaches along the peninsula's western coast, though the lack of a railway and the paucity of local buses means the region is best toured by bike. Make for the medieval frescoes in the eleventh-century churches at **Skibby** or **Dråby**, or keep on northward for **Jægerspris** and its **castle** (May–Sept daily 10am–noon & 1–5pm; 20kr), built during the fifteenth century as a royal hunting seat and last used by the eccentric Frederik VII, who lived here during the mid-1800s with his third wife. She inherited the castle after the king's death and turned it into an institution for "poor and unfortunate girls". The most convenient play to stay in the area is the small *Jægerpris Vandrerhjem* hostel near the Roskilde fjørd bridge – the only bridge that crosses the fjord (as Route 53) from Frederikssund west to Jægerpris – at Skovnæsvej 2, with singles, doubles (①) and family rooms, as well as kitchen facilities (☎47 31 10 32, fax 47 31 28 32).

South from Copenhagen: Køge and around

Not too long ago, **KØGE** was best known for the pollution caused by the rubber factory and chemical works on its outskirts, and despite the town's fine sandy beaches, few ventured here to sample the waters of Køge Bay. In recent years, though, the place has been considerably cleaned up, while an extension of line E of the Copenhagen S-train network has linked the town to the capital, putting its evocatively preserved medieval centre and beaches within easy reach. It's also a good base for touring the **Stevns Peninsula**, which bulges into the sea just south of the town.

The town and beaches

Saturday is the best day to visit Køge: a variety of free entertainment sweeps through the main streets in the morning and the harbourside bars are at their liveliest. Walk from the **train station** along Jernbanegade and turn left into Nørregade for Torvet, which is the hub of the action. On a corner of the square is the **tourist office** (Mon–Fri 9am–5pm; ☎56 65 58 00), while nearby, at Nørregade 4, the **Køge Museum** (June–Aug daily 10am–5pm; Sept–May Mon–Fri 2–5pm, Sat & Sun 1–5pm; 15kr) contains remnants from Køge's bloody past, not least the local executioner's sword. If the tales are to be believed, the beheading tool was wielded frequently on Torvet, a place which, perhaps not surprisingly, has also been the scene of several incidents of witchcraft and haunting. On the site of what is today a clothes shop, the Devil is said to have appeared in the forms of a clergyman, a frog, a dog and a pig, to have thrown a boy from his bed out into the yard, and caused hands to swell – among other unwholesome occurrences.

Once its market stalls are cleared away, a suitably spooky stillness falls over Torvet and the narrow cobbled streets that run off it. One of these streets, Kirkestræde, is lined with sixteenth-century half-timbered houses and leads to **Skt Nikolai Kirke** (mid-June to July daily 10am–4pm; Aug to mid-June Mon–Fri & Sun 10am–noon), where pirates captured in Køge Bay were hung from the tower. Along the nave, some of the carved angel faces on the pew ends lack noses, having been sliced off by drunken Swedish soldiers during the seventeenth century, while the font, an unattractive black-marble and pine item, replaces an earlier one defiled by a woman who performed "an unspeakable act" in it. On a more aesthetic level, the intriguing **Køge Art Museum** of **Sketches**, at Nørregade 29, focuses on the creative process from idea to finished work. Its collection includes drawings, sculptures and models made by important Danish artists of the twentieth century, plus temporary exhibitions of works in progress by both Danish and international artists.

The town's **beaches**, which draw many jaded Copenhageners on weekends, stretch along the bay to the north and south of the town. To take full advantage of the sands, **stay** at one of the two campsites beside the southerly beach: *Køge Sydstrand* (☎56 65 07 69; April–Sept) is virtually on the beach, and *Vallø* (☎56 65 28 51), which also has cabins, is across Strandvejen, close to a pine wood. Further away 2km from the town centre along Ølbyvej, is Køge's youth hostel (☎56 65 14 74; April to mid-Dec) with bunks and some double rooms (②). Take bus #245 from the train station and get off when the bus turns into Ågerskovvej. Staying in the town centre isn't expensive; head for the small and comfortable *Centralhotellet* (☎56 65 06 96; ④), next door to the tourist office at Vestergade 3.

Around Køge: Stevns Peninsula

Stevns Peninsula, easily reached from Køge, is a fairly neglected part of Zealand, mainly because the coastline here is more rugged and less suited to swimming than that immediately around Køge or in North Zealand. The town of **STORE HEDDINGE**, where you'll find a curious octagonal limestone church, is the obvious starting point for explorations; you can get there on the private train line (InterRail and Eurail passes not valid) from Køge in half an hour. In Store Heddinge you'll find a simple **youth hostel** at Ved Munkevænget 1 (☎56 50 20 22; mid-March to Sept), with exceptionally inexpensive doubles (①). There are several **campsites** on the beaches to the south: the nearest to Køge is *Nordstevns*, Strandvejen 29 (☎56 67 70 03), in the woodlands around Strøby, accessible by the frequent bus #209.

Central Zealand: Ringsted

Though now little more than a small farming town, **RINGSTED**'s central location made it one of the most important settlements in Zealand from the end of the Viking era until the Reformation. It was the burial place of medieval Danish monarchs as well as being site of a regional *ting*, the open-air court where prominent merchants and nobles made the administrative decisions for the province.

The three *ting* stones around which the nobles gathered remain in Ringsted's market square, but they're often concealed by the market itself, or the backsides of weary shoppers. It's the sturdy **Skt Bendts Kirke** (May to mid-Sept Mon–Fri 10am–noon & 1–5pm; mid-Sept to April Mon–Fri 10am–noon) that dominates the square, as it has done for over eight hundred years. Erected in 1170 under the direction of Valdemar I, the church was the final resting place for all Danish monarchs until 1341. Many affluent Zealanders also had themselves buried here, presumably so that their souls could spend eternity in the very best company. Four thousand people are said to have been present for the church's consecration, and although these days it receives a mere trickle of visitors compared to those flocking to the royal tombs at Roskilde, it nevertheless represents a substantial chunk of Danish history. During the seventeenth century a number of the coffins were opened and the finds are collected in the **Museum Chapel** within the church. Besides the lead slab found inside Valdemar I's coffin, there are plaster casts of the skulls of Queen Bengård and Queen Sofia, a collection of coins found in the church and a replica of the Dagmar Cross, discovered when Queen Dagmar's tomb was opened in 1697 – the original is in the National Museum in Copenhagen.

Once you've seen the church you've more or less exhausted Ringsted. The town's only other attraction is the **Agricultural Museum** (Mon–Thurs 11am–4pm, Fri

11am–3pm, Sun 1–4pm; 20kr), off Skt Bendtsgade to the rear of the church, an unexpectedly interesting survey of the local farming community, although seeing it won't take up more than half an hour.

For accommodation, the **youth hostel** (☎57 61 15 26) is handily situated across the road from the church – with no campsites nearby, this is the only budget option, and it also has doubles (①). Ringsted does have some pricey hotels, and the **tourist office** (mid-June to Aug Mon–Fri 9am–5pm, Sat 9am–2pm; Sept to mid-June Mon–Fri 10am–5pm, Sat 10am–1pm; ☎57 61 34 00), a few doors along between the hostel and Torvet, can advise on these as well as arranging private rooms (from 100kr per person). One decent choice is the *Scandic* at Nørretorv 57 (☎57 61 93 00, fax 57 67 02 07; ⑤), with sauna, restaurant and children's playground. There's also a simple *kro* between Ringsted and Køge at Hovedgaden 14 (☎57 52 60 12; ④).

Southern Zealand and the islands

Southern Zealand is seriously rural, consisting almost solely of rich, rolling farmland and villages. South from Ringsted, most routes lead to **NÆSTVED**, by far the largest town in the area. Aside from a smartly restored medieval centre and a minor museum, however, Næstved has little to offer except its proximity to unspoilt countryside and the **River Suså**, whose lack of rapids and negligible current makes it a good base for novice **canoe trips** – although busy at weekends, it's free of crowds at other times. Canoes can be rented at Suså Kanoudlejning, Vestbyholmallé 6, in nearby Glumsø (☎55 64 61 44), for around 280kr a day. Off the river, time is best spent strolling amid the town's half-timbered buildings and visiting the **Næstved Museum** at Ringstedgade 4 (Tues–Sun 9am–4pm; 20kr) for its jumble of (mainly religious) oddments and a fairly ordinary selection of historical arts and crafts from the town.

The local **tourist office** (May–Oct Mon–Fri 10am–5pm, Sat 9am–noon; Nov–April Mon–Fri 10am–5pm; ☎55 72 11 22) in the yellow house known as Det Gule Pakkus, Havnen 1, can fill you in on practical details and offer suggestions for **staying over** in Næstved. Or try for a room at the *Vinhuset* (☎ & fax 55 72 08 07, *vinhuset@post4.tele.dk*; ⑤), centrally located on the church square, Skt Peders Kirkeplads. Farther from town but similarly priced is the nicely renovated *Menstrup Kro Resort Hotel* (☎55 44 03 03, fax 55 44 33 63, *menstrup@get2.net.dk*; ⑤), with a sauna, pool and tennis court. The only really cheap spot in town is the **youth hostel** at Frejasevej 8 (☎55 72 20 91; mid-March to mid-Oct) with doubles (①); from the train station (which is about 1km from the centre on Jernbanegade), turn left into Imagesvej and left again along Præstøvej. There's also a **campsite** (also ☎55 72 20 91) beside the hostel, with the same opening season.

If you have the opportunity, take a trip to the island of **Gavnø**, a few miles south of Næstved, to see its eponymous eighteenth-century Rococo palace (May–Aug daily 10am–5pm; 15kr), an imposing structure enhanced by a delightful leafy setting. Parts of the building are still occupied by the descendants of the original owners, and there's a small collection of books and paintings on display. Bus #85 runs about four times a day during the summer between Næstved town centre and the palace.

Falster, Lolland and Møn

Off the south coast of Zealand lie three sizeable islands – **Falster**, **Lolland** and **Møn**. All three are connected to the mainland by road, and Falster and Lolland have rail links too, making them relatively easy to reach, but once there you'll need your own transport – bikes can be rented from virtually all tourist offices and campsites – to do any serious exploration outside the larger communities, since local buses are rare.

Falster

Falster is much the least interesting of the trio. There are some pleasant woods on the eastern side and some good, but very crowded, beaches along its western coast, particularly around the major resort of **MARIELYST**. There's not much to do in Marielyst except enjoy the beach, but it's got plenty of bars, cafés and accommodation. The most affordable **hotel** is the *Marielyst Strand*, near the beach (☎54 13 68 88; ③), or you could ask at the **tourist office** (☎54 13 62 98) for their list of private rooms. There are two **campsites**, *Smedegårdens* (☎54 13 66 17) and *Marielyst Camping* (☎54 78 00 71), both close to the beach.

The island's main town, **NYKØBING** – usually written Nykøbing F – has a major sugar industry and a quaint medieval centre, and is of practical use for its **tourist office** at Østerågade 2 (☎54 85 13 01), which handles enquiries for all three islands. For **accommodation**, try the three-star *Hotel Falster* at Skovalleen (☎54 85 93 93, fax 54 82 21 99; ⑤). There's also the island's only **youth hostel** at Østre Allé 110 (☎54 85 46 99; closed mid-Dec to mid-Jan), about 2km from the Nykøbing train station, with doubles (①) and an adjoining campsite (☎54 85 45 45; May to mid-Sept). If you're here with children, don't miss the **Folkepark Zoo** (daily 9am–4pm; free), which offers the chance to come face to face with a llama, and some native Danish creatures.

If you're ultimately making for the port of **Gedser**, to the south of Falster, for ferries to Warnemünde in Germany, don't bother getting off the train before the ferry dock. Gedser itself doesn't have much to offer except for a decent beach to the east of town.

Lolland

Larger and less crowded than Falster, **Lolland** is otherwise much the same: wooded, with excellent beaches and lots of quiet, explorable corners. A private railway (InterRail and Eurail passes not valid) runs to Lolland from Nykøbing, taking in Sakskøbing, Maribo and finally Nakskov, at the western extremity of the island, near to where ferries cross to Langeland; there's also a DSB train from Nykøbing and Sakskøbing to Rødby on the south coast. Each town has a tourist office, youth hostel and campsite, but **MARIBO**, delectably positioned on the Søndersø lake, is the most scenic setting for a short stay, with a youth hostel at Sdr Boulevard 82b (☎54 78 33 14; doubles ①), a campsite at Bangshavevej 25 (☎54 78 00 71; Easter to Sept), and a good-value two-star hotel, *Ebsens*, near the train station at Vestergade 32 (☎54 78 10 44, fax 54 75 60 44; ④).

After the beaches, the island's top attraction is probably **Aalholm Slot** (July & Aug daily 11am–5pm; Sept–June Sat & Sun 11am–5pm; joint ticket with Automobile Museum 90kr) in the southeast, a twelfth-century castle whose sumptuously furnished rooms and rather less attractive torture chamber are open to the public; next door to the castle is an **Automobile Museum** (same hours and ticket), containing two hundred antique cars. Though Lolland is not the most obvious place to spot big game, you can see antelopes, zebra, giraffes and more at the drive-through **Knuthenborg Safari Park**, 7km north of Maribo (May–Sept 9am–6pm; 70kr).

Møn

Møn is the most difficult of the three islands to get to from Zealand, since it's not connected to it by train, though it's well worth the effort of getting there: take bus #64 from Vordingborg (on the rail line from Copenhagen to Nykøbing F). The island is known for its white chalk cliffs – the only cliffs in Denmark. But what really sets Møn apart are the **Neolithic burial places** which litter the island by the score, and its unique white-washed churches, many of which feature fourteenth-century frescoes depicting rural life – the work, apparently, of one peasant painter. The main town, **STEGE**, is, at least for those without their own transport, the most feasible base, since it's the hub of the island's (minimal) bus service and has a good if pricey **hotel**, the *Præstekilde* (☎55 86

87 88; ⑤), at Klintvej 116 near the beach, and a **campsite** on Falckvej (☎55 81 53 25; May–Aug). Of the four other campsites on the island, *Camping Møns Klint* at Klintvej 544 in **Borre** (☎55 81 20 25), to the east, is the best, while *Ulvshale Camping* (☎55 81 53 25; April–Oct) is right on the beach at the island's northernmost point. If you'd rather sleep in a bed, check out current options with the helpful Stege **tourist office**, by the bus station at Storegade 2 (mid-June to Aug Mon–Sat 9am–6pm, Sun 10am–noon; Sept to mid-June Mon–Fri 9am–5pm, Sat 9am–noon; ☎55 81 44 11).

The best of the Neolithic barrows is **Kong Asker's Høj**, about 20km from Stege near **Sprove**, while the foremost frescoes can be admired at **ELMELUNDE** (bus #51 from Stege) and **FANEFJORD** (take the Vordingborg bus from Stege and get out at Store Damme, then walk), which also has a Neolithic barrow in the churchyard. As for the **cliffs** (Møn Klint), they're at the eastern end of the island and stretch for about 8km. Bus #51 runs between the cliffs and Stege four or five times a day depending on the season. Fifteen minutes' walk from the cliffs, at Langebjergvej 1, is a plain **youth hostel** (☎55 81 20 30; doubles ①; May–Sept).

Bornholm

Although much nearer to Sweden than Denmark, **Bornholm** (shown on the map on p.461) has been a Danish possession since 1522. Once an important Baltic trading post, its population now lives by fishing, farming and, increasingly, tourism. The coastline is blessed with great beaches in the south and some invitingly rugged coastline and hilly landscapes to the north, while the island's centre is covered in woods with good walking possibilities. It's no wonder that Scandinavian and German holiday-makers fill the island each summer, but despite the crowds. It's easily reached by ferry from Copenhagen, and quite feasible as a stopover if you're heading to Sweden or Germany on one of several ferry crossings (see "Travel Details").

Practicalities

To get the most out of Bornholm, you really need to travel around the whole coast – not difficult, since the island is only about 30km across from east to west – and spend three or four days doing it. **Getting around** is easy and best done by **bike**: the island is crisscrossed by some two hundred bike trails, and bikes can be rented in Rønne at Bornholms Cykeludlejning, Nordre Kystvej 5 (☎56 95 13 95), and from most of the island's tourist offices. If this seems too energetic, you can make use of the frequent and extensive **bus** services (all buses are equipped to carry bikes, as well; information on ☎56 95 21 21). **Accommodation** is straightforward, too: there's a youth hostel in each of the main settlements and campsites are sprinkled fairly liberally around the coast. The peak weeks of the summer are very busy, and you should phone ahead to check there's space. But at any other time of year there'll be little difficulty. The nightlife on the island can also be surprisingly lively, although often limited to one spot in each town – invariably the café in the main square.

As for **leaving Bornholm**, if you're not going back to Denmark, ferries to Sweden depart from Rønne for Ystad, and from Allinge, near Sandvig, there's a summer-only catamaran link to Simrishamn. There are also crossings from Rønne to Travemünde and Sassnitz in Germany.

The island

Ferries from Copenhagen arrive in **RØNNE**, the main town on the island, where a **tourist office** (late June–Aug Mon & Fri–Sun 8am–9pm, Tues–Thurs 8am–5pm;

Sept–late June daily 9am–5pm; ☎56 95 08 10) can fill you in on accommodation and transport details, and give you a copy of *Bornholm Denne Uge*, the free weekly listings magazine. If you've arrived on an overnight or early boat, you can celebrate your arrival with breakfast at *Det Røde Pakhus*, Snellemark 30, or with freshly baked bread from the bakery opposite. Otherwise, though, it's best to move on immediately: Rønne lacks the character of many of the other island settlements. If you do need to **stay over**, there are plenty of options: a youth hostel at Arsenalvej 12 (☎56 95 13 40; doubles ②; March–Oct); a campsite at Strandvejen 4 (☎56 95 23 20; mid-May to Aug); private rooms start from around 125kr per person – contact the tourist office, or the quite accurately named *Sverre's Small Hotel* at Skt Snellemark 2 (☎56 95 03 03; ③).

If you're eager to get to the beach, head south to **DUEODDE**, where there's nothing but sand and a string of campsites. In summer Dueodde lighthouse is open to the public (April–Oct 9am–dusk; 5kr), offering superb views. At the other corner of the eastern coast, **SVANEKE** is a quiet place favoured by Danish retirees, but has more spectacular scenery and the beaches are, once again, superb. In the mid-1970s Svaneke won a Council of Europe prize for town preservation and these days upmarket hotels and restaurants occupy some of the renovated old buildings. If you want to **stay**, first choice is the excellent *Siemsens Gaard*, Havnebryggen 9 (☎56 49 61 49, fax 56 49 61 03, *hotel@siemsens.dk*; ⑤), whose front rooms give great views. Otherwise, there's a youth hostel at Reberbanevej 9 (☎56 49 62 42; doubles ②; April–Oct), near the Christiansø ferry landing, and two campsites. The **tourist office** at Staregade 24 (June–Aug Mon–Fri 9.30am–4.30pm, Sat 9am–noon; Sept–May Mon–Wed 10am–4pm, Thurs & Fri 11am–5pm; ☎56 49 63 50) should be able to help with any queries.

Halfway along the north coast, **GUDHJEM** is pretty too, its tiny streets winding their way around the foot of a hill. Buses run the 5km or so north to the **Bornholms Kunstmuseum** (daily 10am–5pm; 30kr), a gallery displaying works from the Bornholm School that thrived here in the first half of the twentieth century. Gudhjem is also a good jumping-off point for the six-kilometre trip inland to **ØSTERLARS**, site of the largest and most impressive of the island's fortified round churches, which date from the twelfth and thirteenth centuries. A similar distance further inland, right in the centre of the island, is Bornholm's largest forest, **Almindingen**; there's a lookout tower for some fabulous views. **SANDVIG**, on the island's northwest corner, is the start of another worthwhile walk, along **Hammeren**, the massive granite headland that juts out towards Sweden. Just south of Sandvig are the remains of the thirteenth-century **Hammershus**, not much in themselves but worth a visit for the views from the tall crag which the castle occupied.

If Bornholm suddenly seems too big, and the weather's good, take one of the daily ferries (from Svaneke, Gudhjem, Sandvig or Allinge; check with any tourist office for the latest details) to the tiny island of **Christiansø**, some 25km northeast of Bornholm – a speck in the Baltic that served as a naval base during the seventeenth century, and later as a prison, though these days the minuscule population prides itself on its spiced herring. From Christiansø there's a footbridge over to the island of **Frederiksø**, a breeding ground for eider ducks. If you want to savour the peace of these little islands, you can stay at the *Gæstgiveriet* (☎56 46 20 15; ③) on Christiansø, one of the few lodgings in these parts.

travel details

Trains
Copenhagen to: Århus (29 daily; 3hr 10min); Esbjerg (25 daily; 3hr 15min); Helsingør (70 daily; 55min); Næstved (74 daily; 35min); Nykøbing F (27 daily; 1hr 45min); Odense (49 daily; 1hr 30min); Ringsted (75 daily; 45min); Roskilde (94 daily; 25min).

Helsingør to: Gilleleje (33 daily; 40min); Hellebæk (34 daily; 12min); Hillerød (40 daily; 30min); Hornbæk (33 daily; 25min).

Køge to: Fakse (21 daily; 38min); Store Heddinge (24 daily; 31min).

Nykøbing F to: Nakskov (28 daily; 45min); Rødby (7 daily; 23min); Sakskøbing (26 daily; 16min).

Roskilde to: Kalundborg (24 daily, connects with ferry to Jutland; 1hr 10min).

Buses

Copenhagen to: Aalborg (2–4 daily; 6hr); Århus (6 daily; 3–4hr); Helsingør (30 daily; 1hr); Hanstholm (1 daily; 6hr 45min).

Ferries

Allinge to: Christiansø (May–Oct Mon–Sat 1 daily; 1hr 10min).

Copenhagen to: Rønne (1–2 daily; 3hr).

Gudhjem to: Christiansø (May–Sept 1 daily; July & Aug 3 daily; 1hr).

Kalundborg to: Århus (15 daily; 1hr 20min–3hr).

Korsør to: Lohals (5 daily; 1hr 30min); Nyborg (15–25 daily; 70min).

Sjællands Odde to: Ebeltoft (12–15 daily; 45min–1hr 40min).

Svaneke to: Christiansø (Mon–Fri 1 daily; 1hr 30min).

Tårs (Langeland) to: Spodsbjerg (16–18 daily; 45min).

International trains

Copenhagen to: Bergen (2 daily; 15–19hr); Gothenburg (9 daily; 5hr); Hamburg (5 daily; 4hr 45min); Helsinki (2 daily, change to ferry in Stockholm; 24hr); Kiruna (2 daily, change in Stockholm; 23hr); Malmö (frequency to be announced; 35min); Narvik (1 daily, change in Stockholm; 24hr 30min); Oslo (3 daily; 9hr 40min); Stockholm (13 daily; 5–8hr); Turku (2 daily, change to ferry in Stockholm; 22hr).

International ferries

Allinge to Simrishamn (3 daily in summer; 2hr).

Copenhagen to: Malmö (catamaran: 18 daily; 45min; boat: 5 daily; 1hr 30min); Oslo (3 daily; 16hr); Swinoujscie (5 weekly; 10hr).

Dragør to: Limhamn (20 daily; 55min).

Gedser to: Warnemünde, Germany (6 daily in summer; rest of year 3 daily; 2hr).

Helsingør to: Helsingborg (Sundbusserne 25–30 daily; 20min; Scandlines 60 daily in summer; 25min).

Rødby to: Puttgarden (30–40 daily in summer; 1hr).

Rønne to: Sassnitz, Germany (1–2 daily in summer; 3hr 30min); Ystad (2–5 daily; 2hr 30min).

CHAPTER TWO

FUNEN

Known as "the garden of Denmark" for the lawn-like neatness of its fields and for the immense amount of fruit and vegetables that comes from them, **Funen** (Fyn), is the smaller of the two main Danish islands, and one which many visitors pass quickly through on their way between Zealand and Jutland. The island's bucolic outlook and coastline draw many, but its attractions are mainly low-profile, such as the various collections of the Funen painters and the birthplaces of writer Hans Christian Andersen and composer Carl Nielsen, who eulogized the distinctive sing-song Funen accent and claimed it inspired his music. If you are still keen, the island's best seen by cycling; otherwise, you'll be getting around on buses more often than trains, which are relatively scarce.

Arriving from Zealand brings you through **Nyborg**, a town with a heavily restored twelfth-century castle, though there's little reason to linger long on the **east coast** and it's preferable to stick to the cross-country railway that continues to **Odense**, Denmark's third-largest city and an obvious base if you want to explore villages by day but would like something other than rural quiet by night. Close by, the former fishing town of **Kerteminde** retains some faded charm, and is a good base for visiting both the **Ladby Boat**, an important Viking relic, and the isolated **Hindsholm Peninsula**. To the **south**, Funen's coastal life centres on maritime **Svendborg** – connected by train with Odense via the island's only branch rail line – with its good beaches and a fragmented archipelago of pretty **islands**: this is vacation territory for the most part, well served by ferries and possibly the top scenic draw on Funen.

East Funen

Travelling from Zealand to Funen takes you over the **Storebælt** ("Great Belt") on the recently completed 18-kilometre road and rail link which now connects the two islands, before bringing you to **Nyborg**, Funen's easternmost town and one that few people see more of than a railway station.

Unless you're in a rush to reach Odense, spare a few hours for Nyborg's strollable old streets and thirteenth-century castle, for two hundred years the seat of Danish political power. While here, you might also visit the Storebælt Exhibition Centre, which details the construction of the mammoth transport link connecting Funen and Zealand. Otherwise, apart from countless lookalike villages, there's little in East Funen to detain you.

ACCOMMODATION PRICE CODES

The hotels and guest houses listed in this chapter have been graded according to the following price bands, based on the **cheapest rate for a double room in summer**.

① Under 300kr   ② 300–400kr   ③ 400–500kr   ④ 500–650kr
⑤ 650–900kr   ⑥ 900–1300kr   ⑦ Over 1300kr

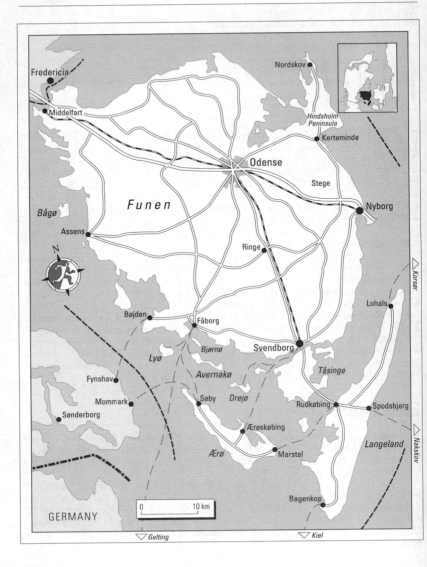

Nyborg

NYBORG is small and easily navigated and you'll have no trouble finding your way to **Nyborg Slot**, built around 1200 by Valdemar the Great as part of a chain of coastal fortresses to guard against Wend piracy. For more than two hundred years, the Danehof – a summertime national assembly involving king, clergy and nobility – met here (and in 1282 drew up the first Danish constitution), which effectively made Nyborg the Danish capital until 1443, when power moved to Copenhagen. The castle bears little evidence of those years, however. Many of the surrounding fortifications have been turned into ordinary homes and all that remains on view is the narrow building holding the living quarters, its distinctive harlequin brickwork a result of 1920s restoration. Inside, the **museum** (daily: June–Aug 10am–5pm; April, May, Sept & Oct 10am–3pm; 25kr) leads through low-beamed chambers and emerges into an expansive attic; the rooms themselves much more evocative of the past than the odd table, chest, or suit of armour with which they are decorated.

With the bright lights of Odense just 25km away to the west, there's little temptation to spend a night in Nyborg. If you decide to do so, though, *Missionshotellet*, on Østervoldgade (☎65 30 11 88; ③), is a fair-priced hotel, while the **youth hostel** is centrally placed at Havnegade 28 (☎65 31 27 04). Bus route #2 (which runs to the Storebælt Exhibition Centre, see below) is the link to the cabin-equipped beachside **campsite** (☎65 31 02 56) at Hjejlegade 99. For further information, drop in to the **tourist office** at Torvet 9 (mid-June to Aug Mon–Sat 9am–5pm; Sept to mid-June Mon–Fri 9am–5pm, Sat 9am–noon; ☎65 31 02 80).

The Storebælt Exhibition Centre

There was a regular ferry between Nyborg and Korsør on Zealand for more than two centuries, and archeological research on the mid-channel island of Spragø suggests that Danes have been boating back and forth for many thousands of years. The latest twist in the saga of Funen–Zealand travel is the multimillion-kroner combined bridge and tunnel that now carries road and rail traffic across the eighteen-kilometre-wide Store Bælt, a task that was completed in 1998.

At Knudshoved, about 5km from Nyborg (bus #2) on Funen's eastern extremity, the **Storebælt Exhibition Centre** (May–Sept daily 10am–8pm; Oct–April Tues–Sun 10am–5pm; 35kr) has robotic models, videos and interactive computer simulations detailing everything you could possibly need to know about the engineering expertise behind the project, the biggest ever seen in Denmark, which involved amongst other things the construction of what at the time was briefly the world's longest suspension bridge. The hour-long gap between Nyborg buses should give you ample time.

Odense

Funen's sole industrial centre and one of the oldest settlements in the country, **ODENSE** – named after Odin, chief of the Norse gods – gained prominence in the early nineteenth century when the opening of the Odense canal linked the city to the sea and made it the major transit point for the produce of the island's farms. Nowadays it's a pleasant provincial town of museums, students, and decent shopping, with a large manufacturing sector hugging the canal bank on the northern side of the city, well out of sight of the compact old centre. The old town houses some fine museums and – thanks to the resident students – a surprisingly vigorous nightlife. Odense is also known, throughout Denmark at least, as the birthplace of Hans Christian Andersen, and although it's all done quite discreetly, the fact is celebrated with souvenir shops and hotels catering for travellers lured by the prospect of a romantic Andersen experience – something they (almost inevitably) won't find.

Arrival, information and accommodation

Long-distance **buses** terminate at the efficient **train station**, a ten-minute walk from the city centre. In the centre you'll find the **tourist office** (mid-June to Aug Mon–Sat 9am–7pm, Sun 10am–5pm; Sept to mid-June Mon–Fri 9.30am–4.30pm, Sat 10am–1pm;

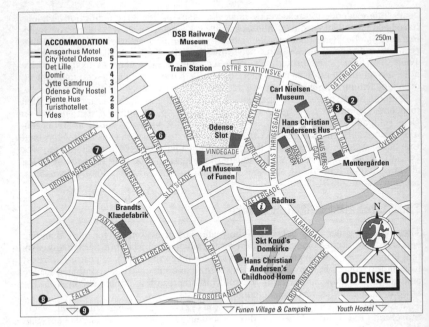

ACCOMMODATION
Ansgarhus Motel 9
City Hotel Odense 5
Det Lille 7
Domir 4
Jytte Gamdrup 3
Odense City Hostel 1
Pjente Hus 2
Turisthotellet 8
Ydes 6

ODENSE

☎66 12 75 20) on the first floor of the nineteenth-century Rådhus. On Odense's **bus** system you pay as you enter: if you have to use more than one bus, ask the driver for a "change ticket" (*omstigning*) to use on the next bus. Better value if you're planning to see Odense's museums is the two-day **Adventure Pass** (Odense Eventyrpas), which for 90kr gets you into all bar the train museum (though there's a discount) and allows unlimited travel on local buses, along with reductions on the Odense Åfart boat and the zoo (see p.119); buy it from any tourist office, most train stations, youth hostels, campsites and hotels on Funen. If you can't face the buses, you can **rent a bike** at City Cykler, Vesterbro 27.

Accommodation

Thanks to Hans Christian Andersen, Odense has a plethora of pricey accommodation, although there are several affordable alternatives. There are also a couple of **hostels**, the *Odense Vandrerhjem* outside town at Kragsbjergvej 121 (☎66 13 04 25; mid-Jan to Nov) – take bus #61 from the train station or cathedral south towards Holluf Pile/Fraugade or Hjallese and get out along Munkebjergvej at the junction with Vissenbjergvej – and the brand-new, brightly coloured *Odense City Hostel* (☎63 11 04 25, fax 63 11 35 20), with good doubles (②), attached to the train station. There are two central and affordable **B&Bs**, both quite close to the Andersen museums: the *Jytte Gamdrup* at Ramsherrud 17 (☎66 13 89 36; ①) and the *Pjente Hus* at Pjentedamsgade 14 (☎66 12 15 55, *pjentehus@teliamail.dk*; ①).

Cheapest among the town's **hotels** are the *Ansgarhus Motel*, Kirkegård Allé 17–19 (☎66 12 88 00; ③), and the friendly *Det Lille Hotel*, Dronningensgade 5 (☎66 12 28 21; ②); also worth trying are *Turisthotellet*, Gerthasminde 64 (☎66 11 26 92; ④), the *Hotel Domir*, Hans Tausens Gade 19 (☎66 12 14 27; ②), and its sister hotel the *Ydes*, close by on the same street (☎66 12 11 31, fax 66 12 17 82; ②); note that breakfast costs extra at all of these. A more upscale choice is the bright yellow *City Hotel Odense* at Hans Mules Gade 5 (☎66 12 12 58, fax 66 12 93 64; ⑨).

The only **campsite** actually in Odense is at Odensevej 102 (☎66 11 47 02; late April to mid-Sept), near Funen Village: take bus #41, #91 or #92 from the Rådhus or train station. The next closest site, which also has a few cabins, is *Blommenslyst*, about 10km from Odense at Middelfartvej 494 (☎66 96 76 41; May to mid-Sept); hourly buses #830 or #832 from the train station get there in twenty minutes.

The Town

Save for two outlying museums a bus ride away, Odense is easily explored on foot. There's a lot to be said for simply wandering around the compact centre with no particular destination in mind, but you shouldn't pass up the chance to visit the Hans Christian Andersen museums – very much what the town is known for – or fail to take in at least one of several absorbing art collections. Two other museums provide more offbeat fare: one celebrates composer Carl Nielsen – after Andersen, Odense's most famous son – and the other eulogizes Danish railways.

The Hans Christian Andersen museums and around

Odense's showpiece museum is the **Hans Christian Andersens Hus** at Hans Jensen Stræde 37–45 (daily: mid-June to Aug 9am–7pm; Sept to mid-June 10am–4pm; 30kr), in the house where the writer was born and which he described in *The Fairy Tale of My Life*. Oddly enough, Andersen was only really accepted in his own country towards the end of his life; his real admirers were abroad, which was perhaps why he travelled widely, and left Odense at the first opportunity. He wrote novels and a few (best-forgotten) plays, but since his death it's his fairy tales that have gained most renown, partly autobiographical tales (not least "The Ugly Duckling") that were influenced by *The Arabian Nights*, German folk stories, and the traditional Danish folk tales passed on by inmates of the Odense workhouse where his grandmother looked after the garden.

Few of the less-than-fairy-tale aspects of Andersen's life are touched upon in the museum, which was founded on the centenary of Andersen's birth, when Odense began to cash in on its famous ex-citizen. The son of a hard-up cobbler, Andersen's first home was a single room that doubled as a workshop in what was then one of Odense's slum quarters. It was a rough upbringing: Hans's ill-tempered mother was fifteen years older than his father, whom she married when seven months pregnant with Hans (she also had an illegitimate daughter by another man); his grandfather was insane; and descriptions of his grandmother, often given charge of the young Hans, range from "mildly eccentric" to "a pathological liar".

There's a nagging falseness about some aspects of the collection, but as Andersen was a first-rate hoarder it's stuffed with intriguing items: bits of school reports, his certificate from Copenhagen University, early notes and manuscripts of his books, chunks of furniture, his umbrella, and paraphernalia from his travels, including the piece of rope he carried to facilitate escape from hotel rooms in the event of fire. A separate gallery contains a library of Andersen's works in seventy languages and headphones for listening to some of his best-known tales read by the likes of Sir Laurence Olivier. Nearby, a sloppy slide-show purports to tell the story of his life, to the accompaniment of a warped pianola soundtrack.

The area around the museum, all half-timbered houses and spotlessly clean, car-free cobbled streets, lacks much character; indeed, if Andersen was around he'd hardly recognize the neighbourhood, which is now one of Odense's most expensive. For more realistic local history, head to the **Møntergården** (daily 10am–4pm; 15kr), a few streets away at Overgade 48–50, where there's an engrossing assemblage of artefacts dating from the city's earliest settlements to the Nazi occupation, plus an immense coin collection – from as long ago and as far afield as England under Danelaw and Danish rule in Estonia – which might engage you for twice as long as the Andersen museum.

There's more, but not much more, about Andersen at Munkemøllestræde 3–5, in the tiny **Hans Christian Andersen's Childhood Home** (daily: mid-June to Aug 10am–4pm; Sept to mid-June 11am–3pm; 10kr), the house where Andersen lived from 1807 to 1819, before moving to Copenhagen, where he spent the rest of his life. More interesting, though, is the nearby **Skt Knud's Domkirke** (April–Oct Mon–Sat 9am–5pm, Sun noon–3pm; Nov–March Mon–Sat 10am–4pm, Sun noon–3pm), whose crypt holds one of the most unusual and ancient finds Denmark has to offer: the **skeleton of Knud II**. Knud was slain in 1086 by Jutish farmers, angry at the taxes he'd imposed on them, in the original Skt Albani Kirke – the barest remains of which were found some years ago in the city park. The king was laid to rest here in 1101, and the miraculous events of following years (see "History", p.57) resulted in his canonization as Knud the Holy. Close to Knud's is another coffin, thought to hold the remains of his brother Benedict (though some claim them to be St Alban, whose body was brought to Denmark by Knud), while displayed alongside is the fading, but impressive, Byzantine-style silk tapestry sent as a shroud by Knud's widow, Edele.

The cathedral itself is noteworthy, too. Mostly late thirteenth-century, it's the only example of pure Gothic church architecture in the country, set off by a finely detailed sixteenth-century wooden altarpiece that's rightly regarded as one of the greatest works of the Lübeck mastercraftsman, Claus Berg.

Odense's art museums

The **Art Museum of Funen**, at Jernbanegade 13 (Fyns Kunstmuseum; daily 10am–4pm, Wed also 7–10pm; 15kr, free on Wed evenings and Sun in winter), a few minutes' walk from the cathedral, gives a good idea of the region's importance to Danish art during the late nineteenth century, when a number of Funen-based painters gave up creating portraits of the rich in favour of impressionistic landscapes and studies of the lives of the peasantry. The collection also contains some stirring works by many Nordic greats, among them Vilhelm Hammershøi, P.S. Krøyer, and Michael and Anne Ancher, but most striking of all is H.A. Benedekilke's enormously emotive *The Cry*. The modern era isn't forgotten, with selections from Asger Jorn, Richard Mortensen and Egill Jacobsen, among many others, drawn from the museum's large collection.

For more modern art, walk along Vestergade to **Brandts Klædefabrik**, a large former textile factory now given over to a number of cultural endeavours: three museums, an art school, a music library and a cinema, along with cafés and restaurants. The **Art Exhibition Hall** here (July & Aug daily 10am–5pm; Sept–June Tues–Sun 10am–5pm; 25kr) is an increasingly prestigious spot for displays of work by high-flying new talent in art and design; close by are the varied displays of the **Museum of Photographic Art** (same hours; 20kr), taken from the cream of modern (and some not so modern) art photography and almost always worth a look. There's also the more down-to-earth **Danish Graphic Museum** (same hours; 25kr), with its bulky machines and devices chronicling the development of printing, bookbinding and illustrating from the Middle Ages to the present. You can buy a combined ticket for all three museums for 40kr.

The Carl Nielsen and railway museums

The **Carl Nielsen Museum**, inside the concert hall at Carls Bergs Gade 11 (June–Aug Tues–Sun noon–4pm; April, May, Sept & Oct Thurs–Sun noon–4pm; Nov–March Thurs & Fri 4–8pm, Sat & Sun noon–4pm; 15kr), celebrates the life and work of Odense's second most famous son. Born in a village just outside Odense in 1865, Nielsen displayed prodigious musical gifts from an early age and joined the Odense military band as a cornet player when just 14 (wearing a specially shortened uniform). From there he went to study at the Copenhagen conservatoire and then on to gain worldwide acclaim as a composer, for his symphonies particularly, the musical cognoscenti in his own country regarding him as having salvaged Danish music from a period of decline. Despite his travels, and long period of residence in Copenhagen, Nielsen continually praised the inspirational qualities of Funen's nature and the island's tuneful dialect, even writing a somewhat sentimental essay romanticizing the landscape in which "even trees dream and talk in their sleep with a Funen lilt". If you've never heard of Nielsen, be assured that his music is nowhere near as half-baked as his prose: in the museum you can listen to some of his work on headphones, including excerpts from his major pieces and the polka he wrote when still a child. The actual exhibits, detailing Nielsen's life and achievements, are further enlivened by the accomplished sculptures of his wife, Anne Marie, many of them early studies for her equestrian statue of Christian IX that now stands outside the Royal Stables in Copenhagen.

The final museum in central Odense is hardly essential viewing unless you've been particularly impressed by the comfort and efficiency of modern Danish trains. The **DSB Railway Museum** (Jernbanemuseet; daily 10am–4pm; 30kr, free to InterRail and Eurail pass holders, half-price with an Adventure Pass), immediately behind the station, houses some of the state railways' most treasured artefacts, which include royal and double-decker carriages and the reconstruction of an entire early twentieth-century station, as well as a feast of otherwise forgotten facts pertaining to the rise and rise of Danish railways.

Funen Village and Funen Prehistoric Museum

A couple of kilometres south of the city centre, the open-air **Funen Village** museum (April to mid-June Tues–Sun 10am–5pm; mid-June to mid-Aug daily 9.30am–7pm; mid-Aug to Oct Tues–Sun 10am–5pm; Nov–March Sun only 11am–3pm; 30kr) comprises a reconstructed nineteenth-century country village which is lent an air of authenticity by its wandering geese and period gardens. From the farmhouse to the poorhouse, all the buildings are originals from other parts of Funen, their exteriors painstakingly reassembled and interiors carefully refurnished. In summer, the old trades are revived in the former workshops and crafthouses, and there are free shows at the open-air theatre. Though often crowded, the village is well worth a call – look out, too, for the village-brewed beer, handed out free on special occasions. Buses #21 and #22 run to the village from the city centre (get out at the Den Fynske Landsby sign), or do what the locals do and rent a boat to float here along the river through Hunderup Skov. Between mid-April and October you can also get here on the Odense Åfart boat (daily 10am–5pm; 45kr) from Munke Mose park in the city centre, stopping off at Odense Zoo on the way.

Also easily reached from the town centre (bus #81) is the **Funen Prehistoric Museum**, some 5km southeast of the city centre (Tues–Sun noon–5pm; 10kr), one of many prehistoric collections in Denmark, but one that at least makes an effort to be different. There is, for example, a simulated TV news broadcast covering events in Bronze Age Denmark, alongside displays describing how ancient symbols are used in modern times. The museum occupies several buildings in the grounds of a sixteenth-century manor house, whose enjoyable landscaped gardens (open dawn–dusk) are decorated by sculptures from the Danish Academy of Fine Arts.

Eating and drinking

Most of Odense's **restaurants** and **snack bars** are squeezed into the central part of town, which means there's a lot of competition and potentially some very good bargains during the day. If the weather is right for outdoor eating, pick up a sandwich from *Raadhusbageriet*, Vestergade 17. Decent, reasonably priced meals can also be had at *Eventyr*, Overgade 18, and at *Restaurant Tinsoldaten*, just around the corner on Frue

Kirkestræde (which is also the place to be at 6am for breakfast after a night's clubbing). Or just get coffee and pie or a quick lunch at the pleasant *Froggys Café*, Vestergade 68. In the evening, relatively inexpensive Danish menus are a feature of *Målet*, Jernbanegade 17. Reliable pizzas and pasta can be found at *Pizza Ristorante Italiano*, Vesterbro 9, and *Mamma's*, Klaregade 4. Mexican dishes make up the menu at *Birdy's Café*, Nørregade 21, while carnivores should head for Odense's branch of the steak restaurant chain, *Jensens Bøfhus* at Kongensgade 10. Other good options include *Den Grimme Ælling* (The Ugly Duckling), across from the Hans Christian Andersens Hus at Hans Jensens Stræde 1 (☎65 91 70 30), for Danish buffets, *Djengis Khan Mongolian Barbecue*, Overgade 24 (☎66 12 88 38) and finally *Carlslund*, Fruens Bøge Skov 7 (☎65 91 11 25), a typical Danish restaurant with the bonus of live jazz on summer Saturdays.

Nightlife and live music

Odense has a plethora of **late-opening cafés** that have usurped the role of nightclubs as evening hangouts. Easily the most fashionable, and decorated with a dazzling display of movie posters, is *Café Biografen* at Brandts Klædefabrik. From there you could move on to *Boogie Dance Café*, downstairs from *Birdy's Café* at Nørregade 21, which is one of the few spots with any life early in the week. For unpretentious drinking, *On-Off*, Vestergade 18, on the western edge of the city centre, and *Carlsens Kvarter*, Hunderupvej 19, south of the Hans Christian Andersen Childhood Home, are the places for knocking back the Carlsberg; *Ryan's of Odense* at Fisketorvet 12, just north of the Rådhus, is a true Irish pub, and there's live music on weekends. If you're in the mood for a gamble, try your luck at the **casino** (7pm–7am; 60kr) in the *SAS Hotel* on Claus Bergs Gade. For details on Odense's **gay and lesbian** scene, contact the Lambda organization (☎66 17 76 92).

Odense's **live music** scene is also worth investigating. Read the free local magazine *Jam* (from most cafés, music shops and the tourist office) for listings. The magazine is based at Rytmeposten, Østre Stationsvej 27a, a converted post office where you'll often find heavy rock bands performing. Another busy spot is the radical politics/arts centre *Badstuen* just opposite, Østre Stationsvej 26. Other likely venues are *Café Oscar*, Vestergade 75 (☎66 14 25 35), with local bands live after 9pm; *Musikhuset*, Vestergade 68; and, for jazz and blues, *Musik Kælderen*, Dronningensgade 2B, and *Kabyssen*, Vindegade 65.

Kerteminde and around

A half-hour bus ride (#890) northeast from Odense, past the huge cranes and construction platforms at Munkebo – until recently a tiny fishing hamlet but now the home of Denmark's biggest shipyard – lies **KERTEMINDE**, itself a place with firm maritime links, originally in fishing and now increasingly in tourism. The town is a centre for sailing and holiday-making, and can get oppressively busy during the peak weeks of the summer. At any other time of year, though, it makes for a well-spent day, split between the town itself and the Viking-era Ladby Boat just outside.

The heart of the town, around the fifteenth-century Skt Laurentius Kirke and along Langegade and Strandgade, is a neat and prettily preserved nucleus of shops and houses. On Strandgade itself, the **town museum** (Farvergården; daily 10am–4pm; 20kr) has five reconstructed craft workshops and a collection of local fishing equipment. On a grander note, Kerteminde was home to the "birdman of Funen", the painter Johannes Larsen – a ten-minute stroll north around the waterfront brings you to his one-time house, now the **Johannes Larsen Museum** (June–Aug daily 10am–5pm; March–May, Sept & Oct Tues–Sun 10am–4pm; Nov–Feb Tues–Sun 11am–4pm; 40kr). During the late nineteenth century, Larsen produced etchings of rural landscapes and birdlife, going against the grain of prevailing art world trends in much the same way as the Skagen artists (see p.158. The house is kept as it was when Larsen lived there, with his furnishings and knick-knacks, many of his canvases and, in the dining room, his astonishing wall paintings. To the chagrin of the pious locals, the house in its day became a haunt of the country's more bacchanalian artists and writers. In the garden is a sculpted female figure by Kai Nielsen, a frequent visitor to the house. A story goes that during one particularly drunken party the piece was dropped and the legs broke off. Someone called the local *falck* (emergency services), but despite much inebriated pleading, the (sober) officer who rushed to the scene refused to take the sculpture to hospital.

Practicalities

The **tourist office**, opposite the Skt Laurentius Kirke, across a small alleyway (mid-June to Aug Mon–Fri 9am–5pm, Sat 9am–2pm; Sept to mid-June Mon–Fri 9am–4pm, Sat 9.30am–12.30pm; ☎65 32 11 21), can give you details on Kerteminde's winter hotel accommodation bargains. If you want to stay over at any other time, the only low-cost option is the **youth hostel** (☎65 32 39 29; mid-Jan to Oct) at Skovvej 46, a twenty-minute walk from the centre (cross the Kerteminde fjord by the road bridge, take the first left and then turn almost immediately right to reach it). There's also a **campsite**, not far from the Larsen museum (☎65 32 19 71; mid-April to mid-Sept) at Hindsholmvej 80, on the main road running along the seafront – a thirty-minute walk from the centre. If you want something more upmarket, try the three-star *Pax*, Klintevej 45 (☎65 32 30 26, fax 65 32 40 26; ⑤).

Around Kerteminde: the Ladby Boat and Hindsholm Peninsula

About 4km from Kerteminde, along the banks of the fjord at Vikingvej 123, is the **Ladby Boat** (Ladbyskibet; May–Oct Tues–Sun 10am–6pm; Nov–April Tues–Sun 10am–3pm; 20kr), a vessel dredged up from the fjord that was found to be the burial ship of a Viking chieftain. The 22-metre craft, along with the remains of the weapons, hunting dogs and horses that accompanied the deceased on his journey to Valhalla, is kept in a tiny purpose-built museum. It's an interesting find, but you'll need only half an hour for a close inspection. Bus #482 runs to the museum several times a day Monday to Friday, and in summer you can also get a motor boat; alternatively, it's pleasant to rent a bike in town and cycle there.

Cycling is also the best way to explore the **Hindsholm Peninsula**, north of Kerteminde, since it's quite small; if this seems too energetic, the tourist office should have the latest bus schedules. There's not actually much to see, save perhaps the ancient **underground burial chamber** (Mårhøj Jættestue) near Martofte, 10km due north of Kerteminde, which is open to the public (though the bodies, of course, are long gone). Outside high season, however, the area becomes an unparalleled spot to pitch a tent and revel in quiet seclusion. Further into the peninsula are two **campsites** *Bøgebjerg Strand* (☎65 34 10 52; April to mid-Sept), on the shore opposite the island of Romsø; and, on the northernmost tip just past Nordskov at Fynshovedvej 748, *Fyns Hoved* (☎65 34 10 14)

Southern Funen and the islands

Southern Funen is noted above all for its many miles of sandy beaches, which during the peak season are packed with tourists. In July and August, the **islands** of the southern archipelago are more enticing: connected by an efficient network of ferries, they range from larger chunks of land such as Tåsinge, Langeland and Ærø – the second two certainly worth a few nights' stay – to minute and sparsely populated places like Lyø, Avernakø, Drejø or Skarø, which are a pleasure to explore, if only for a few hours. From Odense, the simplest plan is to take a train to Svendborg the main centre on the south coast, although you might also find the smaller Fåborg, an hour's bus ride (#960 or #962) from Odense, a good base.

Svendborg

A favourite of the Danish yachting fraternity, with marinas clogging the coastline from here to Fåborg, 24km west, **SVENDBORG** exudes a certain gritty charm, with colourful houses lining cobbled lanes dipping down to the water. It's a pleasant enough place to plot your travels around the archipelago or spend an hour or two meandering around the narrow backstreets, spattered with beautiful bronzes by one of Denmark's best-known sculptors, locally born Kai Nielsen.

A couple of historical collections might occupy a bit of your time. The **County Museum**, Grubbemøllevej 13 (Viebæltegård; May to mid-June daily 10am–4pm; mid-June to Oct daily 10am–5pm; Nov–April Mon–Fri afternoons only; 20kr), has the usual regional collections as well as well-preserved finds from a Franciscan monastery. More entertaining is the **L. Lange & Co. Stove Museum**, Vestergade 45 (mid-May to mid-Aug daily 10am–5pm; 15kr), an eccentric horde of cookers and burners produced by a Svendborg-based firm from 1850 to 1984. Lastly, there's the **Toy Museum**, Skt Nicolajgade 18 (Legetøjsmuseet; daily 10am–4pm; 30kr), with a collection that should appeal to kids and adults alike.

The Lange company's former foundry, next door to the Lange museum at Vestergade 45, is now the town's **youth hostel** (☎62 21 66 99; doubles ①). On Brogade you'll find the reasonably priced, if small, *Hotel Ærø* (☎62 21 07 60; ③), whilst there's also the plain *Hotel Tre Roser*, Fåborgvej 90 (☎62 21 64 26, fax 62 21 15 26; ④). Or ring the **tourist office** on Centrumpladsen (mid-June to mid-Aug Mon–Fri 9am–7pm, Sat 9am–5pm; mid-Aug to mid-June Mon–Fri 9am–5pm, Sat 9am–noon; ☎62 21 09 80), which can provide details of other accommodation, including private rooms (①) and numerous local **campsites**, as well as the latest ferry timetables.

Fåborg

FÅBORG is an alternative base for the south coast, a likeably small and sedate place, rarely as overwhelmed by holiday-makers as Svendborg and with equally good con-

---

THE HELGE STEAMER

Between May and September, the *Helge* steamer (built in 1928) leaves Svendborg three to five times daily for the island of **Tåsinge**, calling at Vindeby, Svendborg's extension just across the Svendborg Sund; the thatched village of Troense, criss-crossed by quiet streets of carefully preserved houses; and the seventeenth-century Valdemar's Slot. The return sailing time is two hours but tickets (50kr round-trip from the harbour; information on ☎62 50 25 00) can be used to get on and off all day.

The *Helge*'s last stop is the best: **Valdemar's Slot**, an imposing pile with Baroque interiors begun by Christian IV and continued by his son, Valdemar, who died before taking up residence. Filled with three centuries of furniture, paintings and tapestries, the castle serves as a **museum** (April–Oct daily 10am–5pm; 50kr). Outside the castle, while waiting for the *Helge* to carry you back to Svendborg, have tea at the reasonably priced *Tea Pavilion*, from where there are great views out to the long, narrow island of Langeland.

Should you want to stay over on Tåsinge, there are four **campsites** on the island, plus a couple of **hotels** – the simple *Det Lille Hotel* (☎62 22 53 41; ③) and the better *Hotel Troense* (☎62 22 54 12; ⑤) – both in Troense.

nections to the archipelago (ferries sail to Søby on Ærø, to Lyø and Avernakø, and to Gelting in Germany). If you've an interest in Danish art, the town's other big attraction is the **Fåborg Museum** at Grønnegade 75 (June–Aug daily 10am–5pm; April, May, Sept & Oct daily 10am–4pm; Nov–March Tues–Sun 11am–3pm; 30kr). The museum opened in 1910 and quickly became the major showcase for the **Funen artists**, particularly the work of Fritz Syborg and Peter Hansen, both of whom studied under the influential Kristian Zhartmann in Copenhagen and typically filled their canvases with richly coloured depictions of Funen landscapes. Apart from the chance to admire the skills of the painters, it's interesting to view the works and realize how little the Funen countryside has changed since they were painted the best part of a century ago.

Almost next door to the museum at Grønnegade 72–73 is one of the country's quaintest **youth hostels** (☎62 61 12 03; April–Oct), with eighteen inexpensive double rooms (①). There's a **campsite** with cabins at Odensevej 140 (☎62 61 77 94), half a mile from town, and a number of other camping areas on the beach as well. Outside Fåborg lies the simple *Mosegaard Inn* at Nabgyden 31 in Astrup (☎62 61 56 91, fax 62 61 56 96; ④), while the equally bare-bones *Hotel Fåborg*, Torvet 15 (☎62 61 02 45, fax 62 61 08 45; ③) is the cheapest choice in town.

For **food** you could splash out and try the fish restaurant *Ved Brønden*, at Torvet 5, or the French-style *Café Chez Patrice* at Torvet 11. Otherwise there's a plethora of pizza places, or stock up on provisions at the Super Brugsen or Føtex markets, which are next to each other on Mellemgade. For **entertainment**, *Kinografen*, Banegårdspladsen 21, is about the liveliest place in town, with live acts and disco nights. You can check local travel details at the **tourist office** at Havnegade 2 (Mon–Fri 9am–5pm, Sat 10am–6pm; ☎62 61 07 07).

Around Fåborg: Egeskov Castle and the smaller islands

In Kværndrup, just ten minutes from Fåborg by bus, is the Renaissance castle **Egeskov Slot** ("Oak-forest Castle"). You're allowed in (daily 10am–5pm; 100kr), though it's really more impressive from the outside, and the price of entry is rather steep. The same ticket also gets you into the nearby **Egeskov Veteranmuseum** (daily 10am–4pm), which displays around three hundred antique cars.

If you're looking for some quiet, it's easy enough to visit one of the three small islands of **Bjørnø**, **Lyø** and **Avernakø**. All are connected with Fåborg by small ferries (at least 5 daily; journey time 10–20min; information on ☎30 66 80 50 or 62 61 23 07). There's not much to do on the islands apart from walking in the beautiful countryside. If you want to stay overnight, contact the tourist office in Fåborg (see above), who can arrange stays with local families for around 125kr per person.

Langeland

You don't need to catch a ferry to reach the largest of the southern islands, **Langeland**, which lies off the southeast coast of Funen, to which it's connected by road bridge. A long, thin, fertile island, Langeland is peaceful and has fine sea views. Frequent buses make the half-hour journey from Svendborg to **RUDKØBING**, the island's main town, from where there are ferry links to Marstal on Ærø; there's also a ferry to Tårs on Lolland (see p.109), leaving from Spodsbjerg, about 6km to the east. Rudkøbing in itself doesn't have a lot to offer except for a pleasant fishing harbour and the historical collection in the **Langelands Museum** (Mon–Thurs 10am–4pm, Fri 10am–1pm; 20kr). The town's **tourist office**, at Torvet 5 (mid-June to Aug Mon–Sat 9am–5pm; Sept to mid-June Mon–Fri 9.30am–4.30pm, Sat 9.30am–12.30pm; ☎62 51 35 05), can give advice on **accommodation**; alternatively, head for the low yellow **youth hostel** at Engdraget 11 (☎62 51 18 30; doubles ②) or one of the two **campsites**, at Spodsbjergvej no. 277

(☎62 50 10 92) and no. 182 (☎62 50 10 06). **Hotel** choices include the budget *Spodsbjergvej Badehotel* at Spodsbjergvej 317 (☎ & fax 62 50 10 64; ③) and the better-located, if more expensive, *Rudkøbing Skudehavn* on the harbour at Havnegade 21 (☎62 51 46 00, fax 62 51 49 40; ⑤).

North of Rudkøbing, the island consists mostly of farmland and the occasional village, with just one sight to head for: the fairy-tale thirteenth-century **Tranekær Slot**, surrounded by a beautiful park dotted with sculptures made from natural materials. There's a **museum** (mid-May to Aug Mon–Fri noon–5pm, Sun 1–5pm; 15kr) in the old water mill opposite, covering the history of the village and its castle. To find the island's best **beaches** – **Ristinge** is the most popular – head for the southern coast, where there are also a couple of **bird sanctuaries**, Gulstav Mose and Tryggelev Nor. Local buses serve all the main sites on the island.

Ærø

For a more varied few days, take the ferry from Svendborg or Rudkøbing to Ærø, a pretty island just north of the coast of Germany. Although getting here can require the better part of a day, it's worth the effort for the island's ancient burial sites, abundant stretches of sandy beach, traditional farms and, in Ærøskøbing, a peach of a medieval merchants' town.

Ærøskøbing

When passing shipping brought prosperity to the island in the nineteenth century, the island historically split into three divisions: fisherfolk resided on the island's windy western tip at Søby; the wealthy shipping magnates and captains resided in Marstal, to the east; while the local middle-classes collected in the town of ÆRØSKØBING. The town's narrow streets, lined with tidy houses, are made for wandering – look out for the oldest building, dating from 1645, at Søndergade 36. If it's raining, you could drop into the **Bottle Ship Collection** and the **Memorial Rooms** (daily: March, April & Oct–Dec 1–3pm; May–Sept 10am–5pm; 15kr) at Smedegade 22, for an eye-straining collection of ships in bottles in the former, and a riot of woodcarvings, furnishings and timepieces from bygone days in the latter.

Ærøskøbing's **tourist office** (June–Aug Mon–Fri 9am–5pm, Sat 9am–2pm, Sun 10am–noon; Sept–May Mon–Fri 9am–4pm, Sat 9am–noon; ☎62 52 13 00), on Torvet, can give information on the island's burial places and other secluded spots. As for **accommodation**, there's a terrific youth hostel with ocean views and friendly management at Smedevejen 13 (☎62 52 10 44; doubles ③; April–Sept), about 2km west of the ferry dock on the road to Marstal. There's also a cabin-equipped campsite at Sygehusvej 40b (☎62 52 18 54; mid-May to mid-Sept), appealingly sited next to the beach. There's a local bus service, but the best way to get around the island is by **bike**, though you'll need to pedal hard to get up some of the hills; the tourist office supplies free bike maps to help plan your route, and bikes can be rented for 40kr a day at Pilebækkens Cykelservice (☎62 52 11 10), about 200m west of the main market place, in a gas station out on Marstal road.

Eating options include *Det Lille Hotel*'s good Danish restaurant at Smedegade 33 (☎62 52 23 00) and the popular *Café Lille Claus*, a burger and fried-fish joint close by the ferry landing. There are fancier places along the main street, often stuffed with vacationing Germans. For provisions there are two small supermarkets, Spar and Merko, in the town centre, and a good little bakery, *Ærøskøbing Bageri*, on the main drag as well. When getting on or off the Svendborg ferry, be sure to look in on the little smoked-fish place, *Ærøskøbing Røgeri*, facing the water at Havnen 15 – the fish is outstanding. **Nightlife** is pretty much limited to the *Strandskoven* bar by the water and the *Arrebo* pub at Vestergade 4, which sometimes hosts live music acts. Summertime brings the occasional open-air concert to the streets of town too.

Marstal and beyond

If you're looking to escape the tourists, then **MARSTAL**, at the east end of the island and reached by bus from Ærøskøbing (or ferry from Rudkøbing), is a good alternative base. Once there, don't miss the superb **Marstal Søfartsmuseum** (July daily 9am–9pm; June & Aug daily 9am–5pm; May & Sept daily 10am–4pm; Oct–April Tues–Fri 10am–4pm, Sat 11am–3pm; 25kr), a collection of maritime paintings and ship models from Marstal's nineteenth-century golden age, when it was one of the busiest harbours in Denmark.

Most people staying here sleep on yachts or in holiday home rentals, but there are a few budget options including the **youth hostel** at Færgestræde (☎62 53 10 64; doubles ①; May–Aug), conveniently close to the town centre and the harbour, and a **campsite**, *Marstal Camping* (☎62 53 36 00; April–Oct), almost on the beach and with cabins too. The nicest reasonably priced choice is the small *Hotel Marstal* (☎62 53 13 52; ②) at Dronningestræde 1A near the harbour, while the *Mejerigården*, Vestergade 30b (☎62 53 32 38; ②), in the centre of town, is another inexpensive choice. For more information, contact the **tourist office** (☎62 53 19 60; summer Mon–Fri 9am–5pm, Sat & Sun 10am–1pm; rest of year Mon–Fri 10am–3pm) on Havnegade, near the youth hostel. **Bikes** can be rented at Nørremark Cykelforretning, Møllevejen 77 (☎62 53 14 77).

The **rest of the island** is speckled with fine *kro*s, B&Bs and working farms, as well, such as Marianne Kristensen's home east of Ærøskøbing in the village of Bregninge (☎62 58 20 10; ②) and the handsome *Vindeballe Kro* (☎62 52 16 13, fax 62 52 23 49; ②) at the centre of the island in Vindeballe, simple but with a good restaurant and bar downstairs.

travel details

Trains

Odense to: Århus (35 daily; 1hr 35min); Copenhagen (48 daily; 1hr 30min); Esbjerg (26 daily; 1hr 45min); Nyborg (39 daily; 15min); Svendborg (24 daily; 40min).

Buses

Kerteminde to: Nyborg (17 daily; 33min).

Odense to: Fåborg (30 daily; 55min–1hr 18min); Kerteminde (42 daily; 30min); Nyborg (14 daily; 1hr 5min); Svendborg (18 daily; 1hr 24min).

Rudkøbing to: Lohals (23 daily; 44min); Spodsbjerg (5 daily; 15min); Svendborg (27 daily; 30min).

Svendborg to: Copenhagen (2–3 daily; 2hr); Fåborg (29 daily; 45min); Rudkøbing (27 daily; 30min).

Ferries

Bøjden to: Fynshav (7 daily; 50min).

Søby to: Mommark (2–4 daily in summer; 1hr).

South coast ferries

Ferry connections are plentiful around the south coast archipelago and it's best to check the fine details locally. Some sailings continue all year, others only operate during the summer. Fares are 30–45kr per person. Frequencies given below are for weekdays; sailings are often reduced on weekends and public holidays.

Fåborg to: Lyø (6 daily via Avernakø; 1hr); Søby (6 daily; 1hr).

Marstal to: Rudkøbing (5 daily; 1hr).

Spodsbjerg to: Tårs (8–10 daily; 45min).

Svendborg to: Ærøskøbing (5 daily; 1hr 15min); Drejø (4 daily via Skarø; 1hr 30min).

International trains

Odense to: Hamburg (6 daily; 4hr 15min).

International ferries

Bagenkop to: Kiel (3 daily; 2hr 30min).

Fåborg to: Gelting (2–3 daily; 2hr)

CHAPTER THREE

JUTLAND

Long ago, the people of **Jutland** (Jylland), the Jutes – pronounced "yutes" – were a quite separate tribe from the more warlike Danes who occupied the eastern islands. In pagan times, the peninsula had its own rulers and wielded considerable power, and it was here that the legendary ninth-century monarch Harald Bluetooth began the process that turned the two tribes into a unified Christian nation. By the dawn of the Viking era, however, the Danes had spread west, absorbing the Jutes, and real power in Denmark gradually shifted towards Zealand.

This is where it has largely stayed, making unhurried lifestyles and rural calm (except for a couple of very likeable cities) the overriding impression of Jutland. This is a friendly land, populated by locals who seem to relish their position outside the national spotlight. Yet there's much to enjoy in the unspoilt towns and villages, and Jutland's comparatively large size and distance from Copenhagen make it perhaps the most distinctive and interesting area in the country.

There are also more regional variations in Jutland than you'll find elsewhere in Denmark. **South Jutland** is a territory long battled over by Denmark and Germany, though beyond the immaculately restored town of **Ribe** it holds little of abiding interest. **Esbjerg**, further north, is fairly dull too, but as a major ferry port you might arrive or leave from here, and it gives easy access to the hills, meadows and woodlands of eastern Jutland, and to some of the peninsula's better-known sights – from the old military stronghold of **Fredericia** and the ancient runic stones at **Jelling** to the modern bricks of **Legoland**.

Århus, halfway up the eastern coast, is Jutland's main urban centre and Denmark's second city, and here, besides a wealth of history and cultural pursuits, you'll encounter the region's best nightlife. It's handy, too, for the optimistically titled **Lake District**, a small but appealing area between **Skanderborg** and **Silkeborg**. Further inland, the retreat of the ice-sheets during the last Ice Age has left a terrain of sharp contrasts: stark heather-clad moors break suddenly into dense forests with swooping gorges and wide rivers – contrasts epitomized by the wild moorland at **Kongenshus** and the grassy vistas of **Hald Ege**. Ancient **Viborg** is a better base for seeing all this than dour **Randers**, and from here you can head north, either to the blustery beaches of **Limfjordslandet** or to old and vibrant **Aalborg**, which sits on the Limfjorden's southern bank.

Across the Limfjorden is Jutland at its most dramatic: a sandy semi-wilderness stretching north to **Skagen**, at the very tip of the peninsula. **Frederikshavn**, on the way, is the port for boats to Norway and Sweden, and is usually full of those countries' nationals stocking up with (what is for them) cheap liquor.

ACCOMMODATION PRICE CODES

The hotels and guest houses listed in this chapter have been graded according to the following price bands, based on the **cheapest rate for a double room in summer**.

   ① Under 300kr   ② 300–400kr   ③ 400–500kr   ④ 500–650kr

     ⑤ 650–900kr   ⑥ 900–1300kr   ⑦ Over 1300kr

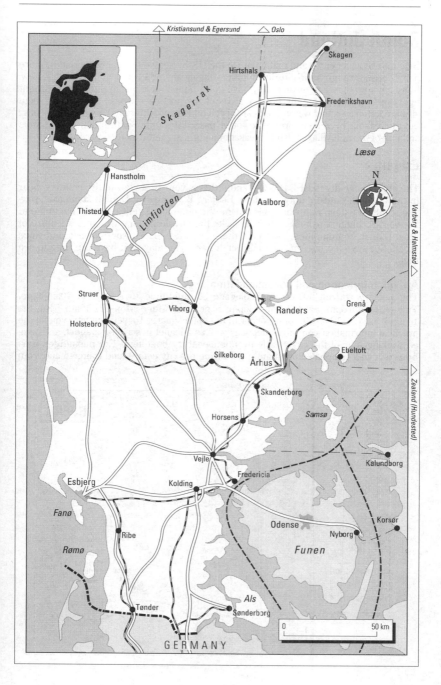

South Jutland

Best known as an entry and exit point (to the UK by sea, to Germany overland), more people pass through **south Jutland** than probably any other part of the country. Few, however, stop here longer than they have to, with most heading straight for the bright lights of Copenhagen or the holiday areas of the northwest coast. This might seem strange for an area that was at the heart of prolonged and bitter international bickering, but the reasons become clearer once you've passed through. South Jutland's landscape and run-of-the-mill villages, while pleasant enough, are not exactly diverting.

Esbjerg

The area's only city is **ESBJERG** – and if this is your first view of the country, bear in mind it's an entirely untypical one. Esbjerg is a baby by Danish standards: purpose-built as a deep-water harbour during the nineteenth century and now home to the world's biggest fish-oil factory, it lacks the visible history which is a feature of most Danish communities. That said, there are a few places worth a visit, and since DFDS Seaways ferries from the UK berth here, you may well have the time to see them.

Arrival, information and accommodation

The Esbjerg **tourist office**, at Skolegade 33 (mid-June to Aug Mon 10am–5pm, Tues–Fri 9am–6pm, Sat 9.30am–6.30pm; Sept to mid-June Mon–Fri 10am–5pm, Sat 10am–1pm; ☎75 12 55 99), on a corner of the main square, Torvet, can give you all the practical information you might need, as well as a leaflet describing a short, self-guided walking tour of the city's early twentieth-century buildings. The **passenger harbour** is a well-signposted ten-minute walk from the city centre, and trains to and from

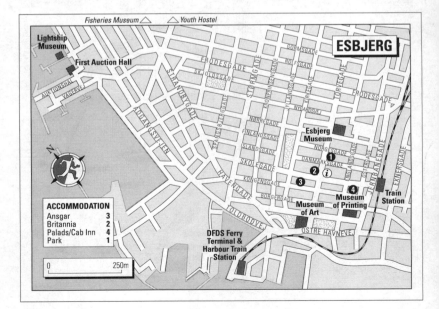

Copenhagen connect directly with the ferries at the harbour station. Otherwise, there are frequent departures to all Danish cities from the main **train station** on Skolegade.

If you're staying, the tourist office can help in finding bed and breakfast-type **accommodation**; otherwise you'll find the cheapest good hotel is the twin-towered *Palads/Cab Inn*, Skolegade 14 (☎75 18 16 00, fax 75 18 16 24; ④), renovated into a mixture of simple, inexpensive cabin-style rooms and more traditional hotel accommodation. Another low-price option is the basic *Park Hotel* at Torvegade 31 (☎75 12 08 68; ④), while the central *Ansgar*, Skolegade 36 (☎75 12 82 44, fax 75 13 95 40; ⑤), is a little more upmarket, as is the excellent *Britannia* on Torvet (☎75 13 01 11, fax 75 45 20 85; ⑤). The **youth hostel** is at Gammel Vardevej 80 (☎75 12 42 58; doubles ②; closed Dec & Jan), 25 minutes' walk from the city centre, or take a bus (#1, #4, #12, #40 or #41) from Skolegade. There's a well-equipped **campsite** with cabins, *Ådalens Camping*, at Guderåvej 20 (☎75 15 88 22), 6km north of the city towards Hjerting and reached by bus #1 from Skolegade.

The Town

The best way to get a sense of the city's newness is by dropping into the **Esbjerg Museum** (June–Aug daily 10am–4pm; Sept–May Tues–Sun 10am–4pm; 20kr) at Torvegade 45, where the meatiest of the few displays recalls the so-called "American period" of the 1890s, when Esbjerg's rapid growth matched that of the US goldrush towns – albeit that the masses came here in search of herring, rather than gold. Also within easy reach of the centre is the **Museum of Art** (Esbjerg Kunstmuseum; daily 10am–4pm; 30kr) at Havnegade 20; its modern Danish artworks are fairly limp affairs, but it sometimes hosts more interesting temporary exhibitions. The nearby **Museum of Printing** (Bogtrykmuseet; June to mid-Sept daily noon–4pm; mid-Sept to May Tues–Fri 1–4pm; 15kr), at Borgergade 6, just off the pedestrianized strip of Kongensgade, has an entertaining assortment of hand-, foot- and steam-operated presses, as well as more recent – and still functioning – printing machines.

With more time to spare, take a bus (#1, #6 or #8 from Skolegade) to the large **Fisheries and Maritime Museum and Sealarium** on Tarphagevej (daily: July–Aug 10am–6pm; Sept–May 10am–5pm; 35kr), where you can cast an eye over the old boats and other vestiges of the early Esbjerg fishing fleet, see a representative of every type of fish found in Danish waters, and clamber around inside a dark and spooky German wartime bunker. The Sealarium is part of a seal research centre; feeding times are 11am and 2.30pm. Just a few minutes' walk from the museum – follow the main road up the hill – is another of Esbjerg's more notable features, the **Sædden Kirke** (Mon–Sat 9am–5pm; ☎75 15 01 51), its completely red-brick interior illuminated by hundreds of hanging lights – a modern reworking of traditional church architecture, made still more unusual by its location inside a shopping centre.

With an hour to kill before your boat leaves, nip around the harbour to the **Lightship Museum** (May–Sept daily 10am–4pm; 10kr), which gives a vivid impression of the North Sea lightshipman's lot.

Eating, drinking and nightlife

Esbjerg's **eating** options are fairly limited if you're on a tight budget, although you can get a decent two-course lunch for around 50kr at the *Park Hotel*, Torvegade 31. For traditional Danish food – and service – try *Sands*, Skolegade 60 (closed Sun). More expensively, for around 120kr you can sample Esbjerg-style *nouvelle cuisine* (basically well-prepared fresh fish with everything) at *Pakhuset*, Dokvej 3, in the dock area. A good place for lunch or an early-evening beer or coffee is the popular *Café Christian IX*, overlooking Torvet and named after the monarch commemorated by the square's equestrian statue – they sometimes have live music at weekends. Also decent value at lunchtime are the dependable chain restaurants *Jensens Bøfhus*, on Kongensgade, for steak and *Den Grimme Ælling* (The Ugly Duckling), Kirkegade 21, with its 75kr lunch special.

What little **nightlife** Esbjerg has is also based around Torvet. If you've just arrived from Britain and want to make the transition to Danish culture (and prices) slowly, sip a beer or two at one of the town's pubs, like the English-style *You'll Never Walk Alone*, Kongensgade 10, or the equally sedate *Kasket-Karl*, Skolegade 17 – the latter shares premises with the livelier *John Wayne Saloon* dance club, which attracts a younger crowd.

Around Esbjerg: Fanø

From Esbjerg it's a straightforward fifteen-minute ferry trip to **Fanø**, a long, flat island with superb beaches that draw German holiday-makers here in droves during the summer. DSB ferries (☎75 12 00 00) run frequently between Esbjerg and the island's main village, **Nordby**, where the **tourist office** at the harbour (June–Aug Mon–Fri 8.30am–6pm, Sat 8am–7pm, Sun 10am–5pm; Sept–May Mon–Fri 8.30am–5.30pm, Sat 9am–1pm; ☎75 16 26 00) can provide information on accommodation and the few sights (a couple of fairly ordinary local museums and a windmill). There are eight **campsites**, of which the best is *Feldberg Familie Camping* (☎75 16 36 80), almost on the beach.

Ribe

Just over half an hour by train south from Esbjerg lies the exquisitely preserved town of **RIBE**. In 856 Ansgar built one of the first Danish churches here as a base for his missionaries arriving from Germany; a hundred years later the town was a major staging post for pilgrims making their way south to Rome. Ribe's proximity to the sea allowed to evolve into a significant trading port, but continued expansion was thwarted by the dual blows of the Reformation and the sanding-up of the harbour. Since then, not much appears to have changed. The surrounding marshlands, which have prevented the development of any large-scale industry, and a long-standing conservation programme have enabled Ribe to keep the appearance and size of medieval times, and its old town is a delight to wander in.

The Town

From Ribe's train station, Dagmarsgade cuts a straight path to Torvet and the **Domkirke** (June–Aug Mon–Sat 10am–6pm, Sun noon–5pm; May & Sept Mon–Sat 10am–5pm, Sun noon–5pm; Oct–April Mon–Sat 11am–4pm, Sun noon–4pm; 10kr), which towers above the town and dominates the wetlands for miles around. A sequel to Ansgar's original church, the cathedral was begun around 1150 using tufa – a suitably light material for the marshy base – brought, along with some of the Rhineland's architectural styles, by river from southern Germany.

Originally raised on a slight hill, the cathedral is now a couple of metres below the surrounding streets, their level having risen due to the many centuries' worth of debris accumulated beneath them. The **interior** is not as spectacular as the cathedral's size and long history might suggest, having been stripped of much of its decoration by Hans Tausen, Bishop of Ribe, during the mid-sixteenth century. The thirteenth-century "Cat's Head Door" on the south side, a good example of the imported Romanesque design, is one of the few early decorative remains. More recent additions that catch the eye are the butcher's-slab altar and the frescoes and mosaics by Carl-Henning Pedersen, added in the mid-1980s. After looking around, climb the 248 steps to peer out from the top of the red-brick **Citizens' Tower**, so named since it doesn't belong to the church but to the people whose taxes pay for its upkeep. In an act worthy of *The Omen*, the tower's predecessor toppled into the nave on Christmas morning, 1283.

Heading away from the cathedral along Overdammen, you cross three streams, channelled around 1250 to provide water for a mill. The houses on the right are the best of Ribe's many half-timbered structures; one of them, **Quedens Gaard**, at the corner

THE NIGHTWATCHMAN OF RIBE

At 10pm every evening between May and mid-September – and also at 8pm from June to August – the **Nightwatchman of Ribe** emerges from the bar of the *Weis' Stue* inn, Torvet 2, and makes his rounds. Before the advent of gas lighting, a nightwatchman would patrol every town in Denmark, looking through windows for unattended candles that might cause fires. The last real nightwatchman of Ribe made his final tour around 1900, but thanks to the early development of tourism in the town, within thirty years the custom had been reintroduced.

Dressed in a replica of the original uniform and carrying an original morning-star pike and lantern (the sharp tip doubling as a weapon), the watchman walks the narrow alleys of Ribe singing songs written by Hans Adolf Brorson, Bishop of Ribe in the mid-eighteenth century (whose statue stands outside the cathedral), and talking about the town's history while stopping at points of interest. One song tells people to go to bed and not light fires – sensible advice, even after 1554 when thatched roofs were officially banned. It's obviously laid on for the tourists, but the tour is free and can be fun.

of Sortebrødregade, is now a museum (June–Aug daily 10am–5pm; March–May, Sept & Oct Tues–Sun 11am–3pm; Nov–Feb Tues–Sun 11am–1pm; 10kr), with sixteenth-century interiors and displays on medieval Ribe. Turn left off Overdammen and walk along the riverside Skibbroen and you'll spot the **Flood Column** (Stormflodssøjlen), a stout wooden pole showing the levels of the numerous floods that plagued the town before protective dykes were built a century ago.

Continuing along Overdammen, Skt Nicolaj Gade cuts right to **Ribe Art Gallery** (mid-June to Aug daily 11am–5pm; Sept to mid-June Tues–Sat 1–4pm, Sun 11am–4pm; 30kr), housing a reasonable display of works by Danish artists in a chronological progression that takes you from noble portraiture through pre-Raphaelite aestheticism to modern verismo. On the first floor the highlight is *The Christening*, by Skagen painter Michael Ancher (see p.158). A handful of accomplished bronze sculptures are supplemented by larger pieces on the back lawn, from where paths and footbridges lead back across the river to the town centre.

Ribe has recently gained a couple of museums celebrating the town's Viking era. The **Ribes Vikinger** (July & Aug daily 10am–6pm, Wed until 9pm; April–June, Sept & Oct daily 10am–4pm; Nov–March Tues–Sun 10am–4pm; 45kr), opposite the train station, displays locally excavated remains, along with a full-size reconstructed Viking ship. If you've not had your fill, head for the **Ribe Vikinge Centre** (July & Aug daily 11am–4.30pm; May, June & Sept Mon–Fri 11am–4pm; 50kr), 3km south of the centre on Lystrupvej, which attempts to re-create the Viking lifestyle, with costumed attendants demonstrating traditional Viking crafts.

That's more or less all there is to Ribe, save for the paltry remains of **Ribehus Slotsbanke**, a twenty-minute walk away on the northern side of the town. The twelfth-century castle that stood here was a popular haunt with Danish royalty for a couple of centuries but was already fairly dilapidated when it was demolished by Swedish bombardment in the mid-seventeenth century. The **statue** of Queen Dagmar, a recent addition to the site and standing in bewitching isolation, is the only visible reward for the trek out here.

Practicalities

Besides the usual services, the **tourist office** (July & Aug Mon–Fri 9.30am–5.30pm, Sat 10am–5pm, Sun 10am–2pm; April–June, Sept & Oct Mon–Fri 9am–5pm, Sat 10am–2pm; Nov–March Mon–Fri 9.30am–4.30pm, Sat 10am–1pm; ☎75 42 15 00), across the road to the rear of the cathedral, offers the free *Denmark's Oldest Town* leaflet, a useful aid to self-guided exploration.

If you intend to stick around for the nightwatchman's tour, you'll need to **stay overnight**. The most intriguing accommodation option is *Den Gamle Arrest*, Torvet 11 (☎75 42 37 00, fax 75 42 37 22; ④). Built originally as a girls' boarding school, it later served as the town's jail – its double rooms are in the former cells, which these days lock from the inside. Alternatively, if you can afford it, try the beautifully restored *Dagmar*, opposite the Domkirke (☎75 42 00 33, fax 75 42 36 52; ⑥), which dates from 1581 and claims to be the oldest hotel in Denmark; its gorgeous doubles come with period furniture and loads of character. There are several cheaper pensions as well, including the bright yellow pub *Frue Mathies* at Saltgade 15 (☎75 42 34 20, fax 75 41 02 44; ④), right in the centre, with en-suite rooms, and the simpler *Restaurant Backhaus*, Grydergade 12 (☎75 42 11 01, fax 75 42 52 87; ④), which has a few rooms above a restaurant. The **youth hostel** at Skt Pedersgade 16 (☎75 42 06 20; doubles ①; May to mid-Sept) is a simple walk over the river from the town centre. The nearest **campsite** (☎75 41 07 77; April–Nov), 2km distant along Farupvej (take bus #771), is equipped with cabins. The tourist office also publishes a list of private rooms for about 175kr per person.

One reputable spot to **eat** close to the cathedral is *Vægterkælderen*, in the basement beneath the *Dagmar* hotel, serving two- (59kr) and three-course (74kr) lunches, and two-course dinners (125kr). *Café Nicolaj*, beside the art gallery, is open late for coffee and drinks and serves 50kr meals from noon to 2pm and from 6pm to 8pm. At night, *Vægterkælderen* (see above) has a lively bar, though the beer is cheaper at *Pepper's* and *Stenbohus*, which face each other just up the street. If you're looking for atmosphere, hit the tiny but distinctive *Strygejernet* pub at Dagmarsgade 1 (☎75 41 13 51), which serves light meals and snacks during the day and popular draught ales at night.

Rømø and Tønder

From Skærbæk, a few kilometres south of Ribe by train, bus #29 heads across 12km of tidal flats to the island of **Rømø**. The actions of sea and wind have given the island a wild and unkempt appearance, as well as creating a wide beach along the eastern side and allowing wildlife to flourish all over. There's a good chance of seeing seals basking during the spring, while at the end of the summer many migratory wading birds can be found, dodging the island's plentiful sheep.

Rømø's **tourist office** (July & Aug daily 11am–4pm; May, June & Sept Mon–Fri 11am–4pm; ☎74 75 51 30), just south of the causeway in the main village of **HAVNE-BY**, can provide details on the island's bus service. There are several spots on Rømø **to stay**: ask at the tourist office for details of private rooms or summer cottages for around 150kr per person. The best hotel on the island is the *Kommandørgården* (☎74 75 51 22, fax 74 75 59 22; ④) in Østerby, a kilometre or so north of Havneby. There's a **youth hostel** in Havneby itself at Lyngvejen 7 (☎74 75 51 88; doubles ③; mid-March to mid-Oct), and just to the north of the town at Havnebyvej 201, on the #29 bus route, is a year-round **campsite** (☎74 75 51 22) with cabins.

Besides enjoying the sands, and the fact that Rømø is a noted **nude bathing** spot, it's possible to **cross the border to Germany** without returning to the Danish mainland by using the ferry that sails from Havneby to List, on the German island of Sylt (information on ☎74 75 53 03).

Tønder

Back on the mainland and heading south brings you to **TØNDER**, the chief town on the Danish side of the border with Germany. Founded in the thirteenth century, the town's cobbled streets still contain many ancient gabled buildings and it makes an attractive and low-key base for a day or two, especially if you're here around the end of August, when there's a terrific annual **jazz and folk festival**. In 1999, performers included Arlo Guthrie, Tom Paxton, Natalie MacMaster and a host of other international performers, plus many free outdoor events. Contact the Tønder Festival office (☎74 72 46 10) for more details. Otherwise, the main sights in town are the **Tønder Museum** (May–Oct Tues–Sun 10am–5pm; Nov–April Tues–Sun 1–5pm; 25kr), in the gatehouse of the sixteenth-century castle, and the adjoining **South Jutland Art Museum** (same hours and ticket), with its changing exhibitions of twentieth-century Danish works. Danish Prince Joachim and Princess Alexandra live 4km to the west of Tønder in **Schackenborg Castle**, in the village of Møgeltønder (bus #66) – there's no entry to the public, but the castle park is good for an hour's strolling and there's the possibility, if you're lucky, of a royal sighting.

First call for local information should be the **tourist office** on Torvet (mid-June to Aug Mon–Fri 9am–5.30pm, Sat 9.30am–3pm; Sept to mid-June Mon–Fri 9am–4pm, Sat 9am–noon; ☎74 72 12 20). There's a **youth hostel** at Sønderport 4 (☎74 72 35 00; closed Christmas & Jan), 1km from the train station, a **campsite** at Holmevej 2a (☎74 72 18 49; April–Sept), the functional *Hotel Tønderhus* at Jomfrustien 1, opposite the Tønder Museum (☎74 72 22 22; ⑤), and the three-star, but somehow cheaper, *Bowler Inn*, Ribelandevej 56 (☎74 72 21 29, fax 74 72 65 11; ④).

Kolding

Even though it's handily placed on the main road and rail axes north of Tønder, **KOLDING** doesn't attract a lot of attention. If you do find yourself here with time to spare, head a short way north from the centre to the Slotsø lake and the imaginatively renovated **Koldinghus** (May–Sept daily 10am–5pm; 45kr), a harmonious mix of ruined and modern structures housing sparsely furnished period rooms. Another worthwhile call in this direction, 3km beyond the lake (bus #4 from the train station), is the **Trapholt Art Museum** (daily 10am–5pm; 40kr), its angular glass walls and shrill white interiors flooding the (mostly) modern art with natural light.

The **tourist office** is at Akseltorv 8 (Mon–Fri 9am–5pm, Sat 9am–noon; closed Sat in winter; ☎75 53 21 00). Predictably, the cheapest **accommodation** option is the youth hostel, Ørnsborgvej 10 (☎75 50 91 40; doubles ①; closed Dec & Jan). Other relatively economical choices include the fairly central *Hotel Tre Roser*, Dyrehavegårdsvej, at Byparken (☎75 53 21 22; ④), and the simple *Bramdrupdam Kro*, about 4km north of the town at Vejlevej 332 in Bramdrupdam (☎75 56 82 88; ③). The *Saxildhus* at Banegårdspladsen, opposite the train station (☎75 52 12 00, fax 75 53 53 10; ⑤), is a more expensive option. The closest **campsite** is at Vonsildvej 19 (☎75 53 47 25), 3km from the town centre by bus #3. Further away are several beachfront campsites – contact the tourist office for details. For a quiet, inexpensive place to **eat**, try the *Café Paraplyen*, Adelgade 10 (☎75 53 85 98), open until 10pm. For Italian, try *Bella Italia*, Jernbanegade 40 (☎75 50 58 07) or *Italiano*, Søndergade 11 (☎75 52 23 43). If you fancy a drink outdoors, go to *Den Blå Café* on Lilletorv at Slotsgade 4; for more excitement, head for the rock bar, *Crazy Daisy Rock 'n' Roll*, Jernbanegade 13, or the *Sci-Fi* disco, both on Jernbanegade.

Sønderborg

Despite lush green landscapes subsiding gently into a peaceful coastline, the eastern section of southern Jutland holds comparatively few spots of interest and is best seen as part of a southerly route to Funen or Ærø (covered in the previous chapter). A lively provincial town in an area laden with campsites, **SØNDERBORG** straddles the once strategically important **Alssund**, a narrow but deep channel dividing the island of Als from the Jutland mainland. The campsites are evidence of the appeal of the region's sandy coastline, while the line of preserved earthworks on the mainland side are testament to the town's crucial place in Danish history. Beside them, the **Battlefield Centre** (Historiecenter Dybbøl Banke; June–Aug daily 10am–6pm; early April, late Sept and late Oct 10am–4pm; 40kr) has multimedia displays that trace the details of the battle that took place here on April 18, 1864, when the Danes were defeated by the Prussians and medieval Sønderborg was all but destroyed. From then until 1918, when a plebiscite returned it to Denmark, northern Schleswig (in which Sønderborg stands) became part of Germany.

The bulk of the town lies across the Alssund, where your attention should focus on **Sønderborg Slot**, which may not be the grandest but is certainly one of Denmark's oldest castles, thought to have been started by Valdemar I in 1170 as a defence against the Wends. Inside the castle, the **Museum of South Jutland** (daily: May–Sept 10am–5pm; April & Oct 10am–4pm; Nov–March 1–4pm; 20kr) comprises room after room of military mementos. One of the more interesting sections tells of the four-day Als Republic of 1918, born as the German Reich's dissenting northern ports – Sønderborg, Bremen, Hamburg and Kiel – rebelled against the Kaiser and, in emulation of the then recent Russian Revolution, raised a red banner over the town's barracks.

Practicalities

Trains go no further than the mainland section of the town, though long-distance **buses** continue across the graceful modern road bridge to Als and the bus station on Jernbanegade. Just downhill from the bus station, you'll find the **tourist office**, on Rådhustorvet (Mon–Fri 9.30am–6pm, Sat 9.30am–1pm; ☎74 42 35 55, fax 74 42 57 47). Of the central **hotels**, the *Arnkilhus*, Arnkilgade 13 (☎74 42 23 36; ③), is best for price, though the grandest place in town is undoubtedly the *Scandic*, Rosengade 2 (☎74 42 19 00; ⑤) – look for deep discounts on weekends. The shiny modern **youth hostel** (☎74 42 31 12; Feb–Nov) is a twenty-minute walk along Perlegade and Alsgade, and a little less centrally placed than the waterfront **campsite** (☎74 42 41 89).

The town's main shopping street is Perlegade, close to the tourist office, which then changes its name twice, first to Store Rådhusgade, then to Lille Rådhusgade, an area that takes on a Mediterranean air on warm evenings as smartly dressed Danes mill from bar to bar. Locals often begin a weekend by shopping in Perlegade, then eating their way down to the other end of the street. For food, *Café Druen*, at Store Rådhusgade 1, has filling, low-cost snacks, and there are good evening meals at *Penny Lane*, a newish English pub just up the street at no.12 – both sometimes host live jazz and other music during July. Further on, there are 50kr pizzas at *Casa Letizia*, while nearby on Bagergade *Tortilla Flats* offers Mexican main courses for 80kr. There's also a branch of the ubiquitous steakhouse chain, *Jensens Bøfhus*, at Løkken 24, and the new *Bella Italia* for cosy Italian meals. **Nightlife** is limited: *Penny Lane*, with beers from all over the world, is your best option. *Maybe Not Bob* is a slightly noisier place, popular with young locals.

Fredericia, Vejle and around

There's little that's unique about **east Jutland**, though its thick forests are a welcome change if you're coming directly from the windswept western side of the peninsula. As the main route between Funen and the big Jutland cities, it's a busy region with good transport links, but the area has only two sizeable towns: **Fredericia** is the more unusual, **Vejle** the more appealing – though neither justifies a lengthy stay.

Fredericia

FREDERICIA – junction of all the rail routes in east Jutland, and those connecting the peninsula with Funen – has one of the oddest histories (and layouts) in Denmark. It was founded in 1650 by Frederik III, who envisaged the town as a strategically placed reserve

capital and a base from which to defend Jutland. Three nearby villages were demolished and their inhabitants forced to assist in the building of the new town – and afterwards they had no choice but to live in it. Military considerations required that the town be built on a strict grid plan, with low buildings enclosed by high earthen ramparts, making it invisible to approaching armies. Even the town's later role as a railway hub hasn't destroyed its soldierly air, with memorials to victorious heroes and the only military tattoo in Denmark – an event that failed elsewhere in the country due to lack of interest.

The half-hour walk from the **train station** along Vesterbrogade into the town centre takes you through Danmarks Port and the most impressive section of the old ramparts. These stretch for 4km and rise 15m above the streets, and walking along the top gives a good view of the layout of the town. But it's the **Landsoldaten statue**, opposite Princes Port, that best exemplifies the local spirit. The bronze figure holds a rifle in its left hand, a sprig of leaves in the right, and its left foot rests on a captured cannon. The inscription on the statue reads "6 Juli 1849", the day the town's battalion made a momentous sortie against German troops in the first Schleswig war – an anniversary celebrated as **Fredericia Day**. The downside of the battle was the five hundred Danes killed; they lie in a mass grave in the grounds of **Trinitatis Kirke** in Kongensgade.

Predictably, three hundred years of armed conflict form the core of the displays in the **Fredericia Museum** at Jernbanegade 10 (mid-June to mid-Aug daily noon–4pm; mid-Aug to mid-June Tues–Sun noon–4pm; 20kr). There are also reconstructions of typical local house interiors from the seventeenth and eighteenth centuries, and a dreary selection of archeological finds only enlivened by a glittering cache of silverware in the crafts section.

Practicalities

Unless you want to laze around on Fredericia's fine **beaches**, which begin at the eastern end of the ramparts, there's little reason to hang around for very long. The cheapest **hotel** is the family-oriented *Sømandshjemmet* on Gothersgade (☎75 92 01 99, fax 75 93 25 90, *fsh@fsh.dk*; ④), near the harbour, which can also lay on meals. There's a modern **youth hostel** west of the town at Vestre Ringvej 98 (☎75 92 12 87; mid-Feb to Nov), with plenty of doubles (②), and a **campsite** (☎75 95 71 83; April–Oct) on the Vejle fjord, though it's 15km north of town and adjacent to a public beach, so can get very crowded during fine weather and at holiday times. You can arrange private rooms with the centrally placed **tourist office** on Danmarksgade (Mon–Fri 9.30am–5pm, Sat & Sun 10am–1pm; ☎75 92 13 77).

For **food**, there's the predictable *Jense's Bøfhus* steak house, Danmarksgade (☎75 91 41 21); *Den Lille Hornblæser*, Jyllandsgade 53 (☎75 93 10 20), with a range of Danish offerings; and the Italian restaurant *Bøf og Vino*, Danmarksgade 12 (☎75 93 08 08). For a **drink**, try the popular *Nelly O'Grady's* pub at Bjergegade 54 (☎75 91 54 88).

Vejle

A twenty-minute train ride north of Fredericia, **VEJLE**, a compact harbour town on the mouth of the Vejle fjord, is home to the Tulip factory, from where 400 million sausages a year begin their journey to British breakfast tables. It's also the best base for exploring the contrasting pleasures of the Viking burial mounds at Jelling and – rather more famously – the Legoland complex at Billund, both within easy reach by bus or train.

The chief attraction in Vejle itself is **Skt Nicolai Kirke** (Mon–Fri 9am–5pm, Sat & Sun 9am–noon) in Kirke Torvet, in which a glass-topped coffin holds the peat-preserved body of a woman found in the Haraldskær bog in 1835. Originally the body was thought to be the corpse of a Viking queen, Gunhilde of Norway, but the claim was disputed and tests carried out in 1977 dated the body to around 490 BC – too old to be a Viking, but nonetheless still the best preserved "bog body" in the country. Unfortunately, it's hidden away behind bars in the north transept; what you can see is mainly the feet. Another macabre feature of the church, though you can't see it, are the 23 skulls hidden in sealed holes in the northern transept. Legend has it that they are the heads of 23 thieves executed in 1630.

The **Museum of Art** and **Vejle Museum** (both Tues–Sun 11am–4pm; free) are conveniently placed next to each other at Flegborg 16 and 18. The art museum specializes in graphics and drawings, has a collection of twentieth-century painting and sculpture, and often hosts innovative temporary exhibitions from around the world; the Vejle Museum has a small collection of local historical and archeological finds. Also run by the museum, and perhaps a better destination on a sunny day, is **Vejle Vindmølle**, a disused windmill which maintains its full complement of ropes, shafts and pinions, and displays a through-the-ages account of milling, from Neolithic blocks to modern roller mills. From the windmill, reached by climbing Kid Desvej (which leads off Søndergade), there are stupendous views across Vejle and its fjord.

Practicalities

Tucked into a small courtyard off the pedestrianized Søndergade, the Vejle **tourist office** (mid-June to Aug Mon–Sat 9am–5.30pm; Sept to mid-June Mon–Thurs 9am–5pm; ☎75 82 19 55) has a list of **accommodation** in private rooms for 250kr per person, but charges a steep 40kr booking fee. Otherwise, try for a room at the *Park* (☎75 82 24 66, fax 75 72 05 39; ④) at O. Lehmannsgade 5, or the pricier four-star *Munkebjerg*, Munkebjergvej 125 (☎76 42 85 00, fax 75 72 08 86; ⑤), which has a casino amongst its attractions. Much less convenient is the **youth hostel** on Gammel Landevej (☎75 82 51

88), a 5km journey on bus #2 from either the bus station on Nørretorv or the Vejle Trafikcentre outside the train station, opposite the tourist office. There's also a **campsite** at Helligkildevej 5 (☎75 82 33 35), a few kilometres east (bus #4).

Central Vejle has plenty of inexpensive places **to eat**. In the same courtyard as the tourist office, *Den Smitske* serves substantial salads and *smørrebrød* through the afternoon and drinks until midnight. Around the corner on Søndergade, the glass-walled *Madværkstedet* has simple food for around 50kr. For a fuller evening meal, make for *Café Biografen*, Klostergade 1, which is also a good place for a drink. There are a number of English-style **pubs** in town: try the *Irish Cat*, Nørregade 61, the *Sevenoaks*, Dæmningen 42, or – perhaps the most popular – the *Tartan Pub*, next door at Dæmningen 40.

Around Vejle: Jelling and Legoland

Twenty minutes by train from Vejle, the village of **JELLING** is known to have been the site of pagan festivals and celebrations, and has two **burial mounds** thought to have contained King Gorm, Jutland's tenth-century ruler, and his queen, Thyra. The graves were found in the early twentieth century and, although only one coffin was actually recovered, there is evidence to suggest that the body of Gorm was removed by his son, Harald Bluetooth, and placed in the adjacent church – which Bluetooth himself built around 960 after his conversion to Christianity. In the grounds of the present church are two big **runic stones**, one erected by Gorm to the memory of Thyra, the other raised by Harald Bluetooth in honour of Gorm. The texts, hewn into the granite, record the era when Denmark began the transition to Christianity.

Train services from Vejle to Struer or Herning stop at Jelling: both run about once an hour on weekdays and less frequently at weekends. There's also a **vintage train** between Vejle and Jelling, running every Sunday in July and on the first Sunday in August. By **bike**, it's a scenic ride through the hamlet of Uhre and along the shores of Fårup Sø – you can rent a bike in Vejle from Buhl Jensen, Gormsgade 14–16 (☎75 82 15 09). If you want to **stay**, the *Jelling Kro*, Gormsgade 16 (☎75 87 10 06; ②), is pleasant and serves filling meals, or head for Jelling's **campsite** (☎75 87 16 53; mid-April to mid-Sept), which also has cabins, about 1km west of the church, on Mølvangsvej.

Legoland Park

Twenty kilometres west of Vejle – to which it's linked by train and bus #211 – the village of **Billund** has been transformed into a major tourist centre, complete with international airport and rows of pricey hotels. It's all thanks to **Legoland Park** (April–Oct daily 10am–8pm, mid-June to Aug until 9pm; 125–140kr depending on time of year), a theme park celebrating the tiny plastic bricks that have filled many a Christmas stocking since a Danish carpenter, Ole Kirk Christiansen, started making wooden toys collectively named "Lego", from the Danish phrase "Leg Godt", or "play well" (which also, by a happy coincidence, means "I study" and "I assemble" in Latin). In 1947 the Lego company began to manufacture its bricks in plastic, becoming the first company in Denmark to use the new plastic moulding-injection techniques – the Lego pieces (or "Automatic Binding Bricks", to be perfectly precise) we know today were first created in 1958. The park itself, featuring a cornucopia of elaborate model buildings, animals, planes and many other weird and wonderful things (such as Titania's Palace – home for the queen of the fairies), is aimed chiefly at kids, but anybody whose efforts at Lego construction have resulted in tears of frustration over missing corner bricks might like to discover what can be achieved when someone has 45 million pieces to play with.

If you want to stay, try the fine modern **youth hostel**, outside town at Ellehammers Allé (☎75 33 27 77, fax 75 33 28 77), which has a good supply of inexpensive double rooms (②) and other family accommodation. Without a car, it's best to take a bus from the city centre to Legoland and walk the remaining 500m to the hostel. The other options in town are rather more expensive, and can be laid out for you at Billund's **tourist office** (☎76 50 00 55, fax 76 35 31 79).

North of Vejle: Horsens

Travelling north from Vejle, there's every chance you'll pass through **HORSENS**, a likeable though hardly exciting town whose Søndergade is claimed to be the widest main street in Denmark. Horsens was also the birthplace in 1681 of **Vitus Bering**, who discovered what became known as the Bering Strait whilst on a mission on behalf of Peter the Great to find an Asian–American land bridge. A memorial to him stands in the park which also bears his name.

In another park, Caroline Amalielunden, just north of Sundvej, are the **Horsens Museum** (July & Aug Tues–Sun 10am–4pm; Sept–June Tues–Sun 11am–4pm; 20kr), which contains a run-of-the-mill collection of local knick-knacks, and the more enticing **Art Museum** (July & Aug Tues–Fri 10am–4pm, Sat & Sun 10am–5pm; Sept–June Tues–Fri 11am–4pm, Sat & Sun 11am–5pm; 20kr), displaying some Danish Golden Age masters and an honourable collection of works by local artists.

There are plenty of **accommodation** options in Horsens, most expensively the fancy pink *Jørgensens Hotel* at Søngergade 17 (☎75 62 16 00, fax 75 62 85 85; ⑥), housed in an eighteenth-century palace. Inexpensive **restaurants** include the Greek eatery *Kikos*, Kippervig 1, near the town's central pedestrian area, the Mexican *Tequila Sunrise*, Smedegad 10, and the lunch place *Teater Cafeen*, Teatertorvet. There's also the usual *Jensens Bøfhus* at Åboulevarden 129 for steaks, with cheap afternoon specials on week-days. During summer, local **bars and cafés** in the centre set chairs and tables outside for alfresco eating and drinking. The best include the new *Corfitz* at Søndergade 23, an elegant place in the heart of town; quiet *Cafe Emma*, Nørregade 10; *Paddy's Dancehall*, an Irish pub right in the centre at Torvet 2A; and another pub, *Camp David*, at Graven 12.

The Lake District

The grandly titled Danish **Lake District** sits within the triangle formed by Vejle, Århus and Viborg, and comprises green, rolling woodlands, several small lakes, and innumerable campsites. If you've seen only Denmark's larger towns, this is a region well worth a couple of days' rural exploration. The north–south rail route passes through **Skanderborg**, which boasts some attractive eighteenth-century houses, many of them built with bricks from the town's medieval castle (of which only the church remains), but it's the Lake District's other main town, **Silkeborg**, spreading handsomely across several inlets of water, which is the area's liveliest centre.

Silkeborg

SILKEBORG has little history of its own – it was still a small village in 1845 when the local river was harnessed to power a paper mill that brought a measure of growth and prosperity – but the well-preserved body of an Iron Age woman, discovered 15km west of Silkeborg in 1928, adds greatly to the appeal of the town's **Culture Museum**, on Hovedgården (daily 10am–5pm; 20kr). As preserved bodies go, however, the so-called Elling Girl has been overshadowed since 1952 by the discovery of the Tollund Man, a corpse of similar vintage also on display at the museum. Gruesome as it may sound, the man's head is in particularly good condition, with stubble still visible on the chin.

An equally worthwhile call is to the excellent collection of abstract works by Asger Jorn and others in the **Museum of Art**, Gudenå 7 (daily 10am–5pm; 30kr). It was to

Silkeborg that Jorn, Denmark's leading modern painter and founder member of the influential CoBrA (Copenhagen-Brussels-Amsterdam) group, came to recuperate from tuberculosis. From the 1950s until his death in 1973, Jorn donated an enormous amount of his own and other artists' work to the town, which displays them proudly in this purpose-built museum.

For something less cultural, the **Aqua** aquarium (June–Aug daily 10am–6pm; Sept–May Mon–Fri 10am–4pm, Sat & Sun 10am–5pm; 55kr), at Vejlsøvej 55 on the southern edge of town, has a variety of freshwater fish – along with numerous water birds and mammals, including some cute otters.

Practicalities

The helpful **tourist office**, Godthåbsvej 4 (mid-June to Aug Mon–Sat 9am–5pm; Sept to mid-June Mon–Fri 9am–4pm, Sat 9am–noon; ☎86 82 19 11), has a lengthy list of affordable accommodation in what's a surprisingly expensive town. The old and atmospheric *Dania*, on Torvet (☎86 82 01 11; ⑥), is a central and typically priced four-star. There are many cheaper *kros* in the outlying countryside, such as *Signesminde Kro* at Viborgvej 145 (☎86 85 54 43; ③), reached by bus #60 from the railway station, and *Linå Kro* (☎86 84 14 43; ②), 8km distant on the road to Århus (bus #113). Budget accommodation is limited to the **youth hostel**, Åhavevej 55 (☎86 82 36 42), which has affordable triples and quads (320–400kr), though no doubles, and several **campsites**: *Indelukkets* (☎86 82 22 01), to the south, and *Silkeborg Sø* (☎86 82 28 24), on the Århus road, are closest to town. To get to the former, walk about 2km from the main square down Christian VII vej and turn left onto Marienlundsvej; for the latter, begin at the square and head down Østergade, through two traffic lights to Århusbakken (also know as Århusvej). The tourist office can also help to organize **canoe trips**, and book you in at campsites along the way. If you want to go it alone, many of the campsites rent out canoes, or try Slusekioskens Kanoudlejning (☎86 80 08 93) at the harbour.

Århus

Geographically at the heart of the country, and often regarded as Denmark's cultural capital, **ÅRHUS** typifies all that's good about Danish cities: it's small enough to get to know in a few hours, yet big and lively enough to have plenty to fill both days and nights. If you're tiring of Copenhagen, this offers a surprising number of sights and a laid-back atmosphere that might keep you around longer than planned. It's also something of an architectural showcase, with several notable structures spanning a century of Danish and international design. A number of these buildings form the city's university campus, whose students contribute to a nightlife that's on a par with that of Copenhagen.

Despite Viking-era origins, the city's present prosperity is due to its long sheltered bay, on which a harbour was first constructed during the fifteenth century, and the more recent advent of railways, which made Århus a nationally important trade and transport centre. It's easily reached by train from all the country's bigger towns, sits at one end of the only direct sea link between Jutland and Zealand (a fast catamaran service linking Århus with Kalundborg), and also has an international airport. There's certainly no better place for a first taste of Denmark.

Arrival, information and city transport

Whichever form of public transport brings you to Århus, you'll be deposited within easy reach of the hotels and main points of interest. **Trains and buses** stop on the southern edge of the city centre, from where it's a short walk to the **tourist office** on the

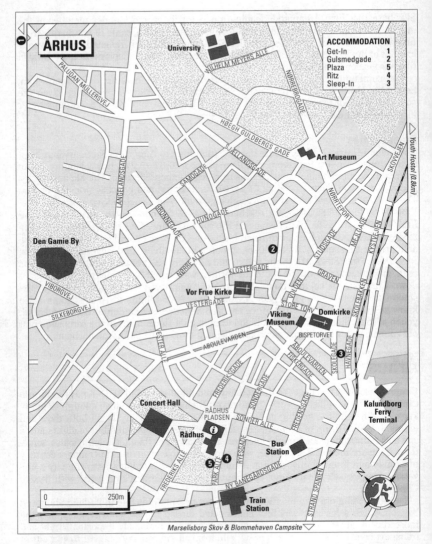

ÅRHUS

University

ACCOMMODATION
Get-In	1
Gulsmedgade	2
Plaza	5
Ritz	4
Sleep-In	3

Art Museum

Den Gamle By

Vor Frue Kirke

Viking Museum   Domkirke

BISPETORVET

Kalundborg Ferry Terminal

Concert Hall

RÅDHUS PLADSEN

Rådhus

Bus Station

Train Station

Marselisborg Skov & Blommehaven Campsite ▽

first floor of the Rådhus (May to mid-June Mon–Fri 9.30am–5pm, Sat 10am–1pm; mid-June to Aug Mon–Fri 9.30am–6pm, Sat 9.30am–5pm, Sun 9.30am–1pm; Sept–April Mon–Fri 9.30am–4.30pm, Sat 10am–1pm; ☎89 40 67 00); **ferries** from Zealand dock just west of the centre, a short distance from the heart of Old Århus. Buses from **Tirstrup Airport**, some 45km northeast of the city, arrive at (and leave from) the train station; the one-way fare for the fifty-minute journey is 50kr.

Getting around is best done on foot: the city centre is compact and you'll seldom need to use **buses** at all unless you're venturing out to the beaches or woods on the city's outskirts. If you do, note that the transport system divides into four zones: zones one and two cover the whole central area; zones three and four reach into the country-side. The basic ticket is the so-called **"cash ticket"**, which costs 13kr from the machine at the rear of the bus and is valid for any number of journeys during the time stamped on it. If you're around for several days and doing a lot of bus hopping (or using local trains, on which these tickets are also valid), it's best to buy either an **Århus Pass**, which costs 85kr for 48 hours and includes entry to numerous museums, including Den Gamle By, or a **multi-ride ticket** (80kr), valid for ten trips within the immediate city area; it can also be used by more than one person at once. These tickets can be bought at newsstands, campsites and shops displaying the "Århus Sporveje" sign. The driver won't check your ticket but a roving inspector might, and there's an instant fine of 150kr if you're caught travelling without one. The **bus information office** is at Banegårdspladsen 20 (Mon–Fri 8am–6pm, Sat 9am–noon; ☎89 43 56 00).

Cycling is another viable way to get around, particularly if you're heading out along the coast to Moesgård. The most central place to rent a bicycle is Gunnar Asmussen Cykler, opposite the bus station at Fredensgade 54 (☎86 19 57 00), which rents out single-speed roadsters for about 50kr a day.

Accommodation

Budget travellers have a tough time of it in Århus – there are a couple of hostels in town, but otherwise, break out your wallet and prepare for the shock. The *Ritz*, on Banegårdspladsen (☎86 13 44 44, fax 86 13 45 87; ⑤), and the central *Guldsmedgade Hotel*, Guldsmedgade 40 (☎86 13 62 96; ⑤), are two of the lowest-priced hotels in town, though neither is especially cheap; the *Plaza*, Bånegardspladsen 14 (☎87 32 01 00, fax 87 32 01 99; ⑤) is equally central but less affordable. Both the Århus Bed & Breakfast network (☎86 27 51 30 or 40 27 90 80) and the tourist office have details of single and double rooms for 175–250kr per person.

For something cheaper, try the *Get-In* guesthouse on the edge of town at Jens Baggesensvej 43 (☎86 10 86 14; ②); a cut above a hostel it's a slightly scruffy but always friendly choice. Even more central, the good *Sleep-In* at Havnegade 20 (☎86 19 20 55) has dorm beds and doubles (①), although guests without their own sleeping bags have to rent sheets and blankets (30kr); other facilities include a games room, café and bike rental (50kr per day). Much more peaceful is Århus's beautifully located **youth hostel**, at Marienlundsvej 10 (☎86 16 72 98, fax 86 10 55 60; closed mid-Dec to mid-Jan), 4km northeast of town in the middle of Risskov wood, close to a popular beach, and served by buses #1, #6 and #9. There's a hotel-style wing with double rooms (①) too.

Two farmhouses some 15km west of the city offer B&B, but you'll need your own transport to reach them. The first of these, *Marskov Mølle*, at Tarskovvej 1 in Harlev (☎86 94 25 44, fax 86 94 25 66; ③), has its own water mill, forest and lake frontage; the other, the half-timbered *Tåstrupgården*, at Tåstrupvej 111, Tåstrup/Harlev (☎86 94 10 13, fax 86 94 29 04; ③), has a beautifully furnished drawing room and the use of a kitchenette.

Of the various **campsites** in the Århus area, the two most convenient for the city are *Blommehaven* at Ørneredevej 35 in Højbjerg (☎86 27 02 07, fax 86 27 45 22, *info@blommehaven.dk*; April–Sept), overlooking the bay about 7km from the city centre (bus #19), and *Århus Nord* (☎86 23 11 33), 8km north of the city (bus #117 or #118). Both campsites have cabins: the cheapest sleep two or three people and cost 330–500kr, depending on the season.

The City

For reasons of simple chronology, Århus divides into two clearly defined parts: even combined, these fill a small and easily walkable area. The old section close to the cathedral, is a tight cluster of medieval streets with several interesting churches and a couple of museums, as well as the bulk of the city's nightlife. The more recent sections of Århus form a collar around the old centre, inevitably with less character, but nonetheless holding plenty that's worth seeing, not least the city's major architectural works.

Old Århus

Søndergade is Århus's main street, a pedestrianized strip lined with shops and overpriced snack bars that leads from the train station (where it's initially called Ryesgade) down into the main town square, Bispetorvet, and the old centre, whose streets form a web around the **Domkirke** (May–Sept Mon–Sat 9.30am–4pm; Oct–April Mon–Sat 10am–3pm; free).

Take the trouble to push open the cathedral's sturdy doors, not just to appreciate the soccer-pitch length – this is easily the longest church in Denmark – but for a view of a couple of features that spruce up the plain Gothic interior, which is mostly a fifteenth-century rebuilding after the original twelfth-century structure was destroyed by fire. At the eastern end is one of few pre-Reformation survivors, a grand tripartite altarpiece by the noted Bernt Notke. Look also at the painted – as opposed to stained – glass window behind the altar, the work of Norwegian Emmanuel Vigeland (brother of Gustav), most effective when the sunlight falls directly on it.

From the time of the first settlement here, in the tenth century, the area around the cathedral has been at the core of Århus life. A number of Viking remains have been excavated on Clemens Torv, across the road from the cathedral, and some of them are now displayed in the Unibank here at Clemens Torv 6 (inside on the left) as the **Viking Museum** (Mon–Fri 9.30am–4pm, Thurs until 6pm; free), including sections of the original ramparts and Viking tools, alongside informative accounts of early Århus. Also close to the cathedral, in a former police station at Domkirkeplads 5, the **Women's Museum** (Kvindemuseet; daily: June to mid-Sept 10am–5pm; mid-Sept to May 10am–4pm; 20kr) is one of Denmark's most innovative, staging temporary exhibitions on aspects of women's lives past and present. After visiting the museums, venture into the small and enjoyable surrounding streets, lined by innumerable old and well-preserved buildings, many of which now house browsable antique shops or chic boutiques. The area is also home to some of the city's most enjoyable drinking spots (see "Nightlife", p.145).

West along Vestergade from the Domkirke, the thirteenth-century **Vor Frue Kirke** (May–Aug Mon–Fri 10am–4pm, Sat 10am–2pm; Sept–April Mon–Fri 10am–2pm, Sat 10am–noon) is actually the site of three churches, the most notable of which is the eleventh-century **crypt church** (go in through the main church entrance and walk straight ahead), which was discovered, buried beneath several centuries' worth of rubbish, during restoration work on the main church in the 1950s. There's not exactly a lot to see, but the tiny, rough-stone church – resembling a hollowed-out cave – is strong on atmosphere, especially during the candle-lit Sunday services. Except for Claus Berg's altarpiece, there's not much to warrant a look in the main church. However, you should make your way through the cloister (to the left of the entrance) that remains from the pre-Reformation monastery – now an old folk's home – to see the medieval frescoes inside the third church, which depict local working people rather than the more commonly found biblical scenes.

Modern Århus

If you've visited the tourist office, you've already been inside the least interesting section of one of the modern city's major sights: the functional **Rådhus**, completed in 1941 and as capable of inciting high passions – for and against – today as it was when it opened. From the outside, it's easy to see why opinions should be so polarized: the coating of Norwegian marble lends a sickly pallor to the building. But on the inside (enter from Rådhuspladsen), the finer points of architects Arne Jacobsen and Erik Møller's vision make themselves apparent, amid the harmonious open-plan corridors and the extravagant quantities of glass. You're free to walk in and look for yourself, but it's worth taking one of the fascinating **guided tours** (in English mid-June to early Aug Mon–Fri at 11am; 10kr). You can also tour the tower at noon and 2pm daily (same months; 5kr).

Above the entrance hangs Hagedorn Olsen's huge mural, *A Human Society*, symbolically depicting the city emerging from the last war to face the future with optimism. In the council chamber, the lamps appear to hang suspended in mid-air (in fact they're held by almost invisible threads), and the shape of the council leader's chair is a distinctive curved form mirrored in numerous smaller features throughout the building, notably the ashtrays in the lifts – though many of these have been pilfered by tourists. Perhaps most interesting of all, however, if only for the background story, are the walls of the small Civic Room, covered by intricate floral designs in which artist Albert Naur, working during the Nazi occupation, concealed various Allied insignia. Finally, a lift (open at 11am, noon, 2pm & 4pm during the summer; 5kr) climbs to the bell tower for a view over the city and across the bay.

A more recent example of Århus's municipal architecture is the glass-fronted **Concert Hall** (Musikhuset), a short walk from the Rådhus, which has been the main venue for opera and classical music in the city since it opened in 1982. It's worth dropping into, if only for the small café where you might be entertained for free by a string quartet or a lone fiddler. A monthly list of forthcoming concerts and events is available from the box office or the tourist office.

It's just a few minutes' walk from the Concert Hall to Viborgvej and the city's best-known attraction, **Den Gamle By** (Jan–March 11am–3pm; April & May 10am–5pm; June–Aug 9am–6pm; Nov & Dec 10am–4pm; Jan–March 40kr, April–Dec 55kr). An open-air museum of traditional Danish life, it consists of sixty-odd half-timbered houses (including a popular Mayor's House of 1597) from all over the country which have been moved here since the museum's inception in 1909. With many of the buildings used for their original purpose, the overall aim of the place is to give an impression of an old Danish market town, complete with bakers, craftsmen and the like. This is done very effectively, although sunny summer days bring big crowds, and the period flavour is strongest outside high season, when visitors are fewer.

If you're at all interested in Danish art, the **Art Museum** (Tues–Sun 10am–5pm; 30kr) in the Vennelystparken, on the northeastern edge of the city centre, gives a good overview of the main national trends, from late eighteenth-century formal portraits and landscapes by Jens Juel, and finely etched scenes of domestic tension by Jørgen Sonne, through to the works of more internationally renowned names, particularly Vilhelm Hammershoi, represented here by some of his moody interiors. There are lots of worthwhile modern pieces too. Besides the radiant canvases of Asger Jorn and Richard Mortensen, don't miss Bjørn Nørgård's sculpted version of Christian IV's tomb: the original, in Roskilde Cathedral, is stacked with riches; this one features a coffee cup, an egg and a ballpoint pen.

Though it's so plain you'd barely notice it, the Art Museum building is often on the itinerary of architects visiting the city. It's reckoned to be a prime example of the modern Danish style: red bricks and white-framed rectangular windows, with no decoration at all. There's much more of this style on the **university campus**, which sprawls across a hillside overlooking the city a short way up Høegh Guldbergs Gade – it's walkable from Den Gamle By, but from the centre take bus #1, #2, #3, #11, #13, #56 or #58. Most of the university buildings were designed by C.F. Møller and completed just after World War II. While on campus, there are two museums that might appeal: the **Natural History Museum** (daily 10am–4pm; 30kr) has a large collection of stuffed birds and animals alongside some exhibits on Danish ecology, while the **Steno Museum** (Tues–Sun 10am–4pm; 30kr) focuses on medical matters and also includes a small planetarium.

Out from the centre

On Sundays Århus resembles a ghost town, with most locals spending the day in the parks, woodlands or beaches on the city's outskirts. If you're around on a Sunday – or, for that matter, any sunny day in the week – you could do much worse than join them. The closest beaches and woods are just **north of the city** at Risskov, near the youth hostel, easily reached on buses #1, #6 or #9, or on any local trains headed for Grenå or Hornslets, some of which halt at the tiny Den Permanente train platform by the beach (but check before boarding, as not all trains stop here). The beach here is narrow but scenic, and clean enough for swimming, while the thick forest behind is criss-crossed with walking and cycling trails.

For a more varied day, head **south** through the thick Marselisborg Skov and on to the prehistoric museum at Moesgård. This is also ideal territory for cycling or hiking – see p.141 for details of bicycle rental. Contact the tourist office for suggestions about routes and maps.

Marselisborg Skov and Dyrehaven

The **Marselisborg Skov**, 4km south of the city centre, is a large park that contains the city's football and horse-trotting stadiums and sees a regular procession of people exercising their dogs. It also holds the diminutive **Marselisborg Slot**, summer home of the Danish royals, whose landscaped grounds can be visited during daylight hours (free) when they're not in residence (usually at all times outside Easter, Christmas and late June to early Aug). Further south, across Carl Nielsen Vej, the park turns into a dense forest, criss-crossed with footpaths but still easy to get lost in.

A simpler route to navigate, and one with better views, is along Strandvejen, which runs between the eastern side of the forest and the shore. Unbroken footpaths run along this part of the coast and there are many opportunities to scamper down to rarely crowded (though often pebbly) beaches. Also on this route, near the junction of Ørneredevej and Thorsmøllevej, is the **Dyrehaven**, or Deer Park – a protected section of the wood that's home to many deer. The animals can be seen (if you're lucky – they're not the most gregarious of creatures) from the marked paths running through the park from the gate on the main road.

Moesgård Prehistoric Museum

Occupying the buildings and grounds of an old manor house 10km south of Århus city centre, **Moesgård Prehistoric Museum** (Jan to mid-March Tues–Sun 10am–4pm; mid-March to Sept daily 10am–5pm; Oct–Dec Tues–Thurs 10am–4pm; 35kr) traces the story of Danish civilizations from the Stone Age onwards with copious finds and easy-to-follow illustrations. It's the Iron Age which is most comprehensively covered and produces the most dramatic single exhibit: the **Grauballe Man**, the remains of a body, dated to 80 BC, which was discovered in a peat bog west of Århus in a state of such excellent preservation that it was even possible to discover what the deceased had eaten for breakfast (burnt porridge made from rye and barley) on the day of his death. Only a roomful of imposing runic stones further on captures the imagination as powerfully, and you'll exhaust the museum in an hour. Bus #6 runs directly to the museum from the city, while bus #19 takes a more scenic route along the edge of Århus Bay, leaving you with at least a two-kilometre walk through woods to the museum.

Outside the museum, the **prehistoric tramway** runs from the far corner of the courtyard to the sea and back again, a distance of about 3km each way, heading past a scattering of reassembled prehistoric dwellings, monuments and burial places – a trail guide is available in English (10kr). On a fine day, the walk itself is as enjoyable as the actual sights, and you could easily linger for a picnic when you reach the coast, or stop for a coffee and a snack at the small but popular *Skovmøllen* restaurant en route. Bus

#19 goes back to the city from a stop about a hundred metres back to the north of the trail's end at the beach.

Eating

Central Århus is loaded with **eating** possibilities and, while nothing is particularly cheap, a good and affordable bite can still be found in the right places. In general, it's wise to follow locals and students away from the heavily touristed Domkirke and Store Torv to streets such as Skolebakken, Nørre Allée, Vestergade or Åboulevarden. You'll find the best **lunch** bargains simply by cruising the cafés and restaurants of the old city and reading the notices chalked up outside them. *Mackie's Pizza*, on Skt Clemens Stræde, by the Viking Museum, has lunchtime specials for around 50kr, while turning the corner into Skolegade turns up a number of unpretentious eateries (so unpretentious, in fact, that they often look closed when they're open). *Pinds Café*, at no. 11, is a case in point, and does excellent *smørrebrød* and set lunches for 50kr, while *Gyngen*, at Mejlgade 53, does filling and healthy dishes at reasonable prices. Takeaway meals in the centre can be found at *Juice Stop*, Gadstuegade, a good sandwich-and-juice place; *Dee Dee's Sandwiches*, Banegårdsplads 8, with tasty breads; and *Capitano Specialiteter*, Tordenskjoldsgade 81, with pizzas from 20kr, sandwiches and salads. A little fancier are *Crêperiet*, Marselisborg Havnevej 24, which turns out crepes, fish soups and onion consommé, and *Café Vestergade Grønnegade* on Vestergade, a little corner café serving up glasses of porter and sandwiches for about 25kr each.

Dinner is going to be much more pricey unless you stick to the pizzerias – *Italia* at Åboulevarden 9 is quite good – or the ethnic restaurants, such as *Det Grønne Hjørne*, Frederiksgade 60, which does Middle Eastern food and a buffet with a good salad bar for 69kr (49kr at lunchtime), or the cheap and good Tunisian cuisine at *Kif Kif Gallorant*, Mejlgade 41, where you can bring your own wine. For Mexican food, *Alimento* at Åboulevarden 46 is the best choice. If you want to splash out a bit, head for the harbour, Marselisborg Havn, where there are a number of fish restaurants – best is the pricey *Seafood* – or walk along Skolegade to *A Hereford Beefstouw* at no. 5 (☎86 13 53 25), an expensive but venerable steak house featuring grilled Australian beef and a French wine list.

If money is tight, or you just want to stock up for a **picnic**, try the *Special Smørrebrød* outlet at Sønder Allé 2. Hjørnet, Mejlgade 24, which sells delicious picnic ingredients – it's next door to a smokers-only bar. For more general food shopping, there's a branch of Brugsen on Søndergade, and a **late-opening DSB supermarket** (8am–midnight) at the train station. There are several other downtown supermarkets of varying quality – try the decent Super Brugsen at Nørre Allé , or the slightly less good Aldi across the way; at the former, local merchants peddle berries and beans fresh from the fields when in season.

Nightlife

Århus is the only place in Denmark with a **nightlife** to match that of Copenhagen. There's a diverse assortment of ways to be entertained, enlightened, or just inebriated, almost every night of the week. And while things sparkle socially all year round, if you visit during the **Århus Festival**, an orgy of arts events held annually over the first week in September (check what's on with the tourist office), you'll find even more to occupy your time.

Cafés and bars

The city has a wonderful endowment of **cafés**, many situated in the recently restored medieval streets close to the cathedral. There's little to choose between the cafés themselves: each pulls a lively and cosmopolitan crowd and the best plan is simply to wander around and try a few. A good place to start is the movie-themed *Casablanca*, at Rosensgade 12, after which you could continue to either *Carlton*, Rosensgade 23, *Café Jorden*, Badstuegade 5, *Drudenfuss*, Graven 30, *Englen*, Studsgade 3, or *Kindrødt*, Studsgade 8. Slightly more upmarket is the classical music-oriented *Café Mozart*, just outside the old centre at Vesterport 10, with good steaks and other meals too. Or try the popular *Café Viggo* in the thick row of cafés on Åboulevarden. All the above stay open until between midnight and 2am depending on the day of the week; if they're not heading for a club, revellers with stamina aim for one of the city's **late-night cafés**, such as *Café Paradis*, at Paradisgade 9 (Thurs & Fri midnight–4am). A better bet are the bars lining both sides of the **Åboulevarden canal** near the central shopping district, whose numerous cafés with chairs spilling out onto the pavement are the places to see and be seen on sunny summer evenings. You pay extra for the ambience, of course – prices drop as you go west out along the canal. Århus's sizeable student population also means that there are plenty of smoky **pubs** to be found, particularly adjacent to the old town along **Skolebakken**, including some Aussie- and British-themed venues – none of them are particularly good, but they're OK for a quick tipple and are relatively cheap.

Live music

There's plenty of **live music** in Århus. You can get basic details of all events from the tourist office, but a better source for rock music news is the Århus Billet Bureau, at Studsgade 44, where you can pick up a variety of free local magazines and flyers advertising forthcoming gigs.

The cream of Danish and international independent **rock** acts can be found at either *Vox Hall*, Vester Allé 15 (☎87 30 97 97) – which has a restaurant and **cinema** almost next door called *Ridehuset* – or *58*, at Vestergade 58 (☎86 13 02 17). Gigs take place at both three or four nights a week; admission runs from 20kr to 100kr, with doors opening at 10pm and the main band on at midnight. More run-of-the-mill Danish bar bands turn up at the pub-cum-piano-bar *Fatter Eskild*, Skolegade 25 (☎86 19 44 11), and *Gyngen*, Fronthuset, Mejlgade 53 (☎86 19 22 55) – only the latter ever charges for entry (20–40kr, free Mon). The small *Æsken*, at Anholtsgade 4 (☎86 13 85 61; closed Sun), features anything from country to rock'n'roll to world music and acid jazz Thursday to Saturday nights.

By far the best **jazz** venue is the smoky, atmospheric pub, *Bent J*, at Nørre Allé 66 (☎86 12 04 92; closed Sun). There are free jam sessions here several nights a week; for a name band expect to pay 50–90kr. On Wednesday nights, **Latin** fans congregate at *Club Havana* in the *Musikcafeen*, Mejlgade 53 (☎86 19 22 55), for free salsa lessons. For **classical music and opera**, check out the regular performances at the Concert Hall on Thomas Jensens Allé in the city centre (☎89 31 82 10).

Clubs and discos

Both *Huset* and *58* (see above) have rock and retro **discos** on nights when they aren't hosting live bands, although the city's coolest club at the moment is *Blitz*, at Klostergade 34 (Fri & Sat only). More mainstream discos are plentiful, the best of which are *Alexis*, Frederiksgade 72 (Thurs–Sat only), *Don Quijote*, Mejlgade 14, *Train*, Toldbodgade 6 (Thurs–Sat only), and *Valdemar Natterdag*, Store Torv 4 – which has the advantage of freshly made pizza available from midnight, and is liveliest early in the week. If you fancy a night of 1950s and 60s nostalgia, the place to go is *Locomotion*, at M.P. Bruuns Gade 15. Early in the week, **admission** to any disco is likely to be free; on Thursday, Friday or Saturday, you'll pay 20–40kr.

Århus doesn't have the wide network of **gay clubs** you'll find in Copenhagen, though the long-established gay social centre *Pan Klubben*, at Jægergårdsgade 42 (☎86 13 43 80), has a café and disco. Thursday nights here are lesbian-only; there's a mixed crowd on Wednesday, Friday and Saturday nights.

Listings

Airlines SAS/Dan Air (domestic ☎70 10 30 00; international ☎70 10 20 00).

Airport Tirstrup (☎86 36 36 00), 44km northeast of the city. Airport buses leave from outside the train station; the fare is 50kr and the journey takes fifty minutes.

Bookshops The English Book Store, Frederiks Allé 53 (☎86 19 54 55, *books@cybernet.dk*; Mon–Fri 11.30am–5.30pm, Sat 11am–2pm), fully lives up to its name.

Bus enquiries Local buses ☎86 12 67 03 or 86 18 17 33. Århus–Copenhagen coach reservations ☎89 46 56 00.

Car rental Avis, Jens Baggesens Vej 88 (☎86 16 10 99); Europcar, Sønder Allé 17 (☎89 33 11 11).

Doctor Between 4pm and 8pm, call ☎86 20 10 22. Outside these hours, contact the Kommunehospital (see "Hospitals" below).

Ferries Hydrofoil to Zealand, Cat-Link ☎86 13 17 00 (car information ☎33 15 15 15, terminal ☎89 41 20 60). DSB ferries ☎86 18 17 78.

Hospitals There's an emergency department at Århus Kommunehospital, Nørrebrogade 44 (☎89 49 33 33).

Late shopping The DSB supermarket at the train station is open daily 8am–midnight.

Market There's a fruit, veg and flower market every Wednesday and Saturday on Bispetorv, beside the cathedral, though the one on Saturday mornings along Ingerslevs Boulevard, south of the centre, is livelier.

Pharmacy Løve Apoteket, Store Torv 5 (☎86 12 00 22), is open 24 hours.

Police Århus Politisation, Ridderstræde 1 (☎86 13 30 00).

Post office Banegårdspladsen, by the train station (Mon–Fri 9am–6pm, Sat 10am–1pm).

Train enquiries Local trains ☎86 12 67 03 or 86 18 17 33. Long-distance trains ☎86 18 17 78.

Travel agents KILROY travels, Fredensgade 40 (☎86 20 11 44).

Central Jutland: Randers, Viborg and around

From rugged windswept heathlands to lush valleys and thick belts of forest, **central Jutland** boasts some of the most varied landscapes in Denmark – these, together with the area's historical remnants, are sufficient ingredients for a couple of days' pleasurable exploration. The region is easily accessed by train, although if coming from Århus you'll need to change at Langå to get straight into the best of it – the patch around Viborg. Failing that, stay on the train and base yourself instead in the countryside close to Randers, seeing the rest by bike or local buses.

Randers

A trading and manufacturing base since the thirteenth century, **RANDERS** is not a promising introduction to central Jutland. Its growth has continued apace over the years, leaving a tiny medieval centre miserably corralled by a bleak new industrial zone. The town's main historical sight is the house at **Storegade 13**, said to be the place where Danish nobleman Niels Ebbesen killed the German count, Gerd of Holstein, in 1340; a shutter on the upper storey is always left open to allow the count's ghost to escape lest the malevolent spirit should cause the house to burn down. But Randers' biggest tourist attraction these days – one of the most popular in Jutland – is the **Randers Regnskov** (Randers Rainforest; May to mid-June daily 10am–5pm; mid-June to Aug daily 10am–6pm; Sept–Dec Sat & Sun 10am–5pm; Jan–April Mon–Fri 10am–4pm, Sat & Sun 10am–5pm; 60kr), a re-creation of a tropical rainforest alongside the River Gudenåen. Visitors wander through the dense, damp foliage, enclosed within two giant domes, watching out for the birds, animals and amphibians, which include a number of rare turtles and a flying fox, not to mention a formidable assortment of vipers, boas, pythons, poison frogs and the like. The best part is undoubtedly the dark and spooky "night zoo", located in a dripping stone cave.

Practicalities

The **bus station** is right in the centre at Dytmærsken 12, while the **train station** is ten minutes' walk out of town at Jernbanegade 29. First stop should be the **tourist office**, near Randers Regnskov at Tørvebryggen 12 (☎86 42 44 77; April to mid-June Mon–Fri 9am–5pm, Sat 9am–noon; mid-June to Aug Mon–Fri 9am–6pm, Sat 9am–3pm; Sept–March Mon–Fri 9am–4.30pm, Sat 9am–noon), which hands out a list of private rooms for rent from 100kr per person – but be aware that some of them are a long way outside town. One of the best-value **hotels** is the *Kronjylland* (☎86 41 43 33, fax 86 41 43 95; ⑤), on Vestergade, close to the train station. More upmarket are the *Randers*, Torvegade 11 (☎86 42 34 22, fax 86 40 15 86; ⑥), and the *Scandic Hotel Kongens Ege* (☎86 43 03 00, fax 86 43 22 73, *randers@scandic-hotels.se*; ⑤), on Gammel Hadsundvej atop a wooded hill above the town, whose rooms give superb views over the city. Randers' **youth hostel**, with dorms and private rooms (①), is only five minutes from the centre at Gethersvej 1 (☎86 42 50 44; closed Jan). The nearest **campsite**, with cabins and a swimming pool, is at Fladbro, 6km west of the town (☎86 42 93 61): take bus #10 to the *Fladbro Kro*, from where it's a ten-minute walk through the woods.

Randers has plenty of relatively cheap **restaurants**: try the Greek dishes at *Hellas*, Vester Kirkestræde 3, or the filling lunchtime deals at *Maren Knudsen, Øl & Vinkælder* on Støregade. As for **nightlife**, Støregade holds a good selection of bars where you can sample the local Thor beer, such as the popular *Tante Olga*, Søndergade 6, which has live rock bands at weekends, or the more peaceful *Café von Hatten*, at Von Hattenstræde 7. In early August the town celebrates **Randers Ugen**, a week packed with all sorts of cultural events; the rest of the year, major rock concerts and theatre performances are put on regularly at Værket Musik & Teaterhus, a converted power station on Mariagervej (ticket office ☎86 43 29 00) – ask at the tourist office for details of what's on.

The best way to see the countryside around Randers is by **bike**. Schmidt Cykler, Vestergade 35 (☎86 41 29 03), rents them for 50kr per day.

East of Randers: Djursland and Mols

East of Randers stretches the peninsula known as **Djursland** (on its north side) and **Mols** (on its south), which, with its hilly, wooded landscape, edged with some fine beaches, attracts an increasing number of tourists every year. **EBELTOFT** is the most popular destination, easily reached by regular bus from Århus, or by frequent ferry services from Odden in Zealand. A thriving market centre in medieval times, it was sacked by the invading Swedes in 1659 and has only recently emerged from economic decline, thanks to tourism: in summer you should aim to get here early, before the cobbled streets are overrun by the hordes shopping for souvenirs. The main sight in town is the **Fregatten Jylland**, a nineteenth-century wooden frigate (daily: mid-June to Aug 10am–7pm; Sept to mid-June 10am–4pm; 50kr). Should you fancy staying in town, the best-value **hotel** is the small one-star *Ebeltoft* on Adelgade (☎86 34 10 90; ④); there's also a **youth hostel** at Søndergade 43 (☎86 34 20 53) with bunks and doubles (①). There are several **campsites** along the bay, the best being *Vibæk Camping* (☎86 34 12 14), right on the beach a little way north of town, which also has cabins.

Over on the southern side of the peninsula, at Jutland's easternmost point, **GRENÅ** grew up around its harbour in the nineteenth century, and it's still an important port, with frequent ferry services to Sweden (Varberg and Halmstad). Though the town centre is pleasant enough, the main draw are the beaches south of town. If you need to stay overnight, try for a room at the yellow *Grenaa Strand*, close to the harbour (☎86 32 68 14, fax 86 32 07 92; ④); alternatively, there's a **youth hostel** with bunks and doubles (②) at Ydesvej 4 (☎86 32 66 22; closed mid-Dec to mid-Jan), while the best of the local **campsites** is *Polderrev Camping*, south of the harbour at Fulgsangvej 58 (☎86 32 17 18). Grenå is reachable by train from Århus (1hr 30min), while bus #214 runs hourly through the day from Randers bus station, the journey taking about ninety minutes.

If it's really the beaches you're after, it's better to head 10km north of Grenå by local bus to **GJERRILD**, a small and quiet village with an inn, bakery, grocery and a small castle (Sostrup Slot). The beach here, **Nordstranden,** is one of the best in the country, far preferable to the pebbly offerings in the opposite direction. Budget accommodation alternatives are pretty much limited to Gjerrild's **youth hostel** (☎86 32 12 00), with bunks and doubles (①), and an excellent **campsite** (☎86 38 42 00; April–Oct), 500m from the sands at Nordstranden.

Viborg

For many years **VIBORG** was one of the most important communities in the country, at the junction of all the major roads across Jutland. From Knud in 1027 to Christian V in 1655, every Danish king was crowned here; Hans Tausen's Lutheran preaching began in Viborg in 1528, eight years before Denmark's official conversion from Catholicism; and until the early nineteenth century the town was the seat of a provincial assembly. As the national administrative axis shifted towards Zealand, however, Viborg's importance waned, and although it's still home to the high court of West Denmark, it's now primarily a market town for local farmers.

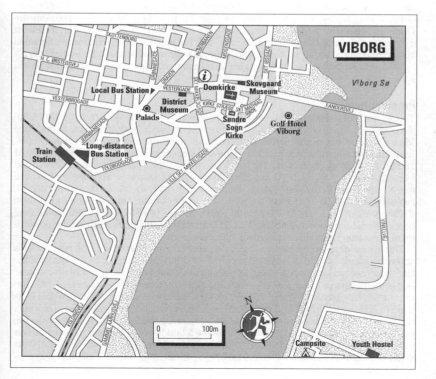

Viborg's centre is concentrated in a small area and most parts of the old town are within a few minutes' walk of each other. The twin towers of the **Domkirke** (June–Aug Mon–Sat 10am–5pm, Sun noon–5pm; April, May & Sept Mon–Sat 11am–4pm, Sun noon–4pm; Oct–March Mon–Sat 11am–3pm, Sun noon–3pm) are the town's most visible feature and the most compelling reminder of its former glories. Begun by Bishop Eskil in 1130, the original building was destroyed by fire in 1726 and rebuilt in the Baroque style by one Claus Stallknecht, though so badly that it had to be closed for two years and the work begun again. The interior is now dominated by the brilliant frescoes of Joakim Skovgaard, an artist commemorated by the **Skovgaard Museum** (daily: May–Sept 10am–12.30pm & 1.30–5pm; Oct–April 1.30–5pm; 10kr July & Aug, rest of the year free) inside the former Rådhus across Gammel Torv – a neat building with which Claus Stallknecht made amends for his botched job of the cathedral. There's a good selection of Skovgaard's paintings in the museum – although they're a little anticlimactic after his splendid work in the cathedral – plus some paintings by other members of his family.

Two minutes' walk away on Kirke Stræde, the late Romanesque **Søndre Sogn Kirke** (Mon–Fri 9am–1pm, Thurs also 3–5.30pm, Sat 9am–noon; free) is all that remains of the cloisters of the Dominican Black Friars, one of four monastic orders in Viborg abolished during the Reformation; get the key from the building just to the right, and note that the opening times given above are not always adhered to. Inside the church, the sixteenth-century Belgian altarpiece is the star turn, with 89 gilded oak figures in high relief around the central Crucifixion scene. If you express sufficient interest, you may be permitted to scramble down into the crypt, which, though now a dusty shell, was once unhygienically used for both burials and food storage.

For a broader perspective of Viborg's past, keep an hour spare for exploring the **District Museum** (Stiftsmuseum; June–Aug daily 11am–5pm; Sept–May Tues–Fri 2–5pm, Sat & Sun 11am–5pm; 15kr), on the northern side of Hjultorvet between Vestergade and Skt Mathias Gade. The museum's three well-stocked floors hold everything from prehistoric and archeological artefacts to clothes, furniture and household appliances.

Practicalities

Trains and long-distance buses arrive on Viborg's western side, roughly 1km from the centre. The **tourist office** is close to the cathedral on Nytorv (mid-May to mid-June Mon–Fri 9am–5pm, Sat & Sun 9.30am–12.30pm; mid-June to Aug Mon–Fri 9am–5pm, Sat & Sun 9am–3pm; Sept to mid-May Mon–Fri 9am–4pm, Sat 9.30am–12.30pm; ☎86 61 16 66). All Viborg's **hotels** are fairly pricey, such as the handsome *Palads Hotel*, Skt Mathias Gade 5 (☎86 62 37 00, fax 86 62 40 46; ⑤); if a lake view appeals, try the even more expensive *Golf Hotel Viborg*, Randersvej 2 (☎86 61 02 22, fax 86 61 31 71, *golfvib@pip.dknet.dk*; ⑥). Close to the same lake, but on the opposite side to the town (a 2km walk or local bus #707), are the **youth hostel** (☎86 67 17 81), with some doubles (①), and a **campsite** (☎86 67 13 11). Contact the tourist office about the possibility of arranging a private room (about 130kr per person).

During the day, you could do worse than pick up some *smørrebrød* (the best outlet is at Jernbanegade 14) and **eat** alfresco in one of the numerous parks or on the banks of the lake. Plenty of reasonably priced eating places can also be found along Skt Mathias Gade; one is the popular *Messing Jens* (closed Sun), with 89kr three-course dinners. A little further out, *Medborgerhuset*, Vesterbrogade 13, serves a 32kr *dagens ret* (daily special) from noon to 8pm on weekdays (Fri until 5pm), as well as cheap coffee and cakes. The cellar restaurant *Brygger Bauers Grotter*, Skt Mathias Gade 61 (☎86 61 45 99), is by far the top spot in town for a candlelit dinner, although you'll find lower prices and a livelier atmosphere at the Mexican restaurant *Tortilla Flats* (closed Mon). For French cuisine, try the small and expensive *Arthur* (☎86 62 21 26), with meals from around 130kr and up.

Around Viborg

The area around Viborg is excellent for cycling, with plenty of pleasant spots within easy reach; there's also a decent local bus service. Leaving Viborg and heading south on Koldingvej brings you to **Hald Ege**, a beautiful area of soft hills and meadows on the shores of Hald Sø. For all its peace, though, the district's history is a violent one. This is where Niels Bugge led a rebellion of Jutland squires against the king in 1351, and where the Catholic bishop, Jorgen Friis, was besieged by Viborgers at the time of the Reformation. Much of the action took place around the manor houses, or *halds*, that stood here, the sites and ruins of which can be reached by following a **footpath** marked by yellow arrows. The path starts close to **Hald Laden**, a restored barn by the side of the road, where an exhibition (June–Aug daily noon–6pm; Sept–May Sat & Sun noon–5pm; free) details the history and geology of the area, and the battle against the pollution that is killing Hald Sø.

About 10km south from Viborg lies the hilly lakeside area of **Dollerup Bakker**, where from June to August rowing boats are available for rent. Just to the south of here, a road leads from the village of Dollerup to **LYSGÅRD** and **E. Bindstouw** (mid-April to mid-Sept Tues–Sun 9am–5pm; 10kr), the old school house where **Steen Steensen Blicher** recorded his famous stories. Blicher would sit here in the evenings while poor locals wove socks beside the stove and told folk tales, which Blicher noted down for posterity. The small building still contains the fixtures and fittings of Blicher's time, including his writing board, stove, and even a few socks. To get here from Viborg, take the #712 bus.

West of Viborg

About 9km west of Viborg, beside the A16 between Mønsted and Raunstrup, the **Jutland Stone** marks the precise geographical centre of Jutland. There's not much to see, just a big inscribed rock and lots of cigarette ends. A few kilometres further, and markedly more interesting, are the **Mønsted Limestone Mines** (mid-May to late Oct daily 11am–5pm, but closed Oct 1–15; 30kr), which wind underground for 35km. The mines stay at a constant temperature, regardless of external weather, and wandering around their cool, damp innards can be magically atmospheric, although a century ago conditions for the workers here were so horrific that when Frederik IV visited the place he was sufficiently appalled to bring about reforms – the mines were subsequently known as "Frederik's Quarries" or, more venomously, "The King's Graves". The caves close in winter, when they're taken over by an enormous colony of hibernating bats. Bus #916 from Viborg runs here.

A few kilometres further west near Daugbjerg is another set of **limestone mines** (times and price as at Mønsted), unlit and narrower than the Mønsted mines – visitors

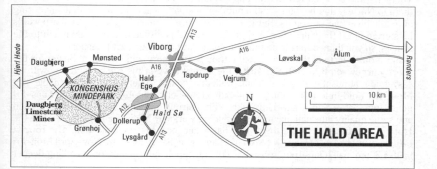

THE HALD AREA

are accompanied by a guide who carries an oil lamp. The entrance to the mines was found by chance fifty years ago and no one has yet charted the full extent of the passages; it's said that work began here at the time of Gorm, the tenth-century King of Jutland, and that the tunnels were used as hideouts by bandits.

A few kilometres south of Daugbjerg is **Kongenshus Mindepark** (early May to mid-Sept daily 10am–6pm; free, 10kr for cars) – three thousand acres of protected moorland on which there have been attempts at agriculture since the mid-eighteenth century, when an officer from Mecklenburg began keeping sheep here. For his troubles, the would-be shepherd received a grant from the king, Frederik V, and built the house that gives the park its name: Kongenshus (King's House). A few years later, a thousand or so German migrants (the so-called "potato Germans") also tried to cultivate the area, but to little avail. In the centre of the park is a memorial to the early pioneers; standing here, as the wind howls in your ears and you look around the stark and inhospitable heath, you can only marvel at their determination. If you're not put off, there are several **campsites** around Kongenshus: *Hessellund-Sø* (☎97 10 16 04; April–Sept), to the south near Karup, and *Haderup* (☎97 45 21 88; April–Sept), off Jens Jensenvej to the west, are just two.

Further west beyond Daugbjerg is one of the most successful of Denmark's heritage tourism projects, the **Hjerl Hedes Frilandsmuseum** (April–Oct daily 9am–5pm; 50kr). This open-air museum attempts to re-create the development of a local village from the years 1500 to 1900, with examples of a forge, an inn, a school, mills, a vicarage, a dairy, a grocer's shop and farms, all relocated here from their original sites around Jutland. By far the best time to come is during summer (mid-June to mid-Aug), when the place is brought to life by a hundred or so men, women and children dressed in traditional costumes, who provide demonstrations of the old crafts and farming methods. To get here from Viborg, take the train to Vinderup (5–10 daily; 30min), from where it's a five-kilometre walk or taxi ride.

Northwest Jutland: Limfjordslandet and around

Limfjordslandet is the name given to the area around the western portion of the **Limfjorden**, the body of water that separates northern Jutland from the rest of the peninsula. In the northwestern half, both the North Sea coast and the coast of the Limfjorden itself – which here resembles a large inland lake – attract legions of holidaying northern Europeans during the summer months, at which time it's best to arrange accommodation in advance. At other times this is a rarely visited quarter of the country. There are fine beaches and plenty of opportunities to mess about in boats – and to catch them to Norway and beyond – and a number of small, neat old towns with a smattering of mildly diverting museums. But the weather here is unpredictable, with sharp winds blustering in off the North Sea, and getting around is difficult: trains only reach to the fringes, so you'll need to rely on buses if you're without your own transport.

For a quick taste of the area, take the train from Viborg and change at Struer for the short journey south to **HOLSTEBRO**, the largest town in the region, and one with an easy-going atmosphere and a small, walkable centre. There's a commendable **Art Museum** (mid-June to mid-Aug Tues–Sun 11am–5pm; mid-Aug to mid-June Tues–Fri noon–4pm, Sat & Sun 11am–5pm; 20kr) with a strong contemporary Danish collection and some quality international pieces, including works by Matisse and Picasso, while the **Holstebro Museum** in the town park has a fair local history collection. The **tourist office** at Brostræde 2 (May–Oct Mon–Fri 9am–5pm, Sat 10am–1pm; Nov–April Mon–Fri 9am–4.30pm, Sat 10am–1pm; ☎97 42 57 00) can supply information on travelling deeper into Limfjordslandet. For **staying overnight**, there's a campsite equipped with cabins at Birkevej 25 (☎97 42 20 68; April to mid-Oct). The cheapest hotel in town by far is the *Borgbjerg Mølle Kro*, Borgbjerg Møllevej 3 (☎97 46 10 10, fax 97 46 16 46; ③).

Also reachable from Struer, **Thisted**, at the end of the local rail line, has access to good beaches and a youth hostel (☎97 92 50 42; doubles ①) and campsite, in Skinnerup, but little else of interest beyond its link (by bus #40) to **Hanstholm**, from where ferries leave for Kristiansand and Egersund in Norway.

Northeast Jutland

Much easier to get to and travel around than Limfjordslandet, **northeastern Jutland** is nonetheless another portion of Denmark often ignored by foreigners. It's a shame, as the region has a highly convivial major city in **Aalborg**, as well as ferries to Sweden and Norway. What's more, once you cross the Limfjorden, it boasts a landscape wilder than anywhere else on the peninsula: lush green pastures giving way to strangely compelling views of bleak moorland and windswept dunes.

Aalborg

The main city of north Jutland and the fourth largest in Denmark, **AALBORG**, hugging the south bank of the Limfjorden, is the obvious place to spend a night or two before venturing into the wilder countryside further on. It's the main transport terminus for the region, and boasts a notable modern art museum, a well-preserved old section, and the brightest (indeed only) nightlife for miles around.

The profits from the seventeenth-century herring boom made Aalborg the biggest and wealthiest Danish town outside Copenhagen, and much of what remains of **old Aalborg** – chiefly the area within Østerågade (commonly abbreviated to Østerå), Bispensgade, Gravensgade and Algade – dates from that era, standing in stark contrast to the new roads that slice through it to accommodate the traffic using the Limfjorden bridge.

Information and accommodation

The **tourist office** is centrally placed at Østerågade 8 (mid-June to mid-Aug Mon–Fri 9am–6pm, Sat 10am–5pm; mid-Aug to mid-June Mon–Fri 9am–4.30pm, Sat 10am–1pm; ☎98 12 60 22). If you want **to stay** in Aalborg, be aware that bargain-priced hotels are hard to find. The three cheapest are the plain-looking *Aalborg Sømandshjem*, Østerbro 27 (☎98 12 19 00, fax 98 11 76 97; ④), just 600m east of the city centre (bus #1, #3, #5, #7 or #9), the *Prinsens*, Prinsensgade 14 (☎98 12 31 33, fax 98 16 52 82; ④), and the *Hotel Krogen*, Skibstedvej 4 (☎98 12 17 05, fax 98 12 86 56; ④), some 2km west of the city centre. If these are too costly, make for the large **youth hostel** (☎98 11 60 44; closed mid-Dec to mid-Jan) to the west of the town on the Limfjorden bank beside the marina, which also has rustic cabins sleeping up to five (295–450kr) – take bus #8 from the centre to the end of its route. The same bus takes you to the **campsite**, *Strandparken* (☎98 12 76 29; mid-May to Sept), about 300m from the youth hostel.

Some years ago, it was officially decreed that the Danish double "Aa" would be written as Å. The mayor of Aalborg, and many locals, resisted this change and eventually forced a return to the previous spelling of their city's name – though you may still see some maps and a few road signs using the "Å" form.

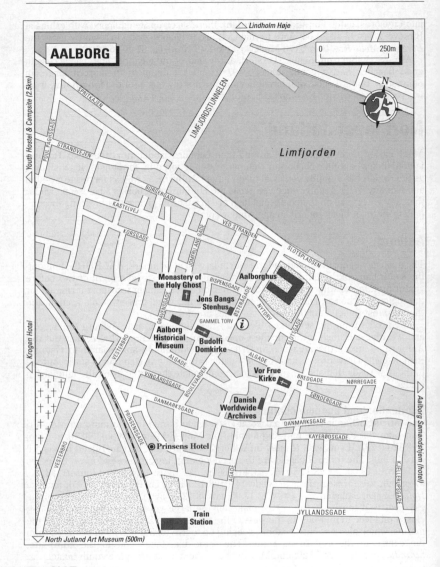

The Old Town

The tourist office is as good a place as any to start exploring, with one of the town's major seventeenth-century structures standing directly opposite. The **Jens Bangs Stenhus** is a grandiose five storeys in Dutch Renaissance style and, incredibly, has functioned as a pharmacy ever since it was built. Jens Bang himself was Aalborg's wealthiest merchant but was not popular with the governing elite, who conspired to keep him off the local council. The host of goblin-like figures carved on the walls allegedly represent the councillors of the time, while another figure, said to be Bang himself, pokes out his tongue towards the former Rådhus, next door.

The commercial roots of the city are further evidenced by portraits of the town's merchants (rather than the more customary portraits of nobles) inside **Budolfi Domkirke** (May–Sept Mon–Fri 9am–4pm, Sat 9am–2pm; Oct–April Mon–Fri 9am–3pm, Sat 9am–noon), easily located by its bulbous spire, just a few steps behind the Jens Bangs Stenhus. The cathedral, a small but elegant specimen of sixteenth-century Gothic, is built on the site of an eleventh-century wooden church, only a few tombs from which remain, embedded in the walls close to the altar. Apart from these, there's little to see inside the cathedral, but plenty to hear when the electronically driven bells ring out each hour – sending a cacophonous racket across the old square of **Gammel Torv**, on which the cathedral stands.

After viewing the cathedral, drop into the **Aalborg Historical Museum**, across the square at Algade 42 (Tues–Sun 10am–5pm; 10kr). The first exhibit here is a dramatic one: the peat-preserved skeleton of a forty-year-old woman who died around 400 AD. In comparison, the rest of the prehistoric section is fairly routine; make instead for the local collections, which provide a good record of Aalborg's early prosperity. The museum also has an impressive glassworks collection illustrating different designs from various Danish glass-working centres – look out for the armadillo-shaped bottle.

Just off Gammel Torv is the fifteenth-century **Monastery of the Holy Ghost** (Helligåndsklostret). Much of the building now serves as a senior citizens' home, and the remainder of the monastery can be seen only on one of the guided tours which run during summer (check details at the tourist office). These take in the monks' refectory, largely unchanged since the monks were thrown out in 1536, and the small Friar's Room, the only part of the monastery into which nuns (from the adjoining nunnery) were permitted entry. Indeed, this was one of the few monasteries where monks and nuns were allowed any contact at all, a fact which accounts for the reported hauntings of the Friar's Room – reputedly by the ghost of a nun who got too friendly with a monk, and as punishment was buried alive in a basement column (the monk was beheaded). Most interesting, however, are the **frescoes** of various biblical characters – dramatically posed images of Jesus, Samson, Mary and St John the Baptist amongst others – that cover the entire ceiling of the chapel. In more recent times, the corridor outside the chapel was used for shooting practice by the so-called "Churchill Gang", a group of local schoolboys who organized resistance to the Nazis.

The rest of old Aalborg lies to the east across Østerågade, and is a mainly residential area - with just a few exceptions. The sixteenth-century **Aalborghus** (castle Mon–Fri 8am–3pm; grounds 8am–sunset; free) is technically a castle but looks much more like a country manor house, and has always had an administrative rather than a military function. Aside from the free theatrical productions staged here in summer, the castle is only worth visiting for the severely gloomy **dungeon**, to the right from the gateway, and the underground passageways that run off it. From the castle, Slotsgade leads to the maze of narrow streets around **Vor Frue Kirke**, a dull church but surrounded by some meticulously preserved houses, many of which have been turned into upmarket craft shops. The best are along the oddly L-shaped Hjelmerstald: notice no. 2, whose ungainly bulge around its midriff has earned it the nickname "the pregnant house".

If you're of Danish descent, or particularly interested in Danish social history, visit the **Danish Worldwide Archives**, nearby at Arkivstræde 1 (Mon–Thurs 9am–4pm, Fri 9am–2pm, Mon May–Sept until 8pm). The story of Danish migration overseas is recorded here through immense stacks of files and books; given enough background facts, details of individual migrants can be traced.

Outside the old centre

The old centre sets the pleasant tone of the city, but just outside it are a couple of other notable targets. One is the **North Jutland Art Museum** (July & Aug daily 10am–5pm; Sept–June Tues–Sun 10am–5pm; 30kr, free on Tues), south from the centre on Kong Christians Allé, close to the junction with Vesterbro (bus #14 or a 15min walk from the centre). Housed in a building designed by the Finnish architect Alvar Aalto, this is one of the country's better modern art collections, strikingly contemporary in both form and content. Alongside numerous Danish contributions, it features works by Max Ernst, Andy Warhol, Le Corbusier and, imposingly stationed next to the entrance, Claes Oldenburg's wonderful *Fag-ends in a Colossal Ashtray*. After leaving the museum, you can get a grand, if pricey, view over the city and the Limfjorden by ascending the **Aalborg Tower** (July daily 10am–7pm; April–June, Aug & mid- to late Oct daily 11am–5pm; 20kr), on the hill just behind.

From the tower, you may be able to spot what looks like a set of large concrete bunkers on a hill to the southeast of the city. This is the **Gug Kirke** (Mon–Fri 9am–4pm), designed by Inger and Johannes Exner and opened in the early 1970s. It's one of the most unusual churches in the country: except for the iron crucifix and the wooden bell tower, the whole thing, including the font, pulpit and altar – decorated by a collage of newspapers – is made of concrete. The idea was to blend the church into the mostly high-rise parish it serves, and for it to function also as a community centre: the perfectly square interior can be turned into a theatre, while the crypt doubles as a café and youth club. It's unique enough to merit a closer look; take bus #5 from the city centre.

Eating, drinking and nightlife

In pursuit of **food, drink** and **nightlife** almost everybody heads for Jomfru Ane Gade, a small street close to the harbour between Bispensgade and Borgergade. Jomfru Ane (literally "young maiden Anne") was a noblewoman and reputed witch who, because of her social standing, was beheaded rather than burnt at the stake – though the street nowadays, at least by night, is more synonymous with getting legless than headless. Around midday, the restaurants crammed together here advertise their daily specials with signs: the most reliable are *Fyrtøjet*, at no. 19, and *Dirch på Regensen*, no. 16, both of which generally have three-course lunches for 75–90kr, or try *Fellini* at no. 23, serving good-value pizzas and pastas. On the weekend, make a beeline for the *Rendez-vous* at nos. 3–5, a bar with sandwiches, coffee and live music on Saturdays. Several other bars along this stretch also host live acts; just walk along, listen, and decide which appeals. For more downtown dining choices, try *Provence*, Ved Stranden 11 (☎98 13 51 33), a cosy French place near the Limfjorden with small, tightly packed tables, or *Jensens Bøfhus*, C.W. Obels Plads 3, with the usual steaks in a half-timbered merchants' house dating from 1585.

The better-known Danish **rock music** acts appear at *Skråen*, Strandvejen 19 (☎98 12 21 89), which also holds a café and multiscreen **cinema**. For less mainstream rock music, make for *Café Tusindfryd* at Kattesundet 10 (☎98 13 22 21). The *Duus* wine bar, in the cellar of the Jens Bangs Stenhus (☎98 12 50 56; closed Sun), is the place for a quiet evening drink.

Around Aalborg: Lindholm Høje and Rebild Bakker

A few kilometres north from Aalborg across the Limfjorden, **Lindholm Høje** (Easter–Oct daily 10am–5pm; Nov–Easter Tues–Sun 10am–4pm; 20kr) was a major Viking and Iron Age burial ground, and is a captivating place, especially at dawn or dusk. There are a number of very rare Viking "ship monuments" here – burial places with stones arranged in the outline of a ship – as well as more than six hundred Iron Age cremation graves. From Aalborg you can get to the site by bus #4 or #11 (every 30min for most of the day), or walk there in under an hour: go over the Limfjorden bridge, along Vesterbrogade into Thistedvej, right into Viaduktvej, and straight on until Vikingvej appears to the left.

About 30km south of Aalborg is **Rebild Bakker**, a heather-covered hill close to some scattered beech woods and the dense conifers of Rold Skov. The area is prime territory for hiking, and has been a **national park** since a group of expatriate Danes in America purchased the land and presented it to the Danish government. It's also the site of the largest American Independence Day celebration outside the USA every July 4, and is home to the somewhat tacky **Lincoln's Log Cabin** (mid-June to mid-Aug daily 11am–4pm; 15kr), a re-creation of Abraham Lincoln's log cabin filled with mundane articles from 49 American states and facts about Danish migration to the USA. The Americana doesn't intrude on the natural beauty of the area, however, and the park can provide a couple of relaxing days. To get there from Aalborg, take a train to Skørping or bus #104 to **Rebild**, where there's a **youth hostel** at Rebildvej 23 (☎98 39 13 40; March–Oct) with dorm beds and doubles (②); the adjacent **campsite** (☎98 39 11 10) is open year-round.

Continue 20km south of Rebild Bakker via either the train or bus #53 from Aalborg and you'll reach the town of **HOBRO**, worth visiting for the 1000-year-old **Fyrkat** (April–Oct daily 10am–5pm; 35kr), a fortress said to have been built by the Viking king, Harald Bluetooth. Fyrkat is a good place to get an impression of life during the Viking era: houses and farms have been reconstructed, and in summer there are demonstrations of traditional Viking activities like bronze casting. Fyrkat is two kilometres' walk from the centre of Hobro, which has a **hostel** at Amerikavej 24 (☎98 52 18 47; closed mid-Dec to mid-Jan) with dorm beds and doubles (②).

Frederikshavn

FREDERIKSHAVN is neither pretty nor particularly interesting, and as a major ferry port it's usually full of Swedes and Norwegians taking advantage of Denmark's liberal drinking laws. There's really not much here of interest except the ferry docks and a small train station with regular services to Skagen, but the town is virtually unavoidable if you're heading north, being at the end of the rail route from Aalborg (if you've an international sailing to meet at Hirtshals, change trains at Hjørring). If you're not catching a boat, speed straight on to Skagen (see overleaf).

There are, however, a couple of things worth seeing. If you have half an hour, visit the **Krudttårnet** (April–Oct daily 10am–12.30pm & 1–5pm; 10kr), the squat, white tower near the train station, which has maps detailing the harbour's seventeenth-century fortifications (of which the tower was a part) and a collection of weaponry, uniforms and military paraphernalia from the seventeenth to the nineteenth centuries. With more time on your hands, take the twenty-minute ride on bus #1 or #2 to the end of the route at Møllehuset and walk on through Bangsboparken to the **Bangsbo-Museet** (April–Oct daily 10.30am–5pm; Nov–March Tues–Sun 10.30am–5pm; 25kr). Here, comprehensive displays chart the development of Frederikshavn from the 1600s, alongside a slightly grotesque, but very engrossing, collection of pictures, bracelets, rings and necklaces – all made of human hair. The museum's outbuildings store an assortment of maritime articles, distinguished only by the twelfth-century *Ellingåskibet*, a ship found north of Frederikshavn, plus a worthwhile exhibition covering the German occupation during World War II and the rise of the Danish resistance movement.

Practicalities

Buses and **trains** both terminate at the train station; crossing Skippergade and walking along Denmarksgade brings you to the town centre in a few minutes. Arriving **ferries** dock near Havnepladsen, also near the centre, and close to the **tourist office** at Brotorvet 1, on the corner of Rådhus Allé and Havnepladsen (April, May & Sept–Dec

Mon–Fri 9am–4pm, Sat 11am–2pm; June–Aug Mon–Sat 8.30am–7pm, Sun 11am–7pm; ☎98 42 32 66). If you're forced to stay, the best-value **hotels** are the *Mariehønen*, Skolegade 2 (☎98 42 01 22, fax 98 43 40 99; ③); the *Sømandshjemmet* at Tordenskjoldsgade 15b (☎98 42 09 77, fax 98 43 18 99, *info@fshotel.dk*; ④); the *Aktivitel*, Knivholtvej 22 (☎98 43 23 77, fax 98 43 89 99; ④); and the central *Hotel 1987*, Havnegade 8E (☎98 43 19 87, fax 98 43 19 42; ④). There's also a **youth hostel** at Buhlsvej 6 (☎98 42 14 75; doubles ①), 1500m from the train station (turn right), and a **campsite** with cabins, *Nordstrand*, at Apholmenvej 40 (☎98 42 93 50; April to mid-Sept), 3km north of the town centre, just off Skagensvej.

Skagen

Forty kilometres north of Frederikshavn, **SKAGEN** perches at the very top of Jutland amid a desolate landscape of heather-topped sand dunes, its houses painted a distinctive bright yellow. It can be reached by bus or privately operated train (Eurail and InterRail not valid), both of which leave from Frederikshavn train station roughly once an hour – the bus is the best choice if you're planning to stay at the Skagen youth hostel.

The Town

Sunlight seems to gain extra brightness as it bounces off the two seas that collide off Skagen's coast, something that attracted the **Skagen artists** in the late nineteenth century. Painters Michael Ancher and Peder Severin (P.S.) Krøyer and writer Holger Drachmann arrived in the small fishing community during 1873 and 1874, and were later joined by Lauritz Tuxen, Carl Locher, Viggo Johansen, Christian Krogh and Oscar Björck. The painters often met in the bar of *Brøndum's Hotel*, off Brøndumsvej, and the owner's stepsister, Anna, herself a skilful painter, married Michael Ancher. The grounds of the hotel now house the impressive **Skagens Museum** (June–Aug daily 10am–6pm; May & Sept daily 10am–5pm; April & Oct Tues–Sun 11am–4pm; Nov–March Tues–Thurs 1–4pm, Fri 11am–4pm, Sat 11am–3pm; 30kr), the most comprehensive collection of these artists' work anywhere. The majority of the canvases depict local scenes, capturing subtleties of colour using the area's strong natural light. Many of the works, particularly those of Michael Ancher and Krøyer, are outstanding; but it's the work of Anna Ancher, though perhaps the least technically accomplished, which often come closest to achieving the naturalism these artists sought.

A few strides away at Markvej 2, the **Michael & Anna Anchers Hus** (mid-June to mid-Aug daily 10am–6pm; May to mid-June & mid-Aug to Sept daily 10am–5pm; April & Oct daily 11am–3pm; Nov–March Sat & Sun 11am–3pm; 30kr) has been restored with the intention of evoking the atmosphere of their time through an assortment of squeezed tubes of paint, sketches, paintings, piles of canvases, books and ornaments. Less essential is **Drachmanns Hus** (June to mid-Aug daily 10am–5pm; mid-Aug to mid-Sept daily 11am–3pm; May & mid-Sept to mid-Oct Sat & Sun 11am–3pm; 20kr), at Hans Baghsvej 21, on the junction with Skt Laurentii Vej, where Holger Drachmann lived from 1902. Inside the house is a large collection of Drachmann's paintings and sketchbooks, although it was for his lyrical poems – at the forefront of the early twentieth-century Danish Neo-Romantic movement – that he was best known. Such was Drachmann's cultural importance that, on his death, the major Danish newspaper, *Politiken*, devoted most of its front page to him; facsimiles are on display.

The arrival and subsequent success of these artists inadvertently made Skagen fashionable, and the town continues to be a popular holiday destination. But it still bears many marks of its past as a fishing community, a history that is well documented in the **Skagen Fortidsminder**, on P.K. Nielsenvej (May–Sept daily 10am–5pm; Oct–April Mon–Fri 10am–4pm; 30kr), a fifteen-minute walk south along Skt Laurentii Vej (or the much nicer Vesterbyvej) from the town centre. This museum – built on the tall dune where townswomen would watch for their husbands returning from sea during storms – examines local fishing techniques in its main displays, reinforced by photos showing millions of fish strewn along the quay before being auctioned. Among the auxiliary buildings are reconstructions of rich and poor fishermen's houses: the rich fisherman's house includes a macabre guestroom kept cool to facilitate the storage of bodies washed ashore from wrecks, while the poor man's dwelling makes plain the contrast in lifestyles: it possesses just two rooms to accommodate the fisherman, his wife, and fourteen children.

Around Skagen: the Buried Church and Grenen

Amid the dunes to the south of town, about twenty minutes' walk along Skt Laurentii Vej and Gammel Kirkestræde and onto a signposted footpath, is **Den Tilsandede Kirke**, or "the Buried Church" (June–Sept daily 11am–5pm; 8kr). The name is misleading since all that's here is the tower of a fourteenth-century church, built in what was then a minor agricultural area. From the beginning of the sixteenth century the church was assaulted by vicious sandstorms; by 1775 the congregation could only reach the church for services with the aid of shovels; and in 1810 the nave and most of the fittings were sold, leaving just the tower as a marker to shipping – while not especially tall, its white walls and red roof are easily visible from the sea. Still under the sands are the original church floor and cemetery. Although part of the tower is open to the public, the great fascination is simply looking at the thing from outside, and appreciating the incredible severity of the storms which covered it.

The forces of nature can be further appreciated at **Grenen**, 4km north of Skagen and served by the Sandormen tractor-drawn bus (April–Oct) from the big parking space, though it's nicer to walk the half kilometre there instead, down Skt Laurentii Vej and then straight ahead along the beach. This is the actual meeting point of two seas – the Kattegat and Skagerrak – and the spectacle of their clashing waves (the seas flow in opposing directions) is a powerful draw, although only truly dramatic when the winds are strong. On the way back, spare a thought for Holger Drachmann (see opposite), a man so enchanted by the thrashing seas that he chose to be buried in a dune close to them. His tomb is signposted from the car park.

Practicalities

Skagen's **train station** is on Skt Laurentii Vej, a short walk from the **tourist office** at Skt Laurentii Vej 18 (mid-June & July Mon–Sat 9am–7pm, Sun 10am–4pm; Aug Mon–Sat 9am–5pm, Sun 10am–2pm; May to mid-June & Sept Mon–Fri 9am–4pm, Sat & Sun 10am–2pm; Oct–April Mon 9am–5pm, Tues–Thurs 9am–4pm, Fri 9am–3pm, Sat 10am–1pm; ☎98 44 13 77). **Staying overnight** in Skagen is infinitely preferable to going back to Frederikshavn, and there are a number of options. For its artistic associations, *Brøndum's Hotel*, Anchervej 3 (☎98 44 15 55, fax 98 45 15 20; ⑤), is by far the most atmospheric spot; the fact that few of the rooms have bathrooms and all are far from luxurious keeps the price of doubles down – but book well ahead in summer. A little cheaper is *Skagen Sømandshjem*, Østre Strandvej 2 (☎98 44 25 88, fax 98 44 30 28; ④). Alternatively, there's the small *Finns Hotel Pension*, Østre Strandvej 63 (☎98 45 01 55; ⑤); the equally pleasant *Clausens Hotel*, Skt Laurentii Vej 35 (☎98 45 01 66, fax 98 44 46 33; ④); and *Badepension Marienlund*, a simpler, beach hotel with all shared facilities right by the water in Old Skagen at Fabriciusvej 8 (☎98 44 13 20; ③). The very good **youth hostel** is at Rolighedsvej 2 (☎98 44 22 00; doubles ②; closed Dec to mid-Feb), a couple of minutes west of the town centre. Of a number of **campsites**, the most accessible are *Grenen* (☎98 44 25 46; May–Aug), which has cabins, to the north along Fyrvej, and *Poul Eeg* (☎98 44 14 70; May–Aug), on Batterivej, left off Frederikshavnvej just before the town centre.

There are plenty of **eating** options in Skagen, though most of them are expensive. For Italian food, try *Italia* or *Alfredo*, both in Havnegade and serving reasonably priced pizza and pasta dishes.

travel details

Trains

Aalborg to: Frederikshavn (20 daily; 1hr 10min).

Århus to: Aalborg (32 daily; 1hr 30min); Copenhagen (29 daily; 3hr 15min); Frederikshavn (19 daily; 2hr 40min); Grenå (8–13 daily; 1hr 30min); Randers (32 daily; 35min); Silkeborg (25 daily; 45min); Viborg (22 daily; 1hr 15min).

Esbjerg to: Århus (21 daily; 2hr 15min); Copenhagen (25 daily; 3hr 15min); Fredericia (25 daily; 1hr 5min); Ribe (25 daily; 35min).

Fredericia to: Århus (38 daily; 1hr 10min); Sønderborg (10 daily; 2hr); Vejle (50 daily; 20min).

Frederikshavn to: Skagen (19 daily; 50min).

Ribe to: Tønder (14 daily; 50min).

Skanderborg to: Århus (53 daily; 15min); Silkeborg (24 daily; 30min).

Sønderborg to: Fredericia (11 daily; 2hr).

Struer to: Holstebro (37 daily; 15min); Thisted (12 daily; 1hr 20min); Vejle (20 daily; 2hr); Viborg (21 daily; 45min).

Tønder to: Ribe (14 daily; 50min).

Vejle to: Silkeborg (33 daily; 1hr 30min).

Viborg to: Struer (21 daily; 45min).

Buses

Århus to: Copenhagen (4–7 daily; 4hr); Ebeltoft (15 daily; 2hr 25min).

Frederikshavn to: Skagen (11 daily; 1hr).

Randers to: Ebeltoft (12 daily; 1hr 15min); Grenå (12 daily; 1hr 15min); Viborg (19 daily; 1hr 15min).

Skærbæk to: Havneby (6–8 daily; 25min).

Sønderborg to: Fynshav (7–8 daily; 30min).

Thisted to: Aalborg (14 daily; 2hr 30min); Hanstholm (14 daily; 45min).

Ferries

Århus to: Kalundborg (ferry: 5 daily; 3hr 10min; hydrofoil: 10 daily; 1hr 30min).

Ebeltoft to: Odden (ferry: 10–15 daily, 1hr; hydrofoil: 5 daily, 45min).

Fynshav to: Bøjden (8 daily; 50min).

Grenå to: Anholt (2 daily; 2hr 45min).

Mommark to: Søby (2–4 daily in summer; 1hr).

International trains

Fredericia to: Flensburg (6 daily; 1hr 50min).

International ferries

Esbjerg to: Harwich (4–5 weekly in summer; 19hr 30min).

Frederikshavn to: Gothenburg (7–11 daily; 3hr 15min); Larvik (1 daily; 6hr); Moss (1 daily; 7hr); Oslo (1–2 daily; 10–14hr).

Grenå to: Halmstad (1–3 daily in summer; 4hr); Varberg (1 daily in summer only; 4hr).

Hanstholm to: Egersund (4–7 weekly; 6hr 30min).

Havneby to: List (June–Oct 4–8 daily; 55min).

Hirtshals to: Oslo (1 daily in summer; 8–12hr).

PART THREE

NORWAY

Introduction

In many ways **Norway** is still a land of unknowns. Quiet for a thousand years since the Vikings stamped their distinctive mark on Europe, the country nowadays often seems more than just geographically distant. Beyond Oslo and the famous fjords, the rest of the country might as well be blank for all many visitors know – and, in a manner of speaking, large parts of it are. Vast stretches in the north and east are sparsely populated and starkly vegetated, and it is, at times, possible to travel for hours without seeing a soul.

Despite this isolation, Norway has had a pervasive influence on the world outside. Traditionally its inhabitants were explorers, from the Vikings – the first Europeans to reach Greenland and North America – to more recent figures like Amundsen, Nansen and Heyerdahl. And Norse traditions are common to many other isolated fishing communities, not least northwest Scotland and the Shetlands. At home, too, the Norwegian people have striven to escape the charge of national provincialism, touting the disproportionate number of acclaimed artists, writers and musicians (most notably Munch, Ibsen and Grieg) who have made their mark on the wider European scene. It's also a pleasing discovery that the great outdoors – great though it is – harbours some lively historical towns.

■ Where to go

Beyond **Oslo**, one of the world's most prettily sited capitals, the major cities of interest – in roughly descending order – are medieval **Trondheim** **Bergen** in the heart of the fjords, hilly, southern **Stavanger** and northern **Tromsø**. All are likeable cities, worth spending time in both for themselves and for the startlingly handsome countryside in which they're set. The perennial draw, though, is the **western fjords** – a must, and every bit as scenically stunning as they're cracked up to be. Dip into the region from Bergen or Åndalsnes, both accessible direct by train from Oslo, or take more time and appreciate the subtleties of the innumerable waterside towns and villages. The **south** of Norway, and in particular the long southern coast, is popular with holidaying Norwegians, with its beaches and whitewashed wooden towns; the central, more remote regions are ideal for hiking and camping.

To the north, Norway grows increasingly barren. The vast lands of **Troms** and **Finnmark** boast wild and untamed tracts of breathtaking proportions. Here you'll find the Sami people and their herds of reindeer, which you'll see on the thin, exposed road up to the North Cape, or **Nordkapp** – the northernmost point of mainland Europe. The Cape is the natural end to the long trek north, although there are still several hundred kilometres to be explored further east, right the way to Kirkenes and the Russian border.

■ When to go

Norway is still regarded as a remote, cold country – spectacular enough but climatically inhospitable. **When to go**, however, is not as clear cut a choice as you'd imagine. There are advantages to travelling during the long, dark **winters** with their reduced everything: daylight, opening times and transport services. If you are equipped and hardy enough to reach the far north, seeing the phenomenal **Northern Lights** (aurora borealis) is a distinct possibility; later, once the days begin to get lighter, **skiing** is excellent; while **Easter** is the time of the colourful Sami festivals. But – especially in the north – it is cold, often bitterly so, and this guide has been deliberately weighted towards the **summer** season, when most people travel and when it is possible to camp and hitch to keep costs down. This is the time of the **Midnight Sun**: the further north you go, the longer the day becomes, until at Nordkapp the sun is continually visible from mid-May to the end of July. The box below lists the dates between which the Midnight Sun is visible in different parts of the north. Something worth noting is that the **summer season** in Norway is relatively short, stretching roughly from the beginning of June to mid-August. Come much later than 16–20 August and you'll find that tourist offices, museums and other sights cut back their hours, while buses, ferries and trains often switch to reduced schedules.

THE MIDNIGHT SUN

(whole sun above the horizon)
Alta: May 16–July 26
Bodø: May 30–July 12
Hammerfest: May 13–July 29
Nordkapp: May 11–July 31
Tromsø: May 18–July 26

As regards **temperatures**, roughly speaking January and February are the coldest months, July and August the warmest; the Gulf Stream makes the north surprisingly temperate during summer.

Getting there from the rest of Scandinavia

There's no problem in reaching Norway from the rest of **Scandinavia**. There are very regular train services from Sweden, year-round ferry connections from Denmark and flights from both countries as well.

■ By train

By train you can reach **Oslo** from both Stockholm (1–3 daily; 6hr) and Copenhagen/Gothenburg (2–4 daily; 4hr/9hr 40min). There are also regular services from Stockholm to **Trondheim** (2 daily; 11hr) and **Narvik** (1 daily; 19hr). From Stockholm to either Oslo, Trondheim or Narvik fares are around 650kr one-way. Under-26s can buy discounted BIJ tickets on these routes, and InterRail, ScanRail and Eurail passes are valid – for train pass details see "Basics", pp.6, 15 and 19.

■ By ferry

Of the several **car ferry** services shuttling across the Skagerrak from **Denmark** to Norway, one of the most useful is DFDS Seaways' ferry from **Copenhagen** to Oslo (1 daily; 16hr). Alternatively, Stena Line links **Frederikshavn** with Oslo (1–2 daily; 8hr 30min) and Color Line ferries depart **Hirtshals** for Oslo (6 weekly; 8hr), Kristiansand (2–3 daily; 4hr 30min) and Moss (1–3 daily; 8hr). Details of sailings and costs can be had from any travel agent or local tourist office. Prices tend to rise sharply in summer, though this is partly offset by all sorts of special deals; rail-pass holders get discounts on some routes. There's also a Color Line ferry service to Norway **from Sweden**, linking Strömstad, north of Gothenburg, with Sandefjord (2–5 daily; 2hr 30min).

■ By plane

Norway has international airports at Oslo (Gardermoen), Sandefjord, Bergen, Stavanger, Kristiansand, Trondheim and Tromsø; most flights from elsewhere in Scandinavia are with SAS. For details of pan-Scandinavian air discounts and deals, see "Getting around" (p.166).

Costs, money and banks

Norway has a reputation as one of the most expensive of European holiday destinations, and in some ways (but only some) this is entirely justified. Most of what you're likely to need – from a cup of coffee to a roll of film – is costly, though on the other hand certain major items are reasonably priced, most notably **accommodation**, which compared with other north European countries can be remarkably inexpensive. Norway's first-rate youth hostels, almost all of which have family, double and dormitory rooms, are particularly good value. **Getting around** is good news too. Most travellers use some kind of rail pass, there are a fistful of discounts and internal deals, and the state subsidizes the more remote and longer bus hauls. Furthermore, **concessions** are almost universally available at attractions and on public transport, with infants (under 4) going everywhere free, children and seniors (over 67, sometimes 60) paying half the standard rate. **Food** is, however, a different matter. With few exceptions – such as tinned fish – it's expensive, while the cost of **alcohol** is enough to make even a heavy drinker contemplate abstinence.

On average, if you're prepared to buy your own picnic lunch, stay in youth hostels, and stick to the less expensive cafés and restaurants, you could get by on around £25/$40 a day excluding the cost of public transport. Staying in three-star hotels, eating out in medium-range restaurants most nights (but avoiding drinking in a bar), you'll get through at least £50/$80 a day – with the main variable being the cost of your room. As always, if you're travelling alone you'll spend much more on accommodation than you would in a group of two or more: most hotels do have single rooms, but they're usually around sixty to eighty percent of the price of a double.

■ Currency and exchange rates

Norwegian currency consists of **kroner**, one of which, a krone (literally "crown"; abbreviated **kr** or **NOK**), is divided into 100 **øre**. Coins in circulation are 50 øre, 1kr, 5kr and 10kr; notes are for 50kr, 100kr, 200kr, 500kr and 1000kr. You can bring in up to 25,000kr in notes and coins (there's no limit on traveller's cheques).

At the time of writing the **exchange rate** was around 12.4kr to the pound sterling; 7.8kr to the US dollar; 5.3kr to the Canadian dollar; 5.2kr to the Australian dollar; 4.2kr to the New Zealand dollar and 0.118 to the euro.

■ Changing money

All but the tiniest of settlements in Norway have a **bank** or **savings bank**, and the vast majority will change foreign currency and traveller's cheques. Banks will also handle Eurocheques, and many give cash advances on credit cards. **Banking hours** in Norway are usually Monday to Friday 8.15am–3pm, though they close thirty minutes earlier during the summer (June–Aug) and are open till 5pm on Thursday all year. All major **post offices** change foreign currency and traveller's cheques at rates that are competitive with those of the banks, and they have longer opening hours too, generally Monday to Friday 8am–5pm and Saturday 9am–1pm. Almost every bank and major post office charges a small commission for changing currency; if commission is waived, it probably means you're getting a poor exchange rate instead.

Outside banking and post office hours, most major hotels, many travel agents and some hostels and campsites will change money at less generous rates and with variable commissions, as will the **exchange kiosks** to be found in Oslo.

■ Tax-free shopping

Taking advantage of their decision not to join the EU, the Norwegians run a **tax-free shopping scheme** for tourists. If you spend more than 308kr at one of three thousand outlets in the tax-free shopping scheme you'll get a voucher for the amount of VAT you paid. On departure at an airport, ferry terminal or frontier crossing, present the goods, the voucher and your passport, and – provided you haven't used the item – you'll get an 11–18kr refund, depending on the price of the item. There isn't a reclaim point at every exit from the country, however – pick up a leaflet at any participating shop to find out where they are – and note that many of the smaller reclaim points keep normal shop hours, closing for the weekend at 2pm on Saturday.

Mail and telecommunications

Postal and telephone systems are both very efficient in Norway, and things are made even easier by the fact that any staff you'll need to deal with nearly all speak good English.

Post offices are plentiful, usual opening hours are Monday to Friday 8am/8.30am–4pm and Saturday 8am/9am–1pm. Some urban post offices open longer hours, especially the post office inside Oslo S station (Mon–Fri 7am–6pm, Sat 9am–3pm). **Postage** costs 5.5kr for either a postcard or a letter under 20g sent within Europe (3.80kr within Scandinavia), and 6kr to countries outside. Mail to the USA takes a week to ten days, two to three days within Europe.

Norway has a reliable **telephone** system, run by Telenor. You can make domestic and international telephone calls with ease from public phones, which are plentiful and almost invariably work – if you can't find one, some bars have payphones. All the more expensive hotel rooms have phones too, but note that they always attract an exorbitant surcharge.

USEFUL NUMBERS

International dialling code for Norway	☎0047
Directory enquiries (Scandinavia)	☎180
Directory enquiries (international)	☎181
Emergencies (fire)	☎110
Emergencies (Police)	☎112
Emergencies (Ambulance)	☎113
International Operator assistance (including collect and reverse-charge calls)	☎115
Domestic operator assistance (including collect and reverse-charge calls)	☎117

Public telephones are of the usual Western European kind, where you deposit the money before you make your call. They take 1kr, 5kr, 10kr and 20kr coins, though coin-operated public phones are gradually being phased out in favour of those that only take **telecards** (*TeleKort*) – these can be purchased at newsstands, post offices, major train stations and some supermarkets, and come in 35kr, 98kr and 210kr denominations. An increasing number of public phones also accept major credit cards. Phone booths have English instructions displayed inside.

Local telephone calls **cost** a minimum of 2kr, while 10kr is enough to start an international telephone call, but not much more. Discount rates on international calls (of around 15 percent) apply from 10pm to 8am. All Norwegian telephone numbers have eight digits and there's no area code.

You can pick up **email** either at one of the country's growing number of Internet cafés (all major cities have at least a couple) or at public libraries, most of which have facilities for getting online.

media

Most British and some American daily **newspapers**, plus the occasional periodical, are sold in most towns from Narvesen kiosks, large train stations and at airports. As for the **Norwegian media**, state advertising, loans and subsidized production costs keep a wealth of smaller papers going that would bite the dust elsewhere. Most are closely linked with political parties, although the bigger city-based papers tend to be indepen-dent. Highest circulations are claimed in Oslo by the independent *Verdens Gang* and the indepen-dent-conservative *Aftenposten*, and in Bergen by the liberal *Bergens Tidende*.

The **television** network has expanded over the last few years, in line with the rest of Europe. Alongside the state channels, NRK and TV2, there are satellite channels like TV Norge, while TV3 is a channel common to Norway, Denmark and Sweden; you can also pick up Swedish TV broadcasts – though pornographic programmes are jammed. Many of the programmes are English-language imports, so there is invariably something on that you'll understand, though much of it is pretty unadventurous stuff. The big global cable and satellite channels like MTV and CNN are commonly accessible in hotel rooms.

Local tourist **radio** giving details of events and festivals is broadcast during the summer months; watch for signposts by the roadside and tune in. Otherwise, English radio broadcasts, featuring news from Norway, are repeated several times daily on FM (93 MHz). The BBC World Service is broadcast to all mainland Scandinavia. Frequencies vary according to area and often change every few months. For the latest details write for the free *Programme Guide* to BBC World Service, Bush House, London WC2B 4PH (☎020/7240 3456).

Getting around

Norway's **public transport system** – a huge mesh of trains, buses, car ferries and passenger express ferries – is comprehensive and reliable. In the winter (especially in the north) services can be cut back severely, but no part of the country is unreachable for long. Bear in mind, however, that Norwegian villages and towns usually spread over a large distance, so don't be surprised if you end up walking a kilometre or two to get where you want to go. It's this sprawling nature of the country's towns and, more especially, the remoteness of many of the sights that encourages visitors to rent a **car**. This is a very expensive business, but costs are manageable if you hire locally for a day or two rather than for the whole trip.

Timetables for most of the principal air, train, bus and ferry services are detailed in the *NRI Guide to Transport and Accommodation*, a free and easy-to-use booklet available in your home country from the Norwegian Tourist Board (see p.27). In Norway itself, almost every tourist office carries a comprehensive range of free local and regional public transport timetables. In addition, all major train stations carry the *NSB Togruter*, a brochure detailing all Norway's train timetables, whilst long-distance bus routes operated by the national carrier, Nor-Way Bussekspress, are listed in the free *Rutehefte* (timetable), available at principal bus stations.

■ Trains

Train services are run by Norges Statsbaner (NSB) – Norwegian State Railways. Apart from a sprinkling of branch lines, they operate on four main routes, linking Oslo to Stavanger in the southwest, to Bergen in the west and to Trondheim and on to Bodø in the north. In places, the rail system is extended by a *TogBuss* (literally train-bus) service, with connecting coaches continuing on from the train terminal. The nature of the country has made most of the routes engineering feats of some magnitude and worth the trip in their own right – the tiny **Flåm line** and the sweeping **Rauma line** from Dombås to Åndalsnes are exciting examples.

Prices are bearable, the popular Oslo–Bergen run, for example, costing around 580kr one way, Oslo–Trondheim 670kr. Both journeys take around six and a half hours. Costs can be reduced by purchasing a **rail pass** in advance (see p.6); note that the Norway Rail Pass (see overleaf) can be purchased either before or after arrival in Norway. Inside Norway, NSB offers a variety of special **discount fares**. There are two main discount schemes. With **Minipris** (mini-price) tickets, you can cut up to fifty percent off the price of long-distance journeys. In general, the further you travel, the more economic they become – the Minipris ticket from Oslo to Bodø, for instance, costs 565kr, compared to a regular fare of 1060kr. The drawback is that they must be purchased at least one day in advance, are not available at peak periods and on certain trains, and stopovers are not permitted (the trains you *can* take are indicated with a green dot on timetables). Alternatively, NSB's **Customer Card** offers a fifty-percent reduction on the normal economy fare on these same "green" departures and a twenty-percent reduction on all other trains. The cards cost around 420kr, are valid for one year and are sold at all staffed railway stations. In addition, NSB offers a variety of special deals and discounts – inquire locally (and ahead of time) for details on any specific route.

In terms of **concessionary fares**, there are group and family reductions; children under 4 travel free provided they don't take up a seat, while under-16s pay half fare, as do senior citizens. It's worth noting that intercity trains and all overnight and international services require an advance **seat reservation** (25kr) whether you have a rail pass or not. In high season it's wise to make a seat reservation on main routes anyway as trains can be packed. **Sleepers** are reasonably priced if you consider you'll save a night's hotel accommodation: a bed in a three-berth cabin costs around 110kr, two-berth from 220kr and one-berth about 600kr.

NSB have two classes: **standard** and **economy** (the former is marketed abroad as "first class" on the reasonable assumption that the term "standard class" might be misunderstood). NSB **timetables** are available free at every train station. The general timetable, the *NSB Togruter*, is supplemented by individual timetables on each of the lines and, in the case of the more scenic routes, by leaflets describing the sights as you go.

For further advance advice about passes, discounts and tickets, either contact the specialist agents listed in "Getting there" (p.7, or NSB direct – see box, below.

see box, below.

NORWEGIAN STATE RAILWAYS AND NOR-WAY BUSSEKSPRESS CONTACTS

The **NSB** Web site is at *www.nsb.no*. Their national number for all enquiries is ☎81 50 08 88.

The **Nor-Way Bussekspress** Web site is *www.nor-way.no*. Their national number for all enquiries is ☎ 23 00 24 40.

Rail passes

Both the **InterRail** and **Eurail** passes (see p.6 and p.15) are valid for the Norwegian railway system, as is the **ScanRail** pass (see p.27). The other alternative is the **Norway Rail Pass**, which allows unlimited travel on the railways of Norway on a specified number of days within a specific period. Three days in one month costs about 1000kr, four days 1270kr, five days 1430kr. These passes can be bought from major train stations inside Norway and from agents abroad (see Basics, p.7). Children under 4 travel free, under-16s get a fifty percent discount and seniors (60+) twenty percent.

All rail pass holders have to shell out a small additional surcharge on certain trains on certain routes and also have to pay the compulsory 25kr seat reservation fee on most intercity trains and all overnight and international services. On the plus side, rail passes are good for travel on the TogBuss, while two of them (ScanRail and InterRail) give a fifty-percent discount on scores of inter-city bus and boat routes.

Buses

Where the train network won't take you, **buses** will – and at no great cost, either: a substantial fjord journey, like the Sogndal–Florø trip, costs 228kr, while the ten-hour bus ride between Ålesund and Bergen is a reasonable 470kr. All tolls and ferry costs are included in the price of a ticket, which can represent a significant saving. You'll need to use buses principally in the western fjords and the far north, though there are also lots of long-distance express buses between major towns. Most long-distance buses are operated by the national carrier, **Nor-Way Bussekspress**, Karl Johans gate 2, N–0154 Oslo (☎23 00 24 40, *ruteinformasjon@nor-way.no*, *www.nor-way. no*).Their services are supplemented by a dense network of local buses, whose timetables are available at most tourist offices and bus stations. In general, most longer-distance routes tend to operate once daily, usually leaving early in the morning, while shorter hauls, although more frequent, often tail off in the late afternoon. **Tickets** are usually bought on board, but travel agents sell advance tickets on the more popular long-distance routes; be sure to keep your ticket till the journey is completed.

In terms of **concessionary fares**, there are group and family reductions, children under three

years travel free provided they don't take up a seat, and youngsters under sixteen pay half fare, as do senior citizens over 67. Nor-Way Bussekspress offers InterRail and ScanRail pass holders a fifty percent reduction on certain bus services, and some local bus companies have comparable deals. Indeed, rail-pass and student-card holders should always ask about discounts when purchasing a ticket.

If you are going to travel much by bus, the Nor-Way Bussekspress **NOR-WAY BusPass** is excellent value. Valid on all their services, the pass offers a guarantee of a seat without advance booking (except for groups of more than eight) – the idea is that if one bus gets full, they will lay on another. It is not, however, valid on the majority of local bus services. There are seven-day (1375kr) and fourteen-day (2200kr) passes, and again any toll and ferry costs are covered. Infants under three travel free; a pass for a child (4–15) is at 75 percent of the adult rate. The pass can be purchased at any of the larger bus stations in Norway, and at the company's head office, Karl Johans gate 2, Oslo; you'll also be given a complimentary timetable detailing all Nor-Way Bussekspress services when you buy the pass.

■ Ferries

Using a **ferry** in Norway is one of the highlights of any visit – indeed among the western fjords and around the Lofotens they are all but impossible to avoid. The majority are roll-on, roll-off **car ferries**. These represent an economical means of transport, with prices fixed on a nationwide sliding scale: short journeys (10–15min) cost foot passengers 15–20kr, whereas the driver of a car will pay in the region of 80kr. Bus tickets include ferry costs where and whenever the bus crosses on a ferry. Ferry procedures are straightforward: foot passengers walk on and pay the conductor, car drivers usually wait in line with their vehicles on the jetty till the conductor comes to the car window to collect the money (although some busier routes have a drive-by ticket office). One or two of the longer car ferries – in particular Bodø–Moskenes – take advance reservations, but the rest operate on a first-come, first-served basis. In the off-season, there's no real need to arrive more than twenty minutes before departure – with the possible exception of the Lofoten Island ferries – but in the summer allow two hours, two and a half to be really safe.

Passenger express boats

Called either **Hurtigbåt** or simply **Ekspressbåt**, Norway's passenger express boats are catamarans which make up in speed what they lack in enjoyment – unlike on ordinary ferries, you're cooped up and view the passing landscape through a window, while in choppy seas the ride can be bumpy too. Nonetheless, they're a convenient time-saving option: it takes just four hours on the Hurtigbåt service from Bergen to Balestrand, for instance, the same from Narvik to Svolvær, and a mere two and a half hours from Harstad to Tromsø. Hurtigbåt services are concentrated on the west coast around Bergen and the neighbouring fjords; the majority operate all year. There's no fixed tariff table, so rates vary considerably, though Hurtigbåt boats are significantly more expensive per kilometre than car ferries – Bergen–Stavanger, for instance, costs 510kr for the four-hour Hurtigbåt journey. There are **concessionary fares** on all routes, with infants up to the age of three travelling free, and children (4–15) and senior citizens (over 67) getting a 50 percent discount. In addition, rail-pass holders and students are often eligible for a fifty percent reduction on the full adult rate.

The Hurtigrute

Norway's most celebrated ferry journey is the long and beautiful haul up the coast from Bergen to Kirkenes on the **Hurtigrute** (literally "rapid route") **coastal ship** – or "coastal steamer" (in honour of its past rather than present means of locomotion). To many, the Hurtigrute remains the quintessential Norwegian experience, and it's certainly the best way to observe the drama of this extraordinary coastline. Eleven ships combine to provide one daily service in either direction and the boat stops off at over thirty ports on the way.

The whole trip lasts eleven days. **Tickets**, which include all meals, go for anything from 8,000kr to 24,000kr depending on whether you're sailing on one of the old or new vessels, where your cabin is on the boat and when you sail – departures between October and March are around forty percent cheaper than those in the summer. There are also **concessionary fares** offering fifty percent discounts for senior citizens (over 67), families, groups of ten or more, students and children (4–15). Infants up to three years old travel free providing they do not occupy a separate berth. Note that these discounts are only valid for a limited number of cabins in the

summertime, which makes pre-booking pretty much essential. If you're over 16 and under 26 and travelling between September and April, another option is a **coastal pass**, which costs 1750kr for 21 days' unlimited travel on the Hurtigrute. Further details are available from, and bookings can be made with, most travel agencies back home. Making a Hurtigrute booking once you've got to Norway is easy too, though this does not apply to the coastal pass and other comparable deals. Contact either a travel agency or the shippers themselves: **OVDS** (☎76 96 76 96, fax 76 96 76 11) and **TFDS** (☎77 64 82 00, fax 77 64 82 40). Most travel agents and local tourist offices have copies of the sailing schedule and there's a Web site at *www.hurtigruten.com*.

A **short hop** along the coast on a section of the Hurtigrute is also well worth considering. Fares are not particularly cheap, especially by comparison with the bus, but they are affordable. The standard, high-season, one-way passenger fare from Kristiansund to Trondheim (7hr), for example, costs 452kr; and from Stamsund to Bodø (4hr 30min), 278kr. Last-minute bargains, however, can bring the rates right down to amazingly low levels. All the tourist offices in the Hurtigrute ports have the latest details and should be willing to telephone the captain of the nearest ship to make a reservation on your behalf.

As for specifics, although it's a cruise ship you don't need to have a cabin, as sleeping in the lounges or on deck is allowed. Bikes travel free. There's a 24-hour cafeteria supplying coffee and snacks and a first-rate restaurant on all Hurtigrute boats.

■ Planes

Internal flights can prove a surprisingly inexpensive way of hopping about the country and are especially useful if you're short on time and want to reach, say, the far north. Tromsø to Kirkenes takes the best part of two days by bus, but it's just an hour by plane. Domestic air routes are serviced by several companies, but the two big players are Braathens (now part of the KLM uk group) and SAS. Regular standard fares are around 1250kr one-way from Oslo to Bergen, 2420kr from Oslo to Tromsø, and 1610kr from Bergen to Trondheim. Both airlines also operate a variety of **discount** schemes, such as Braathens' special fare for under-25s, which knocks 50–75 percent off the full price. The same airline also has special **excursion fares** bookable no less than seven days prior to departure and including a Saturday night away: Trondheim to Tromsø in this scheme costs 1330kr return. Otherwise, check out Braathens' special offers, which often provide some great bargains. In terms of **concessionary fares**, both SAS and Braathens permit infants under 2 to travel free, while children under 16 travelling in a family group including at least one full-fare-paying adult and seniors all pay half-price. The details of these various discounts vary year to year, so it's always worth shopping around.

Both Braathens and SAS have excellent-value **air passes**. Braathens' "Northern Lights Pass" (not available to Scandinavian residents) is valid on all the company's routes from May to September, with short one-way flights within southern or northern Norway costing around 500kr, long one-way flights between south and north costing about 1000kr (the dividing line between north and south is drawn through Trondheim, which is counted as belonging to both zones). The pass can be bought either before you get to Norway or when you're there. Further details direct from Braathens either in Britain (see p.4) or Norway (☎67 58 60 00). The SAS "AirPass" can only be purchased before you arrive in Scandinavia and in conjunction with an SAS flight to the region (and is not available to residents of Scandinavia). It entitles holders to purchase up to six AirPass vouchers for internal flights within Scandinavia for each return flight to Scandinavia you buy. The vouchers are good for all SAS flights within the region and cost about £50 each (£290 for six); airport taxes are extra.

■ Driving

Norway's main roads are excellent, especially when you consider the vagaries of the climate, and now that most of the more hazardous sections have been ironed out or tunnelled through, driving is comparatively straightforward. That said, you still have to be careful on some of the higher sections and in the enormous tunnels. But once you leave the main roads for the narrow byroads that wind across the mountains, you'll be in for some nail-biting experiences – and that's in the summertime. In winter the Norwegians close many roads and concentrate their efforts on keeping the main highways open, but obviously blizzards and ice can make driving difficult to dangerous anywhere even with winter tyres, studs and chains. At any time of the year, the more adventurous the drive, the better equipped you need to be: on remote drives you should pack provisions, have proper hiking gear, check the car thoroughly before departure and carry a spare can of petrol.

Norway's main highways have an E prefix – E6, E18 etc; all the country's other significant roads (*riksvei*, or *rv*) are assigned a number and, as a general rule, the lower the number, the busier the road. In our guide, we've used the E prefix, but designated other roads as Highways, or "Hwy" (followed by the number). Don't be too amazed if the road number we've given is wrong – the Norwegians are forever changing the numbers. **Tolls** are imposed on certain roads to pay for construction projects such as bridges and tunnels. Once the costs are covered the toll is removed. The older building projects levy a fee of around

---

MAJOR MOUNTAIN PASSES OPENING DATES

Obviously enough, there's no preordained date for opening **mountain roads** in the springtime – it depends on the weather, and the threat of avalanches is often much more of a limitation than actual snow falls. The dates below should therefore be treated with caution; if in doubt, seek advice from a local tourist office. If you do head along a mountain road that's closed, you'll sooner or later come to a barrier and have to turn round.

E6: Dovrefjell (Oslo–Trondheim). Usually open all year.

E69: Skarsvåg–Nordkapp. Closed late Oct to early April.

E134: Haukelifjell (Oslo–Bergen/Stavanger). Usually open all year.

Hwy 7: Hardangervidda (Oslo–Bergen). Usually open all year.

Hwy 51: Valdresflya. Closed mid-Dec to early May.

Hwy 55: Sognefjellet. Closed early Dec to early May.

Hwy 63: Grotli–Geiranger–Åndalsnes (Trollstigen). Closed mid-Oct to late May.

20–30kr, but the toll for some of the newer works (like the tunnel near Fjaerland) runs to well over 100kr per vehicle. There's also a modest toll on entering the country's larger cities (between 5–15kr), but whether this is an environmental measure or a means of boosting city coffers is a moot point. To avoid getting flustered at a toll booth, Norwegians carry a supply of coins ready to hand.

Fuel is readily available, even in the north, though here the settlements are so widely separated that you'll need to keep your tank pretty full; if you're using the byroads extensively, remember to carry an extra can. Current fuel prices are around 8–10kr a litre and there are four main grades: unleaded (*blyfri*) 95 octane; unleaded 98 octane; super 98 octane; and diesel. It's worth remembering that many petrol stations don't accept credit cards, so make sure you have enough cash before filling up.

Documentation and rules of the road

EU **driving licences** are honoured in Norway, but other nationals will need an **International Driver's Licence** (available at minimum cost from your home motoring organization). No form of provisional licence is accepted. If you're bringing your own car, you must have vehicle registration papers, adequate insurance, a first-aid kit, a warning triangle and a green card (available from your insurers or motoring organization). Extra insurance coverage for unforeseen legal costs is also well worth having, as is an appropriate **breakdown policy** from a motoring organization. In Britain, for example, the RAC and AA charge members and non-members about £95 for a month's Europe-wide breakdown cover, with all the appropriate documentation, including green card, provided.

Rules of the road are strict: you drive on the right, with dipped headlights required at all times; seatbelts are compulsory for drivers and front-seat passengers (and for back-seat passengers too, if fitted). There's a speed limit of 30kph in residential areas, 50kph in built-up areas, 80kph on open roads and 90kph on motorways and some other main roads. Recently installed cameras monitor hundreds of kilometres of road – watch out for the *Automatisk Trafikk Kontroll* warning signs – they're far from popular and there are folkloric (and largely apocryphal) tales of men in masks returning at night with chain saws to chop them down. **Speeding fines** are so heavy that local drivers stick religiously within the speed limit. If you're filmed breaking the limit in a hire car, expect your credit card to be stung by the car hire company to the tune of at least 700kr. If you're stopped for speeding, large spot fines (700–3000kr) are payable; rarely is any leniency shown to unwitting foreigners. **Drunken driving** is also severely frowned upon. You can be asked to take a breath test on a routine traffic-check; if over the limit, you will have your licence confiscated and may face 28 days in prison.

If you **break down** in a hire car, you'll get roadside assistance from the particular repair company the car hire firm has contracted. The same principle works with your own vehicle's breakdown policy (see above). Two major **breakdown companies** in Norway are Norges Automobil-Forbund (NAF; 24hr assistance on ☎81 00 05 05) and Viking Redningstjeneste (24hr assistance on ☎80 03 29 00). There are emergency telephones along some motorways, and NAF patrols all mountain passes between mid-June and mic-August.

Car rental

All the major international **car rental** companies are represented in Norway – useful addresses are given in the "Listings" sections of larger cities. To rent a car, you'll need to be 21 or over (and have been driving for at least a year), and you'll need a credit card – though the occasional agency will accept a hefty cash deposit. Rental **charges** are fairly high, beginning at around 3600kr per week for unlimited mileage in the smallest vehicle, but include collision damage waiver and vehicle (but not personal) insurance. To cut costs, watch for the special deals offered by the bigger companies – a Friday to Monday weekend rental might, for example, cost you as little as 1000kr. If you go to a smaller, local company (of which there are many, listed in the telephone directory under *Bilutleie*), you should proceed with care. In particular, check the policy for the excess applied to claims and ensure that it includes collision damage waiver (applicable if an accident is your fault). Bear in mind, too, that it's almost always cheaper to rent a car before you leave home – see p.28.

■ Cycling

Cycling in Norway is a great way of taking in the scenery – just be sure to wrap up warm and dry, and don't be over-ambitious in the distances you expect to cover. Cycle tracks as such are few and far between, and are mainly confined to the larger towns, but there's precious little traffic on most of the minor roads and cycling along them is a popular pastime. Furthermore, whenever a road is improved or rerouted, the old highway is usually redesigned as a cycle route. At almost every place you're likely to stay in, you can anticipate that someone will **rent bikes** – either the tourist office, a sports shop, youth hostel or campsite. Costs are pretty uniform and you can reckon on paying between 120kr and 200kr a day for a seven-speed bike plus a refundable deposit of up to 1000kr; mountain bikes are about 30 percent more.

A few tourist offices have maps of recommended cycling routes, but this is a rarity. It is, however, important to check your itinerary thoroughly, especially in the more mountainous areas. Cyclists aren't allowed through the longer **tunnels** for their own protection (the fumes can be life-threatening), so discuss your plans with whoever you hire the bike from. Bikes mostly go free on car ferries and attract a nominal charge on passenger express boats, but buses vary. The national carrier, Nor-Way Bussekspress accept bikes only when there is space and charges the appropriate child fare, whilst local, rural buses sometimes take them free, sometimes charge and sometimes do not take them at all. There's a fee of 50–180kr to take bikes on local trains; on express trains you have to send your bike on ahead at least 24 hours before you yourself set off – the rates are the same.

If you're planning a **cycling holiday**, your first port of call should be the Norwegian Tourist Board (see p.27), who provide general cycling advice and issue a map showing roads and tunnels inaccessible to cyclists. They also have a list of companies offering all-inclusive **cycling tours**. Among several, Erik & Reidar, Kirkegata 34a, Oslo (☎22 41 23 80, fax 22 41 23 90, *erikogreidar@online.no*), run tours of the Hardanger plateau, the Lofotens and Geiranger; and Pedal Nor, Kløverveien 10, Sandnes (☎51 66 40 60, fax 51 66 48 70, *pedal@robin.no*), have a varied programme including fjord and Lofoten island tours. Obviously enough, tour costs vary enormously, but as a baseline reckon on about 5000kr per week all inclusive. The Syklistenes Landsforening, Storgata 20c, Oslo (☎22 41 50 80), the Norwegian Cyclist Association, have an excellent range of specific cycling books and maps. Finally,

www.bike-norway.com has ideas for a dozen routes around the country from 100 to 400km, plus useful practical information about road conditions, repair facilities and places of interest en route.

Accommodation

Inevitably, hotel accommodation is one of the major expenses of a trip to Norway – and if you're after a degree of comfort, it's going to be the costliest item by far. There are, however, budget alternatives, including private rooms, campsites and cabins, and an abundance of youth hostels.

■ Hotels

Almost universally, Norwegian **hotels** are of a high standard, neat, clean and efficient. Summer prices and impromptu weekend deals also make many of them, by European standards at least, comparatively economical. Another plus is that the price of a hotel room always includes a buffet breakfast – these can be sumptuous banquets, in mid- to top-range hotels especially. The only negatives are the sizes of rooms, which tend to be small – singles especially – and their sameness: Norway abounds in mundane concrete and glass skyrise hotels. In addition to the hotels we've detailed in the guide, all Norwegian hotels, their room rates, summer discounts and facilities, are listed in the free booklet *Transport og Overnatting*, available from the Norwegian tourist office.

Summer is the best time to use one of the several **hotel discount and pass schemes** which operate throughout Norway. There are five main ones to choose from; each serves to cut costs, though often at the expense of a flexible itinerary – advance booking is the norm. Most Norwegian hotels are members of one discount/pass scheme or another and you can usually join the scheme at

ACCOMMODATION PRICE CODES

The Norwegian hotels and guesthouses listed in the Guide have been graded according to the following price bands, based on the cost of the **least expensive double room during high season** (late June to Aug). However, almost every hotel offers seasonal and/or weekend discounts, and wherever possible we've given two grades, covering both the regular and the discounted rate.

① Under 500kr   ② 500–700kr   ③ 700–900kr   ④ 900–1200kr   ⑤ 1200–1500kr   ⑥ Over 1500kr

one of the hotels, or at a tourist office; it's also worth checking what's available with your travel agent before leaving home.

■ Pensions and guesthouses

For something a little more informal and less anonymous than the average hotel, **pensions** (*pensjonater*) are your best bet – small, intimate boarding houses which can usually be found in the larger cities and more touristy towns, and which go for about 350–450kr single, 450–550kr double; breakfast is generally extra. A *gjestgiveri* or *gjestehus* is a **guesthouse** or **inn**, charging similar prices. Facilities in all are usually adequate without being overwhelmingly comfortable; at the cheaper establishments you'll share a bathroom with others. Some pensions and guesthouses also have kitchens available for the use of guests. The main advantage is that you're more than likely to meet other residents – a real boon (perhaps) if you're travelling alone – and locals.

■ Youth hostels and private rooms

For many budget travellers, as well as hikers, climbers and skiiers, the country's **youth hostels** (*Vandrerhjem*) provide mainstay accommodation. There are almost a hundred in total, with handy concentrations in the western fjords, the central hiking and skiing regions and in Oslo. The Norwegian hostelling association, **Norske Vandrerhjem**, Dronningens gate 26, Oslo (☎23 13 93 00, fax 23 13 93 50, *hostels@online.no*), issues a free booklet, *Norske Vandrerhjem*, which details locations, opening dates, prices and telephone numbers, or visit their Web site, *www.vandrerhjem.no*, where you can also make online bookings. The hostels themselves are invariably excellent – the only quibble, at the risk of being churlish, is that those occupying schools tend to be rather drab and institutional.

Prices vary, anything from 100kr to 180kr, although the more expensive ones nearly always

include a good breakfast. On average, reckon on paying 120kr a night for a bed, 50kr for breakfast and 80–100kr for a hot meal. Bear in mind also that almost all hostels have a few regular double and family rooms on offer: at 250–450kr a double, these are among the cheapest rooms you'll find in Norway. If you're not a member of Hostelling International (HI) you can still use the hostels, though it will cost you an extra 25kr a night – which can soon mount up, so join HI before you leave home. If you don't have your own sheet sleeping bag, you'll have to rent one for around 40–50kr a time.

It cannot be stressed too strongly that **ringing ahead** to reserve a hostel bed in peak season, summer or winter, will save you lots of unnecessary legwork. Many hostels are only open from mid-June to mid-August and most close between 11am and 4pm. There's sometimes an 11pm or midnight curfew, though this is less of a drawback in a country where carousing is so expensive. Where breakfast is included – as it usually is – ask for a breakfast packet if you have to leave early to catch transport; otherwise note that hostel **meals** are nearly always very tasty and excellent value. Most, though not all, hostels have small **kitchens**, but often no pots, pans, cutlery or crockery, so self-caterers should take their own.

Tourist offices in the larger towns and amongst the more touristy settlements can often fix you up with a **private room** in someone's house, which may include kitchen facilities. Prices are competitive – from around 180–230kr single, 300–350kr double – though there's usually a booking fee (20–30kr) on top, and the rooms themselves are frequently some way out of the centre. Nonetheless, they're often the best bargain available and, in certain instances, an improvement on the local youth hostel. Where this is the case, we've said so. If you don't have a sleeping bag, check the room comes with bedding – not all of them do; and if you're cooking for yourself, a few basic utensils wouldn't go amiss either.

■ Campsites, cabins and mountain huts

Camping is a popular pastime in Norway and there are literally hundreds of campsites to choose from, anything from a field with a few tent pitches through to extensive complexes with all mod cons. The Norwegian tourist authorities detail around 400 campsites in their free *Camping* brochure, classifying them on a one- to five-star grading depending on the facilities offered. Most sites are situated with the motorist (rather than the cyclist or walker) in mind, and a good few occupy key locations beside the main roads. The majority are two- and three-star establishments, where prices are usually per tent, plus a small charge per person; on average expect to pay around 150kr for two people using a tent, with four- and five-star sites around 20 percent more. During peak season it can be a good idea to **reserve ahead** if you have a car and a large tent or trailer; phone numbers are listed in the free camping booklet and throughout the Guide.

Camping rough in Norway, as in Sweden, is a tradition enshrined in law. You can camp anywhere in open areas as long as you are at least 150m away from any houses or cabins. As a courtesy, ask farmers for permission to use their land – it is rarely refused. Fires are not permitted in woodland areas or in fields between April 15 and September 15, and camper vans are not allowed (ever) to overnight on lay-bys. A good sleeping bag is essential, since even in summer it can get very cold, and, in the north at least, mosquito repellent and sunscreen are vital.

The Norwegian countryside is dotted with thousands of timber **cabins/chalets** (called *hytter*), ranging from simple wooden huts through to comfortable lodges. They are usually two- or four-bedded affairs, with full kitchen facilities and sometimes a bathroom or even TV. Some hostels have them on their grounds, there are nearly always at least a handful at every campsite, and in the Lofoten islands they are the most popular form of accommodation, many occupying refurbished fishermen's huts called *rorbuer*. Costs vary enormously, depending on location, size and amenities, and there are significant seasonal variations too. However, a four-bed *hytter* will rarely cost more than 500kr per night – a more usual average would be about 300kr. If you're travelling in a group, they are easily the cheapest way to see the countryside – and in some comfort. Hundreds of *hytter* are also rented out as holiday cottages by the week. The two main agencies produce lavish, detailed brochures of the *hytter* on offer – for further details contact either Den Norske Hytteformidling, P.O. Box 309, Sentrum, N-0105 Oslo (☎22 35 62 70, fax 23 35 62 75, *www.hytte.com*), or Fjordhytter Den Norske Hytteformidling, P.O. Box 103, Lille Markevei 13, N-5005 Bergen (☎55 23 20 80, fax 55 23 24 04), who specialize in western Norway.

One further option for hikers is the chain of **mountain huts** (again called *hytter*) on hiking routes countrywide. Some are privately run, but the majority are operated by **Den Norske Turistforening** (DNT), the Norwegian Mountain Hiking Association, and affiliated regional hiking organizations. Membership of DNT costs around 360kr a year, and although you don't have to be a member of DNT to use their huts, you'll soon recoup your outlay through reduced hut charges for members. For members staying in staffed huts, a bunk in a dormitory costs 70–100kr, 140kr in a family or double room, with meals starting at 60kr for breakfast, 125kr for dinner. At unstaffed huts, where you leave the money for your stay in a box provided, lodging costs about 20 percent less.

Food and drink

At its best, **Norwegian food** can be excellent: fish is plentiful, and carnivores can have a field day trying meats like reindeer steak, elk or even, conscience permitting, seal. Admittedly it's not inexpensive, and those on a tight budget may have problems varying their diet, but by exercising a little prudence in the face of the average menu (which is almost always in Norwegian and English), you can keep costs down to reasonable levels. Vegetarians, however, will have slim pickings, except in Oslo, and drinkers will have to dig very deep into their pockets to maintain much of an intake. Indeed, most drinkers end up visiting the supermarkets and state off-licences so that they can sup away at home (in true Norwegian style) before setting out for the evening.

■ Food

Many travellers exist almost entirely on a mixture of picnic food and by cooking their own meals, with the odd café meal thrown in to boost morale. Frankly, this isn't really necessary (except on the tightest of budgets) as there are a number of ways to eat out inexpensively. To begin with, a

GLOSSARY OF NORWEGIAN FOOD AND DRINK TERMS

Basics and snacks

appelsin-marmelade	marmalade	kaviar	caviar	ris	rice
brød	bread	kjeks	biscuits	rundstykker	roll
eddik	vinegar	krem	whipped cream	salat	salad
egg	egg	melk	milk	salt	salt
eggerøre	scrambled eggs	mineralvann	mineral water	sennep	mustard
flatbrød	crispbread	nøtter	nuts	smør	butter
fløte	cream	olje	oil	smørbrød	open sandwich
grøt	porridge	omelett	omelette	sukker	sugar
iskrem	ice cream	ost	cheese	suppe	soup
kaffefløte	single cream (for coffee)	pannekake	pancakes	syltetøy	jam
		pepper	pepper	varm pølse	hotdog
kake	cake	pommes-frites	chips	yoghurt	yogurt
		potetchips	crisps		

Meat (*kjøtt*) and game (*vilt*)

dyrestek	venison	lammekjøtt	lamb	ribbe	pork rib
elg	elk	lever	liver	skinke	ham
kalkun	turkey	oksekjøtt	beef	spekemat	dried meat
kjøttboller	meatballs	pølser	sausages	stek	steak
kjøttkaker	meatcakes	postei	paté	svinekjøtt	pork
kylling	chicken	reinsdyr	reindeer	varm pølse	frankfurter/hotdog

Fish (*fisk*) and shellfish (*skalldyr*)

ål	eel	kreps	crayfish		(brisling)
ansjos	anchovies (brisling)	laks	salmon	sei	coalfish
		makrell	mackerel	sild	herring
blåskjell	mussels	ørret	trout	sjøtunge	sole
brisling	sprats	piggvar	turbot	småfisk	whitebait
hummer	lobster	reker	shrimps	steinbit	catfish
hvitting	whiting	rødspette	plaice	torsk	cod
kaviar	caviar	røkelaks	smoked salmon	tunfisk	tuna
krabbe	crab	sardiner	sardines		

Vegetables (*grønsaker*)

agurk	cucumber/gherkin/pickle	hvitløk	garlic	poteter	potatoes
		kål	cabbage	rosenkål	Brussels sprouts
blomkål	cauliflower	linser	lentils	selleri	celery
bønner	beans	løk	onion	sopp	mushrooms
erter	peas	mais	sweetcorn	spinat	spinach
gulrøtter	carrots	nepe	turnip	tomater	tomatoes
hodesalat	lettuce	paprika	peppers		

Fruit (*frukt*)

ananas	pineapple	eple	apple	pærer	pears
appelsin	orange	fersken	peach	plommer	plums
aprikos	apricot	fruktsalat	fruit salad	sitron	lemon
banan	banana	grapefrukt	grapefruit	solbær	blackcurrants
blåbær	blueberries	jordbær	strawberries	tyttbær	cranberries
druer	grapes	multer	cloudberries		

continues overleaf . . .

NORWEGIAN FOOD AND DRINK TERMS (contd.)

Terms

blodig	rare, underdone	*marinert*	marinated	*stuet*	stewed
godt stekt	well done	*ovnstekt*	baked/roasted	*sur*	sour, pickled
grillet	grilled	*røkt*	smoked	*syltet*	pickled
grytestekt	braised	*stekt*	fried	*saltet*	cured
kokt	boiled				

Norwegian specialities

brun saus	gravy served with most meats, meatcakes, fishcakes and sausages
fenalår	marinaded mutton, smoked, sliced, salted, dried and served with crispbread, scrambled egg and beer
fiskekabaret	shrimps, fish and vegetables in aspic
fiskeboller	fish balls, served under a white sauce or on open sandwiches
fiskesuppe	fish soup
flatbrød	a flat unleavened cracker, half barley, half wheat
gammelost	a hard, strong smelling, yellow-brown cheese with veins
geitost/ gjetost	goat's cheese, slightly sweet and fudge-coloured. Similar cheeses have different ratios of goats' milk to cows' milk
gravetlaks	salmon marinaded in salt, sugar, dill and brandy
juleskinke	marinaded boiled ham, served at Christmas
kjøttkaker med surkål	homemade burgers with cabbage and a sweet and sour sauce
koldtbord	a midday buffet with cold meats, herrings, salads, bread and perhaps soup, eggs or hot meats
lapskaus	pork, venison (or other meats) and vegetable stew, common in the south and east, using salted or fresh meat, or leftovers, in a thick brown gravy
lutefisk	fish (usually cod) preserved in an alkali solution and flavoured; an acquired taste
multer	cloudberries – wild berries, mostly found north of the Arctic Circle and served with cream (*med krem*)
mysost	brown whey cheese, made from cows' milk
nedlagtsild	marinaded herring
pinnekjøtt	western Norwegian Christmas dish of smoked mutton steamed over shredded birch bark, served with cabbage; or accompanied by boiled potatoes and mashed swedes (*kålrabistappe*)
reinsdyrstek	reindeer steak, usually served with boiled potatoes and cranberry sauce
rekesalat	shrimp salad in mayonnaise
ribbe, julepølse medisterkake	eastern Norwegian Christmas dish of pork ribs, sausage and dumplings
spekemat	various types of smoked, dried meat
Trondhjemsuppe	a kind of milk soup with raisins, rice, cinnamon and sugar

Bread, cake and desserts

bløtkake	cream cake with fruit
fløtelapper	pancakes made from cream, served with sugar and jam
havrekjeks	oatmeal biscuits, eaten with goat's cheese
knekkebrød	crispbread
kransekake	cake made from almonds, sugar and eggs, served at celebrations
lompar	potato scones-cum-tortillas
riskrem	rice pudding with whipped cream and sugar, usually served with *frukt saus*, a slighly thickened fruit sauce
tilslørtbondepiker	stewed apples and breadcrumbs, served with cream
trollkrem	beaten egg whites (or whipped cream) and sugar mixed with cloudberries (or cranberries)
vafle	waffles

Drinks

akevitt	aquavit	*fruksaft*	sweetened	*sitronbrus*	lemonade	*søt*	sweet
appelsin	orange		fruit juice	*te med*	tea with	*tørr*	dry
saft/	squash/	*kaffe*	coffee	*melk/sitron*	milk/lemon	*rød*	red
juice	juice	*melk*	milk	*vann*	water	*hvit*	white
brus	soft, fizzy	*mineralvann*	mineral	*varm*	hot	*rosé*	rosé
	drink		water	*sjokolade*	chocolate	*skål!*	cheers!
eplesider	cider	*øl*	beer	*vin*	wine		

good self-service buffet breakfast, served in almost every hostel and hotel, goes some way to solving the problem whilst special lunch deals will get you a tasty, hot meal for around 60–70kr. Finally, alongside the regular restaurants – which are expensive – there's the usual array of budget pizzerias and cafeterias in most towns.

Breakfast, picnics and snacks

Breakfast (*frokost*) in Norway is a substantial self-service affair of bread, crackers, cheese, eggs, preserves, cold meat and fish, washed down by unlimited tea and coffee. It's usually first-rate at youth hostels, and often memorable in hotels, filling you up for the day for around 50–70kr, on the rare occasions when it's not thrown in with the price of your room.

If you're buying your own **picnic food**, bread, cheese, yogurt and local fruit are all relatively good value, but other staple foodstuffs – rice, pasta, meat, cereals and vegetables – can cost up to around twice the price of British equivalents. Anything tinned is particularly dear, with the exception of tinned fish, but coffee and tea are quite reasonably priced. **Supermarkets** are ten-a-penny – Rema 2000 and Rimi are the two biggest chains.

Fast food offers the best chance of a hot takeaway snack. The indigenous Norwegian stuff, served up from **gatekjøkken** – street kiosks or stalls – in every town, consists mainly of rubbery hotdogs (*varm pølse*), while pizza slices and chicken pieces and chips are much in evidence too. American burger bars are also creeping in – both at motorway service stations and in the towns and cities. A better choice, and usually not much more expensive, is simply to get a sandwich, normally a huge open affair called a **smørbrød** (pronounced "smurrbrur"), heaped with a variety of garnishes. You'll see them groaning with meat or shrimps, salad and mayonnaise in the windows of bakeries and cafés, or in the newer, trendier sandwich bars in the cities. **Cakes and biscuits** are good, too:

watch for doughnuts, Danish pastries (*wienerbrød*), butter biscuits (*kjeks*) and waffles (*vafler*).

Good **coffee** is available everywhere, served black or with cream, rich, strong, and, in some places, particularly at breakfast, free after the first cup. **Tea**, too, is ubiquitous, but the local preference is for lemon tea or a variety of flavoured infusions; if you want milk, ask for it. All the familiar **soft drinks** are also available.

Lunch and dinner

For the best deals, you're going to have to eat your main meal of the day at lunchtime (*lunsj*), when **kafeterias** (often self-service restaurants) lay on daily specials, the *dagens rett*. This is a fish or meat dish served with potatoes and a vegetable or salad, often including a drink, sometimes bread, and occasionally coffee, too; it should go for around 70–80kr. Dipping into the menu is more expensive, but not cripplingly so if you stick to omelettes and such like. Many department stores – including the Domus chain – have *kafeterias*, as does every large railway station. You'll also find them hidden above shops and offices and adjoining hotels in larger towns, where they might be called *kaffistovas*. Most close at around 6pm, and many don't open at all on Sunday. As a general rule, the food these places serve is plain-verging-on-the-ordinary (though there are many excellent exceptions), but the same cannot be said of the continental-style **café-bars** which abound in Oslo and, increasingly, in all of Norway's larger towns and cities. These eminently affordable establishments offer much tastier and much more adventurous meals like pasta dishes, salads and vegetarian options.

In all of the cities, but especially in Oslo, there are first-class **restaurants**, serving dinner (*middag*) in quite formal surroundings. Apart from exotica such as reindeer and elk, the one real speciality is the seafood, simply prepared and wonderfully fresh – whatever you do don't go home without treating yourself at least once. In the smaller towns and villages, gourmets will be harder pressed – many of the restaurants are pretty mundane, though the general standard is improving rapidly. Main courses begin at around 150kr, starters and desserts at around 60kr. If in doubt, smoked salmon comes highly recommended, as does the catfish and monkfish. Again, the best deals are at lunchtime.

In the towns, and especially in Oslo, there is also a sprinkling of **ethnic restaurants**, mostly Italian with a good helping of Chinese and Indian places. Other cuisines pop up here and there too – Japanese, Moroccan and Mongolian to name but three. The most affordable ethnic eateries are the Chinese restaurants and the pizza joints.

Vegetarians

Vegetarians are in for a hard time. Apart from a couple of specialist restaurants in Oslo, you can do little except make do with salads, look out for egg dishes in *kafeterias* and supplement your diet from supermarkets. If you are a **vegan** the problem is greater: when the Norwegians are not eating meat and fish, they are attacking a fantastic selection of milks, cheeses and yogurts. At least you'll know what's in every dish you eat, since everyone speaks English. If you're self-catering, look for **health food shops** (*helsekost*), found in some of the larger towns and cities.

■ Drink

One of the less savoury sights in Norway is the fall-over drunk: you can spot them at any time of the day or night zigzagging along the street, a strangely disconcerting counter to the usual stereotype of the Norwegian as a healthy, hearty figure in a wholesome woolly jumper. For reasons that remain obscure – or at least culturally complex – many Norwegians can't just have a drink or two, but have to get absolutely wasted. The majority of their compatriots deplore such behaviour and have consequently imposed what amounts to alcoholic rationing: thus, although booze is readily available in the bars and restaurants, it's taxed up to the eyeballs (half a litre of beer costs 35kr or over) and the distribution of wines and spirits is strictly controlled by a state-run monopoly, Vinmonopolet. Whether this paternalistic type of control makes matters better or worse is a moot point, but the majority of Norwegians support it.

What to drink

If you decide to lash out on a few drinks, you'll find Norwegian **beer** is lager-like and comes in three strengths (class I, II or III), of which the strongest and most expensive is class III. Brands to look for include Hansa and Ringsnes. There's no domestically produced **wine** and most **spirits** are imported too, but one local brew worth experimenting with at least once is **aquavit**, a bitter concoction served ice-cold in little glasses and, at forty percent proof, real headache material – though it's more palatable with beer chasers: Linie aquavit is one of the more popular brands.

Where to buy drink

Beer is sold in supermarkets and shops all over Norway, though some local communities, particularly in the west, have their own rules and restrictions; it's about half the price you'd pay in a bar. The strongest beer, along with wines and spirits, can only be purchased from the state-controlled shops, known as **Vinmonopolet**. There's generally one in each medium-size town, though there are more branches in the cities (twenty in Oslo). Opening hours are generally Monday to Wednesday 10am–4/5pm, Thursday 10am–5/6pm, Friday 9am–4/6pm, Saturday 9am–1pm, though these times can vary depending on the area, and they'll be closed the day before a public holiday. At these stores, wine is quite a bargain, from around 55kr a bottle, and there's generally a fairly bizarre choice of vintages from various South American countries on offer.

Where to drink

Wherever you **go for a drink**, a half-litre of beer costs between 35kr and 45kr and a glass of wine from 30kr. You can get a drink at most outdoor cafés, in restaurants and at bars, pubs and cocktail bars. That said, only in the towns and cities is there any kind of "European" bar life and in many places you'll be limited to a drink in the local hotel bar or restaurant. However, in Oslo, Bergen, Stavanger, Trondheim and Tromsø you will be able to keep drinking in bars until at least 1am, until 4am in some places.

Directory

BORDERS There is little formality at the Norway–Sweden border, slightly more between Norway and Finland. However, the northern border with Russia is a different story. Despite a recent relaxation of tension in the area following the break-up of the Soviet Union, border patrols (on either side) won't be overjoyed at the prospect of you nosing around. If you have a genuine wish to visit Russia, it's best to sign up for an organized tour from Kirkenes.

KIDS There are no real problems with taking children to Norway. They go for half-price (infants under 3 or 4 go free) on all forms of public transport, and get the same discount on an extra bed in their parents' hotel room. Family rooms are widely available in youth hostels, while many of the summer activities detailed in this book are geared up to cater for kids as well. There are also baby compartments (with their own toilet and changing room) for kids under two and their escorts on most trains, and baby-changing rooms at most larger train stations. Many restaurants have children's menus; where they don't, it's always worth asking if there are cheaper, smaller portions.

LEFT LUGGAGE There are coin-operated lockers in most railway and bus stations and at all major ferry terminals.

PUBLIC HOLIDAYS National public holidays are a noticeable feature of the Norwegian calendar and act as a unifying force in what remains an extremely homogeneous society. There are ten national public holidays per year, most of which are keenly observed, though the tourist industry carries on pretty much regardless. Some state-run museums adopt Sunday hours on the public holidays listed below, except on Christmas Day and New Year's Day (and often December 26) when they close. Otherwise most businesses and shops close, and the public transport system operates a skeleton or Sunday service. Most Norwegians take their holidays in the summer season, between mid-June and mid-August. Public holidays are: New Year's Day; Maundy Thursday; Good Friday; Easter Monday; Labour Day (May 1); Ascension Day (mid-May); National Day (May 17); Whit Monday; Christmas Day; Boxing Day.

SHOPPING HOURS Normal shopping hours are Monday to Friday 9am–4/5pm, with late opening on Thursdays till 6pm or 8pm, plus Saturdays 9am–1/3pm. Some supermarkets stay open much longer – until 8pm in the week and 6pm on Saturdays – and, in addition, the majority of kiosks-cum-newsstands stay open till 9pm or 10pm every night of the week (including Sundays), especially in cities and larger towns. Many petrol stations sell a basic range of groceries and stay open till 11pm daily.

SMOKING Smoking is prohibited in all public buildings, including train stations, and it's forbidden on all domestic flights and bus services. Restaurants have to have non-smoking areas by law, and there are supposed to be dividing walls between smoking and non-smoking sections. Hoteliers have by law to designate fifty percent of their rooms as non-smoking.

TIPPING A service charge is automatically included in hotel and restaurant bills, so any additional tip is not expected.

History

Despite its low contemporary profile, Norway has a fascinating past. As early as the tenth century its people had explored – and conquered – much of northern Europe, and roamed the Atlantic as far as the North American mainland. Though at first an independent state, from the fourteenth century Norway came under the sway of first Denmark and then Sweden. Independent again from 1905, Norway was propelled into World War II by the Nazi invasion of 1940, an act of aggression that transformed the Norwegians' attitude to the outside world. Gone was the old insular neutrality, replaced by a liberal internationalism typified by Norway's leading role in the environmental movement.

■ Early civilizations

The earliest signs of human habitation in Norway date from the end of the last Ice Age, around 10,000 BC. In the Finnmark region of north Norway, the **Komsa** culture was reliant upon seal-fishing, whereas the peoples of the **Fosna** culture, further south near present-day Kristiansund, hunted seals and reindeer. Both these societies were essentially static, dependent upon flint and bone implements. At Alta, the Komsa people left behind hundreds of **rock carvings** and drawings, naturalistic representations of their way of life dating from the seventh to the third millennia BC.

As the edges of the ice cap retreated from the western coastline, so new migrants slowly filtered north. These new peoples, of the **Nøstvet-økser** culture, were also hunters and fishers, but they were able to manufacture stone axes, examples of which were first unearthed at Nøstvet, near Oslo. Beginning around 2700 BC, immigrants from the east, principally the semi-nomadic **Boat Axe** and **Battle-Axe peoples** – so-called because of the distinctive shape of their stone weapons/tools – introduced animal husbandry and agriculture. The new arrivals did not, however, overwhelm their predecessors; the two groups coexisted, each learning from the other how to survive in a land of harsh infertility. These late Stone Age cultures flourished at a time when other, more southerly countries were already using metal. Norway was poor and had little to trade, but the Danes and Swedes exchanged amber for copper and tin from the bronze-making countries. A fraction of the imported bronze subsequently passed into Norway, mostly to the Battle-Axe people, who appear to have had a comparatively prosperous aristocracy. This was the beginning of the Norwegian **Bronze Age** (1500–500 BC).

Around 500 BC Norway was affected by two adverse changes: the climate deteriorated, and trade relations with the Mediterranean were disrupted by the westward movement of the Celts across central Europe. The former encouraged the development of settled, communal farming in an attempt to improve winter shelter and storage; the latter cut the supply of tin and copper and subsequently isolated the country from the early **Iron Age**. Norway's isolation continued through much of the **classical period**, though the expansion of the Roman Empire in the first and second centuries AD did revive Norway's trading links with the Mediterranean. Evidence of these renewed contacts is provided across Scandinavia by **runes**, carved inscriptions dating from around 200 AD whose 24-letter alphabet – the *futhark* – was clearly influenced by Greek and Latin capitals. Initially, runes were seen as having magical powers, but gradually their usage became more prosaic. Of the 800 or so runic inscriptions extant across southern Norway, most commemorate events and individuals: mothers and fathers, sons and slain comrades.

The renewal of trade with the Mediterranean also spread the use of **iron**. Norway's agriculture was transformed by the use of iron tools, and the pace of change accelerated in the fifth century AD, when the Norwegians learnt how to smelt the brown iron ore, limonite, that lay in their bogs and lakes – hence its common name, **bog-iron**. Clearing the forests with iron axes was relatively easy and, with more land available, the pattern of settlement became less concentrated. Family homesteads leapfrogged up the valleys, and a class of wealthy farmers emerged, their prosperity based on fields and flocks. Above them in the pecking order were local **chieftains**, the nature of whose authority varied considerably. Inland, the chieftains' power was based upon landed wealth and constrained by feudal responsibilities, whereas the coastal lords, who had often accumulated influence from trade, piracy, and military prowess, were less encumbered. Like the farmers, these seafarers had also benefited from the iron axe, which made boat-building much easier.

By the middle of the eighth century, Norway had become a country of **small, independent kingships**, its geography impeding the development of any central authority.

■ The Vikings

Overpopulation, clan discord and the lure of commerce all contributed to the sudden explosion that launched the **Vikings** (from the Norse word *vik*, meaning "creek", and -*ing*, "frequenter of") upon an unsuspecting Europe in the ninth century. The patterns of attack and eventual settlement were dictated by the geographical position of the various Scandinavian countries: the Swedish Vikings turned eastwards, the Danes headed south and southwest, while the Norwegians sailed west. Norwegian longships fell upon the Hebrides, Shetland, Orkney, the Scottish mainland and western Ireland. The Pictish population was able to offer little resistance and the islands were quickly overrun, forming the nucleus of a new Norse kingdom, which itself provided a base for further attacks upon Scotland and Ireland.

The Norwegians founded Dublin in 836, and from Ireland turned their attention eastward to northern Britain. Elsewhere, Norwegian Vikings settled the Faroe Islands and Iceland, and even raided as far south as Moorish Spain, attacking Seville in 844. The raiders soon became settlers, sometimes – as in Iceland and the Faroes – colonizing the entire country, but mostly intermingling with the local population. The speed of their assimilation is, in fact, one of the Vikings' most striking features: William the Conqueror (1027–87) was the epitome of the Norman baron, yet he was also the descendant of Rollo, the Viking warrior whose army had overrun Normandy just a century before.

The whole of Norway felt the stimulating effects of the Viking expeditions. The standard of living rose and the economy was boosted by the spoils of war. Farmland was no longer in such short supply; slaves assisted labour-intensive land clearance schemes; cereal and dairy farming extended into new areas in eastern Norway; new vegetables, such as cabbages and turnips, were introduced from Britain; and farming methods were improved by overseas contact – the Celts, for instance, taught the Norwegians how to thresh grain with flails.

The Vikings' brand of **paganism**, with its wayward, unscrupulous deities, underpinned their inclination to vendetta and clan warfare. Nevertheless, institutions slowly developed which helped regulate the bloodletting. Western Norway adopted the Germanic *wergeld* system of cash-for-injury compensation; every free man was entitled to attend the local *Thing* or parliament, while a regional *Lagthing* made laws and settled disputes. Justice was class-based, however, with society divided into three main categories: the lord, the freeman and the thrall or slave, who was worth about eight cows. Viking **decorative art** was pan-Scandinavian, with the most distinguished work being the elaborate and often grotesque animal motifs that adorned their ships, sledges, buildings and furniture. This craftsmanship is seen at its best in the **ship burials** of Oseberg and Gokstad, both on display in Oslo's Viking Ships Museum.

Norway's first widely recognized chieftain was **Harald Hårfagri** (Fair-Hair), who gained control of the coastal region as far north as Trøndelag around 900. This sparked an exodus of minor rulers, most of whom left to settle in Iceland. Harald's long rule was based on personal pledges of fealty; with the notable exception of the regional *Lagthings*, there were no institutions to sustain it, and when he died his kingdom broke up into its component parts. Harald did, however, leave a less tangible but extremely important legacy: from now on every ambitious chieftain was not content to be a local lord, but strove to be ruler of Harald's whole kingdom.

Harald's sons and grandsons warred over their inheritance for the rest of the tenth century, undermining Norway's independence by seeking military support in Denmark and Sweden. Meanwhile, Norwegian settlers were laying the foundations of independent Norse communities in the **Faroes** and **Iceland**, where they established

a parliament, the *Althing*, in 930. Subsequently, Erik the Red, exiled from Norway and then banished from Iceland for three years for murder, set out in 985 with 25 ships, fourteen of which arrived in **Greenland**. The new colony prospered, and by the start of the eleventh century there were about three thousand settlers. This created a shortage of good farmland, making another push west inevitable. The two **Vinland sagas** provide the only surviving account of these further explorations, recounting the exploits of Leif Eriksson the Lucky, who founded a colony he called Vinland on the shore of **North America** (probably Newfoundland) around 1000 AD.

■ The arrival of Christianity

In 1015, a prominent Viking chieftain, **Olav Haraldsson** sailed for Norway from England, intent upon conquering his homeland. Significantly, he arrived by merchant ship with just 100 men, rather than with a fleet of longships and an army, a clear sign of the passing of the Viking heyday. Pledged to him was the support of the yeoman farmers of the interior – a new force in Norway that was rapidly supplanting the old warrior aristocracy – and Haraldsson was soon recognized as king of much of the country.

For twelve years, Olav ruled in peace, founding Norway's first national government. His authority was based upon the regional *Things* – broadly democratic bodies which administered local law – and on his willingness to deliver justice without fear or favour. The king's most enduring achievement, however, was to make Norway **Christian**. Olav had been converted during his days in England and vigorously imposed his new faith on his countrymen.

It was foreign policy rather than pagan enmity, however, that brought about Olav's downfall. By scheming with the Swedish ruler against **King Knut** (Canute) of Denmark and England, Olav provoked a Danish invasion. The Norwegian chieftains who had suffered at the hands of Olav could be expected to help Knut, but even the yeomen failed to rally to the cause. In 1028, Olav was forced to flee, first to Sweden and then to Russia, while Knut's son Svein and his mother, the English Queen Aelfgifu, took the Norwegian crown. Two years later, Olav made a sensational return at the head of a scratch army, only to be defeated and killed by an alliance of wealthy landowners and chieftains at **Stiklestad**, the first major Norwegian land battle.

The petty chieftains and yeoman farmers who had opposed Olav soon fell out with their new king: Svein had no intention of relaxing the royal grip, and his chieftains subsequent rebellion seems also to have had nationalistic undertones – many Norwegians had no wish to be ruled by a Dane. Svein had to flee the country, and Olav's old enemies popped over to Sweden to bring back Olav's young son, **Magnus**, who became king in 1035.

The chastening experience of Svein's short rule transformed the popular memory of Olav. With surprising speed, he came to be regarded as an heroic champion of Norway, and there was talk of miracles brought about by the dead king's body. The Norwegian church, looking for a local saint to enhance its position, fostered the legends and had Olav canonized. The remains of **St Olav** were then reinterred ceremoniously at Nidaros, today's Trondheim, where the miracles increased in scope, hastening the conversion of what remained of heathen Norway.

On Magnus's death in 1047, **Harald Hardråda** (Olav's half-brother) became king. The last of the Viking heroes, Hardråda dominated his kingdom by force of arms for over twenty years. Neither was Hardråda satisfied with being king of just Norway. In 1066, the death of Edward the Confessor presented Harald with an opportunity to press his claim to the English throne. The Norwegian promptly sailed on England, landing near York with a massive fleet, but just outside the city, at Stamford Bridge, his army was surprised and trounced by Harold Godwinson, the new Saxon king of England. Hardråda was killed in the battle and the threat of a Norwegian conquest of England had – though no one realized it at the time – gone forever. Not that the victory did much for Godwinson, whose weakened army trudged back south to be defeated by William of Normandy at the Battle of Hastings.

■ Medieval success

Harald's son, **Olav Kyrre** (the Peaceful) – whose life had been spared after Stamford Bridge on the promise that he never attack England again – went on to reign as king of Norway for the next 25 years. Peace engendered economic prosperity, and treaties with Denmark ensured Norwegian independence. Three native bishoprics were established, and cathedrals built at Nidaros, Bergen and Oslo. It's from this period, too, that Norway's surviving **stave churches** date: wooden structures

resembling an upturned keel, they were lavishly decorated with dragon heads and scenes from Norse mythology, proof that the traditions of the pagan world were slow to disappear.

The first decades of the twelfth century witnessed the further consolidation of Norway's position as an independent power despite internal disorder as the descendants of Olav Kyrre struggled to maintain their influence. Civil war ceased only when **Håkon IV** took the throne in 1240, ushering in what is often called "The Period of Greatness". Secure at home, Hakon strengthened the Norwegian hold on the Faroe and Shetland islands, and in 1262 both Iceland and Greenland accepted Norwegian sovereignty. When his claim to the Hebrides was disputed by Alexander III of Scotland, Håkon assembled an intimidatory fleet, but died in 1263 in the Orkneys. Three years later the Hebrides and the Isle of Man (always the weakest links in the Norwegian empire) were sold to the Scottish crown by Håkon's successor, **Magnus the Lawmender** (1238–80).

Under Magnus, Norway prospered. Law and order were maintained, trade flourished and the king's courtiers even followed a code of etiquette compiled in the *King's Mirror* (*Konungs skuggsja*), in contrast to former rough-and-ready Viking ways. Neither was the power of the monarchy threatened by feudal barons as elsewhere in thirteenth-century Europe. Norway's scattered farms were not susceptible to feudal tutelage and, as a consequence, the nobility lacked local autonomy – castles remained few and far between – and were drawn into the centralized administration of the state. Norwegian **Gothic art** reached its full maturity in this period, as construction began on the nave at Nidaros Cathedral and on Håkon's Hall in Bergen.

Magnus was succeeded by his sons, first the undistinguished Erik and then by **Håkon V** (1270–1319), the last of medieval Norway's talented kings. Håkon continued the policy of his predecessors, making further improvements to central government and asserting royal control of Finnmark by the construction of a fortress at Vardø. His achievements, however, were soon to be swept away along with the independence of Norway itself.

■ Medieval failure

Norway's independence was threatened from two quarters. With strongholds in Bergen and Oslo, the **Hanseatic League** and its merchants had steadily increased their influence, holding a monopoly on imports and controlling inland trade. The power of their international trading links was reinforced in Norway as the royal household grew increasingly dependent on the taxes paid to them by the League. The second threat was **dynastic**. When Håkon died in 1319 he left no male heir and was succeeded by his grandson, the three-year-old son of a Swedish duke. The boy, Magnus Eriksson, was elected Swedish king two months later, marking the virtual end of Norway as an independent country until 1905.

Magnus assumed full power over both countries in 1332, but his reign was a difficult one. When the Norwegian nobility rebelled he agreed that the monarchy should again be split: his three-year-old son, Håkon, would become Norwegian king when he came of age, while the Swedes agreed to elect his eldest son Erik to the Swedish throne. t was then, in 1349, that the **Black Death** struck, spreading quickly along the coast and up the valleys, and killing almost two-thirds of the Norwegian population. It was a catastrophe of almost unimaginable proportions, its effects compounded by the way the country's agriculture was structured. Animal husbandry was easily the most important part of Norwegian farming, and the harvesting and drying of sufficient winter fodder was labour-intensive. Without the labourers, the animals died in their hundreds and famine conditions prevailed for several generations.

Many farms were abandoned and, deprived of their rents, the petty chieftains who had once dominated rural Norway were, as a class, almost entirely swept away. The vacuum was filled by royal officials, the *syslemenn*, each of whom exercised control over a large chunk of territory on behalf of a Royal Council. The collapse of local governance was compounded by the dynastic toing and fro-ing at the top of the social ladder. In 1380, Håkon died and Norway passed under Danish control with Olav, the son of Håkon and the Danish princess **Margaret**, becoming the ruler of the two kingdoms. It was a union that was to last 400 years.

■ The Kalmar union

Despite Olav's early death in 1387, the resourceful Margaret persevered with the union. Proclaimed regent by both the Danish and (what remained of the) Norwegian nobility, she engineered a treaty with the Swedish nobles that not only recognized her as regent of Sweden but also agreed to accept any king she should nominate. Her chosen heir, **Erik of Pomerania**, was foisted on the Norwegians in 1389. When he reached the age of majority in 1397, Margaret organized a grand coronation with Erik crowned king of all three countries at Kalmar in Sweden – hence the **Kalmar Union**.

After Margaret's death in 1412, all power was concentrated in Denmark. In Norway, foreigners were preferred in both state and church, and the country became impoverished by paying for Erik's wars. Incompetent and brutal in equal measure, Erik managed to get himself deposed in all three countries at the same time. In the meantime, Sweden had left the union, and eventually a Danish count, Christian of Oldenburg, was crowned king of Norway and Denmark in 1450. Thereafter, Norway ceased to take any meaningful part in Scandinavian affairs. Literature languished as the Old Norse **language** was displaced as the official language by Danish – and indeed it soon came to be regarded as the language of the ignorant and inconsequential. Only the Norwegian church retained any power, but this itself was overwhelmed by the Reformation.

■ Union with Denmark

In 1536 Christian III declared his kingdom Protestant and, although it was slow to take root among the Norwegian peasantry, **Lutheranism** soon came to be a powerful instrument in establishing Danish influence. The Bible, catechism and hymnal were all in Danish, the bishops were all Danes and, after 1537, so were all the most important provincial Norwegian governors.

In many respects, Norway became simply a source of raw materials – fish, timber and iron ore – whose proceeds lined the royal purse. Naturally enough, the Swedes coveted these materials too, the upshot being a long and inconclusive war (1563–70, which saw much of Norway ravaged by competing bands of mercenaries. Among the Danish kings of the period, **Christian IV** (1588–1648) proved the most sympathetic to Norway. He visited the country often, improving the quality of its administration and founding new towns including Kongsberg, Kristiansand and Christiania (later Oslo).

At last, in the middle of the seventeenth century, the Norwegian economy began to pick up.

The population grew, trade increased and, benefiting from the decline of the Hanseatic League, a native bourgeoisie began to take control of certain parts of the economy, most notably the herring industry. But Norwegian cultural self-esteem remained at a low ebb: the country's merchants spoke Danish, mimicked Danish manners and read Danish pot-boilers. What's more, Norway was a constant bone of contention between Sweden and Denmark, the result being a long series of wars in which its more easterly provinces were regularly battered by the competing armies.

The year 1660 marked a turning point in the constitutional arrangements governing Norway. For centuries, the Danish Council of State had had the power to elect the monarch and impose limitations on his or her rule. Now, a powerful alliance of merchants and clergy swept these powers away to make **Frederik III** an absolute ruler. This was not a reactionary coup, but an attempt to limit the power of the conservative-minded nobility. In addition, the development of a centralized state machine would, many calculated, provide all sorts of job opportunities to the low-born but adept. Norway was incorporated into the administrative structure of Denmark, with royal authority delegated to the *Stattholder*, who governed through what soon became a veritable army of professional bureaucrats. There were positive advantages for Norway: the country acquired better defences, simpler taxes, a separate High Court and doses of Norwegian law, but once again power was exercised almost exclusively by Danes.

■ The eighteenth and early nineteenth centuries

The **absolute monarchy** established by Frederik III soon came to concern itself with every aspect of Norwegian life. The ranks and duties of minor officials were carefully delineated, religious observances tightly regulated and restrictions were imposed on everything from begging and dress through to the food and drink that could be consumed at weddings and funerals. This extraordinary superstructure placed a leaden hand on imagination and invention. Neither was it impartial: there were some benefits for the country's farmers and fishermen, but by and large the system worked in favour of the middle class. The merchants of every small town were allocated the exclusive rights to trade in a particular area and

competition between the towns was forbidden. These local monopolies placed the peasantry at a dreadful disadvantage, nowhere more iniquitously than in the Lofotens, where the fishermen not only had to buy supplies and equipment at the price set by the merchant, but also had to sell their fish at the price set by him too.

In the meantime, there were more wars between Denmark and Sweden. In 1700, **Frederik IV** (1699–1730) made the rash decision to attack the Swedes at the time when their king, Karl XII, was generally reckoned to be one of Europe's most brilliant military strategists. Predictably, the Danes were defeated and only the intervention of the British saved Copenhagen from falling into Swedish hands. Undeterred, Frederik tried again, and this time Karl retaliated by launching a full-scale invasion of Norway. The Swedes rapidly occupied southern Norway, but after Karl was shot dead by a sniper, the two countries agreed the **Peace of Frederiksborg** (1720), which ended hostilities for the rest of the eighteenth century.

Peace favoured the growth of trade, but although Norway's economy prospered it was hampered by the trade monopolies exercised by the merchants of Copenhagen. In the 1760s, however, the Danes did a dramatic U-turn, abolishing monopolies, removing trade barriers and even permitting a free press – and the Norwegian economy boomed. Nonetheless, the bulk of the population remained impoverished and prey to famine whenever the harvest was poor. The number of landless agricultural labourers rose dramatically, partly because the more prosperous farmers were buying up large slices of land, and for the first time Norway had something akin to a proletariat.

Despite this, Norway was one of the few European countries little affected by the French Revolution. Instead of political action, there was a **religious revival**, with Hans Nielson Hauge emerging as an evangelical leader. The movement's characteristic hostility to officialdom caused concern, and Hauge was imprisoned, but in reality it posed little threat to the status quo. The end result was rather the foundation of a fundamentalist movement that is still a force to be reckoned with in parts of fjordland Norway.

The period leading up to the **Napoleonic Wars** was a good time for Norway: overseas trade, especially with England, flourished, with the demand for Norwegian timber and iron heralding a period of unparalleled prosperity.

Denmark and Norway had remained neutral throughout the Seven Years War (1756–63) between England and France, and renewed that neutrality in 1792. However, when Napoleon implemented a trade blockade – the Continental System – against Britain, he roped in the Danes. As a result, the British fleet bombarded Copenhagen in 1807 and forced the surrender of the entire Dano-Norwegian fleet. Denmark, in retaliation, declared war on England and Sweden. The move was disastrous for the Norwegian economy, which had suffered bad harvests in 1807 and 1808, and the English blockade of its seaports ruined trade.

By 1811 it was obvious that the Danes had backed the wrong side in the war, and the idea of an equal union with Sweden, which had supported Britain, became increasingly attractive to many Norwegians. By attaching their coat tails to the victors, they hoped to restore the commercially vital trade with England. They also thought that the new Swedish king would be able to deal with the Danes if it came to a fight – just as the Swedes had themselves calculated when they appointed him in 1810. The man concerned, **Karl XIV Johan**, was, curiously enough, none other than Jean-Baptiste Bernadotte, formerly one of Napoleon's marshals. With perfect timing, he had helped the British defeat Napoleon at Leipzig in 1813. His reward came in the **Treaty of Kiel** the following year when the great powers instructed the Danes to cede all rights in Norway to Sweden (although they did keep the dependencies of Iceland, Greenland and the Faroes). Four hundred years of union had ended.

■ Union with Sweden 1814–1905

The high-handed transfer of Norway from Denmark to Sweden did nothing to assuage the growing demands for greater independence. Furthermore, the Danish Crown Prince Christian Frederik roamed Norway stirring up fears of Swedish intentions. The prince and his supporters convened a Constituent Assembly, which met at Eidsvoll in April 1814 and produced a **constitution**. Issued on May 17, 1814 (still a national holiday), this declared Norway to be a "free, independent and indivisible realm" with Christian Frederik as its king. Not surprisingly, Karl XIV Johan would have none of this and, with the support of the great powers, he invaded Norway. Completely outgunned, Christian Frederik mounted barely any

resistance. In exchange for Swedish promises to recognize the Norwegian constitution and the Storting (parliament), he abdicated as soon as he had signed a peace treaty – the so-called **Convention of Moss** – in August 1814.

The ensuing period was marred by struggles between the Storting and Karl XIV Johan over the nature of the union. Although the constitution emphasized Norway's independence, Johan had a veto over the Storting's actions; the post of *Statthoider* in Norway could be held by a Swede; and foreign and diplomatic matters concerning Norway remained entirely in Swedish hands. Despite this, Karl XIV Johan proved popular in Norway, and during his reign the country enjoyed a fair amount of independence. From 1836 all the highest offices in Norway were filled exclusively by Norwegians and democratic local councils established, in part due to the rise of peasant farmers as a political force.

The gradual increase in prosperity had important **cultural implications**. The layout and buildings of modern Oslo – the Royal Palace, Karl Johans gate and the university – date from this period, whilst Johan Christian Dahl, the most distinguished Scandinavian landscape painter of his day, was instrumental in the moves to establish the National Gallery in Oslo in 1836. Other prominent members of the bourgeoisie championed all things Norwegian. However, under both Oscar I (1844–59) and Karl XV (1859–72) it was **pan-Scandinavianism** that ruled the intellectual roost. This belief in the natural solidarity of Denmark, Norway and Sweden was espoused by the leading artists of the period, including Ibsen and Bjørnstjerne Bjørnson, but died a death in 1864, when the people of Norway and Sweden refused to help Denmark when it was attacked by Austria and Prussia (some of the loudest cries of treachery came from a young writer, Henrik Ibsen, in his poetic drama *Brand*).

Domestic politics changed, too, with the rise to power in the 1850s of **Johan Sverdrup**, who started a long and ultimately successful campaign to wrest executive power from the king and transfer it to the Storting. By the mid-1880s, Sverdrup and his political allies had pretty much won the day, but a further bout of sabre-rattling between the supporters of Norwegian independence and the Swedish king, **Oscar II** (1872–1907), was necessary before both sides would accept a plebiscite. This took place in August 1905, when there was an overwhelming vote in favour of the **dissolution of**

the union, which was duly confirmed by the Treaty of Karlstad. A second plebiscite determined that independent Norway should be a monarchy rather than a republic and, in November 1905, Prince Karl of Denmark (Edward VII's son-in-law) was elected to the throne as **Håkon VII**.

Dissolution came at a time of further economic advance, engendered by the introduction of hydro-electric power. Social reforms also saw funds being made available for unemployment relief, accident insurance schemes and a Factory Act (1909). An extension to the franchise gave the vote to all men over 25 and, in 1913, to women too. The education system was reorganized, and substantial sums were spent on new arms and defence matters. This prewar period also saw the emergence of a strong trade union movement and of a Labour Party committed to revolutionary change.

Culturally, the second half of the nineteenth century was fruitful for Norway, with the rediscovery of the Norwegian language and its folklore by a number of academics who formed the nucleus of the National Romantic movement, which did much to restore the country's cultural self-respect. Following on were famous authors like **Alexander Kielland**, who wrote most of his works between 1880 and 1891, and **Knut Hamsun**, who published his most characteristic novel, *Hunger*, in 1890. In music, **Edvard Grieg** (1843–1907) made his debut in the first concert to consist entirely of works by Norwegian composers and was inspired by old Norwegian folk melodies, composing some of his most famous music for Ibsen's *Peer Gynt*. The artist **Edvard Munch** was also active during this period, completing many of his major works in the 1880s and 1890s, while the internationally acclaimed dramatist **Henrik Ibsen** returned to Oslo after a prolonged, self-imposed exile in 1891.

■ The early years of independence up to 1939

Since 1814 Norway had had little to do with European affairs, and at the outbreak of **World War I** declared herself strictly neutral. Sympathy, though, lay largely with the Western Allies, and the Norwegian economy boomed since its ships and timber were in great demand. By 1916, however, Norway had begun to feel the pinch, as German submarine action hit both enemy and neutral shipping, and by the end of the war Norway had lost half its chartered ton-

nage and 2000 crew. The Norwegian economy also suffered after the USA entered the war because the Americans imposed strict trade agreements in their attempt to prevent supplies getting to Germany, and rationing had to be introduced across Norway. Indeed, the price of neutrality was high: there was a rise in state expenditure, a soaring cost of living and, at the end of the war, no seat at the conference table. In spite of its losses, Norway got no share of the confiscated German shipping, although it was partly compensated by gaining sovereignty of **Spitsbergen** and its coal deposits – the first extension of the Norwegian frontiers for 500 years. In 1920 Norway also entered the new League of Nations.

Later in the 1920s, the decline in world trade led to a decreased demand for Norway's shipping. Bank failure and currency fluctuation were rife, and, as unemployment and industrial strife increased, a burgeoning Norwegian **Labour Party** took advantage. With the franchise extended to all those over 23 and the introduction of larger constituencies, it had a chance, for the first time, to win seats outside the large towns. At the 1927 election the Labour Party, together with the Social Democrats from whom they'd split, were the biggest grouping in the Storting. Nonetheless, because they had no overall majority and because many feared their revolutionary rhetoric, they were manoeuvred out of office after only fourteen days. Trade disputes and lock-outs continued and troops had to be used to protect workers crossing picket lines.

During the war, **Prohibition** had been introduced as a temporary measure, and a referendum of 1919 showed a clear majority in favour of its continuation. But the ban did little to quell – and even exacerbated – drunkenness, and it was abandoned in 1932, to be replaced by the government sales monopoly of wines and spirits that remains in force today. The 1933 election gave the Labour Party more seats than ever. Having shed its revolutionary image, a campaigning reformist Labour Party benefited from the increasing conviction that state control and a centrally planned economy were the only answer to Norway's economic problems. In 1935 the Labour Party, in alliance with the Agrarian Party, took power – an unlikely combination since the Agrarians were profoundly nationalist in outlook, so much so that their defence spokesman had been the rabid anti-Semite **Vidkun Quisling**. Frustrated by the democratic process, Quisling had left the Agrarians in

1933 to found the Nasjonal Samling (National Unification), a fascist movement which proposed, among other things, that both Hitler and Mussolini should be nominated for the Nobel Peace Prize. Quisling had good contacts with Nazi Germany but little support in Norway – local elections in 1937 reduced his local representation to a mere seven, and party membership fell to 1500.

The Labour government under **Johan Nygaardsvold** presided over an improving economy. By 1938 industrial production was 75 percent higher than it had been in 1914; unemployment had dropped as expenditure on roads, railways and public works increased. Social welfare reforms were implemented and trade union membership increased. When war broke out in 1939, Norway was lacking only one thing – adequate defence. A vigorous member of the League of Nations, the country had pursued disarmament and peace policies since the end of World War I and was determined to remain neutral.

■ World War II

In early 1940, despite the threatening rumblings of Hitler, the Norwegians were preoccupied with Allied mine-laying off the Norwegian coast – part of their attempt to prevent Swedish iron ore being shipped from Narvik to Germany. Indeed, such was Norwegian naivety that they made a formal protest to Britain on the day of the **German invasion**. Caught napping, the Norwegian army offered little initial resistance and the south and central regions of the country were quickly overrun. King Håkon and the Storting were forced into a hasty evacuation of Oslo and headed north, eventually taking refuge in Britain where they formed the Norwegian government-in-exile. Norway was rapidly brought under Nazi control, Hitler sending **Josef Terboven** to take full charge of affairs. The fascist Nasjonal Samling was declared the only legal party and the media, civil servants and teachers were brought under their control. As **civil resistance** grew, a state of emergency was declared: two trade union leaders were shot, arrests increased and a concentration camp was set up outside Oslo. In February 1942 Quisling was installed as "Minister President" of Norway, but it was soon clear that his government didn't have the support of the Norwegian people. The church refused to co-operate, schoolteachers protested and trade union members and officials resigned en masse. In response, deportations increased, death sentences

were announced and a compulsory labour scheme was introduced.

Military resistance escalated. A military organisation (MILORG) was established as a branch of the armed forces under the control of the High Command in London. By May 1941 it had enlisted 20,000 men (32,000 by 1944) in clandestine groups all over the country. Arms and instructors came from Britain, radio stations were set up and a continuous flow of intelligence about Nazi movements sent back. Sabotage operations were legion, the most notable being the destruction of the heavy-water plant at **Rjukan**, foiling a German attempt to produce an atomic bomb.

The **government in exile** in London continued to represent free Norway to the world, mobilizing support on behalf of the Allies. Most of the Norwegian merchant fleet was abroad when the Nazis invaded, and by 1943 the Norwegian navy had seventy ships helping the Allied convoys. In Sweden, Norwegian exiles assembled in "health camps" at the end of 1943 to train as police troops in readiness for liberation.

When the Allies landed in Normandy in June 1944, overt action against the Nazis in Norway by the resistance was discouraged, since the Allies couldn't safeguard against reprisals. By late October, the Russians had crossed the border in the far north. The Germans, forced to retreat, burned everything in their path and drove the local population into hiding. To prevent the Germans reinforcing their beleaguered Finnmark battalions, the resistance planned a campaign of mass railway sabotage, stopping three-quarters of the troop movements overnight. As their control of Norway crumbled, the Germans finally **surrendered** on May 7, 1945. King Håkon returned to Norway on June 7, five years to the day since he'd left for exile.

Terboven committed suicide and the Nasjonal Samling collaborators were rounded up. A caretaker government took office, staffed by resistance leaders, and was replaced in October 1945 by a majority **Labour government**. The Communists won eleven seats, reflecting the efforts of Communist saboteurs in the war and the prestige that the Soviet Union enjoyed in Norway after liberation. Quisling was shot, along with 24 other high-ranking traitors, and thousands of collaborators were punished.

■ Postwar reconstruction

At the end of the war, Norway was on its knees: the far north – Finnmark – had been laid waste, half the mercantile fleet lost, and production was at a standstill. Recovery, though, fostered by a sense of national unity, was quick; it took only three years for GNP to return to its prewar level. Norway's part in the war had increased her prestige in the world. The country became one of the founding members of the **United Nations** in 1945, and the first UN Secretary-General, Tryggve Lie, was Norwegian Foreign Minister. With the failure of discussions to promote a Scandinavian defence union, the Storting also voted to enter **NATO** in 1949.

Domestically, there was general agreement about the form that social reconstruction should take. In 1948, the Storting passed the laws that introduced the Welfare State virtually unanimously. The 1949 election saw the government returned with a larger majority and Labour governments continued to be elected throughout the following decade when the dominant political figure was **Einar Gerhardsen**. As national prosperity increased, society became ever more egalitarian, levelling up rather than down. Subsidies were paid to the agricultural and fishing industries, wages increased and a comprehensive social security system helped to eradicate poverty. The state ran the important mining industry, was the largest shareholder in the hydroelectric company and built an enormous steel works at Mo-i-Rana to help develop the economy of the devastated northern counties. Rationing ended in 1952 and, as the demand for higher-level education grew, new universities were approved at Bergen, Trondheim and Tromsø.

■ Beyond consensus: modern Norway

The political consensus began to fragment in the early 1960s. Following changes in the constitution concerning the rural constituencies, the centre had realigned itself in the 1950s, the outmoded Agrarian Party becoming the **Centre Party**. Defence squabbles within the Labour Party led to the formation of the **Socialist People's Party** (the SF), which wanted Norway out of NATO and sought a renunciation of nuclear weapons. The Labour Party's 1961 declaration that no nuclear weapons would be stationed in Norway except under an immediate threat of war did not placate the SF who, unexpectedly, took two seats at the election that year. Holding the balance of power, the SF voted with the Labour Party until 1963, when it helped bring down the government over

the mismanagement of state industries. A replacement coalition collapsed after only one month, but the writing was on the wall. Rising prices, dissatisfaction with high taxation and a continuing housing shortage meant that the 1965 election put a **non-socialist coalition** in power for the first time in twenty years.

The new coalition's programme, under the leadership of **Per Borten** of the Centre Party, was unambitious. However, living standards continued to rise, and although the 1969 election saw a marked increase in Labour Party support, the coalition hung on to power. Also in 1969, **oil and gas** were discovered beneath the North Sea and, as the vast extent of the reserves became obvious, so it became clear that the Norwegians were to enjoy a magnificent bonanza – one which was destined to pay about 25 percent of the government's annual bills. Meanwhile, Norway's politicians, who had applied twice previously for membership of the **European Economic Community** (EEC) – in 1962 and 1967 – believed that de Gaulle's fall in France presented a good opportunity for a third application, which was made in 1970. There was great concern, though, about the effect of membership on Norwegian agriculture and fisheries, and in 1971 Per Borten was forced to resign following his indiscreet handling of the negotiations. The Labour Party, the majority of its representatives in favour of EEC membership, formed a minority administration, but when the 1972 referendum narrowly voted "No" to joining the EEC, the government resigned.

With the 1973 election producing another minority Labour government, the uncertain pattern of the previous ten years continued. Even the postwar consensus on **Norwegian security policy** broke down on various issues – such as the question of a northern European nuclear-free zone and the stocking of Allied material in Norway – although there remained strong agreement for continued NATO membership.

In 1983, the Christian Democrats and the Centre Party joined together in a non-socialist coalition, which lasted only two years. It was replaced in 1986 by a minority Labour administration, led by **Dr Gro Harlem Brundtland**, Norway's first woman prime minister. She made sweeping changes to the way the country was run, introducing seven women into her eighteen-member cabinet, but her government was beset by problems for the three years of its life: tumbling oil prices led to a recession, unemployment rose (though only to four percent) and there was widespread dissatisfaction with Labour's high taxation.

At the **general election** in September 1989, Labour lost eight seats and was forced out of office – the worst result that the party had suffered since 1930. More surprising was the success of the extremist parties on both political wings – the anti-NATO Left Socialist Party and the right-wing, anti-immigrant Progress Party both scored spectacular results, winning almost a quarter of the votes cast, and increasing their representation in the Storting many times over. This deprived the Conservative Party (one of whose leaders, bizarrely, was Gro Harlem Brundtland's husband) of the majority it might have expected, the result being yet another shaky minority administration – this time a **centre-right coalition** between the Conservatives, the Centre Party and the Christian Democrats, led by Jan Syse.

The new government immediately faced problems familiar to the last Labour administration. In particular, there was continuing conflict over joining the **European Community**, a policy still supported by many in the Norwegian establishment but flatly rejected by the Centre Party. It was this, in part, that signalled the end of the coalition, for after just over a year in office, the Centre Party withdrew its support and forced the downfall of Syse. In October 1990, Gro Harlem Brundtland was put back in power at the head of a **minority Labour administration**, remaining in office till her re-election for a fourth minority term in 1993. The 1993 elections saw a revival in Labour Party fortunes and, to the relief of the majority, the collapse of the Progress Party vote. However, it was also an untidy, confusing affair where the main issue, membership of the EU, cut across the traditional left versus right axis of the political parties.

■ Present-day Norway

Following the 1993 election, the country tumbled into a long and fiercely conducted campaign over membership of the EU. Brundtland and her main political opponents wanted in, but despite the near unanimity amongst politicians, the Norwegians narrowly rejected the EU in a **referendum** on November 28, 1994. It was a close call (52.5 percent versus 47.5 percent), but in the end farmers and fishermen afraid of the economic results of joining, as well as womens' groups and environmentalists who felt that Norway's

high standards of social care and "green" controls would suffer, came together to swing opinion against the EU. Afterwards, and unlike the Labour government of 1972, the Brundtland administration soldiered on, wisely soothing ruffled feathers by promising to shelve the whole EU membership issue until at least 2000. Nevertheless, the 1997 election saw a move to the right, the main beneficiaries being the Christian Democratic Party and the ultra-conservative Progress Party. In itself, this was not enough to remove the Labour-led coalition from office – indeed Labour remained comfortably the largest party – but the right was dealt a trump card by the new Labour leader, Thorbjørn Jagland. During the campaign, Jagland had promised that the Labour Party would step down from office if it failed to elicit more than the 36.9 percent of the vote it had secured in 1993. Much to the chagrin of his colleagues, Jagland's political chickens came home to roost when Labour only received 35 per cent of the vote – and they had to go, leaving the government in the hands of an unwieldy right-of-centre, minority coalition. Bargaining with its rivals from a position of parliamentary weakness, the new government has found it difficult to cut a clear path – or at least one very different from its predecessor – apart from in managing to antagonize the women's movement by some of its reactionary social legislation during 1998 and 1999.

In the long term, quite what Norway will make of its splendid isolation from the EU is unclear, though the situation is mitigated by Norway's membership of the European Economic Agreement (EEA), a free-trade deal of January 1994 which covers both Norway and the EU. Whatever happens, and whether or not there is another EU referendum, it's hard to imagine that the Norwegians will suffer any permanent economic harm. They have, after all, a superabundance of natural resources and arguably the most educated workforce in the world. Which isn't to say the country doesn't collectively fret – a modest increase in the amount of drug addiction and street crime has produced much heart-searching, the theory being that an advanced and progressive social policy should be able to eliminate such barbarisms. This thoughtful approach, so typical of Norway, is very much to the country's credit as is the refusal to accept a residual level of unemployment (of about 6–7 percent) that is the envy of other Western governments

A BRIEF GUIDE TO NORWEGIAN

There are two official Norwegian languages: *Riksmål* or *Bokmål* (book language), a modification of the old Dano-Norwegian tongue left over from the days of Danish dominance; and *Landsmål* or *Nynorsk*, which was codified during the nineteenth-century upsurge of Norwegian nationalism and is based on rural dialects of Old Norse provenance. Roughly eighty percent of schoolchildren have *Bokmål* as their primary language, and the remaining twenty percent are *Nynorsk* users, concentrated in the fjord country of the west coast and the mountain districts of central Norway. Despite the best efforts of the government, *Nynorsk* is in decline – in 1944 fully one-third of the population used it. As the more common of the two languages, it is *Bokmål* we use here.

As elsewhere in Scandinavia, you don't really need to know any Norwegian to get by. Almost everyone speaks at least some English, and in the tourist industry most Norwegians are fluent. **Phrasebooks** are thin on the ground, but Berlitz's Norwegian–English mini-dictionary has a useful grammar section and a menu reader, while Routledge's more comprehensive (and much heavier) Norwegian dictionary has much the same. As for **learning the language**, there are tapes and books in the *Teach Yourself Norwegian* course, by Margaretha Danbolt Simons, available in both the UK and US (Hodder Headline).

PRONUNCIATION

Pronunciation can be tricky. A **vowel** is usually long when it's the final syllable or followed by only one consonant; followed by two it's generally short. Unfamiliar ones are:

ae before an r, as in b**a**d; otherwise as in s**ay**
ø as in f**u**r but without pronouncing the r
å usually as in s**aw**

øy between the ø sound and b**oy**
ei as in s**ay**

consonants are pronounced as in English except:

c, q, w, z found only in foreign words and pronounced as in the original
g before i, y or ei, as in **y**et; otherwise hard
hv as in **v**iew
j, gj, hj, lj as in **y**et

rs usually as in **sh**ut
k before i, y or j, like the Scottish lo**ch**; otherwise hard
sj, sk before i, y, ø or øy, as in **sh**ut

BASIC PHRASES

do you speak English?	*snakker du engelsk?*	good morning	*god morgen*
yes	*ja*	good afternoon	*god dag*
no	*nei*	good night	*god natt*
do you understand?	*forstår du?*	goodbye	*adjø*
I don't understand	*jeg forstår ikke*	today	*i dag*
I understand	*jeg forstår*	tomorrow	*i morgen*
please	*vær så god*	day after tomorrow	*i overmorgen*
thank you (very much)	*takk (tusen takk)*	in the morning	*om morgenen*
you're welcome	*vær så god*	in the afternoon	*om ettermiddagen*
excuse me	*unnskyld*	in the evening	*om kvelden*

SOME SIGNS

entrance	*inngang*	cycle path	*sykkelsti*
exit	*utgang*	no smoking	*røyking forbudt*
gentlemen	*herrer* or *menn*	no camping	*camping forbudt*
ladies	*damer* or *kvinner*	no trespassing	*uvedkommende forbudt*
open	*åpen*	no entry	*ingen adgang*
closed	*stengt*	pull/push	*trekk/trykk*
arrival	*ankomst*	departure	*avgang*
police	*politi*	parking fees	*avgift*
hospital	*sykehus*		

QUESTIONS AND DIRECTIONS

where? (where is/are?)	*hvor? (hvor er?)*	good/bad	*god/dårlig*
when?	*når?*	vacant/occupied	*ledig/opptatt*
what?	*hva?*	a little/a lot	*litt/mye*
how much/many?	*hvor mye/hvor mange?*	more/less	*mer/mindre*
why?	*hvorfor?*	can we camp here?	*kan vi campe her?*
which?	*hvilket?*	is there a youth hostel	*er det et vandrerhjem*
what's that called	*hva kaller man det på*	near here?	*i nærheten?*
in Norwegian?	*norsk?*	how do I get to . . . ?	*hvordan kommer jeg*
can you direct me	*kan de vise meg veien*		*til . . . ?*
to . . . ?	*til . . . ?*	how far is it to . . . ?	*avor langt er det*
it is/there is (is it/is there)	*det er (er det)?*		*til . . . ?*
what time is it?	*hvor mange er klokken?*	ticket	*billett*
big/small	*stor/liten*	single/return	*en vei/tur-retur*
cheap/expensive	*billig/dyrt*	can you give me a lift	*kan jeg få sitte på*
early/late	*tidlig/sent*	to . . . ?	*til . . . ?*
hot/cold	*varm/kald*	left/right	*venstre/høyre*
near/far	*i nærheten/langt borte*	go straight ahead	*kjør rett frem*

NUMBERS

0	*null*	7	*sju*	14	*fjorten*	21	*tjueen*
1	*en*	8	*åtte*	15	*femten*	22	*tjueto*
2	*to*	9	*ni*	16	*seksten*	30	*tretti*
3	*tre*	10	*ti*	17	*sytten*	40	*førti*
4	*fire*	11	*elleve*	18	*atten*	50	*femti*
5	*fem*	12	*tolv*	19	*nitten*	60	*seksti*
6	*seks*	13	*tretten*	20	*tjue*	70	*sytti*

80	*åtti*
90	*nitti*
100	*hundre*
101	*hundreogen*
200	*to hundre*
1000	*tusen*

DAYS AND MONTHS

Sunday	*søndag*	January	*januar*	August	*august*
Monday	*mandag*	February	*februar*	September	*september*
Tuesday	*tirsdag*	March	*mars*	October	*oktober*
Wednesday	*onsdag*	April	*april*	November	*november*
Thursday	*torsdag*	May	*mai*	December	*desember*
Friday	*fredag*	June	*juni*		
Saturday	*lørdag*	July	*juli*		

(Note: days and months are never capitalized)

GLOSSARY OF NORWEGIAN TERMS AND WORDS

å	stream or creek	*gate (gt.)*	street	*rabatt*	discount or price
apotek	chemist	*hav*	ocean		reduction
bakke	hill	*havn*	harbour	*rådhus*	town hall
bokhandel	bookshop	*hytte*	cottage, cabin	*sentrum*	city or town centre
bro/bru	bridge	*innsjø*	lake	*sjø*	sea
dal	valley/dale	*jernbanestasjon*	railway station	*skog*	forest
domkirke	cathedral	*KFUM/KFUK*	Norwegian YMCA/YWCA	*slott*	castle, palace
drosje	taxi	*kirke/kjerke*	church	*Storting*	parliament
e.Kr	AD	*klokken/kl.*	o'clock	*tilbud*	special offer
elv/bekk	river/stream	*moderasjon*	discount or price reduction	*torget*	main town square,
ferje/ferge	ferry	*MOMS or MVA*	Value Added Tax		often home to an
fjell/berg	mountain	*museet*	museum		outdoor market
f.Kr	BC	*NAF*	Norwegian Automobile	*vann/vatn*	water or lake
foss	waterfall		Association	*vei/veg/vn.*	road

CHAPTER FOUR

OSLO AND AROUND

O**slo** is an enterprising city. Something of a poor relation to Stockholm until Norway's break with Sweden at the beginning of the twentieth century, it remained dourly provincial until the 1950s, since when it has developed into a go-ahead and cosmopolitan commercial hub of half a million people. The new self-confidence is plain to see in the vibrant and urbane city centre, whose easy-going atmosphere compares favourably with any other capital in Europe. Inevitably, Norway's big companies are mostly based here, as a rash of concrete-and-glass towers testify, though these monoliths rarely interrupt the stately Neoclassical lines of the late nineteenth-century **town centre**. It's here you should head first, as Oslo's handsome older quarters notch up some excellent museums and field a cosmopolitan street-life and bar scene that surprises many first-time visitors – they're also within easy reach of the **Bygdøy peninsula** – home to the world-famous Viking Ships Museum.

Oslo is also the only major metropolis in the country (its nearest rival, Bergen, is less than half its size), a distinction which gives the city an unusually powerful – some say overweening – voice in the nation's affairs, whether political, cultural or economic. The centre itself is compact, but the city's vast boundaries (453 square kilometres) encompass huge areas of forest and coastline, reflecting the deep and abiding affinity which the inhabitants of Oslo have for the wide open spaces that surround their city. The waters of the Oslofjord to the south and the forested hills of the **Nordmarka** inland to the north are immensely popular for everything from boating and hiking to skiing, and on all but the shortest of stays there's ample opportunity to join in. The **island beaches** just offshore in the Oslofjord and the open forest and ski jumps at **Holmenkollen** are obvious targets, both within easy reach by ferry or underground train.

Oslo curves round the northernmost point of the **Oslofjord**, which extends for some 100km from the Skagerrak, the choppy channel separating Norway and Sweden from Denmark. As Norwegian fjords go, Oslofjord is not particularly beautiful, but amongst a string of workaday industrial settlements is Norway's only surviving fortified town, **Fredrikstad**, with its angular bastions and grid-iron of late sixteenth-century streets. It's best visited as a day-trip by train from the capital.

OSLO

The oldest of the Scandinavian capital cities, **OSLO** (the name is made up from Ås, a Norse word for God, and Lo, meaning field) was founded, according to the medieval Norse chronicler Snorre Sturlason, around 1048 by Harald Hardråde. Harald's son, Olav Kyrre, established a bishopric and built a cathedral here, though the kings of Norway continued to live in Bergen – an oddly inefficient division of church and state, considering the difficulty of communications between the two settlements. At the start of the fourteenth century, Håkon V rectified matters by moving to Oslo, where he built himself the Akershus fortress. The town boomed until 1349 when the bubonic plague wiped out almost half the population, initiating a period of slow decline whose pace accelerated after Norway came under Danish control in 1397. No more than a neglected backwater, Oslo's fortunes were ultimately revived by the Danish king Christian IV, who in 1624 moved Oslo lock, stock and barrel, shifting it west to its present site and rechristening it "Christiania". The new city prospered and by the nineteenth century, Christiania (indeed

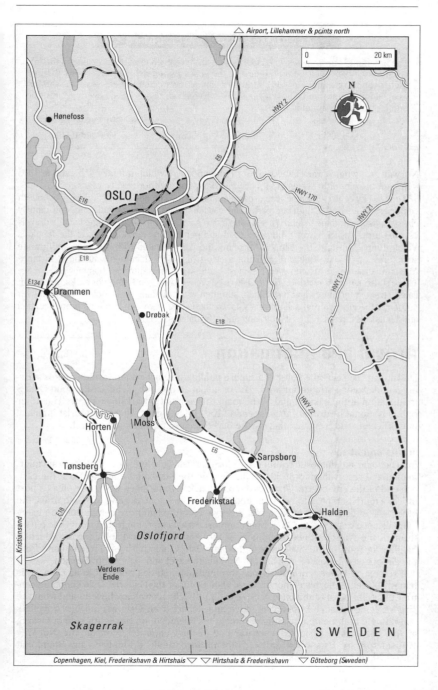

△ Airport, Lillehammer & points north

0   20 km

N

Hønefoss

HWY 2

E6

OSLO

E16

HWY 170

HWY 21

E18

HWY 21

E134

Drammen

Drøbak

E18

HWY 22

Horten

Moss

E6

Sarpsborg

Tønsberg

Frederikstad

Halden

E18

△ Kristiansand

Oslofjord

Verdens
Ende

Skagerrak

S W E D E N

Copenhagen, Kiel, Frederikshavn & Hirtshals ▽ ▽ Hirtshals & Frederikshavn   ▽ Göteborg (Sweden)

ACCOMMODATION PRICE CODES

The hotels and guesthouses listed in this chapter have been graded according to the following price bands, based on the cost of the **least expensive double room during high season** (late June to Aug). However, almost every hotel offers seasonal and/or weekend discounts, and wherever possible we've given two grades, covering both the regular and the discounted rate.

① Under 500kr   ② 500–700kr   ③ 700–900kr
④ 900–1200kr   ⑤ 1200–1500kr   ⑥ Over 1500kr

Norway as a whole) was clamouring for independence, which it finally achieved in 1905 – though the city didn't revert to its original name for another twenty years.

Today's city centre embodies the urban elegance of the late nineteenth and early twentieth centuries: wide streets, dignified parks and gardens, solid buildings and long, consciously classical vistas combine to lend it a self-satisfied, respectable air. Oslo's biggest single draw is its **museums**, which cover a hugely varied and stimulating range of topics: the fabulous Viking Ships Museum, the Munch Museum, the park devoted to the bronze and granite sculptures of Gustav Vigeland, and the moving historical documents of the Resistance Museum are enough to keep even the most battle-weary museumgoer busy for a few days. There's also a decent **outdoor life** – Oslo is enlivened by a good range of parks, pavement cafés, street entertainers and festivals. In summer, when virtually the whole population lives outdoors, the city is a real delight. It's also worth visiting in winter, when its prime location amid hills and forests makes it a thriving and affordable ski centre.

Arrival and information

Downtown Oslo is at the heart of a superb public-transport system, which makes arriving and departing straightforward. The principal arrival hub is the area around Oslo S train station at the eastern end of the main thoroughfare, Karl Johans gate. The other hub is Nationaltheatret at the west end of Karl Johans gate. There's a tourist information office in Oslo S and another by the harbour close to Nationaltheateret.

Trains and buses

International and domestic **trains** use Oslo Sentralstasjon, known as **Oslo S** (train information and reservations ☎81 50 08 88), sited on the Jernbanetorget square at the eastern end of the city centre. There are money-exchange facilities here, as well as a post office, a tourist office, and two train information offices, one dealing with enquiries, the other selling tickets and making seat reservations (the latter are compulsory on many long-distance trains – see p.167). Many domestic trains en route to and from Oslo S pass through the **Nationaltheatret** station, at the west end of Karl Johans gate, which is handier for most of the city-centre sights and Oslo's main harbour. Trains to and from the airport (see opposite) stop at both Nationaltheatret and Oslo Sentralstasjon.

The central **Bussterminalen** (bus terminal), sometimes referred to as Oslo M, is handily placed a short walk northeast of Oslo S, under the Galleriet Oslo shopping centre. It handles most of the bus services within the city as well as those to and from the airport. Long-distance buses also arrive and depart from Oslo M, but bus travellers should note that incoming services sometimes terminate on the south side of Oslo S, at the bus stands beside Havnegata. For all bus enquiries, consult the Nor-Way **Bussekspress Bussterminalen information desk** (Mon–Fri 7am–10pm, Sat 8am–5.30pm, Sun 8am–10pm; ☎23 00 24 40).

Airport

Oslo's gleaming new airport, **Gardermoen**, is a lavish affair very much in the Scandinavian style, with acres of cool wooden floor, softly spoken angles and slender concrete pillars. Departures are processed on the upper and arrivals on the lower level, where there are also currency-exchange facilities, car-rental offices – see p.223 for details – and a tourist information office. Gardermoen is located 45km north of the city off the E6 motorway. If you're **driving** into Oslo, note that there's a 12kr toll on all approach roads into the city. From the airport, **express trains** run south to Oslo, stopping at Oslo S and Nationaltheatret stations (every 20–30min 5.30am–12.30am; 35min; 90kr). There are also ordinary inter-city trains into Oslo (every 1–2hr; 40min; 60kr) and trains north to Lillehammer, Røros and Trondheim. **Flybussen** buses (every 10–15min Mon–Sat 5.30am–1am, Sun noon–midnight; 40min; 65kr) also link the airport with Oslo, departing from outside the arrivals concourse and travelling via the main downtown bus station, Oslo M, to Jernbanetorget, Grensen and the *Radisson SAS Scandinavia* hotel. They will also drop passengers on request at the Haraldsheim youth hostel. Finally, **Nor-Way Bussekspress** operate a variety of other bus services from the airport direct to the small towns surrounding Oslo.

Ferries

DFDS Seaways **ferries** from Copenhagen and Stena ferries from Fredrikshavn, also in Denmark, arrive at the Vippetangen quays, a twenty-minute walk south of Oslo S – take Akershusstranda and Skippergata to Karl Johans gate and turn right, or catch bus #60 marked "Jernbanetorget" (every 20–30min Mon–Fri 6am–midnight, Sat from 7am, Sun from 8am; 10min; 20kr). With Color Line from Kiel in Germany and Hirsthals in Denmark you'll arrive at the Hjortneskaia, some 3km west of the city centre. Bus #56 goes from here to the city centre and Oslo S; services are irregular (every 30min Mon–Fri 6–9.20am & 2.30–5.30pm; 10min; 20kr), but usually coincide with ferry arrivals. Failing that, a taxi to Oslo S will cost about 150kr (for ferry ticket office details see "Listings", p.224). Finally, Hurtigbåt domestic passenger express ferry boats from Arendal and points on the south coast dock at the Palékaia, a five- to ten-minute walk south of Oslo S.

Driving into the city

Arriving **by car**, you'll have to drive through one of eighteen video-controlled toll-points which ring the city: it's 12kr to enter and there are spot fines if you're caught trying to avoid the tolls. Passholder lanes (blue signs inscribed "Abonnement") are always located on the left and are for drivers in possession of toll passes; the "Mynt/Coin" (yellow signs) lanes are for exact cash payments only, and frequently have a bucket-shaped receptacle where you throw your money; the "Manuell" (grey) lanes are also used for cash payments, but provide change. Oslo's ring roads circle and tunnel under the city; if you follow the signs for "Ring 1" you'll be delivered right into the centre and emerge (eventually) at the Ibsen P-hus, a multistorey car park two blocks north of Karl Johans gate.

You won't need your car to sightsee in Oslo. For **car parking**, the above-mentioned Ibsen P-hus, on C.J. Hambros Plass 1 (☎22 33 04 80), is open 24 hours, as is the Aker Brygge P-hus, Sjøgata 4 (☎22 01 94 94). There are half a dozen other multi storey car parks in the centre, though several of them operate restricted hours only. Costs begin at 10kr for 25 minutes during the day and evening, mounting to a maximum charge of 130kr for 24 hours, or 40kr in the evening (6pm–midnight); overnight parking (6pm–9am) costs 80kr. The Ibsen P-hus offers a twenty percent discount to Oslo Card holders.

Alternatively, you can park in **pay-and-display** car parks and metered spaces around the city (up to 15kr per hour, 32kr for two hours). Identified by blue "P" signs, on-street metered spaces are free from Monday to Friday between 5pm and 8am and over the weekend after 2pm Saturday. They're also free for Oslo Card holders at all times (see

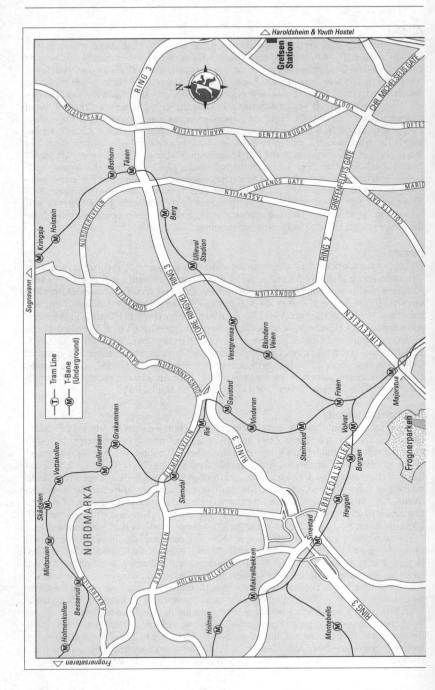

OSLO

Tøyen

Munch Museum

Gamlebyen Ruins

SARS GATE

GATE

Grønland

Jernbane-torget

Oslo S

Stortinget

Nationaltheatret

PILESTREDET

VERGELANDVN

JOHANS GATE

RÅDHUSGATA

OSLO TUNNELEN

AKERHUSKAIA

DRAMMENSVEIEN

RING 1

FRESTRESVET

NYLANDSVEIEN

EKEBERG HEIGHTS

Sjømannsskolen

KARLSBORGV

KONGSVEIEN

MOSSEVEIEN

Vippetangen Pier

Sjømannsskolen

See 'Central Oslo' map

OSLOFJORD

Bleikøya

Hovedøya

Lindøya

Gressholmen Island

Nakholmen & Lindøya Islands

Langøyene (Island)

Denmark

0   500 m

Oslo Bymuseum

Vigeland Museum

Vigelands-parken

HALDVAN SVERRES G.

RING 2

BYGDØY ALLÉ

DRAMMENSVEIEN

FROGNER STRANDA

E18

Dronningen Pier

Bygdøynes Pier

Fram Museum

Maritime Museum

Kon-Tiki Museum

Norwegian Folk-Museum

Viking Ships Museum

BYGDØY

DRAMMENSVEIEN

DRONNING BLANCAS

BYGDØYVEIEN

HUK AVENY

LANGVIKSVN

NSVN

FREDRIKSBORGVN

Lille Herbern

Store Herbern

Nakholmen

Henie Onstad Art Centre

Tokiel & Hirtshals

THE OSLO CARD

The useful **Oslo Card** gives free admission to almost every museum in the city and unlimited free travel on the entire municipal transport system, including local trains, plus free on-street parking at metered parking places. It also provides some useful discounts in shops, hotels and restaurants. Valid for either 24, 48 or 72 hours, it costs 150kr, 220kr and 250kr respectively (children aged 4–15: 50kr, 60kr and 70kr); a 24hr family card for two adults and two children costs 350kr. It's available at the city's tourist offices, most hotels and campsites in Oslo, the Trafikanten office (see below) and downtown Narvesen newsagents. The card is valid from the moment it is first used, at which time it should either be presented and stamped or (for example, if your first journey is by tram) you should ink in the date and time yourself. Bear in mind that in the winter, when opening hours for many sights and museums are reduced, you may have to work hard to make the card pay for itself.

---

box above) – but make sure to write your registration number, date and time on the card in the space provided, and note that you'll still have to observe parking time limits.

Information

The main tourist information office, the **Norges Informasjonssenter** (Norwegian Information Centre; June–Aug daily 9am–7pm; April, May & Sept Mon–Sat 9am–5pm; Oct–March Mon–Fri 9am–4pm; ☎22 83 00 50, *www.oslopro.no*) is housed in what used to be the Oslo Vestbane train station at Brynjulf Bull's plass 1, down by the waterfront at the western end of the city centre. It has some glossy visual displays and an extensive range of brochures relating to Norway as a whole, but also specializes in everything to do with Oslo, providing a full range of information, free city maps, guided tours and an accommodation-booking service. There's also a tourist office inside **Oslo S** (May–Aug daily 8am–11pm; Sept Mon–Sat 8am–11pm; Oct–April Mon–Sat 8am–5pm; ☎22 17 11 24) with similar services. Both offices sell the Oslo Card and have free copies of various booklets and leaflets, including the excellent and very thorough *Oslo Official Guide* and *What's On in Oslo*, an invaluable listings guide to events and services in the city. **Ungdoms Informasjonen**, Møllergata 3 (Mon–Fri 11am–5pm; ☎22 41 51 32, *www.unginfo.oslo.no*) specializes in information for young people aged 16–25. The **Norwegian Youth Hostel Association** (Norske Vandrerhjem) has its main office right in the centre of town, near Oslo S at Dronningens gate 26 (☎23 13 93 00, *www. vandrerhjem.no*). They issue a detailed free booklet on all the country's hostels.

City transport

Compared to other European capitals, Oslo is extremely **safe**, and you're unlikely to be hassled. However, the usual cautions apply to walking around on your own late at night, when you should be particularly careful in the vicinity of Oslo S (where the junkies gather) and on the tougher east side of town along and around Storgata. This sense of safety applies in equal measure to the **city transport** system, which is operated by AS Oslo Sporveier, whose information office, **Trafikanten**, is on Jernbanetorget, beneath the see-through high-tech clock tower outside Oslo S (Mon–Fri 7am–8pm, Sat 8am–6pm; ☎22 17 70 30). Apart from selling Oslo Cards and public transport tickets (see above), they give away a useful **transit route map**, the *Sporveiens hovedkart,* as well as a **timetable** booklet called *Rutebok for Oslo*, which details every timetable for every route in the Oslo system.

Oslo's public transport system consists of buses, trams, a small underground rail system (the Tunnelbanen) and local ferries. Flat-fare **tickets** (bought on board buses, trams or ferries, or at Tunnelbanen stations) cost 20kr and are valid for unlimited travel within the city boundaries for one hour (children 4–16 travel half price; under-4s go free). There are several ways to cut costs, the best being the **Oslo Card** (see box opposite), which is valid on the whole network and on certain routes beyond – but not on trains or buses to the airport. If you're not into museums, however, a straight **travel pass** might be a better buy. A Dagskort, valid for unlimited travel within the city limits for 24 hours, costs 40kr, or there's the Flexikort (8 rides; 115kr), as well as passes for longer stays, available from the Trafikanten office in Jernbanetorget and downtown Narvesen kiosks. On buses, the driver will check your ticket; on trams you're trusted to have one. Flexikort tickets should be cancelled in the machine. Though **fare-dodging** might seem widespread, bear in mind that it is punished by some hefty spot fines.

Buses

Almost all city **bus** services originate at the Bussterminalen beside Oslo S. There are around fifty routes operating within the city limits, and other services out of Oslo too. The vast majority of them pass through Jernbanetorget and many also stop at the Nationaltheatret (National Theatre), towards the west end of the city centre. Most buses stop running at around midnight, though at weekends **night buses** (*nattbussen*) take over on certain routes (flat-rate fare 40kr; Oslo Card and other passes not valid) – for full details see the timetable, *Rutebok for Oslo*.

Trams

The city's **trams** run on eight routes through the city, criss-crossing the centre from east to west, and sometimes duplicating the bus routes. They are a bit slower than the buses, but are a handy and rather more interesting way of getting about. Major stops include Jernbanetorget, Nationaltheatret and Aker Brygge. Most operate regularly throughout the day from 6am to midnight.

Tunnelbanen and local trains

The Tunnelbanen – or **T-bane** – has eight lines, all of which converge to share a common slice of track which crosses the city centre from Majorstuen in the west to Tøyen in the east, with Jernbanetorget, Stortinget and Nationaltheatret stations in between. From this central section, four lines run westbound (*Vest*) and four eastbound (*Øst*). The system mainly serves commuters from the suburbs, but you'll find it useful for trips out to Holmenkollen and Sognsvann – where the trains travel above ground. The system runs from around 6am until 12.30am. A series of **local commuter trains**, run by NSB, link Oslo with Moss, Eidsvoll, Drammen and other outlying towns; departures are from Oslo S, with many also making a stop at Nationaltheatret.

Ferries

Numerous **ferries** shuttle across the northern reaches of the Oslofjord, connecting the city centre with outlying districts and the archipelago. Services to the Bygdøy peninsula (late April to Sept only) leave from the piers behind the Rådhus, while the all-year services to Hovedøya, Lindøya and the other offshore islets (except Langøyene, June–Aug only) leave from the Vippetangen quay, behind Akershus Castle. To get to the Vippetangen quay, take bus #60 from Jernbanetorget. If you're venturing beyond the city limits, there are also boats to Nesodden (all year), and Drøbak (summer weekends only); these leave from the Aker Brygge piers.

Taxis

The speed and efficiency of Oslo's public transport system means that you should rarely have to resort to a **taxi**, which is probably just as well given how expensive they are. Fares are regulated, with the tariff varying according to the time of day: expect to pay around 130kr for a ten-minute, five-kilometre ride at night; about 25 percent less during the day. Taxi ranks can be found round the city centre and outside all the big hotels. For easy reference, there's one at the corner of Karl Johans gate and Akersgata. To call a cab ring Oslo Taxi on ☎22 38 80 90.

Bicycles

Renting a **bicycle** is a pleasant option if you want to get about under your own steam: the city has a reasonable range of cycle tracks, while an increasing number of roads have cycle lanes. Oslo's main bicycle rental shop is Vestbanen, just along from the main tourist office at Brynjulf Bull's plass (☎23 11 51 08); hire charges begin at 90kr for three hours, rising to 180kr for 24 hours and 600kr for a week. Waterproofs and insurance cost extra, as do helmets (25kr per day), and there's a refundable deposit of around 1000kr to pay.

Accommodation

Oslo has the range of hotels you would expect of a capital city, as well as private rooms, a smattering of guesthouses (*pensjonater*) and a quartet of youth hostels, unofficial and official. To appreciate the full flavour of the city, you're best off staying on or near the western reaches of Karl Johans gate – between the Stortinget and the Nationaltheatret – though the well-heeled area to the north and west of Det Kongelige Slott (the Royal Palace) is enjoyable too. Many of the least expensive lodgings are, however, to be found in the vicinity of Oslo S, and this district – along with the grimy suburbs to the north and east of the station – is preferably avoided. That said, if money is tight and you're here in July and August, your choice of location may well be very limited as the scramble for **budget beds** becomes acute – or at least tight enough to make it well worth ringing ahead to check on space. For peace of mind, it is advisable to make an **advance reservation**, particularly for your first night.

One way of cutting out the hassle is to use one of the **accommodation services** provided by the tourist offices inside Oslo S and at the Norges Informasjonssenter (see p.198). Both can give you accommodation lists, or make a booking on your behalf for 20kr per person, a real bargain when you consider that they often get discounted rates – the Oslo S office is especially good for private rooms.

Hotels

The standard charge at the less expensive end of the market will be around 700–900kr. For this you'll get a fairly small and simple en-suite room. You hit the comfort zone at about 900kr, and luxury from around 1000kr. However, **special offers and seasonal deals** often make the smarter hotels more affordable than this. Most of them offer up to forty percent discounts at weekends, while in July and August – when Norwegians leave town for their holidays – prices everywhere tend to drop radically. In addition, nearly all room rates include a good-to-excellent self-service buffet breakfast. To check the best deals, head for either of the two tourist offices, both of which keep lists of the day's best offers, or try the places on the following list – but always ring ahead first.

Ambassadeur, Camilla Colletts vei 15 (☎22 44 18 35, fax 22 44 47 91, *www.bestwestern.com/no/ ambassadeur*). One of a long row of attractive nineteenth-century town houses graced by wrought-iron balconies, though the slightly grimy pink facade doesn't do justice to the elegantly furnished interior. Each of the bedrooms has a different theme, such as "Shanghai" or "Amsterdam", and it's in a great location too, just three blocks west of the Slottsparken. ⑤/④.

Ami, Nordhal Bruns gate 9 (☎22 11 61 10, fax 22 36 18 01). Resembles a *pensjonater* as much as a hotel, with frugal modern rooms and lumpy beds. About ten minutes' walk north of Karl Johans gate, behind the Museum of Applied Art at the east end of St Olavs gate. ③/②.

Anker, Storgata 55 (☎22 99 75 00, fax 22 99 75 20). A large budget hotel in a glum high-rise block beside the murky river at the east end of Storgata. Caters predominantly for visiting Norwegians rather than tourists. The hotel's facilities are perfectly adequate, if somewhat frugal, but the surrounding area is cheerless. Twenty minutes' walk from Oslo S or five minutes by tram #10, #11, #12, #15 or #17. Part of the high-rise which also holds the *Albertine Hostel* – see overleaf – and the *Albert Sommerhotell*. ③.

Bondeheimen, Rosenkrantz gate 8 (☎22 42 95 30, fax 22 41 94 37). One of Oslo's most delightful hotels, handily located just north of Karl Johans gate. Both the public areas and the extremely comfortable bedrooms are tastefully decorated in a modern, Scandinavian style, with polished pine everywhere. The inclusive buffet breakfast, served in the *Kaffistova* (see p.220), is excellent, and there's free coffee, soup and bread in the foyer throughout the evening. Look out for weekend and summer discounts of up to 40 percent. ④/③.

Bristol, Kristian IV's gate 7 (☎22 82 60 00, fax 22 82 60 01, *bristol@online.no*). Plush establishment distinguished by its sumptuous public rooms, with ornate nineteenth-century chandeliers, columns and fancifully carved arches. ⑤/④.

City Hotel, Skippergata 19 (☎22 41 36 10, fax 22 42 24 29). Modest but pleasant hotel, a longtime favourite with budget travellers, located above shops and offices in a traditional Oslo apartment block near the train station. The surroundings are a little seedy, but the hotel is cheerful enough, and the rooms small but perfectly adequate. ②.

Continental, Stortingsgata 24 (☎22 82 40 00, fax 22 42 96 89). One of Oslo's most prestigious hotels, ideally located just steps from Karl Johans gate, with sumptuous public rooms and amazingly comfortable bedrooms furnished in immaculate modern style. ⑥/④.

Frogner House Hotel, Skovveien 8 (☎22 56 00 56, fax 22 56 05 00). Located in one of Oslo's ritziest neighbourhoods, this elegant hotel occupies a handsome Victorian town house. Each of the comfortable bedrooms is individually decorated in tasteful modern style, with stripped wood and thick carpets throughout. It's 1km west of the centre off Frognerveien – trams #12 or #15. ⑤/④.

Gabelshus Hotell, Gabels gate 16 (☎22 55 22 60, fax 22 44 27 30). Delightful and intimate hotel in a smart residential area a couple of kilometres west of the city centre. The beautifully maintained interior boasts ornate fireplaces and antique furnishings. It's off Drammensveien – take tram #10 or #13 from the centre. Highly recommended. ④/③.

Grand, Karl Johans gate 31 (☎23 21 20 00, fax 23 21 21 00, *grand.hotel.oslo@rica.no*). Over 100 years of tradition, comfort and style in a prime position on Oslo's main street translates into stratospheric room rates, though hefty weekend and summertime discounts can make it much more affordable. Breakfasts are sumptuous, the lobby opulent, and the rooms eminently comfortable. ⑥/④.

Nobel House Hotel, Kongensgate 5 (☎23 10 72 00, fax 23 10 72 10, *anne.aanersen@noblehouse.no*). De luxe hotel with style – from the smart wooden floors to the cool, modernist decor. Great downtown location too, footsteps from the restaurants and art museums of Bankplassen. ⑥/④.

Norum Hotel, Bygdøy Allé 53 (☎22 44 79 90, fax 22 44 92 39). With its late nineteenth-century forest of spiky towers, the *Norum* possesses the most imposing hotel façade in the city. Inside, each of the rooms is individually decorated in tasteful modern style and the public rooms are imaginative and engaging. In a busy residential area about 2km west of the centre – take bus #30, #31, #32 or #33. ④/③.

Quality Savoy, Universitetsgata 11 (☎22 20 26 55, fax 22 11 24 80). Attractive and very comfortable choice with pleasant rooms and wood-panelled public areas. In an interesting area too, with bookshops and bars catering primarily for the city's students. ④.

Rainbow Europa, St Olavs gate 31 (☎22 20 99 90, fax 22 11 27 27). Large modern chain hotel in dreary surroundings near the west end of St Olavs gate. Near the bottom end of its price range. ④/③.

Rainbow Norrøna, Grensen 19 (☎22 42 64 00, fax 22 33 25 65). Occupying part of a nineteenth-century apartment block right in the middle of town, this pleasantly renovated hotel offers straightforward modern rooms – nothing exciting but perfectly OK. The buffet breakfast is excellent and the breakfast room offers an attractive city view. At 850kr per double, it's a bargain that's made even more attractive by summer and weekend discounts of 15 percent. ③/②.

Rainbow Stefan, Rosenkrantz gate 1 (☎22 42 92 50, fax 22 33 70 22). Unremarkable but spick-and-span modern hotel with 210 rooms above the first-floor shops of a five-storey high-rise. Near the bottom of its price range, it's one of the city's better deals, and its location, just a couple of minutes' walk north of Karl Johans gate, could hardly be bettered. ④.

Rica Triangel, Holbergs plass 1 (☎22 20 88 55, fax 22 20 78 25, *rica.triangel.hotel.oslo@rica.no*). Despite its grand nineteenth-century facade, this large, chain hotel has a routinely modern interior. Overlooks Holbergs plass, a pint-sized square about 500m to the north of the Slottsparken. ④.

Rica Victoria, Rosenkrantz gate 13 (☎22 42 99 40, fax 22 42 99 43, *rica.victoria.hotel.oslo@rica.no*). Large, smart modern hotel just south of Karl Johans gate, popular with visiting business folk. Verging on the luxurious, its commodious rooms come with every convenience. ⑤.

Hostels, private rooms and guesthouses

There are three HI **hostels** in Oslo, each very popular and open to people of any age, though you'll need to be a member to get the lowest rate (non-members pay a surcharge of 25kr); the fourth hostel is attached to one of the city's budget hotels. Alternatively, the tourist office can book you into a **private room** – the supply rarely dries up. These cost a flat-rate of 170kr a single, and 300kr a double. This is something of a bargain especially as many also have cooking facilities, but they do tend to be out of the city centre, and there is often a minimum two-night stay. Broadly similar to the hostels and private rooms are **guesthouses** (*pensjonater*), which start at around 340kr single, 450kr double. There's only a handful of them, and only one near the city centre. They offer bare but generally adequate accommodation, either with or without en-suite facilities; breakfast is not included, however, and at some places you may need to supply your own sleeping bag.

Albertine Hostel, Storgata 55 (☎22 99 72 00, fax 22 99 72 20). This hostel has plain and simple one- (250kr), two- (340kr), four- (560kr) and six-bedded (690kr) rooms, serves an adequate breakfast and has self-catering facilities – but you have to provide your own utensils. Bed linen and towels are for hire, or bring your own. The hostel occupies part of a glum high-rise block (which also houses the *Anker* hotel) in a cheerless neighbourhood at the east end of Storgata, twenty minutes' walk from Oslo S or five minutes by tram #10, #11, #12, #15 or #17.

Cochs Pensjonat, Parkveien 25 (☎22 60 48 36, fax 22 46 54 02). On the third floor of a drab modern block, this no-frills guesthouse is handily located behind Slottsparken, at the foot of Hegdehaugsveien. Some rooms have en-suite and cooking facilities, and singles, triples and quads are available. ②.

Oslo Ekeberg, Kongsveien 82 (☎22 74 18 90, fax 22 74 75 05). This tiny HI hostel, with just eleven rooms, occupies part of a school complex 4km southeast of Oslo S. Take tram #18 or #19 from outside Oslo S the centre and it's 100m from the Holtet tram stop – ask the driver to put you off.

Oslo Haraldsheim, Haraldsheimveien 4, Grefsen (☎22 22 29 65, fax 22 22 10 25, *haraldsheim@internet. no*). Best of Oslo's three HI youth hostels, 4km northeast of the centre, and open all year except Christmas week. Has 270 beds in 71 rooms, most of which are four-bedded. The public areas are comfortable and attractively furnished and the bedrooms clean and frugal, with about 40 having their own showers and WC. There are self-catering facilities, a restaurant and washing machines. The basic 160kr (non-members 185kr) dorm bed price includes breakfast; single and double rooms are also available (①). The only downside can be the presence of parties of noisy schoolkids. It's a very popular spot, so advance booking is essential throughout the summer. To get there, take tram #10 or #11 from the bottom of Storgata, near the Domkirke, to the Sinsenkrysset stop, from where it's a ten-minute walk along the signposted footpath that cuts across the field. It's also easy to get there by local train from Oslo S to Grefsen – again, follow the signs from the railway station for the fifteen-minute walk. Incidentally, should you miss the Sinsenkrysset stop, the tram's next stop heading out of town is beside Grefsen station. By road, the hostel is situated close to – and signed from – Ring 3.

Oslo Holtekilen, Michelets vei 55, 1320 Stabekk (☎67 51 80 40, fax 67 59 12 30). Another HI hostel, but much smaller than *Haraldsheim* and only open from the end of May to mid-Aug. It's located 10km west of the city centre. From Oslo M, take bus #151 and the hostel is 100m from the Kveldsroveien bus stop. There are kitchen facilities, a restaurant and a laundry. Again, the 160kr price includes breakfast; single and double rooms are also available (①).

Camping and cabins

Camping is a fairly easy proposition: there are sixteen sites within 50km of the city, nearest being just 3km from the centre. If you're out of luck with rooms in town, most sites also offer **cabins**, but ring ahead to ask about availability.

Bogstad, Ankerveien 117 (☎22 51 08 00, fax 22 51 08 50). Large and well-equipped lakeside campsite, with cabins available too (①). Fifteen kilometres northwest of the centre – take bus #32 from Oslo S or Nationaltheatret. It gets crowded, though, so ring ahead first. Open all year.

Ekeberg, Ekebergveien 65 (☎22 19 85 68, fax 22 67 04 36). Large campsite in a rocky, forested parcel of parkland just 3km east of the city centre; bus #34 from Jernbanetorget goes past. Open June–Aug.

Langøyene, Langøyene (☎22 11 53 21). Extremely popular, no-frills campsite, located on one of the islets just offshore from downtown Oslo, close to the city's best beaches and an attractive wooded shoreline. To get there, take ferry #94 from the Vippetangen quay. Open June to mid-Aug.

The City Centre

At the time of their construction, the grand late nineteenth- and early twentieth-century buildings that populate **central Oslo** provided the country's emerging bourgeoisie with a sense of security and prosperity, an aura that survives today. Largely as a result, most of downtown Oslo remains easy and pleasant to walk around, its airy streets and squares accommodating the appealing remnants of the city's early days, as well as a clutch of good museums and dozens of bars, cafés and restaurants.

Despite the mammoth proportions of the Oslo conurbation, the city centre has also stayed surprisingly compact and is easy to navigate by remembering a few landmarks. From the train station **Oslo S**, at the eastern end of the centre, **Karl Johans gate** heads directly up the hill, passing the **Domkirke** en route to the **Stortinget** (parliament building). From here it sweeps down past the **University** to the **Royal Palace**, which sits in parkland (the **Slottsparken**) at the western end of the centre. South of the palace, on the waterfront, is the brash harbourside development of **Aker Brygge** and the distinctive twin-towered **Rådhus** (City Hall). South of the Rådhus, on the lumpy peninsula overlooking the harbour, is the severe **Akershus Slott**, the city's castle. Between the castle, the Stortinget and Oslo S is a tight, slightly gloomy grid of streets and high buildings that was originally laid out by Christian IV in the seventeenth century. For many years this was the city's commercial hub and although Oslo's burgeoning suburbs undermined its position in the 1960s, the district is currently making a comeback, reinventing itself with specialist shops and smart restaurants.

Along Karl Johans gate

Heading west and uphill from Oslo S train station, the city's main thoroughfare, **Karl Johans gate**, begins unpromisingly with a clutter of tacky shops and groups of junkies. Just beyond, at the corner of Dronningens gate is the curious **Basarhallene**, a two-tiered building whose brick cloisters, originally built in the nineteenth century to house the city's food market, have since been revived as a tiny shopping complex complete with art shops and cafés. The adjacent **Domkirke** (cathedral; daily 10am–4pm; free) dates from the late seventeenth century, though its heavyweight tower was remodelled in 1850. Plain and dour from the outside, the cathedral's elegantly restored interior is in delightful contrast, its homely, low-ceilinged nave and transepts awash with maroon, green and gold paintwork, and to either side of the high altar are the stained-glass windows created by Emanuel Vigeland in 1910 (for more on the Vigelands, see p.216). Outside the cathedral, **Stortorvet** was once the main city square, but it's no longer of much account, its nineteenth-century statue of a portly Christian IV now serving merely as the forlorn guardian of a second-rate flower market.

Returning to Karl Johans gate, it's a brief stroll up to the **Stortinget**, the parliament building, an imposing chunk of neo-Romanesque architecture completed in 1866. It's open to the public on free guided tours (July to mid-Aug Mon–Sat 10am, 11.30am &

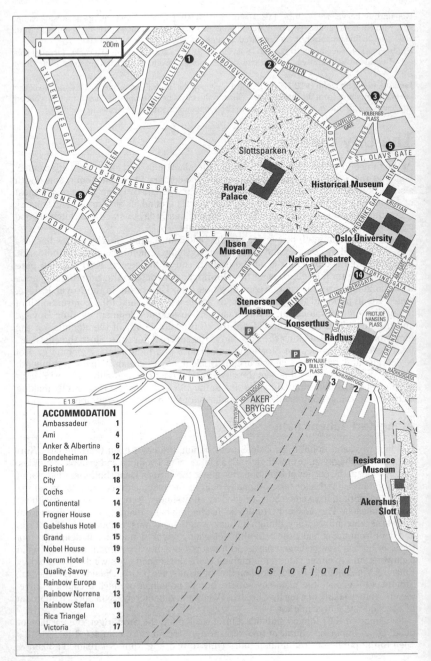

Slottsparken

Royal Palace

Historical Museum

Ibsen Museum

Oslo University

Nationaltheatret

Stenersen Museum

Konserthus

Rådhus

Resistance Museum

Akershus Slott

AKER BRYGGE

Oslofjord

ACCOMMODATION

Ambassadeur	1
Ami	4
Anker & Albertine	6
Bondeheimen	12
Bristol	11
City	18
Cochs	2
Continental	14
Frogner House	8
Gabelshus Hotel	16
Grand	15
Nobel House	19
Norum Hotel	9
Quality Savoy	7
Rainbow Europa	5
Rainbow Norrøna	13
Rainbow Stefan	10
Rica Triangel	3
Victoria	17

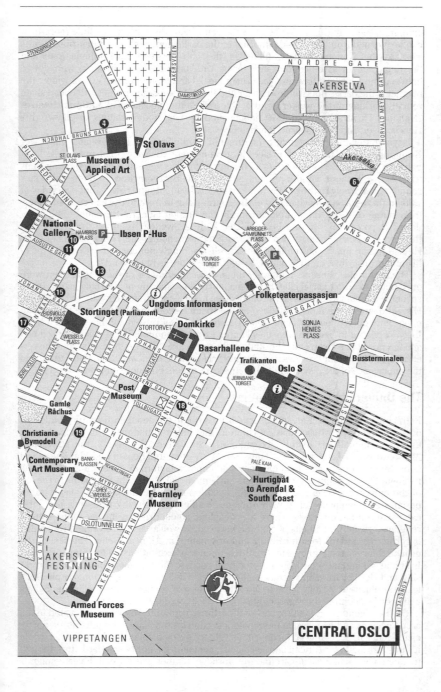

CENTRAL OSLO

1pm; mid-Aug to mid-June Sat 11am & 12.30pm; free), though you see little more than can be gleaned from the outside. In front of the parliament, a narrow **park-piazza** runs west to the Nationaltheatret, filling in the gap between Karl Johans gate and Stortingsgata. In summer, the park brims with promenading city folk, who dodge between the jewellery hawkers, ice-cream kiosks and street performers; in winter the magnet is the park's dinky little open-air and floodlit ice-skating rinks (with cheap skate rental). Lurking at the western end of the park is the Neoclassical **Nationaltheatret** (National Theatre), built in 1899 and flanked by two stodgy statues of playwrights Henrik Ibsen and Bjørnstjerne Bjørnson.

Beyond the theatre, standing on the hill at the end of Karl Johans gate, **Det Kongelige Slott**, the Royal Palace, is a monument to Norwegian openness. Built between 1825 and 1848, at a time when other monarchs were nervously counting their friends, it still stands without railings and walls, the **Slottsparken** grounds which surround it open freely to the public. You can't actually go into the palace, but every day at 1.30pm there's a snappy changing of the guard. Bang in front of the palace is an equestrian statue of **Karl XIV Johan**. Formerly the French General Bernadotte, he abandoned Napoleon and, having been elected king of Sweden, assumed the Norwegian throne when Norway passed from Denmark to Sweden after the Treaty of Kiel in 1814. He had this whopping palace built for himself, seemingly not content with the terms of his motto (inscribed on the statue): "The people's love is my reward".

The grand old mansions bordering the southern perimeter of the Slottsparken were once home to Oslo's social elite. Here, in a fourth floor apartment at Arbins gate 1, Ibsen spent the last ten years of his life, strolling down to the Grand Café every day to hold court. His old quarters are now maintained as the **Ibsen Museum** (Ibsen-museet; Tues–Sun noon–3pm; guided tours at noon, 1pm & 2pm; 30kr). Both Ibsen and his wife died here: Ibsen paralyzed in bed; his wife, unwilling to expire in an undignified pose, dressed and sitting upright in a chair. Only the study looks much like it did in Ibsen's day, but the reverential one-hour tour provides a fascinating background to his work, and helps to explain the importance of the playwright to his emergent nation. For more on Ibsen, see p.246.

The University and its museums

Retracing your steps to Karl Johans gate brings you to the nineteenth-century buildings of the **University**, whose classical columns and imperial pediments fit perfectly with this monumental part of the city centre. Here at Frederiks gate 2, the **Historical Museum** (mid-May to mid-Sept Tues–Sun 11am–3pm; mid-Sept to mid-May Tues–Sun noon–3pm; free) contains the university's hotchpotch historical and ethnographical collections. The highlight is the Viking and early medieval section. In the rooms to the left of the entrance are several magnificent twelfth- and thirteenth-century stave-church porches and gateposts, alive with dragons and beasts emerging from swirling, intricately carved backgrounds. There are weapons, coins, drinking horns, runic stones, religious bric-a-brac and bits of clothing here too, as well as a superb vaulted room, dating from the late thirteenth century and originating in Ål, near Geilo. The rest of the ground floor is taken up by a pretty dire sequence of exhibitions on the Stone, Bronze, Iron and Viking ages. Geared up for school parties, the tiny dioramas are downright silly and detract from the actual exhibits, which (accompanied by long explicatory leaflets) illustrate various aspects of early Norwegian society – from religious beliefs and social structures through to military hardware and trade and craft.

On the second floor, the first part of the **Ethnographical Museum** is devoted to the arctic peoples and features an illuminating section on the Sami, who inhabit the northern reaches of Scandinavia. Incongruously, there's a coin collection here as well, while it's upstairs again for African and Asiatic art and culture – pretty standard stuff, though temporary exhibitions from around the world sometimes prove worth investigating.

The National Gallery

Norway's largest and best collection of fine art is only a step away from the university in the **National Gallery** (Nasjonalgalleriet; Mon, Wed & Fr. 10am–6pm, Thurs 10am–8pm, Sat 10am–4pm, Sun 11am–4pm; free). An approachable collection of works shoehorned into a grand nineteenth-century building, it's short on internationally famous painters – apart from a fine sample of work by Edvard Munch – but there's compensation in the oodles of Norwegian art on display, including examples of the work of all the leading figures up until the end of World War II.

Something of a mishmash, the **first floor** is home to a quirky series of collections, with the large room to the right of the entrance crammed with plaster casts of Greek, Roman and Italian Renaissance sculptures – including a massive and militaristic equestrian statue by Donatello. To the left of the entrance, one room is devoted to Danish and Norwegian nineteenth-century sculpture, another holds a workaday selection of Norwegian paintings from 1870 to 1900, while others are set aside for temporary exhibitions.

Moving on, the wide and gracious stairway – look out for a tortured bronze relief, *Helvete* (Hell), by Gustav Vigeland – leads to the kernel of the gallery's collection on the **second floor**, which broadly divides between Norwegian painting on the right-hand side and European art to the left. The latter section contains an enjoyable sample of work by the **Impressionists**, assorted bursts of colour from Manet, Monet, Degas and Cézanne, as well as a distant, piercing Van Gogh self-portrait, and later works by the likes of Picasso and Braque. There's also a set of Novgorod medieval religious paintings and a rather modest selection of Old Masters, amongst which Lucas Cranach's *The Golden Age* and two warm and melodramatic canvases by El Greco stand out.

To the right of the staircase, the first room of **Norwegian paintings** features the work of the country's most important nineteenth-century landscape painters, **Johan Christian Dahl** (1788–1857) and his pupil **Thomas Fearnley** (1802–42). Dahl's giant-sized canvas *Stalheim* is typical of his work, the soft and dappled hues of the mountain landscape framing a sleepy village dotted with tiny figures. His *Hjelle in Valdres* of 1851 adopts the same approach, though here the artifice suffusing the apparent naturalism is easier to detect: the year before, Dahl had completed another painting of Hjelle, but he returned to the subject to widen the valley and heighten the mountains, sprinkling them with snow. Fearnley often lived and worked abroad, but he always returned to Norwegian themes, painting no fewer than five versions of the *Labrofossen ved Kongsberg* (The Labro Waterfall at Kongsberg), a fine, moody canvas of dark, louring clouds and frothing water.

In Room 23, Gerhard Munthe (1849–1929) and his cosy, folksy scenes are echoed in the paintings of Erik Werenskiold (1855–1938), who is well represented by *Peasant Burial* (1885). During this period, Theodor Kittelsen (1857–1914) defined the appearance of the country's trolls, sprites and sirens in his illustrations of Asbjørnsen and Moe's *Norwegian Folk Tales*, published in 1883. Two modest examples of his other work – a self-portrait and a fairy-tale landscape – are in Room 18. Harald Sohlberg (1869–1935) is represented by a series of sharply observed Røros streetscapes, and by more elemental themes such as the stunning *En blomstereng nordpå* (A Northern Flower Meadow) and *Vinternatt i Rondane* (Winter Night in the Rondane). These are exhibited in Room 31, alongside the comparable *Opptrekkende uvær* (Approaching Storm) by Halfdan Egedius (1877–99).

It's the museum's **Munch** collection, however, which is the star turn, gathering together representative works from the 1880s through to 1916 in one central room, with several lesser pieces displayed elsewhere. His early work is very much in the naturalist tradition of his mentor Christian Krohg, though by 1885 Munch is already pushing the boundaries in *The Sick Child,* a heart-wrenching evocation of his sister Sophie's death from tuberculosis. Other works with this same sense of pain include *Mother and Daughter, Moonlight* and one of several versions of *The Scream,* a seminal canvas of 1893 whose swirling lines and rhythmic colours were to inspire the Expressionists. This sample of Munch's work serves as a good introduction to the artist, but for a more detailed appraisal – and a more comprehensive selection of his work – check out the Munch Museum (p.215).

Setting aside the exceptional Munch, Norwegian art was reinvigorated in the 1910s by a new band of artists who had trained in Paris under Henri Matisse, whose emancipation of colour from naturalist constraints inspired his Norwegian students. **Henrik Sørensen** (1882–1962), the outstanding figure here, summed up the Frenchman's influence thirty years later: "From Matisse, I learned more in fifteen minutes than from all the other teachers I have listened to" – lessons that inspired Sørensen's surging, earthy portrayals of the landscapes of eastern Norway. **Axel Revold** (1887–1962) was trained by Matisse too, but also assimilated Cubist influences – in, for example, his *Sommernatt i Nordland* (Summer Night in Nordland) of 1930 – whilst **Erling Enger** (1899–1990) maintained a gently lyrical approach to the landscape and its seasons. Examples of the work of these and other later artists spreads up from the second to the third floor, where there's also a large collection of paintings from the rest of Scandinavia, mostly dating from the first half of the twentieth century.

The Museum of Applied Art

The **Museum of Applied Art** (Kunstindustrimuseet; Tues–Fri 11am–3pm, Sat & Sun noon–4pm; 25kr) occupies an imposing nineteenth-century building some ten minutes' walk north from the National Gallery, at St Olavs gate 1: continue to the far end of Universitetsgata, veer to the right and it's at the end of the street. Founded in 1876, this was one of the first museums of its kind in Europe, its multifaceted collection (particularly strong on period furniture) spreading over four floors. The **first floor** accommodates temporary exhibitions (which sometimes raise the cost of admission), while on the **second floor** (in the first room to the left of the stairs) is an engaging hotchpotch of Viking tackle from drinking horns, broaches and belts through to religious statuettes and church vestments. The museum's top exhibit is here too, the brightly coloured Baldishol Tapestry, one of the finest early examples of woven tapestry in Europe. Next door, the "Norwegian Gallery" boasts an enjoyable sample of carved wooden furniture, amongst which the cheerily painted chests from Gudbrandsdal are especially fetching. Alongside is a charming selection of bedspreads sporting either religious or folkloric motifs. Upstairs, on the **third floor**, a sequence of period interiors illustrates foreign fashions from Renaissance and Baroque through to Chippendale, Louis XVI and Art Nouveau. The **fourth-floor** displays concentrate on ceramics and glassware from the early nineteenth century onwards, with other exhibits on textiles and fashions. The highlight here is the collection of extravagant costumes worn by Norway's royal family at the beginning of the twentieth century.

To the water: the Rådhus and Aker Brygge

Back in the city centre, rearing high above the waterfront south of the Nationaltheatret, is Oslo's controversial City Hall, the **Rådhus** (May–Aug Mon–Sat 9am–5pm, Sun noon–5pm; Sept–April Mon–Sat 9am–4pm, Sun noon–4pm), a modernist, twin-towered construction of dark-brown brick designed by Arnstein Arneberg and Manus Poulsson. Opened in 1950 to celebrate the city's 900th anniversary, this grandiose statement of civic pride was nearly twenty years in the making. At first, few people had a good word for what they saw as an ugly and strikingly un-Norwegian addition to the city. But with the passing of time, the obloquy has fallen on more recent additions to the skyline such as Oslo S, and the Rådhus has become one of the city's more popular buildings.

Initially, the interior was equally contentious. Many leading Norwegian painters and sculptors contributed to the decorations, which were intended to celebrate all things Norwegian. The **Rådhushallen** (main hall) is decorated with vast stylized – and for some, completely over-the-top – murals. On the north wall, Per Krohg's *From the Fishing Nets in the West to the Forests of the East* invokes the figures of polar explorer Fridtjof Nansen (on the left) and dramatist Bjørnstjerne Bjørnson (on the right) to symbolize, respectively, the nation's spirit of adventure and its intellectual development. On the south wall is the equally vivid *Work, Administration and Celebration,* which took Henrik Sørensen a decade to complete. The self-congratulatory rationalism of these murals is hardly attractive, although the effect is partly offset by the forceful fresco along the east wall in honour of the Norwegian Resistance of World War II.

At the back of the Rådhus a line of six muscular bronze figures represent the trades – builders, bricklayers and so on – who worked on the building, while behind them, over the tram lines, stand four massive granite female sculptures surrounding a central fountain. Beyond that, and shadowed by the Akershus peninsula, is the central **harbour**, always busy with ferries and boats, with Bygdøy and the islands of the Oslofjord filling out the backdrop. This is one of downtown Oslo's prettiest spots, and handy for the **Norges Informasjonssenter**, located steps from the Rådhus in the old, yellow Oslo V railway station. Footsteps away, the old Aker shipyard has been turned into the swish **Aker Brygge** shopping-cum-office complex, a gleaming concoction of circular staircases and glass lifts, trimmed with neon and plastic; the bars and restaurants here are some of the most popular in town.

Rådhusgata and around

Running east from the Rådhus, **Rådhusgata** leads down to the part of the harbour, where ferries from Denmark dock. The grid of streets on either side is a legacy of seventeenth-century Oslo, but it's only the layout that has survived as the old timber buildings were almost entirely demolished and replaced by grander stone structures in the nineteenth century. One block south of Rådhusgata along Kirkegata is **Bankplassen**, arguably the city's most attractive square, framed by Gothic Revival and Second Empire buildings, a perfect illustration of the grand tastes of the Dano-Norwegian elite who ran the country at the beginning of the twentieth century.

The square's proudest building, the 1907 Art Nouveau Norges Bank at no. 4, has been superbly restored to house the enterprising **Museum of Contemporary Art** (Museet for Samtidskunst; Tues, Wed & Fri 10am–5pm, Thurs 10am–8pm, Sat 11am–4pm, Sun 11am–5pm; free). The museum owns work by virtually every major postwar Norwegian artist and by many leading foreign figures too. Each item is allowed a generous amount of space and so – given that some of the pieces are massive, and that the museum also hosts prestigious international exhibitions – only a fraction of the permanent collection can be shown at any one time. Norwegian names to look out for include Bjørn Carlsen, Frans Widerberg, Knut Rose and Bjørn Ransve. There are also three permanent installations, including the weird *Inner Room V*, the fifth in a series of angst-rattling rooms made from recycled industrial junk by the Norwegian Per Inge Bjørlo. Tucked away in a room of its own on the top floor, there's also the peculiar – and peculiarly engaging – *The Man Who Never Threw Anything Away*, the work of Russian Ilya Kabakov, who spent over a decade collecting hundreds of discarded items – bits of toe nail, string, hairs, elastic bands, crumbs – and gathered them together here, each precisely labelled and neatly displayed. Kabakov continues turning up to add bits and pieces to his display, which occupies a sort of parallel reality – its neurotic order a retreat from the chaos of the world outside.

About 200m to the east of the Samtidskunst along Revierstredet at Dronningens gate 4, the **Astrup Fearnley Museum of Modern Art** (Astrup Fearnley Museet for Moderne Kunst; Tues, Wed & Fri noon–4pm, Thurs noon–7pm, Sat & Sun noon–5pm; 30kr), occupies a sharp modern building of brick and glass with six-metre-high steel entrance doors. It's meant to impress – a suitably posh setting for the display of several private collections and for eminent temporary exhibitions. The temporary exhibitions often leave little space for the permanent collection, which includes examples of the work of most major postwar Norwegian artists as well as a smattering of foreign works by celebrated artists such as Francis Bacon, Damien Hirst and Anselm Kiefer.

Akershus Slott and Festning

Though very much part of central Oslo by location, the jutting thumb of land that holds the castle, the **Akershus Slott**, much the most significant memorial to medieval Oslo, is quite separate from the city centre in feel. Built on a rocky knoll overlooking the harbour in around 1300, the original fort was already the battered veteran of several unsuccessful sieges when Christian IV (1596–1648) took matters in hand. The king had a passion for building cities and a keen interest in Norway – during his reign he visited the country about thirty times, more than all the other kings of the Dano-Norwegian union together. So, when Oslo was badly damaged by fire in 1624, he took his opportunity and simply ordered the town to be moved round the bay from its location at the mouth of the river Alna beneath the Ekeberg heights. He had the town rebuilt in its present position, renamed it "Christiania" – a name which stuck until 1925 – and transformed the medieval castle into a Renaissance residence. Around the castle he also constructed a new fortress – the **Akershus Festning** – whose thick earth and stone walls and protruding bastions were designed to combat the threat of artillery bombardment. Refashioned and enlarged on several later occasions – and now bisected by Kongensgate – parts of the fortress have remained in military use to the present day.

There are several entrances to the Akershus complex, but the most interesting is from the west end of Myntgata, where there's a choice of two marked footpaths. One leads to the **Christiania Bymodell** (June–Aug Tues–Sun noon–5pm; 20kr), which illustrates the city's history from 1624 to 1840 by means of an hourly audiovisual performance and a large-scale model of Oslo as it appeared in 1838: drop by to get a better idea of the city's evolution and what the gridded town looked like when it was protected by the fortress. The second footpath leads up to a side gate in the perimeter wall, just beyond which is a cute little pond and a crashingly boring museum-cum-information centre that makes a strange attempt to tie in the history of the castle with modern environmental concerns. There's another choice of signed routes here, with one path offering heady views over the harbour as it worms its way up to the castle. In a separate building just outside the castle entrance is the **Resistance Museum** (Hjemmefrontmuseum; mid-April to Sept Mon–Sat 10am–4pm, Sun 11am–4pm; Oct to mid-April Mon–Sat 10am–3pm, Sun 11am–3pm; 20kr), a particularly apt location as captured Resistance fighters were tortured and sometimes executed in the castle by the Gestapo. Labelled in English and Norwegian, the museum's mostly pictorial displays detail the history of the war in Norway from defeat and occupation through resistance to final victory. There are tales of extraordinary heroism here – the determined resistance of hundreds of the country's teachers to Nazi instructions, and the story of a certain Petter Moen, who was arrested by the Germans and imprisoned in the Akershus, where he kept a diary by picking out letters on toilet paper with a nail: the diary survived, but he didn't. Another section deals with Norway's Jews, of whom there were 1800 in 1939 – the Germans captured 760; 24 survived. There's also an impressively honest account of Norwegian collaboration; fascism struck a chord with the country's petit bourgeois, and hundreds of volunteers joined the Wehrmacht. The most notorious collaborator was Vidkun Quisling: pressing a button brings his radio announcement declaring his assumption of power at the start of the German invasion in April 1940.

Next door, the severe stone walls and twin spires of the **Slott** (May to mid-Sept Mon–Sat 10am–4pm, Sun 12.30–6pm; late April & mid-Sept to Oct Sun only 12.30–4pm; 20kr; guided tours at 11am, 1pm & 3pm, Sun at 1pm & 3pm) perch on a rocky ridge high above the zigzag fortifications that Christian IV added in the seventeenth century. The castle is approached through a narrow tunnel-gateway, beyond which the stone-flagged courtyard is overlooked by the main gate. The interior is, however, a real disappointment, with a series of bare and boring rooms only enlivened by the tapestries and bedspreads of the Romerike Hall. A visit takes in the royal chapel too, as well as the royal mausoleum, the last resting-place of Norway's current dynasty.

Back outside a path leads off the courtyard, running down the side of the castle with the walls pressing in on one side and views out over the harbour on the other. At the foot of the castle, the path swings across a narrow promontory and soon reaches the footbridge over Kongensgate – keep straight for the string of ochre-painted barrack blocks that lead back to the pond and Myntgata.

Out from the centre

From the jetty behind the Rådhus, ferries shuttle southwest from central Oslo to the **Bygdøy peninsula**, home to the city's showpiece museums, whilst other ferries head south from the Vippetangen quay behind Akershus Slott to the string of rusticated **islands** that necklace the inner waters of the Oslofjord. Back on the mainland, **east Oslo** is the least prepossessing part of town, a gritty sprawl housing the poorest of the city's inhabitants whose sole attraction is the superb Munch Museum. **Northwest Oslo** is far more prosperous, with big old houses lining the avenues immediately to the west of the Slottsparken. Beyond is the **Frognerparken**, a chunk of parkland with the stunning open-air sculptures of Gustav Vigeland displayed in the **Vigelandsparken**.

North of the centre is the **Nordmarka**, a massive forested wilderness that stretches inland, patterned by hiking trails and cross-country ski routes. Two T-bane lines provide ready access, clanking their way up into the rocky hills that herald the region. The more westerly grinds on past **Holmenkollen**, a resort whose ski jump forms a crooked finger on Oslo's skyline, before continuing to the **Frognerseteren** terminus, which is still within the municipal boundaries, though the forested hills and lochs around the station feel anything but urban. This atmosphere of remoteness is duplicated in neighbouring **Sognsvann**, at the end of the other T-bane line.

Southwest: the Bygdøy peninsula

Other than the centre, the place you're likely to spend most time in Oslo is the **Bygdøy peninsula**, across the bay to the southwest of the city, where five separate museums make up an absorbing cultural and historical display; it's well worth spending a full day – or, less wearyingly, two half-days – here. The most enjoyable way to reach Bygdøy is by **ferry**. These leave from pier 3 behind the Rådhus (daily: late April & Sept every 40min 9.05am–6.25pm; May–Aug every 40min 9.05am–9.05pm), and call at two places on the peninsula, stopping first at the Dronningen pier, then at the Bygdøynes pier. The two most popular attractions – the Viking Ships and Norwegian Folk museums – are within easy walking distance of the Dronningen pier; the other three are a stone's throw from Bygdøynes. If you decide to walk between the two groups, allow about fifteen minutes: the route is well signposted but dull. The alternative to the ferry is **bus** #30 (every 15min), which runs all year from Jernbanetorget and the Nationaltheatret to the Folk and Viking Ships museums, and, when the ferry isn't running, to the other three museums as well.

Norwegian Folk Museum

About 600m uphill from Dronningen pier, the **Norwegian Folk Museum**, at Museumsveien 10 (Norsk Folkemuseum; mid-June to Aug daily 10am–6pm; mid-May to mid-June & early Sept daily 10am–5pm; Jan to mid-May & mid-Sept to Dec Mon–Sat 11am–3pm, Sun 11am–4pm; 50kr), combines indoor collections focusing on folk art, furniture, dress and customs with an extensive open-air display of reassembled buildings, mostly wooden barns, stables, storehouses and dwellings from the seventeenth to the nineteenth centuries.

At the entrance, pick up a map and English-language guide (10kr) and begin by going upstairs to the Norwegian parliament chamber, a cosy nineteenth-century affair that has been reassembled here, complete with inkwells and quills at the members' seats. The adjoining complex of buildings holds a rather confusing sequence of exhibitions: some are eminently missable, but the **folk art** section has a delightful sample of quilted bedspreads and painted furniture, as well as an intriguing subsection devoted to **love gifts**, with fancily carved love spoons and mangle boards given by the boys, mittens and gloves by the girls. In rural Norway, it was considered improper for courting couples to be seen together during the day, but acceptable (or at least tolerated) at night – parents usually moved girls of marrying age into one of the farm's outhouses to assist the process. The **folk dress** section is excellent too. Rural customs specified the correct dress for every social gathering from cradle to grave, but it's the extravagant and brightly-coloured bridal headdresses that grab the eye. Look out also for the temporary exhibitions – the museum has a well-deserved reputation for imaginative displays.

The open-air collection consists of more than 150 reconstructed buildings. Arranged geographically, they provide a marvellous sample of Norwegian rural architecture, somewhat marred by inadequate explanations. It's worth tracking down the **stave church**, particularly if you don't plan to travel elsewhere in Norway. Dating from the early thirteenth century but extensively restored in the 1880s, when it was moved here from Gol, the church is a good example of its type, with steep, shingle-covered roofs, dragon finials and a cramped, gloomy nave – which can only be viewed from the gallery outside. The interior is decorated with robust woodcarvings and there's a striking *Last Supper* behind the altar. Elsewhere, the cluster of buildings from **Setesdal** in southern Norway holds some especially well-preserved dwellings and storehouses from the seventeenth century, while the **Numedal** section contains one of the museum's oldest buildings, a late thirteenth-century house from Rauland whose door posts are embellished with Romanesque vine decoration. In summer, many of the buildings are open for viewing and costumed guides roam the site to explain the vagaries of Norwegian rural life.

Viking Ships Museum

A five-minute walk south along the main road is the **Viking Ships Museum** (Vikingskipshuset; daily: May–Aug 9am–6pm; Sept 11am–5pm; April & Oct 11am–4pm; Nov–March 11am–3pm; 30kr), a large hall specially constructed to house a trio of ninth-century Viking ships, with viewing platforms to enable you to see inside the hulls. The three oak vessels were retrieved from ritual burial mounds in southern Norway; all were embalmed in a subsoil of clay, which accounts for their excellent state of preservation. The size of the Viking burial mound denoted the dead person's rank and wealth, while the possessions buried with the body were designed to make the afterlife as comfortable as possible. Implicit was the assumption that a chieftain in this world would be a chieftain in the next – slaves were frequently killed and buried with their master or mistress – a fact that would subsequently give Christianity an immediate appeal to those at the bottom of the Viking pile. That much is clear, but quite how the Vikings saw the transfer to the afterlife taking place is less certain. The evidence is contradictory: sometimes the Vikings stuck the anchor on board the burial ship in preparation for the spiritual journey; at other times the vessels were moored to large stones before they were buried. Nor was ship burial the only type of Viking funeral – far from it: the Vikings buried their dead in mounds and on level ground, with and without grave goods, in large and small coffins, both with and without boats – and they practised cremation too.

The star exhibits are the Oseberg and Gokstad ships, named after the places on the west side of the Oslofjord where they were discovered in 1904 and 1880 respectively. The **Oseberg ship**'s ornately carved prow and stern rise high above the hull, where thirty oar-holes indicate the size of the crew. It is thought to be the burial ship of a Viking chieftain's wife, and much of the treasure buried with it was retrieved, and can be seen on display at the back of the museum. The grave goods reveal an attention to detail and a level of domestic sophistication not usually associated with the Vikings: there are marvellous decorative items like the fierce-looking animal-head posts and exuberantly carved ceremonial sleighs, plus a host of smaller, more mundane household items such as agricultural tools and a cooking pot. Here also are finds from another burial mound at Borre in Vestfold, most notably a rare dark-blue glass beaker and a fancifully decorated bridle.

The Oseberg ship is 22m long and 5m wide, and probably represents the type of vessel the Vikings would have used to navigate fjords and coastal waters. The **Gokstad ship** is slightly longer and wider, and quite a bit sturdier and stronger. Its seaworthiness was demonstrated in 1893 when a copy was sailed across the Atlantic to the USA. Like the Oseberg mound, the Gokstad burial chamber was raided by grave robbers long ago – and to greater effect – but a handful of items were unearthed and are exhibited behind the third vessel, the **Tune ship**. Only fragments of this, the smallest of the three vessels, survive; these are displayed unrestored, much as they were discovered in 1867 on the eastern side of the Oslofjord.

The Kon-Tiki, Fram and Maritime museums

A few metres from the Bygdøynes pier, the **Kon-Tiki Museum** (daily: June–Aug 9.30am–5.45pm; April, May & Sept 10.30am–5pm; Oct–March 10.30am–4pm; 30kr) is most unusual. On display inside is the balsawood raft on which, in 1947, Thor Heyerdahl made his now legendary journey across the Pacific from Peru to Polynesia. Heyerdahl wanted to prove the trip could be done: he was convinced that the first Polynesian settlers had sailed from pre-Incan Peru, and rejected prevailing opinions that South American balsa rafts were unseaworthy. Looking at the flimsy raft *Kon-Tiki*, you could be forgiven for agreeing with Heyerdahl's doubters – and for wondering how the crew didn't murder each other after a week in such a confined space. Heyerdahl's later investigations of Easter Island statues and cave graves lent further weight to his ethnological theory, which has now received a degree of acceptance. The whole saga is outlined here in the museum, and if you're especially interested, the story is also told in his book *The Kon-Tiki Expedition*. Preoccupied with trans-oceanic contact between prehistoric peoples, Heyerdahl went on to attempt several other voyages, sailing across the Atlantic in a papyrus boat, *Ra II*, in 1970 to prove that there could have been contact between Egypt and South America. *Ra II* is displayed here and again Heyerdahl recorded the exploit in a book – *The Ra Expeditions*.

Just over the road, in front of the mammoth triangular display hall of the Fram museum, stands the *Gjøa*, the one-time sealing ship in which **Roald Amundsen** made the first complete sailing of the Northwest Passage in 1906. By any measure, this was a remarkable achievement and the fulfilment of a nautical mission that had preoccupied sailors for several centuries. It took three years, with Amundsen and his crew surviving two ice-bound winters deep in the Arctic, but even this epic journey was eclipsed when, in 1912, the Norwegian dashed to the South Pole, famously beating the ill-starred Captain Scott. The ship that carried Amundsen to within striking distance of the South Pole, the *Fram*, is displayed inside the **Fram Museum** (Frammuseet; June–Aug daily 9am–6.45pm; May & Sept daily 10am–4.45pm; March, April & Oct daily 11am–3.45pm; Nov–Feb Mon–Fri 11am–2.45pm, Sat & Sun 11am–3.45pm; 25kr). Designed by Colin Archer, a Norwegian shipbuilder of Scots ancestry, and launched in 1892, the *Fram*'s design was unique, its sides made smooth to prevent the ice from getting a firm grip on the hull, while inside a veritable maze of beams, braces and stanchions held it all together. Living quarters inside the ship were necessarily cramped, but – in true Edwardian style – the Norwegians still found space for a piano. Look out too for the assorted knick-knacks the explorers took with them, including playing cards, maps, notebooks, snowshoes and surgical instruments – although this was as nothing to the clobber carted there by Scott, one of the reasons for his failure. Scott's main mistake, however, was to rely on Siberian ponies to transport his tackle. The animals were useless in Antarctic conditions and Scott and his men ended up pulling the sledges themselves, whereas Amundsen wisely brought a team of huskies.

The adjacent **Norwegian Maritime Museum** (Norsk Sjøfartsmuseum; mid-May to Sept daily 10am–7pm; Oct to mid-May Mon, Wed & Fri–Sun 10.30am–4pm, Tues & Thurs 10.30am–7pm; 30kr) occupies two buildings, the larger of which is a well-designed brick structure with a fairly pedestrian collection of maritime artefacts. Among the assorted models, the only real highlight is an Internet connection to the Oslofjord traffic control system by means of which you can track (but not change!) local shipping movement. The museum's second building, the **Båthallen** (boat hall), is a tad better, with a mildly diverting selection of wooden boats from all over Norway, mostly inshore sailing and fishing craft from the nineteenth century.

South of the centre: the inner Oslofjord

The compact archipelago of low-lying, lightly forested **islands** in the inner Oslofjord is the city's summer playground, and makes going to the beach a viable, if unusual, option for a European capital. Jumping on a ferry is a pleasant way of passing the time, whether in the heat of the day or in the evenings, when the more lightly populated islands become favourite party venues for the city's preening youth. **Ferries** to the islands (20kr each way, Oslo Card & all other transport passes valid) leave from the Vippetangen quay, beside the grain silo at the foot of Akershusstranda – a twenty-minute walk or a five-minute ride on bus #60 south from Jernbanetorget.

Conveniently, **Hovedøya** (ferry #92; mid-March to Sept every hour or ninety minutes 7.30am–7pm; Oct to mid-March 3 daily; 10min), the nearest island, is also the most interesting. Its rolling hills contain farmland and deciduous woods, as well as the overgrown ruins of a Cistercian monastery, built by English monks in the twelfth century, and other remains from the days when the island was garrisoned and armed to protect Oslo's harbour. A map of the island at the jetty helps with orientation, but on an islet of this size – it's just ten minutes' walk from one end to the other – getting lost is pretty much impossible. There are plenty of footpaths to wander, you can swim from the shingle beaches on the south shore, and there's a seasonal café opposite the monastery ruins. Camping is not permitted, however, as Hovedøya is a protected area – that's why there are no summer homes.

The pick of the other islands is H-shaped, wooded **Langøyene** (ferry #94; June–Aug hourly 10am–6pm; 30min), the most southerly of the archipelago and the one with the best beaches. There's a **campsite**, *Langøyene Camping* (☎22 11 53 21; June to mid-Aug), and at night the ferries are full of people with sleeping bags and bottles, on their way to join swimming parties.

East of the centre: the Munch Museum

Nearly everyone who visits Oslo makes time for the **Munch Museum** (Munch-museet) and, if you possibly can, it's worth setting aside a half-day for the experience. In his will, Munch donated all the works in his possession to Oslo city council – a mighty bequest of several thousand paintings, prints, drawings, engravings and photographs, which took nearly twenty years to catalogue and organize for display in this purpose-built gallery.

The **museum** is located to the east of the city centre at Tøyengata 53 (June to mid-Sept daily 10am–6pm; mid-Sept to May Tues–Sun 10am–4pm, Thurs & Sun until 6pm; 50kr) and is reachable by T-bane – get off at Tøyen and it's a signposted, five-minute walk.

The museum

The collection is huge, and only a small part of it can be shown at any one time – an advantage, since you don't feel overwhelmed by what's on display. The space required by visiting exhibitions also often confines the Munch paintings to one large gallery, which can appear cluttered, but at least you can reckon on seeing many of the more highly praised works. There's a basement display on Munch's life and times as well, with oodles of background information.

In the main gallery, the landscapes and domestic scenes of Munch's **early paintings** – such as *Tête à Tête* (1885) and *At the Coffee Table* (1883) – reveal the perceptive, if deeply pessimistic, realism from which Munch's later work sprang. Even more riveting are the great works of the **1890s**, which form the core of the collection and are considered Munch's finest achievements. Among many, there's *Dagny Juel*, a portrait of the Berlin socialite Ducha Przybyszewska, with whom both Munch and his friend Strindberg were infatuated; the searing representations of *Despair* and *Anxiety*; the chilling *Red Virginia Creeper*, a house being consumed by the plant; and, of course, *The Scream* – of which the museum holds several of a total of fifty versions. Consider Munch's words as you view it:

I was walking along a road with two friends. The sun set. I felt a tinge of melancholy. Suddenly the sky became blood red. I stopped and leaned against a railing feeling exhausted, and I looked at the flaming clouds that hung like blood and a sword over the blue-black fjord and the city. My friends walked on. I stood there trembling with fright. And I felt a loud unending scream piercing nature.

EDVARD MUNCH

Born in 1863, Edvard Munch had a melancholy childhood, overshadowed by the early deaths of both his mother and a sister from tuberculosis. After some early works, including several self-portraits, he went to study in Paris, a city he returned to again and again, and where he fell (fleetingly) under the sway of the Impressionists. In 1892 he went to Berlin, where his style moved on and he produced some of his best and most famous work, though his first exhibition there was considered so outrageous it was closed after only a week – his painting was, a critic opined, "an insult to art". Despite the initial criticism, Munch's work was subsequently exhibited in many of the leading galleries of the day. Generally considered the initiator of the Expressionist movement, Munch wandered Europe, painting and exhibiting prolifically. Meanwhile overwork, drink and problematic love affairs were fuelling an instability that culminated, in 1908, in a nervous breakdown. Munch spent six months in a Copenhagen clinic, after which his health improved greatly – and his paintings lost the hysterical edge characteristic of his most celebrated work. It wasn't until well into his career, however, that he was fully accepted in his own country, where he was based from 1909 until his death in 1944.

Munch's style was never static, however. **Later paintings** such as *Workers On Their Way Home* (1913), produced after he had recovered from his breakdown and had withdrawn to the tranquillity of the Oslofjord, reflect his renewed interest in nature and physical work. His technique also changed: in works like the *Death of Marat II* (1907) he began to use streaks of colour to represent points of light. Still later paintings, such as *Winter in Kragerø* and *Model by the Wicker Chair*, reveal at last a happier, if rather idealized, attitude to his surroundings, most evident in works like *Spring Ploughing*, painted in 1919.

The exhibition is punctuated by **self-portraits**, a graphic illustration of Munch's state of mind at various points in his career. There's a palpable sadness in his *Self-portrait with Wine Bottle* (1906), along with obvious allusions to his heavy drinking, while the telling perturbation of *In Distress* (1919) and *The Night Wanderer* (1923) indicate that he remained a tormented, troubled man even in his later years. One of his last works, *Self-portrait by the Window* (1940), shows a glum figure on the borderline of life and death, the strong red of his face and green of his clothing contrasted with the ice-white scene visible through the window.

Munch's **lithographs and woodcuts** are shown in a separate section of the gallery: a dark catalogue of swirls and fogs, technically brilliant pieces of work and much more than simple copies of his paintings – indeed, they're often developments of them. In these he pioneered a new medium of expression, experimenting with colour schemes and a huge variety of materials, which enhance the works' rawness: wood blocks show a heavy, distinct grain, while there are colours like rust and blue drawn from the Norwegian landscape. As well as the stark woodcuts on display, there are also sensuous, hand-coloured lithographs, many focusing on the theme of love (in the form of a woman) bringing death.

Northwest of the centre: Frogner Park, the Vigeland Sculpture Park and Museum

The green expanse of **Frognerparken** (Frogner Park) lies to the northwest of the city centre – take tram #12 from Nationaltheatret and get off at Vigelandsparken, the stop after Frogner plass. The park incorporates one of Oslo's most celebrated and popular cultural attractions, the open-air sculpture park, which, along with the nearby museum, commemorates a modern Norwegian sculptor of world renown, **Gustav Vigeland** (1869–1943). Between them, they display a huge portion of his work, presented to the city in return for favours received in the shape of a studio and apartment during the years 1921–30.

Vigeland began his career as a woodcarver but later, influenced by Rodin, turned to stone and bronze. He started work on the **Vigelandsparken** (open 24hr; free) in 1924, and was still working on it when he died in 1943. It's a literally fantastic work, medieval in spirit and complexity. Here he had the chance to let his imagination run riot and, when unveiled, many city folk were simply overwhelmed – and no wonder. From the monumental wrought-iron gates, the central path takes you into a world of frowning, fighting and posing bronze figures, which flank the footbridge over the river. Beyond, the **central fountain**, part of a separate commission begun in 1907, is an enormous bowl representing the burden of life, supported by straining, sinewy bronze Goliaths while, underneath, water tumbles out around clusters of playing, talking, resting and standing figures.

But it's the twenty-metre-high **obelisk** up on the stepped embankment, and the granite sculptures grouped around it, which really take the breath away. It's a humanistic work, a writhing mass of sculpture which depicts the cycle of life as Vigeland saw it: a vision of humanity teaching, playing, fighting, loving, eating and sleeping – and clambering on and over each other to reach the top. The granite children scattered around the steps are perfect: little pot-bellied figures who tumble over muscled adults, and provide an ideal counterpoint to the real Oslo toddlers who splash around in the fountain, oblivious and undeterred.

A five-minute walk from the obelisk, near the river or. the southern edge of the park, the **Vigeland Museum** (Vigelandmuseet; May–Sept Tues–Sat 10am–6pm, Sun noon–7pm; Oct–April Tues–Sat noon–4pm, Sun noon–6pm; 30kr), at the corner of Halvdan Svartes gate and Nobels gate, was the artist's studio and home during the 1920s. It's still stuffed with all sorts of items related to the sculpture park, including discarded or unused sculptures, woodcuts, preparatory drawings and scores of plaster casts. Here and there are scraps of biographical information, but Vigeland's last decades were defined by his creation: you get the feeling that given half a chance he would have had himself cast and exhibited – as it is, his ashes were placed in the museum's tower.

North of the centre: the Nordmarka

Criss-crossed by hiking trails and cross-country ski routes, the forested hills and lochs of the **Nordmarka** occupy a tract of land that extends deep inland from downtown Oslo, but is still within the city limits for some 30km. A network of byroads provides dozens of access points to this wilderness, which is extremely popular with the capital's outdoor-minded citizens. Den Norske Turistforening (DNT), the Norwegian hiking organization, maintain a handful of staffed and unstaffed huts here, so if you want to spend more than a day in the area, head first for DNT's Oslo branch, in the city centre at Storgata 3 (Mon–Fri 10am–4pm, Thurs until 6pm, Sat 10am–2pm; ☎22 82 28 00). They have detailed maps and will arrange a year's DNT membership for 360kr – a prerequisite if you want to use one of their huts (see p.174 for more on the DNT and hiking in general).

For a day-trip, one of the easiest and most obvious departure points is **Sognsvann** station, the terminus of T-bane line #5, just twenty minutes from the city centre. Maps of the surrounding wilderness are posted at the station and show a network of hiking trails labelled according to the season – red for winter skiing, blue for summer. From the station, it's a signposted five-minute walk to **Sognsvannet**, an attractive loch flanked by forested hills and encircled by an easy four-kilometre hiking trail. The lake is iced-over until the end of May, after which the hardy can go for a dip – though treat Norwegian assurances about the water's pleasant temperature with caution. With the proper hiking equipment (see p.34), it's possible to hike west over the hills to Frognerseteren station (see below), a tough and not especially rewarding trek of about 5km. Locals mostly shun this route in summer, but – approached from the other direction – it's really popular in winter with parents teaching their children to cross-country ski.

T-bane line #1 also delves into the Nordmarka, wriggling up into the hills to the **Frognerseteren** terminus, a thirty-minute ride north of the city centre. From the station, there's a choice of signposted trails across the surrounding countryside. The most popular is the easy but squelchy 2km stroll to the **Tryvannstårnet** TV Tower (daily: June–Aug 10am–6pm; May & Sept 10am–5pm; Oct–April 10am–4pm; 35kr, free with Oslo Card), where a lift whisks you up to an observation platform, from where there are panoramic views over to the Swedish border to the east, Oslo to the south, and the forested hills of the Gudbrandsdal valley to the north – labels inside the platform point everything out for you. This a pointless excursion unless the weather is clear as even a light mist obscures the view. As an alternative to the TV tower, it's just a couple of hundred metres down from the T-bane station to the *Frognerseteren Restaurant* (opens 11am; ☎22 92 40 40), a delightful wooden lodge whose terrace offers splendid views out over the Nordmarka. The self-service restaurant is excellent too, if a little pricey – a sandwich and a coffee will rush you around 80kr.

Moving on, forest footpaths link Frognerseteren with Sognsvannet (see overleaf) or it's a twenty-minute tramp downhill – either along the road or the adjacent footpath – to the flashy chalets and hotels of the **Holmenkollen ski resort**. The latter also has its own T-bane station, located at the very southern end of the resort. Holmenkollen's main claim to fame is its international **ski-jump**, a gargantuan affair that dwarfs its surroundings. At its base, the diligent **Ski Museum** (Skimuseet; daily: June–Aug 9am–8pm; May & Sept 10am–5pm; Oct–April 10am–4pm; 60kr) has a more entertaining display than its name suggests. As well as skis through the ages, the museum has clothes and equipment, from the latest in competition ski-wear to the seemingly makeshift garb of early polar explorers like Nansen and Amundsen. The museum also gives access to the mountain of metal steps which leads up the ski-jump for a peek straight down at what is, for most people, a horrifyingly steep, almost vertical, descent: it seems impossible that the tiny bowl at the bottom could pull the skier up in time – or that anyone could possibly want to jump off in the first place. The bowl is also the finishing point for the 8000-strong cross-country skiing race that forms part of the Holmenkollrennene (ski festival) every March.

Eating and drinking

There was a time when eating out in Oslo hardly set the pulse racing, but things are very different today. At the top end of the market, the city possesses dozens of fine **restaurants** featuring typical Norwegian ingredients, especially fresh fish, along with more exotic dishes such as elk, caribou, and salted and dried cod – for centuries Norway's staple food. Many of these restaurants have also assimilated the tastes and styles of other cuisines – Mediterranean foods are very much in vogue – and there is a light smattering of ethnic restaurants too.

Most of the city's restaurants are fairly formal affairs, with prices to burn your fingers; the city's **cafés** and **café-bars**, by contrast, are much more affordable. These run the gamut from homely family places offering traditional Norwegian stand-bys to student haunts and ultra-fashionable hangouts, serving an imaginative mix of Norwegian and Mediterranean dishes. Nearly all of them serve inexpensive lunches, and many offer excellent, competitively priced evening meals as well, though the self-service cafés amongst them mostly close at 5 or 6pm. Downtown Oslo's vibrant **bar** scene is a noisy, boisterous but generally good-tempered affair which is at its most frenetic on summer weekends when the city is crowded with visitors from all over Norway.

Finally, those carefully counting the kroner will find it easy to buy bread, fruit, snacks and sandwiches from stalls, supermarkets and kiosks across the city centre, while fast-food joints offering hamburgers and *pølser* (hot dogs) are legion.

Restaurants

Dining out at one of Oslo's **restaurants** can make a sizeable dent in most wallets. In most places, a main course will set you back between 180kr and 220kr – not too steep until you add on a couple of beers (at 50kr a throw) or a bottle of wine, which will rush you at least 180kr. The positive side is that Oslo's better restaurants have creative menus marrying Norwegian culinary traditions with those of the Mediterranean – a lousy meal is a rarity. Restaurant decor is often a real feature too, ranging from the (more predictable) fishing nets and fishing photos to sharp modernist places with pastel walls and angular furnishings and fittings.

Engebret Café, Bankplassen 1 (☎22 33 66 94). This smart and intimate restaurant occupies an attractive old building across from the Museum of Contemporary Art. It specializes in Norwegian delicacies such as reindeer and fish, with mouthwatering main courses costing in the region of

250kr. In summer, there's outdoor seating on the pretty cobbled square in front of the restaurant too. Reservations advised. Closed Sun.

Grand Café, Karl Johans gate 31 (☎22 42 93 90). This is the café-restaurant where Ibsen once held court – and the murals prove the point. Now popular with elderly tourists. the old-fashioned formality of the place with its chandeliers, bow-tied waiters and glistening cutlery is the main appeal, plus the reasonably priced set lunches.

Louise, Stranden 3, Aker Brygge (☎22 83 00 60). The interior of this large and reasonably priced restaurant has been done out with great panache in the style of a steamship, complete with funnels, decks, ships' ledgers, ropes, old nautical photos and – bless them – even a seagull mobile. It's all good fun and the food hits the mark too; seafood's the speciality.

L'Opera, Rosenkrantz gate 13 (☎22 42 67 67). Smart Italian restaurant with a stylish modern interior, all varnished wood and tight angles. It divides into two sections – a restaurant (main courses around 200kr) and a "bar-vinothèque", whose three-course set meal at around 300kr is especially delicious and popular. Imaginative pasta dishes and great desserts too.

Det Norske Hus, Prinsengate 18, near junction with Kongensgate (☎22 41 12 10). First-floor and first-rate restaurant serving up traditional Norwegian cuisine, with reindeer at 275kr, salted cod at 175kr. There's a very reasonably priced downstairs lunch bar too – reckon on 80–100kr for a meal. Closed Sun.

Theatercaféen, *Hotel Continental*, Stortingsgata 24–26 (☎22 82 40 50). Eat in splendid Art Nouveau surroundings and watch the city's movers and shakers doing their thing. A classy, pricey menu of mixed provenance makes this restaurant a very popular spot.

Vegeta Vertshus, Munkedamsveien 3b, near junction with Stortingsgata (☎22 83 42 32). Near the Nationaltheatret, this unassuming vegetarian restaurant, with its functional decor, has a self-service buffet with fine salads, mixed vegetables, pizza, potatoes and rice. Small platefuls go for around 80kr, while the all-you-can-eat 125kr buffet includes dessert, a drink and coffee; no alcohol served.

Cafés and café-bars

For sit-down food, **cafés** represent the best value in town. Traditional *kafeterias* (often self-service) offer solid portions of Norwegian food, while more European-style **café-bars** dish up salads, pasta and the like in attractive, often modish surroundings. The best deals are usually at **lunchtime**, when there's normally a good-value dish of the day on offer, but the bulk of the places listed below are also open in the evening until around 8 or 9pm, sometimes later. Note that the distinction between Oslo's café-bars and bars is often very blurred – a number of the places listed below are good venues for a drink too.

Amsterdam, Universitetsgata 11, entrance on Kristian Augusts gate. Done out in the style of a Dutch brown bar, this busy and agreeable café-bar has a moderately priced menu with an international flavour. Offerings include dishes like lasagne, satay, and ciabatta with snellfish. prices are in the 60–80kr range. Open till midnight or later, though the kitchen closes around 9pm.

Arcimboldo, Wergelandsveien 17. Fashionable but unpretentious self-service café-bar located inside the Kunstnernes Hus, the old art gallery facing onto the Slottsparken from near the foot of Linstows gate. The imaginative menu features Mediterranean and Norwegian dishes, with main courses costing in the region of 140kr. Open till midnight (Fri & Sat until 3am, Sun until 6pm).

Bacchus, in the Basarhallene behind the Domkirke. Cramped but cosy café-bar with nineteenth-century decor and a wrought-iron staircase. Attracts a wide-ranging clientele from day-tripping tourists through to art students and city eccentrics. Great cakes and pastries plus tasty sandwiches. Open till midnight.

Celsius, Rådhusgata 19, near junction with Øvre Slottsgate. Hidden away behind a handsome eighteenth-century gateway, this laid-back café-bar occupies one of Oslo's older buildings and offers simply wonderful Mediterranean-inspired food at around 130kr a dish (snacks 40–70kr). It's also a great place for a drink with plenty of seating and an open courtyard in the summer, log fires in the winter. Open till 1 or 2am (Sun 10pm). Closed Mon.

Coco Chalet, Øvre Slottsgate 8, at Prinsens gate. Heavy drapes, soft leather booths and Art Nouveau flourishes characterize this old-fashioned but fashionable café in the city centre. Inexpensive snacks from 25kr.

Ett Glass, Karl Johans gate 33, entrance on Rosenkrantz gate. Trendy, candlelit café-bar awash with platform shoes and tinted hair. The imaginative menu focuses on light meals and lunches with a Mediterranean flavour, moderately priced. Bar open until midnight (Wed–Sat till 2.30am), kitchen till about 10pm.

Falsen, Kongensgate 4. Genial, low-key café favoured by university students. Good Mediterranean-style food with spaghettis at 60kr, moussaka at 65kr. Open till 6pm (Sat 5pm). Closed Sun.

Halvorsen's Conditori, Prinsens gate 26. Long-established, traditional café-cum-teashop across from the Stortinget. Blue rinses abound, but the cakes and pastries – at 25kr to 35kr a slice – are arguably the best in town. Open till 5pm (Sat 4pm). Closed Sun.

Kaffebrenneriet, Grensen 45, near junction with Akersgata. Great coffee, great cakes in this bright, modern coffee house. Open till 7pm (Sat & Sun 5pm). There's another branch at Frognerveien 9, near junction with Skoveien.

Kaffistova, Rosenkrantz gate 8. Part of the *Hotell Bondeheimen*, this spick-and-span self-service café serves tasty, traditional Norwegian cooking at very fair prices. There's usually a vegetarian option, too. Open till 8pm (Sat & Sun 5pm).

Pascal Konditori, Tollbugata 11. Wonderful pastries and tasty coffee in this little café. Occupies an old bakers' shop, delightfully decorated with ceramic tiles of cherubs and fruit. Open till 5pm.

Sjakk Matt, Haakon VII's gate 5. Informal and fashionable café-bar near the Rådhus. Offers delicious, mostly Mediterranean-style, light meals at reasonable prices – around 60–70kr a plate. Highly recommended. Open till 1am (Fri & Sat till 3am).

Bars

The busiest and flashest **bars** are concentrated in the side streets near the Rådhus and down along the Aker Brygge, while other popular but less assertively heterosexual bars are clustered around Universitetsgata and on Rosenkrantz gate. Karl Johans gate weighs in with a string of bars too: some of them staid and stodgy; others – especially those near Oslo S – a fair bit wilder and less conventional. Many of Oslo's bars stay open until well after midnight, sometimes until 3–4am, and a number serve snacks and meals as well as drinks. Drinks are uniformly expensive, so if you're after a big night out, it's a good idea to follow Norwegian custom and have a few warm-up drinks before going out.

Barbeint, Drammensveien 20, near junction with Parkveien. If you're familiar with Scandinavian bands and cult films then you may spot a few faces in this jam-packed, fashionable bar. Loud sounds, everything from rap to rock. About ten minutes' walk west of the Nationaltheatret. Daily 8pm–3.30am.

Beer Palace, Holmensgata 3, Aker Brygge. Cramped and crowded bar with old brick walls and a beamed ceiling. Serves over 50 different brands of beer. Daily noon–3.30am.

Burns Pub, Stortingsgata 28. Deep, dark and busy bar attracting a 30-something clientele. Occasional live music. Daily 10am–4am (Sun from noon).

Cruise Kafé, Stranden 3, Aker Brygge. Standard-issue modern bar done out in shades of brown and cream with photographs of actors hung on the walls. It's all rather contrived, but the rock – and rock'n'roll – background music is excellent, and there are occasional live, often American, acts here too. Open from noon (Fri & Sat 1pm) till around 2am (Sun–Tues 12.30am).

Lipp, Olav V's gate 2. Part of the *Hotel Continental*, this big and brash bar, all wide windows and wood, is popular with the well-heeled of Oslo. Daily 3pm–2.30am (Sun & Mon till 1.30am).

Nichol & Son, Olav V's gate 1. Crowded, pint-sized bar, its walls covered with pictures of Jack Nicholson – an interesting but hardly inspired theme. They do a good line in daytime snacks and sandwiches. Daily 10am–1.30am (Thurs–Sat till 3.30am). In the basement below is *Zipper*, an American-style bar with pool table.

Palace Grill, Solligata 2. A small American-style bar with Irish beers on tap. Roots, rock and jazz background music, plus occasional live acts. Popular with everyone from yuppies to students. A twenty-minute walk west of the Nationaltheatret: follow Drammensveien, turn left down Cort Adelers gate and it's the first on the right. Daily 3pm–2am (Fri & Sat till 3am).

The Scotsman, Karl Johans gate 17, near junction with Nedre Slottsgate. Many visitors to Oslo seek this bar out – though no one is quite sure why. It's an eccentric kind of place, full of incongruities: the *Angus Steakhouse* restaurant in the basement serves Scottish pizzas and the regular live music acts can be unbelievably bad and/or bizarre, but the place is still packed every night. Outdoor seating on the main drag in summer. Daily noon–3.30am (Fri & Sat from 11am).

Stravinsky, Rosenkrantz gate 17. Extremely popular bar with a young clientele; it's a couple of minutes' walk east of the Rådhus, one of several bars on the lower part of this street. Daily 8pm–1.30am (Fri–Sat till 2.30am).

Entertainment and nightlife

Oslo is good for conveniently located downtown **nightclubs**, which is hardly surprising considering the number of Norwegians who flock to Ibiza every year, and tracking down live music is also straightforward, though the domestic **rock** scene is far from inspiring – talent is spread very thin indeed. **Jazz** fans are well served, with several first-rate venues dotted round the city centre, whilst **classical music** enthusiasts can benefit from an ambitious concert programme. For obvious reasons, most **theatre** productions are in Norwegian, but visiting English-language theatre companies are often to be seen, while English-language **films** are shown in their original language, with Norwegian subtitles.

For entertainment **listings** it's always worth checking out the Norwegian-language weekly listings leaflet *Plakaten*, available free from downtown cafés, bars, shops and the tourist office. More detailed information and reviews are provided by *Natt & Dag*, a free Norwegian-language monthly broadsheet, which is also widely available downtown. Alternatively, consult the English-language *What's On in Oslo*, a monthly freebie produced by the tourist office which contains a day-by-day account of all things cultural and entertaining, free or otherwise. Summer is the best time to be in Oslo for events of almost every description, but winter sees a fair range of happenings too.

For **tickets**, larger Norwegian post offices act as agents for Ticket Master (☎81 53 31 33), as does Oslo's Spektrum performance hall, Sonja Henies plass 2 (☎22 05 29 29); otherwise, contact the venue direct.

Nightclubs

Oslo's liveliest and trendiest **nightclubs** are bang in the middle of town on and around Karl Johans gate. Entry will set you back in the region of 100kr – though, surprisingly, drink prices are the same as anywhere else. Nothing gets going much before 11pm; closing times are generally around 3am.

Barock, Universitetsgata 26. Brimming with well-heeled 30-somethings, this smart bar-restaurant is attached to one of Oslo's more popular disco dance floors, kitted out in a sort of modern Baroque, with chandeliers, tall mirrors and frescoes. Just off Karl Johans gate. Closed Mon & Tues.

Castro, Kristian IV's gate 7. Big and busy, this is the city's premier gay-and-lesbian nightspot, with 80s disco sounds plus club and house. Closed Mon.

The Church, Karl Johans gate 10. Opposite the Domkirke, near Oslo S station, this large club spreads over several floors. with Ibiza-inspired sounds – everything from deep house to techno. Fri & Sat only.

Head On, Rosenkrantz gate 11. Well-established student favourite with an emphasis on funk and rap. Closed Sun.

Jazid, Pilestredet 17. Great range of music in this brash, youthful dance club – everything from underground house and Latin through to big beat, soul and jungle. In the city centre, a short walk north from the National Gallery. Closed Sun & Mon.

Rock venues

Big-name **rock** bands often include Oslo in their tours, a necessary leavening to what would otherwise be a pretty dull scene. The most prestigious annual event is

Norwegian Wood, a two-day open-air rock festival held in June at the outdoor amphitheatre at Frogner Park, a ten-minute ride from the city centre on tram #12. It's attracted the likes of Bob Dylan, Lou Reed and Van Morrison, and continues to pull in some of the best, supported by a variety of Norwegian acts. The arena holds around 6000 people, but tickets, costing around 350kr per day (available online at *www.norwegianwood.no*), sell out way in advance.

The following venues host gigs at least once a week.

Blue Monk, St Olavs gate 23 (☎22 20 22 90). Crowded, earthy nightspot noted for its adventurous programme of live music, from blues through to Estonian funk. Below is the equally gritty *Sub Pub*, featuring punk, ska and rock. At the corner of Pilestredet, near the National Gallery. Daily midnight–3am.

Cruise Kafé, Stranden 3, Aker Brygge (☎22 83 64 30). This small modern bar showcases live rock, rock'n'roll and blues bands, many of them American. Open noon–12.30am (Wed–Sat till around 2am).

Oslo Spektrum, Sonja Henies plass 2 (☎22 05 29 00, *www.oslospektrum.no*). Major venue showcasing big international acts – as well as small-fry local bands. Opening times vary with the shows – see press for details.

Rockerfeller Music Hall, Torggata 16, entrance round the back (☎22 20 32 32). With room for 1500 punters, this is one of Oslo's grandest nightspots. Hosts well-known and up-and-coming rock groups, plus reggae and salsa. Opening times vary according to the gig schedule. Also in the same building – entrance on Henrik Ibsens gate – is *John Dee Live* (☎22 20 32 32), a club and pub with more live sounds.

Smuget, Rosenkrantz gate 22 (☎22 42 52 62). Large and popular nightclub with bars, a disco and regular live shows by mostly home-grown jazz, rock or blues bands. Daily 8pm–3.30am.

Jazz venues

Oslo has a strong **jazz** tradition, and its week-long **Jazz Festival** in the middle of August attracts internationally renowned artists as well as showcasing local talent. Concert tickets cost up to 300kr, although there are also many free outdoor performances across the city. In October the comparable **Ultima Contemporary Music Festival** gathers together more Scandinavian and international talent: ticket and programme information from the tourist office. At other times of the year, try one of the following for regular jazz acts.

Herr Nilsen, C. J. Hambros plass 5 (☎22 33 54 05). Small and intimate bar whose brick walls are decorated with jazz memorabilia. Live jazz – often traditional and bebop – most nights. Air-conditioned. Daily 1pm–2.30am.

Original Nilsen, Rosenkrantz gate 11. Popular bar featuring regular live jazz. Daily noon–3.30am.

Stortorvets Gjestgiveri, Grensen 1, near junction with Grubbegata (☎23 35 63 70). Near the Domkirke, this old rabbit-warren of a place, set around a central courtyard, incorporates a jazz café, where there's traditional and modern jazz every Thursday and Friday night, plus Saturday at lunchtime or early evening. Daily 3pm–3am.

Classical music and opera

Oslo's major orchestra, the **Oslo Filharmonien** gives regular concerts in the city's Konserthus, Munkedamsveien 14 (Mon–Fri 10am–5pm, Sat 11am–2pm; ☎23 11 31 11), under its celebrated principal conductor Mariss Jansons. Tickets cost around 400kr, and can be booked online at *http://pluto.no/OFO*. The orchestra traditionally gives a couple of free evening concerts in the Vigeland sculpture park in August and September, and watch out also for good classical programmes at a variety of other venues including the Domkirke, Akershus Slott and the Munch Museum.

   Den Norske Opera, the country's opera company, offers the popular repertoire – Mozart, Richard Strauss and the Italians – but also stages a number of contemporary works each year. Ticket prices start at 180kr and performances are usually held at the Folketeaterpassasjen, Storgata 23 (information ☎22 42 94 75; booking office ☎81 54 44 88 or online at *http://pluto.no/norskopera*).

Cinema

The facility with which the Norwegians tackle other languages is best demonstrated at the **cinema**, where films are shown in their original language with Norwegian subtitles. Given that American (and British) films are the most popular, this has obvious advantages for visiting English speakers. Oslo has its share of mainstream multiscreens, as well as a good art-house cinema. Prices are surprisingly reasonable: tickets average around 60kr and there are reductions of around twenty percent for some matinee and early evening showings. From May to July, Oslo Card holders get a similar discount on any film at any cinema.

Cinema listings – including details of late-night screenings – appear daily in the local press, and the tourist office has programme times too. Central screens include the mainstream Eldorado, Torggata 9 (☎82 03 00 00); Felix, Aker Brygge (☎82 03 00 00); Klingenberg, Olav V's gate 4 (☎82 03 00 00); Saga, Stortingsgata 28 (☎82 03 00 00); and the art-house Filmens Hus, Dronningens gate 16 (☎22 47 45 00).

Theatre

Nearly all **theatre** productions are in Norwegian, making them of limited interest to tourists – there's a full list of venues in the tourist office's *Oslo Guide*. The **Nationaltheatret**, Stortingsgata 15 (☎22 41 27 10), stages an annual Ibsen Festival which sometimes includes performances by visiting English-language theatre companies, who also occasionally appear at the adventurous **Det Norske Teatret**, Kristian IV's gate 8 (☎22 42 43 44, *www.detnorsketeatret.no*).

Listings

Airlines Air France, Haakon VII's gate 9 (☎22 83 56 30); Braathens, at the airport (☎67 58 60 00) and Oslo S (☎64 81 07 30); British Airways, at the airport (☎80 03 31 42); Finnair, Jernbanetorget 4a (☎81 00 11 00); KLM, c/o Braathens; Lufthansa, Haakon VII's gate 6 (☎22 83 65 70); SAS, at the *Radisson SAS Scandinavia* hotel, Holbergs gate 30 and the airport (☎81 00 33 00).

American Express Karl Johans gate 33 (☎22 86 13 00); Fridtjof Nansens plass 6 (☎22 98 37 35). Both Mon–Fri 9am–5pm, Sat 10am–3pm.

Banks and exchange Banks are open Mon–Fri 8.15am–3.30pm (mid-May to mid-Sept 8.15am–3pm), Thurs till 5pm. Among many, Den Norske Bank has downtown branches at Stranden 1, Aker Brygge, and Karl Johans gate 2; Sparebanken at Oslo S, Storgata 1 and Kirkegata 18. Outside normal banking hours, the best bet is the exchange office at Oslo S (Mon–Fri 7am–7pm, Sat & Sun 8am–5pm), where there is also a 24hr automatic exchange machine. There are exchange facilities at the airport – both 24hr machines and offices in the arrival (Mon–Fri 8am–10.30pm, Sat 8.30am–7pm, Sun 10am–10.30pm) and the departure halls (Mon–Fri 5.30am–8pm, Sat 5.30am–6pm, Sun 6.30am–8pm). You can also change money and traveller's cheques at larger post offices, where the rates are especially competitive. There are 24hr cash machines (ATMs) at Oslo S and the airport.

Bookshops Tanum, at Karl Johans gate 37, has the city's widest selection of travel books and a good sample of Norwegian hiking maps. Aker Libris, Fjordalleèn 10, in the Aker Brygge complex, offers a wide selection of travel guides, hiking maps and English-language books. The shop of the Norwegian hiking organization, Den Norske Turistforening (DNT), Storgata 3, have a comprehensive collection of Norwegian hiking maps. The Syklistenes Landsforening (Norwegian Cyclist Association), Storgata 20c (☎22 41 50 80), have cycling books and maps.

Bus enquiries For long-distance services, contact Nor-Way Bussekspress, Bussterminalen information desk (Mon–Fri 7am–10pm, Sat 8am–5.30pm, Sun 8am–10pm; ☎23 00 24 40).

Car rental Avis, Munkedamsveien 27 (☎66 77 11 11) and at the airport (☎64 81 06 60); Bislet Bilutleie, Bedriftsveien 10 (☎22 16 54 00); Budget, Sonja Henies plass 4 (☎22 17 10 50) and at the airport (☎80 03 02 10); Europcar, at the airport (☎64 81 05 60); Statoil, Statoil service station, Sørkedalsveien (☎22 46 34 40). There are many others – see under "Bilutleie" in the yellow pages.

Dentist Oslo Kommunale Tannlegevakt, Tøyen Senter, Kolstadgata 18 (☎22 67 30 00). Daily 7am–10pm (Sat & Sun also 11am–2pm). Otherwise, see under "Tannleger" in the yellow pages.

Email and Internet Internet access is available at the main city library, Henrik Ibsen gate 1 (Mon–Fri 10am–8pm, Sat 9am–3pm).

Embassies and consulates Australia: use UK embassy; Canada, Wergelandveien 7 (☎22 99 53 00); Ireland: use UK embassy; New Zealand: use UK embassy; UK, Thomas Heftyes gate 8 (☎23 13 27 00); US, Drammensveien 18 (☎22 44 85 50). For others, look under "Ambassadeur og Legasjoner" in the yellow pages.

Emergencies Police ☎112; Fire ☎110; Ambulance ☎113. Oslo Kommunale Legevakt, Storgata 40, near junction with Hausmanns gate (☎22 11 70 70), has a 24hr rape and sexual assault counselling service, as well as casualty and outpatient facilities. For a doctor, look in the yellow pages under "Leger".

Ferries DFDS Seaways (to Copenhagen), Vippetangen Utstikker pier #2, beside Akershusstranda (☎22 41 90 90); Stena Line (to Frederikshavn in Denmark), Jernbanetorget 2 (☎23 17 90 00); Color Line (to Kiel, Germany, and Hirtshals, Denmark), Hjortneskaia (☎81 00 08 11). Tickets from the ferry companies direct or from travel agents.

Fishing The freshwater lakes of the Nordmarka are reasonably well stocked with common species such as trout, char, pike and perch. To go freshwater fishing, you need two licences – a national licence, which costs 90kr and is sold at any post office, and a local licence, a fiskekort (165kr), available from sports shops and some campsites. Seawater fishing has different rules: there's no local licence and you only need a national one if you go fishing for salmon, trout or sea char. This licence costs 180kr, can be purchased at any post office, and also includes the freshwater national licence. In addition, there are lots of local rules and regulations regarding what species of fish you can catch where and when – inquire locally for specific information. The Oslomarkas Fiskeadministrasjon, Kongeveien 5 (☎22 49 07 99), near the Holmenkollen ski-jump, provides general information on fishing in the Oslo area. In particular, they can advise about fishing areas and have lists of where local licences can be bought.

Gay Oslo There's not much of a scene in Oslo, primarily because the capital's gays and lesbians are mostly content to share pubs and clubs with heteros. But advice is available and activities and events organized by LLH (Landsforeningen for lesbisk og homofil frigjøring), St Olavs plass 2 (☎22 11 05 09, *www.llh.oslo.no*).

Hiking Den Norske Turistforening (DNT), Storgata 3 (Mon–Fri 10am–4pm, Thurs until 6pm, Sat 10am–2pm; ☎22 82 28 00), sells hiking maps and gives general advice and information on route planning – an invaluable first call before a walking trip in Norway. Join here to use their nationwide network of mountain huts; the subscription fee of 360kr gives a year's membership.

Laundry Majorstua Myntvaskeri, Vibes gate 15 (Mon–Fri 8am–8pm, Sat 8am–5pm); Mr Clean, Parkveien 6, near junction with Welhavens gate (daily 7am–11pm).

Left luggage There are lockers and a luggage office (Mon–Fri 7am–11pm, Sat 7am–3.30pm, Sun 3.30–11pm) at Oslo S.

Lost property Police ☎22 66 98 65; trams, buses and T-bane ☎22 08 40 00; NSB railways ☎23 15 00 00.

Markets and supermarkets Oslo's principal open-air market is on Youngstorget (Mon–Sat 7am–2pm), a brief stroll north of the Domkirke along Torggata. There's everything here from secondhand clothes to fresh fruit and veg – and there are several more handily located fresh produce stalls in the Basarhallene, beside Karl Johans gate. Supermarkets are thick on the ground around the suburbs, but rarer in the city centre. The biggest name is Rimi, who have a downtown outlet at Akersgata 45, near the corner with Grensen (Mon–Sat 8am–8pm, Sun 9am–5/6pm).

Newspapers Many English and American newspapers and magazines are widely available in downtown Oslo's convenience stores and Narvesen kiosks. There's an especially wide selection at Oslo S.

Pharmacy There's a 24hr service at Jernbanetorgets Apotek, Jernbanetorget 4b (☎22 41 24 82). All pharmacies display a rota in their window advising which is the nearest open pharmacy.

Nyhaven, Copenhagen

Climbing wall, Copenhagen

Tivoli Gardens, Copenhagen

Skagen, Denmark

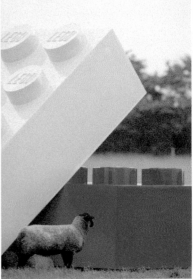

Frederiksborg Slot, Hillerød, Denmark   Legoland, Billund, Denmark

Karl Johans gate, Oslo

Downtown Lillehammer, Norway

Mural of *The Scream*, Oslo

CHRIS COE

Jostedalsbreen glacier, Norway

CHRIS COE

Bryggen at dusk, Bergen, Norway

Police Emergencies ☎112. Otherwise, in case of trouble or lost property (*Hittegods*) go to Oslo Politikammer, a 15min walk east of the centre at Grønlandsleiret 44 (☎22 66 98 65), or T-bane #1–5, Grønland station.

Post offices Main office, Dronningens gate 15 at Prinsens gate (Mon–Fri 8am–6pm, Sat 10am–3pm), with poste restante. There are lots of other post offices dotted across Oslo (usual opening hours Mon–Fri 8am–5pm, Sat 9am–1pm). Downtown locations include Karl Johans gate 22, Universitetsgata 2, Sjøgata 1 in Aker Brygge, and inside Oslo S (Mon–Fri 7am–6pm, Sat 9am–3pm). All post offices exchange currency and cash traveller's cheques at very reasonable rates.

Ride share Shared lifts out of the city are advertised at the youth information office, Ungdoms Informasjon, Møllergata 3 (Mon–Fri 11am–5pm; ☎22 41 51 32).

Train enquiries and bookings on ☎81 50 08 88.

Travel agents For discount flights, train and bus tickets, try either Euro Terra Nova, Dronningens gate 26 (☎22 00 77 30), or KILROY travels, Nedre Slotts gate 23 (☎23 10 23 00). Tourbroker Reisebyrå, Drammensveien 4 (☎22 83 27 15), specialize in Eurolines tickets. For a full list of Oslo travel agents, see under "Reisebyråer" in the yellow pages.

Vinmonopolet Off-licences at Klingenberggaten 4; Møllergaten 10–12; and at the Oslo City shopping complex, Stenersgaten 1.

Winter sports Skiing equipment can be rented from Skiservice Tomm Murstad, Tryvannsveien 2 (☎22 13 95 00), at Voksenkollen T-bane station, the penultimate stop on line #1. Both cross-country and downhill enthusiasts should also call by the Skiforeningen (Ski Society) office, at Kongeveien 5 (☎22 92 32 00), in the ski resort of Holmenkollen, on T-bane line #1. They can tell you more about Oslo's floodlit trails, cross-country routes, downhill and slalom slopes, ski schools (including a children's ski school) and organized excursions to the nearest mountain resorts. Horse-sleigh riding in the Nordmarka can be arranged through either Vangen Skistue, PO Box 29, Klemetsrud, N-1212 Oslo (☎64 86 54 81), or Helge Torp, Sørbråten Gård, Maridalen, Oslo (☎22 23 22 21). Ice fishing is another Nordmarka option, but follow what the locals do as it can be dangerous – and see above for information on fishing licences.

AROUND OSLO

The forested uplands that surround Oslo have little of the splendour of other parts of the country, but if time is pressing you could get a hint of what the Norwegian countryside is about by visiting the narrow straits and chubby basins of the **Oslofjord**, which links the capital with the open sea. This waterway – around 100km from top to bottom – has long been Norway's busiest, an islet-studded channel whose sheltered waters were once crowded with steamers shuttling passengers along the Norwegian coast. Nowadays, the Oslofjord shoreline has been blighted by industry and the only worthwhile destination is **Fredrikstad**, down the eastern side of the fjord on the train route to Sweden, a fortified riverside town whose grid-iron streets and earthen bastions have survived in remarkably good condition.

Fredrikstad

Roughly every two hours, trains leave Oslo to thump down the east side of the Oslofjord on their way to **FREDRIKSTAD**, named after the Danish king, Frederik II, who had the original fortified town built here at the mouth of the River Glomma in 1567. Norway was ruled by Danish kings from 1387 to 1814 and, with rare exceptions, the country's interests were systematically neglected in favour of Copenhagen's. A major consequence was Norway's involvement in the bitter rivalry between the Swedish and Danish monarchies, which prompted a seemingly endless and particularly pointless sequence of wars lasting from the early sixteenth century until 1720. The eastern approaches to Christiania (Oslo), along the Oslofjord, were especially vulnerable to attack from Sweden and the area was ravaged by raiding parties on many occasions. Indeed, Frederik II's fortress only lasted three years before it was burnt to the ground,

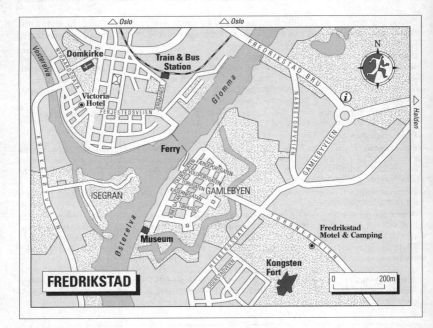

though it didn't take long for a replacement to be constructed – and for the whole process to be repeated again. Finally, in the middle of the seventeenth century, Fredrikstad's fortifications were considerably strengthened. The central grid-iron of cobbled streets was encircled on three sides by zigzag bastions, which allowed the defenders to fire across the flanks and into the front of any attacking force. In turn, these bastions were protected by a moat, concentric earthen banks and outlying redoubts. Armed with 130 cannon, Fredrikstad was, by 1685, the strongest fortress in all of Norway – and it has remained in military use ever since, which partly accounts for its excellent state of preservation. The fort was also left unaffected by the development of modern Fredrikstad, an offspring of the timber industry. This new town was built on the west bank of the Glomma while the old fort – now known as the **Gamlebyen** (Old Town) – was left untouched on the east.

From Fredrikstad **train** and **bus** station, located in the new part of town, it's a couple of minutes' walk to the Glomma river – head straight down Jernbanegata and take the first left along Ferjestedsveien. From the jetty, the **ferry** (Mon–Fri 5.30am–11pm, Sat 7am–11pm, Sun 9.30am–11pm; 5min; 6kr) shuttles over to the gated back wall of the Gamlebyen. Inside, the pastel-painted timber and stone houses of the old town, just three blocks deep and six blocks wide, make for a delightful stroll especially as very few tourists venture this way except in the height of the season. Indeed, on a drizzly day the streets echo with nothing but the sound of your own footsteps plus the occasional army boot hitting the cobbles as the garrison moves about its duties. A **museum** (May–Aug Mon–Fri 11am–5pm, Sat & Sun noon–5pm; 30kr), housed in the Gamle Slaveri (Old Slave House), where prisoners once did hard labour, dutifully outlines the history of the Old Town and displays a model of the fortress in its prime. Elsewhere, the main square holds an unfortunate statue of Frederik II, who appears to have a serious problem with his pantaloons, but it's the general appearance of the place that appeals rather than any specific sight.

Make sure also to take in the most impressive of the town's outlying defences, the **Kongsten Fort**, about ten minutes' walk from the main fortress: go straight ahead from the main gate, take the first right along Heibergsgate and it's clearly visible on the left. Here, thick stone and earthen walls are moulded round a rocky knoll which offers wide views over the surrounding countryside – an amiably quiet vantage point. When you've finished with the fortifications, drop by the *Cewex Konditori* in the Old Town on Voldportgaten for a snack.

Back on the western side of the Glomma, follow Ferjestedsveien in the opposite direction to that taken before for the brief walk round to the small park beside the **Domkirke** (late June to mid-Aug Tues–Sat noon–3pm), a big, brown, brick building with stained glass by Emanuel Vigeland. Beyond the church is the centre of modern Fredrikstad, an uninteresting place plonked on a bend in the river.

Although it's preferable to treat a visit as a day-trip, there are a handful of **hotels** in Fredrikstad, including the *Victoria*, Turngaten 3 (☎69 31 11 65, fax 69 31 87 55; ⑤), a comfortable hotel in a straightforward Art Nouveau building overlooking the park next to the Domkirke. Alternatively, the bargain-basement *Fredrikstad Motel & Camping*, Torsnesveien 16 (☎69 32 05 32, fax 69 32 36 66; ①), is about 300m straight ahead from the main gate of the Gamlebyen; it provides tent space as well as inexpensive rooms.

travel details

Trains

Oslo to: Åndalsnes (2–3 daily; 6hr 30min); Bergen (4–5 daily; 6hr 30min); Dombås (3–4 daily; 4hr 20min); Drammen (4–5 daily; 40min); Fredrikstad (8 daily; 1hr 15min); Geilo (4–5 daily; 3hr 20min); Halden (8 daily; 1hr 45min); Hamar (7 daily; 1hr 40min); Hjerkinn (3 daily; 4hr 45min); Kongsberg (4–5 daily; 1hr 20min); Kristiansand (4–5 daily; 5hr); Larvik (2–7 daily; 2hr 15min); Lillehammer (7 daily; 2hr 30min); Moss (8 daily; 50min); Myrdal (4–5 daily 4hr 30min); Otta (4–5 daily; 4hr 10min); Røros (2–3 daily; 6hr); Stavanger (3 daily; 9hr); Trondheim (3–4 daily; 8hr 15min); Voss (4–5 daily; 5hr 40min).

Buses

Oslo to: Alta via Sweden (3 weekly; 27hr); Arendal (1 daily; 4hr 15min); Balestrand (3 daily; 8hr 15min); Bergen (1 daily; 11hr 40min); Drøbak (hourly; 40min); Fagernes (3 daily; 3hr 20min); Fjaerland (3 daily; 7hr 50min); Grimstad (1 daily; 4hr 40min); Hamar (1 daily; 2hr); Hammerfest via Sweden (3 weekly; 30hr); Haugesund (1 daily; 10hr); Kongsberg (1 daily; 2hr); Kristiansand (1 daily; 5hr 40min); Lillehammer (1 daily; 3hr); Lillesand (1 daily; 5hr); Odda (1 daily; 8hr); Otta (2 daily; 5hr); Risør (1 daily; 3hr 30min); Sogndal (3 daily; 7hr); Stavanger (1 daily; 10hr); Stryn (1 daily; 8hr); Voss (1 daily; 10hr 30min).

Ferries

Horten to: Moss (hourly 6am–1am; 30min).

Oslo to: Dronningen/Bygdøynes (May–Aug every 40min 9.05am–9.05pm; late April & Sept every 40min 9.05am–6.25pm; 10–15min); Hovedøya (mid-March to Sept every 60–90min; Oct to mid-March 3 daily; 10min); Langøyene (June–Aug hourly 10am–6pm; 30min).

Express passenger boats (Hurtigbåt)

Oslo to:Arendal (July to mid-Aug 4 weekly; 6hr 45min); Kragerø (July to mid-Aug 4 weekly; 4hr 30min); Risør (July to mid-Aug 4 weekly; 5hr 10min); Stavern (July to mid-Aug 4 weekly; 3hr 15min).

International trains

Oslo to: Hamburg (1 daily; 14hrs); Copenhagen via Gothenburg (2 daily; 8hr 20min); Stockholm (1–2 daily; 6hr).

International buses

Oslo to: Amsterdam (2–3 weekly; 22hrs); Copenhagen (2–3 daily; 9hr 15min); Gothenburg (2–3 daily; 4hr 45min); London (3–5 weekly; 35hrs); Stockholm (3–4 daily; 10hr). Also services to Germany, Italy, Greece, Hungary, Austria, Russia and Belgium. Further information from Nor-Way Bussekspress, either inside the Oslo M bus station or at Karl Johans gate 2, Oslo (both ☎23 00 24 40).

International ferries

Oslo to: Copenhagen (1 daily; 16hr); Frederikshavn (1–2 daily; 8hr 30min); Hirtshals (6 weekly; 8hr); Kiel (1 daily; 19hr).

CHAPTER FIVE

SOUTH AND CENTRAL NORWAY

P
reoccupied by the fjords and the long road to the Nordkapp, few tourists are tempted to explore **South and Central Norway**. The Norwegians know better. Trapped between Sweden and the fjords, this great chunk of land boasts some of the country's finest scenery, with forested dales trailing north and west from Oslo towards the rearing peaks inland. It's here, within shouting distance of the country's principal train line and the E6 – the main line of communication between Oslo, Trondheim and the north – that you'll find three of Norway's prime **hiking areas**. These are made up of a trio of mountain ranges, each partly contained within a national park – from south to north, Jotunheimen, Rondane and the Dovrefjell. Each park is equipped with well-maintained walking trails and DNT huts; **Otta** and **Kongsvoll**, on both the E6 and the train line, are particularly good starting points for hiking expeditions.

Entirely different, but just as popular with the Norwegians, is the **south coast**, an appealing region whose myriad islets and skerries, beaches and coves punctuate the shoreline that extends west from the Oslofjord, at its prettiest in the east where a handful of old timber ports – **Arendal**, **Lillesand** and **Mandal** – sport bright-white, antique clapboard houses along their harbourfronts. **Kristiansand**, easily the largest town on the coast, is different again, a brisk modern place that successfully combines its roles as a resort and as a major ferry port with connections to Denmark.

Despite these attractions, it's easy to see the whole region as nothing more than a **transport corridor**, especially as two major roads – including the spectacular Hwy 9 to Åndalsnes – branch off the E6 for the fjords. The south coast is traversed by the E18 (and its continuation the E39), linking Oslo with Stavanger. In between the E18/39 and the E6, three major roads – the E16, the E134 and Hwy 7 – cut across the interior from the capital to the central fjords and Bergen. But, whichever way you're heading, it would be a great pity if you didn't allow at least a couple of days for the south coast or the national parks in the north.

ACCOMMODATION PRICE CODES

The hotels and guesthouses listed in this chapter have been graded according to the following price bands, based on the cost of the **least expensive double room during high season** (late June to Aug). However, almost every hotel offers seasonal and/or weekend discounts, and wherever possible we've given two grades, covering both the regular and the discounted rate.

① Under 500kr	② 500–700kr	③ 700–900kr
④ 900–1200kr	⑤ 1200–1500kr	⑥ Over 1500kr

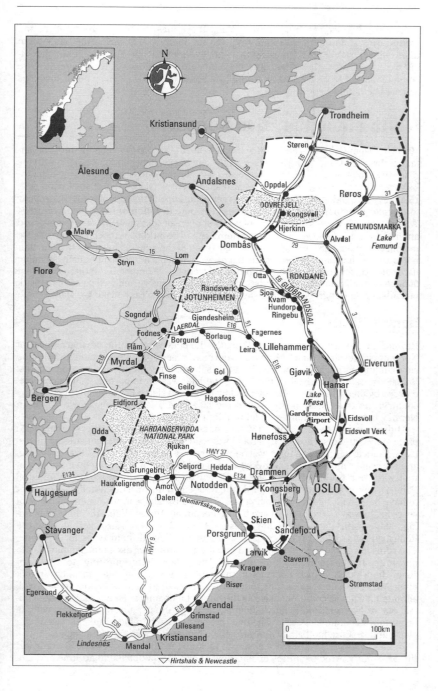

As you might expect, **bus** services along these main highways are excellent and **trains** are fast and frequent too. Away from the highways, however, the bus system thins out and travelling becomes a pain without your own vehicle – it can be worth renting a car locally for a few days. In terms of **accommodation**, roadside campsites are commonplace, there's a reasonable supply of youth hostels and every major town has at least one hotel or guesthouse.

North along the E6 to Kongsvoll

Hurrying from Oslo to Trondheim and points north, the **E6** remains the most important highway in Norway, and is consequently kept in excellent condition – often with the roadworks to prove it. Inevitably, the road is used by many of the region's long-distance **buses**, and for much of its length it's also shadowed by Norway's principal **train** line. Heading out of Oslo, both the E6 and the railway thump northwards across the lowlands to clip along the north bank of Lake Mjøsa en route to **Lillehammer**, site of the 1994 Winter Olympic Games and the country's best open-air folk museum. Thereafter, road and rail wriggle on between the **Jotunheimen** and **Rondane national parks**, whose magnificent mountains are both within easy reach of the amiable town of **Otta**. Further north still is the beautiful **Dovrefjell** range, which forms a third and equally stunning national park, and one that's best approached from tiny **Kongsvoll**. All three parks are famous for their hiking, and are criss-crossed by an extensive and well-planned network of **trails**. From Kongsvoll, Trondheim (see p.302) is within easy striking distance.

North to Hamar

Beyond the flat farmlands north of Oslo, the E6 curves round the northern shore of Norway's largest lake, **Lake Mjøsa**, a favourite retreat for Norwegian families, with the surrounding farmland, woods and pastures harbouring numerous second homes. Before the railroad arrived in the 1880s, the lake was an important transport route, crossed by boats during the summer and by horse and sleigh in winter. It's also halfway country: the quiet settlements around the lake give a taste of small-town southern Norway before the E6 plunges on into wilder regions further north.

Midway round the lake, some 130km from Oslo, lies **HAMAR**, an easy-going little place of 25,000 souls whose marinas and waterside cafés make a gallant attempt to sustain a nautical flavour. The town was once the seat of an important medieval bishopric, and the scant remains of the **Domkirke** (cathedral) – not much more than a chunk of wall with four Gothic arches – are stuck out on the **Domkirkeodden** (Cathedral Point), a low, grassy headland towards the west end of town. The cathedral is thought to have been built by the "English pope" Nicholas Breakspear, who spent a couple of years in Norway as the papal legate before becoming Adrian IV in 1154, but the building, along with the surrounding episcopal complex, was ransacked during the Reformation, and local road-builders subsequently helped themselves to the stone. The ruins have now been incorporated into the **Hedmarksmuseet** (daily: mid-May to mid-June 10am–4pm; mid-June to mid-Aug 10am–6pm; mid-Aug to mid-Sept 10am–4pm; 30kr), which contains an archeological museum and an open-air folk museum. The latter holds fifty buildings collected from across the region and, although it's not as comprehensive as the one in Lillehammer (see p.232), it does contain one or two particularly fine buildings, including the parsonage of Bolstad with its beautifully decorated log walls. The most scenic approach to the headland is along the pleasant lakeshore footpath, which stretches 2km north from the train station.

Hamar is also as good a place as any to pick up the 130-year-old **paddle steamer**, the *Skibladner*, which shuttles up and down Lake Mjøsa between late June and late

August: on Tuesdays, Thursdays and Saturdays the boat makes the return trip across the lake from Hamar to Gjøvik and on up to Lillehammer, while on Mondays, Wednesdays and Fridays it chugs down to Eidsvoll and back; there's no Sunday service. Departure details are available at any local tourist office and from the *Skibladner* office, next door to the tourist office in Hamar on Parkgata (☎62 52 70 85, *www.skibladner.no*). Tickets are bought on board: return trips from Hamar to Eidsvoll cost 200kr and last two and a half hours, those to Lillehammer cost 250kr and last eight hours. One-way fares cost a little over half these rates. Travellers heading north may find the trip to Lillehammer tempting at first sight, but the lake is not particularly scenic, and after four hours on the boat you'll feel like jumping overboard with tedium. The best bet is to take the short bus or train ride instead.

Practicalities

Hamar's **train station** is in the town centre beside the lake; **buses** stop outside. It's here that some trains from Oslo pause before heading up the secondary branch line to Røros (see p.237), a fine three-and-a-half-hour ride over the hills and through huge forests. Some 100m from the train station – turn left out of the terminal building and head along Stangevegen – is the **tourist office**, at Parkgata 2 (mid-June to mid-Aug Mon–Fri 8am–8pm, Sat & Sun noon–6pm; rest of year Mon–Fri 8am–3.30pm; ☎62 51 02 26), and next door is the booking office for the *Skibladner* paddle steamer (see above). The jetty for the *Skibladner* ferry is 500m further north.

There's a fair choice of central **hotel** accommodation, the most attractive option being the lakeshore *First Hotel Victoria*, Strandgata 21 (☎62 53 05 00, fax 62 53 32 23; ⑤), which has a bar and a reasonably good restaurant serving Norwegian favourites. Part of the same complex as a **motel** (②), the **youth hostel**, Åkersvikavegen 10 (☎62 52 60 60, fax 62 53 24 60; doubles ③), occupies smart modern buildings about 2km south along the lakeshore from the train station – it's in the middle of nowhere, just across from the massive skating arena built for the 1994 Winter Olympics in the shape of an upturned Viking ship.

Lillehammer

LILLEHAMMER (literally "Little Hammer"), 50km north of Hamar and 180km from Oslo, is Lake Mjøsa's most worthwhile destination. In **winter**, it's *the* Norwegian ski centre, a young and vibrant place whose rural, lakeshore setting and extensive cross-country ski trails contributed to its selection as venue for the 1994 Winter Olympic Games. In preparation for the games, the Norwegian government spent a massive two billion kroner on the town's sporting facilities, which are now the best in the country. Spread along the hillsides above and near the town, they include a ski-jumping tower and chair lift; a ski-jumping arena with two jumping hills and chairlift; an ice hockey arena; a bobsleigh track and a cross-country skiing stadium which gives access to about 30km of cross-country ski trails. Several local companies, including Saga Arrangement, Gudbrandsdalsvegen 203 (☎61 26 92 44, fax 61 26 24 22), operate all-inclusive winter sports and activity holidays, though if this is what you have in mind, you may as well book your holiday with an agent back home. As you would expect, most Norwegians arriving here in winter come fully equipped, but it's possible to rent (or purchase) equipment when you get here – the tourist office (see overleaf) will advise.

Lillehammer remains a popular holiday spot in **summer** too. Hundreds of Norwegians hunker down in their second homes in the hills, dropping into the town centre for a drink or a meal. Cycling, walking, fishing and canoeing are popular pastimes at this time of year, with all sorts of possibilities for guided tours and equipment hire. But, however appealing the area may be to Norwegians, the countryside round here has little of the wonderful wildness of other parts of Norway, and unless you're someone's guest or bring your own family, you'll probably feel rather out on a limb. That said, Lillehammer is not a bad place to break your journey, and there are a couple of attractions to keep you busy for a day – but not two.

The art gallery and Maihaugen

Lillehammer's briskly efficient centre, just a few minutes' walk from one end to the other, is tucked into the hillside above the lake, the E6 and the railway. It has just one really notable attraction, the municipal art gallery, the **Kunstmuseum**, at Stortorget 2 (mid-June to mid-Aug daily 10am–5pm; mid-Aug to mid-June Tues–Sun 11am–4pm; 40kr; free English guided tours daily in July at 2pm, rest of the year Sat & Sun only at 2pm). Housed in a flashy modern edifice, the gallery's speciality is its temporary exhibitions of contemporary art (which attract an extra admission charge), but the permanent collection is also very worthwhile, with a small but representative sample of the works of most major Norwegian painters from Johan Dahl and Christian Krohg to Munch and Erik Werenskiold.

The much-vaunted **Maihaugen** open-air folk museum – the largest of its type in northern Europe – is located a twenty-minute walk southeast from the town centre along Anders Sandvigsgate (late May & late Aug to Sept daily 10am–5pm; June to mid-Aug daily 9am–6pm; Oct to mid-May Tues–Sun 11am–4pm; 70kr, including free 40min guided tour in English mid-May to Sept; local bus hourly from the Skysstasjon). Incredibly, the whole collection represents the lifetime's work of one man, a magpie-ish dentist by the name of Anders Sandvig. The Maihaugen holds around 140 reconstructed buildings, brought here from all over the region, including a charming seventeenth-century presbytery (*prestegårdshagen*), a thirteenth-century stave church from Garmo, log stores and smokehouses, summer grazing huts and various workshops. The key exhibits, however, are the two **farms** dating from the late seventeenth century, complete with their various outhouses and living areas.

The outside area is stocked with farmyard animals and guides dressed in traditional costume, who give the low-down on traditional rural life, and in the summertime there's often the chance to have a go at homely activities such as spinning, baking, weaving and pottery – good, wholesome fun. The main museum building features temporary exhibitions on folkloric themes. Allow a good half-day for a visit and take advantage of the free guided tour (in English every other hour, on the hour).

Practicalities

The E6 runs along the lakeshore about 500m below the centre of Lillehammer, where the ultramodern **Skysstasjon**, on Jernbanetorget, at the bottom of Jernbanegata, incorporates the **train station** and the **bus terminal**. The **information kiosk** here (Mon–Fri 7.30am–4.30pm, Sat 10am–2pm; ☎61 26 41 99) has public transport timetables and some tourist information. The main **tourist office**, a five-minute walk away up the hill and off the main street, Storgata, at Elvegata 19 (late June to mid-Aug Mon–Sat 9am–7pm, Sun 11am–6pm; mid-Aug to late June Mon–Fri 9am–4pm, Sat 10am–2pm; ☎61 25 92 99 or 81 54 81 70), has bucketloads of free brochures, information on local events and activities, and will help with finding accommodation (though there are no private rooms). **Orientation** couldn't be easier, with all activity focused on the pedestrianized part of Storgata which runs north from Bankgata, across Jernbanegata to the tumbling River Mesnaelva; Anders Sandvigsgate and Kirkegata run parallel on either side to east and west respectively.

For a place to stay, the popular **youth hostel** (☎61 26 25 66, fax 61 26 25 77; doubles ③) is perfect for an overnight visit. It occupies part of the Skysstasjon, and the thirty or so four-bunk rooms are kitted out with smoked-glass windows and smart modern furnishings. If you're around for longer, you may want something rather more cosy: a recommended **guesthouse** is *Gjestehuset Ersgaard*, Nordseterveien 201 (☎61 25 06 84, fax 61 25 31 09; ①), a couple of kilometres above town (in the Nordseter direction), which serves excellent breakfasts in its dining room overlooking the town and lake. For **hotel** accommodation in the centre, the *First Hotell Breiseth*, across from the Skysstasjon at Jernbanegata 3 (☎61 26 95 00, fax 61 26 95 05; ①) is a large chain hotel with comfortable rooms.

Lillehammer has a good supply of downtown **restaurants** and **cafés**. The busy *Bøndernes Hus Kafeteria*, at Kirkegata 68 (Mon–Fri 8.30am–7pm, Sat 8.30am–4pm, Sun noon–6pm), is a big, old-fashioned sort of place with cheap and filling self-service meals. Moving up a rung, the *Vertshuset Solveig*, down an alley off the pedestrianized part of Storgata, is cafeteria-style too, but the meals are first-rate, with main courses averaging around 100kr. For something entirely different, *Teppanyaki*, Storgata 73 (☎61 25 74 44), is a very good and moderately priced Japanese restaurant. If it's sunny, head for the *Terrassen*, a large and moderately priced outdoor restaurant serving all the Norwegian favourites by the river at Storgata 84 (☎61 25 00 49). The town has an animated nightlife, with **bars** clustered around the western end of Storgata. Places come and go pretty fast, but *Nikkers* and *Pipas*, both a stone's throw from the main tourist office, are the liveliest spots at present.

The Gudbrandsdal: Hundorp and Sjoa

Heading north from Lillehammer, the E6 and the railway leave the shores of Lake Mjøsa for the **Gudbrandsdal**, the 160-kilometre-long river valley which was for centuries the main route between Oslo and Trondheim. Enclosed by mountain ranges, the valley has a comparatively dry and mild climate, and its fertile soils have nourished a string of farming villages since Viking times – though there was some industrialization at the beginning of the twentieth century.

The first part of the Gudbrandsdal is fairly uninspiring, but after 70km the road swings past **HUNDORP**, where a neat little quadrangle of old farm buildings has been tastefully turned into a roadside tourist stop, with a café, art gallery and shop. There has been a farm here since prehistoric times, its most famous owner a Viking warrior by the name of Dalegudbrand, who became a bitter enemy of St Olav after his enforced baptism in 1021. With a little time to spare, you could ramble down towards the river from the compound and nose around a couple of Viking burial mounds. Three kilometres further north, amongst the orchards overlooking the E6, is **Sygard Grytting** (☎61 29 85 88, fax 61 29 85 10, *www.grytting.com*; ②; mid-June to mid-Aug), an ancient farmstead whose eighteenth-century buildings are in an almost perfect state of preservation – a beautiful ensemble with assorted barns and outhouses facing onto a tiny courtyard. One barn dates from the fourteenth century, when its upper storey was used to shelter pilgrims on the long haul north to Trondheim – it now offers inexpensive dormitory accommodation (270kr per person), whilst the rooms in the main farmhouse (②) provide some of the most attractive lodgings in the whole of Norway. The nearest train station is Hundorp, which is where long-distance buses will drop you too.

Pressing on, the E6 weaves north along the course of the river to reach, after 35km, **SJOA** train station, which sits beside the E6 at its junction with Hwy 257. The latter cuts west along the Heidal valley, which boasts some of the country's most exciting **whitewater rafting** on the River Sjoa. If you want to come to grips with the Sjoa's gorges and rapids, contact the local specialists Heidal Rafting (☎61 23 60 37, fax 61 23 60 14, *www.heidalrafting.no*). An all-inclusive one-day rafting excursion costs around 700kr; a more strenuous two-day expedition will set you back almost three times that amount inclusive of meals and lodgings. The season lasts from May to September and reservations are recommended, though there's a reasonably good chance of being able to sign up at the last minute. Heidal Rafting are based at the Sjoa youth hostel (☎61 23 62 00, fax 61 23 60 14; doubles ①; May–Sept), which is also where they lodge their customers.

The hostel is itself worth a second look. Perched on a wooded hillside high above the river, the main building is a charming old log farmhouse dating from 1747 and, although visitors sleep elsewhere, they do eat here. Breakfasts are banquet-like and dinners (by prior arrangement only) are reasonably priced if rather less spectacular. The hostel offers no-frills dormitory accommodation and a handful of spacious and comfortable chalets (①). Advance reservations are recommended for the chalets at weekends. The hostel is situated just 1300m west of Sjoa train station near Hwy 257 – note that some trains only stop at Sjoa on request: check with the conductor.

Otta and the Rondane and Jotunheimen national parks

Just 10km beyond Sjoa lies **OTTA**, an unassuming and unexciting little town at the confluence of the rivers Otta and Lågen. It may be dull, but Otta makes a handy base for hiking in the nearby Rondane and Jotunheimen national parks, especially if you're reliant on public transport – though staying in one of the parks' mountain lodges is to be preferred. In Otta, everything you need is within easy reach: the E6 passes within 200m of the centre, sweeping along the east bank of the Lågen, while the **train station, bus terminal** and **tourist office** (mid-June to late Aug Mon–Fri 8.30am–7.30pm, Sat & Sun 10.30am–6pm; late Aug to mid-June Mon–Fri 8.30am–4pm; ☎61 23 66 50, fax 61 23 09 60) are all clumped together on the west bank in the Skysstasjon, itself just 100m from the small grid of streets that pass for the town centre. There are no sights as such, but the stiff hike along the footpath up the forested slopes to the summit of nearby **Pillarguritoppen** (853m), across the Otta River south of the centre, is a popular outing.

Otta tourist office is exceptionally helpful, providing local bus timetables, booking accommodation, reserving boat tickets, selling DNT membership (see p.174) and fishing licences, offering hiking tips and selling a range of hiking maps. They also have a small supply of **private rooms** (①) which they will reserve on your behalf for a booking fee of 25kr. Alternatively, the *Grand Gjestegård* (☎61 23 12 00, fax 61 23 04 62; ②), across from the train station at the corner of Ola Dahls gate, is a large pension-cum-hotel with simple but perfectly adequate rooms furnished in brisk modern style. If they're full, try the *Norlandia Otta Hotell* (☎61 23 00 33, fax 61 23 15 24; ③), which occupies an unenticing concrete block a few metres to the west along Ola Dahls gate. The nearest **campsite**, *Otta Camping* (☎61 23 03 09), occupies a small riverside site with pitches and cabins (②) in a scenic spot on the wooded banks of the River Otta about 1500km from the town centre. To get there, cross the bridge on the south side of the centre, turn right and keep going. Otta doesn't have much in the way of **restaurants**, but the *Pillarguri Café* on Storgata musters a range of Norwegian standbys, as does the popular and inexpensive restaurant of the *Grand Gjestegård*. Both close between 5pm and 6pm.

MOVING ON FROM OTTA TO THE WESTERN FJORDS

Running west from Otta, **Hwy 15** sweeps along the wide and fertile Hjelledal river valley over to Lom (see p.288), where there's a choice of wonderful routes on into the western fjords. From Lom, **Hwy 55** climbs steeply to the south, travelling along the western flank of the Jotunheimen National Park and offering breathtaking views of its jagged peaks before careering down to Sogndal (see p.286). Alternatively, Hwy 15 forges ahead from Lom to Stryn (see p.291), passing the nerve-tingling **Ørnevegen** (Eagle's Highway) – Hwy 63 – turning to **Geiranger** (see p.293). In terms of public transport, the Oslo–Måløy Nor-Way Bussekspress **bus** (3 daily) passes through Otta and Lom en route to Stryn; from mid-June to August, one of these three buses connects at Grotli with the bus down to Geiranger. The journey time from Otta to Lom is one hour, three hours to Stryn. There are no bus services along Hwy 55.

Rondane National Park

Spreading north and east from Otta towards the Swedish border, the **Rondane National Park** (Rondane Nasjonalpark), established in 1962 as Norway's first national park, is now one of the country's most popular hiking areas. Its 580 square kilometres, one-third of them in the high alpine zone, appeal to walkers of all ages and abilities. The soil is poor, so vegetation is sparse and lichens, especially reindeer moss, predominate, but the views across this bare landscape are serenely beautiful, and a handful of lakes and rivers along with patches of dwarf birch forest provide some variety.

Wild mountain peaks divide the Rondane into three distinct areas. To the west of the centrally located lake, **Rondvatn**, are the wild cirques and jagged peaks of Storsmeden (2017m), Sagtinden (2018m) and Veslesmeden (2015m), while to the east of the lake tower Rondslottet (2178m), Vinjeronden (2044m) and Storronden (2138m). Further east still the park is dominated by Høgronden (2115m). Most of the mountains, ten of which exceed the 2000-metre mark, are accessible to any reasonably fit walker via a dense network of trails and hiking huts.

Buses to the park from Otta depart daily in summer (late June to mid-Aug 1 daily; 45min), travelling the 25km to the Spranghaugen car park, the starting point for hikes into the Rondane. Unfortunately, this leaves in the afternoon, meaning you'll almost certainly need to overnight at Rondvassbu hut (see below). There's also a daily morning bus (same dates) terminating at Mysuseter, 5km short of Spranghaugen. The return bus leaves Spranghaugen for Otta in the afternoon. Taking a **taxi** is also a possibility, especially if you're in a group – enquire at the tourist office, who also have details of local **car** rental. If you want to do things yourself, **taxis** are available at the Skysstasjon with Otta Skysstasjon (☎61 23 05 01) and **cars** from Otta Auto (☎61 23 64 50).

Accommodation in the park is limited to the **Rondvassbu hut** (☎61 23 18 66; ①; late June to mid-Sept) at the southern end of Rondvatn. This is a typical DNT staffed lodge, with over one hundred beds, filling meals and pleasant service. If visibility is poor or you don't fancy a climb, there is a charming summer **boat service** (July to late Aug 2–3 daily; 1hr return; 35kr one-way, 50kr return) to the far end of Rondvatn, from where it takes about two and a half hours to walk back to Rondvassbu along the lake's steep western shore.

Jotunheimen National Park

Norway's most celebrated walking area, the national park of **Jotunheimen** ("Home of the Giants") lives up to its name. Pointed summits and undulating glaciers dominate the skyline, soaring high above river valleys and lake-studded plateaux. The park offers an amazing concentration of high peaks, more than two hundred of them rising above 1900 metres, including Norway's and Northern Europe's two highest mountains, Galdhøpiggen (2469m) and Glittertind (2464m), while Norway's highest waterfall, the 275-metre-high Vettisfossen, is here too, a short walk from the Vetti lodge on the west side of the park. A network of footpaths and mountain lodges lattices the park, but be warned that the weather is very unpredictable and the winds can be bitingly cold – be cautious if you're new to mountain hiking and always come well-equipped (see "Basics", p.34).

There are no public roads into the park; visitors usually walk or ski into the interior from Hwy 55 in the west (see opposite) or make the slightly easier approach via **GJENDESHEIM**, off Hwy 51 in the east near Otta. In summer, there's a weekday, early-morning **bus** from Otta to Gjendesheim (late June to Aug Mon–Sat 1 daily; 2hr) and another leaving around noon (late June to early Sept 1 daily; 2hr). Gjendesheim is no more than a couple of buildings, one of which is the excellent DNT **Gjendesheim lodge** (☎61 23 89 44; ①; late June to mid-Sept). It sits at the eastern tip of long and slender Lake Gjende. **Boats** (late June to early Sept 1–3 daily; ☎61 23 85 09) travel the length of the lake, reaching deep into the park to connect with mountain trails and dropping passengerS off at two more lodges, the privately owned **Memurubu** (late June to early Sept; ☎61 23 89 99; ②), halfway along the lake, and the DNT's **Gjendebu** (late June to mid-Sept; ☎61 23 89 44; ①), right at the other end. A single fare from Gjendesheim to Memurubu costs 55kr, to Gjendebu 75kr; returns are double (unless you make the round trip on the same day, in which case they're 75kr and 100kr respectively). It takes the boat twenty minutes to reach Memurubu, forty-five minutes to Gjendebu. Naturally, you can see a slice of the Jotunheimen and avoid a hike by riding the boat and sleeping at the lodges – a useful option in bad weather.

North to the Kongsvoll and the Dovrefjell National Park

If you avoid the temptation of heading west from Otta along Hwy 15 to the fjords, the E6 and the railway lead 45km north to **DOMBÅS**, a mundane crossroads settlement that has a couple of good places to stay, if not much else. Close to the train and bus station and the E6/E136 junction is the *Dombås Hotell* (☎61 24 10 01, fax 61 24 14 61; ④/③), whose distinctive high gables look back down the Gudbrandsdal. A hotel of two halves, most of the bedrooms are tucked away in the modern annexe round the back, but the old main building holds a handsome series of long public rooms dating to the beginning of the twentieth century. The bedrooms in this part of the hotel tend to be a little the worse for wear, but the views down the valley more than compensate. Also offering valley views is Dombås's **youth hostel** (☎61 24 10 45, fax 61 24 13 30; doubles ③), a comfortable complex of mountain huts way up on the hillside above the E6. To get there, head north out of town along the E6 for around 1km and follow the signs up the hill; it's a hard slog from the train and bus station, down in the valley below. Both routes out of Dombås offer tantalizing prospects: E136 leads the 110km west to Åndalsnes and the Romsdalsfjord (see p.294), whilst the E6 plunges north through the mountains towards Trondheim (see p.302); you can complete either journey by rail as well, though the Åndalsnes train only runs a couple of times a day.

Staying on the E6 north from Dombås, it's just 30km to the outpost of **HJERKINN**, stuck out on bare and desolate moorland, its pocket-sized military base battened down against the wind-blasted ice and snow of winter. The base overlooks the E6/Hwy 29 junction, as does the adjacent train station, a perky wooden affair with brightly painted window frames. There's been a mountain inn here since medieval times, a staging post on the long trail to Trondheim, now just 170km away. The present inn, the *Hjerkinn Fjellstue* (☎61 24 29 27, fax 61 24 29 49; ③), continues this tradition in a becoming manner, with two expansive wooden buildings with big open fires and breezy pine furniture. The restaurant is good too – try the reindeer culled from local herds – and there's horse-riding from the stables next door. The inn is set on a hill overlooking the moors just over 2km from the train station beside Hwy 29.

Kongsvoll

Beyond Hjerkinn, the E6 slices across the barren uplands before descending into a narrow ravine, the **Drivdal**. Hidden here, just 12km from Hjerkinn, is **KONGSVOLL**, home of a tiny train station and the delightful *Kongsvold Fjeldstue* (☎72 40 43 40, fax 72 40 43 41, *www.kongsvold.no*; ③), which provides some of the most charming accommodation in the whole of Norway. There's been an inn here since medieval times and the present complex, a huddle of tastefully restored old timber buildings with sun-bleached reindeer antlers tacked onto the outside walls, dates back to the eighteenth century. Dinner is served in the excellent, reasonably priced **restaurant**, and the complex also includes a **café** and a small park **information centre**. The inn is a lovely spot to break your journey and an ideal base for hiking into the Dovrefjell National Park which extends to east and west. If you're arriving by **train**, note that only some of the Oslo–Trondheim trains stop at Kongsvoll station, 500m down the valley from the inn – and then only by prior arrangement with the conductor.

Beyond Drivdal, 35km north of Kongsvoll, **OPPDAL** is a crossroads town where Hwy 70 forks west for Kristiansund and the coast, while the E6 presses on north the 120km to Trondheim (see p.302).

Dovrefjell National Park

Bisected by the railroad and the E6, **Dovrefjell National Park** (Dovrefjell Nasjonalpark) is one of the more accessible of Norway's national parks. A comparative minnow at just 265 square kilometres, it comprises two distinct zones: the marshes, open moors and rounded peaks that characterize much of eastern Norway spread east from the E6, while to the west the mountains become increasingly steep and serrated as they approach the jagged spires of the Romsdal. Beyond the park's western limits, backing on to the Romsdalsfjord, is the greatest concentration of high peaks outside the Jotunheimen; this is a favourite destination for European mountaineers, who clamber perpendicular rock faces reckoned to be some of the world's most difficult.

Hiking trails and **huts** are spread throughout the western part of the Dovrefjell. Kongsvoll makes an ideal starting point: it's possible to hike all the way from here to the coast at Åndalsnes, but this takes all of nine or ten days; a more feasible expedition for most visitors is the two-day hike there and back to one of the four snow-tipped peaks of mighty **Snøhetta**, at around 2200m. There's accommodation five hours' walk west from Kongsvoll at the unstaffed **Reinheim** (mid-Feb to mid-Oct) hut. Further hiking details and maps are available at the park information centre in the *Kongsvold Fjeldstue*.

Røros and around

Located on a treeless mountain plateau 160km east of Kongsvoll, **RØROS** is a blustery place even on a summer's afternoon, when it's full of day-tripping tourists surveying the old part of town, little changed since its days as a copper-mining centre. Røros is a unique and remarkable survivor – until the mining company went bust a decade or so ago, mining had been the basis of life here since the seventeenth century. This dirty and dangerous work was supplemented by a little farming and hunting, and life for the average villager can't have been anything but hard. Furthermore, Røros' wooden houses, some of them 300 years old, have escaped the fires that have devastated so many of Norway's timber-built towns. Røros is now on UNESCO's World Heritage List, and there are firm regulations limiting changes to its grass-roofed cottages. Film companies regularly use the town as a backdrop for their productions – it featured as a labour camp in the film of *One Day in the Life of Ivan Denisovich*.

In the town centre, **Røros kirke** (early to mid-June & mid-Aug to mid-Sept Mon–Sat noon–2pm; mid-June to mid-Aug Mon–Sat 10am–5pm, Sun 2–4pm; mid-Sept to Dec Sat noon–2pm; 15kr) is the most obvious target for a stroll, its heavy tower reflecting the wealth of the eighteenth-century mine owners. Built in 1784, and once the only stone building in Røros, the church is more like a theatre than a religious edifice. A huge structure capable of seating 1600 people, it was designed, like the church at Kongsberg (see p.242), to overawe rather than inspire. Its pulpit is built directly over the altar to emphasize the importance of the priest's word, and a two-tiered gallery runs around the nave. Occasional mine labourers were accommodated in the gallery's lower level, while "undesirables" were compelled to sit above, and even had to enter via a separate, external staircase. Down below, the nave exhibited even finer distinctions: every pew nearer the front was a step up the social ladder, while mine managers vied for the curtained boxes, each of which had a well-publicized annual rent; the monarch (or royal representative) had a private box commanding views from the back. These byzantine social arrangements are explained in depth during the **guided tour** (late June to mid-Aug, 1 daily in English), the cost of which is included in the admission fee.

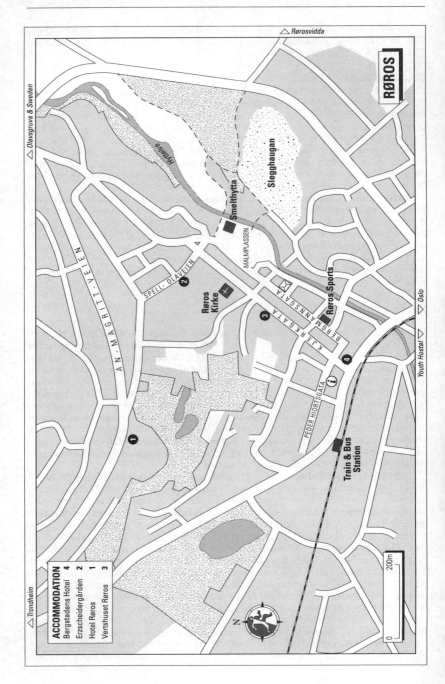

△ *Rørosvidda*

RØROS

△ *Olavsgruva & Sweden*

Hyttelva

Smelthytta

Slegghaugan

MALMPLASSEN

SPELL- OLAVEIEN

Røros Kirke

A·N·MAGRITT·VEIEN

Røros Sports

BERGMANNSGATA

KJERKGATA

▷ *Youth Hostel*

▷ *Oslo*

PEDER HJORTSGATA

Train & Bus Station

△ *Trondheim*

ACCOMMODATION
Bergstadens Hotel 4
Erzscheidergården 2
Hotel Røros 1
Vertshuset Røros 3

N

0   200m

Immediately below the church, on either side of the river, lies the oldest part of Røros. A huddle of sturdy cross-timbered smelters' cottages, storehouses and workshops squat in the shadow of the **slegghaugan** (slagheaps) – more tourist attraction than eyesore, and providing fine views over the town and beyond. Here, next to the river, the rambling main works have been tidily restored and face on to **Malmplassen** ("ore-place"), the wide earthen square where the ore drivers arrived from across the mountains to have their cartloads of ore weighed on the outdoor scales. Also in the square, hung in a rickety little tower, is the smelters' bell, which used to be rung at the start of each shift.

Malmplassen is at the top of Bergmannsgata which, together with parallel Kjerkgata, forms the heart of today's Røros. Conspicuously, the smaller artisans' dwellings, some of which have become **art and craft shops**, are set near the works, away from the rather more spacious dwellings once occupied by the owners and overseers, which cluster round the church. The main works, the **Smelthytta** (literally "melting hut"; late June to mid-Aug Mon–Fri 10.30am–6pm, Sat & Sun 10.30am–4pm; mid-Aug to late June Mon–Fri 11am–3.30pm, Sat & Sun 11am–2pm; 45kr) has been converted into a museum, a large three-storey affair whose most interesting section explains the intricacies of copper production in the cavernous hall which once housed the smelter. Dioramas illuminate every part of the process, and there are production charts, samples of ore and a potted history of the company; pick up the comprehensive English-language leaflet available free at reception. There's actually not that much to look at – the building was gutted by fire in 1975 – and so the museum is perhaps for genuine copper enthusiasts only.

Practicalities

The **train** and **bus stations** are at the foot of the town centre, a couple of minutes' walk from the **tourist office** (late June to mid-Aug Mon–Sat 9am–6pm, Sun 10am–4pm; mid-Aug to late June Mon–Fri 9am–4pm, Sat 10.30am–12.30pm; ☎72 41 11 65), where you can pick up a comprehensive free booklet on Røros and the surrounding region. They also have details of local **hikes** out across the uplands that encircle the town, one of the more popular being the five-hour trek east to the self-service DNT hut at Marenvollen. The uplands are also popular with **cross-country skiers** in the winter, and the tourist office has a leaflet mapping out several possible routes. To get around town, pick up one of the free municipal **bicycles** available at the train station and tourist office; for those venturing further afield, **mountain bikes** can be rented from Røros Sports, on Bergmannsgata (☎72 41 12 18), for around 150kr a day (plus 100kr deposit).

Because of the long drive here and the infrequency of trains to Trondheim and Oslo, you may well want to stay the night. Fortunately, there's a reasonable range of centrally located **accommodation**. Easily the best deal in town is the *Erzscheidergården* guesthouse, Spell-Olaveien 6 (☎72 41 11 94, fax 72 41 19 00, ②), with some charming, unassuming rooms in its wooden main building. Some rooms also have fine views over town, and there's an attractive subterranean breakfast area and a cosy lounge. Also worth considering are the *Hotel Røros*, An-Magritt-veien (☎72 41 10 11, fax 72 41 00 22; ⑤/③), a big modern place on the northern edge of the centre, and *Vertshuset Røros*, Kjerkgata 34 (☎72 41 24 11, fax 72 41 03 64; ②), a guesthouse with cramped doubles that's bang in the centre of town, and at the bottom end of its price category. Less appealing is *Bergstadens Hotel*, Osloveien 2 (☎72 40 60 80, fax 72 41 01 55; ④/③), conveniently located at the foot of Bergmannsgata, but otherwise a routine, modern hotel with workaday double rooms. There's also a **youth hostel**, the unappealing *Røros Vandrerhjem*, Øraveien 25 (☎72 41 10 89, fax 72 41 23 77; ①), about 800m south of the train station next to the sports ground, in a concrete block shared with the *Idrettsparken Hotell* (same details; ②).

When it comes to **food**, Røros is no gourmet's paradise, but there's just enough choice to get by. *Hotel Røros* has a good, if slightly formal, restaurant that's generally reckoned to serve the best meals in town; it's expensive though and closes at 10pm. In contrast, the busy and competent *Papas Pizza*, at the foot of Bergmannsgata in the back of the *Bergstadens Hotel*, is open till late. For substantial meals at fairly reasonable prices there's *Otto's Kro Restaurant*, Peder Hiortsgata 4, just west of the tourist office – try the *entrecôte* at 130kr.

Olavsgruva copper mine and Femundsmarka National Park

Thirteen kilometres east of Røros off Highway 31, the **Olavsgruva**, one of the old copper mines, has been kept open as a museum, and there are daily guided tours of the workings throughout the summer (early June & late Aug to early Sept Mon–Sat 2 daily, Sun 1 daily; late June to late Aug 6 daily; early Sept to May Sat 1 daily; 45kr). Special **buses** timed to coincide with the guided tours make the journey once daily from Røros' train station and Smelthytta to the mine in July and early August (60kr return), returning to town afterwards. The temperature down the mine is a constant 5°C, so remember to take something warm to wear – you'll need sturdy shoes too.

Tucked in tight between the Swedish border and the elongated Lake Femund some 50km east of Røros, the 385 square kilometres that make up the remote **Femundsmarka National Park** encompass a wide variety of terrains. In the north are pine forests, marshes, lakes and rivers, which give way in the south to bare mountains and plateaux. There is no road access into the Femundsmarka itself, but a minor road leads from Røros to **Sørvika**, on the west side of Lake Femund, from where a **passenger boat**, the *M/S Faemund* (mid-June to mid-Oct 2–4 weekly), shuttles around the lake, stopping at several remote outposts and jetties. Among the latter, several give access to the limited network of unstaffed DNT huts and hiking trails which cross the national park; the jetties at **Røa** and **Haugen** are the handiest. Boat schedules and prices are available from Røros tourist office. Several Røros-based operators run three-day canoeing and fishing expeditions in the park – Røros Sports on Bergmannsgata (☎72 41 12 18) is as good as any.

From Oslo to the western fjords

The forested dales and uplands which fill the interior of southern Norway between Oslo and the western fjords rarely inspire: in almost any other European country, these elongated valleys would be attractions in their own right, but here in Norway they simply can't compare with the mountains and fjords of the north and west. Almost everywhere, the architecture is routinely modern and most of the old timber buildings that once lined the valleys are long gone – except in the ten-a-penny open-air museums that are a feature of nearly every town.

Oslo is an easy day's drive, bus or train ride from the fjords. Of the three major trunk roads crossing the region, the **E16** is the fastest, a quick 350-kilometre haul up from Oslo to the fjord ferry point near Sogndal – and there are plans to make it even faster, with an enormous tunnel currently under construction linking the E16 with Hwy 50 near Flåm. Otherwise, the E16's nearest rival, the slower **Hwy 7**, branches off the E16 at Hønefoss and, after a scenic wriggle along the edge of the Hardangervidda plateau, finally reaches the coast at Eidfjord near Hardangerfjord, a distance of 334km. Hwy 7 also intersects with Hwy 50, offering another possible route to Flåm. For most of its length, Hwy 7 is shadowed by the **Oslo–Bergen railway**, though they part company when the train swings north for its spectacular traverse of the coastal mountains. The third road, the **E134**, which stretches the 418km from Drammen near Oslo to Haugesund, passing near Odda on the Sørfjord (323km), is another slower route, and has the advantage of passing through **Kongsberg**, an attractive town that makes for a pleasant overnight stay. There's an enjoyable detour north off the E134 too, via **Rjukan**, a small town whose museum relates the tale of the World War II German heavy water plant and its Norwegian saboteurs. Rjukan is just 60km from Åmot on the E134, but there's a shorter, direct route over the hills from Kongsberg on Hwy 37. There are regular long-distance **buses** along all three major roads.

West along the E16 to Leira and Borgund

Clipping along the **E16** from Oslo, it's 180km up through a sequence of river valleys to ribbon-like **LEIRA**, where you can break your journey economically – if not exactly thrillingly – at the **youth hostel** (☎61 35 95 00, fax 61 35 95 01; doubles ③; June to mid-Aug;), which occupies part of the high-school complex beside the road. Hwy 51 branches north at the next village of **Fagernes**, running along the eastern edge of the Jotunheimen National Park, passing near Gjendesheim and its lodge (see p.235) before finally joining Hwy 15 west of Otta (see p.234).

About 30km west of Fagernes along the E16, the scenery improves as you approach the coast. The road dips and weaves from dale to dale, slipping between the hills until it reaches the valley of **Laerdal**. Here, the stepped roofs and angular gables of the **Borgund stave church** (daily: June–Aug 8am–8pm; May & Sept 10am–5pm; 50kr) are framed by the forested sides of the valley. One of the best preserved stave churches in Norway, Borgund was built beside what was – until bubonic plague wiped out most of the local population in the fourteenth century – one of the major pack roads between east and west. The church has preserved much of its medieval appearance, its tiered exterior protected by shingles and decorated with finials in the shape of dragons and Christian crosses, culminating in a slender ridge turret. A rickety wooden gallery runs round the outside of the church, and the doors sport a swirling abundance of carved animals and foliage. Inside, the dark, pine-scented nave is framed by the upright wooden posts that define this style of church architecture.

STAVE CHURCHES

Of the 29 surviving **stave churches** in Norway, all but a handful are in Southern and Central Norway. Together, they represent the country's most distinctive architectural feature. Their key characteristic is that their timbers are placed vertically into the ground – in contrast to the log-bonding technique used by the Norwegians for everything else. Thus, a stave wall consists of vertical planks slotted into sills above and below, with the sills connected to upright posts – or **staves** (hence the name) – at each corner. The general design seems to have been worked out in the twelfth century and regular features include external wooden galleries, shingles and finials, but the most fetching churches are those where the central section of the nave has been raised above the aisles to create – from the outside – a distinctive, almost pagoda-like effect. In virtually all stave churches, the **door frames** (where they survive) are decorated from top to bottom with surging, intricate carvings – fantastic long-limbed dragons, entwined with tendrils of vine – that clearly relate back to Viking design.

The **origins** of stave churches have attracted an inordinate amount of academic debate. Some scholars argue that they were originally pagan temples, converted to Christian use by the addition of a chancel, whilst others are convinced that they were inspired by Russian churches. In the nineteenth century, they also developed a symbolic importance as reminders of the time when Norway was independent. Many had fallen into a dreadful state of repair and were clumsily renovated – or even remodelled – by enthusiastic medievalists with a nationalistic agenda. Undoing this repair work has been a major operation that continues today. For most visitors, seeing one or two will suffice – two of the finest are those at Heddal (see p.243) and Borgund (see above).

Beyond the church, the valley grows wilder as the E16 travels the 45km down to **Fodnes**, where the car ferry zips over to **Manheller** (departures 24hr, every 30min; 15min; passengers 26kr, car and driver 77kr), some 18km from Sogndal. On the way, you'll pass the entrance to the 24.3km-long tunnel that will, in the next couple of years, link the E16 with Hwy 50 near Flåm.

West along Highway 7 to Geilo

Heading out of Oslo, **Hwy 7** branches off the E16 about 60km from Oslo at **Hønefoss** and then cuts an unexciting course along **Hallingdal**, as does the main Oslo–Bergen railway. Some 180km from Hønefoss, the road forks at **Hagafoss**, with Hwy 50 descending the dales to reach, after 100km, the Aurlandsfjord just round the coast from Flåm. Meanwhile, Hwy 7 presses on west to the winter ski resort of **GEILO**, 250km from Oslo – it's a boring town out of the skiing season, but it does have several inexpensive places to stay, including a **youth hostel** (☎32 09 03 00, fax 32 09 18 96; doubles ①; June–Sept & Nov–April), housed in large barrack-like buildings in the town centre just off the main drag. Details of other accommodation are available from the **tourist office** nearby (July to mid-Aug daily 8.30am–8pm; June & late Aug Mon–Fri 8.30am–6pm, Sat 9am–3pm; Sept–May Mon–Fri 8.30am–4pm; ☎32 09 59 00).

Beyond Geilo, the rail line ceases to follow the road, breaking off to tunnel its way through the mountains to Finse, Myrdal (where you change for the scenic branch line down to Flåm), and points to Bergen. Meanwhile, Hwy 7 continues west for a further 100km, slicing across the upland plateau of the Hardangervidda. It's a lonely, handsome road and on the way you'll pass several places such as Halne and Dyranut where you can pick up the Hardangervidda's network of hiking trails (for more on hiking in the Hardangervidda, see p.276). On the far side of the plateau, Hwy 7 rushes down a steep valley to reach the fjords at **EIDFJORD**, a straggling village with one smashing hotel, the *Eidfjord* (☎53 66 52 64, fax 53 66 52 12; ④/③), a smart, modern, medium-sized place with tastefully furnished rooms perching on a knoll high above the fjord – the restaurant here is very good too. From Eidfjord, it's 10km to the Brimnes car ferry and 19km more to Kinsarvik, which is described on p.275.

West along the E134 – Kongsberg

The third main route west to the fjords from Oslo, the **E134**, leads after an hour or two by train or bus to **KONGSBERG**, one of the most interesting towns in the region. A local story claims that the silver responsible for its existence was discovered by two goatherds, who stumbled across a vein of the metal laid bare by the scratchings of an ox. True or not, Christian IV, his eye on the main chance, was quick to exploit the find, and with the rise of this, his mining centre (the name means "King's Mountain"), the seventeenth-century silver rush began. In the event, it turned out that Kongsberg was the only place in the world where silver was to be found in its pure form, and there was enough of it to sustain the town for a couple of centuries. Indeed, by the 1750s the town was the largest in Norway, with half of its 8000 inhabitants employed in and around the 300-odd mine shafts that littered the area. The silver works closed in 1805, but by this time Kongsberg was also the site of a royal mint and then an armaments factory, which still employs people to this day.

To appreciate the full economic and political clout of the mine owners, it's necessary to visit the church they funded – **Kongsberg Kirke** (mid-May to Aug Mon–Fri 10am–4pm, Sat 10am–1pm; Sept to mid-May Tues–Fri 10am–noon; 15kr), the largest and arguably most beautiful Baroque church in Norway. It dates from 1761, when the mines were at the peak of their prosperity, and sits impressively in a square surrounded on three sides by period wooden buildings. Inside, too, it's a grand affair, with an enormous and showily mock-marbled western wall incorporating altar, pulpit and organ. This arrangement was dictated by political considerations: the pulpit is actually *above* the altar, to ram home the point that the priest's stern injunctions to work harder on behalf of the mine owners were an expression of God's will.

Kongsberg itself is an agreeable if quiet place in summer, with plenty of green spaces. The **River Lågen** tumbles through the centre, and statues on the town bridge at the foot of Storgata commemorate various local activities, including foolhardy attempts to locate new finds of silver – one of them involving the use of divining rods. Enthusiasts will enjoy the **Norwegian Mining Museum**, Hyttegata 3 (Norsk Bergverksmuseet; mid-May to Aug daily 10am–4pm; Sept daily noon–4pm; Oct to mid-May Sun only noon–3pm; 30kr), housed in the old smelting works at the river's edge along with a pocket-sized ski museum and coin collection, but merely pottering around is as enjoyable a way as any of spending time in Kongsberg.

The **silver mines** themselves, the Sølvgruvene, are open for tours and make a fine excursion, especially if you have children to amuse. They're hidden in green surroundings 8km west of town in the hamlet of **SAGGRENDA** – drive (or take the local bus from outside the train station) along the E134 in the Notodden direction and look for the sign leading off to the right. The informative 30-minute **tour** (mid-May to Aug; 50kr) includes a ride on a miniature train through black tunnels to the shafts. There are three or four departures a day; take a sweater as it's cold underground. Back outside, just 350m down the hill, the old ochre-painted, timber workers' compound – the **Sakkerhusene** – has been restored and holds some rather half-hearted displays on the history of the mines, as well as a café.

Practicalities

Kongsberg **tourist office**, at Storgata 53 (late June to mid-Aug Mon–Fri 9am–7pm, Sat & Sun 10am–5pm; mid-Aug to late June Mon–Fri 9am–4.30pm, Sat 10am–2pm; ☎32 73 50 00), is close to the **train and bus station**, and can help with accommodation, not that there's much of a decision to be made: the **youth hostel** at Vinjesgata 1 (☎32 73 20 24, fax 32 72 05 34; doubles ①) is *the* place to stay, with comfortable en-suite rooms in an attractive timber lodge close to the town centre. Drivers need to follow the signs on the E134; train and bus users need to walk south from the station along Storgata, cross the bridge and walk round the back of the church on the right-hand side. At the back of the church, head down the slope and over the footbridge – about a ten-minute walk in all. As for central **hotels**, there is just one appealing option, the *Quality Grand Hotel*, down near the river at Christian Augusts gate 2 (☎32 73 20 29, fax 32 73 41 29; ④/③), which also has a first-class **restaurant**. If the weather's good, the *Gamle Kongsberg Kro* café-restaurant has a pleasant riverside terrace below the church.

West of Kongsberg: Heddal, Seljord and Åmot

A few kilometres west of Kongsberg, the E134 passes into **Telemark**, a county that covers a great forested chunk of southern Norway. Just inside its borders is industrial **NOTODDEN** and, 6km beyond that, beside the main road, is the **stave church of Heddal** (mid-May to mid-June & mid-Aug to mid-Sept Mon–Sat 10am–5pm; late June to early Aug Mon–Sat 9am–7pm; Sun all year open at 1pm only; 25kr). Surrounded by a neat cemetery and rolling pastureland, Heddal is actually the largest surviving stave church in Norway. Its pretty tumble of shingle-clad roofs was restored to something like its medieval appearance in 1955, rectifying a heavy-handed nineteenth-century remodelling. The crosses atop the church's gables alternate with dragonhead gargoyles, a mix of Christian and pagan symbolism that is typical of churches of this type. Inside, the twenty masts of the nave are decorated at the top by masks, and there's some attractive seventeenth-century wall decoration in light blues, browns and whites. Pride of place, however, goes to the ancient bishop's chair in the chancel. Dating from around 1250, the chair carries a relief retelling the saga of Sigurd the Dragonslayer, a pagan story that Christians turned to their advantage by recasting the Viking as Jesus and the dragon as the Devil. Across from the church, there's a café and a modest museum illustrating further aspects of Heddal's history.

There's another fine church around 55km further west just off the E134 in **SELJORD**, a small industrial town of ancient provenance that spreads between the forested hills and lake Seljordsvatnet. Dating from the twelfth century, the church is built of stone (open for guided tours Mon–Sat 10am–4pm, Sun 10am–1pm; 20kr), and as such is something of a medieval rarity. The town also seems to have attracted more than its fair share of "Believe It or Not" stories: a monster is supposed to lurk in the depths of the lake; elves are alleged to gather here for some of their soirées; and the 570kg stone outside the church was, so the story goes, only lifted once, by an eighteenth-century strong man by name of Nils Langedal. Elves and sea serpents apart, there's nothing much to delay you.

Beyond Seljord, it's a further 80km west along E134 to the handsome **Grungedal** valley, home to several antique farmsteads, one of which has been, is not currently, but may well be again in future the *Grungebru* youth hostel – keep your eyes peeled as it's a convenient place to break your journey. Pushing on, the scenery bordering E134 becomes wilder and more dramatic as the road slips across the southern peripheries of the Hardangervidda plateau before tunnelling through the mountains to meet the coastal Hwy 13. Branching off to the north, Hwy 13 passes, in 5km, the waterfalls at **Latefossen**, two huge torrents that empty into the river with a deafening roar. From here, it's a further 14km to Odda, an ugly industrial centre that is a particularly unfortunate introduction to the fjords: try to allow enough time to avoid the place altogether and keep going north to the much more appealing hamlet of Lofthus (see p.275). Alternatively, if you ignore Hwy 13 and keep on along the E134, it's 115km from the crossroads to the coast at Haugesund.

The south coast

Arcing out into the Skagerrak, Norway's **south coast** may have little of the imposing grandeur of other, wilder parts of the country, but the fretted coastline that extends from the Oslofjord to Kristiansand is undeniably lovely. Backed by forests and lakes, it's this part of the coast that attracts Norwegians in droves, equipped not so much with a bucket and spade, but more with a **boat** and navigational aids – these waters, with their narrow inlets, islands and skerries, make for particularly enjoyable sailing. **Camping** on the offshore islands is easy too, the only restrictions being that you shouldn't stay in one spot for more than 48 hours, shouldn't get close to anyone's home or light a fire on bare rock or among vegetation – leaflets detailing further coastal rules and regulations are available at any local tourist office.

If boats and tents aren't your thing, the white-painted clapboard houses of tiny towns like **Lillesand**, **Arendal** and – to a lesser degree – **Grimstad** have an appropriately nautical, almost jaunty air. This portion of the coast is also important for Norway's international trade: it's just a short hop to Denmark from here, and several of the larger towns such as Sandefjord, Larvik and Porsgrunn have kicked over their seventeenth-century traces as rustic timber ports to become industrial centres in their own right. Most of these manufacturing towns are run-of-the-mill, except for the biggest of them, **Kristiansand**, a lively port and resort with enough sights, restaurants, bars and beaches to while away a night or two. Beyond Kristiansand lies **Mandal**, an especially fetching holiday spot with a great beach, but thereafter the coast becomes harsher and less absorbing, heralding a sparsely inhabited region with precious little to detain you before Stavanger.

There are regular **trains** from Oslo to Kristiansand and Stavanger, but the rail line runs inland for most of its journey, only dipping down to the coast at the major resorts – a disappointing ride, the sea views shielded much of the time behind bony, forested hills. The same applies to the main **road** and **bus** route – the **E18/E39** – which also sticks stubbornly inland for most of the 300km from Oslo to Kristiansand (E18) and again for the 250km on to Stavanger (E39). It does, however, make for easy and fast travel to the main destinations, even if exploring the smaller coastal settlements is awkward without your own vehicle. In summer, a third option is to take the **Hurtigbåt passenger express boat** from Oslo to Arendal, which zips along the coast, nipping in between the islands to call at several coastal villages on its six-hour journey. It serves as a good introduction to the south coast, though at 440kr per person it's expensive.

All the places in this section are easily accessed from the E18/E39, and all provide boat trips along the neighbouring coastline and offer accommodation in some form or another. Note, though, that the season is short – from late June to August – at other times of the year many museums are closed and boat trips curtailed.

Arendal

The first place that really merits a stop on the E18 is **ARENDAL**, 260km from Oslo, and one of the most appealing spots on the coast, its sheltered harbour curling right into the town centre, which is itself pushed up tight against the forested hills behind. The town's heyday was in the eighteenth century when its shipyards churned out dozens of the sleek wooden sailing ships that then dominated international trade. There's an attractive reminder of the boom times in the grand **Rådhus** (guided tours in English and Norwegian July & Aug Mon, Tues & Thurs 11am–3pm; 40kr), a four-storey, white timber building from 1812 that faces out over what was once the main city dock. The Rådhus was actually built as a private mansion for a wealthy family of merchants – as the formal rooms inside demonstrate – and there are more elegant old buildings immediately behind it in the oldest part of town, known as **Tyholmen**. You can wander these few blocks and then stroll along the boardwalk flanking **Pollen**, a short rectangular inner harbour bordered by outdoor cafés. For the architectural low-down on Tyholmen, call in at the tourist office (see below) and sign up for one of their city walking tours (late June to early Aug Mon, Tues & Thurs at 4pm; 1hr 30min; 40kr).

Also available at the tourist office are details of all sorts of **boat trips** which leave from Pollen to explore the surrounding coastline; one of the less expensive options is the regular ferry to the offshore islets of **Hisøy** and **Tromøy**, or even better to tiny **MERDØ** (20kr), where you can take a peek at the period interior of the rusticated **Merdøgaard Museum** (guided tours only late June to mid-Aug daily noon–4pm on the hour; 30kr), an eighteenth-century sea captain's house, and have a swim in the Skagerrak. The sheltered channels round Arendal are also ideal for boating; **canoes** can be hired at the town train station, where they will advise on routes too.

Practicalities

From Arendal **train station**, it's a five- to ten-minute walk west to the main square, Torvet – either through the smoggy tunnel or a steep hoof up and over the hill along Bendiksklev, a distinctly more healthy option. Torvet is about 150m north of the inner harbour, Pollen. **Buses** stop in the larger square, west of Pollen across from the huge red-brick church with the copper-green steeple. The **Hurtigbåt express passenger ferry** (late June to mid-Aug 3 weekly) from Oslo arrives at 3.35pm except on Fridays, when it gets here at 10pm. The journey takes almost seven hours and costs 440kr. The return trip leaves at 4pm, reaching Oslo at 11pm.

The Arendal **tourist office** (June to mid-Aug Mon–Sat 9am–7pm, Sun noon–7pm; mid-Aug to May Mon–Fri 8.30am–4pm; ☎37 00 55 44) is at the bus station. Easily the nicest place **to stay** is the luxurious *Tyholmen Hotel*, Teaterplassen 2 (☎37 02 68 00, fax 37 02 68 01; ⑤/④), which occupies a handsome wooden building in the style of an old warehouse on the Tyholmen quayside. The more modest *Scandic Hotel Phonix Arendal*, Friergangen 1 (☎37 02 51 60, fax 37 02 67 07; ⑤/③), is a straightforward modern hotel just off the west side of Pollen. For **food**, there are a couple of inexpensive cafés on Torvet and a string of more tempting places along and around Pollen, including *Madam Reiersen*, which offers delicious seafood and fresh pasta dishes from its harbourside premises at Nedre Tyholmsvei 3. Later on, the café-bars lining Pollen become lively **drinking** haunts till the early hours, especially on a warm summer's night.

Grimstad

From Arendal, it's a short 20km hop south on the E18 by bus or car to **GRIMSTAD**, a brisk huddle of white houses with orange-tiled roofs stacked up behind the harbour. At the beginning of the nineteenth century the town had no less than forty shipyards and carried on a lucrative trade with France. It was not particularly surprising, therefore, that when Henrik Ibsen left his home in nearby Skien in 1844 at the age of sixteen he should come to Grimstad, where he worked as an apprentice pharmacist for the next six years. The careless financial dealings of Ibsen's father had impoverished the family, and Henrik's already jaundiced view of Norway's provincial bourgeoisie was confirmed here in the port, whose worthies Ibsen mocked in poems like *Resignation*, and *The Corpse's Ball*. It was here too that Ibsen picked up first-hand news of the Paris Revolution of 1848, an event that radicalized him and inspired his paean to the insurrectionists of Budapest, *To Hungary*, written in 1849. Nonetheless, Ibsen's stay on the south coast is more usually recalled as providing the setting for some of his better known plays, particularly *Pillars of Society*. The pharmacy where Ibsen lived and worked, just up from the harbour in the centre of town on Henrik Ibsens gate, has been turned into the pocket-sized **Ibsen House and Town Museum** (Ibsenhuset og Grimstad Bymuseet; guided tours May to mid-Sept Mon–Sat 11am–5pm, Sun 1–5pm; mid-Sept to April Mon–Fri 10am–3pm; 30kr). With creaking wooden floors and narrow beamed ceilings, the premises have maintained their nineteenth-century appearance and come complete with various Ibsen memorabilia – look out for the glass case displaying the playwright's hat, coat, umbrella and boots as worn on his daily stroll down to Oslo's *Grand Hotel*. Incidentally, if you wondered what happened to the dining-room furniture from Ibsen's apartment in Oslo, it's here, courtesy of his son.

There's nothing much else to see, but the town is an amiable enough place for a brief stroll. The **bus station** is at the south end of the harbour, a couple of hundred metres along from the **tourist office** (June–Aug Mon–Fri 10am–6pm, Sat & Sun 11am–5pm; Sept–May Mon–Fri 8.30am–4pm; ☎37 04 40 41), which has details of the two-hour **boat cruises** that meander round the skerries offshore every day throughout the summer. They also issue local maps and directions for the most popular **walk** hereabouts: the seven-kilometre jaunt along the old west road which the E18 bypassed. The hike takes about three hours and begins a short drive north of Grimstad at Landvik Manor, from where the footpath threads its way west to meet the E18 at Kaldvell fjord. Grimstad also has an attractive and central **hotel**, the *Grimstad Hotell*, Kirkegaten 3 (☎37 25 25 25, fax 37 25 25 35; ④), in an old, cleverly converted clapboard complex amongst the narrow lanes near the Ibsen house; the hotel has the best **restaurant** in town too.

Lillesand

Bright, cheerful **LILLESAND**, just 20km south of Grimstad, is one of the most popular holiday spots on the coast, with the white clapboard houses of its tiny centre draped prettily round the harbourfront. Although one or two of the buildings (notably the sturdy

Rådhus of 1734) are especially good-looking, it's the general appearance of the place which appeals, best appreciated from the terrace of one of the town's waterfront café-restaurants: choose from either the *Sjøbua* midway round the harbour, or the *Beddingen*, a few metres away.

To investigate Lillesand's architectural nooks and crannies, sign up for one of the hour-long **guided walks** (mid-June to Aug daily at 3pm; 30kr) which leave from the tourist office (see below), located in the old customs house on the waterfront. They also have information on local **boat trips**, including details of fishing excursions and the timetable of the *badebåten* (bathing boat; July only 4 daily; 15min; 25kr), which shuttles over to a bay on the island of **Skaurøya**, where no one seems to notice how chillingly cold the Skagerrak actually is. Alternatively, a dinky little passenger ferry, the *M/S Oya*, makes a three-hour summertime cruise to Kristiansand (late June to mid-Aug Mon–Sat at 10am; 80kr each way; ☎94 58 33 97), following a narrow channel, the Blindleia, as it twists between the skerries and the mainland south from Lillesand. There are other, faster, less poetic (and slightly more expensive) boats which do the trip too – again, further details from the tourist office.

Lillesand cannot be reached by train, but there are regular **bus** connections up and down the coastal E18; the bus stops near the south end of the harbour. The **tourist office** (June–Aug Mon–Fri 10am–6pm, Sat & Sun 11am–5pm; ☎37 27 23 77) is a two-minute walk away along the harbour to the north. Lillesand has one central **hotel**, the first-rate *Hotel Norge*, Strandgaten 3 (☎37 27 01 44, fax 37 27 30 70; ④/②), which occupies a grand old wooden building near the bus stop. Otherwise, the **youth hostel** (☎ & fax 37 27 50 40; doubles ①; mid-June to mid-Aug) is also located in a dignified timber building, although it's an inconvenient 1.5km out of town beside Hwy 402, the road heading inland to Birkeland. For **food**, the *Hotel Norge* has an excellent restaurant, or try the cheaper and less formal *Sjøbua* on the harbourfront (☎37 27 03 66), which serves up excellent fish dishes for around 150kr in breezily naff surroundings – the interior is kitted out like an old sailing ship.

Kristiansand

KRISTIANSAND, some 30km on from Lillesand, is Norway's fifth largest town and part-time holiday resort, a genial, energetic place which thrives on its ferry connections with Denmark, its busy marinas and passable sandy beaches. In summer, the seafront and adjoining streets are a frenetic bustle of cocktail bars, fast-food joints and flirting holiday-makers, and even in winter Norwegians come here to live it up.

Like so many other Scandinavian towns, it was founded by and named after Christian IV, who saw an opportunity to strengthen his coastal defences here. Building started in 1641, and the town has retained the spacious quadrant plan that characterized all Christian's projects. There are few specific sights, but it's worth a quick skirt around, especially when everyone else has gone to the beach and left the central pedestrianized streets relatively uncluttered. Aside from the **Domkirke** (June–Aug Mon–Sat 9am–2pm) on Kirkegata – a modern mock-Gothic edifice seating nearly two thousand – the only real target is the squat **Christiansholm Festning** (mid-May to Sept daily 9am–9pm; free), on Strandpromenaden, a fortress whose sturdy circular tower and zigzagging earth and stone ramparts overlook the marina in the east harbour. Built in 1672, the tower's walls are five metres thick, a precaution that proved unnecessary since it never saw active service. These days it hosts arts and crafts displays.

One of the more enjoyable of Kristiansand's possibilities is to catch a boat for a **cruise** through the offshore skerries. *M/S Maarten* departs from the quay beside Vestre Strandgate, at the foot of Tollbodgaten, for daily two-hour cruises, stopping at several islands which have been designated public (and free) recreation and camping areas – you could always stay overnight and catch the boat back the next day, but check first

with the tourist office (see opposite) for coastal camping rules and regulations. The boat operates once daily from mid-June to mid-August; round-trips cost around 100kr. Another possibility is the *M/S Maarten*'s excursion (late June to early Aug 4 weekly; 3.5hr; 150kr) to **Ny Hellesund**, an islet which is the site of one of the four hundred coastal defences built by the Germans during the occupation. Hitler overestimated both the likelihood of an Allied counter-invasion in the north and Norway's strategic importance, garrisoning the country with nigh on half a million men and building a string of huge coastal artillery batteries. The cruise to Ny Hellesund makes for an enjoyable trip, but actually there are much more substantial military remains at the **Kristiansand Canon Museum** (Kristiansand Kanonmuseet; 30min guided tours May to mid-June Thurs–Sun 11am–6pm; mid-June to Aug daily 11am–6pm; 50kr), situated an easy 10km drive south along the coast at **Møvik**: take Hwy 456 out of Kristiansand, turning down Hwy 457 for the last 3km of the journey. Work began on this coastal artillery battery in 1941, using – like all the other Norwegian sea defences – the forced labour of POWs. Around 1400 men worked on the project, which involved the construction of protective housings for four big guns at the narrowest part of the Skagerrak. Guns on the Danish shore complemented those here, so that any enemy warship trying to slip through the straits could be shelled. Only a small zone in the middle was out of range, and this the Germans mined. The Møvik complex once covered 220 acres, but the principal remains today hog a narrow ridge with a massive, empty artillery casement at one end, and a whopping 38cm-calibre gun in a concrete well at the other. The gun, which could fire a 500kg shell almost 55km, is in pristine condition, and guided tours include a visit to the loading area, complete with the original ramrods, wedges, trolleys and pulleys. Below, and at the start of the tour, is the underground command post and soldiers' living quarters, again almost exactly as they were in the 1940s – including the odd bit of German graffiti. If you've any interest in the war, don't miss it.

Arrival, information and getting around

Train, bus and Color Line **ferry** terminuses are all close to each other, by Vestre Strandgate on the edge of the town grid. The main regional **tourist office** is also here, at Vestre Strandgate 32 (June–Aug Mon–Fri 8am–8pm, Sat 10am–8pm, Sun noon–8pm; Sept–May Mon–Fri 8.30am–3.30pm; ☎38 12 13 14). They can provide a handy town map and information on boat sailing times, as well as island bathing and beaches. They also carry a wide range of leaflets on the whole of the south coast. **Parking** is easy throughout town, with car parks concentrated along Vestre Strandgate. The best way to explore the town centre is on **foot** – it only takes about ten minutes to walk from one side to the other.

Accommodation

Kristiansand has a reasonably good choice of **accommodation**, with a fair sprinkling of hotels, a guesthouse or two, a youth hostel and a campsite, all in or reasonably near the centre.

Bondeheimen Hotel, Kirkegata 15 (☎38 02 44 40, fax 38 02 73 21). Located bang in the middle of town, near the Domkirke, the *Bondeheimen* offers modern and comfortable – if uninspiring – rooms in a converted nineteenth-century town house. ③.

Clarion Ernst Hotel, Rådhusgaten 2 (☎38 12 86 00, fax 38 02 03 07). Located in a flashily modernized old building, this hotel has large doubles with standard-issue modern furnishings and fittings. The air conditioning can be stuffy, so try to get a room where you can open a window – that is, one not facing the enclosed interior courtyard. Summer discounts of around 200kr. ④.

Rainbow Hotel Norge, Dronningens gate 5 (☎38 02 00 00, fax 38 02 35 30). Pleasant modern hotel with attractively furnished rooms in lively colours. A good downtown choice. ④/③.

Roligheden Camping, Framnesveien (☎38 09 67 22). Large and fairly formal campsite 3km east of the town centre behind a dusty gravel car park, which edges a yacht jetty To get there, drive over the bridge at the end of Dronningens gate, turn right along Marvikveien, then right again at the end, and the site is signed. There are also some cabins (③). Open June to mid-Sept.

Villa Frobusdal Hotel, Frobusdalen 2 (☎38 07 05 15, fax 38 07 01 15). This delightful hotel, undoubtedly the best in town, is a family-run affair occupying a shipowner's mansion of 1917. The interior has been sensitively restored and is crammed with period antiques. In particular, look out for some extraordinary wood panelling alive with dragons and snakes. Each of the seven bedrooms has character and is individually decorated. The only problem is location it's tucked away down a hard-to-find side street off the ring road on the edge of the town centre, near the west end of Kirkegata. Drivers should head north along three-lane Festningsgata and, at the traffic lights at the end, follow the sign to Evje. ②.

Youth Hostel, Skansen 8 (☎38 02 83 10, fax 38 02 75 05). At 160kr per person per night this youth hostel is pricey for what you get, which is cramped rooms in ugly, prefabricated 1960s boxes in the middle of an industrial estate; there's a kitchen and cafeteria, however, and it's open all year. The hostel is situated about twenty minutes' walk east of the ferry terminal on the tiny peninsula edging the marina. Take any street up to Elvegata, turn right and keep going: Skansen is near the end of the road on the left. Doubles ①.

Eating and drinking

There are lots of **restaurants** and **cafés** in the centre, but the standard is very variable. There's also a fairly active nightlife based around several **bars** which stay open until 2am.

FRK Larsen, Markens gate 5. Near the corner of Kongensgate, this laid-back café-bar is an appealing, fashionable place. Also serves meals – salted cod (*bacalao*) for instance, is a very reasonable 175kr.

Kick Café Zanzibar, Dronningens gate 8. Arty bar with a terrace at the back, groovy music and coffee and hot chocolate, as well as reasonably cheap beer. Light meals too.

MOVING ON FROM KRISTIANSAND

Moving on from Kristiansand, the obvious route is to push on west to Stavanger, around 210km distant, by train, or by bus or car along the E39. Both the E39 and the train afford glimpses of the coast, but for the most part they travel inland. It's not a gripping journey, but it's certainly a lot more pleasant than the 240km haul north up **Setesdal** on Hwy 9 to join the E134. Note also that there are summertime cruises northeast along the coast from Kristiansand to Lillesand (late June to mid-Aug Mon–Sat at 10am; 80kr each way; ☎94 58 33 97).

Lille-Dampen, Henrik Wergelands gate 15. First-rate and inexpensive bakery, with delicious take-away baguettes.

Royal China Restaurant, Tollbodgaten 7 (☎38 07 02 77). Surprisingly plush Chinese restaurant offering tasty main courses from as little as 90kr.

Sjøhuset, Østre Strandgate 12a (☎38 02 62 60). In an old converted warehouse by the harbour at the east end of Markens gate, this excellent restaurant, the best in town, serves superb fish courses for 170–190kr. Nautical fittings and wooden beams set the scene. Open daily in summer; closed Sun rest of the year.

Mandal

MANDAL, 40km from Kristiansand along the E39, is Norway's southernmost town. This old timber port reached its heyday in the eighteenth century, when pines and oaks from the surrounding countryside were much sought after by the Dutch to support their canal houses and build their trading fleet. Although it's now bordered by a modern mess, Mandal has preserved its quaint old centre, a narrow strip of white-clapboard buildings spread along the north bank of the Mandalselva River just before it rolls into the sea. It's an attractive spot, well worth a few minutes' ramble. You can also drop by the municipal **museum** (July to mid-Aug Mon–Fri 11am–5pm, Sat 11am–2pm, Sun 2–5pm; 20kr), whose rambling collection of local bygones – from agricultural implements to seafaring tackle – occupies an old merchant's house overlooking the river. It's not its antiquities that make Mandal a popular tourist spot, however, but its fine beach, **Sjøsanden**. An 800-metre stretch of golden sand backed by pine trees and framed by rocky headlands, it's touted as Norway's best beach – and although this isn't saying a whole lot, it's a perfectly enjoyable place to unwind for a few hours. The beach is 1.5km from the town centre: to get there, walk along the harbour, past the tourist office to the end of the road and turn left; keep on until you reach the car park at the eastern end of the beach.

Practicalities

Mandal hasn't got a train station, but there's a fast and frequent **bus** service from Kristiansand (Mon–Sat hourly, 6 on Sun; 45min; 60kr). Mandal's ugly modern **bus station** is by the bridge on the north bank of the river; from here it's a brief walk west to the old town centre, just beyond which, facing the river, is the **tourist office**, at Adolf Tidemandsgate 2 (Mon–Fri 9am–4pm; ☎38 27 83 00). There are a couple of good **places to stay**, beginning with the handy and economic *Kjøbmandsgaarden Hotel*, which occupies an old and intelligently renovated timber house in a street of similar buildings across from the bus station at Store Elvegaten 57 (☎38 26 12 76, fax 38 26 33 02; ②). They have six spick-and-span rooms with shared bath and six en suite (an extra 260kr). Moving upmarket, the appealing *First Hotel Solborg*, Neseveien 1 (☎38 26 66 66, fax 38 26 48 22; ⑤/③), is an odd-looking but somehow rather fetching modern structure with every mod con; it's on the west side of the town centre, a good ten-minute walk from the bus station, tight against a wooded escarpment. Alternatively, you can

camp or rent a **cabin** (②) very close to the western end of the beach at the *Sjøsanden Feriesenter*, Sjøsandvei 1 (☎38 26 14 19), a signposted 2km from the town.

The *First Hotel Solborg* has the best **restaurant** in town, but for something less pricey and more informal, head into the centre, where you'll find several places including the lively pizzeria-restaurant, *Jonas B. Gundersen*. The café-restaurant of the *Kjøbmandsgaarden* comes highly recommended too, offering a tasty range of inexpensive Norwegian dishes.

From Mandal, there are daily **express buses** along the E39 to Flekkefjord and Stavanger, 90km and 210km to the west respectively. **Train** travellers have to return to Kristiansand to rejoin the rail network.

West of Mandal: Flekkefjord

Heading west from Mandal on the E39, you'll pass, after 28km, the turning to Lindesnes lighthouse, after which the road weaves near but rarely in sight of the coast on its tortuous route to **FLEKKEFJORD**. This humdrum port, which has traditionally depended on its tanneries and lumber, straddles a narrow inlet, its tiny centre, on the west side of the bridge, mustering a handful of old timber buildings and a **tourist office** (mid-June to mid-Aug Mon–Fri 10am–6pm, Sat 10am–4pm, Sun noon–6pm; mid-Aug to mid-June Mon–Fri 9am–3pm; ☎38 32 43 00). There's precious little to detain you, but for a **snack** head for the harbourside *Selska Pslokaler* café-bar where the home-made soup (55kr) is a good deal tastier than the pizzas. At Flekkefjord, the E39 turns inland for the last 125km into Stavanger (see p.269).

(see p.269)

---

travel details

Trains

Kongsberg to: Kristiansand (4–5 daily; 3hr 30min); Oslo (5–6 daily; 1hr 30min).

Kristiansand to: Kongsberg (4–5 daily; 3hr 30min); Oslo (4–5 daily; 5hr); Stavanger (3–4 daily; 3hr).

Oslo to: Bergen (4–5 daily; 6hr 30min); Dombås (3–4 daily; 4hr 20min); Geilo (4–5 daily; 3hr 20min); Hamar (7 daily; 1hr 40min); Hjerkinn (3 daily; 4hr 45min); Kongsberg (4–5 daily; 2hr); Kongsvoll (3 daily; 4hr 50min); Kristiansand (4–5 daily; 5hr); Lillehammer (7 daily; 2hr 30min); Otta (4–5 daily; 4hr 10min); Sjoa (2 daily; 4hr 30min); Trondheim (3–4 daily; 7hr).

Buses

Kongsberg to: Haugesund (1 daily; 8hr 30min); Kristiansand (1 daily; 8hr 25min); Oslo (4 daily; 2hr); Rjukan (2 daily; 2hr).

Kristiansand to: Åmot (1–2 daily; 5hr); Flekkefjord (2 daily; 2hr 20min); Mandal (Mon–Sat hourly, 6 on Sun; 45min); Oslo (2–3 daily; 5hr 40min); Seljord (1–2 daily; 6hr 30min); Stavanger (2 daily; 4hr 40min).

Lillehammer to: Bergen (1 daily; 10hr 25min); Fagernes (1 daily; 2hr 15min).

Mandal to: Kristiansand (Mon–Sat hourly, 6 on Sun; 45min); Stavanger (1–2 daily; 4hr).

Oppdal to: Kristiansand (1–3 daily; 3hr 30min).

Oslo to: Arendal (2–3 daily; 4hr 15min); Fagernes (3 daily; 3hr 20min); Grimstad (2–3 daily; 4hr 40min); Kongsberg (4 daily; 2hr); Kristiansand (2–3 daily; 5hr 40min); Lillesand (2–3 daily; 5hr); Otta (2 da ly; 5hr); Rjukan (2 daily; 3hr 50min); Sogndal (3 daily; 7hr).

Otta to: Gjendesheim (late June to Aug Mon–Sat 1 daily; 2hr); Lom (3 daily; 1hr).

Rjukan to: Kongsberg (2 daily; 2hr); Oslo (2 daily; 3hr 50min).

Røros to: Oslo (1–3 daily; 6hr); Trondheim (1–3 daily; 3hr 10min).

Express passenger boats (Hurtigbåt)

Oslo to: Arendal (late June to mid-Aug 4 weekly; 7hr).

International ferries

Kristiansand to: Hirtshals (5–6 weekly; 4hr 30min).

Larvik to: Frederikshavn (5–6 weekly; 6hr 15min).

Sandefjord to: Strömstad (2 da ly; 2hr 30min).

CHAPTER SIX

BERGEN AND THE WESTERN FJORDS

I f there's one familiar and enticing image of Norway it's the **fjords**: huge clefts in the landscape running from the coast deep into the interior of the country. Wild, rugged and serene, these water-filled wedges of space are visually stunning; indeed, the entire fjord region elicits inordinate amounts of purple prose from tourist office handouts, and for once it's rarely overstated. The fjords are undeniably beautiful, especially around early May after the brief Norwegian spring has brought colour to the landscape.

The fjords run all the way up the coast to the Russian border, but are most easily – and impressively – seen on the west coast near **Bergen**, the self-proclaimed "Capital of the Fjords". Norway's second largest city, Bergen is a welcoming place with an atmospheric old warehouse quarter, a relic of the days when it was the northernmost port of the Hanseatic trade alliance. It's also a handy springboard for the nearby fjords, including the **Flåmsdal** valley to the east, where an inspiring mountain railway trundles down to the **Aurlandsfjord**, a small arm of the mighty **Sognefjord**. Lined with pretty village resorts, the Sognefjord is the longest, deepest and most celebrated of the country's waterways; it is certainly one of the most beguiling. North of here lies the **Jostedalsbreen** glacier, mainland Europe's largest ice sheet, the relatively uninspiring **Nordfjord**, and the narrow, S-shaped **Geirangerfjord**, perhaps the most scenically impressive of all the fjords, though the tourist hordes can be off-putting. Further north still, towards the **Romsdalsfjord**, the landscape becomes more extreme still, reaching pinnacles of isolation in the splendid **Trollstigen** mountain highway.

BERGEN

As it has been raining ever since she arrived in the city, a tourist stops a young boy and asks him if it always rains here. "I don't know," he replies, "I'm only thirteen." The joke isn't brilliant, but it does tell at least part of the truth. Of all the things to contend with in the western city of **BERGEN**, the weather is the most predictable: it rains relent-

ACCOMMODATION PRICE CODES

The hotels and guesthouses listed in this chapter have been graded according to the following price bands, based on the cost of the **least expensive double room during high season** (late June to Aug). However, almost every hotel offers seasonal and/or weekend discounts, and wherever possible we've given two grades, covering both the regular and the discounted rate.

① Under 500kr	② 500–700kr	③ 700–900kr
④ 900–1200kr	⑤ 1200–1500kr	⑥ Over 1500kr

lessly even in summer, and the surroundings are often shrouded with mist. But despite its dampness, Bergen is one of Norway's most enjoyable cities. Its setting – between seven hills, sheltered to the north, south and west by a series of straggling islands and fjords – is spectacular. There's plenty to see in town too, from sturdy medieval **build-ings** to a whole series of good **museums**, and just outside the city limits is **Troldhaugen**, Edvard Grieg's charming old home.

More than anything else, though, it's the general flavour of the place that appeals. Although Bergen has become a major port and minor industrial centre in recent years, it remains a laid-back, easy-going town with a nautical air. Fishing continues to under-pin the local economy, and the bustling main harbour, **Vågen**, is still very much the focus of attention. If you stay more than a day or two – perhaps using Bergen as a base for visiting the local fjords – you'll soon discover that the city also has the region's best choice of **restaurants**, some impressive art galleries, and a decent nightlife.

Arrival, information and city transport

Bergen's sturdy stone **train station** (☎81 50 08 88) is located on Strømgaten, just along the street from the entrance to the Bergen Storsenter shopping mall, which incorpo-rates the **bus station**. From Strømgaten, it's a five- to ten-minute walk west to Bergen's harbourfront via the pedestrianized shopping street, Marken. If you're heavily laden, a taxi to the harbour will set you back about 60kr. The **airport** is 20km south of the city at Flesland, and is connected to the centre by the Flybussen (Sun–Fri 5.30am–9pm, Sat 5.30am–7pm every 20–30min; 40min; 45kr). This pulls in beside the *SAS Hotel Norge* on Ole Bulls plass and the bus station before carrying on to the harbourfront *SAS Royal Hotel*. Taxis from the rank outside the airport arrivals hall charge around 250kr for the same trip.

Ferry and express boat terminals

As well as being a local hub for ferry links with the fjords, Bergen is also a busy inter-national port. **International ferries** from Denmark, Iceland, Shetland and the Faroe Islands all arrive at Skoltegrunnskaien, the quay just beyond Bergenhus fortress, as do those from Newcastle, which call at Stavanger and Haugesund on the way here. **Hurtigbåt passenger express boats** from Haugesund, Stavanger and the Hardangerfjord, as well as those from Sognefjord and Nordfjord, line up on the oppo-site side of the harbour at the Strandkaiterminalen; most **local ferries** from the islands and fjords immediately north of Bergen arrive here too, though short excursions round the Byforden, adjoining Bergen harbour, leave from beside the Torget.

Bergen is also a terminal port for the **Hurtigrute coastal steamer** (see p.355), which arrives at the Frieleneskaien on the southern edge of the city centre, about 1500m from the train station – beyond the university and close to the Puddefjordsbroen bridge (Hwy 555). City (yellow) bus #5 links the Frieleneskaien with the central Torget (Mon–Sat 6am–midnight every 30min or hourly, Sun 10am–10pm hourly; 17kr). Alternatively, it's a steep 25-minute walk to the centre up through the university and down the other side; the taxi fare for the same journey will rush you about 60kr. Taxis wait by the quayside.

For ferry and boat **ticket and timetable information**, see "Ferries" under "Listings" (p.266).

Driving and parking

If you're **driving** into Bergen, note that a **toll** (10kr) is charged on all vehicles over 50cc entering the city centre from Monday to Friday between 6am and 10pm; pay at

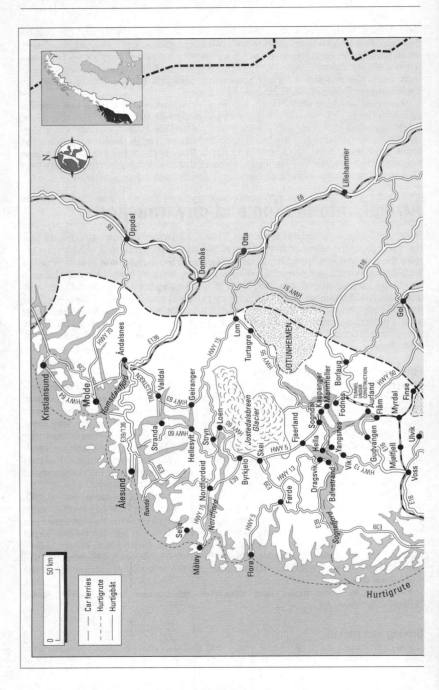

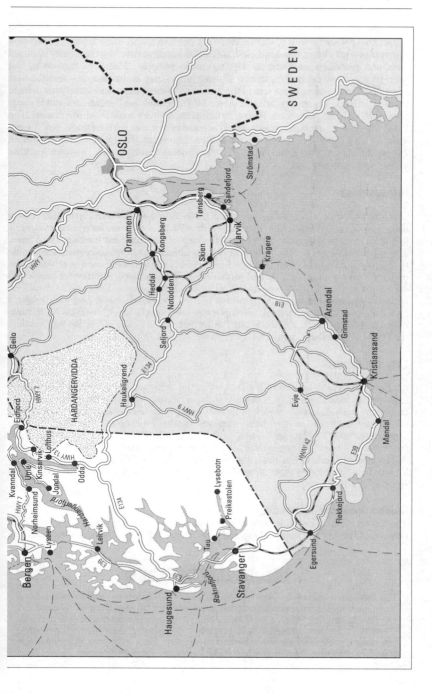

the tollbooths. There's no charge for driving *out* of the city. In an attempt to keep the city centre relatively free of traffic, there's a confusing and none-too-successful one-way and no-entry system in operation, and this is supplemented by rigorously imposed on-street **parking** restrictions. During peak periods (Mon–Fri 8am–6pm, Sat 8am–10am), on-street parking costs 12kr per hour – pay at the meters – and the best advice is to make straight for one of the four central **car parks** and leave your vehicle there. The largest is the Bygarasjen (open 24hr), behind the Bergen Storsenter shopping mall and bus station on Vestre Strømkaien, a short walk from the centre. The Parkeringshuset, on Rosenkrantzgaten, is handier for the harbourfront, but it's not open as long (Mon–Fri 7am–9pm, Sat & Sun 8am–6pm). Tariffs vary, but reckon on 7kr per half-hour up to a maximum of 100kr. Outside peak periods, on-street parking is relatively easy and free.

Information

The **tourist office**, at Vågsallmenningen 1 (June–Aug daily 8.30am–10pm; May & Sept daily 9am–8pm; Oct–April Mon–Sat 9am–4pm; ☎55 32 14 80, *www.bergen-travel.com*), is in a small square across the street from the east end of the main harbour, the Vågen. They give away copies of the *Bergen Guide*, an exhaustive tourist and consumer's guide to the city, and endless other free brochures. You can also book rooms in private houses here, reserve places on guided tours, buy tickets for fjord sightseeing boats, and exchange money. In high season, expect enormous queues. Bergen has two free, bimonthly **news sheets**, the local edition of the Oslo-based *Natt & Dag* and Bergen's own *Filter*, which provide local news, reviews and entertainment listings. Both, naturally enough, are in Norwegian, but the former has an easy-to-use listings section; they're widely available across the city centre.

City transport

All Bergen's main attractions are located in the compact city centre, which is best explored on **foot**. For outlying attractions and accommodation, however, you'll need to take a city **bus**. A dense network of local bus routes criss-crosses Bergen and its surroundings, centred on the **bus station**, in the Storsenter shopping mall on Strømgaten (☎177). Flat-fare tickets, available from the driver, cost 17kr and are valid for an hour; if your journey involves more than one bus, ask the driver for a transfer. Another useful link is the tiny orange **ferry** (Mon–Fri 7am–4.15pm; 10kr) around Vågen, from Munkebryggen along Carl Sundts gate to a point near the *SAS Royal Hotel* on the Bryggen.

Guided tours and sightseeing

The tourist office offers a plethora of **local tours**: city bus tours, a motorized mini-train ride round the city and fjord sightseeing trips are just a few examples of what's on offer

---

THE BERGEN CARD

The **Bergen Card** is a 24-hour (130kr) or 48-hour (200kr) pass valid on all the city's buses and offering free or substantially discounted entry to most of the city's sights and on many sightseeing trips – a handbook listing all the concessions comes with the card. Obviously, the more diligent a sightseer you are, the better value the card becomes, especially if you're staying a bus ride from the centre. The card is sold at a wide range of outlets, including the tourist office, major hotels and the railway station.

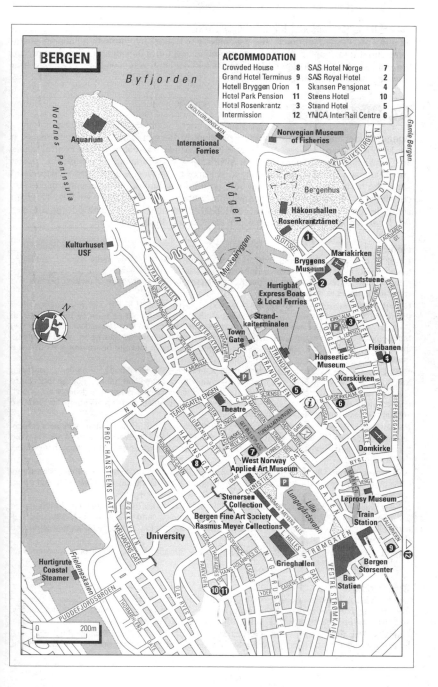

– consult the *Bergen Guide* for full details. However, trips to all the destinations covered by tours are easily and much less expensively arranged by yourself; details are given throughout this chapter. A couple of recommended tours to watch out for, though, are the guided tours of Bryggen (see box, p.260) and the much-vaunted "Norway in a Nutshell" tour to Flåm (see p.280).

Accommodation

Budget **accommodation** is no great problem in Bergen. There are three hostels, a choice of private rooms and *pensjonater* (guesthouses), and some of the central hotels are surprisingly good value. **Rooms** in private houses, bookable through the tourist office, are also good bargains – the vast majority provide self-catering facilities and some are fairly central, though the bulk are in the suburbs. Prices are at a fixed rate, currently 295kr for a double room without a bath and toilet (185kr single), 345kr en suite; there are some apartments too (430kr). They are very popular, during summer you'll need to arrive at the tourist office early to stand much chance.

Hotels

Bryggen Orion, Bradbenken 3 (☎55 31 80 80, fax 55 32 94 14). Deservedly popular mid-range hotel, handily located a stone's throw from the Bergenhus, with unassuming but perfectly comfortable modern rooms. Breakfasts are magnificent banquets with every type of pickled herring you can think of. Hard to beat. ④/③.

Grand Hotel Terminus, Zander Kaaes gate (☎55 31 16 55, fax 55 31 85 76). There was a time when the tweed jackets of prewar England headed straight for the *Grand* as soon as they arrived in Bergen – and not just because the hotel is next door to the train station. Those days are long gone, but the hotel has reinvented itself, making the most of its neo-baronial flourishes, wood panelling, drooping chandeliers and stained glass. Breakfasts are superb and the bedrooms attractive and quiet. ④/③.

Park Pension, Harald Hårfagres gate 35 (☎55 54 44 00, fax 55 54 44 44). This excellent, family-run hotel occupies two handsome late nineteenth-century town houses on the edge of the city centre near the university. The charming interior is painted in soft pastel colours, bedrooms are smart, neat and appealing and the public rooms are cluttered with antiques. It's a very popular place, so advance reservations are advised. A snip at ③/②.

Rosenkrantz, Rosenkrantzgaten 7 (☎55 31 50 00, fax 55 31 14 76). Efficient and extremely competent mid-range hotel in an old building just behind the Bryggen. Has everything you'll need and the rooms are tidy and trim – try not to notice the horrid aluminium windows they've stuck in the attractive facade. ④/③.

SAS Hotel Norge, Ole Bulls plass 4 (☎55 57 30 00, fax 55 57 30 01). Bergen's most central top-class hotel, right in the thick of things and with a full range of facilities from bar to heated swimming pool. ⑥/⑤.

Steens, Parkveien 22 (☎55 31 40 50, fax 55 32 61 22). One of an attractive terrace of high-gabled town houses, overlooking a mini-lake on the edge of the town centre near the university, this well-established hotel offers inexpensive lodgings. The interior has lots of late Victorian flourishes, but the overall effect is a tad gloomy. ③/②.

Strand, Strandkaien 2 (☎55 31 08 15, fax 55 31 00 17). Straightforward but pleasant modern hotel overlooking the Torget. ④/③.

Guesthouses

Bergen YMCA InterRail Centre, Nedre Korskirkealmenning 4 (☎55 31 72 52). Close to Torget, a five- to ten-minute walk from the train station. Facilities include showers, kitchen, sauna and laundry, and there's a supermarket nearby. It has 175 dormitory beds but fills quickly. Open mid-June to Aug.

Crowded House, Håkonsgaten 27 (☎55 23 13 10, fax 55 23 13 30). Traditionally, Bergen's guesthouses have been a little frumpy, but this lively, appealing place is the opposite – from the cactuses in the foyer to the bright and airy (if spartan) bedrooms. There are self-catering facilities; breakfast costs 50kr. Located halfway along traffic-clogged Håkonsgaten, about five minutes' walk from the city centre.

Intermission, Kalfarveien 8 (☎55 31 32 75). Christian-run private hostel east of the train station with beds for 100kr. Open mid-June to mid-Aug.

Montana Vandrerhjem, Johan Blyttsveien 30, Landås (☎55 20 80 70, fax 55 20 80 75). This large and comfortable hostel, popular with school parties, occupies lodge-like premises high up in the hills overlooking the city. Dorm accommodation, plus family rooms and doubles (③), the pick of which are en suite and in a newly added wing. Great views and great breakfasts, as well as self-catering facilities. It's 6km east of the centre – 15min on bus #4 (Montana stop) from Nygaten.

Skansen Pensjonat, Vetrlidsallmenningen 29 (☎55 31 90 80, fax 55 31 15 27). This simple little guesthouse occupies a nineteenth-century stone house of elegant proportions just above – and up the steps from – the terminus of the Fløibanen funicular railway near Torget. It's a great location, in one of the most beguiling parts of town, and although the rooms are comparatively rudimentary, they are perfectly adequate. Of the eight rooms here, one is en suite. A snip at ②.

The City

Founded in 1070 by King Olav Kyrre ("the Peaceful"), **Bergen** was the largest and most important town in medieval Norway, a regular residence of the country's kings and queens and, from the fourteenth century, a Hanseatic League port, connected to other European and Baltic cities by vigorous trading links. The League was controlled by German merchants, however, and although Hansa and local interests initially coincided, the picture slowly changed. Eventually, Germans came to dominate the region's economy, reducing the locals to a state of dependency by fixing the price of fish, the region's main commodity. Their trading station, which flourished on Bergen's main wharf, the Bryggen, became wealthy and hated in equal measure. In the 1550s, with Hansa power evaporating, a local lord, one Kristoffer Valkendorf, finally reasserted Norwegian control. Unfortunately, Valkendorf and his cronies simply took over the monopolies that had enriched their German predecessors, operating a system which continued to pauperize the region's fishermen right down to the nineteenth century.

Very little of medieval Bergen has survived, although parts of the fortress – the **Bergenhus** – which commands the entrance to the harbour, date from the thirteenth century. The rest of the city centre divides into several distinct parts, the most interesting being the wharf area, the **Bryggen**, which houses an attractive ensemble of eighteenth- and nineteenth-century merchants' trading houses. The Bryggen ends at the bottom of the central harbour, **Vågen**, where the **Torget** is home to an open-air fish market. East of here, stretching up towards the train station, is one of the older districts, a mainly nineteenth-century quarter at its prettiest along **Lille Øvregaten** and amongst the narrow lanes that clamber up the adjacent hillside. The main thoroughfare of this quarter, **Kong Oscars gate**, leads to the city's most endearing museum, the Lepramuseet (Leprosy Museum), itself little more than a stone's throw from the modern concrete blocks surrounding the city's central lake, **Lille Lungegårdsvann**. The high-rises here form the cultural focus of the city, holding Bergen's main concert hall and art galleries, whilst the main commercial area is just to the west along pedestrianized **Torgalmenningen**. The steep hill to the south of Lille Lungegårdsvann is crowned by the **university**.

Most of the main sights and museums are concentrated in these areas, but no tour of the city is complete without a stroll out along the **Nordnes peninsula**, where fine timber houses dot the bumpy terrain, and whose old USF sardine factory now contains a first-rate arts complex and café.

Torget

The nineteenth-century traveller Lilian Leland, writing about Bergen in 1890, complained that "Everything is fishy. You eat fish and drink fish and smell fish and breathe fish." Those days are long gone, but even now that Bergen is every inch the go-ahead, modern city, tourists still flock here to seek out all things piscine. The nearest you'll get to those fishy days now is the open-air **fish market** on the **Torget** (Mon–Sat 7am–3pm). It's not a patch on the days when scores of fishing smacks moored up against the quayside to empty their bulging holds, but the stalls still display huge mounds of prawns and crab-claws, buckets of herring and a hundred other varieties of marine life on slabs, in tanks and under the knife. Load up or eat up and hang around for a while to assess the comings and goings of the local boats and ferries and take a peek at the **statue** of the World War II resistance hero Leif Andreas Larsen.

Bryggen

From Torget, central Bergen spears right and left around the Vågen, with **Bryggen**, on the northerly side of the harbour, the obvious historical and cultural target. The site of the original settlement at Bergen, this is the city's best-preserved quarter, containing, among other things, the distinctive wooden gabled trading posts that front the wharf. The area was once known as Tyskebryggen, or "German Quay", after the Hansa merchants who operated their trading station here, but the name was unceremoniously dumped at the end of World War II. Hansa influence, based on an ability to trade grain and beer in return for the fish that came down from northern Norway, dates back to the thirteenth century, but only later did the Germans come to dominate local affairs, much to the consternation of local landowners. By the mid-sixteenth century, however, the League was in decline and although the last German merchant hung on till 1764, economic power had long since passed to Norwegians.

The medieval buildings of Bryggen were destroyed by fire in 1702, to be replaced by another set of wooden warehouses. In turn, many of these were later replaced by high-gabled stone warehouses in a style modelled on that of the Hansa period, but a small section of **timber buildings** has survived and now houses shops, restaurants and bars. It's well worth nosing around here, wandering down the passageways in between wherever you can. Interestingly, these eighteenth-century buildings carefully follow the original building line: the governing body of the Hansa trading station stipulated the exact depth and width of each merchant's building, and the width of the passage separating them – a regularity that's actually best observed from Øvregaten (see opposite). The planning regulations didn't end there. Trade had to be carried out in the front section of the building, with storage rooms at the back; above could be found the merchant's office, bedroom and dining room, and above that, on the top floor, the living quarters of the employees, arranged by rank: merchants, journeymen/clerks and foremen, wharf hands and, last and least, house boys. At the near end of the Bryggen, just off Torget, the **Hanseatic Museum** (Hanseatisk Museum; daily: June–Aug 9am–5pm;

GUIDED TOURS OF BRYGGEN

Guided tours of the Bryggen, in English, are warmly recommended. They start from the Bryggens Museum daily between June and August at 11am and 1pm, cost 60kr, and take roughly an hour and a half. Tickets are on sale at the museum and after the tour you can reuse them to get back into the Bryggens and Hanseatic museums and the Schøtstuene for a longer exploration – but only on the same day.

MOUNT FLØYEN

When the weather's fine, be sure to take the quaint funicular railway (*fløibanen*) to the summit of **Mount Fløyen** ("The Vane"), 320m above sea level. The funicular runs up the hillside close to the Torget, and at the top there's a café-restaurant, a viewing point and colour-coded footpaths heading off through the woods. The funicular departs every thirty minutes (Mon–Fri 7.30am–11pm, Sat 8am–11pm, Sun 9am–11pm, May–Aug until midnight); the return fare is 34kr.

Sept–May 11am–2pm; 35kr) is the best preserved of the early eighteenth-century merchants' dwellings and, kitted out in late Hansa style, gives an idea of how things worked. Among the assorted bric-a-brac are the possessions and documents of contemporary families, including several fine pieces of furniture, but more than anything else it's the gloomy, warren-like layout of the place that impresses, as well as the all-pervading smell of fish.

Along Øvregaten
Walking up past the terminus of the funicular railway (see box below), turn left along **Øvregaten**, which has marked the boundary of the Bryggen for the last 800 years. The Hanseatic warehouses once stretched back from the quayside to this street but no further and, as you stroll along Øvregaten, the old layout of the trading station is still easy to discern – a warren of tiny passages separating warped and crooked buildings. On the upper levels, the eighteenth-century loading bays, staircases and higgledy-piggledy living quarters are still much in evidence, while the overhanging eaves of the passageways were designed to shelter trade goods. Towards the end of the street, at Øvregaten 50, is the **Schøtstuene** (June–Aug daily 9am–5pm; May & Sept daily 11am–2pm; Oct–April Sun 11am–2pm; 35kr), the old Hanseatic Assembly Rooms, where the merchants would meet to lay down the law or just relax – it was the only heated building in the trading post. This made sense – the wooden buildings were a very real fire hazard – but as you explore the comfortable rooms here, it's hard not to believe that the merchants were pleased with their lot and cared not a jot for their employees shivering away nearby.

Just round the corner, the perky twin towers of the **Mariakirken** (late May to mid-Sept Mon–Fri 11am–4pm; mid-Sept to late May Tues–Fri noon–1.30pm; 10kr, free in winter) are the most distinguished features of what is Bergen's oldest extant building, a Romanesque-Gothic church dating from the twelfth century. It's still used as a place of worship and was, from 1408 to 1706, the church of the Hanseatic League merchants, who bought it and subsequently installed a fine and flashy Baroque pulpit and altar, both of which are well worth close examination. In front of the church, the well-conceived **Bryggens Museum** (May–Aug daily 10am–5pm; Sept–April Mon–Fri 11am–3pm, Sat noon–3pm, Sun noon–4pm; 20kr) features all manner of things dug up in the archeological excavations that started on the Bryggen in 1955. A wide range of artefacts – domestic implements, handicrafts, maritime objects and trade goods – forms the basis for a series of lively exhibitions attempting a complete reassembly of local medieval life. The whole caboodle is put into context by a set of twelfth-century foundations, left *in situ* where they were excavated and now forming the museum's centrepiece.

Bergenhus
Just to the west of the Bryggens Museum lies the **Bergenhus**, a large, roughly star-shaped fortification whose stone and earth walls date from the nineteenth century but enclose the remnants of earlier structures. One of these, the **Håkonshallen**, is a routine, largely reconstructed Gothic ceremonial hall built for King Håkon in the mid-thirteenth

century. Across the courtyard is the rather more diverting **Rosenkrantztårnet** tower, whose winding thirteenth-century staircases, medieval rooms, and low, rough corridors were enlarged in 1565 by the lord of Bergenhus, Erik Rosenkrantz, who used the place as a fortified residence. Both buildings were wrecked by the explosion of a German ammunition ship in 1944, and the newness of the rebuilding shows. They can be seen together on a combined guided tour (on the hour every hour mid-May to Aug daily 10am–4pm; Sept to mid-May Sun noon–3pm; 15kr).

Strolling back from the Bergenhus along the Bryggen **waterfront**, you'll pass the assorted restaurants, bars and souvenir shops that pull in the tourist herds with plastic trolls and the like. Frankly, this is not a very appealing prospect, but it only takes a few minutes to regain the relative sanity of the Torget.

Along Lille Øvregaten and Kong Oscars gate

From Torget, return to the Fløibanen funicular railway terminal and head right down **Lille Øvregaten**, lined with an appealing ensemble of old timber houses, all bright-white clapboard planking and dinky little windows. There are more of the same up the hill in the angle between the Fløibanen terminal and Lille Øvregaten, though if anything these are even quainter, with the houses pressing in against steep cobbled lanes intercepted by the odd hunk of stone that was just too bothersome to move. Meanwhile, Lille Øvregaten curves round to the **Domkirken** (mid-May to Aug Mon–Sat 10am–4pm, Sun 10am–1pm; Sept to mid-May Tues–Fri 11am–2pm, Sat 11am–3pm, Sun 10am–1pm; free), a doughty edifice whose stern exterior has been restored and rebuilt so often since its original construction in the thirteenth century that it is now almost entirely without interest.

More promising by far is the fascinating **Leprosy Museum**, just up from the Domkirke at Kong Oscars gate 59 (Lepramuseet; late May to Aug daily 11am–3pm; 20kr). This endearingly antiquated collection is housed in the eighteenth-century buildings of St Jørgens Hospital (St George's Hospital), ranged around a pretty cobbled courtyard, and tells the tale of the Norwegian fight against leprosy. The disease first appeared in Scandinavia in Viking times and became especially prevalent in the coastal districts of western Norway, with around three percent of the population classified as lepers in the early nineteenth century. St Jørgens Hospital specialized in the care of lepers, assuming a more proactive role from 1830 when a series of Norwegian medics tried to find a cure for the disease. The most successful of them was Armauer Hansen, who in 1873 was the first person to identify the leprosy bacillus. The last lepers left St George's in 1946 and the hospital has been left untouched, the small hospital rooms off the central gallery revealing the patients' cramped living quarters. Also on display are medical implements (including cupping glasses for drawing blood) and a few gruesome sketches and paintings of sufferers. Dating from 1702, the adjoining hospital **chapel** is delightful, its rickety timbers holding a lovely folksy pulpit and altarpiece decorated with cherubs and dainty scrollwork. The altar paintings are crude but appropriate: *The Ten Lepers* and *The Canaanite's daughter healed*.

Around Lille Lungegårdsvann

Bergen's central lake, **Lille Lungegårdsvann**, is a focus for summertime festivals and events, and its southern side is flanked by the city's four principal art galleries. The first and most diverting of the quartet, working east to west, is the **Bergen Art Museum Rasmus Meyer Collections** (Bergen Kunstmuseum Rasmus Meyers Samlinger; mid-May to mid-Sept daily 11am–5pm; mid-Sept to mid-May Tues–Sun 11am–5pm; 35kr combined ticket with the Art Society and Stenersen), housed in the big building with the pagoda-like roof at Rasmus Meyers Allé 3. Gifted to the city by one of its old merchant families, the collection contains an extensive collection of Norwegian painting from early landscape painters like Dahl and Fearnley (see p.207), through Christian Krohg to later figures including Alex Revold and Henrik Sørensen. It is, however, for its large sample of the work of Edvard Munch that the museum is usually visited – if you missed out in Oslo (see p.215), this is the place to make amends. There are examples from all of Munch's major periods, with the disturbing – and disturbed – works of the 1890s taking the spotlight from the calmer paintings that followed his recovery from the nervous breakdown of 1908. Apart from the paintings, there's also a substantial collection of his woodcuts and lithographs. The distinctive glass-and-concrete building behind the museum is the **Grieghallen** concert hall, the main venue for the annual Bergen Festival (see p.266).

Just along the street, the **Bergen Fine Art Society** (Bergens Kunstforening; same times and ticket) is noted for its temporary exhibitions of contemporary art, whilst the adjacent **Bergen Art Museum Stenersen Collection** (Bergen Kunstmuseum Stenersens Samling; same times and ticket) features the modern art collection of Rolf Stenersen, gifted to the city in 1971. The collection is especially strong on one of Stenersen's favourites, the Bauhaus painter Paul Klee, and there's a smattering of work by other familiar artists, featuring the likes of Lautrec, Picasso, Miró, Ernst and Léger. Amongst the Norwegians, there are several Munch paintings and a selection of watercolours and oils by the versatile Jakob Weidemann (b. 1923), whose work was much influenced by French Cubists during the 1940s, though he is now best known for the shimmering, pastel abstracts he churned out in the 1960s.

The final gallery of the four, the **West Norway Applied Art Museum** (Vestlandske Kunstindustrimuseum; mid-May to mid-Sept Tues–Sun 11am–4pm; mid-Sept to mid-May Tues–Sat noon–3pm, Thurs till 6pm, Sun till 4pm; 30kr), occupies the Permanenten building, a whopping neo-Gothic structure at the corner of Christies gate and Nordahl Bruns gate. A lively exhibition programme with the focus on contemporary craft and design brings in the crowds, and some of the displays are very good indeed – which is more than can be said for the permanent collection and its Chinese marble statues.

Torgalmenningen and the Nordnes peninsula

The broad sweep of pedestrianized **Torgalmenningen** is the setting for the commercial heart of modern Bergen, lined with shops and department stores and decorated by a vigorous large-scale sculpture celebrating figures from the city's history. Around the corner, **Ole Bulls plass**, also pedestrianized, sports a rock pool and fountain above which stands a rather jaunty statue of local boy Ole Bull, the nineteenth-century virtuoso violinist and heartthrob. Ole Bulls plass stretches up to the municipal **theatre**, Den Nationale Scene, at the top of the hill, worth the short walk for a look at the fearsome, saucer-eyed statue of Henrik Ibsen that stands in front of it. Near here too, just down the hill, at the east end of Strandgaten, is the imposing bulk of an old **town gate**, built in 1628 to control access to the city but soon used by the authorities to increase their revenues by imposing a toll.

Beyond the theatre, the hilly **Nordnes peninsula** juts out into the fjord, its western tip accommodating the **Aquarium** (Akvariet; daily: May–Sept 9am–8pm, 75kr; Oct–April 10am–6pm, 55kr; bus #4) and a pleasant park. It takes about fifteen minutes to walk there from Ole Bulls plass along Klostergaten/Haugeveien, but the effort is much better spent in choosing a different, more southerly route along the peninsula. This takes you past the charming timber villas of Skottegaten and Nedre Strangehagen before it cuts through the bluff leading to the old, waterside United Sardines Factory, imaginatively converted into an arts complex, the **Kulturhuset USF**, aka Verftet, incorporating a groovy café-bar, *Kafe Kippers*.

Out from the centre – Troldhaugen

The lochs, fjords and rocky wooded hills surrounding central Bergen have channelled the city's **suburbs** into long ribbons that trail off in every direction. These urban outskirts are not in themselves appealing, but tucked away among them is **Troldhaugen** (Hill of the Trolls; late April to Sept daily 9am–6pm; early April, Oct & Nov Mon–Fri 10am–2pm, Sat noon–4pm, Sun 10am–4pm; Feb & March Mon–Fri 10am–2pm, Sun 10am–4pm; Jan Mon–Fri 10am–2pm; 40kr), Edvard Grieg's lakeside home and one of the region's most popular attractions. Located about 7km south of downtown off the E39, it's accessible by public transport, though it's a bit of a pain, and there are organized excursions from Bergen too, from about 220kr. Norway's only composer of world renown, Grieg has a good share of commemorative monuments in Bergen – a statue in the city park, the Grieghallen concert hall – but it's here that you get a sense of the man, an immensely likeable and much-loved figure of leftish opinions and disarming modesty: "I make no pretensions of being in the class with Bach, Mozart and Beethoven. Their works are eternal, while I wrote for my day and generation."

A visit begins at the **museum**, where Grieg's life and times are exhaustively chronicled and a short film provides further insights. From here, it's a brief walk to the **house**, a pleasant and unassuming villa built in 1885, and still pretty much as Greig left it, with a jumble of photos, manuscripts and period furniture. Greig didn't, in fact, compose much at home, but preferred to walk round to a tiny **hut** he had built just along the shore. The hut has survived, but today it stands beside a modern concert hall, the **Troldsalen**, where there are **music recitals** (of Grieg) from late June to October – tickets, the cost of which includes transport, are available from Bergen tourist office.

There are regular **buses** (every 20min) to Troldhaugen from the bus station: take any bus leaving from platforms 19, 20 or 21. Get off at the Hopsbroen stop, turn right off the bus (going back upon yourself) and about 200m along the road turn left up Troldhaugsveien for a stiff and uninteresting twenty-minute (700m) walk.

Eating, drinking and nightlife

Bergen has a good supply of **restaurants**, the best of which tend to focus on seafood – the city's main gastronomic asset. The pricier tourist haunts are concentrated on the Bryggen, but should not be dismissed out of hand – several are first-rate. Other less expensive places dot the side-streets behind the Bryggen and the narrow lanes east of Torget. Generally though, the **cafés** and restaurants to the southwest of Ole Bulls plass serve better food in much more fashionable surroundings. The most appealing **bars** are around here too.

The fish market on the Torget (Mon–Sat from 7am) remains *the* place for **takeaway** lunches, offering everything from dressed crab through to smoked-salmon sandwiches and caviar. For a sit-down meal, the town's **cafés** and **café-bars** are easily the most economic option, though you shouldn't leave Bergen without enjoying at least one slap-up, seafood **restaurant** meal. The café-bars mentioned opposite could almost as easily be included in the "Bars" section – the distinction is somewhat arbitrary.

Bergen's **drinkers** have three main choices in terms of ambience and locality: they can plump to join the tourists carousing on the Bryggen; hang around with the high-heeled girls and tattoos on Ole Bulls plass; or seek out the cooler, more studenty places to the southwest of Ole Bulls plass. Several of the more appealing bars offer live music or DJ sounds, and there's a smattering of **clubs** too.

Restaurants

Bryggeloftet & Stuene, Bryggen (☎55 31 06 30). A tad stuffy, but with the widest range of seafood in town – delicious meals featuring every North Atlantic fish you've ever heard of, and some you might not have heard of at all. Main courses around 180kr.

Den Gode Klode, Fosswinckelsgate 18 (☎55 32 34 32). South of the Grieghallen, this is Bergen's only specialist vegetarian restaurant. A wide range of dishes, pleasantly presented and inexpensive. Closes at 7pm (Sat 5pm) and all day Sun.

Enhjørningen, Bryggen (☎55 32 79 19). On the second floor of a superbly restored eighteenth-century merchant's house – all low beams and creaking floors – this smart restaurant serves a mouthwatering range of fish and shellfish with main courses from around 180kr. Worth every kroner for an indulgent evening out. The daily buffet lunch (noon–4pm, Sun from 1pm) is a more affordable alternative, with lashings of salmon, prawns and herring, along with salads, hot dishes, bread, cheese and desserts.

Smauet Mat og Vinhus, Vaskerelvsmuget, off Ole Bulls plass (☎55 23 14 20). This first-rate restaurant offers traditional Norwegian cuisine – including oodles of seafood – and more exotic dishes like ostrich and antelope. Reckon on 180kr for a main course.

To Kokker, Bryggen (☎55 32 28 16). Similar to the *Enhjørningen*, but without the buffet. First-class seafood. Main courses around 200kr, three-course set meals for 500kr. Above the *Baklommen* bar. Closed Sun.

Cafés and café-bars

Café Opera, Engen 24. White wooden building, its windows filled with plants, its interior busy with a fashionable crew drinking beer and good coffee. Tasty, filling snacks from as little as 45kr. DJ sounds on the weekend. West of Ole Bulls plass.

Det Lille Kaffekompaniet, branches at Christies gate 11, close to Lille Lungegårdsvann (Mon–Fri 8am–5pm, Sat noon–5pm), and above the funicular terminal at Nedre Fjellsmug 2 (Mon–Fri 5–11pm, Sat noon–6pm, Sun noon–11pm). These two coffee bars work in tandem during the week one opens as the other closes. They are simple unpretentious places, but locals swear the coffee here is the best in Norway – a recent national poll agreed with them.

Kafe Kippers, Kulturhuset USF, on the Nordnes peninsula. Part of the city's adventurous contemporary arts complex, this laid-back café-bar serves tasty inexpensive food, rustles up great barbecues and, with its sea views and terrace, is *the* place to come on a sunny evening – when the place is jam-packed. Live music too, especially during its own jazz festival in May.

Munkestuen Café, Klostergaten 12. Intimate, cosy café-restaurant noted for its excellent Italian dishes and wine cellar, the best in town. Reckon on 200kr a main course.

Spisekroken, Klostergaten 8. Economical café-bar with delicious daily specials – the mouthwatering catch of the day only costs about 100kr. A fashionable spot.

Bars and clubs

Bryggen Tracteursted, Bryggen. Raucous, earthy bar in one of the old wooden merchants' buildings on the Bryggen. Live music Fri & Sat; closed Sun.

Dickens, Ole Bulls plass 10. One of the busiest of the downtown bars, and a bit of a meat market, with a young clientele spread over two floors and a glass-walled main bar.

Garage, corner of Nygårdsgaten and Christies gate. Very busy place with a mixed crowd. There are two bars on the ground floor, and a live music area downstairs. One of the places in Bergen that seems never to go out of style, even though the interior definitely has.

Hulen, Olav Ryesvei 48. Student hangout in an old air-raid shelter under Nygårdsparken – on the far side of the university from the city centre. Live bands and DJs at weekends. Wed & Thurs 10pm–2am, Fri & Sat 10pm–3.30am.

Kafe Permanenten, corner of Christies gate and Nordahl Bruns gate, in the basement of the building housing the West Norway Applied Art Museum. An indifferent café by day, but an excellent club at night, with DJs from all over the world.

Miles Ahead, Torggaten 7 – look for the very small sign on the wall down this alley. Acid jazz and its relatives, spun by excellent DJs, make this the perfect spot to go dancing, and there's a long and well-stocked bar too. Wed & Thurs 9pm–1am, Fri & Sat 9pm–4am.

Sjøboden, Bryggen. Lively spot situated inside one of the old timber buildings on the Bryggen. Frequent live music, though the quality's very variable.

Festivals and the performing arts

Bergen takes justifiable pride in its **performing arts** and hosts top-notch events throughout the year, especially during the **Bergen International Festival** (Festspillene i Bergen) held around the end of May and presenting a wide-ranging programme of music, ballet, folklore and drama. The principal venue for the festival is the **Grieghallen** (☎55 21 61 50), where you can pick up programmes, tickets and information, as you can at the tourist office. The city's contemporary arts centre, the **Kulturhuset USF**, down on Georgernes Verft on the Nordnes peninsula (☎55 31 55 70), contributes to the main festival with its own international jazz festival, held over the same period. The Kulturhuset is a busy place at other times of the year too, putting on an ambitious programme of concerts, art-house films and contemporary plays.

Throughout the summer, Bergen contrives to have an event of some kind on almost every day of the week – everything from fishing competitions to chamber music recitals. The tourist office details these summer activities in its *Sommer Bergen* promotional leaflet. Otherwise, **entertainment listings** (in Norwegian) are provided in *Natt & Dag*, a free bimonthly news sheet widely available across the city centre.

Listings

Airlines Braathens, Bergen airport (☎55 99 82 50); British Airways inquiries to Braathens; SAS, Bergen airport (☎55 11 43 00).

Bookshop Melvaer No 7, Torgalmenningen 7. Easily the best bookshop in town, with a wide range of English, French, German and Spanish titles. The travel section is especially good, and the staff extremely helpful. Right in the city centre.

Bus enquiries Timetable information on ☎177.

Car parks Of several multistorey car parks, Parkeringshuset, on Rosenkrantzgaten (Mon–Fri 7am–9pm, Sat & Sun 8am–6pm), is central and handy for short-stay parking. For longer stays and/or more flexibility Bygarasjen, beside the Bergen Storsenter shopping mall and bus station on Vestre Strømkaien, is open 24hr.

Car rental All the major international car rental companies have offices in town, including Budget, off the Bryggen at Lodin Lepps gate 1 (☎55 90 26 15), and Avis at Lars Hilles gate 20b (☎55 32 01 30). Statoil Bilutleie has an outlet at the airport (☎55 99 14 90), as does Budget (☎55 22 75 27).

Emergencies Police ☎112; Ambulance ☎113; Fire ☎110. Casualty (24hr) at Vestre Strømkaien 19 (☎55 32 11 20). Emergency dental care is available here too (Mon–Fri 4–9pm, Sat–Sun 3–9pm; ☎55 32 11 20).

Exchange The main post office offers competitive exchange rates for foreign currency and traveller's cheques and its opening hours (mid-May to Aug Mon–Fri 8.15am–3pm, Thurs till 5.30pm; Sept to mid-May Mon–Fri 8.15am–3.30pm, Thurs to 6pm) are longer than those of the banks. The tourist office will also change foreign currency and traveller's cheques but the rates are poor, as they are at the city's big hotels.

Ferries For ferry connections to Norway see Basics, p.8. Fjord Line, Skoltegrunnskaien (☎81 53 35 00), operate car ferry services to Haugesund, Stavanger and Newcastle, and to Egersund and Hantsholm in Denmark. Smyril Line, Slottsgaten 1 (☎55 32 09 70), have car ferry sailings to Shetland, the Faroes and Iceland. Domestic Hurtigbåt passenger express services from the Strandkaiterminalen include HSD (to Haugesund, Stavanger and Hardangerfjord; ☎55 23 87 80), and Fylkesbaatane Reiseservice (to Sognefjord and Nordfjord; ☎55 32 40 15). The Hurtigrute coastal ferry (see p.355) sails daily at 10.30pm from the Frieleneskaien on the southern edge of the city centre, about 1500m from the train station.

Hiking The DNT-affiliated Bergen Turlag, Tverrgaten 4–6 (☎55 32 22 30), will advise on hiking trails in the region, sells hiking maps and arranges guided weekend walks.

Laundry Jarlens Vaskoteque, Lille Øvregate 17 (☎55 32 55 64), near the funicular.

Pharmacy Apoteket Nordstjernen, at the bus station (Mon–Sat 8am–midnight, Sun 9.30am–midnight; ☎55 31 68 84).

Post office Main post office on Olav Kyrres gate at the corner of Rådhusgaten (mid-May to Aug Mon–Fri 8.15am–3pm, Thurs till 5.30pm; Sept to mid-May Mon–Fri 8.15am–3.30pm, Thurs till 6pm). Traveller's cheques and foreign currency exchanged here at competitive rates.

Trains National timetable information on ☎81 50 08 88.

Vinmonopolet Downtown off-licence at Nygårdsgaten 6.

THE WESTERN FJORDS

Heading out from Bergen, the western fjords beckon. The main coastal highway jerks its way south across the mouths of several fjords on its way to **Stavanger**, the region's lively second town, but far more people choose to head east to the closest of the major fjords, **Hardangerfjord**. Northeast from Bergen lie **Voss**, a winter sports resort of some renown, and **Flåm**, at the end of one of the most exciting trips of them all, the train down the Flåmsdal valley to the **Aurlandsfjord**. This is the most popular fjord trip in Norway, and readily done as a day out from Bergen, though it is less expensively undertaken from Voss. But scenic as all this is, the fjord region proper only begins to the north of here, where the Aurlandsfjord joins the **Sognefjord**. One of Norway's greatest and most beautiful fjord systems, the Sognefjord cuts eastwards some 180km inland from the coast. Further north, and running parallel, is the **Nordfjord**, smaller at 90km long, and less intrinsically enticing, though its surroundings are more varied, with patches of the **Jostedalsbreen glacier** visible and visitable beyond. Further north again, the **Geirangerfjord** is a marked contrast – narrow, sheer and rugged – whilst, hopping over a mountain range or two, the **Romsdalsfjord** and its many branches is another of these great inlets, and certainly one of the most beautiful. Here also the terrain begins to splinter into the scattered archipelagos that characterize the north Norwegian coast.

This is not a landscape to be hurried – there's little point in dashing from fjord to fjord. Stay put at least for a while, go for at least one hike or cycle ride, and it's then that you'll really appreciate the western fjords in all their grandeur. The sheer size is breathtaking – but then the geological movements that shaped them were on a grand scale. During the Ice Age, around three million years ago, the whole of Scandinavia was covered in ice, the weight of which pushed the bottom of what would become the fjords down to depths well below that of the ocean floor – the Sognefjord, for example, descends to 1250m, ten times deeper than most of the Norwegian Sea. Later, as the ice retreated, it left huge coastal basins that filled with seawater to become the fjords, which the warm Gulf Stream keeps free of ice.

Where to stay in the fjords

Bergen advertises itself as "Capital of the Fjords", and the tourist office does organize a barrage of excursions from the city. These are an expensive option, however, since most can be done independently and far more cheaply. Also, as Bergen is in fact on the western edge of the fjords, the bulk of the day-trips from here involve too much travelling for comfort. This is doubly true as the main road east from Bergen – the E16 – is prone to congestion and possesses over twenty tunnels, many of which are horribly noxious. Avoid the E16 east of Bergen if you can, and certainly aim to branch off onto the relatively tunnel-free and much more scenic Hwy 7 the first chance you get – about 30km east of the city. For all these reasons, you're much better fixed using one of the small towns that dot the fjords as a base rather than Bergen, especially as distances once you're actually amidst the fjords are – at least by Norwegian standards – quite modest. In the Hardangerfjord, **Ulvik** and **Lofthus** are the most appealing bases, Sognefjord has **Fjærland** and **Balestrand**, while further north **Loen**, **Åndalsnes** and **Ålesund** all have their advantages.

Getting around the fjords

The convoluted topography of the western fjords has produced a dense and complex **public transport** system that is designed to reach all the larger villages and towns at least once every weekday, whether by train, bus, ferry, Hurtigrute coastal boat or Hurtigbåt express passenger boat. By **train**, you can reach Bergen, Stavanger and Flåm in the south and Åndalsnes in the north. For everything in between – the Nordfjord, Jostedalsbreen glacier and Sognefjord – you're confined to buses and ferries, and although virtually all services connect up with each other, it means that there is no set way of reaching or exploring the fjord region. General travel details for this chapter are given on p.298, and in the text itself we've included local connections where they are especially useful; this information should be used in conjunction with the timetables that are widely available across the region. Bear in mind also that although there may be a transport connection to the town or village you want to go to, many Norwegian settlements are scattered and you may be in for a long walk after you've arrived – a particularly dispiriting experience if it's raining.

We've covered the fjords **south to north** – from Stavanger to the Hardangerfjord, Sognefjord, Nordfjord, Geirangerfjord and Romsdalsfjord, to Åndalsnes. There are certain obvious connections – from Bergen to Flåm, and from Geiranger over the Trollstigen to Åndalsnes, for example – but routes are really a matter of personal choice; the text lists the options. It's a good idea to pick up full **bus and ferry timetables** from the local tourist offices whenever you can. The shorter bus routes are often part of a longer chain of linked buses and ferries, so you shouldn't get stranded anywhere.

FJORD FERRIES

Throughout the text there are numerous mentions of fjord **car ferries** and **Hurtigbåt passenger express boats**. The details given in parentheses concern the frequency of operation and the duration of the crossing: for example (hourly; 45min). Hurtigbåt services are usually fairly infrequent – three a day at most – whereas many car ferries shuttle back and forth every hour or two from around 7am in the morning until 10pm at night every day of the week; we've given times of operation where they are either different from the norm or particularly useful. **Hurtigbåt fares** are fixed individually with prices starting at around 70kr for every hour travelled, rising to well over 120kr: the four-hour trip from Bergen to Stavanger, for example, will cost you around 510kr. Rail pass holders (see p.6, 15 & 19) are often entitled to discounts of up to fifty percent and on some routes there are special excursion deals – always ask. **Car ferry fares**, on the other hand, are priced according to a nationally agreed sliding scale, with ten-minute crossings running at around 16kr per person and 37kr per car and driver, 19kr and 52kr respectively for a twenty-minute trip.

South to Stavanger

The skerries and islets which shred the coast **south of Bergen** provide a pleasant introduction to the scenic charms of western Norway – and hint at the sterner beauty of the fjords close by. The intricacies of this shoreline, together with the prevailing westerlies, have long made navigation in these parts difficult, while the region's farmers have always struggled to survive on the thin soils that have accumulated here and there on the leeward side of some of the islands.

With great ingenuity, Norway's road builders have in recent years cobbled together the E39 coastal road, the **Kystvegen**, which traverses the coast from Bergen to Stavanger – with three ferry trips breaking up the journey. Travelling this road by **bus** takes a little under six hours, and you'll get to see far more of the coast this way than by using the **Hurtigbåt passenger express boat**. The bus leaves Bergen for Stavanger two or three times daily. Advance booking is recommended and a one-way ticket costs 350kr, though students and rail pass holders qualify for discounts. By car, drivers should allow six or seven hours for the whole drive, and would be well-advised to pick up car ferry timetables at the tourist office before they depart. Altogether, the various ferry crossings will cost around 280kr per driver and car; 75kr per passenger.

Stavanger and around

STAVANGER is something of a survivor. While other Norwegian coastal towns have fallen foul of the precarious fortunes of fishing, Stavanger has grown and flourished, and is now the proud possessor of a dynamic economy which has swelled the population to around 100,000. It was the herring fishery that first put money into the town, crowding its nineteenth-century wharves with coopers and smithies, net makers and menders. When this industry failed the town moved into shipbuilding and, ultimately, oil: the port builds the rigs for the offshore oilfields and afterwards refines the oil before dispatch.

None of which sounds terribly enticing, and certainly no one could describe Stavanger as picturesque. But if you have arrived here from abroad by ferry or plane, or find yourself at the end of the south coast's railway line, it's an easy city to adjust to and it's worth sparing at least a little time to see the attractive old town before heading onwards. If you stay longer, you can sally out into the surrounding fjords, where the hike to the **Preikestolen** rock is one of the most popular jaunts in the region.

Arrival, information and city transport

Stavanger **airport** is 14km south of the city at **Sola**. There's a Flybussen bus into Stavanger (every 20–30min; 40kr), which stops at the major downtown hotels, the ferry terminals and the bus and train stations. The **bus terminal** and **train station** (☎51 56 96 10) are on the southern side of the town's central lake, Breiavatnet, a pint-sized affair that's the most obvious downtown landmark. Also at the bus station, the Ruteservice Rogaland (Mon–Fri 8am–5pm, Sat 9am–1.30pm; ☎51 56 71 71) provides comprehensive details of buses, boats and trains in the city and surrounding area.

Fjord Line **ferries** (☎51 52 45 45) from Newcastle, Haugesund and Bergen berth on the west side of the harbour, beside Strandkaien, a five-minute walk from the main square, Torget, which is itself immediately to the north of Breiavatnet. Hurtigbåt **passenger express boats** use the terminal at the foot of Kirkegata, around 800m from the city centre. All **local express boats and ferries** for the islands and fjords around Stavanger arrive at and depart from either the Hurtigbåt terminal or the Fiskepiren terminal, about ten minutes' walk southeast along the waterfront. Finally, most pleasure cruises depart from the east side of the main harbour below Torget.

If you arrive by **car**, on-street **parking** is difficult, but not impossible. Central car parks include those beside the bus station, the post office and Skagenkaien.

Information

The **tourist office** overlooks Torget from its bright and breezy premises at Rosenkildetorget 1 (June–Aug daily 9am–8pm; April & May Mon–Fri 9am–5pm, Sat 9am–2pm; Jan–March & Sept–Dec Mon–Fri 9am–4pm, Sat 9am–2pm; ☎51 85 92 00, *www.destinasjon-stavanger.no*). They'll give you the useful free *Stavanger City Guide* and *På Gang*, a free monthly brochure detailing forthcoming cultural events. They also carry a large range of leaflets from elsewhere in Norway, provide local bus and ferry timetables, and can arrange guided tours (see p.271).

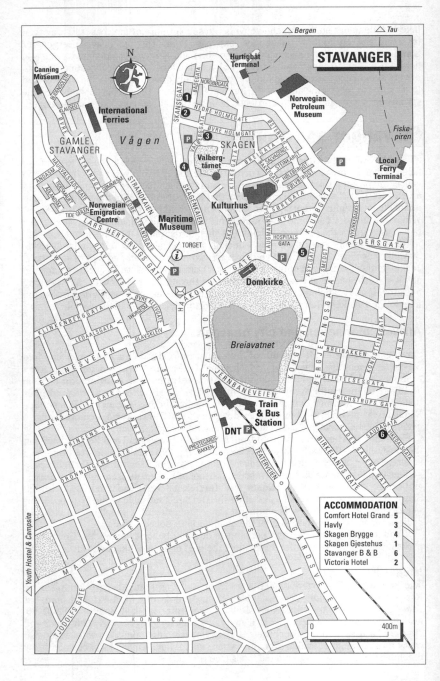

City transport

Just about everywhere in Stavanger is walkable, while the town's surroundings are accessible with a variety of local boats and buses departing from the terminals listed on p.269. For a more formal introduction to the city and surrounding area, consider taking a **guided tour**. There's an enjoyable two-hour walking tour of Stavanger (mid-June to mid-Aug Tues & Thurs at 11am; 105kr), in English and Norwegian, starting at the tourist office and taking in the historic quarter of Gamle Stavanger. The fjords can be seen from sightseeing boats, which depart regularly throughout the summer from Skagenkaien – tickets are available at the quayside from around 200kr.

Accommodation

There's plenty of choice of **accommodation** in Stavanger. Half a dozen hotels are clustered in Stavanger's compact centre, each of which offers substantial summer discounts. Alternatively, there are a couple of convenient, no-frills guesthouses and, further afield, the youth hostel and campsite.

Hotels and guesthouses

Comfort Hotel Grand, Klubbgata 3 (☎51 89 58 00, fax 51 89 57 10). A good central choice, close to all the bars and restaurants. The rooms are smart, modern and spacious, and the price includes a very good buffet breakfast. ④/②.

Havly Hotell, Valberggata 1 (☎51 89 67 00, fax 51 89 50 25). Spick-and-span modern hotel in the narrow side streets off Skagenkaien. Comfortable, quiet rooms. ④/②.

Skagen Brygge Hotell, Skagenkaien 30 (☎51 85 00 00, fax 51 85 00 01). A delightful quayside hotel built in the style of an old warehouse, but with lots of glass and enjoyable views over the harbour. The rooms are modern and tastefully decorated, the buffet breakfast outstanding, and delicious tit-bits – cheese, pickled herring etc – are offered at tea-time as free nibbles. The only quibble is the noise from outside on summer weekends, when your best bet is probably to get a room at the back or on the top floor. ⑤/③.

Skagen Gjestehus, Nedre Holmegate 2 (☎51 89 55 85, fax 51 89 55 86). This utilitarian guest-house occupies an old wooden building on the east side of the harbour. Frugal, basic rooms – but cheap. ②.

Stavanger Bed & Breakfast, Vikedalsgaten 1a (☎51 56 25 00, fax 51 56 25 01). Straightforward, inexpensive modern option in an unexciting residential area a five-minute walk southeast of the central lake. ①.

Victoria Hotel, Skansegata 1 (☎51 86 70 00, fax 51 86 70 10). One of the Rica chain, this large hotel occupies a big old building with a fancy portico overlooking the east side of the harbour. The foyer has kept much of its Victorian appearance, complete with wood panelling, leather sofas and model ships, and the comfortable rooms beyond are in broadly period style. ⑤/③.

Hostels and camping

Mosvangen Camping, Tjensvollveien 1 (☎51 53 29 71, fax 51 87 20 55). By the lake, next door to the youth hostel. Has cabins as well as tent and caravan pitches. Open late May to early Sept.

Mosvangen Youth Hostel, Henrik Ibsens gate 21 (☎51 87 29 00, fax 51 87 06 30). This plain IYHF youth hostel occupies a lakeside setting 3km from the centre: take Madlaveien west from near the station and turn left just beyond Mosvatnet lake on to Tjensvollveien – Henrik Ibsens gate is its continuation. Advance reservations advised. Has self-catering and laundry facilities, plus doubles (①). Breakfasts cost 60kr. Open mid-May to mid-Sept.

The Town

Much of central Stavanger is modern, built with oil money, a flashy but surprisingly likeable ensemble of mini tower-blocks. The only relic of the medieval city is the twelfth-century **Domkirke** (Mon & Tues 11am–2pm, Wed–Sat 10am–3pm; free), up above Torget, whose pointed-hat towers signal a Romanesque church that's suffered from several poorly conceived renovations. The simple interior, built by English craftsmen, has fared badly too, spoilt by ornate seventeenth-century additions including an intricate pulpit and five huge memorial tablets adorning the walls of the aisles – a jumble of richly carved angels, crucifixes, death's heads, animals and apostles.

A brief stroll away, beyond the fresh fish and flower stalls of **Torget**, is the **Skagen** area, built on the bumpy promontory of land which forms the eastern side of the harbour. It's an oddly discordant district, a clumsy mixture of the old and new that incorporates the town's main shopping area, whose mazy street plan is the only legacy of the original Viking settlement. The spiky **Valbergtårnet** (Valberg tower), atop the highest point and guarded by three rusty cannons, is the one specific sight, a nineteenth-century firewatch, offering sweeping views of the city and its industry. Beside the waterfront on the far side of Skagen, the oil industry celebrates its achievements in the gleaming **Norwegian Petroleum Museum** (Norsk Oljemuseum; May–Aug daily 10am–7pm; Sept–April Mon–Wed, Fri & Sat 10am–5pm, Thurs & Sun 10am–7pm; 60kr). Housed in a hangar-like auditorium, the museum has displays on North Sea geology, oil extraction and the like, complete with bits of drills and other oil platform paraphernalia. There are several interactive exhibits too – including a simulated helicopter ride and a step-in diving bell – plus an honest account of the disasters that have occasionally hit the industry. Quite whether the oil industry is of interest to outsiders is another question.

The town's star turn is, however, **Gamle Stavanger** (Old Stavanger), on the western side of the harbour. Though very different in appearance from the modern structures back in the centre, the buildings here were also the product of a boom. From the first decade of the nineteenth century to around 1870, the herring turned up offshore in their millions. Benefiting from this slice of luck, Stavanger flourished and expanded, and the number of merchants and ship owners in the town increased dramatically. Huge profits were made from the exported fish, which were salted and later, as the technology improved, canned. Today, some of the wooden stores and warehouses flanking the western quayside hint at their nineteenth-century pedigree, but it's the succession of narrow, cobbled lanes behind them that show Gamle Stavanger to best advantage. Formerly the home of local seafarers, craftsmen and cannery workers, the area has been maintained as a residential quarter, mercifully free of tourist tat, and the long rows of white-painted clapboard houses are immaculately maintained and come complete with gas lamps, picket fences and tiny terraced gardens.

The **Canning Museum** (Hermetikkmuseet; mid-June to mid-Sept daily 11am–4pm; early June & late Sept Mon–Thurs 11am; Oct–May Sun 11am–4pm; 40kr), right in the heart of Gamle Stavanger at Øvre Strandgate 88, occupies an old sardine-canning factory and gives a glimpse into the industry that saved Stavanger from collapse at the end of the nineteenth century. The herring largely disappeared from local waters in the 1870s, but the canning factories kept the economy afloat and remained Stavanger's main source of employment until as late as 1960: in the 1920s there were seventy different canneries in the town and the last one only closed down as recently as 1983. A visit to an old canning factory may not sound too enticing, but the museum is actually very good; they also smoke their own (very tasty) sardines on the first Sunday of every month and every Tuesday and Thursday from mid-June to mid-August.

Walk back through the old town towards the centre and you'll pass the **Maritime Museum** (Sjøfartsmuseum; same times as Canning Museum; 40kr) at Nedre Strandgate 17. Sited in a restored warehouse, this gives another insight into the history of Stavanger, with exhibits covering the various trades that served the shipping industry. There are some nice touches, like the old sailmaker's room, and some reconstructed shop and office interiors.

Eating

Although prices are marginally inflated by oil workers' business-expense accounts, Stavanger is a great place to **eat**, with several fine seafood restaurants clustered on the east side of the harbour along Skagenkaien. For something less expensive, the best option is to stick to the more mundane cafés and restaurants near the Kulturhus in the heart of the Skagen shopping area.

Akropolis, Sølvberggata 14 (☎51 89 14 54). Near the Kulturhus, this is a medium-priced Greek restaurant housed in a white wooden building on a cobbled street. Closed Mon.

Café Sting, Valberget 3. Right next to the Valbergtårnet, this laid-back café-bar is probably the coolest place in town. Tasty, inexpensive Mediterranean and Norwegian food.

La Piazza, Rosenkildehuset. Above the tourist office, this smart Italian restaurant serves delicious pizzas, pastas and more. Expensive.

Saken er Biff, Skagen 37 (☎51 89 60 80). No self-respecting oil town could do without a steakhouse – and this is it. A couple of stuffed cattle heads remind you what you're eating – from sirloin to tenderloin at around 200kr per main course. Fish dishes, reindeer and ostrich too.

Sjøhuset Skagen, Skagenkaien 16 (☎51 89 51 80). Fine fish and seafood restaurant on the harbour, with monkfish a speciality. Main dishes are around 200kr.

Skagen Bageri, Skagen 18. This pleasant coffee house, with its finely carved antique door and lintel, occupies the prettiest of the old wooden buildings on Skagen, one block up from the quayside. Great pastries, cakes and snacks at reasonable prices.

Drinking and nightlife

Stavanger is lively at night, particularly at weekends when a rum assortment of oil workers, sailors, fishermen, executives, tourists and office workers gather in the **bars and clubs** on and around the harbourside Skagenkaien to live (or rather drink) it up. Most places stay open until 2am or later, with rowdier revellers lurching from one bar to the next.

For more subdued evenings, check out the programme at the **Stavanger Concert Hall** (Konserthus; ☎51 53 70 00) in Bjergsted park, north of the centre beyond Gamle Stavanger, where there are regular concerts by the Stavanger Symphony Orchestra and visiting artists. There's also an eight-screen **cinema**, Stavanger Kinematografer, inside the Kulturhus, on Sølvberggaten (☎51 50 70 30).

Bars and clubs

Hansen Hjørnet, Skagenkaien 18. Whenever the sun pops out, the outside terrace of this bar fills up fast. Good fun. If it's full, try the comparable terrace of **Victoria Terrasse**, along the street at no. 37.

Newsman, Skagen 14. Attractive, busy bar where the newspaper theme means papers to read and a trendy clientele. Open until 2am. One block up from the east side of the harbour.

Taket, Strandkaien. The best club in town, across the harbour from most of the bars and metres from the tourist office. Open midnight–4am (Thurs–Sat from 10pm); don't be surprised if you have to queue.

Timbuktu, Strandkaien. Flashy café-bar beneath *Taket*. Noted for its imaginative decor and groovy atmosphere.

Yank's, Skagenkaien 24. Popular bar-cum-club, with a gold-painted Statue of Liberty above the door and live bands at the weekend. Open until 4am.

Listings

Airlines Braathens (☎51 51 10 00); British Airways (☎80 03 00 77); SAS (☎81 00 33 00). All three have offices at the airport.

Bike rental Sykkelhuset Løkkeveien 33 (☎51 53 99 10).

Car rental Budget, Lagårdsveien 125 (☎51 52 21 33) and at the airport (☎51 65 07 29); Hertz, Olav V's gate 13 (☎51 52 00 00) and at the airport (☎51 65 10 96); Stavanger Bilutleie, Fritjof Nansensveien 45 (☎51 91 09 70).

Dentist Egil Undem, Kannikbakken 6 (☎51 52 84 52).

Emergencies Ambulance ☎113; Police ☎112; Doctor ☎51 53 33 33.

Ferries Fjord Line, Strandkaien (☎51 52 45 45); Ruteservice Rogaland (☎51 56 71 71); Hurtigbåt express boats to Bergen, Flaggruten (☎51 86 87 80).

Hiking The very helpful DNT-affiliated Stavanger Turistforening, Olav V's gate 18 (Mon–Fri 10am–4pm; ☎51 84 02 00), will advise on local hiking routes and sell a comprehensive range of hiking maps. They maintain around 900km of hiking trails and over thirty cabins in the mountains east of Stavanger, as well as organizing ski schools on winter weekends. They also offer general advice about local conditions and weather. You can join the DNT here too.

Laundry Sentralvaskeriet, Breibakken 2, by Breiavatnet. Coin-operated launderette.

Left luggage In the express boat terminal (Mon–Fri 6.30am–10pm, Sat 6.30am–6pm, Sun 9am–10pm); the train station (daily 6.30am–10pm, Sat until 4pm); and the bus station (daily 7am–midnight).

Pharmacy Løveapoteket, Olav V's gate 11 (☎51 52 06 07). Open daily until 11pm (until 8pm on public holidays).

Post Office The main post office is at Haakon VII's gate 9 (Mon–Wed & Fri 8am–5pm, Thurs 8am–6pm, Sat 9am–1pm). Currency exchange at competitive rates.

Taxis Stavanger Taxisentral, Sjøhagen 10 (☎51 90 90 90).

Vinmonopolet Off-licence at Olav V's gate 13.

Around Stavanger: Preikestolen

Stavanger sits on a narrow promontory just to the south of the wide waters of the Boknafjord, a deep indentation in the coast speckled with islets and skerries. Behind the town, longer, narrower fjords drill far inland. The most diverting of these is **Lysefjord**, famous for its precipitous cliffs and an especially striking rock formation, the **Preikestolen** (Pulpit Rock), a distinctive 25m-square table of rock with a sheer 600-metre drop down to the fjord below it on three sides. From the middle of June to late August you can get there by public transport: from Fiskepiren in Stavanger catch the ferry for the forty-minute trip to **TAU**, where a twice-daily bus runs the 20km to the start of the trail to Preikestolen (check at the tourist office to see which ferries coincide with the bus service and to confirm return times). From here, it's a four-hour hike there and back to Preikestolen along a clearly marked trail. The first half is along a comparatively easy, stone-flagged path, but the second half is rocky and awkward. The change in elevation is 350m; take food and water. If you want to hang around, there's a delightful **youth hostel** (June–Aug; ☎94 53 11 11, off season ☎51 84 02 00; fax 51 84 02 14, off season 51 74 91 11; 130kr, doubles ➂) by the start of the trail. Perched high up on a hillside, with great views over the surrounding mountains, the hostel comprises a small complex of turf-roofed lodges, each with a spick-and-span pine interior. It's popular with school groups and reservations are advised.

The Hardangerfjord

To the east of Bergen, the obvious initial target is the 120-kilometre **Hardangerfjord**, whose wide waters are overlooked by a rough, craggy shoreline and a scattering of tiny settlements. At its eastern end, the fjord fractures into a web of lesser fjords and it's here you'll find the district's most appealing villages, **Utne**, **Lofthus** and **Ulvik**, each of which has an attractive fjordside setting and one good place to stay – or several, in the case of Ulvik. To the east of these tributary fjords rises the **Hardangervidda**, a mountain plateau of remarkable, lunar-like beauty and a favourite with Norwegian hikers.

The plateau can be reached from almost any direction; from the Hardangerfjord a favourite starting point is **Kinsarvik**, though this involves a stiff day-long climb up from Sørfjord. Another primary access point is Finse (see p.279).

There are no trains in the Hardanger area, but **buses** are fairly frequent, allowing you to get to the three recommended bases (Utne, Lofthus and Ulvik) without much difficulty, except on Sundays when services are curtailed.

East from Bergen to the Kvanndal ferry

Heading east from Bergen by bus or car to the **Hardangerfjord**, you first have to clear the polluted tunnels of the E16, an unpleasant 30km, before you can fork off onto Hwy 7. In contrast, this is an exhilarating trip, with the road twisting up the valley past thundering waterfalls and around tight bends before chasing down the other side to tiny **NORHEIMSUND**. Sheltered in a bay of the Hardangerfjord, there is precious little to the town – one main street and a pocket-sized harbour – but like many fjord settlements, it's the travel in between that is the real attraction.There are also **Hurtigbåt passenger express** services from Norheimsund to Utne, Kinsarvik, Lofthus and Ulvik.

From Norheimsund, Hwy 7 sticks to the rugged shoreline as it travels east to the ferry dock at **Kvanndal**, another pleasant ride with every turning bringing fresh mountain and fjord views as the Hardangerfjord begins to divide. There's a choice of routes from Kvanndal: you can either press on along the northern shore of the Hardangerfjord towards Ulvik and Voss, or stay with the main, long-distance bus route by taking the Kvanndal ferry (every 1–2hr) over to Utne (20min) or Kinsarvik (50min).

Utne, Kinsarvik and Lofthus

UTNE, the Kvanndal ferry's midway point, is at the head of the peninsula that divides the Hardangerfjord from the slender Sørfjord. It's small, but the wooden houses huddling the hillside behind the jetty are very pretty and include the appealing *Utne Hotel* (☎53 66 69 83, fax 53 66 69 50; ④), whose 25 rooms occupy a cheerful clapboard complex. The older parts of the hotel are stuffed with local bygones, including examples of the brightly painted furniture that was once typical of the district. There's been an inn here since 1722 and Utne's heritage is celebrated at the **Hardanger Folk Museum** (Hardanger Folkemuseum; May, June, Aug & early Sept Mon–Sat 10am–4pm, Thurs till 6pm, Sun noon–4pm; July daily 10am–6pm; early Sept to April Mon–Fri 10am–3pm, Thurs till 6pm; 30kr), just up the hill behind the hotel. The museum has an assortment of old buildings – a grocery, boat and farm houses – in its open-air section, while the exhibitions inside include one featuring traditional folk costume: the headdresses of the Hardanger were amongst the most elaborate in Norway and a popular subject for the romantic painters of the nineteenth century.

From Utne, the car ferry (every 2hr; 30min) bobs over the mouth of the Sørfjord to **KINSARVIK**, a humdrum little town that was once an important Viking marketplace. The Vikings stored their boats in the loft of the town's sturdy stone **church** (May to mid-Sept daily 10am–7pm; free), though this was clumsily restored in the 1880s, leaving only hints of its previous decoration. If you decide to stay in Kinsarvik, there's one **hotel** – the *Best Western Kinsarvik Fjord Hotel* (☎53 66 31 00, fax 53 66 33 74; ④), which occupies a large but quite attractive, ivy-clad modern block by the ferry dock.

Draped beside the Sørfjord, with the Folgefonna glacier glinting in the distance, **LOFTHUS** is an idyllic hamlet of narrow lanes and mellow stone walls where a scattering of old grass-roofed houses sits among the orchards, pinky-white with blossom in the springtime. It's the overall impression which counts, though the **church** (May to mid-Sept daily 10am–7pm; free), dating from 1250, is a good-looking stone structure

---

MOVING ON FROM KINSARVIK AND LOFTHUS

From Kinsarvik and Lofthus there's a choice of three main routes. Heading **north**, Hwy 13 runs the 19km to Brimnes, where a car ferry (every 30min; 10min) shuttles over to Bruravik for Ulvik and Voss (see opposite). Beyond Brimnes, Hwy 13 becomes Hwy 7, which travels **east** across the Hardangervidda for Geilo and, ultimately, Oslo. Alternatively, if you're planning to travel **south** and then east towards Oslo on the E134, you certainly shouldn't set out with the intention of overnighting at the next place along the way, **ODDA**, an eminently missable zinc-producing and iron-smelting town at the head of the Sørfjord. There are **buses** along all these routes.

---

with immensely thick stone walls and several bright but crude wall and wood paintings. A stream gushes through the village, tumbling down the steep escarpment behind it to bubble past the delightful *Ullensvang Gjesteheim* (☎53 66 12 36, fax 53 66 15 19; ②), a huddle of antique timber buildings with thirteen cosy and unassuming rooms and great food. A kilometre north of the village is the plush modern *Hotel Ullensvang* (☎53 66 11 00, fax 53 66 15 20; ⑤/④), a massive, solitary affair plonked on the water's edge.

The Hardangervidda plateau

The **Hardangervidda** is Europe's largest mountain plateau, occupying a 100-square-kilometre slab of land east of the Hardangerfjord and south of the Bergen–Oslo railway. The plateau is characterized by rolling fells and wide stretches of level ground, its rocky surfaces strewn with lakelets and rivers. The whole plateau is above the treeline, and at times has an almost lunar look, although even within this elemental landscape there are variations. To the north, in the vicinity of Finse, there are mountains and a glacier, the **Hardangerjøkulen**, while the west is wetter – and the flora somewhat richer – than the barer moorland to the east. The lichen that covers the rocks is savoured by herds of reindeer, who leave their winter grazing lands on the east side of the plateau in the spring, chewing their way west to their breeding grounds before returning east again after the autumn rutting season.

The Hardangervidda was one of the main crossing points between east and west Norway, with horse traders, cattle drivers and Danish dignitaries all cutting across the plateau along cairned trails. These are often still in use as part of a dense network of trails and tourist huts that has been developed in recent decades. Roughly one third of the plateau has been incorporated within the **Hardangervidda National Park**, but much of the rest is protected too, so hikers won't notice a deal of difference between the park and its immediate surroundings. The entire plateau is also popular for winter cross-country hut-to-hut ski touring. Many hikers and skiers are content with a day on the Hardangervidda, but some find the wide-skied, lichen-dappled scenery particularly enchanting and travel from one end of the plateau to the other, a seven- or eight-day expedition.

In terms of **access**, the Oslo–Bergen train line tracks across the northern edge of the Hardangervidda, pausing at **Finse**, from where hikers and skiers head off across the plateau in all directions. Finse is not, however, accessible by road, so motorists and bus travellers use Hwy 7 (see p.242), which runs across the plateau between Eidfjord and Geilo. There's precious little in the way of human habitation on this 100km-long stretch of road, but you can pick up the plateau's hiking trails at several points: **Dyranut** and **Halne** are two such places, respectively 39km and 47km from Eidfjord. Many hikers prefer to walk onto the Hardangervidda from Kinsarvik and Lofthus on the west side of the Hardangervidda, but this does involve an arduous day-long trek up to the plateau.

Ulvik

Tucked away in a snug corner of the Hardangerfjord, the pocket-sized village of **ULVIK** strings prettily along the shoreline with fruit orchards dusting the green hills behind. There's nothing particular to see: the town's main claim to fame as the place where potatoes were first grown in Norway in 1765 just about sums things up, but it's an excellent place to unwind, and popular small resort with a cluster of good hotels. Hiking trails lattice the surrounding hills, or you can take the 9km-long country road leading east up the Osafjord to the smattering of farmsteads that constitute **OSA**. Here, in the forested hills about 1km above the fjord, is one of the region's more unusual sights, the timber-and-brick **Stream Nest** sculpture (May–Sept daily 11am–5pm; 40kr), built to resemble a gigantic bird's nest and perched above a green river valley rimmed by stern hills. The sculpture was built for the 1994 Lillehammer Winter Olympics and moved here afterwards.

Ulvik is off the main **bus** routes, but there are regular local buses here from Voss and a sparser service from Kinsarvik and Lofthus via the Brimnes–Bruravik ferry. There are also **Hurtigbåt passenger express boats** to Ulvik from Norheimsund via Kinsarvik and Lofthus. Ulvik's jetty is in the centre of the village and buses pull in here too. From the jetty, it's a couple of minutes' walk along the waterfront to the **tourist office** (mid-May to mid-Sept Mon–Sat 8.30am–5pm, Sun 1–5pm; mid-Sept to mid-May Mon–Fri 8.30am–1.30pm; ☎56 52 63 60), which has literature on all local walks and hires out bikes (150kr per day). Among the **hotels**, the big deal hereabouts is the *Rica Brakenes Hotel* (☎56 52 61 05, fax 56 52 64 10; ⑤/③), a large and luxurious modern hotel occupying a lovely fjordside location in the centre of the village. If the *Brakenes* is a bit too big and domineering for your liking, the *Ulvik* (☎56 52 62 00, fax 56 52 66 41; ④/③), another *Rica* hotel a five-minute walk east along the waterfront, is a good deal less overpowering. Again, it's the setting rather than the architecture that appeals, with the fjord stretching out in front of the hotel, overlooked by the balconies of the fifty-odd modern bedrooms. Different again is the *Ulvik Fjord Pensjonat* (May to late Sept; ☎56 52 61 70, fax 56 52 61 60; ③), a well-maintained and appealing pension situated a ten-minute walk west from the centre along the waterfront. The rooms in the main building are plain but comfortable and there's a modern annexe too. Breakfasts are first-rate and evening meals are available by prior arrangement. Otherwise, **eat** at either of the *Rica* hotels – the *Ulvik* edges the other in terms of price and informality.

Voss, Ørneberget and Finse

Without a fjord in sight, **Voss** is primarily a winter ski resort. It's also the first major station east of Bergen on the Bergen–Oslo rail line and a handy base for a day-trip by train up the scenic Raun Valley to the Hardangervidda plateau beyond. The most popular target on this stretch of the line is the **Myrdal** junction, but only because the railway to Flåm meets the main line here. However, you can also disembark at **Ørneberget** (slow trains only) as well as **Finse**, two isolated hiking bases which are ideal for explorations of the Hardangervidda plateau (see opposite). Drivers should note that a mountain road travels east from Voss to Ørneberget, but no further – Myrdal and Finse can't be reached by car.

Voss

Around 100km east of Bergen on the E16, **VOSS** is the first stop for many heading into the fjord region. Impressions are generally favourable, since it's a lakeside town of just 14,000 people, sporting a thirteenth-century church and surrounded by snow-capped

---

SKIING IN VOSS

Skiing in Voss starts in December and continues until mid-April – nothing fancy, but good for an enjoyable few days. From near the train station, a **cable car** – the Hangursbanen – climbs 700m to give access to several short runs as well as the first of two further ski lifts which take you up another 300m. A one-day lift pass costs 200kr, 140kr for half-a-day. There's a choice of downhill ski routes of international standard, or you can take longer and gentler downhill routes through the hills above town.

Full **equipment** for both downhill and cross-country skiing can be hired from Voss Skiskule & Skiutlege (☎56 51 00 32), at the upper station of the Hangursbanen cable car, and costs around 200–300kr per day. They also offer lessons in alpine, telemark and snowboarding techniques. Some trails are floodlit in January and February. More information on skiing in Voss is available from the tourist office.

---

hills, but it's best to remember that Voss is essentially a winter sports haven. Voss has also long been a trading centre on one of the main routes between west and east Norway – though you'd barely guess it from the modern appearance of the town today. In 1023, King Olav visited to check that the population had all converted to Christianity, and stuck a big stone cross here to make his point. Two centuries later another king, Magnus Lagabøte, built a church in Voss to act as the focal point for the whole region. This church, the **Vangskyrkja** (mid-May to mid-Sept daily 10am–4pm; occasionally open in winter, but no set hours; free) still stands, its eccentric octagonal spire rising above stone walls up to two metres thick. The interior is splendid, a surprisingly flamboyant affair with a Baroque reredos and a folksy rood screen showing a crucified Jesus attended by two cherubs. The ceiling is even more unusual, its timbers painted in 1696 with a cotton-wool cloudy sky inhabited by flying angels – the nearer you get to the high altar, the more of them there are. That's pretty much it as far as specific sights go, though you could take a stroll by the **lake**, Vangsvatnet, or wander the central shops and cafés – if you've come from the hamlets and villages further north, the shopping here might seem something of a treat.

Practicalities

Buses stop outside the **train station** at the western end of the town centre; if you're just passing through, there are coin-operated luggage lockers here. From the train station, it's five minutes' walk to the **tourist office** (June–Aug Mon–Sat 9am–7pm, Sun 2–7pm; Sept–May Mon–Fri 9am–4pm; ☎56 52 08 00) on the main street, Uttrågata – veer right round the Vangskyrkja church and it's on the right. They largely concern themselves with hiking and touring in the surrounding area, but pick up a free *Voss Guide*, which has useful listings and any amount of handy information and timetables. If you plan to go to Flåm via Myrdal (see opposite), and don't intend stopping over anywhere on the way, consider buying a **"Norway in a Nutshell"** ticket from Voss tourist office or train station. This inclusive train-bus-ferry ticket for the Voss–Myrdal–Flåm–Gudvangen–Voss route is available all year, costs just over 350kr and is an excellent way of seeing something of the fjords if time is short.

A right turn from the train station and a ten-minute walk along the lake, away from the town centre, brings you to the excellent **youth hostel** (Feb, March & June to mid-Sept; ☎56 51 20 17, fax 56 51 22 05; doubles ①), overlooking the water and complete with its own sauna. It serves large, cheap evening meals (and good breakfasts), though there's no kitchen for guests; you can rent bikes and canoes here, too. The **campsite**, *Voss Camping* (☎56 51 15 97), is by the lake south of the Vangskyrkja church along the Prestegardsalléen footpath – turn left from the train station and take the right fork at the church. It's open all year round and has a few cabins, bicycle and boat rental, and

MOVING ON FROM VOSS

From Voss, the **train route east to Oslo** is one of the most impressive rides in the country, taking in a good number of forests, waterfalls, windy mountains and wild valleys. Some of this route's finest scenery is near the beginning, just east of Voss as the train clambers up the Raun Valley to Myrdal, where you change for the magnificent train journey down to **Flåm**. Beyond Myrdal, continuing on the main line, is **Finse**, perfectly situated for hiking and skiing on the Hardangervidda plateau.

Express buses run north from Voss along the E16, turning down Hwy 13 to reach the Sognefjord at **Vik**. This is another stupendous journey with the road making a dramatic traverse of the bleak wastes of Vikafjell mountain, the snow piled high to either side until at least the end of June. Just beyond Vik, the **Vangsnes** ferry gives ready access to **Balestrand** and the northern shore of the Sognefjord. Also departing Voss is a local bus service (4–6 daily; 1hr 10min) straight along the E16 to **Gudvangen**, connecting with the Hurtigbåt express passenger boats from Gudvangen to Flåm and with car ferries to Kaupanger (2–4 daily; 2hr) – but check connections before you set out. Once daily from late June to mid-September, the bus links with the summertime bus running from Gudvangen to Flåm and Geilo. Flåm and Gudvangen are connected by one of the more spirited pieces of tunnelling on display in the fjords, with two separate stretches of 5km and 11km slicing through the mountains, although even these are pipsqueaks compared with the 24km-long tunnel currently under construction between the Aurlandsdal valley, 8km northeast of Flåm, and the E16 near Fodnes. This monster is scheduled to open in 2001.

washing machines. As you might expect, there are plenty of cheapish (①–②) **pensions** in Voss, and though they'll be fully booked during winter, you should have little trouble in summer, when special rates apply. Ask at the tourist office for the best deals. Easily the best **hotel** is *Fleischer's Hotel* (☎56 52 05 00, fax 56 52 05 01; ⑤/④), next door to the train station. Dating from the 1880s, the hotel's high-gabled and towered facade overlooks the lake and consists of the original building and a modern wing built in the same style. It has the whiff of real luxury: the bedrooms are plush, the **restaurant** is first rate and there's a terrace bar as well. Their all-inclusive food-and-lodging deals are well worth investigating – it's a great place to stay.

East to Ørneberget and Finse

All the trains pulling east out of Voss cut up the Raun Valley, but only some of the slower services stop, after about 45min, at **ØRNEBERGET**, from where it's possible to hike south across the Hardangervidda. Ørneberget also boasts the **Mjølfjell youth hostel** (March, April & mid-June to Sept; ☎56 52 31 50, fax 56 52 31 51; doubles ①), a comfortable mountain lodge in a beautiful, isolated setting beside a rushing river, and with its own heated outside pool. The hostel has single, double and family rooms, several of them en suite, has self-catering and laundry facilities, offers cycle and canoe rental, and is footsteps from several alpine ski runs. You can drive here too – just: the hostel is at the end of a narrow minor road that begins in Voss; but you can't drive any further east to either Myrdal or Finse.

Finse

Beyond Ørneberget, the higher reaches of the railway line are desolate places even in good weather. All trains stop at Myrdal, a remote railway junction in the middle of nowhere where you change for Flåm (see p.280), and then proceed to **FINSE**, the railway's highest point, a solitary outpost glued to the edge of a lock on the northern periphery of the Hardangervidda. Finse is nothing more than its station and a few isolated buildings, bunkered down against the howling winds that rip across the plateau in wintertime. Cross-country skiing is particularly energetic here, with locals buckling up as soon as they leave the station and zipping off into the distance. You can rent cross-country ski gear in Finse if you want to join in; at other times of year it's possible to hike south on the track round the **Hardangerjøkulen** glacier to reach the trails and huts that traverse the main body of the Hardangervidda. From Finse, it takes about eleven hours to reach Hwy 7 at **Dyranut**, so most hikers heading in this direction overnight at the self-service **Kjeldebu** DNT hut (March to mid-Oct), eight hours out.

You can also rent mountain bikes in Finse for the ride along the old construction road, the partly surfaced **Rallarvegen**, originally laid to provide access for men and materials during the building of the mountain section of the railroad. Eighty kilometres long, the Rallarvegen runs west from Haugastøl to Finse and then continues to Flåm; there's also a 43km extension from Myrdal junction to Mjølfjell and Ørneberget. The most popular stretch leads west from Finse to Myrdal, a distance of 38km, though you may have to dispense with the first 21km (to Hallingskeid) as this is the highest part of the Rallarvegen and can be blocked by snow as late as July: check conditions locally. You'll need to be reasonably fit to make the journey too. In Finse, **cycle hire** is available at *Finse 1222* hotel and shop (☎56 52 67 11), who have developed a modified version of the mountain bike ideally suited for the Rallarvegen. At the end of the cycle ride, NSB railways will transport your bike back to the point of departure for 80kr, regardless of the distance involved.

In terms of **places to stay**, DNT operates a fully staffed 150-bed lodge complex at Finse, *Finsehytta* (mid-Feb to mid-May & early July to mid-Sept; ☎56 52 67 32, fax 56 52 67 60; ③) and there's also a hotel, *Finse 1222* (Feb–Sept; ☎56 52 67 11, fax 56 52 67 17; ②). Heading east from Finse, the train takes forty minutes to reach Geilo, three and half hours more to Oslo.

The train to Flåm and Aurlandsfjord

Lonely **MYRDAL**, just forty minutes by train from Voss, is the start of one of Europe's most celebrated branch lines, the 20-kilometre, 900-metre plummet down the **Flåmsdal** – a fifty-minute **train ride** not to be missed under any circumstances. The track, which took four years to lay in the 1930s, spirals down the mountainside through hand-dug tunnels, at one point travelling through a reverse tunnel to drop nearly three hundred metres. The gradient of the line is one of the steepest anywhere in the world, and as the tiny train screeches its way down the mountain, past cascading waterfalls, it's worth remembering that it has five separate sets of brakes, each capable of bringing it to a stop. The service runs all year round, a local lifeline during the deep winter months.

People have in the past risen to the challenge and undertaken the five-hour **walk** from the railway junction at Myrdal down the old road into the valley, instead of taking the train, but much the better option is to disembark about halfway down and walk in from there. **Berekvam** station, halfway along at 343m, will do very nicely, leaving an enthralling two-to three-hour hike through changing mountain scenery down to Flåm.

Flåm

FLÅM village, the train's destination, lies alongside meadows and orchards on the Aurlandsfjord, a slender branch of the Sognefjord. However, having made the exciting journey, you could be excused for wondering why you bothered. The fjordside complex adjoining the train terminus is crass and commercial – souvenir trolls and the like – and on summer days the tiny village heaves with the tourists who pour off the train. But a brief stroll is enough to leave the crowds behind at the harbourside, while out of season, or in the early evening when the day-trippers have all moved on, Flåm remains a pleasant spot, and an especially restful place to spend the night.

The harbourside complex is ugly, but it does hold everything you'll need, from a supermarket and train ticket office to a **tourist office** (June–Aug daily 8.30am–8.30pm; May & Sept Mon–Fri 10.30am–6.30pm; Oct–April Mon–Fri 8am–4pm; ☎57 63 21 06), where you can buy fjord ferry tickets and pick up local transport timetables as well as information on hikes in the Flåmsdal valley. If you do stay, neat and trim *Flåm Camping*, a couple of minutes' signposted walk from the train station, has tent spaces and cabins (①), and also incorporates a small and well-kept **youth hostel** (May–Sept; ☎57 63 21 21, fax 57 63 23 80; doubles ①). Flåm's only **hotel** is the *Fretheim Hotell* (☎57 63 22 00, fax 57 63 23 03; ④, ③ in winter), a rambling structure whose attractive older part, with its high-pitched roofs and white-painted clapboard, is now flanked by ungainly extensions. The gardens are attractive and the rooms are decorated in straightforward modern style. The hotel is set back from the water a couple of hundred metres from the station. The *Heimly Pensjonat* (☎57 63 23 00, fax 57 63 23 40; ②) provides simple but adequate lodgings in a routine modern block overlooking the fjord about 450m east of the train station along the seashore. The only good place to **eat** is the *Fretheim Hotell*.

By boat and bus from Flåm

From Flåm, there are daily **Hurtigbåt passenger express ferries** up the **Aurlandsfjord** and along the Sognefjord to Bergen. Ports of call include Leikanger, Vangsnes, Balestrand and Vik. The one-way trip to Bergen takes five and a half hours and costs 420kr, while Balestrand is two hours and costs 110kr. Hurtigbåt ferries also travel up the first half of the Aurlandsfjord and then down its tributary, the **Nærøyfjord**, four times daily between June and mid-September, once or twice daily the rest of the year. The Nærøyfjord is the narrowest fjord in Europe, its high rock faces keeping out the sun throughout the winter, its stern beauty making for a superb trip. At the end of the cruise, the ferry pulls into **GUDVANGEN**, a forlorn jetty at the southern tip of Nærøyfjord. From here, buses head east back to Flåm and south to Voss and Bergen. For the most part, bus and ferry times are co-ordinated, but confirm connections before you set out. The one-way ferry fare from Flåm to Gudvangen is 135kr, 170kr return, and the journey takes two hours.

Leaving Flåm by **bus**, there are two to four daily services west to Gudvangen, Voss and Bergen, and a sparser service (late June to Sept 1–4 daily) east to Geilo.

Sognefjord and Hwy 55 to Lom

Profoundly beautiful, the **Sognefjord** drills in from the coast for some 200km, its inner recesses splintering into half a dozen tributary fjords. Perhaps inevitably, none of the villages and small towns that dot the fjord quite live up to their setting, but **Balestrand** and **Fjærland** come close and are easily the best bases. Both are on the north side of the fjord which, given the lack of roads on the south side, is where you want (or pretty much have) to be – apart from Flåm, which is described opposite.

The Sognefjord's north bank is hugged by **Hwy 55** for almost the whole of its length and at **Sogndal** this same highway slices northeast, clipping past the **Lustrafjord** before climbing steeply to run along the western side of the **Jotunheimen mountains**. Even by Norwegian standards, this is an extravagantly beautiful journey, with the road eventually thumping down to **Lom** on Hwy 15. What's more, side roads lead off the highway to a pair of top-notch attractions, **Urnes stave church** – via a quick ferry ride

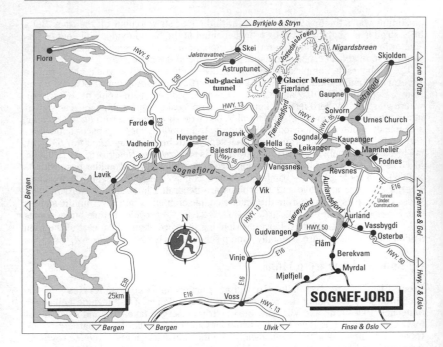

from **Solvorn** – and, further north, to the east side of the **Jostedalsbreen glacier** at **Nigardsbreen** (for more on the glacier, see p.290).

Transport connections to and around the Sognefjord are excellent. Located about halfway along the fjord, perhaps the most useful **car ferry** links Vangsnes, Hella and Dragsvik (for Balestrand), but the 24hr shuttle between Fodnes and Mannheller in the east is useful too, especially if you're arriving from Oslo on the E16 (see p.241). **Hurtigbåt passenger express boats** connect Bergen, Balestrand, Vangsnes and Flåm, and long-distance **buses** come up from Bergen via Voss to scuttle along the north shore between Hella and Sogndal – but not Balestrand, which is most easily reached by changing at Sogndal. Here, some services press on east to Oslo, others run up Hwy 5 to Fjærland and the Nordfjord. There is, however, only a limited local bus service up Hwy 55 between Sogndal and Lom (mid-June to Aug only).

Balestrand

An appealing first stop, **BALESTRAND** has been a tourist destination since the mid-nineteenth century, when it was discovered by European travellers in search of cool, clear air and picturesque mountain scenery. Kaiser Wilhelm II was a frequent visitor, as were the British. These days, the village is used as a touring base for the immediate area, as the battery of small hotels and restaurants above the quay testify. It's still very small in scale, though, and farming remains the principal livelihood among the 2000-strong population. With an hour or so to spare, take a peek at Balestrand's two attractions. The **English Church of St Olav** (free) is a spiky brown-and-beige wooden structure built in the general style of a stave church in 1897 at the behest of a British émigré, a certain Margaret Kvikne. In one of those curious hand-me-downs from Britain's imperial past, the church

---

MOVING ON FROM BALESTRAND

When it comes to moving on from Balestrand you're spoiled for choice. **Buses** travel east along the northern shore of the fjord to Sogndal, the first part of their journey to Oslo. At Sogndal, you can also change for Fjærland and Førde, where you can pick up the bus to Stryn. **Hurtigbåt passenger express boats** leave Balestrand for Bergen, Vik, Flåm and Sogndal, and, best of all, a local **passenger boat** sails north from Balestrand to Fjærland (June to mid-Sept 1 daily; 1hr 25min; 110kr). If you drive to Fjærland, be warned that a toll of 130kr is levied on Hwy 5 just south of the village. Finally, from Balestrand, it's 9km along the fjord to **Dragsvik**, where **car ferries** operate a triangular service sailing south across the fjord to Vangsnes (pedestrians 20kr; car and driver 54kr) and east to Hella (15kr; 36kr).

---

remains part of the Diocese of Gibraltar, which arranges English-language services during the summer. The Germans have left their mark too. About 400m south of the church along the fjord are two large **Viking burial mounds**, supposedly the tombs of King Bele and his wife, next to which the Kaiser has plonked a statue of the king in a heroic pose – there's a statue of his son across the fjord in Vangsnes to match.

There are no car ferries to Balestrand – the nearest you'll get is Dragsvik 9km to the north – but **Hurtigbåt passenger express boats** do call here, docking at the quayside in the town centre. **Buses** stop here too – but not direct from Bergen and Voss: coming from the south the easiest option is to change at Sogndal. From Balestrand's quayside, it's a couple of minutes' walk uphill to the **tourist office** (mid-June to mid-Aug Mon–Fri 7.30am–9pm, Sat 7.30am–6.30pm, Sun 8am–5.30pm; mid-Aug to mid-Sept Mon–Fri 7.30am–1pm & 3.30–5.30pm, Sat 7.30am–1pm & 3.30–6.30pm, Sun 8am–12.30pm & 4.30–5.30pm; mid- to late Sept Mon–Fri 9am–3pm; ☎57 69 12 55). They have a wide range of fjord leaflets, are good for maps showing local hiking routes in the surrounding mountains and rent bikes (100kr a day, no deposit).

For **accommodation**, try the charming *Midtnes Pensjonat* (☎57 69 11 33, fax 57 69 15 84; ③), about 300m from the dock behind the English church. It's a low-key, pleasantly sedate affair with a few plain but commodious rooms in a modern wing adjoining the original clapboard house; make sure to get a room with a fjord view. Another good choice, just 150m uphill from the dock, is the **youth hostel** (☎57 69 13 03, fax 57 69 16 70; doubles ①; late June to late Aug), part of the comfortable *Kringsjå Hotel* (same numbers; doubles ②), whose long veranda overlooks the fjord. The hostel does bike and boat hire and has self-catering facilities. Both the *Kringsjå* and the *Midtnes* serve tasty, excellent-value dinners.

The big deal here, however, is *Kvikne's Hotel* (☎57 69 11 01, fax 57 69 15 02; ④; May–Sept), whose various buildings dominate much of the waterfront. It's worth popping into the bar to take a look at the fancy fittings – some of which are in a sort of Victorian Viking-baronial style – but don't take a room without having a look first: the best rooms are old and overlook the fjord, but many are round the back in a modern annexe. The town **campsite**, *Sjøtun Camping* (☎57 69 12 23), occupies a treeless field just beyond the Viking burial mounds, a kilometre or so south of the dock. Most visitors to Balestrand **eat** in their hotels, but you could try the *Kvikne's* restaurant or, more affordably, *Gekkens Café*, upstairs in the pint-sized shopping centre on the quayside.

North to Fjærland

The most direct route north from Balestrand is the beautiful trip by passenger ferry up to the village of Fjærland. The **Fjærlandsfjord** is a wild place, the mountainsides blanketed with a thick covering of trees extending down to the water's edge, while a succession of waterfalls tumble from vast vertical clefts in the rock. **FJÆRLAND** itself is a gentle ribbon of old wooden houses edging the fjord, one of the region's most picturesque places, saved from the developers by its isolation – it was one of the last settlements on the Sognefjord to be connected to the road system, with Hwy 5 from Sogndal only being completed in 1986. It has eschewed the crasser forms of commercialism moreover to become the self-proclaimed "Norwegian Book Town" (*Den norske bokbyen*), with a dozen old buildings accommodating antiquarian and secondhand bookshops. Naturally enough, most of the books are in Norwegian, but there's a liberal sprinkling of English editions too. The bookselling season runs from mid-May to the end of August, and bookshops are open daily (10am–5pm).

Bookshops aside, the village has two good-looking buildings, the first of which is the **Hotel Mundal** (see opposite), whose nineteenth-century turrets, verandas and pitched roofs overlook the fjord from amongst the handful of buildings that constitute the village centre. Next door, the **church** is a serious affair of 1861, lacking in ornamentation but immaculately maintained; its graveyard hints at the hard and healthy life lived by the district's farmers, most of whom seem to have lived to a ripe old age. Many locals are still farmers, though hardly any of them still herd their cattle up to the mountain pastures in summer, as was the custom until the 1960s. The disused tracks to these summer farms (*støls*) now serve as **hiking trails** of varying length and difficulty – the tourist office will advise.

Around Fjærland

About 2.5km north of the village, along the quiet byroad that links it with Hwy 5, is the **Norwegian Glacier Museum** (Norsk Bremuseum; April, May, Sept & Oct daily 10am–4pm; June–Aug daily 9am–7pm; 60kr; ☎57 69 32 88), which tells you everything you ever wanted to know about glaciers, and a bit more too. It features several lavish hands-on and other displays, including a simulated walk underneath a glacier and a large screen showing glacier-related films; package tourists turn up in droves. The museum is one of the Jostedalsbreen National Park's three information centres (see p.290) and therefore has details of the various **guided glacier walks** on the Jostedalsbreen glacier including, in July and August, those on the nearest hikeable arm, **Supphellebreen** (or, to be precise, that part of it called **Flatbreen**). This is a challenging section of the glacier, however, and walks here last between six and eight hours – unlike Nigardsbreen (see p.287), for example, where there are two-hour and family walks. The Flatbreen starting point is the car park at **Øygarden**, about 4km off Hwy 5 – watch for the sign just 2km north of the Glacier Museum. At the other extreme, you can get close to the glacier without breaking sweat just 7km north of the Glacier Museum on Hwy 5. Here, just before you enter the tunnel, look out for the signed side road on the right leading the 200m to the **Brævasshytta** restaurant. This smart, modern place overlooks the slender glacial lake fed by the **Bøyabreen** nodule up above. It takes a couple of minutes to stroll down from the restaurant to the lake, close to the sooty shank of glacier.

Practicalities

The nearest you'll get by regular **bus** to Fjærland is the Glacier Museum on Hwy 5, from where it's an easy 2.5km stroll south along the fjord to the village. **Passenger ferries** (June to mid-Sept 1 daily; 1hr 25min) arriving from Balestrand and Hella dock in the centre beside the **tourist office** (June to mid-Sept daily 9.30am–4pm; ☎57 69 32 33). A special bus meets the boat to transport passengers onto the Glacier Museum and then the glaciers; the return fare is 80kr. The tourist office will advise on local hiking routes, sells hiking maps and has bus and ferry timetables. **Cycle hire** is available from the S-laget grocery store (Mon–Fri 9am–4.30pm, Sat 9am–2pm; ☎57 69 31 02).

MOVING ON FROM FJÆRLAND

Long distance **buses** travelling along Hwy 5 can be picked up close to the Glacier museum. There are services south to Sogndal and Oslo along the E16 and north to Skei, Førde (change for Stryn) and Florø. If you're heading north, the road **tunnels** under the Jostedalsbreen glacier to meet the E39 at Skei near Astruptunet; this route is covered on p.290. The toll station on Hwy 5 is just south of the Fjærland village turnoff; the charge per car and driver is 130kr. Passenger boats from Fjærland to Hella connect with the regular car ferry over the Sognefjord to Vangsnes.

There are two fjordside **hotels** in Fjærland. The obvious choice is the splendid *Hotel Mundal* (☎57 69 31 01, fax 57 69 31 79; ④; late May to mid-Sept;), a quirky place whose public rooms display many original features, from the parquet floors and fancy wooden scrollwork though to the old-fashioned sliding doors of the cavernous dining room. The rooms are frugal, some well-worn, but somehow it doesn't matter much. If you do stay, look out for the old photos on the walls of men in plus-fours and hob-nail boots climbing round the glaciers – only the softies bothered with gloves. Nearby, the *Fjærland Fjordstue Hotell* (☎57 69 32 00, fax 57 69 31 61; ②) is very different – a well-tended family hotel with smart modern furnishings and a sun room overlooking the fjord. A third option is *Bøyum Camping* (☎57 69 32 52, fax 57 69 31 68) near the Bremuseum; they have cabins (①) as well as tent pitches. Both hotels offer good, wholesome **food**.

Vangsnes and Vik

From Balestrand, Hwy 55 loops for 9km around the Esefjord, an inlet of the Sognefjord, to the quayside at **DRAGSVIK**, from where car ferries cross the mouth of the Fjærlandsfjord to Hella for the road to Sogndal. They also shuttle across the Sognefjord to **VANGSNES**, where local farmers must have had a real shock when Kaiser Wilhelm erected a twelve-metre high **statue** of the legendary Viking chief Fridtjof the Bold on the hilltop above their jetty in 1913. It still stands, an eccentric monument to the Kaiser's fascination with Nordic mythology – Fridtjof the Bold was in love with Ingebjorg, the daughter of King Bele, whose statue stands back across the fjord at Balestrand. You can walk or drive the 500m up from the jetty to take a closer look at Fridtjof, though it's hard not to find the underlying Aryan ideology objectionable, so you might just plod up there for the fine view.

From Vangsnes, it's a straight 12km south along the water's edge to **VIK**, a rather half-hearted village that sprawls up a wide valley. The only reason to stop here is to see the **Hopperstad stave church** (mid-June to mid-Aug daily 9am–7pm; mid-May to mid-June & mid-Aug to mid-Sept daily 10am–5pm; 40kr), sat on a hillock off Hwy 13 – a signed 1500m from the fjord. In the 1880s, the locals were about to knock it down, but a visiting architect and his antiquarian chum persuaded them to change their minds, and then the pair set about repairing the place. They did a good job. The church is one of the best examples of its type, its angular roofing surmounted by a long and slender tower. The interior has its moments too, with a Gothic side-altar canopy, parts of which may have been swiped from France by the Vikings, and a so-called lepers' window through which the infectious listened to church services.

Long-distance buses pass through Vik on their way south to Voss, a dramatic journey over the barren wastes of the Vikafjell mountain, but the best way of visiting is by **bike** from Balestrand – an easy and enjoyable ride.

East to Sogndal

From **Hella**, across the fjord from Dragsvik, the eastbound bus from Balestrand continues for 40km along the water's edge to **SOGNDAL** – bigger and livelier than Balestrand, but still, with a population of just 5000, hardly a major metropolis. Neither is Sogndal as appealing. It does have a pleasant fjord setting, sitting in a broad valley, surrounded by low, green hills dotted with apple and pear trees, but its centre is a rash of modern concrete and glass. Frankly, there are other much more agreeable spots nearby and your best option is to keep going, though bus travellers may find themselves marooned here – Sogndal bus station is a major transfer point.

Buses to Sogndal drop passengers at the station beside the roundabout on the west side of the town centre at the end of Gravensteinsgata, the long main drag. From here, it's about 400m east to the **tourist office** (late June to late Aug Mon–Fri 9am–8pm, Sat 9am–5pm, Sun 3–8pm; late Aug to late June Mon–Fri 9am–4pm; ☎57 67 30 83), housed in one of the flashy modern buildings on Gravensteinsgata. They issue bus and ferry timetables, and have a list of local **accommodation**, though pickings are fairly lean. The nicest place to stay – though it's no great shakes – is the *Hofslund Fjord Hotel* (☎57 67 10 22, fax 57 67 16 30; ③), a stone's throw from the tourist office, which comprises an old wooden building and a modern annexe; ask for a room with a fjord view. Another palatable and certainly economical option is the **youth hostel** (☎57 67 20 33, fax 57 67 31 45; doubles ①; mid-June to mid-Aug), which manages to feel quite homely despite being housed in a residential folk school (*Folkehøgskule*); it's near the bridge 400m beyond the roundabout at the east end of Gravensteinsgata – just follow the signs. Note also that this same roundabout marks the start of Fjørevegen, the town's other main drag, which cuts through the commercial heart of the town. For **food**, the choice is uninspiring, but the restaurant of the *Quality Sogndal Hotell*, Gravensteinsgata 5 (☎57 67 23 11), is reliable, serving tasty Norwegian dishes at reasonable prices.

MOVING ON FROM SOGNDAL

From Sogndal, there are **Hurtigbåt passenger express boats** to Balestrand, Bergen, Vik and Flåm. There are also express **buses** northwest to Fjærland and Førde (for Stryn) and east to Oslo via the E16, a route covered on p.241. Far better than these, however, is the stupendous 140km journey northeast along Hwy 55 to Lom. A **local bus** travels this route, but only in summer (mid-June to late Aug 2 daily; 3hr 30min). Not far out of Sogndal, Hwy 55 also runs past the turnings for Solvorn and the Nigardsbreen glacier. There are local buses to both: Solvorn (mid-June to late Aug 1–3 daily, intermittent weekday services at other times; 20min) and Nigardsbreen (mid-June to late Aug 2–5 daily, intermittent weekday services at other times; 2hr 40min). **Motorists** should note that Hwy 55 is closed by snow from October to late May or thereabouts and that there's a toll of 130kr to use Hwy 5 – the booths are just south of the Fjærland turning. If you're heading to or from Oslo, the Manheller/Fodnes **car ferry** runs round the clock (every 30min; 15min; pedestrians 26kr, car and driver 77kr).

Northeast to Lom

Some 15km northeast of Sogndal on Hwy 55, a steep three-kilometre-long turning leaves the main road to snake its way down to **SOLVORN**, an attractive little place clustered beneath the mountains on the sheltered foreshore of the **Lustrafjord**. The hamlet is the site of the *Walaker Hotell* (☎57 68 42 07, fax 57 68 45 44; ③), the most conspicuous part of which is an ugly motel-style block; don't let this put you off from lunching – maybe even staying – here, since the old house, a comely pastel-painted building with a lovely garden, has first-rate period bedrooms.

From the Solvorn jetty, there's a local **car ferry** (early June to Sept hourly 8am–5pm; 15min) over the fjord to **ORNES**, from where it's a stiff, ten-minute hike up the hill to **Urnes stave church** (June–Aug guided tours only daily 10.30am–5.30pm; 40kr). Magnificently sited against a view of the fjord with the snow-dusted mountains in the background, this is the oldest and most celebrated stave church in Norway. Parts of the church date back to the twelfth century, though it's famous mainly for its **carvings**. On the outside, incorporated into the north wall, are two exquisite door frames, the remains of an earlier church dating from around 1070 and alive with a swirling filigree of strange beasts and delicate vegetation. These forceful, superbly crafted panels witness the sophistication of Viking woodcarving – indeed the church has given its name to this distinctively Nordic art form, found in many countries where Viking influence was felt, and now generally known as the "Urnes" style. Most of the interior is seventeenth century, but there's Viking woodcarving here too, notably the strange-looking figures and beasts carved on the capitals of the staves and the sacred-heart bench ends. The guided tour fills in all the details and a small display in the house-cum-ticket office features a set of photographic enlargements showing carvings it's hard to make out inside the poorly-lit church.

If you're driving, there's a choice of routes from Urnes church. You can head north along the minor road that tracks along the east shore of the Lustrafjord to rejoin Hwy 55 at **Skjolden**. Or you can retrace your steps back to Hwy 55 via Solvorn. The latter is the route you'll need to take if you're heading to the Nigardsbreen glacier.

The Nigardsbreen glacier

On Hwy 55 at **Gaupne**, about 15km north of the Solvorn turning, Hwy 604 veers northwest for the delightful 34-kilometre trip up the wild, forested valley leading to the **Breheimsenteret Jostedal information centre** (daily: mid-June to late Aug 9am–7pm; May to mid-June & late Aug to Sept 10am–5pm; ☎57 68 32 50). This bleak, ultramodern structure fits in well with the bare peaks that surround it and, as you sip a coffee on the terrace, you can admire the glistening **Nigardsbreen** glacier dead ahead. From here, it's an easy three-kilometre drive or walk along the toll road to the shores of an icy green lake where a tiny boat shuttles over to the bare rock slope beside the Nigardsbreen, a great rumpled and seamed wall of ice that sweeps between high peaks. There are two- and four-hour **guided glacier walks** from late June to late August; most start from the car park. The Nigardsbreen is actually an arm of the Jostedalsbreen glacier, for more on which see p.290; further information on glacier walks is given on p.35.

On to Turtagrø

It's beyond Skjolden that the most dramatic part of Hwy 55 begins. First the road wriggles up the hillside, twisting and turning until it reaches a mountain plateau which it traverses, providing absolutely stunning views of the jagged, ice-crusted Jotunheimen peaks to the east. This is Norway's highest mountain crossing and if you want to hang around, easily the best of a series of roadside lodges is the attractive **Turtagrø Hotel** (☎57 68 61 16, fax 57 68 61 07; ④; Easter–Oct), just 17km beyond Skjolden. There's been a lodge here since 1888 and the present structure is a large and attractive red-timber building with a smart, very Scandinavian pine interior. There are eight en-suite rooms (③) and fifty bunk-beds in a Swiss-style chalet. The food is first-rate too. The hotel is a favourite haunt for mountaineers, but it also provides ready access to the hiking trails that lattice the Jotunheimen National Park, and there's summer cross-country skiing in the vicinity as well. Novice hikers shoud be aware however that the terrain is unforgiving, and the weather unpredictable.

Lom

Beyond the plateau, some 60km from Turtagrø on Hwy 55, the crossroads settlement of **LOM** has been a trading and transport centre for centuries, benefiting – in a modest sort of way – from the farms which dot the surrounding valleys. Today, with a population of just 700, it's hardly a boom town, but it does make a comfortable living from the passing tourist trade, with motorists pausing here before the last thump down Hwy 15 to the Geirangerfjord. Lom's eighteenth-century heyday is recalled by its **stave church** (daily: mid-June to mid-Aug 9am–9pm; mid-May to mid-June & mid-Aug to mid-Sept 10am–4pm; 25kr), an enormous structure perched on a grassy knoll above the river. The original church was built here about 1200, but it was remodelled and enlarged after the Reformation, when the spire and transepts were added and the flashy altar and pulpit installed. Its most attractive features are the dinky, shingle-clad roofs, adorned by dragon finials, and the Baroque acanthus vine decoration inside.

Nearby is the town's open-air museum, the **Lom Bygdamuseum Presthaugen** (mid-June to mid-Aug daily 11am–6pm; 20kr), a surprisingly enjoyable collection of old log buildings in a forest setting. Norway teems with this type of museum – and if you stay here long enough you'll scream at the sight of them – but this one is better than most. Museum enthusiasts will also want to visit the **Norwegian Mountain Museum** (Norsk Fjellmuseum; June–Aug Mon–Fri 9am–6pm, Sat & Sun 10am–5pm; May & Sept Mon–Fri 9am–4pm, Sat & Sun 11am–4pm; Oct–April Mon–Fri 9am–4pm; 60kr), a brand new museum which focuses on the Jotunheimen mountains, their flora and flora, landscapes, farmers and mountaineers. A **combined ticket** for all three sights (70kr) is available at each of them, or from the tourist office (see below).

Buses to Lom pull in a few metres west of the main crossroads, and most of what you're likely to need is within easy walking distance of here. The church and open-air museum are across the bridge on the other side of the river, as is the mountain museum, which shares its premises with the **tourist office** (mid-June to mid-Aug Mon–Fri 9am–9pm, Sat & Sun 10am–8pm; early June & late Aug Mon–Fri 9am–6pm, Sat & Sun 10am–5pm; May & Sept Mon–Fri 9am–4pm, Sat & Sun 11am–4pm; Oct–April Mon–Fri 9am–4pm; ☎61 21 29 90). The choicest **accommodation** is in the *Fossheim Hotell* (☎61 21 10 05, fax 61 21 15 10; ③), about 300m east of the crossroads along Hwy 15. The main lodge here is neat and smart, with an abundance of pine, while trailing up the wooded hillside behind are some delightful little en-suite wooden cabins (also ③). The hotel **restaurant** is excellent and reasonably priced. A palatable second-choice hotel is the *Fossberg* (☎61 21 10 73, fax 61 21 16 21; ③), a large, modern and mostly wooden place by the crossroads.

MOVING ON FROM LOM

Moving on from Lom by **bus** is easy. There are regular services east to Otta, Lillehammer and Oslo, west for Grotli, Stryn, Helleslylt and Måløy – amongst many fjord destinations. Hwy 55 southwest to Sogndal is less well served: a **local bus** plies this route, but not very often and only in summer (mid-June to late Aug 2 daily; 3hr 30min).

Nordfjord and the Jostedalsbreen Glacier

Emerge from the Fjærland tunnel (Hwy 5) heading north, and you've just journeyed under the Jostedalsbreen glacier, which somehow seems a bit of a cheek – and environmentally dubious. That said, the highway does put a southerly limb of the glacier within easy reach of Fjærland and, more importantly, is the handiest way to get from Sognefjord to **Nordfjord**, the next great fjord system to the north.

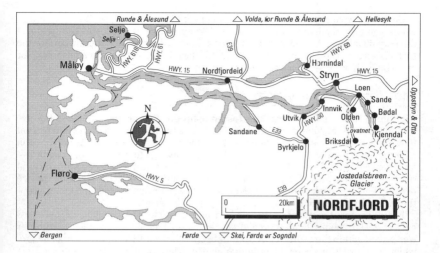

The inner recesses of the Nordfjord are readily explored using Hwy 60, which weaves a tortuous course via a string of unexciting little towns with the fjord on one side and the glacier growling away in the mountains on the other. Two mountain roads lead off Hwy 60 towards outlying sections of glacier, one at **Olden** for **Briksdalsbreen**, the other at **Loen** for **Kjenndalsbreen**. The first is very popular with tourists, the latter slightly more subdued and therefore probably preferable, but to get a real flavour of the ice fields you really have to sign up for a guided **glacier hike**. If you're looking to stay, Loen has a couple of good **hotels**, while the town of **Stryn**, a few kilometres to the northwest, has a pair of less expensive offerings. Stryn is also an important crossroads where Hwy 60 meets Hwy 15. From here, it's north to Hellesylt and east to Geiranger. For access to the glacier's eastern side, see the Nigardsbreen section (p.287).

Long-distance **buses** scuttle along Hwys 5, 15 and 60; the only transport difficulties come when you venture onto the minor roads down to the glacier, where you have to rely on patchy local services.

North from Fjærland to Olden

Heading north from Fjærland on Hwy 5, it's about 30km to the **Kjøsnes** junction, where a bridge begins the country road that slips west along the southern shore of lake **Jølstravatnet**. After 12km you reach the **Astruptunet** (normally June–Aug daily 10am–5pm; Sept Sun only 10am–4pm; 50kr), the farmstead home of **Nikolai Astrup** (1880–1928), one of Norway's more talented artists. Astrup mostly painted romanticized rural scenes in bright colours and soft, flowing forms but, unlike many of his contemporaries he eschewed realism in favour of neoimpressionism. In that regard, he bridged the gap between one generation of Norwegian painters and the Matisse-inspired artists who followed. The Astruptunet looks pretty much the same as it did during the artist's lifetime, comprising a pretty complex of old timber buildings including a sixteenth-century cottage, though a modern gallery, built to house a selection of Astrup's paintings and woodcuts, has replaced the old barn. The Astruptunet is also used for touring art exhibitions with the result that opening hours change – ring ahead to check (☎57 72 67 82).

Back on Hwy 5 at Kjøsnes, it's only a couple of kilometres to the **Skei** crossroads, where you turn north onto the E39 for the 20km cruise up the valley to **Byrkjelo** and the Hwy 60 intersection. From here, it's just 40km to Olden, where you turn off for the Briksdalsbreen, and 7km more to Loen, at the start of the road to Kjenndalsbreen; for more on both of these routes see below.

The Jostedalsbreen glacier

High up in the mountains lurks the **Jostedalsbreen glacier**, the huge sheet of ice, 500km square, that dominates the whole of the inner Nordfjord region and reaches out towards Sognefjord and the Jotunheimen mountains. The glacier stretches northeast in a lumpy mass between Hwy 5 and Hwy 15 with its twenty-four arms – or "nodules" – nudging down into the nearby valleys, the clay particles of its meltwater giving the local rivers and lakes their distinctive light-green colouring. Catching sight of the ice nestling between peaks and ridges and licking its way downwards can be unnerving – the overwhelming feeling is that it really shouldn't be there.

For centuries, the glacier presented an impenetrable east–west barrier, crossed only at certain points by determined farmers and adventurers. In 1991, the glacier was placed within the protected **Jostedalsbreen National Park**, the main benefit of which for tourists has been the proliferation of **guided glacier walks** (*breturar*; June to early Sept only), ranging from two-hour excursions to all-day, fully equipped hikes. Prices start at around 90kr, with a half-day trip weighing in at about 250kr – money well spent if you've never been on a glacier before. A comprehensive leaflet detailing all the various options is available at local tourist offices, some hostels and hotels – like the *Alexandra* in Loen – and at the national park's three **information centres**. Among the latter, the most readily accessible is the Norwegian Glacier Museum (see p.284). The others are the Jostedalsbreen National Park Centre (daily: mid-May to mid-June 9am–4pm, mid-June to mid-Aug 9am–6pm, mid-Aug to mid-Sept 10am–4pm; ☎57 87 72 00; displays 50kr) in Oppstryn, 20km east of Stryn on Hwy 15 – easy to get to by car, but a pain by bus – and the isolated Breheimsenteret Jostedal, up a long byroad north of Sogndal, off Hwy 55 on the east side of the glacier. Each of the three has displays on all things glacial and sells coffee-table glacier books, souvenirs and local hiking maps.

Most of these outlets – and all three information centres – make **bookings** for guided glacier walks, which are taken up to about 6pm the evening before you want to go, though obviously it's best not to leave it until the last minute. **Equipment** is provided, though you'll need to take good boots, waterproofs, warm clothes, gloves and hat, sunglasses, food and drink. With a vehicle, you can get within easy striking distance of the designated **starting points** for all the glacier walks. By **bus** it's a little trickier, but it's usually possible with a bit of pre-planning. Several of these starting points are also near to (or the same as) the places you head for if you just want **to look at the glacier** without actually getting on it; we've described two such routes below – to the Briksdalsbreen and the Kjenndalsbreen. Finally, although it seems a bit of cheat, you can avoid the sweat of a long detour by taking a close peek at a sliver of glacier just off Hwy 5 outside Fjærland (see p.284).

Olden and the Briksdalsbreen

The hamlet of **OLDEN** doesn't have much going for it, except for being at the start of the 24km byroad south to **BRIKSDAL**, a scattering of mountain lodges that serves as the starting point for the easy 45-minute walk to the **Briksdalsbreen**. This is the most visited arm of the Jostedalsbreen glacier, and the easy-to-follow path clambers round waterfalls and weaves up the river until you finally reach the glacier, surprisingly blue, though tarnished by fragments of dust and dirt. It's a simple matter to get close to the ice itself as the only precaution is a flimsy rope barricade and a small warning sign – be careful. Alternatively, you can hire a pony and trap at the café area at the start of the trail, something that will cost you around 175–200kr – though it's a bit of a swindle given that you still have to hike the last bit anyway. Guided glacier walks begin at the café area too.

Local **buses** run from Loen and Stryn via Olden to Briksdal all year (1–2 daily; 1hr/45min).

Loen and the Kjenndalsbreen

LOEN spreads ribbon-like along the fjord's low-lying, grassy foreshore, with snow-capped mountains breathing down its neck. The village is also home to one of Norway's most luxurious hotels, the *Hotel Alexandra* (☎57 87 50 00, fax 57 87 50 51, *www.alexandra.no*; ⑤/④), a big and flashy modern block tucked in beneath the hills and surrounded by carefully manicured gardens. The rooms are spacious, infinitely comfortable and furnished in bright modern style and breakfasts are lavish. For flimsier bank balances, the motel-style *Hotel Loenfjord* (☎57 87 57 00, fax 57 87 57 51; ④/③), across the road, offers less expensive and perfectly adequate rooms – it's actually owned by the same company.

From Loen, the seventeen-kilometre byroad to the **Kjenndalsbreen**, another branch of the Jostedalsbreen, begins innocuously enough, climbing gently up the river valley and slipping between lush meadows before pressing on beside the long and slender lake Lovatnet, which extends right to the end of the valley. After about 10km, however, the road narrows and gets rougher as it zigzags upwards – the last couple of kilometres beyond the toll post (30kr) are quite hairy and should not be attempted after dark. Finally, the road snakes its way down to the lakeshore, petering out at a café and car park, from where it's a rocky twenty-minute walk to the foot of the glacier, whose blue-and-white folds of ice tumble down the rock face, split by fissures and undermined by a furious white-green river fed by plummeting meltwater.

There's a local **bus** service from Stryn and Loen down the first 12km of the valley to **Bødal**, but it's infrequent (1 daily on schooldays only), and anyway you're much better off taking the **boat** (mid-June to Aug 1 daily, extra departures during July; 3hr return). This departs from the **Sande** jetty, 4km up the road from Loen, nudging its way up the lake to the café at the end of the road. The boat is organized by the *Hotel Alexandra*, whose staff issue tickets and take bookings; the return fare, including the return trip by bus, is 110kr.

Stryn

STRYN, just 11km northwest around the fjord from Loen, is the biggest town around here, though with a population of just 1100 that's hardly a major boast. It's a largely humdrum modern sprawl straggling beside its long main street, although there's a pleasant pocket of antique timber houses huddled round the old bridge down by the river just to the south of the main drag – take a few moments to have a look.

Buses stop beside the river to the west of, and a five- to ten-minute walk from, the town centre, where the **tourist office** (June & Aug daily 9am–6pm; July daily 9am–8pm; ☎57 87 23 33) is located in the square just back from the main street behind *Johan's Kafeteria*. The tourist office issues free town maps, has a wide range of local brochures, sells hiking maps and takes bookings for guided walks on the Jostedalsbreen (see opposite). For **accommodation**, look no further than the *Walhalla Gjestgiveri*, Perhusvegen 13 (☎57 87 10 72, fax 57 87 18 94; ①). This provides simple, economic and friendly lodgings plus a tasty breakfast in one of the attractive timber buildings down by the river; it's located about 200m west of the tourist office.

Alternatively, the **youth hostel** (☎57 87 13 36, fax 57 87 11 06; doubles ①; June–Aug) is an inconvenient and difficult-to-navigate 1500-metre walk up the hill to the north of the centre – get a map from the tourist office or keep your eyes peeled for the signs on Hwy 15. The only reasonable **food** in town is served at *Johan's Kafeteria* on the main street, which has sandwiches, pizzas and cafeteria-style meals.

Heading west out of Stryn, Hwys 15 and 60 share the same stretch of road until, after 16km, Hwy 60 forks north to reach, after about 30km, Hellesylt on the Geirangerfjord.

The Geirangerfjord

The **Geirangerfjord** is one of the region's smallest fjords, but one of its most breath-taking. A convoluted branch of the Storfjord, it cuts far inland, with a village at either end of its snake-like profile: **Hellesylt** to the west and **Geiranger** in the east. Of the two it's Hellesylt, away from the tourist crowds of Gerainger, that makes the better **base**.

You can reach Geiranger in dramatic style either from Åndalsnes to the north via the Trollstigen mountain road (see p.295) or from Hwy 15 to the south; the approach to

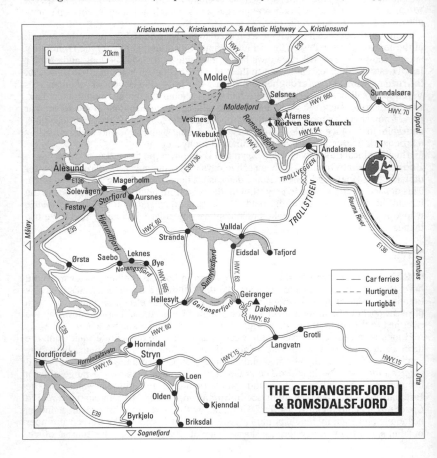

THE GEIRANGERFJORD & ROMSDALSFJORD

Hellesylt via Hwy 60 is a tad more mundane (although this highway as a whole is an especially appealing route between Nordfjord and Ålesund). Long-distance **buses** heading west along Hwy 15 link Otta and Lom with Grotli and Langvatn, at one of which – depending on the service – you change for the local bus north to Geiranger (but note that this connecting service runs only from mid-June to Aug). The same local service pushes on from Geiranger to Åndalsnes. Hellesylt is on the main Bergen–Ålesund bus route, with several services daily. Regular **car ferries** (May–Sept 4 daily, extra departures June to late Aug; 1hr 10min; pedestrians 35kr each way, car plus driver 110kr) run between Hellesylt and Geiranger, turning into the Geirangerfjord itself about 15min after leaving Hellesylt. The journey along the S-shaped fjord is one of the most celebrated trips in the entire region, past a series of plunging waterfalls that drop from heights of up to 250m. The falls are all named, and the multilingual commentary aboard the ferry does its best to ensure that you become familiar with every stream and rivulet. More interesting are the scattered ruins of abandoned farms, built along the fjord's 16km length by fanatically optimistic settlers over the last couple of centuries. The cliffs backing the fjord are almost uniformly sheer, making farming of any description a short-lived and back-breaking occupation – and not much fun for the children either: when they went out to play, they were roped to the nearest boulder to stop them dropping into the fjord.

Hellesylt

In Viking times, **HELLESYLT** was an important and well-protected port. From the village, traders and warriors sallied forth to England, France and Russia, and many old Viking names survive in the area. Nowadays it's primarily a stopoff on tourist itineraries, with most visitors staying just long enough to catch the ferry down the fjord to Geiranger. There's also a tiny **beach** by the ferry quay, the prelude to some very cold swimming – and possibly something worse if you use the rickety old bathing house – or you could splash about (as many do) in the waterfall in the centre of the village. By nightfall, when the visitors have departed, Hellesylt is quiet and peaceful.

Hellesylt is on the main Bergen–Ålesund bus route, which passes along Hwy 60 through Loen and Stryn. The **tourist office** is by the jetty (June–Aug daily 9am–5.30pm; ☎70 26 50 52), as is the c.1900, *Grand Hotel* (☎70 26 51 00, fax 70 26 52 22; ③), whose fancy wooden scrollwork and high-pitched gables have been a local landmark since 1871. The interior has been patchily restored, however, and the rooms are in the modern annexe next door. The hotel's main competitor is the **youth hostel** (☎70 26 51 28, fax 70 26 36 57; doubles ①; June–Aug), pleasantly set on the hillside above the village and Hwy 60 – a 350m walk up the signposted footpath from the jetty. They have cabins (①), which double very nicely as family rooms, self-catering facilities, and also rent out rowing boats (as does the *Grand*). *Hellesylt Camping* (☎70 26 51 88) occupies a shadeless field beside the fjord about 300m from the quay.

Geiranger

Any approach to **GEIRANGER** is spectacular. Arriving by ferry slowly reveals the little village tucked in a hollow at the eastern end of the fjord, while approaching from the north by road involves thundering along a fearsome set of switchbacks on the Ørneveien, the Eagle's Highway, for a first view of the village and the fjord glinting in the distance. Similarly, the road in from Hwy 15 to the south begins innocuously enough, but soon you're squirming round and down the zigzags to arrive in Geiranger from behind. It's a beautiful setting, one of the most magnificent in western Norway, but in the peak season the village is chronically overcrowded, with campers and caravanners filling the over-large fjordside campsite to the gunnels. Frankly, you'll soon want to leave all this behind – or visit in the shoulder season when the true character of the place is more apparent.

Buses to Geiranger stop metres from the waterfront, a stone's throw from the **ferry terminal** and **tourist office** (May–Sept daily 9am–7pm; Oct–April Mon–Fri 9am–5pm; ☎70 26 30 99), which pushes expensive boat tours of the fjord, though the car ferry is perfectly adequate. There are several **hotels** to choose from, but advance reservations are strongly advised in July and August. Both the large and luxurious *Union Hotel* (☎70 26 30 00, fax 70 26 31 61, *www.union-hotel.no*; ⑤/④; March to mid-Dec), high up the hillside on the south side of town, and the ultramodern timber *Grande Fjord Hotel* (☎70 26 30 90, fax 70 26 31 77; ③; May–Sept), by the fjord about 1km north of the centre, have good views and are at a safe distance from the crowds. The *Grande Fjord* also has **cabins** (②) and a **campsite**, which is adjacent to *Grande Turisthytter & Camping* (☎70 26 30 68, fax 70 26 31 17). The restaurant of the over-large *Hotel Geiranger*, not far from the ferry dock, is first class.

The bus service to Geiranger only runs from mid-June to August. It's only a local service, with buses running north into Geiranger from Grotli or Langvatn on Hwy 15 (where they connect with long-distance buses). There are two buses daily, one going straight into Geiranger (50min), the other (2hr) making a dramatic detour up a rough mountain toll road to the Dalsnibba viewpoint, overlooking the Geirangerfjord at 1476m. This same local bus pushes north out of Geiranger heading for Åndalsnes. The journey from Geiranger to Åndalsnes takes just over three hours.

The Romsdalsfjord and around

Easily reached by bus, train or car, small-town **Åndalsnes** is an ideal base for a visit to the **Romsdalsfjord**, a deep gash in the landscape which stretches west of the town, surrounded by some of the wildest mountains in the whole of the fjord country. If you approach the town from the Geirangerfjord, you'll cross the mountains to the south via the knuckle-whitening hairpins of the **Trollstigen**. Travelling up from the southeast, Dombås is where the **E136** and the **Rauma train line** fork west for the thrilling hundred-kilometre-rattle down through the alpine mountains of the **Romsdal** valley to the **Romsdalsfjord** – a spectacular journey by any standard. The area's other prime attraction, and similarly easy to reach by bus or car, is the coastal town of **Ålesund**, whose good-looking centre sports several dozen charming Art Nouveau buildings. Both Åndalsnes and Ålesund possess top-quality **accommodation**.

Åndalsnes

For many travellers **ÅNDALSNES**, connected by train with Oslo, is the first – and sometimes only – contact with the fjord country, a distinction it doesn't really warrant. Despite a wonderful setting between lofty peaks and chill waters, the town itself is unexciting: small (with a population of just 3000), modern and industrial, and sleepy at the best of times. That said, Åndalsnes makes an ideal base for exploring the nearby area, with some wonderful scenery within easy reach by ferry, bus or car, most famously the extraordinary Trollstigen mountain road, which zigzags south to Valldal, or the journey west to Ålesund, another tempting proposition.

Practicalities

Buses stop outside the **train station**, where you'll also find the **tourist office** (late June to late Aug Mon–Sat 10am–7pm, Sun 1–7pm; late Aug to late June Mon–Fri 10am–3.30pm; ☎71 22 16 22). They provide bus timetables, regional guides and a wide range of local information geared to make you use Åndalsnes as a base – which is fair enough. Their free *Dagsturer* (day-trips) booklet gives details of all sorts of motorists' excursions, and most recommendations include a short hike too. They have details of fishing trips (3 daily; 4hr; 250kr), hiking routes, guided climbs (from 1400kr) and sightseeing expeditions with Åndalsnes Taxi (☎71 22 15 55), who charge – for example – 400kr for a brief scoot down the Trollstigen. Better value are the special deals offered by local **car hire** firms: from May to mid-September, *Åndalsnes Camping* (☎71 22 16 29) charge 550kr for 24-hours' car rental, as does Åndal Bil (☎71 22 22 55), who operate all year. The tourist office has all the latest information on local deals. Local **hiking maps** are sold at Romsdal Libris, a couple of minutes' walk from the tourist office in the centre of town.

The tourist office also has a small supply of **private rooms** (①), which go for around 350kr per double (200kr single), en suite, self-catering and with bedding, though most are a good walk from the town centre. Alternatively, Åndalsnes has a delightful **youth hostel** (☎71 22 13 82, fax 71 22 68 35; doubles ①; mid-May to mid-Sept), a two-kilometre hike west out of town. To get there, head up the hill out of the centre, turn right at the island at the major road, go past the E136 turning to Dombås, but keep on E136 in the direction of Ålesund, cross the river and it's on the left. The hostel has a pleasant rural setting and its simple rooms, in a group of modest wooden buildings, are extremely popular, making reservations pretty much essential. They also rent out bikes, and the buffet-style breakfast, with its fresh fish, is one of the best hostellers are likely to get in the whole country. Note that the hostel doesn't do evening meals (though there are cooking facilities) and reception is closed from 10am–4pm. The other excellent choice, the *Grand Hotel Bellevue*, Åndalsgata 5 (☎71 22 75 00, fax 71 22 60 38; ③), occupies a large whitewashed block with attractive Art Deco touches on a hillock just up from the train station. The rooms on the top floors have great views, well worth the extra 100kr or so over the standard room rate. The *Rauma Hotell*, near the station right in the centre of town at Vollan 16 (☎71 22 12 33, fax 71 22 63 13; ③), is a bit cheaper, but it's a routine modern place without much character. Among several local **campsites**, *Åndalsnes Camping og Motell* (☎71 22 16 29, fax 71 22 62 16) has a fine riverside setting about 3km from the town centre – directions are as for the youth hostel, but turn first left immediately after the river. It's a well-equipped site with cabins (①) as well as bikes, boats, canoes and cars available for rent.

For **food**, the *Buona Serà* pizzeria, a brief walk from the station up the hill out of town, serves competent Italian food and reasonably tasty steaks, but much better is the snug *Lille Grand Restaurant* in the basement of the *Grand Hotel*, with main courses at around 190kr.

Over the Trollstigen

The alarming heights of the **Trollstigen**, or "Troll's Ladder", a trans-mountain route **between Åndalsnes and Valldal**, are equally compelling in whichever direction you travel. They are accessible by twice-daily bus from mid-June to August, which takes the sweat out of driving – along with scores of other tourists – round eleven hairpins with a maximum gradient of 1:12. Drivers (and cyclists) should be particularly careful in wet weather; note too that the road is generally closed from early October to mid-May – later if the snows have been particularly heavy.

The Trollstigen, a turning off the E136 just 6km southeast of Åndalsnes, starts gently enough, running up into a valley surrounded by some of the more famous mountain peaks in Norway: to the right, Kongen and Bispen, the "King" and the "Bishop", are the highest. Soon, though, the sheer audacity of the road becomes apparent, climbing its way across the face of the mountain in huge zigzags, before running halfway up directly in front of the tumultuous **Stigfossen Falls** – where the bus stops for photographs. On a clear day the views from here are heart-stopping, the water dropping away 180m under the bridge into the valley.

There is nothing at the top except a bare expanse of mountain and a café – the *Trollstigen Fjellstue* – where the bus makes another stop. From here, it's a five-minute walk to the **Utsikten** (viewpoint), where there's a magnificent panorama over the surrounding mountains and valleys. If you're feeling extremely energetic, this is the place to pick up the Kløvstien, the original **track** over the mountains – abandoned when the road was built – which has been renovated for walkers. It's well-signposted all the way back down towards Åndalsnes, crossing the road in four places, and there's a chain to hang on to on the steeper parts. The walk down the Kløvstien takes around four hours, and then there's an easy ninety-minute stroll down the footpath along the Isterdalen valley, which brings you back to Åndalsnes. You can, of course, shorten the walk by starting (or finishing) at Stigfossen. As usual, come properly equipped, watch for sudden weather changes and be aware of the Trollstigen bus schedules.

Valldal and beyond

On the other side of the mountains, the Trollstigen slips along the Meierdal on its way to **VALLDAL**, a silent, shadowy village sprawled along the water's edge. If you're marooned, there's a small **youth hostel** (☎70 25 70 31, fax 70 25 75 11; doubles ①; mid-June to Aug), 100m from the harbour. You'll almost certainly want to press on, however, heading west along the fjord to either, in 4km, the Linge–Eidsdal ferry (every 30min; 10min) or, 12km further on, the Liabygda–Stranda ferry (every 30min; 15min). Most visitors choose the former, the route to Geiranger, but if you travel to Stranda you'll find yourself on Hwy 60 midway between Hellesylt and Ålesund.

Ålesund

Some 120km west of Åndalsnes, at the end of the E136, the fishing and ferry port of **ÅLESUND** is immediately, and distinctively, different from any other Norwegian town. Neither old clapboard houses nor functional concrete and glass is much in evidence; instead, there's a conglomeration of proud grey-and-white facades, lavishly decorated and topped with a forest of turrets and pinnacles. There are Neoclassical and mock-Gothic facades, dragons and human faces, decorative flowers and even a pharoah or two, the whole ensemble set around the town's meandering harbour. These architectural eccentricities sprang from disaster. In 1904, a dreadful fire left 10,000 people homeless and the town centre destroyed, but within three years a hectic reconstruction programme saw almost the entire area rebuilt in a bizarre Art Nouveau style which borrowed heavily from the German Jugendstil movement. Kaiser Wilhelm II, who used to holiday around Ålesund, footed the bill, and the Norwegian architects, most of whom had learnt their craft abroad, created an engaging hybrid style combining up-to-date foreign influences and folksy local elements.

A walk down pedestrianized **Kongensgate** reveals most of the town's architectural highlights, though many of the other central streets are equally decorative – if you're

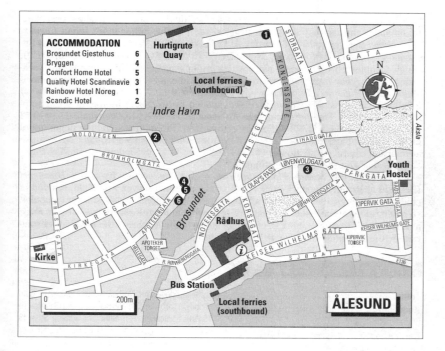

ACCOMMODATION

Brosundet Gjestehus	6
Bryggen	4
Comfort Home Hotel	5
Quality Hotel Scandinavie	3
Rainbow Hotel Noreg	1
Scandic Hotel	2

ÅLESUND

keen to explore every stylistic peccadillo, pick up the free but verbose *On Foot in Åle-sund*. This is available at the tourist office (see below) where – and this is an even better option – you can sign up for one of the **guided walking tours** (mid-June to mid-Aug 3 weekly; 1hr 30min; 50kr). Ålesund's lively centre, draped around its oldest harbour, the **Brosundet**, also makes for a pleasant stroll, with the sight of ferries and Hurtigbåt coming and going to the islands just offshore. The other obvious objective in the town centre is the **park** at the top of Lihauggata. It's a surprise to find monkey puzzle and copper beech trees here, and there's a bust in honour of the town's benefactor, the Kaiser, in which – if you're used to seeing pictures of him as a grizzled older figure in a helmet – he looks disarmingly youthful. The larger statue nearby is of Rollo, a Viking chieftain born and raised in Ålesund, who seized Normandy and became its first duke in 911 – he was an ancestor of William the Conqueror of England. From the park, several hundred steps lead to the top of the **Aksla**, where the view out along the coast and its islands is fabulous.

Practicalities

Ålesund **bus station** is situated on the waterfront across from the **tourist office** in the Rådhus (June to Aug Mon–Fri 8.30am–7pm, Sat 9am–5pm, Sun 11am–5pm; Sept–May Mon–Fri 8.30am–4pm; ☎70 15 76 00). Southbound local ferries depart from beside the bus station, northbound from the other side of the harbour, while beyond that is the quay for the **Hurtigrute coastal steamer** (southbound 12.45am, northbound 3pm).

One of Ålesund's real pleasures is the quality of its downtown **hotels**. The pick of the bunch is the *Brosundet Gjestehus* (☎70 12 10 00, fax 70 12 12 95, *www.brosundet.no*; ③), which occupies an attractively converted waterside warehouse at Apotekergata 5. They have a sauna, washing machines, self-catering facilities and offer an excellent breakfast. In similar premises, just along the street at no.1, is the rather more lavish *Comfort Home Hotel Bryggen* (☎70 12 64 00, fax 70 12 11 80; ⑤/③). Also on the waterfront is the excellent *Scandic Hotel Ålesund*, Molovegen 6 (☎70 12 81 00, fax 70 12 92 10; ⑤/③), which occupies a brisk, modern block with a bright and cheerful interior – ask for a sea-facing room. Away from the waterfront, in the middle of the town centre, the comfortable *Quality Hotel Scandinavie*, Løvenvoldgata 8 (☎70 12 31 31, fax 70 13 23 70; ④/②) inhabits a grand old Art Nouveau edifice, spoiled by an especially horrid set of automatic front doors. The more mundane *Rainbow Hotel Noreg*, Kongensgate 27 (☎70 12 29 38, fax 70 12 66 60; ④/③) suffers by comparison with its rivals, but the upper floors of this modern block offer sea views and the rooms are perfectly adequate. There's also a small and central **youth hostel** (☎70 11 58 30, fax 70 11 58 59; doubles ③; May–Sept) at Parkgata 14, at the top of Rådstuggata.

For **eating**, the *Sjøbua Fiskerestaurant*, round the corner from the *Brosundet Gjestehus* at Brunholmgata 1 (☎70 12 71 00; closed Sun), serves wonderful seafood in chic surroundings, complete with a lobster tank. It's expensive, but still very popular, so reservations are advised. A cheaper if somewhat mundane alternative is *Nilles Pizza* at Kirkegata 1. In sunny weather, everyone flocks to the terrace of the *Metz* café-restaurant by the Brosundet harbour at Notenesgata 1.

travel details

Trains

Åndalsnes to: Dombås (2 daily; 1hr 30min); Oslo (2 daily; 6hr 30min).

Bergen to: Finse (4–5 daily; 2hr 15min); Geilo (4–5 daily; 3hr); Myrdal (4–5 daily; 1hr 50min); Oslo (4–5 daily; 6hr 30min); Voss (4–5 daily; 1hr 10min).

Dombås to: Åndalsnes (2 daily; 1hr 30min); Trondheim (3–4 daily; 2hr 30min).

Myrdal to: Flåm (June to late Sept 11–12 daily; rest of the year 2–4 daily; 50min).

Stavanger to: Kristiansand (3 daily; 4hr); Oslo (3 daily; 9hr).

Buses

Ålesund to: Åndalsnes (3–4 daily; 2hr 20min); Bergen (1–2 daily; 10hr); Hellesylt (1–2 daily except Sat; 2hr 40min); Stryn (1–2 daily except Sat; 4hr); Trondheim (1–2 daily; 8hr 10min).

Åndalsnes to: Ålesund (3–4 daily; 2hr 20min); Geiranger (June–Aug 2 daily; 3–4hr); Valldal (June–Aug 2 daily; 2hr).

Balestrand to: Oslo (3 daily; 8hr 15min); Sogndal (2 daily; 1hr 10min).

Bergen to: Ålesund (1–2 daily; 10hr); Dombås (1 daily; 12hr); Grotli (1 daily; 8hr); Hellesylt (1–2 daily; 8hr 15min); Kinsarvik (2 daily; 2hr 40min); Kristiansand (1 daily; 11hr); Loen (3 daily; 6hr 30min); Lofthus (2 daily; 3hr); Norheimsund (3 daily; 2hr); Oslo (1 daily; 11hr); Skei (3 daily; 5hr); Sogndal (3 daily; 4hr 15min); Stavanger (1–5 daily; 5hr 40min); Stryn (3 daily; 6hr 45min); Trondheim (1 daily; 14hr); Utne (2 daily; 2hr 45min); Voss (4 daily; 1hr 45min).

Geiranger to: Åndalsnes (mid-June to late Aug 2 daily; 3–4hr).

Sogndal to: Balestrand (2 daily; 1hr 10min); Bergen (3 daily; 4hr 15min); Fjærland (3 daily; 35min); Oslo (3 daily; 7hr); Stryn (1–2 daily; 4hr 30min); Voss (3 daily; 3hr).

Stavanger to: Bergen (1–5 daily; 5hr 40min); Haugesund (1–5 daily; 2hr 10min); Kristiansand (2 daily; 4hr 40min).

Stryn to: Bergen (2 daily; 7hr); Hellesylt (1–2 daily; 1hr); Oslo (1 daily; 8hr 30min); Trondheim (1 daily; 8hr).

Ulvik to: Voss (2–4 daily; 1hr).

Voss to: Bergen (3 daily; 4hr); Gudvangen (4–6 daily; 1hr 10min); Norheimsund (3 daily; 2hr); Odda (1 daily; 2hr 30min); Sogndal (2 daily; 3hr); Ulvik (2–4 daily; 1hr).

Hurtigrute boats

The daily Hurtigrute service departs :

Northbound: Bergen at 10.30pm; Florø at 4.45am; Måløy at 7.30am; Ålesund at 3pm; Molde at 6.30pm; Kristiansund at 11pm; Trondheim at noon.

Southbound: Trondheim at 10am; Kristiansund at 5pm; Molde at 9.15pm; Ålesund at 12.45am; Måløy at 5.30am; Florø at 8am; Bergen at 2.30pm. Journey time from Bergen to Trondheim is 31hr 30min.

Ferries

Bruravik to: Brimnes (every 2 hr; 25mins).

Dragsvik to: Hella (every 30min; 10min); Vangsnes (hourly; 25min).

Fodnes (E16) to: Manheller (hourly; 15min).

Geiranger to: Hellesylt (May–Sept 4 daily, rest of the year 2 daily; 1hr 10min).

Gudvangen to: Kaupanger (2 daily; 2hr).

Hella to: Dragsvik (every 30min; 10min); Vangsnes (hourly; 15min).

Stavanger to: Tau (hourly; 45min).

Utne to: Kinsarvik (every 2 hr; 25min).

Express passenger boats (Hurtigbåt)

Bergen to: Balestrand (1–2 daily; 4hr); Flåm (1–2 daily; 5hr 30min); Sogndal (1–2 daily; 5hr); Stavanger (2–5 daily; 3hr 50min).

Bergen by **bus and Hurtigbåt** to: Kinsarvik (1–3 daily; 2hr 20min); Lofthus (1–3 daily; 2hr 35min); Odda (1–3 daily; 3hr 10min); Utne (1–3 daily; 1hr 50min).

Flåm to: Balestrand (1–2 daily; 1hr 30min); Bergen (1–2 daily; 5hr 15min), Gudvangen (1–3 daily; 2hr); Sogndal (Mon–Sat 1–3 daily; 1hr 10min).

Gudvangen to: Flåm (1–3 daily; 2hr).

Stavanger to: Bergen (2–5 daily; 3hr 50min).

Passenger-only ferry

Balestrand to: Fjærland (June to mid-Sept 2 daily; 1hr 30min); Hella (June to mid-Sept 2 daily; 15min).

International Ferries

Bergen and to a lesser extent **Stavanger** and **Haugesund** are international ferry ports. For details of sailings see Basics, p.8.

CHAPTER SEVEN

TRONDHEIM TO THE LOFOTENS

C entral Northern Norway encompasses the city of Trondheim and the elongated stretch of island-studded coast beyond it, and marks the transition from rural southern to blustery northern Norway. **Trondheim**, the capital of what is – in Norwegian terms at least – the fertile **Trøndelag**, is easily accessible from Oslo by train, and with its easy-going air and imposing cathedral remains a highlight of any itinerary. But the express trains that thunder further northwards quickly leave the forested south behind, and you begin to feel far removed from the capital. Travelling becomes more of a slog as the distances between places grow ever greater. As Trøndelag gives way to **Nordland** things get increasingly wild – "Arthurian", thought Evelyn Waugh – though, with the exception of the scenery you can see from the train or the main road, there is little of interest to delay you between Trondheim and the engaging steel town of **Mo-i-Rana**.

Just north of Mo-i-Rana you cross the **Arctic Circle** – one of the principal targets for many travellers – at a point where the cruel scenery seems strikingly appropriate. The circle marks the southernmost point at which for at least one day a year the sun does not sink below the horizon in summer, or rise above it in winter – both the Midnight Sun and Polar Night lengthen the further you travel north. North of the Arctic Circle, the mountains of the interior roll down to a craggy coastline and even the towns, the largest of which is the port of **Bodø**, have a feral quality. The iron ore port of **Narvik**, in the far north of Nordland, has perhaps the wildest setting of them all, and was the scene of some of the fiercest fighting by the Allies and Norwegian Army in World War II. To the west lie the **Vesterålen and Lofoten islands**, strung out along a beautiful chain of mountains and indented with fjords in the north between **Harstad** and **Andenes**. Among a handful of idyllic fishing villages the pick is Å, though **Henningsvaer** and **Stamsund** come a close second.

Transport is good, which is just as well given the isolated nature of much of the region. The **Hurtigrute coastal boat** stops at all the major settlements on its route up the Norwegian coast from Bergen to Kirkenes, while the islands are accessed by a

---

ACCOMMODATION PRICE CODES

The hotels and guesthouses listed in this chapter have been graded according to the following price bands, based on the cost of the **least expensive double room during high season** (late June to Aug). However, almost every hotel offers seasonal and/or weekend discounts, and wherever possible we've given two grades, covering both the regular and the discounted rate.

   ① Under 500kr   ② 500–700kr   ③ 700–900kr
   ④ 900–1200kr   ⑤ 1200–1500kr   ⑥ Over 1500kr

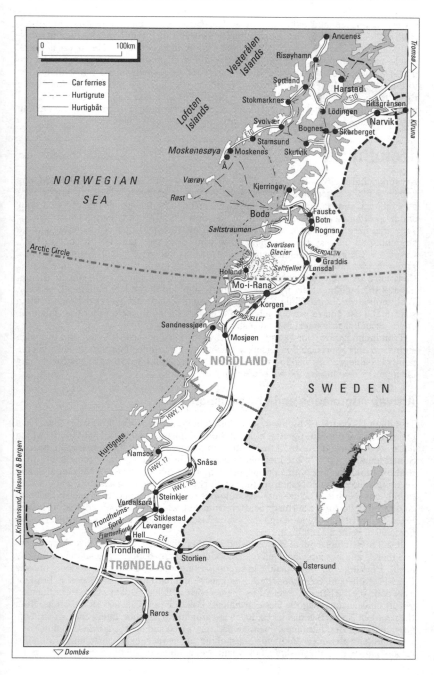

variety of **ferries** and **express boats**. The **E6** – sometimes known as the "Arctic Highway" – is the major road north along the coast from Trondheim; it's kept in excellent condition, though caravans can make the going very slow. The **train** network reaches as far north as Fauske and nearby Bodø, from either of which **buses** make the trip to Narvik, itself the terminal of a separate rail line which runs the few kilometres to the border and then south through Sweden. The only real problem is likely to be **time**. It's a day or two's journey from Trondheim to Fauske, another to Narvik, and without time to spare you should think twice before venturing further: the travelling can be arduous, and in any case it's pointless if done at a hectic pace.

Trondheim

An atmospheric city with much of its antique centre still intact, **TRONDHEIM** was known until the sixteenth century as Nidaros ("mouth of the river Nid"), its importance as a military and economic power base underpinned by the excellence of its harbour and its position at the head of a wide and fertile valley. The early Norse parliament, or *Ting*, met here, and the cathedral was a major pilgrimage centre at the end of a route stretching all the way back to Oslo. After a fire destroyed much of the city in 1681, Caspar de Cicignon, a military engineer from Luxembourg, rebuilt Trondheim on a grid-iron plan, with broad avenues radiating from the centre to act as firebreaks. Cicignon's layout has survived intact, giving the city centre an airy, elegant air, though most of the buildings date from the commercial boom of the late nineteenth century. With timber warehouses lining the river and doughty stone structures dotting the main streets, the city centre is a suitably dignified and prosperous setting for the cathedral, one of Scandinavia's finest medieval structures.

Trondheim is now Norway's third city, but the pace is slow and easy and the main sights are best appreciated in leisurely fashion over a couple of days. A genial and eminently likeable place, a visit to Trondheim is also a pleasant way to wave goodbye to city life if you're heading for the wilds of the north.

Arrival, information and city transport

Trondheim is on the E6 highway, seven or eight hours' drive (540km) from Oslo. It's a major stop for the **Hurtigrute coastal boat** (information on ☎81 03 00 00), which docks at the harbour north of the centre, from where it's a dull fifteen-minute walk to **Sentralstasjon** (☎177), the gleaming bus and train terminal, where there's an **information kiosk** dealing with all transport enquiries. You can save yourself the dull and seemingly interminable walk from the Hurtigrute quay by taking a taxi – it's about 50kr to the city centre. The all-year **Kystekspressen passenger express boat** from Kristiansund docks at the Hurtigbåt Pirterminalen, which is also behind Sentralstasjon. From Sentralstasjon, you simply cross the bridge to reach the triangular island that holds all of central Trondheim.

If you're **driving**, a toll of 20kr is levied in either direction on the E6 near Trondheim, and there's another municipal toll of 12kr (Mon–Fri 6am–6pm) as you approach the city itself. **Parking** can be a pain. On-street parking during restricted periods (mostly Mon–Fri 8am–6pm, Sat 10am–1pm) is expensive and hard to find, so it's best to head for a car park: try the handy Torvet P-hus, in the centre at Erling Skakkes gate 16, or the marginally cheaper (and slightly less convenient) Bakke P-hus, east across the bridge from the centre at Nedre Bakklandet 60. Rates are around 7kr an hour, much cheaper than on-street parking. At other times, on-street parking is free and spaces are easy to find.

Trondheim **airport** is 35km northeast of the city at Vaernes. Airport buses (Mon–Fri & Sun 5am–9pm, Sat 5am–5pm; 50kr) run every fifteen to thirty minutes between the

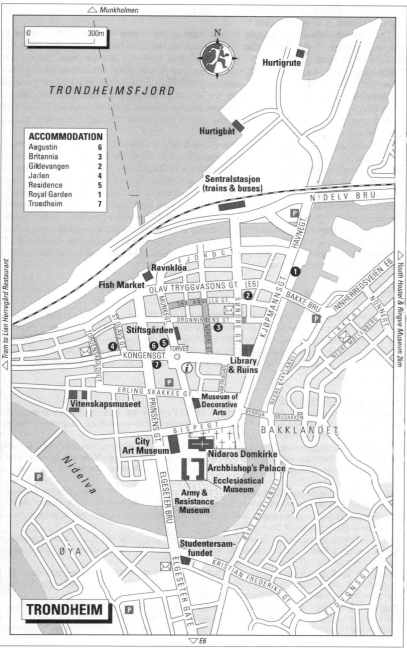

△ *Munkholmen*

0   300m

N

TRONDHEIMSFJORD

Hurtigrute

Hurtigbåt

ACCOMMODATION
Augustin	6
Britannia	3
Gildevangen	2
Jarlen	4
Residence	5
Royal Garden	1
Trondheim	7

Sentralstasjon
(trains & buses)

NIDELV BRU

HAVNEGT.

△ *Tram to Lian Herregård Restaurant*

FJORDGT.

Ravnkloa

Fish Market

OLAV TRYGGVASONS GT. (E6)

MUNKEGT.

IHS. ANGELLS GT.

DRONNINGENS GT.

SØNDRE GT.

BAKKE BRU

KJØPMANNSGT.

INNHERREDSVEIEN E6

NONNEGT.

KIRKEG.

NEDRE MØLLENBERG

△ *Youth Hostel & Ringve Museum 2km*

Stiftsgården

ST OLAVS GT.

TORDENSKJOLDSGT.

❹ ❻❺ TORVET
KONGENSGT.
❼ *i*
Library
& Ruins

NØRRE GT.

VÅR FRUEGT.

NEDRE BAKKLANDET

Vitenskapsmuseet

ERLING SKAKKES GT.

PRINSENS GT.

Museum of
Decorative
Arts

BYBRUA BRUBAKKEN

BAKKLANDET

BISPEGT.

City
Art Museum

ELGESETER BRU

Nidelva

Nidaros Domkirke

Archbishop's Palace

Ecclesiastical
Museum

Army &
Resistance
Museum

ØVRE BAKKLANDET

ØYA

Studentersam-
fundet

ELGESETER GATE

KRISTIAN FREDERIKS GT.

EIDSVQNSGT.

TRONDHEIM

▽ *E6*

airport, Sentralstasjon, the *Radisson SAS Royal Garden Hotel* and the *Britannia Hotel* in the city centre, a 45-minute ride.

The **tourist office**, Munkegata 19, sits right in the centre of town on the corner of the main square, Torvet (mid-May to early June & late Aug Mon–Fri 8.30am–6pm, Sat & Sun 10am–4pm; early to late June & mid-Aug Mon–Fri 8.30am–8pm, Sat & Sun 10am–6pm; early Aug Mon–Fri 8.30am–10pm, Sat & Sun 10am–8pm; Sept to mid-May Mon–Fri 9am–4pm; ☎73 92 94 00, *www.taas.no*). They provide the free and very useful *Trondheim Guide* (also available from the information racks at Sentralstasjon), plus a wide range of other free tourist literature; change money outside banking hours; sell hiking maps; and have a limited supply of private rooms, though these are almost entirely way out in the suburbs.

The best way of exploring the centre is **on foot** – it only takes about ten minutes to walk from one end to the other. Alternatively, the city provides **free bicycle hire**, with brightly coloured municipal bikes available from racks all over the city centre – you pay a small deposit (20kr) to release them. The tourist office issues a map marking the location of the racks, but the bikes are popular, so don't be amazed if the nearest rack is empty. For longer excursions, mountain bikes can be hired from Ila Sikkelsenter, Steinberget 1 (☎73 51 09 40), for about 140kr a day. Otherwise, transport in town is by **buses** and **trams** with flat-fare tickets costing 19kr. If you're going outside town to one of the outlying museums or the campsite, it might be worth buying the unlimited 24-hour public transport ticket, the dagskort, which costs 45kr from the driver and is valid on all local buses and trams.

Accommodation

Accommodation is plentiful in Trondheim, with a choice of private rooms, two hostels, and a selection of reasonably priced hotels and guesthouses (*pensjonater*). Most of the more appealing places are centrally located. **Private rooms**, bookable through the tourist office, are good value too, with a flat-rate charge of 350kr per double per night (250kr single), plus a 30kr booking fee – the only drawback is that they're usually out in the suburbs.

Hotels and guesthouses

Best Western Residence, Torvet (☎73 52 83 80, fax 73 52 64 60). Package-tour favourite on the main square, with standard double rooms. More expensive than most of its competitors, though there's a discount of thirty percent in summer. ④/③.

Britannia, Dronningens gate 5 (☎73 53 53 53, fax 73 51 29 00). Right in the middle of town, this long-established hotel has a magnificent Art Nouveau breakfast room, complete with Moorish water fountain, Egyptian murals and Corinthian columns. Its comfortable rooms are heavily discounted in summer. ⑤/③.

Comfort Hotel Augustin, Kongens gate 26 (☎73 54 70 00, fax 73 55 70 01). Routine chain hotel in a big, old brick building not far from the Torvet. Functional but perfectly adequate rooms. ④/②.

Pensjonat Jarlen, Kongens gate 40 (☎73 51 32 18, fax 73 52 80 80). Guesthouse with basic rooms at bargain prices – handy for the sights. ①.

Rainbow Gildevangen, Søndre gate 22b (☎73 51 01 00, fax 73 52 38 98). In a sturdy Romanesque Revival stone building, a couple of minutes' walk northeast of Torvet, this chain hotel offers eighty comfortable modern rooms at economical prices. ④/③.

Rainbow Trondheim, Kongens gate 15 (☎73 50 50 50, fax 73 51 60 58). Big and popular chain hotel in a plain and chunky modern block right in the centre. Reasonably priced to begin with, there are also summer discounts of twenty-five percent. ④/③.

Radisson SAS Royal Garden, Kjøpmannsgata 73 (☎73 80 30 00, fax 73 80 30 50). Stylish modern hotel with sweeping architectural lines and wonderfully comfortable beds. Good summer deals make this one to check out first if you're looking for upmarket lodgings. Sumptuous breakfasts too. ⑥/③.

Hostels and camping

InterRail Centre, Elgeseter gate 1 (☎73 89 95 38). Operated by the University's student society, this has basic B&B accommodation in a couple of hundred rooms at just 105kr per person per night. There's a cheap, all-day café here too, plus luggage storage. It's a twenty-minute walk from Torvet, half that from the cathedral, or take bus #41, #42, #48, #49, #52 or #63 along Prinsens gate and ask for the *Studentersamfundet* – it's the unusual big, red round house just over the bridge at the south end of Prinsens gate. Open late June to mid-Aug.

Youth Hostel, Weidemannsvei 41 (☎73 87 44 50, fax 73 87 44 55). This HI hostel has twenty six- and thirty four-bedded rooms. It's very institutional – it looks more like a hospital than somewhere you'd want to spend the night – and a dorm bed will set you back 170kr including breakfast, a double room, of which there are just a couple, 440kr. It's a twenty-minute hike east from the centre – out over the Bakke bru (bridge), straight uphill along busy Innherredsveien (the E6), turn right up Wessels gate and it's on the left at the fourth crossroads. Bus #63 from Sentralstasjon and Dronningens gate also runs in that direction. Open all year except Christmas, New Year and Easter.

The City

The historic centre of Trondheim sits on a small triangle of land bordered by the River Nid, with the curve of the long and slender Trondheimsfjord beyond. **Torvet** is the main city square, a spacious open area anchored by a statue of St Olav perched on a tall stone pillar like some medieval Nelson. The broad avenues that radiate out from here were once flanked by long rows of wooden buildings, which served all the needs of the small town and administrative centre. Most of these older structures are long gone, replaced for the most part by uninspiring modern buildings – one notable survivor is the **Stiftsgården**, a fine timber mansion erected in the late eighteenth century. Nevertheless, this is small beer compared with the city's highlight, the **cathedral**, an imposing, largely medieval structure which dominates the southern part of the centre. Close by is the pick of Trondheim's several museums: the **Museum of Decorative Arts** and the **City Art Museum**, while nearby, on the far side of the old town bridge, **Bybrua**, is the pretty clutter of old warehouses and timber dwellings of **Bakklandet**, now the most fashionable part of town and home to its best restaurants and bars.

Nidaros Domkirke

The goal of Trondheim's pilgrims in times past was the colossal cathedral, **Nidaros Domkirke**, Scandinavia's largest surviving medieval building (May to mid-June & late Aug to mid-Sept Mon–Fri 9am–3pm, Sat 9am–2pm, Sun 1–4pm; mid-June to late Aug Mon–Fri 9am–6pm, Sat 9am–2pm, Sun 1–4pm; mid-Sept to April Mon–Fri noon–2.30pm, Sat 11.30am–2pm, Sun 1–3pm; 25kr). Gloriously restored following the ravages of the Reformation and several fires, it remains the focal point of any visit to the city and one of the country's architectural highlights. The building, still known by Trondheim's former name, is dedicated to King – later Saint – Olav. Born in 995, **Olav Haraldsson** followed the traditional life of the Viking chieftain from the tender age of twelve, "rousing the steel-storm" (as the saga writers put it) from Finland to Ireland. He also served as a mercenary to both the duke of Normandy and King Ethelred of England, and it was during this time that he was converted to Christianity. In 1015 he invaded Norway, defeated his enemies and became king, though his zealous imposition of Christianity alienated many of his followers and the bribes of Olav's rival Knut (Canute), King of England and Denmark, did the rest: Olav's retainers deserted him and he was forced into exile in 1028. Two years later, he was back in the Trøndelag, but the army he had raised was far too weak to defeat his enemies, and Olav was killed in battle near Trondheim.

Olav may have lost his kingdom, but the nationwide church he founded had no intention of losing ground. Needing a local **saint** to consolidate its position, the church carefully nurtured the myth of Olav, a beatification assisted by the oppressive rule of the "foreigner" Knut. After the final battle, Olav's body had been spirited away and buried on the banks of the River Nid at what is today Trondheim. There were rumours of miracles in the vicinity of the grave and, when the bishop arrived to investigate these strange goings-on, he exhumed the body and found it uncorrupted. Olav was declared a saint, his body was placed in a silver casket and Olav Kyrre, who became King of Norway in 1066, started work on the grand church that was to house the remains in appropriate style. Over the years the church was altered and enlarged to accommodate the growing bands of medieval tourists. It achieved cathedral status in 1152 and became the traditional burial place of Norwegian royalty.

Best visited in the early morning, when it's reasonably free of tour groups, the cathedral is a magnificent blue- and green-grey soapstone edifice with a copper-green spire and roof and a fancy set of gargoyles on the choir. It's also a true amalgam of architectural styles. The original eleventh-century church was a simple basilica, but subsequent alterations enlarged it considerably. The Romanesque transepts, with their heavy hooped windows and dog-tooth decoration, were built by English stonemasons from Lincoln in the twelfth century, while the early Gothic choir, with its flying buttresses and intricate tracery, is clearly influenced by contemporaneous churches in England. The nave was built in the early thirteenth century, also in the early Gothic style, but was destroyed by fire in 1719; the present structure is a painstakingly accurate late nineteenth-century replica.

Inside the cathedral, the gloomy half-light hides much of the lofty decorative work, but it is possible to examine the striking **choir screen**, whose wooden figures are the work of Gustav Vigeland (see p.216). The other item of particular interest is a famous fourteenth-century **altar frontal** (the front panel of an altar painting) displayed in a chapel off the ambulatory, directly behind the high altar. This is the earliest surviving representation of Olav's life and times, created during a period when few Norwegians could read or write and the saint's cult had to be promoted visually.

In summer there are English-language **guided tours** of the church, included in the admission price (mid-June to mid-Aug at 11am, 2pm & 4pm; 30min), during which you can take a peek at the assorted baubles of the Norwegian **crown jewels** (June to late Aug Mon–Fri 9.30am–12.30pm, Sun 1–4pm; April, May & late Aug to Oct Fri noon–2pm; free), kept at the west end of the church. What you won't see is St Olav's silver casket-coffin: this was taken to Denmark and melted down into coins in 1537. It's also well worth climbing the cathedral **tower** (late June to late Aug Mon–Fri 9am–6pm, Sat 9am–2pm, Sun 1–4pm; 5kr), from where there's a fine view of the city and the forested hills that surround it, with the fjord trailing one way, the river valley the other.

The Archbishop's Palace

Behind the Domkirke lies the heavily restored **Archbishop's Palace** (Erkebispegården). This courtyard complex was originally built in the twelfth century for the third archbishop, Øystein, but two stone-and-brick wings are all that survive of the original quadrangle – the others were added later. After the archbishops were kicked out during the Reformation, the palace became the residence of the Danish governors. It was subsequently used as the city armoury, and many of the old weapons are now displayed in the **Army and Resistance Museum** (Rustkammeret med Hjemmefrontmuseet; June–Aug Mon–Fri 9am–3pm, Sat & Sun 11am–4pm; Feb–May & Sept–Nov Sat & Sun 11am–4pm; free), which occupies the west wing. The first floor gives the broad details of Norway's involvement with the interminable Dano–Swedish wars that wracked Scandinavia from the fifteenth to the nineteenth century. Of more general interest, the second floor describes the German invasion and occupation of Norway during World War II, dealing honestly with the sensitive issue of collaboration: you can turn on the radio to hear Vidkun Quisling's radio speech announcing his coup d'état of April 9, 1940. There are also some intriguing displays on the daring antics of the Norwegian Resistance, notably in an extraordinary – perhaps hair-brained – attempt to sink the battleship *Tirpitz* as it lay moored in an inlet of the Trondheimsfjord in 1942. This escapade, like so many others, involved Leif Larsen, the Resistance hero who is commemorated by a statue on the Torget in Bergen. Larsen worked closely with the Royal Navy, who organized covert operations in occupied Norway from their base in the Shetlands. Supplies and personnel were transported across the North Sea by Norwegian fishing boats – a lifeline known, in that classically understated British (and Norwegian) way, as the "Shetland bus".

Moving on, the south wing holds the smart **Ecclesiastical Museum** (late June to late Aug Mon–Sat 10am–5pm, Sun noon–5pm; late Aug to late June Mon–Sat 11am–3pm, Sun noon–4pm, closed Mon Sept–May; free with cathedral entrance), largely devoted to a few dozen medieval statues originally retrieved and stashed away for safekeeping during the nineteenth-century reconstruction of the nave and west front. Many of the statues are too battered and bruised to be particularly engaging, although they're well displayed, and several are finely carved. In particular, look out for a life-size sculpture of poor old St Denis, his head in his hands (literally), in accordance with the legend that had him beheaded in one spot and carrying his own head to his grave in another. Downstairs, an assortment of finds unearthed during a lengthy archeological investigation of the Archbishop's Palace demonstrates the secular power of the archbishops, who employed all manner of skilled artisans – from glaziers and shoemakers to rope makers, armourers and silver-workers – in the conduct of their worldly affairs, which even included the minting of their own coinage.

From the back of the Archbishop's Palace, you can stroll out onto the grassy lawns beside the **River Nid**. A trio of rusting bastions offer a reminder of the military defences that once protected this side of town, while footpaths snake round to the sturdy old tombs and wild flowers of the **graveyard**, just to the east of the cathedral's main entrance, but it's the setting that really appeals.

The Museum of Decorative Arts and City Art Museum

A couple of museums close to the Domkirke provide some varied entertainment, in particular the delightful **Museum of Decorative Arts** (Nordenfjeldske Kunstindustrimueum; late June to late Aug Mon–Sat 10am–5pm, Sun noon–5pm; late Aug to late June Mon–Sat 10am–3pm, Thurs till 5pm, Sun noon–4pm, closed Mon Sept–May; 30kr), a couple of minutes' walk away at Munkegata 5. The museum's collection is too extensive to be shown in its entirety at any one time, so displays are rotated regularly, and there's also an ambitious programme of temporary exhibitions focusing on contemporary arts, craft and design. Start in the basement, where bourgeois life in Trøndelag from the sixteenth century to 1900 is illustrated via an eclectic assemblage of furniture, faïence, glassware and silver, along with some twentieth-century pieces, notably a fine selection of Art Nouveau ceramics and furniture. The domestic theme is developed on the first floor, where there's a room kitted out by the Belgian designer and architect Henri van de Velde. An unusual display of folkloric tapestries produced in Trondheim in the early years of the twentieth century is also generally on display on this floor – they're modelled on original paintings by the Norwegian Gerhard Munthe, one of whose specialities was the portrayal of medieval folk tales. More modern works can be found on the second floor, but the highlight here is the room devoted to fourteen stunning tapestries by Hannah Ryggen, each done in a naive style with flair and vigour.

The **City Art Museum** (Trondhjems Kunstmuseum; June–Aug daily except Sat 10am–4pm; Sept–May Tues–Sun noon–4pm; 30kr), near the cathedral at Bispegata 7b, is quite small, but features an enjoyable selection of works by Johan Dahl and Thomas Fearnley, the leading figures of nineteenth-century Norwegian landscape painting, as well as the romantic canvases of Hans Gude and his chum Adolph Tidemand. Also displayed is the first overtly political work by a Norwegian artist: *The Strike* (*Streik*) was painted in 1877 by the radical Theodor Kittelsen, better known for his illustrations of the folk tales collected by Jorgen Møe and Pieter Asbjørnsen. If you missed the work of Edvard Munch in Oslo, there's a diverting selection of his woodcuts, sketches and lithographs here, including several of those disturbing, erotically charged personifications of emotions – *Lust, Fear* and *Jealousy* – that were so characteristic of his oeuvre. Munch's works are not clearly labelled, but an inventory is available free at reception. The bad news is that most of the permanent collection is not on view during some of the larger temporary exhibitions – even Munch gets the heave-ho.

From the Stiftsgården to Bakklandet
One conspicuous remnant of old timber-town Trondheim survives in the city centre – the **Stiftsgården** (early to mid-June Mon–Sat 10am–3pm, Sun noon–5pm; late June to late Aug Mon–Sat 10am–5pm, Sun noon–5pm; late Aug to early June open one day monthly – details from the tourist office; guided tours every hour on the hour; 35kr), which stretches out along Munkegata just north of Torvet. Built in 1774–78, this good-looking yellow creation is claimed to be the largest wooden building in northern Europe. These days it serves as an official royal residence – a marked social improvement on its original function as home to the provincial governor. Inside, a long series of period rooms with fanciful Italianate wall-paintings and furniture come in a range of late eighteenth- to early nineteenth-century styles, from Rococo to Biedermeier, that reflect the genteel tastes of the early occupants. The anecdotal guided tour brings a smile – but not perhaps 35kr wide.

From the Stiftsgården, it's a couple of minutes' walk east to the **medieval church ruins** discovered under the library at the far end of Kongens gate. A twelfth-century relic of the days when Trondheim had fifteen or more religious buildings, it is thought to have been a chapel dedicated to St Olav, although the evidence for this is a bit shaky. Excavations revealed nearly 500 bodies in the immediate area, which was once the church graveyard, and the skeletons on display are neatly preserved under glass. Entry is free and the site is accessible during library opening hours (June–Aug Mon–Fri 9am–4pm, Sat 10am–3pm; Sept–May Mon–Thurs 9am–7pm, Fri 9am–4pm, Sat 10am–3pm, Sun noon–4pm).

Following the river south from the library, it's a short walk to the **Bybrua** (Old Town Bridge), an elegant wooden reach with splendid views over the early eighteenth-century gabled and timbered warehouses which flank Kjøpmannsgata. Most of these are now restaurants and offices, and there are more restaurants and several groovy bars at the far end of the bridge in the brightly painted old timber houses of the **Bakklandet** area, Trondheim's own "Left Bank". From the bridge, it's a couple of minutes' walk back to the grounds of the cathedral.

Out from the centre: the Ringve museum
Devoted to musical instruments from all over the world, the **Ringve Museum** (late May daily noon–3pm; June to mid-Aug daily 11am–6pm; mid-Aug to mid-Sept daily 11am–3pm; mid-Sept to late May occasional guided tours, ring for details ☎73 92 24 11; 60kr) occupies a delightful eighteenth-century country house and courtyard complex on the hilly Lade peninsula some two kilometres northeast of the city centre. The museum is divided into two sections: the first, in the main building, focuses on antique European instruments in period settings, with several demonstrations included on a lengthy – and obligatory – guided tour. The second, in the old barn, offers a quick, self-guided zip through some of the key moments of musical history, including topics such as "The Invention of the Piano", "Pop & Rock" and – the real humdinger – "The Marching Band Movement in Norway". Immaculately maintained, the surrounding

botanical gardens make the most of the scenic setting. To get there, take bus #3 or #4 from near the north end of Munkegata to Lade.

Eating and drinking

As befits Norway's third city, Trondheim has a good selection of first-rate **restaurants**, the pick of which are concentrated in Bakklandet and along Kjøpmannsgata, over the river. Chinese and Italian places are popular, but it's the Norwegian restaurants which offer the most distinctive cuisine, with seafood and Arctic specialities, like char and reindeer, a special treat. The best of Trondheim's **café-bars** are also concentrated in Bakklandet and, as in the rest of urban Norway, these laid-back establishments are the most fashionable places to eat and/or drink – well into the early hours. The city's busiest **bars** are concentrated right in the centre around the junction of Dronningens gate and Nordre gate. They heave on the weekend with students, townies and convention-goers, but are a bit too full of people on the pull for many tastes, even if you can ignore the revving of sports cars. Finally, the city's mobile **fast-food** stalls are concentrated around Sentralstasjon and along Kongens gate, on either side of Torvet.

Restaurants and café-bars

Bryggen, Øvre Bakklandet 66 (☎73 52 02 30). Superb seafood restaurant at the east end of the Bybrua. The daily specials, mostly featuring the catch of the day, are a delight. Main courses average about 180kr.

Dromedar, Nedre Bakklandet 3A. A fashionable café-bar with a laid-back, amiable atmosphere located a few metres north of the Bybrua. Tasty, filling and low-price food with a wholefood slant. If it's full, as it often is, try the similar *Bla Bær* just along the street.

Havfruen, Kjøpmannsgate 7 (☎73 53 26 26). An excellent fish restaurant near the cathedral – one of the best in town, with prices to match. Main courses from 180kr. Try to book in advance.

Markens Grøde, Nedre Bakklandet 5 (☎73 53 16 11). The city's main specialist vegetarian restaurant, with tasty food, low prices and a friendly atmosphere.

New China Garden, Kjøpmannsgata 21 (☎73 51 47 77). Excellent Chinese restaurant specializing in Szechuan dishes at reasonable prices.

Ni Muser, Bispegata 9. Just along the street from the City Art Museum, this excellent, relaxed little café-bar serves up tasty snacks and meals from a variety of European cuisines. Prices are low, and many customers have an arty-academic look, perhaps thanks to the small gallery of contemporary art located upstairs. There's a terrace bar at the back.

Posepilten, Prinsens gate 32, at junction with Dronningens gate. Easy-going café-bar with a wide-ranging menu – everything from vegetarian specials through to Mexican tortillas. Tasty, filling and inexpensive food with occasional live music too.

Radisson SAS Royal Garden, Kjøpmannsgata 73 (☎73 80 30 00). Despite its riverside setting, the ground-floor café-restaurant of this plush hotel lacks atmosphere (it serves as the hotel's breakfast area too), but the all-you-can-eat, self-service buffets of good-quality food are outstanding value at around 75kr. They're available most evenings from about 6pm to 9pm.

Zia Teresa Pizzeria, Vår Frue gate 4 (☎73 52 64 22). Easily the best pizzeria in town, with prices from as little as 100kr. The adjacent *Benito's Mat og Vinhus* (same telephone number) is run by the same family and offers traditional Italian dishes in a more formal setting, but still at reasonable prices. East of Torvet, off Kongens gate.

Bars

Bobbys Bar & Snadderi, Søndre gate 22a. Small, intimate and youthful bar in the town centre.

Carl Johan Møteplass, Olav Tryggvasons gate 24. Jam-packed on the weekend, this bar is popular with locals and visitors in equal measure.

Frakken, Dronningens gate, at junction with Nordre gate. Bar and nightclub that sees most of Trondheim's permed hairdos passing through its doors. Popular – and raucous – at the weekend.

Underetg, Kjøpmanns gate 7. On the floor below the *Havfruen* restaurant, this bar caters for the thirtysomething (plus) age range and often has live jazz on Fri and Sat nights.

Listings

Airlines Braathens (☎74 84 32 00); SAS (☎74 80 41 00).

Car rental Avis, Kjøpmannsgata 34 (☎73 52 69 15); Budget, Elgeseter gate 21 (☎73 94 10 25) and at the *Radisson SAS Royal Garden Hotel*, Kjøpmannsgata 73 (☎73 52 69 20).

Dentist ☎73 50 55 00.

Emergencies Police ☎112; Ambulance ☎113; Hospital ☎73 52 25 00.

Hiking Trondhjems Turistforening, Munkegata 64 (Mon–Fri 9am–4pm; ☎73 92 42 00) are the local branch of the DNT and offer advice on the region's hiking trails and huts. They also organize a variety of guided walks and cross-country skiing trips, from one-day excursions to longer expeditions.

Pharmacy St Olav Vaktapotek, Kjøpmannsgata 65 (☎73 52 66 66). Open Mon–Sat 8.30am–midnight, Sun 10am–midnight.

Police Kongens gate 87 (☎73 89 90 90).

Post office Main office at Dronningens gate 10 (Mon–Fri 8am–5pm, Sat 9am–1pm).

Taxis Ranks can be found at Torvet, Sentralstasjon, Søndregata and the *Radisson SAS Royal Garden Hotel*; or call ☎73 50 50 73 (24hr).

Vinmonopolet City centre off-licence at Kjøpmannsgata 32.

North from Trondheim to Fauske

North of Trondheim, it's a long haul up the coast to the next major places of interest: **Bodø**, the main ferry port for the Lofotens, and the gritty but likeable town of **Narvik**, respectively 730km and 908km distant. The easiest way to make the bulk of the trip is by **train**, a rattling good journey with the scenery becoming wilder and bleaker the further north you go – and you'll usually get a blast from the whistle as you cross the Arctic Circle. The train takes nine hours to reach **Fauske**, where the line reaches its northern limit and turns west for the last 65-kilometre dash to Bodø. At Fauske, there are **bus** connections north to Narvik, a further five-hour drive, but many travellers take an overnight break here – though in fact nearby Bodø is a far more pleasant place.

If you're **driving**, you'll find the E6 – which runs all the way from Trondheim to Narvik and points north – too slow to make more than three or four hundred kilometres comfortably in any one day – more, and the journey becomes a tiresome thrash. Fortunately, there are several pleasant places to stop, beginning with Trøndelag's **Snåsa**, a relaxing village beside the E6 with somewhere good to stay. Further on, in Nordland, the next region up, lies **Mo-i-Rana**, once a grimy steel town, but now attractively rehashed and the obvious starting point for a visit to the **Svartisen glacier**, which crowns the coastal peaks close by.

North to Snåsa

Leaving Trondheim, the E6 tunnels and twists its way round the fjord to **HELL**, a busy rail junction, where one line forks north to slice through the dales and hills of Trøndelag en route to Fauske, while the other heads east for the 70km haul to the Swedish frontier, with Østersund beckoning beyond. Just beyond Hell, the road forks too, with the E6 thumping on north and the E14 heading east. Pressing on with the E6, it's about 160km to **SNÅSA**, a sleepy, sprawling hamlet 6km off the main road, with a pretty little hilltop church. On the west side of the village is the *Snåsa Hotell* (☎74 15 10 57, fax 74 15 16 15; ③/②), a modern, rather spartan affair with comfortable bedrooms and a lovely setting overlooking the lake; it's a peaceful spot, ideal if you want to rest up after a long drive. The hotel also operates a small **campsite** (same numbers) with spaces for tents and caravans, as well as huts (②). There's a restaurant here too, serving mundane but filling Norwegian staples – but telephone ahead to check if it will still be open if you expect to arrive late.

Mo-i-Rana and the Svartisen glacier

Beyond Snåsa, the E6 leaves the wooded valleys of the Trøndelag for the wider, harsher landscapes of **Nordland**. The road bobs across bleak plateaux, scuttles along rangy river valleys and eventually – after 300km – reaches **MO-I-RANA** or "Mo", hugging the head of the Ranafjord. A minor port and market town until World War II, Mo was transformed by the construction of a large steel plant in the postwar period. The plant dominated proceedings until the 1980s, when there was some economic diversification and the town began to clean itself up. The fjord shore was cleared of its industrial clutter and the E6 was rerouted to create the pleasantly spacious and surprisingly leafy town centre of today. Most of Mo is resolutely modern, but look out for the pretty **Mo kirke** (church), a good-looking structure of 1832 with a pitched roof and onion dome, perched on a hill on the eastern edge of the town centre.

Mo's **bus** and **train stations** are close together, down by the fjord on Ole Tobias Olsens gate – the compact town centre lies to the east of Ole Tobias Olsens gate, with the foot of the main pedestrianized street, Jernbanegata, opposite the bus station. The **tourist office** is 200m to the south, also by the fjord (late June to early Aug Mon–Fri 9am–8pm, Sat 10am–4pm, Sun 1–7pm; early Aug to late June Mon–Fri 9am–4pm; ☎75 13 92 00).

The pick of the town's several **hotels** is the excellently run and very comfortable *Meyergården Hotell*, at the far end of Ole Tobias Olsens gate (☎75 13 40 00, fax 75 13 40 01; ④/②). Most of the hotel is modern, but the original lodge has survived and is maintained in period style. Mo also has a no-frills **youth hostel** (☎75 15 09 63, fax 75 15 15 30; doubles ①; mid-May to Aug), pleasantly situated on a wooded hillside 2km south of town just off (and signposted from) the E6. The best **restaurant** is at the *Meyergården Hotell*, with main courses from around 130kr.

The Svartisen glacier

Mo-i-Rana is an ideal base for an excursion to the **Svartisen** (literally "Black Ice"), Norway's second largest glacier, which covers roughly 370 square kilometres of mountain and valley between the E6 and the coast. It's actually divided into two sections – east and west – by the Vesterdal valley, though this cleft is a recent phenomenon: when it was measured in 1905, the glacier was one giant block, about 25 percent bigger than it is today. The highest sections of the glacier lie at around 1500m, but parts descend to as little as 170m above sea level – the lowest-lying glacial arms in Europe. To get to the nearest nodule, drive north from Mo on the E6 for about 12km and then take the signed turning to the glacier, a straightforward 23-kilometre drive ending beside the ice-green, glacial lake **Svartisvatnet**. From here, **boats** (late June to late Aug hourly 10am–4pm; 20min each way; 70kr return) shuttle across the lake, but note that services can't begin until the ice has melted – usually by late June, but check with Mo tourist office. From the boat, the great convoluted folds of the glacier look rather like white-blue custard, but close up, after a stiff three-hour hike from the jetty up to the base of the glacier past the rocky detritus left by the retreating ice, the sheer size of the glacier becomes apparent – a mighty grinding and groaning wall of ice edged by a jumble of ice chunks, columns and boulders.

There are no buses to the glacier, but **car hire** is available at relatively reasonable rates in Mo from Bilhuset, at the Statoil gas station, Verkstedveien 1 (☎75 12 76 00); reckon on 600kr per day.

North along the Coast Route

The quickest route north from Mo is along the E6. This is the route taken by long-distance buses and the train and it has several advantages, not least the scenic journey across the barren wastes straddling the Arctic Circle. It is, however, possible to detour west along the E12 from Mo by car to pick up, after 37km, Hwy 17, the **Coastal Route** (Kystriksveien), which extends right along the coast from near Steinker, south of Snåsa, to Bodø. If you opt for this detour, pick up a copy of the **free booklet** on the Coastal Route at Mo tourist office; it contains all Hwy 17's car-ferry timetables. From the E12/Hwy 17 crossroads, it's some 60km to the **Kilboghamn-Jektvik** ferry (Mon–Sat 6 daily, 3 on Sun; 1hr; driver & car 103kr) and a further 30km to the ferry linking **Ågskardet** with **Forøy** (Mon–Sat 12 daily; 10min; driver and car 39kr). The first ferry takes you across the Arctic Circle; after the second you can see an arm of the Svartisen glacier across the slender Holandsfjorden. For a closer look, stop at the information centre in **HOLAND**, 12km beyond Forøy, and catch the **passenger boat** (late May to early Sept daily 8am–7pm; every 45min or 1hr 30min; 15min; 40kr return), which zips across the fjord to meet a connecting bus; this travels the couple of kilometres up to the **Svartisen Tourist Centre** (☎75 75 00 11), a mere 250m from the ice. The Tourist Centre has a café, cabins (②) and is the base for four-hour guided glacier walks (mid-June to mid-Aug) – prior booking is essential. From Holand, it's 170km to Bodø.

The Arctic Circle and Fauske

Given its appeal as a travellers' totem, and considering the amount of effort it takes to actually get here, crossing the **Arctic Circle**, about 80km north of Mo, is a bit of a disappointment. The landscape, uninhabited for the most part, is undeniably bleak, but the gleaming **Arctic Circle Centre** (Polarsirkelsenteret; daily: early to mid-June & Aug 9am–8pm; late June to July 8am–10pm; May & early Sept 10am–6pm) disfigures the scene: a giant lampshade of a building plonked by the roadside and stuffed with every sort of tourist bauble imaginable. You'll whizz by on the bus, the train toots its whistle as it passes by, and drivers can, of course, shoot past too – though the temptation to brave the crowds is strong and, even if you resist the Arctic exhibition (50kr), you'll probably get snared by either the "Polarsirkelen" certificate, or the specially stamped postcards. Outside the centre, a couple of simple stone memorials are poignant reminders of crueller times: they pay tribute to the Yugoslav and Soviet POWs who laboured under terrible conditions to build the Arctic railroad (Nordlandsbanen) to Narvik for the Germans in World War II.

Fauske

But for a brief stretch of line from Narvik into Sweden further north, **FAUSKE** – some 100km north of the Arctic Circle on the E6 – marks the northernmost point of the Norwegian rail network and is, consequently, an important transport hub. Along with Bodø, the town is a departure point of the Nord-Norgeekspressen, the **express bus** service that complements the railway by carrying passengers as far as Nordkapp. Buses leave twice daily from beside Fauske train station and tickets can be purchased from the driver or beforehand at any bus station. There are left luggage lockers at the train station plus information on the region's ferries. There's a fifty percent discount for InterRail and ScanRail pass holders on the first step of the route to Narvik, a gorgeous five-hour run past fjords, peaks and snow.

Most northbound travellers spend the night in Fauske rather than making a quick change onto the connecting bus to Narvik, though Bodø is in fact a more palatable choice. From Fauske **train station**, it's a five- to ten-minute walk down the hill and left at the T-junction to the **tourist office** (Mon–Fri 9am–5pm, Sat 10am–2pm; ☎75 64 33 03) and 24hr gas station. From here, it's only a few metres more to the main drag, Storgata, which doubles as the E6. Storgata runs parallel to the fjord and accommodates the handful of shops that pass for a town centre. At no. 82, you'll also find the better of the town's two **hotels**, the *Fauske* (☎75 64 38 33, fax 75 64 57 37; ④/③), a solid square block whose interior is made slightly sickly by a surfeit of locally quarried salmon-coloured marble. Marble apart, the hotel rooms are comfortable enough, and the big and tasty breakfast is a snip at 60kr – it's handy too for those staying at the spartan **youth hostel** (☎75 64 67 06, fax 75 64 59 95; doubles ①), which doesn't provide meals. The hostel is about 500m west of the hotel and signposted off Storgata. A third, and much more scenic option is the *Lundhøgda* **campsite** (☎75 64 39 66; June–Sept), which occupies a splendid location overlooking the mountains and the fjord about 3km west of the town centre; head out of town along the E80, the Bodø road, and watch for the sign pointing down a country lane, ablaze with wild flowers in the summertime and flanked by old timber buildings. The campsite takes caravans, has pitches for tents and huts too (①).

Bodø and around

BODØ, 63km west of Fauske along the E80, can be reached either by bus from Fauske or on the train from Trondheim, which terminates there. Founded in 1816, Bodø struggled to survive in its early years, but was saved from insignificance by the herring boom of the 1860s. It later accrued several industrial plants and became an important regional centre, but was then heavily bombed during World War II, and nowadays there's precious little left of the proud, nineteenth-century buildings that once flanked the waterfront. Nonetheless, Bodø manages a cheerful modernity, a bright and breezy place within comfortable striking distance of the old trading post of Kjerringøy, one of Nordland's most delightful spots. Bodø is also a regular stop on the Hurtigrute coastal boat route and, importantly, much the best place from which to hop over to the most interesting part of the Lofoten Islands.

In Bodø itself, the most popular tourist attraction is the imaginative **Norwegian Aviation Museum** (Norsk Luftfartsmuseum; June–Aug Mon–Fri & Sun 10am–8pm, Sat 10am–5pm; Sept–May Tues–Fri 10am–4pm, Thurs till 7pm, Sat–Sun 11am–5pm; 70kr), housed in a building constructed in the shape of a two-blaced propeller: one blade houses air force and defence exhibits, the other concerns itself with civilian displays. The hub of the two blades straddles the ring road and is topped by part of the old Bodø airport control tower. Among the planes to look out for are a Spitfire, a reminder that two RAF squadrons were manned by Norwegians during World War II, and a rare example of the Norwegian-made Hønningstad C-5 Polar seaplane. The museum is situated about 2km southeast of the town centre, a dreary walk which you can avoid by catching the city transit Sentrumsbussen #801 (Mon–Sat every 15min 9am–4pm) from the bus station. If you have your own transport, consider driving a further 1km south along Gamle Riksvei to the onion-domed **Bodin kirke** (June–Aug daily 10am–7pm; free), a pretty little stone church which sits snugly among the surrounding meadows. Dating from the thirteenth century, the church was modified after the Reformation by the addition of a tower and the widening of its windows – dark, gloomy churches were then associated with Catholic "superstition". It is, however, the colourful seventeenth-century fixtures that catch the eye, and the lovingly carved Baroque altarboard and pulpit, both painted a century later by an itinerant German artist, Gottfried Ezechiel.

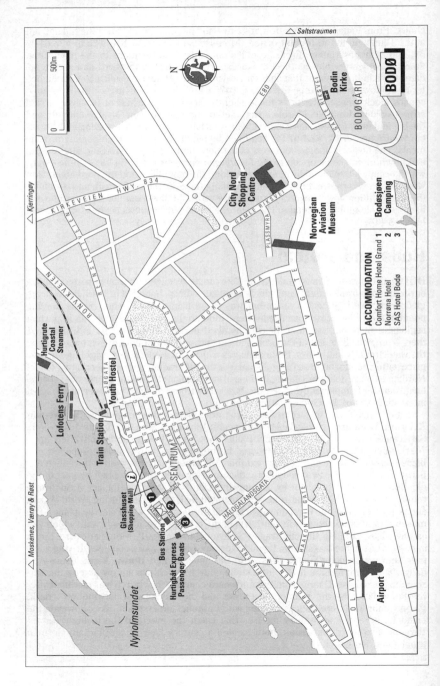

△ Saltstraumen

BODØ

N

500m

△ Kjerringøy

△ Moskenes, Værøy & Røst

KIRKEVEIEN HWY. 834

RØNVIKVEIEN

E80

GAMLE RIKSVEI

BODØGÅRD

Bodin Kirke

City Nord Shopping Centre

GAMLE RIKSVEI

Norwegian Aviation Museum

PLASSMYRA

Bodøsjøen Camping

REINSLI

SJØGATA

Youth Hostel

Hurtigrute Coastal Steamer

Lofotens Ferry

Train Station

BANKGATA

DRONNINGENS GATA

SENTRUM

 i

Glasshuset (Shopping Mall)

Bus Station

Hurtigbåt Express Passenger Boats

Nyholmsundet

BØRTINDGATA

HÅLOGALANDSGATA

HÅKON VII GATE

OLAV V GATE

HÅLOGALANDSGATA

HÅKON VII GATE

PARKVEIEN

HERNESVEIEN

OLAV V GATE

Airport

ACCOMMODATION
Comfort Home Hotel Grand 1
Norrøna Hotel 2
SAS Hotel Bodø 3

Practicalities

The southern **Lofotens ferry** (to Moskenes) and the **Hurtigrute coastal boat** use the docks respectively 500m and 700m northeast along the seafront from the **train station**. From the latter, it's 300m west along Sjøgata to the **tourist office** at Sjøgata 21 (June–Aug Mon–Fri 9am–8.30pm, Sat 10am–4pm & 6–8pm, Sun noon–4pm & 6–8pm; Sept–May Mon–Fri 9am–4pm; ☎75 52 60 00, fax 75 52 21 77, *www.bodoe.com*). The office is good for information on connections to the Lofoten Islands, rents out bikes and issues an excellent town and district guide. The **bus station** is a further 300m west along Sjøgata, beside the gigantic *Radisson SAS Hotel Bodø*. If you're heading further north, note that the same half-price bus deal for InterRail and ScanRail pass holders travelling from Fauske to Narvik operates from Bodø too. Beyond the bus station, at the west end of Sjøgata, another dock deals with **Hurtigbåt** passenger express services to the Lofotens, notably to Svolvær and Stokmarknes. Bodø **airport** is 2km south of the centre; SAS have a ticket office (☎81 00 33 00) there and several authorized agents in the centre – Bennett, Moloveien 20 (☎75 50 60 70), are as good as any. Bodø's local **DNT** branch is Bodø og Omegn Turistforening; for cabin keys and to register, go to Berg Sport, in the town centre at Torvgata 4 (☎75 52 48 90).

Accommodation

There's plenty of accommodation in Bodø. The tourist office has a small supply of **private rooms** in and around the town for 250–300kr per double, plus a 15kr booking fee (25kr outside town). Alternatively, there's a **youth hostel** next door to the station at Sjøgata 55 (☎ & fax 75 52 11 22; doubles ①), although – apart from the convenient location – it has precious little to commend it. Moving up the scale, there are several central **hotels**, including the inexpensive *Norrøna*, in a large modern block close to the bus station at Storgata 4 (☎75 52 55 50, fax 75 52 33 88; ②). A plusher option is the *Comfort Home Hotel Grand*, Storgata 3 (☎75 52 00 00, fax 75 52 27 09; ④/②), where the foyer sports some elegant Art Deco flourishes. The most appealing place in town, however, is the *Radisson SAS Hotel Bodø*, Storgata 2 (☎75 52 41 00, fax 75 52 74 93; ⑥/③), not least because the rooms on the upper floors of this whopping block have great views out to sea. It's not necessarily as pricey as you might think either, since there are substantial summer discounts.

Finally, you can **camp** 3.5km southeast of the centre at *Bodøsjøen Camping* (☎ & fax 75 56 36 80), beside the lake not far from the Bodin kirke – take bus #12 from the bus station. It's open all year and has cabins (②).

Eating and drinking

Bodø is short of good places to eat – indeed, if you don't like pizza your choices are extremely limited, though matters may improve when the next phase of the harbour redevelopment is completed in the next couple of years. Before then, easily the best bet is the *Pizzakjeller'n*, in the basement of the *Radisson SAS Hotel Bodø*, where they serve massive pizzas and a wide variety of daily specials – beef, seafood and so on – from 170kr per main course. Alternatively, the *Neptune Café*, Sjøgata 1, is an unassuming self-service café offering Norwegian standbys from its second-floor premises overlooking the Hurtigbåt terminal. For **drinking**, the *Peacock Pub*, around the corner from the *Radisson SAS Hotel Bodø*, has darts and billiards, while the more fashionable *Paviljongen Bar*, at the east end of the Storgata shopping precinct (the Glasshuset), is an amiable spot to nurse a beer.

Out from Bodø: Kjerringøy, Saltstraumen and the Svartisen glacier

There are three obvious excursions from Bodø: one to the trading station of **Kjerringøy**, another to the tidal current known as the **Saltstraumen**, and a third to the **Svartisen glacier**. The first two can be done by public transport but are much easier with your own vehicle, whilst the third is an organized tour on a passenger express boat. Note that the glacier can also be reached from Mo-i-Rana (see p.311).

Kjerringøy

In summer during the week, it's possible to make a day-trip on the once-daily local bus (65kr return including the Festvåg–Misten ferry) from Bodø bus station 40km north along the coastal Hwy 834 to the old trading station of **KJERRINGØY**, where a superbly preserved collection of nineteenth-century timber buildings stands beside a slender, islet-sheltered channel (daily: late May to late June & Aug noon–5pm; late June to late July 11am–7.30pm; 40kr). This was once the domain of the Zahl family, merchant suppliers of everything from manufactured goods, clothes and farmyard foodstuffs to the fishermen of Lofoten. It was not, however, an equal relationship: the Zahls, who operated a local monopoly until the 1910s, could dictate the price they paid for the fish, and many of the islanders were permanently indebted to them. This social division is still very much in evidence at the trading post, where there's a marked distinction between the guestrooms of the main house and the fishermens' bunkbeds in the boat- and cookhouses. Indeed, the family house is remarkably fastidious, with its Italianate busts and embroidered curtains – even the medicine cabinet is well-stocked with formidable Victorian remedies like the bottle of "Sicilian Hair Renewer."

There are enjoyable, hour-long **guided tours** throughout the summer (late May to late Aug 3–5 daily; 30kr). When you've finished with the tour, you can nose around the reconstructed general store, drop by the café and stroll the fine sandy beach in front of the complex. It's a peaceful and relaxing spot, and if you want to **stay overnight**, the old parsonage, *Kjerringøy Prestegård* (☎75 50 77 10 or 75 51 11 43; ③), about 1km north of the trading post along Hwy 834, has simple double rooms in the main building and slightly pleasanter ones in the renovated cowshed next door.

Saltstraumen

Less interesting, but more widely publicized, is the maelstrom known as the **Saltstraumen**, 33km southeast of Bodø round the bay on Hwy 17. Billions of gallons of water are forced through this narrow channel four times daily, making a headlong rush between inner and outer fjord. The creamy water is at its most turbulent at high tide, and its most violent when the moon is new or full – a timetable is available from Bodø tourist office. But although scores of tourists troop here for every high tide, you can't help but feel they wish they were somewhere else – the scenery is, in Norwegian terms at least, flat and dull, and the view from the bridge which spans the channel unexciting. There's a local **bus** service from Bodø to the Saltstraumen (Mon–Sat 5–7 daily, Sun 1 daily), but the times rarely coincide with high tides, which means you'll end up hanging around, though to pass the time you could drop by the **Saltstraumen Experience Centre** (Saltstraumen Opplevelsessenter; May daily 10am–6pm; June–Aug daily 10am–10pm; 60kr), housed in two adjoining buildings near the east end of the bridge. The centre tells you all you'd ever wanted to know about tidal currents and also has several pools where you can take a close look at local fish, seals and tidepools.

The Svartisen glacier

The easiest way to reach the **Svartisen glacier** from Bodø is on a **passenger express boat trip**. Unfortunately there are only two or three departures a month in June, July and August, but they do allow three hours at the glacier. They depart from the express boat quay in Bodø, last between six and seven hours and cost 290kr per person. Tickets are purchased on board; check times with the Bodø tourist office.

Narvik

The 250km journey north from Fauske to Narvik is spectacular, with the E6 rounding the fjords, twisting and tunnelling through the mountains and rushing over high, pine-studded plateaux. This stretch of the E6 presents two opportunities to catch a **car ferry** to the Lofotens – one at Skutvik, the other at Bognes. The more southerly of the two is **Skutvik**, 37km to the west of the E6, with ferries to Svolvær. At **Bognes**, where the E6 is interrupted by the Tysfjord, there's a choice of ferries. One sails to Lödingen and the E10 on the Lofotens, while a second hops over to **Skarberget** for the E6 and, after a further 80km, Narvik. Long distance **buses** link Bodø, Fauske and Narvik twice daily.

   NARVIK, five hours from Fauske by bus along the E6, is a relatively modern town established less than a century ago to handle the iron ore brought by train from northern Sweden. It makes no bones about its main function: the **iron ore docks** are immediately conspicuous, slap bang in the centre of town and totally overwhelming the whole waterfront. Yet, for all the mess, the industrial complex is strangely impressive, with its rust-coloured cat's cradle of walkways, conveyor belts, cranes, funnels and drive belts.

   Narvik's first modern settlers were the labourers who built the railway line to the mines in Kiruna, over the border in Sweden – a herculean task commemorated every March by a week of singing, dancing and drinking, when the locals dress up in nineteenth-century costume. The town grew steadily up to World War II, when it was demolished by fierce fighting for control of the harbour and iron ore supplies. Rebuilt, the town centre is, perhaps inevitably, rather lacking in appeal, with modern concrete buildings

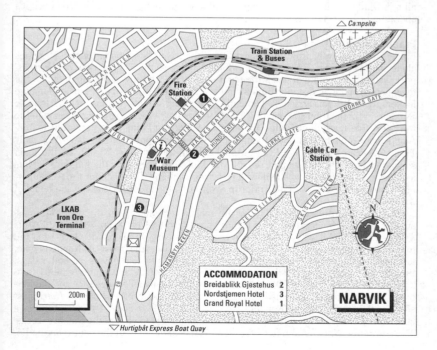

△ Campsite

Train Station & Buses

Fire Station

SNORRES GATE

War Museum

Cable Car Station

LKAB
Iron Ore
Terminal

FJELLVEIEN

N

0   200m

ACCOMMODATION
Breidablikk Gjestehus   2
Nordstjernen Hotel   3
Grand Royal Hotel   1

NARVIK

▽ Hurtigbåt Express Boat Quay

replacing the wooden houses that went before. Nevertheless, try to devote an hour or so to the **War Museum** (Krigsminnemuseum; early June to late Aug Mon–Sat 10am–10pm, Sun 11am–5pm; March to early June & late Aug to Sept daily 10am–4pm; 30kr), in the main town square. Run by the Red Cross, the museum documents the wartime German saturation bombing of the town and the bitter and bloody sea and air battles in which hundreds of foreign servicemen died alongside the local population. In total, the fight for Narvik lasted two months, a complicated campaign beginning with the German invasion of April 1940, followed by an allied counterattack spearheaded by the Royal Navy. The Allies actually recaptured Narvik, driving the Germans into the mountains, but were hurriedly evacuated when Hitler launched the invasion of France. The story is movingly related by the museum, which then tracks through the German occupation of Norway until liberation in 1945 – one display juxtaposes German bullwhips with small toys made by Russian POWs as thanks for food parcels smuggled into the camps by locals, who faced execution if discovered.

If you have a little time to spare, there are also guided tours of the **LKAB ore terminal complex** (1 daily; 30kr), interesting if only for the opportunity to spend ninety minutes amid such giant, ore-stained contraptions. After its arrival by train, the ore is carried on the various conveyor belts to the quayside, from where some thirty million tons of it are shipped out each year. Ask at the tourist office for details.

Located a stiff fifteen-minute walk above the town behind the train station, a **cable car** (mid-June to mid-Aug daily noon–1am; 70kr return), whisks passengers up the first 700m of the mighty **Fagernesfjellet** – on a clear day the Lofoten Islands are visible from the viewpoint at the top. If you stick around and it stays fine, this is also a good spot for observing the Midnight Sun (late May to mid July). The cable car stops running in windy conditions, so you might want to drop by the tourist office to check it's operating before venturing forth.

Practicalities

Fifteen minutes' walk from one end to the other, Narvik's sloping centre straggles along the main street, Kongens gate, which doubles as the E6. Narvik's public transport system is in a state of flux – the **train station** is currently at the north end of the town centre and long-distance **buses** stop outside it. The train station has left-luggage lockers, useful if you arrive by bus and are hanging around waiting for the train to Sweden. From the train station, it's a five- to ten-minute walk along Kongens gate to the **tourist office** (early June Mon–Fri 9am–5pm, Sat & Sun 11am–5pm; early June to mid-Aug Mon–Fri 9am–7pm, Sat 10am–7pm, Sun noon–7pm; mid- to late Aug daily 11am–5pm; late Aug to early June Mon–Fri 9am–4pm; ☎76 94 33 09), on the main square a couple of doors along from the War Museum. They have the full range of bus and ferry timetables and will help with ferry reservations. The dock for the passenger-only **Hurtigbåt express boat** service to Svolvær on the Lofotens is at the south end of the town centre.

As for **accommodation**, you're hardly spoiled for choice, but the pleasant, unassuming *Breidablikk Gjestehus*, Tore Hunds gate 41 (☎76 94 14 18, fax 76 94 57 86; ③) is neat and trim, has views over town and provides a hearty breakfast. It's located at the top of the steps at the end of Kinobakken, a side road leading east off Kongens gate, just up from the main town square. Some of the town's **hotels** have seen better days, though the *Grand Royal Hotel*, just up from the tourist office at Kongens gate 64 (☎76 94 15 00, fax 76 94 55 31; ⑤/③), puts on a show of wood-panelled elegance and has perfectly adequate rooms. Alternatively, the much more modest *Nordstjernen Hotell*, just south of the town square at Kongens gate 26 (☎76 94 41 20, fax 76 94 75 06; ②), has a spacious second-floor breakfast room with an uninterrupted view of the iron-ore works. The **campsite**, *Narvik Camping* (☎76 94 58 10), is 2km north of the centre on the E6. It's open all year and has cabins (①).

MOVING ON FROM NARVIK

There's a choice of several routes on from Narvik. By **bus**, the Nord-Norgeekspressen (2–3 daily) makes the four-hour hop north to Tromsø, before continuing on to Alta and the Nordkapp, while another bus runs direct from Narvik to Alta in ten hours (daily except Sat 1 daily). Both trips are through some wonderfully wild and diverse scenery, from craggy mountains and blue-black fjords to gentle, forested valleys – though it's not perhaps quite as scenic a journey as the E6 from Fauske to Narvik. A third bus service, the Narvik–Lofoten Ekspressen (daily except Sat 1 daily) runs west from Narvik to Sortland, Stokmarknes and Svolvær in the Lofoten Islands. Note that on all these buses, plus the bus trip south from Narvik to either Fauske (for connecting trains to Trondheim) or Bodø, InterRail and ScanRail pass holders get a fifty percent discount. Narvik also has one **Hurtigbåt passenger express boat** service. It operates all year (daily except Sat 1 daily) and takes three to four hours to reach Svolvær. The one-way fare is 267kr, though rail pass holders get a fifty percent discount.

One of the real treats of a visit to Narvik is the **train ride** into the mountains that back the town and spread east across the Swedish border. Called the **Ofotbanen**, the line passes through some wonderful scenery, slipping between hostile peaks before reaching the barren, loch-studded plateau beyond. The trains leave Narvik twice daily (3 daily from late June to mid-Aug) and take fifty minutes to reach the Swedish border settlement of **Riksgrånsen**, a hiking and skiing centre on the plateau; the fare is 108kr return. You can either nose around here before returning by train to Narvik or travel east on to Kiruna and, ultimately, Stockholm; the ride to Stockholm takes around 18 hours.

There's only one really recommendable **restaurant** in Narvik, *Bjørns Mat og Vinhus*, just over the bridge from the town square at Brugata 3 (☎76 94 42 90). This smart, second-floor place offers an inventive and reasonably priced menu with a Mediterranean slant. The **bar** below is good fun too – again the best in town.

The Vesterålen islands

A raggle-taggle archipelago in the Norwegian Sea, the **Vesterålen Islands**, and their neighbours the Lofotens, are like western Norway in miniature: the terrain is hard and unyielding, the sea boisterous and fretful, and the main – often the only – industry is fishing. The weather is temperate but wet, and the islanders' historic isolation has bred a distinctive culture based, in equal measure, on Protestantism, the extended family and respect for the ocean.

The islands were first settled by semi-nomadic hunter-agriculturalists some 6000 years ago, and it was they and their Iron Age successors who chopped down the birch and pine forests that once covered the coasts. It was **boatbuilding**, however, which brought a brief golden age: by the seventh century, the islanders were able to build ocean-going vessels, a skill that enabled them to join in the bonanza of Viking exploration. In the early fourteenth century, the islanders **lost their independence** and were placed under the control of Bergen: by royal decree, all fish caught by the islanders had to be shipped to Bergen for export. This may have suited the economic interests of the Norwegian monarch and the Danish governors who succeeded them, but it put the islanders at a terrible disadvantage. With their monopoly guaranteed, Bergen's merchants controlled both the price they paid for the fish and the price of the goods they sold to the islanders – a system that was to survive, increasingly under the auspices of local merchants, until the early years of the twentieth century. Since World War II, improvements in fishing techniques and, more latterly, the growth in tourism and the extension of the road system have all combined to transform island life.

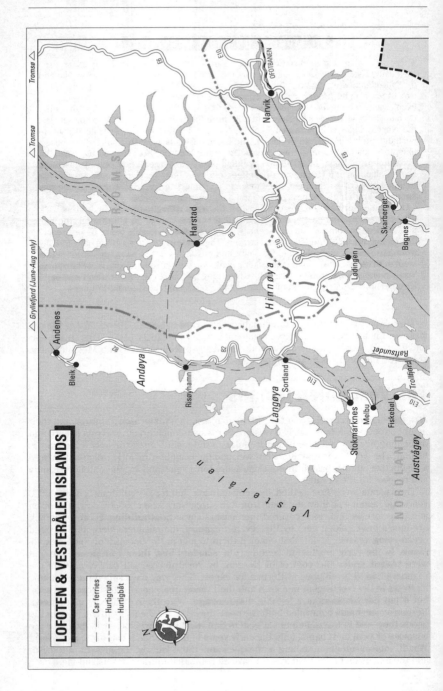

LOFOTEN & VESTERÅLEN ISLANDS

— — Car ferries
— · — Hurtigrute
— — — Hurtigbåt

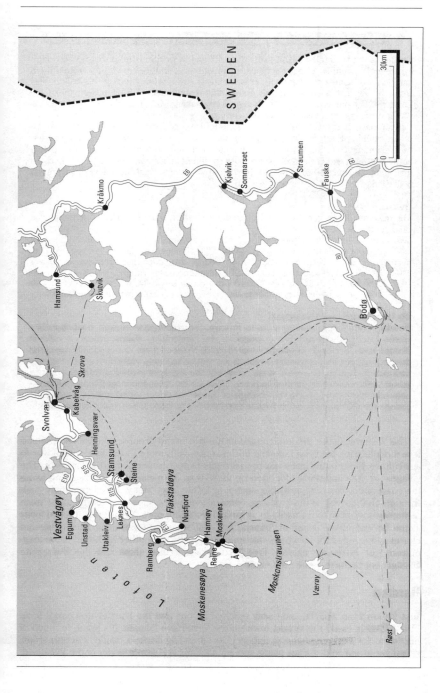

GETTING TO AND AROUND THE VESTERÅLEN ISLANDS

Getting to the Vesterålen Islands from the mainland by **public transport** is easy enough – indeed, the number of permutations is almost bewildering – but getting around them can be more troublesome. The **E10** is the main island road, running the 370km west from the E6 just north of Narvik across the Vesterålens to the southern tip of the Lofotens. The only interruption is the **car ferry** linking Melbu, on the southern edge of the Vesterålens, with Fiskebøl in the Lofotens.

If you have your own **vehicle** it's possible to drive from one end of the islands to the other, catching the ferry from the mainland to Andenes and then driving south across the Vesterålens and the Lofotens to return to the mainland from Moskenes (see p.332) at the southern end of the archipelago. Drivers intent on a somewhat less epic trip could investigate the **car rental** outlets at Harstad, which offer special short deals from around 500kr a day.

By car ferry
The main **car ferry** from the mainland to the Vesterålen Islands departs from the jetty at Bognes, on the E6 between Fauske and Narvik, and sails to Lødingen (6–10 daily; 1hr; pedestrians 37kr, car and driver 118kr). A second, seasonal, car ferry runs from the mainland at remote Gryllefjord, 110km west of the E6 to the north of Narvik, to Andenes at the northern tip of the Vesterålens (June–Aug; 3 daily; 2hr; pedestrians 83kr, car and driver 230kr). Reservations are strongly advised – telephone or fax Andøy Reiseliv in Andenes (☎76 11 56 00, fax 76 11 56 10). A third car ferry links Melbu in the Vesterålens with Fiskebøl in the Lofotens (every 90min; 25min; pedestrians 22kr, car and driver 65kr).

By Hurtigrute and Hurtigbåt
Heading north from Bodø en route to Tromsø, the **Hurtigrute coastal boat** threads a scenic route up through the Lofotens to the Vesterålen Islands, where it calls at Stokmarknes, Sortland, Risøyhamn and Harstad. None of these are especially appealing destinations, though Risøyhamn is well on the way to Andenes, while Harstad is a regional transport hub with a fine old church. Scenically, the highlight is the Raftsundet, a narrow sound between Svolvær and Stokmarknes, off which branches the magnificent Trollfjord – unfortunately, heading north the Hurtigrute leaves Svolvær at 10pm, and only during the period of the Midnight Sun (late May to mid-July) is it possible to see much; heading south,

---

The Vesterålens are the less rugged of the two island groups: greener, gentler and less mountainous than the Lofotens to the south, with more of the land given over to agriculture, though this gives way to vast tracts of peaty moorland in the far north. The villages are less appealing too, often no more than formless ribbons straggling along the coast and across any available stretch of fertile land. Many travellers simply rush through on their way to the Lofotens, demoralized by the sheer mediocrity of the main settlements, a mistake primarily in so far as the fishing port of **Andenes**, tucked away at the far end of the island of Andøya, has a strange but enthralling back-of-beyond charm and is noted for its whale-watching expeditions. The other highlight is the magnificent but extremely narrow **Trollfjord**, where cruise ships and the Hurtigrute coastal boat perform some nifty manoeuvres.

Harstad

Just 120km from Narvik, and easily reached by bus and the Hurtigrute coastal boat, **HARSTAD** is easily the largest town on the Vesterålen Islands. It's home to much of northern Norway's engineering industry, its sprawling docks a tangle of supply ships, repair yards and cold-storage plants spread out along the gentle slopes of the Vågsfjord.

boats leave Stokmarknes at a much more convenient 3.30pm. The journey between Svolvær and Stokmarknes takes three hours and in summer costs 100kr for pedestrians, cars from 280kr.

The Hurtigrute leaves Bodø for the Lofotens and the Vesterålens at 3pm and departs Tromsø heading south at 1.30am daily. In summer, tickets for foot passengers remain reasonably priced, with the journey from Bodø to Harstad (16hr) costing around 590kr, Tromsø to Harstad (6hr 30min), 400kr, but there are discounts off-season. The fare for transporting a car from Bodø to Harstad is 360kr, Tromsø to Harstad 300kr, but there's a fifty percent surcharge on the older vessels, where vehicles have to be hoisted on board. Advance reservations for cars are essential, though these can be made up to a few hours before departure by telephoning the captain – ask at the harbour or at the port's tourist office for assistance. Special deals, which can reduce costs dramatically, are advertised at local tourist offices.

Hurtigbåt passenger express boats provide a speedy and economic alternative to the car ferry and Hurtigrute services. One links Bodø with Stokmarknes, via Svolvær in the Lofotens (Mon–Fri 1 daily; 5hr 30min; 300kr); another links Tromsø with Harstad (1–2 daily; 2hr 45min; 345kr). In both cases, advance booking (via the local tourist office) is recommended.

By bus

A long-distance **bus** leaves Narvik once daily to run along the E6 and then the E10 as far as Sortland, where passengers change (after a 1–2hr wait) for the onward bus to Stokmarknes, the Melbu–Fiskebøl ferry and Svolvær in the Lofotens. Another long-distance bus runs up the E6 from Bodø and Fauske to meet the Bognes–Lødingen car ferry. At Lødingen, there's a choice of two onward connecting buses: one service continues north to Harstad, the other heads west for Stokmarknes, the Melbu–Fiskebøl ferry and Svolvær. As examples of journey times, Narvik to Sortland takes three hours; Bodø to Sortland seven; to Svolvær, ten.

Off these main bus routes, you're reliant on **local buses**, the most useful of which runs from Sortland to Andenes (1–3 daily; 2hr 15min). This bus is a component part of the much longer Hvalrutebussen service (June–Aug only) linking Narvik and Tromsø with Andenes, Risøyhamn and Å at the southern tip of the Lofotens. To avoid getting stuck, make sure you pick up a bus and ferry timetable from any island tourist office or bus station.

This may not sound too enticing, and it's true that Harstad wins few beauty competitions, but the town does have the odd attraction and, if you're tired of sleepy Norwegian villages, it at least provides a bustling interlude.

The main item of interest, the **Trondenes kirke** (guided tours on the hour every 2hr: early June to mid-Aug Mon 10am–4pm, Tues, Fri & Sun 2–6pm; mid-Aug to late Aug daily at 2.30pm; late Aug to early June ask for times at the tourist office; 20kr), occupies a lovely leafy location beside the fjord 3km north of the town centre at the end of a slender peninsula. The original wooden church was built at the behest of King Øystein (cf *rorbuer* fame – see p.330) at the beginning of the twelfth century and had the distinction of being the northernmost church in Christendom for several centuries. The present stone church was erected in the 1300s, its thick walls and the remains of its surrounding ramparts reflecting its dual function as both church and fortress – these were troubled and violent times. After the necessarily stern exterior, the warm and homely interior comes as a surprise. Here the dainty arches of the roodscreen lead into the choir, where each of the three altars is surmounted by a late medieval wooden triptych in bas relief. Of the trio, the central triptych is the most charming: the main panel, depicting the Holy Family, is fairly predictable, but down below is a curiously cheerful sequence of biblical figures, each wearing a turban and sporting a big, bushy and exquisitely carved beard.

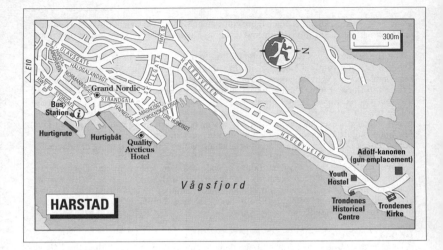

There's a reminder of World War II in the **Adolfkanonen** (Adolf Gun), a massive artillery piece stuck on a hilltop to the north of the church in the middle of the peninsula. It's inside a military zone, and the obligatory **guided tour** (early June to mid-Aug daily at 11am, 1pm, 3pm & 5pm; mid-Aug to late Aug daily at 1pm; 50kr), which begins at the gate of the compound 1km up the hill from the church, stipulates that you have to have your own vehicle to cross from the gate to the gun, a distance of 3km. Near the church, just south along the fjord, is the **Trondenes Historical Centre** (Trondenes Historiske Senter; June to mid-Aug daily 10am–7pm; mid-Aug to May Sat & Sun 11am–5pm; 30kr), a plush new complex with exhibitions on the history of the locality – dioramas, mood music, incidental Viking artefacts and the like.

Downtown Harstad doesn't have much to offer, though the comings and goings of the ferry boats are a diversion, and if you're around in late June the ten-day **North Norway Arts Festival** (Festspillene i Nord-Norge), featuring concerts, theatre and dance, provides a spark of interest (and hotels full to bursting).

Practicalities

Although Harstad is easy to reach by bus or boat from Sortland, Tromsø and Narvik, it's actually something of a cul-de-sac for car drivers, who have to leave the E10 for the final thirty-kilometre drive north into town along Hwy 83. Once you've arrived, however, you'll find almost everything you need close to hand, in the immediate vicinity of the **bus station**, which is metres from the jetties for the **Hurtigbåt express passenger boats** and the **Hurtigrute coastal boat**. Next to the bus station is the **tourist office**, Torvet 8 (early June to mid-Aug Mon–Fri 7.30am–6.30pm, Sat 7.30am–3pm, Sun noon–7pm; mid-Aug to early June Mon–Fri 8am–4pm; ☎77 01 89 89), which has a wide selection of tourist literature on the Vesterålens.

In terms of **accommodation**, the centre is dotted with modern chain hotels. The *Quality Arcticus Hotel* has an attractive quayside location a short walk from the Torvet at Havnegata 3 (☎77 06 50 00, fax 76 06 52 00; ⑨/③), or try the neat and trim *Grand Nordic Hotell*, a couple of minutes' walk from the Torvet at Strandgata 9 (☎77 06 21 70, fax 77 06 77 30; ④/③). The **youth hostel** (☎77 06 41 54, fax 77 06 56 33; doubles ①; reception closed 10.30am–6pm; June to late Aug) has the advantage of a pleasant fjordside location near the church out on the Trondenes peninsula. It's easy to reach by local

---

MOVING ON FROM HARSTAD

From Harstad, the **Hurtigrute coastal boat** sails north for Tromsø at 8.15am and south for points in the Vesterålen and Lofoten islands at 8.45am. Alternatively, there's a **Hurtigbåt express passenger boat** service to Tromsø (1–2 daily; 2hr 45min; 345kr) and frequent **buses** to Narvik, Sortland (for Andenes) and the Lofotens. Several local **car hire** firms offer special short-term deals: try Europcar, Samagata 33 (☎77 01 86 00), or Statoil Bilutleie (☎77 04 02 29), at the Statoil gas station.

---

bus from the station (Mon–Sat 1 hourly; 10min) and the rooms are comfortable, pleasantly furnished and large; the only problem is that the building is a school for most of the year, and has a cold, institutionalized feeling.

When it comes to **eating**, Harstad is no gourmet's paradise. The *Kaffistova*, (Mon–Fri 8am–6pm, Sat 9.30am–2.30pm, Sun 11.30am–4.30pm), across from the Hurtigbåt terminal, serves traditional Norwegian standbys at inexpensive rates, while in the evening *Gallionen*, the restaurant of the *Quality Arcticus Hotel*, has a reasonable line in seafood and offers fjord views too.

Sortland, Stokmarknes, the Trollfjord and Melbu

Back on the E10 south of Harstad, it's 60km southwest along the fjord to the turning for the Lødingen ferry and 40km more to **SORTLAND**, an unappetizing modern sprawl straggling along the shore near the bridge linking the islands of Langøya and Hinnøya. Sortland's location makes it something of a transport centre: bus travellers have to change here for the onward journey south to Stokmarknes and the Lofotens, or to catch the local bus north to Andenes, which originates here. With a little time to spare, the **tourist office** (mid-June to late Aug Mon–Fri 10am–6pm, Sat & Sun 11am–5pm; late Aug to mid-June Mon–Fri 10am–5pm; ☎76 12 15 55), a five-minute walk from the bus station in the centre of town at Kjøpmannsgata 2, has the full range of regional information.

Pushing on south along the E10 from Sortland, the road hugs the shoreline for 30km before shooting over the two bridges that span the straits before **STOKMARKNES** on Hadseløya. The main reason for stopping in Stokmarknes is to catch the Hurtigrute south to Svolvær via the Trollfjord. The boat leaves at 3.30pm, sailing down the narrow sound – the Raftsundet – separating the harsh, rocky shanks of Hinnøya and Austvågøy. Towards the southern end of the sound, the ship usually makes the short detour into the **Trollfjord**, a majestic, two-kilometre-long tear in the landscape. Slowing to a mere chug, the vessels inch up the narrow gorge, smooth stone towering high above and blocking out the light. At its head, the boats effect a nautical three-point turn and then crawl back to rejoin the main waterway. It's very atmospheric, and the effect is perhaps even more extraordinary when the weather is up. One caution: the Hurtigrute does not enter the Trollfjord when there's the danger of a rock fall, but pauses at the fjord's mouth instead. Check locally before you embark, though this is most likely to happen in spring. The Hurtigrute cruise from Sortland to Svolvær takes three hours and costs 100kr per passenger.

If you stay the night in Stokmarknes awaiting the Hurtigrute, you'll find most things conveniently close, with **buses** pulling in near the harbourfront **tourist office** (mid-June to late Aug Mon–Fri 10am–6pm, Sat 10am–4pm, Sun 11am–4pm; ☎76 15 29 55). They have details of local **accommodation**, though there's not much on offer, with the obvious choice being the *Kinnarps Turistsenteret* (☎76 15 29 99, fax 76 15 29 95; ④/②), a brassy hotel with *rorbuer* (fishermen's huts; ③) – it's located on the Børøya islet at the end of the first of the two Langøya bridges. It takes about fifteen minutes to walk there from the tourist office. The nearest **youth hostel** (☎76 15 71 06, fax 76 15 91 30; doubles ③) is a spartan affair in the fishing and industrial port of **MELBU**, 15km to the south on the E10. It's situated 400m from the **car ferry** to Fiskebøl on the Lofotens.

North to Andenes

From Sortland, Hwy 82 begins its 100-kilometre trek north, snaking along the craggy peripheries of the island of Hinnøya before crossing the bridge over to humdrum **RISØYHAMN**, the only Hurtigrute stop on **Andøya**, the most northerly of the Vesterålen Islands. Beyond Risøyhamn, the scenery is much less dramatic, as the mountains give way to hills in the west and a vast, peaty moor in the east. Hwy 82 crosses this moorland and, despite fine panoramic views of the mountains back on the mainland, it's an uneventful journey on to Andenes.

At the old fishing port of **ANDENES** lines of low-slung buildings trail up to the clutter of wooden warehouses and small boat repair yards that edge the harbour and its prominent breakwaters. Andenes is famous for its **whale safaris** (late May to mid-Sept daily at 10.30am, with additional departures depending on demand at 8.30am, 3.30pm & 5.30pm). A "safari" consists of a three- to six-hour cruise off the coast with a marine biologist on board to point out sperm, killer and minke whales and dolphins. There's reckoned to be a ninety percent chance of seeing the whales; tickets are around 625kr each and include lunch and a guided tour of the Whale Centre (see below) beforehand. Booking at least a day in advance is strongly advised as the excursions are popular and some are filled up weeks beforehand; telephone the tourist office at the Whale Centre (☎76 11 56 00, fax 76 11 56 10, *www.whalesafari.no*).

If you can't get on a whale safari, the other recommended **boat trip** (also bookable at the tourist office) is the two-hour cruise round the bird-infested island of **Bleiksøya**, a pyramid-shaped hunk of rock populated by thousands of puffins, kittiwakes, razorbills and, sometimes, white-tailed eagles. Tours costs 250kr, with twice-daily departures from June to late August (when the birds move south). The boats leave from the jetty at **BLEIK**, a comely fishing hamlet of clapboard houses and white picket fences huddling between craggy hills and a long sandy beach. It's around 7km southwest of Andenes; a local bus makes the return trip from Andenes to coincide with sailings.

Back in Andenes, the **Whale Centre** (Hvalsenter; daily: late May to mid-June & mid-Aug to mid-Sept 8am–4pm; mid-June to mid-Aug 8am–8pm; 20kr), close by the harbour, actually makes for a rather disappointing start to the whale trips. Its incidental displays on the life and times of the animal hardly fire the imagination and neither does the massive, deliberately dark and gloomy diorama of a whale munching its way though a herd of squid. Much more diverting is the nearby **Hisnakul** (daily: late May to mid-June & mid-Aug to mid-Sept 1–4pm; mid-June to mid-Aug daily noon–6pm; 20kr), a well-conceived museum-cum-exhibition centre, housed in a refurbished timber warehouse, that explores and explains various facets of Andøya. The centre is short of historical artefacts, plumping instead for imaginative displays such as the 200 facial castings of local people made in 1994 and an assortment of giant imitation bird beaks. There's also a comprehensive explanation of the Northern Lights – Andenes is a particularly good spot for seeing them – illustrated by first-class photographs and a slide show.

Practicalities

Andenes has one long and straight main street, Storgata, which bisects the town and ends abruptly at the seafront. From the end of the street, the **bus station** is just a few metres away to the east; the **tourist office** (late May to mid-Sept daily 8am–8pm; mid-Sept to late May Mon–Fri 8am–4pm; ☎76 11 56 00, fax 76 11 56 10, *www.whalesafari.no*), located in the Hvalsenter some 300m to the west, holds a comprehensive range of local

MOVING ON FROM ANDENES

Moving on from Andenes, the choices are limited. You can take the seasonal **car ferry** (June–Aug 3 daily; 2hr; car and driver 240kr, passengers 83kr; reservation fee 100kr) over to Gryllefjord on the mainland, but this leaves you a good long drive from both Narvik and Tromsø, the nearest worthwhile destinations. Alternatively, you can double back along Hwy 82 en route to the Lofotens. By **bus**, the Hvalrutebussen links Andenes with Risøyhamn, Svolvær and Å to the south, and with Narvik and Tromsø on the mainland (using the Gryllefjord–Andenes ferry). Unfortunately, this very useful service only operates from June to August, and the route breaks up into a number of component parts – study the timetable carefully. This is straightforward on shorter journeys – like Andenes to Sortland – but longer rides are generally impossible at weekends. The Hvalrutebussen also leaves Andenes once daily to meet the southbound **Hurtigrute** in Risøyhamn.

information and makes boat trip and Gryllefjord car ferry reservations (100kr reservation fee). It also has details of local bicycle rental (100kr per day) and of guided walks in the surrounding district, beginning at 250kr for a three- to six-hour hike.

The village has a fair range of inexpensive **accommodation** and several households offer **private rooms** – look out for the signs. But considering how isolated a spot this is, you'd be well advised to ring ahead to make an advance reservation, though if all else fails the tourist office will do their best to help you out. One of the nicer places is the *Sjøgata Gjestehus*, Sjøgata 4 (☎76 14 16 37, fax 76 14 14 53; ②; late May to mid-Sept), which provides simple but inexpensive rooms in a pleasant old timber building just 200m east from the tourist office. Nearby on the seafront is the *Lankanholmen Sjøhus* (☎76 14 28 50, fax 76 14 28 55;), an unenticing modern complex which includes chalet-style huts, apartments and a very small and very frugal **youth hostel** (same number; doubles ①; June–Aug). Andenes has just one **hotel**, the *Norlandia Andrikken*, Storgata 53 (☎76 14 12 22, fax 76 14 19 33; ④/③), whose main building is a routine modern concrete block with rooms to match about 900m from the harbour. More positively, the hotel **restaurant** is easily the best place to eat – the Arctic char is superb – and prices are reasonable. For daytime snacks, head for *Jul Nilsens Bakeri* (Mon–Fri 9am–3pm, Sat 9am–1pm), close to the bus station at Kong Hansgata 1. An alternative to Andenes is to stay in the prettier hamlet of **Bleik**. There are several modern rooms here at *Havhusene Bleik* (☎76 14 57 40, fax 76 14 55 51; ②) and a handful of *rorbuer* (③) too.

The Lofoten Islands

A skeletal curve of mountainous rock stretched out across the Norwegian Sea and fretted by seastacks and skerries, the **Lofoten Islands** are the focal point of northern Norway's winter fishing season. At the turn of every year, cod migrate from the Barents Sea to spawn here, where the coldness of the waters is tempered by the Gulf Stream. The season lasts from January to April, though it impinges on all aspects of the islands' life and is impossible to ignore at any time of year. At almost every harbour stand the massed ranks of wooden racks used for drying the catch; full and odiferous in winter, empty in summer like so many abandoned climbing frames.

Sharing the same history, but better known and more beautiful than their neighbours the Vesterålens, the Lofoten Islands have everything from seabird colonies in the south to beaches and fjords in the north. The traditional approach to the islands by boat from Bodø brings you face to face with their most striking feature, the towering peaks

GETTING TO AND AROUND THE LOFOTENS

The Lofotens can be reached by car ferry, Hurtigbåt passenger express boat and Hurtigrute coastal boat, but once you've got there you'll find **public transport** thin on the ground. What local **bus** services there are stick almost exclusively to the **E10**, the islands' only main road, an ingenious affair with multiple bridges and tunnels which covers the 250km from Fiskebøl to Å. Leave the main highway, however, and you'll mostly have to **walk** – hardly an onerous task in such beautiful surroundings – or go on one of the excellent and plentiful local **sea trips**. Alternatively, **bike hire** is available at the Svolvær tourist office, some youth hostels and many other places you might stay. If you don't have a **car** and want to reach the islands' remoter spots, it's worth considering hiring a vehicle – there are local car rental outlets at Svolvær and Stamsund and special short deals can bring costs down to around 500kr a day.

By Hurtigrute and Hurtigbåt

The **Hurtigrute coastal boat** calls at Stamsund and Svolvær, before nudging through the Raftsundet en route to Stokmarknes. The Hurtigrute leaves Bodø for Stamsund at 3pm daily; from June to September tickets for foot passengers cost 253kr to Stamsund, 271kr to Svolvær (cheaper off-season and free with a Coastal Pass). The fare for taking a car from Bodø to Stamsund is 280kr, 300kr to Svolvær, but there's a fifty percent surcharge on the older vessels, where vehicles have to be hoisted on board. Advance reservations for cars are essential, though these can be made up to a few hours before departure by telephoning the captain – ask at the harbour or at the port's tourist office. Special deals, which can reduce costs dramatically are advertised at local tourist offices.

Hurtigbåt passenger express boats link Bodø with Svolvær (Mon–Fri & Sun 1 daily; 4hr; about 220kr) and Narvik with Svolvær (Sun–Fri 1 daily; 4hr; 255kr per person). In both cases advance booking (via the local tourist office) is recommended.

By car ferry

From the mainland, the principal **car ferry** service connects tiny Skutvik, 40km west of the E6 midway between Fauske and Narvik, with Svolvær (early June to late Aug 8 daily; late Aug to early June 2–3 daily; 2hr); tickets are 55kr for pedestrians, 190kr for a car and driver. Queues are common and it's a first-come, first-served ferry, so drivers need to arrive about two hours before departure to make sure of a place.

A second car ferry (1–2 sailings daily) takes four and a quarter hours to sail from Bodø to the pocket-sized port of Moskenes, a few kilometres from the southern end of the E10. The fare from Bodø to Moskenes is 112kr for pedestrians, 405kr for car and driver. Queues are usual and drivers need to arrive at least two hours before departure to make sure of a place, or to make an advance reservation through Bodø tourist office for a fee of 100kr. If you're driving to the Lofotens on the E10 you'll use the car ferry which links Melbu on the Vesterålen Islands with Fiskebøl on the Lofotens (every 90min; 25min; pedestrians 22kr, driver and car 65kr).

By bus

The only long-distance **bus** services from the mainland to the Lofotens are from Fauske to Svolvær via the Bognes–Lødingen and Melbu–Fiskebøl ferries (1 daily except Sat; 10hr 15min; 379kr one way) and from Narvik to Svolvær via the Melbu–Fiskebøl ferry (1 daily except Sat; 8hr; 321kr).

On the Lofotens, there are at least a couple of **local buses** on weekdays between most of the larger villages, but often nothing at all on Sunday, and sometimes Saturday as well. One useful service links Å, Leknes and Svolvær (Mon–Sat 1–2 daily June–Aug only), part of the much longer Hvalrutebussen service (June–Aug only) which continues all the way to Andenes, at the northern end of the Vesterålen Islands, and links with Narvik and Tromsø on the mainland using the Gryllefjord–Andenes ferry.

of the **Lofotenveggen** (Lofoten Wall), a 160-kilometre chain of mountains which, due to the islands' proximity to each other, appears unbroken. The Lofotens have their own relaxed pace, and are perfect for a simple, uncluttered few days. For somewhere so far north, the weather is exceptionally mild: summer days can be spent sunbathing on the rocks or hiking around the superb coastline; and when it rains, as it does frequently, life focuses on the *rorbuer*, where freshly caught fish are cooked over wood-burning stoves, stories are told and time gently wasted. If that sounds rather contrived, in a sense it is – the way of life here is to some extent preserved like this for tourists. But it's rare to find anyone who isn't less than completely enthralled by it all.

The **E10** weaves a scenic route across the Lofotens, running the 250km from Fiskebøl in the north to Å in the south, hopping from island to island by bridge and causeway and occasionally tunnelling through the mountains. The highway passes through or within a few kilometres of all the islands' main villages, amongst which **Henningsvaer** and **Å** are breathtakingly beautiful, with **Stamsund** coming in just behind – all three make great bases for further exploration. **Boat trips** along the coast (with or without bird-watching and fishing), are popular, as is **mountaineering** – Austvågøy has the best climbing, and the best climbing school at Henningsvaer. There's **walking** too: the islands do not have a well-developed system of huts and hiking trails, but the byroads are quiet and delve into the heart of the scenery.

As regards **accommodation**, the Lofotens have a sprinkling of **hotels** as well as five **youth hostels** and numerous **campsites**, along with the local speciality, the *rorbuer.*

Svolvær

By and large, **SVOLVÆR**, on the east coast of **Austvågøy**, the largest of the Lofotens, is a disappointing introduction to the islands. The administrative and transport centre of the Lofotens, it has all the bustle but little of the charm of the other fishing towns, though it does have more accommodation than its neighbours and, despite the poor aspect of the town itself, Svolvær's surroundings are delightful. Two local **boat trips** provide an excellent introduction. Every day several **cruises** leave Svolvær for the **Trollfjord** (for more on which, see p.325), an impossibly narrow, two-kilometre-long stretch of water up and down which countless excursion boats inch a careful way, wringing gasps from camera-crazy tourists. The excursion takes three hours and costs 220kr. If your tastes are more solitary you may find the ferry ride over to the islet of **Skrova**, just offshore from Svolvær, more to your liking. It's a pretty spot, ideal for a quiet stroll and easily reached on the Svolvær–Skutvik ferry, which calls here a couple of times a day in both directions, Monday to Saturday. The ride takes just thirty minutes and costs about 25kr each way.

Practicalities

Ferries to Svolvær dock on the edge of town, about ten minutes' walk – or a brief taxi ride – from the town centre. The **bus station** is central, a few metres from the busy **tourist office** (late May to mid-June Mon–Fri 9am–4pm, Sat 10am–2pm; mid- to late June Mon–Fri 9am–4pm & 5–7.30pm, Sat 10am–2pm, Sun 4–7pm; late June to mid-Aug Mon–Sat 9am–4pm & 5–8pm, Sun 10am–9.30pm; mid- to late Aug Mon–Fri 9am–7pm, Sat 10am–2pm; late Aug to late May Mon–Fri 8am–4pm; ☎76 07 30 00, fax 76 07 30 01), beside the main town square by the harbour. This has maps, accommodation lists and details of local public transport. They will reserve accommodation anywhere in the Lofotens (for a 35kr booking fee) and also make ferry reservations for a 125kr fee. Svolvær is a good place to **rent a car**, with both Avis and Budget, among others, offering some economic short-term deals from around 500kr per day.

STAYING IN RORBUER

Right across the Lofotens, **rorbuer** (fishermen's shacks) are rented out to tourists for overnight stays and longer periods. The first were built in the twelfth century round the coastline of the island of Austvågøy on the orders of King Øystein, so that fishermen visiting for the winter cod season could be spared from sleeping under their upturned boats. Traditionally, *rorbuer* were built on the shore, often on poles sticking out of the sea, and usually coloured with a red paint based on cod-liver oil. They consisted of two sections, a sleeping and eating room, and a smaller storage area.

Most of the original *rorbuer* disappeared years ago, and nowadays they're mass produced with the tourist trade specifically in mind. At their best, they're comfortable and cosy seashore cabins with bunk beds and wood-fired stoves; at their worst, they're little better than prefabricated hutches dropped off in the middle of nowhere. Most have space for between four and eight guests and cost in the region of 600kr per night – though some charge as little as 400kr, others rise to about 1000kr. Similar rates are charged for the islands' **sjøhus** (literally sea houses), bigger buildings that originated in the quayside halls where the catch was processed and the workers slept. Some of the original *sjøhus* have been cleverly converted into attractive apartments with self-catering facilities, many more into dormitory-style accommodation – though again the quality varies enormously. A full list of *rorbuer* and *sjøhus* is given in several free booklets that you can pick up at any local tourist office.

Accommodation options include the enjoyable wooden *Svolvær sjøhuscamping* (☎ & fax 76 07 03 36; ③), in a snug fishing house by the seashore at the foot of Parkgata; the price includes the use of a well-equipped kitchen and free showers. To get there from the square, turn right up the hill along Vestfjordgata and it's to the right past the library. Alternatively, the *Hotel Havly* (☎76 07 03 44, fax 76 07 07 95; ③), centrally located behind the bus station, occupies a plain modern tower block and has simple but perfectly adequate rooms, while the *Norlandia Royal Hotel* (☎76 07 12 00, fax 76 07 08 50; ④), a few metres up from the main square at the end of Torggata, is similar but a good bit plusher. The town's pride and joy, however, is the flashy, gleaming new *Rica Hotel Svolvær* (☎76 07 22 22, fax 76 07 20 01; ③), whose various buildings, in the style of the traditional *sjøhus*, occupy a prime harbourside location. It's one of the most popular hotels in the Lofotens, but still offers generous summer discounts, with prices for a double room tumbling to as little as 550kr per night.

For **eating**, the self-service café of the Rimi superstore, just up from the harbour, provides Norwegian standbys at inexpensive prices. For something to savour, head for the *Rica Hotel Svolvær*, which has a first-rate restaurant and bar.

Henningsvær

HENNINGSVÆR, 23km southwest of Svolvær and 7km off the E10, is a beguiling headland village, a cobweb of cramped and twisting lanes lined with brightly painted wooden houses. These frame a tiny inlet that literally cuts the place in half, forming a sheltered, postcard-pretty harbour. Almost inevitably, coach parties are wheeled in and out, despite the narrowness of the two high-arched bridges leading into the village. For all the tourist bustle, however, it's well worth an **overnight stay**.

The smartest hotel is the quayside *Henningsvær Bryggehotell* (☎76 07 47 50, fax 76 07 47 30; ④), an attractive modern building in traditional style right on the waterfront, or there's the economical *sjøhus* of *Den Siste Viking* (☎76 07 49 11, fax 76 07 46 46; ①), unadorned but central accommodation which doubles as the home of Lofotens' best

mountaineering school, Nord Norsk Klatreskole (same number). The school operates a wide range of all-inclusive climbing holidays, catering to various degrees of fitness and experience – a three-day, one-climb-a-day holiday costs in the region of 3000kr.

With less time, there are exhilarating **fishing trips**, a morning or afternoon's excursion for around 250kr, or you could visit the **Karl Erik Harr Gallery** (daily: March noon–3pm; late May to mid-June & late Aug 10am–6pm; mid-June to mid-Aug 9am–9pm; 45kr), which exhibits (and sells) the work of the artist himself as well as a small selection of early nineteenth-century Lofoten paintings and photographs. For **food**, the *Bryggehotell* has a first-rate if pricey restaurant, while the café-bar at *Lars Larsen's Rorbuer* features the commonest of all traditional island dishes, dried salted cod.

Henningsvær can be reached by **local bus** from Svolvær (1–4 daily), and from Å (Mon–Fri 1–2 daily).

Stamsund

It's the next large island to the southwest, **Vestvågøy**, that captivates many travellers to the Lofotens. This is due in no small part to the laid-back charm of **STAMSUND**, whose older buildings string along the rocky, fretted seashore in an amiable jumble of crusty wooden houses and *rorbuer*. This is the first port at which the Hurtigrute coastal boat docks on its way north from Bodø, and is much the best place to stay on the island. Getting there by bus from Austvågøy is reasonably easy too, with several buses making the trip daily, though you do have to change at **Leknes**, 16km to the west, the administrative centre of Vestvågøy and site of the airport. The quickest way to Stamsund if you have your own transport is to turn south off the E10 down Hwy 815 shortly after you cross onto Vestvågøy, a scenic 40-kilometre coastal drive.

In Stamsund, the first place to head for is the **youth hostel** (☎76 08 93 34, fax 76 08 97 39; doubles ➀; late Dec to mid-Oct), which comprises several *rorbuer* and a larger *sjøhus* perched over a pin-sized bay, about 1km down the road from the port and 200m from the Leknes bus stop – ask to be put off. The hostel is very friendly and many travellers return time and again. There's a washing machine, bike hire (85kr a day) and the fishing is first-class: the hostel hires out rowing boats and lines to take out on the (usually still) water, or you can head off on an organized fishing trip for 150kr. Afterwards you can cook whatever you've caught on the wood-burning stoves and eat alfresco on the veranda overlooking the bay. The warden is also the best source of **information** on just about everything else to do with Vestvågøy, from fishing through to hiking and cycling. The official village **tourist office** is situated 200m from the ferry dock (mid-June to mid-Aug Mon–Sat 11am–2.30pm & 6–9.30pm, Sun 6–9.30pm; ☎76 08 97 92).

Stamsund hostel is very informal, so even when the place is "full" the warden will usually squeeze you in somewhere, but in the unlikely event you're turned away, push on along the coast to the tiny hamlet of **STEINE**, 3km beyond the ferry harbour, where you'll find the *Steine Rorbuer* (☎ & fax 76 08 92 83; ➀), a comfortable set of *rorbuer* snuggling against the seashore.

South to Nusfjord, Ramberg, Hamnøy and Reine

By any standard the next two islands of the archipelago, **Flakstadøya** and **Moskenesøya**, are extraordinarily beautiful. As the Lofotens taper towards their southerly conclusion, the peaks of the Lofotenveggen rear above a coastline studded with fishing villages and shredded by the sea. The E10 travels along almost the whole of this dramatic shoreline, leaving Leknes to tunnel (toll 65kr) under the sound separating Vestvågøy from Flakstadøya. About 20km from Leknes, an even more improbable byroad manages somehow to worm its way 6km up through the mountains to **NUSFJORD**, an extravagantly picturesque fishing village in a tight and forbidding cove. Unlike many of the fishermen's huts in the Lofotens, the ones here are the genuine nineteenth-century article, and the general store, with its wooden floors and antique appearance, fits in nicely too. Inevitably, it's largely tourism that keeps the local economy afloat, but it's still a beguiling place. **Accommodation** is available in more than thirty comfortably refurbished *rorbuer*. The one-bedroom versions (400kr) hold two to four people, the two-bedroom ones (700kr) have space for five. There's also a **bar-restaurant**. Advance reservations are advised with Nusfjord Rorbuer (☎76 09 30 20, fax 76 09 33 78).

Back on the E10, it's a further 5km to the **Flakstad kirke**, a distinctive onion-domed, red timber church built of Russian driftwood in 1780. The building announces the beginning of **RAMBERG**, the island's administrative centre – if that's what you can call the smattering of services straggling the sandy beach. Pressing on south, over the first of several narrow bridges, you're soon on **Moskenesøya**, where the road squirms across the mouth of the Kirkefjord, hopping from islet to islet to link the fishing villages of **HAMNØY**, on the north side of the inlet, and **REINE** to the south. Reine is an odd little place which manages to look a bit seedy despite its magnificent surroundings, but it is the departure point for many boat trips (see below) and has several *rorbuer* complexes: the neatest of them is *Reine Rorbuer* (☎76 09 22 22 or 76 09 22 25; ②) in the older part of town, at the end of the short promontory just off the E10.

Moskenes and Å

From Reine, it's a couple of kilometres to **MOSKENES**, the main island port from Bodø – not that there's much here apart from a handful of houses dotted round a horseshoe-shaped bay, a **tourist office** (early June Mon–Fri 10am–5pm; mid-June to mid-Aug daily 10am–7pm; ☎76 09 15 99) by the jetty and a basic **campsite** (☎76 09 13 44; ①; June–Aug) up a gravel track a five-minute walk away.

Six kilometres further south the road ends abruptly at the tersely named **Å**, one of the Lofotens' most delightful villages, its huddle of old buildings rambling over a foreshore wedged in tight between the grey-green mountains and the sea. Unusually, so much of the nineteenth-century village has survived that a goodly portion of Å has been incorporated into the **Norwegian Fishing Village Museum** (Norsk Fiskevaersmuseum; late June to late Aug daily 10am–6pm; late Aug to late June Mon–Fri 10am–3.30pm; 40kr), an engaging attempt to re-create life here at the end of the nineteenth century. There are over twenty buildings to examine, including the houses of the two traders who dominated things hereabouts and the fishermen who did their bidding. According to the census of 1900, Å had 91 inhabitants, of whom 10 were traders and their relatives, 18 servants, and 63 fishermen and their families. It was a rigidly hierarchical society underpinned by terms and conditions close to serfdom. The fishermen did not own any land and had to pay rent for the ground on which their houses stood. Payment was made in the form of unpaid labour on the merchant's farmland during the summer harvest. The museum has a series of displays which detail every aspect of village life – and very well presented it is too. Afterwards, you can extend your knowledge of all things fishy by visiting the **Stockfish Museum** (Tørrfiskmuseum; early to mid-June Mon–Fri 11am–4pm; mid-June to late Aug daily 11am–5pm; 35kr) – stockfish being the air-dried and cured fish that was the staple diet of most Norwegians well into the twentieth century.

Both Å and more especially Reine offer a wide variety of **boat trips**. From Å, there are day-long fishing expeditions (June–Aug Mon–Sat 1 daily; 3hr; 260kr), while Reine weighs in with Midnight Sun cruises (late May to mid-July 1 weekly; 5hr; 390kr) and coastal voyages (June to mid-Aug 1 weekly; 4hr; 290kr). There are also, weather and tides permitting, regular cruises (June to mid-Aug 1 weekly; 4hr; 390kr) to the **Moskenestraumen** – the choppy maelstrom created by the conflicting currents just off the island's southern tip.

Practicalities

A local **bus** runs the length of the E10 from Leknes to Å once or twice daily from late June to late August, less frequently the rest of the year. Times do not, however, usually coincide with sailings to and from Moskenes. Consequently, if you're heading from the Moskenes ferry port to Å, you'll either have to walk – an easy 6km – or take a taxi.

As for **accommodation**, the same family owns the assortment of smart *rorbuer* (①–②) that surround the dock as well as the adjacent *sjøhus*, which offers very comfortable and equally smart, hotel-standard rooms (②). They also operate the **youth hostel** (doubles ①), the bar and the only restaurant, where the seafood is very good. Bookings for all these on ☎76 09 11 21, fax 76 09 12 82.

travel details

Trains

Narvik to: Riksgrånsen (2–3 daily; 50min).

Trondheim to: Bodø (2–3 daily; 10hr); Dombås (3–4 daily; 2hr 30min); Fauske (2–3 daily; 9hr 20min); Mo-i-Rana (2–3 daily; 7hr); Oslo (3–4 daily; 7hr); Otta (3 daily; 3hr); Steinkjer (2–3 daily; 1hr 20min).

Buses

Bodø to: Fauske (3 daily; 1hr 10min); Harstad (1 daily; 8hr); Narvik (2 daily; 7hr); Sortland (1–2 daily; 7hr); Svolvær (1 daily; 10hr 20min).

Fauske to: Bodø (2–3 daily; 1hr 10min); Harstad (1 daily; 6hr 30min); Narvik (2 daily; 5hr 30min); Sortland (1–2 daily; 6hr); Svolvær (1 daily; 8hr 30min).

Harstad to: Fauske (1 daily; 6hr 30min).

Narvik to: Alta (1 daily; 14hr); Bodø (2 daily; 7hr); Fauske (2 daily; 5hr 30min); Sortland (1 daily; 3hr 40min); Svolvær (1 daily; 7hr 30min); Tromsø (1–2 daily; 4hr 40min).

Sortland to: Andenes (1–3 daily; 2hr 15min).

Svolvær to: Å (Mon–Fri 1–2 daily; 3hr 20min).

Trondheim to: Ålesund (2–3 daily; 8hr); Bergen (2 daily; 14hr); Kristiansund (2–3 daily; 5hr); Otta (2 daily; 4hr); Stryn (2 daily; 7hr 20min).

Nord-Norgeekspressen

The **Nord-Norgeekspressen** (the North Norway Express Bus) complements the railway system, running north from Bodø and Fauske to the Nordkapp in four leaps: Bodø–Narvik (2 daily; 7hr); Narvik–Tromsø (1–2 daily; 4hr 40min); Tromsø–Alta (1 daily; 6hr 30min); and Alta–Nordkapp (1–2 daily except Sat; 6hr). Permutations allow passengers to omit the detour off the E6 to Tromsø and to travel east from Alta to Kirkenes. If you have the stamina, you can change from one bus to the next at every stop on the main Nord-Norgeekspressen route except Tromsø, where you have to stay the night.

Hurtigrute coastal boat

The daily Hurtigrute service departs

Northbound: Trondheim at noon; Bodø at 3pm; Stamsund at 7.30pm; Svolvær at 10pm; Stokmarknes at 1am; Sortland at 3am; Harstad at 8.15am.

Southbound: Harstad at 8.45am; Sortland at 1.15pm; Stokmarknes at 3.30pm; Svolvær at 7.30pm; Stamsund at 9.30pm; Bodø at 4am; Trondheim at 10am.

Journey time from Trondheim to Harstad 43hr, to Tromsø 51hr.

Car ferries
Bodø to: Moskenes (1–3 daily; 4hr 15min).
Bognes to: Lødingen (5–10 daily; 1hr).
Fiskebol to: Melbu (11–13 daily; 25min).
Skarberget to: Bognes (11–14 daily; 25min).
Svolvær to: Skutvik (early June to late Aug 7–8 daily; rest of year 2–3 daily; 2hr).

Hurtigbåt passenger express boats
Bodø to: Svolvær (1 daily except Sat; 5hr 30min).

Harstad to: Tromsø (1–2 daily; 2hr 45min).
Narvik to: Svolvær (1 daily except Sat; 4hr).
Trondheim to: Kristiansund (1–3 daily; 3hr 30min).

International trains
Narvik to: Stockholm (1 daily; 18hr).
Trondheim to: Stockholm (2 daily; 12hr).

CHAPTER EIGHT

NORTH NORWAY

Baedeker, writing 100 years ago about Norway's remote northern provinces of **Troms** and **Finnmark**, observed that they "possess attractions for the scientific traveller and the sportsman, but can hardly be recommended for the ordinary tourist" – a comment which isn't too wide of the mark even today. These are enticing lands, no question, the natural environment they offer stunning in its extremes, but the travelling can be hard, the specific sights well distanced and, when you reach them, subtle in their appeal.

Troms's intricate, fretted coastline has shaped its history since the days when powerful Viking lords operated a trading empire from its islands. Indeed, over half the population still lives offshore in dozens of tiny fishing villages, but the place to aim for is **Tromsø**, the so-called "Capital of the North" and a lively university town where King Håkon and his government proclaimed a "Free Norway" in 1940 before fleeing into exile. Beyond Tromsø, the long trek north begins in earnest as you enter **Finnmark**, a vast wilderness covering 48,000 square kilometres, but home to just two percent of the Norwegian population. Much of the land was laid waste during World War II, the combined effect of the Russian advance and the retreating German army's scorched-earth policy, and it's now possible to drive for hours without coming across a building more than fifty years old. The first obvious target in Finnmark is **Alta**, a sprawling settlement that is famous for its prehistoric rock carvings. Alta is also an important crossroads. From here, most visitors head straight for the steely cliffs of **Nordkapp** (the North Cape), mainland Europe's northernmost point, with or without a detour to the likeable port of **Hammerfest**, and leave it at that; but some doggedly press on to **Kirkenes**, the last town before the Russian border, which feels as if it's about to drop off the end of the world. From Alta, the other main alternative is to travel inland across the eerily endless scrubland of the **Finnmarksvidda**, where winter temperatures plummet to -25°C. This high plateau is the last stronghold of the **Sami**, northern Norway's indigenous people, many of whom still live a semi-nomadic life tied to the movement of their reindeer herds. You'll spot Sami in their brightly coloured traditional gear all across the region, but especially in the remote Sami towns of **Kautokeino** and **Karasjok**, strange, disconsolate places in the middle of the plain.

ACCOMMODATION PRICE CODES

The hotels and guesthouses listed in this chapter have been graded according to the following price bands, based on the cost of the **least expensive double room during high season** (late June to Aug). However, almost every hotel offers seasonal and/or weekend discounts, and wherever possible we've given two grades, covering both the regular and the discounted rate.

    ① Under 500kr   ② 500–700kr   ③ 700–900kr
    ④ 900–1200kr   ⑤ 1200–1500kr   ⑥ Over 1500kr

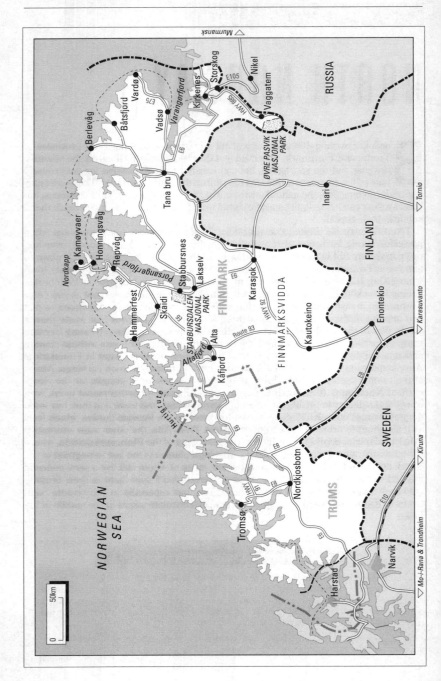

Finally, and even more adventurously, there is the **Svalbard** archipelago, whose icy mountains rise out of the Arctic Ocean 640km north of mainland Norway. Once the exclusive haunt of trappers, fishermen and coal miners, Svalbard now makes a tidy income from adventure tourism – everything from guided glacier walks to snowmobile excursions and whale-watching. You can fly there independently from most of Norway's larger towns, including Tromsø, at prices that are bearable, though most people opt for a package tour.

Transport and accommodation

Public transport in Troms and Finnmark is by bus, Hurtigrute coastal boat and plane – there are no trains. For all but the most truncated of tours, the best idea is to pick and mix these different forms of transport – for example by flying from Tromsø to Kirkenes and then taking the Hurtigrute back, or vice versa. It's best to avoid endless doubling back on the E6, though this is often difficult, as this is the only road to run right across the region. To give an idea of the distances involved, it's 300km from Tromsø to Alta, 500km to Nordkapp and 800km to Kirkenes.

The principal long-distance bus is the seasonal **Nord-Norgeekspressen**, which links Tromsø, Alta, Honningsvåg and Nordkapp in just under fourteen hours (late June to mid-August 1 daily except Sat). During the same period, this service is supplemented by an early-morning weekday service from Alta to Nordkapp; except on Saturday, there's also a daily bus from Tromsø to Alta (April to late Oct). Alta is also where you pick up the bus to Karasjok and Kirkenes; this runs between March and December four or five times weekly with an additional daily (except Sat) service as far as Karasjok. North of Alta, all buses use the E6 and pass through Skaidi, where you change for Hammerfest. There's also a bus linking Hammerfest with Karasjok and Kirkenes (March–Dec 1 daily except Sat). Bus **timetables** are available at most tourist offices and bus stations. On longer rides, it's a good idea to buy tickets in advance.

The **main highways** are all well-maintained, but **drivers** will find the going a little slow as they have to negotiate some pretty tough terrain. You can cover 250–300km in a day without any problem, but much more and it all becomes rather wearisome. One especially appealing option, though this has more to do with comfort than speed, is to combine **car and boat** travel. Special deals on the Hurtigrute can make this surprisingly affordable, and tourist offices at the Hurtigrute's ports of call will make bookings. Incidentally, you may well find that the cost of taking a hired car onto the Hurtigrute is a good deal less than the cost of a one-way rental. In **winter**, driving conditions can be appalling and, although the Norwegians make a spirited effort to keep the E6 open, they don't always succeed. If you're not used to driving in these sort of conditions, don't start here – especially during the Polar Night. If you intend to use the region's **minor roads**, be prepared for the worst and certainly take food and drink, warm clothes and, if possible, a mobile phone.

Much more leisurely is the **Hurtigrute coastal boat**, which takes the best part of two days to circumnavigate the huge fjords between Tromsø and Kirkenes. En route, it calls at eleven ports, mostly remote fishing villages but also Hammerfest and Honningsvåg, where (northbound only) it pauses for a couple of hours so that special buses can cart passengers off to Nordkapp and back. With regard to **air travel**, the

FINNMARK: THE MIDNIGHT SUN AND POLAR NIGHT

On clear nights, the **Midnight Sun** is visible at Alta, Hammerfest and Nordkapp from mid-May until the end of July; the long **Polar Night** runs from the last week in November until the third week in January.

region has several airports including those at Tromsø, Hammerfest, Honningsvåg and Kirkenes. Summer discounts and special offers can make flying an economic possibility – ask for details at any SAS or Braathens office. Both these airlines also fly to Svalbard.

As for **accommodation**, all the major settlements have at least a couple of hotels and the main roads are sprinkled with campsites. If you have a tent and a well-insulated sleeping bag you can, in theory, bed down more or less where you like, but the hostility of the climate and ferocity of the mosquitoes make most people think (at least) twice. There are youth hostels at Tromsø, Alta, Lakselv and Kirkenes.

Tromsø

TROMSØ has been called, rather preposterously, the "Paris of the North", and though even the tourist office doesn't make any pretence to such grandiose titles today, the city is without question the effective capital of northern Norway. Easily the region's most populous town, Tromsø received its municipal charter in 1794, when it was primarily a fishing port and trading station, and flourished in the middle of the nineteenth century when its seamen ventured north to Svalbard to reap rich rewards hunting arctic foxes, polar bears and, most profitable of all, seals. Subsequently, Tromsø became famous as the jumping-off point for a string of arctic expeditions, its celebrity status assured when the explorer Roald Amundsen flew from here to his death somewhere on the Arctic ice cap in 1928. Since those heady days, Tromsø has grown into an urbane and likeable small city with a population of 58,000 employed in a wide range of industries and at the university. Give or take the odd museum, Tromsø is short on specific sights, but its amiable atmosphere and fine mountain and fjord setting more than compensate. It also possesses a clutch of good restaurants, lively bars and several enjoyable hotels.

Arrival, information and accommodation

At the northern end of the E8, 73km from the E6 and 250km north of Narvik, Tromsø's compact centre slopes up from the waterfront on the hilly island of Tromsøya. The island is connected to the mainland by bridge and tunnel. The **Hurtigrute** docks in the town centre at the foot of Kirkegata; **Hurtigbåt** boats arrive at the quay about 150m to the south. Long-distance **buses** arrive and leave from the car park a few metres away. The **airport** is 5km west of the centre on the other side of Tromsøya. From the airport, frequent Flybussen (daily 6am–11pm; 35kr) run into the city, stopping at the *Radisson SAS Hotel Tromsø* on Sjøgata and at several other central hotels; the taxi fare is 70kr.

Tromsø's **tourist office**, Storgata 61 (June to mid-Aug Mon–Fri 8.30am–6pm, Sat & Sun 10am–5pm; mid-Aug to May Mon–Fri 8.30am–4pm; ☎77 61 00 00), is a couple of minutes' walk from the bus station straight up Kirkegata. They issue free town maps and have a small supply of private rooms.

It only takes five minutes to walk from one side of the centre to the other, but for the outlying attractions you can either catch a local bus or **rent a bike** from Sportshuset, Storgata 87 (Mon–Fri 9am–7pm, Sat 10am–4pm; ☎77 66 11 00).

Hotels
Comfort Home Hotel With, Sjøgata 35 (☎77 68 70 00, fax 77 68 96 16). Pleasantly situated down by the harbourfront, this likeable hotel has a nautical air and modern bedrooms. ⑤/③.

Radisson SAS Hotel Tromsø, Sjøgata 7 (☎77 60 00 00, fax 77 68 54 74). Plush downtown sky-rise with smart and comfortable modern rooms and ultraefficient service. ④/③.

Rainbow Polar, Grønnegata 45 (☎77 68 64 80, fax 77 68 91 36). Small, modern rooms decorated in typical chain-hotel style, but summer and weekend discounts make it a real bargain; the central location's a bonus too. ③/②.

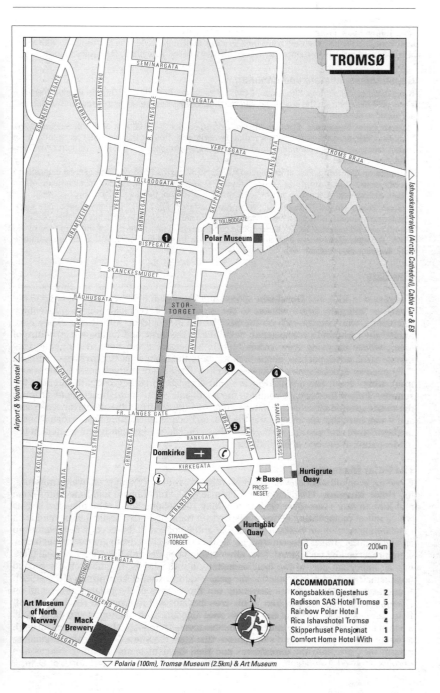

TROMSØ

◁ Ishavskatedralen (Arctic Cathedral), Cable Car & E8

Polar Museum

Airport & Youth Hostel ◁

Domkirke

★ Buses

Hurtigrute Quay

Hurtigbåt Quay

Art Museum of North Norway

Mack Brewery

0   200km

ACCOMMODATION

Kongsbakken Gjestehus	2
Radisson SAS Hotel Tromsø	5
Rainbow Polar Hotel	6
Rica Ishavshotel Tromsø	4
Skipperhuset Pensjonat	1
Comfort Home Hotel With	3

N

▽ Polaria (100m), Tromsø Museum (2.5km) & Art Museum

Rica Ishavshotel Tromsø, Fr. Langes gate 2 (☎77 66 64 00, fax 77 66 64 44). Perched on the harbourfront, this imaginatively designed hotel is partly built in the style of a ship, complete with a sort of crow's-nest bar. Lovely rooms and unbeatable views of the waterfront. Best place in town. ⑤/③.

Guesthouses, hostels and camping

Kongsbakken Gjestehus, Skolegata 24 (☎77 68 22 08, fax 77 68 80 44). This guesthouse has wide views over the city from the hillside behind the town centre. Seventeen simple rooms. Worth booking ahead in summer. ①.

Skipperhuset Pensjonat, Storgata 112 (☎77 68 16 60, fax 77 65 62 92). North of Stortorget, by Bispegata, this guesthouse is a long-standing favourite with budget travellers and has good, cheap rooms. Occupies a large old timber town house. Rooms with showers (②), and without (①). Four-bedded rooms too.

Tromsdalen Camping, Elvestrandvegen (☎77 63 80 37, fax 77 63 85 24). The nearest campsite to the city centre, 1.5km from the Arctic Cathedral (Ishavskatedralen), on the mainland side of the bridge. Several city buses pass nearby – ask at the bus station. Cabins available; open all year.

Tromsø Youth Hostel, Gitta Jønsons vei 4, Elverhøy (☎ & fax 77 68 53 19; late June to late Aug). This barracks-like HI hostel is a basic affair and can be noisy. No food is available, but there's a store close by and self-catering facilities. Reception closed 11am–5pm. It's located about 2km west of the centre. A couple of city buses pass close to it – ask at the bus station– or else it's a stiff thirty-minute walk. Doubles also available (①).

The City

Completed in 1861, the **Domkirke** (June–Aug Tues–Sun noon–4pm; free), bang in the centre on Storgata, bears witness to the prosperity of Tromsø's nineteenth-century merchants, who became rich on the back of the barter trade with Russia. They part-funded the cathedral's construction, resulting in the large and handsome structure of today, whose imposing spire pokes high into the sky. From here, it's a gentle five-minute stroll north past the shops of Storgata to the main square, **Stortorget**, site of a daily open-air knick-knack and flower **market**. The square nudges down to the waterfront, where fresh fish and prawns are sold direct from fishing boats throughout the summer. Follow the harbour round to the north and you're in the heart of old Tromsø: the raised ground close to the water's edge was the centre of the medieval settlement and it was here that the locals built the first fortifications. Nothing now remains of the medieval town, but you can discern the shape of a later, eighteenth-century fort in the modest knoll at the end of Skansegata.

The Polar Museum

Close by, in an old wooden waterfront warehouse, is the city's most enjoyable museum, the **Polar Museum** (Polarmuseum i Tromsø; daily: mid-May to mid-June 11am–6pm; mid-June to Aug 11am–8pm; Sept to mid-May 10am–3pm; 30kr). The museum begins with a rather unappetizing series of displays on trapping in the Arctic, but beyond is an outstanding section on Svalbard, including archeological finds recently retrieved from an eighteenth-century Russian trapping station – most come from graves in which they were preserved by permafrost. Two other sections on the first floor focus on seal hunting, an important part of the local economy until the 1950s. Upstairs, on the second floor, a further section is devoted to the polar explorer **Roald Amundsen** (1872–1928). Amundsen spent thirty years searching out the secrets of the polar regions, and on December 14, 1911, he and four of his crew became the first men to reach the South Pole, famously just ahead of his British rival Captain Scott. The museum exhibits all sorts of oddments used by Amundsen and his men – from long johns and pipes through to boots and ice picks – but it's the photos that steal the show, both for the fascinating insight they give into the expeditions and their hardships, and for their images of a heroically posed Amundsen, complete with the finest set of eyebrows north of Oslo.

The Art Museum of Northern Norway and Polaria

On the other side of the city centre, the profitable **Mack brewery**, at the corner of Storgata and Musegata, proudly lays claim to being the northernmost brewery in the world – and dreams up all sorts of bottle labels with ice and polar bears with which to emphasize the point. Just up Musegata, the **Art Museum of North Norway** (Nordnorsk Kunstmuseum; Tues–Sun 11am–5pm; free), occupies the second and third floors of a large and attractive late nineteenth-century building. It's a small but well-presented collection, containing examples of work by many Norwegian painters, from lesser known figures like Axel Revold (1887–1962) and Christian Krohg (1852–1925) to a few works by Munch. The permanent collection is complemented by frequent loans from the National Gallery in Oslo and a lively programme of temporary exhibitions. Down below, on the first floor and in the basement, is the **Tromsø Art Society** (Tromsø Kunstforening; Tues–Sun 11am–5pm; 20kr), whose temporary exhibitions of Norwegian contemporary art often feature the work of Nordland artists.

Doubling back down Musegata, it's a couple of hundred metres south along Storgata to **Polaria** (daily: May–Aug 10am–7pm; Sept–April noon–5pm; 70kr), a lavish new complex which deals with all things arctic, including an aquarium, a 180-degree cinema showing a film on Svalbard, and exhibitions on polar explorations.

South of the centre: the Tromsø Museum

About 3km from the centre, near the southern tip of Tromsøya, is the **Tromsø Museum** (June–Aug daily 8am–8pm; Sept–May Mon–Fri 8.30am–3.30pm, Sat noon–3pm, Sun 11am–4pm; 20kr), whose varied collections feature nature and the sciences downstairs and culture and history above. Pride of place goes to the medieval religious carvings, crude but evocative pieces retrieved from various Nordland churches. There's also an enjoyable section on the Sami, with displays on every aspect of their lives, from dwellings, tools and equipment through to traditional costume and hunting techniques. To get there take bus #28 (Mon–Sat every 30min, Sun every hour) from the centre.

Eating and drinking

Tromsø has a reasonably good range of places to **eat and drink**, concentrated in the vicinity of the tourist office on Storgata, while most of the livelier bars – many of which sell the local Mack brew – are handily located in the centre too.

Restaurants and cafés

Brankos, Storgata 57 (☎77 68 26 73). Balkan restaurant with good, reasonably priced food and folksy decor. Open evenings only.

Sagatun Café, Richard Withs plass 2. Reasonably priced self-service cafeteria on the first floor of the *Saga Hotell*.

Sjømatresata$uranten Arctandria, Strandtorget 1 (☎77 61 01 01). Easily the best food in town, either in the upstairs restaurant, where main courses start at around 190kr, or downstairs in the café-bar at about twenty percent less. The range of fish in the restaurant is quite superb, with the emphasis on arctic species, plus reindeer and seal. The bar has a tad less variety, but that's not to quibble.

Bars

Blå Rock Café, Strandgata 14. Raucous R&B bar with jukebox and weekend discos.

Ølhallen Pub, Storgata 4. Solid – some would say staid – brewery pub, adjoining the Mack brewery, whose various brews form the house speciality.

Paletten, Storgata 51. This café-bar maintains an arty reputation by hosting occasional exhibitions.

Teaterkafeen, in the *Kulturhus*, Grønnegata 87, on the corner of Stortorget. This arts centre stays open until 1am most days for trendy drinking and snacks.

ROUTES NORTH FROM TROMSØ

Northbound, the **Hurtigrute** leaves Tromsø at 6.30pm, taking 11 hours to reach Hammerfest. From April to late October, the **Nord-Norgeekspressen** bus departs Tromsø for Alta (a 7hr journey) and Nordkapp (14hr) once daily except on Saturday. There's an additional daily service to Alta and another, early in the morning (Mon–Fri), from Alta to Nordkapp. Buses also head east from Alta along the E6 to Kirkenes. To reach Hammerfest by bus, change at Skaidi on the E6.

Into Finnmark: Alta

North of Tromsø, the vast sweep of the northern landscape slowly unfolds, with silent fjords gashing deep into the coastline beneath ice-tipped peaks which themselves fade into the high plateau of the interior. This forbidding, elemental terrain is interrupted by the occasional valley where those few souls hardy enough to make a living in these parts struggle on – often by dairy farming. In summer, cut grass dries everywhere, stretched over wooden poles that form long lines on the hillsides like so much washing drying.

Slipping along the valleys and traversing the mountains in between, the **E8** and then the **E6** follow the coast pretty much all the way to Alta, some 410km – about nine hours' drive – to the north. Drivers can save around 120km (although not necessarily time, and certainly not money) by turning off the E8 25km south of Tromsø onto **Hwy 91**. This cuts across the peninsula and then uses the Breivikeidet–Svendsby and Lyngseidet–Olderdalen **car ferries** (car and driver 55k and 85kr respectively) to rejoin the E6 at Olderdalen, some 220km south of Alta. Both ferries run every hour or so. This is the route used by most long-distance buses.

Whichever route you choose, you enter **Finnmark** around 60km short of a tiny village that bears the name **KÅFJORD**, from where it's just 20km further east to Alta.

Alta

Despite the long haul to get here, first impressions of **ALTA** are not encouraging. With a population of just 16,000, the town spreads unenticingly along the E6 for several kilometres, at its ugliest part in **Alta Sentrum**, now befuddled by a platoon of concrete blocks. Alta was at least interesting once, and for decades was not Norwegian at all, but Finnish and Sami, and host to an ancient Sami fair. World War II polished off the fair and destroyed all the old wooden buildings that once clustered together in Alta's **Bossekop**, where Dutch whalers settled in the seventeenth century.

For all that, Alta does have one remarkable feature: the most extensive area of prehistoric rock carvings in northern Europe. This UNESCO World Heritage site, the **Hjemmeluft Rock Carvings and Museum** (Helleristningene i Hjemmeluft; mid-June to mid-Aug daily 8am–11pm; early June and late Aug daily 8am–8pm; Sept daily 9am–6pm; Oct–April Mon–Fri 9am–3pm, Sat & Sun 11am–4pm; 40kr), is located beside the E6 as you approach Alta from the southwest, 2.5km before Bossekop. A visit begins with the **museum**, which provides a wealth of background information along with a history of the Alta area, covering particularly the salmon-fishing industry and the conflicts around the development of the nearby hydroelectric power station, which involved flooding land used by the local Sami community.

The **rock carvings** themselves spread down the hill from the museum to the fjordside. An easy-to-follow footpath and boardwalk circumnavigates the site, providing thirteen vantage points from which you can observe the carvings close-up, with their recognizable though highly stylized representations of boats, animals and people picked out in red pigment. They form an extraordinarily complex tableau, whose minor variations – there are four identifiable bands – in subject matter and design indicate successive historical periods. The carvings were executed, it's estimated, between 6000 and 2500 years ago, and although the colours have been retouched by scientists, they are indisputably impressive. Stylish, and touching in their simplicity, they provide an insight into a prehistoric culture that was essentially static and largely reliant on the hunting of land animals, with sealing and fishing of lesser importance.

Practicalities

Long distance **buses** usually call at the shopping complex at Bossekop before continuing east along the E6 for another 2km to the main bus station in Alta Sentrum. Get off in Bossekop for the rock carvings (a 2.5km walk back down the E6) and the **tourist office** (early June & late Aug Mon–Fri 10am–5pm, Sat 10am–3pm; mid-June to mid-Aug Mon–Fri 10am–6pm, Sat 10am–4pm, Sun noon–4pm; ☎78 43 79 99), inside the shopping mall. A **local bus** links the bus station with the rock carving site (Mon–Sat, hourly), but doesn't stop in Bossekop.

Alta tourist office will help with finding **accommodation**, a particularly useful service if you're dependent on public transport – the town's hotels and motels are widely dispersed – and in the height of the season when the town gets crowded, so popular is the route to Nordkapp. Alta has two excellent **hotels**, both in Bossekop and within comfortable walking distance of the tourist office. The first, a couple of hundred metres away, is the *Vica Hotell Alta* (☎78 43 47 11, fax 78 43 42 99; ④/③), a cosy, small hotel decorated in the style of a mountain lodge, with lots of pine panelling. Alternatively, the *Altafjord Hotell* (☎78 43 70 11, fax 78 43 70 13; ④), a five- to ten-minute walk to the west, down by the fjord, offers three sorts of rooms – run-of-the-mill in the main building, cottage-style down by the fjord (the best choice), and in spick-and-span modern versions of traditional turf-roofed buildings. Less costly by far is the **youth hostel**, in a plain chalet about 1km north of Alta Sentrum at Midtbakkveien 52 (☎ & fax 78 43 44 09; doubles ①;

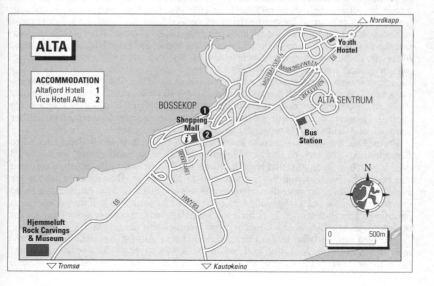

mid-June to mid-Aug). To get there from Alta Sentrum, walk east up the E6 to the next roundabout, then turn left and then first left again – a fifteen-minute stroll. Food isn't available, but there are self-catering facilities. There are also several **campsites** in the vicinity of Alta, the nearest and best-equipped being the four-star *Kronstad Camping* (☎78 43 03 60, fax 78 43 11 55), an all-year site with cabins beside the E6 at the east end of town, some 5km from Alta Sentrum.

Easily the best **restaurant** in town is at the *Vica Hotell Alta*, where they specialize in regional delicacies – cloudberries, reindeer and the like. Prices are very reasonable and traditional Sami dishes are often on the menu too.

The Finnmarksvidda

Venture far inland from Alta and you enter the **Finnmarksvidda**, a vast mountain plateau which spreads southeast up to and beyond the Finnish border. Rivers, lakes and marshes criss-cross the region, but there's barely a tree, let alone a mountain, to break the contours of a landscape whose wide skies and deep horizons are eerily beautiful. Distances are hard to gauge – a dot of a storm can soon be upon you, breaking with alarming ferocity – and the air is crystal-clear, giving a whitish lustre to the sunshine. A couple of roads cross this expanse, but for the most part it remains the preserve of the few thousand semi-nomadic **Sami** who make up the majority of the local population. Many still wear traditional dress, a brightly coloured affair of red bonnets and blue jerkins or dresses, all trimmed with red, white and yellow embroidery. You'll see permutations on this traditional costume all over Finnmark, but especially at roadside souvenir stalls and on Sundays outside Sami churches.

Setting aside the slow encroachments of the tourist industry, lifestyles on the Finnmarksvidda have remained remarkably constant for centuries. The main occupation is reindeer-herding, supplemented by hunting and fishing, and the pattern of Sami life is mostly still dictated by the movements of their animals. During the winter, the reindeer graze the flat plains and shallow valleys of the interior, migrating towards the coast in early May as the snow begins to melt. By October, both people and reindeer are journeying back from their temporary summer quarters. The long, dark winter is spent in preparation for the great **Easter festivals**, when weddings and baptisms are celebrated in Karasjok and Kautokeino, the region's two principal settlements. This is without question the best time to be here – a celebration of the end of the Polar Night and the arrival of spring. There are folk music concerts, church services and traditional sports, including the famed reindeer races. Details of these Easter festivals are available at any Finnmark tourist office or you can telephone or, even better, fax direct to Kautokeino (☎78 48 48 00, fax 78 48 58 90) and Karasjok (☎78 46 80 00, fax 78 46 62 12). Summer visits, on the other hand, can be disappointing, since most families and their reindeer are at coastal pastures in the north and there is precious little activity. In themselves, neither Karasjok nor Kautokeino is especially appealing.

From Alta, the only direct route into the Finnmarksvidda is south along Hwy 93 to **Kautokeino**, a distance of 130km. Thereafter, there's a bit more choice, with Hwy 93 pressing on into Finland, whilst Hwy 92 travels the 130km east to **Karasjok**, where you can rejoin the E6 (but well beyond the road to Nordkapp). **Bus** services across the Finnmarksvidda are no more than adequate: there's one bus daily from Alta to Kautokeino except on Sundays and a twice-daily service along the E6 from Alta to Karasjok except on Saturdays. A further service links Karasjok with Hammerfest once or twice daily except on Saturdays, but there are no buses between Karasjok and Kautokeino.

The best time to **hike** in the Finnmarksvidda is in August and early September – after the peak mosquito season and before the weather turns cold. For the most part the plateau is scrub and open birch forest, which makes the going fairly easy, though

THE SAMI

The northernmost reaches of Norway, Sweden and Finland, and the Kola peninsula of northwest Russia, are collectively known as **Lapland**. Traditionally, the indigenous people were called "Lapps", though in recent years this name has fallen out of favour and been replaced by the term **Sami**, although the change is by no means universal. The new name comes from the Sami word *sámpi*, meaning both the land and its people. There are around 70,000 Sami spread across the whole of the region. Among the oldest peoples in Europe, the Sami are probably descended from prehistoric clans who migrated here from the east by way of the Baltic. Their language is closely related to Finnish and Estonian, though it's somewhat misleading to speak of a "Sami language" as there are, in fact, three distinct versions, and each of these breaks down into a number of markedly different regional dialects. There are, however, many common features, including a superabundance of words and phrases to express variations in snow and ice conditions.

Originally, the Sami were a semi-nomadic people, living in small communities (*siidas*), each of which had a degree of control over the surrounding hunting grounds. They mixed hunting, fishing and trapping, but it was the wild reindeer that supplied most of their needs. This changed in the sixteenth century when the Sami switched over to reindeer herding, with communities following the seasonal movements of the animals.

What little contact the early Sami had with other Scandinavians was almost always to their disadvantage, but these early depredations were nothing compared with the dislocation of Sami culture that followed the efforts of Sweden, Russia and Norway to control and colonize Sami land from the seventeenth century onwards. Things got even worse for the Norwegian Sami towards the end of the nineteenth century, when the government, influenced by the Social Darwinism of the day, embarked on an aggressive policy of "Norwegianization". New laws banned the use of the Sami languages in schools, and stopped them from buying land unless they could speak Norwegian. This policy was only abandoned and slowly replaced by a more considerate and progressive approach in the 1950s.

Since the international anti-colonial struggles of the 1960s, the Norwegians have been obliged to re-evaluate their relationship with the Sami. In 1988, the country's constitution was amended with an article that stated "It is the responsibility of the authorities of the state to create conditions enabling the Sami people to preserve and develop its language, culture and way of life", and the following year the **Sameting** (Sami Parliament) was opened in Karasjok. Certain deep-seated problems do remain and, in common with other aboriginal peoples marooned in industrialized countries, there have been heated debates about land and mineral rights and the future of the Sami as a people, above and beyond one country's international borders. Neither is it clear quite how the Norwegian Sami will adjust to having something akin to dual citizenship – but at least Oslo is asking the right questions.

the many marshes, rivers and lakes often impede progress. There are a handful of clearly marked hiking trails and a smattering of unstaffed huts where you can spend the night; for detailed information, ask at Alta tourist office.

Kautokeino

It's a three-hour bus ride from Alta, deep into the Finnmarksvidda, to **KAUTOKEINO** (Guovdageaidnu in Sami), the principal winter camp of the Norwegian Sami and the site of a huge reindeer market in spring and autumn. Nonetheless, it's still a desultory, desolate-looking place that straggles along the banks of the Kautokeinoelva, though one that has become something of a tourist draw on account of the **jewellers** who have moved here from the south. Every summer, these jewellers line the long main street with souvenir booths, attracting Finnish day-trippers like flies. Their wares are not tourist tack, however, and a visit to **Juhl's Silver Gallery** (daily: June to early Aug 8.30am–10pm; early Aug to May 9am–6pm; ☎78 48 61 89, fax 78 48 69 66) is a must. Located just three kilometres south from the handful of buildings that passes for the town centre – just follow the signs – this smart complex of workshops and showrooms makes and sells exquisitely beautiful, high-quality silverwork, supplemented by a much broader range of quality craftwork influenced by traditional Sami design.

Practicalities

Doubling as Hwy 93, Kautokeino's main street is 1500m long, but most of its facilities, including the **bus stop**, are clustered near the **tourist office** (daily: early June to July 9am–7pm; early to mid-August 9am–4pm; mid- to late Aug 10am–4pm; ☎78 48 65 00), which marks what is effectively the town centre. The tourist office provides town maps and has details of local events and activities from fishing and hiking through to "Sami adventures", characteristically including a boat trip and a visit to a *lavvu* (a Sami tent), where you can sample traditional Sami food and listen to Sami *joik* music. These trips run from late June to mid-August, last about four hours and cost around 300kr per person. The main local provider is Cávso Safari (☎78 48 75 88, fax 78 48 76 39).

With regard to accommodation, the only **hotel** as such is the modest and modern *Norlandia Kautokeino* (☎78 48 62 05, fax 78 48 67 01; ④/③), on the north side of town just off Hwy 93. There are also a couple of **campsites** near the river on the southern edge of town, primarily *Kautokeino Camping og Motell* (☎78 48 54 00, fax 78 48 78 00), with cabins (①) and a few frugal motel rooms (②). The *Norlandia Kautokeino* has a competent **restaurant**.

Karasjok

The only other settlement of any size on the Finnmarksvidda is **KARASJOK** (Kárásjohka), Norway's Sami capital, which straddles the E6 on the main route from Finland to Nordkapp and consequently sees plenty of tourists. Spread across a wooded river valley, it has none of the desolation of Kautokeino, but still conspires to be fairly mundane, despite the siting of the Sami parliament and library here, and the opening of several ethnic jewellery and fine art shops. The busiest place in town is the **Samelandssenteret tourist office** (late June to early Aug, Mon–Sat 9am–6pm, Sun 10am–6pm; mid-Aug to mid-June Mon–Fri 9am–4pm, Sat 10am–2pm; ☎78 46 69 00, fax 78 46 67 35), which incorporates a Sami souvenir shop, replete with authentic arts and crafts, and a café. During the summer there are also displays of various traditional Sami skills in the grounds around the centre, complete with the obligatory reindeers. The tourist office is beside the E6 and Hwy 92 crossroads in what amounts to the town centre. From here, it's a short walk north along the Nordkapp road to the right turn leading along Museumsgata to **Sami Museum** (De Samiske Samlinger; April to early June & mid-Aug to Oct Mon–Fri 9am–3pm, Sat 10am–3pm; early June to mid-Aug Mon–Sat 9am–6pm, Sun 10am–6pm; Nov–March Mon–Fri 9am–3pm, Sat & Sun noon–3pm; 25kr). This attempts an overview of Sami culture and history, with the outdoor exhibits comprising an assortment of old dwellings that illustrate, more than anything, the frugality of Sami life. Inside, a large, clearly presented collection of incidental bygones includes a colourful sample of folkloric Sami costumes. You may also want to take a peek at the **Gamle Kirke**, on the opposite side of the river to the town centre and the only building left standing at the end of World War II. Of simple design, it dates from 1807, making it easily the oldest surviving church in Finnmark.

However diverting these sights may be, you'll only get a feel for the Finnmarksvidda if you venture out of town. The tourist office has the details of local **guided tours**:

options include dog-sledging, a visit to a Sami camp, a boat trip on the Karasjokka river, cross-country skiing and even gold-panning. The region's most popular long-distance **hike** also begins here: a five-day haul across the heart of the Finnmarksvidda to Alta via a string of strategically located huts.

Practicalities

There are only two **buses** a day to Karasjok along the E6 from Alta and Kirkenes and a couple more from Hammerfest, but nothing at all on Saturdays. Schedules mean that it's usually possible to spend a couple of hours here before moving on, which is quite enough to see the sights, but not nearly long enough to get the real flavour of the place. Buses to Karasjok pull in at the **bus station**, on Storgata. From here, it's a signposted five- to ten-minute walk west to the **Samelandssenteret tourist office**, beside the E6/Hwy 92 crossroads. They issue free town maps, provide a full list of local accommodation and have details of all the guided tours on offer.

The best **hotel** in town is the *Rica Hotel Karasjok* (☎78 46 74 00, fax 78 46 68 02; ④/③), a breezy modern establishment a short stroll north of the tourist office along the E6. The hotel also incorporates the unusual *Gammen* **restaurant** (same number), a wooden turf-covered hut where Sami-style meals can be eaten around an open fire. It's good fun, unless you dislike reindeer meat, which is inevitably the staple ingredient. More modest and less expensive accommodation is provided by the unassuming *Annes Overnatting og Motell* (☎78 46 64 32; ②), east of the tourist office along the E6 towards Kirkenes, and by *Karasjok Camping* (☎78 46 61 35, fax 78 46 66 97), where there are cabins (②) as well as tent pitches; it's located a ten-minute walk west from the tourist office on the Alta road.

From Karasjok, it's 130km west to Kautokeino; 240km north to Nordkapp; 220km northwest to Hammerfest and 320km east to Kirkenes.

Hammerfest

HAMMERFEST, some 150km from Alta, is, as its tourist office takes great pains to point out, the world's northernmost town. It was also, they add, the first town in Europe to have its streets lit by electric light. Hardly fascinating facts, but both give a glimpse of the pride that the locals take in making the most of what is, indisputably, an inhospitable location. Indeed, it's a wonder the town has survived at all: a hurricane flattened the place in 1856; it was burnt to the ground in 1890; and the retreating Germans mauled it at the end of World War II. Yet, instead of being abandoned, Hammerfest was stubbornly rebuilt for a third time. Nor is it the grim industrial town you might expect from the proximity of the offshore oil wells, but a bright, cheerful port draped around a horseshoe-shaped harbour sheltered from the elements by a steep rocky hill. But don't get too carried away: Bill Bryson, in *Neither Here Nor There*, hit the nail on the head with his description of Hammerfest as "an agreeable enough town in a thank-you-God-for-not-making-me-live-here sort of way". Neither is the town's main employer, the harbourfront fish-processing plant, the stuff of arctic romance.

Running parallel to the waterfront, **Strandgata**, the town's principal street, is a busy run of supermarkets, clothes and souvenir shops, partly inspired by the town's function as a stopoff for cruise ships on their way to Nordkapp. Most of the activity, however, takes place on the **main quay**, off Sjøgata, with tourists appearing off the liners to beetle around the harbourfront, eating shellfish straight from the stalls along the wharf or buying souvenirs from the small, summertime Sami market. The Hurtigrute coastal boat spends a couple of hours here too, arriving at 11.45am on its way south, 5.30am on its way north (although admittedly Hammerfest at 5.30am hardly sets the pulse racing).

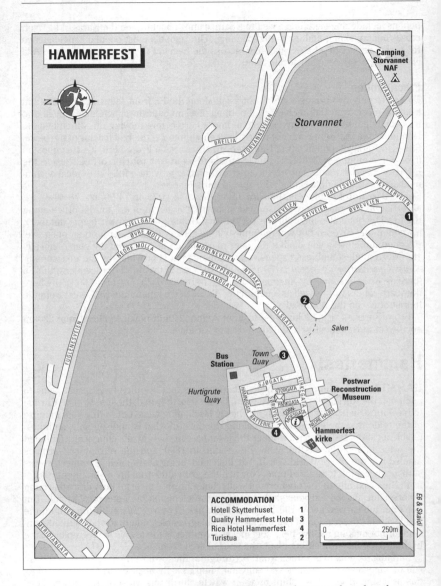

Beyond that, it's the general atmosphere of the place that appeals rather than any specific sight, though the tiny town centre does muster one reasonable attraction, the purpose-built **Postwar Reconstruction Museum** (Gjenreisningsmuseet; mid-June to mid-Aug daily 8am–7pm; mid-Aug to mid-June Mon–Fri 9am–5pm; 40kr), a five-minute walk west of the main quay up Kirkegata. This begins with a fascinating section on the hardships endured by the inhabitants of Finnmark during the German retreat from the advancing Russians in late 1944, then goes on to deal with postwar reconstruction. It's worth acquiring the English guidebook (20kr) as labels are in Norwegian only.

Practicalities

Hammerfest is situated on the island of Kvaløya, which is linked to the mainland by bridge. Buses pull in to the **bus station** at the foot of Sjøgata; the **Hurtigrute coastal boat** docks at the adjacent quay, as does the **Hurtigbåt passenger express boat** from Honningsvåg (early June to mid-Aug 1 daily; 2hr). From here, it's a couple of hundred metres to the main quay halfway up Sjøgata.

The **tourist office** (mid-June to mid-Aug Mon–Fri 9am–7pm, Sat & Sun 10am–5pm; mid-Aug to mid-June Mon–Fri 9am–4pm, Sat & Sun 10am–3pm; ☎78 41 21 85) is just round the back of the Postwar Reconstruction Museum. They issue free town maps and have details of local excursions, easily the most popular of which is the **trip to Nordkapp**. The excursion begins with the Hurtigbåt boat ride to Honningsvåg, where a connecting bus takes passengers to the Nordkapp and back. There's one daily departure from early June to mid-August; it takes nine hours and costs 815kr per person. They do not change money, but the **post office** (Mon–Fri 8.30am–5pm, Sat 10am–2pm), near by on Parkgata, does.

Hammerfest's half dozen **hotels** include the enjoyable *Quality Hammerfest Hotel*, Strandgata 2 (☎78 42 96 00, fax 78 42 96 60; ④/③). This occupies a prime spot, metres from the main quay and, although it's housed in a routine modern block, the cosy interior has a pleasant, slightly old-fashioned air, the rooms equipped with thick wooden fittings. Equally appealing is the *Rica Hotel Hammerfest*, Sørøygata 15 (☎78 41 13 33, fax 78 41 13 11; ④/③), an attractive modern place with sea views that sits on a grassy knoll a couple of minutes' walk west of the main quay. More unusual is the *Turistua* (☎78 41 46 11, fax 78 41 45 55; ④; mid-May to Aug), a modern, low-slung timber complex on top of the Salen hill behind town. Built in the style of a mountain lodge, but with fancy Viking-style carving and turf roofs, the *Turistua* offers extremely comfortable, spick-and-span

---

MOVING ON FROM HAMMERFEST

Except on Saturdays, there's a once- or twice-daily **bus** from Hammerfest to Karasjok and Kirkenes. This passes through Skaidi, on the E6, where you change for the **Nord-Norgeekspressen** service to Honningsvåg and Nordkapp (late June to mid-Aug 1–2 daily). Note, however, that not all the buses make the connection, so be sure to check at Hammerfest bus station before you set out. The other main bus service links Hammerfest with Alta, again once or twice daily except on Saturday. The **Hurtigrute coastal boat** departs Hammerfest heading south at 1.15pm and takes ten and a half hours to reach its next major port-of-call, Tromsø (around 540kr one-way, cars from 320kr). Sailing north, the Hurtigrute departs at 7.45am and reaches Honningsvåg at 5pm (308kr). At Honningsvåg, special connecting buses make the two-hour return trip to Nordkapp. From early June to mid-August, a **Hurtigbåt passenger express boat** leaves Hammerfest for Honningsvåg once daily (2hr; 300kr one-way). Again, connecting buses take passengers on to Nordkapp. Finally, Hammerfest also has several **car-hire** companies offering attractive short-term deals from around 600kr a day. Try Hammerfest Bilsenter, Seilmakerveien 1 (☎78 41 40 66), or ask at the bus station, where the regional bus company, FFR (☎78 41 71 66), is an agent for Hertz. If, however, Nordkapp is your goal, comparable deals are available at Honningsvåg. It's 160km from Hammerfest to Honningsvåg.

bedrooms, and there are great views over town from the restaurant. There's a road there too – head east from the main quay along Strandgata and, after about 400m, watch for the signposted right turn. This 2.5km-long turning leads round lake Storvannet, which lies at the bottom of a steep-sided valley dotted with the houses of Hammerfest's one and only suburb. The road then climbs up the east side of Salen to approach *Turistua* from the rear. On the way, you'll pass the tiny lakeshore *Camping Storvannet NAF* (☎78 41 10 10; June–Aug), with tent spaces (for the hardy) and a few four-bed cabins (①). Unless you're particularly energetic, you'll not want to walk to any of these places from the centre – either take a taxi or a local bus – though these are infrequent – from the bus station.

For **food**, the *Rica Hotel Hammerfest* possesses the best restaurant in town, with sea views and seafood from around 190kr per main course. There are more views from the self-service *Turistua* café, which serves up traditional Norwegian standbys at reasonable rates. More economical still is *Løkkes*, a well-tended, family-run café providing tasty meals across from the Hurtigrute quay on Hamnegata. The liveliest **bar** in town is *Kaikanten*, Sjøgata 19.

Nordkapp

At the northern tip of Norway, the treeless and windswept island of **Magerøya** is mainly of interest to travellers as the location of the **Nordkapp** (North Cape), generally regarded as mainland Europe's northernmost point – though in fact it isn't; that distinction belongs to the neighbouring headland of **Knivskjellodden**. Somehow, everyone seems to have conspired to ignore this simple fact of latitude

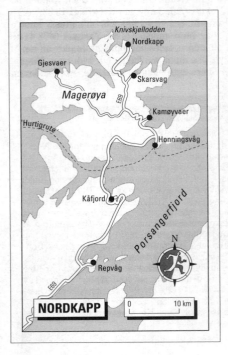

and now, whilst Nordkapp has become one of the most popular tourist destinations in the country, there isn't even a road to Knivskjellodden. Neither has the development of the Nordkapp as a tourist spot been without its critics, who argue that the large and lavish visitor centre – **Nordkapphallen** – is crass and grossly overpriced; their opponents simply point to the huge number of people who visit. Whatever, it's hard to imagine making the long trip to Magerøya without at least dropping by Nordkapp, and the island has other charms too, notably a bleak, rugged beauty that's readily appreciated on the E69 as it threads across the mountainous interior from Honningsvåg, on the south coast, to Nordkapp, a distance of 34km.

The obvious base for a visit to Nordkapp is **Honningsvåg**, the island's main settlement and a middling fishing village with a clutch of chain hotels. More appealing, however, is the tiny hamlet of **Kamøyvaer**, nestling beside a narrow fjord just off the E69 between Honningsvåg and Nordkapp, and with a couple of family-run guest-houses. Bear in mind also that Nordkapp is within easy striking distance of other places back on the mainland including the picturesque fishing station-cum-hotel at **Repvåg** – and maybe even Alta and Hammerfest, respectively 211km and 180km distant.

Arriving from Tromsø, Alta and Skaidi (for Hammerfest), the **Nord-Norgeekspressen** bus stops at both Honningsvåg and Nordkapp twice daily between Monday and Friday and once on Sunday, but only between late June and mid-August. The schedule is such that you can take the first bus to Nordkapp, spend a couple of hours there and then catch the second bus back. At other times of the year (and on Saturdays), the best way of reaching Nordkapp is to hire a **car** or take a **taxi** in Honningsvåg, where special Nordkapp deals are commonplace. In winter, (roughly mid-Oct to mid-May), the road to Nordkapp is closed by snow, but the (fanatically) determined can get there on a guided **snowmobile** excursion. You can also reach Honningsvåg (but not Nordkapp) by boat. There is a seasonal **Hurtigbåt** service from Hammerfest, and the **Hurtigrute** arrives at either 5pm (northbound) or 6.45am (southbound) daily. In both cases, the boats are met by special buses, which cart passengers off to Nordkapp and back.

North from Skaidi to Repvåg and Magerøya island

At the **Skaidi** crossroads near Hammerfest, the E6 veers east to clip across a bleak plateau that brings it, 23km later, to the turning for Nordkapp. This turning, the **E69**, scuttles north along the shore of the **Porsangerfjord**, a deep and wide inlet flanked by bare, low-lying hills whose stone has been fractured and made flaky by the biting cold of winter. After 48km, the E69 zips past the byroad to **REPVÅG**, an old timber fishing station on a promontory 2km off the main highway. A rare and particularly picturesque survivor from prewar days, the buildings here are painted red in the traditional manner and perch on stilts on the water's edge. The whole complex has been turned into the *Repvåg Hotell og Rorbusenter* (☎78 47 54 40, fax 78 47 27 51; May–Oct), with simple, unassuming rooms (③) in the main building, as well as a selection of *rorbuer* (②). It's a charming place to stay and an ideal base from which to reach the Nordkapp. Almost inevitably, the hotel **restaurant** specializes in seafood – and very good it is too.

Back on the E69, it's about 25km to the ambitious – and amazingly expensive – series of tunnels and bridges (110kr toll) that span the straits between the mainland and Honningsvåg, on the island of **Magerøya**, which you'll spy long before you get there, a hunk of brown rock looking like an inverted blancmange.

Honningsvåg

HONNINGSVÅG, 160km from Hammerfest, is officially classified as a village, which robs it of the title of the world's northernmost town – hard luck considering it's barely any smaller or less hardy in the face of adversity than its neighbour. The village straggles along the seashore, sheltered from the blizzards of winter by the surrounding crags – though, given the conditions, sheltered is a comparative term – largely made up of a jumble of well-worn modern buildings. Its prettiest area is at the head of the harbour, where an assortment of timber warehouses, dating back to the days when the village was entirely reliant on fish, make an attractive ensemble. There are also several chain hotels catering primarily for the package tourists who come here en route to the Nordkapp.

Honningsvåg strings along its main drag, Storgata, for about a kilometre. Buses from the mainland, including the long-distance Nord-Norgeekspressen, pull in to the **bus station** at the west end of Storgata. **Hurtigbåt passenger express boats** and the

Hurtigrute coastal boat dock at the adjacent jetty, where they are met by special Nordkapp excursion buses. The **tourist office** is here too (Mon–Fri 8.30am–4pm; ☎78 47 25 99). All Honningsvåg's **hotels** are dotted along or near Storgata. Walking east from the bus station, it's a few metres to the first, the *Rica Hotel Honningsvåg* (☎78 47 23 33, fax 78 47 33 79; ④/③; mid-May to Aug), a routine modern block with nearly 200 rooms. Its sister hotel, the all-year *Rica Bryggen* (☎78 47 28 88, fax 78 47 27 24; ④/③), occupies a similar but slightly smarter concrete high-rise about 500 metres to the east, down at the head of the harbour. Again, the rooms are bright, modern and comfortable, though hardly inspiring. Much more appealing is the adjacent *Best Western Honningsvåg Brygge Hotel* (☎78 47 64 60, fax 78 47 64 65; ④/③), a tasteful and intelligent conversion of a set of wooden warehouses perched on one of the old jetties. The rooms here are smart and cosy – advance reservations are strongly advised. There's cheaper accommodation at *NAF Nordkapp Camping* (☎78 47 33 77, fax 78 47 11 77; May–Sept), a **campsite** and **cabin** (②) complex about 8km from Honningsvåg on the road to Nordkapp – and just 50m from the bus stop.

Back in Honningsvåg, the *Best Western Honningsvåg Brygge* boasts the best **restaurant** by far – the *Sjøhuset* – with main courses, including delicious seafood, from 170kr; it's closed Mondays and Sunday evenings out of season (Oct–May).

Moving on, there are several ways to reach Nordkapp from Honningsvåg. The cheapest option is the **bus** (late June to mid-Aug Mon–Fri 2 daily, Sun 1 daily; 45min; 54kr each way), but if there's a group of you **car hire** can be a reasonably inexpensive option too. FFR, the local bus company, act as agents for Hertz and offer four-hour deals from around 600kr; enquire at the bus station. The taxi fare to Nordkapp, including an hour's waiting time when you get there, is 700kr; contact Nordkapp Taxisentral (☎78 47 22 34). In **winter**, North Cape Adventures (☎78 47 52 48) organize snowmobile trips to Nordkapp from the hamlet of Skarsvåg, 24km north of Honningsvåg; they also arrange transport from Honningsvåg to Skarsvåg. To stand a chance of seeing the Northern Lights, try to pick a cloudless "night".

North from Honningsvåg to Nordkapp

The E69 winds out of Honningsvåg, staying close to the shore to reach, after 9km – just after the conspicuous *Rica Hotel Nordkapp* – the turning for **KAMØYVAER**, a pretty little village tucked in tight between the sea and the hills just 2km from the main road. Here, right on the jetty, the old timber fishing station has been converted into the charming *Havstua Guesthouse* (☎78 47 51 50, fax 78 47 51 91; ②; mid-May to mid-Sept), with twenty simple but smart and extraordinarily cosy rooms. It's a delightful spot and the food is also first-rate – but note that it's advisable to book dinner in advance. A few metres away, just back from the jetty, is the *Árran Nordkapp Gjestehus* (☎78 47 51 29, fax 78 47 51 56; ②; late May to Aug), not quite as appealing perhaps, but still a pleasant family-run guesthouse in a brightly painted and well-tended home.

Beyond the Kamøyvaer turning, the E69 twists up through the hills, making its solitary course across the high tundra plateau, with mountains stretching away on either side. It's a fine run, with snow and ice lingering well into the summer and impressive views over the treeless arctic terrain. From June to October this is pastureland for the herds of reindeer who graze right up to the road, paying little heed to the occasional vehicle unless they get very close. The Sami, who bring them here by boat, combine herding with souvenir selling, setting up camp at the roadside in full costume to peddle clothes, jewellery and antler sets, which some motorists are daft enough to attach to the front of their vehicles. About 29km from Honningsvåg, the E69 passes the start of the **hiking trail** that leads to the real northernmost tip of Europe, the headland of **Knivskjellodden**, stretching about 1500m further north than its famous neighbour. The hike takes between two and three hours each way, but the terrain is too difficult and the climate too unpredictable for the inexperienced or poorly equipped hiker.

Nordkapp

Many visitors, when they finally reach the **Nordkapp**, feel desperately disappointed – it is, after all, only a cliff and, at 307 metres, it isn't even all that high. But for others there's something about this greyish-black hunk of slate, stuck at the end of a bare, wind-battered promontory, that exhilarates the senses – and some such feeling must have inspired the prehistoric Sami when they established a sacrificial site here.

The "North Cape" was actually named by the English explorer Richard Chancellor in 1553, as he drifted along the Norwegian coast in an attempt to find the Northeast Passage from the Atlantic to the Pacific. He failed, though the name stuck, and the visit of the Norwegian king Oscar II in 1873 opened the tourist floodgates. Nowdays the lavish **Nordkapphallen** (North Cape Hall; daily: early April to late May & early Sept to early Oct 2–5pm; late May to early June noon–1am; early June to early Aug 9am–2am; early Aug to late Aug 9am to midnight; late Aug to early Sept noon–5pm; 175kr; ☎78 47 68 60), cut into the rock of the Cape, entertains thousands of visitors, who pay handsomely for the pleasure of standing at mainland Europe's supposed northernmost extremity. Fronted by a statue of King Oscar II, the main building contains a restaurant, cafés, souvenir shops, a post office, where you can get your letters specially stamped, and a cinema showing – you guessed it – films about the cape. There's a viewing area too, but there's not much to see except the sea – and, weather permitting, the Midnight Sun (May 11 to July 31). A **tunnel** runs from the main building to the cliff face. It's flanked by a chapel, where you can get married, and a series of displays detailing past events and visitors, including the unlikely appearance of the King of Siam in 1907, who was so ill that he had to be carried up here on a stretcher. At the far end, the cavernous **Grotten Bar** offers caviar and champagne, long views out to sea through the massive glass wall and (of all things) a mock bird cliff. Alternatively, to escape the hurly-burly, you may decide to walk out onto the surrounding headland, though this is too bleak a spot to be much fun.

East to Kirkenes

East of Nordkapp the landscape is more of the same: a relentless expanse of barren plateau and ocean. Occasionally the picture is relieved by a determined village commanding sweeping views over the fjords that slice into the mainland, but generally there's little for the eyes of a tourist. Nor is there much to do in what are predominantly fishing and industrial settlements, and few tangible attractions beyond the sheer impossibility of the chill wilderness.

The **E6** weaves a circuitous course across this vast territory, travelling close to the Finnish border for much of its length. The only obvious target is the Sami centre of **Karasjok** (see p.346), 240km from Nordkapp and 220km from Hammerfest and easily the region's most interesting town. Frankly, there's not much reason to push on further east unless you're intent on picking up the **Hurtigrute coastal boat** as it bobs along the remote and spectacular shores of the Barents Sea. Amongst the Hurtigrute's several ports of call, the nearest to Karasjok is **Kirkenes**, 320km to the east near the Russian frontier and a town that comes close to defining remoteness. Kirkenes is actually the northern terminus of the Hurtigrute, from where it begins its long journey back to Bergen. Taking the boat also means that you can avoid the long haul back the way you came – and by the time you reach Kirkenes you'll probably be heartily sick of the E6. The other shortcut is to **fly** – SAS operate regular flights between Kirkenes and various Norwegian cities including Alta, Oslo and Tromsø.

Accommodation in this part of Norway is very thin on the ground. Campsites are more frequent and usually have cabins, but they're mostly stuck in the middle of nowhere. Remarkably, the Norwegians keep the E6 open all year, though driving in the Polar Night (late Nov to late Jan) is much too treacherous for most. The main long-distance **bus** service links Alta, Skaidi, Karasjok and Kirkenes three or four times weekly from March to December, and takes eleven hours to do it.

East from Nordkapp: by land

Beyond the junction of the E69 Nordkapp road, the **E6** bangs along the western shore of the **Porsangerfjord**, a wide inlet that slowly shelves up into the sticky marshes and mudflats at its head. After about 45km, the road reaches the hamlet of **STABBURSNES**, which is home to the small but enjoyable **Stabbursnes Natural History Museum** (Stabbursnes Naturhus og Museum; early June & mid- to late Aug daily 10am–5pm; mid-June to early Aug daily 9am–8pm; Sept–May Tues & Thurs noon–3pm, Wed noon–6pm; 25kr), which provides an overview of the region's flora and fauna.

From Stabbursnes, it's about 15km to **LAKSELV**, a fishing port at the head of the Porsangerfjord, and another 70km to Karasjok (see p.346), the best place to spend the night. Pushing on, the E6 weaves its way northeast along the Finnish border to reach, in 180km, **TANA BRU**, a Sami settlement around the suspension bridge over the River Tana, one of Europe's best salmon rivers, which sweeps down to the Tanafjord and the Barents Sea. Beyond the village, the E6 follows the southern shore of the **Varangerfjord**, a bleak, weather-beaten run, all colour and vegetation confined to the opposite coastline with its scattered farms and painted fishing boats. As the road swings inland, it's something of a relief to arrive in Kirkenes.

East from Nordkapp: by sea

Beyond Nordkapp, the **Hurtigrute** steers a fine route round the top of the country, nudging its way between tiny islets and bony bluffs, and stopping at a series of remote fishing villages, the prettiest of which is probably **BERLEVÅG**, set amid a landscape of eerie green and grey rock.

From Berlevåg, it's five hours more to **VARDØ**, Norway's most easterly town, built on an island a couple of kilometres from the mainland, to which it's connected by an underwater tunnel. Like every other town in Finnmark, Vardø was savaged in World War II and subsequently rebuilt. Its present population is just 3000 and its main attraction, located about 500m to the west of the Hurtigrute quay, is the **Vardø Fort** (Vardøhus Festning; daily 8am–10pm; 10kr), a well-preserved star-shaped fortress built in the 1730s at the behest of Christian VI. Vardø's one and only **tree**, a rowan sheltering inside the fortress, is a reminder of what's missing from the flat and barren landscape outside. In fact, Vardø is the only Norwegian town actually within the arctic climatic zone – interesting, but hardly a consolation when you can see your breath on a bright but perishingly cold June afternoon.

Northbound, the **Hurtigrute** reaches Vardø at 5.45am and leaves just thirty minutes later; heading south it docks here at 5pm and departs at 6pm – quite enough time to make it to the fortress and back. If you stay the night, the best bet is the neat and trim *Vardø Hotell* (☎78 98 77 61, fax 78 98 83 97; ④/③), close to the Hurtigrute quay at Kaigata 8. Vardø is at the end of the E75, 76km from Vadsø and 125km from the E6. The only **bus** here is a local service from Vadsø (March–Dec 1–2 daily; 1hr 30min). The sailing time on the Hurtigrute from Vardø to the Kirkenes terminus is six hours.

Kirkenes

During World War II the mining town and ice-free port of **KIRKENES** suffered more bomb attacks than any other place in Europe apart from Malta. What was left was torched by the German army retreating in the face of liberating Soviet soldiers, who found 3500 local people hiding in the nearby iron-ore mines. The mines were finally closed in 1996, threatening the future of the 6000-strong community, which is desperately trying to kindle trade with Russia to keep itself afloat.

Kirkenes is almost entirely modern, with long rows of uniform houses spreading out along the Barents Sea. If that sounds dull, it's not to slight the town, which makes the most of its inhospitable surroundings with some pleasant public gardens, lakes and residential areas – it's just that it seems an awfully long way to come for not very much. That said, once you've finally got here it seems churlish to leave quickly and it's certainly worth searching out the **Savio Museum**, housed in the old library, about 300m south of the tourist office at Kongensgate 10b (Saviomuseet; late June to late Aug daily 10am–6pm; late Aug to late June Mon–Fri 10am–4pm; 20kr). This small museum displays the work of the local Sami artist, **John Savio** (1902–38). Savio's life was brief and tragic – orphaned at the age of three, he was ill from childhood onwards and died in poverty of tuberculosis aged 36 – a fact which lends poignancy to his woodcuts and paintings, with their lonely evocations of the Sami way of life and the overbearing power of nature. The museum also hosts travelling contemporary art exhibitions, some of which are very good indeed.

Practicalities

Kirkenes is the northern terminus of the **Hurtigrute**, which spends two hours here every morning preparing for the return journey to Bergen – boats arrive at 11.15am and depart at 1.45pm from a quay just over 1km east of the town centre. A local bus links the two; failing that, walk or take a taxi. Kirkenes **airport** is 13km west of town. A local bus runs from the airport to the centre, but services are infrequent so you may have to take a taxi. Long-distance and local buses share the same **bus station** in the town centre at the west end of Kirkegata. From here, it's about 300m southeast to the **tourist office** (mid-June to late Aug Mon–Fri 8.30am–6pm, Sat & Sun 10am–6pm; late Aug to mid-June Mon–Fri 8.30am–4pm; ☎78 99 25 44, fax 78 99 25 25), next to the *Rica Arctic Hotel*. They issue free town maps, have lots of ideas as to how to while away time here and provide general information about excursions to Russia.

The town's best **hotel** is the *Rica Arctic*, a smart modern block in the centre at Kongensgate 1 (☎78 99 29 29, fax 78 99 11 59; ④/③). The similarly modern *Rica Hotel Kirkenes* occupies a glum-looking three-storey block about 700m south of the tourist office at Pasvikveien 63 (☎78 99 14 91, fax 78 99 13 56; ④/②). Inexpensive accommodation is provided at the **youth hostel** (☎ & fax 78 99 88 11; doubles ①; late June to late Aug), in a plain prefabricated chalet some 6km out of town on the E6 in Hesseng; beds need to be booked in advance. Much more handy is *Barbara's Bed & Breakfast*, with just two cosy rooms about 500m east of the tourist office at Henrik Lunds gate 13 (☎78 99 32 07; ①).

Svalbard

The **Svalbard archipelago** is one of the most inhospitable places on earth: 640km north of the Norwegian mainland (and just 1300km from the North Pole), two-thirds of the surface is covered by glaciers, the soil frozen up to a depth of 500m. It was probably discovered in the twelfth century by Icelandic seamen, though it lay ignored until 1596 when the Dutch explorer Willem Barents named the archipelago's main island, **Spitsbergen**, after its needle-like mountains. However, apart from a smattering of determined adventurers – from seventeenth-century whalers to eighteenth-century monks – few people ever lived here until, in 1899, rich coal deposits were discovered. The first coal mine was opened by an American seven years later and was passed into Norwegian hands in 1916. Meanwhile, other countries, particularly Russia and Sweden, were getting into the coal-mining act and when, in 1920, Norway's sovereignty was ratified by international treaty, it was on condition that those other countries who were operating mines could continue to do so. It was also agreed that the islands would be a demilitarized zone, which made them sitting ducks for a German squadron, which arrived here to bombard the Norwegian mines in World War II.

Despite the hardships, there are convincing reasons to make a trip to this oddly fertile archipelago. Between late April and late August there's continuous daylight; the snow has virtually all melted by July, leaving the valleys covered in flowers; and there's an abundance of wildlife – over a hundred species of migratory birds, arctic foxes, polar bears and reindeer on land, and seals, walruses and whales offshore. In winter, it's a different story. The Polar Night, when the sun never rises above the horizon, lasts from late October to mid-February; and the record low is a staggering -46°C – not counting the wind-chill factor.

Getting there and around

The simplest way to reach Svalbard is **to fly** to the archipelago's airport at Longyearbyen on Spitsbergen. Braathens operate services from a variety of Norwegian cities including Oslo, Bergen, Trondheim, Tromsø, Alta and – nearest of all – Hammerfest, on average four or five times weekly. SAS also fly to Longyearbyen, but only from Oslo via Tromsø. The Tromsø–Longyearbyen flight takes an hour and forty minutes and a standard fare with Braathens is 2630kr return, though special deals are commonplace and reduce this to around 1500kr. However, before you book your flight, you'll need to reserve accommodation in Longyearbyen (see opposite) and – unless you're happy to be stuck in your lodgings – you'd be well advised to book a place on a guided excursion too. There's a wide range on offer from hiking and climbing to kayaking and snowmobiling, glacier-walking, helicopter rides, boat trips, wildlife "safaris" and ice-caving. In the first instance, further information is available from Info-Svalbard, Postboks 323, N-9170 Longyearbyen (☎79 02 23 03, fax 79 02 10 20, *www.svalbard.com/info*), or try the very good travel and tour agency Svalbard Polar Travel, Postboks 540, N-9170 Longyearbyen (☎79 02 34 00, fax 79 02 34 01, *www.svalbard-polar.com*). You can, of course, take pot luck when you get there, but note that wilderness excursions are often fully booked weeks in advance.

Otherwise, there are adventure **cruises to Svalbard** (polar-bear spotting and the like): an all-inclusive, week-long boat trip from Tromsø will rush you in the region of 7000kr, while a three-day flight, excursion and accommodation deal from Tromsø to Longyearbyen will cost in the region of 4500kr. Contact the Tromsø tourist office (see p.338) for further details. It's also possible to go on a tour from Britain: Arctic Experience (see Basics, p.9) run an excellent range of all-in camping and hiking tours to the archipelago in July and August; prices vary with the itinerary and length of stay, but a ten-day trip costs around £2000.

Finally, if you are determined to strike out into the wilderness **independently**, you first have to seek permission from, and log your itinerary with, the governor's office, Sysselmannen på Svalbard, in Longyearbyen (☎79 02 31 00) – you'll be expected to carry a gun on account of the polar bears. Note also that there are no road connections between any of Svalbard's settlements, though there are about 45km of road around Longyearbyen. The only public transport, apart from the airport bus, is a pricey air service from Longyearbyen to the minuscule settlement of Ny Ålesund.

Spitsbergen

The main island of the Svalbard archipelago, **Spitsbergen**, is the only one that is permanently inhabited; its three Norwegian and two Russian settlements have a total population of around 3000. With just over 1000 inhabitants, the only Norwegian settlement of any size is **LONGYEARBYEN**, which huddles on the narrow coastal plain below the mountains and beside the Isfjorden, roughly in the middle of the island. It was founded in 1906, when John M. Longyear, an American mine owner, established the Arctic Coal Company here, the first to begin mining on the archipelago. Longyearbyen is now well-equipped with services, including shops, cafés, a cinema, post office, bank, swimming pool, several tour companies, a campsite, a couple of guesthouses and three hotels – note that advance reservations are essential for all accommodation

Practicalities

The **airport** is 5km west of town; both Braathens (☎79 02 19 22) and SAS (☎79 02 16 50) have offices there. An airport bus, the Flybussen (March–Sept; 35kr), runs from the airport into town, or you can take a taxi (60kr). Longyearbyen straggles inland from the Isfjorden for a couple of kilometres. Amongst the few buildings that pass for a town centre you'll find the all-year **Info-Svalbard tourist office** (☎79 02 23 03), which is equipped with a full range of leaflets on the archipelago and has information on a wide range of trips, from dog-sledging and ice-caving to snowmobile excursions and glacier walks.

In terms of **accommodation**, options include the unassuming *Svalbard Kro & Hotell* (☎79 02 24 50, fax 79 02 10 05; ④; March–Sept), right in the centre near the tourist office, and the *Nybyen Gjestehus* (☎79 02 24 50, fax 79 02 10 05; ③; mid-Feb to Sept), which offers simple but adequate rooms in refurbished miners' quarters from the 1940s – this is located almost 2km from the tourist office on the southern edge of town. The plushest hotel is the surprisingly swish, modern and central *Svalbard Polar Hotel* (☎79 02 35 00, fax 79 02 35 01; ⑤), or try the spick-and-span *Funken Hotell* (☎79 02 24 50, fax 79 02 10 05; ④), up the hill about 1km south of the tourist office. Finally, there's *Longyearbyen Camping* (☎79 02 24 50, fax 79 02 10 05; late June to Aug), though obviously, you must come fully equipped to survive what can be, at any time of the year, a cruel climate.

The *Svalbard Polar Hotel* possesses the best **restaurant** in town, but it is expensive. Cheaper choices include the straightforward *Café Busen*, near the tourist office, and, across the river at the southern edge of town the *Huset–Longyearbyen Grill og Restaurant* (☎79 02 25 00), which specializes in arctic dishes and is attached to a bar and the cinema. For **drinking**, the liveliest hangout is the *Funken Bar*, part of the hotel from which it takes its name.

The rest of Spitsbergen

There are **four other settlements** on Spitsbergen – two Norwegian and two Russian. The former consist of Ny Ålesund (20 inhabitants), to the northwest of Longyearbyen, and Sveagruva (20) to the southeast; the latter are Barentsburg (950) and Pyramiden (650), to the west and north respectively. However, there are no road connections, and the only public transport, apart from the airport bus, is a pricey air service to Ny Ålesund from Longyearbyen. If you do make it to the Russian settlements, you'll find they accept Norwegian kroner.

travel details

Buses

Alta to: Hammerfest (1–2 daily except Sat; 3hr); Honningsvåg (1–2 daily except Sat; 5hr); Karasjok (Mon–Fri 1 daily; 5hr); Kautokeino (1–2 daily except Sat; 2hr 30min); Kirkenes (Mon–Fri 1 daily; 9hr 45min); Skaidi (1–2 daily except Sat; 1hr 40min); Tromsø (April to late Oct 1–2 daily; 7hr).

Hammerfest to: Alta (1–2 daily except Sat; 3hr); Skaidi (1–2 daily except Sat; 1hr 15min).

Honningsvåg to: Alta (1–2 daily except Sat; 5hr); Lakselv (March to late Oct 1–3 daily except Sat; 4hr); Nordkapp (late June to mid-Aug 2 daily except Sat; 50min).

Karasjok to: Hammerfest (1 daily except Sat; 2hr 30min); Kirkenes (1 daily except Sun; 5hr 30min).

Kautokeino to: Alta (1–2 daily except Sat; 2hr 30min).

Kirkenes to: Alta (5 weekly; 11hr); Hammerfest (1 daily except Sun; 12hr 30min); Karasjok (1 daily except Sun; 5hr 30min).

Lakselv to: Honningsvåg (March to late Oct 1–3 daily except Sat; 4hr).

Tromsø to: Alta (April to late Oct 1–2 daily; 7hr); Nordkapp (late June to mid-Aug 1 daily except Sat; 14hr); Skaidi (for Hammerfest; late June to mid-Aug 1 daily except Sat; 9hr).

Note: With the **Nord-Norgeekspressen**, Bodø–Fauske–Narvik–Tromsø can be made in one journey, change at Narvik.

Hurtigrute coastal boat

The daily Hurtigrute service departs

Northbound: Tromsø at 6.30pm; Hammerfest at 7.45am; Honningsvåg at 5pm; Kirkenes at 11.15am.

Southbound: Kirkenes 1.45pm; Honningsvåg 6.45am; Hammerfest 1.15pm; Tromsø at 1.30am.

Hurtigbåt Express passenger boats

Hammerfest to: Honningsvåg (early June to early Aug 1 daily; 3hr).

Tromsø to: Harstad (1 daily; 2hr 30min).

PART FOUR

SWEDEN

Introduction

In geographical terms, Sweden is easily the biggest of the Scandinavian countries – a massive 450,000 square kilometres, larger than California and twice as big as Britain – although its population numbers barely nine million. Essentially one vast coniferous forest punctuated by some 100,000 crystal-clear lakes, Sweden reposes contentedly within an endless natural beauty. Remote, austere, cold – all these generalizations may be partly true, but Sweden is also friendly and efficient and, as it boasts no single concentration of sights (other than in Stockholm), you're as likely to fetch up on a sunny Baltic beach as camp in the forest or hike through the national parks of Swedish Lapland.

One aspect of the country most likely to impinge on the cluttered eye of Europeans is the sense of space. Away from the relatively densely populated south, it's easy to travel for miles without seeing a soul, and taking in these vast, unpopulated stretches in a limited time can be exhausting and unrewarding. Better, on a short trip, to delve into one or two regions and experience the natural beauty that pervades and shapes the Swedes' attitude to life: once you have broken through the oft-quoted reserve of the people there is a definite emotive feel to the country. And initial contact is easy, as almost everyone speaks.

■ Where to go

The **south and southwest** of the country are flat holiday lands. For so long territory disputed with Denmark (which the landscape closely resembles), the provinces now harbour a host of historic ports – including **Gothenburg**, **Helsingborg** and **Malmö** – and less frenetic beach towns, all old and mostly fortified. Off the **southeast** coast, the Baltic islands of **Öland** and **Gotland** are the country's most hyped resorts – and with good reason, supporting a lazy beach life to match that of the best southern European spots, but without the hotel blocks, crowds and tat.

Central and northern Sweden is the country of tourist brochures: great swaths of forest, inexhaustible lakes ideal for nude bathing and some of the best wilderness hiking in Europe. Two train routes link north with south. The eastern run, close to the **Bothnian coast**, passes old wood-built towns and is handy for the city of Umeå, with its ferry connections to Vaasa in Finland. In the centre of the country, the trains of the **Inland Railway** strike off through some remarkably changing landscapes, lakelands to mountains, clearing reindeer off the track as they go. Both routes meet in Sweden's **far north**, home of the Sami, the oldest indigenous Scandinavian people, and of the Midnight Sun, which in high summer never sets.

Of the cities, **Stockholm** is supreme. A bundle of islands housing regal and monumental architecture, fine museums and the country's most active culture and nightlife, it is a likely point of arrival and a vital stop-off. Two university towns, **Uppsala** and **Lund**, also demand a visit, while nearly all the other major cities, chiefly Östersund, Umeå, Gällivare and Kiruna, can make some sort of cultural claim on your attention. Time is rarely wasted in humbler towns either, the beauty of the local surroundings adequately compensating for any lack of specific sights.

■ When to go

Summer in Sweden is short and hectic. From rowdy Midsummer's Night onwards, accommodation is scarce and trains packed as Swedes head out to the country and onto the beaches. Outside the peak month of **July**, things are noticeably quieter. To avoid the rush, September and late May are both usually bright and warm. The **Midnight Sun** extends the days in June and July, and north of the Arctic Circle it virtually never gets dark. Elsewhere it stays light until very late, up to midnight and beyond. Thanks to the Gulf Stream, temperatures in Sweden are surprisingly high – see the temperature chart on p.xiv – and on the south coast it can be as hot as any southern European resort.

Winter, on the other hand, can be a miserable experience. It lasts a long time (November to April solid) and gets very cold indeed: temperatures of -15°C and below are not unusual even in Stockholm. Further north it is positively arctic. Days are short and dark (in the far north the sun barely rises at all) and biting winds cut through the most elaborate of padded coats. On the plus side, the snow stays crisp and white, the air is clean, the water everywhere frozen solid: a paradise for skaters and skiers. Stockholm too, is particularly beautiful with its winter covering of snow and ice.

Getting there from the rest of Scandinavia

The cheapest Scandinavian connection with Sweden is from Denmark, by bus and ferry, and regular trains and ferries connect other mainland countries.

■ By train

There are four possible **train** routes into Sweden **from Norway**. Cheapest are the five-hour run from Oslo to Gothenburg and the slightly longer route from Oslo to Stockholm; the other options are the twelve-hour ride from Trondheim to Stockholm and the day-long (23hr) haul from Narvik. From the summer of 2000, trains **from Denmark** (Copenhagen and Kastrup airport) to Gothenburg or Stockholm will use the new Öresund bridge between the Danish coast and Malmö. **Rail passes** (InterRail, Eurail and ScanRail) are valid on all these routes. Note that the ScanRail pass gives free or discounted travel on various ferry lines between Denmark or Finland and Sweden.

■ By bus

There are several **bus** routes into Sweden from other Scandinavian cities, though the frequent services **from Denmark** are the only ones that will get you there quickly. The easiest – and cheapest – connection is on one of the several daily buses **from Copenhagen** to Helsingborg, using the ferry from Helsingør – this bus then continues up the southwestern coast of Sweden to Halmstad to connect with trains to Gothenburg. Frankly though, you're better off using the train.

It's a longer haul **from Norway**, and much more expensive, too: there are several daily buses from Oslo to Gothenburg, the journey taking five or six hours, and one daily bus from Oslo to Stockholm, a nine-hour ride. **From Finland** most routes converge upon Helsinki or Turku and then use the ferry crossings to Stockholm.

■ By ferry

Ferry or **fast ferry (HSS)** services to Sweden are plentiful, but can be confusing – not least because several operators run rival services on the same route. To make any sense of the timetables and prices, which change from year to year, check the companies' brochures at any local tourist office. You'll find other details – frequencies and journey times – in the "Travel Details" at the end of each chapter.

In addition, rail passes give **discounts and free travel** on some of the ferry routes. The ScanRail pass currently gives free passage on ferries between Helsingør and Helsingborg, and on the Turku–Stockholm and Frederikshavn–Gothenburg crossings; a fifty percent discount on the routes Helsinki–Stockholm (Silja Line only),

Vaasa–Umeå and Rønne–Ystad; and a 25 percent discount on the Copenhagen–Malmö route.

From Denmark

The shortest and cheapest ferry crossing is **Helsingør–Helsingborg** (25min); just walk on board and go. There are also year-round HSS sailings and slower regular ferry connections to Gothenburg **from Frederikshavn** (2hr and 3hr 15min respectively). Stena Line also sail daily to Varberg **from Grenå**. Quicker (45min) are the catamaran services to Malmö and Helsingborg **from Copenhagen** – though these crossings are often disrupted by frozen sea between November and March.

The other approach from Denmark is to come via the Danish island of **Bornholm**. Ferries and catamarans from Copenhagen run to Rønne (50 percent discount with ScanRail pass), from where you can cross daily to Ystad, on the Swedish coast.

From Finland

Longer ferry journeys link Sweden with Finland, the major crossing being the **Helsinki–Stockholm** route, a fourteen-hour trip with either Silja or Viking. There are also regular crossings **from Turku** and **from Mariehamn** in the Finnish Åland Islands to Stockholm. If you're aiming for the north of Sweden, you might be better off crossing **from Vaasa**: there are year-round services to Umeå, a journey of four hours.

From Norway

There is one crossing from Norway to Sweden, **from Sandefjord** to Strömstad, north of Gothenburg, which operates all year round (4–5 daily; 2hr 30min).

Costs, money and banks

Sweden is no more expensive than, say, France or Germany, and certainly cheaper than neighbouring Norway. If you don't already have a rail pass, flying on standby (at least for under-25s) is a fast and affordable option in cutting travel costs. Elsewhere, regional and city discount travel passes ease what could otherwise be a burden. Accommodation, too, can be good value: well-appointed youth hostels cost an average of just 110kr (£9/$15) a night for members (another 35kr or so for non-members), and are of exceptional quality; campsites are plentiful and cheap. Virtually every hotel in Sweden halves its prices in summer, bringing even the most palatial hotels within reach of most travellers. Eating is made bearable by the three-course daily lunch offers found throughout the country on weekdays – around £6/$9 for a big, all-inclusive meal plus drink.

Put all this together and you'll find you can exist – camping, self-catering, hitching, no drinking – on around £15/$22 a day. Stay in hostels, eat lunch, get out and see the sights and this will rise to at least £25/$40. Add on £3/$5 for a drink in a bar, around £2/$3 for coffee and cake and £40/$65 minimum a night in a hotel (for a double room) and you're looking at a figure of more like £60–75/$90–115 a day. Remember, though, that the countryside (and much of your camping) is free, museums usually have low (or no) admission charges, and that everything everywhere is clean, bright and works.

Swedish **currency** is the krona (plural kronor), made up of 100 öre. It comes in coins of 50 öre, 1kr, 5kr and 10kr; and notes of 20kr, 50kr, 100kr, 500kr, 1000kr and 10,000kr. You can change money in **banks** all over Sweden (open Mon–Fri 9.30am–3pm, Thurs until 5.30pm, though branches in Stockholm and Gothenburg have longer summer hours – see the various city "Listings" sections). Outside normal banking hours you'll also be able to change money in exchange offices at airports and ferry terminals, and in post offices, as well as at Forex exchange offices – again, see the relevant "Listings" sections.

Mail and telecommunications

Communications within Sweden are good, and as most people speak at least some English, you won't go far wrong in the post or telephone office.

Post offices are open Mon–Fri 9am–6pm, Sat 10am–1pm, with some branches closed on Saturday throughout July, Sweden's holiday month. You can buy **stamps** at post offices, most newspaper kiosks, tobacconists and hotels. **Poste restante** is available at all main post offices; take your passport along to claim mail.

For international **telephone calls** dial direct from public **cardphones** – payphones no longer exist in Sweden. This is very easy: buy a card from a Pressbyrå newsagent for 30 units (around 30kr), 60 units (55–60kr) or 120 units (100–120kr). The cards have no fixed price and are sold at whatever the individual retailer decides. English instructions on how to use a cardphone are generally displayed inside each booth. Calls within Europe cost 4.62kr

per minute between 8am and 10pm, 3.88kr per minute at other times. You can also pay for calls using your credit card – look out for phones marked "CCC". Note that numbers prefixed by ☎020 (often transport information numbers) are all toll-free.

International dialling codes for calling **from Sweden** are given on p.22. For reverse-charge international calls, ring the **overseas operator** on ☎020/0018. For **directory enquiries**, dial ☎118 118 for domestic numbers, ☎079 77 for international enquiries.

The media

You'll easily be able to keep in touch with home by tuning into the TV – which relies heavily on English and American programmes – or listening to one of the English-language radio stations. Assuming that you don't read Swedish, you can also keep in touch with world events by buying **foreign newspapers** in the major towns and cities, sometimes on the day of issue, more usually the day after.

Swedish **television**, as in the rest of Scandinavia, is fairly unchallenging. On top of the two Swedish state channels, Kanal 1 and 2, there's a commercial station, TV4, while the cable station TV3 is shared with Denmark and Norway.

On the **radio** there's national (Swedish) news in English on **Radio Sweden**. Their English news programme, *60 Degrees North*, can be heard weekdays in Stockholm at 2.30pm, 3.30pm, 7.30pm, 9.30pm and 12.30am. The evening broadcasts should be audible on 1179kHz medium wave throughout Sweden, although reception can vary considerably. You can also hear BBC World Service on the same frequency (Mon–Fri 6–7.30am; Sat 6–6.30am & 7–7.30am; Sun 5–6.30am) and at all other times by tuning to either 6195, 9410, 12095 or 15070kHz short wave.

Getting around

Sweden's internal transport system is quick and efficient and runs through all weathers. Services are often reduced in the winter (especially on northern bus routes), but it's unlikely you'll ever get stranded anywhere. In summer, when everyone is on holiday, trains and, to a lesser extent, buses are packed, making seat reservations a good idea on long journeys.

All train, bus, ferry and plane schedules are contained within the giant **Rikstidtabellen** (timetable), of which every tourist office and travel agent has a copy. It costs 80kr and isn't worth buying and carrying around; just ask for photocopies of the relevant pages.

Watch out, too, for city and regional **discount cards**. One payment gets a card valid for anything from a day up to a week, and it usually includes **unlimited local travel** (bus, tram, ferry, sometimes train), museum entry and other discounts and freebies. They're often only available during the summer (valuable exceptions being the Stockholm, Gothenburg and Malmö cards), and where useful are detailed in the text. Otherwise it's worth asking at tourist offices, as schemes change frequently.

■ Trains

Apart from flying, **trains** are the quickest way to get around Sweden's vast expanses. The service is excellent, especially on the main routes, and prices not too expensive – a standard-class single from Stockholm to Gothenburg, for example, will cost you 520kr. **Swedish State Railways (SJ** – Statens Järnvägar; from abroad ☎08/696 75 40, in Sweden ☎020/75 75 75, www.sjpersontrafik.sj.se) have an extensive network of routes, running right from the far south of the country up to Östersund in central Sweden. For trains to Swedish Lapland and across the border to Narvik into Norway, services are operated by the private company, **Tågkompaniet** (www.tagkom.com), although rail passes are valid on these services too. Sweden is currently extending its luxurious high-speed train services, the **X2000**, on the main inter-city routes, which can often shave a couple of hours off the normal journey time, particularly on the Stockholm–Gothenburg run, though prices are naturally higher – Stockholm–Gothenburg, for instance, costs a hefty 920kr one-way. Note that one-way train tickets cost half the price of returns, and that you need to make a seat reservation on inter-city services (included in the price).

Buying individual **train tickets** is rarely cost-effective, despite the comprehensive system of discounts, which seem to be in continual flux. If you're planning to travel a lot by train, you're generally better off buying a **train pass**, such as a multicountry InterRail, Eurail or ScanRail pass, which needs to be purchased before you leave home (see Basics for details). If you're planning to travel only in Sweden, then it might be worth considering a Sweden-only rail pass; you need to buy this before arriving in Sweden and it currently

costs £130 ($210) for seven days' economy class travel, £174 ($280) for fourteen days, with supplements payable on inter-city and express services. The pass should be available from the train ticket agents detailed under "Getting There" in Basics – contact the Swedish tourist board (see p.27) if you have difficulties or buy it on the net by emailing swedenbooking@gtsab.se.

If you don't have a pass, check for any special deals that may be available. Alternatively, it's worth being aware of the main discount system for train tickets, the **reslust**. Reslust tickets fall into two varieties: **rosa** (pink) and the cheaper **röd** (red). A restricted number of both pink and red tickets are available on every train, though the cheaper red ones sell out quickly. Both types must be bought at least seven days before departure and be accompanied by a **reslustkort**, which costs 150kr and covers two people for a year. Sample fares between Stockholm and Gothenburg are 390kr for a rosa reslust ticket, 260kr for a röd reslust. They're valid on both X2000 and inter-city trains, including all night trains with couchette or sleeping-car accommodation. **Under-26s** are entitled to a thirty percent discount on all fares, including reslust tickets, but must be able to prove their age, and require a Reslustkort Max 25 card (150kr) to qualify for reslust tickets. On long **overnight** train journeys it's worth paying for a couchette or a sleeping car. Prices are low, with a couchette in a six-berth cabin costing only 90kr on domestic routes, 81kr from Stockholm to Copenhagen, and 117kr from Stockholm to Oslo. Sleepers within Sweden cost 165kr in a three-berth compartment, 280kr in a two-berth.

It's worth picking up the SJ Tågtider **timetable**, free from any train station. Published twice yearly, this is an accurate and comprehensive list of the most useful train services in the country. Otherwise, each train route has its own timetable leaflet, also available free from any station.

The Inlandsbanan

If you're in the country for any length of time at all, then travelling at least a section of the **Inlandsbanan** (Inland Railway) is a must: a single track route, it runs for over a thousand kilometres from central Sweden to arctic Gällivare. The line was saved from closure after it was bought by the local authorities along its length, but it now operates from June to August only. InterRail holders travel free; ScanRail pass holders get a 25 percent discount on the Inlandsbanankort (Inland Railway Card; full price 700kr). Available on board the trains, this card gives unlimited travel on the line for fourteen days. Tickets for short trips cost 50kr per 100km, and seat reservations can be made for 50kr. Timetables vary from year to year: get the latest information by calling ☎063/12 76 95 (fax 10 15 90) or visiting *www.inlandsbanan.se*.

The Pågatåg

In Skåne in southern Sweden, a local company, **Pågatåg**, operate trains between Helsingborg, Lund and Malmö, and Ystad and Simrishamn. These are fully automated and you buy your tickets from a machine on the platform which accepts coins and notes. Prices on the short hops are low, InterRail cards are valid, and ScanRail pass holders get a 50 percent discount.

■ Buses

The main **long-distance bus** companies are Swebus (☎020/64 06 40, *www.express.swebus.se*) and Svenska Buss (☎020/67 67 67, *www.svensksabuss.se*). There are two types of bus: *expressbussar* (express buses) run daily, complementing rather than competing with the train system, while the cheaper *veckoslutsbussar* (weekend buses) often only run at weekends (usually Fri & Sun). For services to the north of Sweden there are a number of smaller companies running only one or two routes, including **Y-Bussen** (☎08/440 85 70 in Stockholm, ☎060/17 19 60 in Sundsvall), the only company operating services from Stockholm to Sundsvall, the High Coast, Örnsköldsvik and Umeå, as well as across to Östersund; and **Lapplandspilen** (☎0951/333 70, *www.lapplandspilen.se*), who operate buses between Stockholm and Hemavan. In the north there are also many regional bus companies, charging 150–200kr for a one- to two-hour journey. Major routes are listed in the "Travel Details" at the end of each chapter, and you can pick up a comprehensive **timetable** at any bus terminal.

Local buses, too, are frequent and regular. Count on using them, as many hostels and campsites are a far distance from town centres. Flat fares cost 15–20kr, with tickets usually valid for an hour. Most large towns operate some sort of discount system where you can buy cheaper books of tickets – these are detailed in the text where useful, or contact the local tourist office.

■ Ferries and cruises

Unlike Norway and Finland, domestic **ferry** services in Sweden are few. The various archipelagos on the southeast coast are served by small ferries, the most comprehensive network being within the **Stockholm archipelago**, for which you can buy a boat pass (see p.418). The other major link is between the Baltic island of **Gotland** and the mainland at Nynäshamn and Oskarshamn, both very popular routes for which you should book ahead in summer. There are discounts for rail pass holders; see p.418 for details on routes. With your own boat it's possible to cross Sweden between Stockholm and Gothenburg on the **Göta Canal** or, alternatively, you can take an expensive cruise along the same route; ticket and journey details are given on p.453. Cheaper day cruises are possible along stretches of the Göta Canal and the Trollhättan Canal.

■ Planes

The **plane** network is operated by SAS and several smaller companies, such as Skyways, and various deals can make flying a real steal, especially those long slogs north. **Under-25s** can fly on standby anywhere in Sweden – the flight from Stockholm to Luleå, for example, currently costs a ridiculously cheap 200kr – while for 350kr you can book yourself onto a particular flight. If you buy eight single standby tickets you also get one return trip within Sweden free. Buy 16 single tickets and you're entitled to a free return ticket from Sweden to any SAS destination north of the Alps. You can avoid lengthy waits at airports by checking seat availability by phone (in Swedish only, ☎020/72 78 88), or on the Internet at *www.sas.se/ungdom*. **Children** under 2 travel free. It's also worth considering an **air pass**, which you'll need to buy in conjunction with your ticket to Scandinavia – SAS and Skyways do one that's valid on all their routes in Sweden, Denmark, Norway and Finland. See Basics for more information.

■ Driving and hitching

Driving presents few problems: roads are good and generally reliable, and the only real danger are the reindeer and elk that wander onto roads in parts of the country. Watch out in bad light particularly – if you hit one, you'll know about it. As for **documentation**, you need a full licence and the vehicle registration document; an international driving licence and insurance "green card" are not essential. **Speed limits** are 110kph on motorways, 90kph and 70kph on other roads, 50kph in built-up areas. It's compulsory to use **dipped headlights** during daylight hours (on rented cars they will probably come on automatically) and, if you are taking your own car from Britain, remember to get the beam of your headlights adjusted to suit **driving on the right**. If you're motoring into northern Sweden then it's recommended that you fit mud flaps to your wheels and stone guards on the front of caravans. Swedish **drink-driving laws** are among the toughest in Europe and random breath tests the norm. Even the smallest amount of alcohol can lead to lost licences (always), fines (often) and prison sentences (not infrequently).

If you **break down**, call either the police or the Larmtjänst (listed in the phone directory), a 24-hour rescue organization run by Swedish insurance companies. You should only use the emergency telephone number (☎112) in the event of an accident.

Car rental and petrol

Car rental is uniformly expensive, though most companies have special weekend tourist rates – from around 500kr, Friday to Monday, for a small car. It's worth checking out local tourist offices in the summer, as they sometimes recommend or operate reasonable weekly deals; otherwise, expect to pay around 3500kr a week, unlimited mileage, for a VW Golf or similar-sized car in the summer months. The major international companies are represented in all the large towns and cities – details under the various city "Listings".

Fuel currently costs around 8.5kr per litre; lead-free fuel is widely available and slightly cheaper. Most filling stations are self-service (*tanka själv*) and lots of them have automatic pumps (*sedel automat*), where you can fill up at any time using 100kr, 50kr and 20kr notes.

■ Cycling

A much better way to get around independently is to **cycle**. Some parts of the country were made for it, the southern provinces (and Gotland in particular) being ideal for a leisurely pedal. Many towns are best explored by bike, and tourist offices, campsites and youth hostels often rent out machines from around 100kr a day, 400kr a week. If you're touring, be prepared for long-distance hauls in the north and for rain in summer. Taking a bike on a train will cost you 150kr and you need to

hand it in three days in advance of your journey, ask to "*pollettera*" it.

The Svenska Cykelsällskapet (Swedish Cycling Association), Box 6006, S-164 06 Kista, Stockholm (☎08/751 62 04, fax 751 19 35), signpost cycle routes in central and southern Sweden and can provide maps of these routes and other information. There's an English-language guidebook, *Cycling in Sweden*, available from Cykelfrämjandet, Box 6027, S-102 31 Stockholm (☎08/32 16 80). Also, contact the STF (see overleaf) for details of cycling package holidays in Sweden, which include youth hostel accommodation, meals and bike rental.

Accommodation

Finding somewhere cheap to sleep is not difficult provided you're prepared to do some advance planning. There's an excellent network of youth hostels and campsites, while private rooms and bed-and-breakfast places are common in the cities. Year-round discounts even make hotels affordable, an option certainly worth considering in the large cities where a city discount card is thrown in as part of the package.

■ Hotels and pensions

Hotels and **pensions** come cheaper than you'd think in Sweden. Although there's little chance of a room under 300kr a night anywhere, you may be lucky during the summer, especially in July, when the Swedes all head south out of the country and hotels drop their prices significantly to attract custom. For the rest of the year, rooms at weekends are much cheaper than midweek, when business travellers push up prices. On average, for a room with TV and bathroom you can expect to pay from 350kr for a single, 500kr a double. Nearly all hotels include a self-service buffet breakfast in the price – which, given its size, can make for a useful saving.

The best **package deals** are those operated in Malmö, Stockholm and Gothenburg, where 300–365kr (minimum) gets you a hotel bed for one night, breakfast and the relevant city discount card thrown in. These schemes are generally valid from mid-June to mid-August and at weekends throughout the year, but see the accommodation details under the city accounts for more detailed information.

The other option to consider is buying into a **hotel pass** scheme, where you pay in advance for a series of vouchers or cheques which then allow discounts or free accommodation in various hotel chains throughout the country. Further details can be found in the free booklet *Hotels in Sweden*, available from the Swedish Tourist Board (see p.27), which also lists every hotel in the country.

■ Youth hostels

The biggest choice (indeed, quite often the only choice) lies with the country's huge chain of **youth hostels** (*vandrarhem*), operated by the Svenska Turistfö·eningen (STF), Box 25, S-101 20 Stockholm (☎08/463 22 70, *info@stfturist.se*). There are over 300 hostels in the country, mainly in southern and central Sweden, but also at regular and handy intervals throughout the north. Forget any preconceptions about youth hostelling: in Sweden rooms are family oriented, modern, clean and hotel-like, existing in the unlikeliest places – old castles, schoolrooms, country manors, and even on boats. Virtually all have well-equipped self-catering kitchens and serve a buffet breakfast; **prices** are low (75–175kr; non-members pay roughly an extra 50kr a night). It would be impossible to l·st every hostel in this guide, so consult the Hostelling International handbook, or the one published by the STF, available from hostels, tourist offices and large bookshops, or directly from STF. Apart from the STF hostels, there are a number of **independently run hostels**, usually charging similar prices, local tourist offices will have details.

Some tips: hostels are used by Swedish families as cheap, hotel-standard accommodation and can fill quickly, so always ring ahead in the summer; family rooms are often available for couples; hostels are sometimes closed between 10am and 5pm and have curfews around 11pm/midnight.

■ Private rooms and B&B

A further option are the **private rooms** in people's houses that most tourist offices can book for you in any reasonably sized town from around 90–140kr per person (plus a 30–50kr booking fee). These are an affordable and pleasant option: all have access to showers and/or baths, sometimes a kitchen too, and hosts are rarely intrusive. Where rooms are available they are mentioned in the text, or look for the words *rum* or *logi* by the roadside.

Farms throughout Sweden offer **B&B** accommodation and self-catering facilities; lists are available from 3o på Lantgård, Box 8, S-668 21 Ed, Sweden (☎0534/120 75, fax 610 11, *bopalant-gard@lrf.se*, *www.bopalantgard.se*), or local tourist offices. It costs roughly 250–300kr a night per person, with discounts for children. If you want to book your B&B accommodation before you leave, the Swedish Tourist Board (see p.27) should be able to point you in the right direction.

■ Campsites

Practically every town or village has at least one **campsite**. These are generally of a high stancard, something that is reflected in the price: pitching a tent costs 80–160kr a night and there's often a small charge per person, too. Most sites are open June to September; some (in winter sports areas) throughout the year. The bulk of the sites are approved and classified by the Swedish Tourist Board and a comprehensive listings book, *Camping Sverige*, is available at larger sites and most Swedish bookshops (or, in advance, try one of the map outlets I sted in Basics). The Swedish Tourist Board also puts out a short free list.

Note that you'll need a **camping card** (49kr from your first stop) at most sites and that **camping gaz** is tricky to get hold of in Sweden – take your own if possible.

Thanks to a tradition known as *Allemansrätt* (Everyman's Right), it's perfectly possible to **camp rough** throughout the country. This gives you the right to camp anywhere for one night without asking permission, provided you stay a reasonable distance (100m) away from other dwellings. In practice (and especially if you're in the north) no one will object to discreet camping for longer periods, although it's as well, and polite, to ask first. The wide open spaces within most town and city borders make free camping a distinct possibility in built-up areas, too.

■ Cabins and mountain huts

Many campsites also boast **cabins**, usually decked out with bunk beds, kitchen and equipment, but not sheets. These make an excellent alternative to camping for groups or couples; cabins go for around 250–350kr for a four-bed affair. Again, it's wise to ring ahead to secure one. Sweden also has a whole series of **chalet villages**, which – on the whole – offer high-standard accommodation at prices to match. If you're interested in a package along these lines, contact the Swedish Tourist Board for more details.

In the more out-of-the-way places, STF operate a system of **mountain huts**, strung along hiking trails and in national parks. Usually staffed by a warden, and with cooking facilities, the huts cost around 100–155kr a night for members. More information and membership details from STF (see p.369).

Food and drink

There's no escaping the fact that eating and drinking is going to take up a large slice of your daily budget in Sweden. However, if you choose to eat your main meal of the day at lunchtime, as the Swedes do, you'll save a small fortune. At its best, Swedish food is excellent. It's largely meat, fish and potato based, but varied for all that, and generally tasty and filling. There are unusual northern Swedish delicacies to look out for as well – reindeer and elk meat, and wild berries – while herring comes in so many different guises that fish fiends will always be content. Drinking is more uniform, the lager-type beer and imported wine providing no surprises, although the local spirit, *akvavit*, is worth trying at least once – it comes in dozens of different flavours.

■ Food

Eating well and cheaply in Sweden are often mutually exclusive aims, at least as far as a sit-down restaurant meal is concerned. The best strategy is to fuel up on breakfast and lunch, both of which offer good-value options. There's also a large number of foreign restaurants – principally pizzerias and Chinese restaurants – which are more likely to serve decently priced evening meals.

Breakfast, snacks and self-catering

Breakfast (*frukost*) in most youth hostels and hotel restaurants is almost invariably a help-yourself buffet; it usually costs around 50kr in hostels, and is free in hotels. If you can eat vast amounts between 7am and 10am, it's nearly always good value. Juice, milk, cereals, bread, boiled eggs, jam, salami, tea and coffee appear on even the most limited tables. Swankier venues will also add herring, porridge, yogurt, paté and fruit. Something to watch out for is the jug of *filmjölk* next to the ordinary milk – it's thicker, sour milk for pouring on cereals. **Coffee** in Sweden is always freshly brewed and very good; often it's free after the first cup, or at least greatly reduced in price – look for the word *påtår*. **Tea** is less exciting – weak Liptons as a rule – but costs around the same, 15kr a cup.

For **snacks** and lighter meals the choice expands, although their availability is inversely related to their health value. A *gatukök* (street kitchen) or *korvstånd* (hot-dog stall) will serve a selection of hot dogs, burgers, pizza slices, chicken bits, chips, ice cream, Coke, crisps and ketchup – something and chips will cost around 50kr. These stalls and stands are on every street in every town and village. A hefty burger and chips meal in a **burger bar** also goes for around 50kr: the local *Clockburger* is cheaper than *McDonalds*, but both are generally the source of the cheapest coffee in town.

It's often nicer to hit the **konditori**, a coffee shop with succulent pastries and cakes. They're not particularly cheap (coffee and cake cost around 35–60kr) but are generally as good as they look, and the coffee is often free after you've paid for the first cup. This is also where you'll come across *smörgåsar*, open **sandwiches** piled high with an elaborate variety of toppings. Favourites include shrimps, smoked salmon, eggs, cheese, paté and mixed salad – around 40–50kr a time.

Restaurants: lunch and dinner

Eating in a **restaurant** (*restaurang*) needn't be out of your price range, but remember that **lunch** is always around a third cheaper than dinner. Most restaurants offer something called the **dagens rätt** (daily dish) at around 50–60kr, an excellent way to sample real Swedish *husmanskost* – "home cooking". Served Monday to Friday between 11am and 2pm, this is simply a choice of main meal (usually one meat, one fish dish) which comes with bread/crispbread and salad, sometimes a soft drink or light beer, and usually coffee. Some Swedish dishes, like *pytt i panna* and *köttbullar* (see p.372), are standards. On the whole, though, more likely offerings in the big cities are pizzas, basic Chinese meals and meat or fish salads. If you're travelling **with kids**, look out for the word *barnmatsedal* (children's menu).

Fjærlandsfjord, Norway

Gamle Stavanger, Norway

Sami elder, Norway

Viking carving, Urnes stave church, Norway

Svalbard, Norway

Millesgården, Stockholm

Royal Palace, Stockholm

T-bana mural, Stockholm

Stockholm archipelago, Sweden

Rural scene, Skåne, Sweden

Kalmar Slott, Sweden

More expensive, but good for a blowout, are restaurants and hotels that put out the **smörgåsbord** at lunchtime for around 150–200kr. Following the breakfast theme, you help yourself to unlimited portions of herring, hot and cold meats, eggs, fried and boiled potatoes, salad, cheese, desserts and fruit. To follow local custom you should start with *akvavit*, drink beer throughout and finish with coffee, although this will add to the bill unless it is a fancier all-inclusive spread (usually found on Sunday). A variation on the buffet theme is the **sillbricka**, a specialist buffet where the dishes are all based on cured and marinaded herring – it might simply be called the "herring table" on the menu.

If you don't eat the set lunch, meals in restaurants, especially at **dinner** (*middag*), can be expensive. Expect to pay at least 400kr for a three-course affair, to which you can add 30–50kr for a beer, and 150kr for the cheapest bottle of house wine. The food in Swedish restaurants is generally *husmanskost*, although the latest trend is for "crossover" cuisine: Swedish cooking with an international edge, it's usually delicious.

Swedes eat early and lunch in most restaurants is served from around 11am, dinner from around 6pm.

Ethnic restaurants

For years the only **ethnic** choice in Sweden was between the pizzeria, and the odd Chinese restaurant and these still offer the best-value dinners. In **pizzerias** you'll get a large, if not strictly authentic, pizza for around 50kr, usually with free coleslaw and bread, and the price generally remains the same whether it's lunch or dinner. Branches of *Pizza Hut* can sometimes be found, though they're much more expensive. **Chinese** restaurants nearly always offer a set lunch for around 50kr, and though pricier in the evenings (from around 80–100kr a dish), a group of people can usually put quite a good-value meal together.

Vegetarians

It's not too tough being **vegetarian** in Sweden, given the preponderance of buffet-type meals, most of which are heavy with salads, cheeses, eggs and soups. The cities, too, have salad bars and sandwich shops where you'll have no trouble feeding yourself, and if all else fails the local pizzeria will always deliver the meat-free goods. At lunchtime you'll find that the *dagens rätt* in many places has a vegetarian option; don't be afraid to ask.

■ Drinking

Drinking is notoriously pricey and there is no way of softening the blow unless you're prepared to forgo bars and buy exclusively in the state liquor shops. Content yourself with the fact that Swedes, too, think it's expensive: you won't find yourself stuck in rounds at the bar that demand a bank loan to pay them off, and it's perfectly acceptable to nurse your drink as long as you like. It's worth noting, though, that some bars have happy hours, when half a litre of beer goes for around half-price.

What to drink

If you drink anything alcoholic in Sweden, a good choice is **beer**, which, while expensive, at least costs the same almost everywhere, be it a café, bar or restaurant. Around 40kr will get you a half-litre of good, lager-type brew – unless you specify, it will be *starköl*, the strongest Class III beer; cheaper will be *folköl*, Class II and weaker; whilst cheapest (around half the price of *folköl*) is *lättöl*, a Class I concoction notable on y for its virtual absence of alcohol. Classes I and II are available in supermarkets, although the real stuff is only on sale in the Systembolaget state-licensed liquor stores – see below – where it's around a third of the price you'll pay in a bar. **Wine** is good value when bought in the Systembolaget but can be expensive in restaurants: a glass in a bar or restaurant costs around 40kr, bottles from 150kr and upwards. **Spirits** are the most expensive; a vodka, for example, costs around 50kr a shot. For experimental drinking, **akvavit** – clear, and tasteless – is a good bet. Served ice cold in tiny shots, it's washed down with beer: hold onto your hat. There are various different "flavours" too, n which spices and herbs are added to the finished brew to produce some unusual headaches. Or try **glögg**: served at Christmas, it's a mulled red wine with cloves, cinnamon, sugar and more than a dash of *akvavit*.

Where to drink

You'll find **bars** in all towns and cities and most villages. In Stockholm and the larger cities the move is towards brasserie-type places – smart and flash. Elsewhere, you still come across more down-to-earth drinking dens, often sponsored by the local union or welfare authority, but the drink's no cheaper and the clientele heavily male and drunk. Either way, the bar is not the centre of Swedish social activity – if you really want to meet people, you'd be better off heading for the campsite or the beach.

In the summer, **café-bars** spread out onto the pavement, better for kids and handy for just a cof-

GLOSSARY OF SWEDISH FOOD AND DRINK TERMS

Basics and snacks

Ägg	Egg	*Mjölk*	Milk	*Smör*	Butter
Bröd	Bread	*Olja*	Oil	*Smörgås*	Sandwich
Glass	Ice cream	*Omelett*	Omelette	*Socker*	Sugar
Grädde	Cream	*Ost*	Cheese	*Soppa*	Soup
Gräddfil	Sour cream	*Pastej*	Paté	*Strips*	Chips
Gröt	Porridge	*Peppar*	Pepper	*Sylt*	Jam
Jus	Fruit juice	*Ris*	Rice	*Te*	Tea
Kaffe	Coffee	*Salt*	Salt	*Våfflor*	Waffles
Knäckebröd	Crispbread	*Senap*	Mustard	*Vinäger*	Vinegar
Mineralvatten	Mineral water	*Småkakor*	Biscuits		

Meat (*Kött*)

Älg	Elk	*Kotlett*	Cutlet/chop	*Oxstek*	Roast beef
Biff	Beef steak	*Köttbullar*	Meatballs	*Renstek*	Roast reindeer
Fläsk	Pork	*Kyckling*	Chicken	*Skinka*	Ham
Kalvkött	Veal	*Lammkött*	Lamb		
Korv	Sausage	*Lever*	Liver		

Fish (*Fisk*)

Ål	Eel	*Krabba*	Crab	*Rödspätta*	Plaice
Ansjovis	Anchovies	*Kräftor*	Freshwater	*Sardiner*	Sardines
Blåmusslor	Mussels		crayfish	*Sik*	Whitefish
Fiskbullar	Fishballs	*Lax*	Salmon	*Sill*	Herring
Forell	Trout	*Makrill*	Mackerel	*Strömming*	Baltic herring
Hummer	Lobster	*Räkor*	Shrimps/	*Torsk*	Cod
Kaviar	Caviar		prawns		

Vegetables (*Grönsaker*)

Ärtor	Peas	*Lök*	Onion	*Spenat*	Spinach
Blomkål	Cauliflower	*Morötter*	Carrots	*Svamp*	Mushrooms
Bönor	Beans	*Potatis*	Potatoes	*Tomater*	Tomatoes
Brysselkål	Brussels sprouts	*Rödkål*	Red cabbage	*Vitkål*	White cabbage
Gurka	Cucumber	*Sallad*	Salad	*Vitlök*	Garlic

Fruit (*Frukt*)

Ananas	Pineapple	*Citron*	Lemon	*Päron*	Pear
Apelsin	Orange	*Hallon*	Raspberry	*Persika*	Peach
Äpple	Apple	*Hjortron*	Cloudberry	*Vindruvor*	Grapes
Aprikos	Apricot	*Jordgrubbar*	Strawberries		
Banan	Banana	*Lingon*	Cranberries		

General terms

Ångkokt	Steamed	*Gravad*	Cured	*Pocherad*	Poached
Blodig	Rare	*Grillat/Halstrad*	Grilled	*Rökt*	Smoked
Filé	Fillet	*Kall*	Cold	*Stekt*	Fried
Friterad	Deep fried	*Kokt*	Boiled	*Ugnstekt*	Roasted/baked
Genomstekt	Well-done	*Lagom*	Medium	*Varm*	Hot

Swedish specialities

Ål	Eel, smoked and served with creamed potatoes or scrambled eggs (*äggröra*).	Hjortron	A wild, northern berry served with fresh cream and/or ice cream.
Ärtsoppa	Yellow pea soup with pork; a winter dish traditionally served on Thursdays.	Köttbullar	Meatballs served with a brown sauce and cranberries.
		Kryddost	Hard cheese with caraway seeds.
		Lövbiff	Sliced, fried beef with onions.
Björnstek	Roast bear meat; fairly rare, but occasionally served at Orsa.	Mesost	Brown, sweet cheese; a breakfast favourite.
		Potatissallad	Potato salad.
Bruna bönor	Baked, vinegared brown beans, usually served with bacon.	Pytt i panna	Cubes of meat and fried potatoes with a fried egg.
Fisksoppa	Fish soup.	Sillbricka	Various cured and marinaded herring dishes; often appears as a first course at lunchtime in restaurants.
Getost	Goat's cheese.		
Gravadlax	Salmon marinaded in dill, sugar and seasoning, and served with mustard sauce.	Sjömansbiff	Beef, onions and potato stewed in beer.

Drinks

Apelsin juice	Orange juice	Mineralvatten	Mineral water	Vatten	Water
Choklad	Hot chocolate	Mjölk	Milk	Vin	Wine
Citron	Lemon	Öl	Beer	Skål!	Cheers!
Frukt juice	Fruit juice	Saft	Squash		
Kaffe	Coffee	Te	Tea		

fee. In out of the way places, when you want a drink and can't find a bar, head for a hotel. Things close down at 11pm or midnight except in Gothenburg and Stockholm where – as long as your wallet is bottomless – you can drink all night.

The Systembolaget

Venturing into a **Systembolaget** (the state off-licence) is a move into a twilight world. Buying alcohol is made as unattractive as possible, with everything behind glass and grilles, and service is often dour and disapproving. There is still a real stigma attached to alcohol and its (public) consumption, and punters sneaking out with a plastic bag full of the hard stuff is not a rare sight. Buying from the Systembolaget is, however, the only option for many budget travellers, although apart from strong beer (15kr or so a third-litre), the only bargain is the wine – from around 50kr a bottle for some surprisingly good European and New World imports. Systembolaget shops are open Monday to Friday only (10am–6pm), although the Swedish government is currently experimenting with limited Saturday opening under pressure from the European Union; minimum age for being served is 20, and you may need to show ID.

Directory

CUSTOMS From outside the European Union your duty-free limit entering Sweden is one litre of spirits, one litre of wine and two litres of beer (or two litres of wine if no spirits are taken in). Other restrictions, if you're taking in a car/caravan are: no potatoes (seriously), fresh, smoked or frozen meat and a limit of 5kg of fruit and veg.

EMERGENCIES Dial ☎112 for police (*polis*), fire brigade (*brandkår*) or ambulance (*ambulans*), free of charge from any phone box.

PUBLIC HOLIDAYS Banks, offices and shops are closed on the following days and may shut early on the preceding day: January 1, January 6 (Epiphany), Good Friday, Easter Monday, May 1 (Labour Day), Ascension Day, Whit Monday, Midsummer's Day, All Saint's Day, Christmas Day, Boxing Day.

SHOPS Open Mon–Fri 9am–6pm, Sat 9am–1pm. Some department stores stay open until 8–10pm in cities, and may open on Sunday afternoons as well.

TIPPING Hotels and restaurants include their service charge (usually ten percent) in the bill. You should tip cloakroom attendants in bars and discos around 10kr a time.

History

Sweden has one of Europe's longest documented histories, but for all the upheavals of the Viking times and the warring of the Middle Ages, during modern times the country has seemed to delight in taking a historical back seat. For one brief period, when Prime Minister Olof Palme was shot dead in 1986, Sweden was thrust into the international limelight. Since then, however, it's regained its poise, even though the current situation is fraught. Political infighting and domestic disharmony is threatening the one thing that the Swedes have always been proud of and that other countries aspire to: the politics of consensus. The passing of this, arguably, is of far greater importance than even the assassination of their prime minister.

■ Early civilizations

It was not until around 6000 BC that the **first settlers** roamed north and east into Sweden, living as nomadic reindeer-hunters and herders. By 3000 BC people had settled in the south of the country and were established as farmers; whilst from around 2000 BC occurred a development in burial practices, with **dolmens** and **passage graves** being found throughout the southern Swedish provinces. Traces also remain of the **Boat Axe People**, named after their characteristic tool/weapon shaped like a boat. The earliest Scandinavian horse riders, they quickly held sway over the whole of southern Sweden.

During the **Bronze Age** (1500–500 BC) the Boat Axe People traded furs and amber for southern European copper and tin. Large finds of ornaments and weapons attest to a comparatively rich culture, exemplified by elaborate burial rites, with the dead laid in single graves under mounds of earth and stone.

The deterioration of the Scandinavian climate in the last millennium before Christ coincided with the advance across Europe of the Celts, which halted the flourishing trade of the Swedish settlers. With the new millennium, Sweden made its first mark upon the classical world when Pliny the Elder (23–79 AD), in the *Historia Naturalis*, mentioned the "island of Scatinavia" far to the north. Tacitus was more specific: in 98 AD he referred to a powerful people, the Suinoes, who were strong in men, weapons and ships: a reference to the **Svear**, who were to form the nucleus of an emergent Swedish kingdom by the sixth century.

The Svear settled in the rich land around Lake Mälaren, rulers of the whole country except the south. From them derives the country's name: "Svear rike", the kingdom of the Svear, or **Sverige** in modern Swedish. More importantly, they gave their first dynastic leaders a taste for expansion, trading with Gotland and holding suzerainty over the Åland Islands.

■ The Viking period

The Vikings – raiders and warriors who dominated the political and economic life of Europe and beyond from the ninth to the eleventh centuries – came from all parts of southern Scandinavia. But there is evidence that the **Swedish Vikings** were among the first to leave home, impelled by a rapid population growth, domestic unrest and a desire for new lands. The raiders (and, later, traders) turned their attention largely eastwards, and by the ninth century trade had developed along well-established routes, with Swedes reaching the Black and Caspian seas and making valuable contact with the **Byzantine Empire**. Although more commercially inclined than their Danish and Norwegian counterparts, Swedish Vikings were quick to use force if profits were slow to materialize. From 860 onwards Greek and Muslim records relate a series of raids across the Black Sea against Byzantium, and across the Caspian into northeast Iran.

But the Vikings were settlers as well as traders and exploiters, and their long-term influence was marked. Embattled Slavs to the east gave them the name **Rus**, and their creeping colonization gave the area in which the Vikings settled its modern name, Russia. Russian names today – Oleg, Igor, Vladimir – can be derived from the Swedish – Helgi, Ingvar, Valdemar.

Domestically, **paganism** was at its height. Freyr was "God of the World", a physically potent god of fertility from whom dynastic leaders would trace their descent. It was a bloody time. Nine **human sacrifices** were offered at the celebrations held every nine years at Uppsala. Adam of Bremen recorded that the great shrine there was adjoined by a sacred grove where "every tree is believed divine because of the death and putrefaction of the victims hanging there".

Viking **law** was based on the Thing, an assembly of free men to which the king's power was subject. Each largely autonomous province had its own assembly and its own leaders: where several provinces united, the approval of each Thing was needed for any choice of leader. For centuries in Sweden the new king had to make a formal tour to receive the homage of each province.

■ The arrival of Christianity

Christianity was slow to take root in Sweden. Whereas Denmark and Norway had accepted the faith by the beginning of the eleventh century, Swedish contact was still with the peoples to the east, who remained largely heathen. Missionaries met with limited success and no Swedish king was converted until 1008, when **Olof Skötonung** was baptized. He was the first known king of both Swedes and Goths (that is, ruler of the two major provinces of Västergötland and Östergötland) and his successors were all Christians. Nevertheless, paganism retained a grip on Swedish affairs, and as late as the 1080s the Svear banished their Christian king, Inge, when he refused to take part in the pagan celebrations at Uppsala. By the end of the eleventh century, though, the temple at Uppsala had gone and a Christian church was built on its site. In the 1130s Uppsala replaced Sigtuna – original centre of the Swedish Christian faith – as the main episcopal seat and, in 1164, Stephen (an English monk) was made the first archbishop.

■ The warring dynasties

The whole of the early Middle Ages in Sweden was characterized by a succession of struggles for control of a growing central power. Principally two families, the Sverkers and the Eriks, waged battle throughout the twelfth century. **King Erik the Holy** was the first notable Sverker king to make his mark: in 1157 he led a crusade to heathen Finland, but was killed in 1160 at Uppsala by a Danish pretender to his throne. Within a hundred years he was to be recognized as patron saint of Sweden, and his remains interred in the new Uppsala Cathedral.

Erik was succeeded by his son **Knut**, whose stable reign lasted until 1196 and was marked by commercial treaties and strengthened defences. Following his death, virtual civil war weakened the royal power with the result that the king's chief ministers, or **Jarls**, assumed much of the executive responsibility for running the country; so much so that when Erik Eriksson (last of the Eriks) was deposed in 1229, his administrator **Birger Jarl** assumed power. With papal support for his crusading policies he confirmed the Swedish grip on the southwest of Finland. His son Valdemar succeeded him, but proved a weak ruler and didn't survive the family feuding after Birger Jarl's death. Valdemar's brother Magnus assumed power in 1275.

Magnus Ladulås represented a peak of Swedish royal power not to be repeated for three hundred years. His enemies dissipated, he forbade the nobility to meet without his consent and began to issue his own authoritative decrees. Preventing the nobility from claiming maintenance at the expense of the peasantry as they travelled from estate to estate earned him his nickname Ladulås or "Barn-lock". He also began to reap the benefits of conversion: the clergy became an educated class upon whom the monarch could rely for diplomatic and administrative duties. By the thirteenth century, there were ambitious Swedish clerics in Paris and Bologna, and the first stone churches were appearing in Sweden, among them the monumental early Gothic cathedral at Uppsala.

The nobility, meanwhile, had come to form a military class, exempted from taxation on the understanding that they would defend the crown. In the country the standard of living was still low, although an increasing population stimulated new cultivation. The forests of Norrland were pushed back, southern heathland was turned into pasture, and crop rotation introduced. Noticeable, too, was the increasing **German influence** within Sweden as the Hansa traders spread. Their first merchants settled in Visby and, by the mid-thirteenth century, in Stockholm.

■ The fourteenth century – towards unity

When Magnus died in 1290, power shifted to a cabal of magnates led by **Torgil Knutsson**. As Marshal of Sweden, he pursued an energetic foreign policy, conquering western Karelia to gain control of the Gulf of Finland and building the fortress at Viborg, which was lost only with the collapse of the Swedish Empire in the eighteenth century.

Magnus's son Birger came of age in 1302 but soon quarrelled with his brothers Erik and Valdemar. They had Torgil Knutsson executed, then rounded on Birger, who was forced to divide Sweden among the three of them. An unhappy arrangement, it lasted until 1317, when Birger had his brothers arrested and starved to death in prison – an act that prompted a shocked nobility to rise against Birger and force his exile to Denmark. The Swedish nobles restored the principle of elective monarchy by calling on the three-year-old **Magnus** (son of a Swedish duke and already declared Norwegian king) to take the Swedish crown. During his minority a treaty was concluded with Novgorod (1323) to fix the frontiers in eastern and northern Finland. This left virtually the whole of the Scandinavian peninsula (except the Danish provinces in the south) under one ruler.

Yet Sweden was still anything but prosperous. The **Black Death** reached the country in 1350, wiping out whole parishes and killing perhaps a third of the population. Subsequent labour shortages and troubled estates meant that the nobility found it difficult to maintain their positions. German merchants had driven the Swedes from their most lucrative trade routes and even the copper and iron-ore **mining** that began around this time in Bergslagen and Dalarna relied on German capital.

Magnus soon ran into trouble, threatened further by the accession of Valdemar Atterdag to the Danish throne in 1340. Squabbles over the sovereignty of the Danish provinces of Skåne and Blekinge led to Danish incursions into Sweden and, in 1361, Valdemar landed on Gotland and sacked **Visby**. The Gotlanders, refused refuge by the Hansa merchants, were massacred outside the city walls.

Magnus was forced to negotiate and his son **Håkon** – now King of Norway – was married to Valdemar's daughter Margrethe. With Magnus later deposed, power fell into the hands of a group of magnates, who shared out the country. Chief of the ruling nobles was the Steward **Bo Jonsson Grip**, who controlled virtually all Finland and central and southeast Sweden. Yet on his death, the nobility turned to Håkon's wife **Margrethe**, already regent in Norway (for her son Olof) and in Denmark since the death of her father, Valdemar. In 1388 she was proclaimed "First Lady" of Sweden and, in return, confirmed all the privileges of the Swedish nobility. They were anxious for union, to safeguard those who owned frontier estates and strengthen the crown against any further German influence. Called upon to choose a male king, Margrethe nominated her nephew, **Erik of Pomerania**, who was duly elected king of Sweden in 1396. As he had already been elected to the Danish and Norwegian thrones, Scandinavian unity seemed assured.

■ The Kalmar Union

Erik was crowned King of Denmark, Norway and Sweden in 1397 at a ceremony in **Kalmar**. Nominally, the three kingdoms were now in union but, despite Erik, real power remained in the hands of Margrethe until her death in 1412.

Erik was at war throughout his reign with the Hanseatic League. Vilified in popular Swedish history as an evil and grasping ruler, the taxes he raised went on a war that was never fought on Swedish soil. He spent his time instead in Denmark, directing operations, leaving his queen Philippa (sister to Henry V of England) behind. Erik

was deposed in 1439 and the nobility turned to **Christopher of Bavaria**, whose early death in 1448 led to the first major breach in the union.

No one candidate could fill the three kingships satisfactorily, and separate elections in Denmark and Sweden signalled a renewal of the infighting that had plagued the previous century. Within Sweden, unionists and nationalists skirmished, the powerful unionist **Oxenstierna** family opposing the claims of the nationalist **Sture** family until 1470, when **Sten Sture** (the Elder) became "Guardian of the Realm". His victory over the unionists at the **Battle of Brunkeberg** (1471) – in the middle of modern Stockholm – was complete, gaining symbolic artistic expression in the **statue of St George and the Dragon** that still adorns the Great Church in Stockholm.

Sten Sture's primacy fostered a new cultural flowering. The first **university** in Scandinavia was founded in Uppsala in 1477, the first printing press appearing in Sweden six years later. Artistically, German and Dutch influences were great, traits seen in the decorative art of the great Swedish medieval churches. Only remote **Dalarna** kept alive a native folk art tradition.

Belief in the union still existed though, particularly outside Sweden, and successive kings had to fend off almost constant attacks and blockades emanating from Denmark. With the accession of **Christian II** to the Danish throne in 1513, the unionist movement found a leader capable of turning the tide. Under the guise of a crusade to free Sweden's imprisoned archbishop Gustav Trolle, Christian attacked Sweden and killed Sture. After Christian's coronation, Trolle urged the prosecution of his Swedish adversaries who, gathered together under an amnesty, were found guilty of heresy. Eighty-two nobles and burghers of Stockholm were executed and their bodies burned in what became known as the **Stockholm Blood Bath**. A vicious persecution of Sture's followers throughout Sweden ensued, a move that led to widespread reaction and, ultimately, the downfall of the union.

■ Gustav Vasa and his sons

Opposition to Christian II was vague and unorganized until the appearance of the young **Gustav Vasa**. Initially unable to stir the locals of the Dalecarlia region into open revolt, he left for exile in Norway, but was chased on skis and recalled after the people had had a change of heart. The chase is celebrated still in the **Vasalopet** race, run each year by thousands of Swedish skiers.

Gustav Vasa's army grew rapidly and in 1521 he was elected regent, and subsequently, with the capture of Stockholm in 1523, king. Christian had been deposed in Denmark and the new Danish king, Frederik I, recognized Sweden's de facto withdrawal from the union. Short of cash, Gustav found it prudent to support the movement towards religious reform propagated by Swedish Lutherans. More of a political than a religious **Reformation**, the result was a handover of church lands to the crown and the subordination of church to state. It's a relationship that is still largely in force today, the clergy being civil servants paid by the State. In 1541 the first edition of the Bible in the vernacular appeared. Suppressing revolt at home, Gustav Vasa strengthened his hand with a centralization of trade and government. On his death in 1560 Sweden was united, prosperous and independent.

Gustav Vasa's heir, his eldest son **Erik**, faced a difficult time, not least because the Vasa lands and wealth had been divided among him and his brothers Johan, Magnus and Karl (an atypically imprudent action of Gustav's before his death). The Danes, too, pressed hard, reasserting their claim to the Swedish throne in the inconclusive **Northern Seven Years War**, which began in 1563. Erik was deposed in 1569 by his brother who became **Johan III**, his first act being to end the war at the **Peace of Stettin**. At home Johan ruled more or less with the goodwill of the nobility, but upset matters with his Catholic sympathies. He introduced the liturgy and Catholic-influenced Red Book, and his son and heir Sigismund was the Catholic king of Poland. On Johan's death in 1592, Sigismund agreed to rule Sweden in accordance with Lutheran practice but failed to do so. When Sigismund returned to Poland the way was clear for Duke Karl (Johan's brother) to assume the regency, a role he filled until declared King **Karl IX** in 1603.

Karl had ambitions eastwards but, routed by the Poles and staved off by the Russians, he suffered a stroke in 1610 and died the year after. The last of Vasa's sons, his heir was the seventeen-year-old Gustav I Adolf, better known as Gustavus Adolphus.

The rule of Vasa and his sons made Sweden a nation, culturally as well as politically. The courts were filled with men of learning and the arts flourished. The **Renaissance** style appeared for the first time in Sweden, with royal castles remodelled – Kalmar being a fine example. Economically, Sweden remained mostly self-sufficient, its few imports being luxuries like cloth, wine and spices. With around 8000 inhabitants, Stockholm was its most important city, although **Gothenburg** was founded in 1607 to promote trade to the west.

■ Gustav II Adolf: the rise of the Swedish empire

During the reign of **Gustav II Adolf** Sweden became a European power. Though still a youth he was considered able enough to rule, and proved so by concluding peace treaties with Denmark (1613) and Russia (1617), the latter isolating Russia from the Baltic and allowing the Swedes control of the eastern trade routes into Europe.

In 1618 the **Thirty Years War** broke out in Germany. It was vital for Gustavus that Germany should not become Catholic, given the Polish king's continuing pretensions to the Swedish crown, and the possible threat it could pose to Sweden's growing influence in the Baltic. The Altmark treaty with a defeated Poland in 1629 gave Gustavus control of Livonia and four Prussian sea ports, and the income this generated financed his entry into the war in 1630 on the Protestant side. After several convincing victories Gustavus pushed through Germany, delaying an assault upon undefended Vienna. It cost him his life. At the **Battle of Lützen** in 1632 Gustavus was killed, his body stripped and battered by the enemy's soldiers. The war dragged on until the **Peace of Westphalia** in 1648.

With Gustavus away at war for much of his reign, Sweden ran smoothly under the guidance of his friend and chancellor, **Axel Oxenstierna**. Together they founded a new Supreme Court in Stockholm (and the same, too, in Finland and the conquered Baltic provinces); reorganized the national assembly into four Estates of nobility, clergy, burghers and peasantry (1626); extended the university at Uppsala (and founded one at Åbo – modern Turku); and fostered the mining and other industries that provided much of the country's wealth. Gustavus had many other accomplishments, too: he spoke five languages and designed a new light cannon, which assisted in his routs of the enemy.

■ The Caroleans

The Swedish empire reached its territorial peak under the **Caroleans**. Yet the reign of the last of them was to see Sweden crumble.

Following Gustav II Adolf's death and the later abdication of his daughter Christina, **Karl X** succeeded to the throne. War against Poland (1655) led to some early successes and, with Denmark espousing the Polish cause, gave Karl the opportunity to march into Jutland (1657). From there his armies marched across the frozen sea to threaten Copenhagen, the subsequent **Treaty of Roskilde**

(1658) broke Denmark and gave the Swedish empire its widest territorial extent.

However, the long regency of his son and heir, **Karl XI**, did little to enhance Sweden's vulnerable position, so extensive were its borders. On his assumption of power in 1672 Karl was almost immediately dragged into war: beaten by a smaller Prussian army at Brandenberg in 1675, Sweden was suddenly faced with war against both the Danes and Dutch. Karl rallied, though, to drive out the Danish invaders, the war ending in 1679 with the reconquest of Skåne and the restoration of most of Sweden's German provinces.

In 1682 Karl XI became **absolute monarch** and was given full control over legislation and *reduktion* – the resumption of estates previously alienated by the crown to the nobility. The armed forces were reorganized too, and by 1700 the Swedish army had 25,000 soldiers and twelve regiments of cavalry; the naval fleet was expanded to 38 ships and a new base built at **Karlskrona** (nearer than Stockholm to the likely trouble spots).

Culturally, Sweden began to benefit from the innovations of Gustav II Adolf's. *Gymnasia* (grammar schools) continued to expand and a second university was established at **Lund** in 1668. A national literature emerged, helped by the efforts of **George Stiernhielm**, "father" of modern Swedish poetry, while the same period saw the work of **Olof Rudbeck** (1630–1702), a Nordic polymath whose scientific reputation lasted longer than his attempt to identify the ancient Goth settlement at Uppsala as Atlantis. Architecturally, this was the age of **Tessin**, both father and son. Tessin the Elder was responsible for the glorious palace at **Drottningholm**, work on which began in 1662, as well as the cathedral at **Kalmar**. His son, Tessin the Younger, succeeded him as royal architect and was to create the new royal palace at Stockholm.

In 1697 the 15-year-old **Karl XII** succeeded to the throne and under him the empire collapsed. Faced with a defensive alliance of Saxony, Denmark and Russia, there was little the king could have done to avoid eventual defeat. However, he remains a revered figure for his valiant (often suicidal) efforts to prove Europe wrong. Initial victories against Peter the Great and Saxony led him to march on Russia, where he was defeated and the bulk of his army destroyed. Escaping to Turkey, where he remained as guest and then prisoner for four years, Karl watched the empire disintegrate. With Poland reconquered by Augustus of Saxony, and Finland by Peter the Great, he returned to Sweden, only to have England declare war on him.

Eventually, splits in the enemy's alliance led Swedish diplomats to attempt peace talks with Russia. Karl, though, was keen to exploit these differences in a more direct fashion. In order to strike at Denmark, but lacking a fleet, he besieged Fredrikshald in Norway in 1718 and was killed by a sniper's bullet. In the power vacuum thus created, Russia became the leading Baltic force, receiving Livonia, Estonia, Ingria and most of Karelia from Sweden.

■ The age of freedom

The eighteenth century saw absolutism discredited in Sweden. A new constitution vested power in the Estates, who reduced the new king **Fredrik I**'s role to that of nominal head of state. The chancellor wielded the real power and under **Arvid Horn** the country found a period of stability. His party, nicknamed the "Caps", was opposed by the hawkish "Hats", who forced war with Russia in 1741, a disaster in which Sweden lost all of Finland and had its whole east coast burned and bombed. Most of Finland was returned with the agreement to elect **Adolf Fredrik** (a relation of the crown prince of Russia) to the Swedish throne on Fredrik I's death, which duly occurred in 1751. During his reign Adolf repeatedly tried to reassert royal power, but found that the constitution was only strengthened against him. The resurrected "Hats" forced entry into the **Seven Years War** in 1757 on the French side, another disastrous venture as the Prussians repelled every Swedish attack.

The aristocratic parties were in a state of constant flux. Although elections of sorts were held to provide delegates for the Riksdag (parliament), foreign sympathies, bribery and bickering were hardly conducive to a democratic administration. Cabals continued to rule Sweden, the economy was stagnant, and reform delayed. It was, however, an age of intellectual and scientific advance, surprising in a country that had lost much of its cultural impetus. **Carl von Linné** (better known by the Latinized version of his name, Linnaeus), the botanist whose classification of plants is still used, was professor at Uppsala from 1741 to 1778. **Anders Celsius** initiated the use of the centigrade temperature scale; **Carl Scheele** discovered chlorine. A royal decree of 1748 organized Europe's first full-scale census, a five-yearly event by 1775. Other fields flourished, too. **Emmanuel Swedenborg**, the philosopher, died in 1772, his mystical works encouraging new theological sects; and the period encapsulated the life of **Carl Michael Bellman** (1740–95), the celebrated Swedish poet, whose work did much to identify and foster a popular nationalism.

W th the accession of **Gustav III** in 1771, the crown began to regain the ascendancy. A new constitution was forced upon a divided Riksdag and proved a balance between earlier absolutism and the later aristocratic squabbles. A popular king, Gustav founded hospitals, granted freedom of worship and removed many of the state controls over the economy. His determination to conduct a successful foreign policy led to further conflict with Russia (1788–90) in which, to everyone's surprise, he managed to more than hold his own. But with the French Revolution polarizing opposition throughout Europe, the Swedish nobility began to entertain thoughts of conspiracy against a king whose growing powers they now saw as those of a tyrant. In 1792, at a masked ball in the Stockholm Opera House, the king was shot by an assassin hired by the disaffected aristocracy. Gustav died two weeks later and was succeeded by his son **Gustav IV**, the country led by a regency for the years of his minority.

The wars waged by revolutionary France were at first studiously avoided in Sweden but, pulled into the conflict by the British, Gustav IV entered the **Napoleonic Wars** in 1805. However, Napoleon's victory at Austerlitz two years later broke the coalition and Sweden found itself isolated. Attacked by Russia the following year, Gustav was later arrested and deposed, his uncle elected king.

A constitution of 1809 established a liberal monarchy in Sweden, responsible to the elected Riksdag. Under this constitution **Karl XIII** was a mere caretaker, his heir a Danish prince who would bring Norway back to Sweden – some compensation for finally losing Finland and the Åland Islands to Russia (1809) after five hundred years of Swedish rule. On the prince's sudden death, however, Marshal Bernadotte (one of Napoleon's generals) was invited to become heir. Taking the name of **Karl Johan**, he took his chance in 1812 and joined Britain and Russia to fight Napoleon. Following Napoleon's first defeat at the Battle of Leipzig in 1813, Sweden compelled Denmark (France's ally) to exchange Norway for Swedish Pomerania.

By 1814 Sweden and Norway had formed an uneasy union. Norway retained its own government and certain autonomous measures. Sweden decided foreign policy, appointed a viceroy and retained a suspensive (but not absolute) veto over the Norwegian parliament's legislation.

■ The nineteenth century

Union under Karl Johan, or **Karl XIV** as he became in 1818, could have been disastrous. He spoke no Swedish and just a few years previously had never visited either kingdom. However, under him and his successor **Oscar I**, prosperity ensued. The **Göta Canal** (1832) helped commercially, and liberal measures by both monarchs helped politically. In 1845 daughters were given an equal right of inheritance, a poor law was introduced in 1847, restrictive craft guilds were reformed and an education act passed.

The 1848 revolution throughout Europe cooled Oscar's reforming ardour, and his attention turned to reviving **Scandinavianism**. There was still a hope, in certain quarters, that closer co-operation between Denmark and Sweden–Norway could lead to some sort of revived Kalmar Union. Expectations were raised with the **Crimean War** of 1854 that Russia – Sweden's main enemy in the eighteenth century – could be weakened for good. But peace was declared too quickly (at least for Sweden) and there was still no real guarantee that Sweden would be sufficiently protected from Russia in the future. With Oscar's death, talk of political union faded.

His son **Karl XV** presided over a reform of the Riksdag that put an end to the Swedish system of personal monarchy. The Four Estates were replaced by a representative two-house parliament along European lines. This, together with the end of political Scandinavianism (following the Prussian attack on Denmark in 1864 in which Sweden refused to offer assistance), marked Sweden's entry into modern Europe.

Industrialization was slow to take root in Sweden. No real industrial revolution occurred, and developments such as mechanization and the introduction of railways were piecemeal. One result was widespread **emigration** amongst the rural poor, who had been hard hit by famine in 1867 and 1868. Between 1860 and 1910 over one million people left for America (in 1860 the Swedish population was only four million). Given huge farms to settle, the emigrants headed for land similar to that they had left behind – to the Midwest, Kansas and Nebraska.

At home, Swedish **trade unionism** emerged to campaign for better conditions. Dealt with severely, the unions formed a confederation (1898) but largely failed to make headway. Even peaceful picketing carried a two-year prison sentence. Hand in hand with the fight for workers' rights went the **temperance movement**. The level of spirit consumption was alarming and various abstinence programmes attempted to educate the drinkers and, where necessary, eradicate the stills. Some towns made the selling of spirits a municipal monopoly – not a big step from the state monopoly that exists today.

With the accession of **Oscar II** in 1872, Sweden continued on an even, if uneventful, keel. Keeping out of further European conflict (the Austro–Prussian War, Franco–Prussian War and various Balkan crises), the country's only worry was a growing dissatisfaction in Norway with the union. Demanding a separate consular service, and objecting to the Swedish king's veto on constitutional matters, the Norwegians brought things to a head, and in 1905 declared the union invalid. The Karlstad Convention confirmed the break and Norway became independent for the first time since 1380.

The late nineteenth century was a happier time for Swedish culture. **August Strindberg** enjoyed great critical success and artists like **Anders Zorn** and **Prince Eugene** made their mark abroad. The historian **Artur Hazelius** founded the Nordic and Skansen museums in Stockholm; and the chemist, industrialist and dynamite inventor **Alfred Nobel** left his fortune to finance the Nobel Prizes. An instructive tale, Nobel hoped that the knowledge of his invention would help eradicate war – optimistically believing that mankind would never dare unleash the destructive forces of dynamite.

■ Two world wars

Sweden declared a strict neutrality on the outbreak of **World War I**, tempered by much sympathy within the country for Germany, sponsored by long-standing language, trade and cultural links. It was a policy agreed with the other Scandinavian monarchs, but a difficult one to pursue. Faced with British demands to enforce a blockade of Germany and the blacklisting and eventual seizure of Swedish goods at sea, the economy suffered grievously; rationing and inflation mushroomed. The **Russian Revolution** in 1917 brought further problems to Sweden. The Finns immediately declared independence, waging civil war against the Bolsheviks, and Swedish volunteers enlisted in the White army. But a conflict of interest arose when the Swedish-speaking Åland Islands wanted a return to Swedish rule rather than stay with the victorious Finns. The League of Nations overturned this claim, granting the islands to Finland.

After the war, a Liberal–Socialist coalition remained in power until 1920, when **Branting** became the first socialist prime minister. By the time of his death in 1924, the franchise had been extended to all men and women over 23 and the state-controlled alcohol system (Systembolaget) set up. Following the Depression of the late 1920s and early 1930s, conditions began to improve after a Social

Democratic government took office for the fourth time in 1932. A **Welfare State** was rapidly established, meaning unemployment benefit, higher old-age pensions, family allowances and paid holidays. The **Saltsjöbaden Agreement** of 1938 drew up a contract between trade unions and employers to help eliminate strikes and lockouts. With war again looming, all parties agreed that Sweden should remain neutral in any struggle and rearmament was negligible, despite Hitler's apparent intentions.

World War II was slow to affect Sweden. Unlike 1914, there was little sympathy for Germany, but neutrality was again declared. The Russian invasion of Finland in 1939 brought Sweden into the picture, providing weapons, volunteers and refuge for the Finns. Regular Swedish troops were refused though, fearing intervention from either the Germans (then Russia's ally) or the Allies. Economically, the country remained sound – less dependent on imports than in World War I and no serious shortages. The position became stickier in 1940 when the Nazis marched into Denmark and Norway, isolating Sweden. Concessions were made – German troop transit allowed, iron ore exports continued – until 1943–44 when Allied threats became more convincing than the failing German war machine. Sweden became the recipient of countless refugees from the rest of Scandinavia and the Baltic. Instrumental, too, by rescuing Hungarian Jews from the SS, was **Raoul Wallenberg**, who persuaded the Swedish government to give him diplomatic status in 1944. Unknown thousands (anything up to 35,000) of Jews in Hungary were sheltered in "neutral houses" (flying the Swedish flag), fed and clothed by Wallenberg. But when Soviet troops liberated Budapest in 1945, Wallenberg was arrested as a suspected spy and disappeared – he was later reported to have died in prison in Moscow in 1947, although unconfirmed accounts had him alive in a Soviet prison as late as 1975.

The end of the war was to provide the country with a serious crisis of conscience. Physically unscathed, Sweden was now vulnerable to Cold War politics. Proximity to the Soviet Union meant that Sweden refused to follow the other Scandinavian countries into **NATO** in 1949. The country did, however, much to Conservative disquiet, return most of the Baltic and German refugees who had fought against Russia during the war into Stalin's hands – their fate is not difficult to guess.

■ Postwar politics

The wartime coalition quickly gave way to a purely **Social Democratic** government committed to welfare provision and increased defence expenditure – non-participation in military alliances didn't mean a throwing down of weapons.

Sweden regained much of its international moral respect (lost directly after World War II) through the election of **Dag Hammarskjöld** as Secretary-General of the United Nations in 1953. His strong leadership greatly enhanced the prestige (and effectiveness) of the organization, participating in the solution of the Suez crisis in 1956 and the Lebanon–Jordan affair in 1958. He was killed in an air crash in 1961, towards the end of his second five-year term.

Throughout the 1950s and 1960s, domestic reform continued unabated. It was in these years that the country laid the foundations of its much-vaunted social security system, although at the time it didn't always bear close scrutiny. A **National Health Service** gave free hospital treatment, but only allowed for a small refund of doctor's fees, medicines and dental treatment – hardly as far-reaching as the British system introduced immediately after the war.

The Social Democrats stayed in power until 1976, when a **non-Socialist coalition** (Centre–Liberal–Moderate) finally unseated them. In the 44 years since 1932, the Socialists had been an integral part of government in Sweden, tempered only by periods of war and coalition. It was a remarkable record, made more so by the fact that modern politics in Sweden has never been about ideology so much as detail. Socialists and non-Socialists alike share a broad consensus on foreign policy and defence matters, and even on the need for the social welfare system.

◼ Olof Palme

The Social Democrats regained power in 1982, subsequently devaluing the krona, introducing a price freeze and cutting back on public expenditure, but lost their majority in 1985, having to rely on Communist support to get their bills through. Presiding over the party since 1969, and prime minister for nearly as long, was **Olof Palme**, probably now one of the world's most famous but least-known foreign leaders. Assassinated in February 1986, his death threw Sweden into modern European politics like no other event. Proud of their open society (Palme was returning home unguarded from the cinema), the Swedes were shocked by the gunning down of a respected politician, diplomat and pacifist. Shock turned to anger and then ridicule as the months passed without his killer being

caught. Police bungling was criticized and despite the theories – Kurdish extremists, right-wing terror groups – no one was charged with the murder.

Then, finally, the police came up with **Christer Pettersson**, who – despite having no apparent motive – was identified by Palme's wife as the man who had fired the shot that night. Despite pleading his innocence, claiming he was elsewhere at the time of the murder, Pettersson was convicted of Palme's murder and jailed. There was great disquiet about the verdict, however, both at home and abroad: the three legal representatives in the original jury had voted for acquittal at the time; and it was believed that Palme's wife couldn't possibly be sure that the man who fired the shot was Pettersson, since by her own admission she had only seen him once, on the dark night in question and then only very briefly. In 1989, on appeal, Pettersson was acquitted and released. The Swedish police appear to believe that they had the right man but not enough evidence to convict; more recent evidence has pointed to South African involvement, Palme having been a vocal opponent of apartheid.

◼ Carlsson and Bildt

Ingvar Carlsson was elected prime minister after Palme's murder, a position confirmed by the **1988 General Election** when the Social Democrats – for the first time in years – scored more seats than the three non-Socialist parties combined. However, Carlsson's was still a minority government, the Social Democrats requiring the support of the Communists to command an overall majority – support that was usually forthcoming but that, with the arrival of the **Green Party** into parliament in 1988, could no longer be taken for granted. The Greens and Communists jockeyed for position as protectors of the Swedish environment, and any Social Democrat measure seen to be anti-environment cost the party Communist support. Perhaps more worryingly for the government, a series of **scandals** swept the country, leading to open speculation about a marked decline in public morality. The Bofors arms company was discovered to be involved in illegal sales to the Middle East, and early in 1990 the Indian police charged the company with paying kickbacks to politicians to secure arms contracts in the subcontinent. In addition, there was insider dealing at the stock exchange and the country's ombudsman resigned over charges of personal corruption.

The real problem for the Social Democrats, though, was the **state of the economy**. With a background of rising inflation and slow economic growth, the government announced an austerity package in January 1990 which included a two-year ban on strike action, and a wage, price and rent freeze – measures whose severity astounded most Swedes. The Greens and Communists would have none of it and the Social Democrat government resigned a month later. Although the Social Democrats were soon back in charge of a minority government, having agreed to drop the most draconian measures of their programme, the problems didn't go away.

The **General Election of 1991** merely confirmed that the consensus model of politics had finally broken down. A four-party centre-right coalition came to power, led by **Carl Bildt**, which promised tax cuts and economic regeneration, but the recession sweeping western Europe didn't pass Sweden by. Unemployment hit a postwar record and in autumn 1992 – as the British pound and Italian lira collapsed on the international money markets – the krona came under severe pressure. Savage austerity measures did little to help: VAT on food was increased, statutory holiday allowances cut, welfare budgets slashed, and – after a period of intense currency speculation – short-term marginal interest rates raised to a staggering 500 percent. In a final attempt to steady nerves, Prime Minister Bildt and the leader of the Social Democratic opposition, Ingvar Carlsson, made the astonishing announcement that they would ignore party lines and work together for the good of Sweden – and then proceeded with drastic public expenditure cuts.

However, it was too little too late. Sweden was gripped by its worst **recession** since the 1930s and unemployment reached record levels of 14 percent. Poor economic growth coupled with generous welfare benefits, runaway speculation by Swedish firms on foreign real estate, and the world recession, all contributed to Sweden's economic woes. With the budget deficit growing faster than that of any other western industrialized country, Sweden also decided it was time to tighten up its asylum laws and introduced controversial new visa regulations to prevent a flood of Bosnian refugees.

■ To the millennium

Nostalgia for the good old days of Social Democracy swept the country in the September of **1994** and Carl Bildt's minority Conservative government was pushed out, allowing a return to power by Sweden's largest party, headed by **Ingvar**

Carlsson. Social Democracy was well and truly back, with Carlsson choosing a cabinet composed equally of men and women. New social reforms were implemented, most significantly the 1995 law allowing gay couples to marry, which gives them virtually equal rights with heterosexual couples.

During 1994, negotiations on Sweden's planned membership of the **European Union** were completed and put to a referendum that saw public opinion split right down the middle. While some thought that EU membership would allow Sweden a greater influence within Europe, others were concerned that the country's standards would be forced downwards, affecting the quality of life Swedes had come to expect. However, in November the vote for membership was won, albeit by the narrowest of margins – just 5 percent – and Sweden joined the Union as of January 1, 1995.

Meanwhile, the welfare state was trimmed back further and new taxes announced to try to rein in the spiralling debt: unemployment benefit was cut to 75 percent of previous earnings, sick leave benefits reduced, and lower state pension payments came into force, though Finance Minister **Göran Persson** did at least reduce taxes on food from a staggering 21 percent to 12 percent to try to retain some public support. Just when everything appeared to be under control, Carlsson announced his resignation in order to spend more time with his family, to be replaced by the domineering Persson.

Following elections in September 1998, Göran Persson clung on to power but with a much reduced majority. The election was a disaster for Sweden's Social Democrats, who recorded their worst result since World War II after losing support to the far left. Many voters complained that the Social Democrats had slashed the welfare state too far in an effort to revive the flagging economy. Debate now rages over whether it is in Sweden's financial interest to join the **single European currency**, the euro, though opposition even to EU membership remains high and recent polls show that a majority of Swedes are in favour of leaving the union. The country's ruling Social Democratic party has long been split over the membership of both the EU and the euro, though despite this, in January 2000, prime minister Göran Persson said Sweden would join the single European currency if approved in a referendum. As the cradle-to-grave pattern of welfare is abandoned and the gap between rich and poor widens, social tensions will continue to pose a major threat to the country's stability. Only renewed economic prosperity is likely to bring about a change in public opinion.

A BRIEF GUIDE TO SWEDISH

Nearly everyone, everywhere in Sweden speaks English, the tourist offices often staffed with what appear to be native Americans (most pick up the accent from films and TV). Still, knowing the essentials of Swedish is useful, and making an effort with the language certainly impresses. If you already speak either Danish or Norwegian you should have few problems being understood; if not, then a basic knowledge of German is a help too. Of the phrasebooks, most useful is *Swedish for Travellers* (Berlitz), or use the section in *Travellers' Scandinavia* (Pan).

PRONUNCIATION

Pronunciation is even more difficult than Danish or Norwegian. A **vowel** sound is usually long when it's the final syllable or followed by only one consonant; followed by two it's generally short. Unfamiliar combinations are:

ej as in m**a**te.

y as in **ewe**.

å when short as in h**o**t; when long as in r**a**w.

ä when before r as in m**a**n; otherwise as in g**e**t.

ö as in f**ur** but without the r sound.

Consonants are pronounced as in English except:

g usually as in **y**et; occasionally as in **sh**ut.

j, dj, gj, lj as in **y**et.

k before i, e y, ä, or ö, like the Scottish lo**ch**; otherwise hard.

qu as **kv**.

sch, skj, stj as in **sh**ut; otherwise hard.

tj like lo**ch**.

z as in **s**o.

BASICS

Hello	Hej	Yes	Ja	Today	I dag
Good morning	God morgon	No	Nej	Tomorrow	I morgon
Good afternoon	God middag	I don't understand	Jag förstår inte	Day after	I övermorgon
Good night	God natt	Please	Var så god	tomorrow	
Goodbye	Adjö	Thank you (very	Tack (så	In the morning	På morgonen
Do you speak	Talar ni	much)	mycket)	In the afternoon	På eftermiddagen
English ?	Engelska ?	You're welcome	Var så god	In the evening	På kvällen

SOME SIGNS

Entrance	Ingång	Closed	Stängt	No smoking	Rökning förbjuden
Exit	Utgång	Push	Skjut	No camping	Tältning förbjuden
Men	Herrar	Pull	Drag	No trespassing	Tillträde förbjudet
Women	Damer	Arrival	Ankomst	No entry	Ingen ingång
Open	Öppen, öppet	Departure	Avgång	Police	Polis

QUESTIONS AND DIRECTIONS

Where is . . . ?	Var är . . . ?	Good/bad	Bra/dålig
When?	När?	Left/right	Vänster/höger
What?	Vad?	Vacant/occupied	Ledig/upptagen
Can you direct me to . . .	Skulle ni kunna visa mig vägen till . . .	A little/a lot	Lite/en mängd
		I'd like	Jag skulle vilja ha . . .
It is/There is (Is it/Is there?)	Det är/det finns (Är det/Finns det?)	A single room	ett enkelrum
		A double room	ett dubbelrum
What time is it?	Hur mycket är klockan?	How much is it?	Vad kostar det?
Big/small	Stor/liten	Can we camp here?	Kan vi tälta här?
Cheap/expensive	Billig/dyr	Campsite	Campingplats
Early/late	Tidig/sen	Tent	Tält
Hot/cold	Varm/kall	Is there a youth hostel	Finns det något van-
Near/far	Nära/avlägsen	near here?	drarhem i närheten?

continued overleaf....

continued from previous page

NUMBERS

0	*noll*	9	*nio*	18	*arton*	70	*sjuttio*
1	*ett*	10	*tio*	19	*nitton*	80	*åttio*
2	*två*	11	*elva*	20	*tjugo*	90	*nittio*
3	*tre*	12	*tolv*	21	*tjugoett*	100	*hundra*
4	*fyra*	13	*tretton*	22	*tjugotvå*	101	*hundraett*
5	*fem*	14	*fjorton*	30	*trettio*	200	*tvåhundra*
6	*sex*	15	*femton*	40	*fyrtio*	500	*femhundra*
7	*sju*	16	*sexton*	50	*femtio*	1000	*tusen*
8	*åtta*	17	*sjutton*	60	*sextio*		

DAYS AND MONTHS

Sunday	*söndag*	January	*januari*	July	*juli*
Monday	*måndag*	February	*februari*	August	*augusti*
Tuesday	*tisdag*	March	*mars*	September	*september*
Wednesday	*onsdag*	April	*april*	October	*oktober*
Thursday	*torsdag*	May	*maj*	November	*november*
Friday	*fredag*	June	*juni*	December	*december*
Saturday	*lördag*				

Days and months are never capitalized

GLOSSARY OF SWEDISH TERMS AND WORDS

Berg	Mountain	*Muséet*	Museum
Bokhandel	Bookshop	*Pressbyrå*	Newsagent
Bro	Bridge	*Rabatt*	Rebate/discount
Cykelstig	Cycle path	*Rea*	Sales (and Vrakpriser, bargain)
Dal	Valley	*Riksdagshus*	Parliament building
Domkyrka	Cathedral	*Sjö*	Lake
Drottning	Queen (as in Drottninggatan, Queen Street)	*Skog*	Forest
		Slott	Castle
		Spår	Platform (at railway station)
Färja	Ferry	*Stadshus*	Town hall
Gamla	Old (as in Gamla Stan, old town)	*Stora*	Great/big (as in Storatorget, main square)
Gata (gt)	Street	*Strand*	Beach
Hamnen	Harbour	*Stugor*	Chalet, cottage
Järnvägsstation	Railway station	*Torg*	Central town square, usually the scene of daily/weekly markets
Klockan (kl)	O'clock		
Kyrka	Church		
Lilla	Little (as in Lilla Torget, small square)	*Universitet*	University
		Väg (v)	Road

CHAPTER NINE

STOCKHOLM AND AROUND

S tockholm is one of the most beautiful cities in Europe. Built on no fewer than four-teen islands, where the fresh water of Lake Mälaren meets the brackish Baltic Sea, fresh air and open space are in plentiful supply here: one-third of the area inside the city limits is made up of water, another third of parks and woodland, and it's

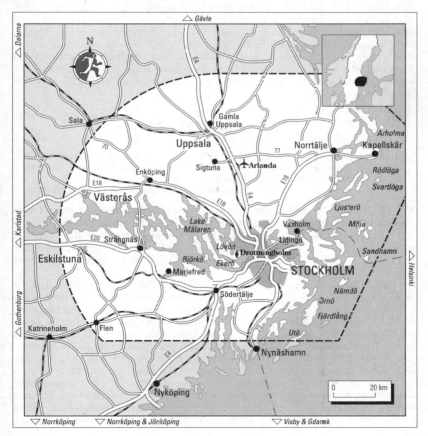

ACCOMMODATION PRICE CODES

The hotels and guesthouses listed in this chapter have been graded according to the following price bands, based on the cost of the **least expensive double room during high season** (late June to Aug). However, almost every hotel offers seasonal and/or weekend discounts, and wherever possible we've given two grades, covering both the regular and the discounted rate.

① Under 500kr   ② 500–700kr   ③ 700–900kr
④ 900–1200kr   ⑤ 1200–1500kr   ⑥ Over 1500kr

---

easy to find a quiet corner to enjoy one of Europe's saner and more civilized capitals. Broad boulevards lined with elegant buildings are reflected in the deep blue water of the Baltic, with rows of painted wooden houseboats moored alongside the city's cobbled waterfront, while the world's first urban national park offers a unique opportunity to swim and fish virtually in the city centre.

You can appreciate Stockholm's unique geography by taking one of a number of boat trips around the city and through the **Stockholm archipelago** – a staggering 24,000 islands, rocks and skerries, as the Swedish mainland slowly dissolves into the Baltic Sea. A boat trip inland along the serene waters of Lake Mälaren is another easy day-trip, with the target either of seventeenth-century **Drottningholm**, the Swedish royal residence, right on the lakeside or, further along the lake, the castle of **Gripsholm** at Mariefred. Also within day-trip range is the ancient Swedish capital and medieval university town of **Uppsala**, easily reached by frequent trains from Stockholm, as well as the odd boat.

STOCKHOLM

"It is not a city at all", he said with intensity. "It is ridiculous to think of itself as a city. It is simply a rather large village, set in the middle of some forest and some lakes. You wonder what it thinks it is doing there, looking so important."

Ingmar Bergman interviewed by James Baldwin.

STOCKHOLM often feels like two cities. Its self-important status as Sweden's most forward-looking commercial centre can seem at odds with the almost pastoral feel of its wide open spaces and expanses of open water. First impressions can be of a distant and unwelcoming place – provincial Swedes call it the Ice Queen – but stick around for the weekend and you'll see another side to Stockholm, when the population really lets its hair down.

Gamla Stan (pronounced "Gam-la Starn", meaning Old Town), was the site of the original settlement of Stockholm. Today it's an atmospheric mixture of pomp and history: ceremonial buildings surrounded by a lattice of medieval lanes and alleyways. Close by to the east is the tiny island of **Skeppsholmen** (pronounced "Shepps-holmen"), with fantastic views of the curving waterfront, while to the north is the modern centre, **Norrmalm**, with its shopping malls, huge department stores and conspicuous wealth, plus the lively Kungsträdgården park and the transport hub of Central Station. East of Norrmalm is the grand residential area of **Östermalm**, southeast of which is the green park island of **Djurgården**, host to two of Stockholm's best-known attractions: the extraordinary seventeenth-century warship, **Vasa**, and **Skansen**, Europe's oldest open-air museum. South of the Old Town lies the island of **Södermalm**, known in English as "the Southside", or as plain "Söder" to its right-on inhabitants.

Traditionally Stockholm's working-class area, it's known today for its cool bars and restaurants and lively streetlife. To the west of the centre is the island of **Kungsholmen**, which is fast coming to rival its southern neighbour with its trendy eateries and drinking establishments.

Arrival and information

Most planes – international and domestic – arrive at **Arlanda airport**, 45km north of Stockholm. A high-speed rail link, the **Arlanda Express**, links the airport with the city every fifteen minutes (5.05am–12.35pm; 20min; 120kr), and is the easiest way to get into Stockholm. A cheaper option is to take the **airport buses**, Flygbussarna (6.30am–11.30pm; 60kr), which run at least once every ten minutes from the airport to the **Cityterminalen** (Stockholm's long-distance bus station), a journey time of about forty minutes; buy your ticket on the bus. **Taxis** into Stockholm should cost around 350kr – an affordable alternative for a group – choose the ones that have prices displayed in their back windows to avoid being ripped off.

Some domestic flights operated by Braathens Malmö Aviation arrive at the more central **Bromma airport**, which is also connected to the Cityterminalen by Flygbussarna – buses run in connection with flight arrivals and departures, leaving from Gate 23 of the Cityterminalen (20min; 60kr). Ryanair flights arrive at **Skavsta airport**, 100km to the south of the capital close to the town of Nyköping; buses operate in conjunction with flight arrivals and departures (80min; 60kr) and arrive in Stockholm at the Cityterminalen.

By **train**, you'll arrive at and depart from **Central Station**, a cavernous structure on Vasagatan in the Norrmalm district. Inside there's a Forex **money exchange** office and a very useful **room-booking service**, Hotellcentralen (see "Accommodation", p.391).

By **bus**, your arrival point will be the huge glass structure known as the **Cityterminalen**, a high-tech bus terminal adjacent to Central Station and reached by a series of escalators and walkways from the northern end of the main hall. It handles all bus services: airport and ferry shuttle services, domestic and international buses all leave from here. There's also an exchange office.

There are two main **ferry** companies connecting Stockholm with Helsinki, Turku and Mariehamn in Finland. **Viking Line** ferries dock at Vikingterminalen on the island of Södermalm, from where you can catch a bus to Slussen for frequent T-bana trains to T-Centralen. **Silja Line** ferries arrive on the northeastern edge of the city at Siljaterminalen; it's a short walk to either Gärdet or Ropsten T-bana stations on the red line, where you can get a train into town. **Estline** sailings from Tallinn in Estonia arrive at Frihamnen at the end of the #41 bus route, which will take you all the way into town. If you're heading for Central Station, get off at the junction of Kungsgatan and Vasagatan and walk the short distance from there; the bus goes directly past the Cityterminalen.

Leaving Stockholm, buses to Arlanda airport leave the Cityterminalen between 4.25am and 10pm; tickets are sold at the booth in the departure area. Buses to Skavsta airport leave from Gate 24 of the Cityterminalen. When leaving Stockholm by ferry, note the Swedish names for destinations: Helsinki is "Helsingfors"; Turku, confusingly, is "Åbo".

Information

You should be able to pick up a map of the city at most points of arrival, but it's still worth dropping in on one of the city **tourist offices**. Each hands out fistfuls of free information, and you'll find a functional (if tiny) **map** in most of the brochures and

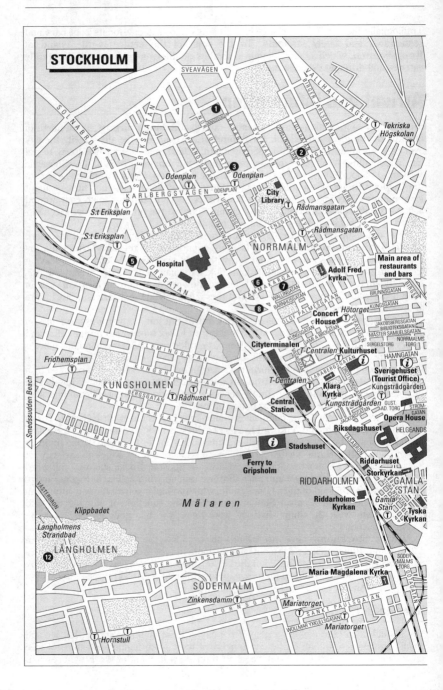

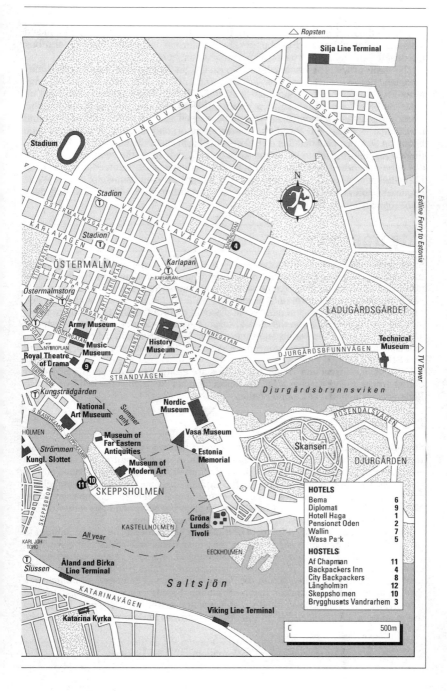

booklets – though it's probably worth paying 15kr for the larger plan of Stockholm and surrounding area produced by the Stockholm Information Service. You can also buy the useful Stockholm Card (see p.390) from any tourist office.

The **main office** is on Hamngatan in Norrmalm, on the ground floor of Sverigehuset (Sweden House; June–Aug Mon–Fri 8am–7pm, Sat & Sun 9am–5pm; Sept–May Mon–Fri 9am–6pm, Sat & Sun 9am–3pm; ☎08/789 24 90, excursion information on ☎08/789 24 15, *info@stoinfo.se, www.stoinfo.se*). Here you can pick up *Stockholm This Week*, a free listings and entertainment guide, as well as any number of brochures and timetables. Upstairs, the **Swedish Institute** has a good stock of English-language books on Sweden, plus detailed factsheets on all aspects of the country for 1kr each – there's also information to be had on working and studying in the country.

There are **other tourist offices** in the Stadshuset at Hantverkargatan 1 on Kungsholmen (May–Oct daily 9am–5pm; Nov–April Fri–Sun 9am–3pm; no telephone enquiries) and at the Kaknäs TV tower on Djurgården (see p.404) (May–Aug daily 9am–10pm; ☎08/789 24 35).

City transport

Stockholm winds its way confusingly across islands, over water and through parkland: the best way to get to grips with it is to equip yourself with a map and walk – it only takes about half an hour to cross central Stockholm on foot. Sooner or later, though, you'll have to use some form of transport and, while routes are easy enough to master, there's a bewildering array of passes and discount cards available. One thing to try to avoid is paying as you go on the city's transport system – a very expensive business. The city is zoned, a trip within one zone costing 14kr, with single tickets valid within that zone for one hour; cross a zone and it's another 7kr. Most journeys worth making cost 21kr.

City bus, local train and T-bana **timetables** are easily obtained from the SL-Center dotted around the city (see p.415); timetables for main-line trains operated by Swedish Railways can be found at Central Station.

City transport

Storstockholms Lokaltrafik (SL) operate a comprehensive system of buses and trains (underground and regional) that extends well out of the city centre. For information and timetables, the main **SL-Center** (Mon–Fri 7am–6.30pm, Sat & Sun 10am–5pm), is at Sergels Torg just by the entrance to T-Centralen (see opposite for other branches), and has timetables for the city's buses, metro, regional trains and archipelago boats. They also sell a useful **transport map** showing all street names and bus routes (35kr); you should be able to buy this from Pressbyrå newsagents too.

The quickest and most useful form of transport both around the centre and out to the suburbs is Stockholm's metro system, the Tunnelbana, or **T-bana**. There are three main lines (red, green and blue) and a smattering of branches; station entrances are marked with a blue letter "T" on a white background. Trains run from early morning until around midnight – all through the night on Friday and Saturday. All branches of the T-bana meet at **T-Centralen**, the metro station directly below Central Station. The regional trains that run throughout Greater Stockholm, the **Pendeltågen**, leave from the main train platforms on the ground level – not from underground platforms. The

For public transport **information**, call ☎08/600 10 00.

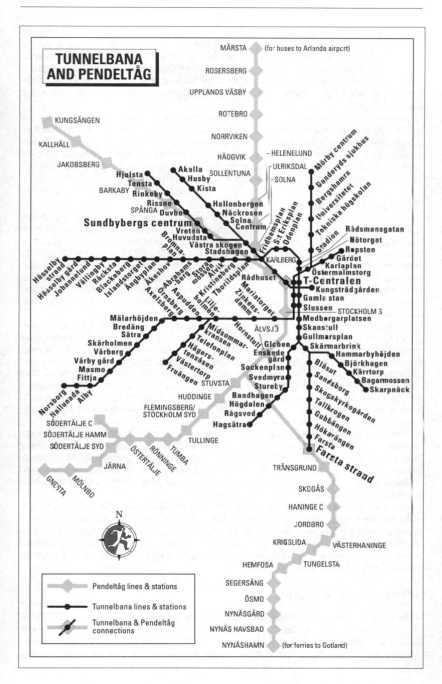

T-bana is something of an artistic venture too: T-Centralen is a huge papier-mâché cave, while Kungsträdgården is littered with statues, spotlights and fountains.

Bus routes can be less direct due to Stockholm's islands and central pedestrianization – consult the route map on the back of the *Stockholms innerstad* bus timetable for help. You board buses at the front, get off at the back or in the middle, and buy tickets from the driver. **Night buses** replace the T-bana after midnight, except on Friday and Saturday nights.

Ferries provide access to the sprawling archipelago from outside the *Grand Hotel* on Strömkajen and also link some of the central islands: Djurgården is connected with Skeppsholmen and Nybroplan in Norrmalm (summer only) and with Skeppsbron in Gamla Stan (all year round). **Cruises** on Lake Mälaren leave from outside the Stadshuset at the southeastern tip of Kungsholmen, and city boat tours leave from outside the *Grand Hotel* and from around the corner on Nybroplan.

Travel passes and tickets

The best pass to have, if you're planning to do any sightseeing at all, is the **Stockholm Card** (Stockholmskortet), which gives unlimited travel on city buses, ferries, T-bana and regional trains, free museum entry, discounts on boat trips and tours, plus free parking and many other discounts. Cards last for 24, 48 or 72 hours (199/398/498kr respectively); each card covers an adult and two children under 18. They're sold undated, then stamped on first use. From mid-May to the end of August the card includes an hour's free sightseeing by boat, though it isn't valid on ferries to Djurgården or airport buses to Arlanda. You can buy the card from any tourist office in the city or from Hotellcentralen (see p.385) in Central Station.

Among the other options, the **tourist card** (Turistkort) is valid for 24 hours (60kr) or 72 hours (120kr) and gives unlimited travel by bus, T-bana and regional train, plus travel on ferries to Djurgården and the city's one tram route; the 72-hour card also gives free admission to most of the city's museums and a 50 percent reduction on the entry price to Skansen. Discounts for under-18s or over-65s bring the cost down to 36kr (24hr) and 72kr (72hr). Tourist cards can only be bought from Pressbyrå newsagents or city tourist offices. Alternatively, you can buy a strip of twenty reduced price SL **ticket coupons** (*rabattkuponger*) for 95kr – you'll have to stamp at least two for each journey. Buy them at any T-bana station.

Finally, if you're staying in Stockholm for a week or more it's worth considering a **monthly card** (Månadskort), which allows unlimited travel on virtually everything that moves throughout the whole of Greater Stockholm for a mere 400kr. If you're spending several months in the city at a time it's probably worth buying a **season card** (Säsongskort) – prices vary depending on the time of year. Both these cards need a photograph and can be bought from any SL-Center.

One-way tickets for the **ferries** linking the central islands cost a basic 20kr, rising to 85kr for the longer trips into the archipelago. Tickets can be bought on board or in advance from the offices of the main ferry company, Waxholms Ångfartygs AB (known as Waxholmsbolaget), on Strömkajen outside the *Grand Hotel*. If you intend to spend a week or so exploring the islands of the archipelago, it may be worth buying a special pass – see p.418 for details.

Bikes, taxis and parking

Bike rental is centrally available from Skepp O'Hoj at Galärvarvsvägen 10 (☎08/660 57 57), just over the bridge to Djurgården, or from the nearby Cykel-och Mopeduthyrningen at Kajplats 24 along Strandvägen (☎08/660 79 59); reckon on paying 180kr per day or 800kr per week for the latest mountain bike, less for a bone shaker.

There are other less central places, too, among them Servicedepån at Kungsholmsgatan 34 on Kungsholmen (☎08/651 00 66), which also rents out tandems.

To get a **taxi**, either try to hail one in the street or more reliably, call one of the three main operators: Taxi Stockholm (☎08/15 00 00), Taxi Kurir (☎08/30 00 00) or Top Cab (☎08/33 33 33). If you do phone for a cab, the meter will show around 28kr before you even get in and will continue to race upwards at an alarming speed – every 10km costs 93kr or thereabouts during the day, 103kr between 7pm and 6am, and 110kr at weekends. A trip across the city centre should add up to around 100–150kr.

If you're driving, be warned that **parking** in Stockholm is a hazardous business. First, it's forbidden to park within ten metres of a road junction, however small; nor can you park within the same distance of a pedestrian crossing; and on one particular night of the week (as specified on the rectangular yellow street signs) no parking is allowed, to permit street cleaning and, in winter, snow clearance. You should never stop in a bus lane or in a loading zone. If your car is towed away (as they are with frightening regularity), go to the compound at Gasverksvägen in Ropsten (Mon–Fri 8am–7pm, Sat 11am–2.30pm; ☎08/651 00 00) – a short walk from the T-bana – where surly staff will demand at least 1500kr for its return, an amount that increases on a daily basis. In short, if in doubt, don't park there: look for the words *Gatukontoret* or *Parkeringsbolaget* to indicate valid spaces. For details on **car rental**, see p.415.

Accommodation

Stockholm has plenty of **accommodation** to suit all tastes and budgets, from elegant hotels with waterfront views to some unusual youth hostels. Demand is high, however, particularly late in the summer, and it's always advisable to book at least your first night's accommodation in advance – this can be done either through the **Sverigehuset tourist office** (see p.388) or by calling the hotel or hostel direct. Alternatively, the excellent **Hotellcentralen**, the room-booking service in the main hall of Central Station (daily: May–Sept 7am–9pm; Oct–April 9am–6pm; ☎08/789 24 25, *hotels@stoinfo. se*), has comprehensive hotel and hostel listings, plus information on the latest special offers; they charge a booking fee of 50kr per hotel room (20kr for a hostel room). Also available here between mid-June and mid-August (and at weekends year round) is the **Stockholm Package**, which gives reduced rates on accommodation plus a free Stockholm Card (normally costing 199kr) for each night's stay: these start at a very economical 485kr per person in a twin room with breakfast, rising to around 700kr in more upmarket hotels; you'll also be charged Hotellcentralen's regular 50kr booking fee. By calling in advance you can choose a particular hotel – on the day, you get whatever's available. For hotels in **Södermalm**, see the map on p.405; for hotels in **Gamla Stan** and **Norrmalm**, see the map on p.395.

Hotels and pensions

In summer, when business trade dwindles, it's a buyer's market in Stockholm, with double rooms going for as little as 500kr. The cheapest choices are generally found to the north of Cityterminalen in the streets to the west of Adolf Fredriks kyrka, but don't rule out the more expensive places either – there are some attractive weekend and summer prices that can make a spot of luxury a little more affordable. All the following hotels and pensions include breakfast in the price unless otherwise stated.

Anno 1647, Mariagränd 3 (☎08/442 16 80, fax 442 16 47), near Slussen. Södermalm; T-bana Slussen. A seventeenth-century building handy for the Old Town, with pine floors and period furniture; not recommended for people with disabilities. ③/②.

Bema, Upplandsgatan 13 (☎08/23 26 75, fax 20 53 58); bus #47 or #69 from Central Station. Small pension-style hotel with 12 en-suite rooms, 10min walk north from the station. Modern Swedish decor, with beechwood furniture. Summer and weekend deals bring the cost down to the bottom of the ② price-code range. ③/②.

Castle, Riddargatan 14 (☎08/679 57 00, fax 611 20 22); T-bana Östermalmstorg. Fine central hotel popular with jazz and blues musicians (there's live jazz on summer evenings). All rooms have baths; good breakfast buffet. ⑤/③.

Central, Vasagatan 38 (☎08/566 208 00, fax 24 75 73); T-bana T-Centralen. Modern hotel, and one of the cheapest of those around the station. ⑤/③.

Columbus Hotell & Vandrarhem, Tjärhovsgatan 11, Södermalm (☎08/644 17 17, fax 702 07 64); T-bana Medborgarplatsen. Simple rooms (not en suite) in a building that looks like a school. ③.

Diplomat, Strandvägen 7C (☎08/459 68 00, fax 459 68 20); T-bana Östermalmstorg or bus #47 or #69. Early twentieth-century town house with top-of-the-range suites and views out over Stockholm's grandest boulevard and inner harbour. It's not cheap, though much better value even so than the cheaper rooms at the *Grand*. Out of season, rooms start at 2095kr, and there are summer and weekend deals too. ⑥.

First Hotel Reisen, Skeppsbron 12 (☎08/22 32 60, fax 20 15 59); T-bana Gamla Stan or Slussen. Traditional hotel with heavy wood-panelled interior. All rooms have baths; some also have excellent views over the Stockholm waterfront. ⑤.

Grand, Södra Blasieholmshamn 8, Norrmalm (☎08/679 35 00, fax 611 86 86); T-bana Kungsträdgården. A late nineteenth-century harbourside building overlooking Gamla Stan, Stockholm's most refined hotel provides the last word in luxury at world-class prices (even with reductions). Only worth it if you're staying in the best rooms – otherwise, the *Diplomat* has suites with a view for the same price. Out-of-season double rooms start at 2700kr, and there are summer and weekend reductions. ⑤.

Haga, Hagagatan 29, Norrmalm (☎08/736 02 00, fax 32 70 75); T-bana Odenplan. Thirty-eight modern and good-value rooms a little out of the centre but in a quiet road within striking distance of the top of Sveavägen. ④/②.

Mälardrottningen, Riddarholmen (☎08/24 36 00, fax 24 36 76); T-bana Gamla Stan. This elegant white ship moored by the side of the island of Riddarholmen was formerly American millionairess Barbara Hutton's gin palace. Its cabin-style rooms are in need of a lick of paint and a bit of a polish, but still represent good value for such a central location. ④/③.

Pensionat Oden, Odengatan 38, Norrmalm (☎08/612 43 49, fax 612 45 01); T-bana Rådmansgatan. Second-floor hotel in a good central location with elegant, excellent-value modern rooms. Recommended. ②.

Pensionat Oden Söder, Hornsgatan 66B, Södermalm (☎08/612 43 49, fax 612 45 01); T-bana Mariatorget. A good-value choice in the heart of Söder, with tastefully decorated rooms at excellent prices. Recommended. ②.

Queen's, Drottninggatan 71A, Norrmalm (☎08/24 94 60, fax 21 76 20); T-bana Hötorget. Good mid-range pension-style hotel, with en-suite rooms and breakfast buffet. Summer and weekend deals. ②.

Rica City Gamla Stan, Lilla Nygatan 25 (☎08/723 72 50, fax 723 72 59); T-bana Gamla Stan. Wonderfully situated, elegant building with rooms to match; all 51 are individually decorated. Really the only halfway affordable Gamla Stan option. ⑤/④.

Scandic Hotel Slussen, Guldgränd 8, Södermalm (☎08/517 353 00; fax 517 353 11); T-bana Slussen. Lots of wooden floors throughout this expensive chain hotel, but worth it if you can get one of the rooms at the front with fantastic views out over Gamla Stan. ⑤/④.

Stockholm, Norrmalmstorg 1 (☎08/440 57 60, fax 611 21 03); T-bana Östermalmstorg or Kungsträdgården. Penthouse hotel on the top floor of a central office building, with good views out over Strandvägen and the harbour. Squeaky wooden floors and faded bathrooms – recommended. ⑤/④.

Tre Små Rum, Högbergsgatan 81, Södermalm (☎08/641 23 71, fax 642 88 08); T-bana Mariatorget. Despite the name, actually seven small rooms (not three). Clean, modern and with a Japanese flavour in the heart of Södermalm. Very popular and often full. Summer and weekend deals. ②.

Wallin, Wallingatan 15, Norrmalm (☎08/506 161 00, fax 791 50 50); bus #47 or #69 from Central Station. Decent central hotel with en-suite rooms; 10min walk from the station. ⑤/③.

Wasa Park, Skt Eriksplan 1, Norrmalm (☎08/34 02 85, fax 30 94 22); T-bana Skt Eriksplan. A clean, simple hotel; a bit out of the centre but cheap. No en-suite rooms. Summer and weekend deals. ②/③.

Zinkensdamm, Zinkens Väg 20, Södermalm (☎08/616 81 10, fax 616 81 20); T-bana Hornstull or Zinkensdamm. Hotel rooms in a separate wing of the youth hostel (see below). ④/③.

Hostels and private rooms

Stockholm has wide range of good, well-run **hostel** accommodation, costing from 70kr to 150kr a night per person. There are several official STF youth hostels in the city, two of which – *Af Chapman* and *Långholmen* – are among the best in Sweden. You'll have to plan ahead if you want to stay at most of the places listed below particularly in summer. For a **private room**, contact Hotelltjänst, Vasagatan 15–17 (☎08/10 44 67), just a few minutes' walk from Central Station. Tell them how much you want to pay, and where you want to stay, and you should land somewhere with a fridge and cooking facilities for around 250kr per person per night.

STF hostels

Af Chapman, Västra Brobänken, Skeppsholmen (☎08/679 50 15, fax 611 98 75, *info@chapman.stf-turist.se*); T-bana Kungsträdgården or bus #65 from Central Station. This square-rigged 1888 ship – a landmark in its own right – has unsurpassed views over Gamla Stan, at least for the price. Without an advance reservation (try a fortnight before you arrive), the chances of a space in summer are slim: the drawbacks to nautical accommodation are no kitchen and a lockout (11am–3pm). Reception 7am–noon & 3–10pm; 2am curfew. Open all year, though restricted Dec–March.

Backpackers Inn, Banérgatan 56, Östermalm (☎08/660 75 15, fax 665 40 39); T-bana Karlaplan (Valhallavägen exit) or bus #41. Reasonably central old school residence with 300 beds in large dorms, plus washing facilities. Open late June to mid-Aug.

Långholmen, Kronohäktet, Långholmen (☎08/668 05 10, fax 720 85 75); T-bana Hornstull and follow the signs. Stockholm's grandest STF hostel is set on the island of Långholmen inside an old prison building (1724), the cells converted into smart hostel rooms with their original (extremely small) windows. It's in a great location too, with fantastic views of Stockholm and Lake Mälaren, beaches nearby, the whole of Södermalm on the doorstep. No lockout.

Skeppsholmen, Västra Brobänken, Skeppsholmen (☎08/463 22 66, fax 611 71 55); T-bana Kungsträdgården or bus #65. Located at the foot of the gangplank to *Af Chapman*, this immensely popular hostel is housed in a former craftsman's workshop, though you're unlikely to get in without a reservation. Again there are no kitchen or washing facilities; though there's no lockout either.

Zinkensdamm, Zinkens Väg 20, Södermalm (☎08/616 81 00, fax 616 81 20); T-bana Hornstull or Zinkensdamm. Huge hostel with 466 beds, kitchen and washing facilities. No lockout.

Independent hostels

Brygghusets Vandrarhem, Norrtullsgatan 12N, Norrmalm (☎08/31 24 24, fax 31 02 06); T-bana Odenplan. Close to the top end of Sveavägen around the lively Odenplan area. Open June to early Sept.

City BackPackers Vandrarhem, Upplandsgatan 2A (☎08/20 69 20, fax 10 04 64); T-bana T-Centralen. Very central all-year hostel with 40 beds.

Columbus Hotell & Vandrarhem, Tjärhovsgatan 11, Södermalm (☎08/644 17 17, fax 702 07 64); T-bana Medborgarplatsen. Friendly hostel-hotel open all year.

Gustav af Klimt, Stadsgårdskajen 153, Södermalm (☎08/640 40 77, fax 640 64 16); T-bana Slussen. This hostel on a boat has rather cramped rooms; if they're full don't be tempted to take one of the more expensive hotel rooms on board instead – they're not worth it. Good central location, just a few minutes' walk from the Old Town.

Camping

With the nearest year-round campsites well out of the city centre, **camping** in Stockholm can prove a bit of a drag. The tourist offices provide free booklets detailing facilities at all Stockholm's campsites. In July and August it costs around 100kr for two people to pitch a tent; half that the rest of the year.

Ängby (☎08/37 04 20, fax 37 82 26); T-bana Ängbyplan on the green line towards Vällingby. West of the city on the lakeshore. Open all year, but phone ahead to book Sept–April.

Bredäng (☎08/97 70 71, fax 708 72 62); T-bana Bredäng on the red line towards Norsborg. Southwest of the city with views over Lake Mälaren. Open all year, but phone ahead to book Nov–April.

Solna Vandrahems Camping, Enköpsvägen 16, Solna, (☎08/655 00 55, fax 655 00 50); T-bana Solna Centrum on the blue line towards Akalla then bus #505 to Råstahem. All-year site set amid the trees 8km from Stockholm.

The City

Visitors have been responding to Stockholm's charms for 150 years, and today the combination of elegant Old Town architecture, wide tree-lined boulevards and great expanses of open water right in the centre all conspire to offer a city panorama unparalleled anywhere in Europe. Seeing the sights is straightforward: everything is easy to get to, opening hours are long, and the city is a relaxed and spacious place to wander. There's also a bewildering range of museums and galleries, the best of which are described in the account below.

Old Stockholm: Gamla Stan and Riddarholmen

Three islands make up the **oldest part of Stockholm** – Riddarholmen, Staden and Helgeandsholmen – a historic cluster of seventeenth- and eighteenth-century Renaissance buildings backed by narrow medieval alleys. Here, on these three adjoining polyps of land, Birger Jarl erected the first fortification in 1255, and for centuries this was the nucleus of the first city of Stockholm. Rumours abound about the derivation of the name Stockholm, but it's generally thought that some sort of wooden drying frames, known as "stocks", were erected on the island that is now home to Gamla Stan thus making it the island, *holm*, of *stock*s. Incidentally, today the word *stock* means log.

Strictly speaking, the **Gamla Stan** (Old Town) area refers only to the streets of the largest island, **Staden**, although in practice the name is usually applied to all three islands. Nowadays Gamla Stan is primarily a tourist city, a rich tableau of cultural history embodied by the royal palace, parliament and cathedral. The central spider's web, especially if you approach it over the bridges of Norrbron or Riksbron, invokes potent images of the past, with sprawling, monumental buildings and airy churches forming a protective girdle around the narrow streets. The tall dark houses in the centre were mostly those of wealthy merchants, still picked out today by intricate doorways and portals bearing coats of arms. Some of the alleys in between are the skinniest thoroughfares imaginable, steeply stepped between battered walls; others are covered passageways linking leaning buildings. It's easy to spend hours wandering around here, although the atmosphere these days is not so much medieval as mercenary: there's a dense concentration of antique shops, art showrooms and chichi cellar restaurants, though the frontages don't really intrude upon the otherwise light-starved streets. Not surprisingly, this is the most exclusive part of Stockholm in which to live.

The Riksdagshuset and the Museum of Medieval Stockholm

Entering or leaving the Old Town, you're bound to pass the Swedish parliament building, the **Riksdagshuset** (June–Aug Mon–Fri guided tours in English at 12.30pm & 2pm; free). Despite the assassination of the former Swedish Prime Minister, Olof Palme, in 1986 (see p.401), Swedish politicians still go freely about their business and you'll often see them nipping in and out of the building or lunching in one of the near-

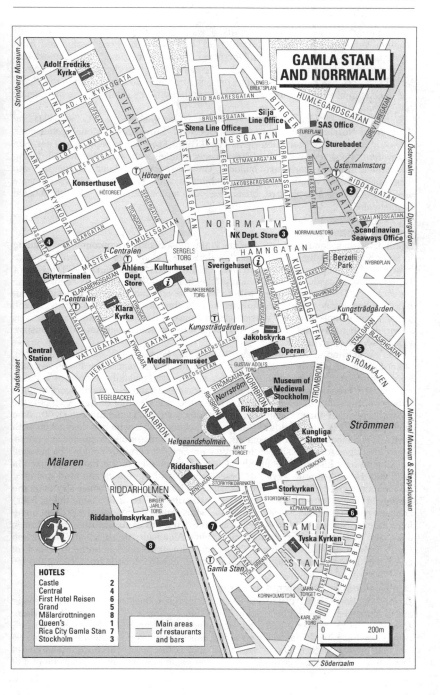

GAMLA STAN
AND NORRMALM

Strindberg Museum

Adolf Fredriks Kyrka

ENGEL-BREKTSPLAN

DAVID BAGARESGATAN

BRUNNSGATAN
Silja Line Office
Stena Line Office
SAS Office
STUREPLAN

Sturebadet

KUNGSGATAN

Konserthuset

Hötorget
HÖTORGET

Östermalmstorg

RIDDARGATAN

JAKOBSBERGSGATAN

SMÅLANDSGATAN

NORRMALM

Cityterminalen

T-Centralen

Åhléns Dept. Store

Kulturhuset

NK Dept. Store

NORRMALMSTORG

Scandinavian Seaways Office

HAMNGATAN

Sverigehuset

Berzelii Park

NYBROPLAN

BRUNKEBERGS TORG

T-Centralen

Klara Kyrka

Kungsträdgården

Kungsträdgården

Central Station

Medelhavsmuseet

Jakobskyrka

Operan

GUSTAV ADOLFS TORG

STRÖMKAJEN

Norrström

Museum of Medieval Stockholm

TEGELBACKEN

Riksdagshuset

Strömmen

Helgeandsholmen

MYNT TORGET

Kungliga Slottet

Mälaren

Riddarshuset

RIDDARHOLMEN

BIRGER JARLS TORG

STORKYRKOBRINKEN

SLOTTSBACKEN

Storkyrkan

STORTORGET

N

Riddarholmskyrkan

KÖPMANGATAN

GAMLA

Tyska Kyrkan

STAN

Gamla Stan

JÄRNTORGET

HOTELS
Castle   2
Central   4
First Hotel Reisen   6
Grand   5
Mälardrottningen   8
Queen's   1
Rica City Gamla Stan 7
Stockholm   3

KORNHOLMSTORG

KARL JOH TORG

0   200m

Main areas of restaurants and bars

Södermalm

by restaurants. The Riksdagshuset itself was completely restored in the 1970s (though only seventy years old even then), and today the grand columned front entrance (seen to best effect from Norrbron) is hardly ever used, the business end being the new glassy bulge at the back – it's round here that the guided tours circulate. This being Sweden, the building contains a crèche, and the seating in the chamber itself is in healthy, non-adversarial rows, with members grouped by constituency rather than party.

In front of the Riksdag (pronounced "Reeks-da"), accessible by a set of steps leading down from Norrbron, the **Museum of Medieval Stockholm** (Medeltidsmuseum; July–Aug Mon, Fri & Sun 11am–4pm, Tues–Thurs 11am–6pm; Sept–June Tues–Sun 11am–4pm; 40kr) features the medieval ruins, tunnels and walls discovered during excavations under the parliament building. These remains have been incorporated into a fascinating walk-through underground exhibition, with reconstructed houses to poke around in, models and pictures, boats, skeletons and street scenes, all with detailed English labels.

Kungliga Slottet

South across a second section of bridges is the most distinctive monumental building in Stockholm, **Kungliga Slottet**, the Royal Palace – a low, yellowy-brown structure whose two front arms stretch down towards the water. Stockholm's old Tre Kronor (Three Crowns) castle burned down at the beginning of King Karl XII's reign, leaving his architect, Tessin the Younger, with a clean slate on which to design his simple but beautiful Renaissance structure. Finished in 1754, the palace is a striking achievement: uniform and sombre from the outside, its magnificent Baroque and Rococo interior is a swirl of state rooms and museums. The sheer size and limited opening hours conspire against seeing everything at once.

The **Apartments** (May–Aug daily 10am–4pm; Sept–April Tues–Sun noon–3pm; 50kr) form a relentlessly linear collection of furniture and tapestries. It's all basically Rent-a-Palace stuff, too sumptuous to take in and inspirational only in terms of its colossal size. The **Treasury** (same times; 50kr), on the other hand, is certainly worthy of the name, with its ranks of jewel-studded crowns: the oldest is that of Karl X (1650); the most charming are those belonging to princesses Sofia (1771) and Eugëne (1860). Also worth catching is the **Armoury** (daily 11am–4pm; 60kr), which is less to do with weapons and more to do with ceremony, featuring suits of armour, costumes and horse-drawn carriages from the sixteenth century onwards. It certainly couldn't be accused of skipping over historical detail. King Gustav II Adolf died in the Battle of Lützen in 1632 and the museum displays his horse (stuffed) and the blood- and mud-spattered garments retrieved after the enemy had stripped him down to his boxer shorts on the battlefield. For those with the energy, the **Museum Tre Kronor** (same times; 50kr) contains part of the older Tre Kronor castle, whose ruins lie beneath the present building, while for real palace junkies there's also the **Museum of Antiquities** (same times; 50kr) and the **Hall of State** (same times; 20kr). Alongside the palace at Slottsbacken 6, the **Royal Coin Cabinet** (daily Tues–Sun 10am–4pm; 45kr) is home to a stash of coins, banknotes and medals, as well as a number of silver hoards from Viking days.

Into Gamla Stan: Storatorget and around

Beyond the Royal Palace you're into Gamla Stan proper, the streets suddenly narrower and darker. Here, the highest point of old Stockholm is crowned by **Storkyrkan**, (May–Aug daily 9am–6pm; 10kr; Sept–April daily 9am–4pm; free), the "Great Church", consecrated in 1306. Pedantically speaking, Stockholm has no cathedral, but this rectangular brick church fulfils the same role and is the place where the monarchs of Sweden are married and crowned. Storkyrkan gained its present shape at the end of the fifteenth century, with a Baroque remodelling in the 1730s. Inside, twentieth-century restoration has removed the white plaster from the red-brick columns and although there's no evidence that this was intended in the original, it gives a warm colouring to the rest of the building. Much is made of the fifteenth-century sculpture of St George and the Dragon, though this is easily overshadowed by the golden, throne-like royal pews and the monumental black-and-silver altarpiece. Organ recitals take place here every Saturday at 1pm.

Stretching south from the church is **Storatorget**, Gamla Stan's handsome and elegantly proportioned main square, fringed by eighteenth-century buildings and surrounded by narrow shopping streets. In 1520 Christian II used the square as an execution site during the "Stockholm Blood Bath", dispatching his opposition en masse with bloody finality. Now, as then, the streets **Västerlånggatan** and **Österlånggatan**, **Stora Nygatan** and **Lilla Nygatan** run the length of the Old Town on either side of the square, although today their time-worn buildings harbour a succession of art and craft shops and restaurants. Happily, though, the consumerism is largely unobtrusive and in summer buskers and evening strollers clog the narrow alleyways, making it an entertaining area to wander – and to eat and drink in. There are few real targets, though at some stage you'll probably pass the copy of the George and Dragon statue in **Köpmantorget** (off Österlånggatan). Take every opportunity too to scuttle up side streets, where you'll find fading coats of arms, covered alleyways and worn cobbles at every turn.

Just of Västerlånggatan, on Tyska Brinken, is the **Tyska kyrkan** (German Church), originally owned by Stockholm's medieval German merchants, when it served as the meeting place of the Guild of St Gertrude. A copper-topped red-brick church atop a rise, it abandoned its secular role in the seventeenth century when Baroque decorators got hold of it: the result, a richly fashioned interior with the pulpit dominating the nave, is outstanding. Sporting a curious royal gallery in one corner, designed by Tessin the Elder, it comes complete with mini palace roof, angels and the three crowns of Swedish kingship.

The Riddarhuset and Riddarholmen

If Stockholm's history has gripped you, it's better to head west from Storatorget towards the handsome Baroque **Riddarhuset** (daily Mon–Fri 11.30am–12.30pm; 40kr), the seventeenth-century "House of Nobles". It was in the Great Hall here that the Swedish aristocracy met during the Parliament of the Four Estates (1668–1865) and their coats of arms – around 2500 of them – are splattered across the walls. Some six hundred of the noble families survive; the last ennoblement was in 1974. Take a look downstairs, too, at the Chancery, which stores heraldic bone china by the shelfload and racks full of fancy signet rings – essential accessories for the eighteenth-century noble-about-town.

From Riddarhuset it takes only a matter of seconds to cross the bridge onto **Riddarholmen** (Island of the Knights), to visit the **Riddarholmskyrkan** (May–Aug daily 10am–4pm; Sept Sat & Sun noon–3pm; 20kr), the burial place for Swedish royalty ever since Magnus Ladulås was sealed up here in 1290. Amongst others, you'll find the tombs of Gustav II Adolf (in the green marble sarcophagus), Karl XII, Gustav III and Karl Johan XIV, plus other innumerable and unmemorable descendants. Walk around the back of the church for stunning views of Stadshuset, the City Hall and Lake Mälaren. Incidentally, the island to the left of Västerbron (the bridge in the distance) is Långholmen; in winter people skate and even take their dogs for walks on the ice along here, as the water freezes solid right up to the bridge and beyond.

Skeppsholmen

A ten-minute walk east from Storatorget lie the islands of **Skeppsholmen** and the microscopic **Kastellholmen**, to which it's connected by a bridge to the south.

Originally settled by the Swedish Navy – some of whose old barracks are still visible – in the nineteenth century, Skeppsholmen is now home to two of the city's youth hostels and an eclectic clutch of museums, the most impressive of them just by the Skeppsholmsbron, the bridge onto the island.

The National Art Museum

As you approach the bridge it's impossible to miss the striking waterfront **National Art Museum** (Nationalmuseum; Tues 11am–8pm, Wed–Sun 11am–5pm; 60kr), looking right out over the Royal Palace. The impressive collection is contained on three floors: the **ground floor** is taken up by changing exhibitions of prints and drawings, and there's a shop and café here too, as well as luggage lockers. So much is packed into the museum that it can quickly become confusing and overwhelming – it's worth splashing out on the guidebook.

The **first floor** is devoted to applied art and if it's curios you're after, this museum has the lot – beds slept in by kings, cabinets leaned on by queens, plates eaten off by nobles – mainly from the centuries when Sweden was a great power. There's modern work alongside the ageing tapestries and furniture, including Art Nouveau coffee pots and vases, and examples demonstrating the intelligent simplicity of Swedish chair design.

It's the **second floor**, however, that's most engaging, featuring a plethora of European and Mediterranean sculpture and some mesmerizing sixteenth- and seventeenth-century Russian icons. The paintings are equally wide ranging and of a similarly high quality, including works by El Greco, Canaletto, Gainsborough and, most notably, Rembrandt's *Conspiracy of Claudius Civilis*, one of his largest monumental paintings, a bold depiction of well-armed Roman chieftains displayed in room 33. There are minor works by other later masters (most notably Renoir and Gauguin) and some fine sixteenth- to eighteenth-century works by **Swedish artists**.

Skeppsholmen's museums

Stockholm's **Museum of Modern Art** (Moderna Muséet; Tues–Thurs 11am–10pm, Fri–Sun 11am–6pm; 60kr), is one of the better modern art collections in Europe, with a comprehensive selection of works by some of the leading artists of the twentieth century. View Dali's monumental *Enigma of William Tell*, showing the artist at his most conventionally unconventional, and Matisse's striking *Apollo*. Look out for Picasso's *Guitar Player* and a whole host of Warhol, Lichtenstein, Kandinsky, Miró and Magritte. Next door, the **Architecture Museum** (Arkitekturmuseet; same times; 45kr) serves up a taste of Swedish architecture in one of the most inspired buildings in the city – all glass and air. Bus #65 here runs from Central Station.

A steep climb up the northern tip of the island brings you to the **Museum of Far Eastern Antiquities** (Östasiatiska Muséet; Tues noon–8pm, Wed–Sun noon–5pm; 40kr), with an array of objects displaying incredible craftsmanship – fifth-century Chinese tomb figures, delicate jade amulets, an astounding assembly of sixth-century Buddhas, Indian watercolours and gleaming bronze Krishna figures – and that's just one room.

Norrmalm and Kungsholmen

Modern Stockholm lies immediately to the north and east of Gamla Stan, and is split into two distinct sections. **Norrmalm**, to the north, is the buzzing commercial heart of the city, packed with restaurants, bars, cinemas and shops, while to the east is the more sedate Östermalm, a well-to-do area of classy boulevards. The island of **Kungsholmen**, linked by bridge to the west of Norrmalm, is a mostly residential and administrative district, though with one positive draw in Stockholm's landmark City Hall.

Around Gustav Adolfs Torg

Down on the waterfront, at the foot of Norrbron, is **Gustav Adolfs Torg**, more a traffic island than a square these days, with the nineteenth-century **Operan** (Opera House) its proudest, most notable – and ugliest – building. It was here in an earlier opera house on the same site, at a masked ball in 1792, that King Gustav III was shot by one Captain Ankarström, an admirer of Rousseau and member of the aristocratic opposition. The story is recorded in Verdi's opera *Un ballo in maschera* and you can see Gustav's ball costume, as well as the assassin's pistols and mask, on display in the Palace Armoury in Gamla Stan. The opera's famous restaurant, *Operakällaren*, is hellishly expensive, the trendy café less so.

A statue of King Gustav II Adolf marks the centre of the square, between Operan and the Foreign Office opposite. Look out hereabouts for fishermen pulling salmon out of **Strömmen**, the fast-flowing tributary that winds its way through the centre of the city. Stockholmers have had the right to fish this outlet from Lake Mälaren to the Baltic since the seventeenth century; it's not as difficult as it sounds and there's usually a group of hopefuls on one of the bridges around the square trying their luck.

Just off the square, at Fredsgatan 2 in the heart of Swedish government land is the **Museum of Mediterranean and Near Eastern Antiquities** (Medelhavsmuséet; Tues 11am–8pm, Wed–Fri 11am–4pm, Sat & Sun noon–5pm; 50kr), a sparkling museum devoted to Mediterranean and Near Eastern antiquities. Its enormous Egyptian section covers just about every aspect of Egyptian life up to the Christian era, with several whopping great mummies and some attractive bronze weapons, tools and domestic objects from the time before the pharaohs. The Cyprus collections are also huge, the largest outside Cyprus itself, spanning a period of over six thousand years, and there are also strong displays of Greek, Etruscan and Roman art. A couple of rooms examine Islamic culture through pottery, glass and metalwork, as well as decorative elements of architecture, Arabic calligraphy and Persian miniature painting.

Walk back towards Operan and continue across the main junction onto Arsenalsgatan to reach **Jakobs kyrka** (daily 11am–5pm), one of the city's many easily overlooked churches. It's the pulpit that draws the eye, a great, golden affair, while the date of the church's consecration – 1642 – is stamped high up on the ceiling in gold figures. There are weekly classical music recitals here, with organ and choir recitals on Saturday at 3pm.

Kungsträdgården

Just beyond the Jacobs kyrka and Operan, Norrmalm's eastern boundary is marked by **Kungsträdgården**, most fashionable and central of the city's numerous squares, reaching from the water northwards as far as **Hamngatan**. The mouthful of a name literally means "the king's gardens", though if you're expecting neatly trimmed flower beds and rose gardens you'll be sadly disappointed – it's actually a great expanse of concrete with a couple of lines of trees. The area may once have been a royal kitchen garden, but nowadays it serves as Stockholm's main meeting place, especially in summer when there's almost always something happening: free evening gigs, theatre and other performances take place on the central open-air stage. Look out too for the park's cafés, packed out in spring with winter-weary Stockholmers soaking up the sun. In winter the park is equally busy, particularly at the Hamngatan end where there's an open-air ice rink, the **Isbanan** (Oct–April daily 9am–6pm; skate rental 35kr). The main tourist office is close by here, in the Sverigehuset, at the corner of Hamngatan (see p.388).

Hamngatan runs east to **Birger Jarlsgatan**, the main thoroughfare that divides Norrmalm from Östermalm, and now a mecca for eating and drinking.

Segels Torg to Hötorget

At the western end of Hamngatan, beyond the enormous NK department store, lies **Segels Torg**, the ugliest part of modern Stockholm. It's an unending free show centred on the five seething floors of **Kulturhuset** (Tues–Thurs 11am–7pm, Fri 11am–6pm, Sat 11am–5pm, Sun noon–5pm; 30kr), whose windows look down upon the milling concrete square. Inside this building devoted to contemporary Swedish culture are temporary art and craft exhibitions together with workshops open to anyone willing to get their hands dirty. The reading room (*Läsesalongen*) on the ground level is stuffed with foreign newspapers, books, records and magazines – a good refuge if it's wet and windy outside. Check the information desk as you come in for details of poetry readings, concerts and theatre performances – admission to Kulturhuset is free, but you have to pay to get into specific exhibitions or performances. Check out the café on the top floor for delicious apple pie and custard and some of the best views of central Stockholm, even if the service often leaves something to be desired. From the café you'll get a bird's-eye view of the tall and singularly ugly wire-like column that dominates the massive open space outside and the surrounding spewing fountain (often obscured by soap suds – the local youth think it's a real wheeze to pour packets of washing powder into the fountain). Down the steps, below Sergels Torg, is **Sergels Arkaden**, a set of grotty underground walkways home to buskers, brass bands and demented lottery ticket vendors; look out for the odd demonstration or ball game too – you may also spot young Stockholmers running around shivering in their skimpy underwear, having tied the rest of their clothes together in a line to see whose is longest, a singularly Swedish pastime. There are also entrances down here into **T-Centralen**, the central T-bana station, and Stockholm's other main department store, Åhléns, not quite as posh as NK and easier to find your way around.

A short walk west from Kulturhuset along Klarabergsgatan will bring you to **Central Station** and **Cityterminalen**, hub of virtually all Stockholm's transport. The area around here is given over to unabashed consumerism, but as you explore the streets around the main drag, **Drottinggatan**, you'll find little to get excited about – run-of-the-mill clothing shops, twee gift shops punctuated by *McDonalds* and the odd sausage stand. In summer the occasional busker or jewellery stall livens up what is essentially a soulless grid of pedestrianized shopping streets. The only point of culture is the **Klara kyrka** (Mon–Fri 10am–6pm, Sat 10am–7pm, Sun 8.30am–6pm), just to the right off Klarabergsgatan, opposite the station. Another of Stockholm's easily missed churches, hemmed in on all sides with only the spires visible from the surrounding streets, it's a particularly delicate example, with a light and flowery eighteenth-century painted interior and an impressive golden pulpit. Out in the churchyard, a memorial stone commemorates eighteenth-century Swedish poet Carl Michael Bellman, whose popular, lengthy ballads are said to have been composed extempore; his unmarked grave is somewhere in the churchyard.

Three blocks further up Drottinggatan, the cobbled square of **Hötorget** hosts an open-air fruit and veg market on weekdays, as well as the wonderful indoor **Hötorgshallen**, an orgy of Middle Eastern smells and sights and a good place to pick up ethnic snacks. Grab something to eat and plonk yourself on the steps of the **Konserthuset** (Concert House), one of the venues for the presentation of the Nobel Prizes, and a good place to hear classical music recitals (often free on Sunday afternoons). The tall building opposite is a former department store where Greta Garbo once worked as a sales assistant in the hat department. If this inspires you to go to the movies, you only have to walk across the square to Filmstaden Sergel, Stockholm's biggest cinema complex; to the east, **Kungsgatan**, which runs down to Stureplan and Birger Jarlsgatan, holds most of the city's other cinemas, interpersed with agreeable little cafés (see p.407).

North to the Strindberg Museum

From Hötorget the two main streets of Drottinggatan and Sveavägen run parallel uphill and north as far as Odengatan and the **Stadsbiblioteket** (City Library), in its own little park. Close by, set in secluded gardens between the two roads, sits the

THE ASSASSINATION OF OLOF PALME

The shooting of Prime Minister Olof Palme in February 1986 sent shockwaves through a society unused to political extremism of any kind. Like most Nordic leaders his fame was his security, and he died unprotected, gunned down in front of his wife on their way home from the cinema on Sveavägen. Sadly, the murder led to a radical rethink of Sweden's long-established policy of open government: ministers no longer walk the streets without bodyguards and security checks now operate in all public buildings. Sweden's biggest ever murder inquiry was launched and as the years went by so the allegations of police cover-ups and bungling grew. When Christer Pettersson was jailed for the murder (see "History", p.381), most Swedes believed that to be the end of the story, but his eventual release only served to reopen the bitter debate. There have been recriminations and resignations within a derided police force, and although in the past the most popular suspects were immigrant Kurdish extremists, right-wing terror groups or even a hitman from within the police itself, more recent theories have suggested that the corrupt regime in South Africa was behind the killing. Palme was an outspoken critic of apartheid, leading calls for an economic blockade against Pretoria, and these recent claims are being treated very seriously in Sweden.

eighteenth-century **Adolf Fredriks kyrka**. Although it has a noteworthy past – the French philosopher Descartes was buried here in 1650 before his body was moved to France – the church would be insignificant today were it not the final resting place for the assassinated Swedish Prime Minister, **Olof Palme**: a simple headstone and flowers mark his grave. A plaque now marks the spot on Sveavägen, near the junction with Olof Palmes Gata, where the prime minister was gunned down; the assassin escaped up the nearby flight of steps (see box above).

Continue north along Drottninggatan and you'll come to the "Blue Tower" at no. 85, the last building in which the writer August Strindberg lived, now turned into the **Strindberg Museum** (Strindbergsmuséet; Tues–Sun 11am–4pm; 35kr), Strindberg lived here between 1908 and 1912, and his house has been preserved to the extent that you must put plastic bags on your feet to protect the floors and furnishings. The study remains as he left it on his death, a dark and gloomy place – he would work with both venetian blinds and heavy curtains closed against the sunlight. Upstairs is his library, a musty room with all the books firmly behind glass, which is a shame because Strindberg wasn't a passive reader: he underlined heavily and made notes in the margins as he read, though these are rather less erudite than you'd expect: "Lies!", "Crap!", "Idiot!" and "Bloody hell!" seem to have been his favourite comments. Good explanatory notes in English are supplied free.

Kungsholmen: Stadshuset

Take the T-bana back to T-Centralen and it takes only a matter of minutes to cross Stadshusbron to the island of **Kungsholmen** and Stockholm's **Stadshuset** (City Hall; June–Aug daily guided tours at 10am, 11am, noon & 2pm; Sept at 10am, noon and 2pm, Oct–May 10am & noon; 40kr). Finished in 1923, the Stadhuset is a landmark of the modern city and one of the first buildings you'll see when approaching Stockholm from the south by train. Its simple, if somewhat drab, exterior brickwork is no preparation for the intricate decor within. If you're a visiting Head of State you'll be escorted from your boat up the elegant waterside steps. For lesser mortals, the only way to view the innards is on one of the guided tours, which reveal the kitschy Viking-style legislative chamber and impressively echoing Golden Hall. The Stadshuset is also the departure point for **boats** to Drottningholm, Mariefred and Uppsala. Venture further into Kungsholmen and you'll discover a rash of excellent bars and restaurants that have sprung up here – see p.410 – and an excellent **beach** at Smedsudden (buses #54 and #62 to Västerbroplan, then a 5min walk). Another attraction is the popular **Rålambshovsparken**, where you can take a swim with fantastic views of the City Hall and Old Town.

Östermalm

East of Birger Jarlsgatan the streets become noticeably broader and grander as you enter the district of **Östermalm**, one of the last areas of central Stockholm to be developed. The first place to head for is the water's edge square, **Nybroplan**, just east along Hamngatan from Sergels Torg, and marked with the white-stone relief-studded **Royal Theatre of Drama** (Kungliga Dramatiska Teatern), Stockholm's showpiece theatre. The curved harbour in front is the departure point for all kinds of archipelago **ferries** and tours (see p.418), and for a summer shuttle service via Skeppsholmen to the Nordic and Vasa museums over on Djurgården (July & Aug every 15min; 25kr). Look out too for the stone pillars near the water with their snaking lines of multicoloured lights – they're an indication of how clean the city's air and water are at the moment.

Behind the theatre at Sibyllegatan 2 is the innovative **Music Museum** (Musikmuséet; Tues–Sun 11am–4pm; 30kr), containing a range of instruments that visitors are allowed to experiment with. The museum charts the history of music in Sweden using photographs, instruments and sound recordings. Best are the sections that deal with the late nineteenth century, a time when *folkmusik* was given fresh impetus by the growing labour movement. The concluding parts on "progressive" and "disco" music are brief and uninteresting, with the merest mention of punk and, astonishingly, nothing on ABBA.

Opposite the Music Museum at Riddargatan 13, the **Army Museum** (Armémuséet; check latest opening times with the tourist office), has displays of precision killing machines, uniforms, swords and medals – not many visitors make it here, and you're likely to be outnumbered by the alert and omnipresent attendants.

Just back from the museums, up the hill of Sibyllegatan, **Östermalmstorg** is an absolute find: the square is home to the **Östermalms saluhallen**, an indoor market hall not unlike Norrmalm's Hötorgshallen, but selling more refined delicatessen – reindeer hearts and the like – and attracting a clientele to match. Wander round at lunchtime and you'll spot any number of fur-coated Stockholmers, sipping Chardonnay and munching shrimp sandwiches.

History Museum

As you plod your way around Östermalm's rich streets, you're bound to end up at the circular **Karlaplan** sooner or later: a handy T-bana and bus interchange, full of media types coming off shift from the Swedish Radio and Television buildings at the end of Karlavägen. From here it's a short walk (or #44 bus ride) down Narvavägen to the impressive **History Museum** (Historiska Muséet; Tues–Sun 11am–5pm; 60kr); from Norrmalm, take bus #56 via Stureplan and Linnégatan. The most wide-ranging historical display in Stockholm, it's really two large collections: a museum of National Antiquities and the new underground Gold Room, with its magnificent fifth-century gold collars and other fine jewellery. Ground-floor highlights include a Stone Age ideal home – flaxen-haired youth, stripped pine benches and rows of neatly labelled herbs – and a mass of Viking weapons, coins and boats, much of it labelled in English. Upstairs there's a worthy collection of medieval church art and architecture, with odds and ends turned up from all over the country, evocatively housed in massive vaulted rooms. If you're heading to Gotland, be sure to look out for the reassembled bits of stave churches uncovered on the Baltic island – some of the few examples that survive in Sweden.

Djurgården

When you tire of pounding the streets, there's respite at hand in the form of Stockholm's so-called National City Park, and in particular the section just to the east of the centre, **Djurgården** (pronounced "Yoor-gorn"). Originally royal hunting grounds from the sixteenth to eighteenth centuries, it is actually two distinct park areas separated by the water of **Djurgårdsbrunnsviken** – popular for swimming in summer and skating in winter when the channel freezes over. Also in Djurgården are some of Stockholm's finest **museums**: the massive open-air **Skansen**, an amazing conglomeration of architecture and folk culture from around the country, and the **Vasa Museum**, the home of a marvellously preserved seventeenth-century warship.

You can walk to Djurgården through the centre out along Strandvägen but it's quite a hike; alternatively, take bus #44 from Karlaplan or buses #47 and #69 from Norrmalm to the bridge, Djurgårdsbron, which crosses over onto the island; alternatively, there are ferries from Skeppsbron in Gamla Stan (all year) and Nybroplan (July & Aug only).

The Nordic Museum, Skansen and Gröna Lunds Tivoli

A full day is just about enough to see everything on Djurgården. Starting with the palatial **Nordic Museum** (Nordiska Muséet; Tues–Sun 11am–9pm; 60kr) just over Djurgårdsbron from Strandvägen, is the best idea, if only because the same cultural themes pop up repeatedly throughout the rest of the island's exhibitions. The displays are a recent attempt to represent Swedish cultural history (from the past 500 years) in an accessible fashion, and the Sami section is particularly good. On the ground floor of the cathedral-like interior is Carl Milles's phenomenal statue of Gustav Vasa, the sixteenth-century king who drove out the Danes and whose inspirational qualities summoned the best from the sculptor (for more on Milles, see p.416).

However, it's for **Skansen** (June–Aug 10am–10pm; 60kr; Sept–May 10am–4pm, May until 8pm; 30kr), that most people come here: a great open-air museum with 150 reconstructed buildings, ranging from an entire town to windmills and farms laid out on a region-by-region basis, with each section boasting its own daily activities – traditional handicrafts, games and displays – that anyone can join in. The best of the buildings are the small Sami dwellings, warm and functional, and the craftsmen's workshops in the old town quarter. You can also potter around a small zoo and a bizarre **aquarium**, fish cheek by jowl with crocodiles, monkeys and snakes. Partly because of the attention paid to accuracy, partly due to the admirable lack of commercialization (a rarity in Sweden), Skansen manages to avoid the tackiness associated with similar ventures in other countries. Even the snack bars dole out traditional foods and in winter serve up great bowls of warming soup.

Immediately opposite Skansen's main gates (and at the end of the #44 bus route; bus #47 also goes by), **Gröna Lunds Tivoli** (May–Sept daily noon–midnight; Oct–April shorter hours – check at the tourist office; 45kr) is not a patch on its more famous namesake, Copenhagen's Tivoli Gardens, though it's decidedly cleaner and less seedy. It's definitely more of a place to stroll through rather than indulging in the rides (not included in the entrance fee) which, frankly, are tame. One notable exception is the Fritt Fall – a hair-raising vertical drop of 80m in just six seconds; do lunch later. At night the emphasis shifts as the park becomes the stomping ground for Stockholm's youth, with raucous music, cafés and some enterprising chat-up lines to be heard.

Vasa Museum

In a brand new building close to the Nordiska Muséet, the **Vasa Museum** (Vasamuséet; daily: mid-June to mid-Aug 9.30am–7pm; mid-Aug to mid-June 10am–5pm, Wed until 8pm; 60kr) is without question head and shoulders above anything else that Stockholm has to offer in the way of museums. Built on the orders of

King Gustav II Adolf, the *Vasa* warship sank in Stockholm harbour on her maiden voyage in 1628 – built to a design that was both too tall and too narrow, it promptly keeled over and sank as soon as it was put afloat. Preserved in mud for over 300 years, the ship was raised along with 12,000 objects in 1961, and now forms the centrepiece of a startling, purpose-built hall on the water's edge.

Impressive though the building itself is, however, nothing prepares you for the sheer size of the **ship** itself: 62m long, with a main mast which was originally 50m above the keel, it sits virtually complete in a cradle of supporting mechanical tackle. Surrounding walkways bring you nose to nose with cannon hatches and restored decorative relief, the gilded wooden sculptures on the soaring prow designed to intimidate the enemy and proclaim Swedish might. Faced with its frightening bulk, it's not difficult to understand the terror that such ships must have generated. Adjacent **exhibition halls** and presentations on several levels take care of all the retrieved bits and bobs. There are reconstructions of life on board, detailed models of the *Vasa*, displays relating to contemporary social and political life, films and videos of the rescue operation, excellent English explanations and regular English-language **guided tours**.

Adjacent to the museum, an altogether more frightening reminder of the power of the sea deserves your attention. Located on the Stockholm waterfront, the three-metre-high granite walls of the **Estonia Memorial**, arranged in the form of a triangle – not unlike the Vietnam memorial in Washington DC – bear the engraved names of the 852 people who died when the *Estonia* ferry sank in the Baltic Sea in September 1994 whilst crossing from the Estonian capital, Tallinn, to Stockholm.

Thiel Gallery

At the far eastern end of Djurgården (take bus #69 from Norrmalm) is one of Stockholm's major treasures, the **Thiel Gallery** (Thielska Galleriet; Mon–Sat noon–4pm; Sun 1–4pm; 40kr), a fine example of Swedish architecture and art. The house was built by Fredinand Boberg at the beginning of the twentieth century for a banker, Ernet Thiel, who then sold it to the state in 1924, when it was turned into an art gallery. Thiel, who knew many contemporary Nordic artists, gathered an impressive collection of paintings over the years, including works by Carl Larsson, Anders Zorn, Edvard Munch, Bruno Liljefors and even August Strindberg. The views are attractive enough to warrant a visit alone.

The Kaknäs TV Tower

Bus #69 from Norrmalm will take you directly to Stockholm's landmark TV tower, in the northern stretch of parkland known as **Ladusgårdsgärdet** (or, more commonly, Gärdet); it's also possible to walk here from Djurgården proper – head northwards across the island on Manillavägen over Djurgårdsbrunnsviken. At 160m, the **Kaknäs TV Tower** (Kaknästornet; daily: May–Aug 9am–10pm; Sept–April 10am–9pm; 25kr) is the highest building in Scandinavia, allowing fabulous views over the city and archipelago; there's also a restaurant about 120m up should you fancy a vertiginous cup of coffee. If you come here by bus, you'll pass a gaggle of sundry museums – Dance, Maritime, Technical and Ethnographical – while beyond Ladusgårdsgärdet, north of the tower, where windmills used to pierce the skyline, lies first Frihamnen, where the Estonia ferry docks and, just beyond that, Värtahamnen and the Silja Line ferry terminal for Finland.

Södermalm and Långholmen

Whatever you do in Stockholm, don't miss the delights of the city's southern island, **Södermalm**, more commonly known simply as Söder, whose craggy cliffs, turrets and towers rise high above the clogged traffic interchange at Slussen. The perched buildings are vaguely forbidding, but venture beyond the main roads skirting the island and

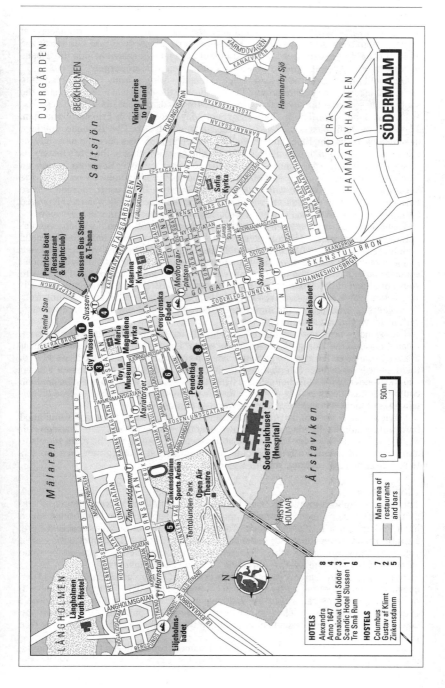

SÖDERMALM

DJURGÅRDEN

BECKHOLMEN

Saltsjön

Viking Ferries to Finland

Patricia Boat (Restaurant & Nightclub)

Slussen Bus Station & T-bana

Sofia Kyrka

Katarina Kyrka

City Museum

Maria Magdalena Kyrka

Forsgrénska Badet

Medborgar-platsen

Toy Museum

Mariatorget

Pendeltåg Station

Erikdalsbadet

Gamla Stan

Slussen

Skanstull

Johanneshovsbron

Södersjukhuset (Hospital)

Mälaren

Zinkensdamm Sports Arena

Open Air Theatre

Tantolunden Park

Hornstull

Liljeholms-badet

Långholmen Youth Hostel

LÅNGHOLMEN

Årstaviken

ÅRSTA HOLMAR

Hammarby Sjö

HAMMARBYHAMNEN

SÖDRA

N

| | | Main area of restaurants and bars |

0   500m

HOTELS
Alexandra	8
Anno 1647	4
Pensionat Oden Söder	3
Scandic Hotel Slussen	1
Tre Små Rum	6

HOSTELS
Columbus	7
Gustav af Klimt	2
Zinkensdamm	5

a lively and surprisingly green area unfolds, one that's emphatically working-class at heart, though Swedish-style – there are no slums here. To get here, take bus #46 or #48 and get off at Bondegatan, or the #53 to Folkungagatan; alternatively, ride the T-bana to Slussen or, to save an uphill trek, Medborgarplatsen or Mariatorget.

On foot, you reach the island over a double bridge from Gamla Stan into Södermalmstorg – the square around the entrance to the T-bana at Slussen. Just to the south of the square is the rewarding **City Museum** (Stadsmuséet; June–Aug Tues, Wed & Fri–Sun 11am–5pm, Thurs 11am–7pm; Sept–May Tues, Wed & Fri–Sun 11am–5pm, Thurs 11am–9pm; 40kr), hidden in a basement courtyard. The Baroque building, designed by Tessin the Elder and finished by his son in 1685, was once the town hall for this part of Stockholm; it now houses a set of collections relating to the city's history as a seaport and industrial centre. Nearby, the Renaissance-style **Katarina kyrka** on Högbergsgatan stands on the site where the victims of the Stockholm Blood Bath – the betrayed nobility of Sweden who opposed King Christian II's Danish invasion – were buried in 1520. Their bodies were burned as heretics outside the city walls and it proved a vicious and effective coup, Christian disposing of the opposition in one fell swoop.

That's about as far as specific sights go on Södermalm, although it's worth wandering westwards towards **Mariatorget**, a spacious square of Art Nouveau-influenced buildings. This is one of the most desirable places to live in the city, within easy reach of a glut of stylish bars and restaurants where trendy Stockholmers simply have to be seen. If you're having a bad hair day, you can escape the latest fashions and regress to your childhood at the **Museum of Toys**, Mariatorget 1C (Leksaksmuseum; Tues–Fri 10am–4pm, Sat & Sun noon–4pm; 40kr, children 20kr), which contains everything from tin soliders to space guns, although there's more to interest big kids than little ones, with few toys you can actually play with.

The island is also home to one of Stockholm's most popular parks, **Tantolunden**, located close to the Hornstull T-bana at the end of Lignagatan, complete with open-air theatre in summer. It's also the place to come for **swimming pools** – there are three of them – Forgrénskabadet (Medborgarplatsen T-bana), Erikdalsbadet (Skanstull T-bana) and the wonderful little Liljeholmsbadet (Hornstull T-bana), a pool in a boat-like pontoon contraption that floats in Lake Mälaren: there's single-sex nude swimming here on certain days of the week and the water is never less than 30°C.

You'll probably end up back on Södermalm after dark, since there are some good bars and restaurants in this quarter of town – though it's best to get your bearings during the day, as finding your way around at night can be confusing. The main streets to aim for are **Götgatan**, **Folkungagatan**, **Bondegatan** and **Skånegatan** (see the sections on eating and drinking, starting opposite).

Långholmen

The name **Långholmen** means "long island" and it's just that, a skinny finger of land off the northwestern tip of Södermalm, crossed by the mighty Västerbron bridge which links Södermalm with Kungsholmen. There are a couple of popular **beaches** here: **Långholmens Strandbad** to the west of the bridge and rocky **Klippbad** to the east; if you don't fancy swimming, take a leisurely stroll through the trees instead for some stunning views over the water towards the City Hall and Gamla Stan.

You may well find yourself staying here as the island's large prison building has been converted into one of the better hostels in Sweden (see p.393). There's a café here in the summer, and you can sit outside and have a drink in what used to be the prison's exercise yard – narrow, bricked-up runs with iron gates at one end. Alternatively, you could nip back over to Södermalm and sample the excellent *Lasse i Parken* café (see p.410).

Långholmen is best reached by taking the T-bana to Hornstull and then following the signs to the youth hostel; bus #4 is also handy as it crosses Västerbron on its way

ELITE HOTELS
OF SWEDEN

575.

Expe At.

Why.   -   Water tower on left

after. ::   turn right. at McDon

Ford & streets on the right.

No. 14 Jord.   Big Yellow. house.

between Södermalm, Kungsholmen, Vasastaden and Östermalm – an excellent way of seeing much of the city for very little cost.

Eating

Eating out in Stockholm needn't be outrageously expensive – observe a few rules and accept a few facts and you'll manage quite well. If money is tight, switch your main meal of the day to lunchtime, at least on weekdays, when almost every café and restaurant offers an excellent-value set menu, or *dagens rätt*, for around 50–60kr. In the evening, look around for the best deals but don't necessarily assume that Italian and Chinese places will be the least expensive; more often than not they're overpriced and the food is tasteless. Having said that, there are plenty of other foreign cuisines on offer, particularly Japanese and Thai, plus, of course, a number of traditional Swedish places.

Breakfast, snacks and shopping for food

Stockholmers don't usually go out for **breakfast**, so there are very few places open in the early morning. Hotels also provide help-yourself buffet breakfasts which go a long way to filling you up for the day. Unless you're desperate, don't bother with **burgers** – you'll pay around 50kr for a large burger and fries at *McDonalds*, only 10kr less than the lunchtime *dagens rätt* elsewhere, though coffee is a bargain both here and at *Clock Burger*, the Swedish burger chain. If the nibbles strike it's much more economical to pick up a *korv*, a grilled or fried sausage in bread, for around 10–15kr from a street vendor.

Of the indoor **markets** (both closed Sun), Hötorgshallen in Hötorget is cheaper and more varied than Östermalmshallen in Östermalmstorg. The former is awash with small cafés and ethnic snacks, but buy your fruit and veg outside where it's less expensive. The latter is posher and pricey – while it's pleasant for a wander, you'll find most things cost less in the city's biggest **supermarket** in the basement of the Åhléns department store, Sergels Torg. Otherwise, try Konsum in Järntorget or Metro in the underground arcade at Sergels Torg; neither is particularly cheap. In summer, **fruit and veg** stalls spring up outside many of the T-bana stations, especially those out of the centre.

Cafés and restaurants

The main areas for decent eating, day or night, are the city-centre area bounded by Norrmalmstorg, Birger Jarlsgatan and Stureplan; Grev Turegatan in Östermalm; and around Folkungagatan, Skånegatan and Bondegatan on Södermalm. Kungsholmen's restaurants are more spread out, so it's best to have a destination in mind before setting out. Several restaurants in Gamla Stan are also worth checking out, though they tend to be expensive. Vegetarians shouldn't have too much difficulty in finding something to eat. Note that in Sweden as a whole there's a fine distinction between cafés, restaurants and bars, with many places offering music and entertainment in the evening as well as serving food throughout the day. Bear in mind too that Swedes eat early: lunch is served from 11am and dinner from 6pm.

Norrmalm

Berns, Berzelii Park, Nybroplan. One of the more chic brasseries in town, with interior design by Britain's Sir Terence Conran. Originally made famous by writer August Strindberg, who picked up character ideas here for his novel, *The Red Room*. Moderate.

Biblos, Biblioteksgatan 9. A wonderfully trendy café and restaurant right in the centre of town – a good place to people-watch. Moderate.

East, Stureplan 13. One of the city's finest restaurants. Trendy to a T and excellent food – lots of fish and Asian-style dishes – but expensive: lunch 74–106kr; dinner around 150kr.

Halv trappa plus gård, Lästmakargatan 3, at junction with Stureplan. Very popular eaterie, with modern European dishes, particularly fish, served outside in summer. Bursting with fashion victims. Moderate.

Hot Wok Café, Kungsgatan 44, in the eclectic Kungshallen food hall. Generous portions of Chinese-style food and the largest glasses of wine anywhere in Stockholm. Inexpensive.

KB, Smålandsgatan 7, Stureplan. Excellent Swedish food in posh surroundings – a favourite haunt of authors and artists. Very expensive.

Köket och en bar, Sturegallerian 30, Stureplan. Very popular place for eats when the nightclubs have turned out – open till 3am Thurs–Sun – but quite pricey.

Konditori Kungstornet, Kungsgatan 28. Popular 1950s-style Swedish coffee house with excellent cakes and sandwiches from 40kr.

Lao Wai, Luntmakargatan 74. Sweden's first Thai and Indonesian restaurant. Decidedly good, though not especially cheap.

Leonardo, Sveavägen 55. Some of the tastiest pizzas (with the only wood-fired oven in town) and pasta in Stockholm – always fresh and delicious. Moderate.

Operakällaren, Operan, Gustav Adolfs Torg. A bill at the famous Opera House restaurant will seriously damage your wallet (starters from 150kr) but the daily *smörgåsbord* (Mon–Sat 11.30am–3pm, Sun noon–6pm) is fabulous and just about affordable – around 250kr per person for a spread beyond compare. A better bet is the *Bakfickan* café around the back where simpler (and much cheaper) dishes are served from the same kitchen.

Peppar, Torsgatan 34. Attractive Cajun restaurant with decent-sized portions. Moderate.

Restaurangen, Oxtorgsgatan 14. Run by one of Stockholm's top chefs, this is the place for Swedish home cooking with an added international flavour. No starters or main courses – you simply put together a meal from three or five excellent smaller dishes. Moderate.

Roberts Coffee, Kungsgatan 44. Just inside the door of the Kungshallen food hall and a popular place to meet friends for a good cup of coffee.

Rolfs Kök, Tegnérgatan 41. Popular central restaurant close to Hötorget with a special line in Asian and Cajun stir-fried food. Fairly expensive.

Sawadee, Olofsgatan 6. Next to Hötorget T-bana. Attractive Thai restaurant with a wonderful 150kr special dinner and reasonably priced drinks.

Svea Bar & Matsal, Sveavägen 53, just by Rådmansgatan T-bana. Excellent place for a cheap and filling lunch (around 60kr). Set menus in the evenings with dishes for around 100kr; cheap beer.

Wayne's, Kungsgatan 14. A popular café for smart city types and trendy young things, who pretend to be reading foreign newspapers whilst sipping cappuccinos.

Östermalm

Aubergine, Linnégatan 38. Upmarket and expensive place on one of Östermalm's busiest streets. Lots of wood and glass. The separate bar menu brings prices within reach – chicken on a skewer for 85kr is good.

Elverket, Linnégatan 69. Tasty international food served up in a restaurant attached to a theatre. Spacious lounge for drinks before dinner or relaxation afterwards. Moderate.

Grevens Bakficka, Fisk och Vilt, Grev Turegatan 7. Affordable and cosy place for lunch, with meat, fish and game dishes for around 100kr.

Grodan, Grev Turegatan 16. Officially called *La Grenouille*, but more usually known by it's Swedish name (it means "the frog"). French cuisine at moderate prices.

Gröna Linjen, 2nd floor, Mäster Samuelsgatan 10. A nineteenth-century building housing Scandinavia's oldest vegetarian restaurant. There's a good buffet here, too. Moderate.

Il Conte, Grev Turegatan 9. Rumoured to be the best Italian in town, with excellent and very good-value pasta.

Meaning Green, Norrlandsgatan 2. Decent food served at one of the city's better vegetarian restaurants with dishes from around 100kr.

Örtagården, Nybrogatan 31. Top-notch vegetarian restaurant, with food dished up under a huge chandelier in c.1900 surroundings. Dozens of different salads, warm dishes and soups. Expensive.

PA & Co, Riddargatan 8. Fashionable restaurant with international dishes, some good old Swedish favourites and a few inventive "crossovers". Moderate.

Saturnus, Erikbergsgatan 6. Café food during the day, including good, moderately priced pasta, huge cakes and massive sandwiches, with more substantial dishes on offer in the evening.

Stockholms Glass och Pastahus, Valhallavägen 155. Excellent fresh pasta at lunchtime and home-made ice cream. Inexpensive.

Stolen, Sibyllegatan 47, close to Östermalmstorg T-bana. The name means "chair", after the dozens of different chairs in the restaurant. Good Italian-style food at reasonable prices – the chicken dishes are especially delicious.

Vassilis Taverna, Valhallavägen 131. Stockholmers say this is the best Greek restaurant in town – try the moussaka, which slips down a treat. Moderate.

Gamla Stan

Bistro Ruby, Österlånggatan 14. French bistro in the heart of the Old Town, tastefully done out in Parisian style, but pricey. Main dishes go for around 150kr, and there's a wide selection of beers.

Costas, Lilla Nygatan 21. Good central Greek restaurant with an ouzo bar, *C2*, next door.

De Fyras Krog, Järntorgsgatan 5. As good a place as any to eat traditional Swedish food – choose between the posh, more expensive restaurant or the simple farmhouse-style section.

Gondolen, Stadsgården 6, at the top of the Katarina lift, opposite Slussen T-bana. Breathtaking views over Stockholm from this high-level restaurant right on the waterfront. Choose the smaller of the two restaurants here and prices fall dramatically. Moderate.

Grill Ruby, Österlånggatan 14. Next door to *Bistro Ruby*, this place serves up American-style grills and weekend brunches.

Den Gyldene Freden, Österlånggatan 51. Stockholm's oldest restaurant, "The Golden Peace" was opened in 1772. Expect to pay around 350kr for just two courses, without drinks, but the atmosphere, food and style are unparalleled in Stockholm.

Hermitage, Stora Nygatan 11. Vegetarian restaurant well worth checking out for hearty dishes. Closes at 8pm (Sun 7pm). Moderate.

Lilla Karachi, Lilla Nygatan 12. Housed in one of Gamla Stan's old cellar vaults, this Pakistani restaurant has vegetarian options and moderate prices; an interesting change for Stockholm.

Mårten Trotzig, Västerlånggatan 79. Known throughout Sweden for its excellent and stylish food served in a beautiful setting – attracts luvvies and business types from across Stockholm. Very expensive.

Södermalm

Blå Dörren, Södermalmstorg 6. Beer hall and restaurant with excellent, but expensive, Swedish food.

Bonden Mat & Bar, Bondegatan 1C. Small and cosy restaurant with rough brick walls; try the delicious fillet of chicken with oyster mushrooms in red wine sauce and potato gratin – a winner every time. Moderate.

Bröderna Olssons, Folkungagatan 84. If you like garlic this is the place for you, with every conceivable dish laced with the white stuff. Expensive.

Creperie Fyra Knop, Svartensgatan 4. A rare treat in Stockholm: excellent crepes at affordable prices (around 50kr).

Dionysos, Bondegatan 56. Over-the-top Greek decor gives this place a friendly feel, and the food is excellent, with moussaka for 85kr, chicken souvlakia for 70kr

Folkhemmet, Renstiernas Gata 30. Very popular place serving Swedish home cooking and international dishes to young trendies and media types. Packed at weekends. Moderate.

Hannas Krog, Skånegatan 80. Crowded and noisy haunt, a firm favourite of Söder trendies, with lunch deals for around 60kr, evening dishes for around 100–150kr. Also a popular drinking haunt – see p.411.

Hosteria Tre Santi, Blekingegatan 32. One of Södermalm's better Italian restaurants and excellent value for money – always busy.

Indigo, Götgatan, near exit from Slussen T-bana. The ideal place to stop off for an afternoon cappuccino. Good pastries, too – the carrot cake is a house speciality. Small evening menu. Moderate.

Indira, Bondegatan 3B. The area's biggest Indian restaurant, with a good tandoori-based menu. Takeaway food too. Inexpensive.

Kvarnen, Tjärhovsgatan 4. Small beer hall with simple Swedish food – lunch for around 50kr. Evening dishes, fish and meat, for 80–90kr. Open till 3am at weekends.

Lasse i Parken, Högalidsgatan 56. Café housed in an eighteenth-century house with a pleasant garden that's very popular in summer; also handy for the beaches at Långholmen. Moderate.

Mellis, Skånegatan 83–85. Another popular restaurant on this busy restaurant street. Greek, French and Swedish dishes – reasonable prices. A nice place for coffee and cakes, too.

Pelikan, Blekingegatan 40. Atmospheric, working-class Swedish beer hall with excellent traditional food, *pytt i panna* for 58kr.

Sjögräs, Timmermansgatan 24. A modern approach to Swedish cooking, influenced by world cuisines; always packed. Moderate.

Snaps/Rangus Tangus, Medborgarplatsen. Good old-fashioned Swedish food in a 300-year-old building. Very popular. Expensive.

Soldaten Svejk, Östgötagatan 15. Lively Czech-run joint that draws in a lot of students. Simple menu at around the 100kr mark. Large selection of Czech beers – Pilsner Urquell goes for 39kr.

String, Nytorgsgatan 38. If you fancy yourself as a brilliant new writer, or if you just fancy yourself, you'll fit in well at this studenty café. Adopt a ponderous air. Good for moderately priced cakes and snacks.

Tre Indier, Möregatan 2. Lively Indian restaurant, slightly tucked away in a tiny street off Åsögatan (take bus #55 in the direction of Södra Hammarbyhamnen), but well worth hunting out. Moderate.

Kungsholmen

Bon Lloc, Bergsgatan 33. Catalan dishes with a hint of Swedish home cooking served up by award-winning chef, Mathias Dahlgren, voted best chef in the world in 1997. Bookings necessary. Expensive.

Carls Bar, Scheelegatan 12. Good Thai food and a reasonable selection of more mainstream European dishes. Worth a look if you're in the area. Moderate.

Hong Kong, Kungbrostrand 23. Popular and good-value Chinese restaurant, one of the best in the city.

La Famiglia, Alströmergatan 45. One of Kungsholmen's better Italian places (even Frank Sinatra once ate here), and a good one for that first date. Expensive.

Mamas & Tapas, Scheelegatan 3. Delicious and reasonably priced Spanish food that deservedly attracts people from across Stockholm. Always packed.

Roppongi, Hantverkargatan 76. The place for sushi and other Japanese delights on Kungsholmen.

Salt, Hantverkaregatan 34. On the island's main road, serving stodgy traditional Swedish fare, including elk burgers. *Salt* is no bad name either – drink a lot of water if you're eating the slabs of pork they serve up. Inexpensive.

Drinking, nightlife and entertainment

There's plenty to keep you entertained in Stockholm, from pubs, gigs and clubs to the cinema and theatre. There's a particularly good **live music** scene in the bars and pubs, but you'll generally have to pay a cover charge of around 60–80kr. Wear something other than jeans and trainers if you don't want to feel very scruffy – many places won't let you in dressed like that anyway – and be prepared to cough up around 10kr to leave your coat in the cloakroom, a requirement at many bars, discos and pubs, particularly in winter. As well as the weekend, Wednesday is a busy night in Stockholm – there's usually plenty going on and queues to get into the more popular places.

Bars, brasseries and pubs

The scourge of Swedish **nightlife** – high alcohol prices – is gradually being neutralized due to increased competition. Over recent years there's been a veritable explosion in the number of bars and pubs in Stockholm, beer prices have dropped considerably, and on Södermalm especially there are some very good deals, though you'll probably still find yourself paying more than at home. Look on the bright side – you no longer need a bank loan to see you through a night out in Stockholm and Swedish beer is stronger than the stuff you're likely to be used to drinking. **Happy hours** also throw up some bargains – look out for signs outside bars and pubs.

Despite the increase in bars, however, it's still the case that many Stockholmers do their drinking over a meal, and several of the places listed below are primarily cafés or restaurants. Almost all are open seven days a week.

Norrmalm and Östermalm

Café Opera, Operan, Gustav Adolfs Torg. If your Katherine Hamnett gear isn't too crushed and you can stand just one more Martini, join the queue outside. Daily till 3am.

Dubliner, Smålandsgatan 8. One of the busiest Irish pubs in town, with live music most evenings.

East Bar, Stureplan. Loud music, loud dress and loud mouths. Great fun.

Lydmar, Sturegatan 10. One of the most popular bars in Stockholm – and very elegant. Dress up a little to get past the beefcakes on the door.

Silver Bar, Birger Jarlsgatan 5. Popular little bar with a nightclub downstairs which attracts big crowds at weekends.

Storstad, Odengatan 41. A popular hangout with Stockholm's media crowd and local celebrities. Crowded at weekends with card-flashing clientele.

Sturecompagniet, Sturegatan 4. Three floors of bars with something for everybody and worth a look, though the beer's expensive.

Svea Bar & Matsal, Sveavägen, by exit to Rådmansgatan T-bana. Cheap beer and an upbeat atmosphere from early evening onwards.

Tranan, Karlbergsvägen 14. Atmospheric old workers' beer hall.

Gamla Stan

Gråmunken, Västerlånggatan 18. Cosy café-pub, usually busy and sometimes with live music to jolly things along.

Kaos, Stora Nygatan 21. DJs at weekends and unpretentious people gather here for a fun time.

Kleins, Kornhamnstorg 51. One of the better bars in Gamla Stan and definitely worth a look.

Magnus Ladulås, Österlånggatan 26. Rough brick walls and low ceilings make this bar-cum-restaurant an appealing place for a drink or two.

Södermalm

Bonden Bar, Bondegatan 1B. Just along from the *Bonden* restaurant and down a sloping walkway. A good choice for an evening beer before strutting your stuff on the adjoining dance floor.

Fenix, Götgatan 40. Cheap and nasty American-style bar that's the place to go if you want some bustle and noise.

Folkhemmet, Renstiernas Gata 30. Trendy hangout for 20- to 30-somethings. Inordinately popular at weekends.

Gröne Jägaren, Medborgarplatsen. Some of the cheapest beer in Stockholm; *storstark* is just 24kr until 9pm – perhaps inevitably the clientele tends to get raucously drunk.

Hannas Krog, Skånegatan 80. A good place for a drink before eating in the excellent restaurant here.

Kvarnen, Tjärhovsgatan 4. Busy beer hall popular with southside football fans.

O'Learys, Götgatan 11–13. Södermalm's most popular Irish pub – great fun and within stumbling distance of the nearby T-bana at Slussen.

Pelikan, Blekingegatan 40. A fantastic old beer hall full of character – and characters.

Sjögräs, Timmermansgatan 24. A wonderful local little bar that is always busy and lively.

WC, Skånegatan 51. Very busy at weekends with people from across town, and handy for the restaurants around Skånegatan and Blekingegatan.

Clubs

The **club scene** in Stockholm is limited, with several places doubling as bars or restaurants (where you have to eat). Entrance charges aren't too high at around 40–50kr, but beer sometimes gets more expensive as the night goes on, reaching as high as 50kr. For gay venues, see opposite.

Aladdin, Barnhusgatan 12–14, Norrmalm. One of the city's most popular dance restaurants, close to the Central Station, often with live bands. Expensive.

Dailys, Kungsträdgården. The *G-Klubben* inside this cheesy nightclub complex complete with striplights on the stairs is where you'll find Stockholm's movers and shakers. Be young, beautiful and trendy.

Fasching, Kungsgatan 63, Norrmalm. Dancing to live jazz from midnight onwards.

Patricia, Stadsgårdskajen, Slussen, Södermalm. Formerly the royal yacht of Britain's Queen Mother, today a restaurant-disco-bar with fantastic views of the city across the harbour and Swedish stand-up comedy nights. The food is quite simply fantastic. Wed–Sun; gay on Sun (see p.414).

Sturecompagniet, Sturegatan 4, Norrmalm. Strut to house and techno and a fantastic light show or work your way through three floors of bars. Very popular.

Live music: rock and jazz

Apart from the cafés and bars already listed, there's no shortage of specific venues that put on **live music**. Most of the performers will be local bands, for which you'll pay around 60–70kr entrance, but nearly all the big names make it to Stockholm, playing at a variety of seated halls and stadiums – naturally, tickets for these are much more expensive. The main big venues are the Stockholm Globe Arena, supposedly the largest spherical building in the world (T-bana Globben; ☎08/725 10 00); Johanneshov (T-bana Gullmarsplan; ☎08/600 34 00); and the Konserthuset in Hötorget (☎08/10 21 10) – ring for programme details or ask at the tourist offices.

Cirkus, Djurgården. Occasional rock and R&B performances.

Daily News, Kungsträdgården, Norrmalm. Part of the Dagens Nyheter complex, this central rock venue hosts the most consistent range of live music in town – everything from grunge to techno.

Engelen, Kornhamnstorg 59, Gamla Stan. Live jazz, rock or blues nightly until 3am, but arrive early to get in; the music starts at 8.30pm (Sun 9pm).

Fasching, Kungsgatan 63, Norrmalm. Local and foreign contemporary jazz; a good place to go dancing too. Closed Sun.

Kaos, Stora Nygatan 21, Gamla Stan. Live pop and rock from 9pm nightly, rock bands on Fri and Sat in the cellar, and reasonable late-night food.

Nallen, Regeringsgatan 74. Once *the* place to hear music in the city (even the Beatles were booked to play here), now offering jazz, swing and big band.

Stampen, Stora Nygatan 5, Gamla Stan. Long-established and rowdy jazz club, both trad and mainstream; occasional foreign names, too.

Tre Backar, Tegnérgatan 12–14, Norrmalm; T-bana Rådmansgatan. Good, cheap pub with a live cellar venue. Rock and blues nightly Mon–Sat until midnight.

Classical music, theatre and cinema

For up-to-date **information** about what's on where, check the special Saturday supplement of the *Dagens Nyheter* newspaper, "På Stan". *Stockholm This Week*, free from the tourist office, is also indispensible for **arts listings**, with day-by-day information about a whole range of events – gigs, theatre, festivals, dance – sponsored by the city, many of which are free and based around Stockholm's many parks. Popular venues in summer are Kungsträdgården and Skansen, where there's always something going on. If

STOCKHOLM WATER FESTIVAL

The annual **Stockholm Water Festival** is a ten-day event in August featuring open-air gigs, street parties, fishing contests, exhibitions, sailing displays and children's events, culminating in a stunning firework display; the tourist office has specific details about each year's events. Book accommodation in advance if you're planning to stay during the festival, sharpen your elbows and prepare to forge your way through the crowds which briefly transform Stockholm into a bustling city. Luckily, the change is brief.

your Swedish is up to it, there's a free monthly paper, *Nöjesguiden*, that details all manner of entertainment – from the latest films to a club guide. You'll see it in bars and restaurants; pick up a copy and get someone to translate.

Classical music and opera
Classical music is always easy to find. Many museums – particularly the History Museum and Music Museum – have regular programmes, and there's generally something on at one of the following venues: Konserthuset, Hötorget, Norrmalm (☎08/10 21 10); Berwaldhallen, Strandvägen 69, Östermalm (☎08/784 18 00); Gamla Musikaliska Akademien, Blasieholmstorg 8, near the National Art Museum (☎08/20 68 18); and Myntet, Hantverkargatan 5 (☎08/652 03 10). **Operan** (☎08/24 82 40) is Sweden's most famous operatic venue; for less rarefied presentations of the classics, check the programme at the Folkoperan, Hornsgatan 72, Södermalm (☎08/658 53 00). If you're after **church music**, you'll find it in Norrmalm at Adolf Fredriks kyrka, Gustav Wasa Kyrka in Odenplan, and at St Jakobs kyrka; in Gamla Stan, try Storkyrkan. For more details consult *Stockholm This Week*.

Theatre and cinema
There are dozens of **theatres** in Stockholm, but only one has regular performances of **English-language productions**: the Regina, Drottninggatan 71 (☎08/20 70 00), which features touring plays. If you want tickets for anything else theatrical, it's often worth waiting for reduced-price standby tickets, available from the kiosk in Norrmalmstorg.

Cinema-going is an incredibly popular pastime in Stockholm, with screenings of new releases nearly always full. The largest venue in the city centre is Filmstaden Sergel in Hötorget, but there's also a good number of cinemas the entire length of Kungsgatan between Sveavägen and Birger Jarlsgatan, always very lively on Saturday night. Tickets cost around 70kr and films are never dubbed into Swedish.

Finally, **Kulturhuset** in Sergels Torg has a full range of artistic and cultural events, most of them free; the information desk on the ground floor gives away programmes.

Gay Stockholm

Stockholm's **gay scene** is disappointingly small and closeted. Attitudes in general are tolerant but you won't see gay couples walking hand in hand or kissing in the street – just one of the false perceptions of Sweden. Until just a few years ago, when the country freed itself from restrictive tax rules imposed on bars and restaurants, there was only one specifically gay hangout in the whole of the city. Thankfully today things have changed and bars are springing up all over the place, although a kneejerk reaction by the government in response to AIDS has forced all gay saunas to close. The main bars and clubs to be seen at are listed below but beware that all are male-dominated – lesbians have an extremely low profile in Stockholm.

Information is available from the **RFSL**, the National Association for Sexual Equality (Riksförbundet för Sexuellt Likaberättigande; ☎08/736 02 12), the city's main gay centre at Sveavägen 57. The centre offers HIV advice (☎08/736 02 11), publishes a free newspaper, and runs a bookstore, a restaurant and radio station. **Gay Pride Week** takes place during the second week of August.

Bars, clubs and restaurants

Häktet, Hornsgatan 82. A wonderful place with two bars, front and back, as well as a quiet sitting room and a beautiful outdoor courtyard – a real haven in summer. It's only open Wed and Fri nights, when it's very popular, especially with women.

Patricia, Stadsgårdskajen. The Queen Mother's former yacht attracts queens from across Stockholm for fun on Sun evenings (no entrance fee if you eat in the restaurant), often with drag acts or stand-up comedy. A great place for romantic evenings staring out across the harbour.

Propaganda, Blekholmsterassen 15. Bar and nightclub on Fri and Sat. The dance floor is particularly hot.

SLM, Wollmar Yxkullsgatan 18. Stockholm's only leather club – very dark and definitely not for the faint hearted. Handy shoe polishing service. Men only.

TipTop, Sveavägen 57 (☎08/30 83 38 or 31 34 80). Stockholm's main gay men's venue – a club, restaurant and bar all rolled into one – and very popular, especially on Fri and Sat nights. Open daily.

Listings

Airlines Aer Lingus, Döbelnsgatan 40 (☎020/79 52 51); Aeroflot, Sveavägen 31 (☎08/21 70 07); Air France, Norrmalmstorg 16 (☎08/679 88 55); Air New Zealand, Kungsbron 1G (☎08/21 91 80); American Airlines, Nybrogatan 3 (☎08/24 61 45); Braathens Malmö Aviation (Arlanda airport ☎797 61 00; Bromma airport ☎08/797 68 74); British Airways, Hamngatan 11 (☎08/679 78 00); Cathay Pacific, Arlanda airport (☎08/797 85 80); Delta Air Lines, Kungsgatan 18 (☎08/796 96 00); Finnair, Norrmalmstorg 1 (☎08/679 93 30); Icelandair, Kungsgatan 38 (☎08/690 98 00); KLM and Northwest, Arlanda airport (☎08/590 799 10); Lufthansa, Norrmalmstorg 1 (☎08/614 15 50); Qantas, Kungsgatan 64 (☎08/24 25 02); SAS Stureplan 8 (international ☎020/72 75 55; domestic ☎020/72 70 00); Singapore Airlines, Grev Turegatan 10 (☎08/611 71 31); United Airlines, Kungsgatan 3 (☎08/678 15 70).

Airport enquiries Arlanda airport, 45km north of Stockholm (airport enquiries ☎08/797 61 00; SAS domestic flight enquiries ☎08/797 50 50); Bromma airport, 8km west of Stockholm (☎08/797 68 00); Skavsta, 100km south of Stockholm (☎0155/28 04 00).

American Express Birger Jarlsgatan 1 (☎08/679 78 80); Mon–Fri 9am–5pm.

Banks and exchange Banks generally stay open later in central Stockholm than in the rest of the country – usually Mon–Fri 9.30am–3pm, though some stay open until 5.30pm; the bank at Arlanda is open even longer hours, and there's also a cashpoint machine in the departures hall. Forex exchange offices offer better value than the banks for changing money; branches can be found in the main hall at Central Station (☎08/411 67 34) and downstairs in the T-bana area (☎08/24 46 02); at Cityterminalen (☎08/21 42 80); Vasagatan 14 (☎08/10 49 90); in the Sverigehuset (☎08/20 03 89); and at Arlanda airport Terminal 2 (☎08/593 622 71). Valutaspecialisten at Kungsgatan 30 (☎08/10 30 00) and at Arlanda Terminal 5 (☎08/797 85 57) also have decent rates.

Bookshops Akademibokhandeln, corner of Regeringsgatan & Mäster Samuelsgatan; Aspingtons secondhand bookshop, Västerlånggatan 54; Hedengrens Bokhandel, Sturegallerian, Stureplan 4; Sweden Bookshop, Sverigehuset, Hamngatan 27.

Bus enquiries For SL bus information see "SL travel information" below; for long-distance bus information call Swebus Express (☎0200/218 218; *www.express.swebus.se*); Svenska Buss (☎020/67 67 67), or visit Busstop inside the Cityterminalen (Mon–Fri 9am–6pm, Sat 9am–4pm, Sun 11am–6pm) for information and tickets on domestic and international services.

Car rental Avis, Vasagatan 10B and at Arlanda and Bromma airports (☎020/78 82 00); Budget, Klarabergsviadukten 92 (☎08/411 15 00), Arlanda airport (☎08/797 84 70); Eurodollar, Klarabergsgatan 33 (☎08/24 26 55); Europcar, Medborgarplatsen 25 and Arlanda airport (☎020/78 11 80); Hertz, Vasagatan 26 and Arlanda airport (☎020/211 211); Holiday Autos, c/o Eurodollar Klarabergsgatan 33 (☎08/24 26 55) and at Arlanda airport; Statoil, service stations throughout Stockholm (information only on ☎08/669 24 45).

Dentist Emergency dental care at St Eriks Hospital, Fleminggatan 22; daily 8am–8.30pm. Out of hours ring the duty dentist (☎08/463 91 00).

Doctor Tourists can get emergency outpatient care at the hospital for the district they are staying in; check with the 24hr medical advice line (☎08/463 91 00).

Embassies and consulates Australia, Sergels Torg 12 (☎08/613 29 00); Canada, Tegelbacken 4 (☎08/453 30 00); Ireland, Östermalmsgatan 97 (☎08/661 80 05); New Zealand – use the Australian Embassy; UK, Skarpögatan 6–8 (☎08/671 90 00); US, Strandvägen 101 (☎08/783 53 00).

Emergencies Ring ☎112 for police, ambulance or fire services.

Ferries Tickets for Finland from Silja Line, Stureplan or Värtahamnen (☎08/22 21 40), and from Viking Line at Resebutik inside the Cityterminalen or Stadsgårdsterminalen (all bookings on ☎08/452 40 00); tickets for Estonia from Estline, Frihamnen (☎08/667 00 01); for cruises, from Birka Cruises, Södermalmstorg 2 (☎08/714 55 20); for the archipelago from Waxholms Ångfartygs AB, Strömkajen (☎08/679 58 30).

Laundry Self-service launderette at Västmannagatan 61, or try the youth hostels.

Left luggage Lockers at Central Station (from 20kr per day), the Cityterminalen bus station and the Silja and Viking ferry terminals. Central Station also has a left-luggage office (☎08/762 25 49).

Lost property Offices at Central Station (☎08/762 20 00); Police, Bergsgatan 39 (☎08/401 07 88); SL, Rådmansgatan T-bana station, (☎08/736 07 80).

News in English BBC and NPR programming can be heard in Greater Stockholm on 89.6 FM at 5–8am. Radio Sweden also provide news in English, about Sweden only, on the same frequency several times during the day – information on ☎08/784 74 00 or look for schedules in the *Dagens Nyheter* newspaper.

Newspapers Kiosks at Central Station, Cityterminalen, and at the Press Center (branches in the Gallerian shopping centre on Hamngatan and at Sveavägen 52). They can be read for free at the Stadsbiblioteket (City Library), Sveavägen 73, or at the Kulturhuset, Sergels Torg.

Pharmacy 24hr service at C. W. Scheele, Klarabergsgatan 64 (☎08/454 81 30).

Police Offices at Agnegatan 33–37, Kungsholmen (☎08/401 00 00), and at Bryggargatan 19, near the train station.

Post office The most useful office is in the Central Station (Mon–Fri 7am–10pm, Sat & Sun 10am–7pm); take your passport if collecting poste restante mail.

SL travel information Bus, T-bana and regional train (*pendeltåg*) information on ☎08/600 10 00. There are SL Centers at Sergels Torg (Mon–Fri 7am–6.30pm, Sat & Sun 10am–5pm); Slussen (Mon–Fri 7am–6pm, Sat 10am–1pm); Gullmarsplan, Södermalm (Mon–Thurs 7am–6.30pm, Fri 7am–6pm, Sat 10am–5pm); Tekniska Högskolan (Mon–Fri 7am–6.30pm, Sat 10am–5pm); and Fridhemsplan, Kungsholmen (Mon–Fri 7am–6.30pm, Sat 10am–5pm).

STF (Svenska Turistföreningen). Information by telephone (☎08/463 21 00) about Sweden's youth hostels, mountain huts, hiking trails, maps and youth hostel membership.

Systembolaget Norrmalm: Klarabergsgatan 62; Regeringsgatan 59; Sveavägen 66; Vasgatan 25; Odengatan 58 and 92. Gamla Stan: Lilla Nygatan 18. Södermalm: Folkungagatan 56 & 101; Götgatan 132; and inside the Söderhallarna shopping centre in Medborgarplatsen.

Toilets There are central public toilets in the Gallerian shopping centre, Åhléns and NK department stores, T-Centralen and Cityterminalen.

Train information Tickets and information for domestic and international routes with SJ (Swedish State Railways) on ☎020/75 75 75; from abroad ring ☎08/696 75 40.

Travel agents KILROY, Kungsgatan 4 (☎08/23 45 15), for discounted rail and air tickets and ISIC cards; Ticket: branches at Kungsgatan 60 (☎08/24 00 90), Sturegatan 8 (☎08/611 50 20) and Sveavägen 42 (☎08/24 92 20); Transalpino Wasteels Resor, Stora Nygatan 37 (☎08/411 22 33); for cheap flights check the travel section of the main *Dagens Nyheter* newspaper.

AROUND STOCKHOLM

Such are Stockholm's attractions, it's easy to overlook the city's surroundings; yet only a few kilometres from the centre the countryside becomes noticeably leafier, the islands less congested, the water brighter. As further temptation, some of the country's most fascinating sights are within easy reach, like the spectacular **Millesgården** sculpture museum and **Drottningholm**, Sweden's greatest royal palace. Further out is the little village of **Mariefred**, containing Sweden's other great castle, **Gripsholm** – like Drottningholm, it's accessible by a fine boat ride on the waters of Lake Mälaren. Other trips from Stockholm – out into the stunning **archipelago** or to the university town of **Uppsala** – really merit more time, although if you're pressed for time it's possible to get there and back within a day.

While the Stockholm Card and turistkort are valid on bus, T-bana and regional train services within Greater Stockholm, you can't use them on the more enjoyable boat services to Drottningholm or in the archipelago. The quickest way to get to Uppsala is by regional train from Central Station – both cards are valid as far as Märsta, where you'll have to buy a supplementary ticket for the final part of the journey (around 50kr). From July to mid-August there's also a boat service to Uppsala, which leaves Stadshusbron (next to City Hall on Kungsholmen) at 9.45am, arriving at Uppsala at 4.30pm. Boats to Mariefred and Drottningholm also leave from Stadshusbron.

Lidingö and Millesgården

Lidingö is where the well-to-do of Stockholm live, a residential commuter island just northeast of the city centre, which you'll already have glimpsed if you arrived from Finland or Estonia on the Silja Line or Estline ferries, as they dock immediately opposite. It's worth a second look, though: eagle eyes may have spotted, across the water, the tallest of the statues in the startling **Millesgården** at Carl Milles Väg 2 (May–Sept daily 10am–5pm; Oct–April Tues–Sun noon–4pm; 60kr), the outdoor sculpture collection of **Carl Milles** (1875–1955), one of Sweden's greatest sculptors and collectors. To **get there**, take the T-bana to Ropsten, then the rickety Lidingöbanan (a cross between a train and a tram) over the bridge to Torsvikstorg, from where it's a short signposted walk down Herserudsvägen.

The statues are placed on terraces carved from the island's steep cliffs, with many of Milles's animated, classical figures perching precariously on soaring pillars, overlooking the distant harbour. A huge *Poseidon* rears over the army of sculptures, the most remarkable of which, *God's Hand*, has a small boy delicately balanced on the outstretched finger of a monumental hand. If you've been elsewhere in Sweden much of the work may seem familiar – copies and casts of the originals adorn countless provincial towns. If this collection inspires, it's worth tracking down three other pieces by Milles in the capital: his statue of *Gustav Vasa* in the Nordic Museum on Djurgården, the *Orpheus Fountain* in Norrmalm's Hötorget and, at Nacka Strand (reached by bus #404 from Slussen or Waxholm boat from Strömkajen), the magnificent *Gud på Himmelsbågen*, a claw-shaped vertical piece of steel topped with the figure of a boy – a stunning marker at the entrance to Stockholm harbour.

The island is also the venue for the world's biggest cross-country running race, the **Lidingöloppet**, held on the first Sunday in October. It's been going since 1965, the thirty kilometre course attracting an international field of around 30,000 runners – quite a sight as they skip or crawl up and down the island's hills. For more information or to find out how to take part, ask at the tourist office in Stockholm.

Drottningholm and Birka

Even if your time in Stockholm is limited, it's worth saving a day for the harmonious royal palace of **Drottningholm** (daily: May–Aug 10am–4.30pm; Sept noon–3.30pm; 50kr), beautifully located on the shores of leafy Lovön island, 11km west of the city centre. The fifty-minute boat trip there is part of the experience, with hourly departures from Stadhusbron (50kr one-way, 70kr return), or take the T-bana to Brommaplan and then any bus numbered between #301 and #323 from there – a less thrilling ride, but one that's covered by the turistkort and Stockholm Card.

Drottningholm is perhaps the greatest achievement of the architects **Tessin**, father and son. Work began in 1662 on the orders of King Karl X's widow, Eleonora, Tessin the Elder modelling the new palace in a thoroughly French style – leading to that tired and overused label of a Swedish Versailles. Apart from anything else it's considerably smaller that its French counterpart, utilizing false perspective and trompe l'oeil to boost the elegant, rather narrow interior. On Tessin the Elder's death in 1681, the palace was completed by his son, already at work on Stockholm's Royal Palace. Inside, good English notes are available to help you sort out each room's detail, a riot of Rococo decoration largely dating from the time when Drottningholm was bestowed as a wedding gift on Princess Louisa Ulrika (a sister of Frederick the Great of Prussia). Since 1981 the Swedish royal family has slummed it out at Drottningholm, using the palace as a permanent home, a move that has accelerated efforts to restore parts of the palace to their original appearance – so that the monumental **Grand Staircase** is now exactly as envisaged by Tessin the Elder.

Nearby in the palace grounds is the **Court Theatre** (Slottsteater; May–Sept guided tours only; 50kr), dating from 1766. Its heyday came a decade later when Gustav III imported French plays and acting troupes, making Drottningholm the centre of Swedish artistic life. Take a guided tour and you'll get a flowery though accurate account of the theatre's decoration: money to complete the building ran out in the eighteenth century, meaning that not everything is quite what it seems, with painted papier-mâché frontages masquerading as the real thing. The original backdrops and stage machinery are still in place though, and the tour comes complete with a display of eighteenth-century special effects – wind and thunder machines, trapdoors and simulated lighting. If you're in luck you might catch a **performance** of drama, ballet or opera here (usually June–Aug): the cheapest **tickets** cost around 100kr, though decent seats are in the region of 300kr – check the schedule at Drottningholm or ask at the tourist offices in the city. With time to spare, the extensive palace grounds also yield the **Chinese Pavilion** (same times; 50kr), a sort of eighteenth-century royal summer house.

Birka

Further into Lake Mälaren lies the island of **Björkö**, known for its rich flora and good swimming beaches. Its real draw, though, are the remnants of Sweden's oldest town, **BIRKA**, founded in around 750 AD. A Viking trading centre at its height during the tenth century, a few obvious remains lie scattered about – including the fragments of houses and a vast cemetery. Major excavations were carried out between 1990 and 1995 and a museum, **Birka the Viking Town** (May to mid-Sept daily 10am–5pm; 50kr), now displays rare artefacts recovered during the excavations as well as scale models of the harbour and craftsmen's quarters. You can get there from Stadshusbron in Stockholm on a Strömma Kanalbolaget boat (departures May to late Sept daily 10am, return trip from Birka at 3.45pm); tickets can be bought on board and cost 200kr, which includes admission to the museum.

The Archipelago

If you arrived in Stockholm by ferry from Finland or Estonia you'll already have had a tantalizing glimpse of the **Stockholm archipelago**. This array of hundreds upon hundreds of pine-clad islands and islets is the only one of its kind in the world. The archipelago can be split into three distinct sections: inner, centre and outer. In the inner archipelago there's more land than sea; in the centre it's pretty much fifty-fifty; while in the outer archipelago distances between islands are much greater – out here, sea and sky merge into one and the nearest island is often no more than a dot on the horizon. It's worth knowing that if it's cloudy in Stockholm, chances are that the sun will be shining somewhere out on the islands. Even if your trip to the capital is short, don't miss the chance to come out here.

Practicalities

Getting to the islands is easy and cheap, with Waxholmsbolaget operating the majority of sailings into the archipelago. Most boats leave from Strömkajen in front of the *Grand Hotel*; others leave from just round the corner at Nybrokajen, next to the Royal Theatre of Drama. Buy tickets either on the boats themselves or from the Waxholmsbolaget office on Strömkajen, where you can also pick up free timetables to help you plan your route – timetables are also posted on every jetty. **Departures** to the closest islands are more frequent (often around 4 daily) than those to the outer archipelago; if there's no direct service connections can often be made at the island of Vaxholm. Ticket prices are very reasonable, ranging from 20kr to 80kr depending on the length of the journey, though if you're planning to visit several islands it might be worth buying the **Interskerries Card** (båtluffarkort), which gives sixteen days' unlimited travel on all Waxholmsbolaget lines for 275kr. Alternatively, if you've already got an SL monthly travel card (see p.390), you can buy a **supplementary Waxholm card** (tillaggskort; 270kr), allowing a month's travel anywhere in the archipelago. Most boats have a cafeteria or restaurant on board.

Though there are few hotels in the archipelago, **accommodation** is most easily available in a number of several well-equipped and comfortable **youth hostels** – the most useful are at **Finnhamn** (☎08/542 462 12; 140kr; open all year), **Gällnö** (☎08/571 661 17; 120kr; May–Sept) and **Utö** (☎08/501 576 60; 140kr; open all year). It's also possible to rent summer **cottages** on the islands – contact the tourist office in Stockholm, though you'll need to book way in advance. **Campsites** are surprisingly hard to find – you'll be much better off camping rough, as a few nights' stay in most places won't cause any problems. Remember, though, that open fires are prohibited all over the archipelago.

Archipelago highlights

Of the vast number of islands in the archipelago, several are firm favourites with Stockholmers, **Vaxholm** in particular; others offer more secluded beaches and plenty of opportunity for lovely walks. The following are a few of the better islands to make for.

Inner and central archipelago

Vaxholm, lying just an hour from Stockholm, is a popular weekend destination. The main settlement on the island, **Vaxholm town**, has an atmospheric wooden harbour with an imposing fortress which once guarded the waterways into the city, successfully staving off attacks from Danes and Russians in the seventeenth and eighteenth centuries; it's now an unremarkable museum of military bits and pieces. Also within easy reach is **Grinda**, two hours or so away, a thickly wooded island typical of the inner archipelago, whose magnificent sandy beaches are much favoured by families.

In the central archipelago, low-lying **Gällnö** is covered with thick pine forest. One of the most beautiful islands, it has been designated a nature reserve, with deer and eider duck the most likely wildlife you'll spot. Ferries take about two hours to get here from Stockholm.

Svartsö lies in what's considered the most beautiful part of the archipelago, some two hours by boat from Stockholm near the island of Möja (see below). Known for its fields of grazing sheep, virgin forest and crystal-clear lakes, the good roads make it ideal cycling or walking territory.

Outer archipelago

If you're heading into the outer archipelago from Stockholm, you can sometimes cut the journey time by taking a bus or train to a further point on the mainland and picking the boat up there – where this is the case, we've given details below.

Three hours from Stockholm, the tiny island of **Finnhamn** lies in the outer archipelago where the islands start to become fewer and where the sea takes over. It's a good place for walking, through forests, meadows and along cliff tops.

Möja (pronounced roughly as "Murr-ya"), three and a half hours from the city, is one of the most popular islands, home to around three hundred people who make their living from fishing and farming. There's a small craft museum in the main town, **Berg**, and even a cinema, though it's not the place to come if you want to go swimming.

In the southern stretch of the archipelago, the beautiful island of **Bullerö** is home to a nature reserve with walking trails and an exhibition on the archipelago's plentiful flora and fauna. The journey takes three hours in total: get the train from Slussen to Saltsjöbaden, and from there a boat to the island of Nämdö, where you can take the shuttle service to Bullerö.

Sandhamn has been a destination for seafarers since the 1700s and remains so today, its tiny harbour packed full of sailing yachts of all shapes and sizes. The main village is a haven of narrow alleyways, winding streets and overgrown verandas. It takes three and a half hours to get here from Stockholm by boat, or you can save time by taking bus #434 from Slussen to Stavsnäs – the furthest point on the mainland – and picking up a boat for the hour-long sailing to Sandhamn.

Lying far out in the southern reaches of the archipelago, **Utö** is ideal for cycling, with the sandy beaches at Ålö storsand perfect for a picnic stop. You can also walk along the cliffs at Rävstavik. The journey time from Stockholm is three hours.

Mariefred and Gripsholm

If you've only got time for one boat trip out from Stockholm, make it to **MARIEFRED**, a tiny village to the west of the city whose peaceful attractions are bolstered by the presence of nearby **Gripsholm**, one of Sweden's most enjoyable castles. To get there in summer, take the *S/S Mariefred* steamboat from Klara Mälarstrand near Stadshuset on Kungsholmen (mid-May to mid-June Sat & Sun 10am; mid-June to mid-Aug Tues–Sun 10am; mid-Aug to mid-Sept Sat & Sun 10am; 3hr 30min each way; 110kr one way, 170kr return); buy your ticket on board. Outside summer, you'll have to travel on an Eskilstuna-bound train as far as **Läggesta**, where connecting buses shuttle passengers to Mariefred, a total journey of around an hour.

Mariefred itself – the name is derived from an old monastery, Pax Mariae (Mary's Peace) – is as quiet, and quintessentially Swedish, as such villages come. Surrounded by clear water, a couple of minutes up from the quayside and you're strolling through narrow streets whose well-kept wooden houses and little squares haven't changed much in decades. The water and enveloping greenery make for a pleasant stroll: if you call in at the central **Rådhus**, a fine eighteenth-century timber building, you can pick up a map from the **tourist office** inside (June–Aug Mon–Fri 10am–6pm; Sept Mon–Fri 10am–4pm; ☎0159/297 90). They also arrange **bike rental** (85kr per day; 400kr per week).

Steam train freaks will love the **Railway Museum** (variable hours; free) in the village – you'll probably have noticed the narrow-gauge tracks running to the quayside. There's an exhibition of old rolling stock and workshops, plus the chance to take one of the hourly trips by steam train from Mariefred to Läggesta (see below).

Gripsholm Castle

Lovely though Mariefred village is, it's really only a preface to **Gripsholm Slott** (May–Aug daily 10am–4pm; April & Sept Tues–Sun 10am–3pm; Oct–March Sat & Sun noon–3pm; 50kr), the imposing red-brick castle built on a round island just to the south: walk up the quayside and you'll spot the path to the castle running across the grass by the water's edge.

In the late fourteenth century, Bo Johnsson Grip, the Swedish High Chancellor, began to build a fortified castle at Mariefred, although the present building owes more to two Gustavs – Gustav Vasa, who started rebuilding in the sixteenth century, and Gustav III, who was responsible for major restructuring a couple of centuries later. Rather than the hybrid that might be expected, the result is rather pleasing – a textbook castle, whose turrets, great halls, corridors and battlements provide the material for an engaging tour. On this you'll be shown a vast portrait collection, which includes recently commissioned works of political and cultural figures as well as assorted royalty and nobility; some fine decorative and architectural work; and, as at Drottningholm, a private theatre, built for Gustav III. It's too delicate to use for performances these days, but in summer plays and events take place out in the castle grounds.

Practicalities

Mariefred warrants a night's stay, if not for the sights – which you can exhaust in half a day – then for the pretty, peaceful surroundings. There's only one **hotel**, *Gripsholms Värdhus*, Kyrkogatan 1 (☎0159/130 20, fax 109 74; ⑤), a wonderfully luxurious option overlooking the castle and the water. The seasonal **youth hostel** (☎0159/361 00; 150kr; mid-June to mid-Aug) is beyond the castle in the Red Cross education centre; there are also better-appointed hotel-style double rooms here too (③).

As for **eating**, treat yourself to lunch in *Gripsholms Värdhus*, a beautifully restored inn (the oldest in Sweden). The food is excellent and around 200kr will get you a turn at the herring table, a main course, drink and coffee – all enhanced by the terrific views over to Gripsholm. Alternatively try *Skänken* at the back of the Värdhus, where lunch goes for around 70kr. Or there's the friendly but basic *Mariefreds Bistro*, opposite the castle.

Leaving Mariefred, one option is to take the **narrow-gauge steam train** that leaves roughly hourly from 11am to 5pm (mid-June to mid-Aug daily; May to mid-June & mid-Aug to Sept Sat & Sun; 32kr single, 36kr return) for **Läggesta**, a twenty-minute ride. Here you can pick up the regular SJ train back to Stockholm; check connections on the timetable at the tourist office before you leave. Of course it's also possible to get to Mariefred from Stockholm this way.

Västerås

Around 100km inland from Stockholm, **VÄSTERÅS** (pronounced "Vest-er-ohs"), Sweden's sixth biggest city and capital of the county of Västmanland, is an immediately likeable mix of old and new. Today the lakeside city carefully balances its dependence on industrial technology giant, ABB, with a rich history dating back to Viking times.

Arrival, information and accommodation

The **train** and **bus stations** are located together on Södra Ringvägen, a ten-minute walk through Vasaparken from the **tourist office** at Stora Gatan 40 (mid-June to mid-Aug Mon–Fri 9am–7pm, Sat 9am–3pm, Sun 10am–2pm; mid-Aug to mid-June Mon–Fri 9.30am–6pm, Sat 10am–2pm; ☎021/10 38 30, *info@westmannaturism.se, www .vastmanland.se*). The **youth hostel** (☎021/18 52 30) is 5km west of the city on Lake Mälaren at Lövudden; take bus #25 from the bus station.

Aaros Metro, Vasagatan 22 (☎021/18 03 30, fax 18 03 37). The cheapest hotel in town, and very centrally located. ③/②.

Arkad, Östermalmsgatan 25 (☎021/12 04 80, fax 83 00 50). New building done out in old-fashioned style. Good value for money in summer. ④/②.

Klipper, Kungsgatan 4 (☎021/41 00 00, fax 14 26 70). Centrally located close to the charming Svartån river in the old town. Charming rooms and good service. ④/②.

SAS Plaza, Karlsgatan 9A (☎021/10 10 10, fax 10 10 91). Known locally as the "skyscraper", this 25-storey glass and chrome structure is the last word in Scandinavian chic, and good value in summer. ⑤/③.

Stadshotellet, Stora Torget (☎021/10 28 00, fax 10 28 10). A Västerås fixture, the hotel has been here as long as anyone can remember. Good-quality modern rooms right in the heart of the city. ⑤/③.

The City

From the tourist office, it's a short stroll up Köpmangatan to the twin cobble squares of **Bondtorget** and **Stora Torget**. A narrow lane leads from the southwestern corner of Bondtorget to the narrow **Svartån river** which runs right through the centre of the city; the bridge across it has great views of the old wooden cottages which nestle eave to eave along the riverside. Although it may not appear so significant, the river was a decisive factor in making Västerås the headquarters of one of the world's largest engineering companies, **Asea-Brown-Boveri** (ABB). North of the two main squares is the thirteenth-century brick **Cathedral** (Mon–Fri 8am–5pm, Sat 9.30am–5pm, Sun 9.30am–7pm), last resting place of Erik XIV, who died an unceremonious death in Örbyhus castle in 1577 after eating pea soup laced with arsenic. His tomb lies to the right of the altar; local rumour has it that his feet had to be cut off in order to fit his body into its coffin. Beyond the cathedral is the most charming district of Västerås, **Kyrkbacken**, a hilly area with steep cobblestone alleys winding between well-preserved old wooden houses where the craftsmen and the petit bourgeoisie lived in the 1700s.

A quick walk past the restaurants and shops of Vasagatan will bring you back to Stora Gatan and eventually to the eye-catching modern **city hall**, a far cry from the Dominican monastery which once stood on this spot. Although home to the city's administration, the building is best known for its 47 bells, the largest of which (known as "The Monk") can be heard across the city at lunchtimes. Across Fiskartorget square, the **Castle** is home to an arrestingly dull collection of local paraphernalia contained within the **county museum** (Tues–Sun noon–4pm; free). The best exhibit lies just inside the entrance: a Viking boat grave from nearby Tuna, Badelunda – the richest female burial yet discovered in Sweden.

Eating and drinking

Västerås has easily the best **restaurants** of any town around Lake Mälaren. Here, you'll find every sort of fare, from Thai to Greek, traditional Swedish to British-style pub food. The city also has a lively **drinking** scene, including one cocktail bar 23 floors up, from where there are unsurpassed views of the lake.

Atrium, corner of Smedjegatan and Sturegatan. Greek favourites from 125kr, and starters from 32kr.

Bill o Bob, Stora Torget 5. Handily located in the main square, with all the usual meat and fish dishes, including lunch from 65kr, and outdoor seating in summer.

Bishops Arms, Östra Kyrkogatan. British-style drinking hole with a large selection of beers, single-malt whisky and pub grub.

Brogården, Stora Gatan 42, next to the tourist office. Riverside café with good views of the water and old wooden houses.

Kalle på Spången, Kungsgatan 2. Great old-fashioned café with outdoor seating close to the river. *The* place for coffee, cakes, grilled baguettes and fresh orange juice.

Karlsson på taket, Karlsgatan 9A. Chichi restaurant and café on the 23rd floor of the Skrapan skyscraper, which also houses the *SAS Plaza* hotel. Expensive, but fantastic views.

Kina Thai, Gallerian 36. Chinese and Thai dishes for around 100kr, and lunch for 59kr. Handily located next to the Filmstaden cinema.

Möller Mat o Musik, Kungsgatan 4. Restaurant serving lunch for 59kr and tapas from 80kr before turning into a nightclub later on in the evening.

Piazza di Spagna, Vasagatan 26. The best pizzeria in town and a very popular place for lunch (59kr). Pizzas and pasta from around 70kr; meat dishes start at 170kr.

Around Västerås: the Anundshög burial mound

Anundshög, 6km northeast of the city, is the largest royal burial mound in Sweden. Dating from the sixth-century, it's thought to be the resting place of King Bröt-Anund and the stash of gold with which he was buried. Several other smaller burial mounds are located close by, suggesting that the site was an important Viking meeting place for several centuries. Beside the main mound lie a large number of **standing stones** arranged end to end in the shape of two ships. To get here take bus #12 from the centre of town to its final stop, Bjurhovda, from where it's a walk of around 1km.

Uppsala

First impressions as the train pulls into **UPPSALA**, less than an hour from Stockholm, are encouraging. The red-washed castle looms up behind the railway sidings, the cathedral dominant in the foreground. A sort of Swedish Oxford, Uppsala clings to the past through a succession of striking buildings connected with and scattered about its cathedral and university. Regarded as the historical and religious centre of the country, it serves as a tranquil daytime alternative to Stockholm – with an active student-oriented nightlife.

Arrival, information and accommodation

Uppsala's **train** and **bus stations** are adjacent to each other, and it's not far to walk down to the **tourist office** at Fyris torg 8 (Mon–Fri 10am–6pm, Sat 10am–3pm, also Sun noon–4pm end June to mid-Aug; ☎018/27 48 00, *tb@utkab.se, www.res.till.uppland.nu*), where you can pick up a handy English guide to the town. This is also the place to rent **bikes** (from 60kr per day). **Boats** to and from Stockholm use the pier south of the centre, at the end of Bävernsgränd. If you're flying in or out of Sweden, you can bypass Stockholm entirely by using the #801 bus link between Uppsala bus station and **Arlanda airport** (daily 3.15am–midnight every 15–30min, calling at Terminals 5, 4 and 2; 40min; 75kr).

Accommodation

Though Uppsala can easily be seen as a day-trip from Stockholm, you may want to stay around a little longer. As well as a fair range of central hotels, there's a **youth hostel** at Sunnerstavägen 24 (☎018/32 42 20; 160kr; May–Aug), 6km south of the centre (bus #20, #25 or #50 from Nybron by Stora Torget). For **camping**, head a few kilometres

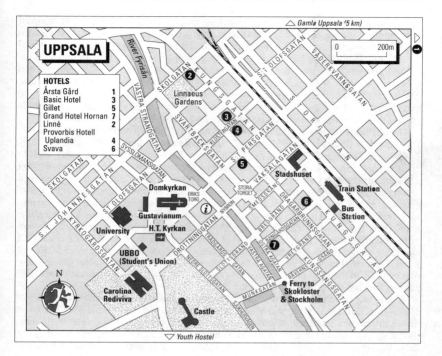

north to the open spaces of Gamla Uppsala (see p.426), or use the regular site at *Sunnersta Camping* by Lake Mälaren in **Graneberg**, 7km from town, near the youth hostel (bus #20).

Årsta Gård, Jordgubbsgatan 14 (☎ & fax 018/25 35 00). This large cottage-style building in the outskirts is the cheapest hotel in town; take bus #7 (daytime) or #56 (evenings) to Södra Årsta (15min). ②.

Basic, Kungsgatan 27 (☎ & fax 018/480 50 00). Simple, bright and clean rooms with en-suite bathrooms and a tiny kitchen. ③.

Gillet, Dragarbrunnsgatan 23 (☎018/15 53 60, fax 15 33 80). A stone's throw from the cathedral but with average, overpriced, shag-piled rooms. Fans of kitsch should head for the restaurant. ⑤/③.

Grand Hotell Hörnan, Bangårdsgatan 1 (☎018/13 93 80, fax 12 03 11). Wonderfully elegant place with large old-fashioned rooms and restaurant. ④/②.

Linné, Skolgatan 45 (☎018/10 20 00, fax 13 75 97). Tiny and completely overpriced rooms – a last resort when everything else is full. ⑤/③.

Provorbis Hotell Uplandia, Dragarbrunnsgatan 32 (☎018/10 21 60, fax 69 61 32). A modern hotel that's gone in for a lot of wood – and small rooms. ⑤/③.

Svava, Bangårdsgatan 24 (☎018/13 00 30, fax 13 22 30). Newly built hotel with all mod-cons, including specially designed rooms for people with disabilities. ⑤/③.

The City

The centre of the medieval town is the great Gothic **Domkyrkan** (daily 8am–6pm; free), Scandinavia's largest cathedral. Built to show the people of Trondheim in Norway that even their mighty church could be overshadowed, it loses out to its competitor by reason of the building material – local brick rather than imported stone – and only the echoing interior remains impressive, particularly the French Gothic ambulatory, sided by tiny chapels and bathed in a golden glow. One chapel contains a lively set of restored fourteenth-century wall paintings that recount the legend of Saint Erik, Sweden's patron saint: his coronation, crusade to Finland, eventual defeat and execution at the hands of the Danes. The Relics of Erik are zealously guarded in a chapel off the nave: poke around and you'll also find the tombs of Reformation rebel Gustav Vasa and his son Johan III, and that of Linnaeus, the botanist, who lived in Uppsala. Time and fire resulted in the rebuilding of the rest of the cathedral, now scrubbed and painted to the extent that it resembles a historical museum more than a thirteenth-century spiritual centre; even the characteristic twin spires are late nineteenth-century additions.

The buildings grouped around the Domkyrkan can all claim a purer historical pedigree. Opposite the towers, the onion-domed **Gustavianum** (mid-May to mid-Sept daily 11am–4pm, Thurs until 7pm; mid-Sept to mid-May Wed–Sun 11am–4pm; 40kr), built in 1625 as part of the university, is much touted by the tourist office for its **Augsburg Art Cabinet**, an ebony treasure chest presented to Gustav II Adolf and its tidily preserved anatomical theatre. The same building houses a couple of small collections of Egyptian, classical and Nordic antiquities, with a small charge for each section. The current **University** building (Mon–Fri 8am–4pm) is the imposing nineteenth-century Renaissance edifice over the way. Originally a seminary, today it's used for lectures and seminars and hosts the graduation ceremonies each May. The more famous of its alumni include Carl von Linné (Linnaeus) and Anders Celsius, inventor of the temperature scale. No one will mind if you stroll in for a quick look, but to see the locked rooms you need to ask in the office inside, to the right of the main entrance (*Vaktmästeriet*), or join a **guided tour** (late June to late Aug daily noon & 2pm; 40kr).

A little way beyond the university is the **Carolina Rediviva** (Mon–Fri 9am–8pm, Sat 10am–4pm, Sun 11am–4pm; mid-May to mid-Sept 10kr, mid-Sept to mid-May free), the university library. On April 30 each year the students meet here to celebrate the first day of spring (usually in the snow), all wearing a traditional student cap, which gives them the appearance of disaffected sailors. This is one of Scandinavia's largest libraries, with around four million books. Adopt a student pose and you can slip in for a wander round and a coffee in the common room. It's also worth taking a look in the **manuscript room**, where there's a collection of rare letters and other paraphernalia. The beautiful sixth-century Silver Bible is on permanent display, as is Mozart's original manuscript for *The Magic Flute*.

After this, the **Castle** (no admission) up on the hill is a disappointment. In 1702 a fire that destroyed three-quarters of the city did away with much of the castle, and only one side and two towers remain of what was once an opulent rectangular palace. But the facade still gives a weighty impression of what's missing, like a backless Hollywood set.

Seeing Uppsala, at least the compact older parts, will take up a good half a day. If the weather holds out, use the rest of your time to stroll along the river that runs right through the centre of town. There are several points worth lingering in and enough greenery to make this stretch more than just pleasant. One beautiful spot is the **Linnaeus Gardens** (daily: May–Aug 9am–9pm; Sept 9am–7pm; voluntary contribution) over the river on Svartbäcksgatan. The university's first botanical gardens, they were relaid by Linnaeus in 1741, and some of the species he introduced and classified still survive. The adjoining **museum** (same times; 20kr) here was once home to Linnaeus and his family and attempts to re-create his life through a partially restored library, writing room and a collection of natural-history specimens.

Gamla Uppsala

Five kilometres to the north of the present city three huge **barrows**, royal burial mounds dating back to the sixth century, mark the original site of Uppsala, **Gamla Uppsala**. This was a pagan settlement, and a place of ancient sacrificial rites. Every ninth year the festival of Fröblot demanded the death of nine people, hanged from a nearby tree until their corpses rotted. The pagan temple where this bloody sacrifice took place is now marked by the Christian **Gamla Uppsala kyrka** (Mon–Fri 8.30am–dusk, Sat & Sun 10am–dusk), built over pagan remains when the Swedish kings were first baptized into the new faith. What survives is only a remnant of what was, originally, a cathedral – look inside for the faded wall paintings and the tomb of Celsius, of thermometer fame. An eleventh-century rune stone is set into the wall outside.

There's little else to Gamla Uppsala, and perhaps that's why the site remains so mysterious and atmospheric. There's an inn nearby, *Odinsborg*, where – especially if you're with kids – you might want to sample the "Viking lunch": a spread of soup, hunks of meat served on a board, and mead, which comes complete with horned helmet, essential equipment if you're considering spending the afternoon pillaging and plundering.

To get to Gamla Uppsala, take **bus** #2 (Mon–Fri every 20min) or #54 (Sat afternoon after 3pm & Sun 6pm–midnight every 30min) from Dragarbrunnsgatan.

Eating, drinking and nightlife

Alexander, Östra Ågatan 59. Completely OTT Greek place with busts of famous personalities from the ancient world at every turn. Lunch deal for 55kr.

Café Katalin, Svartbäcksgatan 19. Reasonably priced veggie food in a similar set-up to *Sten Sture & Co* (see below), and equally popular.

Caroline's, Övre Slottsgatan 12. Cheap pizzeria up by the university, with lunch for 45kr.

Domtrappkälaren, St Eriks Gränd. One of the most chichi places in town – old vaulted roof and great atmosphere. Main courses go for around 200kr, though you can get an excellent lunch upstairs for 60kr.

Elaka Måns, Smedsgränd. A modern bistro-style restaurant with the usual run of fish and meat dishes. Very popular, not too expensive and definitely worth a look.

Fågelsången, Munkgatan 3. Café and lunch place that's full of posey students.

Grisen, Östra Ågatan 11. Very small but oh so trendy restaurant with tiled walls and arty paintings. Moderately priced international fare.

Hambergs fisk o kräft, Fyris Torg 8. Located next to the tourist office and serving very good fish and seafood. Particularly popular at lunchtime.

Kung Krål, Gamla Torget. Across the river from the tourist office in a fantastic old stone building with outdoor seating in summer. Swedish home cooking and international dishes.

Landings, Kungsängsgatan 5. Busy café in the main pedestrian area.

Ofvandahls, Sysslomangatan 3–5. Near the old part of town, this lively café (originally opened in 1878) has old wooden tables and sofas – don't leave town without trying the home-made cakes.

Sten Sture & Co, Nedre Slottsgatan 3. Trendy and inspired cooking at this large, ramshackle wooden house immediately below the castle; there's often live jazz and plenty of young Uppsala folk around. Outdoor tables in summer. A must.

Svenssons åkanten, St Eriks Torg. Outdoor café right by the river; a wonderful place to relax in summer.

Svenssons krog/bakficka, Sysslomangatan 15. A wonderful restaurant decked out in wood and glass with everything from Swedish home cooking to top-class salmon. The cheaper *bakficka* ("back pocket") bar serves good pasta dishes.

Svenssons taverna, Sysslomangatan 14. Large outdoor seating area under the shade of huge beech and oak trees with an international menu and main courses at around 100kr. Recommended.

Wayne's Coffee, Smedgränd 4. The best café in Uppsala – modern and airy with large windows which open right out onto the street.

Nightlife

At night most of the action is generated by the **students** in the "Nations" houses in the grid of streets behind the university, backing onto St Olofsgatan. Not unlike college fraternities, each house organizes dances, gigs and parties of all hues and, most importantly, all boast very cheap bars. The official line is that if you're not a Swedish student you won't get into most of the things advertised around the town; in practice, being foreign and being nice to the people on the door generally yields entrance, while with an ISIC card it's even easier. Since many students stay around during the summer, functions are not strictly limited to term-time. A good choice to begin with is *Uplands Nation*, near the river off St Olofsgatan and Sysslomangatan, which has a summer outdoor café open until 3am.

Otherwise, *Sten Sture & Co* puts on **live bands** in the evenings, while *Café Katalin* is open late and has jazz nights. *Club Dacke* is a student frequented summer-only disco on St Olofsgatan, near the Domkyrkan.

Listings

Banks and exchange Handelsbanken, Vaksalagatan 8; Nordbanken, Stora Torget; SEB, Kungsängsgatan 7–9; Upplandsbanken at the corner of Östra Ågatan and Drottninggatan. There's a Forex exchange at Fyris Torg 8, left of the tourist office (Mon–Fri 8am–7pm, Sat 8am–3pm).

Bus enquiries Uppsalabuss (☎018/27 37 01); city buses leave from Stora Torget; long-distance buses from the bus station adjacent to the train station (see Stockholm "Listings" for phone numbers, p.414).

Car rental Avis, Spikgatan 1 (☎018/10 55 55); Budget, Kungsgatan 80 (☎018/12 43 80); Europcar, Kungsgatan 103 (☎018/17 17 30); Hertz, Kungsgatan 97 (☎018/16 02 00); Statoil, Gamla Uppsalagatan 48 (☎018/20 91 00).

Pharmacy at Bredgränd (Mon–Fri 9am–6.30pm, Sat 10am–3pm).

Police ☎018/16 85 00.

Post office Dragarbrunnsgatan (☎018/17 96 31).

Systembolaget at Svavagallerian (Mon–Wed 10am–6pm, Thurs 10am–7pm, Fri 10am–6.30pm); at Skolgatan 6 (Mon–Wed 10am–6pm, Thurs 10am–7pm, Fri 10am–6.30pm).

Taxis Taxi Direkt (☎018/12 53 60); Taxi Uppsala (☎018/23 90 90).

Train enquiries Information on ☎018/65 22 10.

travel details

Trains

Stockholm to: Boden (2 daily; 14hr); Gällivare (2 daily; 16hr); Gävle (hourly; 1hr 20min); Gothenburg (21 daily; 3hr 10min by X2000, 5hr by Inter-City); Helsingborg (14 daily; 5hr by X2000); Kiruna (2 daily; 17hr); Läggesta (for Mariefred; 32 daily; 45min by X2000); Luleå (2 daily; 14hr); Malmö (11 daily; 4hr 30min by X2000); Mora (11 daily; 3hr 30min by X2000, 5hr by Inter-City); Nynäshamn pendeltåg for ferries to Gotland (hourly; 1hr); Östersund (6 daily; 6hr); Sundsvall (9 daily; 3hr 30min by X2000); Umeå (1 daily; 11hr); Uppsala (50 daily; 40min).

Uppsala to: Gällivare (2 daily; 15hr); Gävle (hourly; 40min); Kiruna (2 daily; 16hr); Luleå (2 daily; 13hr); Mora (11 daily; 2hr 45min by X2000); Östersund (6 daily; 4hr 30 min; Stockholm (50 daily; 40min); Sundsvall (9 daily; 2hr 45 min by X2000); Umeå (1 daily; 10hr).

Buses

Stockholm to: Gävle (1 daily; 2hr 20min); Gothenburg (2 daily Mon–Wed, 3 Thurs, 5 Fri & Sun, 1 Sat; 4hr 30min, or 7hr 20min via Kristinehamn or Jönköping); Halmstad (Fri & Sun 1 daily; 7hr 30min); Helsingborg (1–2 daily except Sat; 8hr); Jönköping (1–2 daily except Sat; 4hr 50min); Kalmar (5 daily; 6hr 30min); Kristianstad (4 weekly; 9hr 30min); Kristinehamn (2–3 daily; 3hr); Malmö (Fri & Sun 1–2 daily; 10hr 20min); Norrköping (2 daily Mon–Wed, 3 Thurs, 5 Fri & Sun, 1 Sat; 2hr); Östersund (1 daily; 8hr 30min); Sollefteå (1 daily; 8hr 15min); Umeå (1 daily; 9hr 20min).

International trains

Stockholm to: Copenhagen (16 daily; 7hr); Narvik (2 daily; 20hr); Oslo (2 daily; 6hr 30min); Trondheim (1 daily; 10hr 30min).

International ferries

Nynäshamn to: Gdansk (3 weekly; 19hr).

Stockholm to: Eckerö on the Åland Islands (3–5 daily; 3hr); Helsinki (1 Viking Line and 1 Silja Line daily; 15hr); Tallinn (1 daily; 13hr); Turku (4 daily; 11–12hr).

CHAPTER TEN

GOTHENBURG AND AROUND

Gothenburg is Sweden's second city and the largest seaport in Scandinavia – facts that have been enough to persuade many travellers arriving here by ferry to move quickly on to the surrounding countryside. But beyond the gargantuan shipyards, Gothenburg's Dutch-designed cityscape of broad avenues, elegant squares, trams and canals is one of the prettiest in Sweden, and with its burgeoning café society and rich cultural life it's worth a lot more time than most visitors give it. The city's image has also suffered from the inevitable comparisons with the capital, and while there is a certain resentment on the west coast that Stockholm wins out in the national prestige stakes, many Swedes far prefer Gothenburg's more relaxed atmosphere and its closer proximity to Western Europe, particularly now that a new rail link has put it within three hours of Copenhagen.

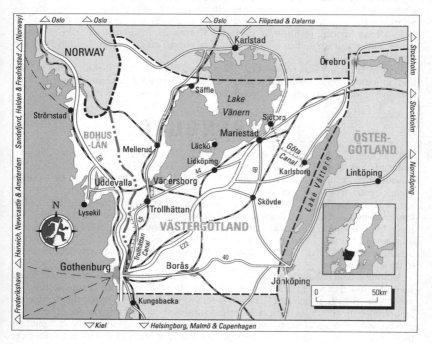

ACCOMMODATION PRICE CODES

The hotels and guesthouses listed in this chapter have been graded according to the following price bands, based on the cost of the **least expensive double room during high season** (late June to Aug). However, almost every hotel offers seasonal and/or weekend discounts, and wherever possible we've given two grades, covering both the regular and the discounted rate.

① Under 500kr	② 500–700kr	③ 700–900kr
④ 900–1200kr	⑤ 1200–1500kr	⑥ Over 1500kr

The counties to the north and east of the city are prime targets for domestic tourists. The closest highlight to Gothenburg is the glorious fortress island of Marstrand, an easy and enjoyable day-trip from Gothenburg, while heading towards Norway, the uninhabited islands, tiny fishing villages and clean beaches of the craggy Bohuslän coastline attract thousands of holiday-makers. To the northeast of city, the vast and beautiful lakes of Vänern and Vättern provide the setting for a number of historic towns, fairytale castles and some splendid scenery, all within an hour's train journey from Gothenburg. The lakes are connected to each other (and to the east and west coasts) by the cross-country Göta Canal, and if you're inspired by the possibilities of water transport you could always make the complete four-day trip by boat from Gothenburg to Stockholm. The first leg of the journey is from the sea up the Trollhättan Canal to Trollhättan, an appealing little town built around the canal and a good place to aim for if you only have time for a short trip out from the city. Beyond here, though, other agreeable lakeside towns vie for your attention, with attractions including the elk safaris on the ancient hills of Halleberg and Hunneberg, near **Vänersborg** at the bottom of Lake Vänern, picturesque medieval **Mariestad**, further up the lake's eastern shore, and the huge military fortress at **Karlsborg**, on the western shore of Lake Vättern.

Regular **train** and **bus** services run across most of the region; the only area you may find difficult to explore without a car is the Bohuslän coast. **Accommodation** is never a problem, with plenty of hotels, hostels and camping sites in each town.

GOTHENBURG

With its long history as a trading centre, **GOTHENBURG** (Göteborg in Swedish, pronounced "Yur-te-boy") is a truly cosmopolitan city. Founded on its present site in the seventeenth century by Gustav Adolf, it was the last in a long line of attempts to create a trade centre free from Danish influence – Denmark had enjoyed control of Sweden's west coast since the Middle Ages, extracting extortionate tolls from all water traffic travelling into Sweden. An original medieval settlement was sited 40km up the Göta River, but was later moved to a location north of the present city in order to avoid these tolls; a third attempt was built on the island of Hisingen, but this fell to the Danes during the battle of Kalmar. Six years later Gustav Adolf founded a new city on the site of today's main square.

Although Gothenburg's reputation as an industrial and trading centre has been severely eroded in recent years – as evidenced by the stillness of the cranes in the shipyards – the British, Dutch and German traders who settled here during the eighteenth and nineteenth centuries left a rich architectural and cultural inheritance. The city is graced with terraces of grand merchant houses, all carved stone, stucco and painted tiles, while the trade between Sweden and the Far East brought an Oriental influence, still visible in the chinoiserie detail on many buildings. This vital trading route was monopolized for over eighty years by the hugely successful Swedish East India Company, whose auction house, selling exotic spices, tea and fine cloth, attracted merchants from all over the world.

Today the city remains a regular port of call for business travellers, though the flashy central hotels that accommodate them say much less about Gothenburg than the restrained opulence of the older buildings, which reflect not only the city's bygone prosperity but also the understatement of its citizens. Gothenburgers may give you the impression they think their surroundings are nothing special, but don't be taken in – they are immensely proud of their elegant city and simply exhibiting a typical Gothenburg modesty.

Arrival and information

From **Landvetter airport**, 25km east of the city, Flygbuss buses run every fifteen minutes via Korsvagan, a junction to the south of the centre, to Central Station. The journey takes around 35 minutes (daily 5am–11.15pm; 45kr, Gothenburg Card not valid). For airline and airport information numbers, see p.445.

All **trains** arrive at Central Station, on Drottningtorget in the centre of the city. There's a Swebus office here too (Mon–Fri 7am–6pm, Sat & Sun 10.30am–6pm; ☎031/10 32 85), where you can buy bus tickets for services to Oslo which stop outside. Otherwise, **buses** to and from destinations north of Gothenburg use **Nils Ericsonsplatsen** (ticket office Mon–Fri 7.30am–5.45pm, Sat 8am–2pm), just behind the train station. Buses from the south arrive at the **Heden** terminal, at the junction of Parkgatan and Sodra Vagen, from where there are easy tram connections to all parts of the city.

DFDS Seaways **ferries** from Newcastle (2 weekly) arrive at Skandiahamn on Hisingen, north of the river (☎031/650 650, fax 53 23 09); special buses shuttle from here to Nils Ericsonsplatsen behind the train station in the city centre (40kr, Gothenburg Card not valid). When leaving, buses return to Skandiahamn from Gate 38 of Nils Ericsonsplatsen ninety minutes before sailings. All DFDS Seaways tickets can be bought through SeaCat (see below). Stena Line ferries from Frederikshavn in Denmark (tickets from their office in the Nordstan Centre, see p.446) dock at a quay twenty minutes' walk or a tram (#3 or #9) ride from the city centre, while those from Kiel in Germany dock 3km outside Gothenburg – take bus #491 or tram #3 or #9 into the centre. Heading back to Germany, Stena Line runs a special bus from Ericsonsplatsen at 5.50pm in time for the 7pm crossing.

SeaCat, with a booking office in Nordstan Centre (☎031/12 60 90, fax 720 08 50), runs high-speed boats to Frederickshavn in Denmark throughout the year.

Information

Gothenburg has two **tourist offices**. Handiest for new arrivals is the **kiosk** in Nordstan, the indoor shopping centre near Central Station (Mon–Fri 9.30am–6pm, Sat 10am–4pm, Sun noon–3pm). The **main office** is on the canalfront at Kungsportsplatsen 2 (May Mon–Fri 9am–6pm, Sat & Sun 10am–2pm; June & mid- to late Aug daily 9am–6pm; July to mid-Aug daily 9am–8pm; Sept–April Mon–Fri 9am–5pm, Sat 10am–2pm; ☎031/61 25 00, fax 61 25 01, *turistinfo@gbg.co.se*). From the train station, it's five minutes' walk across Drottningtorget and down Stora Nygatan: the tourist office is on the right, opposite the statue of the so-called "Copper Mare" (see p.438). Both offices provide information, free city and tram maps, restaurant and museum listings, and offer a room-booking service, as well as selling the Gothenburg Card.

GOTHENBURG

HOTELS
Alleyn	6
City	9
City Ritz	1
Eggers	3
Europa	2
Excelsior	7
Hotel II	10
Lilton	11
Maria Eriksson	8
Robinson	5
SAS Radisson Scandinavia	4

N

HISINGEN

Docks

Stenpiren

Boats to
Elfsborg Fortress

Göta River

Frederikshavn

Stena Line
Terminal

Feskekörkan
('Fish Church')

Fiskhamnen

ANDREEGATAN

Masthuggsterrassen
Youth Hostel

MAST-
HUGGSTORGET

FÖRSTA LÄNGGATAN

JÄRN-
TORGET

SÖDRA

HAGA

HAGA ÖSTER-

HAGA NYGATAN

ANDRA LÄNGGATAN

TREDJE LÄNGGATAN

LINNÉ

PILGATAN

OSKARSLEDEN

BANGÅRD

FJÄLLGATAN

Slottskogens
Youth Hostel

LÅNGSVÄGGATAN

LINNÉGATAN

Skansparken

SKANS-
TORGET

Military
Museum

JUNGMANSGATAN

VEGAGATAN

ÖVRE HUSARGATAN

ROSENGATAN

Natural
History
Museum

Slottskogen

Stena Line Terminal for Kiel, Klippan & Saltholmen & Bay Centre

10

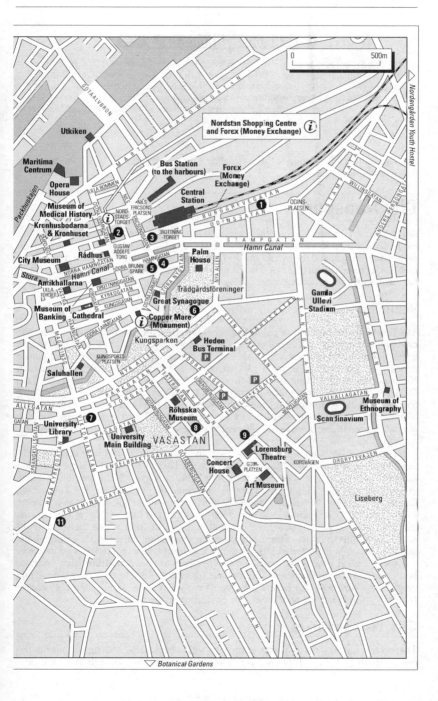

0   500m

Nordengården Youth Hostel

Nordstan Shopping Centre
and Forex (Money Exchange) (i)

Utkiken

Maritima
Centrum

Opera
House

Museum of
Medical History

Kronhusbodarna
& Kronhuset

City Museum

Rådhus

Stora
Antikhallarna

Museum of
Banking   Cathedral

Saluhallen

University
Library

University
Main Building

Packhuskajen

GÖTAÄLVBRON

MÄRTEN KRAKOWSGATAN

LILLA BOMMEN

NILS

DROTTNINGGATAN

Bus Station
(to the harbours)

Forex
(Money
Exchange)

Central
Station

NILS-
ERICSONS-
PLATSEN

NORD-
STADS-
TORGET

DROTTNING-
TORGET

GUSTAV
ADOLFS
TORG

NORRA HAMNGATAN

Hamn Canal

SÖDRA BRUNN
SPARK

VASTRA

LILLA
TORGET

KUNGSGATAN

DROTTNINGGATAN

KYRKOGATAN

SÖDRA LARMGATAN

MAGASINS

HAMNGATAN

KUNGSPORTS
PLATSEN

Palm
House

Trädgårdsföreninger

Great Synagogue

Copper Mare
(Monument)

Kungsparken

Heden
Bus Terminal
P

NYA ALLÉN

PAREGATAN

STORGATAN

GÖTEBORGSGATAN

ALLÉGATAN

GATAN

SPRANGKULLSGATAN

HAGA KYRKGATAN

VASAGATAN

KRIAGATAN

ENGELBREKTSGATAN

FÖRENINGSGATAN

BURGGREVEGATAN

ODINSGATAN

ODINS-
PLATSEN

STAMPGATAN

Hamn Canal

STAMPGATAN

NYA ALLÉN

STEN STURESGATAN

ENGELBREKTSGATAN

VANGANGATAN

Gamla
Ullevi
Stadium

ÅVÄGEN

VALLAALLAGATAN

P

Röhsska
Museum

VASASTAN

Concert
House

Lorensburg
Theatre

GÖTA-
PLATSEN

KORSVÄGEN

Art Museum

Museum of
Ethnography

Scandinavium

ÖRGRYTEVÄGEN

Liseberg

SÖDRA

1
2
3
4
5
6
7
8
9
11

ST

WILLINSGATAN

ANDERS PERSONS GAT.

(i)

▽ Botanical Gardens

THE GOTHENBURG CARD

Buying a **Gothenburg Card** (Göteborgskortet) is a good money-saver if you're planning to do a lot of sightseeing. Available from both tourist offices, Pressbyrån kiosks and hotels, it gives unlimited bus and tram travel within the city, free entry to most of the city museums and the Liseberg Amusement Park (not including rides), free car parking (see below) and boat excursions, plus various other reductions. The card is valid for 24 hours and costs 75kr.

You can also pick up a copy of the fortnightly *Göteborg What's On*, which contains just that in Swedish and English.

City transport

Apart from excursions north of the river or to the islands, almost everywhere of interest in Gothenburg is within easy walking distance of the centre. The wide streets are pedestrian-friendly and the canals and grid layout of the avenues makes orientation simple. If you're staying further out, however, some sort of transport may be necessary. A free **transport map** (*Linje Kartan*) is available from either tourist office.

Public transport

The most convenient form of public transport are the **trams**, which clunk around the city and its outskirts on a colour-coded, eight-line system, passing all the central areas every few minutes – you can tell at a glance which line a tram is on as the route colour appears on the front. The main pick-up points are outside Central Station and in Kungsportsplatsen. During summer, there's the chance to ride on vintage trams from 1902, which trundle through the city centre to Liseberg and Slottskogen. Gothenburg also has a fairly extensive **bus** network, using much the same routes as the trams, although central pedestrianization can lead to some odd and lengthy detours. You shouldn't need to use them in the city centre; routes are detailed in the text where necessary.

If you have a Gothenburg Card, all public transport within the city is free; if not, **tickets** should be bought from tram and bus drivers. There's no zonal system and adult fares cost a flat-rate 16kr. If you're staying for a couple of days, it's cheaper to buy a ticket card from the Tidpunkten (travel information) offices at Brunnsparken, Drottningtorget and Nils Ericsonsplatsen, or from Pressbyrån kiosks – a ten-trip ticket card costs 100kr. Stick these in the machines on a tram or bus, and press twice for an adult, once for a child. Trams run from 5am to midnight, after which there is a night service at double the price. **Fare-dodging** carries an instant fine of 600kr – since all the ticket information is posted in English at bus and tram stops, ignorance is no defence.

Finally, a good way to get to grips with the city is to take a **paddan boat tour**, an hour-long trip around the canals and harbour (daily: late April to early Aug 10am–9pm; early Aug to mid-Sept 10am–5pm; mid-Sept to early Oct noon–3pm; 75kr). Tours leave regularly from moorings on the canal by Kungsportsplatsen.

Cars, taxis and bikes

There's no shortage of **car parks** in the city, with a basic tariff of 20kr per hour in the centre. Buying a Gothenburg Card gets you a free parking card, though this is not valid in privately run or multistorey car parks, or in any car park with attendants. The most useful car parks are the new Ullevigarage at Heden, near the bus terminal, the Lorensbergs near Avenyn, Gamla Ullevi on Alleyn, south of Kungsportsplatsen, and two multistorey car parks at Nordstan near Central Station and Garda-Focus close to Liseberg. The Gothenburg Card is valid in all of these; if you don't have a Gothenburg Card, roadside parking areas marked with blue signs are cheaper than parking meters. Some of the larger hotels offer a discount at the multistorey car parks. For information on **car rental** see p.367.

Taxis can be summoned by calling ☎031/65 00 00. There is a 20 percent reduction for women travelling at night, but check with the driver first.

Cycling is a popular and easy way to get around, since Gothenburg boasts a comprehensive series of cycle lanes and plenty of bike racks. The most central place to **rent a bike** (around 150kr per day) is Millennium Cykel at Chalmersgatan 19 (☎031/18 43 00), just south of Avenyn. You can also rent older bikes from either Slottsskogen or Stigbergssliden youth hostels (see p.434) for just 50kr per day. An excellent *Cykelcarte*, showing all cycle routes through the city and out to the archipelago, is also available from the tourist office.

Accommodation

Gothenburg has plenty of decent accommodation options, with no shortage of comfortable **youth hostels**, a couple of which are very central, along with **private rooms** and a number of big, city-centre **hotels**. Most of these are clustered together around the train station and offer a high standard of service, if with fairly uniform and uninspiring decor. Summer and weekend reductions mean that even the better hotels can prove surprisingly affordable, and most places also take part in the **Gothenburg Package**, which can cut costs further (see below).

Whenever you turn up, you shouldn't have any trouble finding accommodation, though in summer it's a good idea to book ahead if you're aiming to stay in one of the cheaper hotels, or in the most popular youth hostels.

Hotels and pensions

The **Gothenburg Package** scheme, co-ordinated by the tourist office, is a real bargain, as it bundles together accommodation, breakfast and a Gothenburg Card for 390kr per person in a twin bedroom, with discounts for children sharing. Around thirty good central hotels take part in the scheme, which operates every Friday to Monday from early June to the end of August, on all major holidays, winter sports holidays and over Christmas. In some hotels it's valid on Thursdays and in others all year round. At the time of writing all the hotels listed below were involved in the Gothenburg Package, and all include breakfast in the price unless otherwise stated. Note that bookings for the Gothenburg Package have to be made through the tourist office; you can't get this offer by contacting the hotels direct.

Alleyn, Parkgatan 10 (☎031/10 14 50, fax 11 91 60). Very central, sensibly priced hotel close to Avenyn and the old town. Price includes room service and parking. ③/②.

City, Lorensbergsgatan 6 (☎031/708 40 00, fax 708 40 02). Not to be confused with *City Hotel Ritz* (see below), this is a cheapish and popular place, excellently positioned close to Avenyn. For en-suite rooms you'll pay 300kr more. ①.

City Hotel Ritz, Burggrevegatan 25 (☎031/80 00 80, fax 15 77 76). Comfortable hotel close to Central Station; en-suite rooms with cable TV, plus a free sauna and solarium (30kr). ③.

Eggers, Drottningtorget (☎031/80 60 70, fax 15 42 43). The original station hotel, this very characterful establishment has individually furnished bedrooms and a wealth of grand original features.

One of the best-value central hotels, especially if you stay here using the Gothenburg Package. ⑤/④.

Europa, Köpmansgatan 38 (☎031/80 12 80, fax 15 47 55). Reputedly the biggest hotel in Sweden, with 460 rooms and a massive facade attached to the Nordstan shopping centre. Very plush, huge breakfast, and all rooms are en suite with bath tubs. ⑥/③.

Excelsior, Karl Gustavsgatan 9 (☎031/17 54 35, fax 17 54 39). Shabbily stylish 1880 building in a road of classic Gothenburg houses between Avenyn and Haga. It's been a hotel since 1930 and both Greta Garbo and Ingrid Bergman stayed here, as did, more recently, Sheryl Crow. Classic suites with splendid nineteenth-century features cost no more than plain rooms – Garbo's room was no. 535. ④/②.

Hotel 11, Maskingatan 11 (☎031/779 11 11, fax 779 11 10). At the harbour on the site of an old ship-building yard, with views across to Hisingen, this is one of the city's most interesting and stylish places to stay. Take tram #1, #3, #4 or #9 from Järntorget, then the *Älv Snabben* boat (Mon–Fri 6am–11.30pm every 30min, shorter hours on weekends; 16kr, free with Gothenburg Card), in the direction of Klippan from in front of the Opera House at Lilla Bommen – get off at Eriksberg. ⑤/③.

Lilton, Föreningsgatan 9 (☎031/82 88 08, fax 82 21 84). One of Gothenburg's more hidden bed and breakfast hotels, close to the Haga district, this is a small, old, ivy-covered place set among trees with very friendly service. Price includes breakfast. ③/②.

Maria Erikssons Pensionat, Chalmersgatan 27A (☎031/20 70 30, fax 16 64 63). Just ten rooms, but well positioned on a road running parallel with Avenyn. Breakfast not included. ①.

Robinson, Södra Hamngatan 2 (☎031/80 25 21, fax 15 92 91). Facing Brunnspark, this mediocre hotel still boasts its original facade – the building was part of the old Furstenburg Palace (see p.437). Original etched windows on the lift are some of the few features to have survived decades of architectural meddling. All rooms have cable TV; en-suite rooms cost 160kr more. ②.

SAS Radisson Scandinavia, Södra Hamngatan 59–65 (☎031/80 60 00, fax 15 98 88). Opposite the train station and exuding all the usual glitz: the atrium foyer is like a shopping mall with glass lifts and fountains; bedrooms are all pastel shades and birch wood. ⑥/④.

Youth hostels and private rooms

The cheapest accommodation options are either a **private room** (175kr per person in a double, 225kr for a single), bookable through the tourist office (☎031/61 25 00; 60kr booking fee), or a bed in one of the **youth hostels**. All the hostels listed below are run by the STF and are open all year unless otherwise stated. For stays of a week or more, consider renting out a furnished room with a kitchen through SGS Bostader, Utlandgatan 24 (Mon–Fri 11am–3pm); a week's rental costs around 1200kr.

Karralunds Vandrarhem, Olbergsgatan (☎031/84 02 00, fax 84 05 00). Four kilometres from the centre, close to Liseberg Amusement Park – take tram #5 to Welandergatan, direction Torp. Non-smoking rooms available, plus cabins and a campsite (see opposite). Breakfast can only be ordered by groups; book ahead in summer.

Kviberg Vandrarhem, Kvibergsvägen 5 (☎031/43 50 55, fax 43 26 50). In Gamlestad, ten minutes by tram #6 or #7 from Central Station.

Masthuggsterrassen, Masthuggsterassen 8 (☎ & fax 031/42 48 20). A couple of minutes' walk from the Stena Line ferry terminal from Denmark.

M/S Seaside, Packhuskajen (☎031/10 59 70, fax 12 23 69). A moored ship at the harbour next to Maritima Centrum, with twenty cabins sleeping one to four. Single cabins cost 250kr; breakfast and sheets extra. Open April–Sept.

Partille, Landvettervagen, Partille (☎031/44 65 01, fax 44 61 63). Fifteen kilometres east of the city (bus #513 from Heden bus terminal; 30min), this hostel has a solarium and day room with TV.

Slottskogen, Vegagatan 21 (☎031/42 65 20, fax 14 21 02). Superbly appointed, family-run hostel, just two minutes' walk from Linnegatan and not far from Slottskogen Park. Take tram #1 or #2 to Olivedahlsgatan.

Stigbergssliden, Stigbergssliden 10 (☎031/24 16 20, fax 24 65 20). Excellent hostel, well placed for ferries to Denmark, being just west of the Linné area down Först Långgatan. All rooms have basins, disabled access, laundry facilities (20kr) and pleasant back courtyard.

Torrekulla, Kallered (☎031/795 14 95, fax 795 51 40). Pleasantly situated hostel, 15km south of the city, with lots of room, a free sauna and a nearby bathing lake. Bus #705 from Heden or a ten-minute train journey from Central Station, then a fifteen-minute walk.

Campsites and cabins

Two of the following campsites also provide **cabins**, which are worth considering, especially if there are more than two of you. Facilities are invariably squeaky clean and in good working order – there's usually a well-equipped kitchen too – but you'll have to pay extra for bedding. Prices for cabins are given below; if you want to **camp**, you'll pay around 100kr for two people in July or August (50kr the rest of the year).

Askims (☎031/28 62 61, fax 68 13 35). Set beside sandy beaches 12km from the centre: take tram #1 or #2 to Linneplatsen, then bus #83, or the Blo Express (Blue Express; direction Saro) from outside Central Station on Drottningtorget. Open May–Aug (office daily 9am–noon & 3–6pm, slightly later Thurs–Sat); four-bed cabins cost 615kr in high season, 495kr in low.

Karralunds Vandrarhem, Olbergsgatan (☎031/84 02 00, fax 84 05 00). Four kilometres from the centre, close to Liseberg Amusement Park – take tram #5 to Welandergatan, direction Torp. Set among forest and lakes, it's open all year; four-bed cabins cost 615kr; 695kr with your own toilet (50kr discount outside June–Aug).

Lilleby Havsbad (☎031/56 50 66, fax 56 16 05). Take bus #21 from Nils Ericsonsplatsen and change to the #23 at Kongshallavagen. It takes an hour to reach, but has a splendid seaside location.

The City

Everything of interest in Gothenburg lies south of the **Göta River**, and there's rarely any need to cross the water. This is a fairly compact city, and easy to get around, so you can cover most of the sights in just a day or two, although to get the most from your stay give the city a few more days and slow your pace down to a stroll – which will put you in step with the locals.

At the heart of the city is the historic **old town**, and while Gothenburg's attractions are by no means restricted to this area, its picturesque elegance makes it the best place to start. Tucked between the Göta River to the north and the zigzagging canal to the south, old Gothenburg's tightly gridded streets are lined with impressive facades and boast an interesting food market and a couple of worthwhile museums – the **City Museum** and, up by the harbour, the museum of **maritime history**. Just across the canal that skirts the southern edges of the old town is **Trädgårdsforeningen** park, in summer full of picnicking Gothenburgers.

Heading further south into the modern centre, **Avenyn** is Gothenburg's showcase boulevard, alive with showy restaurants and bars. However, it's the roads off Avenyn that hold the area's real interest, with trendy 24-hour café-bars and some of Gothenburg's best museums: in a small area called **Vasastan** to the southwest, you'll find the **Röhsska Museum** of applied arts and, further south in **Götaplatsen**, the city **Art Museum**. For family entertainment day or night, the famous **Liseberg Amusement Park**, just to the southeast of Avenyn, has been pulling in the crowds since the 1920s.

Vasaplan stretches west to **Haga**, the city's old working-class district now thoroughly gentrified and fashionable. Haga Nygatan, the main thoroughfare, leads on to Linnegatan, the arterial road through the **Linné** district. Fast establishing itself as the most vibrant part of the city, Linné is home to the most interesting evening haunts, with new cafés, bars and restaurants opening up alongside long-established antique emporiums and sex shops. Further out, the rolling **Slottskogen** park holds the **Natural History Museum**, but is perhaps most appealing as a place to relax and enjoy the sun.

The old town and harbour

The **old town** is divided in two by the **Stora Hamn Canal**, to the north of which are most of the main sights and the harbour, where the decaying shipyards make for a dramatic backdrop. The streets south of the Stora Hamn, stretching down to the zigzagging southern canal, are perfect for an afternoon's leisurely stroll, with some quirky cafés, food markets and junk shops to dip into, as well as Sweden's oldest synagogue. Straddling the Stora Hamn is Gothenburg's main square, **Gustav Adolfs Torg**, the best place to start your explorations.

North of the Stora Hamn

At the centre of stately **Gustav Adolfs Torg**, a copper statue of the city's founder, Gustav Adolf, points ostentatiously at the ground where he reputedly declared "Here I will build my city." The statue is a copy, however: the German-made original was kidnapped on its way to Sweden and Gothenburgers commissioned a new one rather than pay the ransom.

To the east of the square, with the canal behind you, stands the **Rådhus**. Beyond its rather dull classical colonnaded facade, the interior of its extension was designed by the innovative functionalist architect E.G. Asplund in 1936 and retains its original glass lifts, mussel-shaped drinking fountains and huge areas of laminated aspen. Facing the canal, at right angles to the Rådhus, is the white, double-columned 1842 **Borhuset**, the former stock exchange. If you can persuade the attendants to let you in, you'll be rewarded with magnificent banqueting and concert halls, and smaller rooms with a riot of red and blue stucco inspired by the eighteenth-century excavations at Pompeii.

Head north from the square along the filled-in canal of Östra Hamngatan, past the amorphous **Nordstan Shopping Centre**, Sweden's biggest. Despite several attempts to jazz it up, it remains a depressingly bland complex, although you might venture inside to visit the tourist kiosk or one of the ferry company offices which it houses. If you have time to spare, it's worth taking a short detour along Burggrevegatan to Drottningtorget to see the city's impressive **Central Station**. The oldest in the country, dating from 1856, behind its original facade is a grand and marvellously preserved interior. Look out for the wood beam-ends in the ticket hall, each one carved into the likeness of a city council member of the day.

At its far end, Ostra Hamngatan runs into **Lilla Bommen**. Here Gothenburg's industrial decline comes together with its artistic regeneration to dramatic visual effect: to the west, the cranes of dormant shipyards loom across the sky, a backdrop to industrial-themed sculptures in bronze and pink granite dotted along the waterfront. The new **Opera House** (daily noon–6pm; guided tours ☎031/10 80 50; performance information on ☎031/13 13 00) to the left was designed with conscious industrial styling. To the right, **Utkiken** ("Look out"; mid-May to Aug daily 11am–7pm; Jan to mid-May & Sept to mid-Dec Sat & Sun 11am–4pm; 25kr), designed by the Scottish architect Ralph Erskine in the late 1980s, is an 86-metre-high office block taking the form of a half-used red lipstick. Its top storey offers panoramic views of the city and harbour.

Just west along the quay is the **Maritima Centrum** (Mon–Fri 9am–5pm, Sat & Sun 10am–5pm; 45kr, free with Gothenburg Card), which describes itself as "the largest ship museum in the world". An interesting experience, even for non-enthusiasts, it comprises a dozen boats including a 1915 lightship, a submarine and a fire float, each giving a glimpse of how seamen lived and worked on board. The original toilets and washrooms on board, for public use, are an experience in themselves. There's also a rather good café and restaurant here too.

From the maritime museum it's a short walk south to Gothenburg's oldest secular building, the **Kronhuset** on Kronhusgatan (Tues–Fri 11am–4pm, Sat & Sun 11am–5pm; free). Built by the Dutch in 1642 as an artillery depot for the city's garrison, this was where the five-year-old Karl XI was proclaimed king in 1660. Set in the eighteenth-century wings that flank the original building is the **Kronhusbodarna** (Mon–Fri 11am–4pm, Sat 11am–2pm), a cluster of small, pricey shops specializing in gold, silver and glasswork. You can buy a copy of the city's oldest key from the silversmith here, but your money would be better spent at the atmospheric vaulted café.

A couple of blocks further south, the **City Museum** (Stadsmuseum: May–Aug daily 11am–4pm; Sept–April Tues–Sun 11am–4pm, Wed to 8pm; 40kr) has emerged, after an extensive reshuffling of the city's collections, as Gothenburg's primary museum. Located at Norra Hamngatan 12, it's housed in Ostindiska Huset, the offices, store and auction house that were constructed in 1750 for the enormously influential **Swedish East India Company**. Granted sole Swedish rights to trade with China in 1731, the company monopolized Far East commerce for over eighty years, the only condition being that the spices, silk and porcelain it brought back were to be sold in Gothenburg. The museum itself is well worth a browse, not least for its rich interior, a mix of stone pillars, stained glass and frescoes. Head first to the third floor, where there are exhibitions on the East India Company, allowing a look at the renovated auction hall. The section devoted to industry is also impressive, a well-designed exhibition relating Gothenburg's twentieth-century history with displays on shipping and working conditions in the textile factories at the beginning of the century.

South of the Stora Hamn

Across Stora Hamn just to the west of the Stadsmuseum lies **Lilla Torget**, with its statue of Jonas Alstromer, who introduced the potato to Sweden in the eighteenth century. Walk on to the quayside at **Stenpiren**, the spot where hundreds of emigrants said their last goodbyes before sailing off to the United States. The original granite **Delaware Monument** was carted off to America in the early twentieth century, and it wasn't until 1938 that celebrated sculptor Carl Mille cast a replacement in bronze, which stands here looking out to sea.

Today, boats leave Stenpiren for the popular excursion to the island fortress of **Nya Elfsborg** (early May to Aug hourly 9.30am–3pm; 75kr, free with Gothenburg Card), a twenty-minute ride from the city. Built in the seventeenth century to defend the harbour and the city, the surviving buildings have been turned into a **museum** and café. There are guided tours in English (included in the price of the boat trip) around the square tower, chapel and prison cells.

Back at Lilla Torget, walk down Västra Hamngatn, which leads off the southern side of the square, to the city's cathedral; on the way you'll pass **Antik Hallarna** (Mon–Fri 10am–6pm, Sat 10am–2pm), a clutch of pricey antique shops set in a fantastic building with a gilded ceiling and regal marble stairs leading up to a café. A few blocks south of here, to the left off Västra Hamngatan, is the classically styled **Cathedral** (Mon–Fri 8am–5pm, Sat 8am–3pm, Sun 10am–3pm). Built in 1827 (the two previous cathedrals were destroyed by fires at a rate of one a century), four giant sandstone columns stand at the portico, and inside there's an opulent gilded altarpiece. The plain white walls concentrate the eye on the unusual post-Resurrection cross, devoid of a Jesus, whose gilded grave clothes are strewn below. Another quirky feature are the twin glassed-in verandas that run down either side, designed for the bishop's "private conversations".

Continuing east past the cathedral and north towards Stora Hamn canal, the leafy square known as **Brunnspark** soon comes into view, with Gustav Adolfs Torg just across the canal. The sedate house facing the square (now a snazzy restaurant and nightclub called *The Palace*) was once home to Pontus and Gothilda Furstenburg, the city's leading arts patrons in the late nineteenth century, who converted the top floor into an art gallery, the first in Gothenburg's to be lit with electric as well as natural light. They later donated their entire collection – the biggest batch of Nordic paintings in the country – to the city Art Museum. As a tribute to the Furstenburgs, the museum has made over the top floor into an exact replica of the original gallery (see opposite) – you can still wander upstairs and see the richly ornate plasterwork and gilding much as it was.

Along the southern canal

Following the zigzagging canal that marks the southern perimeter of old Gothenburg – a moat during the days when the city was fortified – makes for a fine twenty-minute stroll, past pretty waterside views and a number of interesting diversions.

Just east of Brunnspark, **Stora Nygatan** wends its way south along the canal's most scenic stretch, with classical buildings stuccoed in cinnamon and cream on one side, and the green expanse of Trädgårdsföreningen park on the other (see below). Among all the architectural finery sits mainland Sweden's oldest synagogue, the **Great Synagogue**, inaugurated in 1855. This simple domed structure hides one of the most exquisite interiors of any European synagogue: the ceiling and walls are a rich mixture of blues, reds and gold, with Moorish patterns stunningly interwoven with Viking leaf designs. Security concerns mean that it can only be visited on a tour – call ☎031/17 72 45.

Heading south from the synagogue, you'll pass **Kungsportsplatsen**, in the centre of which stands a useful landmark, a sculpture known as the "Copper Mare" – though whoever gave it its name obviously didn't see it from below. Also on the square is the main tourist office. A few minutes further on, and a block in from the canal at Kungstorget (the square adjacent to Kungsportsplatsen), is **Saluhallen** (Mon–Fri 9am–6pm, Sat 9am–2pm), a pretty, barrel-roofed indoor market built in the 1880s. Busy and full of atmosphere, it's a great place to wander around; there's a flower market outside.

Five minutes from here is another food market, the neo-Gothic **Feskekörkan**, or "Fish Church" (Tues–Thurs 9am–5pm, Fri 9am–6pm, Sat 9am–1.30pm). Despite its undeniably ecclesiastical appearance, the nearest this 1874 building comes to religion is in the devotion shown by the fish lovers who come to buy and sell here. Inside, every kind of fish lies in gleaming, pungent mounds of silver, pink and black flesh; there's a very small, very good restaurant in a gallery upstairs (see p.441).

Avenyn and around

Across the canal bridge from Kungsportplatsen, the wide cobbled length of Kungportsavenyn runs all the way southeast to Götaplatsen. Known more simply as **Avenyn**, this is the city's liveliest – if mundane – thoroughfare, lined with nineteenth-century buildings, almost all of their ground floors converted into cafés, bars or restaurants. Gothenburg's young and beautiful strut up and down and sip overpriced drinks at tables that spill onto the street from mid-spring till September. It's enjoyable to sit here and watch life go by, but for all its glamour most of the tourist-oriented shops and brasseries are interchangeable and the grandeur of the city's industrial past is better evoked in the less spoiled mansions along roads like Parkgatan, at right angles to Avenyn over the canal. There are a couple of diverting museums here too.

The Trädgårdsföreningen

Before you cross over into the crowds of Avenyn, take time out to visit the **Trädgårdsföreningen**, or Garden Society Park (daily: May–Aug 7am–9pm, 10kr; Sept–April 7am–6pm, free), whose main entrance is just over the canal bridge. For once, this park really does lives up to its blurb – "a green oasis in the heart of the city". Among the trees and lawns are a surprising number of experimental sculptures, designed to blend in with their natural surroundings. Within the park, the **Palm House** (daily: June–Aug 10am–6pm; Sept–May 10am–4pm; 20kr, also gives entry to Botanical Gardens) of 1878 looks like a huge English-style conservatory and contains a wealth of very un-Swedish plant life. Close by is the **Butterfly House** (June–Aug daily 10am–5pm; April, May & Sept Tues–Fri 10am–4pm, Sat & Sun 10am–4pm; Oct–March Tues–Fri 10am–3pm, Sat & Sun 11am–3pm; 35kr), where you can wander among free-flying butterflies from Asia and the Americas. During summer the place goes into overdrive with lunchtime concerts and a special children's theatre.

Vasastan, Götaplatsen and Liseberg

Once you've had your fill of Avenyn, take one of the roads off to the west and wander into the district of Vasastan, where the streets are lined with fine nineteenth-century and National Romantic architecture, and the cafés are cheaper and more laid-back. On Vasagatan, the main street through the area, is the excellent **Röhsska Museum**, Sweden's only museum of applied arts (May–Aug Mon–Fri noon–4pm, Sat & Sun noon–5pm; Sept–April Tues noon–9pm, Wed–Fri noon–4pm, Sat & Sun noon–5pm; 35kr). Built in 1916, this is an aesthete's Aladdin's cave, each floor concentrating on different areas of decorative and functional art, from early dynasty Chinese ceramics to European arts and crafts of the sixteenth century. The first floor holds an especially interesting section devoted to twentieth-century decor and featuring all manner of familiar designs right up to the present – enough to send anyone over the age of 10 on a nostalgia trip.

At the top of Avenyn, **Götaplatsen** is modern Gothenburg's main square, its focal point Carl Milles' **Poseidon**, a giant bronze nude with the physique of a body-builder and a staggeringly ugly face; the size of the figure's penis caused outrage when the sculpture was unveiled in 1930 and it was subsequently dramatically reduced. From the front, Poseidon appears to be squeezing the daylights out of a large fanged fish – a symbol of local trade – but if you climb the steps of the **Concert Hall** to the right, it becomes clear that Milles won the battle over Poseidon's manhood to stupendous effect.

Behind Poseidon looms the impressive **Art Museum** (Konstmuseum; May–Aug Mon–Fri 11am–4pm; Sept–April Tues, Thurs & Fri 11am–4pm, Wed 11am–9pm, Sat & Sun 11am–5pm; 35kr), whose massive, symmetrical facade is reminiscent of 1930s Fascist architecture. One of the city's finest museums, it is easy to spend half a day absorbing the diverse and extensive collections. The **Hasselblad Centre** on the ground floor shows excellent changing photographic exhibitions, while upstairs there's postwar and contemporary Scandinavian paintings, a room full of French Impressionists, and a collection of Italian and Spanish paintings from the sixteenth to eighteenth centuries. Best of all, though, are the **Furstenburg Galleries** on the sixth floor, which celebrate the work of some of Scandinavia's most prolific and revered artists from the early twentieth century. Well-known paintings by Anders Zorn and Carl Wilhelmson depict the seasons and landscapes of the Nordic countries and evoke a vivid picture of life a hundred years ago. Look out for Ernst Josephson's sensitive portraits and a couple of Hugo Birger paintings depicting the interior of the Furstenburg Gallery. Also worth a look is the room of Carl Larsson's fantastical and bright wall-sized canvases.

Just a few minutes' walk southeast from Götaplatsen lies Sweden's largest amusement park, **Liseberg** (late April to June & late Aug daily 3–11pm; July to mid-Aug daily noon–11pm; Sept Sat 1–11pm, Sun noon–8pm; 45kr, under-7s free; all-day ride pass 215kr, or limited-ride tickets for 90kr or 150kr). Dating from 1923, it's a league away from today's neon and plastic entertainment complexes, with flowers, trees, fountains and clusters of lights – more Hansel and Gretel than Disneyland. Old and young dance to live bands, and while at night the young and raucous predominate, it's all good humoured. The newest attraction is an ambitious roller coaster called "Hangover", best avoided if you've got one. If you're here during the day, it's worth dropping into the surprisingly interesting **Museum of Ethnography** (May–Aug Mon–Fri 11am–4pm, Sat & Sun 11am–5pm; 30kr), just over the highway at Avagen 24. The best exhibits are those on native North and South American culture, including some dramatically lit textiles up to 2000 years old, and rather grislier finds, such as skulls deliberately trephined (squashed) to ward off evil spirits.

Haga and Linné

West of Avenyn, and a ten-minute stroll up Vasagatan (or take tram #l, #3, #4 or #9 towards Linnegatan) lies the district of **Haga**, the city's oldest working-class area, now transformed into the Greenwich Village of Gothenburg. Centred on **Haga Nygatan**, Haga is one of Gothenburg's most picturesque quarters, its cobbled streets lined with alternative and pricey cafés and antique clothes shops, frequented by right-on and well-off twenty- and thirty-somethings. Although there are a couple of good restaurants along Haga Nygatan, this is really somewhere to come during the day, when tables are put out on the street and the atmosphere is friendly and villagey, if a little self-consciously fashionable.

Adjoining Haga to the south, **Skansparken** is hardly a park at all, being little more than the raised mound of land where the **Military Museum** (Tues & Wed noon–2pm, Sat & Sun noon–3pm, guided tour 1pm first Sunday of each month; 30kr) occupies one of Gothenburg's two surviving seventeenth-century fortress towers, Skansen Kronan. The steep climb is worth the effort for good views north towards the harbour; the museum itself consists of a rather feeble collection of wax models in military uniforms throughout the ages.

West of Haga is the more cosmopolitan district of **Linné**, named after the botanist Carl von Linné (better known by the Latinized version of his name, Linnaeus), who originated the system of plant classification that's used the world over. Recent years have seen so many new cafés and restaurants spring up along **Linnegatan** – which runs along the western end of Haga Nygatan – that this street of tall, Dutch-style buildings has become a second Avenyn, but without the attitude.

Five minutes' walk south of Linnegatan (or tram #1 or #2 to Linneplatsen) is the huge, tranquil mass of greenery that constitutes the **Slottskogsparken**. Home to farm animals and many varieties of birds, including pink flamingoes in summer, there's plenty here to entertain children. The rather dreary **Natural History Museum** (Tues–Fri 11am–3pm, Sat & Sun 11am–5pm; 30kr) within the grounds prides itself on being the city's oldest, dating from 1833. Its endless cases of stuffed birds seem particularly depressing after the squawking, living ones outside, and the only worthwhile item is the world's only stuffed blue whale, which was killed in 1865 and now contains a Victorian café complete with original red velvet sofas – unfortunately, it's only opened in election years (the Swedish word for whale also means election). On the South side of Slottskogsparken are the large **Botanical Gardens** (daily 9am–dusk; greenhouses May–Aug daily 8am–6pm, Sept–April Mon–Fri 10am–3pm, Sat, Sun & holidays noon–4pm).

Eating

Gothenburg has a multitude of **eating** places, catering for every taste and budget. The city's status as a trading port has brought with it a huge number of ethnic restaurants, everything from Lebanese to Thai, and the only thing you won't see much of, at least at the lower end of the market, is Swedish food. Naturally, there are great fish restaurants, including some of the most exclusive establishments in town, while for less costly eating there is a growing number of low-priced pasta restaurants, along with the staple pizza parlours and burger bars.

Café life has really come into its own in Gothenburg, with a profusion of new places throughout the city joining the traditional **konditori** (bakeries with tearoom attached). Nowadays, it's easy to stroll from one café to another at any time of day or night, and tuck into enormous sandwiches and gorgeous cakes. Cafés also offer a wide range of light meals, and are fast becoming about the best places to go for good food at reasonable prices; the most interesting are concentrated in the fashionable Haga and Linné districts.

Markets and supermarkets

The bustling, historic **Saluhallen** at Kungstorget is a delightful sensory experience, with a huge range of meat, fish, fruit, vegetables and delectable breads; there are also a couple of cheap coffee and snack bars here. A more recent arrival on the market scene is **Saluhall Briggen**, on the corner of Tredje Långgatan and Nordhamsgatan in the Linné area. More continental and much smaller than Saluhallen, this place specializes in high-quality meats, fish and cheese and mouthwatering deli delights. The **Konsum** supermarket on Avenyn (daily till 11pm) sells a wide range of the usual staples, and has a good deli counter.

Cafés and restaurants

If you want to avoid paying over the odds, it's generally a good idea to steer clear of Avenyn itself, where prices are almost double what you'll pay in Haga or Linné, and to eat your main meal at **lunchtime**, when you can fill up on *dagens rätt* deals for 40–60kr. Otherwise, expect to pay 80–120kr for a main dish in most restaurants, a lot higher in the more exclusive places.

The old town

Ahlstroms Konditori, Korsgatan 2. A classic café/bakery of the old school, and although modernization has watered down the original features, it's still worth a visit for its good selection of cakes, plus lunches for 52kr.

Froken Olssons Kafe, Östra Larmgatan 14. Heaps of sandwiches, salads and sumptuous desserts in a rural-style atmosphere. Look out for the mountains of giant meringues on tiered, silver cake trays. Sandwiches 30–50kr.

Gabriel at Feskekorka, Feskekorka fish market (☎031/13 90 51). Excellent fish restaurant, though prices seem particularly high when you can see the real cost of the ingredients below. Closed Sun. It's much cheaper to fill up at the tiny eight-seat *Café Feskekorke* at the opposite end of the market.

Grande E.t.c., Kungsgatan 12 (☎031/701 77 84). Big brother to *E.t.c.* at Vasaplatsen (see below) this one serves similar, very fresh pasta dishes from 85kr.

Greta's, Drottninggatan 35. Stylish, casual bar-restaurant, and a very popular gay venue. The wide-ranging menu has fish, meat and vegetarian options, plus wonderful cakes.

Mat & Dryck, adjoining Saluhallen market. A pleasant, if basic, place for salad and fresh breads. Daily lunch at 58kr and a choice of twenty beers.

Matilda's, adjoining Saluhallen market. A central, friendly café that's good for a bowl of *café au lait* and a cake.

Around Avenyn

Cafe Dali, Vasagatan 42. Friendly, studenty and stylish basement café with sandwiches and cakes.

Café Engelen, Engelbreksgatan. Home-baked, excellent-value food at this friendly studenty café, which is open 24hr. Baked potatoes, lasagne and big sandwiches for 38kr. There's always a vegetarian selection and a good 27kr breakfast. Glorious home-made ice cream and a massive range of fruit teas, too.

E.t.c., Vasaplatsen 4. This cool, white and elegant basement is where to come for superb home-made pasta. Lunch 55kr; dinner also offers meat and fish dishes. Very busy in evenings.

Gothia Hotel, Massansgatan 24 (☎031/40 93 00). Glitzy hotel with panoramic views from the top-floor piano-bar restaurant. Among other fabulously expensive meals, try the superb king-prawn sandwiches at a whopping 110kr.

Java Café, Vasagatan 23. Studenty, Parisian-style coffee house serving a wide range of coffees, and breakfasts for 28kr. Decor includes a collection of thermos flasks dotted among shelves of books. A good Sunday-morning hangout.

Junggrens Café, Avenyn 37. The only reasonably priced Avenyn café, with excellent snacks and sandwiches. Atmospheric and convivial, it's been run for decades by a charismatic old Polish woman and her sulky staff. Coffee for only 10kr, sandwiches 12–20kr.

Lai Wa, Storgatan 11, Vasaplan. One of the better Chinese restaurants with a wide variety of dishes at reasonable prices – try the Peking soup. Good lunches.

Restaurant Frågetecken, Södra Vägen 20. Very popular spot just a minute's walk from Götaplatsen, with a name that translates as "restaurant question mark". Eat out in the conservatory, or inside to watch the chefs at work, carefully preparing Balkan-influenced food. They boast of being "famous for breasts": duck at 219kr is the most expensive thing on the menu. Pasta for under 100kr.

Skåne Café, Södra Vägen 59. Big, freshly made sandwiches – smoked salmon for just 20kr – in a very small, basic café, well worth the five-minute walk from Avenyn or Liseberg.

Smaka, Vasaplatsen 3, off Vasagatan (☎031/13 22 47). Moderately priced traditional Swedish dishes enjoyed by a lively, young crowd in a striking, modern interior.

Tai Pak, Arkivsgatan, just off Avenyn near Götaplatsen. Decent Chinese restaurant serving a two-course special for 69kr. Individual courses around 65–75kr.

Teatergatan Cafe, Teatergatan. Sit at one of the black-and-white swivel chairs and try sandwiches at 50kr and salads at 60kr. A bit posey.

Tintin Café, Engelbrektsgatan 22. Very busy, 24hr café with mounds of food and coffee at low prices (try a big plate of chicken salad for 40kr) in a laid-back, student atmosphere.

28+, Götabergsgatan 28. Very fine French-style gourmet restaurant, whose name refers to the fat percentage of its renowned cheese, sold in the shop (9am–11pm) near the entrance. Specialities include goose-liver terrine. Service is excellent. Closed Sun.

Haga and Linné

Biblos Bar & Restaurant, Andra Långgatan 21 (☎031/42 35 53). Traditional Lebanese food, including a fifteen-dish meze for 195kr (minimum four people) and excellent couscous and lamb dishes. Belly dancing on Fri & Sat nights.

Cyrano, Prinsgatan 7 (☎031/14 31 10) Superb, authentic Provençale bistro specializing in wood-fired pizzas and regional French cooking in a laid-back atmosphere with great service.

Hemma Hos, Haga Nygatan 12 (☎031/13 40 90). Popular restaurant full of quaint old furniture serving upmarket and expensive Swedish food – reindeer and fish dishes among them.

Hos Pelle, Djupedalsgatan 2 (☎031/12 10 31). Sophisticated wine bar off Linnegatan, not cheap, but serving snacks as well as full meals, and decorated with wonderful abstract artwork.

Jacob's Café, Haga Nygatan 10. *The* place to sit outside and people-watch; inside the decor is fabulous, with some fine Jugend (Swedish Art Nouveau) lamps.

Johansson's Café & Curiosity Shop, Andre Långgatan 6. Pleasant café, where you can buy the antique ornaments and furniture around you. Sandwiches from 22kr.

Krakow, Karl Gustavsgatan 28 (☎031/20 33 74). Burly staff serving big, basic and very filling Polish food in a large, dark restaurant. Moderate.

Le Village, Tredje Långgatan 13 (☎031/24 20 03). Lovely candlelit restaurant connected to a big antique shop and serving very well-presented if smallish dishes. The main dining area is expensive – sit in the cheaper bar area where meals start at 65kr.

Linnes Trädgård, Linnegatan 38. This bar and restaurant is a popular, stylish meeting place, with huge windows overlooking the Linnegatan street life. Beautifully presented short menu of fish, meat and pasta (130–170kr). Finish with the blueberry mousse or the deliciously indulgent honey and pecan parfait. Also a good place for a drink.

Louice Restaurant, Värmlandsgatan 18, off Andra Långgatan. Justifiably popular and unpretentious neighbourhood restaurant, with occasional live music. Standard main courses are expensive, but look out for the excellent-value specials at 79kr. There's a full children's menu (35kr) in English too.

Plus (+), at junction of Linnegatan and Landsvägsgatan (☎031/24 08 90). Sit at polished tables beneath chandeliers in a beautifully restored old wooden house nestling in rough-hewn rock. Fish and meat dishes go for 160–180kr, and there's a wide drinks list and terrace seating.

Sjöbaren, Haga Hygatan 27. Small fish and shellfish restaurant on the ground floor of a traditional Governor's house building. Moderate.

Solrosen, Kaponjargatan 4A (☎031/711 66 97). The oldest vegetarian restaurant in Gothenburg with a wide range of dishes at moderate prices.

Solsidan Café, Linnegatan. Lovely café serving delicious cakes; outdoor seating.

Thai Garden, Andra Långgatan 18 (☎031/12 76 60). Nothing special to look at, but big portions and excellent service at good prices.

Drinking, nightlife and entertainment

There's an excellent choice of places to **drink** in Gothenburg, but aside from a small number of British- and Irish-style pubs, even the hippest bars also serve food and have more of a restaurant atmosphere. Listed below are some of the most popular pubs and bar-restaurants in the city, but note that many of the cafés and restaurants listed in the previous section are also good places for a beer, especially those in Avenyn and Linné. Although there are a number of long-established bars in the old town, the atmosphere is generally a bit low-key at night.

There's plenty of other things to do in Gothenburg at night besides drink. The city has a brisk **live music scene** – jazz, rock and classical – as well as the usual cinema and theatre opportunities. The details below should give you some ideas, but it's worth picking up the Friday edition of the *Göteborgs Posten*, which has a weekly listings supplement called "Aveny" – it's in Swedish but not very difficult to decipher. The notice boards in the main hall at the entrance to *Studs*, the student bar in Vasaplan, are also good for gigs, parties and other information on what's going on in the city.

Bars and pubs

Although it is not uncommon for Gothenburgers to drink themselves into oblivion, the atmosphere around the bars isn't generally aggressive. Avenyn, late on a Saturday night, is really the only place where you might feel even slightly unsafe.

The old town

Beefeater Inn, Plantagegatan 1. One of a bevy of British-oriented neighbourhood pubs, very in vogue with Gothenburgers. This one really goes overboard, with a stylistic mishmash of red-tele-phone-box doors, tartan walls and staff in kilts.

Dubliners, Östra Hamngatan 50B. Swedes have for a while been overtaken with a nostalgia for all things old and Irish – or at least a Swedish interpretation of what's old and Irish. This is the most popular exponent.

Gamle Port, Östra Larmgatan 18. The city's oldest watering hole, with British beer in the downstairs pub and an awful disco upstairs (see "Clubs and live music" overleaf).

Norrlands Nation, Västra Hamngatan 20. Open late, with occasional comedy shows and music.

The Palace, Brunnsparken. The rather splendid former home of the Furstenburgs and their art galleries (see p.437), this upmarket bar and restaurant is very popular – but pricey.

Avenyn and around

Brasserie Lipp, Avenyn 8. No longer the hippest place on Avenyn, *Lipp* is expensive and so attracts a slightly older crowd – but a crowd it is, especially during summer. *Bubbles Nightclub* (see "Clubs and live music" overleaf) is connected directly to the brasserie.

Harley's, Avenyn 10. Very loud young crowd. Not a place for a drink and a chat, unless you want to stand out on the street.

Niva, Avenyn 9. Stylish bar that's becoming increasingly popular. The interior's modern, with a mosaic decor and a bar and restaurant on different levels.

Scandic Rubinen, Avenyn 24. Glitzy hotel-foyer type of bar. Always packed with tourists and right at the heart of Avenyn.

Studs, Götabergsgatan, off Engelbrecksgatan behind Vasa Church. This is the hub of Gothenburg student life, with a pub, bar and restaurant. The main advantage of the student bar is its prices, with two-for-one beers before 9pm in summer. If you haven't got student ID, friendly bluffing should get you in.

Haga and Linné

Dog & Duck, Viktoriagatan 5. All-British pub-restaurant which makes a valiant attempt at creating a cosy, nineteenth-century atmosphere. Serves light meals, nachos, burgers and chicken shish kebabs, all at around 65kr. Open till 1am (Fri & Sat till 3am).

Indian Palace Pub, Järntorget 4. Just northwest of Haga Nygatan, this place is rather unappealing from outside, though things improve once you're through the door. There's a restaurant on the ground floor with a basement pub and pool table.

The Irish Rover, Andra Långgatan 12. Run-of-the-mill Anglo-Irish pub selling Boddingtons, with other lagers, ales and cider on tap, plus a wide range of bottled beers. Lamb, steaks and trout dishes for 59–105kr.

1252, Linnegatan. *The* place to be seen in Linné, with reasonably priced food considering the location. Outdoor tables in summer.

Clubs and live music

There are no outstanding **clubs** in Gothenburg. The main venue is the *Valand* nightclub, at Vasagatan 3, just off Avenyn, with three bars and a floor where the clubby crowd strut their stuff. The hip *Trägårn* (☎031/10 20 90) on Nya Alleyn near Heden doesn't look too promising outside, but has a stylish pale-wood interior and a restaurant run by the revered Dahlbom brothers. It's also one of the liveliest haunts, with five bars, a casino, disco and live bands. *Park Lane*, at Avenyn 36, is a hot, crowded club with three bars, a casino and live music. *Yaki Da* (attached to the *Gamle Port* bar – see p.443) has a pretty depressing atmosphere, despite having three bars, a stage and a casino; *Bubbles Nightclub* at *Brasserie Lipp* (see p.443) is similarly disappointing. Sweden's biggest dance floor is said to be at *Rondo*, the dance restaurant at Liseberg Amusement Park – there's always a live band on, and a good atmosphere, with people of all ages dancing.

Live music

Gothenburg's large student community means there are plenty of **local live bands**. The best venue, with the emphasis on alternative and dance music, is *Kompaniet* on Kungsgatan: the top floor is a pub-bar, while downstairs there's dancing to Euro techno. Drinks are half-price between 8pm and 10pm, the place stays open until 3am daily in summer (winter Wed–Sat only) – and you're likely to be the only foreigner there. Jazz enthusiasts should head for the trendy *Neffertiti* **jazz club** at Hvitfeldtsplatsen 6 (Mon–Sat from 9pm) – you may have to queue. *Jazzhuset*, Eric Dahlbergsgatan 3 (Wed–Sat 8pm–2am), puts on trad, Dixieland and swing, but is fairly staid and something of an executive pick-up joint.

International bands perform at some sizeable stadium-type venues in the city, notably Scandinavium (☎031/81 10 20) and the colossal Ullevi Stadium (☎031/61 20 50). Both are off Skånegatan to the east of Avenyn; take tram #1, #3 or #6. Check out the usual listings sources for details of upcoming concerts.

Classical music, cinema and theatre

Classical music concerts are performed regularly in the Konserthuset, Götaplatsen, and the Stora Theatre, Avenyn. Get hold of programme details from the tourist office.

There are plenty of **cinemas** around the city, screening mostly English-language movies with Swedish subtitles. The most unusual is the ten-screen Bio Palatset, on Kungstorget, originally a meat market and then a failed shopping mall, its interior is now painted in clashing fruity colours, and its foyer has been excavated to reveal flood-lit rocks studded with Viking spears. Another multi-screener is Filmstaden, behind the cathedral at Kungsgatan 35. A fine **art-house cinema** is Hagabion on Linnegatan, which shows a wide range of alternative films. If you're around in January or February, look out for the **Gothenburg Film Festival** at Draken cinema on Järntorget, with screenings of a remarkable range of films.

Theatre in Gothenburg is unlikely to appeal to many visitors. Not only are all productions in Swedish, but the city's council-run theatres also put on plays that make Strindberg look like high comedy – the lack of audience is not a big concern.

Gay Gothenburg

Gothenburg's **gay scene** is surprisingly half-hearted, though things have been looking up in the past couple of years, and there's now something approaching choice, though still very limited compared to most cities of this size. Sweden's official gay rights group, the **RFSL** (Riksförbundet för Sexuellt Likaberättigande), have an inconveniently located branch at Karl Johansgatan 31 (☎031/775 40 10; head west towards Klippan, there's a sign when you reach the Karl Johan Church), where you'll find a library and the *Next* café-bar (Thurs 3pm–1am, Fri & Sat 6pm–2am). Far more appealing is the very friendly and well designed *Greta's*, Drottninggatan 35, the city's first gay restaurant and bar. The Greek restaurant *Satyros*, Karl Johansgatan 8 (on the way to the RFSL), is gay on Saturday evenings, while a much younger, hipper and posier crowd head to *XLNT*, the gay club night at *Club Fobi*, Vasagatan 43B, on Fridays and Saturdays.

Listings

Airlines British Airways, at the airport (☎020/78 11 44); Finnair, Fredsgatan 6 (☎020/78 11 00); KLM, at the airport (☎031/94 16 40); Lufthansa, Fredsgatan 1 (☎031/80 56 40); SAS, at the airport, (☎020/91 01 10).

Airport ☎031/94 10 00.

American Express Local agent is Ticket, Östra Hamngatan 35 (☎031/13 07 12).

Banks and exchange Most banks are open Mon–Fri 9.30am–3pm, and are found on Östra Hamngatan, Södra Hamngatan and Västra Hamngatan. There are four Forex exchange offices, which accept American Express, Diners Club, Finax and traveller's cheques: Central Station (daily 8am–9pm), Avenyn 22 (daily 8am–9pm), Nordstan shopping centre (9am–7pm) and Kungsportsplatsen (daily 9am–7pm).

Buses Reservations are obligatory for buses to Stockholm, Helsingborg and Malmö – reserve seats at Bussresebyra, Drottninggatan 50 (☎031/80 55 30).

Car rental Avis, Central Station (☎031/80 57 80) and at the airport (☎031/94 60 30); Budget, Kristinelundsgatan 13 (☎031/20 09 30) and at the airport (☎031/94 60 55) Europcar, Stampgatan 22D (☎031/80 53 90) and at the airport (☎031/94 71 00); Hertz, Stampgatan 16A (☎031/80 37 30) and at the airport (☎031/94 60 20).

Doctor Medical Counselling Service and Information (☎031/41 55 00); Sahlgrenska Hospital at Per Dubbsgatan (☎031/60 10 00). A private clinic, City Akuten, has doctors on duty 8am–6pm at Drottninggatan 45 (☎031/10 10 10).

Emergencies Ambulance and police on ☎90 000.

Laundry At Nordstan Service Centre (see overleaf).

Left luggage at Nordstan Service Centre (see overleaf) or Central Station.

Newspapers International newspapers from the Press Centre in Nordstan shopping centre or Central Station; or read them for free at the City Library, Götaplatsen.

Nordstan Service Centre In the shopping centre near Central Station (Mon–Fri 10am–6.30pm, Sat 10am–4pm); you can leave luggage (10kr), take a shower here (20kr) and use the laundry service (95kr).

Pharmacy Apoteket Vasen, Götagatan 10, in the Nordstan shopping centre, is open 24hr (☎031/80 44 10).

Police Headquarters at Ernst Fontells Plats (Mon–Fri 9am–2pm; ☎031/61 80 00).

Post offices The main office for poste restante is in Drottningtorget (Mon–Fri 10am–6pm, Sat 10am–noon); other offices can be found on Avenyn (Mon–Fri 10am–6pm, Sat 10am–12.30pm) and at the Nordstan shopping centre (Mon–Fri 9am–7pm, Sat 10am–5pm).

Train enquiries Central Station ☎020/75 75 75; international train information ☎031/80 77 10.

Travel agents KILROY Travels, Berzeliigatan 5 (Mon–Fri 9.30am–5pm; ☎031/20 08 60).

AROUND GOTHENBURG

North of Gothenburg, the rugged and picturesque **Bohuslän coast** attracts countless Scandinavian and German tourists each summer. However, the crowds can't detract from the wealth of natural beauty and the many dinky fishing villages that make this stretch of country well worth a few days' exploration. The most popular destination is the island town of **Marstrand**, with its impressive fortress and richly ornamental ancient buildings, but there are several attractions further up the coast that are also worthwhile targets, not least the centre for Bronze Age **rock carvings** at **Tamunshede**, near Strömstad.

Northeast of the city, the county of **Västergötland** encompasses the southern sections of Sweden's two largest lakes, **Vänern** and **Vättern**. Here the scenery is gentler, and a number of attractive lakeside towns and villages make good bases from which to venture out into the forested countryside and onto the **Göta Canal**. The waterway connects the lakes to each other (and, in its entirety, the North Sea to the Baltic), and there are a number of ways to experience it, from cross-country cruises to short hops on rented boats. With energy and time to spare, **renting a bike** offers a great alternative for exploring of Västergötland, using the canal's towpaths, countless cycling trails and empty roads. Nearly all tourist offices, youth hostels and campsites in the region rent out bikes for around 80kr a day or 400kr a week.

The Bohuslän coast

A chain of **islands** linked by a thread of bridges and short ferry crossings make up the county of **Bohuslän** and, despite the summer crowds, it is still easy enough to find a private spot to swim or bathe. Sailing is also a popular pastime among the Swedes, many of whom have summer cottages here, and you'll see yachts gliding through the water all the way along the coast. Another feature of the Bohuslän landscape you can't fail to miss is the large number of **churches** that fill the county – for long stretches these are the only buildings of note. Dating from the 1840s to 1910, these are mostly simple white structures with little variation in design; they're usually open between 10am and 3pm, though the clergyman invariably lives next door and will be happy to open up outside these hours.

Travelling up the coast by **train** is feasible, though they stop only in the main towns, with services from Gothenburg through industrial Uddevalla and on to Strömstad. **Buses** also cover the coast, but services are sketchy and infrequent (on some routes there is only one bus a week). If you really want to explore Bohuslän's most dramatic scenery, you need a **car**. From Gothenburg, the E6 motorway is the quickest route north, with designated scenic routes leading off it every few kilometres.

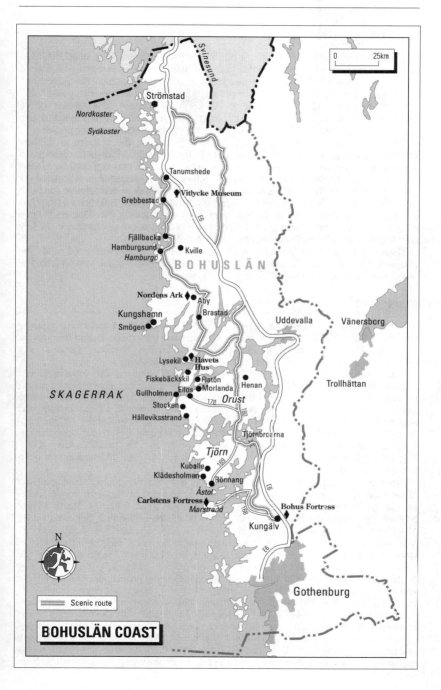

Scenic route

BOHUSLÄN COAST

Kungälv

Just under 20km north of Gothenburg on the E6, the quaint old town of **KUNGÄLV**, overshadowed by the fourteenth-century ruins of Bohus Fortress, is a gem of a place to stop for a few hours. Rebuilt after the Swedes razed it in 1676 to prevent the Danes finding useful shelter, the town now consists of sprawling cobbled streets with pastel-painted wooden houses, all leaning as if on the verge of collapse. The **tourist office** (☎0303/992 00, fax 171 06), in the square below the fortress, will provide you with a map of a walking tour detailing the history of almost every seventeenth-century property.

The main reason most people visit the town is to see the remains of **Bohus Fortress**. The first wooden fort was built here by the Norwegian king in the fourteenth century, on what was then Norway's southern border. This was replaced by a solid stone building, surrounded by deep natural moats, which managed to withstand six Swedish attacks in the 1560s and, once it became Swedish, a remarkable fourteen sieges by the Danes in the following century. Where attack failed, Swedish weather has succeeded, however, and today the building is very much a ruin. The fortress is open from May to September, with guided tours, concerts and opera performances in July and August – for full details contact the tourist office.

There's little else to do here once you've seen the fortress and wandered round the village, but if you do want to stay, there's an STF **youth hostel** a stone's throw from the fortress at Farjevagen 2 (☎0303/189 00, fax 192 95).

Marstrand

About 25km west of Kungälv, the island town of **MARSTRAND** buzzes with summer activity, as holiday-makers come here to sail, bathe and take tours around the impressive castle. With ornate wooden buildings lining the bustling harbour, Marstrand is a delightful place and easily visited on a day-trip from Gothenburg.

Founded under Norwegian rule in the thirteenth century, the town achieved remarkable prosperity through herring fishing in the following century; rich herring pickings, however, eventually led to greed and corruption, and Marstrand became known as the most immoral town in Scandinavia. The murder of a cleric in 1586 was seen as an omen: soon after the whole town burned to the ground and the herring mysteriously disappeared. The fish – and Marstrand's prosperity – eventually returned in the 1770s, only to disappear again for good forty years later. By the 1820s, the old herring salting houses had been converted into bath houses, and Marstrand had been reborn as a fashionable bathing resort.

From the harbour turn left, then it's a lovely walk up the cobbled lane, past the Renaissance-style *Grand Hotel*, to a small square surrounded by exquisite wooden houses, painted in pastel shades. Across the square is the squat, white St **Maria kyrka**; beyond, the streets climb steeply to the castle, **Carlstens Fästning** (June–Sept daily 11am–6pm; 25kr), an imposing sweep of stone walls solidly wedged into the rough rock. You could easily spend half a day clambering around the walls, and down the weather-worn rocks to the sea, where there are always plenty of places to bathe in private. The informal **tours** take an hour and, though none are officially in English, guides are happy to oblige. The most interesting tales are told down in the grim prison cells: Carlstens' most noted prisoner was **Lasse Maja**, a thief who got rich by dressing as a woman and seducing rich farmers. A sort of Swedish Robin Hood, Maja was known for giving his spoils to the poor. Once incarcerated here, Maja ingratiated himself with the officers with his impressive cooking skills, a talent that, after 26 years, won him a pardon from the king.

For 40kr extra, you can take one of the special tours that are run three times a week and lead up through the castle's hundred-metre towers of 1658. The views from the top are stunning, but you'll have to be fit to get there as the steep, spiral climb is quite exhausting. Once a year, around July 20, the fortress hosts a huge **festival**, with an eighteenth-century-style procession and live theatrical performances. It's a colourful occasion and well worth catching.

Practicalities

Gothenburg Card-holders can get a two-for-one ticket deal on the **day-trip by boat** from Gothenburg; boats leave from Lilla Bommen at 9.30am, arriving in Marstrand at 12.30pm (daily in July & Aug; less frequently outside these months). Otherwise, take **bus** #312 from Nils Ericsonsplatsen; buy a 100kr carnet from Tidpunkten, next to the bus terminal, which also covers the ferry journey from the mainland (15min; 13kr return). By car, take the E6 north out of Gothenburg, then Road 168, which leads west right to the ferry. No cars are allowed on the island, and parking on the mainland costs 25kr per day.

The **tourist office** at the harbour (early to mid-June Mon–Fri 10am–4pm, Sat & Sun noon–4pm; late June to early Aug Mon–Fri 9.30am–6pm, Sat & Sun 11am–5pm; early Aug to early June Mon–Fri 10am–4pm; ☎0303/600 87, fax 600 18) can book **private rooms** for a minimum of two people in either an old barracks (370kr per room) or in private homes or cottages (450kr). The island's **youth hostel**, *Båtellet* (☎0303/600 10, fax 606 07) is situated in an atmospheric old bath house overlooking the sea, with a sauna, washing facilities, a swimming pool and a restaurant (see below). Of the several very pleasant **hotels** on the island, the finest is the *Grand Hotel* of 1892, at Paradis Parken (☎0303/603 22, fax 600 53; ⑥), just 50m from the tourist office and left through the park. *Hotel Nautic*, Långgatan 6 (☎0303/610 30, fax 612 00; ③), is a little more basic but perfectly adequate.

About the most interesting place to **eat** on the island is the *American Bar*, close to the harbour, which serves excellent food in huge portions: chicken and cheese salad for 88kr, or brie and bacon salad for 67kr – though coffee is a steep 20kr. Alternatively, you could try the glamorous, if more formal, restaurant at *Oscar's* next door. Another very popular choice is *Maja's Krog* on the harbourfront, whose wide-ranging meat and fish menu has mains at 110–220kr, as well as pizzas at around 80kr. Decent meals are also served in *Drott*, the restaurant connected to the youth hostel: daily pasta dishes cost around 50kr; meat and seafood 90–130kr. Alternatively, try one of the three restaurants in the classic old *Societetshuset*, close to the youth hostel by the water. At night, the *American Bar* and *Oscar's* (which doubles as a nightclub) are good **drinking** haunts.

North to Strömstad

Aside from picturesque scenery and pretty villages, the highlights along this stretch of the coast are the exceptional **marine-life museum** at **Lysekil**, several nature reserves, a wildlife sanctuary and, at **Tanumshede**, an extensive array of Bronze Age **rock carvings**. If you have your own transport, you'll be able to follow the designated **scenic routes** which lead off the E6; otherwise, bus connections from Gothenburg are limited to a few of the main towns. If you have a car, it's easy enough to drive to Strömstad in a day, stopping off at a couple of sights on the way. Although there are plenty of hotels and hostels along the coast, this is one of the most popular parts of the country for **camping** and caravanning, with loads of sites all the way to Strömstad.

Orust to Lysekil

Head north of Marstrand along the E6 for about 25km, then take a left onto the Tjornbroarna, a sequence of three graceful bridges which connect the islands of Tjörn and Orust, affording spectacular views over the fjords. **Orust**, a centre for boat-building since Viking times, is geographically like a miniature Sweden, westerly winds stripping it of trees at the coast, yet with forest running right up to the sea on its eastern shores. The island's STF **youth hostel** (☎0304/503 80), just outside the village of Stocken, occupies a splendid eighteenth-century wooden manor set in vast grounds.

A few kilometres north of here via car ferry is the charming village of **FISKEBÄCKSKIL**. Birthplace and home to Carl Wilhelmson, one of Sweden's best-loved artists, his studio stands proud on granite rocks overlooking the sea – the setting for many of his most famous paintings. The glamorous *Gullmarsstrand* **hotel** (☎0523/222 60, fax 228 05; ③) is just a few metres away. The best place to **eat** is *Kapten Stures Restaurant* (☎0523/221 25) on Kaptensgatan, close to the beautiful church.

On the mainland just opposite Fiskebäckskil (and connected to it by ferry) is **LYSEKIL**, the largest coastal town in the region (also reachable by express bus #840 from Gothenburg). Though it's not as immediately attractive as other coastal towns, Lysekil does still have plenty to recommend it. From the **tourist office** (mid-June to mid-Aug daily 9am–7pm; mid-Aug to mid-June Mon–Fri 9am–5pm; ☎0523/130 50, fax 125 85, *info@lysekil.se*) at Sodra Hamngatan 6, it's just five minutes' walk to the exceptional museum of marine life, **Havets Hus** (Feb–Dec daily 10am–4pm; 50kr). Chief attraction here is the underwater glass tunnel, where massive fish swim over and around you; there's also a special "touch pool" for children to experience the texture of slimy algae and spiky starfish. En route to Havets Hus you'll pass a number of intricately carved villas, a reminder of the nineteenth century when Lysekil was a popular and genteel bathing resort. Today, nude (segregated) bathing and fishing are popular pastimes and much of the shoreline has been turned into a **nature reserve**, with over 250 varieties of plant life – ask at the tourist office about guided botanical and marine walks in summer. Walk up any set of steps from the waterfront and you'll reach the town's **church** (daily 11am–3pm), hewn from the surrounding pink granite. If you want to **stay** in Lysekil, the *Kust Hotel Strand*, Strandvägen 1 (☎0523/101 20, fax 122 02), has both dorm beds and doubles (①) and is well placed on the waterfront in a fancy old house, albeit one showing signs of age. The ugly but central *Hotel Lysekil* at Rosikstorg 1 (☎0523/61 18 60, fax 155 20; ③) offers more comfort.

A possible diversion after visiting Lysekil is to head back along Route 162 and turn left for Nordens Ark **wildlife sanctuary** near Åby (about 25km). On the way you'll pass a couple of notable churches, in particular the one at **Brastad**, an 1870s Gothic affair with an oddly haphazard appearance – every farm in the neighbourhood donated a lump of its own granite, none of which matched. Don't be put off by the yeti-sized inflatable puffin at the entrance to **Nordens Ark** (daily: June–Aug 10am–6pm; Sept–May 10am–4pm; 90–130kr depending on time of year), a wildlife sanctuary for endangered species where animal welfare is prioritized over human voyeurism. Red pandas, lynx, snow leopards and arctic foxes are among the rare animals being bred and reared at the sanctuary, whose densely forested landscape is kept as close as possible to the animals' natural environment.

Fjällbacka and Tanumshede

Thirty-five kilometres north along the coast from Lysekil, the picture-perfect settlement of **FJÄLLBACKA** nestles beneath huge granite boulders, its houses painted in fondant shades, with a wealth of intricate gingerbreading known in Swedish as *snickargladje* ("carpenter's joy"). As you enter Fjällbacka, it will immediately become apparent that a certain celebrated actress holds sway in this little town. There's a **tourist office** (June–Aug erratic hours; ☎0525/321 20, fax 311 43) in a tiny red hut on **Ingrid Bergman's Square**. Here a statue of the big-screen idol looks out to the islands where she had her summer house, and to the sea over which her ashes were scattered. There's not a lot to do, but if you want to stick around there are plenty of **camping** opportunities and a seasonal island **youth hostel** (☎0525/312 34; May–Sept). A more convenient hostel close to the tourist office is at Badholmen (☎0525/321 50).

The area around **TANUMSHEDE**, a few kilometres further north on the E6, has the greatest concentration of **Bronze Age rock carvings** in Scandinavia, with four major sites (now listed as UNESCO World Heritage locations) in the surrounding country-side. Between 1500 and 500 BC, Bronze Age man scratched images into the ice-smoothed rock, and at Tanumshede you'll see some fine examples of the most frequent motifs: the simple cup mark (the most frequent design), boats, humans and animals. When you reach town, head for the **tourist office** (June to mid-Aug Mon–Sat 10am–6pm; mid-Aug to May Mon–Thurs 9am–4.30pm, Fri 9am–3pm; ☎0525/204 00, fax 298 60, *tanum.turist@swipnet.se*), oddly sited in a Texaco filling station, which will provide you with explanatory booklets (10kr) in English. There is also a **rock-carving museum** at nearby Vitlyckehallen (20kr; May to mid-Sept), which explores interpretations of the various images. Tanumshede is reached by five E6 express buses daily from Gothenburg (2hr). There is a smattering of restaurants and a little nightlife at the caravan/camping mecca of **Grebbestad**, a few kilometres southwest of Tanumshede.

Strömstad and the Koster Islands

STRÖMSTAD retains an air of faded grandeur from its days as a fashionable eigh-teenth-century spa resort. Arriving at the train station, everywhere of interest is easily accessible, and with ferry connections on to Sandefjord, Fredrickstad and Halden in Norway, the town makes a good stopover before heading further north. Though its main attraction is its close proximity to the Koster Islands (see p.452), Strömstad does have a couple of interesting public buildings. Behind its plain exterior, the town's **church**, a few minutes' walk from the train and bus stations, is an eclectic mix of dec-orative features, including busy frescoes, model ships hanging from the roof, and gilt chandeliers. More bizarre, however, is the massive, copper-roofed **Stadshus**, the prod-uct of a millionaire recluse. Born to a Strömstad jeweler in 1851, Adolf Fritiof Cavalli-Holmgren became a financial whizz kid, moved to Stockholm and was soon one of Sweden's richest men. When he heard that his poor home town needed a town hall, he offered to finance the building, but only if he had complete control over the project, which was to be situated on the spot where his late parents had lived. By the time the mammoth structure was completed in 1917, he was no longer on speaking terms with the city's politicians, and never returned to see the building he had battled to create, which was topped with a panoramic apartment for his private use. Much later, in 1951, it was discovered that he had designed the entire building around the dates of his par-ents' birthdays and wedding day – January 27, May 14 and March 7 – with the dimen-sions of every room, window or flight of stairs a combination of these numbers. Built entirely from rare local apple granite, the town hall is open to the public, but to view the most interesting areas you have to arrange a free private tour. You can see Adolf's por-trait – dated falsely to include his favourite numbers – in the main council chamber.

Practicalities

Strömstad can be reached by **train** from Gothenburg (9 daily; 3hr), or via the express **bus** between Gothenburg and Oslo (5 daily; 2hr 30min); by **car**, follow Route 176 off the E6 for 12km. Both the train and bus stations are on Södra Hammen, opposite the **ferry** terminal for services to Sandefjord in Norway; ferries to Fredrickstad and Halden leave from Norra Hamnen, 100m to the north on the other side of the rocky promontory, Laholmen, as do ferries to the Koster Islands (full details from the tourist office).

The **tourist office** on the quay (mid-June to mid-Aug Mon–Sat 9am–8pm, Sun 10am–8pm; May to mid-June & late Aug Mon–Fri 9am–6pm, Sat & Sun 10am–4pm; Sept–April Mon–Fri 9am–5pm; ☎0526/623 30, fax 623 35, *info@stromstadtourist.se*) can help with **private rooms** (from 150kr per person plus 50kr booking fee), and **cabins**. The STF **youth hostel** is at Norra Kyrkogatan 12 (☎0526/101 93), 1km or so from the train station along Uddevallavägen; there's also an independent hostel, *Gastis Roddaren Hostel*, at Fredrikshaldsvagen 24 (☎0526/602 01), ten minutes' walk along the road in front of the Stadshus. For a regular, central **hotel** try *Krabban* on Södra Bergsgatan 15 (☎0526/142 00, fax 142 04; ②), or the modern and graceless *Hotel Laholmen* (☎0526/124 00, fax 100 36; ⑤/④), which enjoys fantastic sea views. The nearest **campsite** is 1km from the train station, along Uddevallavägen.

As befits a resort town, there's no shortage of places to **eat and drink**, most of them around the harbour. The best of the bunch are *Backlund's*, a locals' haunt, with sandwiches at 18kr; *Café Casper*, on Södra Hamngatan, with lunch specials for 35kr; and *Kaff Doppet*, a more characterful *konditori* by the station. **Nightlife** in Strömstad boils down to *Skagerack*, a very loud, very young music venue.

The Koster Islands

Sweden's most westerly inhabited islands, the **Koster Islands** enjoy more hours of sunshine than almost anywhere else in the country. **North Koster** is the more rugged, with a grand nature reserve, and takes a couple of hours to walk around. **South Koster** is three times as big, but since no vehicles are allowed on the island, **renting a bike** (ask at the Strömstad tourist office) is the best way to explore its undulating landscape. Both islands are rich in wild flowers, have warm water for swimming, as well as bird- and seal-watching expeditions during the summer. If you want to visit the south island outside high season it's vital to take an early-morning ferry to North Koster (80kr); if you leave later, the only way of making it across is to hitch a lift in a local's boat. **Taxi boats** to the islands cost 500kr and can work out economical if there is a group of you; they're the only option if you miss the last ferry back at 9.30pm.

Camping on North Koster is restricted to *Vettnet* (☎0526/204 66), though there are several sites on South Koster, plus a **youth hostel** (☎0526/201 25; May–Sept) 1500m from the ferry stop at Ekenäs; there are also **apartment** rentals for 250–300kr per apartment a night, excellent value if there are three or more of you. There's just one **hotel** on South Koster, the surprisingly stylish *Skärgårdshotel* at Ekenäs (☎0526/202 50, fax 201 94; ④), with a fine restaurant attached.

The Göta Canal, Trollhättan and Vänersborg

The giant waterway known in its entirety as the **Göta Canal** flows from the mouth of the River Göta to Sweden's largest lake, **Lake Vänern**, via the **Trollhättan Canal**, then cuts across into the formidable **Lake Vättern** and right through southeastern Sweden to the Baltic Sea. If you don't have your own transport then some of the easiest places to see from Gothenburg are the few small towns that lie along the first stretch of the river/canal to Lake Vänern, particularly **Trollhättan**, where the canal's lock system tames the force of the river to dramatic effect. A few kilometres north of Trollhättan,

Vänersborg, at the southernmost tip of Lake Vänern, provides a useful base for exploring the natural beauty of the nearby hills, the home of Sweden's largest herd of elk. From Gothenburg, regular trains stop at Trollhättan; if you have a car take Route 45.

The Göta Canal

Centuries ago it was realized that lakes Vänern and Vättern, together with the rivers to the east and west, could be used to make inland transport easier. A continuous waterway across the country from Gothenburg to the Baltic would provide a vital trade route, both as a means of shipping iron and timber out of central Sweden and of avoiding Danish customs charges levied on traffic though Öresund. It was not until 1810, however, that Baron Baltzar von Platten's hugely ambitious plans to carve a route to Stockholm were put into practice by the Göta Canal Company. Sixty thousand soldiers spent seven million working days over 22 years completing the mammoth task, which was finally opened in 1832, shortly after von Platten's death.

Although the Trollhättan Canal section is still used to transport fuel and timber – the towns on Vänern having their lakeside views blotted by unsightly industrial greyness – this section and the Göta Canal proper, between Vänern and Vättern, are extremely popular tourist destinations, and there's a wide range of canal trips on offer. If cost is not an issue, **Göta Canal Cruises**, at Hotellplatsen 2 in Gothenburg (☎031/80 63 15, fax 15 83 11), offer "golden dollar" cruises aboard historic steamers for glamorous four-, six- or eight-day jaunts across the country to the Baltic, with cabins ranging from 15,100kr for four days in a single cabin or 10,000kr per person in a double. On a smaller budget, **day-trips** can be arranged at any tourist office in the region. You can also **rent a boat** or a bike to follow the towpaths – ask at the tourist offices for further information.

Trollhättan

Seventy kilometres northeast of Gothenburg, **TROLLHÄTTAN** is the kind of place you might end up staying for a couple of days without really meaning to. A small town, it nevertheless manages to pack in plenty of offbeat entertainment along with some peaceful river surroundings. Built around the fast river that for a couple of hundred years powered its flour- and saw-mills, Trollhättan remained fairly isolated until 1800, when the Göta Canal Company successfully installed the first set of locks to bypass the town's furious local waterfalls. River traffic took off and better and bigger locks were installed over the years. The best time to visit is during the **Fallensdagar** on the third Friday in July, a three-day festival of dancing and music based around the waterfalls. Summer is the only time when the sluices are opened and you can see the falls in all their crashing splendour (May & June Sat & Sun 3pm; July & Aug Wed, Sat & Sun 3pm).

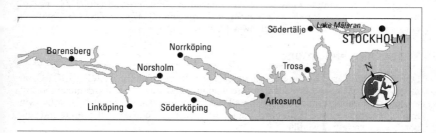

The locks and the steep sides of the falls are the main sights in town, and there are **paths** with orientation maps along the whole system. Strolling south along the path towards the Insikten Energy Centre, the network of canal locks is to your left and the beautiful winding river to your right – it's a splendid half-hour's walk, passing a grand, English-style church perched on rocks between the waterways. **Insikten Energy Centre** itself (mid-June to late Aug daily noon–4pm; by arrangement at other times on ☎0520/888 82; 10kr) is considerably more enjoyable than you might imagine, with none-too-scientific explanations of the workings of the nearby **hydroelectric power station** (June–Aug daily guided tours 10am–5pm), a fine 1910 building containing thirteen massive generators.

A little further down at the upper lock, the **Canal Museum** (mid-June to mid-Aug daily 11am–7pm; mid-Aug to mid-June Sat & Sun noon–5pm; 5kr) puts the whole thing in perspective, with a history of the canal and locks, model ships, old tools and fishing gear. Crossing the canal and heading into the town's industrial hinterland, you'll soon reach the **Saab Museum** (June–Aug daily 10am–6pm; Sept–May Tues–Fri 1–4pm; call to arrange a tour on ☎0520/843 44; 10kr), which holds an example of every model built and miscellaneous extras, such as the demonstration of safety standards in which a simulated elk is depicted running into a large car.

Practicalities

The **tourist office** (mid-June to mid-Aug daily 9am–7pm; mid-Aug to mid-June Mon–Fri 10am–noon & 1.30–4pm; ☎0520/876 54, fax 310 13, *tourist@trollhattan.se*), is next door to the Saab Museum at Åkerssjövägen 10. You can buy the Innovatum Card here (valid mid-June to mid-Aug; 90kr), which gives free entrance to **Innovatum** (mid-June to mid-Aug daily 10am–6pm; by arrangement at other times on ☎0502/48 84 80), a new centre dedicated to exhibitions on Swedish inventors – it's in the same building as the tourist office. The card also gives free cable-car trips and entry to the Insikten Centre and the Saab and Canal museums. From June to August, there are **boats** (☎0520/321 00) up the canal to Vänersborg; the four-hour round-trip costs 100kr. Otherwise, **buses** #600 and #605 ply the route regularly. The tourist office can also book **private rooms** from 130kr (booking fee 26kr). There's an STF **youth hostel** a couple of blocks from the train station at Tingvallavägen 12 (☎ & fax 0520/129 60). The former youth hostel overlooking the river is now a **hotel**, *Stromsberg* (☎0520/129 90, fax 133 11; ③/②), a very pretty place with lots of characterful old features and a lovely restaurant. There's a **campsite**, close to the centre by the river (☎0520/306 13; June–Aug), with a heated swimming pool, bike rental, tennis and golf facilities.

Trollhättan's best **cafés** are mostly along Strandgatan by the canal, notably *Strandgatan*, with a terrace and a young crowd, and *Sluss Caféet,* an outdoor summer café overlooking the locks. The cosy *Café Smulan* on Foreningsgatan is a must and serves delicious cakes as well as terrific and good-value vegetarian meals. The most popular **pubs**, also good for evening meals, are *Oscar's* at Storgatan 44, and *Butler's*, at no. 35, a traditional late-opening Irish-style pub. Nightlife revolves around the **nightclubs** at *Hotel Swania* (entrance in Strandgatan), and *KK's Bar & Nightclub* at Torggatan 3. Trollhättan's **gay** scene is organized by RFSL Trestad (☎0520/41 17 66), who run the friendly *Rainbow Café* at Strindbergsgatan 8 (Wed & Thurs 6–10pm); to get there head down Garvaregatan away from the centre.

Vänersborg and around

Dubbed "Little Paris" by the celebrated local poet Birger Sjoberg, **VÄNERSBORG**, on the tip of Lake Vänern 14km north of Trollhättan, doesn't live up to the comparison, but is a pleasant enough little resort town all the same. Its main sites are the nearby twin hills of **Hunneberg** and **Halleberg**, both of which are of archeological interest and support a wide variety of wildlife.

Vänersborg's old town is compact and pleasant to stroll around – though the grand buildings are all overlooked by a bleak old prison at the end of Residensgatan. **Skracklan Park**, just a few minutes from the centre, is a pretty place to relax, with its 1930s coffee house and promenade. The bronze statue of Sjoberg's muse, Frida, always has fresh flowers in her hand – even in winter, when the lake is solid ice, locals brave the sub-zero winds to thrust rhododendrons through her fingers.

Vänersborg's **museum**, behind the main market square (June–Aug Tues noon–7pm, Wed, Thurs, Sat & Sun noon–4pm; Sept–May Tues, Sat & Sun noon–4pm; 20kr), is worth viewing not so much for its contents (a superabundance of stuffed birds veiled in a century's worth of dust) but because of the sheer antiquity of the displays, which can hardly have changed since the doors first opened to the public in 1891; a living testimony to nineteenth-century museum culture where nothing was meant to be touched and the pervading darkness meant not much more could be seen either.

The **tourist office**'s summer premises have been due to move for several years, but at the time of writing were still at Kungsgatan 15 (June–Aug Mon–Fri 9am–8pm, Sat & Sun 11.30am–4pm; Sept–May Mon–Fri 10am–4pm; ☎0521/27 14 00, fax 27 14 01). If you're here with a car, note that two-hour **parking permits** cost 10kr from kiosks and the tourist office. Apart from the **youth hostel** at Hunneberg (see below), the cheapest place to stay is the friendly and central *Hoglunds* **hotel** at Kyrkogatan 46 (☎0521/71 15 61; ②), or try the *Strand* at Hamngatan 7 (☎0521/138 50, fax 159 00; ③/②). You can **camp** at the lakeside *Ursands Camping* (☎0521/186 66, fax 686 76); get there on **bus** #661, which is really more of a taxi – it makes six journeys a day and you'll need to book a place an hour beforehand on ☎020/71 97 17. For **eating**, try the pleasant bakery-café *Konditori Princess* at Sundsgatan, or make the two-kilometre journey to the excellent hotel restaurant at Värgon (see below). **Nightlife** is pretty limited, the only options being *Club Roccad*, Kungsgatan 23, or *Oslagbar* at Edsgatan 8.

Halleberg and Hunneberg

The 500-million-year-old twin plateaux of **Halleberg** and **Hunneberg**, just a few kilometres east of Vänersborg, are difficult to get to without your own transport, but well worth the trouble. Crossing the Göta River, you'll first reach **VÄRGON**, home to a renowned, ultra-chic restaurant and hotel, *Ronnums Herrgård* (☎0521/26 00 00, fax 26 00 09; ④); there's a set two-course lunch daily from 11.30am to 2pm (200kr). Alternatively, you can save your kronor and get a good pizza and salad for 40kr at *Pizzeria Roma* at Nordkroksvagen 1 (☎0521/22 10 70).

Beyond Värgon, the road cuts through the tree-topped hills. Early human remains have been found here, as well as the traces of an old Viking fort, but the area is best known as the home of Sweden's biggest herd of elk. **Elk safaris** run in midsummer from Vänersborg's central square (150kr), but disease has reduced the stock to just 120, so don't count on seeing any. Probably the easiest way of spotting the creatures is to drive or walk up the five-kilometre lane around Halleberg at dawn or dusk. Take along some apples: these massive creatures have no qualms about eating from your hand.

Regular **buses** run to Värgon from Vänersborg, replaced in summer by a **taxi** service that costs the same; there are just three a day and you need to give an hour's notice (☎020/71 97 17). In addition, bus #619 runs from Trollhättan straight to Hunneberg, while bus #62 goes to Värgon. The excellent **youth hostel**, at Bergagårdsvägen 9 (☎0521/22 03 40, fax 684 97; closed mid-Dec to mid-Jan), is housed in a building at the foot of Hunneberg, dates from 1550 and was used as a base from which Danish soldiers drove the Swedes into the hills. Following the Swedish line of retreat (now a wide path signposted "Naturskola") up Hunneberg brings you to the **Naturskola Nature Centre** (daily: mid-May to mid-Aug 11am–8pm; mid-Aug to mid-May 11am–4pm; free), with a **café** and plenty of information on hand about the wildlife in the hills. A web of nature trails begins here, including special trails for wheelchair users.

Between the lakes: Vastergötland

The county of **Västergötland** comprises much of the region between **lakes Vänern and Vättern** – a wooded landscape that makes up a large part of the train ride between Gothenburg and Stockholm. The most interesting places lie on the southeastern shore of Lake Vänern, notably the pretty town of **Mariestad**, easily reached from Gothenburg, while with more time you can cut south to the western shore of Lake Vättern, and in particular to the colossal fortress at **Karlsborg**. In between the lakes runs the **Göta Canal**, the main regional target for holidaying Swedes in July and August.

Lidköping and around

Although it flanks a grassy banked reach where the River Lidan meets Lake Vänern, **LIDKÖPING**, around 140km northeast of Gothenburg, lacks the charm of other towns in the region. The old town square of 1446 on the east bank of the river faces the new town square, founded by Chancellor Magnus de la Gardie in 1671, on the west; both enjoyed a perfect panorama of Vänern until an unsightly concrete screen of coal-storage cylinders and grain silos was plonked just at the water's edge. The town's claim to fame is the **Rörstrand Porcelain Factory** (Mon–Fri 10am–6pm, Sun noon–4pm; guided tours June & Aug; 15kr), Europe's second oldest, situated at the heart of the bleak industrial zone near the lake. The museum here is pretty uninspiring, but there are some pleasant enough designs on sale at supposedly bargain prices.

Trains arrive at the station by the old square. If you're returning to Gothenburg, change trains at Herrljunga; if you're heading back towards Trollhättan, take **bus** #5, while bus #1 runs directly to Karlsborg (see p.457) in just under two hours. The **tourist office** is in the train station building at Bangatan 3 (May to early June & late Aug Mon–Fri 9am–5pm, Sat 9am–1pm; early to late June & early Aug Mon–Fri 9am–7pm, Sat 10am–7pm, Sun 2–7pm; July Mon–Fri 9am–8pm, Sat 10am–8pm, Sun 2–8pm; ☎0510/77 05 00, fax 77 04 64, *turist@lidkoping.se*) will help with **private rooms** (from 135kr per person; no booking fee), while the cheapest night's stay is at the **youth hostel**, close by at Nicolaigatan 2 (☎0510/664 30). *Park Hotell* (☎0510/243 90, fax 611 50; ②/①) at 24 Mellbygatan – which runs south from Nya Stadens Torg – is a pink-painted 1920s villa **hotel**, with huge rooms and original features. Alternatively, try the *Edward Hotell* at Skaragatan 1 (☎0510/221 10; ③) or the *Stadtshotel* (☎0510/220 85, fax 215 32; ④/③) on Nya Stadens Torg.

For **cafes** and **konditori**, *Garstroms Konditori* at Mellbygatan 2 has been serving cakes and coffee since 1857, or try the attractive *Café Limtorget* on Limtorget, housed in a classic painted wooden cottage in Gamlastad (the old town) and a fine place for gorgeous cakes and waffles. Full meals can be had at *Gotes Festvaning* across the river at Östra Hamnen (☎0510/217 00), or sample the kebabs at *Madonna*, off the main square at Torggatan 6.

Around Lidköping: north to Läckö castle and east to Kinnekulle

Almost everyone heads for **Läckö castle**, 25km north of Lidköping at the tip of the Kalland peninsula. Surrounded by water on three sides, Läckö is everyone's idea of a fairy-tale castle – all turrets and towers, rendered in creamy white. The castle dates from 1290, but was last modified and restructured by Lidköping's Chancellor, de la Gardie, when he took it over in 1652. Inside there's a wealth of exquisite decoration, best appreciated on one of the fairly frequent guided tours in English (daily May–Sept 10am–6pm; 40kr). Be warned, however, that Läckö's charms are no secret, and in summer you should be prepared for the crowds. **Bus** #132 from Lidköping travels out here hourly in summer (20kr), via the tiny village of Spiken.

Twelve kilometres east of Lidköping by train, **KÄLLBY** draws visitors for its ancient burial site (turn left at the road junction), where two impressive stones face each other in an Iron Age cemetery, one carved with a comical, goblin-like figure that's said to be the god Thor. Not far beyond, **Husaby** is a tranquil diversion with great religious and cultural significance. It was here in 1008 that Saint Sigfrid, an English missionary, baptized Olof Skotkonung, the first Swedish king to turn his back on the Viking gods and embrace Christianity. The present three-towered church was built in the twelfth century, just to the west of the well where the baptism is said to have taken place.

Kinnekulle, the "Flowering mountain", is a couple of kilometres on (get off the train at any of the next few stops), an area of woods and lakes interwoven with paths and boasting hundreds of varieties of flowers, trees, birds and other animals. The strange shape of the plateau is due to its top layer of hard volcanic rock, which even four hundred million years of Swedish weather has not managed to wear down, and which makes for something of a botanical and geological treasure trove. There's an STF **youth hostel** (☎0510/406 53, fax 54 00 85) and **campsite** complex nearby in Hellekis (Råbäck station).

Mariestad and around

Smaller, prettier and more welcoming than Lidköping, lakeside **MARIESTAD**, with its splendid medieval quarter and harbour area, is just an hour's train ride to the northeast and an excellent base for a day or two's exploration. It's also worth visiting for the extraordinary range of building styles crammed into its centre – Gustavian, Carolean, Classical, Swiss-chalet style and Art Nouveau – like a living museum of architectural design. Have a look, too, at the **cathedral**, on the edge of the centre, which was built by Duke Karl (who named the town after his wife, Maria of Pfalz) in an attempt to compete with his brother King Johan III's Klara kyrka in Stockholm. To help you explore the town's compact centre, pick up a copy of the walking-tour map from the tourist office, or join one of their free guided **tours** (mid-June to mid-Aug Mon & Thurs).

Mariestad is also an ideal base from which to cruise up Lake Vänern to the start of the Göta Canal's main stretch at **Sjotorp**. There are 21 locks between Sjotorp and Karlsborg, with the most scenic section up to **Lyrestad**, just a few kilometres east of Sjotorp and 20km north of Mariestad on the E20. Lake and canal **cruises** cost 170kr for the day, however long you stay on the boat (contact the tourist office for details).

The **tourist office**, by the harbour on Hamngatan (June–Aug Mon–Fri 8am–7pm, Sat & Sun 9am–6pm; Sept–May Mon–Fri 8am–4pm; ☎0501/100 01, fax 121 40, *turistbyran@mariestad.se*), is opposite the hugely popular STF **youth hostel** (☎0501/104 48; book in advance mid-Aug to mid-June; 120kr). Built after the fire of 1693, the hostel is a former tannery with galleried timber outbuildings and an excellent garden café. For a **hotel**, the *Bergs Hotell* of 1698, in the old town at Kyrkogatan 18 (☎0501/103 24; ①), is very plain inside, but comfortable enough. Other good-value central options include the mundane but cheap *Hotel Aqua*, Viktoriagatan 15 (☎0501/195 15, fax 187 80; ①), or the far cosier and more appealing *Hotel Vänerport*, Hamngatan 32 (☎0501/771 11, fax 771 21; ③). The nearest **campsite** is *Ekuddens*, 2km down the river (☎0501/106 37; May–Sept). Mariestad's trendiest **eating** place is *Café Stroget* at Österlånggatan 10, though the *Garden Café* at the youth hostel is more welcoming, serving baguettes for 30kr. The liveliest **pub-restaurants** are *Buffalo*, at Österlånggatan 3, and *Hjorten*, at Nygatan 21, while the hippest of very few **nightclub-bars** is *Aquavit Blå* at Kungsgatan 5.

Karlsborg and around

Despite the great plans devised for the fortress at **KARLSBORG**, around 70km southeast of Mariestad on the western shores of Lake Vättern, it has survived the years as one of Sweden's greatest follies. By the early nineteenth century, Sweden had lost Finland – after six hundred years of control – and had became jumpy about its own security. In 1818, with the Russian fleet stationed on the Åland Islands and within easy striking distance of Stockholm, Baltzar von Platten persuaded parliament to construct an inland fortress at Karlsborg, capable of sustaining an entire town and protecting the royal family and the treasury – the idea being that enemy forces should be lured into Sweden, then destroyed on home territory. With the town pinched between lakes Vättern and Bottensjön, the Göta Canal – also the brainchild of von Platten and already under construction – was to provide access, but while von Platten had the canal finished by 1832, the fortress was so ambitious a project that it was never completed. It was strategically obsolete long before work was finally abandoned in 1909, and the walls were in any case no longer strong enough to withstand attack from modern weaponry. However, parts are still in use today by the army and air force, and uniformed cadets mill around, lending an air of authenticity.

The complex, which is as large as a town, appears austere and forbidding, but you are free to wander through and to enter the **museum** (mid-May to late June Mon–Fri 10am–4pm; Sat & Sun noon–5pm; late June to early Aug daily 10am–6pm; early Aug to late Aug daily 10am–5pm; Sept to mid-May Mon–Fri 10am–3pm; 30kr) of endless military uniforms; the **guided tour** of the fort (June to late Aug; 60kr), with special sound and smoke effects, is effective enough, though won't be to everyone's taste. A combined tour of the museum and fortress costs 85kr. For further information contact the tourist office (see below).

There is no train service to Karlsborg, though there are regular **bus** services from both Lidköping and Mariestad; if you're driving, take Route 202 from Mariestad. The **tourist office** (June–Aug daily 9am–5pm; Sept–May Mon–Fri 9am–3pm; ☎0505/188 30, fax 188 39), in a lovely old building at the entrance to the fortress during summer (outside the season it's in the big yellow house close by), can book **private rooms** for around 150kr per person. The **youth hostel** (☎ & fax 0506/446 00) is next door, while the **campsite** (☎0505/449 16, fax 449 12; May–Sept) is located on the banks of Lake Bottensjön, two kilometres north. The loveliest **hotel**, and well worth the price, is the *Kanalhotellet,* Storgatan 94 (☎0505/121 30, fax 127 61; ②).

Forsvik

As far back as the early 1300s, the Karlsborg area maintained an important flour mill, 8km north at **FORSVIK**, run by the monastery that was founded by Sweden's first female saint, Birgitta. Using the height differential between lakes Viken and Bottensjon, first over water wheels and later through power-generating turbines, a sizeable industry emerged, working all manner of metal and wood products. During the Reformation, Forsvik was burnt down, but the creation of the Göta Canal gave the place new life, and it once again became a busy industrial centre. Its paper mill continued to operate until the 1940s, and its foundry until the Swedish shipyard crises in the 1970s. Today the mill is a **museum** (June–Aug 9am–5pm; 30kr), which has been restored to its 1940s condition and provides a stimulating picture of Forsvik's industrial past. A bus runs from Karlsborg fairly frequently in summer.

travel details

Trains
Gothenburg to: Kalmar (2–3 daily; 4hr 20min); Karlskrona (1–2 daily; 4hr 40min); Malmö (8–12 daily; 3hr 50min); Stockholm (9–13 daily; 4hr 30min); Strömstad (9 daily; 2hr 40min); Trollhättan (13 daily; 40min); Vänersborg (Mon–Fri 10 daily, 4 on Sat & Sun; 1hr 5min).

Buses

Gothenburg to: Borås (Mon–Fri 13 daily, 3 on Sat, 8 on Sun; 55min); Falun/Gävle (1–3 daily; 10hr 30min); Halmstad (Fri & Sun 3 daily; 2hr); Karlstad (3–5 daily; 4hr); Linköping/Norrköping (3–4 daily, 1 on Sat; 4hr 35min); Mariestad (4–5 daily; 3hr); Oskarshamn (2 on Fri & Sun; 5hr 20min); Oslo (4–5 daily; 4hr 45min); Tanumshede/Strömstad (4–5 daily; 2hr 30min); Trollhättan (2–5 daily; 1hr 5min); Varberg/Falkenberg (2 on Fri & Sun; 50min/1hr 20min).

Lidköping to: Vänersborg/Trollhättan (2 on Fri & Sun; 1hr).

Mariestad to: Gävle (1 daily Mon–Fri; 7hr 30min); Örebro (1–2 daily; 1hr 30min); Skövde/Jönköping (3–4 daily, 1 on Sat; 1hr 30min).

Strömstad to: Svinesund (4–5 daily; 20min).

International ferries

Gothenburg to: Harwich (2 weekly; 24hr); Frederikshavn (ferries: 4–8 daily; 3hr 15min; catamaran: 3–5 daily; 1hr 45min); Kiel (1 daily; 14hr); Newcastle (June to mid-Aug 1 weekly; 24hr).

Strömstad to: Fredrikstad (mid-June to mid-Aug Mon–Sat 5 daily; 1hr 15min); Halden (mid-June to mid-Aug Mon–Sat 3 daily; 1hr 15min); Sandefjord (mid-June to mid-Aug 2 daily; 2hr 30min).

CHAPTER ELEVEN

THE SOUTHWEST

There is a real historical interest to the **southwestern** provinces of **Halland**, **Skåne** and **Blekinge**, not least in the towns and cities that line the coast. The flatlands and fishing ports south of Gothenburg were traded almost constantly between Denmark and Sweden from the fourteenth to seventeenth centuries, and several fortresses today bear witness to the region's medieval buffer status.

Halland, facing Denmark, has a coastline of smooth sandy beaches and bare, granite outcrops, punctuated by a number of small towns. Most charismatic is the old society bathing resort of **Varberg**, dominated by its tremendous thirteenth-century fortress. The small, beautifully intact medieval core of **Falkenberg** is also notable, while for beaches and nightlife, the regional capital, **Halmstad**, is a popular base.

Further south in the ancient province of **Skåne**, the coastline softens into curving beaches backed by gently undulating fields. This was one of the first parts of the country to be settled, and the scene of some of the bloodiest battles during the medieval conflict with Denmark. Although Skåne was finally ceded to Sweden in the late seventeenth century, the Danish influence died hard, and is still evident today in the thick Skåne accent, often incomprehensible to other Swedes, and in the province's architecture. The latter has also been strongly influenced by Skåne's agricultural economy, whose centuries of profitable farming have left the countryside dotted with **castles** – though the continued income from the land means that most of these palatial homes are still in private hands and not open to the public.

The popular perception of Skåne is as a fertile but largely flat and uniform landscape; however, it's worth taking a day or two to appreciate the subtle variety of the countryside – blocks of yellow rape, crimson poppy and lush-green fields interspersed with castles, charming white churches and black windmills. One of the best areas for **walking** and **cycling** is the **Bjäre peninsula**, the thumb of land to the west of the glamorous tennis capital of **Båstad**, where forested hill ranges, spectacular rock formations and dramatic cliffs make for some beautiful scenery. To the south, both **Helsingborg**, with its laid-back, cosmopolitan atmosphere, and Sweden's third city, bustling **Malmö**, are only a stone's throw from Denmark. Between these two centres, and in contrast to Malmö's industrial heritage, the university town of **Lund** has some classic architecture and a unique atmosphere – an essential stop for anyone travelling in the south.

ACCOMMODATION PRICE CODES

The hotels and guesthouses listed in this chapter have been graded according to the following price bands, based on the cost of the **least expensive double room during high season** (late June to Aug). However, almost every hotel offers seasonal and/or weekend discounts, and wherever possible we've given two grades, covering both the regular and the discounted rate.

① Under 500kr	② 500–700kr	③ 700–900kr
④ 900–1200kr	⑤ 1200–1500kr	⑥ Over 1500kr

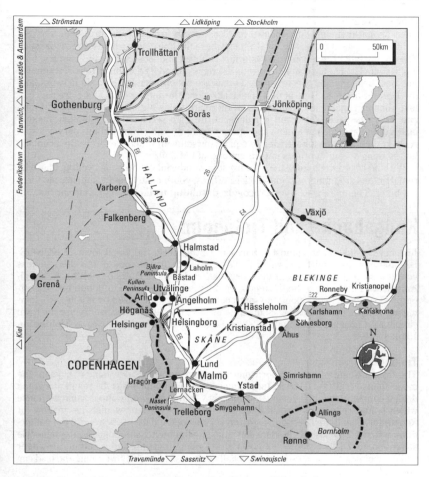

Sweeping east towards the pretty medieval town of **Ystad**, the coast passes some minor resorts with excellent beaches. Beyond here, you enter the splendid countryside of **Österlen**, whose pastoral scenery is studded with Viking monuments, such as the Swedish Stonehenge at **Ales Stennar**, and whose coast is lined with some brilliant white beaches backed by nature reserves. Edging north, the land becomes green and more hilly, while the coast features a number of interesting little places to stop, such as **Kivik**, with its apple orchards and Bronze Age cairn, and the ancient and picturesque resort of **Åhus**. In the northeast of the county, **Kristianstad**, built as a flagship town by the Danes, retains its fine, Renaissance structure.

Beyond here to the east, the ledge of land running to the Baltic is **Blekinge**. Among the province's many small and not particularly distinguished resorts, **Karlskrona** stands out. Centred on a number of islands forming a small archipelago, Sweden's second city in the eighteenth century still exudes an air of regal and naval grandeur.

Getting around

The national **train** network follows the coast south from Gothenburg, with frequent trains stopping at all towns as far as Ystad, where the line cuts northeast to Kristianstad. The comfortable Kustpilen Express trains run east and west across the country, linking Malmö, Helsingborg and Lund with Kristianstad and Karlskrona. However, some of the most beautiful and less-frequented areas are not covered by the train network, and the **bus** service is skeletal at best, especially along the south coast. There are also certain transport anomalies to look out for: there are trains but no buses between Malmö and Ystad; between Ystad and Kristianstad the train service is very limited, making buses the more efficient option; and, more generally, some train and bus services stop early in the day – it's a good idea to equip yourself with timetables from the train and bus stations or tourist offices in Gothenburg and Malmö.

With no really steep hills, the southwest is wonderful country for **cycling**, and bike rental outlets are numerous; most tourist offices, youth hostels and campsites also rent out bikes. There are also several recognized **walking trails**, mentioned in the text.

Kungsbacka and Tjolöholm

Just beyond the southernmost suburbs of Gothenberg, the small town of **KUNGS-BACKA** is a residential backwater that's of no particular interest to travellers, unless you time your trip to arrive on the lively market day (first Thurs of month). Although Kungsbacka dates from the thirteenth century, when it was one of a number of prosperous Hanseatic towns along the south coast, the town was razed by fire in 1846, leaving just a couple of houses as testament to its past. It's altogether better to use the town simply as a means of reaching the splendid manor house on the coast at **Tjolöholm**, 15km south.

Tjolöholm

The dream home of Scottish-born merchant and horse-breeder James Dickson, the manor house at **TJOLÖHOLM** (pronounced "Chewla-home") was the result of a grand design competition in the 1890s. Enormously wealthy, Dickson wanted a unique house which would reflect his British ancestry, the then current Swedish fascination for Romanticism, and the latest domestic innovations of the day. The winner of the competition was the 27-year-old Lars Israel Wahlman, who built a stunning Elizabethan-style stately home. Dickson, however, never saw Tjolöholm completed – cutting his finger while opening a champagne bottle, he fatally poisoned himself by wrapping the lead cap around the wound.

In 1901, a village was built around the house, and its little red-and-white wooden cottages have been immaculately preserved. Along the main driveway, the huge stables and indoor riding track have been converted into an airy café, while the next building contains a **carriage museum** (same times as house – see below), worth a peek to see the bizarre horse-drawn vacuum cleaner. The **interior** of the house (June–Aug daily 11am–4pm; Sept & Oct Sun only 11am–4pm; 45kr) deserves a good hour or so – free pamphlets in English are available (guided tours in English have to be pre-booked on ☎0300/54 42 00). Among the many highlights are the billiard room, whose walls are lined with Belgian marble and punctuated by hot-air vents (part of what was a very new-fangled heating system), and the regal study, which was oak-panelled by Liberty's of London. Sweeping through Blanche Dickson's red boudoir and her four fabulous bathrooms, with sunken baths and showers that sprayed Mrs Dickson from all sides, you're led on to the Charles Rennie Mackintosh-inspired children's nursery, with its simple, white motifs. Once you've had your fill of the mansion, you can while away a pleasant few hours in the grounds, which slope down to a grass-fringed beach.

Practicalities

To get to Tjolöholm, take the **local train** to Kungsbacka from platform 15 at Gothenburg's Central Station (journey time 20min). A special bus runs from here to the house at 11am, returning in the afternoon; if you miss that, **bus** #732 goes to within 3km of the manor, from where you'll have to walk or hitch. In July and August, there's a special SJ bus direct to Tjolöholm from Nils Ericsonsplatsen, by Gothenburg station (Sat, Sun & public holidays). By car, turn off the E6 highway just south of Kungsbacka at Fjärås, and follow the signs to Åsa for 2km, from where there are signs for Tjolöholm.

Kungsbacka has an STF **youth hostel** (☎0300/194 85; mid-June to mid-Aug), 2km from the train station on the road to Sarö – turn left from the station then right onto the main road. **Private rooms** at 170kr per person can be booked at the **tourist office** opposite the station (mid-May to mid-June Mon–Fri 9am–5pm, Sat 10am–2pm; late June Mon–Fri 9am–6pm, Sat 10am–2pm; July Mon–Sat 9am–6pm, Sun 10am–2pm; Aug Mon–Fri 9am–6pm, Sat & Sun 10am–2pm; Sept to mid-May Mon–Fri 9am–5pm; ☎0300/345 95, fax 131 34). The only convenient **hotel** is the reasonable *Hotel Halland* at Storgatan 35 (☎0300/775 30, fax 162 25; ④/②), almost next to the tourist office. The nearest **campsite** (June–Aug ☎0300/148 29; Sept–May ☎0300/346 48) is 3km away at the Kungsbacka Sportscenter – it's a five- to ten-minute walk southwest along Storgatan from the centre of Kungsbacka.

Varberg

More atmospheric than any other town in Halland, the fashionable little nineteenth-century bathing resort of **VARBERG** boasts surprisingly varied sights – most obviously its imposing fortress – plus a laid-back atmosphere, opportunities to swim and plenty of good places to eat.

The Town

All Varberg's sights are concentrated along or near the seafront, with the thirteenth-century moated **fortress**, set on a rocky promontory in the sea, the most prominent attraction. Home to the Swedish king Magnus Eriksson, important peace treaties with Valdemar of Denmark were signed here in 1343. Standing outside, it's easy to imagine how impenetrable the fortress must have appeared to attackers in the past, as the way in is hardly more obvious today: enter on the sea-facing side by climbing the uneven stone steps to a delightful terrace café, or approach through the great archways towards the central courtyard.

Although **tours** in English (July & Aug hourly 11am–4pm; on request at other times; 30kr) take you into the dungeons and among the impressive cocoa-coloured buildings that make up the inner courtyard, it's the **museum** that deserves most of your attention (mid-June to mid-Aug daily 10am–6pm; mid-Aug to mid-June Mon–Fri 10am–4pm, Sat & Sun noon–4pm; summer 40kr, rest of the year 20kr). The most unnerving exhibit is **Bocksten Man**, a 600-year-old murder victim who was garrotted, drowned, impaled and buried in a local bog until 1936, when a farmer dug him up. His entire outfit preserved by the acid bog, Bocksten Man sports the western world's most complete medieval wardrobe, made up of a cloak, a hood, shoes and stockings. His most shocking feature is the thick, red ringletted hair that cascades around his puny skull, while the three stakes thrust through his body were supposed to ensure that his spirit never escaped to seek out his murderers. Much of the rest of the museum is missable, with sections on farming and fishing in Halland, though the room devoted to the works of the so-called **Varberg School** is worth viewing. A small colony of artists – Richard

Bergh, Nils Kreuger and Karl Nordström – who joined together in the last years of the nineteenth century, they developed a national painting style reflecting the moods and atmosphere of Halland, Varberg in particular. Night scenes of the fortress beneath the stars show the strong influence of Van Gogh, but in other paintings, the misty colours create a more melancholy effect.

Overlooking the sea, the cream-painted **fortress prison** from 1850 looks incongruously delicate in the shadow of the looming fortress. The first Swedish prison to be built with individual cells, it housed life prisoners, until the last one ended his days here in 1931. Today you can stay in a private youth hostel in the fortress, which has been carefully preserved to retain most of its original features (see below).

A couple of fine remnants from Varberg's time as a spa resort are within a minute of the fortress. Just behind it, facing the town, is the grand **Societeshuset**, a confection of white-and-pink carved wood where upper-class ladies took their meals after bathing in the splendid (and now beautifully restored) **Kallbadhuset** (cold bathhouse), just to the north of the fortress and overlooking the harbour. This dainty bathhouse has separate-sex naked-bathing areas and is topped at each corner by Moorish cupolas, lending it an imperial air.

Although the Halland coastline is still a little rocky around here, there are several excellent spots for bathing. Head down Strandpromenaden for about five minutes to get to a couple of well-known **nudist beaches**. Goda Hopp, for men, and Kärringhålan for women. Alternatively, a few kilometres further north at **Getterön**, a fist of land jutting into the sea, there's a nature centre and extensive bird reserve, as well as a series of secluded coves, reached by regular buses from town.

Practicalities

Varberg is a handy entry point to southern Sweden, linked by a year-round **ferry** (pedestrians 90–110kr one way; car and up to five people 580kr; 3hr 45min) to Grenå in **Denmark**. Regular **trains** run down the coast from Gothenburg, and local **buses** cover the 45-kilometre trip south from Kungsbacka (bus #732, changing to #615 at Frillesås). From the **train and bus stations**, turn right down Vallgatan and the town centre is off to the left, the harbour to the right. The seasonal **tourist office** in the central square (mid-June to Aug Mon–Sat 9am–7pm, Sun 3–7pm; Sept–March Mon–Fri 8am–5pm; April to mid-June Mon–Fri 8am–5pm, Sat 10am–7pm; ☎0340/887 70, fax 611 195) provides free maps of the town. Varberg is easy to walk around, but to explore the nearby coast it might be worth **renting a bike** from Erlan Cykel och Sport, Västra Vallgatan 41 (☎0340/144 55; 70kr per day, 200kr per week) or from *Getteröns Camping* (see opposite; 50kr per day).

It's worth booking well in advance for the fortress prison **youth hostel** (☎0340/887 88); outside the summer you have to book through the tourist office. Aside from being spotlessly clean, the prison is much as it was, with original cell doors (each has its own key), complete with spy-holes. If it's full, try the other very central hostel, *Platsamas Vandrahem* at Villagatan 13 (☎0340/61 16 40). The cheapest **hotel** is the spartan but clean *Hotel Bergklinten*, close to the station at Västra Vallgatan 25 (☎0340/61 15 45; ①). Alternatively, a couple of excellent-value and appealing family-run hotels are just a few steps away. *Hotel Gåstis*, Borgmästaregatan 1 (☎0340/180 50, fax 138 50; ③), includes an evening meal in the price and offers free cycle hire for guests; there's also a sauna, spa pool and gym. Close by at Norrgatan 16 is *Hotel Varberg* (☎0340/161 25, fax 159 02; ③), which retains some of its nineteenth-century grandeur and serves a great breakfast. The price includes a ticket worth 100kr in the restaurant next door, and service is warm and relaxed. *Hotel Fregatten* (☎0340/770 00, fax 61 11 21; ④/②), in a former cold-storage warehouse overlooking the harbour, is not as stylish as it used to be. There are a number of **campsites** in the area, the nearest being *Apelvikens Camping* (☎0340/141 78, fax

875 38; April–Oct), 3km south of the fortress along Strandpromenaden. To the north, near the nature reserve, is *Getteröns Camping* (☎0340/168 85, fax 104 22). Alternatively, there are plenty of places to put up a tent for free beyond the nudist beaches.

There are plenty of good places to **eat** in Varberg, mostly along Kungsgatan running north of the main square. The best café in town, and great for breakfast, is *Kunst Kafe* on the corner of Norrgatan and Västra Vallgatan. The relaxed *Maja's* at Kungsgatan 28 is where the young locals come. Further down the street, *Harry's Pub & Restaurant* serves a range of pastas (75kr), though service can be less than attentive; they also have a popular happy hour (4–7pm). For lunch, try the *Societen* in Societets Park, directly behind the fortress, where daily specials go for 69kr, or visit on Friday and Saturday evenings, when it comes alive with foxtrotting Swedes.

Falkenberg

It's a twenty-minute train ride south from Varberg to the well-preserved medieval town of **FALKENBERG**, named after the falcons that were once hunted here. With some lively museums and a long beach, it's a likeable little town, though it only really comes alive in July and August. Sir Humphrey Davy, inventor of the mining safety lamp, visited in the 1820s to go **fly-fishing** in the River Ätran that runs through town, and, as the town's reputation for salmon spread, a succession of wealthy English countrymen followed him here, leaving their mark on the town. Today the waters have been so over-fished that it costs relatively little to try your hand in the two-kilometre stretch from the splendid stone **Tullbron** toll bridge of 1756 – permits are available from the tourist office (see overleaf) from March to September, cost 80kr and allow you to catch up to three fish a day.

The **old town**, to the west of the curving river, comprises a dense network of low, wooden cottages and cobbled lanes. Nestling among them is the fine twelfth-century **St Laurentii kyrka**, its interior awash with seventeenth- and eighteenth-century wall and ceiling paintings. When the town acquired a solid new neo-Gothic church in the late nineteenth century, the St Laurentii kyrka was only saved from demolition by being used variously as a shooting range, a cinema and a gymnasium, until being reconsecrated in the 1920s.

Bypassing the pedestrian **Local Museum** on St Lars Kyrkogatan, head straight for the **Falkenberg Museum** (June to mid-Sept Tues–Fri 10am–4pm, Sat & Sun noon–4pm; mid-Sept to May Tues–Fri & Sun noon–4pm; 20kr) in an old grain store near the main bridge. While there are the usual archeological collections, the enthusiastic curator has chosen to devote most of the museum to the 1950s, with displays covering Falkenberg's dance bands, along with original interiors of a shoe repair shop and a stylized café. The town also boasts a rather unusual **Photography Museum** at Sandgatan 13 (late June to mid-Aug Tues–Thurs 1–7pm; mid-Aug to late June Tues–Thurs 5–7pm, Sun 2–6pm; 30kr), housed in what was originally Falkenberg's first purpose-built cinema. Among the thousand or so cameras and other cinematic paraphernalia, there are some superb local peasant portraits, taken in 1898 by Axel Aurelius. Less demanding is a tour of the local **Falken Brewery** (July & Aug Mon–Thurs 10am & 1.15pm; 20kr, bookable at the tourist office): Sweden's most popular beer, Falken, has been brewed here since 1896 and is available for sampling at the end of the tour.

Over the river and fifteen minutes' walk south there's a fine, four-kilometre stretch of sandy beach, **Skrea Strand**. At its northern end is the large bathing and tennis complex of **Klitterbadhuset** (mid-June to mid-Aug Mon–Fri 9am–7pm, Tues & Thurs from 6am, Sat 9am–5pm, Sun 9am–4pm; mid-Aug to mid-June Tues & Thurs 6–9am & noon–8pm, Wed noon–8pm, Fri 9am–noon, Sat 9am–5pm, Sun 9am–3pm; 30kr), which offers a fifty-metre saltwater pool and shallow children's pool, a vast sauna, jacuzzi and steam rooms. If you walk all the way down past the wooden holiday shacks at the southern end of the beach, you'll come across some secluded coves; in early summer, the marshy grassland around here is full of wild violets and clover and is a great place for bird-watching.

Practicalities

Regular **buses** and **trains** drop you close to the centre on Holgersgatan, just a couple of minutes from the **tourist office** in Stortorget (mid-June to mid-Aug Mon–Sat 9am–7pm, Sun 3–7pm; mid-Aug to Sept Mon–Fri 9am–5pm, Sat 10am–2pm; Oct to mid-June Mon–Fri 9am–5pm; ☎0346/174 10, fax 145 26, *falkenberg.tourist@mailbox.colypso.net*). They can book **private rooms** from 120kr per person, plus 30kr booking fee. The comfortable and well-equipped STF **youth hostel** (☎0346/171 11; June to mid-Aug) is in the countryside at Näset, 4km south of town – buses #1 and #2 run there until 7pm. It's just a few minutes' walk through the neighbouring **campsite** (☎0346/171 07) to the south end of the beach. The best-located **hotel** for the beach is the sprawling modern *Hotel Standbaden* (☎0346/71 49 00, fax 161 11; ④); the price includes entry to the Klitterbadhuset complex. Rather more interesting is the riverside *Hvitan* (☎0346/820 90, fax 597 96; ③/②), which has a good restaurant and pub, while the cheapest is *Hotel Steria,* a ten-minute walk from the river up Arvidstorpsvägen (☎0346/155 21, fax 101 30; ①).

About the best place for **lunch** is the atmospheric *Falkmanska Caféet*, Storgatan 42, which serves huge baguettes and decadent cakes. The friendly *D.D.*, at Hotelgatan 3 (closed Sept–May Sun–Tues), is a smallish restaurant and club serving American food and a 55kr lunch; at night it turns into a dance floor. On the main square, *Harry's Bar* is a busy eating place and pub. The poshest restaurant is *Gustav Bratt*, Brogatan 1, near the main square, though its à la carte menu is nothing special. Lunch here costs around 150kr.

Halmstad

The principal town in Halland, **HALMSTAD**, was once a grand walled city and important Danish stronghold. Today, although most of the original buildings have disappeared, the town boasts a couple of cultural and artistic points of interest, most notably the works of the Halmstad Group, Sweden's first Surrealists, extensive, if rather crowded, beaches, and a wide range of really good places to eat.

In 1619, the town's **castle** was used by Danish King Christian IV to entertain the Swedish king Gustav II Adolf; records show that there were seven days of solid festivities. The bonhomie didn't last much longer than that, and Christian was soon building great stone and earth fortifications around the city, surrounded by a moat with four stone gateways. Soon after, a fire all but destroyed the city; the only buildings to survive were the castle and church. Undeterred, Christian took the opportunity to create a modern Renaissance town with a grid of straight streets – the high street, Storgatan, still contains a number of impressive merchants' houses from that time. After the final defeat of the Danes in 1645, Halmstad lost its military significance and the walls were torn down. Today, just one of the great gateways, Norre Port, remains, while Karl XIs Vägen runs directly above the filled-in moat.

The Town

At the centre of the lively market square, **Stora Torg**, is Carl Milles' *Europa and the Bull*, a fountain with mermen twisted around it, all with Milles' characteristically muscular bodies and ugly faces. Flanking one side of the square is the grand fourteenth-century **St Nikolai kyrka** (daily 8.30am–3.30pm), testimony to the town's former importance. Today, the only signs of its medieval origins are the splodges of bare rock beneath the plain brick columns. Leading north from the square, pedestrianized **Storgatan** is a charming street with some creaking old houses built in the years following the 1619 fire, and also the town's main venue for restaurants and nightlife. The great stone arch of **Norre Port** marks the street's end: through here and to the right is the splendid **Norre Katt Park**, a delightful, shady place, with mature beech and horse chestnut trees sloping down to the river bank.

By the river at the northernmost edge of the park is a fine **museum** (June to late Aug daily 10am–7pm, Wed till 9pm; late Aug to May Mon–Fri 10am–4pm, Wed till 9pm; 20kr, 10kr in winter). While the archeological finds are unlikely to set many pulses racing, upstairs there are some home interiors from the seventeenth, eighteenth and nineteenth centuries, including exquisitely furnished dolls' houses and a room of glorious Gustavian harps and square pianos from the 1780s. The top floor contains a decent sample of the work of the Halmstad Group.

A few kilometres north of the town centre heading out along Karlsrovägen past the tiny airport, **Mellby Arts Centre** (July to mid-Aug Tues–Sun 1–6pm; mid-March to June & mid-Aug to Oct Tues–Sun 1–5pm; Nov to mid-Dec Sat & Sun 1–5pm; 40kr) is home to the largest collection of works by the **Halmstad Group**, a body of six local artists who championed Cubism and Surrealism in 1920s Sweden. Their work caused considerable controversy in the 1930s and 40s, and a quick glance shows how strongly they were influenced by Magritte and Dali. Reputedly the only group of its type to have stayed together in its entirety for fifty years, they sometimes worked together on a single project: you can see a good example at the Halmstad City Library, where an impressive fourteen-metre six-section work adorns the wall above the shelves. To get to the centre, take bus #350 or #351 to the airport, from where it's a one-kilometre walk down the road on the right.

Practicalities

From the **train station**, follow Bredgatan to the Nissan River and just by Österbro (East Bridge) is the **tourist office** (June & mid-Aug Mon–Fri 9am–6pm, Sat 10am–3pm; May & late Aug Mon–Fri 9am–6pm, Sat 10am–1pm; July & early Aug Mon–Sat 9am–7pm, Sun 3–7pm; Sept–April Mon–Fri 9am–5pm; ☎035/10 93 45, fax 15 81 15, *info@tourist@halmstad.se*), across the bridge from the main square. They can book **private rooms** (from 120kr per person, plus 25kr booking fee in person, 50kr by phone). Renting a **bike** is a good way to get out to the Mellby Arts Centre or the beaches on the coast hereabouts: there's currently one outlet, Arvid Olsson Cykel, Norra Vägen 11 (Mon–Fri 9.30am–6pm, Sat 9.30am–1pm; ☎035/21 22 51), which charges a steep 95kr per day for a five-speed bike.

There's a central **youth hostel** (☎035/12 05 00; mid-June to mid-Aug) at Skepparegatan 23, 500m to the west of St Nicolai kyrka, which has showers and toilets in all rooms. The best two of the central **hotels** are the very comfortable old *Norre Park Hotel*, Norra Vägen 7 (☎035/21 85 55, fax 10 45 28; ④/③), through the Norre Port Arch north of Storgatan, overlooking the park. The other is the classic *Hotel Continental*, Kungsgatan 5 (☎035/17 63 00, fax 12 86 04; ④/③), just two minutes' walk from the train station and boasting a free sauna and solarium within this National Romantic-style hotel. The nearest **campsite** is *Hägons Camping*, about 3km from the centre (☎035/12 53 63, fax 12 43 65). There are also some **cabins** (3200–4500kr per week for up to eight people).

Eating, **drinking** and **nightlife** possibilities abound along **Storgatan**, although prices can be steep in the swisher places. *Daltons* is a modern bar-restaurant featuring Swedish music and a bar open to the sky in summer. *Kavaljeren* (known locally as "Kavven"), set in the mellow, candlelit vaulted cellars of the seventeenth-century law courts, is a popular nightclub, while *Pio & Co* is a lovely place where the speciality is steaks served on wooden planks with piles of mashed potato at 172kr and a massive drinks list. The best **cafés** are the old-fashioned *Stånska Hembageriet* at Bankgatan 1, just off Storgatan, *Strömbergs Ost & Delikatessen* on Storgatan, which serves great light lunches, and *Tre Hjartan* on Stora Torg, with cakes and sandwiches served in an impressive building with ceiling paintings.

Båstad and the Bjäre peninsula

Although linked together geographically, the town of **Båstad** and the attached **Bjäre peninsula** couldn't be more dissimilar. Båstad is a major Swedish sports resort, geared towards the chic pastimes of yachting, golfing and tennis; the peninsula, on the other hand, is a lot less manicured – with both rugged coastlines and lush meadows, it's an area of outstanding natural beauty.

Båstad

The most northerly town in the ancient province of Skåne, **BÅSTAD** has a character markedly distinct from the other towns along the coast. Cradled by the Bjäre peninsula, which bulges westwards into the Kattegat (the water separating Sweden and Jutland), Båstad is Sweden's elite **tennis centre**, hosting the annual Swedish Open at the beginning of July (tickets 90–310kr), plus another sixty tennis courts, five eighteen-hole golf courses and the well-known Drivan Sports Centre. It's all set in beautiful surroundings, with a horizon of forested hills to the south. Less pleasant, however, is the fact that ever since King Gustav V chose to take part in the 1930 tennis championships, wealthy retired Stockholmers and social climbers from all over Sweden have flocked here to bask in the social glow, something that's reflected in the ostentatiously chic clothes shops and Oriental antique specialists that line **Köpmansgatan**, the main thoroughfare.

Practicalities

From the **train station**, it's a half-hour walk east along Köpmansgatan to the main square, where the **tourist office** (mid-June to mid-Aug Sun–Fri 10am–6pm, Sat 10am–3pm; mid-Aug to mid-June Mon–Sat 10am–4pm; ☎0431/750 45, fax 700 55, *turistbyran@bastad-tourism.se*) can book **private rooms** for 140kr per person. They can also give information on booking tennis courts and renting out sports equipment. The main **bike rental** place is Svenn's Cykel, Tennisvägen 31 (60kr per day). To get to the **harbour and beach**, follow Tennisvägen off Köpmansgatan through a luxury residential district until you reach Strandpromenaden; to the west, the old bathhouses have been converted into restaurants and bars.

The STF **youth hostel** (June–Aug ☎0431/685 00, fax 706 19; Sept–May ☎0431/710 30) is next to the Drivan Sports Centre on Korrödsvagen, signposted off Köpmansgatan. It's open all year, but tends to be reserved for groups in winter, and the number of sporty youngsters here make it one of the noisiest places to stay. The cheaper **hotels** are mostly around the station end of town; note that prices in Båstad increase dramatically during the summer due to the tennis. *Hotel Pension Enehall* at Stationsterrasen 10 (☎0431/750 15, fax 724 09; ②) is an unexciting modern hotel just a few metres from the train station. More atmospheric are the *Bed & Breakfast Malengården*, Åhusvägen 41 (☎ & fax 0431/36 95 67; ①) – take the turning off Köpmansgatan towards the youth hostel – and the *Hotel Pension Furuhem*, close to the train station at Roxmansvägen 13 (☎0431/701 09, fax 701 80; ①); for a harbourside setting, try the *Hotel Skansen* (☎0431/720 50, fax 700 85; ③). **Camping** is not allowed on the dunes; you're best off heading to the Bjäre pensinsula.

Eating and drinking is as much a pastime as tennis in Båstad, and most of the waterside restaurants and hotels both here and on the peninsula offer two-course dinners for around 120kr, with menus changing weekly. *Pepe's Bodega* is a swish pizza place at the harbour; next door is *Fiskbiten*, a busy fish restaurant, set in a c.1900 bathing house. *Slamficken*, in a neighbouring bathing house, has a popular grill from 6pm, and is also open for breakfast and lunch. Although there are a few **nightclubs**, Båstad is much more geared up for wine sipping in restaurants, with only the very young filling the tacky venues along Köpmansgatan.

The Bjäre peninsula

The highlight of the entire region, the magical **Bjäre peninsula** demands a couple of days' exploration. Its varied scenery ranges from open fields of potatoes and strawberries to cliff formations of splintered red rock and remote islands thick with birds and dotted with historical ruins. To help you find your way around, buy a large-scale **map** of the area from Båstad tourist office (40kr). The **Skåneleden walking trail** runs round the entire perimeter of the peninsula, and is equally good for cycling (a few gears help, as the terrain can get quite hilly). **Public transport** around the peninsula is adequate: bus #525 leaves Båstad every other hour on weekdays, running through the centre of the peninsula, via Hov and Karup, to Torekov (20min); at weekends you'll need to call Båstad taxi (☎0431/696 66) an hour before you want to leave – it costs the same as the bus, but be sure to book your return trip. Bus #524 leaves from Förslov, on the peninsula's southern coast, for Hov, which is useful if you've walked this far. If you don't want to head back to Båstad, bus #523 goes regularly from Torekov south to Ängelholm (50min).

Heading north out of Båstad along the coast road, it's just a couple of kilometres to **Norrvikens Gardens** (May to mid-Sept daily 10am–6pm; 35kr), a paradise for horticulturists and also the site in July of Sweden's biggest annual **classic car show** (100kr). Two to three kilometres further on is **KATTVIK**. Once a busy stone-grinding mill village, it's now largely the domain of elderly, wealthy Stockholmers, who snap up the few houses as soon as they appear on the market – it achieved its moment of fame when Richard Gere chose a cottage here for a summer romance. Otherwise, it contains little more than the friendly *Delfin Bed & Breakfast* (☎0431/731 20; ①), an idyllic base for exploring the region, with gourmet vegetarian cooking and breakfast served on the veranda. The sleepy village of **TOREKOV** lies on the peninsula's western coast a few kilometres from Kattvik, and its little harbour is where old fishing boats leave for the nature reserve island of **Hallands Väderö**. Old wooden fishing boats make the fifteen-minute crossing regularly (June–Aug hourly; Sept–May every 2hr; 55kr return), the last one returning at 4.30pm, so it's worth setting off early to give yourself a full day. The island is a glorious mix of trees and sun-warmed bare rocks, with isolated fishing cottages dotted around its edges, while countless birds – gulls, eiders, guillemots and cormorants – fly noisily overhead. If you're lucky, you may be able to make out the seal colony, which lies on the farthest rocks at the southern tip of the island – or ask at Torekov tourist office about organized seal safaris. Check out also the English graveyard, surrounded by mossy drystone walls, which contains the remains of English sailors killed in 1809 when stationed here in order to bombard Copenhagen during the Napoleonic Wars.

Ängelholm and the Kullen peninsula

The best aspects of peacefully uneventful **ÄNGELHOLM** are its 7km of popular golden beach and its proximity to everywhere else in the region – Helsingborg is just thirty minutes away by train, the Bjäre peninsula beckons to the north. It's also the site of a regional airport. With a range of accommodation and some agreeable restaurants, its not a bad base, and there's also a surprisingly lively nightlife too. Ängelholm's efforts to sell itself, however, concentrate not on its beaches but on the town mascot, a musical clay cuckoo (on sale everywhere) and UFOs. The latter have been big business here since 1946, when a railway worker, Gösta Carlsson, convinced the authorities that he had encountered tiny people from another world. Today Ängelholm hosts international UFO conferences, and the tourist board runs tours to the "landing site" of Carlsson's aliens throughout the summer.

From the train station, it's just a few minutes' walk over the Rönneå River to the main square and tourist office. Not far from here, up Kyrkogatan, is a rather unexciting **handicrafts museum** (May–Aug Tues–Fri 1–5pm, Sat 10am–2pm; 10kr), housed in what used to be the town prison. Should you want to see more of the town, the least strenuous way is on a **boat trip** up the river from the harbour (☎0431/203 00; early June to mid-Aug), lasting either forty minutes (45kr) or 2hr (60kr). For more freedom of movement, Skåne Marin, the company which runs the tours, also rents out boats and canoes. If none of this appeals, head left from the station a few kilometres out to the **beaches**. A free bus runs there from the market square (late June to mid-Aug hourly 10am–4pm).

Jutting like a stiletto heel into the Kattegatt, the **Kullen peninsula**, west of Ängelholm, is a highlight along this stretch of coast. It's far flatter than the Bjäre peninsula to the north, and so makes for good cycling. but still undulates enough to ensure there are some great vistas. Head to the picture-perfect village of **Arild**, from where it's just a couple of kilometres northwest to the eighteenth-century farmstead of **Himmelstorp**. From Himmelstorp, it's well worth the twenty-minute scramble to the coast to the remarkable"living" sculpture, **Nimis**. Created by sculptor Lars Vilks out of driftwood, *Nimis* forms corridors and stairways into the sea, providing a spectacular foreground to the backdrop of the Kattegat and the Bjäre peninsula beyond.

To get to Kullen by car or bike, take Järnvägsgatan from Ängelholm, following directions to Höganäs, then take the scenic northern coastal road at Utvälinge. **Bus #225** runs from Ängelholm to Höganäs and on to Mölle bus station almost hourly until after midnight.

Practicalities

There are regular **trains** to Ängelholm from Båstad (25min), plus **buses** from Båstad and Torekov. It's a short distance from the train station to the **tourist office** in the main square (mid-June to mid-Aug Mon–Fri 9am–7pm, Sat 9am–4pm, Sun 11am–3pm; early June & late Aug Mon–Fri 9am–6pm, Sat 9am–2pm; Sept–May Mon–Fri 9am–5pm; ☎0431/821 30, fax 192 07, *turistbyran@engelholm.se*). For **bike rental**, head to Harry's Cykel, Södra Kyrkogatan 9 (☎0431/143 25; 100kr per day). The tourist office can also book hotels (20kr booking fee) or **private rooms** (from 110kr, plus 30kr booking fee). There's an STF **youth hostel** (☎0431/45 23 64; April–Oct) at the beach at Magnarp Strand, 10km north of the train station and reached by local bus. Of several **campsites**, the most convenient for the beach is *Råbocka Camping*, at the end of Råbockavägen (☎0431/105 43, fax 832 45). For a good-value and friendly **hotel**, try *Hotel Lilton* (☎0431/44 25 50, fax 44 25 69; ③/②) at Järnvägsgatan 29, just a few steps from the square and with a great garden café in summer. Another stylish option is the *Kitterhus Pensionat* (☎0431/135 30, fax 135 31; ②), with elegant rooms, big en-suite bathrooms and a gorgeous bar area located in the beautifully renovated premises of the classic old Klitterhus restaurant down by the beach. Failing that, there's the *Hotel Continental* at Storgatan 23 (☎0431/127 00, fax 127 90; ②).

The best place to look for **food** is the harbour. *Hamn Krogen* doesn't look anything special from the outside, but it serves the best fish dishes in Ängelholm – their speciality is "Toast Skagen", shrimps and red caviar on toast. A few metres up the beach, in a whitewashed wartime bunker, is *Bunken* restaurant and bar, serving barbecue food alongside more lavish seafood dishes, and putting on regular live music. The most popular **nightclub** is *Bahnhoff Bar*, a cavernous, industrial-looking place occupying old railway buildings just beyond the present train station. *Club 57*, in the basement of *Hotel Paletten* in the centre, is a smaller alternative.

Helsingborg

Locals used to joke that the most rewarding sight in **HELSINGBORG** is Helsingør, the Danish town whose castle (best known as the "Elsinore" of Shakespeare's *Hamlet*) is clearly visible just 4km away over the Öresund. This had less to do with Helsingborg itself than with the irresistible attractions of Denmark's (comparatively) cheap booze,

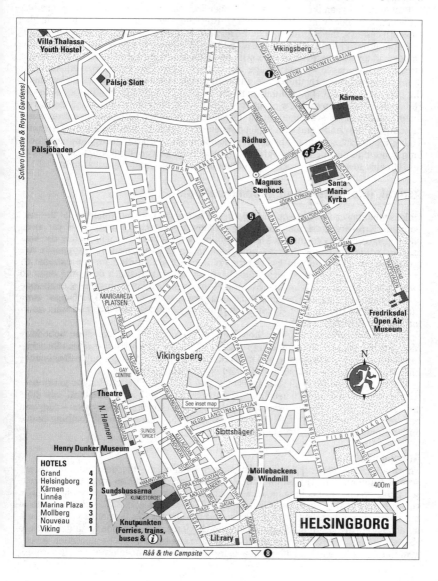

HELSINGBORG

HOTELS	
Grand	4
Helsingborg	2
Kärnen	6
Linnéa	7
Marina Plaza	5
Mollberg	3
Nouveau	8
Viking	1

as trolley-pulling Swedes converged on Helsingborg from all over the country to stock up on beer and to spend entire nights on the ferry-laden waters getting plastered on cut-price alcohol. The opening of the Malmö–Copenhagen bridge is expected to make Helsingborg a less essential destination for thirsty Swedes, although a recent explosion of chic new bars in the regenerated North Harbour area has lent a new vibrancy to this small city and meant that those in search of an invigorating tipple still have plenty of options.

Past links between the two towns have been less convivial – in fact, Helsingborg has a particularly bloody and tragic history. After the Danes fortified the town in the eleventh century, the Swedes conquered and lost it again on six violent occasions, finally winning out in 1710 under the leadership of Magnus Stenbock. By this time, the Danes had torn down much of the town and on its final recapture, the Swedes razed its twelfth-century castle, except for the five-metre-thick walled keep (*kärnen*), that still dominates the centre. By the early eighteenth century, war and epidemics had reduced the population to just 700, and only with the onset of industrialization in the 1850s did Helsingborg wake up to a new prosperity. Shipping and the railways turned the town's fortunes around, as evidenced by the formidable late nineteenth-century commercial buildings in the centre and some splendid villas to the north overlooking the Öresund. Today, a constant stream of Danes, Germans and Swedes pass through, but stay only long enough to change trains, which is a pity, as there is a youthful, Continental feel to this likeable town with its warren of cobbled streets, cafés and historical sights.

Arrival, information and accommodation

Unless you approach by car on the E6, the chances are that you will arrive at the harbourside **Knutpunkten**, the vast, glassy expanses of which incorporate all car, train and passenger **ferry** terminals. On the ground floor behind the main hall is the **bus station**, while the ticket and transport information offices are in front, opposite the tourist office. Below ground level is the combined **train station** for the national SJ trains and the lilac-coloured local Pågatåg trains, which run south down the coast to Landskrona, Lund and Malmö. One floor up brings you to a Forex **currency exchange** office (daily 8am–9pm). The Sundsbussarna passenger-only ferry to Helsingør uses the quayside at Hamntorget, 100m north. For ferry ticket details, bus and train information, see "Listings", p.475.

The **tourist office** (June–Aug Mon–Fri 9am–8pm, Sat & Sun 9am–5pm; Sept–May Mon–Fri 9am–6pm, Sat 10am–2pm; ☎042/12 03 10, fax 12 78 76, *turistbyran@helsingborg.se*) is inside Knutpunkten, and gives out free maps, the listings guide *Helsingborg This Month*, and the excellent English-language *Helsingborg Guide*.

Central Helsingborg is all within easy walking distance, although for the youth hostel and outlying sights you'll need to take a **bus**. Tickets are bought on board, cost 13kr and are valid for two changes within an hour. **Cycling** is an enjoyable option – they can be hired from the tourist office (75kr per day) and Pålsjöbaden, the old bathing house on Drottninggatan, 3km north of the centre.

Accommodation

There are plenty of central **hotel** options in Helsingborg – the best-value places are around Knutpunkten. The tourist office can book **private rooms** from 125kr per person plus a steep 70kr booking fee (rising to a hefty 200kr for three or more nights). The **youth hostel** at Dag Hammarskjöldsväg (☎042/21 03 84, fax 12 87 92), 2.5km north of the town centre, is called *Villa Thalassa* and is superbly set around a c.1900 villa – unfortunately the accommodation isn't in the villa itself, but in cabins behind; there are also some holiday cottages (doubles ①). Bus #7 runs north from Knutpunkten (every 20min) to the Pålsjöbaden bathing house, from where it's a one-kilometre walk through forest; after 7pm, bus #44 runs the same route every thirty minutes till 1am.

Grand, Stortorget 8–12 (☎042/12 01 70, fax 11 88 33). No longer quite as exclusive as it once was. Big summer reductions make it even less so. ⑤/②.

Kärnen, Järnvägsgatan 17 (☎042/12 08 20, fax 14 88 88). Opposite Knutpunkten, this comfortable, recently renovated hotel prides itself on "personal touches", including ominous English-language homilies on each room door (no. 235, for instance, has "He who seeks revenge keeps his wounds open"). There's a small library, cocktail bar and sauna. ④/②.

Linnea, Prästgatan 4 (☎042/21 46 60, fax 14 16 55). Very cheap, central and pleasant. ②.

Marina Plaza, Kungstorget 6 (☎042/19 21 00, fax 14 96 16). Large, modern and well-equipped hotel right at the harbour, next to Knutpunkten. Has a popular restaurant and a lively pub too. ⑤/③.

Mollberg, Stortorget 18 (☎042/37 37 00, fax 37 37 37). Every bit a premier hotel with a grand nineteenth-century facade, elegant rooms and a brasserie. ⑤/③

The Town

The most obvious starting point is the waterfront, by the copper statue of Magnus Stenbock on his charger. With your back to the Öresund and Denmark, the **Rådhus** (July & Aug Mon–Fri 40min tours at 10am) is to your left, a heavy-handed neo-Gothic pile complete with turrets and towers designed by an architect whose admiration for medieval Italy is perhaps a little too obvious. It's worth a look inside to enjoy the extravagances of nineteenth-century provincial wealth and the fabulous stained-glass windows that tell the entire history of the town. The original wall and ceiling frescoes – deemed too costly to restore and therefore painted over in 1968 – are currently being uncovered.

The town hall marks the bottom of **Stortorget** – the central "square", though it's actually so oblong it's more like a boulevard – which slopes upwards to meet the steps leading to the remains of the medieval **castle** (June–Aug daily 10am–8pm; Sept–May Mon–Fri & Sun 10am–6pm, Sat 10am–2pm; 5kr). Take the lift to the top, where the massive castellated bulk of the keep, **Kärnen** (daily: April, May & Sept 9am–4pm; June–Aug 10am–7pm; Oct–March 10am–2pm; 15kr) is surrounded by some fine parkland. Shaped simply as a huge upturned brick, it's worth climbing more for its views than the historical exhibitions housed within. The keep and St Maria kyrka (see below) were the sole survivors of the ravages of war, but the former lost its military significance once Sweden finally won the day. In the mid-nineteenth century it was destined for demolition and only survived because seafarers found it a valuable landmark. What cannon fire failed to achieve, neglect and the weather succeeded in bringing about, and the keep fell into ruin before restoration began in 1894.

From the parkland at the keep's base, you can wander down a rhododendron-edged path, Hallbergs Trappor, to the **St Maria kyrka** (Mon–Sat 8am–4pm, Sun 9am–6pm), which squats in its own square by a very French-looking avenue of beech trees. The square is surrounded by a cluster of quaint places to eat and some excellent shops for picnic food, notably Maratorgets on the south side of the square, which sells fruit, and the adjacent Bengtsons Ost, a cheese shop. The church itself was begun in 1300 and completed a century later; its rather plain facade belies a striking interior, with a clever contrast between the early seventeenth-century Renaissance-style ornamentation of its pulpit and gilded reredos, and jewel-like contemporary stained-glass windows.

Walking back to Stortorget, **Norra** and **Södra Storgatan** (the streets that meet at the foot of the steps to Kärnen) formed Helsingborg's main thoroughfare in medieval times, and are today lined with the town's oldest merchants' houses. Heading south along Södra Storgatan, take the opening to the left of the old cream-painted brick building opposite the modern Maria Församling House and, after a fairly arduous climb of 92 steps, you'll find a handsome nineteenth-century **windmill**. Around the windmill are a number of exquisite farm cottages with low doorways and eighteenth-century peasant interiors – straw beds, cradles and hand-painted grandmother clocks. A further reward for the climb is to be found at *Möllebackens Våffelbruk* (May–Aug daily noon–8pm), which has been serving home-made waffles using the same recipe since 1912.

Out from the centre: Frederiksdal Open-Air Museum and Sofiero

Two kilometres outside the city (take bus #2, #3 or #5 from outside the Rådhus), the **Fredriksdal Open-Air Museum** (May–Sept 10am–6pm; Oct–April reduced hours; 20kr; ☎042/10 59 81) is set around a fine eighteenth-century manor house; there's plenty to look at, with parks, peasant homes and extensive botanical gardens.

Slightly further afield are the gorgeous **Royal Gardens of Sofiero** (May to mid-Sept 10am–6pm; 30kr), easily reached by bus #252 from Knutpunkten, or by cycling the 4km north along the coast. Built as a summer residence by Oscar II in the 1860s, the house itself looks rather like an elaborate train station, but the real reason to come here is the gardens, given by Oscar to his grandson, Gustav Adolf, when he married Crown Princess Margareta in 1905. Margareta created a horticultural paradise and, as a granddaughter of Queen Victoria, was strongly influenced by English garden design. The rhododendron collection in particular is one of Europe's finest, a stunning array of ten thousand plants, with over five hundred varieties making up a rainbow that stretches down to the Öresund.

Eating, drinking and nightlife

Helsingborg has a range of excellent **restaurants**, though these can be expensive. During the day there are some great **cafés** and *konditori*, though things are quiet by night, when locals recommend "taking the boat to Helsingør" – the entertainment is the boat itself, rather than landing in Denmark. Do what the locals do and go back and forth all night. Boats are run by Scandlines, Sundbussarna and Tura and leave from Knutpunkten; tickets (around 30kr) are available from the first-floor office and there are frequent departures.

Cafés and restaurants

Bunker Bar, near the far end of North Harbour. Very crowded eaterie for both lunch and dinner.

Café Annorledes, Södra Storgatan 15. A friendly atmosphere with pleasant 1950s memorabilia, though the cakes are not as special as they used to be.

Ebba's Fik, Bruksgatan 20. The most fun café in town, with authentic 1950s styling and great music to match. A must.

Fahlmans, Stortorget. Helsingborg's classic *konditori*, this has been serving elaborate cakes and pastries since 1914. Try the coconut marzipan confections or the sumptuous apple meringue pie.

Grafitti, first floor, Knutpunkten. Generously filled baked potatoes or baguettes among a young, sometimes rowdy crowd. The ideal place if you're hungry, skint and it's past 9pm.

K & Co, Nedre Långvinkelsgatan. Very friendly, with great muffins, cakes and filling ciabattas and baguettes.

Olson's Skafferi, Mariagatan 6 (☎042/14 07 80). The city's best Italian restaurant, right outside the front of St Maria kyrka. Wonderfully prepared, authentic Italian dishes with fish, meat and pasta options, and zabaglione to drool over.

Pålsjökrog (☎042/14 97 30). Attached to the lovely old Pålasjöbaden bathhouse 2km north of the centre and run by an architect who has designed it to feel like a Swedish country house. It's a special-occasion place serving traditional, well-presented Swedish food with main courses at around 150kr.

Utposten, Stortorget 17. Very stylish decor – a mix of the rustic and industrial – at this great, varied Swedish-food restaurant beneath the post office at the steps to Kärnen. A two-course meal will cost around 140kr. Try the delicate and filling seafood and salmon stew at 90kr. Open till 1am.

Wayne's, Stortorget. One of the hippest cafés in town, with simple modern decor in a grand old building. The cakes, though, can look better than they taste.

Bars and clubs

Jazz Clubben, Nedre Långvinkelsgatan 22. Sweden's biggest jazz club and well worth a visit on Wed, Fri and Sat evenings for live jazz, Dixieland, blues, Irish folk and blues jam sessions.

Le Cardinal, Södra Kyrkogatan 9. Piano bar and nightclub with a steak-oriented restaurant (6pm–1am). The first floor is a popular disco, the second has a quieter piano bar and roulette table (9.30pm–3am). Cover is 60–70kr and you need to be 25 to get in. Often closed during summer.

Marina, *Hotel Marina* by the harbour. A new club with a crowded, Continental atmosphere; minimum age is 24. Thurs–Sat 10pm–3am.

Sailor's Inn, *Hotel Marina* at the harbour. This is a pre-disco or post-dinner drinking spot, and extremely popular too. Regular singers on Fri night.

Tivoli, Hamn Torget. In the main part of the former train station opposite Knutpunkten. Lots of concerts, bands and events at this lively place with its attached restaurant, *Vinyl Baren*, which is indeed filled with red vinyl bench seats and 1960s pop art.

Listings

Airport The nearest airport for domestic flights is at Ängelholm, 30km north of town; take the bus from Knutpunkten (1hr before flight departure). For international services, you'll need to go to Copenhagen's Kastrup airport. Take the Kustlinjen bus from Knutpunkten (two hours).

Buses The daily bus for Stockholm leaves from Knutpunkten; reservations essential (☎0625/240 20), but tickets can only be bought on the bus (Mon–Thurs 250kr, Fri–Sun 355kr). Buses for Gothenburg leave daily (Mon–Thurs 140kr, Fri–Sun 200kr); tickets must be bought from the bus information section at the train booking office.

Car rental Can be arranged at the tourist office or direct: Avis, Garnisonsgatan 2 (☎042/15 70 80); Budget, Gustav Adolfsgatan 47 (☎042/12 50 40); Europcar, Muskötgatan 1 (☎042/17 01 15); Hertz, Bergavägen 4 (☎042/17 25 40).

Exchange Forex in Knutpunkten (1st floor) or Järnvägsgatan 13 (June–Aug 7am–9pm; Sept–May 8am–9pm).

Gay contacts RFSL-run café and pub-bar and occasional discos at Pålsgatan 1 (☎042/12 35 32), close to the concert hall, ten minutes' walk from Knutpunkten.

Pharmacy Björnen, Drottninggatan 14.

Post office Stortorget 17 (Mon–Fri 9am–6pm, Sat 10am–1pm). You can exchange money here but it costs 35kr per transaction.

Trains The Pågatåg trains from Knutpunkten require a ticket bought from an automatic machine on the platform; international rail passes are valid. It's 50kr one-way to Lund and 60kr one-way to Malmö. Fare dodging invites a 600kr spot fine.

Around Helsingborg: Råå

It's just 7km south from Helsingborg to the pretty fishing village of **RÅÅ** (pronounced "Raw-aw"). You can take bus #1A or #1B from the Rådhus, or cycle there along the bike lanes, through the industrial mess of Helsingborg's southern suburbs. Råå's main street, **Rååvägen**, is a subdued place: signs point to the twelfth-century **Raus kyrka** (left up Lybecksgatan, over the highway and along Rausvägen), but it's nothing special. Råå's main attraction is rather its **harbour**, dense with masts and remarkably untouristy. The **Maritime Museum** (free) here is run by a group of Råå residents and shows a comprehensive collection of seafaring artefacts. A fascinating, if somewhat stomach-churning, sight at the harbour is that of eel sorting: the giant, spaghetti-like creatures are slopped into appropriately coffin-shaped boxes to be separated according to size by fishermen using claw-shaped pincers.

There are a couple of good **eating** places at the harbour. Next door to the museum, the long-established *Råå Wärdshus* serves pricey fish dishes at around 150kr, with lighter snacks and various salads for around 50kr. To the left of the museum, on the pier, *Råå Hamnservering* is the best bet for a cheap meal, with an excellent 58kr lunch buffet. If you want to **stay** your choice is limited to the *Råå Camping Site* (☎042/10 76 80, fax 26 10 10), which is advertised as being on the "waterfront". It is, but the dominant view is of Helsingborg's industrial smog.

Lund

Some fifty kilometres south of Helsingborg and a few kilometres inland is the celebrated university cityof **LUND**. Like England's Oxford, with which it is often and aptly compared, there's an eccentric and bohemian atmosphere to the place – a mass of students' bikes will probably be the first image to greet you. Cultural attractions aside, it's the mix of architectural grandeur and the buzz of student life that lends Lund its unique charm, and with its justly revered twelfth-century Romanesque cathedral, its medieval streets, numerous museums and wealth of cafés and restaurants, Lund could well keep you busy for a couple of days.

Arrival, information and accommodation

Frequent **trains** from Helsingborg (40min) arrive at the train station on the western edge of town, which is also the terminus for **buses** and within easy walking distance of

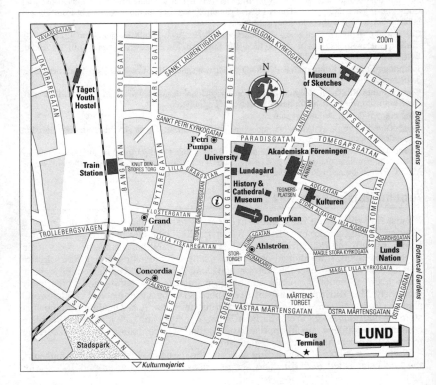

everything of interest. The **tourist office** (June–Aug Mon–Fri 10am–6pm, Sat & Sun 10am–2pm; May & Sept Mon–Fri 10am–5pm, Sat 10am–2pm; Oct–April Mon–Fri 10am–5pm; ☎046/35 50 40, fax 12 59 63, *bitte.saur@lund.se*), opposite the Domkyrkan at Kyrkogatan 11, hands out free maps and copies of *I Lund*, a monthly diary of events with museum and exhibition listings (the summer edition is in English and Swedish).

Though nowhere is no more than ten minutes' walk away, you might want to consider renting a military **bike** – large, sturdy and khaki green, they are almost indestructible, and if you plan to do a lot of cycling around the region, they're excellent value. Ask at the tourist office or try Harry's Cykelaffar, Banvaktsgatan 2 (☎046/211 69 46; 90kr per day).

There is a decent range of **accommodation** on offer in Lund – nearly all of it in the centre. The tourist office can book **private rooms** for 175kr per person, plus a 50kr booking fee. Lund's STF **youth hostel**, *Tåget*, at Vävaregatan 22, through the tunnel behind the train station (☎046/14 28 20, fax 32 05 68), is housed in the carriages of a 1940s train; unfortunately the novelty wears off when you find yourself crammed in three-deep bunks with rope hoists. An alternative is *La Strada*, at Brunnshögsvägen (☎046/32 32 51, fax 521 39): take bus #4 from west of Martens Torget 4km to Klosterängsvägen, then follow the bicycle track under the motorway for 1km.

Hotels

Ahlström, Skomakaregatan 3, just south of the Domkyrkan (☎046/211 01 74). Average, very central cheapie with the option of en-suite rooms. ②.

Concordia, Stålbrogatan 1 (☎046/13 50 50, fax 13 74 22). A couple of streets southwest of Stortorget, this former student hostel has been upgraded into a very homely hotel with attentive service, though it's rather plain inside. There's a guest sauna too. ④/⑤.

The Grand, Bantorget 1 (☎046/280 61 00, fax 280 61 50). This grand nineteenth-century pink-sandstone edifice straddles an entire side of a small, stately and central square. Unpretentious and comfortable, with a fantastic breakfast buffet. ⑥/⑨.

Petri Pumpa, St Petri Kyrkogatan 7 (☎046/13 55 19, fax 13 56 71). An exclusive hotel, although its famous restaurant has now moved to the *Savoy* in Malmö leaving just the *Petri Pumpa* bar, though this is still a very chic and glamorous place for a drink. ⑨/⑨.

The Town

It's only a short walk east from the train station to the magnificent **Domkyrkan** (Mon, Tues & Fri 8am–6pm, Wed & Thurs 8am–7.15pm, Sat 9.30am–5pm, Sun 9.30am–7.30pm; guided tours 3pm), whose storm-cloud charcoal and white stone give it an unusual monochrome appearance. Before entering, head around the back, past the grotesque animal and bird gargoyles over the side entrances; at the very back is the most beautiful part of the exterior: the three-storey apse above the crypt, crowned with an exquisite gallery.

Beyond the great carved entrance, the majestic interior is surprisingly unadorned, an elegant mass of watery-grey, ribbed stone arches and stone-flagged flooring. One of the world's finest masterpieces of Romanesque architecture, the cathedral was built in the twelfth century when Lund became the first independent archbishopric in Scandinavia, laying the foundation for a period of wealth and eminence that lasted until the advent of Protestantism. There are several interesting features, such as the elaborately carved fourteenth-century choir stalls depicting Old Testament scenes, with grotesque carvings hidden beneath the seats, but most striking is the amazing astronomical clock just to the left of the entrance. Dating from the 1440s, it shows hours, days, weeks and the courses of the sun and moon in the zodiac; if you're here at noon or 3pm, you'll get to see an ecclesiastical Punch and Judy show, as two knights pop out and clash swords as many times as the clock strikes, followed by little mechanical doors opening to trumpet-blowing heralds and the three wise men trundling slowly up to the Virgin Mary.

Don't miss the dimly lit and dramatic **crypt**, which has been left almost untouched since the twelfth century. Most of the tombstones are actually memorial slabs, with just one proper tomb containing the remains of Birger Gunnarsson, Lund's last archbishop. A short man from a poor family, Gunnarsson dictated that his stone effigy should be tall and regal. Two pillars are gripped by stone figures – one of a man, another of a woman and child. Legend has it that Finn the Giant built the cathedral for Saint Lawrence; in return, the saint was to guess the giant's name, or failing that, give him the sun, the moon, or his eyes. Preparing to end his days in blindness, Lawrence heard the giant's wife boasting to her baby, "Soon Father Finn will bring some eyes for you to play with". On hearing Lawrence declare his name, the livid giant and his family rushed to the crypt to pull down the columns and were instantly turned to stone.

Just behind the cathedral on Sandgatan, the **History and Cathedral Museum** (Tues–Fri 11am–1pm; free) is rather dull unless you have a particular interest in the subject, although the statues from Scånian churches in the medieval exhibition deserve a look, mainly because of the way they're arranged – a mass of Jesuses and Marys bunched together in groups, with the crowd of Jesuses on crosses looking ominously Hitchcockian.

A few minutes' walk east on Tegnerplatsen is the town's best museum, the open-air **Kulturen** (daily: May–Sept 11am–5pm, Thurs till 9pm; Oct–April noon–4pm, Thurs till 9pm; 40kr). It's easy to spend the best part of a day just wandering around a virtual town of perfectly preserved cottages, farms, merchants' houses, gardens and even churches, brought from seven regions around Sweden and from as many centuries – despite the lack of labelling in English.

Head north from the square along Sandgatan, and then take a right on to Finngatan, in order to reach another rather special museum, the **Museum of Sketches** (Skissernas Museum; Tues–Sat noon–4pm, Sun 1–5pm; free, though special exhibitions cost 30kr). Inside is a fascinating collection of preliminary sketches and original full-scale models of artworks from around the world. One room is full of work by all the major Swedish artists, while in the international room you'll find sketches by Chagall, Matisse, Léger, Mirò and Dufy, and sculptural sketches by Picasso and Henry Moore.

As an antidote to museum fatigue, the **Botanical Gardens** (mid-May to mid-Sept 6am–9.30pm; mid-Sept to mid-May 6am–8pm, greenhouses noon–3pm; free), a few minutes' stroll further southwest down Finngatan,(turn left at the end of the street into Pålsjövågen and right into Olshögsvägen), are as much a venue for picnicking and chilling out as a botanical experience.

Eating, drinking and nightlife

There are plenty of great places to eat and drink in Lund, a great deal of them associated with the university. Certain **cafés** are student institutions and a number of the better **restaurants** are attached to student bodies or museums – which serves to keep prices low, especially for beer. If you want to buy your own provisions, the market at Mortenstorget, **Saluhallen**, sells a range of fish, cheeses and meats, including Lund's own tasty speciality sausage, *knake*. Next door to the *Espresso House* (see opposite) on Skt Petri Kyrkogata, *Widerbergs Charkuteri* is a long-established foodie shop brimming with all the ingredients for a picnic.

When it comes to **nightlife**, it's worth knowing that the university is divided into "nations", or colleges, named after different geographical areas of Sweden and with strong identities. Each nation has its own bar that's active two nights a week, and there are also regular discos. *Lund Nation* is the biggest, based in the red-brick house on Agardhsgatan, while *Smålands Nation* on Kastanjatan, off Mortenstorget, is the trendiest; both are known for hosting **live bands**. Another lively venue is the bright lilac-painted *Mejeriet*, at the end of Stora Södergatan, off the main square. Converted into a music and cultural centre in the 1970s, this century-old dairy now holds a stylish café, concert hall and arts cinema (concert information on ☎046/12 38 11; cinema details on ☎046/14 38 13). The hippest regular club is the more modern *Palladium* (see below).

Cafés and restaurants

Café Ariman, Kungsgatan, attached to the Nordic Law Department. A nineteenth-century brick café, this deliberately shabby place is a classic left-wing coffee house – goatees, pony tails and blond dreadlocks predominate. Cheap snacks and coffee. Closed Sun outside summer.

Café Baguette, Grönegatan. A simple, Mediterranean-style central café, with baguettes from 20kr and fish and meat meals for 70–110kr.

Café Borgen, at the Botanical Gardens. A pleasant café with a basic selection of food, in a castellated building overlooking the waterlily pond. Open June–Aug only, 10am–6pm.

Cafe Stortorget, Stortorget. Housed in a National Romantic-style former bank, with walls covered in dramatic black-and-white shots of actors. Try the big, filled focaccio with crabmeat, cheese or meat for 48kr.

Conditori Lundagård, Kyrkogatan. Classic student *conditori*, with caricatures of professors adorning the walls. Justly famous for its apple meringue pie.

Espresso House, Sankt Petri Kyrkogata 5, opposite the library. Great atmosphere at this stylish new coffee and bagel house. A big range of delicious coffees for 12–20kr, with mellow music setting the mood.

Espresso House (2), Stora Grabrodersgatan. Part of the popular chain, this stylish café is a good place for filled baguettes, cakes and breakfast (8–11am). The decor is contemporary, with lots of lifestyle magazines (in English) to read while munching muffins and pricey ciabatta.

Fellini, opposite the train station (☎046/13 80 20). Stylish and popular Italian restaurant, decked out in dull chrome and stripped wood. Two-course meals for 135kr. Open late.

Gloria's, Sankt Petri Kyrkogata, near the *Espresso House*. Serving American food, and very popular with students and tourists. Local bands play Fri & Sat nights, and there's a big, lively garden area at the back. Open till midnight or later.

I-Internet Cafe, Paradisgatan 1. Check your email (around 1kr per minute) in this almost inappropriately pleasant eighteenth-century former stable set in a charming cobbled courtyard with rudimentary coffee and snacks. Open till midnight or later.

Kulturen, in front of the Kulturen museum. Beneath a giant copper beech and facing ancient runestones, this is a busy café, bar and restaurant. A great place to people-watch, with a youngish crowd drinking cheap beer (28kr). Good lunch with vegetarian choice (59kr), though service can be sluggish.

Stadpark Café, in the park at the end of Nygatan. An old wooden pavilion fronted by a sea of white plastic garden furniture, this place is always busy with families munching on snacks. Big baguettes fill you up for 35–40kr.

Tegners Terass, in the building next to the student union (*Akademiska Föreningen*). Forget any preconceptions about student cafés being tatty, stale sandwich bars. Lunch for 55kr (49kr with student card) is self-service and means as much as you like from a choice of delicious gourmet meals. The main hall is resplendent with gilded Ionic columns; sit inside or on the terrace. Daily 11.30am–2.30pm.

Bars and clubs

Easy, in the Tegners Terass building next to the student union. A new student nightclub (Thurs 7pm–3am; free entry till midnight, then 20kr) with restaurant (same times). With a student card, 18-year-olds and upwards can get in to the club, otherwise it's strictly over-23s only.

John Bull Pub, Bantorget, adjacent to the *Grand Hotel*. Shabby, British-style traditional pub.

Lundia, Knutdenstorestorg. Filled with tourists, the atmosphere in this club is rather soulless. Wed–Sat 11pm–3am.

Palladium, Stora Södergatan 13 (☎046/211 66 60, fax 12 20 90). Hip new place, just a few steps south of Stortorget, with a café, events and concerts, and a huge drinks list (shots at 39kr, cocktails at 53kr). Minimum age is 20. Inside is also a news cafe and American buffet, all very reasonably priced. Closed Sun.

Petri Pumpa Bar, next to *Gloria's* (see p.479). Glamorous place serving beer and excellent continental lunches for 74kr.

Malmö

Founded in the late thirteenth century, **MALMÖ** became Denmark's most important city after Copenhagen. The high density of herring in the sea off the Malmö coast – it was said that the fish could be scooped straight out with a trowel – brought ambitious German merchants flocking to the city, an influence that can be seen in the striking fourteenth-century St Petri kyrka. Eric of Pomerania gave Malmö its most significant medieval boost when, in the fifteenth century, he built the castle and mint, and gave the city its own flag – the gold-and-red griffin of his family crest. It wasn't until the Swedish King Karl X marched his armies across the frozen belt of water to within striking distance of Copenhagen in 1658 that the Danes were forced into handing back the counties of Skåne, Blekinge and Bohuslän to the Swedes. For Malmö this meant a period of stagnation, cut off from nearby Copenhagan and too far from its own uninterested capital. Not until the full thrust of industrialization, triggered by the tobacco merchant Frans Suell's enlargement of the harbour in 1775, did Malmö begin its dramatic commercial recovery.

More recently, Malmö has faced commercial crisis as a series of local miscalculations, added to the nation's overall industrial decline, have stripped it of its wealth – you only have to look at the industrial carcasses left scattered around its environs to realize how misleading the seeming prosperity of the attractive city centre is. Things may yet change with the opening of the sensational new bridge linking Malmö with Copenhagen, however, which brings with it the hope that Malmö will enjoy a renaissance as Sweden's gateway city to and from mainland Europe. Whatever its problems, Malmö makes for a worthwhile visit, although you won't need more than a day to get a feel for the compact centre; there are also delightful parks, a long and popular beach and some interesting cultural diversions south of the centre. The city's lively nightlife is another inducement to stay a while.

THE ÖRESUND BRIDGE

Linking Malmö with Copenhagen in Denmark (and thus Sweden with the rest of continental Europe), the **Öresund bridge** was finally completed in the summer of 1999, an event marked by the symbolic embrace, halfway along the newly finished structure, of Sweden's Crown Princess Victoria and Denmark's Crown Prince Frederick. From Lernacken, a few kilometres south of Mälmo, the bridge runs to a four-kilometre-long artificial island off the Danish coast, from where an immersed tunnel carries traffic and trains across to the mainland – a total distance of 16km. The bridge itself has two levels, the upper for a four-lane highway and the lower for two sets of train tracks, and comprises three sections: a central high bridge, spanning 1km, and approach bridges to either side, each over 3km long.

Whether the bridge should be built at all was debated for some forty years, with protestors pointing to the possible environmental consequences of the project (the late 1990s saw numerous demonstrations in Malmö proclaiming "make love not bridges"). Now that the bridge is a reality, however, even its detractors are proclaiming it Sweden's most significant construction achievement of the twentieth century. Understandably though, Stockholmers have played down the bridge's importance, as it will undoubtedly draw attention to Sweden's west coast, away from the capital.

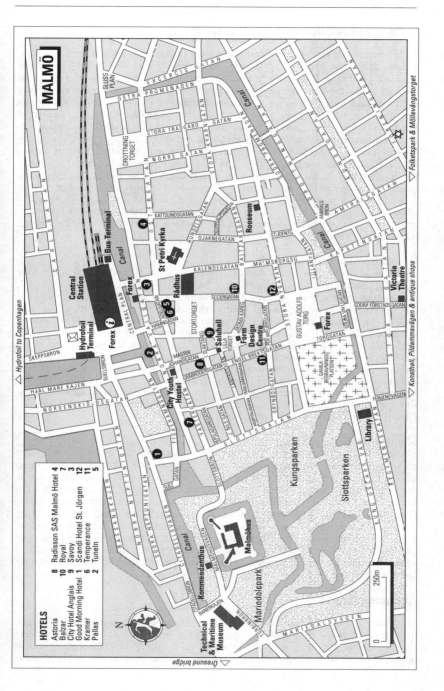

MALMÖ

△ Hydrofoil to Copenhagen

▽ Øresund bridge

▷ Folketspark & Möllevångstorget

▷ Konsthall, Pildammsvägen & antique shops

HOTELS

Astoria	8
Balzar	10
City Hotel Anglais	9
Good Morning Hotel	1
Kramer	6
Pallas	2

Radisson SAS Malmö Hotel	4
Royal	3
Savoy	12
Scandi Hotel St. Jörgen	11
Temperance	5
Tuneln	

Central Station

Bus Terminal

Hydrofoil Terminal

Forex

St Petri Kyrka

Rådhus

Rooseum

Victoria Theatre

Malmöhus

Kommendanthus

Technical & Maritime Museum

Mariedalspark

Kungsparken

Slottsparken

Library

Form Design Centre

Saluhall

City Youth Hostel

250m

Arrival, information and city transport

All passenger-only **ferries** and **catamarans** from Copenhagen dock at the various terminals along the conveniently central Skeppsbron docks (for ticket details see "Listings", p.488). Just up from here is the central **train station**. As well as the SJ national trains, the Danish-built (and very comfortable) Kustpilen trains run hourly from here to Denmark (change at Hässleholm) and east to Kristianstad, Karlskrona and through to Linköping. The frequent local Pågatåg trains to and from Helsingborg/Lund and Ystad use platforms 9–13 at the back. To get to the square outside, Centralplan, site of the main **bus terminal**, either walk through the station or use the exit marked "Lokal stationen". Frequent buses to and from Lund, Kastrup airport (in Copenhagen), Kristianstad/Kalmar and Ystad all stop here. Buses from Stockholm, Helsingborg and Gothenburg arrive at **Slussplan**, east of the station, just over Slussbron at the end of Norra Vallgatan. From Sturup **airport**, to the east of Malmö, take an hourly airport bus (*flygbuss*) into the city centre (Mon–Fri 5.30am–7.30pm, Sat 6.30am–5.30pm; 40min; 60kr). A TT Line bus from the train station heads to Trelleborg to coincide with ferries to **Travemünde** and **Rostock** in Germany, while behind the train station, Polferries make the trip to Poland.

Information and discount cards
The **tourist office** (June–Aug Mon–Fri 9am–7pm, Sat & Sun 10am–2pm; Sept–May Mon–Fri 9am–5pm, Sat 10am–2pm; ☎040/30 01 50, fax 611 18 34, *info@tourism.malmo.com*) is inside Central Station. Here you can pick up a wealth of free information, including several good maps and an events and listings brochure, *Malmö This Month*. You can also buy the very useful **Malmö Card** (Malmökortet; available for 1, 2 or 3 days for 150kr, 275kr or 400kr respectively), which gives free museum entry, car parking, a guided bus tour and up to eight bus journeys, plus various other discounts on transport, cinemas, concerts and trips around the city. It's also worth considering the two-day **Round the Öresund** ticket (Öresund Runt; 149kr), which covers any route (or part of it) by ferry, train and hydrofoil to Lund, Helsingborg, Helsingør and across to Copenhagen. There are Forex **money exchanges** just opposite the tourist office in Central Station (daily 8am–9pm), on Norra Vägen 60 (7am–9pm) and Gustav Adolfs Torg (9am–7pm).

City transport
Although the city centre is easy to walk around, you'll need to use **buses** to reach some of the sights and some accommodation. Individual tickets cost 14kr and are valid for an hour; a 100kr magnetic card is valid for ten trips and can be used by several people at the same time. All tickets are sold on the bus. If you want to use **taxis**, it's worth comparing rates, but for a rough idea of costs: Malmö centre to the airport costs 225kr, Central Station to the soccer stadium 65kr. A one-hour guided **sightseeing tour** (11am & 1pm; 80kr, free with Malmö Card) leaves from the tourist office, but it's pretty slowgoing as it's conducted in Swedish, English and German. Alternatively, you can do your own guided tour on city bus #20, which also leaves from outside the tourist office, where you can buy a brochure pointing out areas of interest for 12kr (several buses an hour; bus ride and brochure free with Malmö Card).

Accommodation

There are some excellent and surprisingly affordable **hotels** in Malmö; the city is eager to attract tourists and competition among hotels can be fierce. It's also worth considering the **Malmö Package**, sold by the tourist office, which provides visitors with a double room in a central hotel with breakfast and a Malmö Card thrown in. The scheme

– similar to those in Stockholm and Gothenburg – runs from June to late August, and on weekends all year; costs range from 365kr to 650kr per person, depending on the hotel. While it's a good deal, the usual summer reductions at many non-participating hotels may prove even better value. All the hotels listed below participate in the scheme, except for the *Hotel Pallas*.

Malmö has two **youth hostels**. The central *City Youth Hostel*, Västergatan 9, comprises student accommodation which is let out as a hostel over summer (☎ & fax 040/23 56 40; single rooms 125kr; June–Aug;); it's friendlier and more convenient than the STF hostel at Backavägen 18 (☎040/822 20; closed mid-Dec to mid-Jan), 5km from the city centre and right by the E6 motorway. To get to the latter, take bus #21A from Centralplan to Vandrarhemmet, cross over the junction past the traffic lights and take the first right; the hostel is signposted to the left. The nearest **campsite**, *Camping Sibbarps* at Strandgatan 101 in Limhamn (☎040/34 26 50), is in a picturesque spot, although the new bridge to Copenhagen is very close by.

Hotels

Astoria, Gråbrödersgatan 7 (☎040/786 60, fax 788 70). A few minutes from the train station across the canal, this is a good, plain hotel, recently upgraded. ③/②.

Balzar, Södergatan 20 (☎040/720 05, fax 23 63 75). Very central hotel between the two main squares. A swanky, traditional place, not remotely Swedish in style. ④/②.

City Hotel Anglais, Stortorget 15 (☎040/660 95 50, fax 660 95 59). A grand, c.1900 hotel in the best central position. Recently renovated and with tasteful rooms. ③/②.

Good Morning, Citadellsvägen (☎040/23 96 05, fax 30 39 68). Five minutes' walk to the right from the train station, towards Malmöhus, this hotel hides a comfortable and pleasant interior behind a 1950s apartment tower facade. Price includes a good breakfast and free parking. ②.

Kramer, Stortorget 7 (☎040/20 88 00, fax 12 69 41). Beautiful white-stuccoed, turreted hotel from the 1870s, once Malmö's top hotel. Very luxurious. ⑤/③.

Pallas, Norra Vallgatan 74 (☎040/611 50 77, fax 97 99 00). Despite its ornate exterior, this is a rather tatty place, and breakfast will cost you an extra 30kr. ①.

Radisson SAS Malmö, Östergatan 10 (☎040/698 40 00, fax 698 40 01). Just beyond the Caroline Church, this hotel's blank and unimposing facade opens into a really delighful interior. The rooms are massive and stylish, and breakfast is eaten inside one of Malmö's oldest houses, cunningly incorporated into the 1960s hotel building. ⑤/③.

Royal, Norra Vallgatan 94 (☎040/97 63 03, fax 12 77 12). Small, family-run hotel just up from the train station. Price includes breakfast served in the garden. ③/②.

Savoy, Norra Vallgatan 62 (☎040/702 30, fax 97 85 51). No longer prohibitively priced during summer, this is the essence of style, with splendid furnishings and excellent Swedish and international food served in the historic elegance of the *Petri Pumpa Restaurant*. Attached is the *Bishop's Arms* pub. ⑥/③.

Temperance, Engelbrektsgatan 16 (☎040/710 20, fax 30 44 06). Pleasant central hotel; price includes sauna, solarium and a big buffet breakfast. ④/②.

Tuneln, Adelgatan 4 (☎040/10 16 20, fax 10 16 25). The finest small hotel in Malmö and very central. Dating from the Middle Ages, it's beautifully furnished. No summer reduction but discounts at weekends. ④/②.

The City

Standing outside the nineteenth-century train station with its ornate red-brick arches and curly-topped pillars, the **canal** in front of you, dug by Russian prisoners, forms a rough rectangle encompassing the **old town** directly to the south and the moated castle, the **Malmöhus**, to the west, surrounded by a series of attractive interconnecting parks. First off, though, head down Hamngatan to the main square. On the way you'll pass the striking sculpture of a twisted revolver, a monument to non-violence, that stands outside the grand former Malmö Exchange building from the 1890s.

The old town

Stortorget, the proud main square, is home to a series of elaborate sixteenth- to nine-teenth-century buildings, amongst which the **Rådhus** of 1546 draws the most attention. A pageant of architectural fiddling and statuary, the building's original design was destroyed during remodelling in the nineteenth century, which left the present, finicky Dutch Renaissance exterior. It's impressive, nonetheless, and to add to the pomp, the red-and-gold Scånian flag, of which Malmö is so proud, hangs from the eaves. There are occasional tours of the interior; check with the tourist office. The cellars, home to *Rådhus Källaven Restaurant* (see p.487), have been used as a tavern for more than four hundred years.

The crumbling, step-gabled red-brick building on the opposite side of the square was once the home of sixteenth-century mayor and Master of the Danish Mint, Jörgen Kocks. Danish coins were struck in Malmö on the site of the present Malmöhus, until irate local Swedes stormed the building and destroyed it in 1534. In the cellars here you'll find the *Kockska Krogan* restaurant, the only part accessible to visitors. In the cen-tre of the square, a statue of Karl X, high on his charger, presides over the city he lib-erated from centuries of Danish rule.

Head a block east, behind the Rådhus, to reach the Gothic **St Petri kyrka** on Göran Olsgatan (Mon–Fri 8am–6pm, Sat 9am–6pm, Sun 10am–6pm), dark and forbidding on the outside, but light and airy within. The church has its roots in the fourteenth century and, although Baltic in inspiration, the final style owes much to German influences, for it was beneath its unusually lofty and elegantly vaulted roof that the German community came to pray – probably for the continuation of the "sea silver", the herrings that brought them to Malmö in the first place. The ecclesiastical vandalism of whitewashing over medieval roof murals started early at St Petri – almost the whole interior turned white in 1553 – consequently your eyes are drawn to the pulpit and four-tiered altarpiece, both of striking workmanship and elaborate embellishment. The only part of the church left with its original artwork was a side chapel, the **Krämare Chapel** (from the entrance, turn left and left again). Added to the church in the late fifteenth century as a Lady Chapel, at the Reformation it was considered redundant and sealed off, thus protecting the paintings from the zealous brushes of the reformers. Best preserved are the paintings on the vault-ed ceiling, mainly depicting New Testament figures surrounded by decorative foliage, while underfoot the chapel floor is a chessboard of tombs in black, white and red stone.

Södergatan, Malmö's main pedestrianized shopping street, leads south of Stortorget down towards the canal. At the Stortorget end there's a jaunty troupe of sculptured bronze musicians, and a collection of lively cafés and restaurants further down. On the corner of the square, take a peak inside **Apoteket Lejonet**. Gargoyled and balconied on the outside, the pharmacy interior is a busy mix of inlaid wood, carvings and etched glass.

Despite the size of Stortorget, it still proved too small to suffice as the sole city square, so in the sixteenth century **Lilla Torg**, formerly marshland, was sewn on to the southeast corner. Looking like a film set, this little square with its creaky old half-tim-bered houses, flowerpots and cobbles, is everyone's favourite part of the city. During the day, people congregate here to take a leisurely drink in one of the many bars and wander around the summer jewellery stalls. At night, Lilla Torg explodes in a frenzy of activity, with people from all over the city converging on the square.

Walk through an arch on Lilla Torg and you'll reach the **Form Design Centre**, housed in a seventeenth-century grain store. Celebrating Swedish design in textiles, ceramics and furniture, its contents are rather less ambitious than you'd expect. From the beginning of the twentieth century until the 1960s, the whole of Lilla Torg was a covered market, and the sole vestige of those days, **Saluhallen**, is diagonally opposite the Design Centre. Mostly made up of specialist fine food shops, it makes for a pleas-ant, cool retreat on a hot afternoon.

A few streets away to the east, but well worth a visit if you're interested in contem-porary art, is the **Rooseum** (☎040/12 17 16; daily except Monday 11am–5pm, Thurs till 8pm, guided tours Tues–Fri 6.30pm, Sat & Sun 2pm: 30kr, free with Malmö Card) on Stora Nygatan. Space is imaginatively used in this elaborate building from 1900, originally constructed to house the Malmö Electricity Company's steam turbines. The main turbine hall forms the central gallery, displaying experimental installations and interesting photographic works. There's also a fine little café here (see p.486).

Malmöhus and around

Take any of the streets running west from Stortorget or Lilla Torg and you soon come up against the edge of **Kungsparken**, within striking distance of the fifteenth-century castle, **Malmöhus** (daily: June–Aug 10am–4pm; Sept–May noon–4pm; 40kr, free with Malmö Card. Free guided tours in English at 3pm). For a more head-on approach, walk west (away from the station) up Citadellsvägen; from here the low castle with its grassy ramparts and two circular keeps is straight ahead over the wide moat.

Originally Denmark's mint, the building was destroyed by the Swedes in 1534. Two years later, a new fortress was built on the site by the Danish King Christian III, only to be of unforeseen benefit to his enemies who, once back in control of Skåne, used it to repel an attacking Danish army in 1677. Serving as a prison for a time (the Earl of Bothwell, Mary Queen of Scots' third husband, its most notable inmate), the castle's importance waned once back in Swedish hands, and it was used for grain storage until opening as a **museum** in 1937.

Passing swiftly through the natural history section – a taxidermal Noah's ark – the most rewarding part of the museum is upstairs, where an ambitious series of furnished rooms takes you from the mid-sixteenth-century Renaissance through Baroque, Rococo, pastel-pale Gustavian and Neoclassical. A stylish Jugend (Art Nouveau) interior is equally impressive, while other rooms feature Functionalist and post-Functionalist interiors. Just as interesting are the spartan but authentic interiors of the castle itself.

Just beyond the castle to the west along Malmöhusvagen is the **Kommendanthuset** (Governor's House), containing a strange combination of military and toy museums. The military section is a fairly lifeless collection of neatly presented medals, rifles and swords, along with the usual dummies sporting eighteenth- and nineteenth-century uniforms. The toy museum is more fun – the link between the two being a brigade of toy British soldiers. A little further west, running off Malmöhusvagen, is a tiny walkway, **Banerkajen**, lined with higgledy-piggledy fishing shacks selling fresh and smoked fish; just beyond is the **Technical and Maritime Museum** (same times as Malmöhus; 15kr). The technical section has displays on transport, power and local industries (sugar, cement), while upstairs in the science section the main display is a model of Tycho Brahe's observatory on the island of Ven.

Once you've had your fill of museums, the castle **grounds** are good for a stroll, peppered with small lakes and an old windmill. The paths lead all the way down to Regementsgatan and the City Library in the southeastern corner of the park. You can continue walking through the greenery as far as Gustav Adolfs Torg by crossing Gamla Begravnings Platsen, a rather pretty graveyard.

Out from the centre

Tourists rarely head further south of the city than the canal banks that enclose the old town, yet with a few hours to spare, the areas around Amiralsgatan (which begins south of the canal near the Rooseum) give an interesting insight into Malmö's mix of cultures. A few hundred metres down Amiralsgatan, the splendid copper-domed Moorish building standing out on Föreningsgatan is the restored **Malmö Synagogue**. Designed and built in 1894, the synagogue is decorated with concentric designs in blue and green glazed brick. Strict security measures mean that to see the unrenovated interior you need to telephone the Jewish Community offices (ask at the tourist office).

Back on Amiralsgatan, it's a ten-minute walk to **Folketspark**, Sweden's oldest working people's park, once the pride and joy of the community. Now rather shabby, Folketspark contains a basic amusement park and, at its centre, the **Moriskan**, an odd, low building with Russian-style golden minarets topped with sickles and housing a ballroom. Amusement park and ballroom are both now privately owned, a far cry from the original aims of the park's Social Democratic founders, carved busts of whom are dotted all over the park.

South of the park, the multicultural character of Malmö becomes apparent. Middle Eastern, Asian and Balkan émigré families predominate, and strolling from the park's southern exit down Möllevången to **Möllevångstorget**, you enter an area populated almost entirely by non-Swedes, with Arabic and Urdu the main languages. The vast Möllevångstorget, boasting a poignant and impressive statue at its centre depicting Malmö workers straining under the weight of their toils, is a haven of cafés (see below) and exotic food shops, along with shops selling pure junk.

Along the beach to Limhamn

Separated from the city centre by the delightful **Öresund park**, Malmö's long stretch of sandy beach reaches all the way to Limhamn, fringed by the Ribersborgs Recreation Promenade. At the town end of the beach is the **Ribersborgs kallbadhuset** (mid-April to mid-Sept Mon–Fri 8.30am–7pm, Sat & Sun 8.30am–4pm; mid-Sept to mid-April Mon–Fri noon–7pm, Sat & Sun 9am–4pm; 28kr), a cold-water bathhouse with a sauna and café. All the beaches along this stretch, known as the Golden Coast because of the grand villas overlooking it, boast shallow water.

LIMHAMN (limestone harbour), 3km to the southwest of the city, has an unusual history and one that will become very apparent if you're staying at the *Sibbarps* campsite or arriving at Lernacken, the Swedish terminal for the bridge. Once a quiet limestone-quarrying village, Limhamn was taken by storm by a local man with big ambitions called Fredryk Berg. At the end of the nineteenth century, Berg had a train line built between the village and Malmö and built up the huge cement works known first as Cementa and later as Euroc. Heading down Limhamnsvägen (the road running parallel with the beach) to Limhamn (or take bus #82), the island of **Ön** will come into view. Another of Berg's creations, he had it built out of waste concrete and constructed apartment houses on it for factory workers and a couple of churches. A strongly religious man, he was fond of saying that the two best things in life were making corporations and attending church, earning him the nickname "Concrete Jesus".

Eating, drinking and entertainment

Most of Malmö's **eating places** are concentrated in and around its central squares (Lilla Torg attracting the biggest crowds). By day, several cafés serve good lunches and sumptuous cakes; at night there are a couple of top places to eat, notably the Italian *Spot Restaurant*. If you want a change of scene, head south of the centre to Möllenvångstorget, the heart of Malmö's immigrant community, for cheaper eats and a very un-Swedish atmosphere. Alternatively, to cut costs, Saluhallen, at the corner of Lilla Torg, is an excellent indoor market with a few specialist food shops.

Cafés and restaurants

Bageri Café, Saluhallen, corner of Lilla Torg. Excellent bagels, baguettes, pies and health foods – with outside seating, too.

Café Horisont, Davidshallgatan 9. An ecological and smoke-free cafe. Very pleasant, quiet place with home-baked cakes, cheap cheesecake, muffins and lots of salads and milkshakes. Try a blueberry, honey and yogurt shake at 24kr.

Café Rooseum, Gasverksgatan 22. Superb chocolate cake is dished up here in the contemporary art museum. A giant generator takes up most of the room, with seats around the edge. Closed Mon.

Café Siesta, Ostindiefararegatan (turn right at the end of Landbygatan, on the first corner on the left). A fun little café specializing in home-made apple cake.

Café Systrar & Bröder, Östra Ronneholmsvägen 26. Looking like a smart transport café, this excellent café has a great-value breakfast buffet at 38kr, and a hip young crowd. Closed Sun.

Conditori Hollandia, Södra Förstadsgatan (south of the canal at Drottninggatan). Traditional, pricey *konditori* with a window full of melting chocolate fondants.

Espresso House, Skomakaregatan 2, close to both Stora and Lilla Torg. Part of the popular chain, with excellent chocolate cake, muffins and ciabattas and a delicious "Oriental latté" (24kr) flavoured with cardamom.

Golden Restaurant, corner of Södra Parkgatan and Simrishamnsgatan, to the south of the city. In the main immigrant area, this spartan place serves cheap crepes, pizza and kebabs.

Green, Södergatan 1. Popular, inexpensive vegetarian fast food, with Thai-style dishes, pizzas or soup and bread for 25–45kr.

Gustav Adolfs, Gustav Adolfs Torg. Popular spot, open late at weekends, serving coffee (18kr) and snacks in a grand, white-stuccoed building with seating outside.

Johan P. Fish Restaurant, Saluhallen (also accessed from Landbygatan). Understated black-and-white-check decor, with fairly pricey fish dishes.

Kockska Krogan, corner of Stortorget and Suellgatan (☎040/703 20). A very fine old cellar restaurant – but rather overpriced – in the former home of Malmö's sixteenth-century mayor, Jörgen Kock. Closed Sun.

Pelles Café, Tegelgårdsgatan 5. Simple café in a quaint period house, serving huge cheap baguettes and playing jolly, dated music. Outside seating too.

Petri Pumpa, *Savoy Hotel*. Elegant fine-dining surrounded by dark panels and a white arched ceiling. Two courses will cost you around 300kr.

Rådhus Källaven, beneath the town hall on Stortorget. Gloriously decorative setting with dishes at around 200kr, though there's also a well-cooked and beautifully served daily economy meal at 65kr. Outside seating in summer.

Rinaldo's, Saluhallen (also accessed from Landbygatan). Big, fresh rainbow-coloured salads and some wicked desserts.

Spot Restaurant, Stora Nygatan 33 (☎040/12 02 03). Chic Italian restaurant with attached charcuterie. All ingredients imported direct from Italy. During the day, light meals based on ciabatta and panini breads are served. There's an evening menu of fish, cheese and meats. Not too expensive, this is a really great place to eat. Closed Sun.

Tempo, Norra Skolgatan 30, near Möllevångstorget to the south of the city. (☎040/12 60 21). A quirky, hip place where journalists and alternative poseurs come to savour very well prepared and intriguing food from the short but inspired menu. Service is friendly if agonisingly slow.

Bars and clubs

Lilla Torg is the place to go in the evenings. The square buzzes with activity, as the smell of beer wafts between the old, beamed houses, and music and chatter fill the air. It's a largely young crowd, and the atmosphere is like a summer carnival. It doesn't make a huge difference which of the six or so bars that you go for (and expect to wait for a seat), but as a basic pointer, *Mellow Yellow* is for the 25-plus age group, *Moosehead* for a younger crowd, and *Victors* even younger and more boisterous, although all are fun. On Möllenvångstorget, south of the centre in the immigrant quarter, the Danish-style *Nyhavn* at no.8 is a laid-back place for a beer.

One striking addition to the nightlife scene is *Club Trocadero*, next door to *Hotel Tuneln* on Adelgatan (Fri & Sat 10pm–3am; 60kr cover). Designed as a futuristic metallic tunnel, it welcomes a wide age range and boasts a cellar bar with a grand piano, a wild dance floor of silver and mirrors, and a restaurant at street level.

Gay Malmö

The city's gay scene is surprisingly lively, though most gay Malmöites still head off to Copenhagen for a really good night out. *Club Trocadero* (see above) is mostly gay on Friday nights, but for an exclusively gay club, try the very friendly *Club Fyran* (Fri & Sat 11pm–3am; 70kr), Sweden's oldest. Head past the St Petri Church, and it's at

Snapperupsgatan 4, above the *Mandarin House* Chinese restaurant. Though it looks permanently closed, ring the buzzer to gain admittance. The RFSL-run **gay centre** is at Monbijougatan 15 to the south of the city centre (head down Amiralsgatan and turn off to the right just before the Folketspark). This is the home of *Club Indigo* (Fri & Sat from 10pm). The first Saturday of the month is women only.

Music and festivals

It used to be that the only entertainment in Malmö was watching rich drunks become poor drunks at the blackjack table in the station bar. Now, if you know where to look, there are some decent **live music** venues and **discos**. A good venue is *Matssons Musikpub*, Göran Olsgatan 1, behind the Rådhus, which puts on a variety of Scandinavian R&B and rock bands (nightly 9.30pm–2am). Check out *Malmö This Month* for the latest nightclubs and other entertainment information.

Classical music performances take place at the Concert Hall, Föreningsgatan 35 (☎040/34 35 00), home of the Malmö Symphony Orchestra, and at the Musikhögskolan, Ystadvägen 25 (☎040/19 22 00); check with the tourist office for programme details. Malmö has two annual **festivals** of differing appeal. The **Folkfesten**, held in Kungsparken near Malmöhus in early June, is a sort of mini-Woodstock, devoted to progressive and classic rock. A far more all-encompassing event is the **Malmö Festival** in August, which takes place mainly in Stortorget. Huge tables are set out and free crayfish tails served, with revellers bringing their own drinks. In Gustav Adolfs Torg, stalls are set up by the immigrant communities, with Pakistani, Somali and Bosnian goodies and dance shows; there are also rowing competitions on the canal.

Listings

Airlines British Airways, Sturup airport (☎020/78 11 44); Finnair, Baltzarsgatan 31 (☎020/78 11 00); KLM, Sturup airport (☎020/50 05 30); Lufthansa, Gustav Adolfs Torg 12 (☎040/717 10); SAS, Baltzarsgatan 18 (☎040/35 72 00).

Buses From Centralplan to Lund (#130), Kristianstad/Kalmar (#805) and Ystad (#330).

Car rental Avis, Skeppsbron 13 (☎040/778 30); Budget, Baltzarsgatan 21 (☎040/775 75); Europcar, Mäster Nilsgatan 22 (☎040/38 02 40); Hertz, Jorgenkocksgatan 1B (☎040/749 55).

Doctor On call daily 7am–10pm, ☎040/33 35 00 (at other times, ☎040/33 10 00).

Exchange Best rates are at Forex, Norra Vallgatan 60 (daily 7am–9am), Gustav Adolfs Torg 12 (Mon–Fri 8am–7pm, Sat 9am–3pm), and by the tourist office at Central Station (daily 8am–9pm).

Ferries and catamarans Flygbåtarna, Skeppsbron (catamaran to Copenhagen; 85kr one-way; ☎040/10 39 30); SAS, Skeppsbron (hovercraft to Kastrup airport: 475kr one-way; ☎040/35 71 00); Pilen (catamaran to Copenhagen; 29kr one-way; ☎040/23 44 11).

Pharmacy 24hr service at Apoteket Gripen, Bergsgatan 48.

Post office Skeppsbron 1 (Mon–Fri 8am–6pm, Sat 9.30am–1pm).

Taxis City Cabs ☎040/710 00.

Telephone office Televerket, Storgatan 23 (Mon–Fri 8am–9pm, Sat 9.30am–3pm).

Train enquiries There's a Pågatåg information office inside the Lokalstationen (Mon–Fri 7am–6pm, Sat 8am–3pm, Sun 9am–3pm).

Southeastern Skåne: the coast to Ystad

The local **Pågatåg train** and the E6 and E14 highways cut directly east towards Ystad, missing out some picturesque minor resorts and a couple of the region's best beaches along Sweden's most southwesterly tip. If you have time to explore, and particularly if you have your own transport, this quieter part of the south makes for a delightful few days' exploration. Thirty kilometres south of Malmö (by car or bus #150), you cross an expanse of heathland to which bird-watchers flock every autumn to spot nesting plovers and terns, as well as millions of migratory birds fleeing the Arctic for the Stevns peninsula, south of Copenhagen.

Skanör and Falsterbro

A few kilometres on, at the fan-shaped southwest tip of the country, lie the seaside resorts of Skanör and Falsterbro. Crossing a canal that was dug by Swedes during the last war to provide a transport alternative to occupied Danish coastal waters, you arrive in the early-medieval town of **SKANÖR**, a Hanseatic centre founded to take advantage of the abundance of herring off this stretch of the coast. In the first years of the twentieth century, Skanör and its neighbour Falsterbro became fashionable bathing resorts for rich Malmö families and, although both have since gone in and out of vogue, they are once again desirable destinations for much the same set. There's not much to see in Skanör, but its beaches are superb, with long ribbons of white sand bordering an extensive bird and nature reserve. From the beach, you can see across the reserve to Skanör's medieval church. Once the herring had moved on to waters new in the sixteenth century, the church never received its intended extensions, making it all the more appealing. From the little harbour, it's a pleasant walk to the town square and the lovely old cottages lining Mellangatan. If you want **to stay** – and the beach is worth it – *Hotell Gässlingen* (☎040/47 30 35, fax 47 51 81; ④/③) at Rådhustorget 6, is a simple but lovely place. If you're **camping**, there are plenty of places to throw down a tent for free, though be careful to avoid the protected bird reserves. The little harbour at Skänor now boasts a gorgeous **restaurant**, *Skänor's Fiskroken* (☎040/47 40 50), where you can sample superb fish dishes in the simple, elegant setting, or choose from a remarkable range of smoked and pickled fish and have them made up into a picnic (around 90kr) – try herring roe marinated in rum and hot smoked salmon with black bread.

FALSTERBRO, just 2km south, is also very picturesque, attracting Swedish yuppies in force. Along with its castle ruin, eighteenth-century lighthouse and church, it also boasts really fine beaches and is slightly livelier than Skanör. A couple of restaurants worth trying are *Kaptensgården* on Stadsalleyn, an elegant establishment with a garden terrace and occasional live jazz, and, just a few steps up the road, *Café Restaurant Allen*, where there's a happy "hour" from noon to 5pm and an afternoon menu of light snacks.

Foteviken Viking Museum

Just to the east of Skänor and Falsterbro, signs point to the **Foteviken Viking Museum** (mid-May to Aug daily 11am–4pm; guided tours in English at 11.30am, 1pm & 2.30pm; 30kr). Forteviken, an ancient coastal village and centre of herring fishing from late Viking times, was the scene of a bloody battle in June 1134 between the Danish king and the would-be king of Skåne. Today, the whole area has been transformed into a working – and remarkably authentic – Viking village which attempts to re-create the way of life here as it existed in 1134. The complex includes houses, workshops, a sacrificial temple and shipbuilding yard, creating a virtually self-sufficient settlement – the atmosphere is like a sort of twelfth-century commune, with unemployed Skånians and others from all over Europe living and working in an 800-year-old time warp. All food, clothes and belongings are cooked, woven and made on site, from curing leather to dying wool, and the houses are built authentically. The most dramatic time to come is June 12–13, when the battle is re-enacted, while from July 2 to 4, hundreds of people engaged in similar Viking-style living projects converge here from all over Northern Europe for an international get together.

Trelleborg

Heading east along the coast, the rolling fields are punctuated by World War II concrete bunkers, some now converted into unlikely looking summer houses. Approaching **TRELLEBORG** by bus from Malmö (35min), a curtain of low-level industry blocks the sea – although this won't bother you too much if you're taking one of the ferries over to the German towns of Rostock, Sassnitz or Travemünde. Yet behind the graceless factories, this is a busy little town, its main attractions an inspired reconstruction of a recently discovered Viking fortress and a gallery of works by the sculptor Axel Ebbe.

From the ferry terminals on the seafront, walk up Kontinengatan, past the tourist office, which supplies a good free leaflet entitled *A Couple of Hours in Trelleborg* in recognition of how long most people stay. A few minutes' further on is the **Axel Ebbe Gallery** (June to early Sept Tues–Sun 11am–5pm; mid-Sept to May Tues–Sun 1–4pm; 20kr) in a compact, 1930s functionalist building that was once the local bank. Ebbe's superb sculptures make for a powerful collection of sensual nudes, all larger than life and in black or white stone. At the beginning of the twentieth century, Ebbe's gently erotic work was celebrated in Paris, though when his graceful, sprawling *Atlas's Daughter* was unveiled in Copenhagen, it caused an outcry. A few steps into the **Stadsparken**, opposite, is Trelleborg's main square, dominated by Ebbe's *Sea Monster*, a fountain comprising a serpentine fiend intertwined with a characteristically sensuous mermaid.

The main shopping promenade, **Algatan**, runs parallel with the seafront, and walking up from the ferry terminal you'll soon come to **St Nicolai's kyrka**, which has some bright ceiling paintings, elaborate memorial tablets, and monks' chairs from a Franciscan monastery destroyed during the Reformation. A couple of minutes' stroll north from here is Trelleborg's most dramatic new attraction, the **Trelle Fortress** (open all year; free), an impressive monument to local Viking life. Surrounded by a moat, the original circular fortress, dating from around 980 AD, was built by King Harald Bluetooth around a seventh-century settlement of pit houses and was composed entirely of earth and wood. Archeologists compared the remains with four almost identical forts in Denmark and, using a certain amount of guesswork, have constructed an impressive replica. Despite the authenticity of location, though, if you're interested in Viking culture, you're still better off heading back west to Foteviken (see p.489) for sheer atmosphere.

Practicalities

The **train station** is close to the ferry terminal; three trains a day run from Malmö to Trelleborg, timed to connect with the Sassnitz ferry, but there are hourly **buses**, stopping at the bus terminal behind the main square. **Ferry** departures to Germany are pretty regular – check "Travel details" at the end of the chapter for details.

The **tourist office**, just off Kontinengatan at Hamngatan 4 (mid-June to mid-Aug Mon–Fri 9am–8pm, Sat 9am–6pm, Sun 1–6pm; mid-Aug to mid-June Mon to Fri 9am–5pm; ☎0410/533 22, fax 134 86), is tucked in behind a hot-dog stand, but boasts its own pleasant café, *Garvaregården*. If you do want to **stay**, they can book **private rooms** for 130kr (plus 35kr booking fee). The cheap *Hotel Standard*, Österbrogatan 4 (☎0410/104 38, fax 71 18 66; ③), is central and somewhat shabby, though better than its entrance suggests. At the other end of the spectrum, *Hotel Dannegården*, Standgatan 32 (☎0410/71 11 20, fax 170 76; ⑤/③), is a beautiful 1910 villa surrounded by scented bushes, with just five double rooms in original Art Nouveau style. Even if you don't stay here, the **restaurant** (closed July) is the finest place for a romantic, though pricey, meal. Otherwise, there are a couple of reasonable **cafés** on Algatan: *Billings* and *Palmblads*.

Smygehuk and Smygehamn

Around a third of the way from Trelleborg to Ystad along coastal Route 9 (bus #183), the tiny harbour village of **SMYGEHUK** has little to it except a particularly cosy youth hostel (see below), among a group of old wooden houses clustered around a nineteenth-century **lighthouse**. Walk through the flowers and nettles along the coast and you'll soon reach the hamlet of **SMYGEHAMN**, less than a kilometre away, which prides itself on being Sweden's most southerly point – it's not much more than a tiny harbour surrounded by a few summertime restaurants, a café and a smoked-fish shop. The harbour itself was built out of a limestone quarry, and lime burning was big business here from Smygehamn's heyday in the mid-nineteenth century right up until the 1950s. Lime kilns are still dotted all around, odd, igloo-like structures with cupola roofs. Back from the harbour, Axel Ebbe's *The Embrace* is a good example of his Romantic style – a female nude rises up from the scrubland, embracing the elements.

Smygehuk's seasonal **tourist office** occupies a fine, early nineteenth-century corn warehouse by the harbour (June–Aug daily 10am–6pm; ☎0410/240 53), and can book **private rooms** from just 90kr per person, plus 35kr booking fee. The **youth hostel** (☎0410/245 83, fax 245 09; mid-May to mid-Sept) is in the lighthouse keeper's house. The nearest **hotels** are in Trelleborg, 13km away, but *Smygehus Havsbad* (☎0410/243 90, fax 293 43), an old bathing house just 500m away, has four-bed cabins for 850kr, including breakfast. There's also a rather fine **bed and breakfast**, *Hedman's* (☎0410/234 73, fax 234 71; ②), three kilometres inland in the hamlet of Boste. The best **restaurant** in the area is *Albinslunds Krog,* Östra Vemmenhog 7 at Skateholm (☎0411/53 23 10, fax 53 23 11), about four kilometres east of Smygehuk, which serves really good international gourmet dishes.

Ystad

An hour by Pågatåg train from Malmö is the exquisitely well-preserved medieval market town of **YSTAD**, with a core of quaint cobbled lanes lined with half-timbered cottages and a central square oozing rural charm. With the stunningly beautiful coastal region of Österlen stretching northwest from town in the direction of Kristianstad and some excellent walking to the north of town, Ystad is a splendid place to base yourself for a day or so. It is also the departure point for **ferries** to the Danish island of Bornholm, and to Poland.

Arrival, information and accommodation

From the **train station**, cross the tracks to St Knuts Torg, where the **tourist office** (mid-June to mid-Aug Mon–Fri 9am–7pm, Sat 11am–7pm, Sun 1–7pm; mid-Aug to mid-June Mon–Fri 9am–5pm; ☎0411/772 79, fax 55 55 85, *turistinfo@ystad.se*) is next door to the Art Museum. St Knuts Torg is also where **buses** from Lund (#X300), Kristianstad (Skåne Express) and Simrishamn (#572) pull in, and where buses leave for destinations along the coast and into the rest of Skåne. However, there's no bus service from Malmö: either take a Pågatåg train or bus #183 from Trelleborg/Smygehamn to Skateholm and then bus #330 to Ystad; to get to Kristianstad by train, you need to return to Malmö and take the inland train. The **ferry terminal** (signposted "Till Färjorna") is a few hundred metres to the east of the train station – turn left out of the station and walk for ten minutes along the quayside. Tickets **to Poland** cost from 220kr one-way (9hr crossing), or you can buy a four-day return for 420kr. One-way tickets and day returns to Bornholm cost 135kr (2hr 30min). **Cycling** is a great way to see the

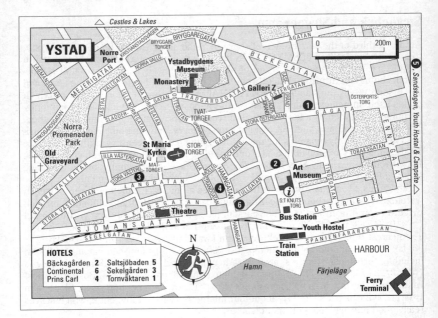

surrounding landscape and bikes can be rented from the tourist office (60kr per day, 300kr per week).

There are several good and reasonably priced **hotels** in town, and one at the beach. There are also two **youth hostels**, one on the beach at Sandskogen (☎0411/665 66), served by buses #572 and #304, but from September to May it's only open to groups. The other is much more conveniently situated in the old station building at the train station (☎0708/57 79 95). There's a **campsite** (☎0411/192 70) with cabins (from 110kr per person) next to the youth hostel at Sandskogen.

Hotels

Bäckagården, Bäckagården 36 (☎0411/198 48, fax 757 15). More a guesthouse than a hotel, in a converted home just behind the tourist office. ②.

Continental, Hamngatan 13 (☎0411/137 00, fax 125 70). Classic hotel touted as Sweden's oldest, with a grand lobby of marble, Corinthian pillars and crystal chandeliers. Rooms are modern Italian-style, and breakfast is a treat. ④.

WALKING AROUND YSTAD

The forested lake region 20km north of Ystad provides plenty of hiking possibilities, either on organized trails or in undeveloped tracts where you can camp rough. Take any bus north in the direction of **Sjöbo** (by car take Route 13), and you'll link with the **Skåneleden** ("Long Trail"), which follows a hundred-kilometre circular route from just outside Ystad. The tourist office (see p.491) can provide route maps as well as details on where to find places to eat and stay along the way. You can also head north on foot from Ystad to Hedeskoga and then follow trails along a chain of forest-fringed lakes – Krageholmsjön, Ellestadssjön and Snogeholmssjön – up to Sövdesjön (a 20km hike).

Prins Carl, Hamngatan 8 (☎0411/737 50, fax 665 30). A mid-range place with rooms reserved for non-smokers, others adapted for people with disabilities or allergies. ④.

Saltsjöbaden, Saltsjöbadsvägen 6 (☎0411/136 30, fax 55 58 35). Renowned for its beachside position, just east of town, this large, 100-year-old hotel (though with endless modern extensions tacked on) has a sauna, pool (summer only) and restaurant in the original saltwater bathing house. ④.

Sekelgården, Stora Västergatan 9 (☎0411/739 00, fax 189 97). The best place to stay in town, this small family-run hotel in a merchant's house of 1793 is friendly and informal, with a cobbled courtyard and flower garden. There are en-suite rooms in both the main house and the old tannery at the back, and excellent breakfasts. ③/②.

Tornväktaven, Stora Östergatan 33 (☎0411/129 54, fax 729 27). Plain and cheap, with breakfast buffet included, this is a reasonable choice if the *Sekelgården* is full. ②.

The Town

Turning left from the station and ferry terminals then right up Hamngatan brings you to the well-proportioned **Stortorget**, a grand old square encircled by picturesque streets. The **St Maria kyrka** is a handsome centrepiece, with additions from nearly every century since it was begun in the thirteenth. In the 1880s, changing tastes saw many of the rich decorative features removed, and only the most interesting ones were returned during a restoration programme forty years later. Inside, the early seventeenth-century Baroque pulpit is worth a look for the fearsome face carved beneath it and, opposite, the somewhat chilling medieval crucifix, which was placed here on the orders of Karl XII to remind the preacher of Christ's suffering.

If you stay in Ystad, you'll soon become acquainted with a tradition that harks back to the seventeenth century: from a room in the church's watchtower, a night watchman blows a haunting tune on a bugle every fifteen minutes from 9.15pm to 3am, as a safeguard against the outbreak of fire. The idea was that if one of the thatched cottages went up in flames, the bugle would sound repeatedly for all to go and help extinguish the blaze. The sounding through the night was to assure the town that the watchman was still awake; until the mid-nineteenth century, if he slept on duty he was liable to be executed.

From Stortorget, it's a short stroll up Garevaregränd, past art and craft workshops, and on up Klostergatan to the **Ystadbygdens Museum** (Mon–Fri noon–5pm, Sat & Sun noon–4pm; 20kr). Set in the thirteenth-century Gråbröder (Greyfriars) Monastery, it contains the usual local history collections, given piquancy here by their preserved medieval surroundings. After the monks were driven out during the Reformation, the monastery was at various times a hospital, a poorhouse, a distillery and finally a dump. A decision to demolish it in 1901 was overturned, and today it's definitely worth a visit.

If you want to explore more of the old town, it's still possible to find your way around using a city map from 1753, copies of which are supplied by the tourist office. Not far from the church on the western side of town, **Norra Promenaden**, a strip of mature horse chestnut trees and parkland, is good for a stroll. Here you'll find *Café Promenaden*, a white pavilion built in the 1870s to house a genteel café and dance hall.

Eating, drinking and nightlife

There is a fair selection of places to eat in Ystad, including some atmospheric **cafés** and fine **restaurants**, most of the latter on Stortorget. To start the day, the *Continental* serves a huge **breakfast buffet** (Mon–Fri 7–9.30am, Sat & Sun 8–10am; 75kr), ideal if you've just come off a morning ferry. Aside from the restaurant-bar *Prince Charles Pub* (see overleaf), **nightlife** is pretty minimal – the only clubs are *Starshine* at Osterportstorg, east from Stortorget along Stora Östergatan (labelled as Gågatan on some maps, meaning pedestrianized street), and the popular *Laura's* disco and casino on Stora Ostergatan (same door as the Konsum supermarket).

Otherwise, locals tend to take a bus thirty minutes north to **Tingballa**, where there are a couple of dance halls.

Cafés, restaurants and pubs

Bruggeriet, Långgatan 20 (☎0411/699 99). Rough, beamed interior dominated by two copper beer casks creates a welcoming ambience at this fine restaurant. Well-cooked fish and meat dishes, with one vegetarian option.

The English Book Café, Gäsegränd. Down a tiny, cobbled street off Stora Östergatan, this precariously leaning wooden house is all old English china and books to read while you feast on home-baked scones and tea. The gardens are delightful too, and retain their 1778 layout.

Lotta's, Stortorget. Justifiably the most popular restaurant in town, packed each evening in summer and serving beautifully presented, scrumptious fish and meat dishes. Closed Sat & Sun. *Lotta's Källare* in the cellars below is a cosy bar with several English beers including the so-called "Manchester United".

Prince Charles Pub, Hamngatan. Next door to the *Prins Carl Hotel*, this English-style pub and restaurant serves meat and fish dishes in the evenings, with live music on Fri and Sat nights.

Rådhuskälleren, in the cellars of the Rådhus. Rather more sedate than *Lotta's* opposite, with candlelit lunch (55kr) and dinners (200kr) in a 700-year-old prison; service can be less than convivial. Closed Sun.

Österlen and the coast to Åhus

It's easy to see how the landscape of the southeastern corner of Skåne, known as **Österlen**, has lured writers and artists to its coastline and plains. Here, yellow fields of rape stand out against a cobalt-blue sky, punctuated by white cottages, blood-red poppy fields and the odd black windmill. Österlen also has a number of engaging sights, notably the Viking ruin **Ales Stennar**, pretty villages and plenty of sandy beaches. Moving further northeast are the orchards of Sweden's apple region, centred on **Kivik**, while **Åhus**, a low-key resort famous for smoked eels, ends this stretch of the coast.

Unfortunately, **getting around** this part of the country isn't easy. The only major road in the area, Route 9 to Kristianstad via Simrishamn, cuts off the main corner of Österlen, the whole area is poorly served by buses and the only train service is the Pågatåg train from Ystad to Simrishamn: if you haven't got a car, you'll need to do some walking and cycling to make the most of this part of Sweden.

Ales Stennar

Twenty kilometres out of Ystad, near the hamlet of Kåseberga, is the Viking site of **Ales Stennar**. Believed to have been a Viking meeting place, this awe-inspiring monument consists of 56 stones forming a 67-metre-long boat-shaped edifice, the prow and stern denoted by two appreciably larger monoliths. The site was hidden for centuries beneath shifting sands, which only cleared in 1958. Buried several metres into the sand, it's difficult to imagine how these great stones, which aren't native to the region, were transported here. Ales Stennar stands on a windy, flat-topped hill, and despite the inevitable tourists snapping away at the ancient site (most of whom don't bother to climb up), there's a majestic timelessness at the top that more than rewards your climb.

There are two ways to get to Ales Stennar from Ystad: either take the infrequent **bus** #322 (20min) or rent a **bike** and follow the coastal cycle track through pine forests and past white sandy beaches, following the signs to Kåseberga.

Simrishamn

There's not much to the little fishing town of **SIMRISHAMN**, around 40km from Ystad, although its old quarter of tiny, fondant-coloured cottages and its church, orginally built as a twelfth-century fisherman's chapel, are pretty enough. The unexceptional **museum** is full of the usual archeological finds, alongside bits and pieces of farm and fishing equipment. You may want to come here, however, for the summer **catamaran** service to the Danish island of Bornholm (3–4 daily). If you do fancy staying, *Hotell Kockska Garden*, Sturgatan 25 (☎0414/41 17 55, fax 41 19 78; ③), is a comfortable **accommodation** option, housed in a renovated tavern. For bike rental, ask at the tourist office, Tulhusgatan 2 (mid-June to mid-Aug Mon–Fri 9am–8pm, Sat noon–8pm, Sun 2–8pm; mid-Aug to mid-June Mon–Fri 9am–5pm ☎0414/41 06 66).

Kivik

Around 20km north from Simrishamn, halfway to Åhus on the coastal road, you'll enter the endless orchards of Sweden's apple-growing region, Kivik. The village of **KIVIK** itself has no real centre, but buses stop outside the *Kivik Vardhus* hotel (see below). The uncommercialized harbour is just a few minutes away down Södergatan; there are a number of sights within a couple of kilometres of here.

Sweden's most notable Bronze Age cairn, **Kungsgraven** (May–Aug daily 10am–6pm; 10kr), is just 500m from the *Kivik Vardhus* hotel. A striking 75-metre upturned saucer of rocks, it lay hidden until discovered by a farmer in 1748. At its centre, the burial chamber is entered by a banked entrance passage, and inside are eight floodlit 3000-year-old runic slabs showing pictures of horses, a sleigh and what look like dancing seals.

Two kilometres from the grave, beyond hilly orchards (follow the signs), is the **Kiviksmusteri** cider factory and the entertaining **Apple House** (April & May 10am–5pm; June–Sept 10am–6pm; 20kr), an apple museum each of whose rooms is infused with a different smell: the room devoted to "Great Apples in History" smells of cider, while a room detailing attempts to create an insect-resistant apple summons up apple pie. Other, wackier exhibitions focus on outlandish topics such as the (alleged) "symphonic soul of apples". Just 200m beyond the Apple House, **Stenshuvuds National Park** is a perfect place to come back to reality. At almost 100m high, the top of this hill laced with walking trails affords superb views. Self-guided walking tours lead around remnants of an ancient fortress, while there are special wheelchair-accessible paths through the forested hillsides.

Frequent Skåne Express **buses** to and from Simrishamn (30min) and Kristianstad (55min) stop outside the *Kivik Vardhus* farmhouse **hotel** (☎0414/700 74, fax 710 20; ②; May–Aug) and restaurant. For cheaper accommodation, the STF **youth hostel** lies in its own attractive gardens on Tittutvägen, north of the harbour, just five minutes' walk from the bus stop (☎0414/711 95). For exploring the region further, **bikes** can be rented at the harbourside in midsummer for 75kr a day.

Åhus

Once a major trading port, and in medieval times a city of considerable ecclesiastical importance, **ÅHUS**, 55km north of Simrishamn, today relies on holidaying Swedes for its income. The town is famed for its eels, which appear on menus all over the country, smoked and usually served with scrambled eggs. From the tourist office (see p.496), it's a short walk up Köpmannagatan to the beautiful old cobbled main square. The twelfth-century **St Maria kyrka**, behind the old Rådhus that houses the town's unexceptional **museum**, is wonderfully preserved, its sheer size attesting to the town's former eminence. However, it's one of the gravestones in the churchyard that really raises the eyebrows: take a look at the headstone of Captain Måns Mauritsson, between the church and the museum. According to the inscription, the captain's wife, Helena Sjöström, was 133 years old when she died, and her daughters were born when she was 82 and 95 respectively. At nearby Västerport (walk to the end of Västergatan from the centre) the **Tobaksmonopolets Lada** (free entry) holds displays of tobacco labels and all the paraphernalia of tobacco processing. For 250 years every garden in Åhus had its own tobacco patch, until the government cancelled its contract with the growers in 1964.

Beyond this, there's little more to do than cut through from the main square down Västra Hamngatan to the waterside, where small pleasure yachts line the harbour, a pretty spot if you avert your eyes from the industrial hinterland to the left. For the **beach**, head out on Järnvägsgatan, behind the tourist office, past a run of old train carriages – there are no trains running now – and left up Ellegatan following signs for **Åhus Strand**.

Practicalities

Unless you're driving, it's easiest to get to Åhus on bus #551 from Kristianstad, 20km to the northwest (see below) – the bus stops outside the **tourist office** at Köpmannagatan 2 (June–Aug Mon–Fri 9am–7pm, Sat 9am–6pm, Sun 2–6pm; Sept, Oct & March–May Mon–Fri 10am–5pm; Nov–Feb Mon–Fri 1–5pm; ☎044/24 01 06, fax 24 38 98, *touristinfo.ahus@kristianstad*). There's a **bike rental** shop on Ellegatan (on the way to the beach) that also rents out double-pedalled buggy bikes at 40kr per hour. The tourist office also rents bikes out for 50kr per day. The **youth hostel** (☎044/24 85 35; book through tourist office Sept–May) is at Stavgatan 3, just a few metres away. Alternatively, stay on the bus a few minutes longer to get to the beach, where there are plenty of hotels and a **campsite** (☎044/24 89 69) in the nearby forest. *Hotel Åhus Strand* (☎044/28 93 00, fax 24 94 80; ②) is a reasonable, if plain, choice among the beach **hotels**.

There are some lovely places **to eat** in Åhus. Down by the harbour, the genteel *Gästgivaregård* specializes in Baltic fish dishes at lunchtime, but for the most enjoyable and relaxed dinner, walk 200m along the waterside to *Ostermans* (May–Sept) at Gamla Skeppsbron, a small wooden restaurant at the water's edge, serving just one item: Greenland prawns. Heading back up Västra Hamngatan, *Gallericaféet* (June–Aug) is a small art gallery and garden restaurant, which again specializes in local seafood.

Kristianstad

Twenty kilometres inland, eminently likeable **KRISTIANSTAD** (for its correct pronunciation, try a guttural "Krwi-chwan-sta") is eastern Skåne's most substantial historic centre – a Renaissance town created in 1614 by Christian IV, Denmark's seventeenth-century "builder-king". A shining example of the king's architectural preoccupations, with beautifully proportioned central squares and broad gridded streets flanking the wide river, it was only to remain in Danish hands for another 44 years.

Arrival, information and accommodation

Local **buses** from Ystad (1hr 30min), Simrishamn (1hr 30min) and Åhus (30min) all stop outside the central bus station on Östra Boulevarden, although the quickest way here is by **train** (1hr 16min from Malmö) on the ultra-comfortable Kustpilen Express between Malmö and Karlskrona. You might also arrive at the sparkling little **airport**, 17km from the city centre, on a domestic service or on one of Ryanair's daily flights from London. Buses leave the airport for the city twenty minutes after each flight arrival (20min; 40kr).

The **tourist office** (mid-June to mid-Aug Mon–Fri 9am–7pm, Sat 9am–3pm, Sun 2–6pm; mid-Aug to mid-June Mon–Fri 10am–5pm and last Sat of each month 11am–3pm; ☎044/12 19 88, fax 12 08 98, *touristinfo@kristianstad.se*) on Nya Boulevarden books **private rooms** from 150kr (plus 40kr booking fee). There's a

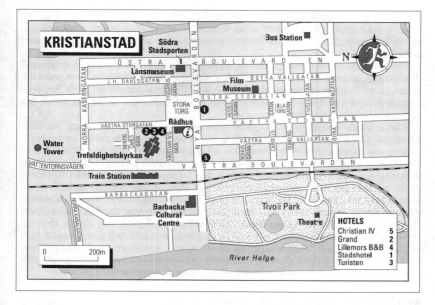

campsite with attached **youth hostel** at *Charlottsborg Camping* (☎044/21 07 67), 2km away (bus #22 or #23).

Three of Kristianstad's **hotels** are side by side, just a few steps from the train station. The cheapest is the very comfortable old *Hotel Turisten*, Västra Storgatan 17 (☎044/12 61 50, fax 10 30 99; ③/②), some of whose rooms have bathtubs; next door is the very cosy *Lillemors B&B* (☎044/21 95 25, mobile 070/521 68 00; ②), built in the 1790s. A few steps away, the modern *Grand Hotel* (☎044/10 36 00, fax 12 57 82; ⑤/③) offers friendly service and very comfortable beds. The most glamorous place to spend the night, though, is *Hotel Christian IV*, Västra Boulevarden 15 (☎044/12 63 00, fax 12 41 40; ⑤/②). A grand, castle-like confection in the old Sparbank building, its beautifully renovated features include original fireplaces and parquet floors.

The Town

The obvious starting point is the **Trefaldighetskyrkan** (Holy Trinity Church; daily 9am–5pm), opposite the train station, which stands as a symbol of all that was glorious about Christian IV's Renaissance ideas. The grandiose exterior has seven magnificent spiralled gables, and the high windows allow light to flood the white interior. Diagonally across from the church, the main square, **Storatorg**, hosts the late nineteenth-century **Rådhus**, itself built in imitation of Christian's Renaissance style. Inside the entrance, a bronze copy of the king's 1643 bust is something of a revelation, with Christian sporting a goatee beard, one earring and a single dreadlock, his one exposed nipple decorated with a flower motif. Back outside in the square, Palle Pernevi's splintered *Icarus* fountain depicts the unfortunate Greek aeronaut falling from heaven into a scaffolded building site.

North of Storatorg on Östra Boulevarden is the **Länsmuseum** (June–Aug Mon–Fri 10am–5pm; Sept–May Tues–Sat noon–5pm; Wed till 8pm year round; free), housed in a building that was begun as a royal palace by Christian in 1616, but soon became an arsenal for Danish partisans during the bloody Scånian wars. Aside from the historical exhibits, there are some interesting textile and art collections on the top floor. If you've time on your hands, it's a pleasant stroll behind the museum to **Södra Stadsporten**, the 1790s southern town gate on Östra Boulevarden, one of the few remaining pieces of fortification.

For a panoramic overview of both the town and the local lakes of Hammarsjön and Aradövssjön, connected by the River Helge, walk a couple of minutes west from the main square to the **water tower** (Mon–Sat 10am–6pm, Sun noon–6pm; free). You take a small lift up the 42 floors (the stairs are kept locked) to the café at the top, which has wall maps to help with orientation.

Walking back through the town centre, a few minutes east of the Storatorg, the **Film Museum**, Östra Storgatan 53 (Tues–Fri & Sun 1–4pm; free), is heralded by a bronze early movie camera outside the door. This was once Sweden's first film studio, where the country's earliest movies were recorded between 1909 and 1911; some of these flickering works can now be viewed on videotape inside. From here, wander down any of the roads to the south and you'll reach **Tivoli Park**, where you can stroll beneath avenues of horse chestnuts; at the park's centre is a green-pained Art Nouveau **theatre**, designed by Kristianstad-born Axel Anderberg, who also created the Stockholm Opera House (see p.413). **Sightseeing boats** (*vattenriket*) splash their way up the river on two-hour trips from behind the theatre (May to mid-June & mid-Aug to mid-Sept 3 daily at 11am, 2pm and 6pm; 70kr, book at the tourist office). At the northern edge of Tivoli Park, there's an art gallery showing temporary exhibitions and housing the **Barbacka Cultural Centre**, which has information about musical events around the town.

Eating, drinking and entertainment

Kristianstad has a number of really good, stylish and fun places **to eat**. Of the **cafés**, best are *Fornstuga House*, an elaborately carved Hansel-and-Gretel lodge in the middle of Tivoli Park, and the more central *konditori, Du Vanders*, Hesslegatan 6. Among the town's **restaurants**, *Restaurant Kippers* on Östra Storgatan is an atmospheric cellar restaurant specializing in pricey steaks, while the nearby *Restaurant Roma*, Östra Storgatan 15, is an inexpensive Italian restaurant serving big pizzas at 65kr. *Bar-B Ko* on Tivoligatan is an inviting place where the speciality is grilled meats, with main courses for 100kr and a huge range of whiskies, spirits, ale and cider. *Restaurant Sparet*, in the charming red-and-cream train station building, is another good bet, with the emphasis on fish dishes at around 100kr and filling staples like *pytt i panni* at 49kr. If money's no object, *Christian Kock*, next to the *Grand Hotel*, serves Swedish delights like nettle soup and interesting combinations of meats, fish and fruits at around 130kr a dish in modern, candlelit elegance.

For a central **drinking** place, check out the 250 or so beers at the *Skänken Pub and Steakhouse* in the old Riksbank on Storatorg, or try the German-owned *Hesslebaren* on Hesslegatan. *Harry's Bar*, Östra Storgatan, is a small but lively place with loud rock music.

The town hosts two annual festivals: **Kristianstadsdagarna**, a huge seven-day cultural festival in the second week of July (during which the tourist office stays open till 10pm). The annual **Kristianstad and Åhus Jazz Festival** runs around the same time – ask for details at the tourist office.

East into Blekinge

The county of **Blekinge** is something of a poor relation to Skåne in terms of tourism, though there are some good beaches, plentiful fishing, some fine walking trails and enough cultural diversions to make for an enjoyable few days. The landscape is much the same as in northeastern Skåne: forests and hills with fields fringing the sea, along with a number of islands and a small archipelago south of Karlskrona that make a picturesque destination for short boat trips. If you only have a day or two in the region, it's best to head to the handsome and lively town of **Karlskrona**, the county capital, from where the tiny, fortified hamlet of **Kristianopel** is just 30km away.

Public transport in Blekinge requires some careful timetable studying to avoid being stranded from early evening onwards. Most locals drive, and on weekend evenings there are unlikely to be any trains or buses between towns, while hitching is nigh on impossible – a fact keenly observed by taxi drivers, who charge as much as 250kr to take you between Ronneby and Karlshamn. The Kustpilen Express **train** runs from Malmö/Lund to Karlskrona and stops at all the towns detailed below.

Karlshamn

An hour's train ride from either Kristianstad or Karlskrona (see p 501), **KARLSHAMN** is a rewarding goal for a day's exploration. After a disastrous fire in 1763, wealthy merchants continued to build ever more grand houses for themselves as replacements, and some are still standing. The town saw its heyday in the nineteenth century, when it manufactured goodies such as punch, brandy and tobacco. Today, margarine and ice-cream factories flank the harbour, but don't be put off, Karlshamn also has some beautiful little streets of pastel-painted houses, a clutch of museums and, within easy reach, some offshore islands that offer a wooded retreat and clean-water swimming.

From the train station, turn left onto Eric Dahlbergsvägen, and right down Kyrkogatan, which is lined with old painted wooden houses. **Karl Gustav kyrka**, an unusual late seventeenth-century church, squats at the junction with Drottninggatan. Walking down this street you are retracing the steps of many nineteenth-century emigrants on their way to "New Sweden" in America. The town's **museums** are all close together at the other end of Drottninggatan, at the junction with Vinkelgatan; best of the bunch is **Skottsbergska Gården**, on Drottninggatan (Tues–Sun noon–5pm; 10kr), an amazingly well-preserved eighteenth-century merchant's house. The ground-floor kitchen is furnished in eighteenth-century style, with an enormous open fireplace, while upstairs there's some splendid Gustavian decoration and wardrobes stuffed with ancient clothes.

On the corner, the **Museum of Local History** (June–Aug Tues–Sun noon–5pm; Sept–May Sat & Sun noon–5pm; 10kr) contains a run-of-the-mill collection of domestic and marine exhibits; more interesting are the various buildings out through the old courtyard, where there's a tobacco-processing works among the authentic interiors. Finally, if you've time on your hands, investigate the intriguing **Punch Museum** (June–Aug Tues–Sun noon–5pm; 10kr or free with entry to Museum of Local History), which displays the workings of Karlshamn Flaggpunch, the factory that blended this potent mixture of sugar, arrack and brandy until forced to close down in 1917.

Practicalities

A short walk from the station, the harbourside **tourist office** is on the corner of Ågatan and Ronnebygatan (mid-June to mid-Aug Mon–Fri 9am–7pm, Sat 10am–6pm, Sun noon–6pm; mid-Aug to mid-June Mon–Fri 9am–5pm; ☎0454/165 95, fax 842 45, *turistbyran@karlshamn.se*) and will book private **rooms** (100kr per person plus 40kr booking fee) and **cottages** (3000kr per week for 2) anywhere in the region. The STF **youth hostel** sits next to the train station at Surbrunnsvägen 1c (☎0454/140 40; May–Sept). The nearest **campsite** (☎0454/812 10; May–Sept) is by the sea at **Kollevik**, 3km out of town, and also has cabins (450kr for 4 people) – take bus #312 from the train station or Stortorget. Of the central **hotels**, the cheapest is the *Bode Hotel*, Södra Fogdelyckegatan (☎0454/315 00; ①); the *Hotel Carlshamn*, Varvsgatan 1 (☎0454/890 00, fax 819 50; ⑤/②), by the harbour, is the luxury option.

Karlshamn has an extraordinarily good **vegetarian restaurant**, *Gourmet Grön*, at Drottninggatan 61, serving a gourmet buffet with as much as you can eat for a remarkable 65kr during the day, 115–185kr in the evening (closed Sun). There's an Italian menu, too, and superb home-made desserts. Alternatively, you can sit outside at the *Terrassen Restaurant*, Ronnebygatan 12, to eat a wide range of fish and meat dishes.

The laid-back and pleasingly dated two-day annual **rock festival** (tickets 300kr) is staged in mid-June at the small village of Norje, 15km west of Karlshamn, when the streets become littered with half-naked (and more than half-inebriated) revellers. Even bigger is the **Baltic Festival** in the third week of July, an impressive, all-consuming town celebration with lots of eating, drinking and merry-making to the sounds of live music.

Ronneby

Much of **RONNEBY** has been destroyed by development and, arriving by train, even the summer sun can't improve the view of banal buildings ahead. There is, however, a tiny **old town**, a few minutes' walk up the hill to the left, testament to the fact that in the thirteenth century this was Blekinge's biggest town, and centre for trade with the Hanseatic League. Only when the county became Swedish four centuries later did Ronneby fall behind neighbouring Karlskrona. Today, the main attraction is the beautifully preserved collection of spa houses, a couple of kilometres over the river at **Ronneby Brunnspark**.

In the town itself, walk uphill to the left of the train station, and turn left again onto the main street, Kungsgatan. There is nothing much of interest here until you reach **Helga Korskyrkan** (Church of the Holy Cross). With its whitewashed walls, blocked-in arched windows and red-tiled roof, the church looks like a Greek chapel presiding over the surrounding modern apartment buildings. Dating originally from the twelfth century, this Romanesque church took quite a bashing during the Seven Years War (1563–70) against the Danes. On the night of what is known as the **Ronneby Blood Bath** in September 1564, all those who had taken refuge in the church were slaughtered – you can still see the gashes in the heavy oak door in the north wall that were made during the carnage.

In 1775 the waters here were found to be exploitably rich in iron, and Ronneby soon became one of Sweden's principal spa towns, centred on **Ronneby Brunnspark**. Fifteen minutes' walk from the train station up the hill and over the river (or take bus #211), the park's houses stand proudly amid blazing rhododendrons and azaleas. One such property is now a fine STF youth hostel (see below), with the wonderful *Wiener Café* next door. There are pleasant **walks** through the beautifully kept park, past a duck pond, and into the wooded hills behind, picking up part of the **Blekingeleden** walking trail. On summer Sunday mornings the park is the site of a giant **flea market**, selling genuine Swedish antiques alongside general tat.

Practicalities

From Karlshamn, there are frequent **train** and **bus** services to Ronneby. The **tourist office** (June–Aug Mon–Fri 9am–7pm, Sat 10am–4pm, Sun noon–4pm; Sept–May Mon, Wed & Fri 9am–5pm, Tues & Thurs 9am–7pm; ☎0457/180 90, fax 174 44) is in the Kulturcentrum, close to the church in the tiny old town. Without a doubt the best place to stay is at the STF **youth hostel** (☎ & fax 0457/263 00; closed Dec to early Jan) in Ronneby Brunnspark, whose owners also run the inaptly named *Grand Hotel* (☎0457/268 80, fax 268 84; ②) in a modern apartment building opposite the train station at Järnvägsgatan 11. Less central is *Strandgården*, Nedre Brunnsvägen 25 (☎0457/661 36; ①), a small, family-run pension near the youth hostel.

For **eating and drinking** in town, try *Nya Wienerbageriet* on Västra Torgatan, off the main square, for filling lunches, including a daily pasta dish for 60kr. At the back is a stylish new **bar** (Thurs–Sat 7pm till late) with occasional live music. Just off Stortorget is the town's best *konditori*, the *Continenta*. There are also a few places near the station: *Restaurant & Pub Piaff*, on Karlskronagatan, is an established pizza restaurant, with outside tables; a few steps away is an intimate, traditional pub, *Jojjes Pub Bar*, though the *Wiener Café* in Ronneby Brunnspark is the most popular place to drink.

Karlskrona

Blekinge's most appealing destination is the regal county capital **KARLSKRONA**, located on the largest link in a chain of breezy islands. Founded by Karl XI in 1680, who picked it as an ice-free southern harbour for his Baltic fleet, the town today revolves around its maritime heritage. The wide avenues and stately squares were built to accommodate the king's naval parades, and cadets in uniform still career around streets named after Swedish admirals and battleships. However, even if you're not a naval fan, Karlskrona has plenty to offer, particularly the picturesque old quarter around the once-busy fishing port at Fisktorget and some short cruises around the islands in the archipelago; however, due to military restrictions no bathing is allowed on them (there's good swimming off the nearby island of **Dragsö** or at the fine bathhouse in town).

Arriving by **train** or **bus**, you'll pass the island of **Hästö**, once home to Karlskrona's wealthiest residents, before arriving a few minutes later in the town centre on **Trossö**, connected to the mainland by the Österleden main road. Climb uphill past Hoglands

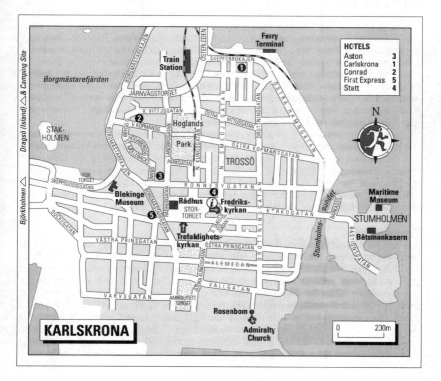

HOTELS

Aston	3
Carlskrona	1
Conrad	2
First Express	5
Statt	4

KARLSKRONA

0   200m

Park to the main square, **Stortorget**, at the highest point and geographical centre of the island. It's a vast and beautiful square, dominated by two complementary **churches**, both designed by Tessin the Younger and stuccoed in burnt orange, with dove-grey stone colonnades. **Fredrikskyrkan** (Mon–Fri 11am–3pm, Sat 9.30am–2pm) is elegant enough, but the interior of the circular domed **Trefaldighetskyrkan** (Mon–Fri 11am–3pm, Sat 9.30am–2pm) holds more interest. Built for the town's German merchant community in 1709, the domed ceiling is its most remarkable feature, painted with hundreds of rosettes and brilliantly shaded to look three-dimensional. The altar is also distinctive, with golden angelic faces peering out of a gilded meringue of clouds.

Head between the churches, down the wide, cobbled Södra Kungsgatan, which is divided down the centre by the walls of a tunnel that once carried trains between the station and the harbour. The leafy square ahead is **Amiralitets Torget** and perched at its centre is the huge, peeling wooden bell tower of the **Admiralty Church**. To get to the church itself, head down Vallgatan on the left of the square and the beautifully proportioned wooden church is up on your right. Built in 1685, it's the oldest entirely wooden church in Sweden. Outside the entrance, take a look at one of the city's best-known landmarks: the wooden statue of **Rosenbom**, a local beggar who one night forgot to raise his hat to thank the wealthy German carver, Fritz Kolbe. When admonished for this, Rosenbom retorted, "If you want thanks for your crumbs to the poor, you can take my hat off yourself!" Enraged, Kolbe struck him between the eyes and sent him away, but the beggar froze stiff and died in a snow drift by the church. Next morning, Kolbe found the beggar's body and, filled with remorse, carved a figure of Rosenbom to stand at the spot where he died, designing it so that you have to raise his hat yourself to give some money.

Karlskrona's best museums are set on the island of Stumholmen, connected to the mainland by road five minutes walk east of Stortorget down Kyrkogatan. The worthwhile **Maritime Museum** (mid-May to mid-Sept daily 10am–6pm, Thurs till 9pm; mid-Sept to mid-May Tues–Sun 11am–5pm, Thurs till 9pm; 40kr) to the left has a facade like a futuristic Greek temple, and its impressive interior is diverting even for those for whom things maritime usually induce yawns. Close by is Karlkrona's good **art gallery** (Tues–Fri noon–4pm, Wed till 7pm, Sat & Sun noon–5pm; free), set in the splendid old Seamen's Barracks (*båtamanskasern*). The highlight is the poignant work of local artist Erik Langemark, who chronicled the city in his paintings and drawings – modern photographs alongside show how the city has changed since.

For more of a feel of old Karlskrona, wander west past the military hardware towards the **Björkhomen** area. Here a couple of tiny wooden early eighteenth-century houses in little gardens survive, the homes built by the very first craftsmen at the naval yard. Nearby **Fisktorget**, originally the site of a fish market, is pleasant for a stroll, and is also the terminal for boat and river trips. The dull **Blekinge Museum** on Fisktorget (Mon–Fri 10am–4pm, Sat & Sun 11am–4pm; free) is worth a visit for the pleasant summertime café rather than the exhibits on shipbuilding and the like.

Practicalities

Karlskrona's **tourist office** (June & Aug Mon–Fri 9am–6pm, Sat 10am–2pm; July Mon–Fri 9am–7pm, Sat 10am–4pm, Sun 10am–6pm; Sept–May Mon–Fri 10am–5pm, Sat 10am–1pm; ☎0455/30 34 90, fax 30 34 94, *turistbyran@karlskrona.se*) is at Stortorget 2. You can book **private rooms** here for around 125kr per person and rent cheap, green military **bikes** for 25kr a day. The best place to rent new bikes (50kr per day) is from the Q8 petrol station near the train station at Järnvägstorget (☎0455/819 93). As usual, the cheapest bed is to be had in the STF **youth hostel**, centrally located at Bredgatan 16 (☎0455/100 20; mid-June to mid-Aug). The nearest **camping** is out on Dragsö island (☎0455/153 54), around 2.5km away: take bus #7 from the bus station to Saltö, from where it's a ten-minute walk. Most appealing of the modern **hotels** is the

Hotel Carlskrona, on Skeppsbrokajen at Fisktorget (☎0455/196 30, fax 259 90; ④/②); alternatively, the *Hotel First Express*, Borgmästaregatan 13 (☎0455/270 00, fax 127 00; ③), is another good choice, or there's the traditional 1890 *Statt Hotel* (☎0455/192 50, fax 169 09; ⑤/②) on the main street at Ronnebygatan 37–39. If these are out of your range, *Hotel Conrad* on Västra Köpmangatan (☎0455/823 35; ③/①), halfway up the hill towards Stortorget, is plain and reasonable, while the *Hotel Aston*, Landbrogatan 1 (☎0455/194 70; ②/①), is more central, though it's closed at weekends in summer.

Most of the town's **konditori** are indistinguishable, two exceptions being the pleasant *Café Tre G* on Landbrogatan, opposite Hoglands Park, which serves baked potatoes, cakes and sandwiches, and *Systrarna Lindkvists Café*, Borgmästaregatan 3, across from the tourist office. The majority of Karlskrona's **restaurants** are along central Ronnebygatan. *Espresso House*, at no. 30, does an exceptional range of well-prepared food, with pizzas (55–75kr), ciabattas, paninis and great cakes and desserts. The Greek *Taverna Santorini*, also on Ronnebygatan, serves all the usual choices, plus several vegetarian options, with no dish over 100kr. Next door is the very pleasant deli and café *Börje Olssons Skafferiet*, good for filled baguettes and luscious meats, cheeses and other exotic delights for picnics.

Ferries to Gdynia in Poland depart from the ferry terminal once daily (10hr 30min); daytime tickets cost 255kr one-way, 510kr return; night-time, 325kr and 535kr.

Kristianopel

Arriving by road at **KRISTIANOPEL**, 30km northeast of Karlskrona, there is not the slightest hint that this idyllic village of just 38 inhabitants was once a strategic fortification with a bloody history; if you're here outside July, you'd also be amazed to know that the place bursts with up to two thousand holiday-makers at that time, contributing to a sense of revelry seldom found in the rest of Sweden.

It's only when you've walked past the minute, untouched cottages in their tumbling gardens and all the way to the tiny harbour that you spot the two kilometres of three-metre-thick **fortified walls** that surround the settlement. A 1970s reconstruction, they were built over the original fortifications erected in 1600 by Danish King Christian IV to protect against Swedish aggression. The walls were finally razed by the Swedes after the little town had spent 77 years changing hands with alarming regularity. There is little in the way of specific sights in Kristianopel, the only building worth a brief look being the **church**, near the village shop, a replacement for a medieval church that burnt to the ground in 1605, killing all the village women, children and elderly, who were huddled inside for protection. Today, the original church is just a grassy mound near the campsite.

Practicalities

Getting to Kristianopel by public transport is tricky. **Bus** #120 from Karlskrona (to Kalmar) only runs along the main E22, stopping at Fågelmara, 6km from the village; from September, bus #122 from Karlskrona goes all the way to the village. Alternatively, **bikes** rented in Karlskrona can be taken on the #120 bus at no extra cost, and **hitching** is easier here than in most places. You can rent a **rowing boat** (10kr per hour, 50kr per day) at the campsite (see below).

For accommodation in the village you are limited to the **youth hostel and campsite** (☎ & fax 0455/661 30), tucked inside the low walls overlooking the sea, or the one **hotel**, a simple eighteenth-century farmhouse called *Gästgiferi* (☎ & fax 0455/36 60 30; ①; April–Sept), a deliciously mellow old place to the left of the main road into the village. *Restaurant Sjöstugan* (☎0455/36 60 88; see below) also has some B&B accommodation (②), though from September to May you'll need to book a couple of days in advance.

There are three **restaurants** in the village. The one at *Gästgiferi* serves well-prepared meals, with main courses from 95kr, in an authentic old farmhouse setting. You'll find a younger crowd at the campsite's *Värdshuset Pålsgården* (Fri 6–9pm, Sat noon–9pm, Sun noon–6pm), which serves food from an appealing menu in cosy surroundings and opens late every night in July as a pub. The nearby *Restaurant Sjöstugan* has a fine menu of fish, meat and pasta dishes at 100–165kr, plus a range of pizzas. If you're around on a Wednesday evening, try the grill buffet (7–10pm), which is excellent value. Every July, the two campsite restaurants are the focus for a wide range of **music** and **night-time entertainment**, ranging from Country and Western via blues, jazz and rock'n'roll to Eurovision Song Contest favourites.

travel details

Express trains
Daily express trains operate throughout the region, in particular **Oslo–Copenhagen** (via Gothenburg, Varberg, Halmstad and Helsingborg) and **Stockholm–Copenhagen** (via Helsingborg). Both routes have a branch service through to Malmö. Despite complicated timetabling, the service is frequent and regular north or south between Gothenburg and Helsingborg/Malmö.

Trains
Helsingborg to: Gothenburg (9 daily; 2hr 40min); Lund (13 daily; 40min); Malmö (13 daily; 50min).

Karlskrona to: Emmaboda for connections to Växjö, Stockholm & Kalmar (1–2 hourly; 40min).

Kristianstad to: Karlshamn (hourly; 50min); Karlskrona (hourly; 1hr 45min); Ronneby (hourly; 1hr 20min).

Malmö to: Gothenburg (8–10 daily; 3hr 45min); Karlskrona (hourly; 3hr 15min); Kristianstad (4 daily; 47min); Lund (3 hourly; 13min); Ystad (Mon–Fri hourly, Sat & Sun 5 daily; 50min).

Buses
Ängelholm to: Torekov (5 daily; 45min).

Båstad to: Torekov (5 daily; 30min).

Helsingborg to: Båstad (16 daily; 55min); Halmstad (6 daily; 1hr 50min).

Karlskrona to: Stockholm (Fri & Sun 1 daily; 7hr 30min).

Kristianstad to: Kalmar (1 daily; 3hr); Lund (1 daily; 2hr 30min); Malmö (1 daily; 2hr 45min).

Malmö to: Falkenberg (2 on Fri & Sun; 2hr 55min); Gothenburg (Mon–Thurs 1 daily, 3 on Fri & Sun; 4hr 25min); Halmstad (2 on Fri & Sun; 2hr 25min); Helsingborg (Mon–Thurs 1 daily, 6 on Fri & Sun; 1hr 5min); Jönköping (Mon–Thurs 1 daily, 3 on Fri & Sun; 4hr 30min); Kalmar (1 daily; 5hr 30min); Kristianstad (1 daily; 2hr); Lund (hourly; 20min); Mellbystrand (1 on Fri & Sun; 2hr); Stockholm (Mon–Thurs 1 daily, 3 on Fri & Sun; 9hr); Trelleborg (hourly; 35min); Varberg (2 on Fri & Sun; 3hr 20min).

Ystad to: Kristianstad (Mon–Fri 5–6 daily, 3 on Sat & Sun; 1hr 55min); Lund (Mon–Fri 3 daily; 1hr 15min); Malmö (3 daily; 1hr); Simrishamn (Mon–Fri 3 daily, 1 on Sat & Sun; 50min); Smygehamn (Mon–Fri 5 daily, 2 on Sat & Sun; 30min).

International ferries, hydrofoils and catamarans
Halmstad to: Grenå (2 daily; 4hr).

Helsingborg to: Helsingør (3 hourly; 25min).

Karlskrona to: Gdynia (1 daily; 10hr 30min).

Malmö to: Copenhagen (Flygbåtarna and Pilen hydrofoils hourly, 45min; Shopping Linjen hydrofoil 5 daily, 45min).

Simrishamn to: Allinge (summer-only 3–4 daily; 1hr).

Trelleborg to: Rostock (3 daily; 6hr); Sassnitz (5 daily; 3hr 45min); Travemünde (2 daily; 7–9hr).

Varberg to: Grenå (2 daily; 4hr).

Ystad to: Rønne (3–5 daily; 2hr 30min); Swinoujscie, Poland (2 daily; 7–9hr).

CHAPTER TWELVE

THE SOUTHEAST

lthough a less obvious target than the coastal cities and resorts of the southwest, Sweden's **southeast** certainly repays a visit. Impressive castles, ancient lakeside sites and numerous glass-making factories hidden amongst forests are some of the mainland attractions, while off the east coast, Sweden's largest Baltic islands offer beautifully preserved medieval towns and fairy-tale landscapes. Train transport, especially between Stockholm and the towns close to the eastern shore of Lake Vättern, is good; speedy, regular services mean that you can even visit some places as day-trips from Stockholm.

Småland county in the south encompasses a varied geography and some strikingly varied towns. The glorious historic fortress town of **Kalmar** is a worthwhile stop, and is also the jumping-off point for the island of **Öland**. Further inland, great swaths of dense forest are rescued from monotony by the many **glass factories** that continue the county's famous tradition of glass production. By the mid-nineteenth century, agricultural reforms and a series of bad harvests in Småland saw mass emigration to America and in **Växjö**, the largest town in the south, the art of glass-making and the history of Swedish emigration are the subject of two superb museums. At the northern edge of the county, **Jönköping** is a great base for exploring the beautiful eastern shore of **Lake Vättern**; it's also worth venturing across the water to visit the island of **Visingsö**, rich with remnants of its royal history.

The idyllic pastoral landscape of **Östergotland** stretches from the shores of the lake east to the Baltic. Popular with domestic tourists, the small lakeside town of **Vadstena** is one of the highlights, its medieval streets dwarfed by austere monastic edifices, a Renaissance palace and an imposing abbey. The **Göta Canal** wends its way through the northern part of the county to the Baltic and a number of fine towns line the route, including **Linköping**, with its unusual open-air museum where people live and work in a re-created nineteenth-century environment. Just to the north, bustling **Norrköping** grew up around the textile industry, a background that's preserved in a collection of handsome red-brick and stuccoed factories.

Outside the fragmented archipelagos of the east and west coasts, Sweden's only two true islands are in the Baltic: Öland and Gotland, adjacent slithers of land with unusually temperate climates. Though they've long been targets for domestic

---

ACCOMMODATION PRICE CODES

The hotels and guesthouses listed in this chapter have been graded according to the following price bands, based on the cost of the **least expensive double room during high season** (late June to Aug). However, almost every hotel offers seasonal and/or weekend discounts, and wherever possible we've given two grades, covering both the regular and the discounted rate.

① Under 500kr	② 500–700kr	③ 700–900kr
④ 900–1200kr	⑤ 1200–1500kr	⑥ Over 1500kr

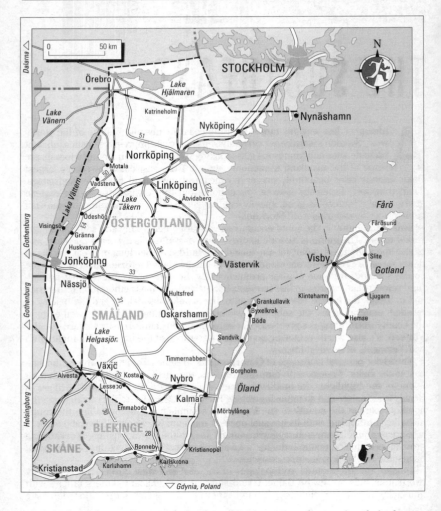

tourists, these days an increasing number of foreigners are discovering their charms – sun, beaches and some impressive historic (and prehistoric) sights. **Öland** – the smaller island and closer to the mainland – is less celebrated, but its mix of dark forest and flowering meadows makes it a tranquil spot for a few days' exploration. **Gotland** is known for its medieval Hanseatic capital, **Visby**, a stunning backdrop to the carnival atmosphere that pervades the town in summer, when ferry-loads of young Swedes come here to sunbathe and party – it's also one of the most popular places for Swedes to celebrate **Midsummer's Night**. The rest of the island, however, is little visited by tourists, and all the more worthwhile for that. Both islands are ideal for cycling, and it's easy to rent **bikes**.

Kalmar

Bright and breezy **KALMAR**, set on a huddle of islands at the southeastern edge of the county of Småland, has treasures enough to make it one of southern Sweden's most delightful towns – a fact that's missed by most visitors, who have their sights set on the Baltic island of Öland, to which Kalmar is joined by a six-kilometre bridge. Surrounded by fragments of ancient fortified walls, the seventeenth-century **New Town** is a mass of cobbled streets and lively squares, lined with some lovely old buildings. Close by is the exquisite castle, **Kalmar Slott**, scene of the Kalmar Union, which brought Sweden, Norway and Denmark together as a single kingdom in 1397, and now one of Scandinavia's most finely preserved Renaissance palaces. Just a short walk in the other direction, there's the fascinating exhibition on the **Kronan**, one of the world's biggest warships, which sunk off Öland over three hundred years ago. Even now, new finds are being discovered, helping to piece together the world's most complete picture of seventeenth-century maritime life.

Arrival, information and accommodation

Kalmar's **tourist office**, at Larmgatan 6 (mid-June to mid-Aug daily 9am–8pm; early June & late Aug daily 9am–7pm; Sept– May Mon–Fri 9am–5pm; ☎0480/153 50, fax 174 53), is within spitting distance of both the **train station** (from where there are several trains daily to Gothenburg and Stockholm) and **bus terminal**. Here you can get a decent map of Kalmar; information on Öland is dealt with on the island itself. Kalmar can be explored easily on foot, but if you want to strike out into the surrounding countryside you can rent a **bike** either from Team Sportia, Södravägen 2, or at the campsite, *Stensö Camping* (see below).

The tourist office arranges **private rooms** from 190kr per person, 300kr for a double, plus a 50kr booking fee. More popular are the cottages which the tourist office rents out by the week from 1800kr for two people to 4000kr for more spacious options. Other budget options include the **youth hostel**, ten minutes' walk away at Rappegatan 1c (☎0480/129 28, fax 882 93), on the next island to the north, Ängö. The nearest **camping** is on Stensö island, 3km from the centre, which also has cheap cabins (☎0480/888 03). Local buses head out this way – check details with the tourist office. Kalmar boasts several attractive central **hotels**, such as the 1906 *Stadshotel*, Stortorget 14 (☎0480/49 69 00, fax 496 10; ⑤/③); and the castle-like *Frimurarehotellet* on Lärmtorget (☎0480/152 30, fax 858 87; ③/②). For something cheaper, try the *Hotel Svarnen* (☎0480/129 28, fax 882 93; ①), next door to the youth hostel, and run by the same staff.

Kalmar Slott

Beautifully set on its own island, a short way from the train and bus stations, the first stones of **Kalmar Slott** (April–Sept daily 10am–6pm; Oct–March, second weekend of each month only 10am–6pm). Guided tours in English 11.30am & 2.30pm; 60kr) were probably laid in the twelfth century. A century later, it became the most impenetrable castle in Sweden under King Magnus Ladulås. The biggest event to take place within its walls was in 1397, when Erik of Pomerania (under the protection of his aunt, the powerful Danish queen, Margarethe) was crowned king of Denmark, Sweden and Norway, instigating the **Kalmar Union**, in which the whole of Scandinavia was united under a single monarch. Subsequently, the castle passed repeatedly between Sweden

and Denmark, but despite eleven sieges remained almost unscathed. By the time
Gustav Vasa became king of Sweden in 1523, Kalmar Slott was beginning to show signs
of stress and strain, and the king set about rebuilding it, while his sons Eric XIV and
Johan III continued with the decoration of the interior. The fine Renaissance palace that
was the eventual result of their efforts well illustrates the Vasa family's concern to maintain Sweden's prestige in the eyes of foreign powers.

Today, if the castle doesn't appear to be defending anything in particular, this is due
to a devastating fire in the 1640s, after which the town was moved to its present site on
the island of Kvarnholmen – though the Old Town (Gamla Stan) beyond the castle still
retains some winding old streets that are worth a look. Unlike many other southern
Swedish castles, this one is picture-perfect, with turrets, ramparts, moat, drawbridge,
dungeon, and a fully furnished interior that's fascinating to wander through. Among the
many highlights is Johan III's bedroom, known as the **Grey Hall**. His bed, which was
stolen from Denmark, is decorated with carved faces on the posts, but all their noses
have been chopped off – the guilty Johan believed that the nose contained the soul and
didn't want the avenging spirits of the rightful owners coming to haunt him. However,
it's King Eric's former bedroom, the **King's Chamber**, which is the most intriguing
room, with its wall frieze of vividly painted animals and a secret door allowing escape

onto the roof – Eric was convinced that his younger brother Johan wanted to kill him. This isn't as paranoid as it sounds: Eric's death in 1569 is widely believed to have been caused by arsenic poisoning.

The rest of the town

Opposite the castle, Kalmar's **Art Museum** (Konstmuseum; May–Aug Mon–Fri 10am–5pm, Sat & Sun noon–5pm; Sept–April Mon–Fri 10am–5pm & 7–9pm, Sat & Sun 11am–5pm; 30kr) displays changing exhibitions of contemporary art, with an emphasis on late 1940s and 50s Expressionism, and a first-floor exhibition devoted to chair design throughout the ages. The top floor contains one largish gallery of nineteenth- and twentieth-century Swedish nude and landscape paintings.

It's worthwhile to head back into the elegantly laid out Renaissance New Town, centred on the grand **Domkyrkan** (daily 9am–6pm) in Stortorget. Designed in 1660 by Nicodemus Tessin the Elder (as was the nearby Rådhus) after a visit to Rome, this vast and airy church in Italian Renaissance style is today a complete misnomer: Kalmar has no bishop and the church has no dome. Inside, the altar, designed by Tessin the Younger, shimmers with gold, as do the sculptures of *Faith* and *Mercy* around it.

The Kronan Exhibition

Housed in a refurbished steam mill on Skeppsbrongatan, a few minutes' walk from the Domkyrkan, the awe-inspring **Kronan Exhibition** is the main attraction of the **County Museum** (Länsmuseum; daily: mid-June to mid-Aug 10am–6pm; mid-Aug to mid-June 10am–4pm; 50kr). The royal ship *Kronan*, built by the British naval designer Francis Sheldon, was one of the world's three largest ships, twice the size of the *Vasa*, which sank off Stockholm in 1628 (see p.403). The *Kronan* went down in 1676, blown apart by an explosion in its gunpowder magazine – 800 of its 842 crew were killed, their bodies preserved for more than three hundred years on the Baltic sea bed.

It wasn't until 1980 that super-sensitive scanning equipment detected the whereabouts of the ship, 26m down off the coast of Öland. A salvage operation was led by a descendant of the ship's captain, Admiral Lorentz Creutz, and the amazing finds are displayed in an imaginative walk-through reconstruction of the gun decks and admiral's cabin, accompanied by sound effects of cannon fire and screeching gulls. While the ship's treasure trove of gold coins is displayed at the end of the exhibition, it's the incredibly well-preserved clothing – hats, jackets, buckled leather shoes and even silk bows and cuff links – that brings this exceptional show to life. Other rooms detail the political background to the wars between the Swedes, Danes and Dutch at the time of the sinking.

Eating and drinking

There's a generous number of good places **to eat** in Kalmar. The liveliest night-time area is **Lärmtorget**, where restaurants, cafés and pubs serve Swedish, Indonesian, Chinese, Greek, Italian and English food. For daytime **snacks** try *Kullzenska Caféet*, Kaggensgatan 26, a charming eighteenth-century *konditori*.

Restaurants and bars

Ernesto Spaghetti & Cocktail Bar, Lärmtorget. Very popular place serving a huge range of very good pizzas and pastas (60–80kr), as well as traditional Italian salads, antipasti and meat dishes (120kr) in quite upmarket surroundings. Live music at weekends.

Ernesto Steakhouse, at the harbour. A glassy building similar in style to its sister restaurant, though this one serves more substantial and expensive meat and fish meals. The daily lunch is reasonable, though, at 55kr.

Krögers, Lärmtorget. Light Swedish meals like *kottbullesmörgås* (meatball sandwiches, 40kr) are served here, along with rather less Swedish fish and chips (66kr), meat dishes and pastas.

Lodbroks Café & Pub, in same building as *Kullzenska Caféet*; enter from Norra Långgatan 20. The romantic dining room is sophisticatedly rustic, though the place is only open for lunch. Try the prawn-and-vegetable pie, or the pie-and-salad buffet (60kr), which is excellent value and includes coffee and cake.

Ming Palace, Fiskaregatan 7. The best Chinese restaurant in town, with a lunch special at 50–60kr. To find it, head towards the base of the old castellated water tower.

O'Keefe's, part of the *Stadshotel*. A pub with a good atmosphere, but closed June–Aug.

Oscars Bar & Brasserie, on Lärmtorget. A pleasant Greek-inspired place serving a three-course meal for 135kr; there's also a well-stocked bar.

T&T, Unionsgatan 20. Kalmar's hippest eaterie, and becoming hugely popular, this place serves unusual (and delicious) pizzas like banana, onion, curry and pineapple (55–75kr), along with meat dishes (sold by weight), plus a big range of wines and some great desserts. Try the *chokladkladd* tart (28kr).

Öland

Linked to mainland Sweden by a six-kilometre bridge, the island of **Öland** is the kind of place a Swedish Famous Five would come on holiday: mysterious forests and flat, pretty meadows to cycle through, miles of mostly unspoilt beaches, wooden cottages with candy-striped canopies, windmills, and ice-cream parlours. Swedes have been coming here in droves for over a century, but since becoming popular with foreign tourists, it's now visited by 55,000 people every July and August. Despite this onslaught, which clogs the road from the bridge north to the main town, Borgholm, this long, splinter-shaped island retains a likeably old-fashioned holiday atmosphere, with a labyrinth of walking trails and bicycle routes and some of the best bathing opportunities in Sweden.

A royal hunting ground from the mid-sixteenth century until 1801, Öland was ruled with scant regard for its native population. Peasants were forbidden from chopping wood or owning dogs or weapons, while Kalmar's tradesmen exploited the trade restrictions to force low prices for the islanders' produce. Danish attacks on Öland saw seven hundred farms destroyed, and following a succession of disastrous harvests in the mid-nineteenth century, a quarter of the population packed their bags for a new life in America. This century, Öland's young are just as likely to migrate to the Swedish mainland.

Today, Öland's attractions include numerous ruined castles, Bronze and Iron Age burial cairns, runic stones and forts, all set amid rich and varied fauna and flora and a striking landscape. To the south is a massive limestone plain known as the Alvaret, whose thin covering of soil is pierced by tiny flowers in summer. In central Öland, the Ice Age left the limestone more hidden and the area is blanketed with forest, while to the north, the coastline is craggy and irregular, with dramatic-looking *rauker* – stone pillars, weathered by the waves into jagged shapes.

Getting to the island

If you're **driving**, take the Ängö link road to Svinö (clearly signposted), just outside Kalmar, which takes you over the bridge to Möllstorp on Öland. **Cycling** over the bridge is forbidden, but there's a free bus from Svinö especially for bikes, which drops you off outside the island's main tourist office in Möllstorp. If you're **hitching**, you can try your luck with the free bus, too, as the bridge has no footpath. **Bus** timetables change with the seasons, but buses #101 and #106 are safe bets, running almost hourly from Kalmar bus station to Borgholm (50min), less regularly in the evenings. Buses also run to Färjestaden, hub of the island's bus network, a couple of kilometres south of Möllstorp.

Information and getting around

Öland's main **tourist office** is in a large pink building in **Möllstorp**, next to the end of the bridge (April & May Mon–Fri 9am–6pm, Sat 10am–5pm, Sun 10am–4pm; June, Aug & Sept Mon–Fri 9am–7pm, Sat 10am–6pm, Sun 10am–4pm; July Mon–Sat 9am–7pm, Sun 10am–6pm; Oct–March Mon–Fri 9am–5pm; ☎0485/390 00, fax 390 10). Pick up a bus timetable and the *Ölands Karten* (49kr), an excellent, if costly, map. While you're at the tourist office, pop into the nature centre, **Naturum**, where a twenty-metre model of the island lights up to show all the areas of interest.

It's worth noting the shape and size of Öland before forming ambitious plans to cover it all by bike; although the island is geared for cycling, with endless cycle tracks along the flat roads, if you want to explore it from north to south, you're looking at 130km. **Bike rental** is available in Kalmar, Borgholm and at most of the island's campsites, hostels and the odd farm, for around 40kr per day, 200kr per week. If you have a **car**, orientation could not be simpler: there is just one main road, Route 136, which runs from the lighthouse at the island's northernmost tip to the lighthouse in the far south; for most of its length it runs close to the west coast. A smaller road runs off the 136 down the east of the island, south from Föra. Though a **bus** network connects most places in Öland, the service is infrequent and you should be prepared for a lot of waiting around, particularly in the south – you need to time trips carefully to avoid being stranded, though **hitching** is not impossible in the far south.

Borgholm

Walking the simple grid of streets that makes up **BORGHOLM**, Öland's "capital", it's clear that tourism is the

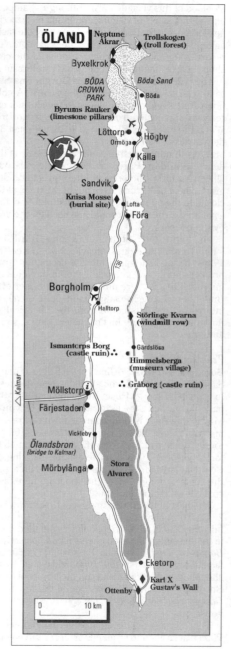

lifeblood of this villagey town. Although swamped well beyond its capacity each July by tens of thousands of visitors, cramming its pizzerias and bars and injecting a riotous carnival atmosphere, Borgholm is in no way the tacky resort it could be. Encircled by the flaking, turreted villas that were the pride of the town during its first period as a holiday resort in the nineteenth century, most of the centre is a friendly, if bland, network of shops and restaurants leading to a very pleasant harbour.

The only real attraction here is **Borgholms Slotts ruin** (May–Aug daily 10am–6pm; free), just to the southwest of the centre. A colossal stone fortification with rows of huge arches and corridors open to the skies, it can be reached either through a nature reserve, signposted from the town centre, or from the first exit south off Route 136. When the town was founded in 1816, with just 33 inhabitants, the twelfth-century castle was already a ruin.

A few hundred metres south of the castle is the present royal family's summer residence, **Solliden Park**, an Italian-style villa built to a design specified by Swedish Queen Victoria (the present king's great-grandmother) in 1903. A huge, austere red-granite bust of Victoria rises out of the trees at the entrance car park. The villa itself is closed to the public but the gardens (mid-May to mid-Sept daily 1–6pm; 35kr) make for a pleasant stroll, or you could just head for the delightful thatch-roofed café, *Kaffetorpet*, by the car park.

Just to the north of the town centre, **Blå Rör** is Öland's largest Bronze Age cairn, a huge mound of stones excavated when a coffin was discovered here in 1849. In the 1920s, burnt bones indicating a cremation grave were also discovered, along with bronze swords and tweezers – common items in such tombs. However, there's nothing much to see there now and you're better off visiting **Forngard**, Köpmangatan 23 (mid-May to Aug Mon–Sat noon–6pm; 20kr), a museum of Öland life whose most interesting exhibits come from the historical sites around the island. The ground-floor displays include bits of ancient skulls, some Viking glass, Bronze Age jewellery and grave finds.

Practicalities

Borgholm's **tourist office** (☎0485/890 00) is tucked away out of the hubbub at Sandgatan 25, though you should expect queues in July. The only place to **rent a bike** in town is Hallbergs Hojar, Köpmangatan 10 (☎0485/890 00; 50kr per day). Set in quiet, park-like gardens, the large and stately STF **youth hostel** at Rosenfors (☎0485/107 56; May to mid-Aug) is 1km from the town centre – ask the bus driver to stop at the Q8 filling station just before Borgholm proper, 100m from the hostel, and walk east. The tourist office will book **private rooms** from 150kr per person (booking fee 25kr, 50kr for stays of 2–5 days; no telephone bookings). The local **campsite**, *Kapelludden's Camping* (☎0485/101 78, fax 129 44), is on a small peninsula five minutes' walk from the centre, though there's no shortage here, as on the rest of the island, of beautiful spots in which to camp rough.

The best of the **hotels** in the centre of town is *Villa Sol*, at Slottsgatan 30 (☎0485/56 25 52; ①). A charming old pale-yellow house set in a fruit tree-filled garden, it's beautifully furnished, with stripped floors, old tiled fireplaces and a sun-filled veranda; rooms in the basement are even cheaper, and perfectly comfortable, though less bright. *Hotel Borgholm*, Trådgårdsgatan 15 (☎0485/770 60, fax 124 66; ③), has smart rooms, while facilities at the vast *Strand Hotel,* Villagatan 4 (☎0485/888 88, fax 888 99; ④), include a shopping mall, disco and nightclub, pool and sauna. Eight kilometres south of Borgholm on Route 136 lies one of the few really fine hotels on the island, *Halltorps Gästgiveri* (☎0485/850 00, fax 850 01; ④), set in a beautiful eighteenth-century manor house.

There is a pronounced summer-holiday feel to the town's **restaurants** and bars. Pizza places abound around Stortorget and down to the harbour, all much the same and

Lake scene near Tärnaby, Sweden

Morning dip at Kalmar, with Öland bridge in the background, Sweden

Chapel at the *Ice Hotel*, Jukkasjärvi, Sweden

Central Station, Helsinki

Helsinki Cathedral

Border post, Treriksröset

Santas for sale, Helsinki

Kerimäki Church, Finland

Lake Region, Finland

Lake and forest near Nurmes, Finland

Smoking salmon, Finland

not cheap at 65–85kr for a pizza. *Mama Rosa*, right at the harbour on Södra Långgatan, is smarter than most and has a more varied menu. On the far side of the harbour, *Skeppet* is a jolly little Italian restaurant open only in summer, hidden behind a group of 1940s industrial silos. For the finest food on the island (with prices to match), head for *Backfickan* at the *Hotel Borgholm*, whose chef is something of a celebrity in Sweden. A real hidden treasure, which goes completely unadvertised, is the lunchtime **vegetarian** restaurant, *Villa Harmoni* (☎0485/100 41; Wed–Fri 11am–2pm), on Storgatan (it's tucked away at the back of the *Ölands Glas Café* ice-cream parlour). Here, behind a vine-strewn terrace and up a flight of stairs, white linen, old china, silver and real crystal chandeliers adorn this excellent establishment run by a cook-cum-aromatherapist. For **drinking**, *Pubben*, Storgatan 18, is a cosy pub with 46 varieties of whisky, while the spacious *O'Keefe's Bar* on Storgatan also fills up nightly throughout summer. One **nightclub** worth checking out is the popular *2001*, on Södralanggatan. Otherwise, a raucous young crowd invariably swarm into the *Strand disco* in the *Strand Hotel* every evening, turning it into a sort of Baltic Ibiza throughout the summer nights.

North Öland

It's the north of the island that has the most varied landscape, with some unexpected diversions to boot. Heading up Route 136, there's no shortage of idyllic villages, dark woods and flowery fields. At **FÖRA**, about 20km north of Borgholm, there's a good example of a typical Öland church, which doubled as a fortress in times of war. About 7km north of here is **KÄLLA**, 2km outside which sits proud, forlorn **Källa kyrka**, empty since 1888 and now sitting in splendid isolation – take care not to confuse it with the present church by the road sign. Surrounded by brightly flowering meadows, this dull-white medieval church is bounded by dry-stone walls, and its grounds littered with ancient, weathered tombs. Inside, the lofty interior has seen plenty of action: built of limestone in 1130 to replace an earlier stave church, it was regularly attacked by heathens from over the Baltic seas. Modernized in the fourteenth century, when Källa was a relatively important harbour and trading centre, and stripped of its furnishings in the nineteenth century, a row of six models of the church in various incarnations are the only interior features.

HÖGBY, a few kilometres on, has the only remaining tied church houses on the island, relics of the medieval Högby kyrka nearby, but there's not a great deal to stop for. At nearby **LÖTTORP** you can engage in an unusual if expensive dining experience: follow the signs east for 4km down country lanes to the *Lammet & Grisen* restaurant, housed in a Spanish hacienda (daily 5.30pm–midnight). The only dishes on the menu are salmon and spit-roasted lamb and pork (hence the restaurant's name), with baked potatoes, flavoured butters and sauces – all you can eat for 230kr.

Continue north and west off Route 136 across the island to the striking **Byrums Rauker**: solitary limestone pillars formed by the sea at the edge of a sandy beach. From here, the north of Öland is shaped like a bird's head, the beak facing east and with a large bite out of its crown. The best **beaches** are along the east coast; the most popular stretch is a couple of kilometres north of Böda Sand at **Kyckesand**; and there's a nudist beach just to the north of here, marked by a large boulder in the sea.

There are some gorgeous areas of natural beauty in the far north. The nature reserve of **Trollskogen** (Trolls Forest) – exactly the kind of place you would imagine trolls to inhabit, with twisted, gnarled trunks of ancient oaks shrouded in ivy – offers some excellent walking. Around the western edge of the north coast, the waters are of the purest blue, lapping against rocky beaches; on a tiny island at the tip stands **Långe Eric Lighthouse**, a handsome obelisk of 1845 and a good goal for a walk or cycle ride. Three kilometres along the western coast to the south is the ridged land formation of **Neptune Åkrar** (Neptune's Ploughland, named by Carl von Linné for its resemblance to ploughed fields), covered with lupin-like flowers during summer which form a sheet of brilliant blue to rival the sea beyond. The only town in this region is **BYXELKROK**, a quiet place with an attractive harbour.

Practicalities

There's not much in the way of proper hotels north of Borgholm, but high-standard **campsites** abound, mostly beside a beach and marked every couple of kilometres off Route 136. The most extensive site is *Krono Camping* at Böda Sand (☎0485/222 00, fax 223 76), 50km north of Borgholm and 2km off the main road at the southern end of the beach. Cabins range from 3400kr per week for four people, up to 5000kr with a water supply. Facilities are extensive, with shops, restaurants and a bakery at the site. The STF **youth hostel**, *Vandrarhem Böda* at Mellböda (☎0485/220 38, fax 221 98), just south of *Krono Camping*, is big and well equipped. An unusual alternative is to stay at the nearby *Bödabaden Öland Square Dance Centre* (☎0485/220 12 or 220 85, fax 220 07; ②), Europe's only square-dancing theme park, with tournaments and courses every day. The en-suite cabins are fairly upmarket, more like basic hotel rooms. Just 6km northwest at **Byxelkrok**, *Solö Värdhus* (☎0485/283 70; ②) is a pleasant enough **hotel**; here you'll find the only decent **nightlife** venue in the north of Öland, at the restaurant, pub and disco *Sjöstugan* (closed Sept–March), right by the shore.

Central Öland

Cutting eastwards from Borgholm (take bus #102), following signs to Räpplinge, brings you to **Störlinge Kvarna**, a row of seven windmills by the roadside. A sign tells you this is the island's longest line of postmill-type windmills, but as you'll probably have already seen several windmills by now, there's no real inducement to stop. A couple of kilometres south, **GÄRDSLÖSA** has the island's best preserved medieval church. Its exterior has been maintained so well that it's almost too pristine, but the inside is worth a look for its 1666 pulpit and thirteenth-century ceiling paintings; these were white-washed over in 1781, but uncovered in 1950.

A few kilometres further south in a gorgeous setting is the preserved village of **Himmelsberga**, now an **open-air museum** (early May to early Sept daily 10am–6pm; 40kr). Since the decline of farming in the middle of the twentieth century, most of Öland's thatched farmhouses have been rather brutally modernized; Himmelsberga, however, escaped, and two of its original farms opened as museums in the 1950s. Buildings were subsequently brought from all over the island, and the collection now includes an extensive assortment of crofters farms, a smithy and a windmill.

East from Himmelsberga, the ancient castle ruin of **Ismantorps Borg** (dating from around 450 AD) only warrants a visit if you fancy a walk along a lovely wooded path. A huge, circular base of stones, you can see the foundations of 88 rooms inside – if you try. **Gråborg**, passed by bus #102, another 10km south of here, is Öland's largest ancient castle ruin, with 640-metre-long walls. Built around 500 AD and occupied throughout the Middle Ages (when the Gothic entrance arch was built), the walls today encircle little more than a handful of hardy sheep.

South Öland

Dominated by **Stora Alvaret**, the giant limestone plain on which no trees can grow, the south of the island is sparsely populated, with its main town the rather dull **Mörbylånga**. You won't see any bare rock, however, only a meadow landscape sprouting rare alpine plant life that has clung on stoically since the Ice Age. **Buses** run so infrequently here that you'll need to check times carefully at Färjestaden, just south of the bridge to the mainland, which is where the few southbound services begin. However, the lack of regular transport means that **hitching** is a feasible option here. There are fewer facilities as a whole than in the north, so it's worth stocking up before you head off. Despite the difficulties of travelling in southern Öland, its great advantage is that summer crowds thin out here, allowing you to explore the most untouched parts of the island in peace.

The prettiest village south along Route 136 is **VICKLEBY**, equidistant between Färjestaden to the north and Mörbylånga to the south, and the site of a remarkable art and design school, **Capella Gården**, the brainchild of furniture designer Carl Malmsten. An idealist, Malmsten's dream was to create a school that stimulated mind, body and soul. In 1959, he bought a range of picturesque farmhouses at Vickleby and opened an art and design school for adults that still runs today. The students' work, including some lovely ceramic and wood pieces, is on sale in a big annual exhibition. If you do want to visit, it's best to call the studios beforehand (☎0485/361 32).

Of all the ruined forts on Öland, the one most worth a visit is at the village of **EKETORP**, reachable by bus from Mörbylånga. The site (May to mid-Sept daily 10am–5pm; guided tours in English 1pm; 50kr) includes an archeological museum containing the finds of a major excavation in the 1970s. Three settlements were discovered, including a marketplace from the fourth century and an agricultural community dating from 1000 AD. The result is a wonderful achievement in speculative archeology, actual physical evidence being thin on the ground. The best of the finds, such as jewellery and weapons, are on show in the museum, and there's a workshop where you can have a go at leatherwork or "authentic" ancient cookery.

If you head south from here, you'll come to a stone wall that cuts straight across the island. Called **Karl X Gustav's Wall**, it was built in 1650 to fence off deer and so improve hunting. A strain of 150 fallow deer still roams about today at **Ottenby**, in the far south of the island. Öland's largest estate, created in 1804, this is now a bird-watcher's paradise, with a huge nature reserve and the Ottenby **bird station**, established in 1946 as a national centre for the study of migrating birds.

Practicalities

The main **tourist office** at Möllstorp (see p.511) will book **private rooms** from 150kr per person per night (plus 25kr booking fee, more for longer stays). *Mörby Youth Hostel* (☎ & fax 0485/493 93), 15km south of the bridge, is a **hostel and hotel** combined, the only difference being that the price of hotel rooms (①) includes sheets and breakfast; bus #105 stops right outside. *Haga Park* (☎0485/360 30), 10km south of the bridge at Haga Park, is a kind of hotel with a **campsite**; the beach here offers good windsurfing. For a **regular hotel**, try *Hotel Kajutan* (☎0485/408 10; ③), a pleasant old place at the harbour behind the bus station in **Mörbylånga**; or the popular *Hotel Bo Pensionat* at Vickleby (☎0485/360 01; ③), in a row of traditional village houses – book ahead in high season.

Småland

Thickly forested and studded with lakes, **Småland County** makes up the southeastern wedge of Sweden – a region of appealing if uniform scenery. It's a part of the country which people frequently travel through – from Stockholm to the southwest, or from Gothenburg to the Baltic coast – yet beneath the canopy of greenery, there are a few spots of interest, along with opportunities for hiking, trekking, fishing and cycling.

Historically, Småland has had it tough. The simple, rustic charm of the pretty painted cottages belies the intense misery endured by generations of local peasants; in the nineteenth century, this led to a massive surge of emigration to America. Subsistence farming had failed, the people were starving and ultimately a fifth of Sweden's population left the country – most of them from Småland. Their plight is vividly retold at the **House of Emigrants** exhibition in **Växjö**, a town that makes an excellent base for exploring the region, but the county's most marketed tourist attraction remains the many **glass factories** hidden away in the forest.

Växjö

Founded by Saint Sigfrid in the eleventh century, **VÄXJÖ** (pronounced "veh-quer") is by far the handiest place to base yourself if you are interested in touring the region's glassworks. Deep in the heart of Småland county (110km from Kalmar), the town itself boasts two superb museums: the beautifully renovated and extensive **Smålands Museum**, notable for being home to the **Swedish Glass Museum**, and the fascinating **House of Emigrants**, which explores the mass emigration from Sweden in the nineteenth and early twentieth centuries. While the town centre doesn't hold much else of appeal, the romantic castle ruin of **Kronoberg** is within easy reach, just 4km to the north of town.

The Town

The enlarged **Smålands Museum**, behind the train station (June–Aug Mon–Fri 10am–5pm, Sat & Sun 11am–5pm; Sept–May Tues–Fri 10am–5pm, Sat & Sun 11am–5pm; 40kr), contains two permanent exhibitions: an intelligently displayed history of Småland's manufacturing industries and the rather more appealing "four hundred years of Swedish glass". The latter's exhibits range from sixteenth-century place settings to eighteenth- and nineteenth-century etched and coloured glass, along with stylish Art Nouveau-inspired pieces. Most appealing, though, are the wide-ranging displays of contemporary glass, all mounted on white wooden plinths. If you're intending to visit any of the glassworks (see opposite), it's a good idea to come here first to gauge the different styles.

The plain building directly in front of the museum contains the inspired **House of Emigrants** (June–Aug Mon–Fri 9am–6pm, Sat & Sun 11am–4pm; Sept–May Mon–Fri 9am–4pm; 30kr), with its moving "Dream of America" exhibition. The museum presents a living picture of the intense hardship faced by the Småland peasant population from the mid-nineteenth century onwards. Due to agricultural reforms and a series of bad harvests, between 1860 and 1930 a million Swedes – a fifth of the population – emigrated to America, most of them from Småland. Most boats left from Gothenburg and, until 1915, sailed to Hull in Britain, where passengers crossed to Liverpool by train to board the transatlantic ships. Conditions on board were usually dire: the steamer *Hero* left Gothenburg in 1866 with 500 emigrants, nearly 400 oxen and 900 pigs, calves and sheep sharing the accommodation.

The attached **Research Centre** (Mon–Fri 9am–4pm; ☎0470/201 20) charges 100kr per day to help interested parties trace their family roots, using passenger lists from ten harbours, microfilmed church records from every Swedish parish, and records of bodies such as the Swedish New York Society, Swedes in Australia and the Swedish Congo Veterans Association. It's worth booking ahead during the peak season of May to mid-August. A vast research site is available at *www.svenskaemigrantinstitutet.g.se*.

There's not much else to see in the centre, but take a quick look at the very distinctive **Domkyrkan** (daily 8am–8pm; June–Aug guided tours 9am–5pm), with its unusual twin green towers and apricot-coloured facade. Regular restorations, the most recent in 1995, together with a catalogue of sixteenth-century fires and a lightning strike in 1775, have left nothing of note except a unique 1775 organ and some brilliant modern glass ornaments by Göran Wärff, one of the best known of the contemporary Glass Kingdom designers. The cathedral is set in the **Linné Park**, named after the Carl von Linné, who was educated at the handsome school next door (closed to the public).

Kronoberg Castle

Set on a tiny island in Lake Helgasjön, the ruins of **Kronoberg Castle** lie 4km north of the town centre in a beautiful and unspoilt setting – follow the signs for Evedal, or take the hourly bus #1B from the bus station. The Bishops of Växjö erected a wooden fortress here in the eleventh century, but it was Gustav Vasa who built the present stone version in 1540. Entered over an old wooden bridge set at a narrow spot in the lake, it's a perfect ruin, leaning precariously and complete with rounded tower and deep-set lookouts. Some new brick archways and a couple of reinforced roofs, added in the 1970s, stop the whole thing collapsing. The grass-roofed *Café Ryttmästargården*, set in an eighteenth-century cottage overlooking the castle, is a good place for snacks, soups and salads, and the old paddle steamer *Thor* makes regular excursions from here around Lake Helgasjön and up to Lake Asassjön – the perfect way to appreciate the lakeland scenery.

Practicalities

The **train** and **bus stations** are alongside one another in the middle of town. The **tourist office**, inside the train station building (mid-June to mid-Aug Mon–Fri 9.30am–6.30pm, Sat & Sun 10am–2pm; mid-Aug to mid-June Mon–Thurs 9.30am–4.30pm, Fri 9.30am–3pm; ☎0470/414 10, fax 478 14), can book **private rooms** from 130kr (25kr extra for sheets, plus a 50kr booking fee). Of the town's **hotels**, the most striking is the *Teater Park*, in the central Concert Hall building (☎0470/399 00, fax 475 77; ④/③). Otherwise, try the no-frills *Esplanad*, Norra Esplanaden 21A (☎0470/225 80, fax 262 26; ②/①), or the good-value *Värend*, Kungsgatan 27 (☎0470/104 85, fax 362 61; ①). The splendid STF **youth hostel** (☎0470/630 70, fax 632 16) is at Evedal, 5km north of the centre, in an eighteenth-century house set in parkland on tranquil Lake Helgasjön (with its own beach). To get there, head north up Linnegatan, following signs for Evedal, or take bus #1C from the bus terminal to the end of the line (last bus is at 4.15pm, 3.15pm on Sat), or bus #1A, which leaves you with a 1.5-kilometre walk, but runs daily till 8.15pm. Next to the hostel is a **campsite**, *Evedal Camping* (☎0470/630 34, fax 631 22), with four-person cabins for 450kr.

One of the pleasures of Växjö and its surrounds is the wealth of really good places to **eat**, though few of them come cheap. For a **café** with strong gourmet leanings, try *Café Momento* in the Smålands Museum, which serves tasty Italian snacks, plus salads and soups. The best **restaurant** is the waterfront *Evedal Vardhus*, next door to the youth hostel on Lake Helga – fish fresh from the lake is the speciality. For a lovely atmosphere, *PM & Friends*, Västra Esplanaden 9 (☎0470/454 45), is very popular and stylish – again the emphasis is on fine modern European cuisine using fish from local lakes. It gets packed on Friday and Saturday nights.

The Glass Kingdom

Within the landscape of dense birch and pine forests, threaded by lakes, that stretches between Kalmar and Växjö, lie the bulk of Småland's celebrated **glassworks**. The area is dubbed **Glasriket**, or the "Glass Kingdom", with each glassworks signposted clearly from the spidery main roads. This seemingly odd and very picturesque setting for the industry is no coincidence. King Gustav Vasa pioneered glass-making in Sweden when he returned from Italy in the mid-sixteenth century and decided to set up a glassworks in Stockholm. However, it was only Småland's forests that could provide the vast amounts of fuel needed to feed the furnaces, and so a glass factory was set up here in 1742, named Kosta after its founders, Koskull and Stael von Hostein – today, under the name Kosta Boda, it's the largest glassworks in Småland.

Visiting the glassworks

Of the twenty or so glassworks still in operation in Småland, thirteen have captivating glass-blowing **demonstrations** on weekdays, several have permanent **exhibitions** of

GLASS-MAKING AND BUYING GLASS

Demonstrations of the **glass-making process**, held in a dozen or so of the glassworks, can be mesmerizing to watch. The process involves a plug being fished out of a shimmering lake of molten glass (heated to 1200°C) and then turned and blown into a graphite or steel mould. In the case of wine glasses, a foot is then added, before the piece is annealed (heated and then slowly cooled) for several hours. It all looks deceptively simple and mistakes are rare, but it nevertheless takes years to become a servitor (glass-maker's assistant), working up through the ranks of stem-maker and bowl-gatherer. In smaller works, all these processes are carried out by the same person, but in many of Småland's glassworks, you'll see the bowl-gatherer fetching the glowing gob for the master blower, who then skilfully rolls and shapes the syrupy substance. When the blower is attaching bases to wine glasses, the would-be stem will slide off or sink right through if the glass is too hot; if too cold, it won't stick – and the right temperature lasts a matter of seconds.

If you want to **buy glassware**, which is marketed with a vengence, don't feel compelled to snap up the first things you see. The same batch of designs appear at most of the glassworks, a testament to the fact that the Kosta Boda and Orrefors companies are the main players nowadays; many of the smaller works have been swallowed up, even though they retain their own names. This makes price comparison easier, but don't expect many bargains; the best pieces go for thousands of kronor. You may find it useful to see the glassware exhibition in Växjö's Smålands Museum (see p.516) first to get an idea of the various styles and where you can find them.

contemporary work or pieces from the firm's history and, without exception, all have a **shop**. Bus services to (or to within walking distance of) the glassworks are extremely limited, and without your own transport it is almost impossible to see more than a couple in a day – although you'll probably find this is enough.

While each glassworks has characteristic individual designs, the Kosta Boda and Orrefors works give the best picture of what is available. **Orrefors** is easiest reached from Kalmar: take Route 25 to Nybro, then Route 31 or a train from Växjö to Nybro, then bus #138, #139 or #140 to the factory (June to mid-Aug; glass-blowing Mon–Fri 8am–3.30pm, Sat 10am–3pm, Sun 11am–3pm; exhibition Mon–Fri 9am–3pm, Sat 9am–4pm, Sun 11am–4pm).

The **Kosta Boda** and **Åfors** glassworks are operated by the same team, with the biggest collection at Kosta (June to mid-Aug; glass-blowing Mon–Fri 10am–3pm, Sat 9am–3pm, Sun 11am–4pm). The historical exhibition here (Mon–Fri 9am–6pm, Sat 9am–4pm, Sun 11am–4pm) contains some delicate c.1900 glassware designed by Karl Lindeberg, while if you're looking for simple modern works, Anna Ehrener's bowls and vases are the most elegant pieces. Some of the most brilliantly innovative creations are by Göran Wärff – examples of his expressive work are found in Växjös Cathedral. These can be bought in the adjacent shop, alongside current designs that tend towards colourful high-kitsch. To get to Kosta from Växjö, take Route 23 in the direction of Oskarshamn, then Route 31 southeast and on to Route 28. By public transport, bus #218 makes the hour-long trip direct from Växjö bus station.

Strömbergshyttan glassworks, near Hormantorp, is the best bet for a short trip from Växjö. With both Kosta and Orrefors displays (June to mid-Aug; shop only Mon–Fri 9am–6pm, Sat 9am–4pm, Sun 11am–4pm), it's more comprehensive than nearby Sandvik, an Orrefors company. To get there, head south down Route 30 from Växjö, or take bus #218 (the Kosta bus; 40min). If you're driving, continue on to the small, traditional **Bergdala** works, 6km north of Hovmantorp, which produces Sweden's distinctive blue-rimmed glassware (mid-June to mid-Aug; glass-blowing Mon–Fri 9am–2.30pm, Sat 10am–3pm, Sun noon–4pm).

To the north, **Rosdala** produces glass for lampshades (mid-June to mid-Aug; glass-blowing Mon–Fri 8am–3pm, though closed most of July), with some of the ugliest 1970s designs on display in its museum (Mon–Fri 9am–6pm. Sat 10am–4pm, Sun 11am–4pm). There's no public transport here: from Växjö, take Route 23 to Norrhult-Klavreström, then Route 31 north. Smaller **Johansfors**, set on the lakeside to the south of the region, specializes in stem-ware (exhibition and shop Mon–Fri 9am–6pm, Sat 10am–4pm, Sun noon–4pm) – take Route 28 from Kosta. Nearby **Skruf** has the most basic, jam jar-style collection, which is also about the cheapest, but is one of the few to charge (5kr) for museum entry.

Jönköping

Perched at the southernmost tip of Lake Vättern, **JÖNKÖPING** (pronounced "Yun-shurp-ing") is one of the oldest medieval trading centres in the country, having won its town charter in 1284. Today it is famous for being the home of the matchstick, the nineteenth-century manufacture and worldwide distribution of which made the town wealthy. Matches are no longer made here: in 1932 the town's match magnate, Ivar Kruger, shot himself rather than face bankruptcy, bringing a swift end to the industry in its home town. Despite the town's bland centre, its location and ample accommodation and eating possibilities make it a viable base for touring the lake. Jönköping's renovated historic core, focused on the match museum, is the most interesting part to explore.

The biggest of the match factories, built in 1844, now houses the **Match Museum** (Tändsticksmuseet; June–Aug Mon–Fri 10am–5pm, Sat & Sun 11am–3pm; Sept–May Tues–Thurs noon–4pm, Sat & Sun 11am–3pm 25kr) at Tändsticksgränd 27, a none-too-thrilling collection of matchbox labels, match-making machines and not much else. Opposite, the **Radio Museum** displays every type of radio from early crystal sets to Walkmans. A couple of metres away, and set in another old match factory, is **Kulturhuset**, a trendy centre with a good cheap café and alternative bookshops; during summer (June–Aug), the centre is converted into a private youth hostel. Next door is the stylish art-house cinema Bio. From September to May, there's also a bustling early-morning Saturday market on the street outside the centre.

The only other museum to bother with is the **County Museum** (Länsmuseum; daily 11am–5pm, Wed till 8pm; 20kr), on Dag Hammarskjölds Plats, across the canal between lakes Vättern and Munksjön. A mishmash of oddities, with exhibits on garden chairs throughout the ages, bonnets, samovars and doll's houses, it is like wandering around a well-stocked junk shop – and there's no English labelling. The best part is the well-lit collection of paintings and drawings by **John Bauer**, a local artist who enthralled generations of Swedes with his Tolkeinesque representations of gnomes and trolls in the *Bland Tomtar och Troll* books.

Practicalities

The **train** and **bus stations** are next to each other on the lake's edge. Just over the bridge, the **tourist office** (mid-June to mid-Aug Mon–Fri 8am–7pm, Sat 10am–2pm, Sun 11am–2pm; mid-Aug to mid-June Mon–Fri 8am–6pm, Sat 9am–1pm; ☎036/10 50 50, fax 12 83 00, *turist@sfk.jonkoping.se*), located in the Djurläkartoget shopping centre, can arrange a **private room** for 200–250kr per person; the town's seasonal **youth hostel** (☎036/19 05 85; mid-June to mid-Aug) is within the Kulturhuset (see above). The *Rosenlund* campsite (☎036/12 28 63) is right on the lakeside, 3km from the town centre on the route of several buses. For style, value and atmosphere, the best **hotel** is the classic *Hotel Victoria* at F.E. Elmgrensgatan 5 (☎036/71 28 00, fax 71 50 50; ⑤/②), which includes afternoon tea and a buffet supper in its price and even boasts its own radio and match museums. Another good bet is the *Familjan Ericcson City Hotel*, just three minutes from the station at Västra Storgatan 25 (☎036/71 92 80, fax 71 88 48; ③/②).

Jönköping has plenty of good and lively places to **eat** and **drink**. However, some close for the summer, when many of the townsfolk head off to the coast, while others are closed on Fridays and Sundays. *Nyfiket Cafe* in the Kulturhus is a friendly, studenty place serving big filled rolls for just 25–30kr. Among the town's **restaurants**, try *Anna-Gretas Matsal & Café*, Västra Torget, an excellent-value place with a friendly atmosphere and an eclectic menu, or splash out at the splendid *Svarta Börsen*, Kyrkogatan 4 (☎036/71 22 22). Many of the town's **bars** also serve food: *Hemma*, Smedjegatan 36, is the town's most popular venue for laid-back live music, with very friendly service and a good menu. *Karlsonn's Salonger*, Västra Storgatan 9, gets very busy and the food is good, while *Rignes*, attached to the *Hotel Savoy* at Brunnsgatan 13–15, is a dark, candlelit pub serving Norwegian beer and playing blues and rock'n'roll. *Solde Bar*, next door to *Trottoaren Restaurant* (which is itself connected to the grand *Stora Hotell* at Hotellplan), is packed out through the summer with people eating out on the terrace.

Along the shore of Lake Vättern

The road heading north along the eastern shore of **Lake Vättern** offers the most spectacular scenery and delightful historical towns in the region. Jönköping can be used as a base for excursions, but there are plenty of other places to eat and stay between here and historic Vadstena (see p.522). It's perfect for **trekking**, too, with several walking paths, the most established being the Södra Vätternleden, John Bauerleden and Holavedsleden.

Six kilometres east of Jönköping on the E4 – initially called Östra Storgatan – is **HUSKVARNA**, originally named "Husqvarna" after the arms factory that was based here, but which now manufactures sewing machines and motorbikes. Buses make the trip in around ten minutes. From Huskvarna, buses #120 and #121 make the trip to Gränna in around an hour, and there's a quicker express bus twice a day too.

Gränna and Visingsö

An excellent target for a day-trip, **GRÄNNA**, 40km north of Jönköping, is for Swedes irrevocably associated with pears, striped candy and hot-air ballooning. It's easy to while away a whole afternoon in the cafés here, while there are several lovely places to stay should you want to linger. Approaching from the south, the Gränna Valley sweeps down to your left, with the hills to the right, most notably the crest of Grännaberget, which provides a majestic foil to some superb views over Lake Vättern and its island, **Visingsö**.

Per Brahe the Elder, one of Sweden's first counts, built the town, using the symmetry, regularity and spaciousness in planning the settlement that he had learnt in Turku while governor of Finland. He also encouraged the planting of pear orchards – the Gränna pear is still one of the best-known varieties in Sweden today – and if you arrive in late spring, the surrounding hills are a confetti of pear blossom. The main roads were all designed so Brahe could look straight down them as he stood at the windows of his now-ruined castle, **Brahehus**.

Next to the tourist office on Brahegatan is the fascinating **S. A. Andree Museum** (same times as tourist office; 30kr), dedicated to Salomon August Andree, the Gränna-born explorer who led a doomed attempt to reach the North Pole by balloon in 1897. Born at Brahegatan 37, Andree was fired by the European obsession of the day to explore and conquer unknown places, and also by the nationalist fervour sweeping through the country, which gained him funding from Alfred Nobel, King Oscar and Baron Oscar Dickson. However, after a flight lasting only three days, the balloon made a forced landing on ice just 470km from its departure point, and after six weeks trekking the men died either from the cold, starvation or poisoning from trichinosis, after eating the raw meat of a polar bear they had managed to spear. It was 33 years before their preserved, frozen bodies and equipment were discovered by a Norwegian sailing ship. Highlights of the poignant displays are the diary of 25-year-old crew member Nils Strindberg, and some film taken by the team, including sequences of them dragging their sledges across the sheets of ice.

Visingsö

From Gränna a twenty-minute ferry crossing (June–Aug every 30min; Sept–May hourly; pedestrians 38kr return, car and driver 150kr) drops you on the diminutive island of **Visingsö**, just 12km by 3km in size. A lagoon at the harbour makes swimming here less chilly than is usually the case in the deep waters of Vättern. During the twelfth and thirteenth centuries, Swedish kings often lived on the island, and five medieval monarchs died here, including Magnus Ladulås in 1290. It was in the mid-sixteenth century that Erik XIV decided that Sweden should follow the example of continental monarchies, and bestow titles and privileges on deserving noblemen. He created the title of Count of Visingsborg, whose lands included Visingsö, and awarded it to Per Brahe the Elder, who enjoyed a spate of castle building here. However, after Brahe the Younger's death in 1680, the Crown took back much of the land, including the island.

Arriving at the dock, you can **rent a bike** from Visingsö's own little tourist office. The bikes have no gears and cost 40kr for three hours, 50kr till 6pm or 65kr for a full day. As Visingsö is entirely flat and there are very few cars around, the whole island can be covered without any strenuous exercise. Even less effort is needed to sit in a horse and trap called a *remmalag*, a tempting way to cover the three-kilometre trip (50–65kr return) to **Kumlaby** church, dating back to the twelfth century, with its beautifully painted ceiling and walls. The church's truncated tower was designed for the astronomy classes organized by Brahe the Younger, whose school was the first in the region to accept women. Between June and August you can climb the steps of the tower for a fine view of the island (daily 9am–8pm) including the remains of **Näs castle**, at the southern tip of the island. This was once a major power centre in Sweden, though there's little sign of its erstwhile glory. **Visingsborg Slott**, near the ferry terminal, is another empty shell of a castle, its roof burned off by Russian prisoners celebrating the death of Karl XII in 1718.

Practicalities

Gränna's **tourist office** (daily: May to mid-June 10am–5pm; mid-June to July 10am–7pm; Aug & Sept noon–4pm; ☎0390/410 10) is on Brahegatan, right beside the S. A. Andree Museum. Two **youth hostels** serve the town: the first (open mid-June to early Aug only) is close to the tourist office, where you can make bookings; the second is right on the beach near the ferry (☎0390/107 06; May–Sept). You can also arrange **private rooms** through the tourist office from 120kr (plus 50kr booking fee). There are a couple of decent **hotels** in town: the charming, antique-filled *Gästgiveri Ribbagården*, just off Brahegatan (☎ & fax 0390/108 20; ③/②), has been a hotel since 1922, and for 970kr you can stay in the room Greta Garbo used. Gränna's other famous hotel is the castle-like *Hotel Gyllene Uttern*, or "Golden Otter" (☎0390/108 00, fax 418 80; ④), 3km south of town close to the main road and with fabulous views of the lake. There are slightly cheaper annexe rooms here too, which have the same views but aren't nearly as special as the rooms in the main building.

There are several excellent **cafés** in Gränna, all on Brahegatan, except for *Café Stugan* (May 10am–9pm; June–Aug 10am–10pm), a steep climb from the market square, heading away from the lake, which specializes in shrimp sandwiches and Swedish cheesecake. Back in town on Brahegatan, *Café Amalia* sells superb lingonberry ice cream, which you can enjoy on a terrace overlooking the rooftops and lake. The best café though, is *Café Fiket*, which serves a big range of savoury and sweet pies, and some luscious cakes. Gränna isn't well endowed with restaurants – your best bet is the *Gränna Pub* at *Café Hjorten*, also on Brahegatan, a very pleasant restaurant and bar, with a beer garden and a pizza parlour downstairs. This is also the place for a **drink**.

Vadstena and Motala

With its beautiful lakeside setting, 60km north of Gränna, **VADSTENA** is the most evocative town in Östergotland and a fine place for a day or two's stay. At one time a royal seat and an important monastic centre, the town's main attraction nowadays is its gorgeous moated castle, **Vadstena Slott**, planned in the sixteenth century by Gustav Vasa as part of his defensive ring to protect the Swedish heartland around Stockholm. The cobbled, twisting streets, lined with cottages covered in climbing roses, also hold an impressive **abbey**, whose existence is the result of the passionate work of fourteenth-century Saint Birgitta, Sweden's first female saint.

The castle and abbey

Vadstena boasts a number of ancient sites and buildings, notably the Rådhus, which contains Sweden's oldest courthouse, but the town's top attraction is its castle, **Vadstena Slott** (May daily 9am–5pm; June & Aug daily 9am–7pm; July daily 9am–8pm; Sept Mon–Fri 9am–5pm, Sat 10am–2pm; Oct–April Mon–Fri 9am–5pm; 45kr). With four seven-metre-thick round towers and a grand moat, it was originally built as a fortification to defend against Danish attacks in 1545, but was then prettified into a palace to house Gustav Vasa's mentally ill third son, Magnus. His elder brother, Johan III, was responsible for its lavish decorations, but fire destroyed it all just before completion, and to save on costs, the post-fire decor was merely painted on the walls, right down to the swagged curtains that can still be seen today.

From the end of the seventeenth century, the building fell into decay and was used as a grain store; the original hand-painted wooden ceilings were chopped up to make into grain boxes. As a result, there wasn't much to see inside until recently, when the acquisition of period furniture from all over Europe has re-created more of an atmosphere. Portraits of the Vasa family have also been crammed in, displaying some very unhappy and ugly faces that make for entertaining viewing.

A few minutes' walk away, at the water's edge, stands Vadstena's **abbey church** (daily: May 9am–5pm; June & Aug 9am–7pm; July 9am–8pm), the architectural legacy of Saint Birgitta. Birgitta came to Vadstena as a lady-in-waiting to King Magnus Eriksson and his wife, Blanche of Namur, who lived at Bjälbo Palace. After being married at the age of 13, and having given birth to eight children, she began to experience visions and convinced her royal employers to give up their home in order to set up a convent and monastery. Unfortunately, she died abroad before her plans could be completed, and the work was continued by her daughter Katarina, with the church finally being consecrated in 1430. Birgitta's specification that the church should be "of plain construction, humble and strong" is fulfilled from the outside, but the sombre, grey exterior hides a celebrated collection of medieval artwork. More memorable than the crypts of various royals is the statue, now devoid of hands, of Birgitta "in a state of ecstasy". To the right, the rather sad "Door of Grace and Honour" was where each Birgittine nun entered the abbey after being professed – the next time she passed through the doorway would be in a coffin on her funeral day. Birgitta's bones are encased in a red velvet box, decorated with silver and gilt medallions, in a glass case down stone steps in the Monk's choir stalls. Although now housing a restaurant and a hotel, the **monastery** and palace-turned-**nunnery** on either side of the abbey are open for tours, though they won't occupy you for long.

Practicalities

Express **bus** #840 runs to Vadstena from Gränna (50min) and Jönköping (90min) twice daily on weekdays, once on Sundays. By car, it's a straight run along the E4 and Route 50 north from Gränna or southwest on Route 50 from Motala (see below). **Bikes** can be rented from Sport Hörnen, on Storgatan by Rådhustorget. The **tourist office** is in the castle itself (May daily 9am–5pm; June & Aug daily 9am–7pm; July daily 9am–8pm; Sept Mon–Fri 9am–5pm, Sat 10am–2pm; Oct–April Mon–Fri 9am–5pm; ☎0143/315 70, fax 315 79, *info@tourist.vadstena.se*). You can buy a **Vadstena Card** here for 75kr, covering a sightseeing tour and entry to the castle, plus a couple of Vadstena's other minor museums, including the Mental Hospital Museum and the Sculpture Museum at Gottfried Larsson's home; it's only worth it if you intend to see the lot.

The tourist office will book **private rooms** (from 160kr, plus a 50kr booking fee), while Vadstena's STF **youth hostel** is close to the lake at Skänningegatan 20 (☎0143/103 02, fax 104 04; it's advisable to book ahead outside midsummer). The town's **hotels**, most of them housed in converted historic buildings, are fairly expensive. The *Vadstena Kloster Hotel*, in the 1369 nunnery next to the abbey (☎0143/315 30, fax 136 48; ④), is still very atmospheric, especially the original Kings Hall, where breakfast (open to non-residents for 50kr) is served, though some of the rooms are surprisingly dated and plain. Alternatively, try the grand and comfortable *Vadstena Slottshotel*, opposite the castle on Ayslen (☎014/103 25; ④/③).

Eating in Vadstena is equally costly. The pick of the **cafés** is *Mi Casa* on Storgatan, where a young, laid-back crowd eat well and relatively cheaply. Also popular is the extremely busy *Gamla Konditori* on Storgatan, while the best **restaurant** in town is *Vadstena Valven*, Storgatan 18, which does lunch for 55kr and fish specialities in the evening (closed Sun outside summer). For decent pizzas, try *Pub No. 1* at Storgatan 13. It's also a pub and **nightclub** of sorts, but is best known as serving filling fare in basic surroundings. *Restaurant Rådhus Källeren,* in the cosy cellars of the sixteenth-century courthouse on Rådhustorget, doubles as a **pub**, particularly busy on Thursday and Saturday evenings, when the locals turn out in force.

Motala

At **MOTALA**, 16km north of Vadstena and reached by regular #16 buses, the Göta Canal tumbles into Lake Vättern through a flight of five locks. The town, designed by the canal's progenitor, Baltzar Von Platen, is one of the most popular spots on the canal – you'll pass Von Platen's grave beside his statue on the canalside walk. It's worth taking the opportunity here to cruise down a stretch of the canal, something that's easiest during the peak summer season (mid-June to mid-Aug), though not impossible at other times of the year. In summer, **boats** run along the canal to Borensburg, 20km east, leaving Motala at 10.30am and taking around five hours for the round trip (180kr; lunch is available on board for 110kr). Alternatively, you could cover the same journey by **bike**; the tourist office can advise about boat tickets and bike rental places.

The town itself is, for the most part, rather bland, although the **Motor Museum** (daily: June–Aug 10am–8pm; May & Sept 10am–6pm; Oct–April 10am–3pm; 40kr) at the harbour edge is much more entertaining than it sounds. A museum of style rather than the usual showroom of shiny vehicles, this is great fun even if you've not much interest in cars. Each of the unusual motors is displayed in context, with music appropriate to the era blaring from radio sets. On the hill behind the town there's a small **Radio Museum** (June–Aug daily 11am–6pm; 25kr), recalling the days during World War II when "Motala Calling" was as evocative to Swedes as "This is London" is to avid BBC World Service listeners. Just up from the Motor Museum is the **Canal and Navigation Museum** (May, June & Aug Mon–Fri 9am–5pm; July daily 9am–6pm; 20kr), which details the canal's construction and demonstrates the operation of a lock.

Just 3km west of the centre, **Varamon Beach**, with its kilometre of golden sand, claims to be Scandinavia's largest inland bathing beach. While that is not strictly true, it does have the warmest waters in Lake Vättern, and on hot summer days the beach is thick with bronzing bodies. It's also a popular windsurfing site.

Practicalities

Trains pull in about a kilometre from the centre of Motala. For the **tourist office**, at Fokets Hus (June to mid-Aug daily 10am–7pm; mid-Aug to May Mon–Fri 10am–5pm; ☎0141/22 52 54, fax 521 03, *turistbyran@motala.se*), turn left along Östermalmsgatan, right along Vadstenavägen and left into Repslagaregatan. This brings you past the central Stora Torget and the **bus station**; the tourist office is on the right, close to the harbour. You can **rent a bike** from Velosipede at the harbour (☎0141/521 11 or 070/564 07 36) for 95kr per day.

Private rooms for around 250kr per person can be booked through the main tourist office. The STF **youth hostel** at Varamon (☎ & fax 0141/225 285) is right on the beach – take bus #301 from Stora Torget. There's a popular summer café here, too. There's also a well-equipped **campsite** on the beach, *Z-Parkens Camping* (☎0141/21 11 42), next door to *Varamon Chalet Colony*, which has some pretty wooden cabins overlooking the lake (book through the tourist office). The main town-centre **hotels** are entirely business-oriented, but are the only option if you want an en-suite bathroom. *Stadshotellet*, on Storatorget (☎0141/21 64 00, fax 21 46 05; ④/③), has large if worn rooms, and *Palace Hotel,* Kungsgatan 1, just off Storatorget (☎0141/21 66 60, fax 57 221; ④/③), is much the same.

Most of Motala's nondescript **restaurants**, grouped around Stora Torget, offer daily lunches for around 50kr. Most of the **pubs** cater for a very young crowd; a more stylish alternative for all-day food and drink is the *Hallen* bar-restaurant, housed in an old market hall just off Stora Torget near the *Stadshotellet*.

Örebro

Beyond Motala, Lake Vättern runs out of decent-sized towns and it isn't until **ÖREBRO** – 60km north of the lake – that you reach a significant settlement. Strategically located on the main route from southwest Sweden to Stockholm, its light industrial hinterland promises little, and even Örebro's proudest boasts are anticlimatic: it's Sweden's sixth most populous city, lying on the shores of Hjälmaren, the country's fourth largest lake. Yet the heart of Örebro comes as a pleasant surprise, the much fortified thirteen-century **castle** forming a magnificent backdrop for the water lily-studded **River Svatån**. Aside from the town's attractions, **Lake Tysslingen**, a few kilometres west, makes for a good afternoon excursion by bike, while in spring the several thousand whooper swans that settle here on their way to Finland make for spectacular viewing.

Arrival, information and accommodation

Örebrö is just three hours from Stockholm on the main east–west train line. From the train and bus stations it's a short walk to the helpful tourist office in the castle

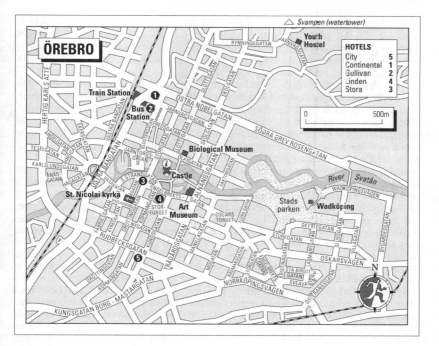

(June–Aug Mon–Fri 9am–7pm, Sat & Sun 10am–5pm; Sept–May Mon–Fri 9am–5pm, Sat & Sun 11am–3pm; ☎019/21 21 21, fax 10 60 70, *destination@orebro.se*). The town centre is easy to see on foot, but if you want to get out into the countryside, you can rent a bike from Hamnplatsen on the way to the Stadsparken (☎019/21 19 09 or 070/318 30 13) for 40kr per day or 180kr per week. Another option is take a boat trip around nearby Lake Hjälmaren on *M/S Linnea* or *M/S Gustav Lagerbjelke* (2hr, 70kr; 3hr, 200kr).

Private rooms can be booked at the tourist office for 135kr per person, plus a 25kr booking fee. The STF **youth hostel** (☎019/31 02 40, fax 31 02 56), is in an old army barracks (though very appealing ones), just to the north of the centre; take bus #31 to Rynninge and get off one stop before the end of the line. If you're **camping**, the nearest site is 2km south of town at **Gustavsvik** (☎019/19 69 50, fax 19 69 90; May to mid-Sept) – take bus #31. Of Örebrö's rather uninspiring **hotels**, the oldest and most luxurious is the central *Stora Hotellet*, Drottninggatan 1 (☎019/15 69 00, fax 15 69 50; ⑤/②), which is supposedly haunted by the ghost of a young woman and her mother. *City Hotel*, Kungsgatan 24 (☎019/601 42 00, fax 601 42 09; ④/②), and *Hotel Continental*, opposite the train station at Järnvägsgatan 2 (☎019/611 95 60, fax 611 73 10; ④/③), are similiar mid-range hotels; while *Hotel Gullvivan*, Järnvägsgatan 20 (☎019/611 90 35, fax 18 94 50; ③/②), is a cheaper option. Finally, there's the basic but perfectly adequate *Hotel Linden*, Köpmangatan 5 (☎019/611 87 11, fax 13 34 11; ①).

The Town

A fort has defended the town ever since a band of German merchants settled here in the thirteenth century, attracted by the presence of iron ore in the area. Enlarged by

King Magnus Eriksson, **Örebro Castle** was further fortified by Gustav Vasa, whose son Karl IX did what Vasa's sons invariably did and turned it into a splendid Renaissance palace, raising the walls to the height of the medieval towers and plastering them in cream stucco. After the town lost its importance, the castle fell into disuse and was turned into a storehouse and prison.

The fairy-tale exterior you see today is the result of renovation in the 1890s, when the castle was carefully restored to reflect both its medieval and Renaissance grandeur. The same cannot be said for the interior: valiant **tour guides** (May–Sept 6 daily; English tour at 2pm; 45kr) face a real challenge as there is no original furniture, and today many of the rooms are used by the county governor or for conferences. If you do join a tour, the few features of interest are some finely inlaid doors and floors dating from the 1920s, depicting historical events at Örebrö, and a large portrait of Karl XII and his family, all their faces painted to look the same – all have popping eyes, the result of using arsenic to whiten their faces. On the top floor there are a few local exhibits moved here from the old county museum.

Nearby, at the top of the very oblong Stortorget, **St Nicolai kyrka** originates from 1260, but lost most of its original medieval character during extensive restoration in the 1860s. Recent renovations have tried to undo the damage, but today it's the contemporary art exhibitions on show here that catch the eye. Historically, however, the church is significant, as it was here in 1810 that Napoleon's unknown marshal, Jean Baptiste Bernadotte, was elected successor to the Swedish throne. The present royal family are descendants of this new king, Karl Johan, who never spoke a word of Swedish.

Following the river eastwards brings you to the **Art Museum** (daily 11am–5pm, Wed till 9pm; 25kr), a spacious series of galleries housed in what was formerly the county museum. Much of the work on show is mediocre, the best room showing a collection by the late nineteenth-century local artist, Axel Borg. A little further up the river, past the appealing Stadsparken, stands **Wadköping** (daily May–Aug 11am–5pm; Sept–April 11am–4pm; shops and exhibitions closed Mon), an entire village of centuries-old wooden cottages and shops brought to the site to form a living open-air museum. It's all extremely pretty, but very staged. Some of the cottages have been reoccupied, and the twee little shops sell pastel-coloured wooden knick-knacks.

Eating and drinking

There are plenty of atmospheric places in Örebro in which to enjoy a wide range of good **food**. If you're here in July, though, be prepared for some of the smaller restaurants to be closed for the holidays. In the daytime, delicious organic home-baked goodies are served at *Café Stadsträdgården*, in the greenhouses at the entrance to Stadsparken. For sheer fun, the *Medeltidspuben, Drottning Blanka* (Queen Blanka's Medieval Pub) serves medieval-style meals, such as wild boar, in the windowless, candlelit depths of the castle's torture chamber and prison – a main course and drink costs around 100kr. The hippest bar and restaurant in town is *Babar*, at Kungsgatan 4 (☎019/10 19 00), while *Björnstugan* (☎019/13 58 90), just opposite, is also very popular. For a quiet drink and dinner in a superb rustic pub the finest choice is *Stallyktan*, Södra Strandgatan 3B (☎019/10 33 23), a couple of minutes' walk west of the castle, which serves freshly cooked chicken, salmon and steak dishes for a very reasonable 89kr. Alternatively, *Drången*, Oskarstorget 9 (☎019/32 32 96), is a good, unpretentious local's pub and restaurant.

Linköping

Sixty kilometres east of Lake Vättern in the county of Östergötland, **LINKÖPING**'s range of appealing buildings stands as testament to its 900-year history. The architectural highlights are the remarkable **Domkyrkan** and, a few kilometres to the west, **Gamla Linköping**, an entire village caught in a late nineteenth-century time warp. Linköping's best-kept secret, however, missed by all but a handful of visitors, is a unique **art exhibition** that reveals more about eighteenth-century Swedish society than any number of old houses could hope to do.

The Town and around

With its soaring, 107-metre-high spire, the elegant **Domkyrkan** (June & July Mon–Sat 9am–7pm, Sun 9am–6pm; Aug–May Mon–Sat 9am–6pm, Sun 10am–6pm), set in a swath of greenery, dates from 1232 – though the bulk of the present sober building was completed around 1520 – and is built entirely of local hand-carved limestone. Stonemasons from all over Europe worked on the building and, with a belfry and the west facade added as late as 1885, you can make out a number of styles from Romanesque to Gothic. The venerable old buildings around the Domkyrkan include the much-rebuilt thirteenth-century castle which, like so many others, was fortified by Gustav Vasa and beautified by his son Johan III.

Five minutes' down Ågatan in the direction of the Stångån River is the town's most unexpected cultural diversion, housed in the unlikely setting of the **Labourers' Educational Association** (ABF) at Snickaregatan 22. On the fourth floor is a priceless collection of 85 brilliantly executed pictures by the celebrated artist **Peter Dahl**, illustrating all the *Epistles of Bellman*. Carl Michael Bellman was an eighteenth-century poet-songwriter who sought to expose the hypocrisies of contemporary Swedish society, telling of life in pubs, of prostitutes, and of the wild and drunken sexual meanderings of high-society men and women, all set against fear of the Church and final damnation. Officially, the ABF closes for July, but if you walk round the corner onto Storgatan and to the left of the Spar Bank, a set of elevators leads to a second entrance, where someone should let you in.

One block back along St Larsgatan, **St Lars kyrka** (Mon–Thurs 11am–4pm, Fri 11am–3pm, Sat 11am–1pm) is frequently overlooked, standing as it does within a few metres of the great Domkyrkan. Consecrated by Bishop Kol in 1170, the present interior has had too many facelifts to show many signs of its age. However, it was a plan to reinforce the floor that led to the discovery of a number of twelfth-century engraved stone and wood coffins. There are no signs to direct you, but beneath the church, in candlelit half light, complete twelfth-century skeletons reside in new glass coffins, alongside some remarkably preserved wood coffins and the exposed remains of the original church, rebuilt in the 1730s. To see it all, just ask whoever is selling postcards to unlock the door leading to the basement.

Gamla Linköping

Just 3km west of Linköping proper, **Gamla Linköping** (Mon–Fri 10am–5.30pm, Sat & Sun noon–4pm; free) is a remarkable open-air museum, essentially different from the others you may have seen in that it is a true living environment. An entire town of houses, shops and businesses has been brought here from Linköping, along with street-lighting, fences, signs and even trees, to re-create the town as an identical copy of its nineteenth-century incarnation – even the street plan is exactly the same. Fifty people live here, and there's a massive waiting list for eager new tenants, despite the drawbacks of not being allowed to alter the properties and the fact that tourists trundle through year-round. Craftsmen work at nineteenth-century trades, and most shops are open every day, including a small chocolate factory, gold- and silversmiths, a woodwind workshop and linen shops; there's a cafeteria and an open-air theatre, with performances throughout the summer. Buses #203 and #205 run here from Resecentrum (Sept–May every 20min).

Canal trips

Linköping is riddled with waterways, and a number of trips offer the chance to explore them. The **Göta Canal** (for a map of which see p.452) is the most obvious target, wending its way from Motala through Borensberg to the seven-sluice Carl Johan Lock at Berg, just north of Linköping, where it meets Lake Roxen. South of the city, the less well-known **Kinda Canal** has a manually operated triple lock at Tannefors, and you can head south for 35km through a mix of canal and river to Rimforsa.

There are endless combinations of canal and river trips, with mystifying ticket and price permutations, from a basic cruise up and down the Göta Canal for two adults or an adult and two children for 295kr (245kr one-way), to a more glamorous spree on the *M/S Nya Skärgården* to Söderköping (35km east) and back in a steamer from 1915 (bookings on ☎070/637 17 00). For a less ambitious trip, boats also head down the Kinda Canal and Stångån River to a pleasant outdoor café at Tannefors.

Practicalities

All **trains** and **buses** arrive at and leave from the **Resecentrum** (travel centre) in the north of the town centre. Linköping is easy to walk around, with the reference point of the Domkyrkan spire rarely out of sight. The **tourist office** (☎013/20 68 35, fax 12 19 03, *info@ekoxen.se*) is at the *Quality Ekoxen Hotel*, Klostergatan 68, and, uniquely in Sweden, is open 24 hours a day all year. They can supply a list of **private rooms** (from around 150kr), but they won't book them for you. Every room in Linköping's STF **youth hostel**, Klostergatan 52A (☎013/14 90 90, fax 14 83 00), has its own mini-kitchen and en-suite shower and toilet. *Glyttinge Camping*, a modern **campsite** with four-bed cabins, is 3km east of town at Berggårdsvägen (☎013/17 49 28; mid-April to Sept); take bus #201. Linköping is not a popular holiday destination with Swedes, and several of the smaller **hotels** close for July – the plus side is that some of those that stay open drop their prices dramatically. Best value and cheapest is the *Hotellet Östergyllen,* Hamngatan 2 (☎013/10 20 75, fax 12 59 02; ①), which also operates **cycling and canoeing packages**. For more luxury, try the *Quality Ekoxen,* Klostergatan 68 (☎013/14 60 70, fax 12 19 03; ⑤/②), which has every facility, including a pool.

Linköping is a likeable spot to spend an evening, and the liveliest and most appealing places to **eat and drink** after dark are mostly on Ågatan, running up to the Domkyrkan. Some of them are open during the day, too. The best cakes and sandwiches in town are served at a couple of **café-konditori** around Storatorget: *Lind's,* on the edge of the square, is the best of the bunch. For bigger meals, try *B.K.* on Ågatan, a fun place with a huge cocktail bar and an elegant **restaurant** serving mostly meat, plus a couple of fish and vegetarian dishes. *Amore Mio,* on the corner of Ågatan and Snickaregatan, serves up very cheap pasta and pizza – it's very plain, but pasta, with a choice of four filling toppings and coffee, salad and bread, costs only 29kr. Rather more stylish are *Chiccolatta,* a very popular Italian café on Storatorget, and *PM & Co,* a trendy (though overpriced) hangout where the Kinda Canal meets the River Stånga. *Gula Huset,* on Ågatan, is a good bet for vegetarian choices, serving an extensive vegetarian buffet for 55kr at lunchtime and big portions of Swedish meat and fish dishes or pizzas (74kr) later on – it's also the cheapest place **to drink**. The RFSL run a **gay bar,** *Joy Café* at Nygatan 58 (Tues 7–10pm only, closed July; ring ☎013/13 20 22 for exact times).

Norrköping and around

It is with good reason that the dynamic, youth-oriented town of **NORRKÖPING** calls itself Sweden's Manchester. Like its British counterpart, Norrköping's wealth came from its textile industry, which thrived in the eighteenth and nineteenth centuries (the

Swedish word for corduroy is *manchester*). The legacy from this period is the town's most appealing feature: it is one of Europe's best-preserved industrial urban landscapes, with handsome red-brick and stuccoed mills reflected in the waters of Motala Ström.

It was this small, rushing river that attracted the Dutch industrialist **Louis De Geer** to the town in the late seventeenth century, and his paper mill, still in operation today, became the biggest factory in the city, to be followed by numerous wool, silk and linen factories. Today, many buildings are painted a strong, tortilla-chip yellow, as are the trams – De Geer's favourite colour has become symbolic of the town. Textiles kept Norrköping booming until the 1950s, when foreign competition began to sap the market, and the last big textile mill closed its doors in 1992.

Like Manchester, Norrköping has also become a nucleus for music-inspired **youth culture**, popularized by Ulf Lundell, one of Sweden's most famous singer-songwriters, and home to the country's best-known working-class rock band Eldkvarn. In addition, the city has one of the highest immigrant populations in Sweden The first to come here were the Jews in the mid-eighteenth century. Today's immigrant communities are mostly from Asian and Arab countries, though in the past few years there's been a considerable influx from the former Yugoslavia.

Arrival, information and accommodation

The helpful **tourist office**, in an old cotton warehouse opposite the gates of the paper mill at Dalsgatan 16 (June to mid-Aug daily 10am–7pm, Sat 10am–5pm, Sun 10am–2pm;

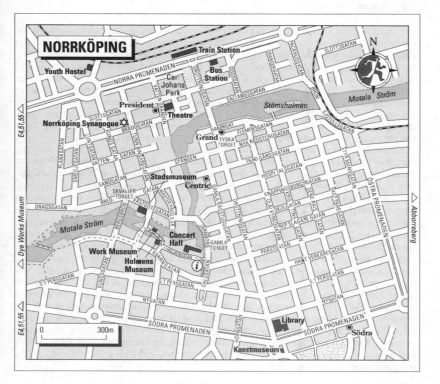

mid-Aug to May Mon–Fri 10am–6pm, Sat 10am–2pm; ☎011/15 50 00, fax 15 50 74, *info@norrkoping.se*), is five minutes' walk from the **train** and **bus** terminals. There is a range of cards and packages available to help cut the cost of sightseeing and accommodation. Ask at the tourist office too about the 1902 **vintage tram**, which circles around the city on a sightseeing tour during summer. Ordinary yellow trams run on two lines all over the town centre, with tickets costing a flat 15kr, including any tram changes made within the hour.

The tourist office can book **private rooms** from 150kr per person, plus a 60kr booking fee, or can just supply you with the list. The cheapest central **hotel**, *Hotel Centric,* Gamla Rådstugugatan 18–20 (☎011/12 90 30, fax 18 07 28; ③/①), is reasonable enough, or for a more upmarket experience, try for a room at the c.1900 *Hotel,* bang in the centre at Tyska Torget 2 (☎011/36 41 00, fax 18 11 83; ⑤/③). The *President Hotel,* next to the theatre at Vattengränden 11 (☎011/12 95 20, fax 10 07 10; ⑤/③), is very pleasant too, with special touches like electrically adjustable beds. There are two STF **youth hostels**. *Turistgården*, Ingelstadsgatan 31 (☎011/10 11 60, fax 18 68 63), is just a few hundred metres north of the train station, or there's the more picturesque hostel at Abborreberg, 5km east of town (take bus #111 from Repslagaregatan, just off Drottninggatan, to Lindö, and ask the driver to drop you off at the hostel). The closest **campsite** is by the rock carvings at Himmelstalund, *City Camp,* on Utställningsvägen (☎011/17 11 90, fax 17 09 87) – walk west along the river or take bus #118 from the bus station.

The Town

The main avenue, **Drottninggatan**, runs north–south from the train station through the city centre. Just a few steps down from the station, the small but pretty **Karl Johans Park** boasts the unusual feature of 25,000 cacti, all formally arranged in thematic patterns. Continuing over the river and following the tram lines up Drottninggatan, a right turn into Repslagaregatan leads into **Gamla Torget**, overlooked by a charismatic sculpture of Louis De Geer by Carl Milles. From here, the steely modern riverside **Concert Hall** is fronted by trees, providing a lovely setting for the *Kråkholmen Louis De Geer* café. It's worth stepping inside the Concert Hall for a moment, as its surface modernity belies the fact that this was once one of De Geer's paper factories. You can also pick up information on the symphony orchestra's weekly concerts while you're here.

Through the impressive, eighteenth-century paper mill gates to the left of the concert hall and across a wooden bridge behind the hall is the **Work Museum** (Arbetetsmuseum; daily 11am–5pm; free), housed in a triangular, yellow-stuccoed factory from 1917. Known as "The Iron" – though its shape and colour are more reminiscent of a wedge of cheese – the building was considered by Carl Milles to be Europe's most beautiful factory. It's a splendid place, with seven floors of exhibitions on living conditions, workers' rights and daily life in the mills. Take the stairs down, rather than the lift, to see a touching exhibition in the stairwell about the life of Alva, a woman who spent 35 years as a factory worker here. Next door, over another little bridge, is the excellent **City Museum** (Stadsmuseum; Tues–Fri 10am–4pm, Thurs till 8pm, Sat & Sun 11am–5pm; free). Set in an interconnecting (and confusing) network of old industrial properties, the most engaging of the permanent exhibitions is a trade street featuring the workplaces of a milliner, confectioner, chimney sweep and, in a backyard, a carriage maker. Three streets north of the Stadsmuseum, on Bråddgatan, stands the beautiful **Norrköping synagogue**, spiritual home to Sweden's oldest Jewish community. The present synagogue, the city's third, was built in 1858. Recently beautifully restored, highlights of this grand old building include an enormous central chandelier and the pulpit, finely painted in blues, reds and yellows, and with a magnificent ark. To see inside, call the tourist office.

Head back south across the river and follow the bank west for ten minutes into the countryside to reach **Färgargården**, an open-air dyeworks museum (May–Aug Tues–Sun noon–4pm; free), ranged in a huddle of wooden nineteenth-century houses. A better reason to come here than the exhibitions, or the garden of plants used to make dyes, is the outdoor café, open during summer whenever the weather is good.

Any interest you have in Swedish art can be satisfied at Norrköping's **Art Museum** (Konstmuseum; May–Aug Tues–Sun noon–4pm, Wed till 8pm; Sept–April Tues–Sun 11am–5pm, Tues & Thurs till 8pm; 30kr), at the southernmost tip of Drottninggatan, which is full of some of the country's best-known modernist works. Founded by a local snuff manufacturer around the beginning of the twentieth century, the galleries offer a fine, well-balanced progression from seventeenth-century Baroque through to up-to-the-minute contemporary paintings. Coming out of the art museum, the bunker-like, concrete building to the right is the town **library**, more interesting and user-friendly than most, with a big range of international newspapers and free Internet access.

Eating and drinking

There's a fair selection of eating places in Norrköping, most of them doubling as bars. However, it's the Norrköping custom to have a drink at home before heading out to the pubs, so the city only starts coming alive from 10pm or so.

For an old fashioned neighbourhood **café**, try *Café Curiosa,* Hörngatan 6 (in the centre of town east of Drottninggatan), which serves home-baked cakes, savoury pies and ice cream in an old living room-style environment. The most sensational **restaurant** in town is *Pappa Grappa,* Gamla Rådstugugatan 24 (☎011/18 00 14), a terrific Italian restaurant not to be missed if you enjoy inventive and original combinations of searingly fresh ingredients in a mellow atmosphere, or try *Guskelov,* Dalsgatan 13 by the Concert Hall (☎011/13 44 00; closed Sun), an Art Deco-style restaurant specializing in fish dishes. *Pub Wasa* and *Tegelvalvet Bar,* at Gamla Rådstugugatan, along with nearby *Källaren Bacchus* at Gamla Torget 4, provide plenty of scope for **drinking** and dancing. *Källaren Bacchus* has a cellar restaurant and gardens and boasts a long cocktail, whisky and beer list, while *Pub Wasa* is in an old, ornate building, serves lots of beers and cheap food and has **live music** every night from 11pm. The *Tegelvalvet Bar* (closed July) is in the basement and also has live singers every Friday and Saturday till 3am and a dance floor. It's a restaurant during the rest of the week.

Around Norrköping

The following are both easy trips from Norrköping; within even closer reach are the rock carvings at **Himmelstalund**, a couple of kilometres west of the centre. These carvings date from around 1500 BC and show with unusual clarity ships, weapons, animals and men; while burial mounds, though nothing much to look at, attest to Iron Age and Viking settlements in the area. To get there take bus #113 from Norrköping.

Löfstad Manor

Just 10km southwest of town, **Löfstad Manor** (May Sat & Sun noon–4pm; June to mid-Aug daily noon–4pm; late Aug noon–2pm; tours hourly, on the hour; 40kr) dates from the 1650s but was rebuilt a hundred years later after a fire ravaged all but its shell. The same family owned Löfstad until the last, unmarried daughter, Emily Piper, died in 1926. She willed the house, its contents and the whole estate to the Museum of Östergotland, which has kept it untouched since her death. Generations of ancestors before Emily all made their mark, and there's a splendid collection of eighteenth- and nineteenth-century Baroque and Rococo furniture and pictures. Emily's most notable ancestor was Axel Fersen, who, during the French Revolution, tried in vain to save King Louis XVI and Queen Marie-Antoinette. His motives may not have been entirely political – rumoured to have been the queen's lover, it's thought that he fathered the daughter of Marie Antoinette whose portrait hangs in the drawing room. The areas with the most authentic and lived-in feel are the kitchen and servants quarters, while in the servant's quarters you can see Miss Piper's bathroom, with her ancient bathrobe still hanging from the door. The tour whisks you round pretty quickly and it's a good idea to ask the guide for English translations before the tour gets underway.

Bus #481 runs from Norrköping bus terminal to Löfstad (ask for Löfstad Slott). Getting back can be a problem, especially on weekend afternoons, but you may be able to get a ride from another visitor. There's a pleasant **restaurant** in one wing of the house, serving traditional Swedish food, plus a cheaper café in the stables.

Kolmården Djurpark

Around 30km northeast of Norrköping, **Komården Djurpark** is one of the country's biggest tourist attractions. A combined zoo, safari park and dolphinarium, it's understandably popular with children, who have their own zoo, as well as access to a gaggle of other diversions and enclosures. If your views on zoos are negative, it's just about possible to be convinced that this one is different; there are no cages, but instead sunken enclosures, rock barriers and moats to prevent the animals from feasting on their captors. Attractions include a cable-car ride over the safari park, a tropical house, working farm and dolphin shows.

If you're interested in just one or two specific attractions in the park, it might be as well to call first (☎011/24 90 00), as the safari park can be closed in bad weather. Generally, though, most things are open daily (from 10am until around 4–6pm). Entrance charges vary according to what you want to see, but a combined ticket for everything runs from 195kr to 235kr, depending on the season. If you don't have your own transport, take bus #432 from Norrköping bus terminal (hourly; 50min). Should you want to stay, there's a **hotel**, the *Vidmarkshotellet* (☎011/15 71 00, fax 39 50 84; ④), at the park, or you can **camp** at *Kolmården Camping* (☎011/39 82 50, fax 39 70 81), close by at the water's edge.

Nyköping and around

The county of Södermanland – known as Sörmland – cuts diagonally to the northeast of Norrköping above Bråviken bay. Its capital, the very small historic town of **NYKÖPING**, has had a lively past, but today is used by most visitors simply as a springboard for the picturesque coastal islands to the east. This is a pity, as its underrated charms include an excellent museum, set in and around the ruins of its thirteenth-century castle, and a harbour that bustles with life in summer.

A late twelfth-century defensive tower, built to protect the trading port at the estuary of the Nyköping River, was converted into a fortress by King Magnus Ladulås, and it was here in 1317 that the infamous **Nyköping Banquet** took place. One of Magnus's three sons, Birger, invited his brothers Erik and Valdemar to celebrate Christmas at Nyköping and provided a grand banquet. Once the meal was complete, and the visiting brothers had retired to bed, Birger had them thrown in the castle's dungeon, threw the key into the river and left them to starve to death (whether the rusting key on display, found by a boy fishing in the river in the nineteenth century, is the genuine item, no one knows). Gustav Vasa fortified the castle with gun towers in the sixteenth century, and his son Karl, Duke of Södermanland, later had it converted into a regal Renaissance palace. The following century all but the King's Tower was devastated by fire, and never rebuilt.

Today, the riverside tower and connected early eighteenth-century house built for the county governor form a **museum complex** (daily noon–4pm, closed Mon in July; 20kr). Wandering through the original gatehouse beneath Karl's heraldic shield, you reach the extensively restored **King's Tower**. Climbing up to the first floor you'll pass carefully stacked bits and pieces excavated from Karl's palace – most notably some spectacular Ionic column tops. On the first floor, a model of the fortress fronted by a dashboard of buttons allows you to follow the events of the Nyköping Banquet – complete with gory details. The top floor has some evocative exhibits, including a bizarre 3-D cameo depicting the dead King Gustavus Adolfus lying in state, with his widow and six-year-old Queen Kristina looking on. It's the old **Governor's Residence**, however, that has the most exquisite collections. Here you can climb the stairs, lined with menacing portraits, to an exceptional run of magnificently decorated rooms from a variety of periods. Among the highlights is the Jugend room – probably the finest example of this style you'll see in Sweden.

Once you've seen the castle and museum, take the pleasant walk along the river bank, lined with people fishing, to the popular harbour and marina, a regular goal for the Stockholm yachting set – the capital being just 100km away by road or train; the flat water inside the 1500-metre-long breakwater is also an important venue for canoe racing.

Practicalities

The **train station**, which is where buses also stop, is at the opposite end of town from the harbour, though the distance is easily walkable. The central **tourist office**, in the Rådhus, Storatorget (June to mid-Aug Mon–Fri 8am–6pm, Sat & Sun 10am–5pm; mid-Aug to May Mon–Fri 8am–5pm; ☎0155/24 82 00, fax 24 81 36, *turism@nykoping.se*), will book **private rooms** from 125kr (no booking fee). The delightful **youth hostel** (no longer part of the STF) is set in the castle grounds at Brunnsgatan 2 (☎0155/21 18 10). The nearest **camping site**, which also has cheap cabins, is *Oppeby Camping* (☎0155/21 13 02; May–Sept), 2km northwest of the centre near the E4. Among the **hotels**, *Kompaniet*, on Folkungavägen by the harbour (☎0155/28 80 20, fax 28 16 73; ⑤/③), is stylish and excellent value, since breakfast, afternoon tea and a buffet dinner are included in the price. Otherwise, try the cheap but adequate *Hotel Wictoria*, Fruängsgatan 21 (☎0155/21 75 80, fax 21 44 47; ②/①).

Most of the town's **eating and drinking**, unsurprisingly, is done at the harbour, but for the best daytime **café**, head for *Café Hellmans* on Västra Trädgårdgatan 24 (Mon–Fri 7.30am–6pm, Sat 9am–4pm, Sun 10am–4pm), just off Stora Torget, where you can sit outside in the courtyard in summer. *Tova Stugen*, behind the castle grounds close to the harbour, serves light lunches in low, grass-roofed fifteenth-century cottages brought here from around Södermanland. Nyköping's lively **restaurant** and **bar** scene is based around the old wooden storage buildings along the harbourside. Try the popular *Kapten Krook Bistro* at the harbour, the first warehouse you'll see. It serves a range of beers, whiskies and schnapps, and the menu, in English runs from not-very-Swedish Cajun shrimp to more traditional gravadlax with mustard sauce. It's not cheap, with steaks and seafood at 120–170kr, though sandwiches and salads are more like 65kr. Serving similar food, *Café Aktersnurran*, just a few buildings up, is more laid-back and cheaper.

If you're **driving** from Nyköping to Stockholm, it's a straight run on the E4; it's also a quick **train** journey (1hr 15min). The **bus** route is convoluted, involving one of five buses to either Trosa or Vagnhärad, then bus #782 to Liljeholmen, followed by a subway trip to the city centre.

Around Nyköping

Hundreds of **islands** are accessible from Nyköping, served by regular boat trips from town. The most popular excursion is to the nature reserve on **Stendörren**, around 30km west of town, which offers some fine walking between the islands, which are connected by footbridges. From Stendörren boats continue to the idyllic little island settlement of **Trosa** (also reachable by road, 40km along the E4) – ideal for tranquil riverside walks, with forested trails and picture-perfect, red wooden cottages around the old centre.

In summer, *M/S Labrador* leaves the dock at Nyköping for Stendörren and Trosa at 9am (mid-June to mid-Aug Tues & Thurs); it costs 80kr to Stendörren, 120kr to Trosa, and the return boat leaves at 2pm. Alternatively you can stay on Trosa in the STF **youth hostel** (☎015/653 21 00; June to mid-Aug). If you don't want to return to Nyköping, take bus #702 from Trosa bus terminal to Liljeholmen (1hr), where you can connect with public transport to Stockholm. **Camping** near Trosa is possible at *Nynäs Camping* (☎015/64 10 09; mid-April to mid-Oct). There's only one cabin, so it's worth booking well in advance. A bigger site is *Trosa Havsbaden* (☎015/61 24 94), which has nine cottages, bookable through Trosa tourist office (☎015/65 22 22).

Gotland

Rumours about good times on **Gotland** are rife. Wherever you are in Sweden, one mention of this ancient Baltic island will elicit a typically Swedish sigh followed by an anecdote about what a great place it is. You'll hear that the short summer season is an exciting time to visit; that it's hot, fun and lively. Largely, this is all true: the island has a distinctly youthful feel as young, mobile Stockholmers desert the capital for a boisterous summer spent on the island's beaches. The flower-power era also makes its presence felt with a smattering of elderly VW camper vans lurching off the ferries, but shiny Saabs outnumber them fifty to one. During summer, bars, restaurants and campsites are packed, the streets swarm with revellers, and the sands are awash with bodies. It's not everyone's cup of tea: to avoid the hectic summer altogether, come in late May or September when, depending on your bravado, you can still swim.

Gotland itself, and in particular its capital, **Visby**, has always seen frenetic activity of some kind. A temperate climate and fortuitous geographical position attracted the Vikings as early as the sixth century, and the lucrative trade routes they opened, through to Byzantium and western Asia, guaranteed the island its prosperity. With the ending of Viking domination, a golden age followed, during which Gotland's inhabitants sent embassies, maintained trading posts and signed treaties with European and Asian leaders. However, by the late twelfth century the island's autonomy had been undermined by the growing power of the Hanseatic League, under whose influence Visby became one of the great cities of medieval Europe, famed for its wealth and strategic power. A contemporary ballad had it that "The Gotlanders weigh their gold with twenty pound weights. The pigs eat out of silver troughs and the women spin with golden distaffs."

This romantic notion of the island's prosperity persisted right into the twentieth century, when Gotlanders began relying on tourism to prop up the traditional industries of farming, forestry and fishing. Modern hype makes great play of the sun, and it's true that the flowers that give Gotland its "Island of Roses" tag have been known to bloom at Christmas. It's not all just tourist brochure fodder, however: nowhere else in Scandinavia is there such a concentration of unspoilt medieval country churches, 93 of them still in use and providing the most permanent reminder of Gotland's ancient wealth.

Getting there: ferries and planes

Ferries to Gotland are numerous and, in summer, packed, so try to plan well ahead. Destination Gotland run a range of ferries to the island (reservations on ☎0498/20 10 20, fax 20 13 90 in Visby; ☎08/20 10 20 in Stockholm); crossings take five hours from Nynäshamn or four hours from Oskarshamn during the day (on night-time trips you have to stay on the boat until 8am). Night-time sailings in summer get packed, so a

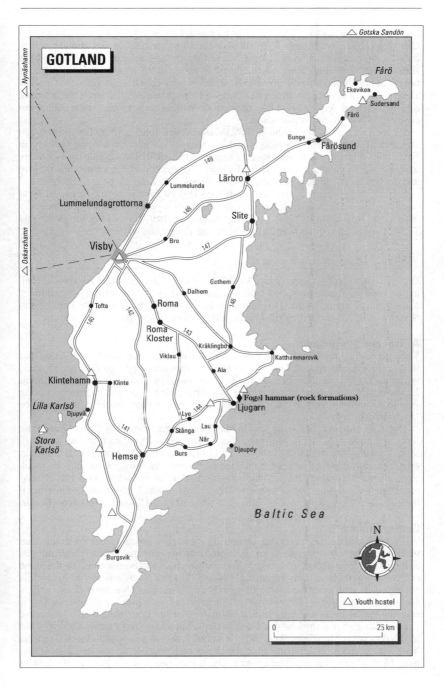

GOTLAND

△ Gotska Sandön

△ Nynäshamn

Fårö

Ekeviken

△ Sudersand

Fårö

Bunge

Fårösund

149

Lummelunda

Lärbro

Lummelundagrottorna

148

Slite

△ Oskarshamn

Bro

147

Visby

Gothem

Dalhem

146

Tofta

142

Roma

140

Roma Kloster

143

Kräklingbo

Viklau

Ala

Katthammarsvik

Klintehamn

Klinte

Fogel hammar (rock formations)

Lilla Karlsö

Djupvik

Lye

144

Ljugarn

△

Stora Karlsö

141

Stånga

Lau

När

Hemse

Burs

Djaupdy

Baltic Sea

N

Burgsvik

△ Youth hostel

0   25 km

cabin may be worthwhile. A return ticket for two in a cabin in high season costs 1016kr. Carrying a bike across costs 35kr. As phone lines to Destination Gotland are notoriously busy, another option is to try Gotland City (☎08/406 15 00, fax 406 15 90), at Kungsgatan 57 in Stockholm, who can provide plenty of information and sell advance tickets at prices roughly equivalent to Destination Gotland. One-way fares cost around 135kr (195kr at weekends) during high season (June to mid-Aug). There's also a brand-new **high-speed ferry** (205–430kr one-way depending on season), which makes the crossing in just two and a half hours.

The nearest port to Stockholm is **NYNÄSHAMN**, which has a youth hostel (☎09/520 208 34) not far from the train station at Nickstbadsvägen 17 – advance booking is essential. From Gothenburg or the southwest of the country, **OSKARSHAMN**, a little over six hours by train from Gothenburg, may well be the more convenient port. Be warned that the limited food on board the ferries is expensive, so it's worth stocking up before you leave.

Recent competition between the two **airlines** (Flying Enterprise and Skyways) serving the island has made flying an economical option if you're under 26, with one-way fares from Stockholm to Visby on Flying Enterprise (☎020/95 95 00) for as little as 270kr. The lowest regular over-26 fare is around 1200kr one way.

Visby

Undoubtedly the finest approach to **VISBY** is by ship, when you can see the old trading centre as it should be seen – from the sea. If you sail on one of the busy summer night-time crossings, it's good to get out on deck for the early sunrise. By 5am the sun is above the city, silhouetting the towers of the cathedral and the old wall turrets.

Arrival and information

Visby **airport** is 3km from town, a five-minute ride on the airport bus (30kr). A **taxi** into the centre will cost around 75kr. All the huge **ferries** serving Visby dock at the same terminal, just outside the city walls (and off our map). Just turn left and keep walking for the centre. Alternatively, a short way to the right along the harbourfront will bring you to **Gotlandsresor** at Färjeleden 3, which has a room-booking service (see "Accommodation", p.538).

The main **tourist office** (mid-April to May Mon–Fri 8am–5pm, Sat & Sun 10am–4pm; June to mid-Aug Mon–Fri 7am–7pm, Sat & Sun 10am–7pm; mid-Aug to mid-April Mon–Fri 9am–4pm; ☎0498/20 17 00, fax 20 17 17) is within the city walls at Hamngatan 4, conveniently en route between the ferries and the old city. Here you can buy the excellent *Turistkarta Gotland* (25kr), a map with descriptions of all the island's points of interest. There's also a selection of **tours** available, some of which are worth considering if time is short, the walking tour of Visby (May–Aug daily at 11.30am; 70kr) in particular.

Getting around

Visby itself is best explored on foot. Despite its warren-like appearance, it's a simple matter to find your way around the narrow, cobbled streets. The main square, **Storatorget**, is signposted from almost everywhere, and early arrivals will be rewarded by the smell of freshly baked bread from the square's bakery. Modern Visby has spread beyond its old city walls, and today the new town sprawls gently out past **Österport** (East Gate), a few minutes' walk up the hill from Storatorget. From here, the **bus terminal** in the Östercentrum serves the rest of the island; the tourist office has free timetables.

For getting around the island, it's best to rent a **bike**. Most ferry arrivals at Visby are plagued by people hustling bikes, and if you don't have one you might as well succumb here. Bike rental is also available from the kiosks on Korsgatan or, less helpfully, Österport. Most places charge around 50kr a day; if you want to try a tandem, it's best to

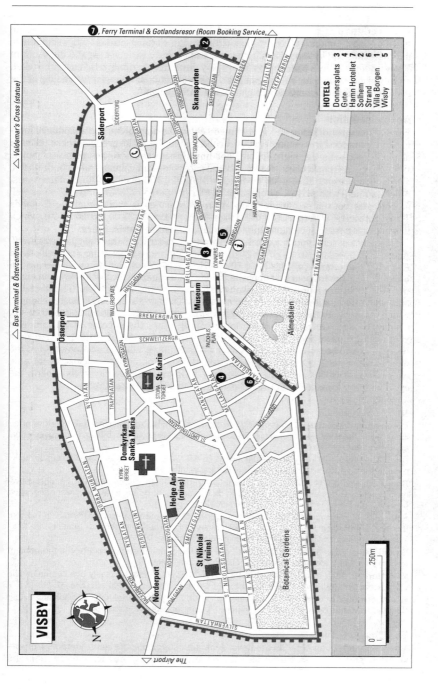

VISBY

N

△ Valdemar's Cross (statue)

△ Bus Terminal & Östercentrum

⑦ , Ferry Terminal & Gotlandsresor (Room Booking Service, △

HOTELS
Donnersplats 3
Gute 4
Hamn Hotellet 7
Solhem 2
Strand 6
Villa Borgen 1
Wisby 5

Söderport

Skansporten

②

①

⑤

⑦

③

Museum

Donners Plats

Almedalen

St. Karin

④

⑥

Domkyrkan
Sankta Maria

Helge And
(ruins)

St Nikolai
(ruins)

Österport

Norderport

Botanical Gardens

▽ The Airport

250m

0

arrive early as they're extremely popular. If you intend striking out into the countryside beyond Visby – undiscovered by most of the young summer crowd – it's worth knowing that bikes can be rented easily, and more cheaply, at various towns to the south of Visby, though Visby's bike outlets like to play down this possibility. Bikes can be taken on the island's buses for a flat fee of 20kr. Ask at the tourist office for a free map of the **cycle route** that circumnavigates almost the entire island.

Accommodation

Finding **accommodation** in Visby should seldom be a problem; the abandoned-looking souls wrapped in sleeping bags and collapsed in the parks are only there through alcoholic excesses the night before, not homelessness. There are plenty of hotels (though few are particularly cheap), several campsites and cabins, and a youth hostel. The Gotlandsresor office, at Färjeleden 3 (☎0498/20 12 60, fax 20 12 70), and the tourist office can help with **private rooms** from 240kr per person (380kr for doubles) as well as **cottages** both in or outside Visby. More information is available at the Gotlands Turist Service at Österport (Mon–Fri 9am–6pm; ☎0498/20 33 00, fax 20 33 90), which has better access to accommodation information than the tourist office.

Of Visby's several **youth hostels**, the two most central are the *Visby Jernvägshotell*, Adelsgatan 9 (☎0498/27 17 07 or 21 98 32), and the more interesting and well-placed *Fångelset Sjumastam* (☎0498/20 60 50 or 070/426 57 60), situated in a former prison building near the harbour just opposite the ferry terminal. Beds cost 100kr in an eight-bed cell, 150kr in a four-bed cell, or you can have your own cell for 300kr. There's a café and sauna here, and it's lively in the evenings. The town's only STF hostel changes venue regularly. To track it down, call *Visby Vandrarhem* (☎0498/26 98 42, fax 20 42 90). Chiefly, though, Gotland is a place for **camping**. After the success of Ulf Lundell's youth-culture novel *Jack*, which extolled the simple pleasure of getting wasted on a beach, Gotland became the place to go for wild summer parties: at many campsites, the most exercise you'll get is cycling to and from the Systembolaget. The closest campsite, *Nordenstrands* (☎0498/21 21 57; May–Sept), is 1km outside the city walls – follow the cycle path that runs through the Botanical Gardens along the seafront.

HOTELS

Donnersplats, Donnersplats 6 (☎0498/21 49 45, fax 21 49 44). A popular, central hotel also offering two- and three-bed apartments for 950kr, and suites for six people for 1800kr. Booking essential in July and Aug. ③.

Gute, Mellangatan 29 (☎0498/24 80 80, fax 24 80 89). Very central and reasonably comfortable; reductions may be possible if you appear at the last minute. ④/③.

Hamn, Färjeleden 3 (☎0498/20 12 50, fax 20 12 70). Opposite the harbour, this is the most convenient hotel for early-morning ferries back to the mainland. All rooms have TV, shower and toilet; breakfast (included) is served from 5am. Open May–Sept. ②/③.

Solhem, Solhemsgatan 3 (☎0498/27 90 70, fax 21 95 23). Just outside the city walls at Skansporten, this large comfortable hotel has recently been renovated, the better to justify its grand price. It has a basement sauna and is quieter than the more central hotels. ④.

Strand, Strandgatan 34 (☎0498/25 28 00, fax 25 88 11). A rather glamorous place in the heart of town, with a sauna, steam bath, indoor pool and a stylish atmosphere. ⑤.

Villa Borgen, Adelsgatan 11 (☎0498/27 99 00, fax 24 93 00). Attractive family hotel in the middle of the action, yet with lovely, peaceful gardens. En-suite rooms, sauna and solarium. ④.

Wisby, Strandgatan 6 (☎0498/25 75 00, fax 25 75 50). Splendid, central hotel in a building dating back to the Middle Ages. Fine breakfasts (open to non-residents for 65kr). ⑥.

The City

Visby is much older than its medieval remnants suggest – the name derives from its status as a Stone Age sacrificial site: "the settlement" (*by*) at "the sacred place" (*vi*). The magnificent **defensive wall** that encircles Visby is the most obvious manifestation of its previous importance. It was hardly a new idea to fortify trading centres against outside attack, although this land wall, built around the end of the thirteenth century, was actually constructed to separate the city's foreign traders from the island's own locals. Annoyed at seeing all their old trade monopolized, the Gotlanders saw something sinister in the wall's erection. They didn't have to wait long to be vindicated: in 1361, during the power struggle between Denmark and Sweden, the Danish king, Valdemar III, took Gotland by force and advanced on Visby. The burghers and traders, well aware of the wealth of their city, shut the gates and sat through the slaughter outside. Excavations during the twentieth century revealed the remains of two thousand bodies, more than half of them women, children and invalids. **Valdemar's Cross**, a few hundred metres east of Söderport (South Gate), marks their mass grave. Erected by the survivors of the carnage, it reads: "In 1361 on the third day after St James, the Goths fell into the hands of the Danes. Here they lie. Pray for them."

Back inside the city walls, the merchants surrendered, and a section of the wall near Söderport was broken down to allow Valdemar to ride through as conqueror. Valdemar's Breach is recognizable by its thirteen crenellations representing, so the story goes, the thirteen knights who rode through with the Danish king. Valdemar soon left clutching booty and trade agreements, and Visby continued to prosper while the island's countryside around it stagnated, its people and wealth destroyed.

The old **Hanseatic harbour** at Almedalen is now a public park and nothing is much more than a few minutes' walk from here. Pretty **Packhusplan**, the oldest square in the city, is bisected by curving Strandgatan, which runs southwards to the fragmentary ruins of **Visborg Castle**, overlooking the harbour. Built in the fifteenth century by Erik of Pomerania, the castle was blown up by the Danes in the seventeenth century. In the opposite direction, Strandgatan runs northwest towards the sea and the lush **Botanical Gardens**, just beyond which is the **Jungfrutornet** (Maiden's Tower), where a local goldsmith's daughter was walled up alive – reputedly for betraying the city to the Danes.

Strandgatan itself is the best place to view the impressive merchants' houses looming over the narrow streets, with storerooms above the living quarters and cellars below, notably **Burmeisterska house** (June–Aug daily 11am–6pm; free). One of the most picturesque buildings is the old pharmacy, **Gamla Apoteket** (June–Aug Mon–Fri 2–6pm, Sat 10am–1pm; 10kr), a lofty place with gloriously higgledy-piggledy windows. Strandgatan's small **Natural History Museum** (June–Aug daily 11am–5pm; free) is largely missable, unlike the fine **Gotlands Fornsal Museum**, next door at Strandgatan 14 (mid-May to Sept daily 10am–5pm; Oct to mid-May Tues–Sun noon–4pm; 40kr). Housed in a mid-eighteenth-century distillery, it holds five storeys of exhibition halls covering eight thousand years of history, plus a good café and bookshop. Among the most impressive sections is the **Hall of Picture Stones** in Room 1, a collection of richly carved keyhole shaped stones dating mostly from the fifth to seventh centuries. The **Hall of Prehistoric Graves** is equally fascinating, its glass cases displaying skeletons dating back six thousand years. Rooms 9 to 13 trace the history of **medieval Visby**, with exhibits including a trading booth, where the burghers of Visby and foreign merchants dealt in commodities – furs, lime, wax, honey and tar – brought from all over Northern Europe. A series of tableaux bring the exhibition up to 1900, starting with Erik of Pomerania, the first resident of Visborg Castle, and leading on through the years of Danish rule, up to the island's sixteenth-century trading boom. There's a wax model of influential businesswoman Anna Margareta Donner, a member of the eighteenth-century trading dynasty whose name you'll spot all over town. A couple of streets up on St Hansgatan, the **Visby Art Museum** at no. 21 (May to mid-Sept 10am–5pm; 30kr) has some very innovative temporary exhibitions of contemporary painting, sculpture and installations which really tease the eye. The permanent work on the top floor is not so exciting, but does include some twentieth-century Gotlandic art.

MEDIEVAL WEEK

During the first week of August, Visby becomes the backdrop for a boisterous re-enactment of the conquest of the island by the Danes in 1361. **Medieval Week** sees music in the streets, medieval food on sale in the restaurants (no potatoes – they hadn't yet been brought to Europe) and, on the first Sunday, a procession re-creating Valdemar's triumphant entry through Söderport to Stortorget. Here, modern-day burghers are stripped of their wealth before the procession moves onto the Jungfrutornet. Locals and visitors to Gotland really get into this festival – you'll see crowds on the boats over to Visby already dressed in home-made clothes and specially created medieval garb, and at least half the people on the streets of the town will be dressed up in period costume. It's great fun and a visual feast.

Strolling aimlessly around the twisting streets and atmospheric walls is rewarding enough in itself, but if you need a focus, aim for **Norra Murgatan**, above the cathedral, once one of Visby's poorest areas. At the end nearest Norderport you'll be treated to the best view of the walls and city rooftops, along with a rare opportunity to climb onto the ramparts. **Kruttornet**, the dark, atmospheric tower on Strandgatan (June–Aug daily 10am–6pm), affords grander views, while the roof of the **Helge And** church ruin (May–Sept daily 10am–6pm), which has been reinforced to allow access to the second floor, provides another central vantage point. Alternatively, head for **Studentallén** on the water's edge, from where the sunsets are magnificent.

VISBY'S CHURCHES

At the height of its power, Visby maintained sixteen **churches**, and while only one, the Domkyrkan, is still in use, the ruins of eleven others can be seen. The **Domkyrkan** (Mon–Fri & Sun 8am–9pm, Sat 8am–6.30pm) was built between 1190 and 1225 and as such dates from just before the great age of Gothic church-building on the island. Used as both warehouse and treasury in the past, it's been heavily restored, and about the only original fixture left is the thirteenth-century sandstone font. Most striking are its towers, a square one at the western front and two slimmer ones to the east; each was originally topped by a spire, but since an eighteenth-century fire they've been crowned with fancy Baroque cupolas, giving them the appearance of inverted ice-cream cones. Inside, have a look beneath the pulpit, decorated with a fringe of unusually hideous angels' faces.

Seventeenth- and eighteenth-century builders and decorators found the smaller churches in the city to be an excellent source of free limestone, tiles and fittings – which accounts for the fact that most are today in ruins. Best of what's left is the great **St Nikolai** ruin, just down the road from the Domkyrkan, once the largest church in Visby. Destroyed in 1525, its part-Gothic, part-Romanesque shell hosts a week-long **chamber music festival**, starting at the end of July; tickets range from 150kr to 300kr and are available from the tourist office – which also gives away a reasonably informative guide, *The Key to all of Gotland's Churches*.

Eating, drinking and nightlife

Visby's centre is small enough to wander around and size up the eating options. **Wallersplats** and adjoining **Hästgatan** are both busy at lunchtime, while neighbouring **Adelsgatan** is lined with cafés and snack bars. For good, cheap food all day, try **Saluhallen**, the market opposite the harbour: here you can buy fresh baked bread, fish and fruit and eat it at tables overlooking the water. Visby's restaurants and bars see plenty of life during the day, but at night they positively heave with young bodies – many of them drunk. **Strandgatan** is the focus of Visby's evening parade, while

Donnersplats, midway along it, has lots of takeaway food stalls. Alternatively, head down to the **harbour,** where forests of masts make a pretty backdrop to the loud, happy beat of music and revellers grooving away on the dance floors. Note that many of Visby's discos and clubs open in the late afternoon, from around 4pm onwards, for "After Beach" sessions of relatively cheap beer.

Gotlanders also enjoy a unique licence from the state to brew their own **beer,** the recipe differing from household to household. It's never on sale, but summer parties are awash with the murky stuff – be warned, it is extremely strong. There are central off-licences in Storatorget and at Östervägen 3; the island's other Systembolagets are found at Hemse, Slite, Klintehamn, Färösunds and Burgsvik.

DAYTIME CAFÉS

Björkstugan, Späksgränd. In a fabulous, lush garden on the prettiest central cobbled street, this little café serves pies and coffee. Open till 10pm.

Gula Huset, Tranhusgatan 2, near the Botanical Gardens. This is the place Visby locals choose: a cosy place serving delighful home-baked port-wine cake and concoctions of almonds, chocolate and fruit in an unspoiled garden setting outside a vine-covered cottage.

Ryska Gården, Storatorget. Rustic place specializing in *saffranspanskakka,* a saffron-yellow rice pie, rather stronger in colour than taste, along with Gotland's own salmberry (a sweet, hybrid berry) jam and cream.

Skafferiet, Adelsgatan. A lovely eighteenth-century house turned into a cosy café boasting a lush garden at the back. Baked potatoes and great cakes.

Vinäger Café Bar, Hästgatan 3. Great place for giant muffins, terrific cakes and pies and a relaxed, mellow atmosphere, all in an anachronistically modern, laid-back building in a former 1896 pharmacy. Open daily till 9pm.

RESTAURANTS AND BARS

Bakfickan, corner of St Katarinegatan and Storatorget. A quiet, relaxed little restaurant, with a tiled interior. Also a good place for a drink.

Barbeque Garden, Strandgatan 15. On the site of Visby's medieval town hall, this huge garden pizza restaurant has indoor and outdoor seating, lots of cocktails, and a bright if not exactly trendy atmosphere.

Burmeister, Strandgatan. Busy place serving a full à la carte menu with starters around 80kr, pasta 90kr and main courses at 160kr. Expect long queues.

Café Boheme, Hästgatan 9. A mellow but lively candlelit place, serving inexpensive salads, sandwiches and pizzas and lots of cakes, including a rather good *kladdkaka* (gooey chocolate pie).

Clematis Medeltidskrogen, Strandgatan 20. Set in the vaulted cellars of a thirteenth-century house, this is Visby's most brilliantly atmospheric and evocative restaurant by far. Lit with candles only, with mead served in flagons and food in rough ceramic bowls and on wooden platters. Try the pear cake with lavender cream.

Friheten, Donnersplats. A lively pub attached to the *Wisby Hotel.* Loud, live bands reverberate on Fri & Sat evenings.

Gutekällaren, Lilla Torggränd. This restaurant, fronting onto Storatorget, is less frenetic than the other nearby eateries, and cleverly designed with striking primary-colour paintings to complement the vivid harlequin chairs. Excellent food, but quite costly, with mains from 140kr.

Munk Källeren, Lilla Torggränd, opposite *Gutekällaren.* Massively fashionable, and subsequently crowded. There's an extensive à la carte menu, entirely in English.

The rest of the island

There's a real charm to the rest of Gotland – rolling green countryside, forest-lined roads, fine beaches and small fishing villages, and everywhere the rural skyline is dominated by churches, the remnants of medieval settlements destroyed in the Danish invasion. Yet perhaps because of the magnetic pull of Visby, very few people bother to go and explore. The **south** of the island, in particular, boasts numerous wonderful and untouched villages and beaches; the **north**, though pretty, can be adequately seen on a day-trip from the capital.

Cycling around the island is immensely enjoyable, since the main roads are free of traffic and minor roads are positively deserted. Gotland's **buses**, though regular, are very few indeed. Outside Visby, they tend to run only twice daily – morning and evening. **Hitching**, however, is an accepted means of transport, and unless you have a specific destination in mind, it's often just as well to go wherever the driver is heading. As you go, keep an eye out for the waymarkers erected in the 1780s to indicate the distance to "Wisby" (the old spelling).

The South

The so-called "capital" of the south, **HEMSE**, around 50km from Visby (buses ply the route), is little more than a main street, but there are a couple of banks and a good local café, *Bageri & Conditori Johansson*, on Storgatan – if you're camping or without your own transport, this is the place to stock up with food. You can rent **bikes** from two places on Ronevägen, off Storgatan: Hemse Krog is a general rental shop with bikes, although you'd do better to avail yourself of the incredibly cheap rates of Ondrell's, next door (40kr per day, 20kr each day after or 160kr per week). There's not a lot else to Hemse, except a summer-only **swimming pool** (signposted "simhall"; June–Aug Mon–Thurs 2–8pm, Fri 5–8pm; 35kr), off Storgatan at the north end of town. Hemse **bus station**, parallel with Storgatan (head down Ronevägen for one block and turn left), is oddly sited in a boarded-up and vandalized house.

Along Route 144 west towards Burs, the countryside is a glorious mix of meadows, ancient farms and dark, mysterious forest. **BURS** itself has a gorgeous thirteenth-century saddle church, so called because of its low nave and high tower and chancel. Inside there's a fabulously decorated ceiling, medieval stained-glass windows and ornately painted pews. Nearby, *Burs Café* is a friendly locals' joint serving cheap, filling meals. Heading east out of Burs, the scenery is a paradise of wild, flowering meadows and medieval farmholdings with ancient windows and carved wooden portals. The next place you come to is the tranquil and pretty hamlet of **NÄR**, notable for its church, set in an immaculate churchyard. The tower originally served as a defensive fortification in the thirteenth century, but more arresting are the bizarre portraits painted on the pew ends right the way up the left side of the church. All depict women with demented expressions and bare, oddly placed breasts. A couple of kilometres north, just beyond the village of **LAU**, *Garde* **youth hostel** (☎ & fax 49 11 81; pre-booking necessary Nov–April) provides some of Sweden's strangest accommodation: the cluster of buildings is situated right by the local football pitch, and the clean bathroom facilities are shared with anyone doing football practice. There's a food shop around the corner from the hostel reception and a café-bar in the village.

For beaches, and the nearest thing Gotland has to a resort, the lively and charming town of **LJUGARN**, on the coast north of När, makes a good base. The **tourist office** (daily: June 9am–6pm; July to mid-Aug 9am–7pm; May & mid-Aug to mid-Sept 11am–4pm) is just off the main road as you approach town and has plenty of information about the southeast of the island. Though full of touristy restaurants, the village manages to retain an authentic feel and is famous for its *rauker* – tall limestone pillars rising up from the sea. A delightful cycle or stroll down Strandvägen follows the coastline through woods and clearings carpeted in *blåeld*, the electric-blue flowers for which the area is known. This is one place where it's easy to find a range of eating places to suit most tastes, and accommodation, unlike most of the island, is not restricted to camping or hostels. "*Rums*" are advertised in appealing-looking cottages all over the little town – the tourist office can also make bookings from 125kr per person (plus 10 percent booking fee) – and there's a **youth hostel** (☎0498/49 31 84) on

Strandridaregården. Gotland's oldest **B&B**, *Badpensionatet* (☎0498/49 32 05; ②) is here too; it opened its doors in 1921. All rooms are en suite and there's also a restaurant, the only one in town that's open all year. Some of the best cakes in Sweden are to be found in Ljugarn at *Café Espegards* on Storvägen, where there's a permanent queue. Finally, *Brunna Dorren* is a pleasant old stuccoed house which is now home to a pizza restaurant, with a big garden where beer is served overlooking the sea.

Heading back west from Ljugarn, Route 144 passes through **LYE**, a charming if sleepy hamlet with an antique shop and café. **STÅNGA**, just a few kilometres on, is worth stopping at for its fourteenth-century church with its unusual wall tablets running down the facade. By the golf course outside is *Gumbalda Golf* (☎0498/48 28 80, fax 48 28 84; ①, including breakfast), a stylish **place to stay** at a very reasonable price; special golf packages are offered here, and the green fee for the eighteen-hole course is 200kr per day.

Stora and Lilla Karlsö

The two **islands** of Stora Karlsö and Lilla Karlsö, lying 6km off the southwest coast, have been declared **nature reserves**, and both have bird sancturaries where razorbills, guillemots, falcons and eider duck breed relatively undisturbed. **Stora Karlsö** is reached from Klintehamn: tickets are available from the harbour office for sailings at 9am and 11am (200kr return; 45min). The only accommodation is in the tiny, very basic fishermen's huts that comprise the STF **youth hostel** (☎0498/24 05 00, fax 24 52 60; 200–280kr per hut for four). No camping is allowed on either island.

Lilla Karlsö is reached from Djupvik, 7km south of Klintehamn (no buses). Boat tickets (120kr return) are available from the harbour office, and there are also tours from Visby (May–Aug daily, occasionally in Sept; 250kr per person). You can book both boat and tour tickets on ☎0498/24 05 00. It's possible to stay on the island in hostel-style accommodation (☎0498/24 11 39; 100kr), but you'll have to book all meals in advance.

The north: Visby to Slite

Thirteen kilometres north of Visby are the **Lummelundagrottorna** (daily: late June to mid-Aug 9am–6pm; May to late-June & mid- to late Aug daily 9am–4pm; late Aug to mid-Sept 10am–2pm; 45kr), limestone caves, stalagmites and stalactites that make for a disappointingly dull and damp stop. There's a more interesting natural phenomenon 10km to the north, where you'll see the highest of Gotland's coastal **limestone stacks**, the remnants of reefs formed over four hundred million years ago (the fact that they're well above the tide line is taken as proof of earlier, higher sea levels). This stack, 11.5 metres high and known as **Jungfruklint**, is said to look like the Virgin and Child – something you'll need a fair bit of imagination to deduce.

Instead of taking the coastal road from Visby, you could head inland instead towards **BRO**, which has one of the island's most beautiful churches. Several different building stages are evident from the Romanesque and Gothic windows in the tower, but the most unusual aspect is the south wall with its flat-relief picture stones, carved mostly with animals, that were incorporated from a previous church on the site.

On the whole, it's far better to press on north, where many of the secluded cottages serve as summer holiday homes for urban Swedes. The peninsula north of **Lärbro** is no longer prohibited to foreign tourists now the army has left. At **BUNGE** it's worth visiting the bright fourteenth-century fortified church and open-air museum (mid-May to mid-Aug daily 10am–6pm; 30kr). **SLITE**, just to the south of Lärbro, is the island's only really ugly place – day-trip buses travel right past its cement factories, quarries and monumentally dull architecture. Beyond this though, Slite has a sandy beach and good swimming. If you don't mind paying for your camping, then the campsite (☎0498/22 08 30; May–Sept) isn't a bad choice, right on the beach.

Fårö

The tourist office in Visby, has, for the present at least, ceased arranging special day-long bus trips to Fårö (Sheep Island), at the northern tip of Gotland, although it's possible to travel to it independently, taking a bus to the town of Fårösund and making the ten-minute ferry crossing (departures every 30min) from the quay ten minutes' walk to the south, on the main road. There's a down-at-heel but surprisingly good working-men's café in town, *Färösund Grill*, which serves excellent sandwiches (25kr) and almond tart (10kr), with good, cheap coffee. Just opposite is *Bungehallen*, a very well-stocked supermarket (open daily till 10pm).

Most of Fårö island itself is flat limestone heath, with shallow lakes and stunted pines much in evidence. In winter (and sometimes in summer, too) the wind whips off the Baltic, justifying the existence of the local windmills – and of the sheep shelters, with their steeply pitched reed roofs, modelled on traditional Fårö houses. Examples of both line the road as you leave the ferry. The best place to head for (and the target of most of the Swedish holiday-makers who visit) is the five-kilometre white sand arc at **Sundersandsviken**; much of the rest of the swimming is done at **Ekeviken**, on the other side of the isthmus. The remainder of the coastline is rocky, spectacularly so at **Lauterhorn** and, particularly, **Langhammars**, where limestone stacks are grouped together on the beach. At Lauterhorn you can follow the signs for Digerhuvud, a long line of stacks leading to the tiny fishing hamlet of **Helgumannen**, which has no more than a dozen shacks on the beach, now used as holiday homes. Continuing along the same rough track brings you to a junction; right runs back to the township of Fårö; left, a two-kilometre dead-end road leads to Langhammars.

travel details

Trains

Hallsberg to: Gothenburg (hourly; 2hr 40min); Stockholm (hourly; 1hr 30min).

Jönköping to: Falköping (for Stockholm and Gothenburg; hourly; 45min); Nässjo (for Stockholm and Malmö; hourly; 35min).

Kalmar to: Emmaboda (16 daily; 35min); Gothenburg (5 daily; 4hr 15min); Malmö (8 daily; 3hr 40min); Stockholm (5 daily; 6hr 30min); Växjo (10 daily; 1hr 15min).

Motala to: Hallsberg (for Örebro, Stockholm and Gothenburg; 6 daily; 45min); Mjölby (for Malmö and Stockholm; 2 daily; 1hr 15min).

Norrköping to: Linköping (1–2 hourly; 25min); Malmö (11 daily; 3hr 15min); Nyköping (5 daily; 40min); Stockholm (hourly; 1hr 40min).

Örebro to: Gävle (6 daily; 3–4hr); Hallsberg (for Stockholm and Gothenburg; 1–2 hourly; 20min); Motala (6 daily; 1hr 30min); Stockholm (7 daily; 3hr 10min).

Oskarshamn to: Gothenburg (3 daily; 5hr 30min); Nässjo (3 daily; 2hr 25min); Jönköping (3 daily; 3hr 20min).

Växjö to: Gothenburg (8 daily; 3hr 20min); Kalmar (6 daily; 1hr 40min); Karlskrona (2 daily; 1hr 30min).

Buses

Jönköping to: Gothenburg (Mon–Fri 2–3 daily; 2hr 15min); Gränna/Vadstena/Motala/Örebro (up to 2 daily; 30min/1hr 20min/1hr 40min/3hr 5min); Växjö (1 on Fri & Sun; 1hr 20min).

Kalmar to: Gothenburg (1 daily; 6hr); Lund/Malmö (1 daily; 5hr 30min/5hr 45min); Oskarshamn/Västervik/Stockholm (3 daily; 1hr 25min/2hr 35min/6hr 50min).

Motala to: Norrköping/Stockholm (2 on Fri & Sun; 1hr 35min/3hr 25min).

Norrköping to: Linköping/Jönköping/Gothenburg (6 daily; 30min/2hr 40min/4hr 55min); Kalmar (5 daily; 4hr 15min); Stockholm (5 daily; 2hr 10min).

Växjö to: Jönköping/Linköping/Norrköping/Stockholm/Uppsala (1 on Fri & Sun; 1hr 20min/3hr 30min/4hr/6hr 30min/7hr 30min).

Ferries

Nynäshamn to: Visby (mid-June to mid-Aug 3 daily; 5hr day, 6hr night; rest of the year night sailings only; 5–6hr).

Oskarshamn to: Visby (mid-June to mid-Aug 1 daily plus one night sailing; rest of the year night sailings only; 4hr day, 6hr night).

Fast ferries

Nynäshamn to: Visby (1 daily; 3hr).

Oskarshamn to: Visby (1 daily; 2hr 30min).

CHAPTER THIRTEEN

THE BOTHNIAN COAST: GÄVLE TO HAPARANDA

Facing Finland across the waters of the Gulf of Bothnia, Sweden's **east coast** forms a corridor of land that, with its jumble of erstwhile fishing towns and squeaky-clean modern cities, is quite unlike the rest of the north. The coast is dominated by towns and cities, the endless forest so characteristic of other parts of northern Sweden having been felled here to make room for the settlements that dot almost the entire coastline. Some, like **Gävle** and **Hudiksvall**, still have their share of old wooden houses, offering evocative images of the past, though much was lost during the Russian incursions in the eighteenth century. Others, like **Sundsvall**, **Umeå** and **Luleå**, are more typical – modern, bright and airy, they rank as some of Sweden's liveliest and most likeable destinations. Throughout the north you'll also find traces of the religious fervour that swept the region in centuries past: **Skellefteå** and, particularly, **Luleå** all boast excellently preserved *kyrkstäder*, or parish villages, clusters of gnarled old wooden cottages dating from the 1700s, where villagers from outlying districts would spend the night after making the lengthy journey to church in the nearest town.

The highlight of the Bothnian Coast, however, is undoubtedly the **Höga Kusten**, or High Coast, between Härnösand and Örnsköldsvik – an indented stretch of shimmering fjords, tall cliffs and a string of pine-clad islands on which it's possible to island-hop up the coast. There's also good hiking to be had here in the **Skuleskogen National Park**. The weather may not be as reliable as further south but you're guaranteed clean beaches – often all to yourself – crystal-clear waters and some fine walking.

Getting around

The **train** line hugs the coast until just beyond Härnösand, where SJ InterCity services terminate. From here a branch line swings inland, joining up in Långsele with the main line north to Swedish Lapland and on to the Norwegian port of Narvik. There are regular services between Stockholm and Sundsvall, stopping at Gävle, Söderhamn and Hudiksvall; from Sundsvall a handful of trains continue on to

---

ACCOMMODATION PRICE CODES

The hotels and guesthouses listed in this chapter have been graded according to the following price bands, based on the cost of the **least expensive double room during high season** (late June to Aug). However, almost every hotel offers seasonal and/or weekend discounts, and wherever possible we've given two grades, covering both the regular and the discounted rate.

① Under 500kr	② 500–700kr	③ 700–900kr
④ 900–1200kr	⑤ 1200–1500kr	⑥ Over 1500kr

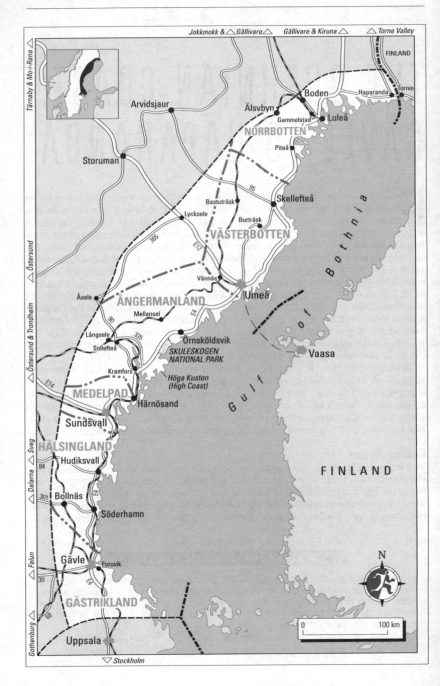

Jokkmokk & △ Gällivare △   Gällivare & Kiruna △   △ Torne Valley

FINLAND

△ Tärnaby & Mo-i-Rana

Arvidsjaur

Boden

Haparanda   Tornio

Älsvbyn

Gammelstad   Luleå

NORRBOTTEN

Piteå

Storuman

95

Basuträsk   Skellefteå

△ Östersund

Lycksele

Burträsk

365

VÄSTERBOTTEN

E12

Vännäs

Åsele   ÄNGERMANLAND   Umeå

△ Östersund & Trondheim

Mellansel

90

E4

Långsele   335

Sollefteå   Örnsköldsvik

SKULESKOGEN
NATIONAL PARK

Kramfors   Höga Kusten
(High Coast)

E14   MEDELPAD

Härnösand

Sundsvall

HÄLSINGLAND

△ Sveg

84   Hudiksvall

△ Dalarna

E4

301   Bollnäs

FINLAND

Söderhamn

△ Falun

Gävle   Furuvik

N

30

E4

GÄSTRIKLAND

0   100 km

68

Uppsala

▽ Stockholm

Gulf of Bothnia

Vaasa

Härnösand, sometimes with a direct connection from Stockholm. There's also a handy train connection to Sundsvall from the inland town of Östersund. Beyond Härnösand things get trickier, and it's easier to continue by **bus** from Härnösand up the High Coast towards Örnsköldsvik and on to connect with the main train line at Umeå, Boden or Luleå. Island-hopping by **ferry** along the High Coast is a wonderful way to make your way north and to take in one of northern Sweden's most beautiful regions. There are frequent bus services north from Örnsköldsvik via Umeå and Skellefteå to Luleå and Boden.

Over recent years the number of ferry services between the Bothnian coast and **Finland** has shrunk dramatically. The only remaining service operates all year between Umeå and Vaasa (4hr).

Gävle and around

It's only two hours north by train from Stockholm to **GÄVLE** (pronounced "Yev-luh"), capital of the county of Gästrikland and the southernmost city in Norrland, the region that makes up two-thirds of Sweden and covers more or less everything north of Uppsala. Gävle is an old city – its town charter was granted in 1446 – although this is hardly obvious from the modern, sophisticated centre, with its large squares, broad avenues and proud monumental buildings. Almost completely rebuilt after a devastating fire in 1869, the spacious layout of present-day Gävle reflects its industrial success in the late nineteenth century, when it was the export centre for locally produced iron and timber. Today the city is more famous as the home of Gevalia coffee, which you're certain to taste during your time in Sweden.

Arrival, information and accommodation

The city centre is concentrated in the grid of streets that spreads southwest from the **train station** on Stora Esplanadgatan. You'll find left-luggage lockers (15kr) on the main platform. The **bus station**, for both local and long-distance services, is on the east side of the train station – use the subway that runs under the train tracks. The **tourist office** is a two-minute walk from the train station at Drottninggatan 37 (June–Aug Mon–Fri 9am–6pm, Sat 9am–2pm, Sun 11am–4pm; Sept–May Mon–Fri 9am–5pm; ☎026/14 74 30, *turistbyran@gavletourism.se, www.gavle.se*). It will book private **apartments** from 345kr per person per night (cheaper by the week or month). Gävle has two **youth hostels**: one is superbly located in the old quarter at Södra Rådmansgatan 1 (☎026/62 17 45, fax 61 59 90); the other is on the coast at Bönavägen 118 in Engeltofta, 6km northeast of the city on bus #5 from Rådhuset (☎026/961 60, fax 960 55; May–Aug). The nearest **campsite** is at *Furuvik Amusement Park*, a twelve-kilometre ride southeast on bus #821, #832 or #838.

Hotels

Aveny, Södra Kungsgatan 31 (☎026/61 55 90, fax 65 15 55). Small and comfortable family-run hotel south of the river. ③/②.

Boulogne, Byggmästargatan 1 (☎ & fax 026/12 63 52). Cosy basic hotel with breakfast on a tray. Close to Boulognerskogen park. ①.

Grand Central, Nygatan 45 (☎026/12 90 60, fax 12 44 99). One of the smartest hotels in town, with old-fashioned en-suite rooms. ④/②.

Nya Järnvägshotellet, Centralplan 3 (☎026/12 09 90, fax 10 62 42). The cheapest hotel in Gävle, with toilet and shower in the corridor but quite ok. ②/①.

Winn, Norra Slottsgatan 9 (☎026/64 70 00, fax 10 59 60). Another smart hotel with its own pool, sauna and sunbeds. ⑤/③.

CENTRAL GÄVLE

HOTELS
Aveny 5
Boulogne 4
Grand Central 1
Nya Järnvägshotellet 2
Winn 3

0   250m

The City

Central Gävle is easy to navigate, with the broad, straight streets of the modern city bisected by a stretch of park that runs roughly north–south. To the south, cut off by the river, lies Gamla Gefle, the only part of the city that survived the fire of 1869, and the first place to head for.

Gamla Gefle

The part of the city known as **Gamla Gefle** passes itself off today as the old town, though unfortunately there's not much left of it. If you stay in the youth hostel you'll be right on the edge of the few remaining narrow cobbled streets – notably Övre Bergsgatan, Bergsgränd and Nedre Bergsgränd – with their pastel-coloured wooden cottages complete with window boxes bursting with summer flowers. For a glimpse of social conditions a century ago, visit the **Joe Hill-Gården** (June–Aug daily 11am–3pm; free; other times by arrangement on ☎026/61 34 25) at Nedre Bergsgatan 28. Joe Hill, born in the house as Johan Emanuel Hägglund in 1879, emigrated to the United States in 1902, where with a new name he went on to become a working-class hero whose songs and speeches served as rallying cries to comrades everywhere. Framed for murder in Salt Lake City, he was executed in 1915. The syndicalist organization to which he belonged runs the museum, a collection of standard memorabilia – pictures and belongings – given piquancy by the telegram announcing his execution.

On the other side of Gamla Gefle, on the canalside at Södra Strandgatan 20, is the county museum, **Länsmuséet Gävleborg** (Tues–Sun noon–4pm; Wed until 9pm; 25kr). Its extensive displays of artworks by most of the great Swedish artists from the 1600s to the present day, including Nils Kreuger and Carl Larsson, make this a rarity among provincial museums, and attract visitors from across the country. Also on show are displays on the area's ironworks and fisheries, as well as work by local artist Johan-Erik Olsson (popularly known as Lim-Johan), whose vivid imagination and naive technique produced some strangely childlike paintings.

The rest of the city

The modern city lies over the river, its broad streets and tree-lined avenues designed to prevent fires from spreading. A central boulevard of parks, trees and fountains runs from the sculpture-spiked **Rådhus** up to the beautiful nineteenth-century theatre, neatly dividing the city into two, while the roomy **Storatorget** has the usual open-air market (Mon–Sat from 9am), selling good-quality fruit and veg.

Gävle's other main sights – none of them major – are out of the centre but close enough to reach on foot. Back at the river by the main double bridge, **Gävle Slott**, the seventeenth-century residence of the county governor, lost its ramparts and towers years ago and now lurks behind a row of trees like some minor country house. You can't go inside, although you can arrange a visit to the **Fängelsemuséet** (Prison Museum) on the premises by contacting the tourist office. From Gävle Slott a short walk along the river leads to a wooden bridge, across which is Kaplansgatan and the **Heliga Trefaldighets Kyrka**, the Church of the Holy Trinity, a seventeenth-century masterpiece of wood-carved decoration. Check out the pulpit, towering altarpiece and screen – each the superb work of a German craftsman, Ewardt Friis. Cross back over the river and take a stroll down **Kungsbäcksvägen**, a narrow street lined with old wooden houses painted yellow, green and orange, with tulips and wild roses growing outside their front doors. Keep going west alongside the riverside path from here and in about fifteen minutes you'll come to **Silvanum** (Tues, Thurs & Fri 10am–4pm, Wed 10am–7pm, Sat & Sun 1–5pm; free) at Kungsbäcksvägen 32, northern Europe's largest forestry museum – interesting only if you're desperate to learn more about the unforgiving forest that you'll become well acquainted with as you travel further north. Continue and you'll come to the rambling **Boulognerskogen**, which opened in the mid-nineteenth century and still provides an oasis of trees, water and flowers just outside the city centre – a good place for a picnic and a spot of sunbathing.

On a rainy day you may find yourself contemplating the **Sveriges Järnvägsmuséet**, the national railway museum at Rälsgatan 1 (June–Aug daily 10am–4pm; Sept–May Tues–Sun 10am–4pm; 30kr, free with InterRail pass), a fifteen-minute walk south from the station following the train tracks. Now housed in an old engine shed, the fifty or so locomotives, some of them over 100 years old, are of limited appeal to non-enthusiasts. If you walk here from the train station along Muréngatan, you'll pass the old dockside **warehouses** off Norra Skeppsbron, a reminder of the days when ships unloaded coffee and spices in the centre of Gävle. Today, strolling past the red wooden fronts with fading company names, it feels as though you're wandering around an old Hollywood movie set rather than the backstreets of a northern Swedish city.

Eating, drinking and entertainment

There's a fair choice of **eating places** in Gävle, but for the best options stick to the central grid of streets around Stortorget and spots up and down the central esplanade between the Rådhus and the theatre. Nearly all cafés and restaurants double up as bars, and some also mutate into nightclubs too.

Cafés, bars and restaurants

Bali Garden, corner of Nygatan and Norra Kopparslagergatan. Good Indonesian food with dishes from 85kr.

Brända Bocken, Stortorget. Young and fashionable, with outdoor seating in summer. Lunch for 63kr, and beef and pork dishes, hamburgers and salmon from around 80kr. Also a popular place for a drink.

Café Artist, Norra Slottsgatan 9. Trendy hangout offering fish and meat dishes for around 150kr, and smaller dishes such as *pytt i panna* for 62kr; in the evenings this is a relaxed place for a beer or two on cosy sofas.

Heartbreak Hotel, Norra Strandgatan 15. Pub, bistro-style bar and nightclub – worth checking out.

Herman, opposite the Rådhus on Norra Kungsgatan. This trendy eaterie is a good place for lunch (59kr), or choose from a series of snacks (40–60kr) or meat dishes (from 120kr).

Kungshallen, Norra Kungsgatan 17, next to the theatre. Mammoth-sized pizzas for 44–60kr and cheap beer.

O'Leary's, Södra Kungsgatan 31. A good 20min walk south from the centre, but still incredibly busy. Catering for a young crowd, this is *the* place to do your boozing and boogying. Closed Mon.

Österns Pärla, Ruddammsgatan 23. Fairly standard Chinese restaurant, serving all the usual favourites for 80–90kr.

Tennstoppet, Nygatan 38. Cheap and cheerful hamburger restaurant close to the station with sausage and chips, egg and bacon and a mixed grill.

Listings

Bank FöreningsSparbanken and Handelsbanken on Nygatan and Nordbanken at Norra Kungsgatan 3–5 all have cash machines.

Bus enquiries Local buses are operated by XTrafik (☎020/91 01 09); long-distance buses to Bollnäs, Uppsala and Stockholm are operated by Swebus (☎0200/218 218).

Car rental Budget (☎026/65 40 00); Europcar (☎020/78 11 80); Hertz (☎026/51 18 19); Statoil (☎020/25 25 25).

Pharmacy Drottninggatan 12 (Mon–Fri 9am–6pm, Sat 9am–2pm, Sun 11am–3pm; ☎026/14 92 01).

Police Södra Centralgatan 1 (☎026/65 50 00).

Post office Drottninggatan 16 (☎026/12 13 90).

Systembolaget Södra Kungsgatan, near Gävle Slott, and at Nygatan 13 (Mon–Thurs 10am–6pm, Fri 9.30am–6pm).

Taxis Gävle Taxi (☎026/12 90 00 or 10 70 00).

Around Gävle

If the sun's shining, you'll find locals catching the rays at the nearby sandy beach of **Rullsand**, which stretches for about 3km. There should be a bus there in the morning, returning in the evening, with one change in Skutskär, but it's worth checking with the tourist office. If you miss the bus you could head out instead for the beaches at either **ENGELTOFTA** (near the youth hostel) or **ENGESBERG**; take bus #5 from the Rådhus (12 daily). From here the bus continues to **BÖNAN**, where there's more good swimming to be had and an old lighthouse that now holds a small museum. There are other enjoyable beaches on the island of **Limön**, which is also a pleasant place for some gentle walks, with paths criss-crossing the island. It can be reached by summer ferry from Skeppsbron (three daily; 30kr), with one departure making a stop in Engeltofta on the way.

In the other direction is the **Furuvik Amusement Park** (May–June Mon–Fri 10am–4pm, Sat & Sun 10am–5pm; July daily 10am–6pm; early Aug daily 10am–5pm; adults 95kr, children 55kr; rides cost 12–24kr, or you can buy a day-pass for 95kr), featuring a zoo, fairground, parks and playgrounds. Buses #821, #832 and #838 run here roughly every half-hour from the bus station. There's also a **campsite** (☎026/980 28 or 19 90 00) nearby with cabins.

Söderhamn and Hudiksvall

On the first leg of the coastal journey further into Norrland the railway sticks close to the coast. If you are in no great rush, **Söderhamn** and **Hudiksvall** are both worth a leisurely stop, though Hudiksvall's distinctive wood-panel architecture gives it the edge over Söderhamn.

Söderhamn

It's easy to see that **SÖDERHAMN** was once much more important than it looks nowadays. Founded in 1620 at the head of a ten-kilometre-long fjord, its glory days came several decades later – the seventeenth-century **Ulrika Eleonora kyrka** that towers over the Rådhus hints at the wealth the city once had, which was earned primarily from fishing. Relics from an earlier church on the same site are kept in the **Söderhamn Museum** (late June to early Aug Tues–Sun noon–5pm; free), halfway up Oxtorgsgatan from the main square, Rådhustorget. The museum is housed in a former rifle factory, from the days when Söderhamn supplied the weapons that helped Sweden to dominate northern Europe.

A number of fires have taken their toll on Söderhamn, the most devastating, in 1876, destroying virtually everything in its path. As a result the modern town is built on the familiar grid pattern, with space for central parks. For an overview of the town and its surroundings, climb up the white 23-metre-high **Oskarsborg tower** (follow the path signposted from down by the railway tracks), from where you can look out across the forests that enclose the town, stretching away as far as the eye can see. To explore further, a series of **walking paths** strike out from near the hospital – go up Kyrkogatan from under the railway bridge near Rådhustorget and continue up the hill onto the footpath, turn left into Krongatan and head for the hospital, past the helipad, and turn right into the forest.

If you've time to spare, it's easy to take a **boat trip** out among the five hundred islands of the Söderhamn archipelago. The largest, Storjungfrun (The Great Virgin), has given its name to the stretch of coast around Söderhamn and Hudiksvall: **Jungfrukusten**, or The Virgin Coast. Boats (info on ☎0270/122 54) leave from the opposite end of town to Rådhustorget – walk down the main street and along the canal for about fifteen minutes to reach the jetty.

Practicalities
Söderhamn's **train** and **bus stations** and **tourist office** (June to early Aug Mon–Fri 7am–7pm, Sat & Sun noon–5pm; mid-Aug to May Mon–Fri 7am–5pm; ☎0270/753 53) are located together in the Resecentrum. The tourist office can provide information on boat trips and hiking routes in the area. If you're planning on **staying** overnight you

won't be overwhelmed with choices: the central *First Hotel Statt*, Oxtorgsgatan 17 (☎0270/414 10, fax 135 24; ③/②), is the luxury option. If money is tight, you'll be better off at the **youth hostel** (☎0270/42 52 33, fax 42 53 26; June–Aug) and year-round **campsite** (same phone & fax numbers) 13km west of town at **MOHED**, beautifully located beside a lake in deep pine forest. To get there take bus #64 or #100 (hourly); the #100 continues to **Bollnäs**, about thirty minutes' ride away and handy for main-line trains north to Swedish Lapland.

A fair number of decent bars and restaurants have opened in Söderhamn in recent years. **Eating** places are mostly to be found along the main pedestrian street, Köpmangatan. At the Rådhus end of the street, *Mosquet Restaurant* has pizzas and pasta for 40–55kr, fish dishes from 100kr. For a more upmarket culinary experience, at prices to match, try the *Stadsrestaurang* inside the *First Hotel Statt* on Oxtorgsgatan. The Chinese restaurant *Mandarin Palace*, in Köpmantorget, has *dagens rätt* for 53kr. For coffee and cakes, *TeWe's Konditori* on Köpmangatan can't be beaten. **Drinking** is best done at *Dino* on Oxtorgsgatan 17 or at the *King's Road Café* on Kungsgatan.

Hudiksvall

One of the oldest towns in Norrland, **HUDIKSVALL** was originally founded in 1582 around the Lillfjärden bay at the mouth of the River Hornån. At the beginning of the seventeenth century the harbour silted up and Hudiksvall was forced to move to its present location. An important commercial and shipping centre, it bore the brunt of the Russian attacks on the northeast Swedish coast in 1721 and to this day its church is pockmarked with cannon holes; every other building was razed to the ground. The oldest part of the city is split into two main sections. Turn right out of the train station and cross the narrow canal, Strömmingssundet (Herring Sound), and you'll soon see the small old **harbour** on the right. This area is known as **Möljen**, and is a popular place for locals to while away a couple of hours in the summer sunshine along the wharfside flanked by a line of red wooden fishermen's cottages and storehouses. The back of the warehouses hide a run of bike and boat repair shops, handicraft studios and the like.

More impressive and much larger than Möljen, **Fiskarstan** (Fishermen's Town), down Storgatan beyond the *First Hotel Statt*, contains neat examples of the so-called "Imperial" wood-panel architecture of the late eighteenth and nineteenth centuries. It was in these tightly knit blocks of streets with their fenced-in plots of land that the fishermen used to live during the winter. Take a peek inside some of the little courtyards – all window boxes and cobblestones. The history of these buildings is put into perspective in the excellent **Hälsinglands Museum** (Tues, Thurs & Fri 9am–4pm, Wed 9am–8pm, Sat & Sun 11am–3pm; 20kr, free on Sat) on Storgatan, which traces the development of Hudiksvall as a harbour town. Have a look at the paintings by **John Sten** upstairs: born near Hudiksvall, his work veered strangely from Cubism to a more decorative and fanciful style.

The best time to visit Hudiksvall is July 5–21, when the town hosts the **Musik vid Dellen**, a multifarious cultural festival including folk music and other traditional events; information and tickets from the tourist office.

Practicalities

Hudiksvall's **train** and **bus stations** are conveniently located opposite each other, and it's just two minutes' walk along the main road to the town centre. The **tourist office** (mid-June to mid-Aug Mon–Fri 9am–7pm, Sat & Sun 10am–5pm; mid-Aug to mid-June Mon–Fri 9am–4pm; ☎0650/191 00, *turist@hudiksvall.se*, *www.hudiksvall.se*) is behind the old warehouses near the wharf. As for **accommodation**, the *First Hotel Statt* at Storgatan 36 (☎0650/150 60, fax 960 95; ④/②) is the priciest hotel in town, though good value in midsummer, or there's the cheaper *Hotell Temperance* near the station at

Håstagatan 16 (☎ & fax 0650/311 07; ②/①). The nearest **youth hostel** (☎0650/132 60) is located out at the Malnbaden **campsite**, 3km from town – bus #5 runs there hourly (10am–6pm) in summer; otherwise you'll need to take a taxi from the bus station (80kr each way). Sited on the bay, it has a large sandy beach and offers bike rental.

Oddly enough, Hudiksvall has fewer **eating and drinking** opportunities than smaller Söderhamn. The one and only **bar** in town is the *Pub Tre Bockar* at Bankgränd, opposite the fishermen's warehouses at Möljen. A popular eating place is *Bolaget* at Storgatan 49, with main dishes at around 85kr, pizzas at 45kr. Alternatively, try the smarter *Le Bistro* on Hamngatan, which has a 3–10pm happy hour for food and drink, or the town's top restaurant, *Stadts Bar o Kök*, attached to *First Hotel Statt* on Storgatan.

Sundsvall

The capital of the tiny province of Medelpad, **SUNDSVALL**, known as "Stone City", is immediately and obviously different. Once home to a rapidly expanding nineteenth-century sawmill industry, the whole city burned to the ground in June 1888, and nine thousand people lost their homes. Rebuilding began at once, and within ten years a new centre constructed entirely of stone had emerged. The result is a living document of early twentieth-century urban architecture, based around wide esplanades intended to serve as fire breaks and designed and crafted by the same architects who were involved in rebuilding Stockholm's residential areas at the same time. However, the reconstruction was achieved at a price: the workers who had laboured on the new stone buildings were shifted from their homes in the centre and moved south to a poorly serviced suburb, highlighting the glaring difference between the wealth of the new centre and the poverty of the surrounding districts.

Arrival, information and accommodation

From the **train station** it's a five-minute walk to the city centre: turn left and go under the road bridge. The helpful **tourist office** (June–Aug Mon–Fri 10am–6pm, Sat & Sun 10am–3pm; Sept–May Mon–Fri 11am–4pm; ☎060/67 18 00) is in the main square, Storatorget. The **bus station** is at the bottom of Esplanaden, though if you want information or advance tickets for the express buses south to Stockholm, north to Örnsköldsvik or inland to Östersund, visit Y-Bussen at Sjögatan 7 (☎060/17 19 60). For other bus information contact the tourist office. The airport is 20km north of town, linked by an airport bus to connect with flights to and from Stockholm.

There's no shortage of reasonably priced **hotels** in Sundsvall. For budget accommodation, try the slightly grotty **youth hostel** (☎060/61 21 19, fax 61 78 01) a 30min walk from town at Norra Berget, the mountain overlooking the city. The nearest **campsite**, *Fläsians Camping* (☎060/55 44 75; May to mid-Sept), also has cabins for 200–400kr for up to four people; it's outside town – ask at the tourist office for directions.

Hotels

Baltic, Sjögatan 5 (☎060/15 59 35, fax 12 45 60). Centrally located near the Kulturmagasinet and the harbour, with perfectly adequate rooms. ④/②.

Continental, Rådhusgatan 13 (☎060/15 00 60, fax 15 75 90). A fairly cheap hotel centrally located with all rooms en suite. Sun terrace and cable TV. ③/②.

First Hotel Strand, Strandgatan 10 (☎060/12 18 00, fax 61 92 02). The smartest hotel in town; there are 200 rooms, an indoor pool and a wicked breakfast buffet. ⑤/③.

Good Morning, Trädgårdsgatan 31–33 (☎060/15 06 00, fax 12 70 80). Worth trying if the other cheap hotels are full. All rooms en suite and some have a bath. ②/①.

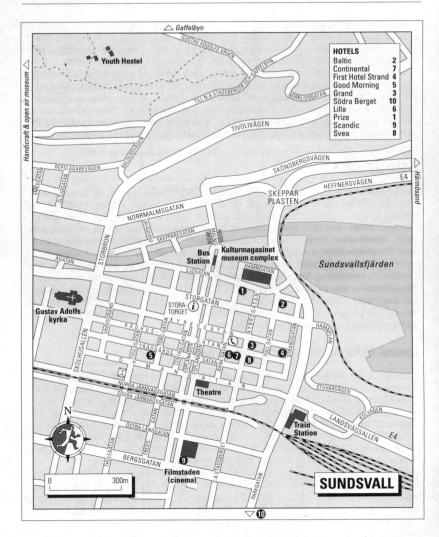

Grand, Nybrogatan 13 (☎060/64 65 60, fax 64 65 65). Not a bad choice if you get the summer or weekend reduction, and there's an excellent sauna and jacuzzi suite in the basement. ④/②.

Lilla, Rådhusgatan 15 (☎060/61 35 87). One of the cheapest hotels in town, with just eight rooms, all en suite and with cable TV. ②/①.

Prize, Sjögatan 11 (☎060/15 07 20). Mid-range hotel each of whose comfortable rooms is named after a particular village in the province of Medelpad. ③/②.

Scandic Hotel Sundsvall City, Esplanaden 29 (☎060/17 16 00, fax 12 20 32). International hotel boasting eight cinemas, saunas, sunbeds and a golf simulator, with prices to match the opulence. ⑤/③.

Södra Berget, on the hill south of the city (☎060/67 10 00, fax 67 10 10). Popular in winter with skiers, this has fantastic views, plus solarium, steam room and a jacuzzi. Good value in summer. ⑤/②.

Svea, Rådhusgatan 11 (☎060/61 16 05). The cheapest hotel in Sundsvall, but its ten rooms soon fill up in summer. ②/①.

The City

The sheer scale of the rebuilding that followed the fire of 1888 is clear as you walk into town from the train station. The style is simple, uncluttered limestone and brick, the dimensions often overwhelming, with palatial four- and five-storey houses, most of which served as offices as well as homes. As you stroll the streets you can't help but be amazed by the tremendous amount of space right in the heart of the city – it's hard to believe that Sundsvall is the most densely populated city in northern Sweden.

Several of the buildings in the centre are worth a second look, not least the sturdy bourgeois exterior of the **Sundsvall Museum** (Mon–Thurs 10am–7pm, Fri 10am–6pm, Sat & Sun 11am–4pm; June–Aug 20kr, Sept–May free), housed within four nineteenth-century warehouses down by the harbour. The buildings stood empty for twenty years before being turned into what's now the **Kulturmagasinet** (Culture Warehouse), comprising the museum, a library and a café. Magasinsgatan, an old street complete with railway tracks, still runs between the warehouses, a reminder of the days when coffee and rice were transported to the harbour for export. Inside, the regional museum is worth a quick look, as is the nearby art exhibition. Towards the other end of town, follow the main pedestrian street, Storgatan to its far end and you'll come across **Gustav Adolfs kyrka** (daily: June–Aug 11am–4pm; Sept–May 11am–2pm), which marks one end of the new town, a soaring red-brick structure whose interior resembles a large Lego set.

Beyond the city's design, the most attractive diversion is the tiring three-kilometre climb to the heights of **Gaffelbyn**, the hill that overlooks the city to the north; walk up Storgatan, cross over the main bridge and follow the sign to the youth hostel. If you'd prefer to spare your legs, buses for Norra Berget will take you there. The view on a clear day is fantastic, giving a fresh perspective on the city's planned structure and the restrictive nature of its location, hemmed in on three sides by hills and the sea. From here you can see straight across to Södra Berget, the southern hill, with its winter ski slopes. Also here is the **Norra Bergets Hantverks och Friluftsmuseum** (June–Aug Mon–Fri 9am–4pm, Sat & Sun 11am–3pm; Sept–May Mon–Fri 9am–4pm; free), an open-air handicrafts museum with the usual selection of twee wooden huts and assorted activities, though you can try your hand at baking some *tunnbröd*, the thin bread that's typical of northern Sweden.

Eating, drinking and entertainment

Over the last couple of years **restaurants** have mushroomed in Sundsvall, and you'll find a good choice – something you may want to make the most of if you're heading further north. The town's **bars** generally have a good atmosphere, though nightclubs are rather thin on the ground.

Cafés and restaurants

Åhlénsrestaurangen, inside the Åhléns department store on Storgatan. Good lunchtime vegetarian buffet.

Athena restaurang och pizzeria, Köpmangatan 7. All the Greek favourites from tzatziki to souvlakia, as well as pizzas, from 100kr.

Cactus, Trädgårdsgatan 17, just off Esplanaden. Mexican food including chicken enchilladas and nachos from 100kr.

Café Charm, branches at Storgatan 34 and in Världshuset shopping centre on Sjögatan. A good choice for coffee and cakes, with free refills and naughty-but-nice cream concoctions.

China Restaurant, Esplanaden, near bus station. Dishes from 72kr to eat in or take away.
La Spezia, Sjögatan 6. Perfectly acceptable bargain-basement pizzas from 35kr.
Restaurang Sevilla, Rådhusgatan 7. Spanish food, including a reasonable selection of moderately priced tapas.
Saigon Palace, Trädgårdsgatan 5. Vietnamese and Chinese restaurant, handily placed for the train station with some well-priced dishes, including lunch for 50kr and chicken in peanut sauce for 89kr.
Skeppsbrokällaren, next to *Hotell Baltic* on Sjögatan. Limited choice of meat and fish dishes plus a strong beer for 100kr.
Wayne's Coffee, Storgatan 13. Located in an atmospheric old building on the main drag, this is *the* coffee house in Sundsvall, with dozens of varieties of coffee and excellent sandwiches and cakes.

Bars and nightlife

Dublin, Nybrogatan 16. Irish pub with a broad selection of different beers, including Caffreys and Kilkennys, Irish food, music and darts.
Hoagy's, Strandgatan 10, in the *First Hotel Strand*. A tasteful piano bar, where well-oiled locals can be found rounding off an evening's boozing. It's open till 3am, with cheap beer during the 8–11pm happy hour.
JOP's, Trädgårdsgatan 35. Popular place for a mid-evening tipple.
Marley's, Sjögatan 25. Attracts a younger crowd with its dark corners and reggae music.
Mercat Cross, Esplanaden 27, in the Filmstaden complex. Scottish pub with staff in kilts serving just about every variety of whisky you can think of.
O'Bar, Bankgatan 11. Good, lively bar. Try the excellent cocktails, if your pocket can take the strain. Staff are happy to make up any concoction you can think of.
O'Leary's, Storgatan 40. Sports pub with a good choice of beer and pub grub with a Tex-Mex flavour. Big screens show the latest football and hockey matches.
Spegelbaren, Nybrogatan 10. One of the biggest bars in Norrland and a good place to start the evening off. Large glass mirrors, a glass ceiling and nineteenth-century paintings add to the atmosphere.

Listings

Airlines SAS ☎060/18 80 00; Skyways ☎060/18 80 10.
Airport Information on ☎060/18 80 10.
Banks Handelsbanken, Storgatan 23; Nordbanken, Kyrkogatan 15; SEB, Storgatan 19.
Bus enquiries ☎020/51 15 13.
Car rental Bilbolaget, Bultgatan 1 (☎060/18 08 00); Budget, at the airport (☎060/57 80 06).
Hospital Lasarettsvägen 19 (☎060/18 10 00).
Newspapers in English Sundsvall library in the Kulturmagasinet; or buy them from Sundsvalls Tobaksaffär, Storgatan 20B.
Pharmacy Storgatan 18 (Mon–Fri 9.30am–6pm, Sat 10am–3pm; ☎060/18 11 17).
Police Storgatan 37 (☎060/18 00 00).
Post office Köpmangatan 19 (☎060/19 60 00).
Systembolaget Torggatan 1 (Mon–Wed 10am–6pm, Thurs 10am–7pm, Fri 9.30am–6pm; ☎060/61 36 69).
Taxis Taxi Sundsvall (☎060/19 90 00).
Train enquiries ☎060/18 30 00.

Härnösand

From Sundsvall it's an hour's train trip north along the coast to **HÄRNÖSAND**, a pleasant little place at the mouth of the River Ångerman. Founded in 1585, the town has had its fair share of disasters – two great fires in 1710 and 1714, followed by a thorough ransacking by invading Russians in 1721 – yet despite this it preserves a host of architectural delights, and is definitely worth a stop on the way north. Härnösand also marks the beginning of the stunningly beautiful province of Ångermanland, one of the few areas in Sweden where the countryside resembles that of neighbouring Norway, with its low mountains, craggy coastlines and long fjords reaching far inland. The town is a good base from which to explore the nearby High Coast (see p.558), or from which to head inland to connect with the main train line north at Långsele.

The Town and around

For such a small and provincial place, the proud civic buildings of Härnösand reek of grandeur and self-importance. The town centre is on the island of **Härnön**, and its main square, **Stora Torget**, was once chosen by local worthies as the most beautiful in Sweden. From the square, take a stroll up Västra Kyrkogatan to the Neoclassical **Domkyrkan** (daily 10am–4pm), which dates from the 1840s, though it incorporates bits and pieces from earlier churches which stood on the site (the Baroque altar is eighteenth-century, as are the VIP boxes in the nave). The building is notable both for being the smallest cathedral in Sweden, and the only one which is white.

Turn right from here and follow the road round and back down the hill until you come to the narrow old street of **Östanbäcksgatan**, with its painted wooden houses that date back to the 1700s. For a taste of the town's architectural splendour, take a walk up the main street, **Nybrogatan**, where the grand building with the orange facade that houses the Länsstyrelsen (County Administration) and Mitt Sverige Turism (a good source of information on the High Coast; see p.558) is particularly beautiful. From the top of the hill here some good views can be had back over the town and the water.

Nearby beaches and the Murberget open-air museum

The long, sandy **beaches** in nearby **Smitingen**, fifteen minutes away by bus #14 (4 daily from the bus station) are regarded as some of the best in Norrland. Closer to town, there are pebble beaches near the *Sälstens* campsite. Continue round the coast from here and you'll eventually reach the **open-air museum** (June–Aug daily 11am–5pm; free) at **Murberget**, the second biggest in Sweden after Skansen (see p.403). Bus #2 runs there hourly from Nybrogatan in front of the Rådhuset. Around eighty buildings have been transplanted here, including traditional Ångermanland farmhouses and the old Murberg church which is popular for local weddings. The worthy exhibits in the nearby **County Museum** (Länsmuseet; daily 11am–5pm; free) demonstrate how people settled the area two thousand years ago, alongside desperately dull displays of birds' feet, silver goblets and spectacles from more modern times, and a collection of armoury.

Practicalities

The **tourist office** (June–Aug Mon–Fri 8am–6pm, Sat & Sun 10am–2pm; Sept–May Mon–Fri 8am–5pm; ☎0611/881 40, *turistinfo@ebox.tninet.se, www.turism.harnosand.se*) is near the train station at Järnvägsgatan 2, inside the building marked Spiran, where the helpful staff can advise on transport and accommodation in the area. Härnösand's **youth hostel** (☎0611/104 46; mid-June to early Aug), where you're likely to get your own self-contained apartment, is a fifteen-minute walk from the centre up Nybrogatan and then left. The nearby **Sälstens Camping** (☎0611/181 50) is around 2km from the centre, next to a string of pebble beaches; it also has a small selection of four-bed cabins for 250kr per night and rents out bikes to guests. Of the town's three **hotels**, *Hotell Royal*, close to the train station at Strandgatan 12 (☎0611/204 55; ③/②), is the cheapest, although *Hotell City* at Storgatan 28 (☎0611/277 00; ③/①) is only marginally more expensive at standard rates, and cheaper when discounted. The *First Hotell Härnösand*, Skeppsbron 9 (☎0611/105 10; ⑤/②), is much bigger and a lot plusher, but can be worth it in summer, when a double costs only 100–200kr more than in the other two hotels.

The town's most popular **pub-restaurant** is *Kajutan* on pedestrianized Storgatan, which links Stora Torget and Nybrogatan: the eat-all-you-can lunch goes for 89kr; otherwise reckon on 90kr for pasta, 140kr for meat dishes; beer costs from 30kr. If you feel like splashing out on some northern Swedish delicacies, *Restaurang Apothequet*, located in an old pharmacy at Nybrogatan 3, is the place: two courses go for 179kr, three courses for 209kr. Other eateries include the neighbouring *Nybrokällaren*, which serves lunch from 11am to 2pm; the popular pizzeria *Matverkstaden* at Storgatan 5; and the *Rutiga Dukan* café, near the cathedral at Västra Kyrkogatan 1, which does good-value lunches and delicious home-baked pastries and pies. For **drinking**, try the popular Scottish-theme pub *Highlander*, at Nybrogatan 5 (Tues–Sat evenings only).

North to Örnsköldsvik: the Höga Kusten

North of Härnösand as far as Örnsköldsvik is the **High Coast** (Höga Kusten), the beautiful stretch of Bothnian coastline characterized by rolling mountains and verdant valleys that plunge precipitously into the Gulf. The rugged shoreline is composed of sheer cliffs and craggy outcrops of rock, along with some peaceful sandy coves. Offshore are dozens of islands, some no more than a few metres in size, others much larger and covered with dense pine forest – it was on these that the tradition of preparing the foul-smelling *surströmming* (fermented Baltic herring) is thought to have first started. The coastline is best seen from the sea, and a trip out to one of the islands gives a perfect impression of the scale of things; however, it's also possible to walk virtually the entire length of the coast on the **Höga Kusten leden**, a long-distance hiking path that extends 130km from the Golden Gate-style bridge just north of Härnösand to Varvsberget in Örnsköldsvik.

There are two options for seeing the coast from Härnösand: either take one of the Norrlandskusten **buses** from the bus station for Örnsköldsvik – these pass through the tiny villages of Ullånger and Docksta (jumping-off points for the island of Ulvön) and skirt round the Skuleskogen National Park – or take the Norrlandskusten bus part of the way up the coast from Härnösand to Bönhamn (see p.574 for details), from where a small boat leaves for the island of Högbonden.

The islands

A trip out to the islands off the High Coast has to rank as the highlight of any trip up the Bothnian coast. Using a combination of buses and boats you can make your way to three of the most beautiful islands in the chain: **Högbonden**, **Ulvön** and **Trysunda**. Only Högbonden has connections to the mainland, which means doubling back on yourself a little to take the bus up the coast to reach the boat which sails out to Ulvön from Ullånger and Docksta.

Högbonden

After just ten minutes' boat ride from the mainland, the steep sides of the tiny round island of **Högbonden** rise up in front of you. There are no shops (bring all provisions with you), no hotels, no flush-toilets – in fact the only building on Högbonden is a lighthouse situated at the highest point on a rocky plateau where the pine and spruce trees have been unable to get a foothold. The lighthouse has now been converted into a youth hostel (☎0613/230 05; mid-May to end-Sept, groups only outside mid-June to mid-Aug), with stunning views and just thirty beds. To make the most of it you need to stay a couple of nights, exploring the island's gorge and thick forest by day, and relaxing in the traditional wood-burning **sauna** down by the sea in the evenings.

To **get there**, take the 11.55am Luleå-bound bus from Härnösand, get off at Gallsäter and get the bus to Nordingrå, then change again to get to Börhamn, from where the *M/F Högbonden* (mid-June to mid-Aug daily every two hours 10am–6pm; 60kr return) makes the ten-minute trip out to the island. Tell the bus driver you're taking the boat over to Högbonden and he'll ring the skipper to ask him to wait for the bus; the same applies on the trip back to the mainland.

Ulvön

The largest island in the chain, **Ulvön** is really two islands: Norra Ulvön and, across a narrow channel, the uninhabited Södra Ulvön. Before the last war Ulvön boasted the biggest fishing community along the High Coast but many islanders have since moved to the mainland, leaving around forty permanent residents.

All boats to the island dock at the main village, **Ulvöhamn**, a picturesque one-street affair with red-and-white cottages and tiny boathouses on stilts. The island's only **hotel**, *Ulvö Skärgårdshotell* (☎0660/22 40 09, fax 22 40 78; ③; May to mid-Oct), is at one end of the street, just to the right of where the *M/S Kusttrafik* from Ullånger and Docksta puts in. Walk a short distance to the left of the quay and you'll come to a tiny wooden hut that functions as a summer **tourist office** (mid-June to mid-Aug daily 11am–3.30pm; ☎0660/23 40 93) – you can also rent bikes here for 30kr for four hours. Continue and you'll soon reach a seventeenth-century fisherman's chapel, decorated with flamboyant murals; the road leading uphill to the right just beyond here leads to the **youth hostel** (☎0660/22 41 90; June to mid-Aug). Another 7km on is the old fishing village of **Sandviken**, now a minuscule holiday village renowned for its long sandy beach (*M/S Otilia II* to Örnsköldsvik also puts in here). Back in Ulvöhamn at the other end of the main street is the village shop; *M/F Ulvön* to Trysunda and Köpmanholmen leaves from the quay just in front, while *M/S Otilia II*, for Örnsköldsvik, docks just on the other side of the jetty. The shop also looks after the keys for the pine **cabins** on the island (☎0660/22 40 14 or 22 41 57).

To **get to Ulvön**, make your way to **Docksta** on the Norrlandskusten bus, from where *M/S Kusttrafik* (☎0613/105 50, *info@hkship.se*, *www.hkship.se*; 135kr same-day return) leaves daily from June to August at 10.15am, arriving in Ulvöhamn at 11.30am, and returning at 3pm. A year-round boat, the *M/F Ulvön*, runs to Trysunda and Ulvön from Köpmanholmen, fifteen minutes south of Örnsköldsvik: out of summer there's generally one departure daily, depending on ice – check at the tourist office. To get to Docksta from Högbonden, take the bus from Bönhamn via Nordingrå back to Gallsäter, where you can connect with the frequent Norrlandskusten buses that stop there on their way between Sundsvall and Umeå (for bus information, ring Din Tur on ☎020/51 15 13 or visit *www.dintur.se*). There are frequent bus services to Docksta **from Härnösand**. From late June to early August it's also possible to reach Ulvön from Örnsköldsvik on the *M/S Otilia II* (☎0660/22 34 31; 70kr single; 1 daily at 9.30am, returning 3pm).

Trysunda

Boats from Ulvön, just an hour away, dock in **Trysunda**'s narrow U-shaped harbour, around which curves the island's tiny village. This is the best preserved fishing village in Ångermanland: a charming little spot with forty or so red-and-white houses right on the waterfront and a seventeenth-century chapel with wonderful murals. The island's gently shelving rocks make it ideal for bathing and there's no shortage of secluded spots. Trysunda is also criss-crossed with walking paths leading through the gnarled and twisted dwarf pines. You can stay on the island in one of seven simple **rooms** (☎0660/430 11 or 430 38; ①; June–Sept) at the service building of the small marina at the harbour entrance. There's a kitchen and a sauna in the same building. **Getting here** from Ulvöhamn is simple: the *M/F Ulvön* (☎070/651 92 65; 40kr one-way) makes the trip at least once a day year round, before continuing on to **Köpmanholmen** back on the mainland (30kr; 50min), where there's a youth hostel (☎0660/22 34 96; May–Sept) plus regular buses to Örnsköldsvik.

The High Coast Trail and Skuleskogen

The **High Coast Trail** (Höga Kusten Leden) stretches 130km from Veda, near Härnösand, to Varvsberget, virtually in the centre of Örnsköldsvik, and is divided up into thirteen stages (each 7–12km long) with free overnight cabins. It takes in the magnificent **Skuleskogen National Park**, noted for its dense forests, coastal panoramas and sharp-edged ravines. The park is home to the unusual long-beard lichen *(Usnea longissima)*, which grows on spruce trees, as well as many varieties of bird, such as woodpecker (including the rare whitebacked woodpecker), capercaillie, hazel and black grouse, wren, coal tit and crested tit; other residents include elk, roe deer, lynx, fox, badger, ermine, marten, mink, mountain hare and squirrel. A number of well-marked paths lead through the park in addition to the trail. It's also possible to do some **climbing** in the park. Trails of varying difficulty lead up **Skuleberget** (285m) near Docksta, and anyone in reasonable shape can make it safely to the summit for some magnificent views. If you're out to do some serious climbing, you can rent equipment at Skule Naturum, on the route of buses between Härnösand and Örnsköldsvik. For more **information**, contact the tourist offices in Härnösand or Örnsköldsvik, who also sell a small map book about the High Coast for 40kr.

Örnsköldsvik

About 120km north of Härnösand beyond the High Coast lies the port of **Örnsköldsvik** (usually shortened to **Övik**), an ugly modern city stacked behind a superbly sheltered harbour. The town's only saving grace is its **museum** at Läroverksgatan 1 (mid-June to mid-Aug daily noon–4pm; mid-Aug to mid-June Tues–Sun noon–4pm; 10kr). From the long-distance bus station, walk up the steps on the other side of Strandgatan, which will bring you out on Storgatan, then continue east along either Läroverksgatan or Hamnagatan to get to the museum. Ignore the typical collections of prehistoric finds and dreadful nineteenth-century furniture and ask to be let into the adjacent workshop, which conceals an interesting account of the work of locally born artist, **Bror Marklund**. Most of his art was commissioned by public bodies: his *Thalia*, the goddess of the theatre, rests outside the City Theatre in Malmö, and his figures adorn the facade of the Historical Museum in Stockholm. Inside the workshop, look for the brilliantly executed jester plaster casts, one of Marklund's most easily identifiable motifs. The only other vaguely interesting thing to do in town is to take a stroll along the harbourside past the old warehouses and the impressive culture and business centre known as Arken.

Practicalities

Approaching Övik by **train**, you'll have to alight at Mellansel on the main line from Stockholm to Swedish Lapland, about 30km to the northwest; to get into town from here take one of the frequent buses. This is also the arrival and departure point for the Norrlandskusten **buses** that run along the coast between Sundsvall and Luleå, as well as services from Östersund (☎020/51 15 13, *www.dintur.se*). Boats to and from Ulvön dock at the Arken quay in front of the bus station along Strandgatan.

The **tourist office**, at Nygatan 18 (mid-June to mid-Aug Mon–Fri 9am–7pm, Sat 9am–3pm, Sun 10am–3pm; mid-Aug to mid-June Mon–Fri 10am–5pm; ☎0660/125 37 or 880 15, *turism@ovik.se, www.ovik.se*), can provide information on the High Coast islands. Budget **accommodation** options include the *Strand City Hotell*, right in the centre at Nygatan 2 (☎0660/106 10, fax 21 13 05; ③/①), a cheap and cheerful hostel-like establishment; and the small *Hotell Park* (☎0660/103 60, fax 21 17 79; ③/②) close to the swimming pool at Örnsköldsgatan 7. Best, however, is the plain and functional *Hotell Focus* up the hill at Lasarettsgatan 9 (☎0660/821 00, fax 838 67; ④/②). Don't be misled by the swanky exterior of the *First Hotell Statt* at Lasarettsgatan 2 (☎0660/101 10, fax 837 91; ⑤/③); its expensive rooms are down at heel and its fittings and decor Soviet-inspired. The **youth hostel** (☎0660/702 44) is 7km southwest of town in **Över-hörnäs** – take the bus marked Köpmanholmen and ask the driver to let you off.

For daytime **eating**, sandwiches and cakes are available from *Café Brittas II* in the pedestrianized Storgatan, or check out the snacks at *Brittas Delikatessen*, Skolgatan 4. For more substantial fare, head for the lively harbourside, where many restaurants have outside tables overlooking the waters of the Örnsköldsviksfjärden: try the brasserie-style *Arkenrestaurangen*, next to the harbour, where lunch costs 85kr and main dishes go for around 120kr. More upmarket are *StrandKaj 4*, also on the harbourside, serving up local delicacies from 89kr, and the nearby *Fina Fisken*, with fish dishes from 130kr, although lunch (recommended) is just 65kr. Of the pizzerias, the best are *Il Padrino* on Läroverksgatan, just off Stora Torget, and *Restaurangen Mamma Mia* on Storgatan. Off Storatorget, between Hemköp and the Sparbanken, is the *China Tower restaurangen*, which doubles as a pub. *Pub Nr. 1*, on the harbourside next to the *Arkenrestaurangen* restaurant, is the best place to go **drinking**, while for **nightlife** you're confined to *Hamncompagniet* on the corner of Viktoriaesplanaden and Strandgatan, a bar and disco popular with 18- to 25-year-olds.

Umeå

UMEÅ is the biggest city in northern Sweden, with a population of around 104,000. Demographically it's probably Sweden's most youthful city, with an average age of just 36, no doubt influenced by the presence of Norrland University and its 25,000 students. Strolling around the centre, you'll notice that those who aren't in pushchairs are pushing them, while the cafés and city parks are full of teenagers. With its fast-flowing river and wide, stylish boulevards, Umeå is a distinctly likeable city, and it's no bad idea to spend a couple of days here sampling some of the bars and restaurants – the variety of which you won't find anywhere else in Norrland.

Arrival, information and accommodation

It's a ten-minute walk from either the **train station** or **long-distance bus station** to the centre, down one of the many parallel streets that lead in the general direction of the river. The bus station will also be your point of arrival if you come to Umeå by Silja Line **ferry** from Vaasa in Finland – these dock at nearby Holmsund, from where connecting buses run to Umeå. A good first stop is the **tourist office** (mid-June to mid-Aug Mon–Fri 8am–7pm, Sat 10am–5pm, Sun 11am–5pm; mid-Aug to mid-June Mon–Fri 10am–6pm, Sat 10am–2pm; ☎090/16 16 16, *umeturist@umea.se, www.umea.se*) in the ugly concrete square of Renmarkstorget. The staff here are very helpful and dish out among other things a free newspaper with detailed listings; they also have a supply of **private rooms** from 150kr per night (booking fee 25kr). Umeå's bright and modern

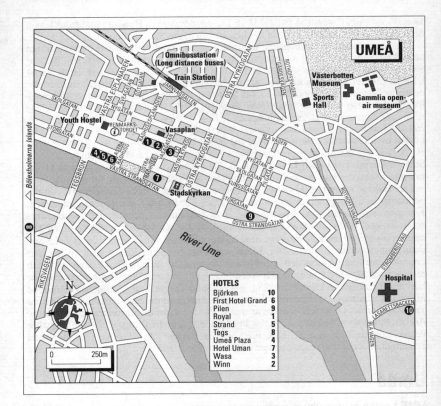

HOTELS	
Björken	10
First Hotel Grand	6
Pilen	9
Royal	1
Strand	5
Tegs	8
Umeå Plaza	4
Hotel Uman	7
Wasa	3
Winn	2

youth hostel (☎090/77 16 50, fax 77 16 95) is in the centre at Västra Esplanaden 10. The nearest **campsite** is the lakeside *Umeå camping stugby* (☎090/70 26 00, fax 70 26 10), 5km out of town on the E4 at Nydala; it also has **cabins** for four to six people for 610kr, individual double rooms in other cabins (250kr) and *trätält* (tiny two-bed huts) for 185kr per night; facilities include washing machines and bike rental. Take bus #2, #6, #7 or #82 (no service Sun), get off at Nydala and the campsite is about a five-minute walk towards Nydalabadet.

Hotels

Björken, Lasarettsbacken 10 (☎090/10 87 00). Next to the hospital, and popular with its patients, but with good-quality rooms. ④/②.

Comfort Home Hotel Uman, Storgatan 52 (☎090/12 72 20, fax 12 74 20). Home from home, with evening coffee and newspapers for all guests. ④/③.

First Hotel Grand, Storgatan 46 (☎090/77 88 70, fax 13 30 55). Newly renovated and rather chic, right in the heart of town. ④/③.

Pilen, Pilgatan 5 (☎090/14 14 60). One of the cheaper smaller hotels with clean and basic rooms, and weekend and summer doubles for 500kr. ③/②.

Provobis Umeå Plaza, Storgatan 40 (☎090/17 70 00, fax 17 70 50). Voted the fourth best hotel in Sweden, this is a very smart place to stay, with marble washbasins in the bathrooms and superb views from the sauna suite on the fourteenth floor with free light beer. Weekend and summer discounts make it worth the indulgence. ④/③.

Royal, Skolgatan 64 (☎090/10 07 30). Good, centrally located hotel with sauna, whirlpool and solarium. Cheap summer deals. ④/②.

Strand, Västra Strandgatan 11 (☎090/70 40 00, fax 12 18 40). Another low-budget but perfectly adequate hotel. ③/②.

Tegs, Verkstadsgatan 5 (☎090/12 27 00, fax 13 49 90). The cheapest hotel in town – in summer doubles are as little as 440kr – though it's south of the river and some way from the action. ②/①.

Wasa, Vasagatan 12 (☎090/77 85 40, fax 77 85 49). A comfortable hotel in a lively central location. ③/②.

Winn, Skolgatan 64 (☎090/71 11 11, fax 12 54 28). Close to the city bus station and good for nearby restaurants and bars. ④/②.

The City

Umeå is known as the "City of Birch Trees" for the trees that were planted along every street following a devastating fire in 1888. Most of the city was wiped out in the blaze, but rebuilding began apace, and two wide esplanades were constructed to act as firebreaks should a similar disaster occur again. You'll be hard pushed to find any of the original wooden buildings, but around the little park in front of the former **Rådhus**, lingering bits of c.1900 timber architecture still look out over the river responsible for the town's name: *uma* means "roar" and refers to the sound of the rapids along the River Ume, now put to use by the hydroelectric power station further upstream.

Umeå also offers one terrific museum complex, **Gammlia**, which merits a good halfday. The original attraction around which everything else developed is the **Open Air Museum** (Friluftsmuseum; late June to Aug daily 10am–5pm; free), an open-air group of twenty regional buildings, the oldest the seventeenth-century gatehouse on the way in. As usual, the complex is brought to life by people dressed in period costume – in the bakery you can watch them preparing traditional unleavened *tunnbröd* – while cows, pigs, goats, sheep and geese are kept in the yards and farm buildings. The main collection is housed in the indoor **Västerbotten Museum** (late June to Aug Mon–Fri 10am–5pm, Sat & Sun noon–5pm; Sept to mid-June Tues–Fri 9am–4pm, Sat noon–4pm, Sun noon–5pm; free): three exhibitions that canter through the county's development, from prehistory (including the oldest ski in the world, dated at 5200 years old) to the Industrial Revolution. It's all good stuff, well laid out and complemented by an array of videos and recordings, with a useful English guidebook available. Linked to the Västerbotten Museum is the **Pictorial Museum** (Bildmuseum; late June to Aug daily noon–5pm; Sept to mid-June Tues–Sat noon–4pm, Sun noon–5pm; free), which houses the university art collection, featuring contemporary Swedish work by artists such as Carl Larsson and Anders Zorn and a cobbledtogether set of old masters. Back outside, county history continues in the separate **Fish and Maritime Museum** (Fiske och Sjöfartsmuseum; late June to Aug daily noon–5pm; Sept to mid-June Tues–Sat noon–4pm, Sun noon–5pm; free), an attempt at a maritime museum which is really no more than a small hall clogged with fishing boats.

If you've a bike (see "Listings", overleaf, for rental details), it's a gentle day's cycle along the riverside cycle track (*Umeleden*) to Norrfors and its 5000-year-old rock carvings in the dried-up river bed. Back down the southern side of the river, the path leads past the massive hydroelectric station and **Bölesholmarna**, two islands that can also be reached easily on foot from the city centre in about fifteen minutes, an ideal spot for picnics and barbecues, as well as a quick dip in the small lake in the middle of the islands. The route is detailed on a free map available from the tourist office.

Eating and drinking

Eating and drinking possibilities are enhanced in Umeå by the number of students in the city: most of the restaurants can be found around the central pedestrianized Kungsgatan and Rådhusesplanaden. For a quick bite, the best **café** in town is *Konditori*

Mekka, close to the train station at Rådhusesplanaden 17, serving heavenly pastries and free coffee refills. Otherwise, try *Wayne's Coffee*, Storgatan 50, another branch of the highly successful chain currently sweeping Sweden; *Kafé Station*, Östra Rådhusgatan 2L, next to the Filmstaden cinema, with its rough brick walls and wooden floors; or on board the *Vita Björn*, the white boat moored down from the Rådhus.

Restaurants

Blå, corner of Rådhusesplanaden and Västra Norrlandsgatan. Stylish evenings-only restaurant popular with a young crowd for its summer eat-until-you-drop buffet at 99kr.

Great Eastern, Magasinsgatan 17, close to the railway and bus stations. Reputed to be the best Chinese restaurant north of Stockholm. Lunch for 60kr, evening chicken and beef dishes from 86kr.

K-A Svenssons kök och matsalar, Vasaplan. In an old, blue wooden bus station with 1960s design and check tablecloths. Small dishes for 79kr, fish, seafood or meat for 100kr. The service and the quality of food can vary.

Lottas Krog, Nygatan 22. A good place for lunch, with a 75kr special of entrecote and potatoes.

Restaurang Il Fratello, corner of Nygatan and Rådhusesplanaden. Probably the priciest place in town: reindeer, duck, sole, lamb from 250kr per head. The interior is mostly wood, with heavy tablecloths, delicate lighting and soft music.

Rex Bar och Grill, Rådhustorget. Probably the most popular – and stylish – place to eat in Umeå. Everything from spaghetti bolognaise (69kr) to reindeer noisettes in madeira sauce (168kr).

Sjöbris, boat moored off Västra Strandgatan at Kajplats 10. An excellent fish restaurant on board an old white fishing boat with dishes from 100kr.

Skytten, Järnvägstorget, near the train station. Two restaurants – an upmarket place and a cheaper brasserie – in one. Good choice of food at reasonable prices.

Listings

Airlines SAS at the airport (☎090/18 30 08); Braathens Malmö Aviation at the airport (☎090/10 62 80). For other airlines call the airport on ☎090/728 30 10.

Banks Föreningsbanken, Renmarkstorget 9; Handelsbanken, Storgatan 48; Nordbanken, Rådhusesplanaden 3; SEB, Kungsgatan 52; FöreningsSparbanken, Rådhustorget.

Bike Bike, Storgatan 38 (Mon–Fri 11am–6pm, Sat 11am–2pm); Cykel & Mopedhandlar'n, Kungsgatan 101 (Mon–Fri 9.30am–5.30pm, Sat 10am–1pm; ☎090/14 01 70); Oves Cykelservice, Storgatan 87 (Mon–Fri 8am–5pm, Sat 10am–2pm; ☎090/12 61 91). Count on around 50kr per day.

Bus enquiries Long-distance buses leave from the station at Järnvägstorget 2 (☎020/91 00 19, *www.lanstrafikeniac.se*); city buses from Vasaplan (☎090/16 22 50).

Newspapers in English English-language newspapers are sold at the Pressbyrån at the railway station, and at Press Stop, Skolgatan 51, or read them at the library (*stadsbiblioteket*) at Rådhusesplanaden 6.

Pharmacy Renmarkstorget 6 (☎090/77 05 41) or at the hospital, Norrlands Universitetssjukhus (☎090/785 00 00).

Police Ridvägen 10 (☎090/15 20 00).

FERRIES TO FINLAND

Silja Line operate a year-round service between Umeå and **Vaasa in Finland**, with a crossing time of around 4 hours – if you want to make the return journey as a day-trip it's usually possible to leave Umeå at 9am, returning on the 4.30pm sailing from Vaasa, but note that times vary depending on the time of year. The normal one-way fare is 340kr, 680kr return, though in summer (mid-June to mid-Aug) day returns go for 340kr. Boats sail from the port of **Holmsund**, southeast of Umeå; buses leave the long-distance bus station an hour before boat departures. Tickets and information from Silja Line in Renmarkstorget (Mon–Fri 9am–5pm; ☎090/71 44 00, *www.silja.se*).

Post office Vasaplan (Mon–Fri 8am–6pm, Sat 10am–2pm).
Systembolaget Kungsgatan 50A (Mon–Fri 10am–6pm); Vasagatan 11 (Mon–Fri 9.30am–6pm, Thurs until 7pm).
Taxis City Taxi (☎090/14 14 14); Taxi Lillebil (☎090/441 44); Taxi Umeorten (☎090/13 20 00); Umeå Taxi (☎090/77 00 00).
Train enquiries ☎090/15 58 00 or 020/75 75 75.

Skellefteå and around

"In the centre of the plain was Skellefteå church, the largest and most beautiful building in the entire north of Sweden, rising like a Palmyra's temple out of the desert." So enthused the nineteenth-century traveller Leopold von Buch, for there used to be a real religious fervour about **SKELLEFTEÅ**. In 1324 an edict in the name of King Magnus Eriksson invited "all those who believed in Jesus Christ or wanted to turn to Him" to settle between the Skellefte and Ume rivers. Many heeded the call and parishes mushroomed on the banks of the Skellefte. By the end of the eighteenth century a devout township was centred on the monumental church, which stood out in stark contrast to the surrounding plains and wide river. Nowadays more material occupations support the town, and the tourist office makes the most of modern Skellefteå's gold and silver refineries, while admitting that the town centre doesn't have much to offer: concentrate instead on the church and its nearby *kyrkstad*, or parish village.

Skellefteå's church and parish village, **Bonnstan**, are within easy striking distance of the centre: head west along Nygatan and keep going for about fifteen minutes. On the way you'll pass the **Nordanå Kulturcentrum**, a large and baffling assortment of buildings that's home to a theatre, a twee period grocer's shop (*lanthandel*) and a dire **museum** (Mon noon–7pm, Tues–Thurs 10am–7pm, Fri–Sun noon–4pm; free) containing three floors of mind-numbing exhibitions on everything from the region's first settlers to swords. Tucked away to the side of the *lanthandel* is *Nordanå Gårdens Värdshus*, a pleasant restaurant serving lunches for around 60kr.

Bonnstan's **kyrkstad** consists of five long rows of weatherbeaten log houses with battered wooden shutters (the houses are protected by law and any modernization is forbidden, including the installation of electricity). Take a peek inside, but bear in mind that they're privately owned by local people who use them as summer cottages. Beyond the parish village you'll find the **kyrka** (daily: mid-June to Aug 10am–6pm; Sept to mid-June 10am–4pm), a proud white Neoclassical building with four mighty pillars supporting the domed roof. Inside there's an outstanding series of medieval sculptures

PARISH VILLAGES

Parish villages – consisting of rows of simple wooden houses grouped tightly around a church – are common throughout the provinces of Västerbotten and Norrbotten. After the break with the Catholic Church in 1527, the Swedish clergy were determined to teach their parishioners the Lutheran fundamentals. Church services became compulsory: in 1681 it was decreed that those living within 10km of the church should attend every Sunday, those between 10km and 20km every fortnight and those between 20km and 30km every three weeks. Within a decade parish villages had appeared throughout the region to provide the travelling faithful with somewhere to spend the night after attending church. The biggest and most impressive is at Gammelstad near Luleå (see p.569), and another good example can be seen in Öjebyn near Piteå (p.566). Today they're no longer used in their traditional way, but many people still live in the old houses, especially in summer, and sometimes even rent them out to tourists.

including the 800-year-old Virgin of Skellefteå, a walnut carving near the altar and one of the few remaining Romanesque images of the Virgin in the world.

Practicalities

Skellefteå's small centre is based around a modern paved square flanked by Kanalgatan and Nygatan; at the top of the square is the **bus station** and a seasonal **tourist office** (end June to early Aug Mon–Fri 10am–7pm, Sat & Sun 10am–3pm; ☎0910/73 60 20, *skelleftea@turist.se*, *www.skelleftea.se*), which can provide all the usual information and help with accommodation. The main tourist office, in Mossgatan (Mon–Fri 8am–5pm; same number as above), handles enquiries out of season.

There are four central **hotels** to choose from: cheapest is the *Hotell Viktoria* at Trädgårdsgatan 8 (☎0910/174 70; ②/①), a family-run establishment on the top floor of a block on the south side of the main square; virtually next door at Torget 2, *Hotell Malmia* (☎0910/77 73 00, fax 77 88 16; ④) has perfectly adequate rooms and is also the centre of Skellefteå's nightlife; nearby at Stationsgatan 8 is the dingy *First Hotel Statt* (☎0910/141 40, fax 126 28; ④/②); the smartest hotel is the *Scandic* (☎0910/383 00; ④/③) at Kanalgatan 75, across Viktoriagatan. The **youth hostel**, at Elevhemsgatan 13 (☎0910/372 83; mid-June to mid-Aug) – a smart yellow building by the southern bank of the River Skellefte, half an hour's walk from the centre – is well worth seeking out. Head east on either Storgatan or Nygatan, turn right onto Viktoriagatan, cross the river over Viktoriabron and take the first left, Tubölegatan, to its end, then keep to the gravel path rather than the main road and the hostel is on the left. For **campers**, *Skellefteå campingplats* (☎0910/188 55) is 1500m north of the centre on Mossgatan, just off the E4; it also has **cabins** for 250kr per night for up to four people.

The best spot for **lunch**, if you can catch it when it's open, is *Urkraft*, at the corner of Nygatan and Tjärhovsgatan. Good cakes can be had at *Café Carl Viktor*, Nygatan 40, or the twee *Lilla Mari* at Köpmangatan 13. Skellefteå's **restaurants** aren't exactly impressive, though the restaurant on the veranda at the *Scandic Hotel* offers northern Swedish specialities for around 150kr. Among the usual cluster of pizzerias, the best are *Pizzeria Pompeii* at Kanalgatan 43, where pizzas cost 60kr, and *Pizzeria Dallas* at Köpmangatan 9, which serves fourteen different varieties at 35kr. **Drinking** is best done at *MB* (Malmiabaren) in the *Hotell Malmia* on the main square; in summer there's outdoor seating and a lively atmosphere.

North from Skellefteå: Piteå

With no train station – the nearest is at Bastuträsk (4 buses daily) – the easiest way to continue north from Skellefteå is by using one of the frequent Norrlandskusten **buses**, which stop in the small town of **PITEÅ** before terminating in Luleå.

Located in Sweden's most northerly county, Norrbotten, Piteå's history goes back to the beginning of the fourteenth century, when it was situated at what is today the nearby village of **Öjebyn**. When granted its town charter in 1621, the town was still situated 20km west of its current location, but an extensive fire razed much of the settlement and the decision was taken to up sticks and move to the coast. Modern Piteå is an anodyne mix of squares and pedestrianized shopping streets, as well as being home to one of Sweden's biggest paper producers, and the sole reason to stop here is to visit the parish village, **Öjebyns kyrkstad**, 6km out of town (bus #1 runs there hourly until 4.15pm from the bus station at the end of pedestrianized Prästgårdsgatan). The village's small wooden cottages, grouped around a fifteenth-century stone church on Kyrkovägen, are privately owned, and most of them still have no electricity. Debate continues as to whether this parish village is the oldest in Sweden – a title that's also claimed by nearby Luleå's parish village.

Practicalities

If you want to stay, the **tourist office** at Noliagatan 1 (June–Aug Mon–Sat 9am–8pm, Sun noon–8pm; Sept–May Mon–Fri 8am–5pm; ☎0911/933 90, *pitea.turistbyra@swipnet.se, www.pitea.se*) can fix up **private rooms** for 200–600kr per person per night. Other than that you're looking at the town's two **hotels**, the comfortable, olde-worlde *Stadshotellet* at Olof Palmes gata 1 (☎0911/197 00, fax 122 92; ④/③), or the less characterful *Skoogs City Hotell*, off the main square at Uddmansgatan 5 (☎0911/100 00, fax 100 01; ③/②). The **youth hostel** (☎0911/158 80) is located in the old hospital 2km out of town at Storgatan 3. For **eating**, your best bet is *Pentryt* at Sundsgatan 29 (closed Fri), which has lunch deals for around 50kr – it serves food until 8pm then mutates into a bar and disco. Another reasonable choice is *Pigalle*, across the road at Sundsgatan 36. The best pizzeria is *Ängeln*, at Källbogatan 2. **Drinking** dens can be found downstairs at the *Stadshotellet* in the *Cockney Pub*, and at the popular *Karls Källa*, where beer costs slightly less, in Sundsgatan.

Luleå

Last stop on the Norrlandskusten bus line, **LULEÅ** lies at one end of the Malmbanan, the iron-ore railway that connects the ice-locked Gulf of Bothnia with the ice-free Norwegian port of Narvik in the Norwegian Sea. The town's wide streets and lively atmosphere have an immediate appeal, making this a much better stopoff than nearby Boden (see p.570), 25 minutes down the train line. If you're heading north for the wilds of the Torne valley, Gällivare and Kiruna, or indeed to the sparsely populated regions inland, it's a good idea to spend a day or so here enjoying the sights and the impressive range of bars and restaurants: Luleå is the last oasis in a frighteningly vast area of forest and wilderness spreading north and west.

Luleå was founded in 1621 around the medieval church and parish village of nearby Gammelstad (meaning Old Town; see p.569). Even in those days trade with Stockholm was important, and Gammelstad's tiny harbour soon proved inadequate to the task. In 1649, by royal command, the city was moved lock, stock and barrel to its present site – only the church and parish village remained. Shipping is still an important part of the local economy, but over recent years Luleå has become the high-tech centre of northern Sweden, specializing in metallurgy, research and education.

Arrival, information and accommodation

The **train** and **bus** stations are about five minutes' walk apart at one end of the grid of parallel streets that make up the city centre. Luleå's **tourist office** is a good ten minutes away in the Kulturcentrum Ebeneser at Storgatan 43B (mid-June to mid-Aug Mon–Fri 9am–7pm, Sat & Sun 10am–4pm; mid-Aug to mid-June Mon–Fri 10am–6pm, Sat 10am–2pm; ☎0920/29 35 00 or 29 35 05, *turistbyra@lulea.se, www.norrbotten.se*). Ask here about boat trips to some of the hundreds of mostly uninhabited islands in the archipelago off the coast.

The tourist office has a very small number of **private rooms** for about 200kr per person. Unfortunately, the nearest **youth hostel** (☎0920/25 23 25, fax 25 24 19), fifteen minutes out at **Gäddvik** (Pike Bay), is too close to the main E4 for a quiet night's sleep; to get there, take hourly bus #6 from outside the train station and tell the bus driver to let you off at the hostel. The nearest **campsite** (☎0920/25 00 60), also reached on bus #6, is another five minutes on from the hostel.

Hotels

Amber, Stationsgatan 67 (☎0920/102 00, fax 879 06). Small and cosy family-run place in an old wooden building near the train station. ④/②.

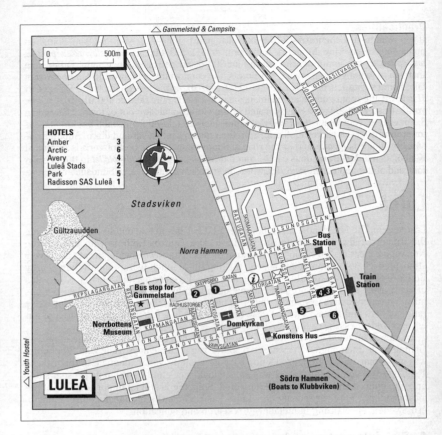

Arctic, Sandviksgatan 80 (☎0920/109 80, fax 607 87). A smart little hotel with en-suite rooms and very handy for the train station. ⑤/②.

Aveny, Hermelinsgatan 10 (☎0920/22 18 20). Small, modern and comfortable hotel, with reasonable prices in summer. ④/②.

Park, Kungsgatan 10 (☎0920/21 11 49). The cheapest of Luleå's hotels, basic but perfectly adequate, with doubles (not en suite) in summer for just 400kr. ③/①.

Provobis Luleå Stads, Storgatan 15 (☎0920/670 00, fax 670 92). The oldest and smartest of the city's hotels, right in the centre of town, with tasteful, old-fashioned rooms and a huge breakfast buffet. ⑤/③.

Radisson SAS Luleå, Storgatan 17 (☎0920/940 00). A modern hotel with heavy colours and gloomy wooden interiors. Not worth the money, though it might have rooms if the city's other hotels are full. ⑤/③.

The City

There's only really one main street, the long **Storgatan**, south of which, past the main square, Rådhustorget, is the **Domkyrkan**. The medieval original disappeared centuries ago and the current edifice, built in 1893, contains a modern barrage of copper chandeliers hanging like Christmas decorations. Walking west up Köpmangatan from the

Domkyrkan you'll find the **Norrbotten Museum** (Mon–Fri 10am–4pm, Sat & Sun noon–4pm; free) at Storgatan 2. Among the usual dull resumé of county history are some good displays on the Sami culture that begins to predominate northwest of Luleå. Just south of the Domkyrkan, **Konstens Hus**, at Smedjegatan 2, (Tues, Thurs & Fri 11am–6pm, Wed 11am–8pm, Sat & Sun noon–4pm; free) is worth a look for some interesting works by local and not-so-local artists and sculptors.

If the weather's good, the next stop should be the **Gültzauudden** – a wooden promontory with a sandy beach; its odd name derives from the German shipbuilder, Christian Gültzau, who helped to make Luleå a shipbuilding centre. For more room to stretch out, you're better off taking the *M/S Stella Marina* out to the island of **Klubbviken**, the prettiest of the score of tiny islets that lie in the archipelago offshore. Here you'll find an enormous sandy beach and enough privacy to satisfy even the most solipsistic of souls. Boats leave from the southern harbour (Södra Hamnen) from the end of June to early August; information from the tourist office or on ☎0920/22 38 90 or 010/225 07 61 (mobile).

Gammelstad

The original settlement of Luleå, **GAMMELSTAD**, is 10km northwest of the city centre. When the town moved to the coast a handful of the more religious stayed behind to tend the church, and the attached **parish village** remained in use. One of the most important places of historical interest north of Uppsala, the site is set to become the latest addition to the UNESCO World Heritage List. The church itself (June–Aug Mon–Fri 8am–5pm, Sat 8am–2pm, Sun 8am–5pm; Sept–May Mon–Fri 10am–2pm) was completed at the end of the fifteenth century and adorned with the work of church artists from far and wide: both the decorated choir stalls and the ornate triptych are medieval originals, while the sumptuous pulpit is a splendid example of Bothnian Baroque, trimmed with gilt cherubs and red and gold bunches of grapes. Look out for the opening above the south door, through which boiling oil was generously poured over unwelcome visitors.

Around 450 cottages are gathered around the church, making this the biggest parish village in Sweden, though nowadays they're unoccupied except during important religious festivals. Guided walks can be arranged with Gammelstad's **tourist office** (mid-June to mid-Aug daily 9am–6pm; mid-Aug to mid-June Mon–Fri 11am–4pm; ☎0920/25 43 10, *worldheritage.gammelstad@lulea.se*), located in one of the cottages. Down the hill from the tourist office is the **Hägnan Open-Air Museum** (Friluftsmuséet Hägnan; June to mid-Aug daily noon–5pm), an open-air heritage park whose main exhibits are two old farmstead buildings from the eighteeenth century. During the summer there are demonstrations of rural skills such as sheep husbandry, the crafting of traditional wooden roof slates and the baking of *tunnbröd*, northern Sweden's unleavened bread.

Getting to Gammelstad from Luleå is straightforward. **Bus** #32 operates from June to August (Mon–Fri every 30min, reduced service at weekends); buses #8 and #9 run every half-hour outside the summer period. Services leave from Hermelinsparken, at the west end of Skeppsbrogatan.

Eating and drinking

While the restaurants on Storgatan may be a little pricier than those in the side streets, you'll probably find that the extra kronor are worth it for the livelier atmosphere. As usual, you can happily do an evening's drinking in the restaurants listed below.

Ankaret, Köpmangatan 16, near the Domkyrkan. Delicious fish dishes from 100kr make this a deservedly popular place.

Cook's Krog, inside *Radisson SAS Luleå* hotel at Storgatan 17. An intimate and cosy place to enjoy the best steak in Luleå, cooked over a charcoal grill for around 200kr.

Fiskekyrkan, in Södra Hamnen. One of the cheaper restaurants in town, with pasta and other simple dishes for around 100kr. Walk down Nygatan, cross Sandviksgatan, and it's located in the orange warehouse building by the sea. Popular drinking hole in the evenings.

Margaretas Wärdshus, Lulevägen 2 in Gammelstad. Fine food, including Norrbotten delicacies, served in a beautiful old wooden house close to the old church.

O'Leary's, Skomakargatan 22. Tex-Mex food for around 120kr and a good choice of beer. Definitely *the* place to watch the summer sun set over the northern harbour from the adjoining terrace.

Oliver's Inn, Storgatan 11. Pub grub and a good selection of beer. Known for its 1970s and 1980s music, which attracts a large crowd at weekends.

Pasta Restaurangen, Magasinsgatan 5. Hefty pizzas from around 60kr, but reckon on the place being pretty empty.

Pimpinella, Storgatan 40. The liveliest bar in town, with good-value food and tables out in the street during summer catering to a young crowd with attitude.

Restaurang Corsica, Nygatan. Dark and dingy interior but good for a change, with some traditional Corsican dishes, along with lots of steak and pizzas.

Tegel, Storgatan 27. Another of Luleå's attitude bars. Wear your sharpest clothes, darkest shades and sip a chilled foreign beer before going clubbing. Predictably stylish – yet surprisingly good value – menu.

Waldorf, inside the Wasa City shopping centre at Storgatan 33. Renowned for its pizzas (from 60kr), and also serves Chinese and Japanese food.

Listings

Airlines Aeroflot, contact the airport (☎0920/58 71 00); SAS, close to the bus station on Storgatan (☎0920/24 31 00).

Airport Kallax airport (☎0920/58 71 00), 10km from the city; buses from the bus station (40kr); taxis 145kr. Direct flights to Gällivare, Kiruna, Sundsvall and Umeå with Skyways; Östersund and Umeå with Swedeways; Stockholm Arlanda with SAS and Braathens Malmö Aviation (Arlanda and Bromma); also to Murmansk and Arkhangelsk in Russia with Aeroflot.

Banks Handelsbanken, Storgatan, between the *Provobis Luleå Stads* hotel and tourist office; Nordbanken, Köpmangatan.

Bus enquiries City bus times on ☎0920/24 11 00; long-distance bus information on ☎020/47 00 47, or visit *www.ltnbd.se*.

Car rental Avis, Kallax airport (☎0920/22 83 55); Budget, Robertviksgatan 3 (☎0920/131 11); Hertz, Gammelstadsvägen 23 (☎0920/873 44); Englunds Hyrcenter, Hummergatan 8 (☎0920/24 44 74); Europcar, Kallax airport (☎0920/101 65); Statoil, Stationsgatan 30 (☎0920/186 22).

Hospital Luleå Lasarett, Repslagaregatan 6–8 (☎0920/710 00).

Pharmacy Köpmangatan 36c (Mon–Fri 9am–6pm, Sat 9am–2pm, Sun 1–4pm).

Police Skeppsbrogatan 37 (☎0920/29 50 00).

Post office Storgatan 53 (Mon–Fri 8am–6pm, Sat 10am–2pm).

Systembolaget Köpmangatan (Mon–Fri 10am–6pm, Thurs until 7pm).

Taxis Taxi Luleå (☎0920/100 00); 6:ans Taxi (☎0920/666 66); Taxi Kurir (☎0920/22 26 66).

Train station Prästgatan. For train times call ☎0920/22 23 33 or 020/75 75 75.

Boden

Twenty-five minutes by train from Luleå, **BODEN** is a major transport junction for the entire north of the country; from here trains run northwest to Gällivare and Kiruna and eventually on to Narvik in Norway, south to Stockholm and Gothenburg, and east to Haparanda and across the border to Tornio in Finland. Its strategic location means that in summer Boden's tiny train station can be filled with backpackers; if you've got time, it's well worth stepping out into the town.

Boden's position, roughly halfway along the coast of Norrbotten at the narrowest bridging point along the Lule River, was no doubt one of the reasons that the **Överluleå kyrka** (daily: mid- to late June & early Aug 1–7pm; rest of the year 10am–2pm) and its **parish village** were founded here in 1826. The church is a twenty-minute walk from the train station, down the modest main street, **Kungsgatan**, over the bridge and right along Strandplan – it impresses most by its location, perched on a hillock overlooking the water, surrounded by whispering birch trees. The surrounding cottages of the parish village once spread down the hill to the lake, Bodträsket, complete with their stables and narrow little alleyways. Nowadays they're rented out as superior **hostel accommodation** during the summer (see below).

Today Boden is Sweden's largest military town and everywhere you look you'll see spotty-faced young men kitted out in camouflage gear and black boots strutting purposefully (if somewhat ridiculously) up and down the streets; there are infantry, tank, artillery and air corps here. The first garrison was established in 1901 and a fortress completed in 1907. Atop a hill about 3km southeast of the centre – a forty-minute walk from the train station – is the hilltop fortress of **Svedjefortet** (June–Aug daily 11am–5pm; 20kr), offering good views of the town. Blasted out of the hill there's an underground section with old cannons from 1894 and 1917, plus a selection of military uniforms. On the southwest edge of town lies the **Garrison Museum** (Garnisonsmuséet; June–Aug daily 11am–4pm; free), proudly displaying the largest collection of military uniforms north of Stockholm.

Practicalities

Ask at the **tourist office** at the train station (June–Aug daily 8am–9pm; Sept–May Mon–Fri 9am–5pm; ☎0921/624 10, *bodens.turistbyra@boden.se*, *www.boden.se*) about staying in the **parish cottages** close to the church. Although these usually book up months in advance, particularly for July, it's always worth checking availability (☎0921/198 70). In June and August the cottages cost around 300kr for two people, 420kr for three or four, slightly more in July. The **youth hostel** (☎0921/133 35) is just 100m from the train station at Fabriksgatan 6. There are also dormitory beds at the cheap-and-cheerful *Standard Hotell*, at Stationsgatan 5 (☎0921/160 55, fax 175 58; dormitory beds 100kr, doubles ②), which is the first thing you'll see when coming out of the station building. For more comfort and style, there's *Hotell Bodensia* in the centre of town at Kungsgatan 47 (☎0921/177 10, fax 192 82; ④/③). The **campsite** (☎0921/624 07), a few minutes' walk from the church following the path along the lakeside to Björknäs, also has six-bed **cabins** (700kr per night), four-bed cottages (450kr per night) and rents **canoes** (30kr an hour, 150kr a day) and **bikes** (50kr a day).

Eating in Boden, you won't be overwhelmed by choice. For a solid meal, try *Panelen* at the station end of Kungsgatan, whilst finer food is served up across the road at the excellent and unexpectedly chic *Pär och Mickes Kök* at Kungsgatan 20. For pizza or pasta you're best off at *Restaurang Romeo* in the pedestrianized centre, with pizzas from 58kr. Opposite, *Café Ollé* at Drottninggatan 4 does a 50kr lunch deal and tasty open sandwiches. Boden's best **drinking** spots are *Oliver's Inn*, on Kungsgatan just before the bridge, and the oddly-named *Puben med stort P* ("Pub with a capital P") closer to the station at Kungsgatan 23.

Haparanda and around

Hard by the Finnish border and at the very north of the Gulf of Bothnia, **HAPARAN-DA** is hard to like. The train station sets the tone of the place – an austere and rather grand-looking building reflecting Haparanda's aspirations to be a major trading centre. That never happened, and walking up and down the streets around the main square, Torget, can be a pretty depressing experience. The signpost near the bus station doesn't help matters either, reinforcing the feeling that you're a very long way from anywhere: Stockholm is 1100km, the North Cape 800km, and Timbuktu 8386km.

To fully understand why Haparanda is so grim, you need to know a little history: the key is the neighbouring Finnish town of **Tornio** (Torneå in Swedish). From 1105 until 1809 Finland was part of Sweden and Tornio was an important trading centre, serving markets across northern Scandinavia. But things began to unravel when Russia attacked and occupied Finland in 1807; the Treaty of Hamina then forced Sweden to cede Finland to Russia in 1809 – thereby losing Tornio. It was decided that Tornio had to be replaced, and so in 1821 the trading centre of Haparanda was founded, on the Swedish side of the new border along the River Torne. However, it proved to be little more than an upstart compared to its neighbour across the water. Nearly two hundred years on, with Sweden and Finland both now members of the European Union, Haparanda and Tornio have declared themselves a "Eurocity" – one city made up of two towns from different countries.

There are only a couple of sights in town: the train station building from 1918 and the peculiar **Haparanda kyrka**, a monstrous modern construction that looks like a cross between an aircraft hangar and a block of flats topped off in dark-coloured copper. When the church was finished in 1963 it caused a public scandal and has even been awarded a prize for being the ugliest church in Sweden.

Practicalities

There are no **border formalities** and you can simply walk over the bridge to Finland and wander back whenever you like; it's worth remembering that Finland is an hour ahead of Sweden.

Haparanda's **tourist office** (June to mid-Aug Mon–Fri 8am–8pm, Sat & Sun 10am–8pm; mid-Aug to May Mon–Fri 8am–4pm; ☎0922/120 10, *info.tourism@haparanda.se*, *www.haparanda.se*) is actually in Finland, just over the bridge to Tornio in the Green Line Welcome Center. From June to August it's also possible to get basic information from the *Stadshotel* in the main square. Haparanda's **youth hostel** (☎0922/611 71) is a smart riverside place at Strandgatan 26 and has the cheapest beds in town, with good views across to Finland. Alternatively, there's the cheap-and-cheerful pension, *Resandehem*, in the centre of town at Storgatan 65B (☎0922/120 68; ①). *Haparanda Stadshotel*, at Torget 7 (☎0922/614 90, fax 102 23; ⑤/②), is the only **hotel** in town. The **campsite**, *Sundholmens Camping* (☎0922/618 01) is at the opposite end of town from the youth hostel at Järnvägsgatan 1 – walk along the river down Strandgatan, take a right onto Storgatan, cross the train lines and follow the signs. There are four-bed cabins here, too, for 270kr.

Tornio (see p.716) has many more **bars** and **restaurants** than its Swedish neighbour, so you may want to do what the locals do and nip over into Finland for a bit of high life, especially at the weekend. For **lunch**, try the plastic-looking *Prix Restaurant* at Norra Esplanaden 8, which charges 50kr; it's OK, if not particularly inspiring. Otherwise *dagens rätt* is also available from the restaurant at the youth hostel for 55kr, but your best bet is *El Paso Pizzeria* at Storgatan 88, close to Torget, which has lunch for 43kr. Lunch (61kr) and pizzas are also served at the Chinese restaurant *Lei-Lane*, Köpmangatan 15, as well as a range of Chinese and Thai dishes. *Nya Konditoriet* on Storgatan is good for coffee and cakes; for open sandwiches (16–28kr) try *Café Rosa* in the Gallerian shopping centre on Storgatan. For **drinking** in Haparanda head for the pub *Ponderosa* at Storgatan 82, or try the *Gulasch Baronen* pub attached to the *Stadshotel*.

MOVING ON FROM HAPARANDA

Swedish buses head north on the Swedish side of the border through the beautiful Torne valley to Pajala (Mon–Fri 3–4 daily, 1 on Sun), from where connections can be made to either Gällivare or Kiruna, or with a change at Vittangi to Karesuando. Alternatively, if you're heading on into Finland, Finnish buses connect Haparanda with Tornio and Kemi roughly every hour – times are displayed at the bus station in Haparanda. There's also a direct afternoon bus from Haparanda to Rovaniemi (Mon–Fri 1 daily; 3hr).

Around Haparanda: Kukkolaforsen

If you're stuck in Haparanda for a day or two, it's worth making the trip 15km north to **KUKKOLAFORSEN**. On the last weekend in July the impressive rapids here are the scene of the **Sikfesten** or Whitefish Festival. This local delicacy is caught in nets at the end of long poles, fishermen dredging the fast, white water and scooping the whitefish out onto the bank, then grilling them on large open fires. Originally a centuries-old fisherman's harvest festival, it's now largely an excuse to get plastered, with a beer tent, evening gigs and dancing the order of the day. It costs 100kr to get in on the Saturday, 60kr on the Sunday, although if you're staying in the adjacent campsite (☎0922/310 00, fax 310 30), which also has cabins (from 420kr), you should be able to sneak in for free.

River rafting down the rapids can also be arranged here, either through the campsite or at the tourist office in Haparanda – 180kr gets you the gear, helmet and life jacket, and pays for a short trip downriver plus a certificate at the end. Finally, the **sauna** at Kukkolaforsen has been declared the best in the country by the Swedish Sauna Academy; after boiling yourself in temperatures of over 100°C, step out onto the veranda with a cool beer, breathe the crisp air heavy with the scent of pine, and listen to the roar of the rapids. And don't forget to wave to Finland across the river.

travel details

Trains

Boden to: Gällivare (3 daily; 2hr); Gävle (2 daily; 11hr); Gothenburg (1 daily; 16hr); Haparanda (mid-June to mid-Aug 1 daily; 3hr); Kiruna (3 daily; 3hr); Luleå (5 daily; 25min); Stockholm (2 daily; 13hr); Uppsala (2 daily; 12hr).

Gävle to: Boden (2 daily; 11hr); Falun (4 daily; 1hr); Gällivare (2 daily; 13hr 30min); Härnösand (2 daily; 3hr); Hudiksvall (8 daily; 1hr 15min); Kiruna (2 daily; 15hr); Luleå (2 daily; 12hr); Örebro (6 daily; 3hr); Östersund (4 daily; 4hr); Söderhamn (8 daily; 40min); Stockholm (hourly; 1hr 30min); Sundsvall (8 daily; 2hr); Umeå (1 daily; 9hr); Uppsala (hourly; 45min).

Härnösand to: Gävle (2 daily; 3hr); Hudiksvall (2 daily; 2hr); Långsele (2 daily; 1hr 45min); Sollefteå (2 daily; 1hr 30min); Stockholm (3 daily; 4hr 30min); Sundsvall (3 daily; 1hr).

Hudiksvall to: Gävle (8 daily; 1hr 15min); Härnösand (2 daily; 2hr); Söderhamn (8 daily;

30min); Stockholm (8 daily; 2hr 30min); Sundsvall (8 daily; 45min); Uppsala (8 daily; 2hr).

Luleå to: Boden (5 daily; 25min); Gällivare (3 daily; 2hr 30min); Gävle (2 daily; 12hr); Gothenburg (1 daily; 16hr 45min); Haparanda (mid-June to mid-Aug 1 daily; 4hr); Kiruna (3 daily; 3hr 30min); Stockholm (2 daily; 14hr); Umeå (1 daily; 4hr 15min); Uppsala (2 daily; 13hr).

Söderhamn to: Gävle (8 daily; 40min); Härnösand (2 daily; 2hr 30min); Hudiksvall (8 daily; 30min); Stockholm (8 daily; 2hr); Sundsvall (8 daily; 1hr 30min); Uppsala (8 daily; 1hr 30min).

Sundsvall to: Gävle (8 daily; 2hr); Härnösand (3 daily; 1hr); Hudiksvall (8 daily; 45min); Östersund (5 daily; 2hr 20min); Söderhamn (8 daily; 1hr 30min); Stockholm (8 daily; 3hr 30min).

Umeå to: Gävle (1 daily; 9hr); Gothenburg (1 daily; 13hr 30min); Luleå (1 daily; 4hr 15min); Stockholm (1 daily; 11hr 15min); Uppsala (1 daily; 10hr 30min).

Buses

Boden to: Haparanda (4–6 daily; 3hr); Luleå (Mon–Fri 43 daily, Sat & Sun 9 daily; 50min).

Haparanda to: Boden (4–6 daily; 3hr); Kiruna (1–2 daily; 6hr); Luleå (Mon–Fri 12 daily, Sat & Sun 5 daily; 2hr 30min); Pajala (Mon–Fri 3–4 daily, 1 on Sun; 3hr 30min).

Luleå to: Arvidsjaur (1–2 daily; 3hr); Boden (Mon–Fri 43 daily, Sat & Sun 9 daily; 50min); Gällivare (1–3 daily; 3hr 15min); Haparanda (Mon–Fri 11 daily, Sat & Sun 5 daily; 4hr); Jokkmokk (1–3 daily; 2hr 45min); Kiruna (1–3 daily; 5hr); Pajala (1–2 daily; 3hr 30min).

Örnsköldsvik to: Östersund (1–2 daily; 4hr 30min).

Piteå to: Arvidsjaur (1 daily except Sat; 2hr).

Skellefteå to: Arvidsjaur (1 daily except Sat; 2hr).

Umeå to: Storuman (Mon–Sat 3–4 daily, 1 on Sun; 3hr 40min); Tärnaby/Hemavan (Mon–Sat 3–4 daily, 1 on Sun; 6hr).

Norrlandskusten buses

Norrlandskusten buses run four times daily between Sundsvall and Luleå, generally connecting with trains to and from Sundsvall. Buy your tickets from the bus driver before boarding. From Sundsvall, buses call at Härnösand (45min); Gallsäter (1hr 35min); Docksta (1hr 50min); Örnsköldsvik (2hr 30min); Umeå (4hr); Skellefteå (6hr 15min); Piteå (7hr 30min); and Luleå (8hr 30min).

International trains

Boden to: Narvik (2 daily; 6hr).

Luleå to: Narvik (2 daily; 6hr 30min).

International buses

Haparanda to: Rovaniemi (Mon–Fri 1 daily; 3hr).

Skellefteå to: Bodö (1 daily except Sat; 9hr); Fauske (1 daily except Sat; 7hr 30min).

Umeå to: Mo-i-Rana (1 daily; 8hr).

International ferries

Umeå to: Vaasa (1–2 daily; 3hr 30min).

CHAPTER FOURTEEN

CENTRAL AND NORTHERN SWEDEN

n many ways the long wedge of land that comprises **central and northern Sweden** – from the shores of **Lake Vänern** up to the Finnish border north of the Arctic Circle – encompasses all that is most typical of the country. Rural and underpopulated, it fulfils the image most people have of Sweden: lakes, pine forests, wooden cabins and reindeer – a vast area of land which is really one great forest broken only by the odd village or town.

Folklorish **Dalarna** province is the most intensely picturesque region. Even a quick tour around one or two of the more accessible places gives an impression of the whole: red cottages with white doors and window frames, sweeping green countryside, summer festivals and water which is bluer than blue. Dalarna's inhabitants maintain a cultural heritage (echoed in contemporary handicrafts and traditions) that goes back to the Middle Ages. And the county is *the* place to spend midsummer, particularly Midsummer's Eve, when the whole region erupts in a frenzy of celebration.

The privately owned **Inlandsbanan**, the great inland railway, cuts right through central and northern Sweden and links virtually all the towns and villages covered in this chapter. Running from **Mora** to **Gällivare**, above the Arctic Circle, it ranks with the best European train journeys, an enthralling two-day, 1100km adventure. It's certainly a much livelier approach to the north than the east coast run up from Stockholm. Buses connect the rail line with the **mountain villages** that snuggle alongside the Norwegian border – the Swedish *fjäll*, or fells, not only offer some of the most spectacular scenery in the country but also some of the best, and least spoilt, hiking in Europe. North of Mora, **Östersund** is the only town of any size, situated by the side of Storsjön, the "Great Lake", reputed to be home to Sweden's very own Loch Ness Monster. From here trains head in all directions: west to Norway through the country's premier ski resort, **Åre**, south to Dalarna and Stockholm, east to Sundsvall on the Bothnian coast and north to Swedish Lapland.

The wild lands of the **Sami** make for the most fascinating trip in northern Sweden. Omnipresent reindeer are a constant reminder of how far north you are, but the

---

ACCOMMODATION PRICE CODES

The hotels and guesthouses listed in this chapter have been graded according to the following price bands, based on the cost of the **least expensive double room during high season** (late June to Aug). However, almost every hotel offers seasonal and/or weekend discounts, and wherever possible we've given two grades, covering both the regular and the discounted rate.

① Under 500kr	② 500–700kr	③ 700–900kr
④ 900–1200kr	⑤ 1200–1500kr	⑥ Over 1500kr

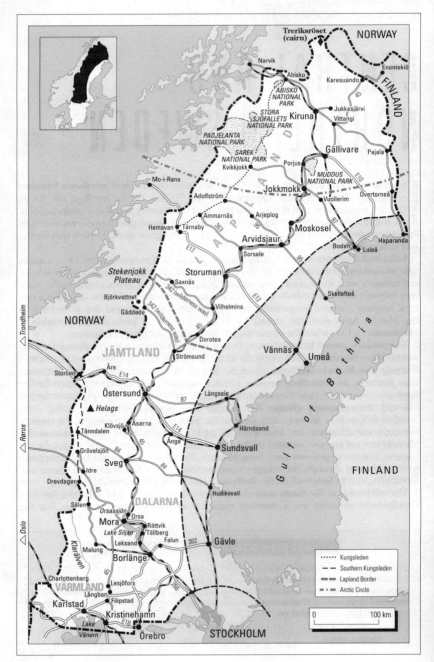

enduring Sami culture, which once defined much of this land, is now under threat. The problems posed by tourism are escalating, principally the erosion of grazing land under the pounding feet of hikers, making the Sami increasingly economically dependent on selling souvenirs and handicrafts. The Chernobyl nuclear accident in 1986 led to a fundamental change in living patterns, the result of the fallout affected grazing lands and even today reindeer in certain parts of the north are unfit for human consumption. Further north, around industrial **Gällivare** and **Kiruna**, and as far as the Norwegian border at **Riksgränsen**, the rugged **national parks** offer a chance to hike and commune with nature in the last great wilderness in Europe.

Karlstad

Capital of the province of Värmland, **KARLSTAD** is named after King Karl IX, who granted the place its town charter in 1584. The town has had its fair share of disasters: devastating fires ripped through the centre in 1616, 1729 and, most catastrophically, in 1865, when a fire started by a bakery on the corner of Östra Torggatan and Drottninggatan burnt virtually the entire town, including the cathedral, to the ground. Rebuilding began apace, with an emphasis on wide streets and large open squares to guard against another tragedy. The result is an elegant and thoroughly likeable town.

Arrival, information and accommodation

Elegantly sited along the shores of Lake Vänern roughly halfway between Stockholm and Oslo, Karlstad is served by inter-city **trains** between the two capitals as well as the faster X2000 to and from Stockholm. Direct services also run along the western side of the lake from Gothenburg. Karlstad is also linked by Swebus Express **bus** to Gothenburg, and by **air** to Stockholm and Copenhagen with SAS; the airport (☎054/455 50 10), 18km from the centre, is served by bus (40kr) and taxi (200kr). The **tourist office** is located in the Carlstad Conference Centre on Tage Erlandergatan 10D (June–Aug Mon–Fri 9am–7pm, Sat 10am–7pm, Sun 11am–4pm; Sept–May Mon–Fri 9am–5pm; ☎054/14 90 55, *tourist@karlstad.se*, *www.karlstad.se* or *www.varmland.org*). Ask here about **boat trips on Lake Vänern**.

Karlstad's **youth hostel** (☎054/56 68 40) is located 3km from the centre in a rambling old three-storey house, Ulleberg, served by buses #11, #21 and #32 towards Bellevue. The nearest **campsites** are a nine-kilometre drive out of town west along the E18: *Skutbergets Camping* (☎054/53 51 39) is open all year, whereas *Bomstad Badens Camping* (☎054/53 50 68) next door, and beautifully situated on the lakeshore, is only open from June to August. From mid-June to mid-August the campsites can be reached on the daily Badbussen (#18; 10.30am–5.30pm hourly; 25min) which runs from Stora Torget via Drottninggatan to the beaches at Bomstad.

Hotels

In summer all hotels in Karlstad charge 550kr for a double room if booked at least two days in advance.

Carlton, Järnvägsgatan 8 (☎054/21 55 40, fax 18 95 20). Located in the pedestrianized centre, this is the cheapest hotel in Karlstad. ②.

Drott, Järnvägsgatan 1 (☎054/10 10 10, fax 18 99 30). Smart, elegant hotel dating from 1908; it's next to a busy main road just 50m from the railway station. ④.

First Hotel Plaza, Västra Torggatan 2 (☎054/10 02 00, fax 10 02 24). Large, modern and plush hotel with fantastic views over the city from its panoramic sauna. ⑤.

Freden, Fredsgatan 1A (☎054/21 65 82). Cheap-and-cheerful place close to the bus and train stations. ②.

Good Morning Hotel Karlstad City, Västra Torggatan 20 (☎054/21 51 40, fax 21 94 43). Good-value hotel in the centre of town with a large breakfast buffet and free evening parking. ②.
Nya Solsta, Drottninggatan 13 (☎054/15 68 45). Cheap central hotel with cable TV and some rooms adapted for the disabled. A good choice. ②.
Stadshotellet, Kungsgatan 22 (☎054/21 52 20, fax 18 82 11). Beautifully located next to the river. Men's sauna with plunge pool, women's sauna with solarium and spa. Great value in summer. ⑤.

The Town

It's best to start your wanderings around town from the airy main square, Stora Torget, one of the largest market squares in the country. The rather austere **Peace Monument** in front of the Town Hall commemorates the peaceful dissolution of the union between Sweden and Norway in 1905, which was negotiated in Karlstad. Unveiled fifty years after this event it portrays an angry woman madly waving a broken sword whilst planting her right foot firmly atop a dismembered soldier's head: "feuds feed folk hatred, peace promotes people's understanding" reads the inscription. The Neoclassical **Town Hall** was the cause of much local admiration upon its completion in 1867, just two years after the great fire – local worthies were particularly pleased with the two fearsome Värmland eagles which adorn the building's roof, no doubt hoping they would ward off another devastating blaze. Across Östra Torggatan, the nearby **Cathedral** was consecrated in 1730, although only its arches and walls survived the flames of 1865. Its most interesting features are the altar, made from Gotland limestone with an Orrefors crystal cross, and the crystal font.

Continuing east along Kungsgatan and over the narrow Pråmkanalen, the road swings left and changes its name to Nygatan ahead of the longest arched stone bridge in Sweden, **Östra Bron**. Completed in 1811, this massive construction spans 168m across the eastern branch of the Klarälven river. It's claimed that the builder, Anders Jacobsson, threw himself off the bridge and drowned, afraid his life's work would collapse – his name is engraved on a memorial stone tablet in the centre of the bridge. On sunny days (and Karlstad is statistically one of the sunniest places in Sweden) the nearby wooded island of **Gubbholmen**, reached by crossing the stone bridge and turning right, is a popular place for catching the rays; take a picnic and dip your toes in the refreshing waters of the river.

Back in town, at the junction of Norra Standgatan and Västra Torggatan, the two-storey yellow wooden building with the mansard roof dates from 1781, one of the handful of dwellings which wasn't destroyed in the great fire. This building, the **Bishop's Residence** (Biskopsgården), owes its survival to the massive elm trees on its south side which formed a natural firebreak and the sterling firefighting efforts of the bishop of the time. The only other houses which survived are located in the **Almen district**, next to the river at Älvgatan; the oldest parts of these wooden buildings date from the 1700s, but their facades are all nineteenth century.

A half-hour walk along Jungmansgatan, Hööksgatan and Rosenborgsgatan will bring you to **Mariebergsskogen** (June–Aug daily 7am–10pm; free). Originally modelled on the Skansen open-air museum in Stockholm, this contains a number of old wooden buildings from across Värmland. There's also a **leisure park** (June–Aug daily) here with a funfair and children's animal park.

Cafés, bars and restaurants

Eating and **drinking** in Karlstad is a joy. There's a good selection of restaurants specializing in everything from Spanish to vegetarian dishes. For a Swedish provincial town, **bars** are also thick on the ground – the *Bishop's Arms* and the *Woolpack Inn* are particularly popular.

Bishop's Arms, Kungsgatan 22. Classic British-style pub with a wide range of beers and enjoying a great location overlooking the river, with outdoor seating in summer.

Casa Antonio, Drottninggatan 7. Good Spanish restaurant with tapas from 30kr and paella for two for 190kr.

Glada Ankan, Kungsgatan 12. Lively first-floor restaurant and bar with a balcony overlooking the main square. It serves mostly Swedish dishes (from 130kr) and is a nice place for coffee.

Gröna Trädgården, Västra Torggatan 9. First-floor vegetarian restaurant with a small balcony overlooking the pedestrian street below. Large salad buffet and home-made bread included with all meals. Open lunchtime only.

Harrys, Kungsgatan 16. American-style bar, café and restaurant in the main square, popular with drinkers in the evening, and with open-air seating in summer. The small menu has pub grub from 75kr.

Jäger, Västra Torggatan 8. Buzzing evening restaurant open till 2am. Also serves lunches for 59/79kr.

Kebab House, Västra Torggatan 7. Small but pleasant pizza and kebab place with outdoor seating in summer. From 40kr.

La Baguette, Kungsgatan 14. A good choice for a quick bite at lunchtime, with baguettes featuring every imaginable filling for 35kr and coffee. Outdoor seating available in summer.

Rådhuscafeet, Tingvallagatan 8. Elegant café in the town hall; enter from the left side of the building.

Woolpack Inn, Järnvägsgatan 1. Just across the road from the station, this is another pub doing its best to create a traditional British drinking atmosphere in central Sweden. Very popular.

Listings

Airline SAS, at the airport (☎054/55 50 00).

Banks FöreningsSparbanken, Kungsgatan 10; Handelsbanken, Tingvallagatan 17; Nordbanken, Tingvallagatan 11–13; S-E Banken, Drottninggatan 24.

Beaches Sundstatjärnet, in the centre of town by the swimming pool on Drottning Krisitinas väg; Mariebergsviken, take bus #20 and #31; Bomstad, take bus #18.

Bus station Drottninggatan. Information on buses in Värmland on ☎020/22 50 80 or at *www.kollplatsen.com.*

Car rental Avis, Hamngatan 24 (☎054/15 26 60); Budget, Gjuterigatan 26 (☎054/85 35 50); Hertz, Körkarlsvägen 7 (☎054/56 15 00).

Newspapers Hanssons Tabak, Järnvägsgatan 1.

Police Drottninggatan 4 (☎054/14 50 00).

Post Office Järnvägsgatan 2 (Mon–Fri 8am–6.30pm, Sat 10am–2pm).

Systembolaget Drottninggatan 26 (Mon–Thurs 10am–6pm, Fri 8am–6pm).

Taxi Karlstad Taxi (☎054/15 02 00); Taxi Kurir (☎054/101 101).

Train station Hamngatan. For information call ☎054/14 33 50 or 020/75 75 75.

Dalarna

The large province of Dalarna, stretching from **Lake Siljan** up to the ski resorts of **Sälen** and **Idre**, holds a special place in the Swedish heart. Around Lake Siljan the idyllic landscape is one of verdant cow pastures, gentle rolling meadows sweet with the smell of summer flowers, and tiny rural villages, rising slowly to the west to meet the chain of mountains that forms the border with Norway. **Leksand** and **Mora** are the best of the lakeside towns, and **Rättvik** may also be worth a visit if you've time. If you're here for more than a couple of days, the nearby industrial towns of **Falun** and **Borlänge** can be a relief after the folksiness of the lakeside and the tourist hordes that dominate the area in summer. North of Mora the county becomes more mountainous and less populous, and the only place of any note is **Orsa**, with its fascinating **bear park**.

Trains operated by the national rail company, SJ, call at all the towns around the lake and terminate in Mora; Falun can be reached by changing at Borlänge; north from Mora, services are taken over by the privately operated **Inlandsbanan** railway. Orsa, Sälen and Idre can all be reached by **bus** from Mora. Another good way to get about, especially around Lake Siljan, is to rent a **bike** from one of the tourist offices – this region is a popular Swedish holiday destination so there's no shortage of accommodation.

Around Lake Siljan

Things have changed since Baedeker, writing in 1889, observed that "Lake Siljan owes much of its interest to the inhabitants of its banks, who have preserved many of their primitive characteristics . . . In their idea of cleanliness they are somewhat behind the age". Today it's not the people who captivate but the scenery: **Lake Siljan** is what many people come to Sweden for, its gentle surroundings, traditions and local handicrafts weaving a subtle spell. There's a lush feel to much of the region, the vegetation enriched by the lake, which adds a pleasing dimension to the small and low-profile towns and villages. Only Mora stands out as being bigger and busier, with the hustle and bustle of holiday-makers and countless caravans in summer.

Mora

If you've only got time to see part of the lake, then **MORA**, the largest of the settlements, is the place to head for, especially if you're travelling further north, as it's the starting point of the Inlandsbanan (see box opposite). Mora's main draw is the work of Sweden's best-known artist, **Anders Zorn** (1860–1920), who moved here in 1896 and whose paintings are exhibited in the excellent **Zorn Museum** at Vasagatan 36 (mid-June to mid-Sept Mon–Sat 9am–5pm, Sun 11am–5pm; mid-Sept to mid-June Mon–Sat noon–5pm, Sun 1–5pm; 30kr) – look out for the self-portrait and the especially pleasing *Midnatt* (Midnight) from 1891, which depicts a woman rowing on Lake Siljan, her hands blue from the cold night air. You might also want to wander across the lawn and take in his home, **Zorngården** (mid-June to mid-Sept Mon–Sat 10am–4pm, Sun 11am–4pm; mid-Sept to mid-June Mon–Sat noon–3pm, Sun 1–5pm; 35kr), where he lived with his wife, Emma. Also on Vasagatan, but on the other side of the church, is the **Vasaloppet Museum** (Vasaloppsmuséet; mid-June to mid-Aug daily 10am–5pm; mid-Aug to mid-June Mon–Fri 10am–5pm; 30kr). Here you'll find an exhibition on the history of the Vasaloppet (see p.585), a ski race that started 500 years ago with the attempts of two Mora men to catch up with King Gustav Vasa, who was fleeing from the Danes. Once you've covered the town's sights, you might want to take a **cruise** on the lake aboard the lovely old steamship *M/S Gustaf Wasa* (timetables vary; info on ☎010/252 32 92 or 070/542 10 25); count on 120kr for a round-trip to Leksand or 80kr for a two-hour lunch cruise.

Mora's **tourist office** (mid-June to mid-Aug Mon–Fri 9am–8pm, Sat & Sun 10am–7pm; mid-Aug to mid-June Mon–Fri 9am–5pm, Sat 10am–1pm; ☎0250/56 76 00, *siljan.turism@stab.se, www.siljan-dalarna.com*), is at Stationsvägen in the same building as the train station.

The cheapest place to stay is the **youth hostel** (☎0250/381 96), at Fredsgatan 6; get off the train at Mora station, turn left, and keep walking for about five minutes along the main street, Vasagatan. Mora's **campsite**, *Mora Camping* (☎0250/153 52), is a ten-minute walk from the centre along Hantverkaregatan, which begins near the bus station: there's a good beach nearby, as well as a lake for swimming. Among the **hotels**, the biggest and best is the *First Resort Mora* at Strandgatan 12 (☎0250/717 50, fax 189 81; ③/②), opposite Mora Strand train station, with a choice of modern and old-fashioned rooms. *Hotell St Mikael*, Fridhemsgatan 15 (☎0250/159 00, fax 380 70; ②), is small with tasteful rooms, while *Hotell Kung Gösta*, Kristinebergsgatan 1, is handy for the main train station (☎0250/150 70, fax 170 78; ③/②).

INLANDSBANAN PRACTICALITIES

The **Inlandsbanan**, the great inland railway that links Dalarna with Swedish Lapland, is today a mere shadow of its former self. Spiralling costs and low passenger numbers forced Swedish Railways to sell the line in 1992, at which point services on the southern section between Mora and Kristinehamn had already been abandoned. The railway was bought by the fifteen municipalities the route passes through, and the private company, Inlandsbanan AB, was launched. It now operates only as a tourist venture in summer – generally from mid-June to the end of August. InterRail passes give free travel; see p.6 for details of other discounts. Timetables are approximate and the train is likely to stop whenever the driver feels like it; maybe for a spot of wild strawberry picking or to watch a beaver damming a stream. It's certainly a fascinating way to reach the far north of the country, but isn't recommended if you're in a rush. Taken in one go the whole journey lasts two days, with an overnight stop in Östersund. Take it easy and make a couple of stops along the route and you'll get much more out of it. Special guides available on board contain commentaries and information about places along the route. For **timetables** and other **information** ask at any tourist office around the lake or contact Inlandståget AB, Kyrkgatan 56, S-831 34 Östersund (☎063/12 76 95 or 10 15 90, fax 51 99 80, *www.inlandsbanan.se*).

As for **eating and drinking**, all the hotels serve up a decent *dagens rätt* for around 55kr – there's little to choose between them. *Wasastugan*, a huge log building at Tingnäsvägen between the main train station and the tourist office, also does good lunches, but it's particularly lively in the evenings, with meat and fish dishes from 80kr. Alternatively, *Pizzeria Primo* in Fridhemplan or *Pizzeria Torino* in Älvgatan serve up virtually any pizza you can imagine, all at reasonable prices. In summer, coffee and cakes can be enjoyed outside at *Helmers Konditori* and at *Mora Kaffestugan*, virtually next door to each other on Kyrkogatan. *Terassen* bar, inside the *First Resort Mora* on Strandgatan, is one of the liveliest places in the evening besides *Wasastugan*.

Rättvik

Situated at the eastern bulge of Lake Siljan, 37km from Mora, **RÄTTVIK** is altogether much smaller and quieter: one tiny shopping street, a massive jetty out into the lake (reputed to be the longest in the world) an outdoor swimming pool and that's about the sum of it. While there's not much in the way of sights, what Rättvik does have is access to plenty of gorgeous countryside. Get out of the village as soon as you can and head up for the viewing point at **Vidablick** – about an hour's walk and a stiff climb, but the view is worth it – you can see virtually all of Lake Siljan and the surrounding hillsides, covered in forests broken only by the odd farm. You can get to the viewing point by walking on marked trails through the forests above Rättvik: pick up a free map of town from the tourist office. In the forest itself there are a couple of information boards showing different walking trails, while Vidablick has a small café and a shop to reward your efforts. The quickest way back down to Rättvik is to take one of the steep roads down the hill (ask the staff in the shop to point out the correct one); go left at the end onto Wallenkampfvägen and then right along Mårsåkervägen towards Lerdal, and you'll see some of the most beautifully located residential houses in Dalarna – all wood logs and flowers and with a view out over the lake.

Rättvik's **tourist office** (mid-June to mid-Aug Mon–Fri 9am–8pm, Sat & Sun 10am–7pm; mid-Aug to mid-June Mon–Fri 9am–5pm, Sat 10am–1pm; ☎0248/702 00, *siljan.turism@stab.se, www.siljan-dalarna.com*) is handily situated in the train station. The best and cheapest place to stay is the **youth hostel** on Centralgatan (☎0248/105 66), built in traditional Dalarna style out of large pine logs and surrounded by trees; to get there, follow Domarbacksvägen 1km from the train station. There are two **campsites** in town, one opposite the youth hostel (☎0248/561 10), the other right on the lakeside behind the railway tracks (☎0248/516 91). When it comes to **hotels** there's not much choice: the best in town is the average *Hotell Lerdalshöjden* (☎0248/511 50, fax 511 77; ③) on Bockgatan, or there are some comfortable pine cabins at *Hotell Vidablick* (☎0248/302 50, fax 306 60; ②), about 3km out of Rättvik at Faluvägen.

There's a dearth of good places to **eat and drink** in Rättvik and most people head off to Leksand or Mora for a night out. A decent bet is *Restaurant Anna* on Vasagatan – a cosy restaurant with lunch for 55kr and local specialities in the evening from 100kr; otherwise you're looking at *Krögar'n* on pedestrianized Storgatan, which serves burgers for around 40kr and meat dishes from 80kr; or *Bella Pizza* at Ågatan 11, where pizzas go for around 55kr.

Leksand

LEKSAND is perhaps the most popular and traditional of the Dalarna villages and is certainly worth making the effort to reach at Midsummer, when festivals recall age-old dances performed around the maypole (Sweden's maypoles, incidentally, aren't erected until June: spring comes late here, and in May there are few leaves on the trees and often some lingering snow). Celebrations culminate in the **church boat races**, an aquatic procession of sleek wooden longboats that the locals once rowed to church every Sunday. The race starts on Midsummer's Day in nearby Siljansnäs and continues for ten days around the lake, reaching Leksand on the first Saturday in July. Between twenty and twenty-five teams take part in the races, all cheered on by villagers at the water's edge. Check the latest details at the tourist office. Another event worth coming here for is **Music by Lake Siljan** (Musik vid Siljan) in the first week of July: nine days of nonstop classical, jazz and dance-band music performed in churches, on the lakeside and at various locations in the surrounding forest – check with the tourist office for the latest details.

At other times there's little to do in Leksand other than to rest up and take it easy for a while. Stroll along the riverside down to **Leksands kyrka**, which enjoys a magnificent setting overlooking the river and the lake. One of the biggest churches in the country, it has existed in its present form since 1715, although the oldest parts date back to the thirteenth century.

All trains between Mora and Börlange stop in Leksand; the **tourist office** (mid-June to mid-Aug Mon–Fri 9am–8pm, Sat & Sun 10am–7pm; mid-Aug to mid-June Mon–Fri 9am–5pm, Sat 10am–1pm; ☎0247/803 00, *siljan.turism@stab.se, www.siljan-dalarna.com*) is at the train station. Leksand's comfortable **youth hostel**, one of the oldest in Sweden, is over the river, around 2.5km from the train station in Parkgården (☎0247/152 50). Otherwise, there are two hotels to choose between: *Hotell Moskogen*, at Insjövägen 50 (☎0247/146 00, fax 144 30; ③), and the beautiful *Hotell Korstäppen* at Hjortnäsvägen 33 (☎0247/123 10, fax 141 78; ③) tastefully done out in traditional Dalarna colours and styles. The tourist office can also book four-bed **cabins** in the area from 450kr per night. If you're camping, the nearest **campsite**, *Leksands Camping*, is a twenty-minute walk from the tourist office along Tällbergsvägen (☎0247/803 13 or 803 12). The best place to **eat** is at *Café Kulturhuset*, just up from the tourist office on Norsgatan – in summer there are tables in the garden at the back. Alternatively, try *Bosporen*, an OK place serving pizzas and meat and fish dishes in the tiny pedestrianized centre of town, which does lunch for 60kr. This is also the place to come for a **drink**.

Borlänge

BORLÄNGE, the biggest town in Dalarna, is ugly and dull. It originally developed as a steel and papermill centre, industries that still dominate the town today. If it's a rainy day, you might want to investigate the three museums. The best of these is the **Jussi**

Björling Museum, at Borganäsvägen 25 (mid-May to mid-Sept Mon–Fri 11am–6pm, Sat 10am–2pm, Sun noon–5pm; mid-Sept to mid-May Tues–Fri noon–5pm; 20kr), which commemorates Borlänge's most famous son and world-famous tenor. It's a toss up as to which of the other two is the more dull: the **Geological Museum** at Floragatan 6 (Geologiska muséet; Mon–Fri 11am–2pm, Sat 11am–5pm; 10kr) has mind-numbing displays of rocks, minerals and fossils, whereas the **Museum of the Future** at Jussi Björlingsvägen 25 (Framtidsmuséet; Mon 1–5pm, Tues–Fri 10am–5pm, Sat & Sun noon–5pm; 25kr) features a planetarium amongst its attractions. Weather permitting, it's much more fun to take a stroll round the river starting at the open-air craft village on Stenhålsgatan, **Gammelgården**, with its small collection of old wooden houses.

From the centrally located train station, walk past the green Liljekvistska parken to get to the **tourist office** on Borganäsvägen (mid-June to mid-Aug daily 9am–7pm; mid-Aug to mid-June Mon–Fri 10am–6pm; ☎0243/665 66, *turistbyra@borlange.se*, *www.borlange.se*). There's a **youth hostel** (☎0243/22 76 15) within easy walking distance of the centre at Kornstigen 23A, while the **campsite**, *Mellsta Camping*, is more of a trek out, but is beautifully located by the river on Mellstavägen. There are a number of identikit **hotels** in the centre of town, all with pleasant modern rooms. The *Hotel Gustaf Wasa*, Tunagatan 1 (☎0243/810 00, fax 806 00; ④/②), has the only bathtubs in town. Otherwise, try *Hotel Brage* (☎0243/22 41 50, fax 871 00; ④/②) at Stationsgatan 1, or the smaller and cheaper *Hotell Saga* (☎0243/21 18 40; ①) at Borganäsvägen 28.

When it comes to **eating**, you can't fail to notice Borlänge's proliferation of pizzerias: best of the bunch is *La Pizza* on Tunagatan. Greek specialities are served up at *Akropolis* on Vattugatan, Chinese food at *Le Mandarin* in Svea Torget, and Mexican and Cajun delights at *Broken Dreams* inside the *Hotel Gustaf Wasa*. The best food in town, though, is served up at the smart restaurant in the *Hotel Brage,* while traditional Swedish dishes can also be sampled at the intimate *Balders Krog* on Målaregatan. The most popular **pubs** in town are the *Flying Scotsman* in the Museum of the Future building on Jussi Björlingsvägen, and the *Hotel Brage*'s bar.

Falun

Twenty minutes by train from Börlange, the copper-mining town of **FALUN** is another essentially industrial settlement, though a pleasant one at that. At their peak in the seventeenth and eighteenth centuries the mines here produced two-thirds of the world's copper ore and the town acquired buildings and a layout commensurate with its status as Sweden's second largest town. In 1761, however, two devastating fires wiped out virtually all of central Falun – the few old wooden houses to survive can be found in the areas of Elsborg (southwest of the centre), Gamla Herrgården and Östanfors (north of the centre), which are worth seeking out for an idea of the cramped conditions the mineworkers had to live in.

The **mines** themselves, out of town at the end of Gruvgatan, were said by the botanist Carl von Linné to be as dreadful as hell itself. An unnerving element of eighteenth-century mining was the omnipresence of copper vitriol gases, a strong preservative: one case is recorded of a young man known as Fat Mats whose body was found in the mines in 1719. He'd died 49 years previously in an accident, but the corpse was so well preserved that his erstwhile finacée, by then an old woman, recognized him immediately. Hour-long **guided tours** (May–Aug daily 10am–4.30pm; March, April & Sept to mid-Nov Sat & Sun 12.30–4.30pm; 60kr), begin with a lift ride that takes you down 55m to a network of old mine roads and drifts – be warned that the temperature drops to around 6–7°C. Make sure you also peer into the "Great Pit", **Stora Stöten**, which appeared on Midsummer Day in 1687 – the result of a huge underground collapse caused by extensive mining and the unplanned driving of galleries and shafts.

Apart from the mines, Falun's attractions boil down to **Dalarnas Museum** at Stigaregatan 2–4 (May–Aug Mon–Thurs 10am–5pm, Fri–Sun noon–5pm; Sept–April Mon, Tues, Thurs 10am–5pm, Wed 10am–9pm; Fri–Sun noon–5pm; 20kr) which includes sections on the county's folk art, and, on the hill overlooking town, Sweden's **National Ski Stadium** (Riksskidsstadion; ask for directions from the tourist office), where you can take a lift up to the top of the ninety-metre ski jump for a terrifying peer down.

Practicalities

From the **train** and **bus stations**, east of the centre, take the underpass beneath the main road and head towards the shops in the distance to reach Stora Torget and Falun's **tourist office** (mid-June to mid-Aug Mon–Sat 9am–7pm, Sun 11am–5pm; mid-Aug to mid-June Mon–Fri 9am–6pm, Sat 10am–2pm; ☎023/830 50, *turist@welcome.falun.se, www.welcome.falun.se*), opposite the *First Hotel Grand* in Trotzgatan. The nearest **youth hostel** (☎023/105 60), a modern affair, is about 3km from the train station at Hälsinggårdsvägen 7 in Haraldsbo – take bus #701 or #704 from the centre. The **campsite** (☎023/835 63) is up at Lungnet by the National Ski Stadium, about fifteen minutes' walk from town. Central **hotels** include the swanky *First Hotel Grand* at Trotzgatan 9–11 (☎023/79 48 80, fax 141 43; ④/②), and the more homely *Hotell Winn*, near the train station at Bergskolegränd 7 (☎023/636 00, fax 225 24; ④/②).

In terms of **eating and drinking** places, Falun far outstrips the towns around Lake Siljan – in quality as well as choice. Most popular is the trendy *Banken Bar & Brasserie* at Åsgatan 41, housed in an old bank building decorated with bank notes and serving burgers, baked potatoes, and fish from around 80kr. Next door is the posh but cosy *Två rum och kök*, where meat and fish dishes start at 150kr. Another popular spot is *Rådhuskällaren*, a cellar under the town hall in Stora Torget serving delicious, if somewhat pricey, food – reckon on 120kr upwards, and at least 200kr for a bottle of wine. The *Firefly* **bar** next door is the place to hang out among Falun's trendy young things. Other drinking establishments include the excellent *Pub Engelbrekt*, at Stigaregatan 1, and the average English-themed *King's Arms* at Falugatan 3. For entertainment value, the best time to be in Falun is mid-July, when musicians from all over the world take over the town for a four-day **International Folk Music Festival** (check latest dates with the tourist office).

Sälen and Idre

The major ski resort of **SÄLEN** also in effect encompasses the surrounding slopes and mountains of Lindvallen, Högfjället, Tandådalen, Hundfjället, Rörbäcksnäs and Stöten. Each site has its own slope but looks to the village of Sälen for shops and services – not least the Systembolaget. **Buses** call at each resort in turn, terminating in Stöten. In summer there's just one bus a day from Mora (#95; 1hr 40min).

There are no sights as such: like neighbouring Idre (see opposite), Sälen is a base for outdoor activities during the summer and skiing in winter. In **summer** fishing, canoeing and beaver safaris are all available through the tourist office, plus there's some fantastic **hiking** to be had in the immediate vicinity. In **winter** snow is guaranteed from November to May, making Sälen the biggest ski centre in the Nordic area, with over a hundred pistes. However, unless you've booked a package in advance, prices are high and hotels may be full up.

Your first port of call should be the **tourist office** (late June to mid-Aug & Dec to late April Mon–Fri 9am–6pm, Sat & Sun 10am–4pm; late April to late June & mid-Aug to Nov Mon–Fri 9am–6pm; ☎0280/202 50, *turist.saelen@malung.se, www.salen.nu*) on the one straggly main street that runs through the village. The best bet for summer **accommodation** is the wonderfully situated *Högfjällshotellet* (☎0280/870 00, fax 211

61; ④/②) at Högfjället – right on the tree line with good views of the surrounding hills – a bus runs there twice a day. If you really want to be out in the wilds and get away from it all, head for the **youth hostel** (☎0280/820 40) at Gräsheden, near Stöten. The hostel staff will pick you up from the bus stop in Stöten if you call ahead.

Idre

A twice-daily bus from Mora follows the densely forested valley of the Österdalälven on its almost three-hour journey to another of Sweden's main ski resorts, **IDRE**, before continuing up the mountain to the ski slopes at Idrefjäll. In winter the place is buzzing – not just with people but also with the reindeer who wander down the main street at will. Idre is a tiny one-street affair, with a bank, supermarket and post office. The **tourist office** (mid-June to mid-Aug Mon–Fri 8am–7pm, Sat 8.30am–7pm, Sun 9am–7pm; mid-Aug to mid-June Mon–Fri 9am–5pm, Sat & Sun 10am–2pm; ☎0253/207 10) is at the far end of the main street when approaching from Mora. It can help arrange all sorts of activities, from fishing to horse-riding, and has plenty of information on hiking in the area.

For **accommodation** try the small and comfortable *Hotell Idregården* (☎0253/200 10, fax 206 76; ③/①) on the main road in from Mora – its **bar** is a popular spot at weekends. When it comes to **eating** there's precious little choice – either *Idregården*, which is famous for its ostrich and wild game, or *Kopparleden*, complete with plastic flowers, which does simple fry-ups. In the ski resort of **Idrefjäll** there's just one **hotel**, *Idre Fjäll* (☎0253/410 00, fax 401 58; ⑤/②), which organizes skiing and other activities, but for all practical matters you'll need to go down to the village. It's essential to book ahead.

Hiking around Sälen and Idre

The best **hiking route** is the southern **Kungsleden** which starts at the *Högfjällshotellet* above Sälen and runs to Storlien. It's an easy path to walk, with overnight cabins along its length, the majority operated by Svenska Turistföreningen, plus three fell stations at the Storlien end. From Idre you can join the path near the border at **Grövelsjön**, renowned for its stark and beautiful mountain scenery (bus from Mora via Idre, 1–2 daily), where there's also accommodation at an **STF Fell Station** (☎0253/230 90; Feb–April, mid-June to Sept, Christmas & New Year). Latest information from the tourist office in Idre or from the fell station in Grövelsjön. See p.604 for more on the Kungsleden.

An alternative is to follow the ninety-kilometre **Vasaloppssleden** to Mora. This footpath traces the route taken by skiers on the first Sunday in March during the annual Vasaloppet race (see p.580). A detailed map of the route, which starts just outside Sälen in **Berga**, is available from the tourist offices in Sälen and Mora.

The Inlandsbanan: Orsa to Östersund

First stop for the Inlandsbanan on its long way north is the tiny town of **ORSA**, 21km from Mora. If you get off the train here you're entering bear country: it's reckoned that there are a good few hundred **brown bears** roaming the dense forests around town, though few sightings are made, except by the hunters who cull the steadily increasing numbers. Your best chance of seeing one is to visit the **Orsa Grönklitt björnpark** (mid-May to late June & early Aug to early Sept daily 10am–3pm; late June to early Aug daily 10am–5pm; 65kr), the biggest bear park in Europe, 13km outside town (reached by twice-daily bus #118 from Mora, which you can pick up at Orsa train station). The bears here are not tamed or caged, but wander around the 900 square kilometres of the forested park at will. It's the humans who are restricted, having to clamber up viewing towers and along covered-in walkways. Funny, gentle and vegetarian for the most part, the bears are occasionally fed the odd dead reindeer or elk that's been killed on the roads. Out of season they hibernate in specially constructed lairs that are monitored by closed circuit television cameras.

From the train station on Järnvägsgatan it's a short walk to the **tourist office** on Centralplan (mid-June to mid-Aug Mon–Fri 9am–8pm, Sat & Sun 10am–7pm; mid-Aug to mid-June Mon–Fri 9am–5pm, Sat 10am–1pm; ☎0250/55 21 63). If you need to stay over, the best bet is the **youth hostel** (☎0250/421 70; closed late April to mid-May & Nov), beautifully located on Moravägen by the side of Lake Orsa, 1km east of the centre. There's also a second, well-equipped **youth hostel** at the bear park (☎0250/462 00).

Härjedalen province: Sveg and Klövsjö

A sparsely populated fell region stretching north and west to the Norwegian border, **Härjedalen** is excellent terrain for walking. Until 1645 the county belonged to Norway, something that has left its mark in the local dialect. Some of Sweden's most magnificent scenery can be seen here – more than thirty mountains exceed the 1000-metre mark, the highest peak being **Helags** (1797m), whose icy slopes support Sweden's southernmost glacier. Härjedalen is also home to the largest single population of bears in the country, as well as a handful of shaggy musk oxen, ferocious creatures that have wandered over the border from Norway.

Härjedalen's main town – and the first major stop on the Inlandsbanan after Orsa – is **SVEG** (pronounced "Svay-gg"), site of a 1273 parliament called to hammer out a border treaty between Sweden and Norway. Since then things have quietened down considerably and even on a Friday night in midsummer you're likely to find yourself alone in the wide streets lined with grand old wooden houses. A graceful river runs right through the centre of town and there are some delightful meadows and swimming spots just a few minutes' walk from the centre.

Sveg's **tourist office** (☎0680/107 75, *www.haerjedalen.se*) is in the centre of town in the Folkets Hus building at Ljusnegatan 1. If you're keen to **stay overnight**, try the ramshackle **youth hostel**, a fifteen-minute walk from the station at Vallervägen 11 (☎0680/103 38; advance booking required Oct–May). In the same building is the rather shabby *Hotell Härjedalen* (same phone number; ①); or try the more upmarket *Hotell Mysoxen* (☎0680/71 12 60, fax 100 62; ③/②), the other side of Torget on the corner of Fjällvägen and Dalagatan. The **campsite** (☎0680/130 25) is located right on the riverside. Your best chances of not **eating** alone are at the greasy-spoon *Inlandskrogen* café next to the bus and train stations on Järnvägsgatan, or at the *Knuten* pizzeria in the main square, Torget.

Klövsjö

A thoroughly charming place with log cabins set in rolling pastures, **KLÖVSJÖ** has gained the reputation of being Sweden's most beautiful village. There's some justification to this – the distant lake and the forested hills that enclose the village on all sides create the feeling that it's in a world of its own. Ten farms continue to work the land much as in days gone by – ancient grazing rights still in force mean that horses and cows are free to roam through the village at will. Flowering meadows, trickling streams, wooden barns and the smell of freshly mown hay drying on frames in the afternoon sun cast a wonderful spell. Once you've taken a look at the old wooden buildings of the seventeenth-century farm estate, **Tomtangården** (July to mid-Aug daily; free), there's not much else to do except breathe the bitingly clean air and admire the beauty – you won't find anywhere as picturesque as this. Unfortunately you can't stay here because there are no rooms to let, but the **tourist office** on the main road (mid-June to mid-Aug Mon–Sat 9am–7pm, Sun noon–7pm; mid-Aug to mid-June

Mon–Fri 9am–5pm; ☎0682/212 50) has cabins to rent in the vicinity (375–500kr for up to four people).

To **reach Klövsjö**, get off the train at Åsarna, a skiing centre, from where buses make the twenty-minute trip to the village four times a day. In summer at least it's fairly easy to find accommodation in Åsarna. There's a well-equipped **campsite** (☎0687/302 30, fax 303 60) and three four-berth **cabins** from 490kr per day. Opposite the train station, the *Åsarna Hotell* (☎0687/300 04; ②) is smarter, with a restaurant and bar. The skiing centre itself is on the one and only main road, a few minutes from the train station; there's a **tourist office** in the same complex (June–Aug daily 8am–9pm; Sept–May daily 8am–7pm; ☎0687/301 93).

Östersund

Having reached **ÖSTERSUND**, it's worth stopping at what is the last large town until Gällivare, inside the Arctic Circle – if you're heading north this is your last chance to indulge in a bit of high life, since the small towns and villages beyond have few of the entertainment or culinary possibilities available here. Östersund is also a major **transport hub**: the E14 runs through town on its way to the Norwegian border, while as well as the summer Inlandsbanan service there are trains west to Åre and Storlien (the latter with connections to Trondheim in Norway), east to Sundsvall and south to Stockholm and Gothenburg, plus express buses north to Gällivare, which run all year and are a better option than the Inlandsbanan if you're in a hurry.

Arrival, information and accommodation

From the **train station** on Strandgatan it's a five-minute walk north to the town centre; the **bus station**, on Gustav III's Torg, is more central. A couple of blocks to the north, the helpful **tourist office** (June and early to mid-Aug Mon–Sun 9am–7pm; July Mon–Sat 9am–9pm, Sun 9am–7pm; late Aug to May Mon–Fri 9am–5pm; ☎063/14 40 01, *turistbyran@ostersund.se*, *www.ostersund.se/turist*), is opposite the minaret-topped Rådhus at Rådhusgatan 44.

For accommodation, the modern STF **youth hostel** (☎063/13 91 00; late-June to early Aug) is ten minutes' walk from the train station at Södra Gröngatan 34. More atmospheric, though, is a night spent inside *Jamtli* (☎063/10 59 84), another STF hostel set amid the old buildings in the open-air museum grounds. **Campers** can stay either at *Östersunds Camping* (☎063/14 46 15), a couple of kilometres south down Rådhusgatan; or over on Frösön at *Frösö Camping* (☎063/14 46 15; June–Aug) – take bus #3 or #4 from the centre.

Hotels

Älgen, Storgatan 61 (☎063/51 75 25). Small central hotel, handy for the train station, with plain yet comfortable en-suite rooms. ③/②. Also has hostel-style accommodation for 180kr per person in rooms sleeping up to four people.

Asken, Storgatan 53 (☎063/51 74 50). Only eight rooms – all en suite but rather plain and simple – one room is for the use of people with allergies. ③/①.

Aston, Köpmangatan 40 (☎063/51 08 51). The cheapest hotel in town, small with plain rooms – some en suite. Entrance in Postgränd. ②/①.

Emma, Prästgatan 26 (☎063/51 78 40). Nineteen garishly decorated tiny rooms, mostly en suite. ④/②.

Gamla Teatern, Thoméegränd 20 (☎063/51 16 00, fax 13 14 99). Without doubt the best hotel in town, in an atmospheric early twentieth-century theatre with sweeping wooden staircases, tall doorways and wide corridors, but disappointingly plain rooms. ⑤/③.

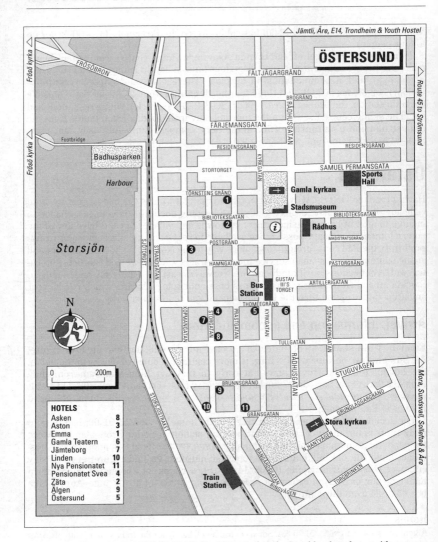

△ Jämtli, Åre, E14, Trondheim & Youth Hostel

ÖSTERSUND

Fröså kyrka
FRÖSÖBRON
FÄLTJÄGARGRÄND
BROGRÄND
RÅDHUSGATAN
Route 45 to Strömsund
FÄRJEMANSGATAN
Footbridge
RESIDENSGRÄND
RESIDENSGRÄND
Fröså kyrka
Badhusparken
STORTORGET
KYRKGATAN
SAMUEL PERMANSGATA
Sports Hall
Harbour
TÖRNSTENS GRÄND ❶
Gamla kyrkan
Stadsmuseum
BIBLIOTEKSGATAN ❷
(i)
BIBLIOTEKSGATAN
Rådhus
SJÖTORGET
STRANDGATAN
Storsjön
POSTGRÄND ❸
MAGISTRATSGRÄND
HAMNGATAN
PASTORGRÄND
⊠
Bus Station
GUSTAV III'S TORGET
ARTILLERIGATAN
N
KÖPMANGATAN
❼
STORGATAN
PRÄSTGATAN
❹ ❺
THOMEEGRÄND
KYRKGATAN
❻
SÖDRA GRÖNGATAN
STUGUVÄGEN
❽
TULLGATAN
0   200m
RÅDHUSGATAN
Mora, Sundsvall, Sollefteå & Åre
STORGSJÖSTRÅKET
BRUNNSGRÄND ❾
❿ ⓫
GRÄNSGATAN
GRUNDLÄGGARGRÄND
Stora kyrkan

HOTELS
Asken	8
Aston	3
Emma	1
Gamla Teatern	6
Jämteborg	7
Linden	10
Nya Pensionatet	11
Pensionatet Svea	4
Zäta	2
Älgen	9
Östersund	5

N HANTVÄGEN
Train Station
RINGVÄGEN
BANGÅRDSGATAN
TORGBRINKEN

Jämteborg, Storgatan 54 (☎063/51 01 01). Tasteless, drab and miserable – but cheap, with summer doubles from 400kr. ②/③.

Linden, Storgatan 64 (☎063/51 73 35). Cramped and basic rooms all with en-suite facilities. ③/①.

Nya Pensionatet, Prästgatan 65 (☎063/51 24 98). Near the train station, this tastefully decorated house, dating from around 1900, has just eight rooms, with toilet and shower in the corridor. Summer doubles from just 330kr. ①.

Östersund, Kyrkgatan 70 (☎063/57 57 00, fax 57 57 11). A massive modern hotel with 126 rooms; high on quality, but low on charm. ④/②.

Pensionat Svea, Storgatan 49 (☎063/51 29 01). Seven tweely decorated rooms with shared toilet and shower. Discounted rates for long-term stays. ①.

Zäta, Prästgatan 32 (☎063/51 78 60). Simple, plain but comfortable, with cable TV and sauna. ④/②.

The Town

Östersund sits on the eastern shore of the mighty **Storsjön** (Great Lake), lending the town a seaside holiday atmosphere, unusual this far inland. It's an instantly likeable place, made up of the familiar grid of parallel streets lined with modern quadruple-glazed apartment blocks designed to keep the winter freeze at bay (temperatures regularly plummet as low as -20°C). Strolling through the pedestrianized centre is a relaxed experience; take time out and sip a coffee around the wide open space of Stortorget and watch Swedish provincial life go by, or amble down one of the many side streets that slope down to the still, deep waters of the lake. Here you may be lucky enough to spot Sweden's own Loch Ness monster, **Storsjöodjuret**, a vast dog-headed creature of which sightings are numerous if unsubstantiated.

The main attraction in town is **Jamtli Historieland** (late June to mid-Aug daily 11am–5pm; 80kr), an impressive open-air museum a quarter of an hour's walk north of the centre along Rådhusgatan. For the first few minutes it's a bit bewildering, full of people milling around in traditional country costume, farming and milking much as their ancestors did. They live here throughout the summer and everyone is encouraged to join in – baking, tree-felling, grass-cutting. Kids, naturally, love it, and you'd have to be pretty cynical not to enjoy the enthusiastic atmosphere. Some intensive work has been done on getting the settings right: the restored and working interiors are gloomy and dirty, with no hint of the usual pristine historical travesty. In the woodman's cottage, presided over by a bearded lumberjack who makes pancakes for visitors, shoeless and scruffy children snooze contentedly in the wooden cots. Outside, even the planted crops and roaming cattle are historically accurate, while an old-fashioned local store, Lanthandel, has been set up among the wooden buildings around the square near the entrance. The **Provincial Museum** (Länsmuséet; late June to mid-Aug 11am–5pm; mid-Aug to late June Tues–Sun 11am–5pm; 50kr) on the same site shows off the county collections: a rambling houseful of local exhibits that includes monster-catching gear devised by nineteenth-century lakeside worthies. The museum's prize exhibits are the awe-inspiring Viking **Överhögdal tapestries**, which date from the ninth or tenth centuries – discovered in an outhouse in 1910, the tapestries are crowded with brightly coloured animals and buildings.

Back in the centre, apart from the **City Museum** (Stadsmuseum; Mon–Fri noon–4pm, Sat & Sun 1–4pm; free) – a crowded two hundred years of history in a building the size of a shoebox – on Rådhusgatan, and the neighbouring **Gamla Kyrkan** (June–Aug 8am–8pm; Sept–May Mon–Fri 1–3pm), there's not a vast amount in the way of sights. Take a look though, at the **harbour**, with its fleet of tiny boats and a couple of light aircraft bobbing about on the clean water. Immediately to the right of the harbour is the tiny **Badhusparken** – an inordinately popular spot in summer for catching a few rays.

Finally, it's possible to go monster-spotting on a **lake cruise** on board *S/S Thomée* – a creaking old wooden steamship built in 1875. Routes and timetables vary but always include a two-hour trip around the lake (65kr), amongst other destinations; for more information contact the tourist office.

Frösön

Take the foot- or road bridge across the lake from Badhusparken and you'll come to the island of **Frösön**. People have lived here since prehistoric times – Frösön's name derives from the Viking settlement on the island and its association with the pagan god of fertility, Frö. There's plenty of good walking here, as well as a couple of historical stops. Just over the bridge in front of a red-brick office block, look out for the eleventh-century **rune stone** that tells of a man called Östmadur (East Man), son of Gudfast, who brought Christianity to the people of Jämtland – presumably from some point to the east. From here you can clamber up the nearby hill of Öneberget, where you'll find the fourth-century settlement of Mjälleborgen – the most extensive in Norrland.

Follow the main road west and up the hill for about 5km to the beautiful **Frösö kyrka** (or take bus #3 from the centre of Östersund), an eleventh-century church with a detached bell tower. In 1984 archeologists digging under the church's altar came across a bit of birch stump surrounded by the bones of bears, pigs, deer and squirrels – evidence of the cult of ancient gods, the *Aesir*, and an indication that the site has been a place of worship for almost two thousand years. Today the church is one of the most popular in Sweden for marriages – especially at Midsummer, for which you have to book years in advance.

Eating, drinking and nightlife

Gastronomically there's more choice in Östersund than for a very long way north. For **breakfast**, the train station café is good value and always busy. For **coffee** and cakes try *Wedemarks Konditori*, Prästgatan 27, where you can also make up your own sandwiches.

Restaurants and bars

Athena, Stortorget 3. Pompously decorated but tasty pizza restaurant tucked away in one corner of Stortorget.

Brunkullans Krog, Postgränd 5. Östersund's premier eating place, this old-fashioned, home-from-home restaurant, with polished lanterns and a heavy wooden interior, offers traditional Swedish fare as well as more international fish and meat dishes. It's expensive, although in summer there are tables in the garden at the rear with a cheaper menu.

Captain Cook, Hamngatan 9. A selection of delicious Australian-style grilled delights that really draws in the crowds – also one of the most popular places for a drink with its extensive beer and whisky selection. Moderate.

Kvarterskrogen, Storgatan 54. Upmarket restaurant, with tables decked out in fresh linen and high prices to match. Lamb, entrecôte, beef and sole dishes, as well as northern Swedish delicacies, start at 160kr.

Ming Palace, Storgatan 15. The town's best Chinese, with the usual dishes at moderate prices.

O'Leary's, Storgatan 28. Popular Irish-style pub offering a large selection of beer and a Tex-Mex inspired menu.

Paviljon Thai, Prästgatan 50B. The only Thai and Indonesian restaurant in central northern Sweden – make the most of it. Excellent green curry and tiger prawn soup. Main courses go for around 95kr, or there's a lunch for 65kr.

Restaurang G III/Pub Köket, inside the *Hotel Östersund*, Kyrkgatan 70. The first is a standard, fairly expensive à la carte restaurant; the second (right beside it) is one of the town's popular drinking holes.

Restaurang Volos, Prästgatan 38. Cheap pizzas and a few authentic Greek dishes. Look out for special offers on beer.

Simon & Viktor, Prästgatan 19. An English-style watering hole with upmarket pub grub. It's at the top end of Stortorget.

Listings

Airlines SAS, at the airport (☎063/635 10 10).

Airport on Frösön (☎063/635 10 00). Direct flights to Stockholm Arlanda with SAS. Buses (45kr) connect with all planes to and from Stockholm (information ☎0708/86 77 20). Taxis cost 130kr.

Banks Handelsbanken, Sparbanken and FöreningsSparbanken are all on Prästgatan.

Bike rental Cykelogen at Kyrkogatan 45, with mountain bikes from about 100kr per day.

Bus enquiries For information on all buses call ☎020/61 62 63 or visit *www.lanstrafiken-z.se*. The express bus, Inlandsexpressen (#45), leaves from the bus station south to Mora (2 daily) and north to Gällivare (1 daily). You can't book seats, just pay on board, but there is usually enough room – though it's always wise to get there early. For information on the Y-Bussen express service to Stockholm call ☎063/15 55 65.

Car rental Avis, at the airport (☎063/448 70) or at Bangårdsgatan 9 (☎063/10 12 50); Budget, Köpmangatan 25 (☎063/10 44 10); Europcar, Hofvallsgränd 1 (☎063/57 47 50); Hertz, Köpmangatan 25 (☎063/10 21 12); Statoil, Krondikesvägen 97 (☎020/75 75 75).

Doctor Health Centre Z-gränd (Mon–Fri 8am–5pm; ☎063/14 20 00).

Left luggage Lockers at the train station for 15kr.

Pharmacy Prästgatan 51 (Mon–Fri 9am–6pm, Sat 9am–4pm, Sun 11am–4pm).

Police (☎063/15 25 00).

Post office Kyrkgatan (☎063/14 16 10).

Systembolaget Prästgatan 18 (Mon–Fri 10am–6pm); Kyrkgatan 82 (Mon–Wed & Fri 10am–6pm, Thurs 10am–7pm).

Taxi Taxi Östersund (☎063/51 72 00).

Trains Information from the station on Strandgatan (information on ☎020/75 75 75). The Inlandsbanan leaves daily heading south for Mora at 2.45pm and north to Gällivare at 7am.

West from Östersund

The E14 and the train line follow the route trudged by medieval pilgrims on their way to Nidaros (now Trondheim) over the border in Norway, a twisting route that threads its way through sharp-edged mountains rising high above a bevy of fast-flowing streams and deep, cold lakes. Time and again the eastern Vikings assembled their armies beside the holy Storsjön lake to begin the long march west, most famously in 1030 when King Olaf of Norway collected his mercenaries for the campaign that led to his death at the Battle of Stiklestad. The Vikings always crossed the mountains as quickly as possible and so today – although the scenery is splendid – there's nothing much to stop for en route, other than the winter-skiing and summer-walking centres of Åre and Storlien.

Åre

ÅRE (pronounced "Or-ruh"), two hours by train from Östersund, is Sweden's most prestigious ski resort, with 44 lifts and snow guaranteed between December and May. During the snowbound season rooms are like gold dust and prices sky-high: if you do come to ski, book accommodation well in advance through the tourist office or, better still, come on a package tour. Equipment rental isn't too expensive: downhill and cross-country gear costs 100–150kr per day, around 600kr per week – contact the tourist office.

In summer the Alpine village is a quiet haven for ramblers, sandwiched as it is between the river and a range of craggy hills overshadowed by the mighty 1420-metre-high Åreskutan mountain. A network of **walking tracks** criss-crosses the hills or, for a more energetic scramble, take the **Kabinbanan**, Sweden's only cable-car (80kr return), up to a viewing platform from where it's a thirty-minute clamber to the summit. The view is stunning – on a clear day you can see over to the border with Norway and a good way back to Östersund. Beware that even the shortest walk back to Åre takes two hours and requires some stamina.

The **tourist office** (late June to Aug & mid-Dec to April daily 9am–6pm; May to late June & Sept to mid-Dec Mon–Fri 9am–3pm; ☎0647/177 20) is in the square, 100m up the steps opposite the train station. It has detailed mountain maps and endless information on hiking in the nearby mountains and further afield – ask for the excellent *Hiking in Årefjällen* booklet. They can also help with mountain biking in the area.

The tourist office can help fix up a **private room** from around 125kr in summer, almost all of them with kitchen, shower and TV. Otherwise, the cheapest option is the unofficial **youth hostel** known as *Åre Backpackers Inn* (☎0647/177 31), in the park below the square; the **campsite** (☎0647/136 00; closed Sept–Nov) is five minutes' walk from the station – head to the right.

Åre's **eating** possibilities aren't up to much, but there are several cheap places around the square: try the cheerful *Café Bubblan*, which does reasonable lunches of pies and sandwiches, or the more substantial dishes served at nearby *Wersens*. At the cable-car terminus, *Bykrogen* serves decent main meals from 100kr, but note that it closes at 7pm.

Storlien

Just 6km from the Norwegian border and a favourite feasting spot for the region's mosquitoes, **STORLIEN** is the place to stop if you plan to do some hiking, which is good and rugged around here. The countryside hereabouts is also prime berry-picking territory, the rare cloudberry grows here, and mushrooms, in particular canterelles, can be found in great number. There's not much else here though, apart from a **tourist office** in an old train carriage at the station (June–Aug daily 10am–5pm; Sept–May telephone inquiries only on ☎0647/701 70), a couple of hotels, a supermarket, and mile upon mile of open countryside.

Storlien's **youth hostel** (☎0647/700 50; closed mid-June to mid-July) is a four-kilometre walk across the railway tracks to the E14 and then left down the main road towards Storvallen. If you're merely after a bed for the night, then **ÅNN**, halfway between Åre and Storlien, is the best bet: all trains between Östersund and Åre and Storlien stop there and the **youth hostel** (☎0647/710 70) is right opposite the station. Of Storlien's **hotels**, *Hotell Storlien* (☎0647/701 51, fax 705 22; ①), right by the train station, has mega-cheap rooms in summer – from 95kr per person in a double room. **Eating and drinking** is not easy, with just two options, the better of which is the *Le Ski* restaurant, nightclub and bar at the train station; otherwise, coffee, waffles and sandwiches are available at *Café Storliengården* (Tues–Sun 9am–5pm), a two-minute walk from the station.

Moving on from Storlien, two trains operated by Norwegian Railways leave for Trondheim in Norway. In the opposite direction there are services to Stockholm and Gothenburg via Östersund, while the afternoon train from Trondheim to Storlien connects with sleeper services to both these destinations.

North to Swedish Lapland

After Östersund the **Inlandsbanan** slowly snakes its way across the remote Swedish hinterland, a vast and scarcely populated region where the train often has to stop for elk and reindeer – and occasionally bears – to be cleared from the tracks. On the other occasions that the train comes to a halt with no station in sight, it's usually for a reason – a spot of berry-picking, perhaps – while at the Arctic Circle everyone jumps off for photos.

Route 45, the **Inlandsvägen**, sticks close to the train line on its way north to Gällivare – if you're not bound to the train this should be your preferred road north. It's easy to drive and well surfaced for the most part, though watch out for suicidal reindeer – once they spot a car hurtling towards them they'll do their utmost to throw themselves underneath it. **Bus** travellers on the daily Inlandsexpressen from Östersund to Gällivare will also take this route.

Vilhelmina and Storuman

Three and a half hours up the Inlandsbanan from Östersund, **VILHELMINA** is a pretty little town that once was an important forestry centre. The timber business has since moved out of town, however, and the main source of employment nowadays is a telephone-booking centre for Swedish Railways. Despite the grandeur hinted at by the town's name (from Fredrika Dorotea Vilhelmina, the wife of King Gustav IV Adolf), Vilhelmina remains a quiet little place with just one main street. The principal attraction is the **parish village**, nestling between Storgatan and Ljusminnesgatan, whose thirty-odd wooden cottages date back to 1792 when the first church was consecrated. It's since been restored and today the cottages can be rented out via the **tourist office** (mid-June to mid-Aug Mon–Fri 8am–8pm, Sat & Sun noon–6pm; mid-Aug to mid-June Mon–Fri 8am–5pm; ☎0940/152 70, *tuby@vilhelmina.se*, *www.vilhelmina.se*) on the main street, Volgsjövägen, a five-minute walk up Postgatan from the **train station**, which also serves as the **bus** station.

Vilhelmina's **campsite**, *Rasten Saiva Camping* (☎0940/107 60), is about ten minutes' walk from the centre and has four-berth cabins for rent for 250–525kr, as well as a great sandy **beach**; head down Volgsjövägen from the centre and take the first left after the youth hostel. There are two central **hotels** in town: the ostentatious *Hotell Wilhelmina* (☎0940/554 20, fax 101 56; ④/②), at Volgsjövägen 16, and the friendly *Lilla Hotellet* (☎0940/150 59; ②) at Granvägen 1.

There isn't exactly a multitude of **eating and drinking** options: try the à la carte restaurant at the *Hotell Wilhelmina* for traditional northern Swedish dishes and 60kr lunches, or the plain *Pizzeria Quinto*, Volgsjövägen 27. For coffee and sandwiches head for *Kyrkstands Café & Data* next to the parish village, which also has Internet access. In the evenings locals gravitate towards *Krogen Besk* in the main square for a drink or two.

Storuman

STORUMAN, an hour and a half up the line from Vilhelmina, is a transport hub for this part of southern Lapland. **Buses** run northwest up the E12, skirting the Tärnafjällen mountains, to Tärnaby and Hemavan, before wiggling through to Mo-i-Rana in Norway and, in the opposite direction, down to Umeå via Lycksele, where there are connections on to Vindeln and Vännäs on the main coastal rail line. A direct bus, the Lapplandspilen, also links Storuman with Stockholm.

There's not much to Storuman itself – the centre consists of one tiny street supporting a couple of shops and banks. The **tourist office** (mid-June to mid-Aug 8am–8pm; mid-Aug to mid-June Mon–Fri 9am–5pm; ☎0951/333 70) is 50m right of the **train station** on Järnvägsgatan. While it's possible to stay here – the seasonal **youth hostel** (☎0951/777 00; June–Aug) and the luxurious *Hotell Toppen* (☎0951/777 00, fax 121 57; ④/②) are both only a ten-minute walk up the hill at Blå Vägen 238 – it's much better to head off into the mountains for some good **hiking** and **fishing**.

If you do stay, try the **restaurant** at *Hotell Toppen*, which has a lunch buffet for 60kr, or alternatively there's the basic, reasonably priced *Cleo Bar* in the main square. Better is *Restaurang Storuman*, opposite the train station, which does Chinese food, pizzas and lunch deals.

Tärnaby and Hemavan

Four **buses** daily make the two-hour drive northwest from Storuman to the tiny mountain village of **TÄRNABY**, birthplace of Ingemar Stenmark, double Olympic gold medallist and Sweden's greatest skier. It's a pretty place, with flower-decked meadows running to the edge of the mountain forests, and great swaths of world-class ski slopes. At the eastern edge of the village as you approach from Storuman, the **Samigården** (late June to mid-Aug daily 10am–4pm; 10kr) is a pleasant introduction to Sami history, culture and customs. The museum recalls older times when, after a kill in a bear hunt, the gall bladder was cut open and the fluid drunk by the hunters. The **tourist office** (mid-June to mid-Aug daily 9am–8pm; mid-Aug to mid-June Mon–Fri 8.30am–5pm; ☎0954/104 50, *info@tarnaby.se*, *www.tarnaby.se*) on the main street can provide information on fishing and hiking in the area. One popular walk is across the nearby Laxfjället mountain, with its fantastic views down over the village – it can be reached by chair lift from either of the two hotels mentioned below. If it's sunny, head for the **beach** at Lake Laisan, where the water is often warm enough to swim – take the footpath which branches off right from Sandviksvägen past the **campsite**. There are several inexpensive places **to stay** – try the *Tärnaby Fjällhotell*, Östra Strandvägen 16 (☎0954/104 20, fax 106 27; ②/①), which also has four-bed apartments for 445kr per day; or the *Fjällvindens Hus* (☎0954/104 25, fax 106 80; ②/①) on Skyttevägen, which also rents out two- to six-berth cabins for 545kr per day.

Buses continue on from Tärnaby to **HEMAVAN**, which marks the beginning and the end of the 500-kilometre Kungsleden trail – see p.604. If you need to stay, head for the *FBU-Gården* **youth hostel** (☎0954/305 10; mid-June to Sept) on Blå Vägen, the main road into the village from Tärnaby. If you have your own transport, you could continue along the E12 towards Norway to the *Hotell Sånninggården* (☎0954/330 00, fax 330 06; ③), dramatically located next to a range of craggy mountains and renowned for its excellent food. It's also the last stop for the Lapplandspilen bus from Stockholm.

Sorsele

SORSELE (pronounced "Sosh-aye-le") is the next major stop on the Inlandsbanan, although major is perhaps a misleading word to use for this dreary, pint-sized town. On the Vindel River, Sorsele became a cause célèbre among conservationists in Sweden when they forced the government to abandon its plans to regulate the flow here by building a hydroelectric power station. The river remains in its natural state today – seething with rapids – and is one of only four in the entire country that haven't been tampered with in some form or other. During the last week in July the river makes its presence felt with the **Vindelälvsloppet**, a long-distance race held over four days (Wed–Sat) that sees hundreds of competitors flog themselves over the 350km from nearby Ammarnäs down to Vännäsby near Umeå. It's quite a spectacle – though, needless to say, accommodation at this time is booked up months in advance. The other big event is the **Vindelälvsdraget**, a dog-sleigh race held over the same course in the second week of March (Thurs–Sun). The town is also an ideal base for **fly-fishing** – the Laisälven and Vindelälven are teeming with grayling and brown trout and a number of local lakes are stocked with char; more details from the **tourist office** at the train station on Stationsgatan (end June to end Aug Mon–Fri 9am–6pm, Sat & Sun 10am–6pm; end Aug to end June Mon–Fri 8.30–11.30am; ☎0952/140 90). In the same building there's a small **museum** (same times; 20kr) detailing the life and times of the Inlandsbanan – worth a look if you're using the train at any time, though unfortunately all labelling is in Swedish.

Accommodation in Sorsele boils down to a rather drab hotel, *Hotell Gästis* (☎0952/107 20, fax 551 41; ④/②) at Hotellgatan 2; a riverside **campsite** (☎0952/101 24) with **cabins** (from 285kr per day); and a small **youth hostel** at Torggatan 1–2 (☎0952/100 48; mid-June to early Aug), just 500m from the train station. **Eating** options are similarly scant: at lunchtime head for the hotel, which has simple dishes for around 60kr, or the dreary pizzeria *La Spezia* on Vindelvägen. Other than that you're left with *Grillhörnan* near the train station, with its greasy burgers and pizzas (40–60kr); the bakery in the same building is the place to buy fresh bread. There are no **bars** in Sorsele, like many of the villages in this part of Sweden, but you can find expensive beer at all the restaurants mentioned above.

Arvidsjaur and the Arctic Circle

An hour and a quarter north of Sorsele on the Inlandsbanan, **ARVIDSJAUR** is by far the largest town you'll have passed since Östersund – though that's not saying much.

Drab housing areas spread out either side of a nondescript and indeterminate main street, Storgatan. For centuries this was where the region's Sami gathered to trade and debate, until their agenda was hijacked by the Protestant missionaries who established their first church here in 1606. The settlement's success was secured when silver was discovered in the nearby mountains and the town flourished as a staging point and supply depot. Despite these developments, the Sami continued to assemble here on market days and during religious festivals, building their own parish village, the **Lappstaden** (daily tours in July at 6pm, 25kr; at other times you can walk in for free), of simple wooden huts at the end of the eighteenth century. About eighty of these have survived, clumped unceremoniously towards the north end of town next to a modern yellow apartment block; they're still used today for the Storstämningshelgen festival over the last weekend in August, as well as for auctions and other events throughout the year. There are still around twenty Sami families in Arvisdjaur, making their living from reindeer husbandry. For more of this, visit the **reindeer enclosure** (late June to mid-Aug daily 5–7pm; 60kr) off Järnvägsgatan. There are generally 10–40 animals in the enclosure, although numbers sometimes increase when hungry reindeer out in the forest drop in for an unexpected visit (they get free and easy food here). **Get there** by walking along Järnvägsgatan towards the campsite, cross the railway lines opposite Sandbackaskolan and take the footpath through the trees towards Lillberget. Arvidsjaur also has some of the best **white-water rafting** in northern Sweden, on the Piteälven river. The price of a trip (260kr per person in July, 350kr at other times; minimum 10 people) includes two hours on the water plus return transport to Arvidsjaur. Bookings can be made at the tourist office. After the trip it's possible to continue north to Jokkmokk and Gällivare by taking the Inlandsbanan from nearby **Moskosel**.

There's no real reason to tarry, but if you want to stay, head for the **tourist office** (mid-June to mid-Aug daily 8.30am–6.30pm; mid-Aug to mid-June Mon–Fri 9am–5pm; ☎0960/175 00, *info@arvidsjaurturism.se, www.arvidsjaurturism.se*) is at Garvaregatan 4, just off Storgatan and five minutes' walk from the station up Lundavägen. They'll fix you up with a **private room** for around 110kr, plus a booking fee of 25kr. The best place to stay however is *Rallaren* (☎0960/216 02; ①; June–Aug), a wonderful old wooden house tastefully restored by a local artist. There's also a cosy private **youth hostel**, *Lappugglans Turistviste*, conveniently situated at Västra Skolgatan 9 (☎0960/124 13); or you could try *Camp Gielas* (☎0960/556 00), which also has **cabins** from 375kr for up to four people set beside Tvättjärn, one of the town's dozen or so lakes, a few minutes' walk along Strandvägen and Järnvägsgatan from the tourist office. The only **hotel** in town is *Hotell Laponia* at Storgatan 45 (☎0960/555 00; ④/③), with comfortable, modern en-suite rooms and a swimming pool. Be warned that in winter much of the town's accommodation is full of test drivers from Europe's leading car companies, who come to the area to experience driving on the frozen lakes – book well in advance to secure a room.

For **snacks** and **coffee** try *Kaffestugan* at Storgatan 21, which has sandwiches and salads for 40–50kr. There's a small choice of **restaurants**: for pizzas and Italian food try *Athena* at Storgatan 10, which has a 60kr lunch deal. Next door at Storgatan 8, *Cazba* serves up pizzas for the same price but has less atmosphere. For finer food, head for the restaurant at the *Hotell Laponia*, where delicious à la carte meals, including local reindeer, go for 100–150kr. The **bar** here is the place to be seen of an evening, but be prepared to shell out 49kr for a beer.

The Arctic Circle

A couple of hours north of Arvidsjaur the Inlandsbanan finally crosses the **Arctic Circle**. This is occasion enough for a bout of whistle-blowing as the train pulls up to allow everyone to take photos of the hoardings announcing the crossing: due to the earth's uneven orbit the line is creeping northwards at a rate of up to 15m a year and the circle is now around 1km north, but for argument's sake this spot is as good as any.

Painted white rocks curve away over the hilly ground, a crude but popular representation of the Circle: one foot on each side is the standard photographic pose.

Jokkmokk

During his journey in Lapland, the botanist Carl von Linné said, "If not for the mosquitoes, this would be earth's paradise"; his comments were made after journeying along the river valley of the Lilla Luleälven during the short summer weeks when the mosquitoes are at their most active. The town's Sami name comes from one particular bend (*mokk*) in the river (*jokk*), which runs through a densely forested municipality the size of Wales with a minuscule population of just 6500; needless to say, **JOKKMOKK** is a welcome oasis, though not an immediately appealing one. Once wintertime Sami quarters, a market and church heralded a permanent settlement by the beginning of the seventeenth century. Today, as well as being a well-known handicrafts centre, the town functions as the Sami capital and is home to the Samiras Folkhögskola, the only further education college teaching handicrafts, reindeer husbandry and ecology in the Sami language.

Jokkmokk's fantastic **Ájtte Museum** (*ájtte* means storage hut in Sami), a brief walk east of the centre on Kyrkogatan, off the main Storgatan (mid-June to late Aug Mon–Fri 9am–7pm, Sat & Sun 11am–6pm; late Aug to mid-June Mon–Fri 9am–4pm, Sat & Sun noon–4pm; 40kr) is the place to really mug up on the Sami. Displays and exhibitions recount the tough existence of the original settlers of northern Scandinavia and show how things have slowly improved over time – today's Sami are more dependent on snow scooters and helicopters to herd their reindeer than on the age-old methods employed by their ancestors. There are some imaginative temporary exhibitions on Sami culture and local flora and fauna, and the museum staff can also arrange day-trips into the surrounding marshes for a spot of mushroom-picking (and mosquito-swatting). Close to the museum on Lappstavägen, the **alpine garden** (late June to mid-Aug Mon–Fri 10am–7pm, Sat & Sun 10am–3pm; other times by arrangement on ☎0971/101 00; 25kr) is home to moor-king, mountain avens, glacier crowfoot and other vegetation to be found on the fells around Jokkmokk.

Have a look, too, at the **Lapp kyrka**, off Stortorget, a recent copy of the eighteenth-century church that stood on this site. The octagonal design and curiously shaped tower betray a Sami influence, but the surrounding graveyard wall is all improvisation: the space in between the coarsely hewn timbers was used to store coffins during winter until the thaw in May, when the Sami could go out and dig graves again – temperatures in this part of Sweden regularly plunge to -30°C and below in winter.

THE JOKKMOKK WINTER MARKET

The great **Jokkmokk winter market** (Jokkmokks marknad), still survives, now nearly 400 years old, held in the first week of February (Thurs–Sun), when 30,000 people force their way into town, increasing the population almost tenfold. It's the best and coldest time of the year to be in Jokkmokk – there's a Wild West feeling in the air – with lots of drunken stall holders trying to flog reindeer hides and other unwanted knick-knacks to even more drunken passers-by – and all in, literally, Arctic temperatures. The **reindeer races** can be a real spectacle: held on the frozen Talvatissjön lake behind the *Hotell Jokkmokk*, man and beast battle it out on a specially marked out track on the ice; however, the reindeer often have other ideas and frequently veer off with great alacrity into the crowd, sending spectators fleeing for cover. Staying in town at this time of year means booking accommodation a good year in advance (although some private rooms become available in the autumn before the market). A smaller and less traditional autumn fair is held at the end of August (around the 25th) – an easier though poorer option.

During summer, Talvatissjön is the preferred spot for catching Arctic char and rainbow trout, though to **fish** here you need a fishing permit (*fiskekort*), available from the tourist office.

Practicalities

Coming by train from Stockholm, get off at Murjek, from where buses run west to Jokkmokk four times a day. Jokkmokk's **tourist office**, at Stortorget 4 (mid-June to mid-Aug daily 9am–7pm; mid-Aug to mid-June Thurs–Sat 8.30am–4pm; ☎0971/121 40, *jokkmokk.turistbyra@jokkmokk.se*, *www.jokkmokk.se/turism*), is a five-minute walk from the train station along Stationsgatan. The **youth hostel** (☎0971/559 77) is located in a wonderful old house with a garden at Åsgatan 20, behind the tourist office. To get to the *Jokkmokks Turistcenter* **campsite** (☎0971/123 70), 3km southeast of town on the Lule River, off the main E97 to Luleå and Boden, you're best off renting a bike from the tourist office (50kr per day). Of the town's two **hotels**, *Hotell Jokkmokk* has a convenient and attractive lakeside setting at Solgatan 45 (☎0971/553 20, fax 556 25; ④/②), though its en-suite rooms are very ordinary and the restaurant a 1970s throwback; *Hotell Gästis* at Herrevägen 1 (☎0971/100 12; ③/②) is nothing to write home about either, with simple modern en-suite rooms.

Jokkmokk has a limited number of **eating** and **drinking** possibilities. The cheap and cheerful *Restaurang Milano* at Berggatan has lunch for 50kr and pizzas for around 60kr at other times. Pizzas are also on the menu at the rather nicer *Restaurang Opera* at Storgatan 36, along with the usual range of meat and fish dishes. If you're gagging for a burger or some Swedish home cooking, head for *Smedjan* on Föreningsgatan. For traditional Sami dishes, such as reindeer, head for the restaurant at the Ájtte Museum, where lunch costs 50kr – the cloudberries and ice cream here is simply divine. The best place to drink is the *Restaurang Opera*; failing that, try *Restaurang Milano* and, in the evenings, the bar inside the *Hotell Jokkmokk* – if you've drunk your way round Jokkmokk this far you won't mind the inebriated late-night company here.

Southeast of Jokkmokk: Vuollerim

Forty-five kilometres southeast of Jokkmokk on Route 97 to Boden and Luleå lies **VUOLLERIM**, site of a 6000-year-old Stone Age winter settlement. Archeological digs have uncovered evidence of habitation in the area – the well-preserved remains of houses, storage pits, tool and weapon shards, fires, rubbish dumps and drainage works. A small and excellent **museum** (mid-June to mid-Aug Mon–Fri 9am–6pm; mid-Aug to mid-June Mon–Fri 9am–4pm; 50kr) covers the development of the various sites and a slide show takes you on a local journey through time, reconstructing the probable life of the inhabitants. The whole thing really comes alive when a minibus carts you off to the digs themselves, with archeologists providing a guided tour in English – without them the whole thing would be nothing more than a mudbath to the untrained eye. The museum is on the edge of tiny Vuollerim at Murjeksvägen 31. To get here from Jokkmokk, either take the #44 Boden/Luleå bus and get off at the Statoil filling station, from where it's a one-kilometre walk up the road towards the village, or take bus #94 to Murjek, which goes right to the museum. The site sits on a narrow, wooded promontory that juts out into the lake – a great place for a picnic.

Gällivare

Last stop on the Inlandsbanan and by far the biggest town since Östersund, **GÄLLIVARE** is far more pleasant than you'd imagine from its industrial surroundings. Strolling around its open centre, heavily glazed and insulated against the biting cold of winter, is a great antidote to the small inland villages along the train route. There's a gritty ugliness to Gällivare that gives the place a certain charm: a steely grey mesh of modern streets that has all the hallmarks of a city, although on a scale that's far too modest for the title to be applied with any justification. It's also an excellent base for hiking in the nearby national parks (see p.600).

Arrival, information and accommodation

Gällivare's **train station**, on Lasarettsgatan, is five minutes' walk from the **tourist office** at Storgatan 16 (June to mid-Aug Mon–Fri 9am–8pm, Sat & Sun 10am–6pm; mid-Aug to May Mon–Fri 9am–4pm; ☎0970/166 60, *turistinfo@gellivare.se*, *www.lappland.se* and *www.gellivare.se*), which provides good free maps and hiking information; downstairs in the same building there's a café and upstairs a simple **museum** dealing with Sami history and forestry. The tourist office can fix you up with a **private room** for around 130kr per person, plus a booking fee of 10kr, or you could sample the town's **youth hostel** (☎0970/143 80; open all year but bookings required Sept–May), behind the train station – cross the tracks by the metal bridge; because of the town's position

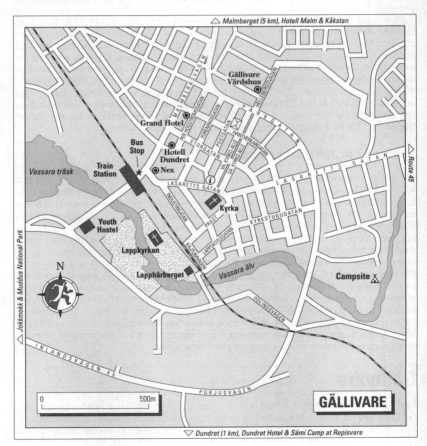

△ Malmberget (5 km), Hotell Malm & Kåkstan

Gällivare Värdshus

Grand Hotel

Bus Stop

Hotell Dundret

Nex

Train Station

Vassara träsk

LASARETTS GATAN

Kyrka

KYRKSTUGUGATAN

Youth Hostel

Lappkyrkan

Lapphärberget

Vassara älv

Campsite

Jokkmokk & Muddus National Park

N

INLANDSVAGEN 45

PORJUSVAGEN

△ Route 45

GÄLLIVARE

0   500m

▽ Dundret (1 km), Dundret Hotel & Sámi Camp at Repisvare

on routes north to Kiruna and Narvik (and south to Stockholm and Gothenburg), book-ing ahead in summer is advised. This is a wonderful place to stay in winter when the Vassara träsk lake is frozen – snow scooters whizz up and down its length under the eerie Northern Lights, clearly visible in Gällivare. If the hostel's full, try the small and rather less friendly **private hostel**, *Lapphärberget* (☎0970/125 34), near the Lappkyrkan. There's also a **campsite** (☎0970/165 45; mid-May to mid-Sept) by the river and off the main E45 between Porjusvägen and Jokkmokk. If you've your own transport, undoubtedly the most interesting place to stay is in the simple wooden huts at the reconstructed shantytown, **Kåkstan**, up at Malmberget, the hill 1km to the north of the town (☎0970/183 96 or book through the tourist office). A four-berth hut costs 360kr; cheaper dormitory accommodation in an eight-bed room goes for just 90kr.

Hotels

Dundret (☎0970/145 60, fax 148 27). The best hotel around, but it's at the top of the Dundret moun-tain south of the town, so you'll need your own transport to get here. Not to be confused with the *Hotell Dundret* in town. ⑤/⑤.

Hotell Dundret, Per Högströmsgatan 1 (☎0970/550 40). Actually a small pension, with just seven rooms and shared shower and toilet. ②/①.

Gällivare Värdshus, Klockljungsvägen 2 (☎0970/162 00, fax 155 45). A central German-run cheap-ie; it looks dreadfully grotty on the outside, but inside is perfectly OK. ③/①.

Grand, Per Högströmsgatan 9 (☎0970/164 20, fax 164 25). The second-best hotel in town with decent rooms and handily situated for the *Kilkenny Inn* which shares the same building. ③/②.

Malm, Torget 18, in Malmberget, 1km north of Gällivare (☎0970/244 50). Rooms here are basic, without bathrooms, but reasonable all year round. ①.

Nex, Lasarettsgatan 1 (☎0970/550 20, fax 154 75). The best in town, with smart, tastefully decorat-ed rooms and a good restaurant (see p.600), and handy for the station. ④/③.

The Town

Gällivare is one of the most important sources of **iron ore** in Europe, and if you've any interest in seeing a working mine, don't wait until Kiruna's tame "tourist tour" (see p.602). The modern mines and works are distant, dark blots, tucked away up at Malmberget, the hill overlooking Gällivare. There are two separate tours (book at the tourist office), both running from June to August: one is of the underground **iron-ore mine** (Mon–Fri 9.30am & 1.30pm; 160kr); the other of the open cast **copper mine** (Mon–Fri 2pm; 160kr), which is the biggest in Europe (and also, incidentally, Sweden's biggest gold mine – gold is recovered from the slag produced during the extraction of the copper). The ear-splitting noise produced by the mammoth-sized trucks in the iron-ore mine (they're five times the height of a man) can be quite disconcerting in the con-fined darkness. This tour also takes in **Kåkstan**, the shantytown where the miners lived over a hundred years ago – rows of reconstructed wooden huts either side of an unmade street (it's also possible to stay here – see above).

Gällivare occupies the site of a Sami village and one theory has it that the town's name comes from the Sami language – *djelli* (a crack or gorge) *vare* (in the mountain). Down by the river near the train station, you'll come across the Sami church, **Lappkyrkan** (mid-June to late Aug 10am–3pm), a mid-eighteenth-century construc-tion. It's known as the "Ettöreskyrkan" (One Öre Church) after the one öre subscrip-tion drive throughout Sweden that paid for it.

Walks around Gällivare

There's precious little else to see or do in Gällivare and you'd be wise to use your time exploring the marshes and forests of one of the nearby **national parks**: Padeljanta,

Stora Sjöfallet or, especially, **Muddus** (for more on which, see below), which lies south of town, hemmed in by the Inlandsbanan on one side and the train line from Boden to Gällivare on the other. The park is easy to reach with your own car; public transport will only take you to within 12km – take the bus to Ligga and then walk to Skaite and the beginning of the network of trails (see below).

Train travellers unfortunately barely catch a glimpse of the park, which is shrouded by dense forest, and will have to be satisfied with the **Dundret** mountain, overshadowing the town, which is the target of Midnight Sun spotters. You can walk up to the *Björnfällan* restaurant (the name means "bear trap"), about a four-kilometre hike on a well-marked path, and the views are magnificient, though this isn't the very top. Buses head up the winding road specially for the Midnight Sun, leaving daily at 11pm from the train station (mid-June to mid-July), returning at 1am; tickets, available from the tourist office, cost 160kr return and include the ubiquitous Swedish waffle covered with cloudberries and cream.

Eating and drinking

If you're arriving from one of the tiny villages on the Inlandsbanan, the wealth of **eating and drinking** possibilities in Gällivare will make you quite dizzy; if you're coming from Luleå, grit your teeth and bear it. A good place for lunch is the *Restaurang Peking* at Storgatan 21B, which has reasonable Chinese food from 60kr, plus pizzas. The best pizzeria in town is *Pizzeria Dylan* in the Arkaden shopping centre, which also does takeaways but is closed in the evening. The restaurant in the *Nex Hotell* on Lasarettsgatan does good lunches for 50–60kr. Coffee and cakes can be consumed at *Centralskolans Café* under the tourist office. As for **drinking**, the place to be seen is the Irish-theme pub, *Kilkenny Inn* at Per Högströmsgatan 9, or the *Wassara Pub* inside the *Nex Hotel* opposite the train station.

National parks around Gällivare

Muddus is the place recommended for beginnners, a pine forest and marshland park between Jokkmokk and Gällivare, home to bears, lynx, martens, weasels, hares, elk and, in summer, reindeer; the whooper swan is one of the most commonly sighted

---

HIKING IN THE NATIONAL PARKS

It's not a good idea to go **hiking in the national parks** of northern Sweden on a whim. Even for experienced walkers, the going can be tough and uncomfortable in parts, downright treacherous in others. Mosquitoes are a real problem: it's difficult to imagine the utter misery of being covered in a blanket of insects; your eyes, ears and nose full of the creatures. Yet this is one of the last wilderness areas left in Europe: the map of this part of the country shows little more than vast areas of forest and mountains; roads and human habitation are the exception rather than the norm. Reindeer are a common sight since the parks are breeding grounds and summer pasture, and Sami settlements are dotted throughout the region – at Ritsem and Vaisaluokta, for example. Although there are some good short trails in the national parks, suitable for beginners, the goal for more ambitious hikers is the northern section of the **Kungsleden** trail, which crosses several of the parks.

The best **time** to go hiking in the Swedish mountains is from late June to September. During May and early June the ground is very wet and boggy due to the rapid snow melt. Once the snow has gone wild flowers burst into bloom to make the most of the short summer months. The **weather** is very changeable – one moment it can be hot and sunny, the next it can be cold and rainy – snow showers are by no means uncommon even in summer. It goes without saying that you'll need to be **well equipped** with hiking gear, a sleeping bag, decent boots and of course a map.

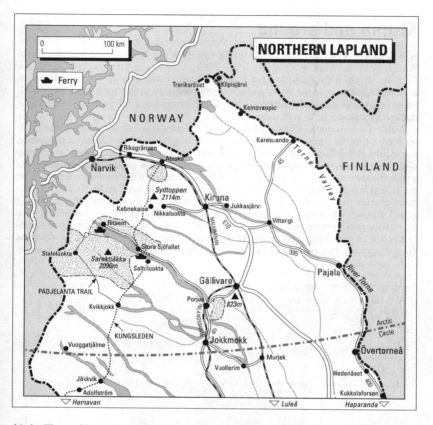

birds. The park's western edges are skirted by Route 45 and the easiest approach is to leave the highway at Liggadammen (buses from Gällivare) and then follow the small road to Skaite. You can also reach the park from the southeast via Nattavaara and Messaure. An easy hiking trail of 50km starts at Skaite, with cabins along the route and a campsite by the Muddus falls.

Beginning about 120km northwest of Gällivare, the tract of wilderness edging Norway contains no fewer than three national parks, with the low fells, large lakes and moors of Padjelanta and Stora Sjöfallet parks framing the sheer face of the mountainous and inhospitable Sarek park. **Padjelanta** is the largest national park in Sweden; the Sami name means "the higher country", an apt description for a high tableland almost exclusively above the treeline and home to thousands of reindeer. A 150-kilometre trail, the **Padjelanta Trail**, runs from Kvikkjokk (reached by bus from Jokkmokk) north through Stora Sjöfallet to Vaisaluokta (across the lake from Ritsem) and is good for inexperienced walkers – allow at least a week. From Ritsem there are buses back to Gällivare.

The real baddie is **Sarek**, the terrain being officially classed as "extremely difficult". There are no tourist facilities, trails, cabins or bridges; the rivers are dangerous and the weather rotten – definitely not for anyone without Chris Bonington-type experience.

Kiruna and around

KIRUNA was at the hub of the battle for the control of the iron-ore supply during World War II. From here ore was transported north by train to the great harbour at Narvik over the border in Norway. Much German fire power was expended in an attempt to interrupt the supply to the Allies and wrest control for the Axis. In the process, Narvik suffered greviously, whilst Kiruna – benefiting from supposed Swedish neutrality – made a packet selling to both sides.

Today the train ride to Kiruna rattles through sidings, slag heaps and ore works, a bitter contrast to the surrounding wilderness. Brooding reminders of Kiruna's prosperity, the **mines** still dominate the town, and much more depressingly than in neighbouring Gällivare, two hours back down the train line: despite the new central buildings and open parks, the town retains a gritty industrial air. **Guided tours** of the mines are arranged by the tourist office (July to mid-Aug 3 daily; late June and late Aug 2 daily; 125kr). A coach takes visitors through the underground road network and then stops off at a "tourist mine", a closed-off section of a leviathan structure containing service stations, restaurants, computer centres, trains and crushing mills. All the other sights in town are firmly wedded to the all-important metal in one way or another. The tower of the **Rådhus** (June–Aug daily 9am–6pm; Sept–May Mon–Fri 9am–5pm) is obvious even from the train

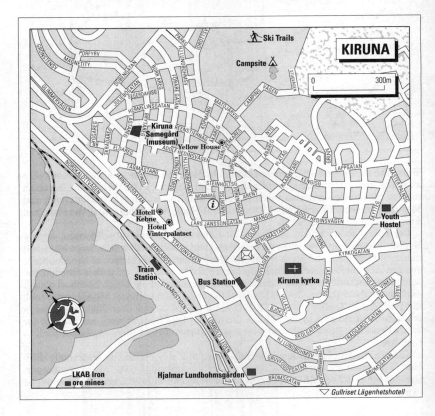

station, a strident metal pillar harbouring an intricate latticework clock face and sundry bells that chime raucously at noon. It was designed by Bror Marklund and the whole hall unbelievably won the 1964 award for the most beautiful Swedish public building. Inside there's a tolerable art collection and Sami handicraft displays in summer.

Only a few minutes up the road, **Kiruna kyrka** (daily 11am–5pm; July till 10pm) causes a few raised eyebrows. Built in the style of a Sami hut, it's a massive origami creation of oak beams and rafters the size of a small aircraft hangar. LKAB, the iron-ore company that to all intents and purposes *is* Kiruna, and which paid for its construction, was also responsible for the nearby **Hjalmar Lundbohmsgården** (June–Aug daily 10am–5pm; Sept–May Mon–Fri 10am–4pm; 30kr), a country house once used by the managing director of the company and "founder" of Kiruna. Displays inside mostly consist of early twentieth-century photographs featuring the man himself and assorted Sami in their winter gear. Visit before going down the mine and everything will take on an added perspective – without the mine, Kiruna would be a one-reindeer town instead of the thriving place it is today.

The **Kiruna Samegård**, at Brytaregatan 14 (mid-June to Sept daily 10am–6pm; Oct to mid-June Mon–Fri 10am–4pm; 20kr), is the most rewarding exhibition of Sami culture in town. The handicrafts may be familiar but what won't be is the small display of really very good Sami art. There's a café and souvenir shop where you can buy a piece of antler bone or reindeer skin to take home.

Practicalities

Arriving by **train**, it's a brisk ten-minute walk from the station up the steep hill to the **tourist office** in Folkets Hus, in the central square off Mommagatan (mid-June to Aug Mon–Fri 9am–8pm, Sat & Sun 9am–6pm; Sept to mid-June Mon–Fri 9am–5pm; ☎0980/188 80, *lappland@kiruna.se, www.lappland.se*). Kiruna's **youth hostel** (☎0980/171 95) is 900m from the train station at Bergmästaregatan 7. It fills quickly in summer, as does the **campsite** (☎0980/131 00), a twenty-minute walk north on Campingvägen, in the Högalid part of town; cabins (②) are available here too. Kiruna also has a number of central **hotels** – try *Hotell Vinterpalatset* at Järnvägsgatan 18 (☎0980/677 70, fax 130 50; ⑨/③), which has a superb sauna and jacuzzi suite on the top floor. Round the corner at Konduktörsgatan 7, *Hotell Kebne* (☎0980/681 80; ④/②) is also handy for the train station and has good-quality rooms. A cheap alternative is *Yellow House* (☎0980/137 50, fax 137 51) at Hantverkaregatan 25, which has hostel-style rooms sleeping up to four with shared bathrooms for 120kr per person.

Kiruna's hardly a centre of haute cuisine, but **eating** at the inordinately popular *Mats & Mums,* Bergmästaregatan 10, is the best bet – the window through into the adjacent swimming pool makes an unusual setting for a meal of burgers or Arctic specialities (100–150kr). Good food is also served at the *Restaurang Lapplandia,* Bergmästaregatan – don't be put off by the ugly brown facade. The best pizza in town is found at *Pizza & Pasta Plus* in Mangigatan. Next door at no. 26, *Nan King* is the northernmost Chinese restaurant in Sweden. Coffee and cakes are served up at *Safari* in Geologgatan. Kiruna's most popular **bar** is the *3nd Baren* at Föreningsgatan 11, an old wooden building with coarsely hewn floorboards. The Western-style *Mommas* in the main square, alongside the tourist office, is also worth a look. The grotty drinking den that is *Restaurang Arran,* across the square at Föreningsgatan 9, often serves staggeringly cheap beer before 11pm and attracts a corresponding clientele – go in with a friend.

Around Kiruna: Jukkasjärvi

The tiny village of **JUKKASJÄRVI** is a mecca for any tourist travelling in Lapland in winter: the **Ice Hotel** (☎0980/668 00, fax 668 90, *rec@icehotel.com, www.icehotel.com*;

850kr per person in a double room; a decorated suite is 1250kr per person) that is built here late every October is also the world's biggest igloo and stands proudly by the side of the Torneälven river until it melts in May. Ten thousand tons of ice and thirty thousand tons of snow are used to make the igloo, whose exact shape and design changes from year to year. There is usually a bar in the entrance hall, several bedrooms with compacted snow beds covered with reindeer hides, an exhibition hall, cinema and a chapel where local couples can marry. Winter temperatures are generally around -20 to -30°C, which means that inside the igloo it's normally around -5°C. Guests are provided with specially made sleeping bags as used by the Swedish army, who do their Arctic survival training here – don't wear pyjamas or you'll sweat. If you chicken out, there are also cabins for rent on the site (⑤/④); all bookings are handled by *Jukkas AB* at Marknadsvägen 63. Undoubtedly the best way to arrive at the *Ice Hotel* is by **dog sled** from the airport; for a hefty 3500kr you can be met from your plane and pulled to your room. You can **eat** across the road at *Jukkasjärvi Wärdhus*, where lunch goes for around 100kr.

In **summer** Jukkasjärvi is a good place to commune with nature: river-rafting, fishing and hiking are all possible – ring the *Ice Hotel* number for details.

From Kiruna to the Norwegian border

Since 1984 there's been a choice of ways to continue your journey towards Norway: by train on the last leg of the long run from Stockholm or Luleå towards Narvik, or on the **Nordkalottvägen** road, which runs parallel to the railway, threading its way across barren plateaux (the lakes up here are still frozen in mid-June) before slicing through the mighty Norwegian mountains. It's an exhilarating run that passes the start of the **Kungsleden** trail at Abisko: get off the train at Abisko Turiststation (not Abisko Ö, which is the village) and the adjoining fell station offers all sorts of useful advice for hikes from half a day upwards. The **cable car** (*linbanan*; 85kr return) offers fantastic views of the surrounding wilderness, including the spectacular U-shaped peaks of Lapporten (used as landmark by the Sami for guiding reindeer between their summer and winter grazing land), the 70km-long Torneträsk lake and the vast wooded expanses of Abisko National Park. Both train line and road continue on to Riksgränsen, the last settlement in Sweden, where it's possible to ski right up to late June. There's a **hotel** here, the *Hotell Riksgränsen* (☎0980/400 80, fax 431 25; ④/③), opposite the train station, which has information about **hiking, mountain biking** and **canoeing** in the area. Remember though that this is the wettest spot in Sweden.

THE KUNGSLEDEN

The **Kungsleden** is the most famous and popular of Sweden's hiking trails, a 500-kilometre route from **Abisko** in the north to **Hemavan**, near Tärnaby (see p.594), in the south. From Abisko to Kvikkjokk, north of the Arctic Circle, and in the south between Ammarnäs and Hemavan there are STF cabins and fell stations. Huts are placed at intervals of 15–20km, a distance that can be covered in one day, while shelter from the wind is provided at various places along the route. The Kungsleden is an easy trail to walk: it's well-marked; all the streams en route are crossed by bridges and patches of marshy ground overlaid with wooden planks; and there are also boat services or rowing boats for crossing the several large lakes on the way.

If you're looking for total isolation this is not the trail for you – it's the busiest in the country. One handy tip is to go against the flow: most people start from Abisko, but if you walk the route in reverse you'll find it easier going – or avoid July.

The Torne Valley

The gently sloping sides of the lush **Tornedalen** (Torne Valley) are one of the most welcoming sights in northern Sweden. Stretching over 500km from the mouth of the Gulf of Bothnia to Sweden's remote northern tip, the three rivers, Torne, Muonio and Könkämä mark out the long border between Sweden and Finland in the far north of Scandinavia. The valley is refreshingly different from the coast; the villages here are small and rural, often no more than a couple of wooden cottages surrounded by open flower meadows running down to the river's edge; and different too from the heavily wooded inland regions of the country, the open plains here providing much needed grazing land for the farmers' livestock. **Buses** run from Haparanda up the valley and you can break the journey whenever you feel like it to take in one of the many lakes swirling in mist.

Pajala

The valley's main village is pretty **PAJALA** (pronounced "py-allah") – a place which has earned itself something of a reputation in Sweden. To celebrate the village's recent 400th anniversary, the local council placed ads in Swedish newspapers inviting women from the south of the country up to Lapland to take part in the birthday festivities; the predominance of heavy-labouring jobs in the north of Sweden has produced a population imbalance – around three men to every woman – and explains the ridiculously macho behaviour that prevails in these parts. Journalists outside Sweden soon heard about the ads and before long busloads of women from across Europe were heading north to take part in a drunken, debauched bash. The plan worked, however, with dozens of east European women losing their hearts to gruff Swedish lumberjacks and beginning new lives north of the Arctic Circle. However, it remains to be seen whether the effects of several winters of 24-hour darkness, coupled with temperatures of -25°C, will tip the balance back.

The third week of September, the **Römpäviiko** – the "romp week" – as this ongoing cultural festival is called, is undoubtedly the liveliest time to be in the village. At any other time Pajala is a great place to rest up for a day or so, take a walk along the riverside or head off in search of the great grey owl (*strix nebulosa*) that sweeps through the nearby forests; the huge wooden model in the bus station will give you an idea of what the bird looks like: lichen grey with long slender tail feathers and a white crescent between its black and yellow eyes.

Pajala's **tourist office** (mid-June to Sept Mon–Fri 9am–6pm, Sat & Sun 11am–5pm; Oct to mid-June Mon–Fri 9am–5pm; ☎0978/100 15) is located in the bus station and can provide information on the surrounding area. Close by at Soukolovägen 2, *Bykrogen Hotell* (☎0978/712 00, fax 714 64; ④/②) has cosy little **rooms**, or there's the similar *Hotell Smedjan* at Fridhemsvägen 1 (☎0978/108 15, fax 717 75; ④/②). But the best place to stay is right at the other end of the village: *Pajala Camping* (☎0978/718 80; May–Sept) offers stunning views over the lazy Torne river, plus some simple **cabins** with cold water.

For **eating and drinking**, head for the *Bykrogen Hotell* at lunchtime for the cheapest meals – *dagens rätt* goes for 60kr; for traditional northern Swedish delicacies count on at least 120kr. At weekends there's also a popular **disco** in the basement. Plain *Bykrogen*, just round the corner, is a cheap and cheerful pizzeria.

Heading north: Karesuando and Treriksröset

Two buses leaves Pajala once daily (except Sun) for Sweden's northernmost village, **KARESUANDO** (change in Vittangi), a surprisingly likeable place where the land is in the grip of permafrost all year round and life is pretty tough. Karesuando is 250km north of the Arctic Circle and deep in Sami country – here national borders carry little significance, people cross them without as much as a bat of an eyelid as they go about their everyday business.

If you're heading for **Treriksröset** – a cairn where Sweden, Norway and Finland meet – you can spend the night here and travel on the next day; *Karesuando Camping* (☎0981/201 39) with **cabins** from 275kr for up to four people is your only choice of **accommodation**. Alternatively there's a **youth hostel** across the river in Finnish Kaaresuvanto (from Sweden call ☎00 358/167 7771). For **eating** you're limited to self-catering or the nameless greasy-spoon grill restaurant between the OK and Statoil filling stations.

The seasonal **tourist office** (mid-June to mid-Aug daily 10am–7pm; ☎0981/202 05) is located in the village school, to the left of the bridge across to Finland. The only sight to speak of in Karesuando is the wooden cabin beyond the tourist office which was once home to revivalist preacher, **Lars Levi Laestadius**. The rectory, complete with simple wooden pews, was used as a meeting place whilst Laestadius was rector in Karesuando. Also worth a quick look is the **Sámiid Viessu** (July to mid-Aug daily 10am–7pm) photography and handicraft exhibition along the road to the campsite, which has some atmospheric black-and-white shots of local Sami.

To continue to Treriksröset, cross the River Könkämä to **Kaaresuvanto** in Finland (remember Finnish time is an hour ahead), from where buses leave in summer for Kilpisjärvi, the settlement closest to the border junction. From Kilpisjärvi there are two choices: an eleven-kilometre hike down a track to the Treriksröset cairn or a twenty-minute **boat** ride across the lake which shortens the hike to just 3km.

travel details

Trains

Borlänge to: Falun (11 daily; 15min); Gävle (4 daily; 1hr 30min); Mora (7 daily; 1hr 20min); Örebro (4 daily; 2hr); Stockholm (8 daily; 2hr 20min); Uppsala (8 daily; 1hr 45min).

Falun to: Borlänge (11 daily; 15min); Gävle (4 daily; 1hr); Örebro (4 daily; 2hr 30min); Stockholm (10 daily; 2hr 40min); Uppsala (10 daily; 2hr 20min).

Gällivare to: Boden (3 daily; 2hr); Gävle (2 daily; 14hr); Gothenburg (1 daily; 19hr 30min); Kiruna (3 daily; 1hr); Luleå (3 daily; 2hr 20min); Stockholm (2 daily; 16hr 30min); Umeå (1 daily; 7hr); Uppsala (2 daily; 15hr 30min).

Karlstad to: Stockholm (5 daily; 2hr 40min).

Kiruna to: Abisko (3 daily; 1hr 20min); Boden (3 daily; 3hr); Gothenburg (1 daily; 20hr 30min); Luleå (3 daily; 3hr 20min); Narvik (3 daily; 3hr); Riksgränsen (3 daily; 2hr); Stockholm (2 daily; 17hr 30min); Uppsala (2 daily; 16hr 30min).

Mora to: Borlänge (8 daily; 1hr 20min); Leksand (8 daily; 40min); Rättvik (8 daily; 25min); Stockholm (6 daily; 4hr); Uppsala (8 daily; 3hr 40min).

Östersund to: Åre (4 daily; 1hr 45min); Gothenburg (1 daily; 11hr); Stockholm (6 daily; 6hr); Storlien (4 daily; 3hr); Sundsvall (5 daily; 2hr 15min); Trondheim (3 daily; 5hr 30min); Uppsala (6 daily; 5hr 40min).

The Inlandsbanan

Timetables change slightly from year to year, but the following is a rough idea of **Inlandsbanan** services and times. The Inlandsbanan runs from Mora to Gällivare via Östersund from late June to mid-Aug. **Northbound** trains leave Mora daily at 7.35am calling at Orsa and Sveg and many other wayside halts en route for Östersund. From Östersund, trains leave daily for Gällivare at 7.05am calling at Ulriksfors (for Strömsund), Dorotea, Vilhelmina, Storuman, Sorsele, Arvidsjaur, the Arctic Circle, Jokkmokk and Gällivare. **Southbound** trains leave Gällivare daily at 6.45am for stations to Östersund. From Östersund a train leaves at 2.45pm daily for Mora.

Buses

The **Inlandsexpressen** (#45) runs **north** from Mora to Gällivare via Orsa, Sveg, Åsarna, Östersund, Strömsund, Dorotea, Vilhelmina, Storuman, Sorsele, Arvidsjaur, Moskosel and Jokkmokk. It operates daily all year, leaving Mora at 8am and 2pm for Östersund, from Östersund at 7am for Gällivare, at 1.40pm for Arvidsjaur and at 4.55pm for Storuman. Heading **south**, a bus leaves Gällivare at 9.30am for Östersund, from Arvidsjaur at 8.35am for Östersund and from Storuman for Östersund at 7.10am. From Östersund two buses leave for Mora at 6.50am and 12.30pm.

Åsarna to: Klövsjö (3 daily; 15min); Östersund (5 daily; 1hr 20min).

Gällivare to: Jokkmokk (5 daily; 1hr 30min); Kiruna (4 daily; 2hr); Luleå (4 daily; 3hr 15min); Pajala (3 daily; 2hr 20min); Ritsem (3 daily; 3hr 30min).

Jokkmokk to: Gällivare (5 daily; 1hr 30min); Kvikkjokk (2 daily; 1hr 50min).

Kiruna to: Gällivare (3 daily; 2hr); Karesuando (2 daily; 3hr); Luleå (2 daily; 4hr 45min); Pajala (2 daily; 3hr 15min).

Kvikkjokk to: Jokkmokk (2 daily; 1hr 50min).

Mora to: Idre (2 daily; 2hr 30min); Orsa (26 daily; 20min); Sälen (1 daily; 2hr 30min).

Östersund to: Arvidsjaur (1 daily; 7hr); Gällivare (1 daily; 11hr); Mora (2 daily; 5hr); Storuman (1 daily; 4hr 30min); Umeå (2 daily; 6hr).

Storuman to: Hemavan (3 daily; 2hr 20min); Tärnaby (4 daily; 2hr).

International trains
Karlstad to: Oslo (2 daily; 3hr).

Flights
There are fairly regular flights, operated mainly by SAS and Skyways between Stockholm Arlanda and the main northern cities. Timetables are subject to constant change, however, so it's advisable to check with a travel agent.

PART FIVE

FINLAND

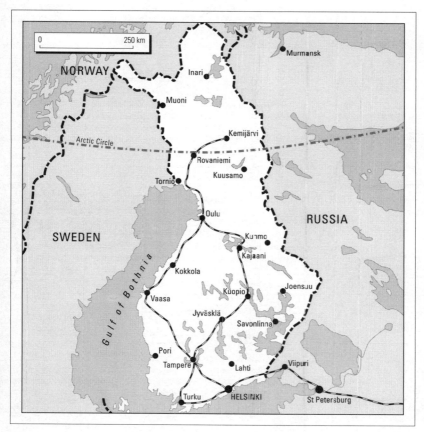

Introduction

Main and Scandinavia's most culturally isolated and least understood country, **Finland** has been independent only since 1917, having been ruled for hundreds of years by imperial powers: first the Swedes and then the tsarist Russians. Much of its history involves a struggle simply for recognition and survival.

During the Swedish period, the Finnish language (one of the world's strangest and most difficult) was regarded as fit only for peasants – which the majority of Finns were – and attempts were later made to forcibly impose Russian. All publications were in Swedish until the *Kalevala* appeared in the early nineteenth century. A written collection of previously orally transmitted folk tales telling of a people close to nature, living by hunting and fishing, the *Kalevala* instantly became regarded as a truly Finnish history, and formed the basis of the **National Romantic** movement in the arts that flourished from the mid-nineteenth century, stimulating political initiatives towards Finnish nationalism.

It's not surprising therefore that modern-day Finns have a well-developed sense of their own culture, and the legacy of the past is strongly felt – in the still widely popular Golden Age paintings of Gallen-Kallela, Edelfelt and others; the music of Sibelius; the National Romantic architecture (which paved the way for modern greats like Alvar Aalto); or in the fact that the scars of the 1918 Civil War, which split the nation following independence, have yet to heal fully. Equally in evidence, even among city dwellers, are the deeply ingrained, down-to-earth values of rural life, along with a sense of spirituality epitomized by the sauna, which for Finns is a meaningful ritual rather than an exercise in health. A small but significant proportion of Finns actually come from Karelia – a large tract of land now scythed in two by the Finnish–Russian border and sparsely inhabited, but historically a homeland distinct from Finland and Russia, and one whose traditional peasant culture is highly revered.

Some elderly rural dwellers are prone to suspicion of anything foreign, but in general the Finnish population is much less staid than its Nordic neighbours, and the disintegration of its once powerful neighbour, the Soviet Union, has allowed it to form closer ties with Europe through membership of the European Union. By the end of the 1990s Finland's economy was buoyant enough to allow it to join the first wave of countries in the European Monetary Union, and with the success of Finnish telecommunications giant Nokia and a flourishing IT sector, the country reached the millennium with renewed confidence and self-belief. However, unemployment is still high in some places, particularly in rural areas, and some sections of the country's society are being left behind in Finland's drive to become a technological world leader.

■ Where to go

Finland is mainly flat, and filled by huge forests and lakes – you'll need to travel around a lot to appreciate the country's wide regional variations. The **south** contains the least dramatic scenery, but the capital, **Helsinki**, more than compensates, with its brilliant architecture and superb museum collections. Stretching from the Russian border in the east to the industrial city of **Tampere**, the water systems of the **Lake Region** provide a natural means of transport for the timber industry – indeed, water here is a more common sight than land.

Ostrobothnia, the upper portion of the west coast, is characterized by near-featureless farmlands and long sandy beaches which are – to Finns at least – the region's main draw. Here too you'll also find the clearest Swedish influence: in parts up to a third of the population are Swedish-speaking – known as "Finland-Swedes" – and there's a rich heritage from the days of Swedish trading supremacy. **Kainuu** is the thickly forested heart of the country, much of its small population spread among scattered villages. The land begins to rise as you head north from here, folding into a series of fells and gorges that are ripe for spectacular hiking. **Lapland**, completely devoid of large towns, contains the most alluring terrain of all, its stark and haunting landscapes able to absorb any number of visitors on numerous hiking routes. This region is home to the Sami people, semi-nomadic reindeer herders whose traditional way of life remains relatively untainted by modern culture.

■ When to go

The official Finnish **holiday season** is early July to mid-August, and during these weeks there's an exodus from the towns to the country. The best time to visit the rural regions is either side of these dates, when things will be less crowded and hectic – though no cheaper.

In **summer**, regarded as being from June to early September, Helsinki, the south and the Lake

Region enjoy mild and sunny weather. Temperatures are usually 18–24°C (65–75°F), sometimes reaching 32°C (90°F) in the daytime, but they drop swiftly in the evening, when you'll need a light jacket. The north is always a few degrees cooler and often quite cold at night, so carry at least a thick jumper. The Midnight Sun can be seen from Rovaniemi northwards for two months over midsummer; the rest of the country experiences a night-long twilight from mid-June to mid-July.

Winter, roughly from late October to early April in the south, plus a few weeks more on either side in the north, is painfully cold. Helsinki generally fluctuates between 0°C and -20°C (32°F and -4°F), the harshest months being January and February; in the north it's even colder, with just a few hours of daylight; and in the extreme north the sun doesn't rise at all. The snow cover generally lasts from November to March in the south, a few weeks longer in the north. On the plus side, Finland copes easily with low temperatures and transport is rarely disrupted.

The best time for **hiking** is from May to September in the south and from June to September in the north. You'll need a good-quality tent, a warm sleeping bag, rainwear, spare warm clothing, thick-soled waterproof boots, a compass and detailed maps. Maps and other equipment can be bought in tourist centres close to the hiking routes. See p.34 for more on hiking.

Getting there from the rest of Scandinavia

Finland's geographical position – effectively separated from the rest of Scandinavia by the Gulf of Bothnia – means that except in the extreme north of the country the easiest approaches are usually by ferry or plane. Crossing from the east coast of Sweden is easy, with regular **ferry** crossings from a number of points and usually good onward links once you've arrived. Further north, Sweden and Norway both have land borders with Finland and these are no fuss to cross by **bus**, although in a few spots you may have to wait several days between connections. From Denmark, it's impossible to get to Finland without passing through Sweden unless you **fly**, although there's a direct bus–ferry service and fairly frequent trains.

■ By bus

In the Arctic North, buses connect the Norwegian–Finnish border towns of **Karasjok–Karisganiemi**

and **Skipbotn–Kilpisjärvi**, as well as the Finnish border villages of **Polmak** and **Nuorgam**; fares and schedules, beyond what we've included under the Travel Details at the end of the relevant chapters, can be checked at any tourist office or bus station. There are also regular services from points in northern Sweden via the twin border towns of **Haparanda-Tornio**, at the northern end of the Gulf of Bothnia – see the Travel Details on p.574 for more information.

Long-distance bus-and-ferry connections to Finland are also fairly frequent. The service **from Copenhagen** to Finland runs four times a week to Helsinki, via **Stockholm** and **Turku**. Naturally, it's a fairly exhausting journey, taking 25 hours.

■ By train

There are no direct train connections between Finland and other Scandinavian countries. The nearest railhead is at Luleå in Sweden, at the northern end of the Gulf of Bothnia, around 100km before the Finnish border at Haparanda-Tornio (rail passes are valid on buses from Luleå to Haparanda). Other train connections, such as those between Helsinki and **Stockholm** or **Copenhagen** (1–2 daily; 25hr) make use of ferry crossings for part of their route.

■ By ferry

The most frequent ferries from Sweden to Finland run between **Stockholm** and Helsinki and are operated by the Silja and Viking lines. Each company has a year-round overnight service, leaving at 6pm and arriving at 9am. Both lines also run a twice-daily service from Stockholm to **Turku**, which takes ten or eleven hours. Quicker still (6–10hr) are the daily services between Stockholm and **Mariehamn**, run by Silja, Viking and Birka Line.

For current details on timetables and the numerous discounts available – ranging from 50 percent reductions to free passage for holders of InterRail or Eurail cards, plus reductions for children and senior citizens – check with a travel agent or the relevant ferry office.

■ By plane

Finnair have nonstop flights to Helsinki from **Copenhagen** (3 daily), **Stockholm** (15 daily) and **Oslo** (3 daily). There are also fourteen flights a week **to Tampere** from Stockholm, although getting to Tampere from Copenhagen or Oslo involves going via

Helsinki. **Turku** is served by twice-daily flights from Stockholm – from elsewhere you need to change at Helsinki. Check with a travel agent for occasional bargain fares between Scandinavian cities.

Costs, money and banks

Though the cost of a meal or the bill for an evening's drinks can come as a shock, for the most part prices in Finland are comparable with those in most European capitals, and there is no shortage of places catering for those on tighter budgets. Bargain lunchtime "specials" are common and travelling costs, in particular, can come as a pleasant surprise.

There are ways to cut **costs**, which we've detailed where relevant, but as a general rule you'll need £20–30/$30–45 a day even to live fairly modestly – staying mostly at youth hostels or campsites, eating out every other day and supplementing your diet with food from supermar-

THE EURO

Finland is one of the eleven European Union countries who, on January 1, 1999, entered into economic and monetary union (EMU) and began using a single currency, the **euro**. Initially it will only be possible to make paper transactions in the new currency (if, for example, you have a euro bank or credit-card account), and the national currencies will remain, in effect, the normal unit of tender. However, many prices will be quoted in both euros and markka. Euro notes and coins will be issued at the beginning of 2002, and will replace the markka entirely by July of that year.

kets, visiting only a few selected museums and socializing fairly rarely. To live well and see more, you'll be spending closer to £50/$75.

Finnish **currency** is the markka (plural markkaa), which divides into 100 penniä. Notes come as 1000mk, 500mk, 100mk and 50mk; coins are 10mk, 5mk, 1mk, 50p, 20p and 10p. The **exchange rate** at the time of writing was around 9mk to £1, 6mk to US$1.

As usual, one of the best ways to carry money is as traveller's cheques. These can be changed at most **banks** (Mon–Fri 9.15am–4.15pm), the charge for which is usually 15mk (though several people changing money together need only pay the commission once). You can also change money at hotels, though normally at a much worse rate than at the banks. In a country where every markka counts, it's worth looking around for a better deal: in rural areas some banks and hotels are known not to charge any commission at all. Outside normal banking hours, the best bet for changing money are the currency exchange desks at transport terminals which open to meet international arrivals.

Major **credit and charge cards** – Amex, MasterCard, Visa, Diner's Club – are usually accepted by hotels, car rental offices, department stores, restaurants and sometimes even by taxis. However, it's still advisable to check beforehand.

There are no restrictions on the amount of money you can take in or out of Finland.

Mail and telecommunications

In general, communications in Finland are dependable and quick, although in the far north, and in some sections of the east, minor delays arise due simply to geographical remoteness.

Unless you're on a hiking trek through the back of beyond, you can rest assured your letter or postcard will arrive at its destination fairly speedily. The cost of mailing anything weighing under 20g to other parts of Europe is 3.20mk priority class, 2.60mk for economy; to the rest of the world prices are 3.40mk or 2.80mk respectively. You can buy **stamps** from **post offices** (Mon–Fri 9am–5pm; longer hours at the main post office in Helsinki), street stands or R-Kiosks, and at some hotels. **Poste restante** is available at the main post office in every large town.

An out-of-order **public phone** is virtually unheard of in Finland. Most, however, only take **phonecards**, which you can buy in denominations of 30mk, 50mk and 100mk from the R-Kiosk chain and some other outlets. If you intend to use the phone frequently, it may be worth stocking up on phonecards, since it can sometimes be impossible to buy them in out-of-the-way places or late at night. Also note that each municipality runs its own phonecard system – which may or may not be compatible with systems in other areas. Your best bet is probably to invest in a Sonera phonecard, since their telephones can be found pretty much everywhere. The minimum cost of a **local call** is 2.3mk. Phones that accept money take 1mk and 5mk coins, and a few older ones also accept two 50p coins (which run out rapidly – have a supply of small change to hand). **International calls** are cheapest between 10pm and 8am. The bill for using a hotel phone is often dramatically more expensive.

Finland comes second only to the USA in terms of per-person Internet use, a fact borne out by the amount of free public **Internet and email** access that is available in even the most out-of-the-way places. The first point of call should be any public library – in the busier ones you may need to book a slot the day before, although most have short-use walk-up terminals. You'll need to show some kind of ID when booking a terminal, which you may also have to leave as a deposit while using it. Another source of free Internet access are tourist offices, a number of which have terminals, while some towns also have cafés with free Internet access.

Tourist office Web pages normally provide links to all the **accommodation** available in their area that is online, allowing you to book via email before you travel. Most of the better-run hotels, guesthouses and hostels will maintain Web pages; these normally accept online bookings.

The media

The biggest-selling **Finnish newspaper**, and the only one to be distributed all over the country, is the daily *Helsingin Sanomat* (10mk). Most of the others are locally based and sponsored by a political party, except for the second most popular daily rag, *Uusi Suomi* (10mk), an independent paper that publishes an English-language resumé of the day's news. All newspapers carry entertainment listings; only the cinema listings – where the film titles are translated into Finnish – present problems for non-Finnish speakers. A better source of information about **what's on**, if you're in Helsinki, Tampere or Turku, is the free *City* (appearing fortnightly in Helsinki, monthly in Turku and Tampere), which carries regional news, features and entertainment details in Finnish and English. For **rock music** listings, the fortnightly *Rumba* (15mk) has a rundown of forthcoming gigs and festivals throughout the country.

Overseas newspapers, including most British and some US titles, can be found, often on the day of issue, at the Academic Bookstore, Pohjoisesplanadi 39, in Helsinki. Elsewhere, foreign papers are harder to find and less up-to-date, though they often turn up at the bigger newsagents and train stations in Helsinki, Turku, Tampere and, to a lesser extent, Oulu.

Finnish **television**, despite its three channels (one of which is called MTV, but is unrelated to the round-the-clock music station), isn't exactly inspiring and certainly won't keep you off the streets for long. Moderately more interesting is the fact that, depending on where you are, you might be able to watch Swedish, Estonian and Russian programmes. A few youth hostels have TV rooms, and most hotel room TVs have the regular channels plus a feast of cable and satellite alternatives. As with films shown in the cinema, all TV programmes are broadcast in their original language with Finnish subtitles.

Getting around

Save for the fact that traffic tends to follow a north–south pattern, you'll have few headaches getting around the more populated parts of Finland. The chief form of public transport is the train, backed up, particularly on east–west journeys, by long-distance coaches. For the most part trains and buses integrate well, and you'll only need to plan with care when travelling through sparsely inhabited areas such as the far north and east. Feasible and often affordable variations come in the form of boats, planes, bikes, and even hitching – though car rental is strictly for the wealthy.

The complete **timetable** (*suomen kulku-neuvot*) for train, bus, ferry and air travel within the country is published every two months and costs 95mk from stations and kiosks. This is essential for plotting complex routes; for simplified details of the major train services, pick up the *Taskuaikataulu* booklet (5mk) from any tourist office or train station.

■ Trains

The swiftest land link between Finland's major cities is invariably the reliable **train service**, operated by the national company, VR. Large, comfortable express trains (and a growing number of "ICs", super-smooth state-of-the-art intercity trains) serve the principal **north–south** routes several times a day, reaching as far north as Kemijärvi and Kolari in southern Finnish Lapland. Elsewhere, especially on east–west hauls through sparsely populated regions, rail services tend to be skeletal and trains are often tiny one- or two-carriage affairs. The Arctic North has a very limited network of services. More details on Finnish Railways can be found at *www.vr.fi*.

InterRail, **BIJ** and **ScanRail** passes are valid on all trains; if you don't have one of these and are planning a lot of travelling, get a **Finnrail Pass** before arriving in Finland (the pass cannot be pur-

chased in Finland itself) from a travel agent or Finnish Tourist Office (for addresses, see p.27). This costs around £65/$100 for three days' unlimited travel within a month, £90/$135 for five days, or £120/$180 for ten days.

Otherwise, train **fares** are surprisingly reasonable. As a guide, a one-way, second-class ticket from Helsinki to Turku (a trip of around 200km) costs around 96mk; Helsinki to Kuopio (465km) costs around 210mk, and Helsinki to Rovaniemi (900km) around 328mk. If you've brought a car with you, car sleeper services are a convenient way of covering long distances. A one-way trip from Helsinki to Rovaniemi for a car and up to three passengers costs around 1160mk, including sleeping berths.

Tickets are valid for a month, while some allow you to break your journey en route – check when you buy. You should **buy tickets** from station ticket offices (*lippumyymälä*), although you can also pay the inspector on the train. If there are three or more of you travelling together, **group tickets**, available from a train station or travel agent, can cut the regular fares on journeys over 80km by at least 20 percent (25 percent for parties of 11 or more). **Senior citizens** with Rail Europ cards are entitled to a 30 percent discount on regular tickets, or 50 percent if they are over 65 and buy a Finnish Senior Citizens railcard (50mk). **Seat reservations**, costing 35mk (35–80mk supplement on ICs), can be a good idea if you're travelling over a holiday period or on a Friday or Sunday evening.

■ Buses

Buses – run by local private companies but with a common ticket system – cover the whole country, and are often quicker and more frequent than trains over the shorter east–west hops, and essential for getting around the remoter regions. In the Arctic North there is a very limited railway network, so almost all public transport is by road. The free bus **timetable**, *Suomen Pikavuorot*, lists all the routes in the country and can be picked up at most long-distance bus stations. Information on travel in Finland by coach and bus can also be found at *www.matkahuolto.fi*.

Fares are fixed according to distance travelled: Helsinki to Lahti (100km) costs around 88mk, Helsinki to Kuopio (400km) around 220mk. Express buses charge a supplement of 12–15mk. All types of ticket can be purchased at bus stations or at most travel agents; only ordinary one-way tickets can be bought on board the bus, though on journeys of 80km or less there's no saving in buying a return anyway. On return trips of over 80km, expect a reduction of 10 percent. To cut costs, there is a slightly bewildering array of **discounted tickets** available: three or more people travelling 80km or more qualify for a **group reduction** of 20 percent; holders of YIEE/FIYTO cards (but not ISIC cards) can get a 30 percent reduction on trips of similar length. Another discount option is to purchase **through-tickets** with prearranged stopoffs, A through-ticket from Vaasa to Turku with stopoffs at Pori and Rauma, for example, will work out about 20 percent cheaper than buying individual tickets for each leg of the journey. **Students** can also buy a bus travel discount card for 50mk, which gives 35–50 percent reductions on journeys of 80km or more; these are available from bus stations on presentation of a photo and proof of full-time education. Similar reductions can be claimed by those **over 65**. If you're going to travel a lot by bus, it's cheapest to get a **Coach Holiday Ticket**, available from any long-distance bus station, which gives 1000km of bus travel over any two-week period for 390mk, though exactly how much money it saves you will obviously depend on your itinerary.

■ Ferries

Lake travel is aimed more at holidaying families than the budget-conscious traveller. **Prices** are high considering the distances, and progress is slow as the vessels chug along the great lake chains. If you have the time, money and inclination, though, it can be worth taking one of the shorter trips simply for the experience. There are numerous routings and details can be checked at any tourist office in the country and at Finnish Tourist Offices abroad.

■ Planes

With their range of discounts, domestic **flights** can be comparatively cheap as well as time-saving if you want to cover long distances, such as from Helsinki to the Arctic North. That said, travelling by air means you'll miss many interesting parts of the country; another point to bear in mind is that flights from smaller towns to the bigger centres – Helsinki, Tampere and Oulu – tend to depart at around 6am. Finnair run a variety of off-

peak summer reductions which can be checked at travel agents and airline or tourist offices in Finland.

■ Cycling

Cycling can be an enjoyable way to see the country at close quarters since the only appreciable hills are in the far north and extreme east. Villages and towns may be separated by several hours' pedalling, however, and the scenery can get monotonous. Finnish **roads** are of high quality in the south and around the large towns, but are much rougher in the north and in isolated areas; beware the springtime thaw when the winter snows melt and sometimes cover roads with water and mud. All major towns have bike shops selling spares – Finland is one of the few places in the world where you can buy bicycle snow tyres with tungsten steel studs. Most youth hostels, campsites and some hotels and tourist offices offer **bike rental** from 70mk per day, 200mk per week; there may also be a deposit to pay of 150–200mk.

■ Driving and hitching

With such a good public-transport network, **renting a car** is only worth considering if you're travelling as a group of four or five as it's extremely expensive (as is petrol). The big international companies such as Avis, Budget, EuropCar and Hertz, and the similarly priced Finnish company, Oy Polarpoint, have offices in most Finnish towns and at international arrival points. They all accept major credit cards; if paying by cash, you'll need to leave a substantial deposit. You'll also need a valid driving licence, at least a year's driving experience, and to be a minimum of 19–23 years old, depending on the company you rent from.

Rates for a medium-sized car are 200–400mk per day, with reductions for longer periods, down to around 2400mk for a fortnight's use. On top of this, there's a surcharge of up to 5mk per kilometre (which may be waived on long-term loans) and a drop-off fee of around 350mk if you leave the car somewhere other than the place from which it was rented. For more details on car rental before arriving in Finland, visit an office of one of the international companies mentioned above, or ask at a Finnish Tourist Board office.

If you **bring your own car** to Finland, it's advisable (though not compulsory) to have a Green Card as proof that you are comprehensively insured in the event of an accident. Some insurers in EU countries will offer you a Green Card for free as part of your insurance package, whilst others will charge a premium. Further information about driving in Finland can be obtained from the Automobile and Touring Club of Finland, Hameentie 105A, FIN-00550 Helsinki (☎09/774 761, fax 7747 6444).

Once underway, you'll find the next financial drain is **fuel**, which costs 6mk a litre (unleaded). **Service stations** are plentiful (except in the far north, where they are few and far between) and usually open from 7am to 9pm from Monday to Saturday, often closed on Sunday – although in summer many stay open round the clock in busy holiday areas. Though **roads** are generally in good condition there can be problems with melting snows, usually during April and May in the south and June in the far north. Finnish **road signs** are similar to those throughout Europe, but be aware of bilingual place names (see p.637); one useful sign to watch for is *Keskusta*, which means "town centre". **Speed limits** vary between 40kph and 60kph in built-up areas to 100kph – if it's not signposted, the basic limit is always 80kph. On motorways the maximum speed is 120kph in summer, 100kph in winter.

Other **rules of the road** include using headlights all the time when driving outside built-up areas, as well as in fog and in poor light, and the compulsory wearing of seatbelts by drivers and all passengers. As elsewhere in Scandinavia, penalties for drunk driving are severe – the police may stop and breathalyse you if they think you've been driving erratically. In some areas in the north of the country, reindeer and elk are liable to take a stroll across a road, especially around dusk. Although these are sizeable creatures, damage (to the car) is unlikely to be serious; still, all such collisions should be reported at the nearest police station.

Hitching is generally easy, and sometimes the quickest means of transport between two spots. Finland's large student population has helped accustom drivers to the practice, and you shouldn't have to wait too long for a ride on the busy main roads between large towns. Make sure you have a decent road map and emergency provisions/shelter if you're passing through isolated regions. While many Finns speak English, it's still handy to memorize the Finnish equivalent of "let me out here" – *jään pois tässä*.

■ **City transport**

It's only in and around very small towns and villages that you may struggle to get about. In cities and larger towns, **public transport** takes the form of a comprehensive bus network (together with trams in Helsinki) with fares of 8–15mk for a single journey. After midnight, a **taxi** (*taksi*) may be your only option. These can be hailed in the street, found at taxi ranks or phoned for (look under *Taksiasemat* in the phone book). Taxis are cheaper in the north than the south, and most expensive of all in Helsinki. Basic charges are normally around 14mk plus 6–7mk per kilometre, with additional charges at night and at weekends. With several people sharing, taxis can be an affordable way to travel between isolated towns when public transport is scarce.

Accommodation

Whether you're at the end of a long-distance hiking trail or in the centre of a city, you'll find at least some kind of **accommodation** in Finland to

---

ACCOMMODATION PRICE CODES

The hotels and guesthouses listed in the Finland chapters of this Guide have been graded according to the following price bands, based on the cost of the **least expensive double room in summer**. However, many hotels offer summer and/or weekend discounts, and in these instances we've given two grades, covering both the regular and the discounted rate.

① Under 275mk   ② 275–350mk   ③ 350–450mk   ④ 450–550mk   ⑤ 550–750mk   ⑥ Over 750mk

suit your needs. You will, however, have to pay dearly for it: prices are high, and only by making use of special offers and travelling during low season will you be able to sleep well on a budget.

■ Hotels

Finnish **hotels** (*hotelli*) are rarely other than polished and pampering: TV, phone and private bathroom are standard fixtures, breakfast is invariably included in the price, and there's often free use of the sauna and swimming pool too. Costs can be formidable – frequently in excess of 500mk for a double – but planning ahead and taking advantage of various discount schemes and seasonal reductions can cut prices, often to as little as 300mk.

In major cities, particularly Helsinki, there can be bargains in business-oriented hotels during July and August, and on Fridays, Saturdays and Sundays throughout the year. Exact details of these change frequently, but it's worth checking the current situation at a local tourist office. Reductions are also available to holders of Helsinki Cards and the similar card issued for Tampere. Otherwise, between July and August you're unlikely to find anything under 350mk by turning up on spec. Hotels in country areas are no less comfortable than those in cities, and often a touch less costly, typically 250–300mk. However, space is again limited during summer.

Expense can be trimmed a little by using the **Finncheque** system: you buy an unlimited number of 200mk vouchers, each valid for a night's accommodation for one person in any of the 200 participating hotels from mid-May to September. There are three price categories, depending on the quality of room. You can only buy the Finncheque outside Finland at a Finnish Tourist Board office (see p.27) or a specialist travel agent, who will also supply addresses of the hotels involved. Don't worry about buying more vouchers than you might need – they are refundable at the place of purchase. Another discount is offered by the Scanhotel chain's "Scandic Holiday Cheque" vouchers. They're valid at all Scandic hotels in Finland throughout the year and cost from 450mk per room including breakfast, though beware that some hotels add on a "quality surcharge". The cheques are widely available from travel agents outside Finland.

In many towns you'll also find **tourist hotels** (*matkustajakoti*), a more basic type of family-run hotel. They charge 200–300mk per double room,

but may well be full throughout the summer. The facilities of **summer hotels** (*kesähotelli*), too, are more basic than regular hotels, since the accommodation is in student blocks which are vacated from June to the end of August: there are universities in all the major cities and in an impressive number of the larger towns. Reservable with any Finnish travel agent, summer hotel prices are around 225mk per person. Bear in mind that identical accommodation – minus the bed linen and breakfast – comes a lot cheaper in the guise of a youth hostel.

■ Youth hostels

Often the easiest and cheapest place to rest your head is a **youth hostel** (*retkeilymaja*). These exist throughout the country, in major cities (which will have at least one) and isolated country areas. It's always a good idea to phone ahead and reserve a place, which many hostel wardens will do for you. If you're arriving on a late bus or train, say so when phoning and your bed will be kept for you; otherwise bookings are only held until 6pm. Things are quieter after mid-August, although a large number of hostels close soon after this date – check that the one you're aiming for doesn't. Similarly, many hostels don't open until June.

Overnight **charges** vary between 60mk and 150mk, depending on the type of accommodation, with hostels ranging from the basic dormitory type to those with two- and four-bed rooms and at least one bathroom for every three rooms. Bed linen, if not already included, can be rented for an extra 20–30mk. With a Hostelling International Card (not obligatory) you can get a 15mk reduction per person per night. The Finnish hostel association's office in Helsinki sells International Guest Cards (90mk) that do the same job. Their guide, *Suomen Retkeilymajat*, available directly from them at Suomen Retkeilymajajärjestö, Yrjönkatu 38B, 00100 Helsinki (☎09/694 0377), lists all Finnish hostels, and the very helpful staff there can also provide a free Finland map showing locations.

All youth hostels have wardens to provide general assistance and arrange **meals**: most hostels offer breakfast, usually for 22–28mk, and some serve dinner as well (around 45mk). Hostel breakfasts, especially those in busy city hostels, can be rationed affairs and – hunger permitting – you'll generally be better off waiting until you can find a cheapish lunch somewhere else (see "Food and Drink", p.620). The only hostel breakfasts really worth taking advantage of are those offered at summer hotels, where hostellers can mingle with the hotel guests and, for 25–30mk, partake of the help-yourself spread.

■ Campsites and camping cottages

There are some 200 official **campsites** (*leirintäalue*) in Finland, and around 150 more operating on a less formal basis. Most open from May to September, although around seventy stay open all year. The approved sites, marked with a blue and white tent sign in a letter C, are classified by a star system: one-star sites are in rural areas and usually pretty basic, while on a five-star site you can expect excellent cooking and laundry facilities and sometimes a well-stocked shop. The cost for two people sharing is 30–90mk, depending on the site's star rating. Campsites outside major towns are frequently very big (a 2000-tent capacity isn't uncommon), and they're very busy at weekends during July and August. Smaller and more remote sites (except those serving popular hiking routes) are, as you'd imagine, much less crowded.

Holiday villages have been sprouting up throughout Finland in the last few years and there are now around 200 of them. Standards vary considerably, with accommodation ranging from basic cabins to luxurious bungalows. All provide fuel, cooking facilities, bed linen and often a sauna – but you'll need to bring your own towels. Costs range from 700mk to 3000mk per week, though for a luxury bungalow you might be paying up to 6000mk. Camping cottage cheques, available from travel agents for 700mk per cabin per night, can be used at some ninety campsites and holiday villages throughout the country from May 15 to September 15 – an economical option if there are enough of you.

Without an International Camping Card (see p.30) you'll need a National Camping Card, available at every site for 20mk and valid for a year. If you're considering **camping rough**, remember it's illegal without the landowner's permission – though in practice, provided you're out of sight of local communities, there shouldn't be any problems.

■ Hiking accommodation

Hiking routes invariably start and finish close to a campsite or a youth hostel, and along the way there will usually be several types of basic accommodation. Of these, a *päivätupa* is a cabin with cooking facilities which is opened during the day for free use; an *autiotupa* is an unlocked hut which can be used by hikers to sleep in for one night only – there's no fee but often no space either during the busiest months. A *varaustupa* is a locked hut for which you can obtain a key at the Tourist Centre at the start of the hike – there's a smallish fee and you'll almost certainly be sharing. Some routes have a few *kämppä* – cabins originally erected for forest workers but now used mainly by hikers; check their exact location with the nearest tourist centre. On most hikes there are also marked spots for pitching your own tent and building fires.

Food and drink

Finnish food is full of surprises and demands investigation. It's pricey, but you can keep a grip on the expenses by indulging most often at markets and at the many down-to-earth dining places, saving restaurant blowouts for special occasions. Though tempered by many regulations, alcohol is more widely available here than in much of Scandinavia: there are many places to drink but also many people drinking, most of them indulging moderately but some doing it to excess on a regular basis, regarding themselves as the last true Finns.

■ Food

Though it may at first seem a stodgy, rather unsophisticated cuisine, **Finnish food** is an interesting mix of western and eastern influences. Many dishes resemble those you might find elsewhere in Scandinavia – an enticing array of delicately prepared fish (herring, whitefish, salmon and crayfish), together with some exotic meats like reindeer and elk – while others bear the stamp of Russian cooking: solid pastries and casseroles, strong on cabbage, pork and mutton.

All Finnish restaurants will leave a severe dent in your budget, as will the foreign places, although the country's innumerable pizzerias are relatively cheap by comparison. The golden money-saving rule is to treat **lunch** (*lounas*, usually served 11am–2pm) rather than the much dearer **dinner** (*päivällinen*, usually from 6pm) as your main meal. Also, eke out your funds with stand-up snacks and by selective buying in supermarkets. If you're staying in a hotel, don't forget

GLOSSARY OF FINNISH FOOD AND DRINK TERMS

Basics

Juusto	Cheese	Maito	Milk	Riisi	Rice
Kakku	Cake	Makeiset	Sweets	Voi	Butter
Keitto	Soup	Perunat	Potatoes	Voileipä	Sandwich
Keksit	Biscuits	Piimä	Buttermilk		
Leipä	Bread	Piirakka	Pie		

Meat (Lihaa)

Häränfilee	Fillet of beef	Kinkku	Ham	Sianliha	Pork
Hirvenliha	Elk	Lihapyörykat	Meatballs	Poro	Reindeer
Jauheliha	Minced beef	Nauta	Beef	Vasikanliha	Veal
Kana	Chicken	Paisti	Steak		

Seafood (Äyriäisiä) and Fish (Kala)

Ankerias	Eel	Rapu	Crayfish	Silakat	Baltic herring
Graavilohi	Salted salmon	Sardiini	Sardine	Silli	Herring
Hauki	Pike	Savustettu	Smoked	Suolattu	Pickled herring
Hummeri	Lobster	lohi	salmon	Taimen	
Katkaravut	Shrimp	Savustettut	Smoked	or forelli	Trout
Lohi	Salmon	silakat	Baltic herring	Tonnikala	Tuna
Makrilli	Mackerel	Siika	Large, slightly oily,	Turska	Cod
Muikku	Small whitefish		whitefish		

Egg dishes (Munaruoat)

Hillomunakas	Jam omelette	Kinkkumunakas	Ham omelette	Perunamunakas	Potato omelette
Hyydytetty muna	Poached egg	Munakas	Omelette	Sienimunakas	Mushroom
Juustomunakas	Cheese	Munakokkeli	Scrambled eggs		omelette
	omelette	Paistettu muna	Fried egg		
Keitetty muna	Boiled eggs	Pekonimunakas	Bacon omelette		

Vegetables (Vihannekset)

Herneet	Peas	Pavut	Beans	Sipuli	Onion
Kaali	Cabbage	Peruna	Potato	Tilli	Dill
Kurkku	Cucumber	Pinaatti	Spinach	Tomaatti	Tomato
Maissintähkät	Corn on the cob	Porkkana	Carrot		
Paprika	Green pepper	Sieni	Mushroom		

Fruit (Hedelmä)

Appelsiini	Orange	Luumu	Plums	Pähkinä	Nuts
Aprikoosi	Apricot	Mansikka	Strawberry	Persikka	Peach
Banaani	Banana	Meloni	Melon	Raparperi	Rhubarb
Greippi	Grapefruit	Omena	Apple	Sitruuna	Lemon
Kirsikka	Cherries	Päärynä	Pear	Viinirypäle	Grapes

Sandwiches (Voileipä)

Kappelivoileipä	Fried French bread with bacon and topped by a fried egg	Oopperavoileipä	Fried French bread with hamburger and egg
Muna-anjovisleipä	Dark bread with slices of hard-boiled egg, anchovy fillets and tomato	Sillivoileipä	Herring on dark bread, usually with egg and tomato

Finnish specialities

Kaalikääryleet	Cabbage rolls: cabbage leaves stuffed with minced meat and rice	Merimiespihvi	Casserole of potato slices and meat patties or minced meat
Kaalipiirakka	Cabbage and mincemeat pie	Piparjuuriliha	Boiled beef with horseradish sauce
Karjalanpaisti	Karelian stew: beef and pork with onions	Porkkanalaatikko	Carrot casserole; mashed carrots and rice
Kurpitsasalaatti	Pickled pumpkin served with meat dishes	Poronkäristys	Sautéed reindeer stew
Lammaskaali	Mutton and cabbage stew or soup	Sianlihakastike	Gravy with slivers of pork
Lasimestarin silli	Pickled herring with spices, vinegar, carrot and onion	Silakkalaatikko	Casserole with alternating layers of potato, onion and Baltic herring, with an egg and milk sauce
Lihakeitto	Soup made from meat, potatoes, carrots and onions	Stroganoff	Beef with gherkins and onions, browned in a casserole, braised in stock with tomato juice and sour cream
Lindströmin pihvi	Beefburger made with beetroot and served with a cream sauce	Suutarinlohi	Marinated Baltic herring with onion and peppers
Lohilaatikko	Potato and salmon casserole	Tilliliha	Boiled veal flavoured with dill sauce
Lohipiirakka	Salmon pie		
Makaroonilaatikko	Macaroni casserole with milk and egg sauce	Venäläinen silli	Herring fillets with mayonnaise, mustard, vinegar, beetroot, gherkins and onion
Maksalaatikko	Baked liver purée with rice and raisins	Wieninleike	Fried veal cutlet

Drinks

Appelsiinimehu	Orange juice	Konjakki	Cognac	Tonic vesi	Tonic water
Gini	Gin	Limonaati	Lemonade	Vesi	Water
Kahvi	Coffee	Olut	Beer	Viini	Wine
Kivennäisvesi	Mineral water	Tee	Tea	Viski	Whisky

to load up on the inclusive **breakfast** (aamiainen) – often an open table laden with herring, eggs, cereals, porridge, cheese, salami and bread.

Snacks, fast food and self-catering

Economical **snacks** can be found in market halls (kauppahalli), where you can find basic foodstuffs along with local and national specialities. Adjoining these halls are cafeterias, where you will be charged by the weight of food on your plate. Look out for karjalan piirakka – oval-shaped Karelian pastries containing rice and mashed potato, served not with a mixture of finely chopped hard-boiled egg and butter for 5–10mk. Also worth trying is kalakukko, a chunk of bread with pork and whitefish baked inside it – legendary around Kuopio but available almost everywhere. Expect to spend around 15mk for a chunk big enough for two. Slightly cheaper but just as filling, lihapiirakka are envelopes of pastry filled with rice and meat – ask for them with mustard

(sinappi) and/or ketchup. Most train stations and the larger bus stations and supermarkets also have cafeterias proffering a selection of the above and other greasier nibbles.

Less exotically, the big **burger** franchises are widely found, as are the Grilli and Nakkikioski roadside fast-food stands turning out burgers, frankfurters and hot dogs for 14–20mk; they're always busiest when the pubs shut.

Finnish **supermarkets** – Sokos, K-Kaupat, Pukeva and Centrum are widespread names – are fairly standard affairs. In general, a substantial oval loaf of dark ryebread (ruisleipä) costs about 7–10mk, ten karjalan piirakkas 14mk, a litre of milk 7mk, and a packet of biscuits around 12–14mk. Finnish tinned **soup** (keitto) can be an excellent investment for self-catering, a usually flavoursome option containing hunks of meat and vegetables.

Coffee (kahvi) is widely drunk and costs 7–12mk per cup; in a baari or kahvila (bar or coffee shop) it's sometimes consumed with a *pulla* – a kind of doughy bun. It's normally drunk black, although milk is always available if you want it; you'll also commonly find espresso and cappuccino, although these are more expensive. **Tea** (*tee*) costs 5–10mk, depending on where you are and whether you want to indulge in some exotic brew. In rural areas, though, drinking it is considered a bit effete. When ordering tea, it's a good idea to insist that the water is boiling before the teabag is added – and that the bag is left in for more than two seconds.

Mensas, ravintolas and pizzerias

If you're in a university town, the campus cafeteria or **student mensa** is the cheapest place to get a hot dish. Theoretically you have to be a student, but you are unlikely to be asked for ID. There's a choice of three meals: *Kevytlounas* (KL), the "light menu", which usually comprises soup and bread; *Lounas* (L), the "ordinary menu", which consists of a smallish fish or meat dish with dessert; and *Herkkulounas* (HL), the "delicious menu" – a substantial and usually meat-based plateful. All three come with bread and coffee, and each one costs 15–22mk. Prices can be cut by half if you borrow a Finnish student ID card from a friendly diner. The busiest period is lunchtime (11.30am–12.30pm); later in the day (usually 4–6pm) many mensas offer price reductions. Most universities also have cafeterias where a small cup of coffee can cost as little as 3mk.

If funds stretch to it, you should sample at least once a **ravintola**, or restaurant, offering a lunchtime buffet table (*voileipäpöytä* or *seisova pöytä*), which will be stacked with tasty traditional goodies that you can feast on to your heart's content for a set price of around 75mk. Less costly Finnish food can be found in a **baari**. These are designed for working people, generally close at 5pm or 6pm, and serve a range of Finnish dishes and snacks (and often the weaker beers; see "Drink", opposite). A good day for traditional Finnish food is Thursday, when every *baari* in the country dishes up *hernekeitto ja pannukakut*, thick pea soup with black rye bread, followed by oven-baked pancakes with strawberry jam, with buttermilk to wash it down – all for around 35mk. You'll get much the same fare from a *kahvila*, though a few of these, especially in the big cities, fancy themselves as being fashionable and may charge a few markkaa extra.

Although *ravintola* and *baaris* are plentiful, they're often outnumbered by **pizzerias**, as var-

ied in quality here as they are in any other country, but especially worthwhile for their lunch specials, when a set price of 35–55mk buys a pizza, coffee and everything you can carry from the bread and salad bar. Many of the bigger pizza chains offer discounts for super-indulgence – such as a second pizza for half-price and a third for free if you can polish off the first two. **Vegetarians** are likely to become well acquainted with pizzerias – specific vegetarian restaurants are thin on the ground, even in major cities.

■ Drink

Finland's **alcohol laws** are as bizarre and almost as repressive as those of Norway and Sweden, although unlike those countries, boozing is tackled enthusiastically, and is even regarded by some as an integral part of the national character. Some Finns, men in particular, often drink with the sole intention of getting paralytic; younger Finns are more inclined to regard the practice simply as an enjoyable social activity.

What to drink

Finnish spirits are much the same as you'd find in any country. **Beer** (*olut*), on the other hand, falls into three categories: "light beer" (*I-Olut*) – more like a soft drink; "medium-strength beer" (*Keskiolut, III-Olut*) – more perceptibly alcoholic and sold in many food shops and cafés; and "strong beer" (*A-Olut* or *IV-Olut*), which is on a par with the stronger international beers, and can only be bought at the ALKO shops and fully licensed (Grade A) restaurants and nightclubs.

The main – and cheapest – outlet for alcohol of any kind is the **ALKO** shop (Mon–Thurs 10am–5pm, Fri 10am–6pm, Sat 9am–2pm). Even the smallest town will have one of these, and prices don't vary. In an ALKO shop, strong beers like Lapin Kulta Export – an Arctic-orginated mind blower – and the equally potent Karjala, Lahden A, Olvi Export, and Koff porter, cost 7.90–8.40mk for a 300ml bottle. Imported beers such as Heineken, Carlsberg and Becks go for 9.90–10.20mk a bottle. As for **spirits**, Finlandia vodka and Jameson's Irish Whiskey are 150mk and 190mk respectively per litre. There's also a very popular rough form of vodka called Koskenkorva, ideal for assessing the strength of your stomach lining, which costs 140mk. The best bargain in **wine** is reputedly the Hungarian variety, which changes hands for around 35mk per bottle, though you can buy bottles in ALKO for under 30mk. French wines range from 42mk to 285mk a bottle.

■ Where to drink

Most **restaurants** have a full licence, and some are actually frequented more for drinking than eating; it's these that we've listed under "Drinking" throughout the text. They're often also called bars or pubs by Finns simply for convenience. Just to add to the confusion, some so-called "pubs" are not licensed; neither are *baari*, mentioned opposite.

Along with ordinary restaurants, there are also **dance restaurants** (*tanssiravintola*). As the name suggests, these are places to dance rather than dine, although most do serve food as well as drink. They're popular with the over-40s, and before the advent of discos were the main places for people of opposite sex to meet. Even if you're under 40, dropping into one during the (usually early) evening sessions can be quite an eye-opener. Expect to pay a 14–35mk admission charge.

Once you've found somewhere to drink, there's a fairly rigid set of **customs** to contend with. Sometimes you have to queue outside the most popular bars since entry is permitted only if a seat is free – there's no standing. Only one drink per person is allowed on the table at any one time except in the case of porter – a stout which most Finns mix with regular beer. There's always either a doorman (*portsari*) – whom you must tip (5–7mk) on leaving – or a cloakroom into which you must check your coat on arrival (again 5–7mk). Bars are usually open until midnight or 1am and service stops half an hour before the place shuts. This is announced by a winking of the lights – the *valomerkki*.

Some bars and clubs have **waitress/waiter service**, whereby you order, and pay when your drinks are brought to you. A common order is *iso tuoppi* – a half-litre glass of draught beer, which costs 15–25mk (up to 35mk in some nightclubs). This might come slightly cheaper in **self-service** bars, where you select your tipple and queue up to pay at the till.

Wherever you buy alcohol, you'll have to be of **legal age**: at least 18 to buy beer and wine, and 20 or over to have a go at the spirits. ID will be checked if you look too young – or if the doorman's in a bad mood.

Directory

CANOEING With many lakes and rivers, Finland offers challenges to every type of canoe enthusiast, expert or beginner. There's plenty of easy-going paddling on the long lake systems, innumerable thrashing rapids to be shot, and abundant sea canoeing around the archipelagos of the south and southwest coast. Canoe rental (available wherever there are suitable waters) costs around 20mk per hour, 50–165mk per day, or 400mk per week, with prices dependent on the type of canoe. Many tourist offices have plans of local canoeing routes, and you can get general information from the Finnish Canoe Association, Radiokatu 2, 00240 Helsinki (☎09/158 2363).

CUSTOMS There are few, if any, border formalities when entering Finland from another Scandinavian country by land [although the crossing from Norway at Näätämö is – at least in theory – closed to non-Scandinavians from 10pm to 7am). The same applies when crossing by sea; only by air do you usually need to show your passport.

DENTIST Seeing a dentist can be very expensive: expect to spend a minimum of 100mk. Look under *Hammaslääkari* in the phone book, or ask at a tourist office.

DOCTOR Provided you're insured, you'll save time by seeing a doctor at a private health centre (*lääkäriasema*) rather than queueing at a national health centre (*terveyskeskus*). You are required to present a doctor's referral and a written statement confirming that you will pay the bill in order to stay in hospital.

EMERGENCIES ☎112.

FISHING Non-Scandinavians need a General Fishing Licence if they intend to fish in Finland's waterways; this costs 20mk for a seven-day period from post offices. In certain parts of the Arctic North you'll need an additional licence costing 30mk and obtainable locally. Throughout the country you'll also need the permission of the owner of the particular stretch of water, usually obtained by buying a permit on the spot. The nearest campsite or tourist office will have details of this, and advise on the regional variations on national fishing laws.

MARKETS In larger towns, these usually take place every day except Sunday from 7am to 2pm. There'll also be a market hall (*kauppahalli*) open

FINNISH AND SWEDISH PLACE NAMES

On most maps and many transport timetables cities and towns are given their Finnish names followed by their Swedish names in parentheses. Both Swedes and Finland-Swedes will frequently use the Swedish rather than the Finnish names. The main places in question are listed below, with the Finnish name first.

Helsinki (Helsingfors)   Tampere (Tammerfors)   Kokkola (Gamlakarleby)
Porvoo (Borgå)   Mikkeli (St Michel)   Oulu (Uleåborg)
Turku (Åbo)   Savonlinna (Nyslott)
Pori (Björneborg)   Vaasa (Vasa)

weekdays 8am–5pm. Smaller places have a market once or twice a week, usually including Saturday.

NUDE BATHING Sections of some Finnish beaches are designated nude bathing areas, sometimes sex-segregated and occasionally with an admission charge of around 10mk. The local tourist office, or campsite, will have the facts.

PHARMACIES *Kemikaalikauppa* sell only cosmetics; for medicines you need to go to an *apteekki*, generally open daily 9am–6pm.

PUBLIC HOLIDAYS January 1, May 1, December 6, December 24, 25 and 26. Variable dates: Epiphany (between Jan 6 and 12), Good Friday and Easter Weekend, the Saturday before Whit Sunday, Midsummer's Eve, All Saint's Day (the Saturday between Oct 31 and Nov 6). Shops and banks close on these days and most public transport will operate a Sunday schedule; museum opening hours may also be affected.

SAUNAS These are cheapest at a public swimming pool, where you'll pay 10–20mk for a session. Hotel saunas, which are sometimes better equipped than public ones, are more expensive (30–40mk) but free to guests. Many Finnish people have saunas built into their homes and it's common for visitors to be invited to share one.

SHOPS Supermarkets are usually open Mon–Fri 9am–8pm, Sat 9am–6pm. Some in cities keep longer hours, for example 8am–10pm. In Helsinki the shops in Tunneli are open until 10pm. In the weeks leading up to Christmas some stores and markets are open on Sunday too.

History

Finland's history, inextricably bound with the medieval superpowers, Sweden and Russia, and later with the Soviet Union, is a stirring tale of a small people's survival – and eventual triumph – over what have often seemed impossible odds. It's also a story that's been full of powerful contemporary resonances, as the other Baltic nations have successfully striven to regain their own independence.

■ First settlements

As the ice sheets of the last Ice Age retreated, parts of the Finnish Arctic coast were settled by tribes from eastern Europe. They hunted bear and reindeer, and fished the well-stocked rivers and lakes: relics of their existence have been found and dated to around 8000 BC. Pottery skills were introduced around 3000 BC, and trade with Russia and the east flourished. At the same time, other peoples were arriving and merging with the established population. The **Boat Axe** culture (1800–1600 BC), which originated in central Europe, spread as Indo-Europeans migrated into Finland. The seafaring knowledge they possessed enabled them to begin trading with Sweden from the Finnish west coast, as indicated by **Bronze Age** findings (around 1300 BC) concentrated in a narrow strip along the seaboard. The previous settlers withdrew eastwards and the advent of severe weather brought this period of occupation to an end.

■ The arrival of the Finns

The antecedents of the Finns were a race from central Russia, from where they moved outwards in two directions. One tribe went south, eventually to Hungary; and the other westwards to the Baltic, where it mixed with Latgals, Lithuanians and Germans. The latter, the "**Baltic Finns**", were migrants who crossed the Baltic around 400 AD to form an independent society in Finland. In

100 AD the Roman historian Tacitus described a wild and primitive people called "the Fenni". This is thought to have been a reference to the earliest **Sami**, who occupied Finland before this. With their more advanced culture, the Baltic Finns absorbed this indigenous population, although some of their customs were maintained. The new Finns worked the land, utilized the vast forests and made lengthy fishing expeditions on the lakes.

■ The pagan era

The main Finnish settlements were along the west coast facing Sweden, with whom trade was established, until the Vikings' opening up of routes further to the east forced these communities into decline. Meanwhile the Finnish south coast was exposed to seaborne raiding parties and most Finns moved inland and eastwards, a large number settling around the huge Lake Ladoga in **Karelia**. Eventually the people of Karelia were able to enjoy trade in two directions – with the Varangians to the east and the Swedes to the west. Groups from Karelia and the more northern territory of Kainuu regularly ventured into Lapland to fish and hunt. At the end of the pagan era Finland was split into three regions: Varsinais-Suomi ("Finland proper") in the southwest, Häme in the western part of the lake region, and Karelia in the east. Although they often helped one another, there was no formal cooperation between the inhabitants of these areas.

■ The Swedish era (1155–1809)

At the start of the tenth century, pagan Finland was caught between two opposing religions: Catholicism in Sweden on one side and the Orthodox Church of Russia on the other. The Russians wielded great influence in Karelia, but the west of Finland began to gravitate towards Catholicism on account of its high level of contact with Sweden. In 1155, King Erik of Sweden launched a "crusade" into Finland – although its real purpose was to strengthen trade routes – which swept through the southwest and established Swedish control, leaving the English **Bishop Henry** at **Turku** to establish a parish. Henry was killed by a Finnish yeoman, but became the patron saint of the Turku diocese and the region became the administrative base of the whole country. Western Finland generally acquiesced to the Swedes, but Karelia didn't, becoming

a territory much sought after by both the Swedes and the Russians. In 1323, under the **Treaty of Pähkinäsaari**, an official border was drawn up, giving the western part of Karelia to Sweden while the Russian principality of Novgorod retained the eastern section around Lake Ladoga. To emphasize their claim, the Russians founded the Orthodox **Valamo Monastery** on an island in the lake.

Under the Swedish crown, Finns still worked and controlled their own land, often living side by side with Swedes, who came to the west coast to safeguard sea trade. Finnish provincial leaders were given places among the nobility and in 1362 King Håkon gave Finland the right to vote in Swedish royal elections. When the Swedish throne was given to the German Albrecht of Mecklenburg, in 1364, there was little support for the new monarch in Finland, and much violent opposition to his forces who arrived to occupy the Swedish-built castles. Once established, the Mecklenburgians imposed forced labour and the Finnish standard of living swiftly declined. There was even a proposal that the country should be sold to the Teutonic Order of Knights.

In a campaign to wrest control of the Swedish realm, a Swedish noble, **Grip**, acquired control of one Finnish province after another, and by 1374 was in charge of the whole country. In doing this he was obliged to consider the welfare of the Finns and consequently living conditions improved. Another effect of Grip's actions was to underline Finland's position as an individual country – under the Swedish sovereign but distanced from Sweden's political offices.

Grip had intended to ensure that Finnish affairs would be managed by the Swedish nobility irrespective of the wishes of the monarch. The nobility, however, found themselves forced to look for assistance to Margrethe, Queen of Denmark and Norway. She agreed to come to the Swedes' aid provided they recognized her as sovereign over all the Swedish realm including Finland. This resulted in the **Kalmar Union** of 1397.

While the Finns were barely affected by the constitution of the Union, there was a hope that it would guarantee their safety against the Russians, whose expansionist policies were an increasing threat. Throughout the fifteenth century there were repeated skirmishes between Russians and Finns in the border lands and around the important Finnish Baltic trading centre of Viipuri (now Russian Vyborg).

The election of King Charles VIII in 1438 caused a rift in the Union and serious strife between Sweden and Denmark. He was forced to abdicate in 1458 but his support in Finland was strong, and his successor, Christian I, sent an armed column to subdue Finnish unrest. While Turku Castle was under siege, the Danish noble **Erik Axelsson Tott**, already known and respected in the country, called a meeting of representatives from every Finnish estate where it was agreed that Christian I would be acknowledged as king of the Union.

Tott went on to take command of Viipuri Castle and was able to function almost independently of central government. Although he planned to make Viipuri the major centre for east–west trade, resources had to be diverted to strengthening the eastern defences. During the 1460s Novgorod was sucked into Moscow's sphere of influence and finally absorbed altogether. This left Finland's eastern edge more exposed than ever before. Novgorod had long held claims on large sections of Karelia, and the border situation was further confused by the Finnish peasants who had drifted eastwards and settled in the disputed territories. Part of Tott's response to the dangers was to erect the fortress of **Olavinlinna** (in the present town of Savonlinna) in 1475, actually inside the land claimed by Russia.

Tott died in 1481 and **Sten Sture**, a Swedish regent, forced the remaining Axelssons to relinquish their family's domination of Finland. By 1487 Sture had control of the whole country, and appointed bailiffs of humble birth – instead of established aristocrats – to the Finnish castles in return for their surplus revenue. These monies were used to finance Sture's ascent through the Swedish nobility. As a result nothing was spent on maintaining the eastern defences.

Strengthened by an alliance with Denmark signed in 1493, Russia attacked Viipuri on November 30, 1495. The troops were repulsed by the technically inferior Finns, an achievement perceived as a miracle. After further battles it was agreed that the borders of the Treaty of Pähkinäsaari would remain. However, the Swedes drew up a bogus version of the treaty in which the border retained its fifteenth-century position, and it was this forgery which they used in negotiations with the Russians over the next hundred years.

Within Finland a largely Swedish-born nobility became established. Church services were conducted in Finnish, although Swedish remained the language of commerce and officialdom. Because the bulk of the population was illiterate, any important deed had to be read to them. In the thirteenth and fourteenth centuries, any Finn who felt oppressed simply moved into the wild lands of the interior – out of earshot of church bells.

By the time **Gustav Vasa** took the Swedish throne in 1523, many villages were established in the disputed border regions. Almost every inhabitant spoke Finnish. but there was a roughly equal division between those communities who paid taxes to the Swedish king and those who paid them to the Russian tsar. In the winter of 1555, a Russian advance into Karelia was quashed at Joutselkä by Finns using skis to travel speedily over the icy roads, a victory that made the Finnish nobility confident of success in a full-scale war. While hesitant, Vasa finally agreed to their wishes: 12,000 troops from Sweden were dispatched to eastern Finland, and an offensive launched in the autumn of 1556. It failed, with the Russians reaching the gates of Viipuri, and Vasa retreating to the Åland Islands, asking for peace.

In 1556 Gustav Vasa made Finland a Swedish Grand Duchy and gave his son, Johan, the title Duke of Finland. It was rumoured that **Duke Johan** not only spoke Finnish but was an advocate of Finnish nationalism. These claims were exaggerated, but the duke was certainly pro-Finnish, surrounding himself with Finnish nobles and founding a chancery and an exchequer. He moved into Turku Castle and furnished it in splendour. However, the powers of his office, as defined by the Articles of Arboga, were breached by a subsequent invasion of Livonia and he was sentenced to death by the Swedish Diet in 1563, although the king's power of pardon was exercised. Finland was divided between loyalty towards the friendly duke and the need to keep on good terms with the Swedish crown, now held by Erik XIV. The Swedish forces sent to collect Johan laid siege to Turku castle for three weeks, executing thirty nobles before capturing the duke and imprisoning him.

The war between Sweden and Denmark over control of the Baltic took its toll on Erik. He became mentally unbalanced, slaying several prisoners who were being held for trial, and, in a moment of complete madness, released Johan from detention. The Swedish nobles were incensed by Erik's actions and rebelled against him – with the result that Johan became king in 1568.

In 1570 Swedish resources were stretched when hostilities again erupted with Russia, now ruled by the aggressive Tsar Ivan ("the Terrible") IV. The conflict was to last 25 years, a period known in Finland as **"The Long Wrath"**. It saw the introduction of a form of conscription instead of the reliance on mercenary soldiers, which had been the norm in other Swedish wars. Able-bodied men aged between 15 and 50 were rounded up by the local bailiff and about one in ten selected for military service. Russia occupied almost all of Estonia and made deep thrusts into southern Finland. Finally the Swedish–Finnish troops regained Estonia and made significant advances through Karelia, capturing an important Eastern European trading route. The war was formally concluded in 1595 by the **Treaty of Täyssinä**. Under its terms, Russia recognized the lands gained by Sweden and the eastern border was altered to reach up to the Arctic coast, enabling Finns to settle in the far north.

Sweden was established as the dominant force in the Baltic, but under Gustav II, who became king in 1611, Finland began to lose the special status it had previously enjoyed. Its administration was streamlined and centralized, causing many Finnish nobles to move to Stockholm. Civic orders had to be written rather than passed on orally, and many ambitious Finns gave themselves Swedish surnames. Finnish manpower supported Swedish efforts overseas – the soldiers gaining a reputation as wild and fearless fighters – but brought no direct benefit to Finland itself. Furthermore, the peasants were increasingly burdened by the taxes needed to support the Swedish wars with Poland, Prussia and Germany.

Conditions continued to decline until 1637, when **Per Brahe** was appointed governor-general. Against the prevailing mood of the time, he insisted that all officers should study Finnish, founded Turku University – the country's first – and instigated a successful programme to spread literacy among the Finnish people. After concluding his second term of office in 1654 he parted with the terse but accurate summary: "I was highly satisfied with this country and the country highly satisfied with me."

A terrible harvest in 1696 caused a **famine** that killed a third of the Finnish population. The fact that no aid came from Sweden intensified feelings of neglect and stirred up a minor bout of Finnish nationalism led by **Daniel Juslenius**. His

book, *Aboa Vetus Et Nova*, published in 1700, claimed Finnish to be a founding language of the world, and Finns to be descendants of the tribes of Israel.

In 1711 Viipuri fell to the Russians. Under their new tsar, Peter ("the Great"), the Russians quickly spread across the country, causing the nobility to flee to Stockholm and Swedish commanders to be more concerned with salvaging their army than saving Finland. In 1714, eight years of Russian occupation – **"The Great Wrath"** – began. Descriptions of the horrors of these times have been exaggerated, but nonetheless the events confirmed the Finns' longtime dread of their eastern neighbour. The Russians saw Finland simply as a springboard to attack Sweden, and laid waste to anything in it which the Swedes might attempt to regain.

Under the **Treaty of Uusikaupunki**, in 1721, the tsar gave back much of Finland but retained Viipuri, east Karelia, Estonia and Latvia, and thus control of the Baltic. Finland now had a new eastern border that was totally unprotected. Russian occupation was inevitable but would be less disastrous if entered into voluntarily. The Finnish peasants, with Swedish soldiers forcibly billeted on them, remained loyal to the king but with little faith in what he could do to protect them.

The aggressive policies of the Hats in the Swedish Diet led to the 1741 declaration of war on Russia. With barely an arm raised against them, Russian troops again occupied Finland – the start of **"The Lesser Wrath"** – until the **Treaty of Turku** in 1743. Under this, the Russians withdrew, ceded a section of Finland back to Sweden but moved their border west.

■ The Russian era (1809–1917)

In an attempt to force Sweden to join Napoleon's economic blockade, Russia, under Tsar Alexander I, attacked and occupied Finland in 1807. The **Treaty of Hamina**, signed in September of that year, legally ceded all of the country to Russia. The tsar had needed a friendly country close to Napoleon's territory as a reliable ally in case of future hostilities between the two leaders. To gain Finnish favour, he had guaranteed beneficial terms at the Diet (based in Porvoo) in 1809, and subsequently Finland became an **autonomous Russian Grand Duchy**. There was no conscription and taxation was frozen, while realignment of the northern section of the Finnish–Russian border gave additional land to Finland. Finns could freely occupy positions in the Russian empire, although Russians were denied equal opportunities within Finland. The long period of peace that ensued saw a great improvement in Finnish wealth and well-being.

After returning Viipuri to Finland, the tsar declared Helsinki the **capital** in 1812, regarding Turku as too close to Sweden for safety. The "Guards of Finland" helped crush the Polish rebellion and fought in the Russo-Turkish conflict. This, along with the French and English attacks on Finnish harbours during the Crimean War, accentuated the bond between the two countries. Many Finns came to regard the tsar as their own monarch.

There was, however, an increasingly active **Finnish-language movement**. A student leader, the future statesman **Johan Vilhelm Snellman**, had met the tsar and demanded that Finnish replace Swedish as the country's official language. Snellman's slogan "Swedes we are no longer, Russians we cannot become, we must be Finns" became the rallying cry of the **Fennomen**. The Swedish-speaking ruling class, feeling threatened, had Snellman removed from his university post and he retreated to Kuopio to publish newspapers espousing his beliefs. His opponents cited Finnish as the language of peasants, unfit for cultured use – a claim undermined by the efforts of a playwright, **Aleksis Kivi**, whose works marked the beginning of Finnish-language theatre. In 1835, the collection of Karelian folk tales published in Finnish by **Elias Lönnrot** as the **Kalevala** became the first written record of Finnish folklore, and a focal point for Finnish nationalism.

The liberal tsar Alexander II appointed Snellman to Turku University, from where he went on to become minister of finance. In 1858 Finnish was declared the official language of local government in areas where the majority of the population were Finnish speaking, and the Diet, convened in 1863 for the first time since the Russian takeover, finally gave native-tongued Finns equal status with Swedish speakers. The only opposition was from the so-called **Svecomen**, who sought not only the maintenance of the Swedish language but unification with Finland's westerly neighbour.

The increasingly powerful Pan-Slavist contingent in Russia was horrified by the growth of the Finnish timber industry and the rise of trade with

the west. They were also unhappy with the special status of the Grand Duchy, considering the Finns an alien race who would contaminate the eastern empire by their links with the west. Tsar Alexander III was not swayed by these opinions but, after his assassination in 1894, Nicholas I came to power and instigated a **Russification process**. Russian was declared the official language, Finnish money was abolished and plans were laid to merge the Finnish army into the Russian army. To pass these measures the tsar drew up the unconstitutional **February Manifesto**.

Opposition came in varying forms. In 1899, a young composer called **Jean Sibelius** wrote *Finlandia*. The Russians banned all performances of it "under any name that indicates its patriotic character", causing Sibelius to publish it as Opus 26 No. 7. The painter **Akseli Gallen-Kallela** ignored international art trends and depicted scenes from the *Kalevala*, as did the poet **Eino Leino**. Students skied to farms all over the country and collected half a million signatures against the manifesto. Over a thousand of Europe's foremost intellectuals signed a document called "Pro-Finlandia".

But these had no effect, and in 1901 the **Conscription Law** was introduced. This forced Finns to serve directly under the tsar in the Russian army. A programme of civil disobedience began, the leaders of which were soon obliged to go underground, where they titled themselves the Kagel – borrowing a name used by persecuted Russian Jews. The Finnish population became divided between the "compliants" (acquiescent to the Manifesto) and the "constitutionalists" (against the Manifesto), splitting families and even causing the rival sides to do their shopping in different stores.

The stand against conscription was enough to make the Russians drop the scheme, but their grip was tightened in other ways. A peaceful demonstration in Helsinki was broken up by cossacks on horseback, and in April 1903 the tsar installed the tough **Bobrikov** as governor-general, giving him new and sweeping powers. The culmination of sporadic acts of violence came on June 16, 1904, when the Finnish civil servant **Eugen Schauman** climbed the Senate staircase and shot Bobrikov three times before turning the gun on himself. After staggering to his usual Senate seat, Bobrikov collapsed and died – and his assassin became a national hero.

In 1905, the Russians suffered defeat in their war with Japan and the general strike that broke out in their country spread to Finland, the Finnish labour movement being represented by the Social Democratic Party. The revolutionary spirit that was moving through Russia encouraged the conservative Finnish Senate to reach a compromise with the demands of the Social Democrats, and the result was a gigantic upheaval in the Finnish parliamentary system. In 1906, the country adopted a single-chamber parliament (the Eduskunta) elected by national suffrage – Finnish women being the first in Europe to get the vote. In the first election under the new system the Social Democrats won eighty seats out of the total of two hundred, making it the most left-wing legislature seen so far in Europe.

Any laws passed in Finland, however, still needed the ratification of the tsar, who now viewed Finland as a dangerous forum for leftist debate (the exiled Lenin met Stalin for the first time in Tampere). In 1910, Nicholas II removed the new parliament's powers and reinstated the Russification programme. Two years later the **Parity Act** gave Russians in Finland status equal to Finns, enabling them to hold seats in the Senate and posts in the civil service. The outspoken anti-tsarist parliamentary speaker **P.E. Svinhufvud** was exiled to Siberia for a second time.

As World War I commenced, Finland was obviously allied with Russia and endured a commercial blockade, food shortages and restrictions on civil liberties, but did not actually fight on the tsar's behalf. Germany promised Finland total autonomy in the event of victory for the Kaiser and provided clandestine military training to about two thousand Finnish students – the Jäger movement who reached Germany through Sweden and later fought against the Russians as a light infantry battalion on the Baltic front.

■ Towards independence

When the tsar was overthrown in 1917, the Russian provisional government under Kerensky declared the measures taken against Finland null and void and restored the previous level of autonomy. Within Finland there was uncertainty over the country's constitutional bonds with Russia. The conservative view was that prerogative powers should be passed from the deposed ruler to the provisional government, while socialists held that the provisional government had no right to exercise power in Finland and that supreme authority should be passed to the Eduskunta.

Under the **Power Act**, the Eduskunta vested in itself supreme authority within Finland, leaving only control of foreign and military matters residing with the Russians. Kerensky refused to recognize the Power Act and dissolved the Finnish parliament, forcing a fresh election. This time a bigger poll returned a conservative majority.

The loss of their parliamentary majority and the bitterness felt towards the bourgeois-dominated Senate, who happily complied with Kerensky's demands, made the Social Democrats adopt a more militant line. Around the country there had been widespread labour disputes and violent confrontations between strikers and strike-breaking mobs hired by landowners. The Social Democrats sanctioned the formation of an armed workers' guard, soon to be called the **Red Guard**, in response to the growing **White Guard** – a right-wing private army operating in the virtual absence of a regular police force. A general strike was called on November 13, which forced the Eduskunta into reforms after just a few days. The strike was called off, but a group of dissident Red Guards threatened to break from the Social Democrats and continue the action.

After the Bolsheviks took power in Russia, the conservative Finnish government became fearful of Soviet involvement in Finnish affairs and a de facto **statement of independence** was made. The socialists, by now totally excluded from government, declared their support for independence but insisted that it should be reached through negotiation with the Soviet Union. Instead, on December 6, a draft of an independent constitution drawn up by **K.J. Ståhlberg** was approved by the Eduskunta. After a delay of three weeks it was formally recognized by the Soviet leader, Lenin.

■ The civil war

In asserting its new authority, the government repeatedly clashed with the labour movement. The Red Guard, who had reached an uneasy truce with the Social Democratic leadership, were involved in gun-running between Viipuri and Petrograd, and efforts by the White Guard to halt it led to full-scale fighting. A vote passed by the Eduskunta on January 12, 1918, empowered the government to create a police force to restore law and order. On January 25, the White Guard was legitimized as the Civil Guard.

In Helsinki, a special committee of the Social Democrats took the decision to resist the Civil Guard and seize power, effectively pledging themselves to **civil war**. On January 27 and 28, a series of occupations enabled leftist committees to take control of the capital and the major towns of the south. Three government ministers who evaded capture fled to Vaasa and formed a rump administration. Meanwhile, a Finnish-born aristocrat, **C.G.E. Mannerheim**, who had served as a cavalry officer in the Russian army, arrived at the request of the government in Ostrobothnia, a region dominated by right-wing farmers, to train a force to fight the Reds.

Mannerheim, who had secured a 15 million markkaa loan from a Helsinki bank to finance his army, drew on the German-trained Jäger for officers, while the Ostrobothnian farmers – seeking to protect their landowning privileges – along with a small number of Swedish volunteers, made up the troops. Their initial task was to mop up the Russian battalions remaining in western Finland, which had been posted there by the tsar to prevent German advancement in World War I, and which by now were politicized into Soviets. Mannerheim had achieved this by the beginning of February, and his attention then turned to the Reds.

The Whites were in control of Ostrobothnia, northern Finland and parts of Karelia, and were connected by a railway from Vaasa to Käkisalmi on Lake Ladoga. Although the Reds were numerically superior they were poorly equipped and poorly trained, and failed to break the enemy's line of communication. Tampere fell to the Whites in March. At the same time, a German force landed on the south coast, their assistance requested by White Finns in Berlin (although Mannerheim opposed their involvement). Surrounded, the leftists' resistance collapsed in April.

Throughout the conflict, the Social Democratic Party maintained a high level of unity. While containing revolutionary elements, it was led mainly by socialists seeking to retain parliamentary democracy and believing their fight was against a bourgeois force seeking to impose right-wing values on the newly independent state. Their arms, however, were supplied by the Soviet Union, causing the White taunt that the Reds were "aided by foreign bayonets". Many of the revolutionary socialists within the party fled to Russia after the civil war, where they formed the Finnish Communist Party. The harsh treatment of the

Reds who were captured – 8000 were executed and 80,000 were imprisoned in camps where more than 9000 died from hunger or disease – fired a resentment that would last for generations. The Whites regarded the war as one of liberation, ridding the country of Russians and the Bolshevik influence, and setting the course for an anti-Russian Finnish nationalism. Mannerheim and the strongly pro-German Jäger contingent were keen to continue east, to gain the whole of Karelia from the Russians, but the possibility of direct Finnish assistance to the Russian White Army – who were seeking to overthrow the Bolshevik government – came to nothing thanks to the Russian Whites' refusal to guarantee recognition of Finland's independent status.

Later that year, a **provisional government of independent Karelia** was set up in Uhtua. Its formation was masterminded by Red Finns, who ensured that its claims to make Karelia a totally independent region did not accord with the desires of the Finnish government. The provisional government's congress, held the following year, also confirmed a wish for separation from the Soviet Union and requested the removal of the Soviet troops, which was agreed, with a proviso that Soviet troops retained a right to be based in eastern Karelia. The eventual collapse of the talks caused the provisional government and its supporters to flee to Finland as a Finnish battalion of the Soviet Red Army moved in and occupied the area. Subsequently the Karelian Workers' Commune, motivated by the Finnish Communists and backed by Soviet decree, was formed.

A few days later, the state of war which existed between Finland and Russia was formally ended by the **Treaty of Tartu**. The existence of the Karelian Workers' Commune gave the Soviet negotiators a pretext for refusing Finnish demands for Karelian self-determination, claiming the new set-up to be an expression of the Karelian people's wishes. The treaty was signed in an air of animosity. A bald settlement of border issues, it gave Finland the Petsamo area, a shoulder of land extending to the Arctic coast.

■ The republic

The White success in the civil war led to a right-wing government with a pro-German majority, which wanted to establish Finland as a monarchy rather than the republic allowed for under the 1917 declaration of independence. Although twice defeated in the Eduskunta, Prime Minister

J.K. Paasikivi evoked a clause in the Swedish Form of Government from 1772, making legal the election of a king. As a result, the Finnish crown was offered to a German, Friedrich Karl, Prince of Hessen. Immediately prior to German defeat in World War I, the prince declined the invitation. The victorious Allies insisted on a new Finnish government and a fresh general election if they were to recognize the nation's independent status. Since the country was now compelled to look to the Allies for future assistance, the request was complied with, sealing Finland's future as a republic. The first president was the liberal **Ståhlberg**.

The termination of the monarchists' aims upset the unity of the right and paved the way for a succession of centrist governments. These were dominated by two parties, the **National Progressives** and the **Agrarians**. Through a period of rapidly increasing prosperity, numerous reforms were enacted. Farmers who rented land were given the opportunity to buy it with state aid, compulsory schooling was introduced, laws regarding religious freedom were passed and the provision of social services strengthened. As more farmers became independent producers, the Agrarians, claiming to represent the rural interests, drew away much of the Social Democrats' traditional support.

Finnish economic development halted abruptly following the world slump of the late 1920s. A series of strikes culminated in a dock workers' dispute which began in May 1928 and continued for almost a year. It was settled by the intervention of the Minister for Social Affairs on terms perceived as a defeat for the strikers. The dispute was seen by the right as a communist-inspired attempt to ruin the Finnish export trade at a time when the Soviet Union had re-entered the world timber trade. It was also a symbolic ideological clash – a pointer to future events.

Moves to outlaw communist activity had been deemed an infringement of civil rights, but in 1929 the Suomen Lukko was formed to legally combat communism. It was swiftly succeeded by the more extreme and violent **Lapua Movement** (the name coming from the Ostrobothnian town, where a parade of communist youth had been brought to a bloody end by "White" farmers). The Lapuans rounded up suspected communists and communist sympathizers, and drove them to the Russian border, insisting that they walk across. Even the former president, Ståhlberg, was kid-napped and dumped at the eastern town of Joensuu. The Lapuans' actions were only half-heartedly condemned by the non-socialist parties, and in private they were supported. But when the Lapuans began advocating a complete overthrow of the political system, much of this tacit approval dried up.

The government obtained a two-thirds majority in the elections of October 1930 and amended the constitution to make communist activity illegal. This was expected to placate the Lapuans but instead they issued even more extreme demands, including the abolition of the Social Democrats. In 1932, a coup d'état was attempted by a Lapuan group who prevented a socialist member of parliament from addressing a meeting in Mäntsälä, 50km north of Helsinki. They refused to disperse, despite shots being fired by police, and sent for assistance from Lapuan bases around the country. The Lapuan leadership took up the cause and broadcast demands for a new government. They were unsuccessful because of the loyalty of the troops who surrounded the town on the orders of the then prime minister, Svinhufvud. Following this, the Lapuans were outlawed, although their leaders received only minor punishments for their deeds. Several of them regrouped as the Nazi-style Patriotic People's Movement. But unlike the parallel movements in Europe, there was little in Finland on which Nazism could focus mass hatred, and, despite winning a few parliamentary seats, it quickly declined into insignificance.

The Finnish **economy** recovered swiftly, and much international goodwill was generated when the country became the only nation to fully pay its war reparations to the USA after World War I. Finland joined the League of Nations hoping for a guarantee of its eastern border, but by 1935 the League's weakness was apparent and the Finns looked to traditionally neutral **Scandinavia** for protection as Europe moved towards war.

■ World War II

The Nazi–Soviet Non-Aggression Pact of August 1939 put Finland firmly into the Soviet sphere. Stalin had compelled Estonia, Latvia and Lithuania to allow Russian bases on their land, and in October was demanding a chunk of the Karelian isthmus from Finland to protect Leningrad, as well as a leasing of the Hanko peninsula on the Finnish Baltic coast. Russian troops were heading towards the Finnish border from Murmansk, and on November 30 the

Karelian isthmus was attacked – an act that triggered the **Winter War**.

Stalin had had the tsarist military commanders executed, and his troops were led by young communists well versed in ideology but ignorant of war strategy. Informed that the Finnish people would welcome them as liberators, the Soviet soldiers anticipated little resistance to their invasion. They expected to reach the Finnish west coast within ten days and therefore carried no overcoats, had little food, and camped each night in open fields. The Finns, although vastly outnumbered, were defending their homes and farms as well as their hard-won independence. Familiarity with the terrain enabled them to conceal themselves in the forests and attack through stealth – and they were prepared for the winter temperatures, which plunged to -30°C (-18°F). The Russians were slowly picked off and their camps frequently surrounded and destroyed.

While Finland gained the world's admiration, no practical help was forthcoming and it became simply a matter of time before Stalin launched a better-supplied, unstoppable advance. It came during February 1940 and the Finnish government was forced to ask for peace. This was granted under the **Treaty of Moscow**, signed in March by President **Kyösti Kallio**, who cursed "let the hand wither that signs such a paper" as his hand put pen to paper. The treaty ceded 11 percent of Finnish territory to the Soviet Union. There was a mass exodus from these areas, with nearly half a million people travelling west to the new boundaries of Finland. Kyösti Kallio was later paralyzed on his right side.

The period immediately following the Winter War left Finland in a difficult position. Before the war, Finland had produced all its own food but was dependent on imported fertilizers. Supplies of grain, which had been coming from Russia, were halted as part of Soviet pressure for increased transit rights and access to the important nickel-producing mines in Petsamo. Finland became reliant on grain from Germany and British shipments to the Petsamo coast, which were interrupted when Germany invaded Norway. In return for providing arms, Germany was given transit rights through Finland. Legally, this required the troops to be constantly moving, but a permanent force became stationed at Rovaniemi.

The Finnish leadership knew that Germany was secretly preparing to attack the Soviet Union, and a broadcast from Berlin had spoken of a "united front" from Norway to Poland at a time when Finland was officially outside the Nazi sphere. Within Finland there was little support for the Nazis, but there was a fear of Soviet occupation. While Finland clung to its neutrality, refusing to fight unless attacked, it was drawn closer and closer to Germany. Soviet air raids on several Finnish towns in June 1941 finally led Finland into the war on the side of the Nazis. The ensuing conflict with the Russians, fought with the primary purpose of regaining territory lost in the Winter War, became known as **the Continuation War**. The bulk of the land ceded under the Treaty of Moscow was recovered by the end of August. After this, Mannerheim, who commanded the Finnish troops, ignored Nazi encouragement to assist in their attack on Leningrad. A request from the British prime minister, Winston Churchill, that the Finns cease their advance, was also refused, although Mannerheim didn't cut the Murmansk railway which was moving Allied supplies. Even so, Britain was forced to acknowledge the predicament of its ally, the Soviet Union, and declared war on Finland in December 1941.

In 1943, the German defeat at Stalingrad, which made Allied victory almost inevitable, had a profound impact in Finland. Mannerheim called a meeting of inner-cabinet ministers and decided to seek a truce with the Soviet Union. The USA stepped forward as mediators but announced that the peace terms set by Moscow were too severe to be worthy of negotiation. Germany meanwhile had learned of the Finnish initiative and demanded an undertaking that Finland would not seek peace with Russia, threatening to withdraw supplies if it was not given. (The Germans were also unhappy with Finnish sympathy for Jews. Several hundred who had escaped from central Europe were saved from the concentration camps by being granted Finnish citizenship.) Simultaneously, a Russian advance into Karelia made Finland dependent on German arms to launch a counterattack. An agreement with the Germans was signed by President **Risto Ryti** in June 1944 without the consent of the Eduskunta, thereby making the deed invalid when he ceased to be president.

Ryti resigned the presidency at the beginning of August and Mannerheim informed Germany that the agreement was no longer binding. A peace with the Soviet Union was signed in Moscow two weeks later. Under its terms, Finland was forced to give up the Pestamo region and the border was restored to its 1940 position. The Hanko peninsula was returned but instead the Porkkala peninsula, nearer to Helsinki, was to be leased to the Soviet Union for fifty years. There were stinging reparations. The Finns also had to drive the remaining Germans out of the country within two weeks. This was easily done in the south, but the bitter fighting that took place in Lapland caused the total destruction of many towns. It was further agreed that organizations disseminating anti-Soviet views within Finland would be dissolved and that Finland would accept an Allied Control Commission to oversee war trials.

■ The postwar period

After the war, the Communist Party was legalized and, along with militant socialists expelled from the Social Democratic Party, formed a broad leftist umbrella organization – the **Finnish People's Democratic League**. Their efforts to absorb the Social Democrats were resisted by that party's moderate leadership, who regarded communism as "poison to the Finnish people". In the first peace-time poll, the Democratic League went to the electorate with a populist rather than revolutionary manifesto – something that was to characterize future Finnish communism. Both they and the Social Democrats attained approximately a quarter of the vote. Bolstered by two Social Democratic defections, the Democratic League narrowly became the largest party in the Eduskunta. The two of them, along with the Agrarian Party, formed an alliance ("The Big Three Agreement") that held the balance of power in a coalition government under the premiership of Paasikivi.

Strikes instigated by communist-controlled trade unions allowed the Social Democrats to accuse the Democratic League of seeking to undermine the production of machinery and other goods destined for the Soviet Union under the terms of the war reparation agreement, thereby creating a scenario for Soviet invasion. Charges of communist vote-rigging in trade union ballots helped the Social Democrats to gain control of the unions. The Democratic League won only 38 seats in the general election of 1948, and rejected the token offer of four posts in the new government, opting instead to stay in opposition. Their electoral campaign wasn't helped by the rumour – almost certainly groundless – that they were planning a Soviet-backed coup.

To ensure that the terms of the peace agreement were adhered to, the Soviet-dominated Allied Control Commission stayed in Finland until 1947. Its presence engendered a tense atmosphere both on the streets of Helsinki – there were several incidents of violence against Soviet officers – and in the numerous clashes with the Finnish government over the war trials. Unlike the Eastern European countries under full Soviet occupation, Finland was able to conduct its own trials, but had to satisfy the Commission that they were conducted properly. Delicate manoeuvring by the Chief of Justice, **Urho Kekkonen**, resulted in comparatively short prison sentences for the accused, the longest being ten years for Risto Ryti.

The uncertain relationship between Finland and the Soviet Union was resolved, to some extent, by the signing of the **Treaty of Friendship, Cooperation and Mutual Assistance** (FCMA) in 1948. It confirmed Finnish responsibility for its own defence and pledged the country not to join any alliance hostile to the Soviet Union. In the suspicious atmosphere of the Cold War, the treaty was perceived by the Western powers to place Finland firmly under Soviet influence. The Soviet insistence that the treaty was a guarantee of neutrality was viewed as hypocritical while they were still leasing the Porkkala peninsula. When it became clear that Finland was not becoming a Soviet satellite and had full control over its internal affairs, the USA reinstated credit facilities – carefully structured to avoid financing anything that would be of help to the Soviets – and Finland was admitted to Western financial institutions such as the IMF and World Bank.

The postwar **economy** was dominated by the reparations demand. Much of the bill was paid off in ships and machinery, which established engineering as a major industry. The escalating world demand for timber products boosted exports, but inflation soared and led to frequent wage disputes. In 1949 an attempt to enforce a piece-work rate in a pulp factory in Kemi culminated in two workers being shot by police, a state of emergency being declared in the town, and the arrest of communist leaders. Economic conflicts reached a climax in 1956 after right-wingers in the Eduskunta had blocked an annual extension of government controls on wages and prices. This caused a sharp rise in the cost of living and the trade unions demanded appropriate pay increases. A general strike followed, lasting for three weeks until the strikers' demands were met. Any benefit, however, was quickly cancelled out by further price rises.

In 1957, a split occurred in the Social Democrats between urban and rural factions, the former seeking increased industrialization and the streamlining of unprofitable farms, the latter pursuing high agricultural subsidies. By 1959 a group of breakaway ruralists had set up the Small Farmers' Social Democratic Union, causing a rift within the country's internal politics that was to have important repercussions in Finland's dealings with the Soviet Union. Although the government had no intention of changing its foreign policy, the Social Democrat's chairman, **Väinö Tanner**, had a well-known antipathy to the Soviet Union. Coupled with a growing number of anti-Soviet newspaper editorials, this precipitated the "**night frost**" of 1958. The Soviet leader, Khruschev, suspended imports and deliveries of machinery, causing a rise in Finnish unemployment. **Kekkonen**, elected president in 1956, personally intervened in the crisis by meeting with Khruschev, angering the Social Democrats, who accused Kekkonen of behaving undemocratically; meanwhile, the Agrarians were lambasted for failing to stand up to Soviet pressure.

In 1960, Tanner was re-elected as chairman and the Social Democrats continued to attack Kekkonen. The Agrarians refused to enter government with the Social Democrats unless they changed their policies. As global relations worsened during 1961, the Soviet Union sent a note to Kekkonen requesting a meeting to discuss the section of the 1948 treaty dealing with defence of the Finnish–Soviet border. This was the precursor to the "**note crisis**". The original note went unanswered, but the Finnish foreign secretary went to Moscow for exploratory talks with his opposite number. Assurances of Soviet confidence in Finnish foreign policy were given, but fears were expressed about the anti-Kekkonen alliance of conservatives and Social Democrats formed to contest the 1962 presidential election. Kekkonen again tried to defuse the crisis himself: using his constitutional powers he dissolved parliament early, forcing the election forward by several months and in so doing weakened the alliance. Kekkonen was re-elected and foreign policy remained unchanged. This was widely regarded as a personal victory for Kekkonen and a major turning point in relations with the Soviet

Union. Through all subsequent administrations, the maintenance of the **Paasikivi-Kekkonen line** on foreign policy became a symbol of national unity.

Following Tanner's retirement from politics in 1963, the Social Democrats ended their stand against the established form of foreign policy, making possible their re-entry to government.

Throughout the early 1960s there was mounting dissatisfaction within the People's Democratic League towards the old pro-Moscow leadership. In 1965, a moderate non-communist was elected as the League's general secretary, and two years later he became chairman; a similar change took place in the communist leadership of the trade unions. The new-look communists pledged their desire for a share in government. The election of May 1966 resulted in a "popular front" government dominated by the Social Democrats and the People's Democratic League, under the prime ministership of **Rafael Paasio**.

This brought to an end a twenty-year spell of centre-right governments in which the crucial pivot had been the Agrarian Party. In 1965, the Agrarians changed their name to the Centre Party, aiming to modernize their image and become more attractive to the urban electorate. A challenge to this new direction was mounted by the **Finnish Rural Party**, founded by a breakaway group of Agrarians in the late 1950s, who mounted an increasingly influential campaign on behalf of "the forgotten people" – farmers and smallholders in declining rural areas. In the election of 1970 they gained 10 percent of the vote, but in subsequent years lost support through internal divisions.

The communists retained governmental posts until 1971, when they too were split – between the young "reformists" who advocated continued participation in government, and the older, hard-line "purists" who were frustrated by the failure to implement socialist economic policies, and preferred to stay in opposition.

■ Modern Finland

Throughout the postwar years Finland promoted itself vigorously as a **neutral country**. It joined the United Nations in 1955 and Finnish soldiers became an integral part of the UN Peace-Keeping Force. In 1969 preparations were started for the European Security Conference in Helsinki, and in 1972 the city was the venue for the **Strategic Arms Limitation Talks (SALT)**, underlining a

Finnish role in mediation between the superpowers. But an attempt to have a clause stating Finland's neutrality inserted into the 1970 extension-signing of the FCMA Treaty was opposed by the Soviet Union, whose foreign secretary, Andrei Gromyko, had a year earlier defined Finland not as neutral but as a "peace-loving neighbour of the Soviet Union".

In 1971 the revelations of a Czech defector, General Sejna, suggesting that the Soviet army was equipped to take over Finland within 24 hours should Soviet defences be compromised, brought a fresh wave of uncertainty to relations with its eastern neighbour; as did the sudden withdrawal of the Soviet ambassador, allegedly for illicit scheming with the People's Democratic League.

The stature of Kekkonen as a world leader guaranteed continued support for his presidency. But his commitment to the Paasikivi-Kekkonen line ensured that nothing potentially upsetting to the Soviet Union was allowed to surface in Finnish politics, giving – as some thought – the Soviet Union a covert influence on Finland's internal affairs. Opposition to Kekkonen was simply perceived as an attempt to undermine the Paasikivi-Kekkonen line. Equally, the unchallengeable nature of Kekkonen's presidency was considered to be beyond his proper constitutional powers. A move in 1974 by an alliance of right-wingers and Social Democrats within the Eduskunta to transfer some of the presidential powers to parliament received a very hostile reaction, emphasizing the almost inviolate position that Kekkonen enjoyed. Kekkonen was re-elected in 1978, although forced to stand down through illness in 1981.

Because Finland is heavily dependent on foreign trade, its well-being has closely mirrored world trends. The international financial boom of the 1960s enabled a range of social legislation to be passed and created a comparatively high standard of living for most Finns – albeit not on the same scale as the rest of Scandinavia. The global **recession** of the 1970s and early 1980s was most dramatically felt when a fall in the world market for pulp coincided with a steep increase in the price of oil. Although the country tackled the immediate problems of the recession, industry remained heavily concentrated in the south, causing rural areas further north to experience high rates of unemployment and with few prospects for economic growth – save through rising levels of tourism.

The election of 1987 saw a break with the pattern of recent decades. Non-socialist parties made large gains, mainly at the expense of the Rural Party and Communists. The new government of **Harri Holkeri**, however, appeared inept – particularly in its hesitant reaction to events in the Soviet Union and continued deference to Moscow, whether real or apparent. Public disillusionment resulted in large gains for the Centre Party in the election of March 1991. The Centre Party chairman, 47-year-old **Eske Aho**, subsequently became prime minister, leading a new coalition in which many of the members reflected the comparative youth and fresh ideas of its leader.

In 1992, celebrations to mark 75 years of Finnish independence were muted by the realization that the country was entering a highly critical period, facing more problems (few of its own making) than it had for many decades. The end of the Cold War had diminished the value of Finland's hard-won neutrality, the economic and ethnic difficulties in Russia were being watched with trepidation, while another global **recession** hit Finland just as the nation lost its major trading partner – the Soviet Union – of the last fifty years.

Throughout the early 1990s Finland's economic depression was among the worst in the industrial west, with its banking system in crisis and unemployment figures almost the highest in Europe. Such events forced Finland to pin its hopes on closer links with Western Europe. On January 1, 1995, Finland became a full member of the **European Union**, and the same year the Social Democratic Party's **Martti Ahtisaari** was elected as president, with the general election resulting in a coalition win for the Social Democrats, their Chairman Paavo Lipponen forming a majority government that includes conservatives, socialists, the Swedish Folk Party and the Green Party.

By the Millennium, as Russia descended into farce, Finland had become more firmly linked to the European Union and its economy had recovered sufficiently for it to be accepted into the first wave of countries to join European Monetary Union. In 1999, for the first time, it assumed the presidency of the European Union, while President Ahtisaari established himself as an important international statesman through his interventions in the war in Kosovo. Economically, the country's highly educated populace and technological expertise have made it a powerful player in the world IT market, while EU membership

A BRIEF GUIDE TO FINNISH

Finnish has nothing in common with the other Scandinavian languages. It belongs to the **Finno-Ugric** group, and its grammatical structure is complex: with fifteen cases alone to grapple with, it's initially a tricky language to learn, although once a basic vocabulary is attained things become less impenetrable. Usefully, compared to other languages, there are very few actual words in Finnish – the majority of terms being compounded. English is widely spoken, particularly by young people and around the main towns. Swedish is a common second language and the first of the Finland-Swedes, who live mainly in the western parts of the country.

Of the few available phrasebooks, *Finnish For Travellers* (Berlitz) is the most useful for practical purposes; the best Finnish–English dictionary is *The Standard Finnish Dictionary* (Holt, Rinehart and Winston).

PRONUNCIATION

In Finnish, words are pronounced exactly as they are written, with the stress always on the first syllable: in a compound word the stress is on the first syllable of each part of the word. Each letter is pronounced individually, and doubling a letter lengthens the sound: double "kk"s are pronounced with two "k"sounds and the double "aa" pronounced as long as the English "a" in "car". The letters b, c, f, q, w, x, z and å are only found in words derived from foreign languages, and are pronounced as in the language of origin.

a as in f**a**ther but shorter
d as in ri**d**ing but sometimes soft as to be barely heard
e between the e in p**e**n and the i in p**i**n.
g (only after "n") as in si**ng**er
h as in **h**ot
i as in p**i**n
j like the y in **y**ellow
np like the m in **m**other

o like the aw in l**aw**
r is rolled
s as in **s**aid but with the tongue a little further back from the teeth
u as in b**u**ll
y like the French u in "s**u**r"
ä like the a in h**a**t
ö like the ur in F**ur** but without any "r"sound.

BASICS

Do you speak English?	*Puhutteko englantia?*	Good day	*hyvää päivää (*usually shortened to *päivä)*
Yes	*kyllä/joo*		
No	*ei*	Goodnight	*hyvää yötä*
I don't understand	*En ymmärrä*	Goodbye	*näkemiin*
I understand	*Ymmärrän*	Yesterday	*eilen*
Please	*olkaa hyvä*	Today	*tänään*
Thank you	*kiitos*	Tomorrow	*huomenna*
Excuse me	*anteeksi*	Day after tomorrow	*ylihuomenna*
Good morning	*hyvää huomenta*	In the morning	*aamulla/aamupäivällä*
Good afternoon	*hyvää päivää*	In the afternoon	*iltapäivällä*
Good evening	*hyvää iltaa*	In the evening	*illalla*

SOME SIGNS

Entrance	*Sisään*	Pull	*Vedä*
Exit	*Ulos*	Arrival	*Saapuvat*
Gentlemen	*Miehille/Miehet/Herrat*	Departure	*Lähtevät*
Ladies	*Naisille/Naiset/Rouvat*	Police	*Poliisi*
Hot	*Kuuma*	Hospital	*Sairaala*
Cold	*Kylmä*	No Smoking	*Tupakointi kielletty*
Open	*Avoinna*	No Entry	*Pääsy kielletty*
Closed	*Suljettu*	No Trespassing	*Läpikulku kielletty*
Push	*Työnnä*	No Camping	*Leiriytyminen kielletty*

QUESTIONS AND DIRECTIONS

Where's…?	*Missä on…?*	How much?	*Kuinka paljon?*
When?	*Koska/milloin?*	How much is that?	*Paljonko se maksaa?*
What?	*Mikä/mitä?*	I'd like	*Haluaisin*
Why?	*Miksi?*	Cheap	*Halpa*
How far is it to…?	*Kuinka pitkä matka on …n ?*	Expensive	*Kallis*
Where is the railway		Good	*Hyvä*
station?	*Missä on rautatieasema?*	Bad	*Paha/Huono*
Train/bus/boat/ship	*Juna/bussi (or) linja-auto/*	Here	*Täällä*
	vene/laiva	There	*Sie'lä*
Where is the youth		Left	*Vasen*
hostel?	*Missä on retkeilymaja?*	Right	*Oikea*
Can we camp here?	*Voimmeko leiriytyä tähän?*	Go straight ahead	*Ajakaa suoraan eteenpäin*
Do you have anything	*Onko teillä mitään*	Is it near/far?	*Onko se lähellä/kaukana?*
better/bigger/	*parempaa/isompaa/*	Ticket/ticket office	*Lipputoimisto*
cheaper?	*halvempaa?*	Train/bus station/	*Rautatieasema/linja-*
It's too expensive	*Se on liian kallis*	bus stop	*autoasema/bussipysäkki*

NUMBERS

0	*nolla*	9	*yhdeksän*	18	*kahdeksantoista*	80	*kahdeksankymmentä*
1	*yksi*	10	*kymmenen*	19	*yhdeksäntoista*	90	*yhdeksänkymmentä*
2	*kaksi*	11	*yksitoista*	20	*kaksikymmentä*	100	*sata*
3	*kolme*	12	*kaksitoista*	21	*kaksikymmentäyksi*	101	*satayksi*
4	*neljä*	13	*kolmetoista*	30	*kolmekymmentä*	151	*sataviisikymmentäyksi*
5	*viisi*	14	*neljätoista*	40	*neljäkymmentä*	200	*kaksisataa*
6	*kuusi*	15	*viisitoista*	50	*viisikymmentä*	1000	*tuhat*
7	*seitsemän*	16	*kuusitoista*	60	*kuusikymmentä*		
8	*kahdeksan*	17	*seitsemäntoista*	70	*seitsemänkymmentä*		

DAYS AND MONTHS

Monday	*maanantai*	January	*tammikuu*	August	*elokuu*
Tuesday	*tiistai*	February	*helmikuu*	September	*syyskuu*
Wednesday	*keskiviikko*	March	*maalisku*	October	*lokakuu*
Thursday	*torstai*	April	*huhtikuu*	November	*marraskuu*
Friday	*perjantai*	May	*toukokuu*	December	*joulukuu*
Saturday	*lauantai*	June	*kesäkuu*		
Sunday	*sunnuntai*	July	*heinäkuu*		

GLOSSARY OF FINNISH TERMS AND PHRASES

Järvi	Lake	*Museo*	Museum
Joki	River	*Pankki*	Bank
Katu	Street	*Posti*	Post office
Kauppahalli	Market hall	*Puisto*	Park
Kauppatori	Market square	*Rautatieasema*	Train station
Kaupungintalo	Town hall	*Sairaala*	Hospital
Keskusta	Town centre	*Taidemuseo*	Art museum
Kirkko	Church	*Tie*	Road
Kylä	Village	*Tori*	Square
Linja-autoasema	Bus station	*Torni*	Tower
Linna	Castle	*Tuomiokirkko*	Cathedral
Lipputoimisto	Ticket office	*Yliopisto*	University
Matkailutoimisto	Tourist office		

has given the country a new sense of security and confidence. However, the picture is not entirely rosy: high unemployment and the chaos of Russia's gangster economy on the doorstep provide major worries, as do continuing debates around membership of NATO and the role of the welfare state. Other pressing issues include the need to diversify an economy that is over-reliant on the Nokia phone company (which by 1999 had become the world leader in its field and the provider of a staggering fifty percent of Finland's GDP) and how to continue development in rural areas without the support of big government subsidies. How these problems are addressed will be the major concerns of Finland in the first years of the new millennium.

CHAPTER FIFTEEN

HELSINKI AND THE SOUTH

The southern coast of Finland is the most populated, industrialized and richest part of the country, centred around the capital, **Helsinki**, a city of half a million people with the friendliness of a peasant village on market day. Helsinki's innovative architecture and batch of fine museums and galleries collectively expose the roots of the national character, while at night the pubs and clubs strip it bare. It may seem the perfect prelude to exploring the rest of Finland, and in the practical sense it is, being the hub of the country's road, rail and air traffic routes. However, if you can, try to arrive in Helsinki *after* seeing the rest of the country. Only with some prior knowledge of Finland does the significance of the city as a symbol of Finnish self-determination become clear.

A couple of towns **around Helsinki** evince the change from ruralism to modernism even further. **Porvoo** sits placidly locked in the nineteenth century, while the suburban area of **Espoo** forms a showpiece of twentieth-century design. Further away, in the country's southeastern extremity, the only community of significant size and importance between Helsinki and the Russian border is the shipping port of **Kotka** – not wildly appealing in itself, but at the heart of a historically intriguing coastal region.

Helsinki only became the capital in 1812, after Finland had been made a Russian Grand Duchy and Tsar Alexander I had deemed the previous capital, **Turku**, too close to Sweden for comfort. Today Turku, facing Stockholm across the Gulf of Bothnia, handles its demotion well. Both historically and visually it's one of Finland's most enticing cities; indeed, the snootier elements of its Swedish-speaking contingent still consider Åbo (its Swedish name) the real capital, and Helsinki just an uncouth upstart.

Between Helsinki and Turku, along the entire southern coast, only small villages and a few slightly larger towns break the continuity of the forests. Beyond Turku, though, things are more interesting, with the two most southerly of the Finland-Swedish communities: **Rauma**, with its unique dialect and well-preserved town centre; and the likeably downbeat **Pori**, famous for its annual jazz festival.

ACCOMMODATION PRICE CODES

The hotels listed in this chapter have been graded according to the following price bands, based on the cost of the **least expensive double room in summer**. However, many hotels offer summer and/or weekend discounts, and in these instances we've given two grades, covering both the regular and the discounted rate.

① Under 275mk	② 275–350mk	③ 350–450mk
④ 450–550mk	⑤ 550–750mk	⑥ Over 750mk

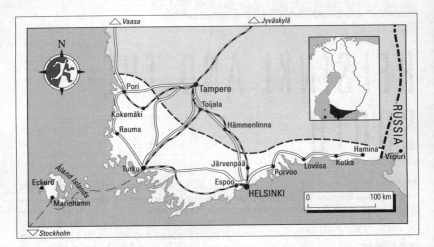

Where this corner of Finland meets the sea it splinters into an enormous archipelago, which includes the curious **Åland Islands** – a grouping of thousands of fragments of land, only about half a dozen of which are inhabited, connected by small roadways skirting the sea. There's a tiny self-governing population here, Swedish-speaking but with a history that's distinct from both Sweden and Finland.

Much of the region is most easily reached from Helsinki, from where there are frequent bus and rail services to Turku. Rauma and Pori are best reached by bus from Turku, and from Pori there are easy connections to Tampere and the Lake Region (covered in the following chapter). Daily ferries also connect Turku to the Åland Islands.

HELSINKI AND AROUND

HELSINKI has a character quite different from the other Scandinavian capitals, and in many ways is closer in mood (and certainly in looks) to the major cities of Eastern Europe. For years an outpost of the Russian empire, its very shape and style was originally modelled on its powerful neighbour's former capital, St Petersburg. Yet throughout the twentieth century the city was also a showcase for independent Finland, much of its impressive **architecture** drawing inspiration from the dawning of Finnish nationalism and the rise of the republic. Equally the **museums**, especially the National Museum and the Art Museum of the Ateneum, reveal the country's growing awareness of its own folklore and culture.

Much of central Helsinki is a succession of compact granite blocks, interspersed with more characterful buildings, alongside waterways, green spaces and the glass-fronted office blocks and shopping centres you'll find in any European capital. The city is hemmed in on three sides by water, and all the things you might want to see are within walking distance of one another – and certainly no more than a few minutes apart by tram or bus. The streets have a youthful buzz, and the short summer is acknowledged by crowds strolling the boulevards, cruising the shopping arcades and socializing in the outdoor cafés and restaurants; everywhere there's prolific **street entertainment**. At night the pace picks up, with a great selection of pubs and clubs, free rock concerts in the numerous parks, and an impressive quota of fringe events. It's a pleasure just to be around, merging with the multitude and witnessing the activity.

Arrival, information and city transport

However you arrive you'll be deposited somewhere close to the heart of town. Helsinki's **airport**, Vantaa, 20km to the north, is served by frequent airport buses (30min; 25mk). These stop at the new suburb of Pasila, and at the Finnair terminal behind the *Inter-Continental Hotel*, halfway between the city centre and the Olympic Stadium, before continuing to the train station. A cheaper, if slightly slower, airport connection is city bus #615; this costs 15mk and runs roughly every twenty minutes from the airport to the bus terminal beside the train station. City bus #614 runs from the airport to the other bus station, Simonkatu, but only a few times a day.

The Viking and Silja **ferry** lines have their terminals on opposite sides of the South Harbour (at docks known respectively as Katajanokka and Olympic), and disembarking passengers from either have a walk of less than 1km to the centre. The **train station**, equipped with luggage lockers, is right in the heart of the city, next door to one of the two city bus terminals. All trams stop immediately outside or around the corner in Mannerheimintie. Just across Mannerheimintie, behind the Lasipalatsi, and a short way up Simonkatu is the second city bus terminal and the **long-distance bus station**.

Information

The **City Tourist Office**, at Pohjoisesplanadi 19 (May–Sept Mon–Fri 9am–7pm, Sat & Sun 9am–3pm; Oct–April Mon–Fri 9am–5pm, Sat 9am–3pm; ☎09/169 3757, fax 169 3839, *www.hel.fi*), supplies free street and transport maps, along with the useful free tourist magazine *Helsinki This Week* and the stylish *Helsinki Happens* (20mk). While here, try to get hold of the excellent free brochure, *Helsinki On Foot*, useful even if it tends to mix Finnish and Swedish street names on its maps. If you're staying for a while and plan to see as much of the city and its museums as possible, consider purchasing a **Helsinki Card** (available from the tourist office), which gives unlimited travel on public transport and free entry to over forty museums. The three-day card (180mk) is the best value, although there are also two-day (150mk) and one-day (120mk) versions.

For information on the rest of the country, visit the **Finnish Tourist Board**, just south of the City Tourist Office at Eteläesplanadi 4 (May–Sept Mon–Fri 9am–5pm, Sat & Sun 10am–2pm; Oct–April Mon–Fri 9am–5pm; ☎09/4176 9300, fax 4176 9301, *www.mek.fi*). Next door is Edita, the best place for **maps** of Finland, the Baltic and Scandinavia generally; there's a second branch at Annankatu 44 (both open Mon–Fri 9am–5pm).

City transport

The central area and its immediate surrounds are covered by an integrated transport network of buses, trams and a small metro system. A single-journey **ticket** for the system costs 10mk when bought from the conductor or driver, 8mk if purchased in advance from an R-Kiosk or other outlet, with unlimited transfers allowed within one hour. A **multi-trip** ticket gives ten rides for 75mk. You can also buy a **tourist ticket** covering the city and surrounding areas such as Espoo and Vantaa for one (45mk), three (90mk) or five days (135mk), which permits travel on buses and trams displaying double arrows (effectively all of them); obviously, this is only a cost-cutter if used frequently. If you don't intend to leave the city proper, you're better off with a **Helsinki-only tourist ticket**, again available in one- (25mk), three- (50mk) and five-day (75mk) versions. All these tickets can be bought from R-Kiosk stands, the long-distance bus station or the City Tourist Office.

On **buses** you enter at the front, where you must either buy or show your ticket. On **trams**, get on at the front or back, and stamp your ticket in the machine. It's unlikely

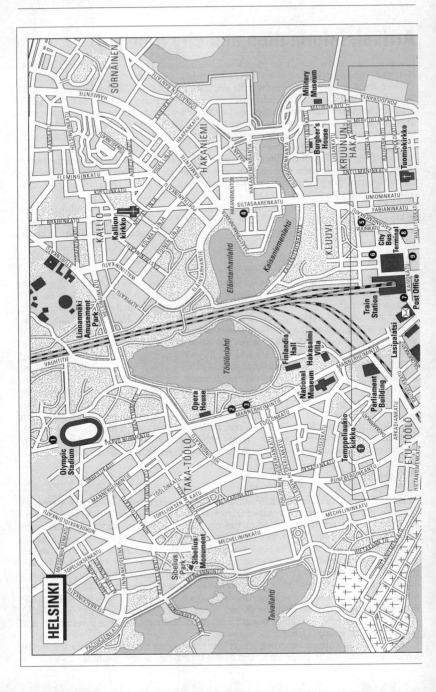

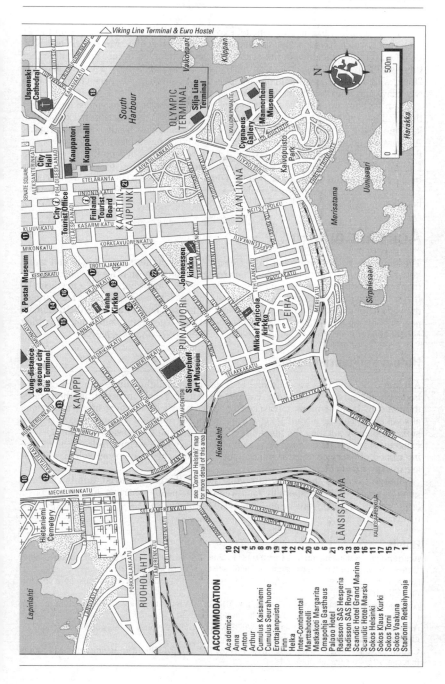

△Viking Line Terminal & Euro Hostel

N

500m

0

ACCOMMODATION

Academica	10
Anna	22
Anton	4
Arthur	5
Cumulus Kaisaniemi	8
Cumulus Seurahuone	9
Erottajanpuisto	19
Finn	14
Helka	12
Inter-Continental	2
Marttahotelli	20
Matkakoti Margarita	6
Omapohja Gasthaus	6
Palace Hotel	21
Radisson SAS Hesperia	3
Radisson SAS Royal	13
Scandic Hotel Grand Marina	18
Scandic Hotel Marski	16
Sokos Helsinki	11
Sokos Klaus Kurki	15
Sokos Torni	17
Sokos Vaakuna	7
Stadionin Retkeilymaja	1

that you'll be asked to show your ticket except on some of the old vehicles on the #1 tram route, which have a seated conductor instead of a machine. **Metro** tickets can be bought from the machines in the stations. If you're tempted to fare-dodge, note that there's a 250mk on-the-spot fine on buses and trams. **Taxis** have a basic charge of 20mk, with a further 7mk per kilometre, plus a 10mk surcharge between 8pm and 6am weekdays and from 4pm Saturday to 6am Monday.

Tram **#3T** follows a figure-of-eight route around the city, and if you're pushed for time will take you past the most obvious attractions. For a more leisurely exploration, join one of the two-hour guided **walking tours** (30mk) run by the Helsinki Tourist Association, Lönnrotinkatu 7B (☎09/603 417), and you'll finish up knowing more about the city than most of its residents do. For details, phone the above number or ask at the City Tourist Office. There are also numerous **boat sightseeing tours** from the harbour costing around 40mk for an hour or 60mk for two hours. These run from around 11am to 7pm, and brochures are available at the tourist office, or from touts at the harbour itself.

Accommodation

There's plenty of **accommodation** in Helsinki, although the bulk of it is in mid-range hotels. Various discounts (see below) can reduce costs in these places, or alternatively there are a couple of cheaper summer hotels, several tourist hotels and a few hostels. If you arrive without a reservation, it's possible to book a room for a 12mk fee through the very helpful **Hotel Booking Centre** in the train station, to the left of the platforms near the left-luggage office (June–Aug Mon–Sat 9am–7pm, Sun 10am–6pm; Sept–May Mon–Fri 9am–5pm; ☎09/2288 1400, fax 2288 1499, *hotel@helsinkiexpert.fi*).

Hotels and tourist hotels

Although the cost of a room in one of Helsinki's top-flight **hotels** can be high, the better hotels aren't necessarily completely out of reach: many drop their rates dramatically in the summer tourist season, while nearly everywhere offers reductions at weekends. To take advantage of any bargains, it's essential to book as early as possible – either by phoning the hotel directly or by making a reservation through a travel agent. However much you pay, it's unlikely that you'll leave any Helsinki hotel feeling ripped off: service and amenities – such as the inclusive help-yourself breakfast – are usually excellent.

Though they lack the luxury of regular hotels, the city's **tourist hotels** can be a good-value alternative, especially for three or four people sharing. All provide basic accommodation in private rooms without bathrooms, and usually offer inexpensive meals as well.

Hotels

Academica, Hietaniemenkatu 14 (☎09/1311 4334, fax 441 201). A well-placed summer hotel (June–Aug only) with morning sauna and pool; see also "Hostels, p.646. ②.

Anna, Annankatu 1 (☎09/616 621, fax 602 664). Small, central and with a cosy atmosphere, in a former Christian mission. ⑤.

Anton, Paasivuorenkatu 1 (☎09/750 311, fax 701 4527). A bit out of the way, just north of the centre close to Hakaneimentori, but good value at weekends. ④.

Arthur, Vuorikatu 19 (☎09/173 441, fax 626 880). You can save money in this good-quality hotel by getting a room without a bathroom – but do it early. ④.

Cumulus Kaisaniemi, Kaisaniemenkatu 7 (☎09/172 881, fax 605 379). Ageing but clean rooms that can be good value at weekends. ⑥.

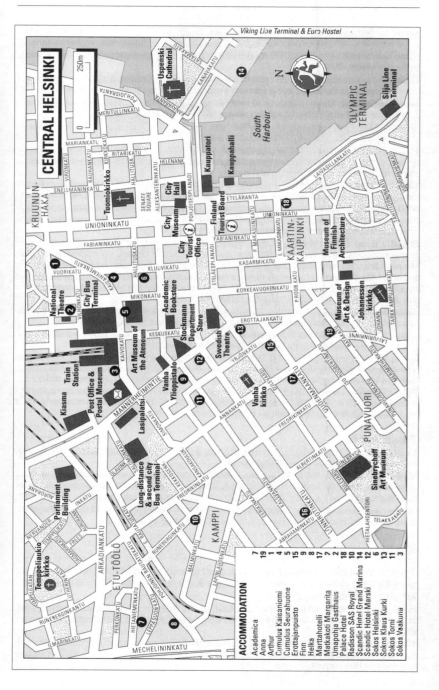

CENTRAL HELSINKI

△ Viking Line Terminal & Euro Hostel

250m

0

KRUUNUN-HAKA

Uspenski Cathedral

Tuomiokirkko

SENATE SQUARE

Kauppatori

Kauppahalli

South Harbour

OLYMPIC TERMINAL

Silja Line Terminal

National Theatre

City Bus Terminal

City Hall

City Museum

City Tourist Office ⓘ

Finland Tourist Board ⓘ

Academic Bookstore

Stockmann Department Store

KAARTIN-KAUPUNKI

Museum of Finnish Architecture

Swedish Theatre

Museum of Art & Design

Johannessen kirkko

Train Station

Kiasma

Post Office & Postal Museum

Art Museum of the Ateneum

Lasipalatsi

Vanha Ylioppilastalo

Vanha kirkko

Parliament Building

Long-distance & second city Bus Terminal

KAMPPI

PUNAVUORI

Sinebrychoff Art Museum

Temppeliaukio kirkko

ETU-TÖÖLÖ

ACCOMMODATION

Academica	7
Anna	19
Arthur	1
Cumulus Kaisaniemi	4
Cumulus Seurahuone	5
Erottajanpuisto	15
Finn	9
Helka	8
Marttahotelli	17
Matkakoti Margarita	2
Umapohja Gasthaus	2
Palace Hotel	18
Radisson SAS Royal	10
Scandic Hotel Grand Marina	14
Scandic Hotel Marski	12
Sokos Helsinki	6
Sokos Klaus Kurki	13
Sokos Torni	11
Sokos Vaakuna	3

Cumulus Seurahuone, Kaivokatu 12 (☎09/69 141, fax 691 4010). A stylish, classic hotel opposite the train station, with the historic *Café Socis* attached. Big, splendid rooms with original features. ⑥.

Finn, Kalevankatu 3b (☎09/640 904, fax 640 905). A modern, compact and peaceful place, virtually in the city centre. ③/②.

Helka, Pohjoinen Rautatiekatu 23 (☎09/613 580, fax 441 087). Rather plain-looking exterior but very welcoming on the inside; and within easy reach of everything. Some weekend reductions. ⑤.

Inter-Continental, Mannerheimintie 46 (☎09/40 551, fax 4055 3255). Next door to the *Radisson SAS Hesperia* and slightly less expensive, though the service is equally excellent. ⑥.

Marttahotelli, Uudenmaankatu 24 (☎09/618 7400, fax 618 7401). A clean and cosy hotel, though the rooms are on the small side. No alcohol served. ⑤.

Palace, Eteläranta 10 (☎09/134 561, fax 654 786). Luxurious and overlooking the Olympic Harbour. A quiet day in summer can bring substantial reductions, although it's difficult to get discounts on rooms with a sea view unless you're really pushy. ⑥.

Radisson SAS Hesperia, Mannerheimintie 50 (☎09/43 101, fax 431 0995). Swish and business-oriented, this is one of the major hotels just past the parliament building; weekend reductions. ⑥/⑤.

Radisson SAS Royal, Runeberginkatu (☎09/69 580, fax 6958 7100). Five-star, white-tiled and glamorous, resembling buildings like the Opera House and Finlandia Hall, this is not surprisingly expensive; visit in summer, when rates are cut by half. ⑥/⑤.

Scandic Hotel Grand Marina, Katajanokanlaituri 7 (☎09/16 661, fax 664 764). The vast former harbour customs house from the 1930s, now transformed into an elegant, very Scandinavian-looking hotel just a few strides from the arrival point of Viking Line boats from Sweden. ⑥/④.

Scandic Hotel Marski, Mannerheimintie 10 (☎09/68 061, fax 642 377). Opposite the Stockmann department store and named after Marski (Marshal) Mannerheim, this is one of the best hotels in the city, though less atmospheric than the *Palace*, above. ⑥/⑤.

Sokos Helsinki, Kluuvikatu 8 (☎09/131 401, fax 176 014). The best aspect of this place is its location, a stone's throw from Senate Square in one of the city's prime central streets. ⑥/④.

Sokos Klaus Kurki, Bulevardi 2–4 (☎09/618 911, fax 6189 1234). Recently renovated and perfectly situated for exploring the city. Usually offers weekend rates. ⑥/④.

Sokos Torni, Yrjönkatu 26 (☎09/131 131, fax 131 1361). Next door to the classic sauna and pools on Yrjönkatu. On a clear day, the thirteenth-floor bar gives views, so the locals claim, all the way to Estonia, but the drinks are pricey, as are the rooms – though weekend rates can drop dramatically. ⑥/⑤.

Sokos Vaakuna, Asema-Aukio 2 (☎09/131 181, fax 1311 8234). In the heart of the city facing the train station, built for the 1952 Olympic Games, this smartly refurbished hotel still contains many of its original, quintessentially Finnish architectural features. ⑥/⑤.

Tourist hotels

Erottajanpuisto, Uudenmaankatu 9 (☎09/642 169, fax 680 2757). Usefully positioned, and especially good value for several people sharing. ①.

Matkakoti Margarita, Itäinen Teatterikuja 3 (☎09/622 4261). Fairly basic place set in a quiet street close to the train and bus stations, and quite adequate for a night's rest. It also rents rooms cheaply by the day for those arriving in the city early and leaving later the same day. ①.

Omapohja Gasthaus, Itäinen Teatterikuja 3 (☎09/666 211). Downstairs from *Matkakoti Margarita*, this tourist hotel has en-suite rooms with colour TVs and other mod-cons. ②.

Hostels

Though the staple accommodation option of budget travellers, Helsinki's **hostels** are not without drawbacks: curfews are common in dormitories, and there is sometimes a limit imposed on the length of stay during the peak summer period.

Academica, Hietaniemenkatu 14 (☎09/1311 4334, fax 441 201). Dormitory accommodation is available in this summer hotel (see "Hotels", p.644) on production of an IYHF or student card. June–Aug only.

Euro, Linnankatu 9 (☎09/622 0470, fax 655 044). Comfortable place in a clean modern building with free morning sauna. It's in the up-and-coming but quiet Katajanokka area, close to the Viking Line arrival point; take tram #4.

Stadionin retkeilymaja, in the Olympic Stadium (☎09/496 071, fax 496 466). A three-kilometre hike from the city centre up Mannerheimintie; the hostel entrance is on the far side of the stadium complex. With its own *Café Pinja*, this is a great venue for a youth hostel, though breakfast (25mk) is not served in very sporting quantities and the place is often crowded. You'll be asked to vacate the premises from noon to 4pm. Trams #3T, #4, #7A and #10 from Mannerheimintie stop outside.

Campsites

Of Helsinki's two **campsites**, only one makes a reasonable base if you're planning to spend time in the city. This is *Rastila* (☎09/316 551, fax 344 1578), 13km to the east in Itäkeskus, on the metro line (Itäkeskus station) and also served by buses #90, #90A, #965 and #98 from Mannerheimintie. It's open all year and there's always plenty of space. The other site is *Oittaa* (☎09/863 2585), about 30km to the west, which is open from June to mid-August; take a train to Espoo and then a bus.

The City

Following a devastating fire in 1808, and the city's elevation to capital in 1812, Helsinki was totally rebuilt in a style commensurate with its status: a grid of wide streets and Neoclassical, Empire-style brick buildings, modelled on the then Russian capital, St Petersburg. This grid forms the basis of the modern city, and it's a tribute to the vision of planner Johan Ehrenström and architect Carl Engel that in and around **Senate Square** the grandeur has endured, often quite dramatically. The square itself, overlooked by the gleaming Lutheran Cathedral, is still the city's single most eye-catching feature; and, just a few blocks away, past the South Harbour and the waterside market, **Esplanadi** remains a handsome tree-lined avenue. Meeting the western end of Esplanadi, the great artery of **Mannerheimintie** – the main route into the centre from the suburbs – carries traffic and trams past Finlandia Hall and the Olympic Stadium on one side, and the National Museum and the streets leading to Sibelius Park and the vast Hietaniemi Cemetery on the other. The bulge of land that extends **south of Esplanadi** has long been one of the most affluent sections of town. Dotted by palatial embassies and wealthy dwellings, it rises into the rocky **Kaivopuisto** park, where the peace is disturbed only by the rumble of the trams and the summer rock concerts.

West of Kaivopuisto are the narrow streets of the exclusive **Eira** quarter, while to the north of the city centre and divided by the waters of Kaisaniemenlahti, the districts of **Kruununhaka** and **Hakaniemi** contain what little is left of pre-seventeenth-century Helsinki – in the small area up the hill behind the cathedral, compressed between the botanical gardens and the bay; over the bridge is a large marketplace and the hill leading past the formidable **Kallion kirkko** towards the modern housing districts further north. Helsinki also has innumerable offshore islands, the biggest of which are **Suomenlinna** and **Seurasaari**. Both of these, despite their location close to the city centre, offer untrammelled nature and a rewarding crop of museums.

Senate Square and Esplanadi

The heart of Helsinki lies in and around **Senate Square**, a compact area of broad bustling streets, grand buildings, famous (to Finns) shops, and, in Esplanadi, the most popular promenading spot in the entire country. Most of the streets leading into Senate Square are fairly narrow and unremarkable, however, a fact that simply serves to increase the impact as the square comes into view and you're struck by the sudden burst of space, by the graceful symmetry of the buildings, and most of all by the exquisite form of the **Tuomiokirkko**, or Lutheran Cathedral (June–Aug Mon–Sat 9am–6pm,

Sun noon–8pm; Sept–May Mon–Fri 10am–4pm, Sat 10am–6pm, Sun noon–6pm), raised on granite steps that support it like a pedestal. Designed, like most of the other buildings on the square, by Engel, its construction was overseen by him until his death in 1840, before being finally completed, with a few variations, in 1852. Among the post-Engel additions are the statues of the twelve apostles that line the roof, which may seem familiar if you've visited Copenhagen: they're copies of Thorvaldsen's sculptures for Vor Frue Kirke. After the Neoclassical extravagances of the exterior, the spartan Lutheran interior comes as a disappointment; better is the gloomily atmospheric **crypt**, which is now used as a café (June–Aug daily 10am–4pm; entrance on Kirkkokatu).

The buildings around the square contribute to the pervading sense of harmony, and although none is open to the public, some are of great historical significance. The **Government Palace** (Valtioneuvosto), known as the Senate House until independence and seating the Senate from 1822, consumes the entire eastern side. It was here that an angry Finnish civil servant, Eugen Schauman, became a national hero by assassinating the much-hated Russian governor-general Bobrikov in 1904. Opposite are the Ionic columns of **Helsinki University** (Helsingin Yliopisto), next door to which is the **University Library** (Yliopiston Kirjasto), considered by many to be Engel's finest single building, although only students and bona-fide researchers are allowed in.

Just north of the square between Kirkkokatu and Rauhankatu is **The House of Scientific Estates** (Säätytalo), the seat of the Diet that governed the country until 1906, when it was abolished in favour of a single-chamber parliament elected by universal suffrage (at the time, Europe's most radical parliamentary reform). In the small park behind the Government Palace is the **House of Nobility** (Ritarihuone), where the upper crust of Helsinki society rubbed shoulders a hundred years ago.

Directly opposite the cathedral at Aleksanterinkatu 18 is Helsinki's oldest stone building, **Sederholm House** (June–Aug daily 11am–5pm; Sept–May Wed–Sun 11am–5pm; 20mk), dating from 1757. It now houses a small museum concentrating on aspects of eighteenth-century life in the city, with particular reference to industrialist Johan Sederholm. There are exhibitions on trade, education and construction, but what makes it perhaps most enjoyable is the eighteenth-century music collection – you can ask to hear a range of classical CDs while you wander around. A more high-tech record of Helsinki life can be found one block south from Sederholm House at the new **City Museum**, Sofiankatu 4 (Mon–Fri 9am–5pm, Sat & Sun 11am–5pm; 20mk), where a permanent exhibition entitled "Time" gives glimpses of Helsinki from its origins as a country village right up to the present day. It's an impressive show, beautifully lit with fibreoptics and halogen lamps, though the chronology jumps around disconcertingly.

The square at the eastern end of Aleksanterinkatu is overlooked by the red-and-green onion-shaped domes of the Russian Orthodox **Uspenski Cathedral** (May–Sept Mon & Wed–Sat 9.30am–4pm, Tues 9.30am–6pm, Sun noon–3pm; Oct–April Tues–Fri 9.30am–4pm, Sat 9.30am–2pm, Sun noon–3pm; tram #4) on Katajanokka, a wedge of land extending out to sea between the North and South harbours and currently the scene of a dockland development programme, converting the area's old warehouses into pricey new restaurants and apartments. In contrast to its Lutheran counterpart, the cathedral is drab outside, but inside has a rich display of icons and other sumptuous adornments.

Esplanadi and around

Walking from the Uspenski Cathedral towards the South Harbour along Aleksanterinkatu takes you past the **President's Palace**, noticeable only for its conspicuous uniformed guard, and the equally bland **City Hall**, used solely for administrative purposes. There's more colour and liveliness among the stalls of the **kauppatori**, or market square (Mon–Thurs 8am–5.30pm, Fri 8am–6pm, Sat 8am–3pm), along the waterfront, laden with fresh fruit and vegetables; you can buy fresh fish directly from the boats moored around the edge of the harbour and, if your principles allow it, the market is also the best place to buy fur – mink and fox hats and coats are cheaper here than in the city's many fur salons. A bit further along, the **kauppahalli** (market hall) with its interior of original carved mahogany and carved pediments (Mon–Fri 8am–5pm, Sat 8am–2pm), is a good place for snacks such as reindeer kebab and Russian caviar.

Across a mishmash of tram lines from here lie the twin thoroughfares of Pohjoisesplanadi and Eteläesplanadi, known collectively as **Esplanadi**. At the height of the Swedish/Finnish language conflict that divided the nation during the mid-nineteenth century, this neat boulevard was where opposing factions demonstrated their allegiance – the Finns walking on the south side and the Swedes on the north. Nowadays it's dominated at lunchtime by office workers, later in the afternoon by buskers, and at night by strolling couples. Musical accompaniment is provided free on summer evenings from the hut in the middle of the walk – expect anything from a Salvation Army band to rock groups. Entertainment of a more costly type lies at the far end of Esplanadi in the dreary off-white horseshoe of the **Swedish Theatre** building – its main entrance is on Mannerheimintie.

Around the Stockmann Department Store

If you think Esplanadi is crowded, wait until you step inside the brick Constructivist **Stockmann Department Store**, at the junction of Mannerheimintie and Aleksanterinkatu. Europe's largest department store, this is the place to buy everything from bubble gum to a Persian rug. Also part of Stockmann's (though it has its own entrance on Aleksanterinkatu), the **Academic Bookstore** allegedly holds more titles than in any other bookstore in Europe, including many English-language paperbacks and a sizeable stock of foreign newspapers and magazines. Directly across Mannerheimintie is the massive Forum shopping mall, which has been cutting into the Stockmann profits in recent years.

Opposite Stockmann's main entrance is a statue by Felix Nylund, the *Three Smiths*, which commemorates the workers of Finland who raised money to erect a building for the country's students. This building is the **Vanha Ylioppistalo** – the old Students' House – its main doors facing the statue. The Finnish Students' Union is based here, owning what is now some of the most expensive square metres of land in Finland and renting them out at considerable profit. In the Vanha, as it's usually known, is the **Vanhan Galleria** (during exhibitions usually 10am–6pm; free), a small gallery with frequent modern art events. It's worth becoming acquainted with the building's layout, as it contains a couple of lively bars which are well worth an evening visit. Taking a few strides further along Mannerheimintie brings you to the Bio cinema; beside it, steps lead down into a little modern courtyard framed by burger joints and pizzerias, off which runs the entrance to **Tunneli**, an underground complex containing shops, the central metro station and a pedestrian subway to one of the city's most striking structures – the train station.

The train station and National Theatre

Erected in 1914, **Helsinki train station** ranks among architect Eliel Saarinen's greatest achievements. In response to criticism of his initial design, Saarinen jettisoned the original National Romantic features and opted for a style more akin to late Art Nouveau. Standing in front of the huge doors (so sturdy they always give the impression of being locked), it's hard to deny the sense of strength and solidity the building exudes. Yet this power is tempered by gentleness, a feeling symbolized by four muscular figures on the facade, each clasping a spherical glass lamp above the heads of passers-by. The interior details can be admired at leisure from either one of the station's two restaurants. Later, Saarinen was to emigrate to America; his son in turn became one of the best-known postwar American architects, whose most famous creation is the TWA terminal building in New York.

Just northeast of the station is the imposing granite form of the **National Theatre**, home of Finnish drama since 1872. Under the country's then governing Swedish-speaking elite, "Finnish culture" was considered simply a contradiction in terms, while later under the tsars it was felt (quite rightly) to pose a nationalist, anti-Russian threat – Finnish theatre during the Russification process became so politically charged that it had to be staged away from the capital in the southwest coastal town of Pori. At the forefront of Finnish drama during its early years was Aleksis Kivi, who died insane and impoverished before being acknowledged as Finland's greatest playwright. He's remembered here by Wäinö Aaltonen's bronze sculpture. Interestingly, nobody knows for sure what Kivi actually looked like, and this imagined likeness, finished in 1939, has come to be regarded as a true one.

Just across from the train station inside the city's main post office is the surprisingly enjoyable **Posti Museo** (Postal Museum; Mon–Fri 10am–7pm, Sat & Sun 11am–4pm; free), a remarkably innovative collection, displaying the unlikely-looking implements connected with more than 350 years of Finnish postal history, along with interactive computer games, multiscreen displays and a special crayoning area for toddlers.

The Art Museum of the Ateneum

Just southeast of the train station is the **Art Museum of the Ateneum** (Tues & Fri 9am–6pm, Wed & Thurs 9am–8pm, Sat & Sun 11am–5pm; 15mk, 45mk for special exhibitions). Chief among the museum's large collection of Finnish paintings is the stirring selection of works from the late nineteenth century, the so-called Golden Age of Finnish painting, when the spirit of nationalism was surging through the country and the movement towards independence gaining strength; indeed, the art of the period was a contributing factor in the growing awareness of Finnish culture, both inside and outside the country. Among the prime names of this era were **Akseli Gallen-Kallela** and **Albert Edelfelt**, particularly the former, who translated onto canvas many of the mythic scenes of the *Kalevala* (all but one of Gallen-Kallela's works, however, the unrepresentative *Kallervo Goes To War*, have been moved to Turku – see p.672). Slightly later came **Juho Rissanen** with his moody and evocative studies of peasant life, and **Hugo Simberg**, responsible for the eerie *Death and the Peasant* and the powerful triptych *Boy Carrying a Garland*. Cast an eye, too, over the works of **Helene Schjerfbeck**, for a long time one of the country's most underrated artists but now enjoying an upsurge in popularity – and collectability. Among the best examples of pure Finnish landscape are the works of **Pekka Halonen**: *Pioneers in Karelia* is typical, with soft curves expressively denoting natural scenes.

This cream of Finnish art is assembled on the first floor, appropriately placed directly off the main landing of the grand staircase that leads up from the entrance. Continue to the second floor and you'll find the provocative expressionism of **Tyko Sallinen** and the November Group, most active around 1917, some token **foreign** masters – a couple of large Munchs, a Van Gogh, a Chagall and a few Cézannes – and several much more recent installations by innovative contemporary Finnish artists. Before you leave, check out the excellent art bookshop on the ground floor.

North along Mannerheimintie

Mannerheimintie is the logical route for exploring north of the city centre. The wide thoroughfare is named after the military commander and statesman C.G.E. Mannerheim, who wielded considerable influence on Finnish affairs in the first half of the twentieth century. He's commemorated by a statue near the busy junction with Arkadiankatu, a structure on which the city's bird population has left its mark.

The Lasipalatsi

Opposite the Postal Museum is the recently renovated **Lasipalatsi**, the old Olympic transit and entertainment building. Reopened in 1998, the functional two-storey building is typical of late 1930s Finnish Art Nouveau design, and now contains some 25 shops, galleries, exhibition sites, cafés and a media centre embodying the Finns' faith in publicly accessible new technology – enough to feed mind and body for a few hours at least. On the glass-fronted lower level check out the **Skenet Café** (Mon–Fri 8.30am–1am, Sat 10am–1am, Sun 11.30am–9pm), with Internet terminals inset into glasstop tables, and the glass-fronted studio of **MTV3**, one of the main Finnish TV companies – it overlooks the street and is often surrounded by hordes of teenagers anxious to catch a glimpse of the stars at work inside. Also on the ground floor is **Bio Rex**, a cinema that specializes in screening independent films that you probably won't find anywhere else in the city. Upstairs, the **Cable Book Library** (Mon–Thurs 10am–midnight, Sat & Sun noon–6pm) has magazines and a couple of dozen more free Internet terminals. For more details, check out the centre's Web site at *www.lasipalatsi.com*.

Museum of Contemporary Art: the Kiasma

Just beyond the Lasipalatsi at Mannerheiminaukio 2 is the new **Museum of Contemporary Art: the Kiasma** (Tues 9am–5pm, Wed–Sun 10am–10pm; 25mk), a slightly forbidding, steel-clad and tube-like structure that looks from the side like a mix of the Sydney Opera House and the Guggenheim in Bilbao – a rather pretentious building for the usually functionalist Finns. Inside the catacomb-like interior are sweeping curves and well-lit hallways. On the ground floor natural light pours in from a variety of angles onto a brilliant-white interior that looks like it gets a new coat of paint on a weekly basis. Entry to this floor is free , and there's a decent café, Internet access, one of the best art bookshops in Finland and an interactive children's play room.

The Kiasma draws its exhibition material from an archive of four thousand pieces of contemporary art, as well as works by visiting artists. Nothing is permanently on display, although as you explore you begin to feel that it's the building itself – with its play on space, light and technology – that is the principal exhibit. Some rooms are blacked out completely; others have high overhanging arches through which the light spills into the display area, giving the place an almost religious feel. Various touchscreen terminals built into the wall at strategic points tell you all need to know about the works on display, and there's also a room in which about ten state-of-the-art computers are set up with numerous CD-ROMs on art and culture; one about the Kiasma itself is projected continuously onto the wall. Exhibitions change every two to three months – check the museum's Web site at *www.kiasma.fi* for details.

The Parliament Building and National Museum

The section of Mannerheimintie north from the Kiasma passes a number of outstanding buildings, the first of which is the **Parliament Building**, on the left (guided tours July & Aug Mon–Fri 2pm, Sat 11am & noon, Sun noon & 1pm; Sept–June Sat & Sun only; when in session, access is to the public galleries only; free). The work of J.S. Sirén, the porridge-coloured building, with its pompous columns and choking air of solemnity, was completed in 1931. Intended to celebrate the new republic, its style was drawn from the revolutionary Neoclassicism that dominated public buildings from Fascist Italy to Nazi Germany, and its authoritarian features can appear wildly out of place in Helsinki, though it's worth a look nonetheless.

North of here things improve with the **National Museum** (Tues & Wed 11am–8pm, Thurs–Sun 11am–6pm), whose design was the result of an early twentieth-century competition won by the three Young Turks of Finnish architecture – Armas Lindgren, Herman Gesellius and Eliel Saarinen. With National Romanticism at its zenith, they steeped their plan in Finnish history, drawing on the country's legacy of medieval churches and granite castles (even though many of these were built under Swedish domination), culminating in a weighty but slender tower that gives the place a cathedral-like profile. The entrance is guarded by Emil Wikström's sculptured bear and the interior ceilings are decorated by Gallen-Kallela with scenes from the *Kalevala*.

The museum may seem the obvious place to discover what Finland is all about but, especially if you've spent hours exploring the copiously stocked national museums of Denmark and Sweden, you might well find the collections disappointing. Being dominated by other nations for many centuries, Finland had little more than the prerequisites of peasant life to call its own up until the mid-1800s (when moves towards Finnish nationalism got off the ground), and the rows of farming and hunting tools alongside endless displays of bowls and spoons from the early times do little to fire the imagination. The most interesting sections of the museum are those relating to the rise of Finnish self-determination and the early years of the republic. Large photographs show the enormous crowds that massed in Helsinki's streets to sing the Finnish anthem in defiance of their (then) Russian rulers, and cabinets packed with small but intriguing objects outline the left–right struggles that marked the early decades of independence and the immediate postwar years – periods when Finland's political future teetered precariously in the balance, a long way from the stability and prosperity enjoyed in more recent times.

Finlandia Hall to the Olympic Stadium

Stylistically a far cry from the National Museum building but equally affecting, **Finlandia Hall** (guided tours when not in use; ring☎09/40 241 or check at the City Tourist Office) stands directly across Mannerheimintie, partially hidden by the roadside foliage. Designed by the country's premier architect, **Alvar Aalto**, a few years before his death in 1976, Finlandia Hall was conceived as part of a grand plan to rearrange the entire centre of Helsinki. Previously, Eliel Saarinen had planned a traffic route from the northern suburbs into a new square in the city centre, to be called Vapaudenkatu (Freedom Street) in celebration of Finnish independence. Aalto plotted a continuation of this scheme, envisaging the removal of the rail-freight yards, which would enable arrivals to be greeted with a fan-like terrace of new buildings reflected in the waters of Töölönlahti. Finlandia was to be the first of these, and only by looking across from the other side of Töölönlahti do you perceive the building's soft sensuality and the potential beauty of the greater concept. Inside the hall, Aalto's characteristic wave pattern (the architect's surname, as it happens, means "wave") and asymmetry are in evidence. From the walls and ceilings through to the lamps and vases, the place has a quiet and graceful air. But the view from the foyer is still of the rail-freight yards, and the great plan for a future Helsinki is still under discussion.

Next door is **Hakasalmi Villa** (Wed–Sun 11am–5pm; 20mk), one of four satellite museums belonging to the new City Art Museum (see p.656). An Italian-style Neoclassical villa built in the 1840s by a councillor and patron of the arts whose collection inspired the founding of the museum, it houses long-term temporary exhibitions, often strikingly designed and worth a peek. Finland's **Opera House** (Mon–Fri 9am–6pm, Sat 3–6pm, Sun open 2hr before performances), a little way beyond Finlandia, is, like so many contemporary Finnish buildings, a Lego-like expanse of white-tiled facade. Its light-flooded interior is enlivened by displays of colourful costumes though, and its grounds and entrance spiked with minimalist black-granite sculptures.

From this point on, the decisive outline of the **Olympic Stadium** becomes visible. Originally intended for the 1940 Olympic Games, the stadium eventually staged the second postwar games, in 1952. From the **Stadium Tower** (Mon–Fri 9am–8pm, Sat & Sun 9am–6pm; 10mk) there's an unsurpassed view over the city and a chunk of the southern coast. If you're a stopwatch-and-spikes freak, ask at the tower's ticket office for directions to the **Sport Museum** (Mon–Fri 11am–5pm, Sat & Sun noon–4pm; 20mk), whose mind-numbing collection of track officials' shoes and swimming caps overshadows a worthy attempt to present sport as an integral part of Finnish culture. The nation's heroes, among them Keke Rosberg and Lasse Virén, are lauded to the skies. Outside, Wäinö Aaltonen's sculpture of Paavo Nurmi captures the champion runner of the 1920s in full stride, and full nudity – something that caused a stir when the sculpture was unveiled in 1952.

West of Mannerheimintie

As there's little of note north of the stadium, it's best to cross Mannerheimintie and follow the streets off it leading to **Sibelius Park** and Eila Hiltunen's monument to the composer made from 24 tons of steel tubes, like a big silver surrealist organ, and, next to it, an irrefutably horrid sculpture of Sibelius's dismembered head. The shady and pleasant park is rudely cut by a main road called Mechelininkatu. Following this back towards the city centre brings you first to the small Islamic and Jewish cemeteries, and then to the expanse of tombs comprising **Hietaniemi Cemetery** (usually open until 10pm). A prowl among these is like a stroll through a "Who was Who" of Finland's last 150 years: Mannerheim, Engel and a host of former presidents are buried here, while just inside the main entrance lies Alvar Aalto, his witty little tombstone consisting partly of a chopped Neoclassical column; behind it is the larger marker of Gallen-Kallela, his initials woven around a painter's palette. It's to the cemetery that local school kids head when skipping off lessons during warm weather, not for a smoke behind the gravestones but to reach the **beaches** that line the bay just beyond its western walls. From these you can enjoy the best sunset in the city.

On the way back towards Mannerheimintie, at Lutherinkatu 3, just off Runeberginkatu, is **Temppeliaukio kirkko** (Mon–Fri 10am–8pm, Sat 10am–6pm, Sun noon–1.45pm & 3.15–5.45pm; closed Tues 1–2pm and during services; tram 3B). Brilliantly conceived by Timo and Tuomo Suomalainen and finished in 1969, the church is built inside a large lump of natural granite in the middle of an otherwise ordinary residential square. Try and see it from above if you can (even if you have to shin up a drainpipe), when the copper dome that pokes through the rock makes the thing look like a ditched flying saucer. The odd combination of man-made and natural materials has made it a fixture on the tourist circuit, but even when crowded it's a thrill to be inside. Classical concerts frequently take place here, the raw rock walls making for excellent acoustics – check the notice board at the entrance for details.

South of Esplanadi: Kaivopuisto and Eira

From the South Harbour it's a straightforward walk past the Silja terminal to Kaivopuisto, but it's more interesting to leave Esplanadi along Kasarmikatu, for some small, offbeat museums. First of these is the **Museum of Finnish Architecture** (Tues–Sun 10am–4pm, Wed until 7pm; 10–20mk) at no. 24, which is aimed at the serious fan: architectural tours of less accessible buildings both in Helsinki and around the country can be arranged here. Combined with an extensive archive, it's a useful resource for a nation with an important architectural heritage.

A block from Kasarmikatu is Korkeavuorenkatu, with the excellent **Museum of Art and Design** at no. 23 (Mon–Fri noon–7pm, Sat & Sun noon–6pm; 50mk), which traces the relationship between art and industry in Finnish history. There are full explanatory texts and period exhibits, from Karelianism – the representations of nature and peasant life from the Karelia region in eastern Finland that dominated Finnish art and design in the years just before and after independence – to the modern movements, along with the postwar shift towards the more familiar, and less interesting, pan-Scandinavian styles.

Kaivopuisto park

Kasarmikatu ends close to the base of a hill, from where footpaths lead up to the Engel-designed **Astronomical Observatory**. Down on the other side and a few streets on is the large and rocky **Kaivopuisto** park. In the 1830s this was developed as a health resort, with a spa house that drew Russian nobility from St Petersburg to sample its waters. The building, another of Engel's works (although greatly modified), can be found in the middle of the park's central avenue, today pulling in the crowds as a restaurant.

Off a smaller avenue, Itäinen Puistotie, runs the circular Kallionlinnantie, which contains the house where Gustaf Mannerheim spent the later years of his life, now maintained as the **Mannerheim Museum** (Fri–Sun 11am–4pm, other times by appointment; 40mk, includes guided tour; ☎09/635 443). A Finnish-born, Russian-trained military commander, Mannerheim was pro-Finnish but had a middle-class suspicion of the working classes: he led the right-wing Whites during the Civil War of 1918 and two decades later the Finnish campaigns in the Winter and Continuation wars (for more on which, see the "Military Museum", opposite). His influence in the political sphere was also considerable, and included a brief spell as president. While acknowledging his importance, the regard that Finns have for him these days, naturally enough, depends on their own political viewpoint.

Ideology aside, the house is intriguing. The interior is left much as it was when the man died in 1951, and the clutter is astounding. During his travels Mannerheim raided flea markets at every opportunity, collecting a remarkable array of plunder – assorted furniture and antiques, ornaments and books from all over the globe. Upstairs is the camp-bed which Mannerheim found too comfortable ever to change, and in the wall is the vent inserted to keep the bedroom as airy as a field-tent.

If he had lived a few decades earlier, one of Mannerheim's Kallionlinnantie neighbours would have been Frederik Cygnaeus, art patron and Professor of Aesthetics at Helsinki University. In 1860 Cygnaeus built a summer house at no. 8, a lovely yellow-turreted affair, and filled it with an outstanding collection of art. Later he donated the lot to the nation and today it's displayed as the **Cygnaeus Gallery** (Wed 11am–7pm, Thurs–Sun 11am–4pm; 15mk). Everything is beautifully laid out in the tiny rooms of the house, with whole walls of work by the most influential of his contemporaries. The von Wright brothers (Ferdinand, Magnus and Wilhelm) are responsible for the most touching pieces – the bird and nature studies. Look out, too, for a strange portrait of Cygnaeus by Ekman, showing the man sprouting sinister wings from under his chin.

The edge of Kaivopuisto looks out across a sprinkling of little islands and the Suomenlinna fortress. You can follow one of the pathways down into **Merikatu**, along which lie several of the Art Nouveau villas lived in by the big cheeses of Finnish industry during the early part of the twentieth century. Easily the most extreme is no. 25, the Enso-Gutzeit villa, now portioned off into offices and with a lingering air of decay hanging over its decorative facade.

Eira

Inland from Merikatu, the curving alleys and tall elegant buildings of the **Eira** district are landmarked by the needle-like spire rising from the roof of **Mikael Agricola kirkko**, named after the translator of the first Finnish Bible but making no demands on your time. A few blocks northeast, the twin-towered Johanessen kirkko is again not worth a call in itself but functions as a handy navigation aid. Following Yrjönkatu northwards from here takes you past the partly pedestrianized Iso Roobertinkatu, before reaching Bulevardi and the square containing **Vanha kirkko**, or Old Church. A humble wooden structure, and another example of Engel's work, this was the first Lutheran church to be erected after Helsinki became the Finnish capital, predating that in Senate Square by some years but occupying a far less glamorous plot – a plague victim's burial ground dating from 1710.

Heading left along Bulevardi for a couple of hundred metres brings you to the Sinebrychoff brewery which, besides bestowing a distinctive aroma of hops to the locality, also finances the **Sinebrychoff Art Museum** at no. 40 (Mon, Thurs & Fri 9am–6pm, Wed 9am–8pm, Sat & Sun 11am–5pm; 10mk, 35mk for special exhibitions). This rather precious museum houses mostly seventeenth-century Flemish and Dutch paintings, along with some excellent miniatures, delicately illustrated porcelain and refined period furniture. Continuing east along Bulevardi to the waterfront brings you to the wide **Hietalahdentori**, a concrete square that perks up with a daily morning flea market and, in summer, an evening market between 3.30pm and 8pm.

Kruununhaka and Hakaniemi

North of Senate Square is the little district of **Kruununhaka**. Away from the city hubbub, its closely built blocks shield the narrow streets from the sunlight, evoking a forlorn and forgotten mood. At Kristianinkatu 12, the single-storey wooden **Burgher's House** (Wed–Sun 11am–5pm; 20mk) stands in vivid contrast to the tall granite dwellings around it – and gives an indication of how Helsinki looked when wood was still the predominant building material. The interior has been kitted out with mid-nineteenth-century furnishings, the period when a city burgher did indeed reside here.

Kristianinkatu meets at right-angles with Maurinkatu, a short way along which is the **Military Museum** (Mon–Fri & Sun 11am–4pm; 20mk), a rather formless selection of weapons, medals and glorifications of armed-forces life, but with some excellent documentary photos of the Winter and Continuation wars of 1939–44. Finland was drawn into World War II through necessity rather than choice. When Soviet troops invaded eastern Finnish territories in November 1939, under the guise of protecting Leningrad, they were repelled by technically inferior but far more committed Finns. The legends of the "heroes in white" were born then, alluding to the Finnish soldiers and the camouflage used in the winter snows. Soon after, however, faced with possible starvation and a fresh Soviet advance, Finland joined the war on the Nazi side, mainly in order to continue resisting the threat from the east. For this reason, it's rare to find World War II spoken of as such in Finland: much more commonly it's divided into these separate conflicts.

Hakaniemi

The western edge of Kruununhaka is defined by the busy Unioninkatu (if it's a sunny day, take a stroll around the neat **botanical gardens**, just off Unioninkatu), which continues northwards across a slender body of water into **Hakaniemi**, a district chiefly visited for its **kauppahalli** (Mon–Fri 8am–5pm, Sat 8am–2pm).

Although the square of Hakaniementori is surrounded by drab storefronts and office blocks, the indoor market is about the liveliest in the city – mainly due to its position near a major junction for city buses and trams, as well as a metro station. From the square you can see right up the hill to the impressive Art Deco brickwork of the **Kallion kirkko**, beyond which is the busy Sturenkatu and the open green area partly consumed by **Linnanmäki amusement park**. After crossing Sturenkatu, on the way to the **Museum of Workers' Housing** at Kirstinkuja 4 (May–Sept Wed–Sun 11am–5pm; 20mk), for some fascinating social history. The series of wooden buildings that now hold the museum were built during the early 1900s to provide housing for the impoverished country folk who moved to the growing, increasingly industrialized city to work as street cleaners and refuse collectors. Six of the one-room homes where the new arrivals settled have been re-created with period furnishings, and a biography on the door describes each flat's occupants – woeful tales of overcrowding, overwork, and sons who left for America and never returned.

Suomenlinna

Built by the Swedes in 1748 to protect Helsinki from seaborne attack, the fortress of **Suomenlinna** stands on five interconnected islands, reached by half-hourly ferry from the South Harbour, which make a rewarding break from the city centre – even if you only want to laze around on the dunes. (These were created by the Russians with sand shipped in from Estonia to strengthen the new capital's defences after they'd wrested control of Finland.) For information, head to the **Inventory Chambers Visitors Centre** (April & Oct Mon–Fri 11am–4pm, Sat & Sun 11am–5pm; May–Aug daily 10am–6pm; Sept Mon–Fri 11am–4pm, Sat & Sun 10am–5pm; Nov–March daily 11am–4pm), housed in a former naval stores. Here you'll also find the **Suomenlinna Museum and Experience** (April & Oct Sat & Sun 11am–5pm; May–Aug daily 10am–6pm; Sept daily 10am–5pm; 30mk), which charts the history of the fortress. If you're feeling inquisitive, there are hour-long summer **guided walking tours** (June–Aug daily 10.30am, 1pm & 3pm in English; 25mk), beginning close to the ferry-landing stage. Suomenlinna has a few museums, none particularly riveting, although the **Nordic Arts Centre** (Tues–Sun 11am–5.45pm; closed Aug; free), with its small displays of contemporary arts from the Nordic countries, is worth a browse. Of the others, the **Ehrensvärd Museum** (May–Aug daily 10am–5pm; Sept Mon–Fri 10am–5pm, Sat & Sun 10am–4.30pm; Oct–April Sat & Sun 11am–4.30pm; 15mk) occupies the residence used by the first commander of the fortress, Augustin Ehrensvärd. He oversaw the building of Suomenlinna and now lies in the elaborate tomb in the grounds; his personal effects remain inside the house alongside displays on the fort's construction. The **Armfelt Museum** (June–Aug daily 11am–5pm; 10mk) contains the eighteenth- and nineteenth-century family heirlooms of the Armfelt clan, who lived in the Joensuu Manor at Halikko. Finally, the **Coastal Artillery Museum** (Aprilto mid-May & Oct Sat & Sun 11am–3pm; mid-May to Aug daily 10am–4.45pm; Sept daily 11am–3pm; 10mk) records Suomenlinna's defensive actions and – for an extra 20mk – visitors can clamber around the darkly claustrophobic World War II submarine *Vesikko*.

Seurasaari and around

A fifteen-minute tram (#4) or bus (#24) ride from the city centre (get off one stop after the big hospital on the left, from where it's a one-kilometre walk) lies **Seurasaari**, a small wooded island delightfully set in a sheltered bay. The three contrasting museums on or close by the island make for a well-spent day. Access to the island proper is by a bridge at the southern end of Tamminiementie, conveniently close to the **Helsinki City Art Museum** (Wed–Sun 11am–6.30pm; 15–45mk). Though one of the best collections of modern Finnish art, with some eerily striking work, the museum is hardly a triumph of layout, with great clumps of stuff of differing styles scattered about the walls. But the good pieces shine through. Be warned, though, that during temporary exhibitions the permanent stock is locked away.

A few minutes' walk from the art museum, towards the Seurasaari bridge, is the long driveway leading to the **Urho Kekkonen Museum** (mid-May to mid-Aug daily 11am–5pm; mid-Aug to mid-May Tues–Sun 11am–5pm; 20mk, includes guided tour), the villa where the esteemed president lived until his death in 1986. Whether they love him or loathe him, few Finns would deny the vital role Kekkonen played in Finnish history, most significantly by continuing the work of his predecessor, Paasikivi, in the establishment of Finnish neutrality. He accomplished this largely through delicate negotiations with Soviet leaders – whose favour he would gain, so legend has it, by taking them to a sauna – narrowly averting major crises and seeing off the threat of a Soviet invasion on two separate occasions. Kekkonen often conducted official business here rather than at the Presidential Palace in the city. Yet the feel of the place is far from institutional, with a light and very Finnish character, filled with birchwood furniture, its large windows giving peaceful views of surrounding trees, water and wildlife.

Close by, in another calm setting across the bridge on Seurasaari itself, is the **Open-Air Museum** (second half of May Mon–Fri 9am–3pm, Sat & Sun 11am–5pm; June–Aug daily 11am–5pm; first half of Sept Mon–Fri 9am–3pm, Sat & Sun 11am–5pm; mid-Sept to mid-Nov Sat & Sun 11am–5pm; 20mk), a collection of vernacular buildings assembled from all over Finland, connected by the various pathways that extend around the island. There are better examples of traditional Finnish life elsewhere in the country, but if you're only visiting Helsinki this will give a good insight into how the country folk lived until surprisingly recently. The old-style church is a popular spot for city couples' weddings.

Aside from the museums and the scenery, people also come to Seurasaari to strip off. Sex-segregated **nudist beaches** (10mk) line part of the western edge – also a popular offshore stop for the city's weekend yachtsmen, armed with binoculars.

Outlying museums

Helsinki has a few other **museums** outside the centre that don't fit into any walking tour. All are within fairly easy reach with public transport, and sometimes a little legwork.

Gallen-Kallela Museum

The **Gallen-Kallela Museum**, Gallen-Kallelantie 27, Tarvaspää peninsula (mid-May to Aug Mon–Thurs 10am–8pm, Fri–Sun 10am–5pm; Sept to mid-May Tues–Sat 10am–4pm, Sun 10am–5pm; 35mk), is housed inside the Art Nouveau studio of the influential painter Akseli Gallen-Kallela, who lived and worked here from 1913. Sadly, it's a bit of an anticlimax, lacking either atmosphere or a decent display of the artist's work. There are a few old paints and brushes under dirty glass coverings in the studio, while in an upstairs room are the pickled remains of reptiles and frog-like animals collected by Gallen-Kallela's family. Inscribed into the floor is a declaration by Gallen-Kallela: "I Shall Return". Unless you're a huge fan, it's probably not worth the bother. To get there, take tram #4 from the city centre to the end of its route (on Saunalahdentie), then walk 2km along Munkkiniemi on the bay's edge to a footbridge which leads over the water and towards the poorly signposted museum. Alternatively, bus #33 runs from the tram stop to the footbridge about every twenty minutes.

The Cable Factory museums (Kaapelitehdas)

The former cable factory to the west of the city centre at Tallberginkatu 1F is now home to a clutch of museums, accessible on tram #8 (all open Tues–Fri noon–6pm, Wed until 8pm, Sat & Sun noon–5pm; 20mk combined ticket). The **Hotel and Restaurant Museum** is specifically designed for aficionados of the catering trade, although the photos on the walls of its two rooms reveal a fascinating social history of Helsinki, showing hotel and restaurant life from both sides of the table, alongside a staggering selection of matchboxes, beer mats emblazoned with the emblems of their establishments, and menus signed by the rich and infamous.

Despite its grand title, the **Photographic Museum of Finland** comprises a shabby herd of old cameras that suggest Finnish photography never really progressed beyond the watch-the-birdie stage. Amends are made by the innovative temporary collections of photos that regularly adorn the walls. The third museum in the complex is the city's **Theatre Museum**, displaying a permanent collection of costumes, stage sets and lights. Frequent temporary exhibitions focus on different aspects behind the scenes in Finnish theatre.

Eating and drinking

Eating in Helsinki, as in the rest of the country, isn't cheap, but there is plenty of choice and, with careful planning, plenty of ways to stretch out funds. Other than all-you-can-eat **breakfast** tables in hotels (hostel breakfasts in the city tend to be rationed), it's best to hold out until **lunch**, when many restaurants offer a reduced fixed-price menu or a help-yourself table, and in almost every pizzeria you'll get a pizza, coffee, and all you can manage from the bread and salad bar for under 40mk. **Picnic food**, too, is a viable option. Use the markets and market halls at the South Harbour or Hakaniementori for fresh vegetables, meat and fish. Several supermarkets in Tunneli, by the train station, stay open until 10pm. The popular **Forum** shopping centre, a somewhat downtrodden version of the Stockmann (which it's directly opposite), has a number of popular, inexpensive eateries on two floors, while the **precinct** opposite the train station contains a range of mid-standard, filling eateries open till late.

Throughout the day, up until 5pm or 6pm, you can also get a coffee and pastry, or a fuller snack, for 10–25mk at one of the numerous **cafés**. The best cafés are stylish, atmospheric affairs dating from the beginning of the twentieth century. Alternatives include myriad multinational hamburger joints and the slightly more unusual *grilli* roadside stands, which sell hot dogs and the like; if you're tempted, experts claim the *Jaskan Grilli*, in Töölönkatu behind the National Museum, to be the best of its kind. If you're hungry and impoverished (and are, in theory at least, a student), you can get a full meal for 12–15mk from one of the **student mensas**, two of which are centrally located in the main university buildings at Aleksanterinkatu 5, and at Hallituskatu 11–13. One or the other will be open during the summer; both are open during term time. The mensas can be cheaper still in the late afternoon, from 4pm to 6pm, and are also usually open on Saturdays from 9am to 1pm. As for **evening eating**, there are plenty of restaurants serving reasonably priced ethnic foods, as well as a number of Finnish *haute cuisine* places.

Cafés

Aalto, in the Academic Bookstore, Pohjoisesplanadi 39. Designed by the world-famous Finnish architect whose name it bears, and well worth a visit after a morning's book-browsing.

Avec, Stockmann Department Store. Cakes, stylish sandwiches and drinks in pleasant surroundings.

Caramelle, by Hakasalmi Villa, Karamzininkatu 2. A small, intimate café serving gorgeous gooey cakes.

Ekberg, Bulevardi 9. Nineteenth-century fixtures and a deliberately *fin de siècle* atmosphere, with starched waitresses bringing the most delicate of open sandwiches and pastries to green-marble tables.

Eliel, on the ground floor of the train station. An airy, vaulted Art Nouveau interior with a good-value self-service breakfast (Mon–Sat 7–10am, Sun 8–10am) – and a roulette table.

Engel, Aleksanterinkatu 26. Named after the Berlin-born designer of all the buildings you can see from its window, this is a haven of fine coffee, pastries, cakes and intellectual chit-chat, just across from Senate Square. Try the smoked-fish salad.

Esplanad, Pohjoisesplanadi 37. The best place for cheaper food. Filled baguettes, a choice of fresh soups daily and always a queue.

Fazer, Kluuvikatu 3. Helsinki's best-known bakery, justly celebrated for its lighter-than-air pastries; there's another branch in the Forum Shopping Centre, opposite Stockmann. At either, try the speciality "Bebe", a praline cream-filled pastry for 8mk.

Kappeli, Esplanadi Park, Esplanadi. An elegant glasshouse with massive wrought-iron decorated windows overlooking Esplanadi and the harbour, with lots of live entertainment outside and in during the summer. The cellar is also a great spot for an evening drink – see *Kappelin Olutkellari,* p.661. Open daily until 4am.

Mini Succes, Korkeavuorenkatu 2. Freshly baked bread, doughnuts and pastries every day.

Socis, Kaivokatu 12. Big, cosmopolitan and very beautiful – though also very expensive. Open till midnight (Sun until 10pm).

Strindberg, Pohjoisesplandi 33. Stylish outdoor coffee sipping – though it's expensive if you want to eat, with a menu listing such items as smoked reindeer with Lapland cheese followed by glow-fried grayling and arctic cloudberry. Open till midnight.

Tamminiementie, Tamminiementie 8. A good stopoff when visiting the nearby City Art Museum or Seurasaari Island, for high-quality tea or coffee served in elegant surroundings, with Chopin playing in the background.

Tomtebon Kahvila, opposite the Kekkonen Museum at Seurasaari. Coffee served with home-made cookies and cakes in a lovely old wooden villa set in a lush garden.

Ursula (1), Ehrenströmintie 3. On the beach at the edge of the Kaivopuisto park, with a wonderful sea view from the outdoor terrace.

Ursula (2), Pohjoisesplanadi 21. Elegant place for good cakes and tarts. There's courtyard eating at the back, near the entrance to a beautiful interior design shop. Daily 9am–10pm.

Victor, 32 Bulevardi. Enticing selection of reasonably priced lunch dishes that attract a regular local clientele; large windows for watching the world go by.

Restaurants

Foreign restaurants are reasonably plentiful in Helsinki, and in a typical **pizzeria** you can expect to pay 60–70mk per person for dinner, provided you don't drink anything stronger than mineral water. There are also a few **vegetarian** restaurants, which charge about the same. **Finnish** restaurants, on the other hand, and those serving **Russian** specialities, can be terrifyingly expensive; expect to spend around 150mk each for a night of upmarket overindulgence. Restaurants are usually open daily until around 1am, though the kitchens close at about 11pm. It's best to check first if you want to eat late, especially at the more expensive places, which tend to close a little earlier.

Finnish and Russian

Alexander Nevski, Pohjoisesplanadi 17. A very fine, classic Russian restaurant with live music. Closed Sun lunchtime.

Bellevue, Rahapajankatu 3, behind the Uspenski Cathedral. A superb Russian restaurant opened, ironically, in 1917, the year Finland won independence from Russia. Expensive but gourmet Russian food. Try Marshal Mannerheim's favourite of minced lamb flavoured with herring. Closed Sat & Sun lunchtime.

Havis Amanda, Unioninkatu 23. An excellent fish restaurant, albeit pricey and somewhat staid.

Holvari, Yrjönkatu 15. Specializes in mushrooms, personally picked by the owner and providing the basis of tasty soups and stews.

Hullu Kukko, Simonkatu 8. Nothing special to look at, but great fish soup, excellent pizzas and one of the best wine lists in town.

Iso-Ankkuri, Pursimiehenkatu 16. Fairly downbeat, and favoured mostly by locals for its filling, unextravagant menu.

Kannu, Punavuorenkatu 12. Much of the original interior, designed by Alvar Aalto, remains in this locals' haunt, where the staff dish up stodgy, down-to-earth Finnish food.

Kasakka, Meritullinkatu 13. Over-the-top spirit-of-the-tsars atmosphere and great food in this old-style Russian restaurant.

Katajanokan Kasino, Laivastokatu 1. Just east of the Uspenski Cathedral, this gourmet and theme restaurant offers you the chance to feast on à la carte elk or reindeer in anything from a mock wartime bunker to the "Cabinet Room", decorated with markers to Finnish independence. A great place if someone else is paying.

Kuu, Töölönkatu 27. Between the Opera House and Sibelius Park, this is an unpretentious place to consume equally unpretentious and inexpensive Finnish food.

Kynsilaukka Ravintola Garlic, Fredrikinkatu 22. Pricey, but the ultimate if you like garlic, as its name suggests.

Ravintola Lappi, Annankatu 22. A fine, though not cheap Finnish restaurant specializing in real Finnish foods like pea soup and oven pancakes, as well as Lapish specialities of smoked reindeer and warm cloudberries.

Ravintola Perhon, Mechelininkatu 7 (near corner of Hietaniemenkatu). The restaurant of the Finnish Culinary College and an excellent choice for lunch, which is normally a three-course buffet for around 40mk. Prices are much lower than normal and service impeccable.

Sea Horse, Kapteeninkatu 11. Serves a range of fairly inexpensive Finnish dishes, and is renowned for its Baltic sprats.

Sipuli, Kanavaranta 3. A tastebud-thrilling, formal and glamorous – though financially ruinous – choice of gourmet dishes, several based on traditional Sami fare. A few metres west of the Uspenski Cathedral.

Terrace Bar, Stockmann Department Store, sixth floor. Situated on the top floor and with bright, relaxed Lloyd loom-style seating. A small salad and soup costs 42mk, or go for dishes from the grill (11am–7pm) such as potato and anchovy bake (42mk) or grilled chicken (47mk).

Ethnic and vegetarian

Ani, Telakkakatu 2. Turkish food at its best from the 40mk open table laid out at lunchtime.

Aurinkotuuli, Lapinlahdenkatu 25a. A good range of vegetarian dishes at prices to suit all but the tightest of budgets.

Kasvis, Korkeavuorenkatu 3. Literally a "vegetable restaurant", and one of the oldest and best (though not the cheapest) in the country. Good vegetarian shop attached.

Mai Thai, Annankatu 32. The least expensive and quite possibly the best of the city's crop of Thai restaurants.

Namaskar, Mannerheimintie 100. Currently the most expensive Asian restaurant in the city, and the pick of a slowly growing band of Indian restaurants struggling to make an impression on Helsinki eating habits.

Wienerwald, Kaivokatu, opposite the train station. A sort of Austrian-style *Pizza Hut* with good-value Austrian fish and meat dishes and wide range of Austrian sausages. Try half a roasted chicken and potato salad for 37mk.

Zucchini, Fabianinkatu 4. A friendly and stylish vegetarian restaurant.

American

Cantina West, Kasarmikatu 23. Fiery Tex-Mex food in a lively, western-themed restaurant spread over several floors. Gets loud late at night.

Chico's, Mannerheimintie 68. Very friendly, inexpensive all-American eatery with pizzas and burgers starting at around 50mk, alongside specialities from the Deep South and Mexico.

La Havanna, Uudenmenkatu 9–11. Pioneering Cuban eaterie doing great things with seafood, but make sure you come at lunchtime – at night it's packed with boozers.

Planet Hollywood, Mikonkatu 9. Much-hyped American diner crammed with movie memorabilia.

Italian and pizzas

Mama Rosa, Runeberginkatu 55. A classic pizzeria also serving fish, steaks and pasta. One of the best mid-priced restaurants in the city – not surprisingly it's generally full.

Pasta Factory, Mastokatu 6. Intimate, discreetly stylish and quite affordable Italian place.

Pizza No.1, Mannerheimintie 18, second floor of the Forum shopping centre. Standard pizzas, but good deals at lunchtime and an entertaining selection of English cricket memorabilia on the walls.

Drinking

Although never cheap, alcohol is not a dirty word in Finland, and **drinking**, especially beer, can be enjoyed in the city's many café-like pubs, which are where most Helsinki folk go to socialize. You'll find one on virtually every corner, but the pick of the bunch are listed below. Only the really swanky places have a dress code, and they are usually too elitist – and expensive – to be worth bothering with anyway. Sundays to Thursdays are normally quiet; on Fridays and Saturdays on the other hand, it's best to arrive as early as possible to get a seat without having to queue. Most drinking dives also serve food, although the grub is seldom at its best in the evening (where it's good earlier in the day, we've included it under "Restaurants"). If you want a drink but are feeling anti-social, or just very hard-up, the cheapest method, as ever, is to buy from the appropriately named ALKO shop: there are self-service ones at Fabiankatu 7 and Vuorikatu 7.

Pubs and bars

Angleterre, Fredrikinkatu 47. Utterly Finnish despite the flock wallpaper and Dickensian fixtures – good for a laugh and cultural disorientation.

Aseman Yläravintola, second floor of the train station. Socially much more interesting than the *Eliel* downstairs (see "Cafés", p.658), this is a lively and diverse place for a drink, surrounded by architect Saarinen's fabulous features. Don't risk it if you've a train to catch.

Ateljeebaari, *Hotel Torni*, Yrjönkatu 26. On the thirteenth floor of a plush hotel: great views, great posing – but be warned that the women's toilet has bizarre ceiling-to-floor windows. Drinks are pricey.

Bulevardia, Bulevardi 34. Many customers are technicians or singers from the neighbouring Opera House who swoop in after a concert. Join them for the Art Deco decor – matt-black furniture designed by 1930s architect Pauli Blomstedt, and burr-birch walls.

Corona, Eerikinkatu 11, Famous pool hall-cum-bar, very popular with Helsinki's alternative set. It's owned by the Kaurismaki brothers, creator of the Leningrad Cowboys.

Elite, Etläinen Hesperiankatu 22. Northwest of the National Museum, this was once the haunt of the city's artists, many of whom would settle the bill not with money but with paintings – a selection of which lines the walls. Especially good in summer, when you can drink on the terrace.

Happy Days, Pohjoisesplanadi 2. Spend a few hours in this sometimes rowdy summer-only bar and you'll encounter a cross-section of Helsinki characters – some coming, some going, others falling over.

Juttutupa, Säästöpankinranta 6. Once the HQ of the Social Democrats, who built it with a tower to allow their red flag to fly above the neighbouring church spires. The decision to take up arms, which culminated in the 1918 civil war, was made here, and photos commemorate the fact. Apolitical entertainment is provided on Wed, Fri and Sat by an accordian and/or violin player, encouraging enjoyable singalongs.

Kaarle XII, Kasarmikatu 40. Fine Art Nouveau features hewn into the red-granite walls make this the most traditional-looking of the city's bars; not that the customers allow the surroundings to inhibit their merrymaking.

Kappelin Olutkellari, Esplanadi Park, Esplanadi. The entrance is to the side of this distinctive multipurpose building of glass and fancy ironwork (see also *Kappeli*, p.658). A garrulous and gloriously eclectic clientele.

Kosmos, Kalevankatu 3. This is where the big media cats – TV producers, PR people, the glitzier authors – hang out and engage in loud arguments as the night wears on. The wonderful interior is unchanged since the 1920s, but you'll only see it if you get past the officious doorman.

Kultainen Härkä, Uudenmaankatu 16–20. Load your plate from the inexpensive salad bar by day; drink, and heckle the singer tinkling the piano, by night.

La Havanna, Uudenmaankatu 9–11. A Cuban restaurant, though there's much more boozing than dining in the evenings, and not much space to move as Latin American music fills the smoky air. A must.

Ma Baker's, Mannerheimintie 12. A good place to initiate yourself into drinking Helsinki-style; open until 3am, it has a reputation as a last-chance pick-up spot.

Meri Makasiini, Hietalahdenranta 4. Slightly out-of-the-way, on a street running off Hietalahdentori towards the waterfront, but worth sampling on a Fri or Sat night when the customers spill onto the terrace to drink and gaze at the cranes of the city's cargo harbour.

Moskova, Eerikinkatu 11. An anonymous looking entrance gives way to the Kaurismaki brothers' quirky Soviet-themed bar.

Mulligans, Mannerheimintie 10. Live Irish music every night at this likeable pub.

No Name, Töölönkatu 2. Looks like an American cocktail bar and pulls an intriguing cross-section of Finns on the razzle.

Salve, Hietalahdenranta 11. Filled with nautical paraphernalia but no longer the seedy sailors' haunt that it was. Worth a call, to eat or drink, although the recently hiked-up prices suggest the place has ideas above its station. On same street as *Meri Makasiini* (see above).

St Urho's Pub, Museokatu 10. Close to the National Museum, this is one of the most popular student pubs – which accounts for the lengthy queue that forms from about 9pm on Fri and Sat.

Vanhan Kahvila, Mannerheimintie 3. A self-service and hence comparatively cheap bar. It fills quickly, so try to arrive early for a seat on the balcony overlooking the bustle of the streets below.

Vanhan Kellari, Mannerheimintie 3. Downstairs from the *Vanhan Kahvila*, its underground setting and bench-style seating help promote a cosy and smoky atmosphere. Rumour has it that this is where the Helsinki Beat poets of the early 1960s drank, and where they now bring their children.

Vastarannan Kiiski, Salomonkatu 15. A crowded pub with a wide selection of beers both on tap and bottled.

William K, Mannerheimintie 72. A cosy, locals' pub with old Indian carpets for tablecloths and every beer you could want, though the imported ones are expensive.

Zetor, Kaivopiha, near the train station. A loud, country-themed bar designed by the people who run the Leningrad Cowboys rock group.

Nightlife and entertainment

Helsinki probably has a greater number of ways to spend the evening than any other Scandinavian city; there is, for example, a steady diet of **live music**. Finnish rock bands, not helped by the awkward metre of their native language, often sound absurd on first hearing, but at least seeing them is relatively cheap at 20–35mk – around half the price of seeing a British or American band – and sometimes even free. The best gigs tend to be during term-time, but in summer there are dozens of free events in the city parks, the biggest of which take place almost every Sunday in Kaivopuisto. Many bands also play on selected nights in one of the growing number of surprisingly hip **clubs and discos**, in which you can gyrate, pose or just drink into the small hours – admission is usually 20–30mk.

For up-to-the-minute details of **what's on**, read the entertainment page of *Helsingin Sanomat* or the free fortnightly paper *City* (found in record shops, bookshops and department stores), which has listings in English covering rock and classical music, clubs, cinema, theatre and opera. The Lasipalatsi (see p.651) has a youth service centre with information on festivals, concerts and events, or else simply watch out for posters on the streets. **Tickets** for most events can be bought at the venue or, for a small commission, at a couple of agencies: City, at the central City Tourist Office (see p.641) (☎0600/10 495 or 10 020; although note that these are premium-rate lines), and Tiketti, Yrjönkatu 29c (Mon–Fri 9am–5pm; ☎0600/11 616; also premium rate).

Clubs and music venues

Clubs in Helsinki change ownership, style and format with baffling rapidity and the listings below are only a pointer to what may be on offer. For up-to-the-moment information, check out the city's listings magazines.

Bar 52, Fabiankatu 29. Live 1950s music in a cool, laid-back atmosphere.

Botta, Museokatu 10. Joined to *St Urho's Pub* (see "Drinking", above). Vibrant dance music of various hues most nights.

Helmi, Eerikinkatu 14. The only non-gay venue on this street – very crowded and loud, with a good bar selection.

Kaivo, Kaivopuisto Park. One of the city's longest established late-night party spots; come here to dance, drink and join the very long taxi queues for home.

KY-Exit, Pohjoinen Rautatiekatu 21. Sometimes has visiting foreign bands, more often lively disco nights for clubbers in their early twenties.

Manala, Dagmarinkatu 2. Two floors and long queues for anything from ballroom dancing to grinding to MTV's latest offerings.

Nylon, Kaivokatu 12. Slightly pretentious but hip small club run by the city's Live Music Association. Popular very late at night.

Olutkellari, *Merihotelli*, John Stenberginranta 6. Acoustic blues on Mon & Tues.

Orfeus, Eerikinkatu 3. Free live jazz and blues on Thurs, Fri & Sat.

Soda, Uudenmaankatu 16–20. One of the hippest places in town – at least for the time being. All varieties of dance music downstairs; standard bar with guest DJs upstairs.

Storyville, Museokatu 8. Buzzing jazz joint, with live dixieland, swing or bebop on stage every night. Open till the small hours.

Tavastia, Urho Kekkosenkatu 4–6. A major showcase for Finnish and Swedish bands. Downstairs has the stage and self-service bar; the balcony is wait-ess service.

Vanha Maestro, Fredrikinkatu 51–53. Legendary venue among the country's enthusiasts of *humpa* – a truly Finnish dance, distantly related to the waltz and tango. Afternoon and evening sessions most days (entry 10–30mk).

Vanha Ylioppilastalo, Mannerheimintie 3. The main venue for leading indie bands from around the world; see also the *Vanhan* bars under "Drinking" opposite.

Gay Helsinki

The **gay scene** in Helsinki, though it's still small, has really blossomed during the past few years, gaining a much higher profile and wider acceptance, at least among the city's younger and more cosmopolitan population. Most of the gay **cafés/bars** are within a couple of minutes' walk of each other around **Eerikinkatu**, the most hip being *H2O* at no. 14, a dark and stylish Continental-style café-bar. On the other side of the road, *Stonewall* (Tues–Thurs & Sun 5pm–2am, Fri 5pm–3am, Sat 2pm–3am) is a more traditional basement bar serving good food in a slightly less welcoming atmosphere – go before 9pm for happy hour, when beers are 15mk. A street away is the popular nightclub *DTM*, at Annankatu 32, and next door to that is *Café Escale*, a gay boozer's hangout with little charm. Newest on the scene is *Lost & Found*, Annankatu 6 (Mon–Fri 2pm–4am, Sat & Sun 1pm–4am), a very stylish gay drinking and eating place with a sweeping bar – try the fine salmon and herb soup (36mk). Back on Eerinkatu is Finland's one and only gay **bookstore**, the well-stocked Baffin Books (Mon–Fri noon–7pm, Sat 10am–3pm). For information and advice, contact the national gay and lesbian organization **SETA**, Oikokatu 3 (✆09/135 8303), during office hours.

Cinema

Both the latest blockbusters and a good selection of fringe **films** are normally showing somewhere in Helsinki. A seat is usually 30–45mk, although some places offer a 25mk matinee show on Mondays; this isn't loudly advertised but discreetly indicated by handwritten notices outside the venue. Check the listings in *City* or pick up a copy of *Elokuva-Viikko*, a free weekly leaflet that lists the cinemas and their programmes. English-language films are shown with Finnish subtitles – there's no overdubbing. If you're at a loose end, the three-screened *Nordia*, Yrjönkatu 36 (✆09/1311 9250), commonly has an excellent programme of new art-house films and cult classics – at cheap prices.

Listings

Airlines British Airways, Aleksanterinkatu 21a (✆09/650 677); Finnair, Töölönkatu 21 (✆09/818 800); SAS, Keskuskatu 7a (✆09/228 021).

Airport Enquiries ✆9600 1800; Finnair terminal for airport buses (✆09/818 7793).

American Express Mikonkatu 2 (Mon–Fri 9am–4pm; ✆09/628 728).

Banks and exchange Outside banking hours at the airport 6.30am–11pm, and slightly more cheaply at Katajanokka harbour (where Viking and Finnjet dock) daily 9–11.30am & 3.45–6pm. Also Forex in the central train station (daily 8am–9pm), though it doesn't accept Visa; and Postipankki, opposite the station (Mon–Fri 8am–8pm, Sat 10am–6pm), which handles cash advances on all major cards.

FINLAND'S LINKS WITH ESTONIA

Following Estonia's regaining of its independence, a growing number of passenger vessels are plying the 85-kilometre route across the Baltic between Helsinki and the Estonian capital, Tallinn. The situation with visas is changing all the time as the former Soviet bloc loosens its previous restrictions – check the latest situation at the tourist office in Helsinki.

Estonia and Finland have similar languages, a common ancestry, and histories which had largely run parallel up until the Soviet Union's annexation of Estonia in 1940. Despite the decades of Soviet occupation, **Tallinn**, within its medieval walls, is a beautifully maintained Hanseatic city with many museums and some fine old churches just a few minutes' walk from the harbour. If you have time, take a look, too, at the enormous Song Festival Grounds just outside the old centre, scene of the much-publicized pro-independence rallies of the late 1980s.

While independence has brought Estonians many new freedoms, it hasn't brought them any money. The introduction of the kroon (rhymes with "prawn", not "prune"), a new version of the pre-Soviet currency, did little to ease the uphill struggle faced by the country's economy.

Crossings (2–3hr) are offered by Tallink Finland OY (tickets from South Harbour booking office; ☎09/2282 1277); Linda Line, Makasiini Terminal (☎09/668 9700, *www.lindaline.fi*); Nordic Jet Line, Kanavaterminaali (☎09/681 770). Expect to pay 80–130mk for a one-way ticket; cars cost 140–200mk.

Bookshops The Academic Bookstore at Keskuskatu 1 has several floors containing thousands of books in various languages on all subjects, including a large stock of English paperbacks.

Bus enquiries Long-distance buses ☎0200 4000; city buses ☎09/765 966.

Car rental Avis, Pohjoinen Rautatiekatu (☎09/441 155); Budget, Malminkatu 24 (☎09/686 6500); Europcar, Mannerheimintie 50 (☎09/4780 2220).

Dentist Dentarium (24hr), 6th floor, 7a Mikonkatu (☎09/622 1533). Expect to pay 500mk.

Doctor ☎10 023.

Embassies Canada, Pohjoisesplanadi 25B (☎09/171 141); UK, Itäinen Puistotie 17 (☎09/2286 5100); USA, Itäinen Puistotie 14 (☎09/171 931). Citizens of Australia and New Zealand should contact the Australian Embassy in Stockholm (see p.415).

Emergencies Ambulance ☎112; Police ☎10 022.

Ferries Reservations and information: Silja Line ☎9800/74 552 (daily 8am–8pm); Tallink ☎09/2282 1277 (Mon–Sat 8.30am–7pm); Viking Line ☎09/123 577 (daily 7am–9.30pm).

Hitching Radio City on 96.2MHz has a phone-in lift service each Thursday (☎09/694 1366) – and they speak English.

Hospital Töölö Hospital, Topeliuksenkatu 5 (☎4711), has a first-aid unit; Meilahti Hospital, Haartmaninkatu 4, has an emergency department (same phone number).

Late shopping The shops in Tunneli, the underground complex by the train station, are open Mon–Sat 10am–10pm, Sun noon–10pm.

Laundry Runeberginkatu 47 (Mon–Thurs 10am–8pm, Fri 10am–6pm, Sat & Sun 10am–4pm; closed Sun in Aug).

Left luggage For 10mk at the long-distance bus station (Mon–Thurs & Sat 9am–6pm, Fri 8am–6pm), or in the train station (Mon–Fri 7am–10pm).

Libraries (*kirjasto*) Central branches at Topeliuksenkatu 6 in Töölö, at Rikhardinkatu 3 near Esplanadi, and at Viides linja 11, close to Kallio kirkko (all Mon–Fri 9.30am–8pm, Sat 9.30am–3pm).

Lost property (*löytötavaratoimisto*) 3rd floor, Päivänteentie 12A (Mon–Fri 8am–4.15pm and Wed until 5.30pm; ☎09/189 3180).

News in English There's a daily English-language free paper available from some hostels, hotels, the railway station and airport called *Metro* that provides a succinct breakdown of the day's international news and sport.

Newspapers Almost every central Helsinki newsstand stocks some UK or US papers. Try at the train station, the airport, or inside Stockmann Department Store.

Pharmacy Yliopiston Apteeki, Mannerheimintie 96 (☎09/4178 0300), is open 24hr; its branch at Mannerheimintie 5 is open daily 7am–midnight.

Police Pieni Roobertinkatu 1–3 (☎1891).

Post office The main office is at Mannerheiminaukio 1a (Mon–Fri 9am–6pm); poste restante at the rear door (Mon–Fri 7am–9pm, Sat 9am–6pm, Sun 11am–9pm). Stamps from post offices or the yellow machines in shops, which take 1mk and 5mk coins.

Train enquiries ☎09/707 5700 or 010 800 100.

Travel agents KILROY Travels, Kaivokatu 10D (☎09/680 7811), is the Scandinavian youth travel agent, specializing in discounted tickets for students and young people. Suomen Matkutoimisto (SMT), the Finland Travel Bureau, Aleksanterinkatu 17 (☎09/18 261), organizes trips to Russia and the necessary visas.

What's on Listings in *Helsinki This Week* (monthly), and the *Helsinki Guide* (issued each summer), from the City Tourist Office, hotels and hostels.

Around Helsinki

To be honest, there's little in Helsinki's outlying area that's worth venturing out for. But three places, all an easy day-trip from the city, merit a visit: the visionary suburbs of **Espoo**; the home of the composer Sibelius at **Järvenpää**; and the evocative old town of **Porvoo**, which also serves as an obvious access point to the underrated southeastern corner of the country.

The Espoo area

Lying west of Helsinki, the suburban area of **Espoo** comprises several separate districts. The one nearest to Helsinki, directly across the bay, is the "garden city" of **TAPIOLA**. In the 1950s Finnish urban planners attempted to blend new housing schemes with the surrounding forests and hills, frequently only to be left with a compromise that turned ugly as expansion occurred. Tapiola was the exception to this rule, built as a self-contained living area rather than a dormitory town, with alternating high and low buildings, abundant open areas, parks, fountains and swimming pools. Much praised on its completion by the architectural world, it's still refreshing to wander through and admire the idea and its execution. The **tourist office** at Itätuulenkuja (☎09/8164 7230, fax 8164 7238) handles enquiries about the whole Espoo area.

About 3km north of Tapiola, past the traffic-bearing Hagalundintie, brings you to the little peninsula of **Otaniemi** and a couple more notable architectural sites. One of these is the Alvar Aalto-designed campus of Helsinki University's technology faculty; the other – far more dramatic – is the Dipoli student union building on the same campus. Ever keen to harmonize the artificial with the natural, architects Reimi and Raili Pietilä here created a building which seems fused with the rocky crags above, the front of the structure daringly edging forward from the cliff face.

Though the town of Espoo itself has little to delay you, just beyond lies the hugely absorbing **Hvitträsk** (June–Aug Mon–Fri 10am–7pm, Sat & Sun 10am–6pm; April, May, Sept & Oct Mon–Fri 11am–6pm, Sat & Sun 11am–5pm; 15mk), the studio home built and shared by Eliel Saarinen, Armas Lindgren and Herman Gesellius until 1904, when their partnership dissolved amid the acrimony caused by Saarinen's independent (and winning) design for Helsinki's train station. Externally, this is an extended and romanticized version of the traditional Finnish log cabin, the leafy branches that creep around making the structure look like a mutant growth emerging from the forest. Inside are frescoes by Gallen-Kallela and changing exhibitions of Finnish art and handicrafts. Eliel Saarinen and his wife are buried in the grounds.

Buses run throughout the day from Helsinki **to Tapiola**, but you usually need specifically to request them to stop there; check details and times at the bus station or the City

Tourist Office. To get from central Helsinki **to Hvitträsk**, take the local (line L) train to Louma (10 daily; 37min) and follow the signs for 3km, or take bus #166 from Helsinki (3 daily; 55min). Four-hour guided tours of Hvitträsk plus Sibelius's home (see below) start every Saturday at 1pm from Fabiankatu, in the city centre, costing 210mk, or 40mk with Helsinki Card, and lasting four hours (call ☎09/2288 1222 for reservations).

Järvenpää: Ainola

Around 40km north of Helsinki in **JÄRVENPÄÄ**, easily reached by either bus or train, is **Ainola** (May & Sept Wed–Sun 11am–5pm; June–Aug Tues–Sun 11am–5pm; for guided tours combined with Hvitträsk, see above) – the house where Jean Sibelius lived from 1904 with his wife, Aino (sister of the artist Eero Järnefelt), after whom the place is named.

Though now regarded as one of the twentieth-century's greatest composers, **Jean Sibelius**, born in Hämeenlinna in 1865, had no musical background, and by the age of nineteen was enrolled on a law course at Helsinki University. He had, however, developed a youthful passion for the violin and took a class at the capital's Institute of Music. Law was soon forgotten as Sibelius's real talents were recognized, and his musical studies took him to the cultural hotbeds of the day, Berlin and Vienna. Returning to Finland to teach at the Institute, Sibelius soon gained a government grant, which enabled him to begin composing full time, the first concert of his works taking place in 1892. His early pieces were inspired by the Finnish folk epic, the *Kalevala*, and by the nationalist movement of the times; in 1899 the country's Russian rulers banned performances of Sibelius's rousing *Finlandia* under any name that suggested its patriotic sentiment – it was instead published simply as "Opus 26 No. 7".

While the overtly nationalistic elements in Sibelius's work mellowed in later years, his music continued to reflect a very Finnish obsession with nature: "Other composers offer their public a cocktail," he said, "I offer mine pure spring water". He is still revered in his own land, although he was also notorious for his bouts of heavy drinking, and a destructive quest for perfection which fuelled suspicion that he had completed, and destroyed, two symphonies during his final thirty years. This was an angst-ridden period when no new work appeared, which became known as "the silence from Järvenpää". Sibelius died in 1957, his best-known symphonies setting a standard younger Finnish composers have yet to live up to.

The house is just the kind of home you'd expect for a man who included representations of flapping swans' wings in his music: a tranquil place, close to lakes and forests. The wood-filled grounds are as atmospheric as the building, which is a place of pilgrimage for devotees, although books, furnishings and a few paintings are all there is to see. His grave is in the grounds, marked by a marble stone inscribed simply with his name. For more tangible Sibelius memories, and more of his music, visit the Sibelius Museum in Turku (see p.673).

While in Järvenpää, it would be a pity to miss out on a visit to the **Halosenniemi Museum** (May–Aug Tues–Sun 11am–6pm; Sept–April Tues–Sun 11am–4pm; 25mk). On the Tuusula Lakeside road, just a few minutes' walk from Ainola, this is the rustic home of Pekka Halonen, one of Finland's most renowned artists. A beautifully serene place, its National Romantic decor has been painstakingly restored and now houses some of Halonen's pictures and painting materials in their original setting.

Porvoo

One of the oldest towns on the south coast, **PORVOO**, 50km northeast of Helsinki, with its narrow cobbled streets lined by small wooden buildings, gives a sense of the Finnish life that predated the capital's bold squares and Neoclassical geometry. This, coupled with its elegant riverside setting and unhurried mood, means you're unlikely to be alone. Word of Porvoo's peaceful time-locked qualities has spread.

First stop should be the newly built **tourist office** at Rihkamakatu 4 (July & Aug Mon–Fri 10am–6pm, Sat & Sun 10am–4pm; Sept–June Mon–Fri 10am–4.30pm, Sat 10am–2pm; ☎019/580 145, fax 582 721, *www.porvoo.fi*), for a free map of the town. For something more historic, look in at the preserved **Johan Ludwig Runeberg House**, at Aleksanterinkatu 3 (May–Aug Mon–Sat 10am–4pm, Sun 11am–5pm; Sept–April Wed–Sat 10am–4pm, Sun 11am–5pm; 10mk), where the man regarded as Finland's national poet lived from 1852 while a teacher at the town school. Despite writing in Swedish, Runeberg greatly aided the nation's sense of self-esteem, especially with *Tales of Vänrikki Ståhl*, which told of the people's struggles with Russia in the 1808–09 conflict. The first poem in his collection *Our Land* later provided the lyrics for the national anthem. Across the road, the **Walter Runeberg Gallery** (May–Aug Mon–Sat 10am–4pm, Sun 11am–5pm; Sept–April Wed–Sun 11am–3pm; 15mk) displays a collection of sculpture by Runeberg's third son, one of Finland's more celebrated sculptors. Among many acclaimed works, he's responsible for the statue of his father that stands in the centre of Helsinki's Esplanadi.

The old town (follow the signs for "Vanha Porvoo") is built around the hill on the other side of Mannerheimkatu. Near the top, its outline partially obscured by vegetation, is the fifteenth-century **Tuomiokirkko** (May–Sept Mon–Fri 10am–6pm, Sat 10am–2pm, Sun 2–5pm; Oct–April Tues–Sat 10am–2pm, Sun 2–4pm). It was here in 1809 that Alexander I proclaimed Finland a Russian Grand Duchy, himself Grand Duke, and convened the first Finnish Diet. This, and other aspects of the town's past, can be explored in the **Porvoo Museum** (May–Aug daily 10am–4pm; Sept–April Wed–Sun noon–4pm; 15mk) at the foot of the hill in the old town's main square. There are no singularly outstanding exhibits here, just a diverting selection of furnishings, musical instruments and general oddities, largely dating from the years of Russian rule.

Practicalities

Buses run all day from Helsinki to Porvoo from the long-distance bus station; a one-way trip costs around 40mk. Idling around the town is especially pleasant late in the day as the evening stillness descends; the last bus back to the city conveniently departs around midnight. There are also a couple of **boats** from Helsinki in summer: the *J. L. Runeberg* (June–Aug Tues, Wed, Sat & Sun, plus Fri July to mid-Aug & Mon July at 10am, arriving 1.15pm; returns to Helsinki at 4pm; 150mk day-trip), and the quicker *MS Queen* (July to mid-Aug Tues–Thurs, Sat & Sun at 11am, arriving 1.30pm; leaves Porvoo at 3.30pm; 95mk single). Tickets for both boats can be bought from their respective ticket offices in the kauppatori in Helsinki.

If you've exhausted Helsinki, **spending a night** in Porvoo leaves you well placed to continue into Finland's southeastern corner (see below). If possible, try to arrange accommodation while in Helsinki, particularly if you're after hotel bargains – rates in Porvoo are steep. There is, however, a **youth hostel**, open all year, at Linnankoskenkatu 1 (☎019/523 0012), and a **campsite** (☎019/581 967), open from June to mid-August, 2km from the town centre.

THE SOUTHEAST

As it's some way from the major centres, foreign tourists tend to neglect the extreme **southeastern corner** of Finland; Finns, however, rate it highly, flocking here to make boat trips around the islands and to explore the many small communities, which combine a genuine rustic flavour with sufficient places of minor interest to keep boredom at bay. For Finns, the region also stirs memories: its position on the Soviet border means it saw many battles during the Winter and Continuation wars, and throughout medieval times it was variously under the control of Sweden and Russia. It's an intriguing area, worth two or three days of travel – most of it will be by bus, since rail lines are almost nonexistent.

East to Kotka

If Porvoo seems too tourist-infested, make the 40km journey east to **LOVIISA**, an eighteenth-century fishing village pleasantly free from Helsinki day-trippers. The village, whose 8000-strong population divides into equal numbers of Finnish- and Swedish-speakers, is overlooked by the two old **fortresses** of Rosen and Ungern, both worth exploring. The **tourist office** (Mon–Fri 8.30am–4pm; ☎019/555 234, fax 532 322), on the market square, can supply details of how to get to them; off the square, a row of prettily preserved houses points the way to the **Municipal Museum** (June–Aug Tues–Sun 11am–4pm; Sept–May Tues–Sun noon–4pm; 10mk), containing, besides the usual local hotchpotch of bits and pieces, a fine stock of romantic postcards. Later on, if you have the cash, spend it on a slap-up meal at *Degerby Gille*, Sepänkuja 4, a restaurant set in a seventeenth-century house that's one of the town's most important historical sights; if you don't, poke your head around the restaurant's door anyway to marvel at the wonderfully maintained interior.

In the bay off Loviisa there's a less welcome modern sight – one of the country's two **nuclear power stations**. Finland's Cold War balancing act between East and West led to the country buying its nuclear hardware from both power blocs; this one has spent the past thirty years producing plutonium for (allegedly) Soviet nuclear weapons. The other, Western-backed, at Olkiluoti (near Rauma), is newer and still the subject of much argument. The Finnish public is divided over the merits of nuclear power in general: the country takes about forty percent of its energy from nuclear sources, but the growing anti-nuclear movement is calling for a switch to hydroelectric power. Whatever the outcome of the debate, mindful of the design flaws in Soviet-built reactors, the view is an unnerving one.

If you have the time, a couple of smaller settlements between Loviisa and Kotka can comfortably consume half a day. In 1809, the Swedish–Russian border was drawn up in this area, splitting the region of Pyhää in two. Some 20km from Loviissa is **RUOTSINPYHTÄÄ** (**Stromfors** in Swedish), whose local **tourist office** (☎019/618 474, fax 618 475) is diplomatically positioned on the bridge over the inlet that once divided the two feuding empires. Historical quirks aside, the main attraction here is the seventeenth-century **ironworks**, now turned into craft studios, with demonstrations of carpet-weaving, jewellery-making and painting – all quite enjoyable to stroll around on a sunny day. You should also visit the oddly octagonal-shaped **wooden church** (June–Sept Mon–Fri 10am–6pm, Sat & Sun 8am–4pm; Oct–May, book with tourist office) to admire Helene Schjerfbeck's beautiful altarpiece. It was here, incidentally, that a Finnish TV company filmed a very popular soap opera, *Vihreän Kullanmaa* ("The Land of the Green Gold"), making good use of the contrast between the spacious millowners' houses and the cramped workers' cottages.

The village of **PYHÄÄ** is a twenty-minute bus ride further east. There's a **stone church** here (June–Sept daily noon–3pm; Oct–May Sun noon–3pm), one of the oldest in the country, dated at around 1300. Its interior frescoes are primitive and strangely moving, and were discovered only recently when the Reformation-era whitewash was removed. From the quay on the other side of the village's sole street there's a ferry service to the nearby islands, including Kaunissaari ("Beautiful Island"), where you can connect with an evening motorboat straight on to Kotka.

The land route to Kotka takes you through **SILTAKYLÄ**, a small town significant only for the hills around it and its **tourist information** counter at the town hall, beside the main road, which has information on walks in the district. The hills afford great views over a dramatic legacy of the Ice Age: spooky Tolkienesque forests and many miles of a red-granite stone known as *rapakivi* that's unique to southeast Finland, covered by a white moss. A number of marked hiking trails lead through the landscape, strewn with giant boulders, some as big as four-storey buildings and supporting their own little ecosystem of plant and tree life. After a day's trek, you can reward yourself with food and drink – or even a swim – at the not too pricey *Pyhtään Motelli* (☎05/343 1661), which despite its name is situated on the edge of Siltakylä.

Kotka to the Russian border

After the scattering of little communities east of Porvoo, **KOTKA**, a few kilometres on from Siltakylä, seems immense. Built on an island in the Gulf of Finland, Kotka's past reflects its closeness to the sea. Numerous battles have been fought off its shores, among them the Sweden–Russia confrontation of 1790, the largest battle ever seen in Nordic waters: almost 10,000 people lost their lives. Sixty-odd years later, the British fleet reduced Kotka virtually to rubble during the Crimean War. In modern times the sea has been the basis of the town's prosperity: sitting at the end of the Kymi river with a deep-water harbour, the town makes a perfect cargo transit point – causing most locals to live in fear of a major accident occuring in the industrial section, or in the freight yards. Only two roads link Kotka to the mainland and a speedy evacuation of its inhabitants would be almost impossible.

The town itself has little to delay you; it's more a place to eat and sleep than anything else. Only the eighteenth-century Orthodox **St Nicolai kirkko** (June–Aug Tues–Fri noon–3pm, Sat & Sun noon–6pm) survived the British bombardment, and even that is not particularly interesting, although it's worth visiting the **Langinkoski Imperial Fishing Lodge** (May–Aug daily 10am–7pm; Sept & Oct Sat & Sun 10am–7pm; 15mk), off the main island, about 5km north of the town centre (take bus #12). It was here that Tsar Alexander III would relax in transit between Helsinki and St Petersburg; the wooden building, a gift to him from the Finnish government, is most striking for its simplicity and the attractive setting in the woods near the fast-flowing Kymi river.

Practicalities

Rail and road connections bring you right into the compact centre, where the **tourist office** at Keskuskatu 7 (June–Aug Mon–Fri 9am–5pm, Sat 10am–2pm; Sept–May Mon–Fri 9am–5pm; ☎05/234 4424, fax 234 4407) will fill you in on local bus details – essential for continuing around the southeast.

Grumbling stomachs can be quietened in *Kairo*, Satamakatu 7, an authentic seamen's **restaurant**, popular with Eastern European sailors, while excellent cuisine can be found at the gourmet *Kesäravintola Meriniemi* at Kaivokatu 16. A good-value **hotel** is the pleasant *Hotelli Merikotka*, Satamakatu 9 (☎05/215 222, fax 215 414; ②), or there's the more upmarket *Seurahoune*, Keskuskatu 21 (☎05/35 035, fax 350 0450; ⑤/③). The nearest youth hostel, *Kärkisaari*, is 6km north of Kotka in Mussalo (bus #27), overlooking a spectacular bay (☎05/260 4804; mid-May to mid-Sept). There's also a campsite in Mussalo (☎05/260 5055 or 0400/415 815; May–Sept) and, next door, the *Hotel Santalahti* (same phone number; ②) which also has a cheapish cafeteria open to non-residents.

Hamina and east to the Russian border

Twenty-six kilometres east of Kotka is **HAMINA**, founded in 1653 and sporting a magnificently bizarre town plan, the main streets forming concentric circles around the centre. It was built this way to allow the incumbent Swedish forces to withstand attack – the town being the site of many Swedish–Russian battles. Besides the layout, however, there's not an awful lot to amuse, although you can pick up suggestions and local information from

TRIPS TO RUSSIA

Overland from Helsinki

Two trains – one Russian and one Finnish – leave Helsinki every day for the six-hour trip to St Petersburg; there's also a Russian overnight service. All border formalities are carried out on the train, but you must have a Russian visa before you leave – the tourist office has a list of travel agencies that can arrange these, though be warned that they take a week to process. A one-way second-class ticket costs 278mk, including seat reservation, first-class tickets are 441mk, or 493mk for a sleeping compartment.

Day cruises

If sailing to St Petersburg for a short visit sounds more attractive, you could book a place on one of the four cruises a year operated by Kristina Cruises: there's one in June, one in July and two in August. All leave Helsinki at 5.30pm, arrive in St Petersburg 9am the following morning and return at 10.30pm the next day; all-inclusive packages with cabin start at 1600mk. You don't strictly need a visa for one of these excursions, although if you want to come and go as you please from the boat once it has docked in Russia you will need to get one a week in advance from the tour operator. If you don't have one you'll have to either see the city with a guided tour or pay 55mk for a transfer ticket. For more information, contact Kristina Cruises, Korkeavuorenkatu 2, Kotka (☎ & fax 05/21 144).

the **tourist office** at Rautatienkatu 8 (Mon–Fri 8am–4pm; ☎05/749 525, fax 749 5381).

The tourist office can also give you the latest schedule of the bus that runs to Virolahti, 31km east, and within a few kilometres of the **Salpalinjan Bunkkerit** or Salpa Line Bunkers – fortifications that stretched from here to Lapland and were intended to protect Finland from Soviet attack during the run-up to the Winter War of 1939. Massive hunks of granite blocked the way of advancing tanks. These days Finnish war veterans are eager to show off the bunker's details and lead visitors to the seats (and controls) of ageing anti-tank guns. Buses from Helsinki to Viipuri, the formerly Finnish town now on the Russian side of the border (see p.695), pass through Hamina; again, details are best checked at the tourist office.

THE SOUTHWEST

The area between Helsinki and Finland's **southwestern** extremity is probably the blandest section of the whole country. By road or rail the view is much the same, endless forests interrupted only by modest-sized patches of water and virtually identical villages and small towns. Once at the southwestern corner, however, things change considerably, with islands and inlets around a jagged shoreline, and the distinctive Finland-Swedish coastal communities.

Turku

There is very little in Åbo which has entertained me in the survey, or can amuse you by the description. It is a wretched capital of a barbarous province. The houses are almost all of wood; and the archiepiscopal palace, which has not even a single storey, but may be called a sort of barrack, is composed of no better materials, except that it is painted red. I inquired if there was not any object in the university, meriting attention; but they assured me that it would be regarded as a piece of ridicule, to visit it on such an errand, there being nothing within its walls except a very small library, and a few philosophical instruments.
A Tour Round The Baltic, Sir N.W. Wraxall, 1775.

TURKU (or **Åbo** as it's known in Swedish) was the principal town in Finland when the country was a province of Sweden, losing its status in 1812, along with most of its buildings in a ferocious fire soon after – occurrences that clearly improved the place, if the above quotation is to be believed. These days Turku is small and highly sociable – thanks to the boom years under Swedish rule and the number of students from its two universities – bristling with history and culture, and with a sparkling nightlife to boot.

Arrival, information and accommodation

The River Aura splits the city, its tree-lined banks forming a natural promenade as well as a useful landmark. The cathedral and castle stand at opposite ends of the river, while the main museums are found along its edge. There are gleaming department stores, banks and offices on the northern side of the river in Turku's central grid, where you'll also find the **tourist office** at Aurakatu 4 (Mon–Fri 8.30am–6pm, Sat & Sun 9am–4pm; ☎02/233 6366, fax 233 6488, *www.turkutourist.fi*). Outside banking hours you can **change money** at Forex, Eerikinkatu 12 (Mon–Sat 8am–7pm, Sun 10am–4pm). Both the **train station** and **bus station** are within easy walking distance of the river, just north of the centre.

Accommodation

If you turn up at the weekend having made an early reservation, there can be some good deals in Turku's mid-range **hotels**: *Scandic Hotel Julia*, Eerikinkatu 4 (☎02/336 311, fax 251 1750; ⑨/④); *Ramada Hotel Turku*, Eerikinkatu 28 (☎02/338 211, fax 338

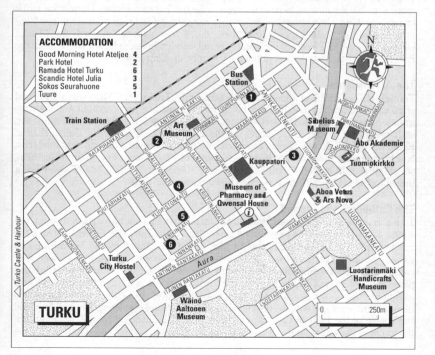

2299; ⑤/③); or the *Sokos Hotel Seurahuone*, Eerikinkatu 23 (☎02/337 301, fax 251 8051; ⑤/③). If you feel like splashing out on something with a bit more character, try the *Park Hotel* (☎02/273 2555, fax 251 9696; ⑥/⑤), built in 1902 at Rauhankatu 1, a five-minute walk from the train station. Also near the train station at Humalistonkatu 7 is the *Good Morning Hotel Ateljee* (☎02/336 111, fax 233 6699; ④), housed in a rather drab building designed by Alvar Aalto. Its themed rooms copy the style of Finnish designers – including a nice Aalto-style room among them.

At the budget end of the market, Turku has an excellent official **youth hostel**, *Turku City Hostel*, open all year and beautifully situated by the river in the city centre at Linnankatu 39 (☎02/231 6578, fax 231 1708) – take bus #30 from the train station or #1 from the airport and bus station. There's also a decent **bed and breakfast**, *Tuure*, near the bus and train stations at Tuureporinkatu 17c (☎02/233 0230; ①). The nearest **campsite** (☎02/258 9100) is on the small island of Ruissalo, overlooking Turku harbour. It's open from June to mid-August and takes about fifteen minutes to reach on bus #8. Ruissalo is a good place to visit anyway, for its two sandy beaches, a botanical garden sporting a host of rare and spectacular plants, and fine views to the archipelago.

The City

Arriving in Turku by train, you'll quickly make the pleasing discovery that the town's major places of interest unintentionally arrange themselves into a very logical pattern. By beginning at the Art Museum, a few strides from the station, and from there moving south through the town centre and heading westwards along the river's edge, you'll be able to see everything worth seeing in a day – although allowing two days might be more sensible if you want to have energy left for the Turku nightlife. During the 1970s and 80s parts of Turku were subjected to some thoughtless redevelopment, resulting in a number of really hideous buildings, and a new national byword, the "Turku Disease". However, streets of intricately carved wooden houses still survive around the Port Arthur area, a lovely part of town for simply strolling around.

The Art Museum

Though it's not much of a taster for the actual city, **Turku Art Museum** (times and price varies according to exhibition; 20–40mk), housed in a purpose-built Art Nouveau granite structure close to the train station, is one of the better collections of Finnish art, with works by all the great names of the country's Golden Age – Gallen-Kallela, Edelfelt, Pekka Halonen, Simberg and others – plus a commendable stock of moderns. Not least among these are the wood sculptures of Kain Tapper and Mauno Hartman, which stirred up heated debate on the merits of carefully shaped bits of wood being presented as art when they were first shown during the 1970s.

The Cathedral and around

To get to grips with Turku itself, and its pivotal place in Finnish history, cut through the centre to the river, and the tree-framed space that, before the great fire of 1879, was the bustling heart of the community, and which is still overlooked by the **Tuomiokirkko** (9am–7pm daily except during services; free guided tours in English available). The cathedral, erected in the thirteenth century on the "Knoll of Sheep", a pre-Christian place of worship, was at the centre of the Christianization process inflicted by the crusading Swedes on the pagan Finns, and grew larger over the centuries as the new religion became stronger and Swedish involvement in Finland escalated. The building, still the centre of the Finnish Church, has been repeatedly ravaged by fire, although the thickness of the walls enabled many of its medieval features to survive. Of these, it's the tombs that catch the eye: Torsten Stålhandske, commander of the Finnish cavalry during the seventeenth-century Thirty Years War, in which Sweden sought to protect its domination of the Baltic and the Finns confirmed their reputation as wild and fearless fighters, lies in a deliriously ornate coffin (to the right as you enter) opposite Samuel Cockburn and Patrick Ogilvie, a couple of Scots who fought alongside him. On the left-hand side, Catharine Månsdotter, the commoner wife of the Swedish king Erik XIV, with whom, in the mid-sixteenth century, she was imprisoned in Turku Castle, is as popular in death as she reputedly was in life, judging by the numbers who file past her simple black-marble sarcophagus. The window behind it carries her stained-glass image – and if you crane your neck to the left, you can see a wall plaque bearing the only known true likeness of her. For 10mk you can visit the **cathedral museum** upstairs (same times as cathedral), which gives a stronger insight into the cathedral's past. There's an assortment of ancient jugs, goblets, plates and spoons, though more absorbing are the collections of church textiles – funeral flags and the like – at the far end.

Immediately outside the cathedral is a statue to **Per Brahe**, governor-general of Finland from 1637 and the first Swedish officer to devote much attention to the welfare of the Finns, encouraging a literacy programme and founding the country's first university. The site of this is within the nearby yellow Empire-style buildings, although the actual seat of learning was moved to Helsinki during the era of Russian rule. Next to these are the oldest portions of the **Åbo Akademie** – Finland's only remaining Swedish-language university – while the modern, Finnish-language **Turku University** is at the other end of Henrikinkatu: these days both are more notable as places for eating rather than sightseeing.

Turku's newest and most splendid museum is the combined **Aboa Vetus** and **Ars Nova** (May–Aug daily 10am–7pm; Sept–April times vary; 35mk, or 50mk for both) on the bank of the Aurajoki river just a few steps from the university. Translating as "Old Turku, New Art", the place was intended to be simply a modern art gallery, but when the building's foundations were dug a warren of medieval lanes and cellars came to light, an unmissable opportunity to present the history and archeology of the city. Glass flooring allows a near-perfect view of the remains. The New Art part comprises a striking collection of 350 works, alongside frequent temporary exhibitions. There's a great café too: prepare yourself here by browsing through the museum's English-language brochure, since the guided tours are in Finnish only.

Back past the cathedral and across Piispankatu is the sleek low form of the **Sibelius Museum** (Tues–Sun 11am–3pm, Wed also 6–8pm; 15mk). Although Sibelius had no direct connection with Turku, this museum is a fitting tribute to him and his contribution to the emergence of an independent Finland. Chances are that the recorded strains of *Finlandia* will greet you as you enter: when not the venue for live concerts (which usually take place during the winter), the small but acoustically perfect concert area pumps out recorded requests from the great man's oeuvre; take your place beside dewy-eyed Finns for a lunch hour of Scandinavia's finest composer. Elsewhere, the Sibelius collection gathers family photo albums and original manuscripts along with the great man's hat, walking stick and even a final half-smoked cigar. Other exhibits cover the musical history of the country, from intricate musical boxes and the frail wooden *kantele* – the instrument strummed by peasants in the *Kalevala* – to the weighty keyboard instruments downstairs.

The Observatory and Maritime Museum

On the other side of the cathedral from the Sibelius museum, you'll see a small hill topped by the wooden dome of the **Observatory**, designed – rather poorly – by Carl Engel, who had arrived in Turku seeking work in the days before his great plan for Helsinki made him famous. Originally the building was intended to serve the first

Turku University as an observatory, but disputes between Engel and his assistants and a misunderstanding of scientific requirements rendered the place useless for its intended purpose. To make things worse, the university moved to Helsinki, and the building was then turned into a navigational school. The **Maritime Museum** formerly housed in the Observatory is due to move to a new purpose-built site near the harbour in 2000 – check with the tourist office for further information.

The Luostarinmäki, Aaltonen and pharmacy museums

From the water tower, head directly down the side of the hill to the far more engrossing **Luostarinmäki Handicrafts Museum** (May–Sept daily 10am–6pm; Oct–April Tues–Sun 10am–3pm; 15mk), one of the best – and certainly the most authentic – open-air museums in Finland. Following a severe fire in 1775, rigorous restrictions were imposed on the town's new buildings, but due to a legal technicality they didn't apply in this district. The wooden houses here were built by local working people in traditional style and evolved naturally into a museum as descendants of the original owners died and bequeathed their inherited homes to the municipality. The unpaved streets run between tiny wooden houses, which once had goats tethered to their chimneys to keep the turfed roofs cropped. The chief inhabitants now are the museum volunteers who dress up in period attire and demonstrate the old handicrafts.

A short walk from the handicrafts museum, on the southern bank of the river, is another worthwhile indoor collection: the **Wäinö Aaltonen Museum** (daily 11am–7pm, closed Mon in winter; 13mk, more during special exhibitions). Unquestionably the best-known modern Finnish sculptor, Wäinö Aaltonen, born in 1894, grew up close to Turku and studied for a time at the local art school. His first public show, in 1916, marked a turning point in the development of Finnish sculpture, introducing a freer, more individual style to a genre struggling to break from the restraints of the Neoclassical tradition and French realism. Aaltonen went on to dominate his field totally throughout the 1920s and 30s and his influence is still felt today; the man's work turns up in every major town throughout the country, and even the parliament building in Helsinki was designed with special niches to hold some of his pieces. Much of his output celebrates the individuals who contributed to the growth of the Finnish republic, typically remembering them with enormous heads, or as immense statues that resemble massive social-realist chunks. But Aaltonen, who died in 1966, really was an original, imaginative and sensitive sculptor, as the exhibits here demonstrate. There's also a roomful of his paintings, some of which show perhaps why he concentrated on sculpture.

Across the river from the Aaltonen museum, there's a sign in the grass which spells out TURKU:ÅBO. Not far away from this is a wooden staircase running up to the front door of the **Museum of Pharmacy and Qwensel House** (mid-April to mid-Sept daily 10am–6pm; mid-Sept to mid-April Tues–Sun 10am–3pm; 10mk). Qwensel was a court judge who moved to the house in 1694, and it later became the home of Professor Josef Gustaf Pipping – the "father of Finnish medicine" – in 1785. Period furnishings remain, proving just how wealthy and stylish the life of the eighteenth-century bourgeoisie actually was. Many chemists' implements from around the country are on show, among them some memorable devices for drawing blood.

Turku Castle

The town's museums, and its cathedral and universities, are all symbols of Turku's elevated position in Finnish life, though by far the major marker to its many years of importance stands at the western end of Linnankatu. Follow the signs for "Turun Linna", or take bus #1 from the harbour, and you'll eventually see, oddly set among the present-day ferry terminals, the relatively featureless and unappetizing exterior of **Turku Castle** (mid-April to mid-Sept daily 10am–6pm; mid-Sept to mid-April Mon 2–7pm, Tues–Sun

10am–3pm; 20mk). Fight any dismay though, since the compact cobbled courtyards, maze-like corridors and darkened staircases of the interior make the castle a good place to wander – and to dwell on the fact that this was the seat of the government of the country for centuries; and that much of Finland's (and a significant portion of Sweden's) medieval history took shape within these walls. Unless you're an expert on the period, you'll get a migraine trying to figure out the importance of everything that's here, and it's a sensible idea to buy one of the guide leaflets on sale at the entrance.

The castle probably went up sometime around 1280, when the first bishop arrived from Sweden; gradual expansion through the following years accounts for the patchwork effect of its architecture – and the bewildering array of finds, rooms and displays. The majority of the fortification took place during the turbulent sixteenth century, instigated by Swedish ruler Gustavus Vasa for the protection of his son, whom he made Duke Johan, the first Duke of Finland. Johan pursued a lavish court life but exceeded his powers in attacking Livonia and was sentenced to death by the Stockholm Diet. Swedish efforts to seize Johan were successful only after a three-week siege, and he was removed to Stockholm. The subsequent decision by the unbalanced Erik XIV to release Johan resulted not only in Johan becoming king himself, but also in poor Erik being imprisoned here – albeit with a full quota of servants and the best food and wine. The bare cell he occupied for a few weeks contrasts strongly with the splendour from Johan's time, offering a cool reminder of shifting fortunes. There's a gloomy nineteenth-century painting here, by Erik Johan Löfgren, of Erik with his head on the lap of his queen (Catharine Månsdotter), while the lady's eyes look askance to heaven.

Eating, drinking and entertainment

You'd need to be very fussy not to find somewhere to **eat** in Turku that's to your liking. Walking around checking the lunchtime offers can turn up many bargains, plus there's the usual selection of economical pizzerias. Floating restaurants are popular among tourists, if not with too many locals, and the boats change each summer, though the names *Papa Joe*, *Svarte Rudolf* and *Lulu* reappear year after year: all have decent enough restaurants, and often put on live music.

Cafés and restaurants

Angel, Kauppiaskatu 16. Wonderful cakes and coffee.

Café Qwensel, in a courtyard behind the Museum of Pharmacy. Fabulous cakes in atmospheric eighteenth-century surroundings.

Foija, Aurakatu 10. Good pizzas for under 50mk.

Gadolinia, Henrikenkatu. This student mensa is part of Åbo Akademie – look for the sign saying "Rouka" – and the cheapest option in town.

Herman, Läntinen Rantakatu 37 (☎02/230 3333, fax 230 3334). On the riverside, set in a bright and airy storehouse dating from 1849. Since Turku hosted the Tall Ships Race in 1996, the whole area has been renovated – ask to reserve the table for two overlooking the river. Fantastic food that comes at a price, with main courses running from 60mk to 150mk.

Italia, Linnankatu 3. Sizeable pizzas at very affordable prices.

Pinella, Porhaninpuisto. Café in an antique wooden pavilion, serving decadent chocolate brownies and ice cream (15mk), as well as main dishes such as cold smoked reindeer pancakes (60mk).

Pizzeria Dennis, Linnankatu 17. Decent, well-priced pizzeria.

Toilet, Puutori. Bizarre restaurant housed in a former public toilet, and worth a visit if only for its location.

Turun Hotelli Ravintola Oppilaitos, in the Data Centre close to Turku Hospital and Sports Hall – take the train one stop to Kupittaa. Run by the catering college, the service here is almost too efficient and the food usually excellent.

Bars and entertainment

The riverside restaurant *Samppalinna*, on Itäinen Rantakatu, is a good night-time **drinking** venue, as well as being a wonderful restaurant. Other popular bars are *Olavinkrouvi*, Hämeenkatu 30, which draws numerous students, and *Erik XIV*, Eerikinkatu 6, which also serves decent food. Consider also the "English-style" pub, *Hunter's Inn*, part of *Hotel Julia* but with its own entrance at Brahenkatu 3. One drinking hole which attracts a young crowd is *Pharmacy*, Kaskenkatu 1, housed in an old chemist's shop, with drug and pill bottles scattered about the place. It allegedly predates Damian Hirst's famous London bar-restaurant of the same name by a year. The floating restaurants mentioned on p.675 are also good for a beer.

If you want to fill your nights with something more energetic than boozing, there are several **discos**, most of them within the bigger hotels. *Börs Night Club* in the *Hotel Hamburger Börs,* Kauppiaskatu 6, is one of the best known. *Puuteri*, Eerikinkatu 12 is one of the trendiest in town, while not far behind are *Opera*, Aurakatu 8, and *Forte* on Kristiinankatu. More sedate, and with a slightly older clientele, are *Kilta*, Humalistonkatu 8, and *Hotel Ateljee*, Humalistonkatu 7, which sometimes holds Finnish tango nights.

During August, the **Turku Music Festival** packs thousands into a number of venues for performances in a wide range of musical genres (information on ☎02/251 1162, *www.turkumusic.netti.fi*). If your tastes are for classical music, try and get a ticket for the **Turku Philharmonic Orchestra**, founded in 1790 and thus one of the oldest orchestras in Europe. It's now based in the Concert Hall at Aninkaistenkatu 9, which hosts symphonic and chamber-music concerts. The box office telephone line (☎02/262 0800) opens in mid-August, one month before concerts begin. Alternatively, check with the tourist office for a rundown of the week's films: Turku has five **cinemas**, the largest, with five screens, being the Julia, Eerikinkatu 4. There are usually two screenings a night, at 6.30pm and 8.30pm.

Around Turku – and moving on

NAANTALI, 16km from Turku is famous as the home of **Moomin World** (mid-June to mid-Aug daily 10am–7pm; adults 80mk, children 60mk), a theme-park set on an island and based on Tove Jansson's famous creations. It's a must-see if you have kids in tow, and many tour operators run buses to the park from Turku. Naantali itself is pleasant enough, with its wooden buildings and slight passageways, but hardly worth hanging around for more than a few hours, and with regular buses there's no need to stay, though there's a tourist office should you need further information (☎02/850 850).

Moving on from Turku

Continuing from Turku **north along the coast**, there are direct bus services to the nearest main towns, Rauma and Pori. It's also possible to reach Pori by train, although this takes virtually a whole day and involves going via Tampere and changing at least once, possibly three times. From **Turku harbour** ferries sail through the vast archipelago to the Åland Islands, and on to Sweden. The harbour is 3km from the city centre and bus #1 covers the route frequently.

Rauma and Pori

RAUMA, 90km north of Turku, is one of the oldest towns in Finland, its historic importance reflected by its designation as a UNESCO World Heritage Site. Its cobbled eighteenth- and nineteenth-century streets are becoming increasingly touristy, but the town still retains plenty of charm. Strangely for the west coast, it's a mainly Finnish-speaking community, although with an archaic dialect that many other Finns find hard to understand. This past is documented in the **History Museum** in the eighteenth-century town hall at Kauppakatu 13 (mid-May to Aug daily 10am–5pm; Sept to mid-May Tues–Fri 10am–5pm, Sat 10am–2pm, Sun 10am–5pm; 20mk), with further evidence on show at **Marela**, Kauppakatu 24 (same times as History Museum; 20mk), a house preserved in the style of a rich shipowner's home from the beginning of the twentieth century. Combined entry to Marela and the History Museum costs 20mk with a day pass available from either museum. If you want to plunge even further into local history, the **Old Rauma Renovation Centre** at Vähäkirkkokatu 8 (June–Aug daily 10am–6pm; free) runs evening classes (unfortunately, all in Finnish) covering activities such as Rauma-style community singing, lessons in how to tie seafarers' knots and instruction in the local Rauma dialect.

There's a **tourist office** at Valtakatu 2 (June–Aug Mon–Fri 8am–6pm, Sat 10am–3pm, Sun 11am–2pm; Sept–May Mon–Fri 9am–4pm; ☎02/834 4551, fax 822 4555, *www.satanet.fi/rsm*) and there's free Internet access at Rauma public library, Ankkarikatu 1 (Mon–Fri 10am–7pm). If you need to stay, it's just 1km along Poroholmantie from the town centre to *Poroholma*, the combined **youth hostel** and **campsite** (☎02/8388 2500, fax 8388 2502; mid-May to Aug); otherwise, the *Cumulus, Aittakarinkatu 9* (☎02/837 821, fax 8378 2299; ⑤/③), boasts two saunas, a pool and summer terrace. There is also the *Kesähotelli Rauma*, Satamakatu 20 (☎02/824 0130; ②; June–Aug) which offers student-style accommodation, and allows use of a sauna for a small fee (5mk). For a filling lunch, try the *Villa Tallbo*, in a shipowner's restored *fin-de-siècle* summer villa at Petäjäksentie 178 (☎02/8220 7333).

Pori

Due to its yearly jazz festival – increasingly rock- and pop-oriented in recent years – **PORI** has become one of the best-known towns in Finland. For two weeks each July, its streets are full of music and the 150,000 people who come to hear it. Throughout the rest of the year Pori reverts to being a small, quiet industrial town with a worthy regional museum and a handful of architectural and historical oddities. The central section, despite its spacious grid-style streets, can be crossed on foot in about fifteen minutes.

In the centre of Pori at Hallituskatu 14, just across the road from the tourist office (see overleaf), stands the recently renovated **Pori Theatre**, the temporary home of Finnish-language theatre during the period of Russification, when Finnish drama was considered too provocative to appear in a larger centre like Turku or Helsinki. Built in 1884, it has a striking Renaissance facade, and the tiny interior – seating just 300 – is heavy with opulent frescoes and sculptured chandeliers. To see inside, ask at the tourist office. A few steps away, at Hallituskatu 11, the **Satakunta Museum** (Tues–Sun 11am–5pm; 10mk) has three well-stocked floors which trace the life of both Pori and the surrounding Satakunta region through medieval findings, late nineteenth-century photos and shop signs, and typical house interiors, alongside interesting memorabilia from the powerful labour movement of the 1930s.

Pori's strangest sight, however, is in the big Käppärä cemetery, a twenty-minute walk along Maantiekatu. In the cemetery's centre is the Gothic-arched **Juselius Mausoleum** (May–Aug daily noon–3pm; Sept–April Sun noon–2pm; free), erected in 1898 by a local businessman, F.A. Juselius, as a memorial to his daughter, Sigrid, who died aged 11. The leading Finnish church architect of the time, Josef Steinbäck, was called on to design the thing, while Gallen-Kallela decorated the interior with some of his best large-scale paintings. The artwork was adversely affected by both fire and the local sea air, but has been restored by Gallen-Kallela's son from the original sketches, enabling the structure to fulfil its purpose as powerfully, and as solemnly, as ever.

Practicalities

It's a short walk from either the **bus station** – into Isolinnankatu and straight on – or the **train station** – follow Rautatienpuistokatu – into the centre of town, where the **tourist office** is opposite the theatre in the opulent old town hall at Hallituskatu 9a (June to mid-Aug Mon–Fri 8am–6pm, Sat 10am–3pm; mid-Aug to May Mon–Fri 8am–4pm; ☎02/621 1273, fax 621 1275, *www.pori.fi*). There's free **Internet** access at the municipal offices (*yhteipalvelupiste hööveli*), Yryönkatu 15 (Mon–Fri 10am–6pm, Sat 10am–4pm). The nearest **youth hostel**, the *Terkunkorpi Hostel,* is about 5km from the centre, at Tekniikantie 4 (☎02/637 8400, fax 637 8125; May–Aug) – buses #30M, #31, #32, #40M and #41 stop nearby. The city's **campsite**, *Isomäki* (☎02/641 0620), is a little closer, just 2km from the centre in the Isomäki Sports Centre, next to the outdoor swimming pool, but it's only open during the jazz festival; buses #7 and #8 run from the centre to the hospital (*sairaala*) close by. During the festival the Porin Linojen Jazzliikenne bus links the main festival sites, the town square and campsite (10am–4am, every 20min). At other times of year, the nearest campsite is the *Yyteri*, 20km distant (☎02/638 3778), though it does have a shop, café, sauna and many cabins; the #32 bus heads that way. Among the **hotels**, you could try the *Cumulus*, Itsenäisyydenkatu 37 (☎02/550 900, fax 550 9299; ③), one of the larger places and with its own restaurant. A smarter option is the *Vaakuna*, Gallen-Kallenkatu 7 (☎02/528 100, fax 528 182; ④), a business-oriented hotel with good weekend discounts.

In the **evening** most people gravitate to the town centre and watch a procession of highly polished cars heading aimlessly up and down the main streets. Cafés and bars fall in and out of favour quite rapidly, although one of the most consistently popular is *Anton's* on Antinkatu, where a 10mk cup of coffee comes with a cloudberry liqueur chocolate. *Anton's* also offers a decent lunch, though in the evening it's primarily a place to drink beer. Otherwise, for eating there are numerous fast-food outlets – particularly *grillis*, which tend to serve a local speciality called the *porilainen*, a large thick slice of grilled onion sausage that is served hamburger style in a roll with pickles, ketchup and some chopped onion. If you fancy something more substantial try the excellent *Raatinhuoneen Kellari* in the cellar of the old town hall, the same building as the tourist office. Check out also the all-year spin-off from the jazz festival, the *Jazz-Café*, at Eteläranta 6 on the banks of the Kokemäenjoki.

If you're planning to come here for the **jazz festival**, it's best to have accommodation fixed up at least six months in advance – hotels, hostel and campsite fill very quickly, although the tourist office endeavours to house as much of the overspill as possible in private homes (about 200mk per person) or on mattresses in local schools (100mk). It's easiest to purchase festival **tickets** online at *www.porijazz.fi*, the main festival Web site; alternatively, contact the Pori tourist office. A third of the festival's 150-odd concerts are free, in any case. If you plan to stay the whole week it's best to buy a pass (costing up to 680mk; on sale from the beginning of April). Individual tickets range from 30mk to 220mk for the bigger acts (in 1999 these included Ray Charles, George Clinton, Marianne Faithfull and UB40). During the festival there's a Festival Centre at Pohjoisranta 11, in an old cotton mill on the left-hand side just after you cross the main Pori bridge heading away from the town centre. Here you can buy any tickets that haven't already been sold and pick up festival programmes and information.

The Åland Islands

The **Åland Islands**, all 6000-plus of them, lie scattered between Finland's southwest coast and Sweden. Politically Finnish but culturally Swedish, the islands cling to a weird form of independence, with their own parliament and flag (a red and yellow cross on a blue background). The currency is Finnish but the language is Swedish – which explains why the main and only sizeable town is more commonly known by its Swedish name of **MARIEHAMN** than by the Finnish **Maarianhamina**.

The Ålands (**Ahvenanmaa** in Finnish) were in Swedish hands through the Middle Ages, but, coveted by the Russians on account of their strategic location on the Baltic, they became part of the Russian Grand Duchy of Finland in 1807. When Finland gained independence, the future of the Ålands was referred to the League of Nations (though not before several Åland leaders had been imprisoned in Helsinki on a charge of high treason). As a result, Finnish sovereignty was established, in return for autonomy and complete demilitarization: the Ålanders now regard themselves as a shining example of Nordic co-operation, and living proof that a small state can run its own affairs while being part of a larger one.

The Ålands' ancient history is as interesting as the modern: many Roman coins have been found and there are scores of Viking burial mounds, plus the remains of some of the oldest Finnish churches. The excellent **Åland Museum** (May–Aug daily 10am–4pm, Tues until 8pm; Sept–April Tues–Sun 11am–4pm, Tues also 6–8pm; 15mk) in Mariehamn's Stadshusparken tells the full story, and is complemented by the ship-shaped **Åland Maritime Museum** on Hamngatan (daily: June–Aug 10am–5pm; Sept–May 10am–4pm; 20mk), 1km away at the other end of Storagatan, which celebrates the fact that, despite their insignificant size, the Ålands once had the world's largest fleet of wooden sailing ships.

Smaller local history museums in the Åland's other communities reflect the surprisingly strong regional differences among the islands; it seems the only thing that's shared are the ubiquitous Åland maypoles – which stand most of the year round – and the fact that specific sights generally take a back seat to the various forms of nature. There are, however, several things worth making for. To the northeast of Mariehamn, in Tosarby Sund, are the remains of **Kastelholm**, a fourteenth-century fortress built to consolidate Swedish domination of the Baltic. Strutted through by numerous Swedish monarchs, it was mostly destroyed by fire in the mid-nineteenth century and is now being restored. In summer guided tours run several times a day (20mk) from the gate to the nearby open-air **Jan Karlsgården Museum**. The Russians also set about building a fortress, **Bomarsund**, but before it could be completed the Crimean War broke out and an Anglo-French force stormed the infant castle, reducing it to rubble; just the scattered ramparts remain. Both would-be castles are on the same bus route from Mariehamn.

Elsewhere, you can trace the route of the old **post road**, the only mail link from Stockholm to what was then tsarist St Petersburg. To their long-lasting chagrin, the Åland people were charged with seeing the safe passage of the mail, including taking it across the frozen winter sea – and quite a few died in the process. The major remnant of these times is the nineteenth-century Carl Engel-designed **Post House** in **ECKERÖ**, at the islands' western extremity. Standing on the coast facing Sweden, the building was intended to instil fresh arrivals with awe at their first sight of the mighty Russian empire. Despite retaining its grandeur, it now looks highly incongruous amid the tiny local community.

History besides, the Ålands have sea, sun and beckoning terrain in unlimited quantities – which is precisely their appeal. Nowadays the islands' primary source of income is summer tourists, especially Swedes on day-trips to Mariehamn. Elsewhere the flat and thickly forested islands contain plenty of secluded spots to search out and enjoy.

Practicalities

Ferries from Finland and Sweden (see "Travel Details" p.680) stop in Mariehamn's West Harbour and there's a **tourist office** a few minutes away at Storagatan 11 (June–Aug daily 9am–6pm; Sept–May Mon–Sat 10am–4pm; ☎018/27 300), which can provide the latest details regarding travel and accommodation. You're going to have a hard time finding **accommodation** if you turn up in summer on spec and without a tent: there are no official youth hostels on the islands and, although there are a number of cheapish guesthouses, some of which offer hostel-type facilities, these fill quickly. If you're at a loose end in Mariehamn, try *Kronan* at Neptunigatan 52 (☎018/12 617; ②), or *Kvarnberget*, Parkgatan 28 (same phone number; ①). The wise option, though, is to camp: there are plentiful **campsites** (in isolated areas you should be able to camp rough with no problems) and a fairly thorough **bus service** covering the main islands. **Cycling** is a sound alternative to the buses, offering not only more freedom but also rental rates slightly cheaper than on the mainland. Most of the islands not linked by road bridge can be reached by small and often free local ferries. If you're feeling lazy, or don't have much time, get a feel of the place by taking one of the **guided bus tours** that leave Mariehamn most weekdays from June to August. They cost 60mk, and last a few hours – check schedules with the tourist office.

travel details

Trains
Helsinki to: Espoo (30 daily; 30min); Järvenpää (38 daily; 30min); Jyväskylä (9 daily; 4hr); Kajaani (4 daily; 7hr 30min); Kuopio (7 daily; 5hr 30min); Lahti (13 daily; 1hr 30min); Luoma (30 daily; 37min); Mikkeli (7 daily; 3hr 30min); Oulu (7 daily; 6hr 30min); Rovaniemi (4 daily; 9hr 30min); Tampere (19 daily; 2hr); Turku (12 daily; 2hr).

Pori to: Tampere (7 daily; 1hr 40min).

Turku to: Helsinki (12 daily; 2hr); Tampere (8 daily; 1hr 50min).

Buses
Hamina to: Virolahti (2–3 daily; 35–55min).

Helsinki to: Joensuu (4 daily; 8hr 55min); Jyväskylä (8 daily; 5hr); Kotka (7–9 daily; 1hr 30min–2hr 10min); Lahti (26 daily; 1hr 30min); Mikkeli (8 daily; 4hr); Porvoo (18 daily; 1hr); Tampere (16 daily; 3hr); Tapiola (4 daily; 35min); Turku (21 daily; 2hr 30min).

Kotka to: Hamina (3 daily; 35min); Helsinki (7–9 daily; 1hr 30min–2hr 10min); Porvoo (8–10 daily; 40min).

Mariehamn to: Bomarsund (5 daily; 30min); Eckerö (5 daily; 45min); Kastelholm (5 daily; 30min).

Pori to: Rauma (4 daily; 45min); Turku (7 daily; 2hr).

Porvoo to: Helsinki (18 daily; 1hr); Kotka (8–10 daily; 40min); Loviissa (8–10 daily; 1hr); Pyhtää (8–10 daily; 1hr 40min).

Rauma to: Pori (4 daily; 45min); Turku (10 daily; 1hr 30min).

Turku to: Helsinki (21 daily; 2hr 30min); Pori (7 daily; 2hr); Rauma (10 daily; 1hr 30min).

Ferries
Helsinki to: Mariehamn (2 daily; 9hr 45min).

Mariehamn to: Helsinki (2 daily; 9hr 45min); Turku (4 daily; 5hr 20min).

Turku to: Mariehamn (4 daily; 5hr 20min).

International trains
Helsinki to: Moscow (1 daily; 16hr 30min); St Petersburg (2 daily; 10hr).

International buses
Hamina to: St Petersburg (1 daily; 5hr 30min); Viipuri (1 daily; 2hr 30min).

International ferries
Helsinki to: Stockholm (2 daily; 15hr); Tallinn (3–4 daily; 3–5hr).

Mariehamn to: Kappellskär (3 daily; 7hr); Stockholm (Mon–Thurs 3 daily, Fri–Sun 2 daily; 6hr).

Turku to: Stockholm (4 daily; 12hr).

CHAPTER SIXTEEN

THE LAKE REGION

T he **Lake Region** is unique in Finland, and indeed in Scandinavia. Extensive lake chains, chiefly the Päijanne and Saimaa systems, consume a third of the region, particularly its easternmost part, near the border with Russia. Each chain features countless bays, inlets and islands, interspersed with dense forests. The settlements that flourished here grew up around the paper mills, which used natural waterways and purpose-built canals to transport timber to pulping factories powered by gushing rapids.

Wherever you go, water is never far away, further pacifying an already tranquil and verdant landscape. Even **Tampere**, Finland's major industrial city, is likeable as much for its lakeside setting as for its cultural delights. It's also the most accessible of the region's cities, being on the railway line between Helsinki and the north. Also reachable by train from Helsinki, **Lahti** comes into its own as a winter sports resort; during summer the town is comparatively lifeless. Diminutive **Mikkeli** has more character, and makes a good stopover en route to the atmospheric eastern part of the Lake Region, where slender ridges furred with conifers link the few sizeable areas of land. Its regional centre, **Savonlinna**, stretches delectably across several islands, and boasts a superbly preserved medieval castle. To get a sense of Karelian culture (for more on which, see p.625) visit **Joensuu**, or **Lappeenranta** or the city of **Kuopio**, three towns where many displaced Karelians settled after World War II. In the heart of the region lies **Jyväskylä**, whose wealth of buildings by Alvar Aalto draws modern architecture buffs to what is otherwise a typically sleepy town. Down-to-earth **Iisalmi** is effectively a bridge between the Lake Region and the rougher, less watery terrain further north.

Unless you want total solitude (which is easily attained), it's best to spend a few days in the larger towns and make shorter forays into the more thinly populated areas. Although the western Lake Region is mostly well served by **trains**, rail connections to – and within – the eastern part are awkward and infrequent. With daily services between the main towns and less frequent ones to the villages, **buses** are handier for getting around. Slow, expensive **ferries** also link the main lakeside towns, while practically every community runs short pleasure cruises, but to really explore the countryside, you'll need to rent a **car** or **bicycle**.

ACCOMMODATION PRICE CODES

The hotels listed in this chapter have been graded according to the following price bands, based on the cost of the **least expensive double room in summer**. However, many hotels offer summer and/or weekend discounts, and in these instances we've given two grades, covering both the regular and the discounted rate.

① Under 275mk	② 275–350mk	③ 350–450mk
④ 450–550mk	⑤ 550–750mk	⑥ Over 750mk

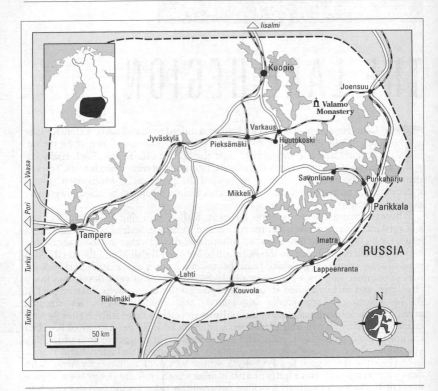

Tampere and around

"Here it was as natural to approve of the factories as in Mecca one would the mosques," wrote John Sykes of **TAMPERE** in the 1960s and you soon see what he meant. Although Tampere is Finland's biggest manufacturing centre and Scandinavia's largest inland city, it's a highly scenic place, with leafy avenues, sculpture-filled parks and two sizeable lakes. The factories that line the Tammerkoski rapids in the heart of the city actually accentuate its appeal, their chimneys standing as bold monuments to Tampere's past – it's no coincidence that the town is known colloquially as Finland's Manchester. Its rapid growth began just over a century ago, when Tsar Alexander I abolished taxes on local trade, encouraging the Scotsman James Finlayson to open a textile factory here, drawing labour from rural areas where traditional crafts were in decline. Metalwork and shoe factories soon followed, their owners paternalistically supplying culture to the workforce by promoting a vigorous local arts scene. Free outdoor rock and jazz concerts, lavish theatrical productions and one of the best modern art collections in Finland maintain such traditions to this day.

Arrival, information and accommodation

Almost everything of consequence is within the central section of the city, bordered on two sides by the lakes Näsijärvi and Pyhäjärvi. The main streets run off either side of

Hämeenkatu, which leads directly from the **train station** across Hämeensilta – the bridge over Tammerkoski, famous for its weighty bronze sculptures by Wäino Aaltonen, representing four characters from local folklore. Although there's little call to use local **buses**, most routes begin from the terminal on Hämeenkatu. At Hämeenkatu 1 there's a useful late-opening **exchange** office (Mon–Fri 8am–7pm, Sat 9am–5pm, Sun 10am–4pm, closed Sun Sept–May). Tampere's **tourist office**, Verkatehtaankatu 2 (June–Aug Mon–Fri 8.30am–8pm, Sat 8.30am–6pm, Sun 11am–6pm; Sept–May Mon–Fri 8.30am–5pm; ☎03/3146 6800, fax 3146 6463, *www.tampere.fi*), hands out copies of the excellent, free *Key to Tampere* guide and also offers free Internet access. From June to August they also organize two-hour sightseeing tours (daily at 2pm; 40mk).

Accommodation

Budget travellers are catered for best during the summer, when both the main **youth hostels** are open. *NNKY Hostel* (the Finnish YWCA, open to both sexes) stands opposite the cathedral at Tuomiokirkkokatu 12A (☎03/254 4020, fax 254 4022; June to late Aug); *Uimahallin Maja*, centrally located at Pirkankatu 10–12 (☎03/222 9460, fax 222 9940), 1km from the train station, is a superb, cheap hotel-style hostel open all year, with rooms sleeping one to four people (50mk per person, extra for bedding), plus dorm beds. Of Tampere's regular **hotels**, the *Victoria*, Itsenäisyydenkatu 1 (☎03/242 5111, fax 242 5100; ④/③), and *Sokos Hotel Villa*, Sumeliuksenkatu 14 (☎03/262 6267, fax 262 6268; ⑤/③), are both handily placed and well priced, or an early booking might get you some luxury beside the lake at the *Rosendahl*, Pyynikintie 13 (☎03/244 1111, fax 223 3375; ⑤/④), a couple of kilometres from the city centre. As usual, however, the least expensive lakeside option is a **campsite** – *Härmälä* (☎03/265 1355; mid-May to late Aug; bookings at other times of year on ☎09/6138 3210), 5km to the south and accessible by bus #1. Tents can be pitched for 90mk, while cabins for three people cost 170mk, those sleeping five 310mk.

The City

Short, broad streets make central Tampere very easy to explore. From the train station, Hämeenkatu runs across the Tammerkoski into the heart of the city, and almost everything of interest lies within a few minutes' walk of this busy thoroughfare. You'll need to cross back over the river (most easily done by following Satakunnankatu), however, to reach Tampere's historic cathedral – and to get the best view of the Finlayson factory, on which the city's fortunes were founded.

Hämeenkatu and north

Walking the length of Hämeenkatu from the train station leaves you in front of the upwardly thrusting neo-Gothic **Aleksanterin kirkko** (daily: May–Aug 10am–5pm; Sept–April 11am–3pm). With its riot of knobbly ceiling decorations, the effect inside is something like an ecclesiastical train station, with an unusually unpleasant artexed altar. To the left, following the line of greenery south down Hämeenpuisto, is the Tampere Workers' Theatre and, in the same building, the **Lenin Museum** (Mon–Fri 9am–6pm, Sat & Sun 11am–4pm; 15mk). After the abortive 1905 revolution in Russia, Lenin lived in Finland and attended the Tampere conferences, held in what is now the museum. It was here that he first encountered Stalin, although this is barely mentioned in the displays, one of which concentrates on Lenin himself, the other on his relationship with Finland. For a detailed explanation, borrow the English-language brochure from reception.

Several blocks north of Hämeenkatu, the Amuri district was built during the 1880s to house Finlayson's workers. Some thirty homes have been preserved as the

Workers' Museum of Amuri at Makasiininkatu 12 (mid-May to mid-Sept Tues–Sun 10am–6pm; 20mk; during the rest of the year only the museum shop is open, same times), a simple but affecting place that records the family life of working people over a hundred-year period. In each home is a description of the inhabitants and their jobs, and authentic articles from the relevant periods – from beds and tables to family photos, newspapers and biscuit packets.

Just around the corner at Puutarhakatu 34 is the **Art Museum of Tampere** (Tues–Sun 10am–6pm; 20mk, 40mk during special exhibitions; guided tours by arrangement on ☎03/3146 6580), whose first floor holds powerful if staid temporary exhibitions featuring Finnish and international artists; the large basement galleries are filled with contemporary local work. If you're looking for older Finnish art, head instead for the far superior **Heikka Art Museum**, a few minutes' walk away at Pirkankatu 6 (Wed & Thurs 3–6pm, Sun noon–3pm; other times by arrangement ☎03/212 3973; 20mk). Kustaa Heikka was a gold- and silversmith whose professional skills and business acumen made him a local big shot around 1900. The art collection he bequeathed to Tampere reflects his interest in traditional lifestyles; borrow a catalogue from reception, since most pieces are identified only by numbers. Amongst the most notable work (including sketches by Gallen-Kallela and Helene Schjerfbeck) are two of Heikka's own creations: a delicately wrought brooch marking the completion of his apprenticeship, and a finely detailed bracelet with which he celebrated becoming a master craftsman. Well worth the diver-

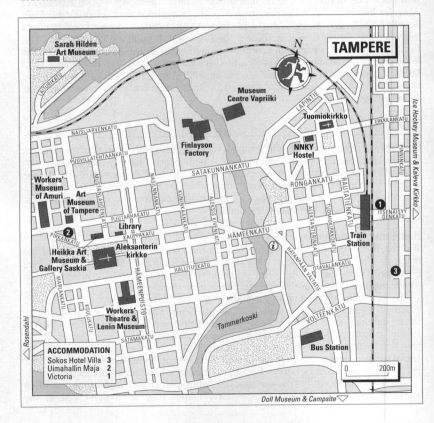

sion, and free too, is the next-door **Gallery Saskia** (daily noon–6pm), showing intriguing new work that you won't catch elsewhere.

Nearby stands the **Tampere Library**, Pirkankatu 2 (June–Aug Mon–Sat 9.30am–7pm; Sept–May Mon–Fri 9.30am–8pm, Sat 9.30am–3pm), an astounding feat of user-friendly modern architecture. The work of Reimi and Raili Pietilä (who also designed the epic Kalevala kirkko – see p.686), and finished in 1986, the library's curving walls give it a warm, cosy feel; believe it or not, the building's shape was inspired by a certain type of grouse (a stuffed specimen of which sits in the reception area). Strolling around is the best way to take in the many small, intriguing features, and will eventually lead you up to the top-floor café, which gives a good view of the cupola, deliberately set eleven degrees off the vertical – to match the off-centre pivot of the earth. In the basement of the library, with its own entrance at Hämeenpuisto 20, **Moomin Valley** (June–Aug Mon–Fri 9am–5pm, Sat & Sun 10am–6pm; Sept–April Tues–Fri 9am–5pm, Sat & Sun 10am–6pm; 20mk) re-creates with dolls and 3-D displays scenes from the incredibly popular children's books by Finnish author Tove Jansson.

The Näsijärvi lakeside

Just north of Tampere's central grid-plan streets, the tremendous **Sara Hildén Art Museum** (daily 11am–6pm; 20mk), built on the shores of Näsijärvi, displays Tampere's premier modern art collection by means of changing exhibitions. The museum is on the other side of Paasikiventie from Amuri (take a #16, or the summer-only #4 bus from the town centre or train station).

Occupying the same waterside strip as the Hildén collection is **Särkänniemi**, a tourist complex incorporating a dolphinarium, aquarium, planetarium and observation tower. Seen from the tower – an unmistakeable element of Tampere's skyline – the city seems insignificant compared to the trees and lakes that stretch to the horizon. The rapids that cut through them can be identified from afar by the factory chimneys alongside. The tower is open from 10am to 8pm during summer, and there's a 15mk admission charge, waived if you're using the tower restaurant; the other diversions cost 20–30mk apiece and are usually crowded with families. To make a day of it, buy the 140mk Särkänniemi Passport, valid for all parts of the complex. There's a café here too, serving uninspired pizza and quiche.

The Cathedral and around

Cross to the eastern side of the Tammer River along Satakunnankatu and you'll not only see – foaming below the bridge – the rapids that powered the **Finlayson Factory**, but also the factory itself, still standing to the north and now home to several crafts workshops.

Immediately ahead, the **Tuomiokirkko** stands in a grassy square, a picturesque cathedral in the National Romantic style, designed by Lars Sonck and finished in 1907 (daily: May–Aug 9am–6pm; Sept–April 11am–3pm). It's most remarkable for the gorily symbolic frescoes by Hugo Simberg – particularly the *Garden of Death*, where skeletons happily water plants, and *The Wounded Angel*, showing two boys carrying a bleeding angel through a Tampere landscape – which caused an ecclesiastical outcry when unveiled. So did the viper (a totem of evil) which he placed amongst the angel wings on the ceiling; Simberg retorted that evil could lurk anywhere – including a church.

Out from the centre

To learn more about Tampere's origins, visit the **Museum Centre Vapriiki** (Tues–Sun 11am–5pm; 10mk), housed in a converted factory just across the river from the great Finlayson factory. Its most interesting section deals with the early twentieth century – a turbulent time for both Tampere and Finland. As an industrial town with militant workers, Tampere instigated a general strike against the Russification of Finland, filling the streets with demonstrators and painting over the Cyrillic names on trilingual street signs. After independence the city became a Social Democratic stronghold, and one ruthlessly dealt with by the right-wing government following the civil war of 1918 – yet the municipal administration remains amongst the most left-leaning in Finland. A brand new permanent exhibition is due to open in late 2000 – contact the tourist office for details.

Away to the east of the centre, Itsenäisyydenkatu runs uphill behind the train station to meet the vast concrete folds of the **Kaleva kirkko** (daily: May–Aug 9am–6pm; Sept–April 11am–3pm). Built in 1966, it was a belated addition to the neighbouring **Kaleva estate**, which was heralded in the 1950s as an outstanding example of high-density housing. Though initially stunning, the church's interior lacks the subtlety of the city library, despite being designed by the same team of Reimi and Raili Pietilä – who this time based their plan on a fish.

Continuing past the church, follow the signs for *Jäähalli* (Ice Hall) to the ice hockey stadium just off the city ring road (or take bus #18, #19, #25 or #27 from the centre). The **Ice Hockey Museum** here at Keltinkatu 2 (Tues–Thurs noon–4pm, 1hr before matches, or by special request on ☎03/212 4200 or 050/561 1195; 10mk), accords due honour to the local teams Ilves and Tappora, which have won more national championships than all of Finland's other teams combined. Other exhibits include a vast collection of hockey sticks from around the world, and a white puck used during the immediate postwar period, when artificial ice was unavailable and matches were played on the blue ice of frozen lakes.

Eating

Tampere boasts an eclectic range of restaurants and cafés to suit most pockets. Several places in the *Koskikeskus* shopping mall, Hatanpään valtatie 1, offer cheap lunchtime specials, but, as usual, the cheapest **places to eat** are the student mensas – in the university at the end of Yliopistonkatu, just over the railway line from the city centre – where full meals can cost as little as 15mk with a student card, 20mk without. There are all the usual pizza places: *Rosso* has two outlets, one just across the bridge on Hämeenkatu and another on the pedestrianized Kuninkaankatu. For quiet posing, *Café Strindberg* opposite the train station serves fine cakes, pies and excellent filled baguettes (40mk), as well as breakfasts and more substantial lunches. For carnivores, *Tiiliholvi*, Kauppakatu 10, is known for its good but pricey steaks, while *Henricks*, Satamakatu 7, serves up French cuisine in a more intimate atmosphere. If you want to try a Tampere speciality, head for the Laukontori open-air market, by the rapids, where the local black sausage, *mustamakkara*, is sold.

There are numerous **supermarkets** at which to stock up on provisions. Two central options are the big Sokos store at Hämeenkatu 21 or Anttila, Puutarhakatu 10. Slightly further out, and cheaper, are City Market, Sotilaankatu 11, and Sokos Market at Sammonkatu 73. There's also a large **kauppahalli** at Hämeenkatu 19 (Mon–Thurs 8am–5pm, Fri 8am–5.30pm, Sat 8am–2pm), and the open-air markets at Laukontori (Mon–Fri 6am–2pm, Sat 6am–1pm), Keskustori (first Mon of month 6am–6pm) and Tammelantori (Mon–Fri 6am–2pm, Sat 6am–1pm).

Drinking and entertainment

Tampere at night is very much alive and buzzing, with numerous late-night bars, cafés and clubs. One of the most popular **pubs** is the Irish *Dublinin Ovet* ("Doors of Dublin") at Kauppakatu 16, though the best place for Guinness is in fact *Pikilinna* on Pinninkatu, to the east of the city centre, a small football fans' pub with an ambience all its own. Another summertime favourite is *Falls*, down by the rapids. For live **jazz**, try the laid-back *Tullikamari*, a nightclub set in an old customs house behind the train station on

Itsenasyydenkatu, or *Paapankapakka,* a swing-style jazz club with up-and-coming bands almost opposite the tourist office. *Café Europa* on Aleksanterinkatu is more of a meeting place than an all-night hangout, though it does have live music, while on the same street, the extremely popular rock disco *Doris* in the basement of *Restaurant Katupoika* is the place where locals go to drink beer and dance till morning. On warm nights the locals head out to the Pyynikki area, a natural ridge on the edge of Tampere, beside Pyhäjärvi. Tickets for the **Pyynikki Summer Theatre** cost around 120mk, but it's worth trekking out just to look at the revolving auditorium which slowly rotates the audience around during performances, blending the surrounding woods, rocks and water into the show's scenery.

There are a couple of good **gay bars**, the friendliest and most laid-back in the country being *Mixei* on Otavalankatu 3. Entrance is just 10mk and – unusually for Finland – there's no compulsory cloakroom charge. The town also possesses Finland's only **lesbian bar**, *Nice Place,* Hämeenpuisto 29 – though open to anyone, the customers are usually women relaxing over coffee.

Around Tampere – and moving on

Half an hour from Tampere on the busy rail line to Helsinki, **HÄMEENLINNA** is revered both as the birthplace of Sibelius and as Finland's oldest inland town. The major attraction is **Häme Castle** (daily May to mid-Aug 10am–6pm; mid-Aug–April 10am–4pm; 20mk), the sturdy thirteenth-century castle from which the town takes its name. Next comes the **Sibelius Childhood Home** (daily: May–Aug 10am–4pm; Sept–April noon–4pm; 10mk) at Hallituskatu 11, where the great composer was born, now reverentially restored to how it was during the first years of his life. A few blocks away at Viipuriintie 2, the **Art Museum** (Tues–Sun noon–6pm, Thurs until 8pm; 10mk) musters a mundane collection of minor works by major Finnish names, among them Järnefelt, Gallen-Kalela and Halonen.

Seeing all this won't take long, and any spare hours are better spent in the outlying area of **Hattula**, roughly 5km from the centre of Hämeenlinna. The local **Hattulan kirkko** (daily May to mid-Aug 11am–5pm; other times by appointment on ☎03/672 3383; 15mk) is probably the finest medieval church in Finland – outwardly plain, with an interior totally covered by 180 sixteenth-century frescoes of biblical scenes. En route to the church, a combined **youth hostel** (☎03/682 8560; May to mid-Aug) and **campsite** (same number; June–Aug) face Hämeenlinna across the river, 4km from the town centre.

Moving on from Tampere

Tampere has excellent **train and bus links** to the rest of Finland. To reach the rest of the Lake Region, however, there are two main choices. Aiming for Jyväskylä (simplest by train) also puts you within comparatively easy reach of Varkaus, Joensuu and Kuopio. Alternatively, heading for Lahti (to which there are direct buses; by train change at Hyvinkää) makes more sense if you want to press on to Mikkeli, or see more of the eastern Lake Region.

Jyväskylä

JYVÄSKYLÄ is the most low-key and provincial of the main Lake Region towns, despite the industrial section that takes up one end and a big university which consumes the other – though the latter does provide something of a youthful feel. Jyväskylä also has more than its fair share of buildings by **Alvar Aalto**. The legendary architect grew up here and opened his first office in the town in 1923, and his handiwork – a collection of buildings spanning his entire career – litters the place.

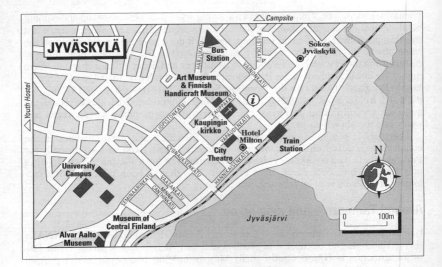

After some minor projects, Aalto left Jyväskylä in 1927 for fame, fortune and Helsinki, but returned in the 1950s to work on the teacher-training college. By the 1970s this had grown into the **Jyväskylä University**, whose large campus halts traffic where the main road gives way to a series of public footpaths, leading to a park and sports ground. Although Aalto died before his ambitious plan for an Administration and Cultural Centre was complete, the scheme is still under construction along Vapaudenkatu. Across the road from the (perhaps intentionally) uninspiring police station – unveiled in 1970 – stands a **city theatre** resembling a scaled-down version of Helsinki's Finlandia.

Two of the town's most important museums are situated close together on the hill running down from the university towards the edge of the lake, Jyväsjärvi. At the request of the town authorities rather than through vanity, Aalto built the **Alvar Aalto Museum** at Alvar Aallon Katu 7 (Tues–Sun 11am–6pm, Aug until 8pm; 30mk, free on Fri). The architect's best works are obviously out on the streets, making this collection of plans, photos and models seem rather superfluous. But the Aalto-designed furniture makes partial amends. The first floor hosts temporary art exhibitions and the ground floor has a pleasant if unexciting café. Aalto also contributed to the exterior of the nearby **Keski-Suomen Museo** (Museum of Central Finland; Tues–Sun 11am–6pm, Aug until 8pm; 20mk, free on Fri), which contains two separate exhibitions: one devoted to Middle Finland – well designed but with no English translations – and the other representing each decade of the twentieth century through the car numberplates, music and kitchen gadgetry of the day. The collection of room interiors is worth the visit alone.

Jyväskylä also hosts an impressive **Art Museum** (Tues–Sun 11am–6pm, Aug until 8pm; 20mk, free on Fri) at Kauppakatu 25 which is split into two exhibition sites. The main site houses the permanent collection of the Ester and Jalo Sihtola Fine Arts Foundation, plus that of the Association of Finnish Printmakers. The site next door houses temporary exhibitions reflecting the latest trends in modern art from Finland and the rest of the world. In summer 2000 both the **Finnish Handicraft Museum**, with displays ranging from bell-making to spectrolite jewellery, and the **National Costume Centre**, which holds the Finnish National Costume Council's collection will be moving here too. Also worth a look is the nineteenth-century **Kaupungin kirkko**

(June–Aug Mon–Fri 11am–6pm, Sat & Sun 11am–2pm; Sept–May Wed–Sun 11am–2pm), opposite the tourist office. The church was the centrepiece of Jyväskylä life a century ago, but declined in importance as the town gained new suburbs and other churches. Despite recent restoration – when the interior was repainted in its original pale yellow and green – the church looks authentically dingy.

Practicalities

From the train and bus stations, right in the centre, it's a short walk to the **tourist office**, in a beautiful wooden building at Asemakatu 6 (June–Aug Mon–Fri 8am–6pm, Sat & Sun 9am–3pm; Sept–May Mon–Fri 9am–5pm, Sat 9am–2pm; ☎014/624 903, fax 624 904, *www.jkl.fi*), which can supply a useful free leaflet on the local buildings designed by Aalto. There's free **Internet** access in the pubic library at Vapaudenkatu 39–41 (June–Aug Mon–Fri 11am–7pm; Sept–May Mon–Fri 11am–8pm, Sat 11am–3pm), though you'll need to book in advance. For **accommodation**, the central, family-run *Hotel Milton*, Hannikaisenkatu 27–29 (☎014/213 411, fax 631 927; ③), is a good choice, right by the train station, while for a bit more luxury, try the *Sokos Jyväskylä* at Vapaudenkatu 73 (☎014/330 3000, fax 616 996; ⑥/④) – some rooms have their own private saunas. The local **youth hostel**, *Laajari* (☎014/624 885, fax 624 888), is a state-of-the-art affair, 4km from the centre, at Laajavuorentie 15 – take bus #25 from Vapaudenkatu. The nearest **campsite**, *Tuomiojärven* (☎014/624 895; June–Aug), is 2km north off the E4 – take Puistokatu and then continue along to Taulumäentie 47, or take bus #8.

Eating options veer from the pizza establishments along the main streets to the more upscale *Kissanviikset* ("The Cat's Whiskers") at Puistokatu 3, which serves some sizeable and just-about-affordable fish dishes at lunchtime. The most popular place is the light and airy *Sohwi* at Vaasankatu 21, which doubles as a tapas bar. Among the cafés, *Kahvila Ruustinna* at Kauppakatu 11 serves deliciously calorific cakes, while *Book Café Beckers* at Seminaarinkatu 28 occupies a maze of old wooden carved buildings holding art galleries and a bookshop.

The university hosts events in and out of term-time, so it's always worth checking the student mensas for posters. The neighbourhood around the university is also a focus for the town's **nightlife**, such as it is. Two notable haunts are *Ilokivi*, Keskussairaalantie 2, often featuring art exhibitions and live bands; and the smoky *Ruthin ravintola*, Seminaarinkatu 19, where members of the philosophy and politics departments get down to chess and/or hard drinking. *Nice Time*, at Kauppakatu 30, is a more central hangout with its own microbrewery; the relaxed bar *Freetime* is just a couple of doors away.

There is quite a strong **gay** scene in town; for information on local gay events, call in at SETA, Yliopistonkatu 26 (☎014/310 0660).

Lahti

LAHTI doesn't know if it's a Lake Region town or a Helsinki suburb. Its entire growth took place in the twentieth-century (mostly since Alvar Aalto opened several furniture factories, which kept him going between architectural commissions) and although it's now the major transport junction between the Lake Region and the south, it lacks any lake-area atmosphere, while local cultural life is diminished by the relative proximity of Helsinki. Lahti's one compensation is its status as a **winter sports** centre of international renown: three enormous ski jumps hang over the town, and there's a feeling of biding time when summer grass rather than winter snow covers their slopes.

Unless you're here to ski, Lahti isn't a place you'll need or want to linger in – the town can easily be covered in a day. Head first for the **observation platform** on the highest ski jump (May–Sept daily 9am–6pm; chairlift open same days 10.30am–5.30pm; 20mk), whose location is unmistakeable. From such a dizzying altitude the lakes and forests around Lahti stretch dreamily into the distance, and the large swimming pool below resembles a puddle (when frozen in winter it's used as a landing zone).

The only structures matching the ski jumps for height are the twin radio masts atop Radiomäki hill, between the train station (a 15min walk away) and the town centre. Steep pathways wind uphill towards the **Radio Ja TV Museo** (Radio and Television Museum; Mon–Fri 10am–5pm, Sat & Sun 11am–5pm; 20mk), inside the original transmitting station at the base of one of the masts. Here, two big rooms are packed with bulky Marconi valves, crystal sets, antiquated sound-effect discs, room-sized amplifiers and intriguing curios. Look out for the Pikku Hitler – the German-made "little Hitler", a wartime portable radio that forms an uncanny facsimile of the dictator's face.

At Radiomäki's foot, the distinctive red brickwork of Eliel Saarinen's **Town Hall** injects some style into the concrete blocks that make central Lahti so dull and uniform. Built in 1912, many of its Art Nouveau features were considered immensely daring at the time, and although most of the originals were destroyed in World War II, careful refurbishment has re-created much of Saarinen's design. Viewable during office hours, the interior is definitely worth seeing. Lahti's other notable building is at the far end of Mariankatu, which cuts through the town centre from the town hall: the **Ristinkirkko** (daily 10am–3pm), whose white roof slopes down from the bell tower in imaginative imitation of the local ski jumps. Interestingly, this was the last church to be designed by Alvar Aalto: he died during its construction and the final work was overseen by his wife. Outside, Wäinö Aaltonen produced one of his most discreetly emotive sculptures to mark the war graves in the cemetery.

By now you've more or less exhausted Lahti, although Hämeenkatu, running parallel to the far more hectic Aleksanterinkatu, contains a number of little art galleries owned by local artists and a few secondhand bookshops. The **Art Museum** (Mon–Fri 10am–5pm, Sat & Sun 11am–5pm; 20mk), just around the corner at Vesijärvenkatu 11, exhibits nineteenth- and twentieth-century works, most notably by Gallen-Kallela and Edelfelt.

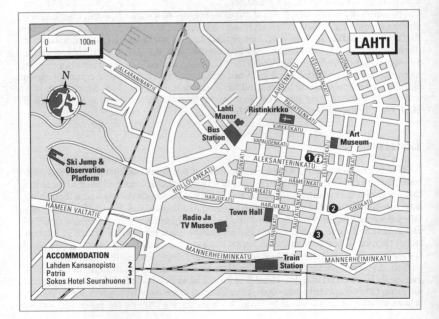

Finally, near the hazardous web-like junction by the bus station is the wooden nineteenth-century **Lahti Manor**, hidden behind a line of trees. Now a historical museum (Mon–Fri 10am–5pm, Sat & Sun 11am–5pm; 20mk), it contains regional paraphernalia, numerous Finnish medals and coins, plus an unexpected hoard of French and Italian paintings and furniture.

Practicalities

The **tourist office** is at Aleksanterinkatu 16 (June–Aug Mon–Fri 9am–5pm, Sat & Sun 10am–4pm; Sept–May Mon–Fri 9am–5pm; ☎03/814 4566 or 814 4568, fax 814 4564). The library (Mon–Fri 10am–6pm, Sat 10am–3pm), at Kirkkokatu 31, provides reservable free **Internet** access. There are some good budget **accommodation** options in Lahti. A decent choice is the *Patria* hostel at Vesijärvenkatu 3 (☎03/782 3783, fax 782 3793), near the train station, which also has double rooms. In summer, try the excellent *Kesähotelli Lahden Kansanopisto* (☎03/878 1181, fax 878 1234; June to mid-Aug; ①) in a very central position at Harjukatu 46. For more luxury the *Sokos Hotel Seurahuone*, Aleksanterinkatu 14, boasts a sauna and pool, and TV and video in all rooms (☎03/85 111; ④). About 4km to the north of Lahti at **Mukkula** is a lakeside **campsite** with cottages (☎03/874 1442; June–Aug; 200mk), reached directly by bus #30 from the bus station at the end of Aleksanterinkatu.

Low-priced **eating** options include *Grilli Serdika* at Hämeenkatu 21, which claims to be the cheapest steakhouse in Lahti, while the best place for cakes and pastries is the central *Café Sinuhe*, Mariankatu 21. You'll find the larger **supermarkets** clustered along Savonkatu. Though hardly remarkable for its nightlife, Lahti holds its own compared to smaller towns in the Lake Region. For an evening **drink**, try the lively *Memphis* in the *Sokos Hotel Seurahuone* (see above), or *Diva*, at Hämeenkatu 16. The terrace-style café on Mariankatu offers a more refined venue.

Train and bus connections onwards from Lahti are fairly good. Mikkeli, to the north, is the sensible target if you're ultimately making for Kuopio, while Lappeenranta is a better destination if you're keen to discover the small towns and glorious scenery of the eastern Lake Region.

Mikkeli

In 1986 a Helsinki bank robber chose the market square in **MIKKELI** as the place in which to blow up himself, his car and his hostage. This, the most violent event seen in Finland for decades, was perhaps an echo of Mikkeli's blood-spattered past. In prehistoric times the surrounding plains were battlegrounds for feuding tribes from east and west, the Finnish Infantry has a long association with the town, and it was from Mikkeli that General Mannerheim conducted the campaign against the Soviet Union in the Winter War.

Military matters are a strong local feature, but you don't need to be a bloodthirsty warmonger to find interest in the town's military collections – the insights they provide into Finland's recent history can be fascinating. More generally, Mikkeli lacks the heavy industry you'll find in some Lake Region communities, functioning instead as a district market town (the daily crowds and activity within its kauppatori seem out of all proportion to its size), while sporting a handsome cathedral and a noteworthy art collection.

The military museums

Older Finns visiting Mikkeli tend to make a beeline for the office used by Mannerheim, preserved as the **Headquarters Museum**, Päämajankatu 1–3 (mid-May to Aug daily

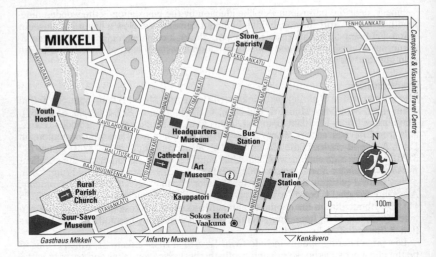

10am–5pm; rest of the year by appointment only ☎015/194 2424; 10mk). It's not so much the exhibits – the centrepiece is Mannerheim's desk, holding his spectacles and favourite cigars – but the fact that the Winter War, which effectively prevented a Soviet invasion of Finland in 1939 (see p.632), was waged and won from this very room that gives the museum its significance. An adjoining room has photo displays and a short slide show about Mannerheim's days in Mikkeli.

Mannerheim spent some of those days in the **Mikkeli Club**, a cross between a speakeasy and a masonic lodge, which still exists, occupying what is now part of the Sokos department store on Hallituskatu, facing the kauppatori. The club's walls are lined with photos of Mannerheim and his staff, although less prominence is given to the snaps of the Marshal riding with Hitler during the Führer's birthday visit (these are in an unmarked folder usually lying on a side table). The club is not strictly open to the public but the tourist office (see opposite) can arrange for interested individuals to be shown around.

A few minutes' walk south from the town centre is the **Infantry Museum**, Jääkärinkatu 6–8 (mid-May to mid-June & mid-Aug to mid-Sept Tues–Sun 10am–5pm; mid-June to mid-Aug daily 10am–5pm; mid-Sept to mid-May Wed, Sat & Sun noon–5pm; 15mk), which records the key armed struggles that marked Finland's formative years as an independent nation. Assorted rifles, artillery pieces and maps of troops' movements provide the factual context, but it's the scores of frontline photos and display cases of troops' letters and lucky charms that reveal the human story. A second, substantially less interesting, section of the museum concentrates chiefly on the Finnish role in the United Nations Peace-Keeping Force.

The rest of the town

Raised in 1897, Mikkeli's Gothic Revival **Tuomiokirkko** (daily: June–Aug 10am–6pm; Sept–May 10–11am) sits primly on a small hill in the middle of Hallituskatu. Inside, Pekka Halonen's 1899 altarpiece attracts the eye, a radiant Christ against a dark, brooding background. Take a close look, too, at Antii Salmenlinna's stained-glass windows and you'll spot depictions of three Finnish towns (Viipuri, Sortavala and Käkisalmi) ceded to Russia after World War II.

Opposite the cathedral, the excellent **Art Museum**, at Ristimäenkatu 5A (Tues–Fri & Sun noon–6pm, Sat noon–3pm; 15mk), stages some stimulating temporary exhibitions of the latest Finnish art and has two permanent displays of artworks bequeathed to the town. The Martti Airio Collection is a forceful selection of early twentieth-century Finnish Impressionism and Expressionism – Tyko Saalinen's *Young American Woman* and *On the Visit* are particularly striking. The museum's other benefactor was the Mikkeli-born sculptor Johannes Haapasalo, who left nearly three hundred finished works and over a thousand sketches to the museum. One of Haapasalo's better works can be seen beside the cathedral: called *Despair*, it marks the graves of Mikkeli's Civil War dead.

If you've ever wondered how vergers in eighteenth-century Finland kept their church congregations awake, the answer (a big stick) can be seen at the tiny **Stone Sacristy**, to the north at Porrassalmenkatu 32a (July daily 11am–5pm; other times by appointment on ☎015/194 2424; free); the church which the sacristy served was demolished in 1776. Several other historic items from the Mikkeli diocese sit in the room, a wooden pulpit, a "shame bench" (for women deemed unvirtuous) and a wood-framed Bible among them.

A fifteen-minute walk from the town centre along Otavankatu (easily combined with a visit to the Infantry Museum) leads to the **Rural Parish Church** (mid-June to mid-Aug Mon–Fri 10am–5pm, Sun 11am–5pm), believably claimed to be one of the largest wooden churches in Finland. Size aside, the church is a modest sight, but is a more satisfying time-filler than the small stone building in its grounds which houses the **Suur-Savo Museum** (April–Sept Tues–Sun 11am–3pm, Wed until 6pm; Oct–March Wed 4–6pm, Sun 11am–3pm; free), a hotchpotch of broken clocks, cracked crockery, and even a bent-wheeled penny-farthing bicycle, which purports to be a record of regional life.

Kenkävero and Visulahti

Should the urge to weave, sew or create something in clay suddenly strike, **Kenkävero**, Pursialenkatu 6 (June–Aug Sun–Fri 10am–6pm, Sat 10am–4pm; Sept–May daily 11am–4pm; 20–35mk in summer, 10mk in winter), run by the local handicrafts association, has several workshops that can provide the necessary tools and instruction. Even if artistic urges don't stimulate a call, Kenkävero's historical associations might: the workshops occupy the buildings of Finland's oldest vicarage, most of it dating from 1869 – and the main building holds a very nice café. It's just south of the train station.

Another good place to occupy young hands and minds is the less traditional **Visulahti Travel Centre**, 5km from Mikkeli (bus #1) on the road to Kuopio (mid-May to mid-Aug daily 10am–7pm; 15–45mk for each section, 80mk for a combined day ticket), which includes a waxworks display, motor museum and dinosaur theme park with a host of displays and rides.

Practicalities

The **train and bus stations** are both within a few minutes' walk of Mikkeli's centre, where the **tourist office** faces the kauppatori at Hallituskatu 3a (June to mid-Aug Mon–Fri 9am–5.30am, Sat 9am–2pm; mid-Aug to May Mon 9am–5pm, Tues–Fri 9am–4.30pm; ☎015/151 444, fax 151 625, *www.travel.fi/Mikkeli*). Free **Internet** access is available at the Enter Net shop on Porrassalmenkatu 18 (Mon–Fri 11am–7pm, Sat 11am–3pm).

Of Mikkeli's **hotels**, the top-notch *Sokos Hotel Vaakuna*, Porrassalmenkatu 9 (☎015/20 201, fax 202 0421; ⑤/④), is a good bet, or if that's too pricey, try *Gasthaus Mikkeli*, Nuijamiestenkatu 63 (☎015/150 225 or 0400/956 290; ①) about 1.5km south of the centre. The nearest official **youth hostel**, one of the most beautiful in the country, is *Löydön kartano* (☎015/664 101, fax 664 109), 20km to the south at Kartanontie 71 in **Ristiina** (5 or 6 Kouvola-bound buses a day stop there). This family-run hostel occupies a large, atmospheric pink-painted wooden house, for two hundred years home to an aristocratic Russian general and his descendants, who bought it in 1752. Beds are 70mk and a generous breakfast costs 30mk. Mikkeli also has a couple of **campsites** within striking distance: *Visulahti* (☎015/18 281; mid-May to Aug), 5km from the centre beside the Visulahti Travel Centre on local bus #1, and *Mäntyniemi*, Ihastjärventie 40B (☎015/174 220), 7km from the centre (no public transport).

When it comes to **eating**, a tasty range of pizzas, fish and pasta dishes are served up by the mid-priced *Hyvä Naapuri*, Raatihuoneenkatu 4, and *Café Sole* on Porrassalmenkatu, opposite the kauppatori, serves filling, cheap lunches. You'll sacrifice atmosphere but save a few markkaa by eating at *Rosso*, Maaherrankatu 13, but if you want excellent pizza try *Angela*, a Turkish-run place opposite the kauppahalli. The main square hosts a particularly good daily market selling fresh breads, fish, fruit and snacks.

Lappeenranta

Likeable **LAPPEENRANTA** provides an excellent first taste of the eastern Lake Region, conveniently sited on the main rail line between Helsinki and Joensuu and along all the eastern bus routes. It's a small, slow-paced town where summer evenings find most of the population strolling around the linden tree-lined harbour. Once holding a key position on the Russian border, Lappeenranta boasts historical features that its neighbouring towns don't share and provides an eye-opening introduction to political conflicts that not only affected medieval Finland but also had an impact on recent generations.

The town and fortress

It's a twenty-minute walk from the train station, ten minutes from the bus station, through the town centre to the harbour, where the main activity is strolling and snacking from the numerous stands selling the local specialities – spicy meat pastries called *vetyjä* and *atomeja*. If you're feeling more energetic, climb the steep path on the harbour's western side, which brings you to the top of the town's old earthen ramparts and into the Russian-built fortress area, where Lappeenranta's past soon becomes apparent. Its **origins** as a trading centre reach back to the mid-seventeenth century, but it was with the westward shift of the Russian border in 1721 that the town found itself in the front line of Russian–Swedish conflicts. After the Peace of Turku in 1743, the border was again moved, this time leaving Lappeenranta inside Russian territory. Subsequently, a garrison of the Tsar's army arrived and, by 1775, had erected most of the stone buildings of the **fortress** on the short headland that forms the western wall of the harbour. You can buy a joint ticket for both the South Karelian museums (30mk; see opposite) inside the fortress.

Several of these structures still line the cobblestoned Kristiinankatu, which leads across the headland before descending to the shores of the lake, three of them housing museums. Unless you've a particular interest in the military role of horses and the uniforms worn by their riders, however, the collections of the **Cavalry Museum** (June–Aug Mon–Fri 10am–6pm, Sat & Sun 11am–5pm; rest of the year by appointment on ☎05/616 2261; 15mk) can safely be ignored. A better quick stop is the **Orthodox Church** (June to mid-Aug Tues–Sun 10am–4pm; rest of the year by appointment on ☎05/451 5511), just opposite, where the glow of beeswax candles helps illuminate the icons of what is Finland's oldest Orthodox church, founded in 1785.

Step back across Kristiinankatu and you're outside the **South Karelian Art Museum** (June–Aug Mon–Fri 10am–6pm, Sat & Sun 11am–5pm; Sept–May Tues–Thurs, Sat & Sun 11am–5pm; 20mk), which rotates its permanent stock of paintings with south Karelian connections – mostly a mundane bunch of landscapes and portraits, although some important Finnish artists are represented – and stages exhibitions of emerging regional artists in an adjoining building. More rewarding, however, is the **South Karelian Museum** (same hours; 20mk) at the end of Kristiinankatu. Surprisingly, it isn't collections from Lappeenranta that form the main displays here, but ceramics, souvenirs and sporting trophies from Viipuri, the major Finnish town 60km from Lappeenranta that was ceded to the Soviet Union after World War II (see the box on p.695). Many of those who left Viipuri to stay on the Finnish side of the border began their new lives in Lappeenranta, and it's mostly they who shed a tear when looking at these reminders (including a large-scale model) of their home town. Elsewhere in the museum are numerous Karelian costumes, subtle differences in which revealed the wearer's religion and (for women) marital status, and worthy displays on hunting, farming and traditional handicrafts.

Practicalities

The **tourist office** is due to move in the summer of 2000 to an as yet undecided location – try phoning or checking their Web site for details (☎05/667 788, *www.travel.fi/int/Lappeenranta*). There should also be a small tourist booth open by the harbour in summer (daily June to mid-Aug 9am–9pm). There's free **Internet** access at the town library, Valtakatu 47 (Mon–Fri 10am–6pm).

Reward yourself after a tour of the fortress area with coffee and a home-baked pie or cake at *Café Majurska*, close to the Orthodox church on Linnoitus. Sour rye bread and the softer *rieska* bread are easily found in Lappeenranta's marketplace or by the

---

VIIPURI

Before it was ceded to the Soviet Union in 1944, **VIIPURI** (still shown on most maps as "Vyborg") was one of Finland's most prosperous and cosmopolitan towns. Once a major port, being the Saimaa waterway's main link to the Baltic Sea, with a mixed population of Finns, Swedes, Russians and Germans, the town's fortunes declined under Soviet administration. Lack of investment (Viipuri was never allowed to challenge Leningrad's place as the USSR's major western seaport) resulted in a dearth of new construction, and allowed many of the town's once elegant structures to reach advanced states of dilapidation.

Viipuri today has a strange time-locked quality – a crumbling reminder both of the conflicts that have enveloped the region and of the fading power of the Soviet Union. There's still a host of medieval buildings, the magnificent Alvar Aalto public library, and an enthralling covered market, while Lenin's statue continues to stand in the town's Red Square. But the depths to which the great Russian Bear has fallen are self-evident, with the town's entire infrastructure seemingly in danger of imminent collapse and aggressive-looking moneychangers clutching wads of hard currency on street corners.

From Lappeenranta, there's a **daily bus** to Viipuri (120mk return), which continues to St Petersburg (320mk return). Russian visas, which can take up to ten days to acquire, are needed for this journey. An alternative is a **visa-free day-trip by boat** from Lappeenranta (150mk), with roughly two sailings daily in summer (Mon–Sat) run by Karelia Lines (☎05/453 0380). It's best to reserve as far in advance as possible as these trips get booked up weeks in advance; if you do call with the hope of a last-minute booking try asking if there has been any cancellations, but remember all bookings must be finalized the night before the cruise.

harbour, where you'll also find stuffed waffles and *atomeja* and *vetjäy* pastries, both local favourites. For more substantial **eating**, try the fair-priced pizzas at *Kebab Pizzeria*, Kirkkokatu 8, or the tasty fish dishes at *Majakka*, Satamatie 4, facing the harbour. A good choice for affordable pizzas, meat, fish and vegetarian dishes is *Huvi Retki* at Valtakatu 31. Should you be in Lappeenranta on a Sunday, the traditional Finnish lunches served at *Pitotalo Miekkala*, Partalantie 136, are enough to satisfy a huge appetite, though it's advisable to book (☎05/458 1882). In fact, as traditional South Karelian cookery relies on lengthy oven baking and roasting, if you want to try local specialities, it's often necessary to reserve a table and order your food in advance.

Lappeenranta is easily covered in a day, though you may well need to stay overnight between transport links. The pick of several high-standard **hotels** is *Lappee*, Brahenkatu 1 (☎05/67 861; ⑤/④), and *Hotel Cumulus*, Valtakatu 31 (☎05/677 811; ⑤/④), which contains the *Huvi Retki* restaurant (see above). There are also some cheaper **guesthouses**, such as *Gasthaus Turistilappee*, Kauppakatu 52 (☎05/415 0800; ②). The town's two **youth hostels** are 2km west of the centre: *Karelia Park*, Korpraalinkuja 1 (☎05/675 211, fax 452 8454), and *Huhtiniemi*, Kuusimäenkatu 18 (☎05/453 1888), which is also where you'll find the local **campsite** (same phone number).

Savonlinna and around

Draped across a series of tightly connected islands, **SAVONLINNA** is one of the most relaxed towns in Finland. Formerly sustained by its woodworking industries and position at a major junction on the Saimaa route, the town nowadays prospers on the income generated from tourism and the cultural kudos derived from its annual international opera festival. It's packed throughout July (when the opera festival takes place) and early August, but on either side of the peak season the town's streets and numerous small beaches are uncluttered. The easy-going mood, enhanced by the slow glide of pleasure craft in and out of the harbour, makes Savonlinna a superb base for a two- or three-day stay, giving ample time to soak up the mellow atmosphere, discover the local sights and curiosities – such as a remarkable modern art centre and a huge nineteenth-century church – that lie within the town's idyllic surrounds.

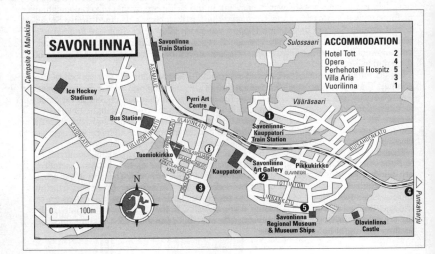

The Town

Savonlinna's centrally placed passenger harbour and kauppatori are pleasant spots to mingle with the crowds and enjoy a snack from one of the numerous food stalls. Within a few strides, you might poke your head inside the **Savonlinna Art Gallery**, Olavinkatu 40 (Tues–Sun 11am–5pm, July also Mon same hours; 10mk), which provides a spacious home for temporary shows usually mounted in tandem with those at the Savonlinna Regional Museum (see below), or the smartly restored **Pikkukirkko** (June to mid-Aug daily 10am–6pm), a Lutheran church which began life serving the Greek Orthodox faithful.

Fine as these places may be, however, none of them holds a candle to Savonlinna's greatest possession: the engrossing **Olavinlinna Castle** (daily: June to mid-Aug 10am–5pm; mid-Aug to May 10am–3pm; 20mk), a fifteen-minute walk from the harbour, at the end of Linnankatu. Perched on a small island and looking like some great, grey sea monster surfacing from the deep, the castle was founded in 1475 to guard this important lake-transport junction at the eastern extremity of what was then the Swedish empire – a region being eyed by an expansionistic Russia. The Swedes built walls 5m thick to resist attack on the eastern side, but the castle was to switch hands fairly frequently in later years; the last change saw the Russians moving in after the westward shift of the border that followed the 1743 Peace of Turku. They added the incongruous Adjutant's Apartment which, with its bright yellow walls and curved windows, resembles a large piece of Emmenthal cheese. With military importance lost when Finland became a Russian Grand Duchy in 1809, the castle ended its prerestoration days rather ignominiously as the town jail.

The castle can only be visited on guided **tours** (in English), included in the admission fee, which begin on the hour from the entrance. The guides' commentary is a vital aid to comprehending the complex historical twists and turns that the castle endured, and for pointing out the numerous oddities, such as the sole original indoor toilet, in the maiden's chamber, through which there's a sheer drop to the lake below.

Occupying an 1852 granary a stone's throw from the castle, the **Savonlinna Regional Museum** (July daily 10am–6pm; Aug daily 11am–5pm; Sept–June Tues–Sun 11am–5pm; 20mk, ticket also covers the art gallery – see above) is among the Lake Region's better accounts of the evolution of local life, beginning with an intriguing display on the prehistoric rock paintings found near Savonlinna. The bulk of the museum charts hunting and farming techniques, and the birth of the area's tar and logging industries, although the upper level holds temporary art exhibitions, often culled from the country's most interesting private collections.

Outside, docked at the end of a jetty, are three c.1900 steamers known as the **Museum Ships** (June–Aug only, same times as Regional Museum; admission with same ticket), which earned their keep plying the Saimaa waterways, sometimes travelling as far as St Petersburg and Lübeck.

THE SAVONLINNA OPERA FESTIVAL

Begun in 1912, and an annual event since 1967, Savonlinna's **Opera Festival** lasts the whole of July. The major performances take place in the courtyard of the castle and there are numerous spin-off events all over the town. **Tickets**, priced 70–650mk, go on sale the preceding November and sell out rapidly, although the tourist office keeps some back to sell during the festival. For further details contact the **Opera Office**, Olavinkatu 27 (☎015/476 750, fax 476 7540, *www.operafestival.fi*).

Practicalities

While there are very few trains to Savonlinna, there is a choice of **train stations**: Savonlinna-Kauppatori is by far the most central, although if you're making straight for the *Malakias* youth hostel (see below), get off at Savonlinna, 1km to the west. The **bus station**, served by three buses a day from Mikkeli and Helsinki, is also a short distance west of the centre, just off Olavinkatu. The **tourist office**, Puistokatu 1 (June–Aug daily 8am–6pm, until 10pm during festival; Sept–May Mon–Fri 9am–4pm; ☎015/517 510, fax 517 5123, *www.travel.fi/fin/Savonlinna*), faces the passenger harbour. They can point you in the right direction to rent out bicycles and also supply useful route maps for cycling in the area. Free **Internet** access is available at the main library (Mon–Fri 11am–7pm), but must be booked in advance.

Savonlinna has several budget **accommodation** possibilities and some good hotels, but don't expect the big discounts you might find elsewhere, as the hotels have no shortage of summer business. The stylish, summer-only *Hotel Tott*, Satamakatu 1 (☎015/575 6390, fax 514 504; ③, ⑥ during festival), is a sound choice, with apartments on offer (440–680mk) as well as rooms. Other summer hotels include *Villa Aria* (☎015/476 7515; advance bookings when closed ☎015/515 555; ②/⑤), a recently renovated c.1900 building on Puistokatu 15, just down the street from the tourist office; and the summer-only *Hotel Opera* (☎015/476 7515; advance bookings when closed on ☎015/521 116; ②/③), just past the castle near the road to Punkaharju at Kryönniemenkesja 9. Two of Savonlinna's other summer hotels also have **dormitory** accommodation: *Malakias*, Pihlajavedenkatu 6 (☎015/533 283; ③), 2km west of the centre, and the handier *Vuorilinna* (☎015/739 5494; same phone number as *Malakias* during winter; ③) on Vääräsaari, the island linked by a short bridge to the kauppatori – though the hostel section here is closed in July. *Perhehotelli Hospitz*, Linnankatu 20 (☎015/515 661, fax 515 120; ③/④ in July), also has good-value rooms, but you'll need to book ahead as it's very popular. There's a marked absence of **campsites** in Savonlinna: the nearest is *Vuohimäki* (☎015/537 353, fax 272 524; June to late Aug), 7km west of the centre and served by bus #4.

When it comes to **eating**, the usual pizza joints line Olavinkatu – *Pizza Capero*, at no. 51, is as good as any of them – while with a bit more to spend you might try the Chinese restaurant at Olavinkatu 33 (main courses 70–80mk). For **Finnish food**, sample the 45mk lunches at *Snellman*, Olavinkatu 31, or the better but pricier (60mk) *Majakka*, Satamakatu 11. The most adventurous place to dine, however, is *Paviljonki*, Rajalahendenkatu 4, where Finland's top trainee chefs serve up their latest creations. The service is excellent, the food imaginative and well prepared. Lunch here costs 50mk, or 60mk on Sundays.

North of Savonlinna: Villa Rauhalinna

Completed in 1900 in the village of Lehtiniemi, 17km north of Savonlinna, **Villa Rauhalinna** was built by a high-ranking officer in the Russian army as a silver-wedding present to his wife. The villa is a phenomenal example of intricate and ornate carpentry, and is decorated throughout with many of its original fixtures and fittings. It's not a museum, however, and while visitors are free to explore most of the villa, and the tree-filled grounds that extend to the lakeside, most people make the day-trip from Savonlinna to partake of the slap-up Russian lunch buffet (July daily, 135mk; June & Aug Sun only, 75mk) served in the dining room.

If eating in the villa is beyond your means, bring a picnic to consume beside the lake and take the opportunity to discover something of the privileged lifestyles of well-heeled Russians in early twentieth-century Finland. Regular **buses** run from Savonlinna to Lehtiniemi, but it's more in keeping with the spirit of the place to arrive by **boat** (at 40mk return, only slightly pricier than the bus) from the passenger harbour. If you can't face leaving the villa, a few double rooms are available (☎015/517 640; ③).

East of Savonlinna: Punkaharju Ridge and beyond

According to local belief, the **Punkaharju Ridge** is the healthiest place to breathe in the world, thanks to an abundance of conifers that super-oxygenate the air. This narrow seven-kilometre-long thread of land between lakes Puruvesi and Pihlalavesi begins 27km east of Savonlinna, and three roads and a railway line are squeezed onto it. With the water never more than a few metres away on either side, this is the Lake Region at its most beautiful, and easily reached on any train heading this way from Savonlinna.

Along the ridge, at the centre of things, you'll find **Lusto**, the national forest museum (May–Sept daily 10am–6pm; Oct–April Tues–Fri 10am–5pm; 35mk). Designed, predictably, from wood, its permanent exhibits examine how forests function and survive; there's also a shop stocked with wooden items, though perhaps the best part is the restaurant-café, where you can fill up on sauteed reindeer, fillet of elk and *kuusenkerkkä*, a gloriously rich cake of *smetana*, pine kernels and Lapish berries. For exploring the area further, you can rent bikes here for 35mk a day.

The most atmospheric **place to stay** is *Punkaharjun Valtionhotelli*, Punkaharju 2 (☎015/739 611, fax 441 784; summer ④, winter ②), an ornate wooden house on the ridge that still summons up the Tsarist era, despite an insipid restoration. Only a little cheaper in season but decidedly ugly is *Gasthaus Punkaharju*, Palomäentie 18 (☎015/441 371 or 473 123, fax 441 771; ③).

Retretti Arts Centre

About 25km southeast from Savonlinna, just before reaching the village of Punkaharju, the main road passes the extraordinary **Retretti Arts Centre** (June & Aug 10am–5pm; July 10am–6pm; 68mk), a place devoted to the visual and performing arts. The unique element is the setting – man-made caves gouged into three-billion-year-old rock – it cost so much to build that the project bankrupted the original owner. Outside, in the large sculpture park, fibreglass human figures by Finnish artist Olavi Lanu entwine cunningly with the forms of nature; tree branches suddenly become human limbs and plain-looking boulders slowly mutate under your gaze into a pile of male and female torsos. Inside the caves, the exhibitions are changed every year, with artists developing site-specific projects to complement the dramatic setting. The interior also features underground streams, whose gushings and bubblings underpin the music piped into the air. There are also several above-ground sites that show work from well-known European masters – the last few years have seen major displays by Matisse, Chagall, Kandinsky and Munch.

The few daily **trains** between Savonlinna and Parikkala call at Retretti train station; their timings can be very inconvenient, however, and **buses** provide a more reliable alternative. Another option, though an expensive one (130mk return), is to travel by **boat** from Savonlinna's passenger harbour. All these transport details should be checked at the tourist office as the details fluctuate frequently. One way to enjoy the art without keeping an eye on your watch is to stay virtually next door at *Punkaharjun Lomakeskus* (☎015/739 611, fax 441 784), an extensive camping area with simple huts (from 215mk) and fully equipped cottages (from 675mk) as well.

Kerimäki church

Though, like Retretti, it lies to the east of Savonlinna (23km distant), without independent transport the village of **Kerimäki** is nearly impossible to reach without first returning to Savonlinna, from where there are several daily buses and a summer boat service (check the latest details at the tourist office). The reason to come to this otherwise unremarkable village on the shores of Lake Puruvesi is to see the **Kerimäki kirkko** (June to late Aug daily 10am–6pm; closed rest of year), an immense wooden church, built in 1848 to hold 3000 people and claimed to be the largest wooden church in the world. Complete with double-tiered balconies, and a yellow- and white-painted exterior beaming through the surrounding greenery, it's a truly astonishing sight. Kerimäki can be a pleasant place to spend a quiet couple of days: there's a nice little place to swim and a decent guesthouse, the *Kerihovi* (☎015/541 225; ②), which has a traditional bar/restaurant that offers home-cooking and alcoholic beverages.

Varkaus, Valamo Monastery and Joensuu

Due to the preponderance of water in the vicinity, **train connections** around Savonlinna are extremely limited, only running east to Parikkala to link with Helsinki-bound express trains. The express train from Helsinki also calls at Parikkala on the way north to **Joensuu** (a major town of the eastern lake region) but if arriving from Savonlinna, you're left with a wait of several hours for the northbound connection. Unless you want to spend half a day drinking coffee at tiny Parikkala's train station, a sensible alternative is to travel by bus to the industrial town of **Varkaus** and pick up a train on the Turku–Joensuu line. In all cases, the latest timetables should be carefully checked before making plans.

Valamo Monastery, which lies between Varkaus and Joensuu, makes for an intriguing stop, but one fraught with difficulties unless you have your own transport.

Varkaus

The sawmills and engineering factories that dominate diminutive but commercially important **VARKAUS** sit amid gentle hills and dense forests. On a good day, the billowing chimneys and steel pipes are artily mirrored in the placid waters of the town's lakes; on a bad day, unwelcome smells fill the air and there can be few Finnish towns where nature seems so obviously to be losing the battle against heavy industry. Even if you hate Varkaus on arrival, stick around long enough to see the canal and mechanical music museums: both, in their very different ways, are unique.

The Town

In such a place, it seems appropriate that **Varkaus kirkko**, on Savontie (June–Aug daily 11am–6pm; rest of the year by appointment only on ☎017/578 5205), should be designed in a severe functional style. Inside, the church is notable less for its architecture than an immense altar fresco, measuring almost 300 square metres, painted – with the aid of several helpers and a large amount of scaffolding – by revered Finnish artist Lennart Stegerstråle.

A short walk from the church, a group of yellow wooden buildings from 1916 holds the **Museum of Workers' Housing**, Savontie 7 (June–Aug Wed 3–7pm, Thurs, Fri & Sun 11am–3pm; Sept–May by appointment only on ☎017/579 4440; 20mk), comprising a briefly interesting succession of single rooms furnished to show typical living conditions from the 1920s (when Varkaus factory labourers kept pigs and cows to remind them of their country origins) to the 1960s. The **Museum of Esa Pakarinen**, also in the workers' housing complex (same times as above; same ticket valid), remembers a tremendously popular Finnish comic actor of the postwar years who was a Varkaus resident. Pakarinen's forte was playing the fool (he rejoiced in the on-screen nickname "wood head") and singing with his false teeth removed. Besides assorted mementos of his glittering career, a TV runs videos of Pakarinen's finest films – though the subtleties are well and truly lost on non-Finnish speakers.

A fifteen-minute walk from Savontie along factory-dominated Ahlströminkatu brings you to the **Varkaus Museum**, Wredenkatu 5A (Wed 11am–7pm, Thurs 9am–4pm, Fri & Sat 9am–3pm, Sun 10am–6pm; 10mk), which provides some proof – with displays on the beginnings of local settlements and early agricultural life – that Varkaus did exist before the discovery of iron ore in local river beds set the town on course to becoming an engineering powerhouse. Much of the museum, however, charts the rise and rise of the local firm founded in 1909 by Walter Ahlström (after whom most things in the town appear to be named); by the 1950s, the company was – and continues to be – among the world's leading innovators in industrial machinery.

The canal and mechanical music museums

Leaving the town centre on Taipaleentie takes you over the rapids that made lake transport around Varkaus difficult until 1835, when a rough canal was built a kilometre east of the ferocious waters (look for the tower above the locks of the modern-day Taipale Canal). Following successive poor harvests, emergency labour was used to build a second, wider canal in 1867. Before this task was completed, 227 labourers had died from hunger or disease and been buried in mass graves; their final resting places can still be seen at the end of a rough track on Varkausmäki hill, some 7km from Varkaus. Rather than make the long and morbid trek to the grave sites, however, a visit to the **National Central Canal Museum**, inside a former warehouse beside the modern canal (June–Aug daily 10am–6pm; Sept–May by appointment on ☎017/579 4440; 10mk), provides all the background you'll need on the building of the Varkaus canals and the growth of canals generally in Finland. It's less drab than you might expect: the early canals not only opened up important new transport routes in the pre-motorized days, but had strategic importance in the border disputes between Finland and Russia.

Close to the canal museum, the bizarre and superb **Museum of Mechanical Music**, Pelimanninkatu 8 (July daily 10am–6pm; Aug to mid-Dec & March–June Tues–Sat 11am–6pm, Sun 11am–5pm; 50mk) is really more of a personal show than a museum, with the eccentric German curator and his family singing along with his extraordinary collection of music-making devices – from an ancient pianola to a prototype stereo gramophone – gathered from all over Europe and restored to working order.

Practicalities

From the **bus and train terminals** on Relanderinkatu, it's a walk of just a few minutes to Kauppakatu, Varkaus's main street. To reach the **tourist office** at Kauppatori 6 (Mon–Fri 9am–4.30pm; ☎017/579 4944, fax 579 4949, *www.varkaus.fi/kongressikeskus*), however, you'll need to walk for a further ten minutes along Taipaleentie – note that there's no sign outside. The well-stocked library (Mon–Thurs 10am–7pm, Fri 10am–6pm) on Osmajoentie has free **Internet** access.

There's little incentive to spend longer than you have to in Varkaus, but if you do need to **stay overnight**, try the adequate but old-fashioned (and receptionless) *Keskus Hotelli*, Ahlströminkatu 18 (③/②), which has a wonderful mirrored entrance hall. If you want to get in touch with the *Keskus* then you need to contact the more modern *Oscar*, around the corner at Kauppatori 4 (☎017/579 011, fax 579 050; ⑤/④), which handles reservations for both hotels. A more basic alternative is *Joutsenkulma*, Käämeniementie 20 (☎017/366 9797, fax 366 9798; ②). The only truly budget accommodation in town is the *Taipale* **campsite** (☎017/552 6644; June–Aug) on Leiritie.

Varkaus isn't the nation's culinary hot spot, and **eating** cheaply is limited to the simple menu of the café in the *Joutsenkulma* hotel (see above), or the local branch of *Rosso*, Ahlströminkatu 21, plying the usual pizzas.

Valamo Monastery

The original **Valamo Monastery**, on an island in Lake Ladoga, was the spiritual head-quarters of Orthodox Karelia from the thirteenth century onwards. In 1940, however, with Soviet attack imminent, the place was abandoned and rebuilt well inside the Finnish border, roughly halfway between Varkaus and Joensuu.

Volunteer workers arrive each summer to assist the monks in their daily tasks, and shorter-term visitors are welcome to imbibe the spiritual atmosphere and enjoy the tranquillity of the setting, though the somewhat austere regime won't suit everyone. Without transport of your own, **getting to the monastery** is not easy. There's a once-daily bus from Varkaus in the summer leaving at 1.45pm for the hour-long journey. To get there from other destinations try contacting the monastery direct. It is possible **to stay** overnight in dormitories or private rooms (☎017/570 1504, fax 570 1510; ②/①).

Joensuu

JOENSUU, the capital of what was left of Finnish Karelia after the eastern half was ceded to the Soviet Union in 1944, has attracted attention for all the wrong reasons in recent years due to several well-documented racist attacks on refugees. However things have quietened down of late and the town appears to be making a considered effort to welcome all visitors.

Whether you arrive by bus or train (the terminals are adjacent to one another), the kilometre-long walk into the centre of Joensuu is one of the most enjoyable introductions to any Lake Region town: the route crosses the broad Pielisjoki River and then the narrow Joensuu Canal before reaching Eliel Saarinen's epic Art Nouveau town hall and the wide kauppatori. Pleasing first impressions apart, compact and modestly sized Joensuu doesn't have too much beyond the usual round of local museums and churches to fill your time – a day will cover it with ease.

The Town

The newly opened culture and tourist centre, **Carelicum** (Mon–Fri 9am–6pm, Sat & Sun 10am–4pm; free), in the centre of town at Koskikatu 5, houses the **tourist office** (all year Mon–Fri 9am–6pm; summer only Sat & Sun 10am–4pm; ☎013/267 5223, fax 267 5216, *www.jns.fi*), an excellent source of information (plus free **Internet** access), a **box office** (☎013/610 0670) selling tickets for all the town's theatrical and musical performances, and a decent café and a gift shop. Also housed in the centre is the **North Karelian Museum** (same times as Carelicum; 25mk), focusing on Karelia's historical position in the middle of an East–West power struggle.

Considering the devastation caused by World War II, Joensuu has a surprising number of nineteenth-century buildings intact. These include the wood-framed structure that used to house the tourist office at Koskikatu, and the red-brick former schoolhouse which holds the **Art Museum**, at Kirkkokatu 23 (Tues & Thurs–Sun 11am–4pm, Wed 11am–8pm; 15mk). The museum's minor pieces and an unexpected crop of Far Eastern and Greek antiquities fail to divert attention from Edelfelt's finely realized portrait, *The Parisienne* – worth the admission fee alone. Some of Finland's more radical new artists get a showing a hundred metres down the road at Rantakatu 23 at the **Avant Art Gallery** (Mon–Fri 10am–4pm, Sun noon–3pm; free).

Leaving the art museum and glancing either way along the aptly named Kirkkokatu, you'll spot Joensuu's major churches standing at opposite ends. To the right, the neo-Gothic **Lutheran Church** (June to mid-Aug Mon 11am–7pm; other times by arrangement through tourist office) can seat a thousand worshippers but, aside from Antti Salmenlinna's impressive stained-glass windows, it's not wildly different from its counterparts in other towns. A few years older, the icon-rich **Greek Orthodox Church** (mid-June to mid-Aug Mon–Fri 10am–4pm; other times by arrangement on ☎013/122 564) is more deserving of a swift peek inside.

If you find yourself with time to spare, take a trip through the cactus-filled greenhouses of Joensuu University's **Botanical Gardens**, Heinäpurontie 70 (April–Aug daily except Tues 10am–6pm; Sept–March Wed–Sun 10am–4pm; 25mk). In summer the gardens are also home to flocks of tropical butterflies which are flown in weekly from Malaysia. Afterwards, you could explore the gardens themselves, which are claimed to hold a specimen of every plant native to northern Karelia – there are many more of these than you might expect.

Practicalities

For an overnight stay, you'll find some very good summer rates at the central and comfortable *Hotel Vaakuna*, Torikatu 20 (☎013/277 511, fax 277 3210; ④/③). Elsewhere, there are **dorm beds** as well as regular double rooms at the central summer hotel *Elli*, Länsikatu 18 (☎013/225 927, fax 225 763; ①). The *Partiotalo*, a **youth hostel** run by the Scouts organization (☎013/123 381; June–Aug), is located 1km north of the town centre, at Vanamokatu 25; the town **campsite** is beside the Pyhäselka lake in Linnunlahti (☎013/126 272, fax 123 933; June–Aug).

Besides the tasty morsels which can be picked up for a few markkaa inside the kauppahalli (beside the kauppatori), Joensuu's bargain **eating** options include the usual pizza joints – *Rosso*, Siltakatu 8, is the most dependable. For something more extravagant, try the French and Finnish cuisine and subdued atmosphere provided by an old-fashioned live orchestra at the *Hotel Kimmel* restaurant, Itäranta 1. For good Hungarian food, head for *Astoria*, overlooking the river at Rantakatu 32, where you can eat outside in warm weather.

Two major festivals enliven the town's entertainment calendar. The last weekend of July sees the **Gospel Festival**, when thousands of singers turn up from all around Europe. Even bigger, however, is the annual **Iisaarirock Festival** (middle of July), attracting top Finnish and international acts as well as hordes of thrill-seeking Finnish youths. If you're in any doubt as to the sheer scale of these events, take a look at the huge **Song Bowl**, which sits beside the Pyhäselkä lake, just southwest of Joensuu's centre. Tickets to both festivals can be booked via the box office in the Carelicum.

North from Joensuu: Nurmes

Should Joensuu be as rural as you want to get, swing inland (you'll have to do this by bus) to the more metropolitan Kuopio (see p.704). Otherwise, continue north from

---

CROSSING THE RUSSIAN BORDER: SORTAVALA

If you've visited the Carelicum in Joensuu, you'll have seen a scale model of **Sortavala**, one of the many Finnish towns to come under Soviet control following the postwar realignment of the border. Since the collapse of the Soviet Union, it's now possible for Finns (and indeed any other Westerners equipped with Russian visas) to visit the town with comparative ease. Despite occupying a scenic position on the shores of Lake Ladoga, Sortavala itself has no intrinsic appeal whatsoever. The **journey from Joensuu to Sortavala** takes nearly four hours and several local tour companies go there in the summer; get the latest details from the Joensuu tourist office.

Joensuu into some of the eastern Lake Region's least populated but scenically most spectacular sections, where there are hilltop views out above the tips of fir trees across watery expanses that stretch far into Russia. The small town of **NURMES**, 120km from Joensuu and linked to it by daily train, is the obvious base for exploration, though you'll need private transport – or a lot of careful juggling with local timetables and costly sightseeing trips – to find the best of the forested and lake-studded landscape. There's a useful **tourist office** on Lomatie (daily: June to mid-Aug 8am–midnight; mid-Aug to May 8am–9pm; ☎013/481 770, fax 481 775). Budget **accommodation** in Nurmes can be found at two hostels, *Pompannappi* (☎049/806 725), Koulukatu 16, and *Hyvärilä* (☎013/481 770), on Lomatie, which is also the location of the town's campsite. There's also an exceedingly ordinary, central **hotel**, *Nurmeshovi*, Kirkkokatu 21 (☎013/480 750; ②/③).

Kuopio

Sited on a major inland north–south rail route and the hub of local long-distance bus services, **KUOPIO** has the feel – and, by day, much of the hustle and bustle – of a large city, although it is in fact only marginally bigger than most of the other Lake Region communities. Nonetheless, it's an important Finnish town and, especially if you're speeding north to Lapland, provides both a break in the journey and an enjoyable taste of the region.

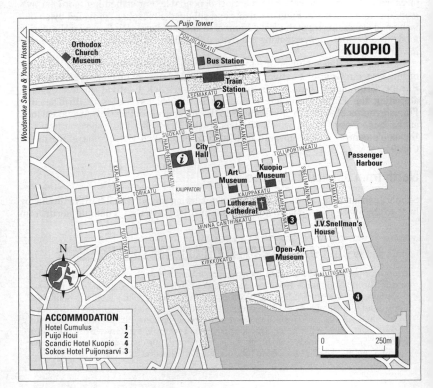

Arrival, information and accommodation

Adjacent to one another at the northern end of Puijonkatu, Kuopio's **train and long-distance bus stations** are an easy walk from the town centre. There are good bus and train connections north from Kuopio to Iisalmi (see p.707) and on to Kajaani and Oulu (see the following chapter), as well as with Helsinki and all the main southern towns. The **tourist office** faces the kauppatori at Haapaniemenkatu 17 (June to mid-Aug Mon–Fri 9am–6pm, Sat 9am–4pm; mid-Aug to May Mon–Fri 9am–5pm; ☎017/182 584, fax 261 3538).

The rock-bottom budget **accommodation** options are both some distance from the centre of town: the **youth hostel** *Hostelli Rauhalahti* is a four-kilometre trek to the south at Katiskaniementie 8 (☎017/473 473, fax 473 470), while the **campsite** (☎017/312 244; May–Aug) is 500m further south from the hostel to get there take bus #6 (summer only), #16 or #20. Staying centrally costs more, although there are no-frills double rooms (and a few dorm beds) at *Puijo Hovi*, Vuorikatu 35 (☎017/261 4943; ①). More luxurious accommodation, with lake views and private saunas, can be found at the *Sokos Hotel Puijonsarvi*, Minna Canthinkatu 16 (☎017/170 111, fax 170 117; ⑤/④). Otherwise, try the *Hotel Cumulus*, Puijonkatu 32 (☎017/617 711, fax 617 7299; ⑤/③), which has a pool, or the glitzier and recently refurbished *Scandic Hotel Kuopio*, Satamakatu 1 (☎017/195 111, fax 195 170; ⑤).

The Town

Kuopio's broad kauppatori, overlooked by the nineteenth-century city hall, is very much the heart of the town, with live jazz and rock music issuing from its large stage in summer. Walk the kilometre eastwards from here along Kauppakatu, towards the busy passenger harbour on the Kallavesi lake, and you'll pass most things worth seeing in town – with the exception of the extraordinary Orthodox Church Museum (see overleaf).

At Kauppakatu 35, the **Kuopio Art Museum** (Mon–Sat 9am–4.30pm, Wed until 8pm, Sun 11am–6pm; 15mk; for guided tours call ☎017/182 633) fills a sturdy granite building with an enterprising assortment of contemporary exhibitions, and, on the upper floor, keeps a less stimulating stock of twentieth-century Finnish painting with local connections. Further along the same street at no. 23, the **Kuopio Museum** (Mon–Sat 9am–4pm, Wed until 8pm, Sun 11am–6pm; Sept–April closed Sat; 15mk) charts the evolution of local settlements, from motley Stone Age findings to the thousand-and-one uses that tree bark was put to in pre-industrial Finland. The switch from rural to urban life caused great changes in Finnish society, but one thing that remained constant was a dependency on coffee: using the original fittings, the museum re-creates a Kuopio institution: *Alli Karvonen's* coffee shop, which dispensed the beverage from 1933 to 1969 in cups etched with Finnish landscapes. Unless stuffed reindeer munching plastic lichen and a bleak collection of painted wooden insects set your pulse racing, the rest of the museum can be ignored, but keep an eye out for Juho Rissanen's study of naked Nordic men building a wall, on the staircase – a fresco that turns many heads. Also within the Kuopio Museum, and included in the entrance fee, the **Museum of Natural History** houses a spectacular, full-size reconstruction of a woolly mammoth.

Leave the museum and cross the road to the **Lutheran Cathedral** (June–Aug Mon, Tues & Thurs 10am–6pm, Wed & Fri 10am–midnight; Sept–May Mon–Thurs 10am–3pm, Fri 10am–midnight), a handsome creation erected in 1815 using local stone. Although spacious, the cathedral's interior could hardly be described as opulent, but years ago it did contrast dramatically with the cramped living quarters of most Kuopio folk. Walk south along Kuninkaankatu until you reach Kirkkokatu and the

Kuopio Open-Air Museum (mid-May to mid-Sept daily 10am–5pm, Wed until 7pm; mid-Sept to mid-May Tues–Sun 10am–3pm; 15mk), where the stock of mostly wooden dwellings reveals the up-against-it domestic conditions that prevailed, at least for Kuopio's poorer inhabitants, from the 1840s to the 1930s.

Another old house, interesting for a quite different reason, stands at Snellmaninkatu 19, preserved as **J.V. Snellman's Home** (mid-May to Sept daily 10am–5pm, Wed until 7pm; rest of the year by appointment on ☎017/182 624, in winter ☎017/182 625; 10mk). From 1844, when the 39-year-old Snellman (for more on whom, see p.628) married his 17-year-old bride, the couple spent several years in this large but far from grand home. At the time, Snellman was earning a living as head of Kuopio's elementary school after the country's Swedish-speaking ruling class had booted him out of his university post, angry at his efforts to have Finnish made an official language. Aided by a few original furnishings and a colour scheme devised by Snellman, the house may be fairly authentic, but there isn't actually a lot to see – though that shouldn't deter anyone with an interest in Finnish history from paying their respects.

Set on the brow of the hill at Kuopio's northwest corner, the enormously impressive **Orthodox Church Museum**, Karjalankatu 1 (May–Aug Tues–Sun 10am–4pm; Sept–April Mon–Fri noon–3pm, Sat & Sun noon–5pm; 20mk), draws the Orthodox faithful from many parts of the world. Even if the workings of the Orthodox religion are a complete mystery to you, there's much to be enjoyed: elaborate Russian-made icons, gold-embossed Bibles, gowns and prayer books, and lots more. The placing of the museum in Kuopio is no accident. This part of Finland has a large Orthodox congregation, many of them (or their parents) from the parts of eastern Finland that became Soviet territory after World War II. Many objects from the original Valamo Monastery (see p.702), likewise caught on the wrong side of the border, are also on display here.

One of the highlights of Kuopio is a visit to the **world's biggest wood smoke sauna** (50mk) at the *Rauhalahti* hostel (see p.705), an enormous unisex affair which can hold up to sixty people. Its size is such that it takes 24 hours just to heat up – consequently, it's only open on Tuesdays and Fridays. For about 85mk you can avail yourself of an inclusive deal combining sauna and a traditional Finnish feast – visit the tourist office or call the hostel for more details.

Situated about 2km behind the train station on a ridge is the 75-metre-high **Puijo Tower** (June & July daily 9am–10pm, Aug & Sept daily 9am–9pm; Oct–May Mon–Sat noon–8pm, Sun noon–5pm; 15mk), with fantastic views over the surrounding countryside, a revolving restaurant (closed during winter) and a small goblin theme park for the kids.

Eating, drinking and nightlife

The **evening market**, held nightly during summer at the passenger harbour, is a good place to sample *kalakukko* – a kind of bread pie, baked with fish and pork inside it. While it's to be found all around the country, Kuopio is *kalakukko*'s traditional home and at least one stall here will be selling it, warm and wrapped in silver foil; a fist-sized piece costs about 15mk. You can also buy *kalakukko* hot from the oven at the Hanna Partanen in a backyard on Kasamikatu (5am to 9pm), reckoned the best place in town, if not the whole of Finland, to sample it. A kilo loaf costs about 70mk.

Away from the harbourside market, it's the usual pizza joints that provide nourishment at the most reasonable prices: *Rosso*, 24–26, or *Pamukkale*, on the side of the kauppatori, are just two of many. The town's finest restaurant is undoubtedly the *Musta Lammas*, down in the cellar vaults at Satamakatu 4 (Mon–Sat 5pm–midnight; ☎017/262 3494), which has been in business since 1862. Another excellent and popular choice is *Isä Camillo*, Kauppakatu 25–27 (☎017/581 0450), which serves a range of Mediterranean cooking. Several of the pubs mentioned below also offer good-value lunches; for something more exotic, try the Mexican food at *Amarillo*, Kirjastokatu 10, where lunches cost around 35mk.

Kuopio has a reputation for being the stamping ground of some of Finland's best rock musicians, and the town has a number of **pubs** where you can hear live music. *Henry's Pub*, Kauppakatu 18, sees jam sessions and some live bands; *Freetime* (part of *Amarillo*; see above) at Kirjastokatu 10, and *Emigrant's*, Kauppakatu 16, are less music-oriented but are usually enjoyable drinking spots. For a more mellow evening out, try the upmarket *Sampo*, Kauppakatu 13, noted for its fine fish restaurant. Out of central Kuopio (but close to the campsite), the *Yölintu* bar at *Hotel Rauhalahti* stages some wild bashes on Friday nights, and often lays on free transport from the town centre. Find out what's happening there by asking at the tourist office, or try phoning the hotel itself on ☎017/473 473.

Iisalmi

The farmland around **IISALMI**, an hour north of Kuopio by bus, makes a welcome break from pine forests and marks the centre of northern Savolax, a district that, in public opinion polls, is regularly voted the least desirable place to live in Finland. The reason for this is slightly mysterious – the modestly sized town looks nice enough – but might be due to the locals' reputation for geniality mixed with low cunning. Whether this is innate, or a defensive reaction by country folk who've been pitchforked into urban life, is debatable.

Whatever the truth, two museums give a very good insight into local life. The **District Museum** (daily June–Aug noon–6pm; 10mk), at Kivirannantie 5 on the shores of the Palosvirta river – cross the river from the centre of town and turn left – reveals the down-at-heel life of the peasantry; while the **Juhani Aho Museum** (by arrangement on ☎017/830 1388; free) in Mansikkaniemi, 5km along the Kajaani road by local bus, shows how the other half lived. Juhani Aho was a major influence on Finnish literature as it emerged around the beginning of the twentieth century, and the simple buildings filled with the author's possessions manage to convey the commitment of the artists who came together in the last years of Russian rule.

Aside from a few hotels, such as *Artos* on Kyllikinkatu (☎017/812 244, fax 814 941; ③/②) and the tiny *Hotel Restentti*, Puistotie 21 (☎017/862 660, fax 862 535; ③), accommodation in the town is limited. However, the **tourist office** at Kauppakatu 22 (June–Aug Mon–Fri 9am–6pm; Sept–May Mon–Fri 9am–5pm; ☎017/830 1391, fax 826 760), on the corner with the main street, Pohjolankatu, can point you towards summertime budget options on the outskirts, and to **campsites** with cabins, such as *Koljonvirta Camping*, Ylemmäisentie (☎017/825 252; mid-May to mid-Aug).

travel details

Trains

Iisalmi to: Kajaani (4 daily; 1hr); Oulu (3 daily; 3hr 30min).

Joensuu to: Helsinki (4 daily; 4hr).

Jyväskylä to: Tampere (9 daily; 2hr).

Kuopio to: Iisalmi (5 daily; 1hr); Jyväskylä (5 daily; 1hr 50min); Kajaani (4 daily; 2hr 15min); Mikkeli (6 daily; 1hr 45min).

Lahti to: Helsinki (10 daily; 1hr 45min); Mikkeli (5 daily; 1hr 45min).

Lappeenranta to: Helsinki (8 daily; 2hr 40min); Lahti (8 daily; 1hr 15min).

Mikkeli to: Kuopio (5 daily; 1hr 30min); Lahti (5 daily; 1hr 45min).

Savonlinna to: Parikkala (4 daily; 50min).

Tampere to: Hämeenlinna (21 daily; 53min); Helsinki (12 daily; 2hr 15min); Jyväskylä (9 daily; 2hr); Oulu (7 daily; 5hr); Pori (6 daily; 1hr 45min); Savonlinna (2 daily; 4hr); Turku (7 daily; 2hr 15min).

Varkaus to: Joensuu (3 daily; 1hr 30min).

Buses

Joensuu to: Kuopio (5 daily; 2hr 30min); Valamo Monastery (1 daily; 1hr 10min).

Kuopio to: Jyväskylä (3 daily; 2hr 15min).

Lahti to: Mikkeli (6 daily; 2hr 15min); Savonlinna (2 daily; 3hr 45min).

Lappeenranta to: Imatra (hourly; 37min).

Mikkeli to: Savonlinna (4 daily; 1hr 45min).

Savonlinna to: Kuopio (4 daily; 3hr 40min); Parikkala (2 daily; 1hr 20min); Punkaharju (2 daily; 50min); Varkaus (4 daily; 2hr 20min).

Tampere to: Helsinki (5 daily; 2hr); Pori (5 daily; 1hr 45min); Turku (5 daily; 2hr 30min).

Varkaus to: Joensuu (2 daily; 2hr); Kuopio (8 daily; 1hr 15min).

International buses

Joensuu to: Sortavala (1 daily in summer; 3hr 45min).

Lappeenranta to: St Petersburg (2 weekly; 4hr); Viipuri (1 daily; 1hr 30min).

CHAPTER SEVENTEEN

OSTROBOTHNIA, KAINUU AND LAPLAND

B etween them, these three regions take up nearly two-thirds of Finland, but unlike the populous south or the more industrialized sections of the Lake Region, they're predominantly rural, with small and widely separated communities. Despite this or perhaps because of it, each region has a very individual flavour.

Living along the coast of **Ostrobothnia** are most of the country's Swedish-speaking Finland-Swedes, a small subsection of the national population whose culture differs from that of both Swedes and Finns. Towns hereabouts are known as often by their Swedish names as by their Finnish, while their distance from the ravages of World War II enabled them to retain some of their old wooden architecture. Much of the region's affluence stems from its flat and fertile farmlands, although the coastal area's fortunes are changing as the numerous ferry connections from Sweden – the "booze cruises" – are shutting down as European law does away with duty-free alcohol, the main reason for the ferries' existence. **Vaasa** remains one of the region's few entry points, although new routes may still emerge, depending on future demand. Overall, though, given the lack of exciting scenery – save for a few fishing settlements scattered along the jagged shoreline – and the region's social insularity, you'd be generous to devote more than a couple of days to it. Even busy and expanding **Oulu**, the region's major city, has a surprisingly anodyne quality, although you could always join the Swedes drinking their way into oblivion slightly further north at the border town of **Tornio**.

Kainuu is the thickly forested, thinly populated heart of Finland. It's traditionally peasant land – something perhaps felt more strongly here than anywhere else in the country – and over recent decades has suffered a severe economic decline as wealth has become concentrated in the south. There's still a surprising level of poverty in some parts, although tourism is beginning to help alleviate this. The only sizeable town, **Kajaani** is a good base for wider explorations by foot, bike or canoe, and, since no railways serve the area, it's also the hub of a bus network which connects the region's far-flung settlements. **Kuhmo**, east of Kajaani, is at the centre of a notable web of nature trails and hiking routes, while heading north through **Suomussalmi** and on past

---

ACCOMMODATION PRICE CODES

The hotels listed in this chapter have been graded according to the following price bands, based on the cost of the **least expensive double room in summer**. However, many hotels offer summer and/or weekend discounts, and in these instances we've given two grades, covering both the regular and the discounted rate.

| ① Under 275mk | ② 275–350mk | ③ 350–450mk |
| ④ 450–550mk | ⑤ 550–750mk | ⑥ Over 750mk |

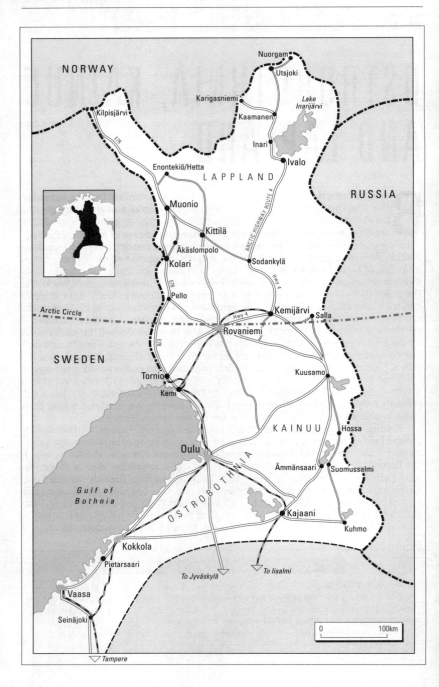

NORWAY

Nuorgam

Utsjoki

Karigasniemi

Lake
Inarijärvi

Kilpisjärvi

Kaamanen

Inari

Ivalo

Enontekiö/Hetta

LAPPLAND

RUSSIA

Muonio

Kittilä

Äkäslompolo

Kolari

Sodankylä

Pello

Arctic Circle

Kemijärvi

Salla

Rovaniemi

SWEDEN

Tornio

Kuusamo

Kemi

KAINUU

Hossa

Oulu

Ämmänsaari

Suomussalmi

Gulf of
Bothnia

OSTROBOTHNIA

Kajaani

Kuhmo

Kokkola

Pietarsaari

To Jyväskylä

To Iisalmi

Vaasa

Seinäjoki

0   100km

Tampere

Kuusamo, the landscapes become wilder, with great gorges, river rapids and fells on which reindeer are as common as people. Hikers here are well catered for by a number of marked tracks, in addition to totally uninhabited regions traversable only with map, compass and self-confidence. The villages have little to offer beyond accommodation and transport to and from the end-points of the hikes, so stay away if you're not the hiking type.

Much the same applies to **Lapland**, one of the most thrilling places to hike in the world. **Rovaniemi**, the main stopover en route, is useful mainly for its transport connections and information on the area beyond. Beyond Rovaniemi, two roads lead into the **Arctic North**. Here you'll find wide open spaces that are great for guided treks through gold-panning country and along the edges of mountain chains which continue far into Sweden and Norway. Elsewhere you can be totally isolated, gazing from barren fell-tops into Russia. But while the Arctic settlements are small, and few and far between, the whole region is home to several thousand Sami (for more on whom, see p.625), who've lived in harmony with this special, often harsh environment for millennia. Discovering their culture and way of life can be as exciting as experiencing the Arctic North itself.

Vaasa

There's little reason to visit **VAASA**, although it's a useful stopover if you're travelling along the coast and has good travel connections with Oulu to the north and Pori to the south. The lifeblood of the town is its harbour, through which the produce of southern Ostrobothnia's wheat fields is exported and the lucrative tourist traffic from Sweden arrives. Years of steady income have given the town a staid, commercial countenance, and its wide avenues (the old centre was obliterated by fire a century ago) are lined by shipping offices, consulates and a plethora of boozing venues aimed at Swedes from Umeå, who come here to get smashed.

Eighty-odd years ago, Vaasa was briefly the seat of the provisional government after the Reds (an alliance of Communists and Social Democrats who had taken up arms against Finland's repressive Civil Guard) had taken control of Helsinki and much of the south at the start of the Civil War in 1918; it was among Ostrobothnia's right-wing farmers that the bourgeois-dominated government drew most of its support. This barely endearing fact is recalled by the reliefs of the then president Svinhufvud, and Mannerheim, who commanded the Civil Guard, on the front of the town hall and by the monument outside it.

Since then, it seems, little besides drunkenness has broken the peace. The pinnacle of local cultural activity is represented by the **Ostrobothnia Museum** (daily 10am–5pm, Wed until 8pm; 10mk) at Museokatu 3, which recounts the history of the town and boasts an enjoyable collection of sixteenth- and seventeenth-century Dutch, Italian and Flemish art.

Practicalities

The **bus** and **train** stations are located at the northern end of the town centre, within walking distance of the **tourist office**, which is located in part of the town hall at Raastuvankatu (June–Aug Mon–Fri 8am–6pm, Sat & Sun 10am–6pm; Sept–May Mon–Fri 8am–4pm; ☎06/325 1145, fax 325 3620, *www.vaasa.fi*). There's free **Internet** access just across the road from the tourist office in the Rewell Centre shopping complex at both the library (Mon–Fri 11am–8pm, Sat 10am–3pm), where you must book terminals in advance, and also at the Kansalais Info office. If you have to stay overnight before moving on, **hostels** are your best bet. The official hostel (open all year) is part of the summer hotel *Tekla* at Palosaarentie 58 (☎06/327 6411, fax 321 3989), and lies about 3km from the town centre; take bus #3. Slightly more central but also pricier is the *Olo* hostel, Asemakatu 12 (☎06/317 4558), whilst further out is the better-value *EFO/Summer Hotel*, Rantakatu 21–22 (☎040/066 8521; ①; mid-June to mid-Aug). Just up the road from *EFO* at Korsholmanpuistikko 6–8 is the *Kenraali Wasa Hostel* (same phone number; ①), situated in an old army barracks. In the summer months, there's the further option of the **campsite**, *Wasa Camping* (☎06/317 3852, winter bookings ☎06/312 5888, fax 312 5989), which is 2km from the town centre but close to the ferry harbour. The most pleasant central **hotel** is the small *Astor*, Asemakatu 4 (☎06/326 7611, fax 326 9484; ⑤/④), where for 100mk extra you can get a room with its own sauna; the newest is the *Silveria*, Ruutikellarintie 4 (☎06/326 7611, fax 326 7510; ⑤/③), with morning sauna, swimming and breakfast included in the room price.

Onward from Vaasa

Ferries currently run from Vaasa to **Umeå** in Sweden, twice-daily in summer, less often in winter, although these may be under threat following the EU's abolition of duty-free goods – the main incentive for the hundreds of Swedes who make the journey in search of cheap booze.

Heading **south from Vaasa** there are trains direct to Tampere, although it's actually quicker to change at Seinäjoki (which all southbound trains from Vaasa pass through), on the main line between Helsinki and Oulu. There are numerous buses to Pori and Turku. About 70km south of Vaasa, these pass through Kaskinen (in Swedish, Kaskó) and neighbouring Kristiinankaupunki (Kristinestad), notable for its surviving seventeenth-century layout.

Travelling **north from Vaasa** by bus to the major coastal city of Oulu involves a mildly scenic journey passing fishing hamlets along the archipelago, and the small and still largely wooden towns of Uusikaarlepyy (Nykarleby) and Pietarsaari (Jakobstad). En route you'll pass through the uninspiring port of **KOKKOLA**. If you feel like hanging around, the **tourist office** on Mannerheiminaukio (June–Aug Mon–Fri 9am–5pm, Sat 9am–1pm; Sept–May Mon–Fri 8am–4pm; ☎06/831 1902, fax 831 0306) can help sort out accommodation and point you towards the only remotely interesting local sight: the **English Park**, at one end of Isokatu, which contains a boat captured when the British fleet tried to land here during the Crimean campaign in 1854. A much more welcome sight, though, is the **train station** at Isokatu's other end. **Travelling on** from Kokkola is straightforward since the town is on the main rail line between Oulu and Helsinki.

Oulu

Despite **OULU**'s role as national leader in the computing and microchip industries, the city still has sufficient remnants from the past to remind visitors of its nineteenth-century status as a world centre for tar. The black stuff was brought by river from the forests of Kainuu, and the international demand for its use in ship- and road-building helped line the pockets of Oulu's merchants. Their affluence and quest for cultural refinement made the town a vibrant centre, not only for business, but also for education and the arts. Today, a handsome series of islands, a couple of highly conspicuous old buildings, and a nightlife fuelled by the university's fun-hungry students bring colour into an otherwise pallid city. Though it has its share of faceless office blocks, there's an ancient feel to the place, too, as seen in tumbledown wooden shacks around the intricately carved kauppahalli.

ACCOMMODATION
Apollo 2
Kesähotelli Oppimestari 1
Turisti 3

Arrival and accommodation

Oulu is handy for **trains** in various directions, most usefully the direct services to and from Helsinki, Kajaani in the east (see p.717) and Rovaniemi in the north (see p.721). Arriving here, you'll find the platforms of the **train station** feed conveniently into an underground walkway with two exits: one runs to the nearby **bus station** (with regular services to and from Kuusamo), while the other leads directly into the compact city centre, just a few minutes' walk from the **tourist office** (July Mon–Sat 9am–6pm, Sun 10am–4pm; Aug–June Mon–Fri 9am–4pm; ☎08/5584 1330, fax 5584 1711, *www.ouka.fi*), which is close to the City Hall at Torikatu 10.

Low-cost **accommodation** is, unfortunately, limited. The **youth hostel** is at Kajaanintie 36 (☎08/880 3311, fax 880 3754; June–Aug), a fifteen-minute walk east from the train and bus stations. The very central *Turisti*, Rautatienkatu 9 (☎08/375 233, fax 311 0755; ③), has the cheapest year-round **hotel** beds. If you arrive in June or July the *Kesähotelli Oppimestari*, Nahkatehtaankatu 3 (☎08/884 8527, fax 884 8529; ①), can provide well-kept rooms, while the best summer discounts can be found at the *Apollo Hotel*, Asemakatu 31–33 (☎08/374 344, fax 372 060; ④/③). If you're looking for luxury, the *Eden*, on the island of Nallikari (☎08/550 4100, fax 554 4103; ⑤), won't disappoint – it's got a superb pool and offers spa treatments and steam rooms, as well as a fine restaurant. Bus #5 runs there, as well as to the cabin-equipped **campsite** (☎08/558 61351), 4km from town on Heitissaari Island; nearby is the sliver of sand that locals call a beach.

The City

Leaving either the bus or train station, it's just a few minutes' walk straight ahead to the **harbour** and the neighbouring **kauppatori** and **kauppahalli** (Mon–Fri 8am–6pm, Sat 8am–3pm), an appealing and ornate place, good for cheap eats. Nearby, the sleekly modern **library** and **theatre** rise on stilts from the waters of Rommakonselkä. The library frequently stages **art and craft exhibitions**, which are usually worth a look.

The **City Hall**, a few minutes' away on Kirkkokatu, retains some of its late nineteenth-century grandeur, when it was built as a luxury hotel symbolizing the affluent and cosmopolitan tar-rich town. A local newspaper called it "a model for the whole world. A Russian is building the floor, an Austrian is doing the painting, a German is making the bricks, an Englishman is preparing the electric lighting, the Swede is doing the masonry, the Norwegian is carving the relief and the Finn is doing all the drudgery." Nowadays, the drudgery is performed by local government officials, who've become accustomed to visitors stepping in to gawp at the wall-paintings and enclosed gardens that remain from the old days. While inside, venture up to the second floor, where the Great Hall still has its intricate Viennese ceiling paintings and voluminous chandeliers.

Further along Kirkkokatu, the copper-domed, yellow-stuccoed **Tuomiokirkko** (summer daily 10am–7pm; reduced hours rest of the year; free) was built in the 1770s following a great fire that more or less destroyed the city, and underwent a full and successful restoration in 1996. Within the cathedral is a portrait of Swedish historian Johannes Messinius, supposedly painted by **Cornelius Arenditz** in 1612. Restored and slightly faded, it's believed to be the oldest surviving oil painting in Finland, despite the efforts of the Russian cossacks, who lacerated the canvas with their sabres in 1714. The small park outside the cathedral is part of a former cemetery, and bits of clothing and bone found nearby beneath the floor of the seventeenth-century cellar in the pleasant *Franzen Café*, on the corner of Kirkkokatu and Linnankatu, have been reburied beneath the cafe's tiled floor – the barman can point out the spot.

Cross the small canal just north of the cathedral to reach **Ainola Park**, a pleasantly wooded space which makes a nice spot for a picnic or a late evening stroll. In the park, the **North Ostrobothnia Museum** (Mon–Thurs 10am–7pm, Sat & Sun 11am–5pm; 10mk) is packed with tar-stained remnants from Oulu's past and an interesting Sami section. There's no English labelling, but the displays are mostly self-explanatory.

If the future does more to excite your imagination than the past, head for **Tietomaa**, the Science Museum, a few minutes' walk away at Nahkatehtaankatu 6 (May, June & Aug daily 10am–6pm; July daily 10am–8pm; Sept–April Mon–Fri 10am–4pm, Sat & Sun 10am–6pm; 60mk). Housed in an old powerstation, this is a great place if you like exploring the bounds of technological possibility, with several floors of gadgets to test mental and physical abilities as well as video games, holograms, a ski jump simulator, a giant-screen IMAX cinema and a glass elevator that takes you to the top of a tower from which you can get unparalleled views of Oulu.

Just around the corner, the **City Art Gallery** (Tues & Fri–Sun 11am–6pm, Wed 11am–8pm; 15mk, free on Fri), Kasarmintie 7, is located in a renovated glue factory. One of the largest galleries in Finland, it houses permanent and visiting international and Finnish contemporary art collections, plus a pleasant café – a good place to kill a few hours on a cold day.

Koskikeskus, the University and Botanical Gardens

A pleasant way to pass a few hours is to set off for the four small islands across the mouth of Rommakonselkä, collectively known as **Koskikeskus**. The first island, Linnansaari, has the inconsequential remains of Oulu's sixteenth-century castle; next comes Raatinsaari, followed by Toivonsaari, and the rapids that drive a power station designed by Alvar Aalto, with twelve fountains added by the architect to prettify the plant. Pikisaari, the fourth island, is much the best to visit, reached by a short road bridge from Raatinsaari. A number of tiny seventeenth-century wooden houses here have survived Oulu's many fires, and Pikisaari has become the stamping ground of local artists and trendies, with several **art galleries** and **craft shops**.

The islands can also be glimpsed through the windows of buses #22 and #30, both of which pass through Koskikeskus during the twenty-minute ride to the **University**. It's not a bad destination if you're at a loose end, if only for the opportunity to gorge in the student mensa. To work up an appetite, try finding the **Geological Museum** (Mon–Fri & Sun 11am–3pm; free) or the **Zoological Museum** (Mon–Fri 8.30am–3.30pm, Sun 11am–3pm; free), both secreted within the university's miles of corridors. The former is much as you'd expect, with a large collection of rare gems; the latter's best feature are the painstakingly hand-painted habitats created for each of the numerous specimens of stuffed Finnish wildlife.

Once you've ventured onto the campus you may as well take a look at the tropical and Mediterranean flora inside the two glass pyramidal structures that make up the **Botanical Gardens** (June–Aug Tues–Fri 8am–4pm, Sat & Sun 10am–4pm; Sept–May Tues–Fri 8am–3pm, Sat & Sun noon–3pm; 10mk).

Eating, drinking and nightlife

Oulu boasts some delightful **cafés** for lunch or the odd snack, the best of which include *Sokeri Jussi*, set in an old salt warehouse on Pikisaari, and, just over the bridge from the mainland, the *Café Pilvikirsikka*, in an old greenhouse in Hupisaari park; *Café Koivuraranta*, a wooden café on the riverside, is also popular, while *Café Saara* is a peaceful place to stop off for a coffee, right in the centre at Kirkkokatu 2. For **cakes**, the finest outlet in Oulu is *Katri Antell* on Rotuaari, while the more basic *Bisketti* is just opposite. If you're stuck for somewhere to go on a Sunday, NUKU, the youth cultural centre, has a laid-back café in an atrium courtyard at Hallituskatu 7. Finally, for a little more class, venture into the Concert Hall on Lintulammentie, a short walk south of the bus station. A coffee in the hall's café isn't cheap, but it does allow you to admire the gleaming Italian marble interior, with the bonus of live classical music at lunchtimes during the summer (Mon–Sat 12.30–1pm).

For a waterside **meal**, try the central *Neptunus*, which serves good fish and meat dishes in a boat moored by the kauppatori. Another place to fill up with good food is the *Franzen Café*, in a charismatic old building opposite the Tuomiokirkko at Kirkkokatu 2, in the same building as *Café Saara* (☎08/311 3224) – as well as the ultraswish street-level restaurant, there's a cellar bar serving German beers and sausages. Otherwise, load up in any of Oulu's pizzerias – one of the the best is *Fantasia* at Isokatu 23. *Oskarin Kellari*, at Rautatienkatu 9 near the train station, and in the same block as the *Hotel Turisti*, is a good choice for a reasonably priced meal with a stuff-your-face buffet lunch for about 40mk.

Nightlife and entertainment

Oulu's **nightlife** revolves around its numerous **cafés** and **pubs**, the best of the bunch being the friendly *Rauhala*, in the Ainola Park at Mannenkatu 1 (daily 2pm–2am), which has live music on Wednesday, Friday and Saturday from 10pm. One of the trendiest bars, with occasional live music, is *V.P.K.* in the old fire station on Uusikatu – you need to be 20 or over to get in. The most popular Irish pub is *Leskinen*, near Akateeminen Kirjakauppa, while *Never Grow Old* at Hallituskatu 13 is a long-standing reggae pub. For a changing atmosphere, with a different kind of music each night, try the *Foxia*, Pakkohuoneenkatu 19. Otherwise, head for the string of nightclubs opposite the *Apollo Hotel* (inside which there's also a popular karaoke club).

On to Tornio: Kemi

If you want to cross overland into Sweden, the place to make for is Tornio, 130km northwest of Oulu – reached by bus from **Kemi**, a small town on the Oulu–Rovaniemi train route around 110km northwest of Oulu. Although otherwise undistinguished, in Kemi you can join a four-hour "cruise" on a genuine **arctic ice-breaker** between January and April, which costs 780mk. Details from the tourist office on Torikatu (☎016/259 465, fax 259 708), or from Sampo Tours (☎016/256 458), at Ajos Harbour, 15km from Kemi.

Tornio

Situated on the extreme northern tip of the Gulf of Bothnia, **TORNIO** makes a living by selling booze to fugitives from Sweden's harsh alcohol laws, and catering to the Finns who come here to enjoy the beach, to fish, or shoot the Tornionjoki Rapids. After the Swedish–Russian conflict of 1808–09, the border between Sweden and Finland was drawn around **Suensaari**, an oval piece of land jutting from the Swedish side into the river, on which central Tornio now sits. With no formalities at the customs post on the bridge linking the two countries, the traffic in liver-damaged Swedes from nearby Haaparanta (in Swedish, Haparanda) is substantial. If you're **arriving by bus** the journey will terminate in Suensaari.

The dominant features of the town are its bars and restaurants, so numerous that it's pointless to list them. Simply stroll around Hallituskatu and Kauppakatu and drop into the ones with the most promising noises. Always lively are *Pub Tullin*, Hallituskatu 5, and *Aarninholvi*, Aarnintie 1, while everyone who sets foot in Tornio seems to visit *Pizzeria Dar Menga*, Kauppakatu 12–14, one of the cheapest spots for solid nourishment. For coffee and fresh bread and cakes, it's hard to beat *Karkiaisen Leipomo*, Länsiranta 9. Alternatively, you can buy a bag of salted and smoked whitefish along the banks of the rapids (roughly 12mk for a meal's worth).

If you find the boozy atmosphere unappealing, try visiting the seventeenth-century **Tornionkirkko** (summer Mon–Fri 9am–3pm) on the edge of the town park, or climbing the **observation tower** (June to mid-Aug daily 11am–8pm). Otherwise there's only the **Tornio River Valley Historical Museum** (Mon–Fri noon–5pm, Sun noon–3pm; 10mk), near the corner of Torikatu and Keskikatu, or the possibility of some diversion suggested by the **tourist office**, in the Green Line Centre at the Swedish border (June to mid-Aug Mon–Fri 8am–8pm, Sat & Sun 10am–8pm; mid-Aug to May Mon–Fri 8am–4pm; ☎016/432 733, fax 480 048, *www.tornio.fi*).

It might be slightly cheaper to join the drunken legions staggering back across the border to sleep in Haaparanta (see p.571), but should you choose to stay in Tornio, there's a decent enough summer hotel, *Joentalo* (☎016/482 144; ②; June to mid-Aug) about 2km out from the centre at Kiyrannantie 13 plus a **campsite** on Matkailijantie (☎016/445 945, fax 480 048), with cottages going for around 200mk a night. Among the town's other hotels, *Kaupunginhotelli*, Itäranta 4 (☎016/43 311, fax 482 920; ③), boasts a trio of restaurants and five saunas.

Kajaani and around

KAJAANI, 178km southeast of Oulu by bus, could hardly be more of a contrast to the communities of the Bothnian coast. Though small and pastoral, the town is by far the biggest settlement in this very rural part of Finland, where trains and buses are rare and the pleasures of nature take precedence over everything else. Obviously there's little bustle or nightlife, but the place offers some insight into Finnish life in one of its less prosperous regions. Fittingly, it was in Kajaani that Elias Lönnrot completed his version of the *Kalevala*, the nineteenth-century collection of Finnish folk tales that extolled to the hilt the virtues of traditional peasant life. At the beginning of July Kajaani also hosts Finland's biggest annual **poetry festival**, during which the main street, Kauppakatu, turns into a bustling market.

From the gloriously Art Nouveau **train station**, Kauppakatu leads directly into Kajaani's minuscule centre, but first turn left into Asemakatu and you'll spot the decorative exterior of the **Kainuun Museum** at no. 4 (Mon–Fri noon–3pm, Wed until 8pm, Sun noon–5pm; 10mk, free Wed 4–8pm). Inside, the engrossingly ramshackle collection of local art and history says a lot about the down-to-earth qualities of the area. Heading for the centre, you'll find the **Old Town Hall**, designed by Carl Engel, at the junction of Kauppakatu and Linnankatu. Slightly further on stands the dramatic **Kajaani kirkko** (summer daily 10am–8pm; winter Mon–Sat 5–7pm), whose wooden frame, weird turrets and angular arches were heralded as the epitome of the neo-Gothic style when the church was completed in 1896. Resembling a leftover from a *Munsters* set, its spectral qualities are most intense by moonlight.

More historically significant, perhaps, but far less thrilling, is the ruined **Kajaani Castle**. Built in the seventeenth century to forestall a Russian attack, it later served as a prison where, among others, Johannes Messenius, the troublesome Swede,

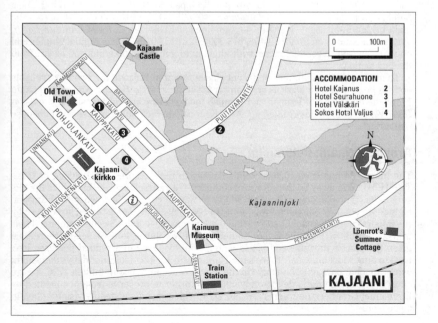

was incarcerated. Although there's constant talk of schemes to rebuild it, the castle was ruined so long ago that nobody's sure what it actually looked like, and the present heap of stones is only worth seeing if you're already idling along the riverside beside it.

Given the lack of other evening activities, idling is what you're likely to be doing if you stay here overnight. The problem of complete boredom is no less severe for the local youth, who've taken to lining the pavements of Kauppakatu in their hundreds, waiting for something to happen. About the only other way to pass the sunset hours is to take a quiet walk along the riverside footpath, from the corner of Ämmäkoskenkatu and Brehenkatu. Heading west, the path passes the **open-air theatre**, and also provides a chance to gaze at logs sliding blissfully towards destruction at the pulp mill ahead. Following the river eastwards leads to **Lönnrot's summer cottage**. Built by Elias Lönnrot for his wife, the small wooden structure now stands totally empty, isolated and seemingly insignificant; the only acknowledgement of its existence is in the name of the neighbouring *Elias Restaurant* – an odd neglect for a man whose life's work was so influential, and revered.

Practicalities

The official **youth hostel**, at Pohjolankatu 4 (☎ & fax 08/622 254; ①) is open all year, and though the town's only campsite recently closed there are plans to open a new one – check with the **tourist office** at Pohjolankatu 16 (June–Aug Mon–Fri 9am–6pm, Sat 9am–1pm; Sept–May Mon–Fri 9am–5pm; ☎08/615 5555, fax 615 5664). There are a number of adequate choices in the town centre, and rates drop during the summer and at weekends. Two of these, *Sokos Hotel Valjus*, Kauppakatu 20 (☎08/615 0200, fax 629 005; ⑤/④), and *Hotel Seurahuone* (☎08/623 076, fax 613 4495; ③/②) Kauppakatu 11, have cheaper rooms in so-called "traditional" sections, though tradition here amounts simply to a less recent lick of paint. The *Sokos Hotel Valjus* also hires out rooms at the *Hotel Välskäri* (②) 200m down the street at Kauppakatu 21. If you can afford it the best hotel in town is the *Scandic Hotel Kajanus* (☎08/61 641, fax 616 4505; ⑤/④) across the main bridge in pleasant riverside surroundings at Koskikatu 3. *Hotel Kainuun Portti*, 4km south of town on Route 5 (☎08/613 3000, fax 613 3010; ③) has regular singles and doubles, as well as rooms for five with kitchen; to get there, take bus #50 or #51 from the bus station.

There's not a huge number of decent places to **eat** in Kajaani, the two most reliable options being as much pizza as you can eat for 40mk at *Casa Bianca*, Koivukoskenkatu 17, or the odd blend of Finnish and Spanish food at *Fransmanni*, upstairs at the *Sokos Hotel Valjus*. Other options lined up along Kauppakatu include a Chinese and Lebanese restaurant.

Around Kajaani: Paltaniemi

The hourly #4 bus from Kajaani winds its way to the well-preserved village of **PALTANIEMI**, 9km away on the shores of Oulujärvi – an attractive place but, since the closure of its campsite, one without anywhere to stay. In contrast to down-at-heel Kajaani, eighteenth-century Paltaniemi was home to Swedish-speaking aesthetes lured here by the importance of Kajaani Castle during the halcyon days of the Swedish empire. Their transformation of Paltaniemi into something of a cultural hotbed seems incredible given the place's tiny size and placid setting, but evidence of a refined pedigree isn't hard to find. Most obviously there's the **Paltaniemi kirkko** (summer daily 10am–6pm; winter guided tours only, bookable in the tourist office in Kajaani), built in 1726, a large church whose interior is deliberately chilled in order to preserve **frescoes** painted by Emmanuel Granberg between 1778 and 1781, which include a steamy vision of hell in a gruesome *Last Judgement*.

It's also fun to ferret around behind the pews, trying to decipher centuries-old graffiti. Even Tsar Alexander I paid a visit to Paltaniemi after Finland had become a Russian Grand Duchy, and his impromptu meal in a stable is reverentially commemorated in the **Tsar's Stable** by the church. **Hövelö**, the old cottage across the road, was the birthplace of **Eino Leino**, whose poems captured the increasingly assertive mood of Finland at the beginning of the twentieth century: his life and the history of Kajaani Castle form the subject of a rather dull exhibition.

Moving on to Kuhmo

Buses provide the easiest way of **moving on** from Kajaani. The only rail links are west to Oulu (4 daily via Kontiomäki), plus the four daily connections for Iisalmi, Kuopio and beyond. The best direction to head for more rural delights is east towards Kuhmo, where the scenery becomes increasingly spectacular, especially around the town of Sotkamo (39km from Kajaani) and the acclaimed beauty spot of **Vuokatti** – a high pine-clad ridge commanding views all the way to Russia. The rolling hills make this Finland's premier ski-training area.

Kuhmo

With belts of forests, hills and lakes, and numerous nature walks and hikes within easy reach, **KUHMO** makes a fine base for exploring the countryside. The terrain is in some ways less dramatic than that further north, but then again it's also far less crowded.

You can get details of hiking routes, maps and other practical information from the **tourist office**, Kainuuntie 126 (June–Aug Mon–Fri 8am–6pm, Sat 9am–4pm; Sept–May Mon–Fri 8am–5pm; ☎08/655 6382, fax 655 6384). The tourist office can also explain how best to reach the **Kalevala Village** on the outskirts of the town. This re-creation of a wooded Karelian village provides an illuminating account of traditional building methods, plus it's a good excuse to indulge in some pricey souvenirs – and interesting handicrafts – which are sold to the many genuine Karelians who visit. It's also the only thing close to Kuhmo of appeal to non-hikers.

Low-budget **accommodation** options in Kuhmo include the **youth hostel** *Piilolan Koulu* (☎08/655 6245, fax 655 6139), which has rooms as well as dorms, though it's only open July. *Hotel Kalevela*, 3km from the centre (☎08/655 4100, fax 655 4200; ⑤), is a fair bet for a clean, modern room and also rents out **canoes** and **bikes**. The town **campsite** (☎08/655 6388, fax 655 6384; June–Aug) is 4km from the centre along Koulukatu.

HIKING ROUTES AROUND KUHMO

The local section of the several hundred kilometres of track that make up the **UKK hiking route** starts from the Kuhmo Sports Centre and winds 70km through forests and the Hiidenportti canyon. Several other hikes begin further out from Kuhmo and can be reached by bus from the town. **Elimyssalo**, to the east, is a 15km track through a conservation area, and also to the east is **Kilpelänkankaan**, where a cycle path runs 3.5km across heathland, passing a number of Winter War memorials. To the north, **Sininenpolku** is a hike of more than 20km over a ridge, past small lakes and rivers. In the northwest, **Iso-Palosenpolku** has two paths through a thickly forested area, where there are overnight shelters. Additionally, several **canoeing routes** trace the course of the old tar-shipping routes between Kuhmo and Oulu.

Continuing northwards from Kuhmo leads only to more hiking lands, and if you need urbanity, nightlife and easy living, now's the time to own up and duck out. If not, and your feet are itching to be tested over hundreds of kilometres of untamed land, simply clamber on the bus for Suomussalmi.

Around Suomussalmi

Divided by a lake, Kiantajärvi, SUOMUSSALMI falls into two distinct parts: one the older, more traditional village of Suomussalmi proper; the other, Ämmänsaari, a newer administrative centre. Ämmänsaari is on the main road, Route 5, about 100km from Kajaani, while the smaller Route 41 covers the similar distance from Kuhmo to Suomussalmi. The villages themselves are connected by a more or less hourly bus service. Ämmänsaari, which serves as the administrative centre of the whole of northern Kainuu, is a good place to gather details on hiking and accommodation: contact the **tourist office**, Jalloniemi, by Route 5 (summer Mon–Fri 8am–8pm, Sat 11am–7pm, Sun noon–7pm; winter Mon–Fri 8am–4pm; ☎08/719 1243, fax 711 189). There's also a **campsite** (☎08/711 209 or 050/566 4252; June–Aug) and a tourist hotel, the *Kianta-Baari*, at Ämmankatu 4 (☎08/711 173; ②). Buses from both parts of Suomussalmi run to the main hiking areas in the province, usually on a daily basis.

To the east, something of the old Karelian culture can still be felt in the tiny villages of Kuivajärvi and Hietajärvi, close to the Russian border. Near Kuivajärvi is the **Saarisuo Nature Reserve**, where an eight-kilometre hiking trail traverses a protected forest and marshy areas that are home to a wide variety of bird life. Adjacent to the reserve is a youth hostel (☎08/723 179, fax 711 189; April–Sept), which serves breakfast (30mk) and other meals to order.

A few kilometres north of Suomussalmi, in the Ruhtinansalmi area, is the **Martinselkonen Nature Reserve**, known locally as the "last wilderness". A solitary marked path passes through the reserve, and there are some open cabins and *laavu* shelters – crude slope-roofed huts open to the elements on one side, which were used by early lumber workers and based on the design of peasant hunters. It's best to contact the Martinselkonen Wilds Centre in the reserve (☎08/736 160, fax 736 150) before you venture forth, which as well as offering the usual information on the local area also can provide accommodation and meals.

Heading north from Suomussalmi along Route 843 to Kuusamo brings you to **HOSSA**, situated close to a network of hiking paths graded according to difficulty and ranging in length from 1km to 25km, which pass through pine forests and over ridges between limpid lakes. Dotted about are old tar pits, lumber camps and a few traditional *laavu* shelters. Various cabins are also available on the trails, some with open access, others which have to be booked in advance. Hossa also offers about 100km of excellent canoeing routes and some great fishing. All the hikes begin 8km from the village, which has a **campsite** (☎ & fax 08/732 310) that's open all year, and a **holiday village** (☎08/732 322, fax 732 307), both with affordable cabins. If you travel 5km north of Hossa you'll find the Hossa Information Centre (☎08/732 366, fax 732 367), which has a café, an activity service to help you get the most out of the local area and an adjacent campsite.

Kuusamo and around

KUUSAMO, 120km north of Suomussalmi, is reached by daily express buses from Oulu, plus regular services from Rovaniemi. For full details of local hiking and accommodation, and the many summer events that bring some life to the town, call in at the

Karhuntassu Tourist Centre at Torangintaival 2 (☎08/850 29⁣0, fax 850 2901). For accommodation, try the **youth hostel** across the street from the bus station at Kitkantie 35 (☎08/852 2132, fax 852 1134; June–Aug).

Kuusamo is the starting point for the **Kuusamo Bear Circuit** (*Karhunkierros*), one of the most popular hiking routes in Finland: a seventy-kilometre trek weaving over the summit of Rukatunturi, dipping into canyons and across slender log suspension bridges over thrashing rapids. Herds of hikers are a far more common sight than bears, but the hike is still a good one and there are several interesting shorter routes off the main track. From Kuusamo, take the bus to **Ristikallio** for the start of the hike. Wilderness huts are placed roughly at ten-kilometre intervals along the route, though during peak months these are certain to be full. Fortunately there's no shortage of places to pitch your own tent, and about halfway along the route are three **campsites**, *Juuma* (☎08/863 212), *Jyrävä* (☎08/863 236) and *Retkietappi* (☎08/863 218), all open from June to August.

Heading north again, the tougher **Six Fells Hiking Route** starts at **Salla**. A bus runs here from Kuusamo two times a day from Monday to Friday, pulling up at the Salla Tourist Centre (☎016/839 651, fax 839 657), which marks the beginning of the trail. Should you need to stay, there's a **hotel** here, *Hotel Revontuli* (☎016/879 711, fax 837 760; ③), plus some nearby **cabins** (with showers) costing 245mk a night (☎016/831 931, fax 837 765). The 35-kilometre hike includes some stiff climbs up the sides of spruce-covered fells, with spectacular views from their bare summits. **Niemelä**, close to the road between Kuusamo and Salla, marks the other end of the trail. From Salla you can continue by bus into the Arctic North (see p.724), or to Kemijärvi to meet the train for Rovaniemi.

Rovaniemi and around

Easily accessible by train or bus, **ROVANIEMI** is touted as the capital of Lapland. Just south of the Arctic Circle it may be, but tourists who arrive on day-trips from Helsinki expecting sleighs and tents will be disappointed by a place that looks about as Lapish as a palm tree. The wooden huts of old Rovaniemi were razed to the ground by departing Germans at the close of World War II, and the town was completely rebuilt during the late 1940s. Alvar Aalto's bold but impractical design has the roads forming the shape of reindeer antlers – which is fine if you're travelling by helicopter, but makes journeys on foot take far longer than they need to. It's now really quite dismal, with its uniform greyish-white buildings and an unnerving newness to everything – even the smattering of antique shops contain nothing older than 1970s junk. Most visitors use it only as a short-term stopover, or as a base for studies in Lap culture.

The Town

An essential stop if you have any interest in Lapish culture is **Arktikum**, in the northern part of town at Pohjoisranta 4 (May–Aug daily 10am–6pm; Sept–April Tues–Sun 10am–6pm; 50mk), by far the most fascinating museum in Rovaniemi. Its great arched atrium emerges from the ground like a U-boat, with almost all the exhibition areas submerged beneath banks of stone. The centre contains both the **Provincial Museum of Lappland** and the **Arctic Centre**, which together provide a varied insight into the history and present-day lives of the peoples of the Arctic North. Taking an intelligent, unsentimental approach, the museum superbly evokes the remarkable Sami culture and is well worth a couple of hours. Displays range from raincoats made of seal intestine, polar bear trousers, arctic fox and caribou hide, to superb photographic displays on reindeer husbandry today – modern technology has made its mark, with cellular

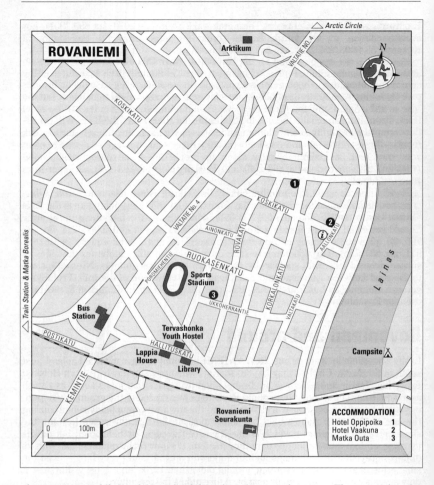

phones, snowmobiles and four-wheel-drive buggies now the norm. There are also pictures of the horrific devastation caused by German soldiers in 1944, when they were forced to retreat, burning every building in sight.

Back in the town centre, **Lappia**, an Aalto-designed building a short distance from the bus and train stations at Hallituskatu 11, contains a theatre and concert hall, plus an excellent **library** (June to mid-Aug Mon–Fri 11am–7pm, Sat 10am–3pm; mid-Aug to May Mon–Fri 11am–8pm, Sat 10am–4pm), with several free Internet terminals (bookable in advance). There's also a **Lappland Department** (situated at the bottom of the stairwell from the main lending section), housing a staggering hoard of books, magazines and newspaper articles in many languages covering every conceivable Sami-related subject. This constantly growing collection is already the largest of its kind in the world, and probably the best place anywhere for undertaking Lap-related research.

Other points of interest in Rovaniemi are few. At Rauhankatu 70, **Rovaniemi Seurakunta** (daily mid-May to early Aug 9am–9pm; Sept 9am–7pm), the parish church, repays a peek on account of its jumbo-sized altar fresco, *Fountain of Life* by Lennart Segerstråle, an odd work that pitches the struggle between good and evil into a Lapland setting. In winter the church also hosts concerts. About the only other thing meriting a look is the **J. Martiinni Knife Factory** (Mon–Fri 8am–4pm) at Marttinintie 6 (walk or take bus #4). In the kingdom of the sharp edge the Martinni multipurpose knife reigns supreme, and if you're looking for one the prices in the factory shop are cheaper than anywhere else – plus you can have your name inscribed on the blade. Prices range from a few markkaa up to 300mk for the latest model.

If you have more time to kill and the weather isn't too cold (Rovaniemi's prone to chilly snaps even in summer), visit one of the two outdoor museums that lie near each other just outside town, accessible by bus #6. The **Ethnographical Museum** in Pöykkölä, 3km outside town (June–Aug Tues–Sun noon–4pm; 10mk), is a collection of farm buildings that belonged to the Pöykkölä family between 1640 and 1910, and forms part of a potpourri of objects pertaining to reindeer husbandry, salmon-fishing and rural life in general. About 500m up the road is the **Lappish Forestry Museum** (June to mid-Sept Tues–Sat noon–6pm; 10mk) where the reality of unglamorous forestry life is remembered by a reconstructed lumber camp.

The Arctic Circle

Some people are lured to Rovaniemi solely for the dubious thrill of crossing the **Arctic Circle**. While the "circle" itself doesn't remain constant (it's defined as the area where the midnight sun can be seen, which shifts a few hundred metres every year), its man-made markers do – 8km north of town along Route 4. Bus #8 goes to the circle from the bus station around every half-hour, and also calls at the stops in town with "Arctic Circle" emblazoned on them.

Near the circle and served by the same bus is the **Santa Claus Village** (daily: mid-Jan to June 10am–5pm; June to mid-Aug 11am–7pm; mid-Aug to Sept 9am–6pm; Oct–Nov 10am–5pm; Dec to mid-Jan 9am–7pm; free). Considering its tourist pitch, the place – inside a very large log cabin – is quite within the bounds of decency: you can meet Father Christmas all year round, contemplate the reindeer grazing in the adjoining farm and leave your name for a Christmas card from Santa himself (although it may take anything up to a decade to arrive). Within the village is the ticket office for **Santa Park** (June to mid-Aug, Dec to mid-Jan, mid-Feb to mid-Mar daily 11am–6pm; Fri–Sun 1–6pm only at other times; closed mid-Sept to mid-Oct; ☎016/333 0000; 95mk) from which a train connects to the park itself. A collection of themed fairground rides within a cavern inside a granite hill, Santa Park is predominantly aimed at those who believe the big guy with the white beard is real. For those without children, it's probably worth missing, unless you want to pretend you're four again.

Practicalities

Rovaniemi's bus and train stations are just a couple of minutes' walk from each other and from the city centre. The **tourist office** (June to mid-Aug Mon–Fri 8am–6pm, Sat & Sun 11.30am–4pm; mid-Aug to May Mon–Fri 8am–4pm; ☎016/346 270, fax 322 2767) is to the northeast at Koskikatu 1, a few minutes' walk from the basic but friendly all-year **Tervashonka youth hostel** at Hallituskatu 16 (☎ & fax 016/344 644). It's always crowded in summer, so try to book in advance. Other budget options include the weirdly decorated *Matka Outa* guesthouse, at Ukkoherrantie 16 (☎016/312 474; ②), or the excellent value *Matka Borealis*, Asemieskatu 1 (☎ & fax 016/342 0130; ②). With a little more money to spend, try the *Oppipoika*, Korkalonkatu 33 (☎016/20 321, fax 16 969; ④/③), in the same building as the hotel and catering school (see p.724) and boasting a pool and two saunas, as well as good food. Swankier still is the *Hotel Vaakuna*, Koskikatu 4 (☎016/332 211, fax 332 2199; ⑤/④), just opposite the tourist office. Rovaniemi's **campsite** is at Jäämerentie 1 (☎016/345 304), on the far bank of Ounasjoki, and equipped with a café and sauna.

There are a few pleasant **cafés** in town, the best being the small *Antinkaapo*, just a few buildings up from *Valentina Conditoria*, Rovakatu 21, another good spot for sticky buns. For filling food at very reasonable prices, *Café Kisälli*, Korkalonkatu 35 (Mon–Fri 8.30am–5pm), and the neighbouring *Oppipoika Restaurant* (daily 11am–11pm) are both run by the local hotel and catering school. At the café you can fill up on delicious schnitzels or perch with potatoes and vegetables for 30mk. The restaurant at the *Hotel Cumulus* is also good, specializing in reindeer dishes (try the 30mk reindeer soup).

In the **evening** the few students of the Lappland University can usually be found socializing in *Lapinpaula* (often known by its nickname *Tupsu*) at Hallituskatu 24, *Tivoli*, Valtakatu 19, or *Paha Kurki*, Koskikatu near the *Hotel Vaakuna*. The *Rio Grande Rock Cafe*, Korkalonkatu 32, plays host to serious drinkers, while a more relaxed atmosphere prevails at the *Roy Club*, Maakuntakatu 24. Drinking is one of the few things to do here other than watching logs float downriver. The hotels tend to host any **nightlife** there is: *Scandic Rovaniemi*, Koskikatu 23, is popular, while *Doris*, at the *Hotel Vaakuna*, attracts an older crowd. The town wakes up a bit when ROPS, the Rovaniemi **football team**, are playing at home. You'll hear the cheering all over town and be able to see the game for free through gaps in the fencing – the stadium is on Pohiolankatu and the season runs through the summer. Despite what you might assume from the modest facilities, ROPS is one of the country's best teams.

The Arctic North

Squeezed inland by the northern tip of Norway, Finland's **Arctic North** mixes forests, lakes and rivers with tracts of desolate upland that rise high above the tree line. In these uncompromising latitudes, some of the indigenous Sami population still herd their reindeer and maintain their traditions despite serious threats from a number of sources – most dramatically, in recent years, the fallout from Chernobyl. The Sami tend to remain far from the prying eyes of the tourist, though their angular *tipis* (tents), wreathed in reindeer antlers, skins, and all sorts of Arctic trinkets, are to be found along the region's main roads during the summer, in what can seem a rather crass and commercially inspired conformity. This racial stereotyping is intended to appeal to the wallets of the thousands of motorists who use the **Arctic Highway**, the E75/4, the fastest approach to the Nordkapp (see p.350). But don't let this put you off: the Arctic wilderness is a ready escape, its stark and often haunting landscapes easily accessible.

Two main roads lead north from Rovaniemi: the Arctic Highway, which services the **northeast**, linking the communities of Sodankylä, Ivalo, Inari and Kargasniemi; and Route 79/E78, which crosses the **northwest**, connecting Muonio and Kilpisjärvi. Inari and Sodankylä are the only settlements worth a second look, but the landscape which surrounds the Arctic North's minuscule communities will hold your gaze for much longer – provided you take the trouble to do at least some **hiking**. If you're planning to travel north from Rovaniemi on one route then back on the other, be warned that there are no roads in between, only rough tracks – with no facilities – traversing some desolate landscape. For safety, you need either to retrace your steps to Rovaniemi before taking the other route, or travel in an arc into Norway and over the other side, a journey by car of around four hours.

Buses are the only form of public transport in the Arctic North; they run far less frequently here than elsewhere in Finland, but services along the Arctic Highway are quite good and all the larger settlements are reached by bus at least once a day. Other buses run

HIKING IN THE ARCTIC NORTH

The best way to experience the Arctic North is to get off the bus and explore slowly, which means on foot. The rewards for making the physical effort are manifold. There's a tremendous feeling of space here, and the wild and inhospitable terrain acquires a near-magical quality when illuminated by the constant daylight of the summer months (the only time of year when hiking is feasible).

Many graded **hiking routes** cover the more interesting areas; most of the more exhilarating of them are distributed among the region's four national parks: **Pyhätunturi**, southeast of Sodankylä; **Urho Kekkonen** and **Lemmenjoki**, further north off the Arctic Highway; and **Pallas-Ounastunturi**, near Muonio in the northwest. There are challenges aplenty for experienced hikers, though mere novices need have nothing to fear, provided basic common sense is employed. The more popular hikes can become very busy and many people find this an intrusion into their contemplation of the natural spectacle – others enjoy the camaraderie. If you are seeking solitude you'll find it, but you'll need at least the company of a reliable compass, a good-quality tent, and emergency supplies.

We've assembled a broad introduction to the major hikes and described the type of terrain that you'll find on them. Bear in mind that these aren't definitive accounts as conditions and details often change at short notice; always gather the latest information from the nearest tourist centre or park information office.

Hiking rules and tips

Obviously you should observe the **basic rules** of hiking, and be aware of the delicate ecology of the region: don't start fires in any old place (most hikes have marked spots for this), and don't pitch your tent out of specified areas on marked routes. You should always check that you have maps and adequate supplies before setting out, and never aim to cover more ground than is comfortable. Bathe your feet daily to prevent blisters, and carry some form of mosquito repellent – the pesky creatures infest the region.

Hiking accommodation

To be on the safe side, you shouldn't go anywhere without a good-quality **tent**, although the majority of marked hikes have some form of basic shelter (see p.30) and most have a **youth hostel** and **campsite** (plus comfy hotels for those who can afford them) at some point on the trail. These fill quickly, however, and few things are worse than having nowhere to relax after a long day's trek – so make an advance reservation whenever possible.

to schedules designed to deliver and collect hikers from either end of the busier trails. Be sure to check timetables carefully and plan several days ahead: get the special northern bus timetable from the tourist office in Rovaniemi if possible, or refer to the more general nationwide timetable, *Pikavuoro Aikataulut*, available at the bigger bus stations. Forward planning applies equally to accommodation (see box above). On your way northwards, you'll almost certainly meet people returning from hikes, whose advice can be very useful.

The northeast: Sodankylä and the Arctic Highway

North of Rovaniemi, it's an uneventful 130-kilometre drive along the Arctic Highway to **SODANKYLÄ**, a modest, comfortable town, whose modern appearance belies its ancient foundation. From the late seventeenth century, Finnish settlers and Christian Sami gathered here on high days and holidays to trade and to celebrate religious festivals. Unusually, their wooden **church** of 1689 has survived intact (summer daily 10am–6pm), its rough-hewn timbers crowding in upon the narrowest of naves with the

SODANKYLÄ'S MIDNIGHT SUN FILM FESTIVAL

The only time accommodation is likely to be at a premium in Sodankylä is during the Midnight Sun Film Festival, which draws film-loving Finns – and a remarkable number of top directors and their latest cinematic offerings – to the tiny town for a week each June. For more information about the event, contact the festival office at Jäämerentie 9 (☎016/614 524, fax 618 646, *www.msfilmfestival.fi*).

pulpit pressing intrusively into the pews. The old church nestles beside the Kitinen River in the shadow of its uninspiring nineteenth-century replacement and a stone's throw from the **Alariesto Art Gallery** (June–Aug Mon–Sat 10am–5pm, Sun noon–6pm; Sept–May Mon–Fri 10am–5pm, Sat 10am–4pm, Sun noon–4pm; 20mk). The gallery features the work of Andreas Alariesto, a twentieth-century Sami artist of some renown. Each canvas is an invigorating representation of traditional native life and custom, notably a crystalline *View from the Arctic Ocean* embellished with chaotic boulders, predatory fish jaws and busy Sami. A useful catalogue available at reception explains the background to the exhibits.

Sodankylä is little more than an elongated main street: Jäämerentie. The bus station, post office and petrol stations are within a few metres of each other, while the **tourist office** (☎016/618 168) is in the centre of the village, about 1.5km from the bus station. Of the handful of **hotels**, the most convenient are the *Hotelli Kultaisen Karhun Majatalo* (☎016/613 801, fax 613 810; ③), a five-minute walk from the bus station at Sodankyläntie 10, and the nearby *Hotel Sodankylä*, Unarintie 15 (☎016/617 121, fax 613 545; ④/③), both of which are open year round. There's also a **campsite** (☎016/612 181; early June to mid-Aug) and a **youth hostel** (☎016/612 218, fax 611 503; same dates), a ten- to fifteen-minute walk from the centre: cross the bridge, veer left along Savukoskentie and follow the signs. As for **meals**, the pizzas served up at *Poronsarvi*, Jäämerentie 52, are the best in town, while for a wider choice of meat and fish dishes try *Ravintola Revontuli* on the same street. *Matkanuisto Kahvio*, Sompiontie 4, is a reasonable café, though stuffed with tacky souvenirs.

Around Sodankylä: Pyhätunturi National Park

Off the Arctic Highway some 65km southeast of Sodankylä lies **Pyhätunturi National Park**, and the steep slopes and deep ravines of the most southerly of Finland's fells. Here, the 45-kilometre **Pyhätunturi and Luostotunturi hiking route** rises from marshlands and pine woods and rounds five fell summits. Five kilometres from the start is the impressive waterfall of the Uhrikuru gorge, after which the track circles back for a short stretch, eventually continuing to Karhunjuomalampi (The Bear's Pool). There's a *päivätupa* (cabin) here, but the only other hut on the route is by the pool at Pyhälampi.

Near the hike's starting point are an **information centre** (☎016/882 773, fax 882 824), a **campsite** (☎016/852 103, fax 852 140), and two reasonably priced hotels: the *Pyhätunturi* (☎016/856 111, fax 882 740; ③) and *Pyhän Asteli* (☎016/852 141, fax 852 149; ③). The hike ends at Luostotunturi, where accommodation includes the *Luosto Hotel* (☎016/624 400, fax 624 410; ④/③) and the more basic *Luostonhovi* (☎016/624 421, fax 624 297; ①). The daily **bus** between Sodankylä and Kemijärvi (on the rail line from Rovaniemi) stops close to both ends of the trail.

Continuing north: Urho Kekkonen National Park

Travel north by car from Sodankylä on the Arctic Highway for 110km and you'll arrive at **Koilliskaira Visitor Centre** (June–Sept daily 9am–6pm; Oct–May Mon–Fri 9am–4pm; ☎016/626 251, fax 626 113), where you can reserve cabin beds, get information on dozens of hikes and watch a film about the local terrain. Just 100m from the centre lurks a gaggle of tourist establishments: the **Gold Museum and Panning Centre** (40mk), the *Gold Prospector* restaurant, serving Lapish specialities for 45–100mk (reindeer omelette is the cheapest), and a guesthouse, the *Korundi* (☎ & fax 016/626 158; ②) with **cabins** (①).

Twenty kilometres further north (130km from Sodankylä) is the turning for Tuntura Kaapää, a popular and well-equipped fell-walking centre on the edge of the **Urho Kekkonen National Park**. The park is one of the country's largest, incorporating the uninhabited wilderness that extends to the Russian border – pine moors and innumerable fells scored by gleaming streams and rivers. With regular bus connections to north and south, the fell centre is easily the most convenient base for exploring the park. It's at the head of several walking trails, from the simplest of excursions to exhausting expeditions using the park's chain of wilderness cabins. The *Fell Resort* (☎016/667 101, fax 667 121; ⑤/③) with en-suite rooms can provide information and sells detailed trail maps for 40–65mk, rents out mountain bikes (110mk per day; 500mk per week), organizes guided walks, and also arranges accommodation in the adjoining, year-round **youth hostel** (same phone number). There's also a good restaurant and a sauna (30mk).

Ivalo and Inari

Try not to get stuck in **IVALO**, on the Arctic Highway 40km north of the fell centre, a town of singular ugliness. If you do have to stay, however, the riverside *Hotel Kultahippu*, Petsamontie 1 (☎016/661 825, fax 662 510; ③), is the most palatable overnight option, with breakfast and sauna included in the price. There's no longer an official **tourist office** here, the nearest being in Inari (see below), though in summer there's a small information area in the shop called "Porotuote" on the main road through the village.

The road heading north to Inari winds around numerous lakes dotted with islands – it's a spectacular route if you can time your trip with the glorious Lapish **Ruska**, a season that takes in late summer and autumn, when the trees take on brilliant citrus colours that reflect in the still waters. **INARI** itself, 35km away, is slightly more amenable than Ivalo, straggling along the bony banks of the Juutuanjoki River as it tumbles into the freezing-cold, islet-studded waters of Lake Inarijärvi. There's nothing remarkable about the village itself, but it's a pretty little place with several appealing diversions. The bus stops outside the **tourist office** in Inari House (June–Aug Mon–Fri 9am–7pm, Sat & Sun 10am–4pm; Sept–May Mon–Fri 9am–5pm; ☎016/661 666). As well as accommodation information, you can get a fishing licence (39mk) here, and visit the building's permanent Sami handicrafts exhibition (free), whose exhibits show a marked contrast in quality with the tourist souvenirs that pop up everywhere here. Close by lies the **Sami Museum** (daily except Mon in winter 9am–8pm; 35mk), featuring a re-sited nineteenth-century village, a cluster of old *tipis* and various reconstructions illustrating aspects of Sami life – principally handicrafts and hunting and fishing techniques. Beginning about 2km from the museum, the five-kilometre **Pielppajärvi Wilderness Church hiking trail** leads to the isolated remains of a 1752 church.

From the river bridge you can take a two-hour **lake cruise** in summer (June to mid-Sept 1–2 daily; ☎016/358 400 or 391 017; 60mk), as well as similarly priced fishing trips. You can rent a twelve-seat boat and a guide for two and a half hours for three to eleven people (150mk flat fee).

Many travellers pass through Inari during the summer, so it's best to reserve accommodation during this period. There's a **campsite**, *Uruniemi Camping* (☎016/671 331; March, April & June to late Sept; late Sept to Feb open only by prior arrangement), on the southern outskirts of the village, with cottages to rent; the *Inarin Kultahovi* hotel (☎016/671 221, fax 671 250; ④) offers comfortable rooms with river views, plus an excellent, reasonably priced **restaurant**. If money's tight, stick to the popular *Terassikavla Café*, beside the bus stop.

Around Inari: Lemmenjoki National Park
A vast tract of birch and pinewood forest interrupted by austere, craggy fells, marshland and a handful of bubbling rivers, **Lemmenjoki National Park**, about 40km southwest of Inari, witnessed a short-lived gold rush in the 1940s. A few panners remain, eking out a meagre living.

The park's most breathtaking scenery is to be found on its southeastern side along the Lemmenjoki river valley. To get there, take the daily bus from Inari to **Njurgalahti**, a tiny settlement on the edge of the park about 12km off Route 955 (the district's main road), which is where the 55-kilometre, two-day hike down the river valley begins; taking the twice-daily boat (June–Aug) from Njurgalahti to Kultasatama cuts 20km off the hike's full distance.

At **Härkäkoski**, hikers cross the river by a small boat, pulled by rope from bank to bank; the track then ascends through a pine forest to **Morgamoja Kultala**, the old gold-panning centre, where there's a big unlocked hut. There are a couple of other huts set aside for those walking the trail, but the nearest **campsite** (☎ & fax 016/673 001), with cottages, is back on the main road at **Menesjärvi**. The holiday village (☎ & fax 016/673 435) in the hamlet of **Lemmenjoki** is far closer, with four-berth **cabins** from around 230mk per cabin per day. At present there's no information centre in the park; enquiries should be directed to the Ylä-Lappi district forestry office on ☎0205/647 701.

North from Inari: crossing into Norway
Travelling north from Inari is rather pointless unless you're aiming for Norway. The Finnish section of the Arctic Highway continues to dreary **KAAMANEN**, though on the way, just past a sign for the *Jokitörmä Hostel*, is a bold, stark and deeply evocative memorial in rusty red metal to World War II in Finland. In simple words, it states "the battles of the light infantrymen in the wilds of Lapland were brought to an end in Kaamanen, Inari at the end of October 1944. 774 killed, 262 missing, 2904 wounded". In Kaamanen there's a **campsite** with cottages that's open all year (☎016/672 713). The route then swings westwards on its way to the Nordkapp, exiting Finland at **KARIGASNIEMI**, an unprepossessing hamlet that has a restaurant (*Soarve Stohpu*) and pleasant rooms in the small and basic *Kalastajan Majatalo* hotel next door (☎ & fax 016/676 171; ②), though its bar is permanently full of drunken locals. There are also two **campsites**: *Lomakylä* (☎016/676 160; June–Sept), and the *Tenorinne* (☎016/676 113; early June to mid-Sept).

From Kaamanen, a minor road branches due north to **UTSJOKI**, a small border village beside the Tenojoki River. The nearest **campsite** (☎016/678 803; mid-June to Aug) is a few kilometres away, by the river's edge in Vetsikko. The road on from Utsjoki runs parallel to the Norwegian border, then crosses it just beyond the hamlet of **Nuorgam**, where there's a guesthouse, the *Matkakoti Suomenrinne* (☎016/678 620; mid-June to mid-Aug), and a year-round **campsite** (☎016/678 312). Once across the border, it's a 160-kilometre journey to Kirkenes in Norway (see p.355).

The northwest

Heading northwest from Rovaniemi, Route 79 sticks close to the banks of the Ounasjoki River before it reaches the straggling settlement of **KITTILÄ**, a distance of 150km. There's little to detain you here – the departing German army burnt the place to the ground in 1944 and the rebuilding has been uninspired – though both the **youth hostel**, Valtatie 5 (☎016/648 508; mid-June to early Aug), and neighbouring **campsite** are conveniently located beside the main road.

It's a further 20km to the dishevelled ski resort of **SIRKKA**, whose surrounding hills boast seven hiking (or, in winter, cross-country skiing) routes, including the enjoyable river and fell walking of the eighteen-kilometre Levi Fell trail. All seven tracks begin in or near the centre of Sirkka, where you should find a whole range of places to stay, though nearly all are open only during the winter.

Muonio and Pallas-Ounastunturi National Park
Modest **MUONIO** lies 60km northwest of Sirkka beside the murky river that separates Finland from Sweden. What passes for the town centre falls beside the junction of the E78, the main north–south highway, and Route 79. Despite a rash of green tourist information signs, outside the high season you'll be lucky to find any form of information office. Muonio's summertime **tourist office** (June–Aug Mon–Fri 10am–6pm, July also Sat & Sun noon–4pm; ☎016/534 370) is attached to a small snack bar; in winter there's just a telephone service (☎016/534 312). You're better off asking about the surrounding area at the year-round **youth hostel** *Lomamaja Pekonen* (☎ & fax 016/532 237; ①) close by. If you carry on south 3km towards Tornio you'll come to the well organized and equipped *Harriniva Holiday Centre* (open all year except for Oct and May, when they only take group bookings; ☎016/532 491, fax 532 750, *harrinivan.lomakeskus@co.inet.fi*). Here you can pitch a tent, hook up your campervan or stay in a range of accommodation that runs from basic cabins (①) to fully equipped, more expensive, apartments (④). They also run a variety of summer and winter programmes, including activities such as helicopter tours and white-water rafting through to two-day dog-sled safaris in the middle of winter.

From Muonio, buses leave for Kilpisjärvi (see p.730) and (once-daily) to Enontekiö/Hetta, skirting the **Pallas-Ounastunturi National Park**, a rectangular slab of mountain plateau whose bare peaks and coniferous forests begin about 30km northeast of Muonio. A bus leaves Muonio at 9.30am Monday to Friday for the National Park, stopping outside the **information office** (☎016/532 451, fax 532 929; summer Mon–Fri 11am–6pm, Sat & Sun 9am–4pm). The best places to camp around here are south of Muonio on Route 21 – ask for details at the information office or in Muonio.

Pallastunturi marks the start of the **Pallas-Hetta hiking route**, an arduous 56-kilometre trail that crosses a line of fell summits with several *autiotupa* and *varastupa* (locked and unlocked huts) and camping areas en route, as well as a sauna about halfway along in the hut at **Hannukuru**. The highest point is the summit of Taivaskero, near the start. The track ends at Lake Ounasjärvi, which you'll need to cross by **ferry** (7am–11pm); if the boat isn't there, raise the flag to indicate that you want to cross.

On the other side of the lake are the unremarkable adjoining villages of **ENONTEKIÖ/HETTA** – hardly an inspiring place, although the thrice-weekly flights to and from Helsinki can make it an accessible starting point for exploring Lapland. The services on offer are also excellent, including Enontekiö Flights (☎016/521 230), whose air taxis can take you quickly (and expensively) into the depths of Lapland, and Lapland Guiding (☎016/521 230), who offer four-day organized treks. There's also the **Fell-Lapland Nature Centre** (April–Sept Mon–Fri 9am–6pm; Oct–March Mon–Fri 9am–4pm), where you can buy maps and make reservations for a host of cottages in the Pallas-Ounastunturi National Park. There are some reasonable **accommodation** options including a **youth hostel** (☎016/521 361, fax 521 049; mid-Feb to April & June to mid-Sept; rooms ①) and a trio of **campsites**: *Hetan Lomakylä* (☎016/521 521, fax 521 293; March–Sept), which also has some cabins, *Kotatieva* (☎016/521 062; June to mid-Aug) and *Ounasloma* (all year, but call ahead ☎016/521 055). Among the settlement's hotels a good choice is the *Hetan Majatalo* (☎016/521 351, fax 521 362; ②/①), which offers excellent en-suite rooms, along with cheaper and more basic accommodation. In winter they organize a whole host of activities such as ice-fishing, reindeer safaris and dog-sleigh tours. In summer you can rent boats, bikes and go on fishing trips. They also do a highly recommended traditional Lapish dinner. The *Hetta Hotel* (☎016/521 361, fax 521 049; ③) offers a plush alternative, with several rooms overlooking the lake.

If you're driving north through Enontekiö towards Norway, 6km before you get to the border on the Alta road is **PALOJÄRVI**, where the log cabins of *Galdotieva* (☎016/528 630; ②) offer a reasonable overnight spot.

OTHER HIKES IN THE PARK: THE PALLAS-OLOS-YLLÄS TRAIL
Although the Pallas-Hetta trail is the Pallas-Ounastunturi National Park's most impressive walk, and the one with the best transport links, there are several other options. Of these, the most notable is the 87-kilometre **Pallas-Olos-Ylläs hiking trail**, which also begins from Pallastunturi. With several unlocked huts en route, this track twists south past fells and lakes until it leaves the park and reaches the Muonio–Sirkka road close to the swanky *Olostunturi Hotel* (☎016/536 111, fax 536 444; ⑤). The hotel is open only for winter skiing between September and April but the hills that surround it are crisscrossed by a number of shorter walking trails. The reception desk has all the details on the slower services, the bus stops here after it's been to Pallastunturi.

From the hotel, the Pallas-Olos-Ylläs trail continues south, soon reaching the dam on the Särkijoki river before proceeding down to Lake Äkäkasjärvi, where there's a café in a former grain mill. From here, the track heads onto the eastern slopes of Äkäkero, passing the remarkably good-value *Äkäskero Hotel* (☎016/533 077, fax 533 078; ③) and continuing for 4km to the tiny settlement of **ÄKÄSLOMPOLO**, on the upper slopes of Yllästunturi.

The **bus service** on from Äkäslompolo is dreadful: there's a once-weekly summer service to Kolari, eventually reaching Tornio on the E78, but to reach Muonio, 76km north of Kolari, you'll have to hitch.

Continuing north from Muonio: Kilpisjärvi and around

The thumb-shaped chunk of Finland that sticks out above the northern edge of Sweden is almost entirely uninhabited, a hostile arctic wilderness whose tiny settlements are strung along the only road, the E78. For the most part this seems a gloomy route of desolate landscapes and untidy villages, comparing poorly with the splendour of the parallel road to the south that connects Sweden's Kiruna and Norway's Narvik. However, the E78 does have its moments as it approaches the Norwegian frontier, with the bumpy uplands left behind for dramatic snow-covered peaks.

From the E78, you might cross into Sweden via **KAARESUVANTO**, a dreary village 95km north of Muonio, to reach the Kiruna–Narvik road. Otherwise there's little reason to cross the border here or stay longer than you need to in Karesuvanto – if you do, use the all-year **campsite** (☎016/522 079), which has some smart, green-painted cabins (160mk for a twin-bed cabin). Otherwise, try the *Ratkin Hotel* (☎016/522 101, fax 522 104; ④/②), which has fully equipped cabins and a good restaurant.

There's more to be said for continuing for 110km on the E78 to the hamlet of **KILPISJÄRVI** on the Norwegian frontier. On the way, about 25km south of Kilpisjärvi,

---

BUSES INTO NORWAY AND SWEDEN

Once a day, the Rovaniemi/Muonio to Kilpisjärvi bus continues to Skibotn in **Norway**. From Skibotn, there's a daily service along the coastal highway – north to Alta and south to Tromsø. Unfortunately, the bus schedules rarely connect, so you'll almost certainly have to hitch to avoid a night in Skibotn. Similarly, the Finnish bus to Karesuvanto usually arrives too late for passengers to cross the bridge to **Sweden**'s Karesuando and catch the early-morning bus to Kiruna.

you'll pass the welcoming *Peeran Retkeilykeskus* **youth hostel** (☎ & fax 016/532 659), which also serves good food. At Kilpisjärvi itself, perched beside the coldest of lakes in the shadow of a string of stark tundra summits, the *Kilpisjärvi Tourist Hotel* (☎016/537 761, fax 537 767; ③) has a gorgeous location which means it gets booked up months ahead for the March to mid-June period; however, 5km further down the road, the tourist hotel *Kilpisjärvi Tourist Centre* (☎016/537 771, fax 537 702; ②) offers rooms and cottages in just as fine a setting. Both places sell maps covering a number of **local hikes**, the most popular of which are the brace of ten-kilometre trails running to the top of the neighbouring Saanatunturi, 1029m high. The main way up (and down) is the track on the steep north side, although another route runs behind the fell to the northern shore of Saanijärvi, where there's a *päivätupa* (cabin).

Another option is the 24-kilometre loop trail, beginning and ending at Kilpisjärvi, that runs north through the **Malla Nature Reserve** to the **Three Countries Frontier** where Finland, Norway and Sweden meet. The track crosses by footbridge the rapids of Siilajärvi, after which a secondary track ascends to the summit of Pikku Malla. The main route continues to Iso Malla. There's a steep and stony section immediately before the waterfalls of Kihtsekordsi, and then a reindeer fence marking the way down to an *autiotupa* cabin beside the Kuokimajärvi lake. From the tourist office, a stone path leads to the cairn marking the three national borders. There's a **campsite** at the tourist centre (mid-March to mid-May & mid-June to mid-Sept) and, nearby, a private **guesthouse**, *Saananmaja* (☎016/537 746; ①).

travel details

Trains
Kokkola to: Helsinki (9 daily; 5hr); Oulu (8 daily; 2hr 30min); Tampere (9 daily; 3hr 45min).

Oulu to: Kajaani (3 daily; 2hr 20min); Kemi (9 daily; 1hr 10min); Kokkola (8 daily; 2hr 30min); Rovaniemi (7 daily; 2hr 30min) Tornio (2 daily; 2hr).

Rovaniemi to: Kemijärvi (1 daily; 1hr 15min); Oulu (7 daily, 2hr 30min).

Vaasa to: Helsinki (4 daily via Seinajöki; 4hr 30min); Kokkola (3 daily; 2hr 30min); Oulu (3 daily; 5hr 30min); Tampere (4 daily; 2hr 30min).

Buses
Inari to: Kaamanen (6 daily; 1hr 45min); Kargasneimi (2 daily; 1hr 45min); Utsjoki (2 daily; 3hr 45min).

Kajaani to: Ämmänsaari (1 daily; 2hr 30min direct, longer by slower indirect routes); Kuusamo (1 daily; 4hr 10min direct, also slower indirect routes).

Kemi to: Tornio (4 daily; 30min).

Kolari to: Äkäslompolo (1 weekly; 55min).

Kuusamo to: Ristikallio (1 daily; 1hr 15min); Salla (2 daily; 3hr).

Muonio to: Kilpisjärvi (1 daily; 3hr 45min).

Oulu to: Kuusamo (6 daily; 4hr).

Pallastunturi to: Enontekiö (1 daily; 2hr 30min); Muonio (1 daily; 40min).

Pietarsaari to: Kokkola (6 daily; 40min).

Rovaniemi to: Enontekiö/Hetta (2 daily; 5hr 15min); Inari (2 daily; 6hr); Ivalo (3 daily; 5hr); Kiilopää (1 daily; 4hr); Kilpisjärvi (2 daily; 7hr 45min); Kittilä (4 daily; 2hr 30min–2hr 50min); Muonio (2 daily; 4hr); Pallastunturi (1 daily; 4hr 45min); Sodankylä (4 daily; 1hr 40min).

Sodankylä to: Kemijärvi (5 daily; 2hr).

Suomussalmi to: Kuusamo (3 daily; 2hr 45min).

Tornio to: Äkäslompolo (1 weekly; 3hr 45min).

Utsjoki to: Nuorgam (2 daily; 55min).

Vaasa to: Pori (5 daily; 2hr 45min); Turku (6 daily; 5hr).

International ferries
Vaasa to: Umeå (2 daily in summer; 4hr).

INDEX

ROUGH GUIDES: Travel

Amsterdam
Andalucia
Australia

Austria
Bali & Lombok
Barcelona
Belgium &
 Luxembourg
Belize
Berlin
Brazil
Britain
Brittany &
 Normandy
Bulgaria
California
Canada
Central America
Chile
China
Corfu & the
 Ionian Islands
Corsica
Costa Rica
Crete
Croatia
Cyprus
Czech & Slovak
 Republics
Dodecanese &
 the East Aegean

Dominican
 Republic
Ecuador
Egypt
England
Europe
Florida
France
French Hotels &
 Restaurants
 1999
Germany
Goa
Greece
Greek Islands
Guatemala
Hawaii
Holland
Hong Kong &
 Macau
Hungary
India
Indonesia
Ireland
Israel & the
 Palestinian
 Territories
Italy
Jamaica
Japan
Jordan

Kenya
Lake District
Laos
London
Los Angeles
Malaysia,
 Singapore &
 Brunei
Mallorca &
 Menorca
Maya World
Mexico
Morocco
Moscow
Nepal
New England
New York
New Zealand
Norway
Pacific
 Northwest
Paris
Peru
Poland
Portugal
Prague
Provence & the
 Côte d'Azur
The Pyrenees
Rhodes & the
 Dodecanese

Romania
St Petersburg
San Francisco
Sardinia
Scandinavia
Scotland
Scottish
 highlands and
 Islands
Sicily
Singapore
South Africa
South India
Southwest USA
Spain
Sweden
Syria

Thailand
Trinidad &
 Tobago
Tunisia
Turkey
Tuscany &
 Umbria
USA
Venice
Vienna
Vietnam
Wales
Washington DC
West Africa
Zimbabwe &
 Botswana

AVAILABLE AT ALL GOOD BOOKSHOPS

ROUGH GUIDES: Mini Guides, Travel Specials and Phrasebooks

MINI GUIDES

Antigua
Bangkok
Barbados
Big Island of
  Hawaii
Boston
Brussels
Budapest

Dublin
Edinburgh
Florence
Honolulu
Jerusalem
Lisbon
London
  Restaurants
Madrid
Maui
Melbourne
New Orleans
Rome
Seattle
St Lucia

Sydney
Tokyo
Toronto

TRAVEL SPECIALS

First-Time Asia
First-Time
  Europe
Women Travel

PHRASEBOOKS

Czech
Dutch

Egyptian Arabic
European
French
German
Greek
Hindi & Urdu
Hungarian
Indonesian
Italian
Japanese

Mandarin
  Chinese
Mexican
  Spanish
Polish
Portuguese
Russian
Spanish
Swahili
Thai
Turkish
Vietnamese

AVAILABLE AT ALL GOOD BOOKSHOPS

ROUGH GUIDES:
Reference and Music CDs

REFERENCE
Classical Music
Classical:
  100 Essential CDs
Drum'n'bass
House Music
Jazz
Music USA

Opera
Opera:
  100 Essential CDs
Reggae
Reggae:
  100 Essential CDs
Rock
Rock:
  100 Essential CDs
Techno
World Music
World Music:
  100 Essential CDs
English Football
European Football

Internet
Millennium

ROUGH GUIDE MUSIC CDs
Music of the
  Andes
Australian
  Aboriginal
Brazilian Music
Cajun & Zydeco

Classic Jazz
Music of
  Colombia
Cuban Music
Eastern Europe

Music of Egypt
English Roots
  Music
Flamenco
India & Pakistan
Irish Music
Music of Japan
Kenya & Tanzania
Native American
North African
Music of Portugal

Reggae
Salsa
Scottish Music
South African
  Music
Music of Spain
Tango
Tex-Mex
West African
  Music
World Music
World Music Vol 2
Music of
  Zimbabwe

AVAILABLE AT ALL GOOD BOOKSHOPS

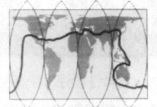
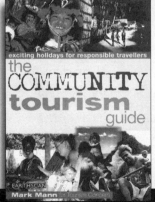